College Football Awards

Also by Dave Blevins and from McFarland

Television Networks: More Than 750 American and Canadian Broadcasters and Cable Networks (2006; paperback 2011)

American Political Parties in the 21st Century (2006)

Halls of Fame: An International Directory (2004)

UFO Directory International: 1,000+ Organizations and Publications in 40+ Countries (2003)

College Football Awards

All National and Conference Winners Through 2010

DAVE BLEVINS

McFarland & Company, Inc., Publishers
Jefferson, North Carolina, and London

Library of Congress Cataloguing-in-Publication Data

Blevins, David.
College football awards : all national and conference winners through 2010 / Dave Blevins.
p. cm.
Includes index.

ISBN 978-0-7864-4867-8
softcover : acid free paper ♾

1. Football — Awards — United States.
2. College football players — United States.
1. Title.
GV959.B54 2012 796.332'63 — dc23 2012020029

British Library cataloguing data are available

Cover art by Henry Alonzo "Lon" Keller (Wood River Gallery)

Manufactured in the United States of America

McFarland & Company, Inc., Publishers
Box 611, Jefferson, North Carolina 28640
www.mcfarlandpub.com

Contents

Preface

College Football Awards: All National and Conference Winners Through 2010 lists more than 575 awards and trophies presented to college football players and coaches across the United States each year. Three types of awards are highlighted in this book: (1) those that are level-specific (such as the NCAA Division I Lou Groza Award); (2) those for which all players and coaches are eligible (regardless of school location or conference, such as the Heisman Trophy); and (3) those that are conference-related (such as the Pacific-10 Conference Offensive Player of the Year Award).

This book focuses only on conferences and colleges that maintain football programs. It details the awards presented to players and coaches in the following levels of competition:

(1) Major Awards (generally open to all players and/or coaches)
(2) National Collegiate Athletic Association (NCAA) Division I — Football Bowl Subdivision (FBS)
(3) National Collegiate Athletic Association (NCAA) Division I — Football Championship Subdivision (FCS)
(4) National Collegiate Athletic Association (NCAA) Division II
(5) National Collegiate Athletic Association (NCAA) Division III
(6) National Association of Intercollegiate Athletics (NAIA)
(7) National Christian College Athletic Association (NCCAA)
(8) Community and junior college football championships, including:
    - California Community College Athletic Association (CCCAA)
    - National Junior College Athletic Association (NJCAA)
    - Northwest Athletic Association of Community Colleges (NWAACC)

Each section is divided into two parts: (1) the name and description of the award and (2) a listing of all past winners (through 2010). Listings include the year of the award, the winner's name, and his school.

The awards and listing of winners do not take into account some of the major football conference realignments announced in 2011. A school that participates in multiple football conferences is listed under each conference.

I do not provide a complete football-related history of each conference, a detailed listing of all schools that have joined or left each conference, or the success of each school within a particular conference. Also not included are any awards or trophies presented by each particular team to its own players, which would be outside the scope of this book. You'll find here a yearly listing of schools that have won their particular conference championship as well as a listing of award winners for each honor within the conference (such as Coach of the Year, Offensive Player of the Year, Defensive Player of the Year, etc).

The details of each award and the listing of winners have been provided by each sponsoring conference or organization.

Major Awards

Unlike the other chapters of this book, the awards and trophies presented in this section are all non-conference related and can be won by players across the country from any number of schools and conferences. This section includes the college football awards that are best-known by most college football fans, such as the Heisman Trophy.

Amos Alonzo Stagg Award

Sponsored by the American Football Coaches Association (100 Legends Drive, Waco, TX 76706; Telephone: 254-754-9900; Fax: 254-754-7373; http://www.afca.com), the Amos Alonzo Stagg Award is presented annually to an individual who has made outstanding contributions to college football. The award is named in honor of Amos Alonzo Stagg (born: August 16, 1862, in West Orange, NJ, died: March 17, 1965, in Stockton, CA), who was instrumental in founding the AFCA in the 1920s.

As a coach, Stagg is credited with some of college football's early innovations, including the tackling dummy, the huddle, the reverse play, man in motion, numbering plays and players, and the awarding of letters. According to National Collegiate Athletic Association information, his 57-year record as a college head coach was 314–199–35 (.573) while he coached at the School of Christian Workers (now known as Springfield College in Massachusetts); the University of Chicago (1892–1932 in Illinois, one of the longest tenures in the history of college football); and the College of the Pacific (now known as the University of the Pacific, from 1933 to 1946 in Stockton, CA).

As a student, he attended Yale University (New Haven, CT) and was named by Walter Camp to the first-ever All-American team in 1886 as an end for the school's team. At Springfield College, the center of his first team was James A. Naismith, who later founded/invented the game of basketball. Stagg was elected to the College Football Hall of Fame as both a player and a coach in the charter class of 1951 and his contributions to the early game of basketball eventually led to his induction in the charter class of the Naismith Memorial Basketball Hall of Fame in 1959. Additionally, the NCAA Division III Championship is decided in the Amos Alonzo Stagg Bowl.

The Amos Alonzo Stagg Award Committee presents the nominee to the Board of Trustees, which then endorses the winner.

Some of the more well-known winners of this award include Grantland Rice, Pop Warner, Eddie Robinson, Paul "Bear" Bryant, Woody Hayes, Keith Jackson (from ABC Television), Joe Paterno, Bill Walsh (more well-known as the coach of the National Football League's San Francisco 49ers), and John Gagliardi (college football's winningest coach).

Year	***Name***	***School*** *(or Other Identification)*
1940	Donald Herring, Jr.	Princeton University (NJ); player
1941	William H. Cowell	University of New Hampshire (NH)
1942	No Winner Named	
1943	No Winner Named	
1944	No Winner Named	
1945	No Winner Named	
1946	Grantland Rice	Sportswriter
1947	William A. Alexander	Georgia Institute of Technology (GA)
1948	Gilmour Dobie	North Dakota State University (ND) / University of Washington (WA) / United States Naval Academy (MD) / Cornell University (NY) / Boston College (MA)
1948	Glenn S. "Pop" Warner	University of Georgia (GA) / Cornell University (NY) / Carlisle Indian Industrial School (PA) / University of Pittsburgh (PA) / Stanford University (CA) / Temple University (PA)

Year	*Name*	***School** (or Other Identification)*
1948	Robert C. Zuppke	University of Illinois (IL)
1949	Richard C. Harlow	Pennsylvania State University (PA) / Colgate University (NY) / Western Maryland College (MD) / Harvard University (MA)
1950	No Winner Named	
1951	DeOrmond "Tuss" McLaughry	Westminster College (PA) / Amherst College (MA) / Brown University (RI) / Dartmouth College (NH)
1952	A.N. "Bo" McMillin	Centenary College of Louisiana (LA) / Geneva College (PA) / Kansas State University (KS) / Indiana University (IN)
1953	Lou Little	Georgetown University (Washington, D.C.) / Columbia University (NY)
1954	Dana X. Bible	Mississippi College (MS) / Louisiana State University (LA) / Texas A&M University (TX) / University of Nebraska (NE) / University of Texas at Austin (TX)
1955	Joseph J. Tomlin	Founder, Pop Warner Football
1956	No Winner Named	
1957	General Robert R. Neyland	University of Tennessee (TN)
1958	Bernie Bierman	University of Montana (MT) / Mississippi State University (MS) / Tulane University (LA) / University of Minnesota (MN)
1959	Dr. John W. Wilce	Ohio State University (OH)
1960	Harvey J. Harman	Haverford College (PA) / Sewanee: The University of the South (TN) / University of Pennsylvania (PA) / Rutgers, the State University of New Jersey (NJ)
1961	Ray Eliot	University of Illinois (IL)
1962	E.E. "Tad" Wieman	University of Michigan (MI) / Princeton University (NJ) / University of Maine (ME)
1963	Andrew Kerr	Stanford University (CA) / Washington & Jefferson College (PA) / Colgate University (NY) / Lebanon Valley College (PA)
1964	Don Faurot	University of Missouri (MO)
1965	Harry Stuhldreher	Villanova University (PA) / University of Wisconsin, Madison (WI)
1966	Bernie H. Moore	Mercer University (GA) / Louisiana State University (LA)
1967	Jess Neely	Rhodes College (TN) / Clemson University (SC) / Rice University (TX)
1968	Abe Martin	Texas Christian University (TX)
1969	Charles A. "Rip" Engle	Brown University (RI) / Pennsylvania State University (PA)
1970	Lynn "Pappy" Waldorf	Oklahoma A&M University (OK) / Kansas State University (KS) / Northwestern University (IL) / University of California, Berkeley (CA)
1971	Bill Murray	University of Delaware (DE) / Duke University (NC)
1972	Jack Curtice	West Texas A&M University (TX) / University of Texas, El Paso (TX) / University of Utah (UT) / Stanford University (CA) / University of California, Santa Barbara (CA)
1973	Lloyd Jordan	Amherst College (MA) / Harvard University (MA)
1974	Alonzo S. "Jake" Gaither	Florida A&M University (FL)
1975	Gerald B. Zornow	Business Executive
1976	No Winner Named	
1977	Floyd "Ben" Schwartzwalder	Muhlenberg College (PA) / Syracuse University (NY)
1978	Tom Hamilton	United States Naval Academy (MD) / University of Pittsburgh (PA)
1979	H.O. "Fritz" Crisler	University of Minnesota (MN) / Princeton University (NJ) / University of Michigan (MI)
1980	No Winner Named	
1981	Fred Russell	Sportswriter
1982	Eddie Robinson	Grambling State University (LA)
1983	Paul W. "Bear" Bryant	University of Maryland (MD) / University of Kentucky (KY) / Texas A&M University (TX) / University of Alabama (AL)
1984	Charles B. "Bud" Wilkinson	University of Oklahoma (OK)
1985	Duffy Daugherty	Michigan State University (MI)
1986	Woody Hayes	Denison University (OH) / Miami University (Ohio) / Ohio State University (OH)
1987	Field Scovell	Cotton Bowl Athletic Association
1988	G. Herbert McCracken	Allegheny College (PA) / Lafayette College (PA)

Year	*Name*	***School*** *(or Other Identification)*
1989	David Nelson	Hillsdale College (MI) / University of Maine (ME) / University of Delaware (DE)
1990	Len Casanova	Santa Clara University (CA) / University of Pittsburgh (PA) / University of Oregon (OR)
1991	Bob Blackman	Denver University (now known as the University of Denver) (CO) / Dartmouth College (NH) / University of Illinois (IL) / Cornell University (NY)
1992	Charles McClendon	Louisiana State University (LA)
1993	Keith Jackson	ABC-TV Announcer
1994	Bob Devaney	University of Wyoming (WY) / University of Nebraska, Lincoln (NE)
1995	John Merritt	Jackson State University (MS) / Tennessee State University (TN)
1996	Chuck Neinas	College Football Association Executive
1997	Ara Parseghian	Miami University (Ohio) / Northwestern University (IL) / University of Notre Dame (IN)
1998	Bob Reade	Augustana College (IL)
1999	Bo Schembechler	Miami University (Ohio) / University of Michigan (MI)
2000	Tom Osborne	University of Nebraska (NE)
2001	Vince Dooley	University of Georgia (GA)
2002	Joe Paterno	Pennsylvania State University (PA)
2003	LaVell Edwards	Brigham Young University (UT)
2004	Ron Schipper	Central College (IA)
2005	Hayden Fry	Southern Methodist University (TX) / North Texas State University (TX) / University of Iowa (IA)
2006	Grant Teaff	McMurry University (TX) / Angelo State University (TX) / Baylor University (TX)
2007	Bill Curry	Georgia Institute of Technology (GA) / University of Alabama (AL) / University of Kentucky (KY) / Georgia State University (GA)
2008	Bill Walsh	Stanford University (CA) / San Francisco 49ers (NFL)
2009	John Gagliardi	Carroll College (MT) / St. John's University (MN)
2010	Darrell Royal	University of Texas (TX)

Archie Griffin Award

The Archie Griffin Award, named after the only two-time Heisman Trophy winner (1974 and 1975) as of this writing, was first presented to Virginia Tech quarterback Michael Vick in 1999. It is one of the few college football awards presented after all bowl games are completed and recognizes college football's Most Valuable Player for the entire season. The trophy is presented by the Touchdown Club of Columbus (Ohio, http://www.touchdownclubof columbus.com) and some of the more well-known winners are Michael Vick, Matt Leinart, Vince Young, and Colt McCoy.

Sam B. Nicola (who died in 1993) founded the Touchdown Club of Columbus in 1956 and was president of the Athletic Club of Columbus when the initial All-Sports Banquet was held in January 1956. Although a local organization, its range has always been national (not limited to the Columbus, Ohio area) and athletes from all sports have been recognized. Honored athletes are selected by the appropriate Touchdown Club's committees, consisting of coaches, sportswriters, and former players.

Archie Mason Griffin (born: August 21, 1954 in Columbus, OH) was a running back for the Ohio State Buckeyes (Columbus, 1972–1975); helped the team win four consecutive Big Ten Conference titles; is the only running back to lead the Big Ten in rushing for three straight years; and was the first player to start in four Rose Bowls. Earlier, he had led Eastmoor High School (Ohio) to the Columbus City League championship as a senior and was later inducted into the High School Hall of Fame (1996).

Griffin is one of two players to win the Big 10 Most Valuable Player Award twice (1973–1974); named United Press International Player of the Year twice (1974–1975); Walter Camp Foundation Player of the Year twice (1974–1975); inducted into the College Football Hall of Fame (1986); inducted into the Rose Bowl Hall of Fame (1990); and was named one of ESPN's Top 25 players in College Football History (2007). In professional football, Griffin was a first-round draft pick (24th overall selection) in the National Football League of the Cincinnati Bengals in 1976; played in Super Bowl XVI in 1982 (losing 26–21 to the San Francisco 49ers); and played for the Jacksonville Bulls of the United States Football League.

As of this writing, only Ken Dorsey (University of Miami) and Matt Leinart (University of Southern California) have won this award multiple times.

Year	*Player*	*School*	*Note*
1999	Michael Vick	Virginia Tech University (VA)	NFL First-Round Draft Pick
2000	Josh Heupel	University of Oklahoma (OK)	2000 NCAA Quarterback of the Year
2001	Ken Dorsey	University of Miami (FL)	2001 NCAA National Championship
2002	Ken Dorsey	University of Miami (FL)	Two-Time NCAA Quarterback of the Year
2003	Matt Leinart	University of Southern California (CA)	Two-Time Quarterback of the Year
2004	Matt Leinart	University of Southern California (CA)	2004 BCS National Championship
2005	Vince Young	University of Texas (TX)	First-Round NFL Draft Pick
2006	Troy Smith	Ohio State University (OH)	2006 Heisman Trophy Winner
2007	Pat White	West Virginia University (WV)	NCAA QB Rushing Leader, 4,385 Yards
2008	Colt McCoy	University of Texas (TX)	2008 Big 12 Offensive Player of the Year
2009	Toby Gerhart	Stanford University (CA)	2009 Jim Brown Trophy Winner
2010	Andrew Luck	Stanford University (CA)	2010 Pac 10 Offensive Player of the Year

Associated Press College Football Coach of the Year Award

Address: 450 West 33rd Street, New York, NY 10001; Telephone: 212-621-1500; Web site: http://www.ap.org

Since 1998, the Associated Press College Football Coach of the Year Award has been presented annually to the top NCAA college football coach. The award is determined by the Associated Press voters who participate in the weekly college football AP Poll.

Year	*Coach*	*School*
1998	Bill Snyder	Kansas State University (KS)
1999	Frank Beamer	Virginia Polytechnic Institute and State University (VA)
2000	Bob Stoops	University of Oklahoma (OK)
2001	Ralph Friedgen	University of Maryland (MD)
2002	Kirk Ferentz	University of Iowa (IA)
2003	Nick Saban	Louisiana State University (LA)
2004	Tommy Tuberville	Auburn University (AL)
2005	Joe Paterno	Pennsylvania State University (PA)
2006	Jim Grobe	Wake Forest University (NC)
2007	Mark Mangino	University of Kansas (KS)
2008	Nick Saban	University of Alabama (AL)
2009	Gary Patterson	Texas Christian University (TX)
2010	Chip Kelly	University of Oregon (OR)

Associated Press College Football Player of the Year Award

Address: 450 West 33rd Street, New York, NY 10001; Telephone: 212-621-1500; Web site: http://www.ap.org

The Associated Press College Football Player of the Year Award has been presented annually since 1998 to the most outstanding NCAA collegiate football player. The winner is chosen by a vote of AP sportswriters and sports editors throughout the country.

Year	*Player*	*School*	*Note*
1998	Ricky Williams	University of Texas (TX)	1998 Hiesman Trophy Winner
1999	Ron Dayne	University of Wisconsin (WI)	1999 Hesiman Trophy Winner
2000	Josh Heupel	University of Oklahoma (OK)	2000 NCAA Quarterback of the Year
2001	Rex Grossman	University of Florida (FL)	2001 AP National Player of the Year
2002	Brad Banks	University of Iowa (IA)	2002 Big Ten Player of the Year
2003	Jason White	University of Oklahoma (OK)	2003 Hesiman Trophy Winner
2004	Matt Leinart	University of Southern California (CA)	2004 Heisman Trophy Winner
2005	Reggie Bush	University of Southern California (CA)	2005 Heisman Trophy Winner
2006	Troy Smith	Ohio State University (OH)	2006 Heisman Trophy Winner
2007	Tim Tebow	University of Florida (FL)	2007 Heisman Trophy Winner
2008	Sam Bradford	University of Oklahoma (OK)	2008 Heisman Trophy Winner
2009	Ndamukong Suh	University of Nebraska (NE)	2009 Outland Trophy Winner
2010	Cameron Newton	Auburn University (AL)	2010 Heisman Trophy Winner

Associated Press National Championship Trophy

Address: 450 West 33rd Street, New York, NY 10001; Telephone: 212-621-1500; Web site: http://www.ap.org

Presented since 1936, the Associated Press National Championship Trophy is awarded annually by the AP to the team that finishes the season at the number one spot in the organization's poll. The trophy consists of a silver or gold football mounted on a base that has the letters "AP" (Associated Press), along with the information on the team that won the award that particular season.

This trophy does not reflect the winner of the annual Bowl Championship Series and can be awarded to a team that does not win the BCS National Championship Game. This last happened in the 2003 season when Louisiana State University won the BCS title game, but the University of Southern California received a higher total of votes in the AP Poll, and won the Trophy.

Year	*School*
1936	University of Minnesota (MN)
1937	University of Pittsburgh (PA)
1938	Texas Christian University (TX)
1939	Texas A&M University (TX)
1940	University of Minnesota (MN)
1941	University of Minnesota (MN)
1942	Ohio State University (OH)
1943	University of Notre Dame (IN)
1944	United States Military Academy (NY)
1945	United States Military Academy (NY)
1946	University of Notre Dame (IN)
1947	University of Notre Dame (IN)
1948	University of Michigan (MI)
1949	University of Notre Dame (IN)
1950	University of Oklahoma (OK)
1951	University of Tennessee (TN)
1952	Michigan State University (MI)
1953	University of Maryland (MD)
1954	Ohio State University (OH)
1954	University California, Los Angeles (CA)
1955	University of Oklahoma (OK)
1956	University of Oklahoma (OK)
1957	Auburn University (AL)
1958	Louisiana State University (LA)
1959	Syracuse University (NY)
1960	University of Minnesota (MN)
1961	University of Alabama (AL)
1962	University of Southern California (CA)
1963	University of Texas (TX)
1964	University of Alabama (AL)
1965	University of Alabama (AL)
1966	University of Notre Dame (IN)
1967	University of Southern California (CA)
1968	Ohio State University (OH)
1969	University of Texas (TX)
1970	University of Nebraska (NE)
1971	University of Nebraska (NE)
1972	University of Southern California (CA)
1973	University of Notre Dame (IN)
1974	University of Oklahoma (OK)
1975	University of Oklahoma (OK)
1976	University of Pittsburgh (PA)
1977	University of Notre Dame (IN)
1978	University of Alabama (AL)
1979	University of Alabama (AL)
1980	University of Georgia (GA)
1981	Clemson University (SC)
1982	Pennsylvania State University (PA)
1983	University of Miami (FL)
1984	Brigham Young University (UT)
1985	University of Oklahoma (OK)
1986	Pennsylvania State University (PA)
1987	University of Miami (FL)
1988	University of Notre Dame (IN)
1989	University of Miami (FL)
1990	University of Colorado (CO)
1991	University of Miami (FL)
1992	University of Alabama (AL)
1993	Florida State University (FL)
1994	University of Nebraska (NE)
1995	University of Nebraska (NE)
1996	University of Florida (FL)
1997	University of Michigan (MI)
1998	University of Tennessee (TN)
1999	Florida State University (FL)
2000	University of Oklahoma (OK)
2001	University of Miami (FL)
2002	Ohio State University (OH)
2003	University of Southern California (CA)
2004	University of Southern California (CA)
2005	University of Texas (TX)
2006	University of Florida (FL)
2007	Louisiana State University (LA)
2008	University of Florida (FL)
2009	University of Alabama (AL)
2010	Auburn University (AL)

AT&T ESPN All-America Player of the Year

Awarded since 2004, the AT&T ESPN All-America Player is a weekly and annual award given to college football's player of the week and player of the year. The award was previously known as the Cingular All-America Player before AT&T acquired Cingular. The winners are decided from cellular telephone polls conducted jointly by AT&T and ESPN.

Year	Player	School	Note
2004	Cedric Benson	University of Texas (TX)	2004 Doak Walker Award Winner
2005	Vince Young	University of Texas (TX)	2005 Manning Award Winner
2006	Brady Quinn	University of Notre Dame (IN)	2006 Johnny Unitas Golden Arm Award
2007	Michael Crabtree	Texas Tech University (TX)	Two-Time All-American
2008	Graham Harrell	Texas Tech University (TX)	2008 Johnny Unitas Golden Arm Award
2009	Colt McCoy	University of Texas (TX)	2009 Johnny Unitas Golden Arm Award
2010	LaMichael James	University of Oregon (OR)	2010 Doak Walker Award

Best College Football Player ESPY Award

Awarded by the Touchdown Club of Columbus (Ohio, http://www.touchdownclubofcolumbus.com), the Best College Football Player ESPY Award was presented annually between 1993 and 2001 to the collegiate American football player voted to be the best in the United States. The award was superseded in 2002 by the Best Male College Athlete ESPY Award.

Sam B. Nicola (who died in 1993) founded the Touchdown Club of Columbus in 1956 and was president of the Athletic Club of Columbus when the initial All-Sports Banquet was held in January 1956. Although a local organization, its range has always been national (not limited to the Columbus, Ohio area) and athletes from all sports have been recognized. Honored athletes are selected by fans and the appropriate Touchdown Club's committees, consisting of coaches, sportswriters, and former players, as well as various ESPN personalities selected by the ESPN Select Nominating Committee.

Year	Player	School	Note
1993	Garrison Hearst	University of Georgia (GA)	Led nation in touchdowns (21) as a junior
1994	Charlie Ward	Florida State University (FL)	2006 College Football Hall of Fame inductee
1995	Rashaan Salaam	University of Colorado (CO)	1994 Heisman Trophy Winner
1996	Eddie George	Ohio State University (OH)	1995 Heisman Trophy Winner
1997	Danny Wuerffel	University of Florida (FL)	1996 Heisman Trophy Winner
1998	Peyton Manning	University of Tennessee (TN)	Super Bowl XLVI Most Valuable Player
1999	Ricky Williams	University of Texas (TX)	1998 Heisman Trophy Winner
2000	Michael Vick	Virginia Tech University (VA)	1999 Big Eight Rookie of the Year
2001	Chris Weinke	Florida State University (FL)	2000 Heisman Trophy Winner

Best Male College Athlete ESPY Award

Replacing the Best College Football Player ESPY Award, the Best Male College Athlete ESPY Award has been presented annually (since 2002) to the best National Collegiate Athletic Association male college athlete of the year. This award also replaces the Best Male College Basketball Player ESPY Award (awarded through 2004).

Year	Winner	School	Note
2002	Non Football Winner		
2003	Non Football Winner		
2004	Non Football Winner		
2005	Matt Leinart	University of Southern California (CA)	2004 Heisman Trophy Winner
2006	Reggie Bush	University of Southern California (CA)	2005 Heisman Trophy Winner
2007	Non Football Winner		
2008	Tim Tebow	University of Florida (FL)	2007 Heisman Trophy Winner
2009	Tim Tebow	University of Florida (FL)	2008 SEC Offensive Player of the Year
2010	Non Football Winner		

Bill Willis Trophy

Presented by the Touchdown Club of Columbus (Ohio, http://www.touchdownclubofcolumbus.com) since 1991, the Bill Willis Trophy is presented annually to college football's best defensive lineman.

Sam B. Nicola (who died in 1993) founded the Touchdown Club of Columbus in 1956 and was president of the Athletic Club of Columbus when the initial All-Sports Banquet was held in January

1956. Although a local organization, its range has always been national (not limited to the Columbus, Ohio area) and athletes from all sports have been recognized. Honored athletes are selected by fans and the appropriate Touchdown Club's committees, consisting of coaches, sportswriters, and former players.

An Ohio State University football player, Willis (born: October 5, 1921 in Columbus, OH, died: November 27, 2007, in Columbus, OH) was the first lineman and first defensive player to have his jersey number (99) retired at Ohio Stadium (November 3, 2007). A Buckeye lineman from 1942 to 1944, Willis (6'2", 215 pounds) was a three-year starter on both offense and defense; earned All-America honors in 1943 and 1944 (Ohio State's first African American player to do so); and was part of the school's 1942 national championship team. After college, Willis played eight years (1946–1953) in the All-America Football Conference for the Cleveland Browns and is widely considered to be the first African American starter in professional football.

He was inducted into the College Football Hall of Fame in 1971 and into the Pro Football Hall of Fame in 1977.

Year	*Player*	*School*	*Note*
1991	Steve Emtman	University of Washington (WA)	Elected to College Football Hall of Fame in 2006
1992	Michael Barrow	University of Miami (FL)	Played in the National Football League for 13 years
1993	Dan Wilkinson	Ohio State University (OH)	Number One draft pick in the NFL
1994	Warren Sapp	University of Miami (FL)	Won Super Bowl XXXVII
1995	Tedy Bruschi	University of Arizona (AZ)	Played in 13 NFL seasons
1996	Grant Wistrom	University of Nebraska (NE)	Elected to College Football Hall of Fame in 2009
1997	Andre Wadsworth	Florida State University (FL)	NFL First-Round Draft Pick in 1998
1998	Tom Burke	University of Wisconsin (WI)	1998 All-American
1999	Corey Moore	Virginia Tech University (VA)	1999 All-American
2000	Jamal Reynolds	Florida State University (FL)	First-Round NFL Draft Pick
2001	Julius Peppers	University of North Carolina (NC)	2002 NFL Defensive Rookie of the Year
2002	Terrell Suggs	Arizona State University (AZ)	2003 NFL Defensive Rookie of the Year
2003	Tommie Harris	University of Oklahoma (OK)	2003 Lombardi Award Winner
2004	Erasmus James	University of Wisconsin (WI)	2004 All-American
2005	Elvis Dumervil	University of Louisville (KY)	2005 Big East Defensive Player of the Year
2006	Quinn Pitcock	Ohio State University (OH)	2006 All-American
2007	George Selvie	University of South Florida (FL)	2007 Big East Defensive Player of the Year
2008	Brian Orakpo	University of Texas (TX)	2008 Big 12 Defensive Player of the Year
2009	Ndamukong Suh	University of Nebraska (NE)	2009 AP Player of the Year
2010	Ryan Kerrigan	Purdue University (IN)	2010 Big Ten Defensive Player of the Year

Bobby Dodd Coach of the Year Award

Address: Bobby Dodd Coach of the Year Foundation, P.O. Box 15908, Chattanooga, TN 37415; Telephone: 423-875-5868; Fax: 423-875-6573; Email: info@bobbydoddfoundation.com; Web site: http://www.bobbydoddfoundation.com

The Bobby Dodd Coach of the Year Award is presented annually by the Bobby Dodd Coach of the Year Foundation to the NCAA FBS head coach whose team excels on the field, in the classroom, and in the community. The award was established in 1976 to honor the values that Coach Dodd exemplified and recipients are chosen by a selection committee composed of college football experts and all previous recipients. As of this writing, the winner of the award is announced during half-time of the Chick-fil-A Bowl on Dec. 31 in Atlanta, Georgia.

Bobby Dodd (Robert Lee Dodd, born on November 11, 1908 in Galax, VA, and died on June 21, 1988, in Atlanta, GA) played college football at the University of Tennessee (Knoxville, quarterback, 1928–1930) and began his coaching career with Georgia Tech (Atlanta, GA) as an assistant in 1931. After 14 years under coach William A. Alexander, Dodd replaced him in 1945 and over the next 22 seasons, led the Yellow Jackets to a 165–64–8 record (.696). Later, he was inducted into the Georgia Sports Hall of Fame (1965), the Tennessee Sports Hall of Fame (1966), and the College Football Hall of Fame (1993).

As of this writing, Pennsylvania State University's Joe Paterno is the only coach to receive this award twice (1981, 2005).

Year	*Coach*	*School*	*Note*
1976	Vince Dooley	University of Georgia (GA)	1994 College Football Hall of Fame
1977	Bo Schembechler	University of Michigan (MI)	1993 College Football Hall of Fame
1978	Tom Osborne	University of Nebraska (NE)	1999 College Football Hall of Fame
1979	LaVell Edwards	Brigham Young University (UT)	2004 College Football Hall of Fame
1980	Bobby Bowden	Florida State University (FL)	2006 College Football Hall of Fame
1981	Joe Paterno	Penn State University (PA)	2007 College Football Hall of Fame
1982	George MacIntyre	Vanderbilt University (TN)	Lost 1982 Hall of Fame Bowl
1983	Ken Hatfield	United States Air Force Academy (CO)	Played on 11–0 1964 Arkansas Team
1984	Jim Wacker	Texas Christian University (TX)	Lost 1984 Bluebonnet Bowl
1985	Fisher DeBerry	United States Air Force Academy (CO)	South Carolina Sports Hall of Fame
1986	Dick Sheridan	North Carolina State (NC)	1985 Division 1-AA Coach of the Year
1987	Dick MacPherson	Syracuse University (NY)	2009 College Football Hall of Fame
1988	Don Nehlen	West Virginia University (WV)	2005 College Football Hall of Fame
1989	Bill Curry	University of Alabama (AL)	1989 SEC Coach of the Year
1990	Bobby Ross	Georgia Institute of Technology (GA)	Lost Super Bowl XXIX (1995)
1991	George Welsh	University of Virginia (VA)	2004 College Football Hall of Fame
1992	Eddie Robinson	Grambling State University (LA)	1997 College Football Hall of Fame
1993	Barry Alvarez	University of Wisconsin-Madison (WI)	Winningest Coach in School History
1994	Fred Goldsmith	Duke University (NC)	1992 Sports Illustrated Coach of the Year
1995	Gary Barnett	Northwestern University (IL)	Two-Time Big Ten Coach of the Year
1996	Bob Sutton	United States Military Academy (NY)	Ranked 24th in the country in 1996
1997	Mike Price	Washington State University (WA)	Lost the 2003 Rose Bowl
1998	Bill Snyder	Kansas State University (KS)	Won the 1993 Copper Bowl
1999	Frank Beamer	Virginia Tech (VA)	Made 16 Consecutive Bowl Appearances
2000	George O'Leary	Georgia Institute of Technology (GA)	Two-Time ACC Coach of the Year
2001	Ralph Friedgen	University of Maryland (MD)	Made Six Bowl Appearances
2002	Jim Tressel	Ohio State University (OH)	2002 National Championship
2003	Bob Stoops	University of Oklahoma (OK)	2000 National Championship
2004	Paul Johnson	United States Naval Academy (MD)	Won the 2005 Poinsettia Bowl
2005	Joe Paterno	Penn State University (PA)	Two-Time NCAA Championship
2006	Jim Grobe	Wake Forest University (NC)	2006 ACC Coach of the Year
2007	Lloyd Carr	University of Michigan (MI)	1997 AP National Champion
2008	Mack Brown	University of Texas(TX)	2005 1-A National Champion
2009	Gary Patterson	Texas Christian University (TX)	2009 Eddie Robinson Coach of the Year
2010	Chris Petersen	Boise State University (ID)	2008 & 2009 Paul "Bear" Bryant Award

Bronko Nagurski Award

Since 1993, the non-profit Charlotte Touchdown Club (7725 Ballantyne Commons Parkway, Suite 103, Charlotte, NC 28277; Telephone: 704-347-2918; Fax: 704-362-0411; Email: jrocco@touchdownclub.com; Web site: http://www.touchdownclub.com) has presented the annual Bronko Nagurski Award to the nation's best National Collegiate Athletic Association defensive player, as voted on by the Football Writers Association of America and about 850 members of various print and Internet media outlets.

The award is named after the 6'2", 226-pound Bronko Nagurski (born: November 3, 1908, in Rainy River, Ontario, Canada; died: January 7, 1990, in International Falls, MN), who played football for the University of Minnesota (Twin Cities, 1927–1929) and for nine seasons with the National Football League's Chicago Bears (1930–1937, 1943). He was inducted into the College Football Hall of Fame in 1951 and into the Pro Football Hall of Fame in 1963.

As of this writing, Pat Fitzgerald (linebacker from Northwestern University in Evanston/Chicago, Illinois) is the only two-time winner of this award (1995–1996).

Year	*Winner*	*School*	*Note*
1993	Rob Waldrop	University of Arizona (AZ)	1993 UPI Lineman of the Year
1994	Warren Sapp	University of Miami (FL)	1994 Lombardi Award Winner
1995	Pat Fitzgerald	Northwestern University (IL)	2008 College Football Hall of Fame
1996	Pat Fitzgerald	Northwestern University (IL)	1995 Chuck Bednarik Award Winner
1997	Charles Woodson	University of Michigan (MI)	1997 Heisman Trophy Award Winner

Year	*Winner*	*School*	*Note*
1998	Champ Bailey	University of Georgia (GA)	Won the 1998 Peach Bowl
1999	Corey Moore	Virginia Tech University (VA)	1999 Lombardi Award Winner
2000	Dan Morgan	University of Miami (FL)	2000 Dick Butkus Award Winner
2001	Roy Williams	University of Oklahoma (OK)	2001 Jim Thorpe Award Winner
2002	Terrell Suggs	Arizona State University (AZ)	2002 Lombardi Award Winner
2003	Derrick Strait	University of Oklahoma (OK)	2003 Jim Thorpe Award Winner
2004	Derrick Johnson	University of Texas (TX)	2004 Dick Butkus Award Winner
2005	Elvis Dumervil	University of Louisville (KY)	2005 Bill Willis Award Winner
2006	James Laurinaitis	Ohio State University (OH)	2007 Dick Butkus Award Winner
2007	Glenn Dorsey	Louisiana State University (LA)	2007 Outland Trophy Winner
2008	Brian Orakpo	University of Texas (TX)	2008 Lombardi Award Winner
2009	Ndamukong Suh	University of Nebraska (NE)	2009 Outland Trophy Winner
2010	Da'Quan Bowers	Clemson University (SC)	2010 ACC Defensive Player of the Year

Broyles Assistant Coach of the Year Award

The Broyles Award (more often known as the Broyles Assistant Coach of the Year Award) is presented annually to the best assistant coach in college football. First awarded in 1996, it is named after former University of Arkansas men's athletic director Frank Broyles and is presented by the Downtown Rotary Club in Little Rock, Arkansas (1501 North University Avenue, Little Rock, AR 72207; Telephone: 501-663-0063; Web site: http://www.broylesaward.com).

Each year, approximately 1,500 assistant coaches (representing all Division One college football programs) vote and the top five Broyles Award finalists are chosen from these ballots. Each head coach can nominate one assistant coach from his staff and all nominations are reviewed by a selection committee composed of former head coaches. The five finalists receive $1,000.00 and the winner receives $2,500.00 and the trophy.

John Franklin "Frank" Broyles (born: December 26, 1924, in Decatur, Georgia) is a former American football player and coach, athletics administrator, and broadcaster. He served as the head football coach at the University of Missouri (Columbia, MO) in 1957 and at the University of Arkansas (Fayetteville, AR) from 1958 to 1976. He also served as Arkansas' athletic director from 1974 until 2007; won a college national title in 1964; and was inducted into the College Football Hall of Fame in 1983.

As a head coach, he compiled an overall 149–62–6 record (.687) and his 144–58–5 record (.696) in 19 seasons at Arkansas makes him the winningest coach in Razorbacks history. Broyles was later a color commentator for nine years with the ABC network and worked with college football announcers Chris Schenkel and Keith Jackson.

Year	*Coach*	*School*	*Note*
1996	Mickey Andrews	Florida State University (FL)	1994 West Alabama Hall of Fame
1997	Jim Herrmann	University of Michigan (MI)	Coach for the NFL's New York Giants
1998	David Cutcliffe	University of Tennessee (TN)	2003 SEC Coach of the Year (Ole Miss)
1999	Ralph Friedgen	Georgia Tech Institute (GA)	Coached with the NFL's San Diego Chargers
2000	Mark Mangino	University of Oklahoma (OK)	2007 AP National Coach of the Year (Kansas)
2001	Randy Shannon	University of Miami (FL)	University of Miami Head Coach
2002	Norm Chow	University of Southern California (CA)	1999 AFA Assistant Coach of the Year
2003	Brian VanGorder	University of Georgia (GA)	Currently coaches in the NFL
2004	Gene Chizik	Auburn University (AL)	Head Coach at Auburn (2008–Present)
2005	Greg Davis	University of Texas (TX)	Helped Coach the 2005 National Champions
2006	Bud Foster	Virginia Polytech Institute (VA)	Helped Coach Three ACC Champions
2007	Jim Heacock	Ohio State University (OH)	Also Coached at the University of Washington
2008	Kevin Wilson	University of Oklahoma (OK)	2008 Offensive Coordinator of the Year
2009	Kirby Smart	University of Alabama (AL)	1st Alabama Assistant to Win This Award
2010	Gus Malzahn	Auburn University (AL)	2006 National Offensive Coordinator of the Year

Buck Buchanan Award *see* NCAA — I — Football Championship Subdivision

Burlsworth Trophy

First presented in 2010, the Burlsworth Trophy is awarded to the most outstanding college football player who began his career as a walk-on and is presented by the Rotary Club of Springdale, Arkansas (http://www.springdale rotary.org).

The mission of the Brandon Burlsworth Foundation (117 West Central Avenue, Harrison, AR 72601; Telephone: 866-534-2875, 870-741-1443; Fax: 870-741-0094; Web site: http://burlsworthtrophy.com/) is to support the physical and spiritual needs of children, especially those who have limited opportunities.

The award is named for Brandon Burlsworth, a walk-on at the University of Arkansas (Fayetteville) in 1994 after receiving no Division 1 scholarship offers. He eventually earned a football scholarship; became team captain; named All-SEC twice (1997–1998), was First Team All-SEC (1998); and was the first All-American from the University of Arkansas in a decade.

Eleven days after being drafted by the Indianapolis Colts as the 63rd overall pick in the 1999 NFL draft, he was killed in a car accident near Alpena, Arkansas.

In 2010, the Burlsworth Trophy was created to honor the achievements and successes of the Walk-On athlete, defined as a player who begins his football career with no financial assistance or aid of any kind from his university's athletic department. Nominees are limited to players from universities in the Division I Football Bowl Subdivision (FBS) of the National Collegiate Athletic Association (NCAA) who must have completed their first entire season of active participation as a member of the football team without financial assistance of any kind from the university's athletic department. Players will be eligible if they have received financial support from the athletic department of a school from a division lower than FBS before transferring to an FBS school.

Year	*Player*	*Position*	*School*	*Notes*
2010	Sean Bedford	Center	Georgia Tech	2009 First Team All-ACC

Bulger Lowe Award

Since 1939, the Bulger Lowe Award (sometimes referred to as "New England's Heisman Trophy") has been presented each season by the Gridiron Club of Greater Boston (9 Broadway, Unit 320, Saugus, MA 01906; Web site: http://www.gridclubofgreaterboston.com/) to the best Division I FBS / FCS player in the New England area, and in 1982, the award was divided into both offensive and defensive categories. Founded in 1932, the Gridiron Club promotes the game of football and honors players, coaches, and officials at all levels.

The George H. "Bulger" Lowe Award (Bulger Lowe Award) is the second-oldest honor of its kind after the Heisman Trophy and is named after George Henry "Bulger" Lowe Jr., a military hero who died at age 43. His football career began in 1909 as a 14-year-old guard at Arlington High School; he later captained the team as a senior, and went on to captain teams at Phillips Exeter Academy (Exeter, NH), Lafayette College (Easton, PA), and Fordham University (New York, NY). He was later awarded the Croix de Guerre for service with the Ambulance Corps in 1917.

Year	*Winner*	*School*	*Note*
1939	Gene Goodreault	Boston College (MA)	College Football Hall of Fame, 1982
1940	Charlie O'Rourke	Boston College (MA)	College Football Hall of Fame, 1972
1941	Endicott "Chub" Peabody	Harvard College (MA)	Governor of Massachusetts (1963–1965)
1942	Mike Holovak	Boston College (MA)	College Football Hall of Fame, 1985
1943	George Connor	College of the Holy Cross (MA)	College Football Hall of Fame, 1963
1944	Paul Walker	Yale University (CT)	1944 All-American
1945	Stan Kozlowski	College of the Holy Cross (MA)	Played One Season in the NFL
1946	Levi Jackson	Yale University (CT)	First African American Team Captain
1947	Bob Sullivan	College of the Holy Cross (MA)	Holy Cross Hall of Fame, 1973
1948	Joe Sullivan	Dartmouth College (NH)	Record for Interception Return Yards, 212
1949	John Clayton	Dartmouth College (NH)	Threw 26 Total Touchdowns
1950	Bob Spears	Yale University (CT)	1951 Team Captain
1951	Harry Agganis	Boston University (MA)	College Football Hall of Fame, 1974
1952	Charles Malloy	College of the Holy Cross (MA)	1969 Holy Cross Hall of Fame Inductee

Year	*Winner*	*School*	*Note*
1953	Dick Clasby	Harvard University (MA)	Longest Run From Scrimmage, 96 Yards
1954	Sam Pino	Boston University (MA)	Boston University Hall of Fame, 1974
1955	Charles Sticka	Trinity College (CT)	5th All-Time School Rushing, 2,292 Yards
1956	Dennis McGill	Yale University (CT)	1956 All Ivy First Team
1957	Joseph Palermo	Dartmouth College (NH)	1957 All Ivy First-Team
1958	Frank Finney	Brown University (RI)	1950s Brown University All-Decade Team
1959	Chet Boulris	Harvard University (MA)	Harvard Varsity Club Hall of Fame
1960	Tom Singleton	Yale University (CT)	2X All-Ivy (1959–1960)
1961	Pat McCarthy	College of the Holy Cross (MA)	1971 Holy Cross Hall of Fame Inductee
1962	Don McKinnon	Dartmouth College (NH)	1962 All-Ivy First-Team
1963	Jack Concannon	Boston College (MA)	First Selection in 1964 AFL Draft
1964	Jerry Whelchel	University of Massachusetts (MA)	UMass Athletic Hall of Fame, 2005
1965	Robert Hall	Brown University (RI)	Member Brown University 125th Anniversary Team
1966	Bobby Leo	Harvard University (MA)	2X All-Ivy (1965–1966)
1967	Greg Landry	University of Massachusetts (MA)	All-Yankee Conference (1967–1968)
1968	Brian Dowling	Yale University (CT)	Nils V. "Swede" Nelson Award, 1967
1969	Bruce Taylor	Boston University (MA)	College Football Hall of Fame, 1997
1970	Fred Willis	Boston College (MA)	Played Six Seasons in the NFL
1971	Bruce Laird	American International College (MA)	Played in 12 NFL Seasons
1972	Dick Jauron	Yale University (CT)	3X All-Ivy League First-Team
1973	Mike Esposito	Boston College (MA)	BC Varsity Club Athletic Hall of Fame, 1980
1974	Pat McInally	Harvard University (MA)	5th Round NFL Draft Pick
1975	Mike Kruczek	Boston College (MA)	1975 All-American
1976	Tim Whelan	Tufts University (MA)	2nd in School Rushing Yards, 2,617
1977	William Burnham	University of New Hampshire (NH)	2nd in School Rushing Yards, 3,773
1978	Dan Ross	Northeastern University (MA)	College Football Hall of Fame, 2004
1979	Mal Najarian	Boston University (MA)	1st Team Player to Rush > 1,000 Yards
1980	Jim Budness	Boston College (MA)	1980 Team Captain
1981	Rich Diana	Yale University (CT)	Played One Season in the NFL
1982	Doug Flutie	Boston College (MA)	11th Round NFL Draft Choice
1982	Garry Pearson	University of Massachusetts (MA)	Led NCAA in Kickoff Return Avg Yards, 1979
1983	Joseph Azelby	Harvard University (MA)	1984 Team Captain
1983	Brian Brennan	Boston College (MA)	Played in Nine NFL Seasons
1984	Mike Ruth	Boston College (MA)	Recorded 102 Tackles in 1984
1984	Doug Flutie	Boston College (MA)	1984 Heisman Trophy Winner
1985	Mike Ruth	Boston College (MA)	Only BC Player to Win the Outland Trophy, 1985
1985	Tom Ehrhardt	University of Rhode Island (RI)	Played in the NFL for the New York Jets
1986	John Bosa	Boston College (MA)	1st Round NFL Draft Choice
1986	Gordie Lockbaum	College of the Holy Cross (MA)	2X All-American (1986–1987)
1987	Bill Romanowski	Boston College (MA)	Played 16 Seasons in the NFL
1987	Gordie Lockbaum	College of the Holy Cross (MA)	College Football Hall of Fame, 2001
1988	Robert McGovern	College of the Holy Cross (MA)	Played Four Seasons in the NFL
1988	Dave Palazzi	University of Massachusetts (MA)	2nd in Career Total School Offense, 6,728 Yards
1989	Mike Buck	University of Maine (ME)	Played Five NFL Seasons
1989	Dave Murphy	College of the Holy Cross (MA)	4X Team Interception Leader (1986–1989)
1990	Matt Kelley	Boston College (MA)	1989 New England All-Star
1990	Matt DeGennaro	University of Connecticut (CT)	Set School Record for Total Offense
1991	Tom Ciaccio	College of the Holy Cross (MA)	2001 Holy Cross Hall of Fame Inductee
1991	Tom McManus	Boston College (MA)	Played Five Years in the NFL
1992	Charlie Brennan	Boston College (MA)	1991 New England All-Star
1992	Chuckie Dukes	Boston College (MA)	School Record 1,387 Rushing Yards in 1992
1993	Stephen Boyd	Boston College (MA)	1994 ECAC Player of the Year
1993	Rob Dougherty	Boston University (MA)	2000 Boston University Hall of Fame Inductee
1993	Glenn Foley	Boston College (MA)	Won 1993 Blockbuster Bowl
1994	Pete Mitchell	Boston College (MA)	2X All-American
1994	Rob Dougherty	Boston University (MA)	Boston University 2000 Hall of Fame Inductee

Year	*Winner*	*School*	*Note*
1994	Mike Mamula	Boston College (MA)	1994 All-Big East Selection
1995	Mike Foley	University of New Hampshire (NH)	2003 UNH Hall of Fame Inductee
1995	Rene Ingoglia	University of Massachusetts (MA)	2007 UMass Hall of Fame Inductee
1996	Stalin Colinet	Boston College (MA)	Played Six NFL Seasons
1996	Chris Bresnahan	University of New Hampshire (NH)	4,085 School Career Passing Yards
1997	Jim Murphy	Northeastern University (MA)	2003 Northeastern University Hall of Fame
1997	Eric Storz	Boston College (MA)	Played Three NFL Seasons
1998	Kahri Samuel	University of Massachusetts (MA)	Played Three NFL Seasons
1998	Jerry Azumah	University of New Hampshire (NH)	Had Four 1-A Rushing 1,000 Seasons
1999	James Perry	Brown University (RI)	3X First-Team All-Ivy League Section
1999	Chris Hovan	Boston College (MA)	3X All-Big East
2000	Kole Ayi	University of Massachusetts (MA)	Played Two NFL Seasons
2000	Stephen Campbell	Brown University (RI)	2X All-American (1999–2000)
2001	Scott Bradley	Boston College (MA)	2001 Scanlan Award Winner
2001	Neil Rose	Harvard University (MA)	2001 All-Ivy Selection
2002	Derrick Knight	Boston College (MA)	BC's All-Time Leading Rusher
2002	Stephen Cooper	University of Maine (ME)	2002 Atlantic-10 Defensive Player of the Year
2003	Derrick Knight	Boston College (MA)	2003 Big East Rushing Leader
2003	Dante Balestracci	Harvard University (MA)	4X All-Ivy Selection
2004	Liam Ezekiel	Northeastern University (MA)	2X First-Team All-American (2003–2004)
2004	Ryan Fitzpatrick	Harvard University (MA)	7th-Round NFL Draft Pick
2005	Mathias Kiwanuka	Boston College (MA)	2004 Big East Defensive Player of the Year
2005	Ricky Santos	University of New Hampshire (NH)	2006 Walter Payton Award Winner
2006	David Ball	University of New Hampshire (NH)	Holds 1-AA Record for Touchdown Receptions (58)
2006	DeJuan Tribble	Boston College (MA)	2008 6th-Round NFL Draft Choice
2007	Matt Ryan	Boston College (MA)	2007 ACC Player of the Year
2007	Jamie Silva	Boston College (MA)	2007 First-Team All-American
2008	Bobby Abare	Yale University (CT)	2008 First-Team All-American
2008	Dominic Randolph	College of the Holy Cross (MA)	2009 ECAC Player of the Year
2008	Mark Herzlich	Boston College (MA)	2009 ACC Defensive Player of the Year
2009	Mark "Buddy" Farnham	Brown University (RI)	First-Team All-Ivy
2009	Mike McLaughlin	Boston College (MA)	Team Defensive Captain
2010	Montel Harris	Boston College (MA)	All-Time BC Leader in Carries (756)
2010	Luke Kuechly	Boston College (MA)	Fastest BC Eagle to Ever Record 200 Tackles

Butkus Award

The Butkus Award, first presented in 1985, is presented annually to the top football linebackers at the high school, collegiate, and professional levels. This Award is named in honor of Dick Butkus (Richard Marvin "Dick" Butkus, born: December 9, 1942, in Chicago, Illinois), widely considered the best linebacker of his generation, who played football at the University of Illinois (Urbana-Champaign, 1962–1964) and for nine seasons (1965–1973) with the NFL's Chicago Bears. He was a two-time All-American selection (1963–1964); won the Chicago Tribune Silver Football in 1963 as the Big Ten's Most Valuable Player; named the American Football Coaches Association Player of the Year in 1964; and was inducted into both the Pro Football Hall of Fame (1979) and the College Football Hall of Fame (1983).

The Butkus Award (sometimes called the Dick Butkus Award) was created in 1985 and was originally sponsored by the Downtown Athletic Club of Orlando, Florida. Since 2008, the Award has been sponsored and presented by the non-profit Butkus Foundation (18920 NE 227th Avenue, Brush Prairie, WA 98606; Telephone: 360-601-2991; Email: rarp@butkusfoundation.org; Web site: http://www.thebutkusaward.com; headquarters in Chicago, Illinois) and winners are selected by a group of national coaches and sportswriters.

Originally intended to honor only college linebackers, the Butkus Award was expanded in 2008 to include high school and professional recipients.

As of this writing, Brian Bosworth (University of Oklahoma) is the only two-time collegiate winner.

Year	Player	School	Note
1985	Brian Bosworth	University of Oklahoma (OK)	2X All-American
1986	Brian Bosworth	University of Oklahoma (OK)	#30 Best College Players of All-Time
1987	Paul McGowan	Florida State University (FL)	All-American as a senior
1988	Derrick Thomas	University of Alabama (AL)	1988 All-American
1989	Percy Snow	Michigan State University (MI)	Won both the Butkus & Lombardi Awards
1990	Alfred Williams	University of Colorado (CO)	Captain of 1990 Championship Team
1991	Erick Anderson	University of Michigan (MI)	2nd in School Career Tackles (286)
1992	Marvin Jones	Florida State University (FL)	2000 FSU Hall of Fame Inductee
1993	Trev Alberts	University of Nebraska (NE)	1993 Consensus All-American
1994	Dana Howard	University of Illinois (IL)	1993 & 1994 Consensus All-American
1995	Kevin Hardy	University of Illinois (IL)	1995 Consensus All-American
1996	Matt Russell	University of Colorado (CO)	Played One Season (1997) in NFL
1997	Andy Katzenmoyer	Ohio State University (OH)	First Butkus Winner from OSU
1998	Chris Claiborne	University of Southern California (CA)	1998 First-Team All-American
1999	LaVar Arrington	Pennsylvania State University (PA)	2X All-American
2000	Dan Morgan	University of Miami (FL)	1st Sophomore Captain in Team History
2001	Rocky Calmus	University of Oklahoma (OK)	3X All–Big 12 Selection
2002	E.J. Henderson	University of Maryland (MD)	2002 Chuck Bednarik Award Winner
2003	Teddy Lehman	University of Oklahoma (OK)	2X First-Team All-American (2002 & 2003)
2004	Derrick Johnson	University of Texas (TX)	2004 Bronko Nagurski Trophy Winner
2005	Paul Posluszny	Pennsylvania State University (PA)	2X First-Team All-American (2005 & 2006)
2006	Patrick Willis	University of Mississippi (MS)	2006 Conerly Trophy Winner
2007	James Laurinaitis	Ohio State University (OH)	2006 Bronko Nagurski Trophy Winner
2008	Aaron Curry	Wake Forest University (NC)	2008 First-Team All-American
2009	Rolando McClain	University of Alabama (AL)	2009 All-American
2010	Von Miller	Texas A&M University (TX)	2009 NCAA Sacks Leader (18)

Charlie Conerly Award *see* Conerly Trophy

Chic Harley Award

The Chic Harley Award is presented by the Touchdown Club of Columbus (Ohio; http://www.touchdownclubofcolumbus.com) to the College Football Player of the Year. The winner is selected by a committee of college football coaches and is named after Ohio State University (Columbus, Ohio) All-America football legend, Chic Harley. First presented in 1955, it is the longest-standing award of the Touchdown Club.

Chic Harley (Charles William Harley, born: September 15, 1894, in Chicago, IL; died: April 21, 1974, in Columbus, Oh) was the major player who brought the Ohio State University football program to national attention. He was the school's initial consensus first-team All-America selection; first three-time All-America selection; and was a charter member of the College Football Hall of Fame (1951).

Sam B. Nicola (who died in 1993) founded the Touchdown Club of Columbus in 1956 and was president of the Athletic Club of Columbus when the initial All-Sports Banquet was held in January 1956. Although a local organization, its range has always been national (not limited to the Columbus, Ohio area) and athletes from all sports have been recognized. Honored athletes are selected by the appropriate Touchdown Club's committees, consisting of coaches, sportswriters, and former players.

As of this writing, four players have won this award twice: Billy Cannon (Louisiana State University), Archie Griffin (Ohio State University), Ken Dorsey (University of Miami), and Reggie Bush (University of Southern California).

Year	Player	School	Note
1955	Howard Cassady	Ohio State University (OH)	1955 Heisman Trophy Winner
1956	Paul Hornung	University of Notre Dame (IN)	1956 Heisman Trophy Winner
1957	John David Crow	Texas A&M University (TX)	1957 Heisman Trophy Winner

Chic Harley

1958	Billy Cannon	Louisiana State University (LA)	1959 Heisman Trophy Winner
1959	Billy Cannon	Louisiana State University (LA)	2008 College Football Hall of Fame
1960	Joe Bellino	U.S. Naval Academy (MD)	1960 Heisman Trophy Winner
1961	Ernie Davis	Syracuse University (NY)	1961 Heisman Trophy Winner
1962	Terry Baker	Oregon State University (OR)	1962 Heisman Trophy Winner
1963	Roger Staubach	U.S. Naval Academy (MD)	1963 Heisman Trophy Winner
1964	Bob Timberlake	University of Michigan (MI)	Won the 1965 Rose Bowl
1965	Mike Garrett	University of Southern CA (CA)	1965 Heisman Trophy Winner
1966	Steve Spurrier	University of Florida (FL)	1966 Heisman Trophy Winner
1967	Gary Beban	University of California, Los Angeles (CA)	1967 Heisman Trophy Winner
1968	O.J. Simpson	University of Southern California (CA)	1968 Heisman Trophy Winner
1969	Steve Owens	University of Oklahoma (OK)	1969 Heisman Trophy Winner
1970	Jim Plunkett	Stanford University (CA)	1970 Heisman Trophy Winner
1971	Pat Sullivan	Auburn University (AL)	1971 Heisman Trophy Winner
1972	John Rodgers	University of Nebraska (NE)	1972 Heisman Trophy Winner
1973	John Cappelletti	Penn State University (PA)	1973 Heisman Trophy Winner
1974	Archie Griffin	Ohio State University (OH)	1974 Heisman Trophy Winner
1975	Archie Griffin	Ohio State University (OH)	1975 Heisman Trophy Winner
1976	Tony Dorsett	University of Pittsburgh (PA)	1976 Heisman Trophy Winner
1977	Earl Campbell	University of Texas (TX)	1977 Heisman Trophy Winner
1978	Billy Sims	University of Oklahoma (OK)	1978 Heisman Trophy Winner
1979	Charles White	University of Southern California (CA)	1979 Heisman Trophy Winner
1980	George Rogers	University of South Carolina (SC)	1980 Heisman Trophy Winner
1981	Marcus Allen	University of Southern California (CA)	1981 Heisman Trophy Winner
1982	Herschel Walker	University of Georgia (GA)	1982 Heisman Trophy Winner
1983	Mike Rozier	University of Nebraska (NE)	1983 Heisman Trophy Winner
1984	Doug Flutie	Boston College (MA)	1984 Heisman Trophy Winner
1985	Bo Jackson	Auburn University (AL)	1985 Heisman Trophy Winner
1986	Jim Harbaugh	University of Michigan (MI)	Won the 1986 Fiesta Bowl
1987	Chris Spielman	Ohio State University (OH)	1987 Lombardi Trophy Winner
1988	Barry Sanders	Oklahoma State University (OK)	1988 Heisman Trophy Winner
1989	Anthony Thompson	Indiana University (IN)	2007 College Football Hall of Fame
1990	Greg Lewis	University of Washington (WA)	Inaugural Doak Walker Award Winner
1991	Desmond Howard	University of Michigan (MI)	1991 Heisman Trophy Winner
1992	Gino Torretta	University of Miami (FL)	1992 Heisman Trophy Winner
1993	Charlie Ward	Florida State University (FL)	1993 Heisman Trophy Winner
1994	Rashaan Salaam	University of Colorado (CO)	1994 Heisman Trophy Winner
1995	Eddie George	Ohio State University (OH)	1995 Heisman Trophy Winner
1996	Troy Davis	Iowa State University (IA)	Ran for 378 Yards in a College Game
1997	Charles Woodson	University of Michigan (MI)	1997 Heisman Trophy Winner
1998	Ricky Williams	University of Texas (TX)	1998 Heisman Trophy Winner
1999	Ron Dayne	University of Wisconsin, Madison (WI)	1999 Heisman Trophy Winner
2000	Josh Heupel	University of Oklahoma (OK)	AP Player of the Year in 2000
2001	Ken Dorsey	University of Miami (FL)	Won 2001 NCAA National Title
2002	Ken Dorsey	University of Miami (FL)	Co-MVP of the 2002 Rose Bowl
2003	Larry Fitzgerald	University of Pittsburgh (PA)	Won the 2003 Walter Camp Award
2004	Reggie Bush	University of Southern California (CA)	USC 2004 MVP
2005	Reggie Bush	University of Southern California (CA)	2005 Heisman Trophy Winner
2006	Troy Smith	Ohio State University (OH)	2006 Heisman Trophy Winner
2007	Tim Tebow	University of Florida (FL)	2007 Heisman Trophy Winner
2008	Sam Bradford	University of Oklahoma (OK)	2008 Heisman Trophy Winner
2009	Colt McCoy	University of Texas (TX)	2009 Maxwell Award Winner
2010	Cameron Newton	Auburn University	2010 Heisman Trophy Winner

Chicago Tribune Silver Football *see* Big Ten Conference

Chuck Bednarik Award

The Chuck Bednarik Award is presented annually to the best defensive college football player as voted on by the Maxwell Football Club. Voters for the various honors sponsored by the Maxwell Club Awards include NCAA head college football coaches, sportswriters and sportscasters from across the country, and members of the Maxwell Football Club.

The Maxwell Football Club (P.O. Box 1225, Southampton PA 18966; Telephone: 215-643-3833; Web site: http://www.maxwellfootballclub.org) presents its awards in honor of Robert W. "Tiny" Maxwell (born: September 8, 1883, in Chicago, IL; died: June 30, 1922, in Norristown, PA), college player, official, and sports columnist. He played football at the University of Chicago (IL, 1902), at Swarthmore College (Swarthmore, PA in 1904 and 1905), and was inducted into the College Football Hall of Fame in 1974.

He later played professional football for the Canton Bulldogs and Massillon Tigers (both of the Ohio League); was a sports editor for the *Philadelphia Public Ledger*; served as a football official; and was an assistant coach at both Swarthmore and the University of Pennsylvania (Philadelphia).

The Maxwell Football Club (originally called the Maxwell Football Club of Philadelphia) was established in 1935 in his honor to promote safety in the game of American football and is physically located in King of Prussia, Pennsylvania.

Chuck Bednarik (Charles Philip Bednarik) was born on May 1, 1925, in Bethlehem, Pennsylvania) and was a two-way player (center, linebacker) in the National Football League for the Philadelphia Eagles (1949–1962). He is best remembered for his tackle on Frank Gifford (running back for the New York Giants) in 1960 that forced Gifford out of the league for 18 months and shortened his career. Bednarik was a member of two NFL championship teams (1949, 1960) and was inducted into the Pro Football Hall of Fame in 1967 and the College Football Hall of Fame in 1969.

As of this writing, only Pat Fitzgerald (Northwestern University) and Paul Posluszny (Pennsylvania State University) have won the award twice.

Year	*Player*	*School*	*Note*
1995	Pat Fitzgerald	Northwestern University (IL)	2008 College Football Hall of Fame Inductee
1996	Pat Fitzgerald	Northwestern University (IL)	Current Coach at Northwestern
1997	Charles Woodson	University of Michigan (MI)	1997 Heisman Trophy Winner
1998	Dat Nguyen	Texas A&M University (TX)	1998 Lombardi Award Winner
1999	LaVar Arrington	Pennsylvania State University (PA)	1999 Dick Butkus Award Winner
2000	Dan Morgan	University of Miami (FL)	1st to win Butkus, Nagurski, & Bednarik Awards
2001	Julius Peppers	University of North Carolina (NC)	Won 2001 Lombardi & Bill Willis Awards
2002	E. J. Henderson	University of Maryland (MD)	2002 ACC Defensive Player of the Year
2003	Teddy Lehman	University of Oklahoma (OK)	Won the 2003 Butkus Award
2004	David Pollack	University of Georgia (GA)	Won 2004 Lott Trophy & Lombardi Award
2005	Paul Posluszny	Pennsylvania State University (PA)	Won the 2005 Dick Butkus Award
2006	Paul Posluszny	Pennsylvania State University (PA)	2006 All-American
2007	Dan Connor	Pennsylvania State University (PA)	2X First-Team All-American (2006, 2007)
2008	Rey Maualuga	University of Southern California (CA)	2008 Pac-10 Defensive Player of the Year
2009	Ndamukong Suh	University of Nebraska (NE)	2009 Lombardi Award Winner
2010	Patrick Peterson	Louisiana State University (LA)	2010 SEC Defensive Player of the Year

Conerly Trophy (officially known as the Cellular South Conerly Trophy)

Since 1996, the Charlie Conerly Award (officially known as The Cellular South Conerly Trophy) has been presented annually to the top college player in the State of Mississippi and is given by the Mississippi Sports Hall of Fame (1152 Lakeland Drive, Jackson, MS 39216; Telephone: 601-982-8264, 800-280-FAME (3263); Fax: 601-982-4702; Email: generalinfo@msfame.com; Web site: http://www.msfame.com/contact.html). Sixty media representatives from across the state vote on recipients and all players at Mississippi's four-year college football programs are eligible.

The Conerly Trophy is bronze, 19" high × 11" long × 7.5" wide, and weighs 18.5 pounds. The original trophy is on permanent display at the Mississippi Sports Hall of Fame and Museum. A replica of the trophy is presented to the winner each year at the announcement dinner. As of this writing, Eli Manning from the University of Mississippi is the only player to win this award twice.

Charles Albert Conerly, Jr. (born: September 19, 1921, in Clarksdale, Mississippi; died: February 13, 1996, in Memphis, Tennessee) was a quarterback in the National Football League for the New York Giants from 1948 through 1961. He was inducted into the College Football Hall of Fame in 1966.

Conerly played college football at the University of Mississippi (Oxford) in 1942, but left to serve in the U.S. Marines in the South Pacific during World War II. After the war, he returned to the school in 1946 and led the team to its first-ever Southeastern Conference championship in 1947, during which he was an All-American and named Player of the Year by the Helms Athletic Foundation.

He was inducted into the Ole Miss Athletic Hall of Fame in 1987 and the Mississippi Sports Hall of Fame in 1966, while also being a member of the Ole Miss Team of the Century (1893–1992). Although Conerly was selected in the 11th round of the 1945 National Football League Draft by the Washington Redskins; he played his entire career with the New York Giants as a quarterback; was a two-time Pro Bowl selection (1950, 1956); and was named the NFL's Most Valuable Player in 1959 by the Newspaper Enterprise Association.

After being named the NFL Rookie of the Year in 1948, he led the Giants to three NFL Championship games in four seasons (1956, 1958–1959).

Year	*Name*	*Position*	*School*
1996	Tregnel Thomas	Running Back	Delta State University (MS)
1997	Stewart Patridge	Quarterback	University of Mississippi (MS)
1998	J. J. Johnson	Running Back	Mississippi State University (MS)
1999	Deuce McAllister	Running Back	University of Mississippi (MS)
2000	Josh Bright	Quarterback	Delta State University (MS)
2001	Eli Manning	Quarterback	University of Mississippi (MS)
2002	Rod Davis	Linebacker	University of Southern Mississippi (MS)
2003	Eli Manning	Quarterback	University of Mississippi (MS)
2004	Michael Boley	Linebacker	University of Southern Mississippi (MS)
2005	Jerious Norwood	Running Back	Mississippi State University (MS)
2006	Patrick Willis	Linebacker	University of Mississippi (MS)
2007	Damion Fletcher	Running Back	University of Southern Mississippi (MS)
2008	Juan Joseph	Quarterback	Millsaps College (MS)
2009	Anthony Dixon	Running Back	Mississippi State University (MS)
2010	Chris White	Linebacker	Mississippi State University (MS)

Dave Rimington Trophy *see* Rimington Trophy

Davey O'Brien Award

Since 1981, the Davey O'Brien Award (officially called the Davey O'Brien National Quarterback Award) has been presented annually to the collegiate football player voted by the Davey O'Brien Foundation (306 West Seventh Street, Suite 305, Fort Worth, TX 76102; Telephone: 817-338-3488; Fax: 817-335-7737; Email: info@DaveyObrien.org; Web site: http://www.daveyobrien.com) to be the best collegiate NCAA quarterback.

O'Brien (Robert David O'Brien, born: June 22, 1917, in Dallas, TX; died: November 18, 1977, in Fort Worth, TX) played college football at Texas Christian University (Fort Worth, Texas); won the Heisman Trophy, Maxwell Award, and the Walter Camp Award in 1938; led his team to the 1938 national title; played two seasons in the NFL with the Philadelphia Eagles (1939–1940); was inducted into the College Football Hall of Fame in 1955; and was inducted into the Texas Sports Hall of Fame in 1956.

Retiring from the NFL in 1940, he then joined the FBI, where he stayed for 10 years.

After his death in 1977, the award was initially established as the Davey O'Brien Memorial Trophy and was presented to the most outstanding football player in the now-defunct Southwest Conference. In 1980, the trophy was renamed the Davey O'Brien Award.

As of this writing, three players have won this award twice: Ty Detmer (Brigham Young University), Danny Wuerffel (University of Florida), and Jason White (University of Oklahoma).

Year	*Player*	*School*	*Note*
1981	Jim McMahon	Brigham Young University (UT)	2X All-American (1980, 1981)
1982	Todd Blackledge	Pennsylvania State University (PA)	Won 1982 NCAA National Championship
1983	Steve Young	Brigham Young University (UT)	2001 College Football HOF Inductee
1984	Doug Flutie	Boston College (MA)	1984 Heisman Trophy Winner
1985	Chuck Long	University of Iowa (IA)	1999 College Football HOF Inductee
1986	Vinny Testaverde	University of Miami (FL)	1986 Heisman Trophy Winner
1987	Don McPherson	Syracuse University (NY)	2008 College Football HOF Inductee
1988	Troy Aikman	University of California, Los Angeles (CA)	2008 College Football HOF Inductee
1989	Andre Ware	University of Houston (TX)	1989 Heisman Trophy Winner
1990	Ty Detmer	Brigham Young University (UT)	1990 Heisman Trophy Winner
1991	Ty Detmer	Brigham Young University (UT)	Tied 1991 Holiday Bowl
1992	Gino Torretta	University of Miami (FL)	1992 Heisman Trophy Winner
1993	Charlie Ward	Florida State University (FL)	1993 Heisman Trophy Winner
1994	Kerry Collins	Pennsylvania State University (PA)	1994 Maxwell & Sammy Baugh Award Winner
1995	Danny Wuerffel	University of Florida (FL)	1995 Sammy Baugh Trophy Winner
1996	Danny Wuerffel	University of Florida (FL)	1996 Heisman Trophy Winner
1997	Peyton Manning	University of Tennessee (TN)	1997 SEC Championship MVP
1998	Michael Bishop	Kansas State University (KS)	1998 All-American
1999	Joe Hamilton	Georgia Tech (GA)	2002 Member ACC 50th Anniversary Team
2000	Chris Weinke	Florida State University (FL)	2000 Heisman Trophy Winner
2001	Eric Crouch	University of Nebraska (NE)	2001 Heisman Trophy Winner
2002	Brad Banks	University of Iowa (IA)	2002 Big Ten Player of the Year
2003	Jason White	University of Oklahoma (OK)	2003 Heisman Trophy Winner
2004	Jason White	University of Oklahoma (OK)	2004 Johnny Unitas Golden Arm Award Winner
2005	Vince Young	University of Texas (TX)	2005 Manning & Archie Griffin Award Winner
2006	Troy Smith	Ohio State University (OH)	2006 Heisman Trophy Winner
2007	Tim Tebow	University of Florida (FL)	2007 Heisman Trophy Winner
2008	Sam Bradford	University of Oklahoma (OK)	2008 Heisman Trophy Winner
2009	Colt McCoy	University of Texas (TX)	Won 2009 Big 12 Conference Championship
2010	Cameron Newton	Auburn University (AL)	2010 Manning Award Winner

Disney Sports Spirit Award (Disney's Wide World of Sports Spirit Award)

First awarded in 1996 to a high school recipient, the Disney Sports Spirit Award is now presented to college football's most inspirational individual or team and is awarded by the National College Football Awards Association (c/o Sports Media Director, Disney Destinations, LLC, P.O. Box 10000, Lake Buena Vista, FL 32830; Telephone: 407-566-5339; Fax: 407-566-5320; Email: tony.morreale@disney.com; Web site: http://www.ncfaa.org/spirit/index.html.) The Award is not based on statistics or other specific on-field records or achievements, but for bravery, courage, and overcoming adversity.

For the 10th anniversary of the Award, the trophy was completely redesigned and is now 15 inches high and displays the characteristics of a football and a flame.

Year	*Winner*	*School*	*Note*
1996	Daniel Huffman	Rossville High School (IL)	Donated Kidney to his Grandmother
1997	Dwight Collins	Central Florida University (FL)	Deaf Football Player
1998	Matt Hartl	Northwestern University (IL)	Died of Hodgkin's Disease

Year	Winner	School	Note
1999		East Carolina University, Greenville, North Carolina (NC)	Overcame Hurricane Floyd
2000	Hameen Ali	College of William & Mary (VA)	Overcame a Troubled Youth
2001		United States Air Force Academy, Colorado Springs, Colorado (CO)	In Honor of September 11, 2001
2001		United States Military Academy, West Point, New York (NY)	In Honor of September 11, 2001
2001		United States Naval Academy, Annapolis, Maryland (MD)	In Honor of September 11, 2001
2002	Dewayne White	University of Louisville (KY)	Overcame Youthful Obstacles
2003	Neil Parry	San Jose State University (CA)	Right Leg Amputated
2004	Tim Frisby	University of South Carolina (SC)	Walk-On Receiver at Age 39
2005		Tulane University, New Orleans, Louisiana (LA)	Overcame Hurricane Katrina
2006	Patrick Henry Hughes	University of Louisville (KY)	Overcame Physical Handicaps
2007	Zerbin Singleton	United States Naval Academy (MD)	Overcame a Car Wreck
2008	Tim Tebow	University of Florida (FL)	Honored for Humanitarian Efforts
2009	Mark Herzlich	Boston College (MA)	Overcame Bone Cancer
2010	D.J. Williams	University of Arkansas (AR)	Overcame an Abusive Childhood

Doak Walker Award

Named after the Southern Methodist University (Dallas, Texas) and Detroit Lions football player, the Doak Walker Award (first presented in 1990) honors the nation's best college football running back and in presented by SMU (Guaranty Bank SMU Athletic Forum, P.O. Box 750460, Dallas, TX 75275; Telephone: 214-768-4314; Fax: 214-768-3570; Email: dwilcox@smu.edu (Dana Wilcox) or lockhart@smu.edu (Jeff Lockhart); Web site: http:///www.doakwalkeraward.com).

Award winners receive a sculpture of Doak Walker (created by J. Blair Buswell of Provo, Utah, who has sculpted the busts of some Pro Football Hall of Fame [Canton, Ohio] inductees), which is cast in bronze and mounted on a wooden base.

Doak Walker (Ewell Doak Walker, Jr.; born: January 1, 1927, in Dallas, Texas; died: September 27, 1998, in Steamboat Springs, Colorado) was an All-American and won the Heisman Trophy is 1948 (as a junior). He played six seasons with the Detroit Lions (1950–1955) and helped the team win two National Football League championships (1952–1953). He was inducted into the College Football Hall of Fame in 1959 and into the Pro Football Hall of Fame in 1986.

As of this writing, there have only been two multiple winners: Ricky Williams (University of Texas) and Darren McFadden (University of Arkansas).

Year	Winner	School	Note
1990	Greg Lewis	University of Washington (WA)	1990 All-American
1991	Trevor Cobb	Rice University (TX)	Played One Season in the NFL
1992	Garrison Hearst	University of Georgia (GA)	Led Nation in TDs as a Junior
1993	Byron "Bam" Morris	Texas Tech University (TX)	2nd in Nation in Rushing Yards (1993)
1994	Rashaan Salaam	University of Colorado (CO)	1994 Heisman Trophy Winner
1995	Eddie George	Ohio State University (OH)	1995 Heisman Trophy Winner
1996	Byron Hanspard	Texas Tech University (TX)	All-Time School Leader in Rushing Yards
1997	Ricky Williams	University of Texas (TX)	2X Jim Brown Trophy Winner (1997 & 1998)
1998	Ricky Williams	University of Texas (TX)	1998 Heisman Trophy Winner
1999	Ron Dayne	University of Wisconsin (WI)	1999 Heisman Trophy Winner
2000	LaDainian Tomlinson	Texas Christian University (TX)	2000 Jim Brown Trophy Winner
2001	Luke Staley	Brigham Young University (UT)	2001 All-American
2002	Larry Johnson	Pennsylvania State University (PA)	2002 Jim Brown Award Winner
2003	Chris Perry	University of Michigan (MI)	2003 Jim Brown Trophy Winner
2004	Cedric Benson	University of Texas (TX)	2X First-Team All-Big 12 (2003 & 2004)

Year	*Winner*	*School*	*Note*
2005	Reggie Bush	University of Southern California (CA)	2005 Heisman Trophy Winner
2006	Darren McFadden	University of Arkansas (AR)	2006 1st-Team All-American
2007	Darren McFadden	University of Arkansas (AR)	2X All-American (2006 & 2007)
2008	Shonn Greene	University of Iowa (IA)	2008 Jim Brown Trophy Winner
2009	Toby Gerhart	Stanford University (CA)	School Record in Career Touchdowns (44)
2010	LaMichael James	University of Oregon (OR)	2010 NCAA Rushing Leader (1,682 Yards)

Draddy Trophy (Vincent dePaul Draddy Trophy) *see* William V. Campbell Trophy

Dudley Award

The Dudley Award, named after former University of Virginia (Charlottesville, VA) running back Bill Dudley, is presented annually by the *Richmond Times-Dispatch* newspaper (300 East Franklin Street, Richmond, VA 23219) to the best NCAA Division I football player in the state of Virginia.

Bill Dudley (William McGarvey Dudley; born: December 24, 1921, in Bluefield, VA; died: February 4, 2010, in Lynchburg, VA) played college football at the University of Virginia and, as a junior (1941), he became the first Virginia player to earn All-America honors and won the Maxwell Award as the best college football player of the year.

He later played nine seasons in the NFL with the Pittsburgh Steelers (1942, 1945–1946), the Detroit Lions (1947–1949), and the Washington Redskins (1950–1951, 1953) and led his team in scoring all of his nine years. Dudley is the only professional player with a rushing touchdown, touchdown reception, punt return for touchdown, kickoff return for touchdown, interception return for touchdown, fumble return for touchdown, and a touchdown pass. He was elected to the College Football Hall of Fame in 1956, the Pro Football Hall of Fame in 1966, and the Virginia Sports Hall of Fame in 1972.

As of this writing, Lee Suggs (Virginia Polytechnic Institute and State University) is the only two-time winner of the Award.

Year	*Player*	*School*	*Note*
1990	Shawn Moore	University of Virginia (VA)	Played in the NFL and the CFL
1991	Matt Blundin	University of Virginia (VA)	1991 ACC Player of the Year
1992	Cary Perkins	Emory and Henry College (VA)	1993 E & H Sports Hall of Fame
1993	Jim Pyne	Virginia Tech University (VA)	1st Virginia Tech All-American
1994	Mike Frederick	University of Virginia (VA)	Played Five Years in the NFL
1995	Cornell Brown	Virginia Tech University (VA)	Won 1995 Sugar Bowl
1996	Tiki Barber	University of Virginia (VA)	1st School Back-to-Back 1,000 Seasons
1997	Anthony Poindexter	University of Virginia (VA)	School Record 98 Tackles (1996)
1998	Marc Megna	University of Richmond (VA)	1997 First-Team Atlantic-10 Selection
1999	Corey Moore	Virginia Tech University (VA)	1999 Bronko Nagurski Winner
2000	Lee Suggs	Virginia Tech University (VA)	Holds NCAA FBS Season Record, Games W/TD (14)
2001	Billy McMullen	University of Virginia (VA)	2nd All-Time ACC Conference Receiver (210)
2002	Lee Suggs	Virginia Tech University (VA)	Played Four Years in the NFL
2003	Kevin Jones	Virginia Tech University (VA)	2nd On School All-Time List for TDs (35)
2004	Bryan Randall	Virginia Tech University (VA)	2004 ACC Offensive Player of the Year
2005	Darryl Tapp	Virginia Tech University (VA)	2X First-Team All-ACC (2004 & 2005)
2006	Vince Hall	Virginia Tech University (VA)	2006 First-Team All-ACC Selection
2007	Chris Long	University of Virginia (VA)	2007 First-Team All-American
2008	Rodney Landers	James Madison University (VA)	2008 CAA Offensive Player of the Year
2009	Cody Grimm	Virginia Tech (VA)	Seventh Round NFL Draft, Tampa Bay
2010	Tyrod Taylor	Virginia Tech (VA)	2010 ACC Player of the Year

Fred Biletnikoff Award

The Fred Biletnikoff Award (presented annually since 1994) is given to the top college football receiver by the non-profit Tallahassee Quarterback Club Foundation, Inc. (P. O. Box 14473, Tallahassee, FL 32317; http//www.tallahasseeqbclub.com/; http://www.biletnikoffaward.com/). A national selection committee of more than 150 journalists, sports commentators, broadcasters, and former players selects the Award winner. Any college player who receives the football in a game through the forward pass is eligible for the Award.

Fred Biletnikoff (Frederick S. Biletnikoff; born: February 23, 1943, in Erie, PA) played football as a wide receiver with the NFL's Oakland Raiders (1965–1978) and the Canadian Football League's Montreal Alouettes (1980). After his playing days, Biletnikoff went into coaching. Before joining the NFL, he played at Florida State University (Tallahassee, FL), where he was the first consensus All-American football player in the school's history. With Oakland, he won Super Bowl XI (1977) and was named the game's Most Valuable Player. He was inducted into the Pro Football Hall of Fame in 1988 and the College Football Hall of Fame in 1991.

As of this writing, Texas Tech University's Michael Crabtree is the only two-time winner.

Year	*Player*	*School*	*Note*
1994	Bobby Engram	Pennsylvania State University (PA)	1994 Citrus Bowl MVP
1995	Terry Glenn	Ohio State University (OH)	1995 First-Team All-Big Ten
1996	Marcus Harris	University of Wyoming (WY)	4,518 college receiving yards
1997	Randy Moss	Marshall University (WV)	2X First-Team All-American (1996 / 1997)
1998	Troy Edwards	Louisiana Tech University (LA)	27 season touchdowns
1999	Troy Walters	Stanford University (CA)	Played eight years in the NFL
2000	Antonio Bryant	University of Pittsburgh (PA)	2nd Round NFL Draft Choice
2001	Josh Reed	Louisiana State University (LA)	Consensus First-Team All-American (2001)
2002	Charles Rogers	Michigan State University (MI)	Consensus All-American (2002)
2003	Larry Fitzgerald	University of Pittsburgh (PA)	2003 Walter Camp Award winner
2004	Braylon Edwards	University of Michigan (MI)	2004 Big Ten Offensive Player of the Year
2005	Mike Hass	Oregon State University (OR)	2X First-Team All Pac 10 (2004 / 2005)
2006	Calvin Johnson	Georgia Institute of Technology (GA)	2006 Paul Warfield Trophy Winner
2007	Michael Crabtree	Texas Tech University (TX)	2X Consensus All-American (2007 / 2008)
2008	Michael Crabtree	Texas Tech University (TX)	2X Paul Warfield Trophy winner
2009	Golden Tate	University of Notre Dame (IN)	10th All-Time in School's TD Receptions
2010	Justin Blackmon	Oklahoma State University (OK)	2010 Big 12 Offensive Player of the Year

Freshman of the Year

Simply named the Freshman of the Year, this award has been presented since 2001 to the best freshman college football player. The award is presented by the Touchdown Club of Columbus (Ohio, http://www.touchdownclubofcolumbus.com).

Sam B. Nicola (who died in 1993) founded the Touchdown Club of Columbus in 1956 and was president of the Athletic Club of Columbus when the initial All-Sports Banquet was held in January 1956. Although a local organization, its range has always been national (not limited to the Columbus, Ohio area) and athletes from all sports have been recognized. Honored athletes are selected by the appropriate Touchdown Club's committees, consisting of coaches, sportswriters, and former players.

Year	*Name*	*School*	*Note*
2001	Anthony Davis	University of Wisconsin (WI)	Played in the Canadian Football League
2002	Maurice Clarett	Ohio State University (OH)	Won 2002 BCS National Championship
2003	Chris Leak	University of Florida (FL)	Named to 2003 SEC All-Freshman Team
2004	Adrian Peterson	University of Oklahoma (OK)	2004 Jim Brown Trophy Winner
2005	Tyrell Sutton	Northwestern University (IL)	2005 Big Ten Freshman of the Year
2006	Colt McCoy	University of Texas (TX)	2006 Valero Alamo Bowl Offensive MVP
2007	Michael Crabtree	Texas Tech University (TX)	2X All-American (2007–2008)
2008	Julio Jones	University of Alabama (AL)	2008 SEC Freshman of the Year

2009	Dion Lewis	University of Pittsburgh (PA)	New Jersey Prep Offensive Player of the Year
2010	Marcus Lattimore	University of South Carolina (SC)	2010 SEC Freshman of the Year

Gagliardi Trophy *see* NCAA Division III

Gene Upshaw Award (Gene Upshaw Division II Lineman of the Year Award) *see* NCAA Division II

George H. "Bulger" Lowe Award

Since 1939, the George H. "Bulger" Lowe Award has been presented annually to New England's best Division I collegiate football player and is presented by the Gridiron Club of Greater Boston (9 Broadway, Unit 320, Saugus, MA 01906; Web site: http://www.gridclubofgreaterboston.com/). Beginning in 1982, separate awards have been presented for both offense and defense.

Year	*Player*	*School*
1939	Gene Goodreault	Boston College
1940	Charlie O'Rourke	Boston College
1941	Endicott "Chub" Peabody	Harvard University
1942	Mike Holovak	Boston College
1943	George Connor	Holy Cross
1944	Paul Walker	Yale University
1945	Stan Kozlowski	Holy Cross
1946	Levi Jackson	Yale University
1947	Bob Sullivan	Holy Cross
1948	Joe Sullivan	Dartmouth College
1949	John Clayton	Dartmouth College
1950	Bob Spears	Yale University
1951	Harry Agganis	Boston University
1952	Charles Malloy	Holy Cross
1953	Dick Clasby	Harvard University
1954	Sam Pino	Boston University
1955	Charles Sticka	Trinity College
1956	Dennis McGill	Yale University
1957	Joseph Palermo	Dartmouth College
1958	Frank Finney	Brown University
1959	Chester Boulris	Harvard University
1960	Thomas Singleton	Yale University
1961	Pat McCarthy	Holy Cross
1962	Don McKinnon	Dartmouth College
1963	Jack Concannon	Boston College
1964	Jerry Whelchel	University of Massachusetts
1965	Robert Hall	Brown University
1966	Bobby Leo	Harvard University
1967	Greg Landry	University of Massachusetts
1968	Brian Dowling	Yale University
1969	Bruce Taylor	Boston University
1970	Fred Willis	Boston College
1971	Bruce Laird	American International College
1972	Richard Jauron	Yale University
1973	Mike Esposito	Boston College
1974	Pat McInally	Harvard University
1975	Mike Kruczek	Boston College
1976	Timothy Whelan	Tufts University
1977	William Burnham	University of New Hampshire
1978	Dan Ross	Northeastern University

Year	*Player*	*School*
1979	Mal Najarian	Boston University
1980	Jim Budness	Boston College
1981	Rich Diana	Yale University
1982	Offense: Doug Flutie	Boston College
1982	Offense: Garry Pearson	University of Massachusetts
1983	Offense: Brian Brennan	Boston College
1983	Defense: Joe Azelby	Harvard University
1984	Offense: Doug Flutie	Boston College
1984	Defense: Mike Ruth	Boston College
1985	Offense: Tom Ehrhardt	University of Rhode Island
1985	Defense: Mike Ruth	Boston College
1986	Offense: Gordie Lockbaum	Holy Cross
1986	Defense: John Bosa	Boston College
1987	Offense: Gordie Lockbaum	Holy Cross
1987	Defense: Bill Romanowski	Boston College
1988	Offense: Dave Palazzi	University of Massachusetts
1988	Defense: Robert McGovern	Holy Cross
1989	Offense: Mike Buck	University of Maine
1989	Defense: Dave Murphy	Holy Cross
1990	Offense: Matt DeGennaro	University of Connecticut
1990	Defense: Matt Kelley	Boston College
1991	Offense: Tom Ciaccio	Holy Cross
1991	Defense: Tom McManus	Boston College
1992	Offense: Chuckie Dukes	Boston College
1992	Defense: Charles Brennan	Boston College
1993	Offense: Rob Dougherty	Boston University
1993	Offense: Glenn Foley	Boston College
1993	Defense: Stephen Boyd	Boston College
1994	Offense: Rob Dougherty	Boston University
1994	Offense: Pete Mitchell	Boston College
1994	Defense: Mike Mamula	Boston College
1995	Offense: Rene Ingoglia	University of Massachusetts
1995	Defense: Mike Foley	University of New Hampshire
1996	Offense: Chris Bresnahan	University of New Hampshire
1996	Defense: Stalin Colinet	Boston College
1997	Offense: Jim Murphy	Northeastern University
1997	Defense: Erik Storz	Boston College
1998	Offense: Jerry Azumah	University of New Hampshire
1998	Defense: Khari Samuel	University of Massachusetts
1999	Offense: James Perry	Brown University
1999	Defense: Chris Hovan	Boston College
2000	Offense: Steve Campbell	Brown University
2000	Defense: Kole Ayi	University of Massachusetts
2001	Offense: Neil Rose	Harvard University
2001	Defense: Scott Bradley	Boston College
2002	Offense: Derrick Knight	Boston College
2002	Defense: Steve Cooper	University of Maine
2003	Offense: Derrick Knight	Boston College
2003	Defense: Dante Balestracci	Harvard University
2004	Offense: Ryan Fitzpatrick	Harvard University
2004	Defense: Liam Ezekiel	Northeastern University
2005	Offense: Ricky Santos	University of New Hampshire
2005	Defense: Mathias Kiwanuka	Boston College
2006	Offense: David Ball	University of New Hampshire
2006	Defense: DeJuan Tribble	Boston College
2007	Offense: Matt Ryan	Boston College
2007	Defense: Jamie Silva	Boston College

Year	*Player*	*School*
2008	Offense: Dominic Randolph	Holy Cross
2008	Defense: Bobby Abare	Yale University
2008	Defense: Mark Herzlich	Boston College
2009	Offense: Buddy Farnham	Brown University
2009	Defense: Mike McLaughlin	Boston College
2010	Offense: Montel Harris	Boston College
2010	Defense: Luke Kuechly	Boston College

George Munger Award

The George Munger Award (presented annually since 1989) is given to the NCAA Division I college football coach of the year by the Maxwell Football Club (P.O, Box 1225, Southampton, PA 18966; Telephone: 610-277-8900; Fax: 610-277-2239; Email: info@maxwellfootballclub.org; Web site: http://www.maxwellfootballclub.org). Winners are selected by NCAA head coaches, members of the Maxwell Club, and sportswriters from around the country.

The Award is named in honor of former University of Pennsylvania (Philadelphia, PA) head football coach George Munger.(George Almond Munger), who served from 1939 to 1954; compiled an overall record of 52–7–4 (0.825); and won nine Ivy League titles. He passed away in 1994. In March 2010, the Maxwell Football Club announced that the award would be renamed the Joseph V. Paterno Award.

As of this writing, Joe Paterno (Pennsylvania State University) is the only coach to receive the honor multiple times, with three wins. In 2010, this honor was replaced by the Joseph V. Paterno Award.

Year	*Winner*	*School*	*Note*
1989	Bo Schembechler	University of Michigan (MI)	1993 College Football Hall of Fame Inductee
1990	Joe Paterno	Pennsylvania State University (PA)	2X National Champion (1982, 1986)
1991	Don James	University of Washington (WA)	1997 College Football Hall of Fame Inductee
1992	Gene Stallings	University of Alabama (AL)	1992 National Champion
1993	Terry Bowden	Auburn University (AL)	Paul "Bear" Bryant Award Winner
1994	Joe Paterno	Pennsylvania State University (PA)	Walter Camp Coach of the Year Winner
1995	Gary Barnett	Northwestern University (IL)	2X Big Ten Coach of the Year (1995, 1996)
1996	Bruce Snyder	Arizona State University (AZ)	1996 Pac 10 Coach of the Year
1997	Lloyd Carr	University of Michigan (MI)	1997 Catholic League Hall of Fame Inductee
1998	Phil Fulmer	University of Tennessee (TN)	1998 SEC Coach of the Year
1999	Frank Beamer	Virginia Tech University (VA)	3X Big East Champion (1995, 1996, 1999)
2000	Bob Stoops	University of Oklahoma (OK)	2000 Walter Camp Coach of the Year
2001	Ralph Friedgen	University of Maryland (MD)	2001 Atlantic Coast Conference Champion
2002	Tyrone Willingham	University of Notre Dame (IN)	Scripps College Coach of the Year Winner
2003	Pete Carroll	University of Southern California (CA)	2X National Champion (2003, 2004)
2004	Urban Meyer	University of Utah (UT)	2004 Eddie Robinson Coach of the Year
2005	Joe Paterno	Pennsylvania State University (PA)	2007 College Football Hall of Fame Inductee
2006	Greg Schiano	Rutgers University (NJ)	2006 Big East Coach of the Year
2007	Mark Mangino	University of Kansas (KS)	2007 Woody Hayes Coach of the Year
2008	Mike Leach	Texas Tech University (TX)	2008 Big 12 Coach of the Year
2009	Gary Patterson	Texas Christian University (TX)	2X Mountain West Conference Winner (2005, 2009)

Grantland Rice Award

The Grantland Rice Award (Trophy) has been presented annually since 1954 to the collegiate national champion as decided by voting of the Football Writers Association of America (http://www.

sportswriters.net/fwaa/; http://www.sportswriters.net/fwaa/awards/rice/index.html). Since 2002, the organization began issuing weekly polls and the winner of its final yearly poll has been presented the Award.

The Award honors former sportswriter and radio broadcaster Grantland Rice (born: November 2, 1880, in Murfreesboro, Tennessee; died: July 13, 1954, in New York, New York), who is well-known for being the successor to Walter Camp in selecting college football All-America teams (beginning in 1925) and for being the writer who named the backfield of the Notre Dame football team of 1924 the "Four Horsemen" (a biblical reference to the Four Horsemen of the Apocalypse). He was often called the "Dean of American Sports Writers."

Year	*School*	*Conference*	*Coach*	*Record*
1954	University of California, Los Angeles (CA)	Pacific Coast	Red Sanders	9–0
1955	University of Oklahoma (OK)	Big 7	Bud Wilkinson	11–0
1956	University of Oklahoma (OK)	Big 7	Bud Wilkinson	10–0
1957	Ohio State University (OH)	Big Ten	Woody Hayes	9–1
1958	University of Iowa (IA)	Big Ten	Forest Evashevski	8–1–1
1959	Syracuse University (NY)	Independent	Ben Schwartzwalder	11–0
1960	Mississippi State University (MS)	Southeastern	John Vaught	10–0–1
1961	Ohio State University (OH)	Big Ten	Woody Hayes	8–0–1
1962	University of Southern California (CA)	AAWU	John McKay	11–0
1963	University of Texas (TX)	Southwestern	Darrell Royal	11–0
1964	University of Arkansas (AR)	Southwestern	Frank Broyles	11–0
1965	University of Alabama (AL)	Southeastern	Paul "Bear" Bryant	9–1–1
1965	Michigan State University (MI)	Big Ten	Duffy Daugherty	10–1
1966	University of Notre Dame (IN)	Independent	Ara Parseghian	9–0–1
1967	University of Southern California (CA)	AAWU	John McKay	10–1
1968	Ohio State University (OH)	Big Ten	Woody Hayes	10–0
1969	University of Texas (TX)	Southwestern	Darrell Royal	11–0
1970	University of Nebraska (NE)	Big 8	Bob Devaney	11–0–1
1971	University of Nebraska (NE)	Big 8	Bob Devaney	13–0
1972	University of Southern California (CA)	Pac-8	John McKay	12–0
1973	University of Notre Dame (IN)	Independent	Ara Parseghian	11–0
1974	University of Southern California (CA)	Pac-8	John McKay	10–1–1
1975	University of Oklahoma (OK)	Big 8	Barry Switzer	11–1
1976	University of Pittsburgh (PA)	Independent	Johnny Majors	12–0
1977	University of Notre Dame (IN)	Independent	Dan Devine	11–1
1978	University of Alabama (AL)	Southeastern	Paul "Bear" Bryant	11–1
1979	University of Alabama (AL)	Southeastern	Paul "Bear" Bryant	12–0
1980	University of Georgia (GA)	Southeastern	Vince Dooley	12–0
1981	Clemson University (SC)	Atlantic Coast	Danny Ford	12–0
1982	Pennsylvania State University (PA)	Independent	Joe Paterno	11–1
1983	University of Miami (FL)	Independent	Howard Schnellenberger	11–1
1984	Brigham Young University (UT)	Western Athletic	LaVell Edwards	13–0
1985	University of Oklahoma (OK)	Big 8	Barry Switzer	11–0
1986	Pennsylvania State University (PA)	Independent	Joe Paterno	12–0
1987	University of Miami (FL)	Independent	Jimmy Johnson	12–0
1988	University of Notre Dame (IN)	Independent	Lou Holtz	12–0
1989	University of Miami (FL)	Independent	Dennis Erickson	11–1
1990	University of Colorado (CO)	Big 8	Bill McCartney	11–1–1
1991	University of Washington (WA)	Pac-10	Don James	12–0
1992	University of Alabama (AL)	Southeastern	Gene Stallings	13–0
1993	Florida State University (FL)	Atlantic Coast	Bobby Bowden	12–1
1994	University of Nebraska (NE)	Big 8	Tom Osborne	12–1
1995	University of Nebraska (NE)	Big 8	Tom Osborne	12–0
1996	University of Florida (FL)	SEC	Steve Spurrier	12–1
1997	University of Michigan (MI)	Big Ten	Lloyd Carr	12–0
1998	University of Tennessee (TN)	Southern	Phil Fulmer	13–0
1999	Florida State University (FL)	Atlantic Coast	Bobby Bowden	12–0

Year	*School*	*Conference*	*Coach*	*Record*
2000	University of Oklahoma (OK)	Big 12	Bob Stoops	13–0
2001	University of Miami (FL)	Big East	Larry Coker	12–0
2002	Ohio State University (OH)	Big Ten	Jim Tressel	14–0
2003	University of Southern California (CA)	Pac-10	Pete Carroll	12–1
2004	University of Southern California (CA)	Pac-10	Pete Carroll	13–0
2005	University of Texas (TX)	Big 12	Mack Brown	13–0
2006	University of Florida (FL)	Southern	Urban Meyer	13–1
2007	Louisiana State University (LA)	Southern	Les Miles	12–2
2008	University of Florida (FL)	Southern	Urban Meyer	13–1
2009	University of Alabama (AL)	SEC	Nick Saban	14–0
2010	Auburn University (AL)	SEC	Gene Chizik	14–0

Harlon Hill Trophy *see* NCAA Division II

Heisman Memorial Trophy

Easily the most well-known college football award, the Heisman Memorial Trophy (more commonly known as the Heisman Trophy) is presented annually to college football's best player (The Heisman Memorial Trophy, 17 Battery Street, Suite 943, New York, NY 10004; Telephone: 212-425-7000; Fax: 212-269-4547; Web site: http:///www.heisman.com). As of this writing, all winners have come from FBS schools. It honors John William Heisman (born: October 23, 1869, in Cleveland, Ohio; died: October 3, 1936, in New York, New York) who played football at Brown University (Providence, Rhode Island; 1887–1889) and at the University of Pennsylvania (Philadelphia; 1890–1891). After his playing career ended, Heisman coached at several colleges, including Oberlin College (Ohio; 1892 and 1894); Auburn University (Alabama; 1895–1899); Clemson University (South Carolina; 1900–1903); Georgia Institute of Technology (Atlanta; 1904–1919); University of Pennsylvania (Philadelphia; 1920–1922); Washington & Jefferson College (Washington, Pennsylvania; 1923); and Rice University (Houston, Texas; 1924–1927).

Heisman introduced football's forward pass; the team's "hike" function; and was an early proponent of the game being divided into quarters instead of halves. He was inducted into the College Football Hall of Fame in 1954.

He served as the athletics director of the Downtown Athletic Club (Manhattan, New York) and in 1935, the club began awarding a Downtown Athletic Club trophy to the best football player east of the Mississippi River. In December 1936, the trophy was renamed the Heisman Memorial Trophy. Today, voters include media representatives and prior winners.

The Trophy is a replica in bronze of a football player striving to attain more yardage and was sculpted by Frank Eliscu. The trophy is 14 inches long, 13.5 inches high, and weighs 25 pounds. Beginning in 1997, the top three candidates are invited to New York City for the announcement, which is made on live television.

The Heisman Trophy Trust decides the policies and procedures of determining the annual winner and selects six Sectional Representatives (Far West, Mid Atlantic, Mid West, North East, South, Southwest), who then each appoint State Representatives (who are responsible for selecting the voters within their particular state). The amount of votes for each state is determined by its size and the number of media outlets within its borders.

Each Section within the United States has 145 media votes (for a total of 870 votes across the country) and every living former Heisman Trophy winner has a vote. In 1999, The Heisman Committee decided to allow the public at large one vote in the process. The actual voting ballot allows electors to designate three potential winners, with the first choice receiving three points, the second choice garnering two points, and the third choice getting one point. The candidate with the most points is awarded the Trophy. To be eligible for the award, each candidate must be an actual student of an accredited college or university, including the United States Military Academies.

During World War II, Heisman winners did not receive a trophy because wartime restrictions prevented the use of metal and each winner during this time received a certificate. After the war, previous winners who had been presented with certificates received an actual trophy.

The 1938 winner (quarterback Davey O'Brien from Texas Christian University) is the smallest winner (5'5", 140 pounds); 1945 winner Felix "Doc" Blanchard (United States Military Academy in West Point, New York) was the first junior to win the trophy; 1949 winner Leon Hart (University of Notre Dame) is the biggest man to win the Trophy (6'5", 260 pounds); 1952 winner Billy Vessels was the first Heisman winner to play in the Canadian Football League; 1961 winner Ernie Davis (Syracuse University in Syracuse, New York) was the first African American player to win the Heisman; 1965 winner Mike Garrett (University of Southern California) was the first Californian to win the Heisman; and 1966 winner Steve Spurrier (University of Florida in Gainesville) became the first head coach to have one of his player also win the Heisman Trophy (Danny Wuerffel).

Archie Griffin (Ohio State University in Columbus) is the only man to win two Heisman trophies (1974–1975). As of this writing, Reggie Bush (University of Southern California) is the only winner (2005) to relinquish his Trophy (he was accused of off-field NCAA rules violations years after he left the school).

Year	*Winner*	*School*	*Position*	*Class*	*Points*
1935	Jay Berwanger	University of Chicago (IL)	Running Back	Senior	84
1936	Larry Kelley	Yale University (CT)	End	Senior	219
1937	Clint Frank	Yale University (CT)	Quarterback	Senior	524
1938	Davey O'Brien	Texas Christian University (TX)	Quarterback	Senior	519
1939	Nile Kinnick	University of Iowa (IA)	Running Back	Senior	651
1940	Tom Harmon	University of Michigan (MI)	Running Back	Senior	1,303
1941	Bruce Smith	University of Minnesota (MN)	Running Back	Senior	554
1942	Frank Sinkwich	University of Georgia (GA)	Running Back	Senior	1,059
1943	Angelo Bertelli	University of Notre Dame (IN)	Quarterback	Senior	648
1944	Les Horvath	Ohio State University (OH)	Quarterback	Senior	412
1945	Doc Blanchard	U.S. Military Academy at West Point (NY)	Fullback	Junior	860
1946	Glenn Davis	U.S. Military Academy at West Point (NY)	Running Back	Senior	792
1947	John Lujack	University of Notre Dame (IN)	Quarterback	Senior	742
1948	Doak Walker	Southern Methodist University (TX)	Running Back	Junior	778
1949	Leon Hart	University of Notre Dame (IN)	End	Senior	995
1950	Vic Janowicz	Ohio State University (OH)	Running Back	Junior	633
1951	Dick Kazmaier	Princeton University (NJ)	Running Back	Senior	1,777
1952	Billy Vessels	University of Oklahoma (OK)	Running Back	Senior	525
1953	John Lattner	University of Notre Dame (IN)	Running Back	Senior	1,850
1954	Alan Ameche	University of Wisconsin (WI)	Fullback	Senior	1,068
1955	Howard Cassady	Ohio State University (OH)	Running Back	Senior	2,219
1956	Paul Hornung	University of Notre Dame (IN)	Quarterback	Senior	1,066
1957	John David Crow	Texas A&M University (TX)	Running Back	Senior	1,183
1958	Pete Dawkins	U.S. Military Academy at West Point (NY)	Running Back	Senior	1,394
1959	Billy Cannon	Louisiana State University (LA)	Running Back	Senior	1,929
1960	Joe Bellino	U.S. Naval Academy (MD)	Running Back	Senior	1,793
1961	Ernie Davis	Syracuse University (NY)	Running Back	Senior	824
1962	Terry Baker	Oregon State University (OR)	Quarterback	Senior	707
1963	Roger Staubach	U.S. Naval Academy (MD)	Quarterback	Junior	1,860
1964	John Huarte	University of Notre Dame (IN)	Quarterback	Senior	1,026
1965	Mike Garrett	University of Southern California (CA)	Running Back	Senior	926
1966	Steve Spurrier	University of Florida (FL)	Quarterback	Senior	1,679
1967	Gary Beban	University of California, Los Angeles (CA)	Quarterback	Senior	1,968
1968	O.J. Simpson	University of Southern California (CA)	Running Back	Senior	2,853
1969	Steve Owens	University of Oklahoma (OK)	Fullback	Senior	1,488
1970	Jim Plunkett	Stanford University (CA)	Quarterback	Senior	2,229
1971	Pat Sullivan	Auburn University (AL)	Quarterback	Senior	1,597
1972	Johnny Rodgers	University of Nebraska (NE)	Running Back	Senior	1,310
1973	John Cappelletti	Pennsylvania State University (PA)	Running Back	Senior	1,057

Year	Winner	School	Position	Class	Points
1974	Archie Griffin	Ohio State University (OH)	Running Back	Junior	1,920
1975	Archie Griffin	Ohio State University (OH)	Running Back	Senior	1,800
1976	Tony Dorsett	University of Pittsburgh (PA)	Running Back	Senior	2,357
1977	Earl Campbell	University of Texas (TX)	Running Back	Senior	1,547
1978	Billy Sims	University of Oklahoma (OK)	Running Back	Junior	827
1979	Charles White	University of Southern California (CA)	Running Back	Senior	1.695
1980	George Rogers	University of South Carolina (SC)	Running Back	Senior	1,128
1981	Marcus Allen	University of Southern California (CA)	Running Back	Senior	1,797
1982	Herschel Walker	University of Georgia (GA)	Running Back	Junior	1,926
1983	Mike Rozier	University of Nebraska (NE)	Running Back	Senior	1,801
1984	Doug Flutie	Boston College (MA)	Quarterback	Senior	2,240
1985	Bo Jackson	Auburn University (AL)	Running Back	Senior	1,509
1986	Vinny Testaverde	University of Miami (FL)	Quarterback	Senior	2,213
1987	Tim Brown	University of Notre Dame (IN)	Wide Receiver	Senior	1,442
1988	Barry Sanders	Oklahoma State University (OK)	Running Back	Junior	1,878
1989	Andre Ware	University of Houston (TX)	Quarterback	Junior	1,073
1990	Ty Detmer	Brigham Young University (UT)	Quarterback	Junior	1,482
1991	Desmond Howard	University of Michigan (MI)	Wide Receiver	Junior	2,077
1992	Gino Torretta	University of Miami (FL)	Quarterback	Senior	1,400
1993	Charlie Ward	Florida State University (FL)	Quarterback	Senior	2,310
1994	Rashaan Salaam	University of Colorado (CO)	Running Back	Junior	1,743
1995	Eddie George	Ohio State University (OH)	Running Back	Senior	1,460
1996	Danny Wuerffel	University of Florida (FL)	Quarterback	Senior	1,363
1997	Charles Woodson	University of Michigan (MI)	Cornerback	Junior	1,815
1998	Ricky Williams	University of Texas (TX)	Running Back	Senior	2,355
1999	Ron Dayne	University of Wisconsin (WI)	Running Back	Senior	2,042
2000	Chris Weinke	Florida State University (FL)	Quarterback	Senior	1,628
2001	Eric Crouch	University of Nebraska (NE)	Quarterback	Senior	770
2002	Carson Palmer	University of Southern California (CA)	Quarterback	Senior	1,328
2003	Jason White	University of Oklahoma (OK)	Quarterback	Junior	1,481
2004	Matt Leinart	University of Southern California (CA)	Quarterback	Junior	1,325
2005	Reggie Bush*	University of Southern California (CA)	Running Back	Junior	2,541
2006	Troy Smith	Ohio State University (OH)	Quarterback	Senior	2,540
2007	Tim Tebow	University of Florida (FL)	Quarterback	Sophomore	1,957
2008	Sam Bradford	University of Oklahoma (OK)	Quarterback	Sophomore	1,726
2009	Mark Ingram	University of Alabama (AL)	Running Back	Sophomore	1,304
2010	Cameron Newton	Auburn University (AL)	Quarterback		2,263

*Reggie Bush, a running back from the University of Southern California (Los Angeles, CA), won the Heisman Trophy in 2005 by the second largest margin ever (after O.J. Simpson's margin of victory in 1968). However, after he left college and joined the National Football League, stories arose about him and his family accepting inappropriate gifts and support from agents. Although it was commonly agreed that his controversial actions did not affect his on-field performance for that season, in 2010 he was ruled ineligible for the Trophy and returned it to the Heisman Trust, becoming the first player to ever do so. After deliberation, the Heisman Trophy Trust decided not to conduct a re-vote, but to leave the award vacant for that year (2005).

Helms Athletic Foundation National Champion

Founded in 1936, the Helms Athletic Foundation was based in Los Angeles, California, and started by Bill Schroeder and Paul Helms. It assembled a panel of experts that selected college National Champion teams and All-America teams in numerous sports, the most well-known being football and basketball. The panel voted on national football champions until 1982, retroactively ranked football teams back to 1883, and ran a football hall of fame.

After Paul Helms died in 1957, the United Savings and Loan bank took over the Helms Foundation and when the bank merged with the Citizen Savings Bank in 1973, the Foundation became known as the Citizens Savings Athletic Foundation. It was again renamed in 1982 when the First Interstate Bank assumed the Foundation. When the Helms Foundation was finally dissolved in 1982, its documents and awards were absorbed into the collection of the Amateur Athletic Foundation.

Helms Foundation NCAA National Champions (Football)

Year	Team
1883	Yale University (CT)
1884	Yale University (CT)
1885	Princeton University (NJ)
1886	Yale University (CT)
1887	Yale University (CT)
1888	Yale University (CT)
1889	Princeton University (NJ)
1890	Harvard University (MA)
1891	Yale University (CT)
1892	Yale University (CT)
1893	Princeton University (NJ)
1894	Yale University (CT)
1895	University of Pennsylvania (PA)
1896	Princeton University (NJ)
1897	University of Pennsylvania (PA)
1898	Harvard University (MA)
1899	Harvard University (MA)
1900	Yale University (CT)
1901	University of Michigan (MI)
1902	University of Michigan (MI)
1903	Princeton University (NJ)
1904	University of Pennsylvania (PA)
1905	University of Chicago (IL)
1906	Princeton University (NJ)
1907	Yale University (CT)
1908	University of Pennsylvania (PA)
1909	Yale University (CT)
1910	Harvard University (MA)
1911	Princeton University (NJ)
1912	Harvard University (MA)
1913	Harvard University (MA)
1914	United States Military Academy (NY)
1915	Cornell University (NY)
1916	University of Pittsburgh (PA)
1917	Georgia Institute of Technology (GA)
1918	University of Pittsburgh (PA)
1919	Harvard University (MA)
1920	University of California (Berkeley) (CA)
1921	Cornell University (NY)
1922	West Virginia University (WV)
1923	University of Illinois (IL)
1924	University of Notre Dame (IN)
1925	University of Alabama (AL)
1926	Stanford University (CA)
1926	University of Alabama (AL)
1927	University of Illinois (IL)
1928	Georgia Institute of Technology (GA)
1929	University of Notre Dame (IN)
1930	University of Notre Dame (IN)
1931	University of Southern California (CA)
1932	University of Southern California (CA)
1933	University of Michigan (MI)
1934	University of Minnesota (MN)
1935	University of Minnesota (MN)
1936	University of Minnesota (MN)

Year	Team
1937	University of California (Berkeley) (CA)
1938	Texas Christian University (TX)
1939	Texas A&M University (TX)
1940	Stanford University (CA)
1941	University of Minnesota (MN)
1942	University of Wisconsin (WI)
1943	University of Notre Dame (IN)
1944	United States Military Academy (NY)
1945	United States Military Academy (NY)
1946	United States Military Academy (NY)
1946	University of Notre Dame (IN)
1947	University of Michigan (MI)
1947	University of Notre Dame (IN)
1948	University of Michigan (MI)
1949	University of Notre Dame (IN)
1950	University of Oklahoma (OK)
1951	Michigan State University (MI)
1952	Michigan State University (MI)
1953	University of Notre Dame (IN)
1954	Ohio State University (OH)
1954	University of California, Los Angeles (CA)
1955	University of Oklahoma (OK)
1956	University of Oklahoma (OK)
1957	Auburn University (AL)
1958	Louisiana State University (LA)
1959	Syracuse University (NY)
1960	University of Washington (WA)
1961	University of Alabama (AL)
1962	University of Southern California (CA)
1963	University of Texas (TX)
1964	University of Arkansas (AR)
1965	Michigan State University (MI)
1966	Michigan State University (MI)
1966	University of Notre Dame (IN)
1967	University of Southern California (CA)
1968	Ohio State University (OH)
1969	University of Texas (TX)
1970	University of Nebraska (NE)
1971	University of Nebraska (NE)
1972	University of Southern California (CA)
1973	University of Notre Dame (IN)
1974	University of Oklahoma (OK)
1974	University of Southern California (CA)
1975	Ohio State University (OH)
1975	University of Oklahoma (OK)
1976	University of Pittsburgh (PA)
1977	University of Notre Dame (IN)
1978	University of Alabama (AL)
1978	University of Oklahoma (OK)
1978	University of Southern California (CA)
1979	University of Alabama (AL)
1980	University of Georgia (GA)
1981	Clemson University (SC)
1982	Pennsylvania State University (PA)
1982	Southern Methodist University (TX)

Jack Lambert Trophy

Awarded since 1991 by the Touchdown Club of Columbus (Ohio, http://www.touchdownclubof columbus.com), the Jack Lambert Trophy is presented annually to college football's best linebacker.

Sam B. Nicola (who died in 1993) founded the Touchdown Club of Columbus in 1956 and was president of the Athletic Club of Columbus when the initial All-Sports Banquet was held in January 1956. Although a local organization, its range has always been national (not limited to the Columbus, Ohio area) and athletes from all sports have been recognized. Honored athletes are selected by the appropriate Touchdown Club's committees, consisting of coaches, sportswriters, and former players.

The Trophy honors Jack Lambert (John Harold "Jack" Lambert; born: July 8, 1952, in Mantua, Ohio), who played football at Kent State University (Kent, Ohio) and won four Super Bowls (IX [1975], X [1976], XIII [1979], XIV [1980]) during his 11-year career with the NFL's Pittsburgh Steelers (1974–1984). He was the 1974 NFL Defensive Rookie of the Year; 1976 NFL Defensive Player of the Year; named to the NFL 1970s All-Decade Team; named to the NFL 1980s All-Decade Team; and was selected to the NFL 75th Anniversary All-Time Team. He was inducted into the Pro Football Hall of Fame in 1990.

As of this writing, only James Laurinatis (Ohio State University) has won the award twice.

Year	*Winner*	*School*	*Note*
1991	Eric Anderson	University of Michigan (MI)	1991 All-American
1992	Marvin Jones	Florida State University (FL)	1992 Butkus Award Winner
1993	Trev Alberts	University of Nebraska (NE)	1993 All-American
1994	Derrick Brooks	Florida State University (FL)	2X All-American (1993–1994)
1994	Dana Howard	University of Illinois (IL)	2X All-American (1993–1994)
1995	Simeon Rice	University of Illinois (IL)	2X All-American (1994–1995)
1996	Pat Fitzgerald	Northwestern University (IL)	2008 College Football Hall of Fame Inductee
1997	Andy Katzenmoyer	Ohio State University (OH)	1997 Dick Butkus Award Winner
1998	Dat Nguyen	Texas A&M (TX)	1st Vietnamese Player in the National Football League
1999	LaVar Arrington	Pennsylvania State University (PA)	2X All-American (1998–1999)
2000	Dan Morgan	University of Miami (FL)	1st Sophomore Captain in Team History
2001	Rocky Calmus	University of Oklahoma (OK)	2001 Butkus Award Winner
2002	Eric Henderson, Jr.	University of Maryland (MD)	2002 Butkus Award Winner
2003	Jonathan Vilma	University of Miami (FL)	3X Academic A, Big East Conference
2004	Derrick Johnson	University of Texas (TX)	2004 Bronko Nagurski Trophy Winner
2005	Aaron Hawk	Ohio State University (OH)	2005 Lombardi Award Winner
2006	Patrick Willis	University of Mississippi (MS)	2006 Butkus Award Winner
2007	James Laurinaitis	Ohio State University (OH)	2007 Butkus Award Winner
2008	James Laurinaitis	Ohio State University (OH)	2008 Lott Trophy Winner
2009	Rolando McClain	University of Alabama (AL)	2009 Butkus Award Winner
2010	Von Miller	Texas A&M University (TX)	2010 Butkus Award Winner

Jack Tatum Trophy

Named after Ohio State University All-American and 2004 College Football Hall of Fame inductee, the Jack Tatum Trophy has been presented since 1991 by the Touchdown Club of Columbus (Ohio, http//www.touchdownclubofcolumbus.com) to college football's best defensive back.

Sam B. Nicola (who died in 1993) founded the Touchdown Club of Columbus in 1956 and was president of the Athletic Club of Columbus when the initial All-Sports Banquet was held in January 1956. Although a local organization, its range has always been national (not limited to the Columbus, Ohio area) and athletes from all sports have been recognized. Honored athletes are selected by the appropriate Touchdown Club's committees, consisting of coaches, sportswriters, and former players.

The Trophy is named after Jack Tatum (John David Tatum; born: November 18, 1948, in Cherryville, North Carolina) who played in the NFL for the Oakland Raiders (1971–1979) and the Houston Oilers (1980). Commonly known as "The Assassin," he was voted to three Pro Bowls (1973–1979) and helped the team win Super Bowl XI (1977). He is also remembered as the defensive back whose hit paralyzed Darryl Stingley (New England Patriots) during a 1978 pre-season game.

At Ohio State University, he was a three-time First-Team All-Big Ten selection (1968–1970); a 1970 All-American selection and National Defensive Player of the Year; and helped the school win the 1968 national championship in his first year.

As of this writing, only Eric Berry (University of Tennessee) has won the Trophy twice.

Year	*Winner*	*School*	*Note*
1991	Terrell Buckley	Florida State University (FL)	1991 Jim Thorpe Award Winner
1992	Deon Figures	University of Colorado (CO)	1992 Jim Thorpe Award Winner
1993	Antonio Langham	University of Alabama (AL)	1993 Jim Thorpe Award Winner
1994	Bobby Taylor	University of Notre Dame (IN)	1994 All-American
1995	Lawyer Milloy	University of Washington (WA)	1995 All-American
1996	Chris Canty	Kansas State University (KS)	Played in the NFL and American Football League
1997	Charles Woodson	University of Michigan (MI)	1997 Jim Thorpe Award Winner
1998	Antoine Winfield	Ohio State University (OH)	1998 Jim Thorpe Award Winner
1999	Tyrone Carter	University of Minnesota (MN)	1999 Jim Thorpe Award Winner
2000	Jamar Fletcher	University of Wisconsin (WI)	2000 Jim Thorpe Award Winner
2001	Roy Williams	University of Oklahoma (OK)	2001 Bronko Nagurski Trophy Winner
2002	Mike Doss	Ohio State University (OH)	3X All-Big Ten (2000–2002)
2003	Sean Taylor	University of Miami (FL)	Won 2001 National Championship
2004	Antrel Rolle	University of Miami (FL)	2004 All-American
2005	Jimmy Williams	Virginia Tech University (VA)	2005 All-American
2006	Reggie Nelson	University of Florida (FL)	2006 All-American
2007	Aqib Talib	University of Kansas (KS)	2007 All-American
2008	Eric Berry	University of Tennessee (TN)	2008 SEC Defensive Player of the Year
2009	Eric Berry	University of Tennessee (TN)	2009 Jim Thorpe Award Winner
2010	Patrick Peterson	Louisiana State University (LA)	2010 SEC Defensive Player of the Year

Jacobs Blocking Trophy *see* Atlantic Coast Conference (NCAA Division I FBS), Southeastern Conference (NCAA Division I FBS), Southern Conference (NCAA Division I FCS), South Atlantic Conference (NCAA Division II)

Jim Brown Trophy

Presented annually by the Touchdown Club of Columbus (Ohio; http:www.touchdownclubofcolumbus.com) since 1991, this Trophy is awarded to the NCAA's best running back, and is named for college and professional football hall of famer Jim Brown (Syracuse University, NFL's Cleveland Browns).

Sam B. Nicola (who died in 1993) founded the Touchdown Club of Columbus in 1956 and was president of the Athletic Club of Columbus when the initial All-Sports Banquet was held in January 1956. Although a local organization, its range has always been national (not limited to the Columbus, Ohio area) and athletes from all sports have been recognized. Honored athletes are selected by the appropriate Touchdown Club's committees, consisting of coaches, sportswriters, and former players.

Jim Brown (James Nathaniel "Jim" Brown; born: February 17, 1936, in St. Simons Island, Georgia) was a legendary athlete at Syracuse University (Syracuse, New York, 1954–1956) and a hall of fame player for the NFL's Cleveland Browns (1957–1965). He has been inducted into the Pro Football Hall of Fame (1971), the Lacrosse Museum and National Hall of Fame (1983), and the College Football Hall of Fame (1995). Often considered one of the greatest players ever in the game, he was a three-time Most Valuable Player (1957–1958, 1965); elected to the NFL 1960s All-Decade Team; and was selected to the NFL 75th Anniversary All-Time Team. When he retired from the NFL, Brown held league records for single-season (1,863 in 1963) and career rushing (12,312) yards; rushing touchdowns (106); total touchdowns (126); and all-purpose yards (15,549). He was the first player in league history to score 100 rushing touchdowns (in 93 games) and the only rusher to average more than 100 yards per game for a career (104.3, with a career average of 5.2 yards per carry).

In 1988, Brown founded the Amer-I-Can Program and currently works with gang members in Los Angeles, California and Cleveland.

As of this writing, Ricky Williams (University of Texas) and Darren McFadden (University of Arkansas) are the only multiple winners.

Year	*Name*	*School*	*Note*
1991	Vaughn Dunbar	Indiana University (IN)	1991 All-American
1992	Marshall Faulk	San Diego State University (CA)	3X All-American (1991–1993)
1993	Brent Moss	University of Wisconsin (WI)	1993 Big Ten Offensive Player of the Year
1994	Rashaan Salaam	University of Colorado (CO)	1994 Heisman Trophy Winner
1995	Eddie George	Ohio State University (OH)	1995 Heisman Trophy Winner
1996	Troy Davis	Iowa State University (IA)	1st in NCAA History to gain 2,000 in two seasons
1997	Ricky Williams	University of Texas (TX)	2X Doak Walker Award Winner (1997–1998)
1998	Ricky Williams	University of Texas (TX)	1998 Heisman Trophy Winner
1999	Ron Dayne	University of Wisconsin (WI)	1999 Heisman Trophy Winner
2000	LaDainian Tomlinson	Texas Christian University (TX)	2000 Mobile Alabama Bowl MVP
2001	Luke Staley	Brigham Young University (UT)	2001 Doak Walker Award Winner
2002	Larry Johnson	Pennsylvania State University (PA)	2002 Maxwell Award Winner
2003	Chris Perry	University of Michigan (MI)	2003 Doak Walker Award Winner
2004	Adrian Peterson	University of Oklahoma (OK)	2004 All-American
2005	Reggie Bush	University of Southern California (CA)	2005 Heisman Trophy Winner
2006	Darren McFadden	University of Arkansas (AR)	2006 Doak Walker Award Winner
2007	Darren McFadden	University of Arkansas (AR)	2007 Walter Camp Award Winner
2008	Shonn Greene	University of Iowa (IA)	2008 Big Ten Most Valuable Player
2009	Toby Gerhart	Stanford University (CA)	2009 Doak Walker Award Winner
2010	LaMichael James	University of Oregon (OR)	2010 Doak Walker Award Winner

Jim Parker Trophy

Presented by the Touchdown Club of Columbus (Ohio, http://www.touchdownclubofcolumbus.com) annually since 1991, the Jim Parker Trophy is awarded to the best collegiate offensive lineman.

Sam B. Nicola (who died in 1993) founded the Touchdown Club of Columbus in 1956 and was president of the Athletic Club of Columbus when the initial All-Sports Banquet was held in January 1956. Although a local organization, its range has always been national (not limited to the Columbus, Ohio area) and athletes from all sports have been recognized. Honored athletes are selected by the appropriate Touchdown Club's committees, consisting of coaches, sportswriters, and former players.

This Trophy is named after Ohio State University football player Jim Parker (James Thomas "Jim" Parker, born: April 3, 1934, in Macon, Georgia; died: July 18, 2005, in Columbia, Maryland) from 1954 to 1956 and helped the team win the national title in 1954. He later played for the NFL's Baltimore Colts for 11 seasons (1957–1967); was named to the NFL 1950s All-Decade Team; and was selected to the NFL's 75th Anniversary All-Time Team.

He was inducted into the Pro Football Hall of Fame in 1973 (the first full-time offensive lineman to be inducted) and into the College Football Hall of Fame in 1974.

As of this writing, no player has won this award twice.

Year	*Winner*	*School*	*Note*
1991	Greg Skrepenak	University of Michigan (MI)	1991 Big Ten Offensive Lineman of the Year
1992	Lincoln Kennedy	University of Washington (WA)	2X Morris Trophy Winner (1991–1992)
1993	Aaron Taylor	University of Notre Dame (IN)	2X All-American (1992–1993)
1994	Zach Wiegert	University of Nebraska (NE)	1994 Outland Trophy Winner
1995	Jonathan Ogden	University of California, Los Angeles (CA)	1995 Outland Trophy Winner
1996	Orlando Pace	Ohio State University (OH)	2X Lombardi Award Winner (1995–1996)
1997	Aaron Taylor	University of Nebraska (NE)	1997 Outland Trophy Winner
1998	Matt Stinchcomb	University of Georgia (GA)	2X All-American (1997–1998)
1999	Chris McIntosh	University of Wisconsin (WI)	1999 All-American

Year	Winner	School	Note
2000	Steve Hutchinson	University of Michigan (MI)	4X All-Big Ten Selection (1997–2000)
2001	Bryant McKinnie	University of Miami (FL)	2001 Outland Trophy Winner
2002	Brett Romberg	University of Miami (FL)	2002 Dave Rimington Trophy Winner
2003	Shawn Andrews	University of Arkansas (AR)	2003 All-American
2004	Jammal Brown	University of Oklahoma (OK)	2004 Outland Trophy Winner
2005	Greg Eslinger	University of Minnesota (MN)	2005 Outland Trophy Winner
2006	Joe Thomas	University of Wisconsin (WI)	2006 Outland Trophy Winner
2007	Jake Long	University of Michigan (MI)	2X All-American (2006–2007)
2008	Andre Smith	University of Alabama (AL)	2008 Outland Trophy Winner
2009	Russell Okung	Oklahoma State University (OK)	2X First-Team All-American (2008–2009)
2010	Gabe Carimi	University of Wisconsin (WI)	2010 Big Ten Offensive Lineman of the Year

Jim Thorpe Award

The Jim Thorpe Award, named in honor of the multi-sport legend Jim Thorpe, has been awarded annually since 1986 to the top defensive back in college football and the winner is voted on by the Jim Thorpe Association (Jim Thorpe Museum / Oklahoma Sports Hall of Fame, 4040 North Lincoln Boulevard, Oklahoma City, Oklahoma 73105; Telephone: 405-427-1400; Web site: http://www.jimthorpe assoc.org/).

The Award is named after the legendary Jim Thorpe (Jacobus Franciscus "Jim" Thorpe; born: May 28, 1888, in Prague, Oklahoma; died: March 28, 1953, in Lomita, California), one of America's greatest sports legends. He played professional football for numerous teams (Canton Bulldogs (1915–1917, 1919–1920, 1926); Cleveland Indians (1921); Oorang Indians (1922–1923); Rock Island Independents (1924–1925); New York Giants (1925); Tampa Cardinals (1926); and the Chicago Cardinals (1928)), and was selected to the NFL's 1920s All-Decade Team.

Additionally, Thorpe played Major League Baseball for the New York Giants (1913–1915, 1917, 1918–1919); Cincinnati Reds (1917); and Boston Braves (1919), retiring with a .252 career batting average in 289 games.

Before becoming a professional athlete, he won two gold medals at the 1912 Stockholm, Sweden, Summer Olympics (Decathlon, Pentathlon).

Derived from Native American ancestry, Thorpe grew up in the Sac and Fox nation in Oklahoma; attended school (and played in early athletics) at the Carlisle Industrial School in Carlisle, Pennsylvania; played on several All-American Indian teams (various sports); and barnstormed as a professional basketball player with a team composed entirely of Native Americans.

He was inducted into the College Football Hall of Fame in 1951 and the Pro Football Hall of Fame in 1963.

As of this writing, no player has won this award twice.

Year	Winner	School	Note
1986	Thomas Everett	Baylor University (TX)	2006 College Hall of Fame Inductee
1987	Bennie Blades	University of Miami (FL)	Won 1987 NCAA National Championship
1987	Rickey Dixon	University of Oklahoma (OK)	1987 All-American
1988	Deion Sanders	Florida State University (FL)	2X First-Team All-American (1986–1987)
1989	Mark Carrier	University of Southern California (CA)	USC's 1st and Only Jim Thorpe Winner
1990	Darryll Lewis	University of Arizona (AZ)	1991 Houston Oilers 2nd Round Draft Pick
1991	Terrell Buckley	Florida State University (FL)	1991 Jack Tatum Trophy Winner
1992	Deon Figures	University of Colorado (CO)	Won 1990 National Championship
1993	Antonio Langham	University of Alabama (AL)	1993 Jack Tatum Trophy Winner
1994	Chris Hudson	University of Colorado (CO)	3rd Round NFL Draft Pick
1995	Greg Myers	Colorado State University (CO)	5th Round NFL Draft Pick
1996	Lawrence Wright	University of Florida (FL)	Won 1996 National Championship
1997	Charles Woodson	University of Michigan (MI)	1997 Heisman Trophy Winner
1998	Antoine Winfield	Ohio State University (OH)	1998 Jack Tatum Trophy Winner

Year	*Winner*	*School*	*Note*
1999	Tyrone Carter	University of Minnesota (MN)	1999 Jack Tatum Trophy Winner
2000	Jamar Fletcher	University of Wisconsin (WI)	2000 Jack Tatum Trophy Winner
2001	Roy Williams	University of Oklahoma (OK)	2001 Bronko Nagurski Trophy Winner
2002	Terence Newman	Kansas State University (KS)	2002 All-American
2003	Derrick Strait	University of Oklahoma (OK)	2003 Bronko Nagurski Trophy Winner
2004	Carlos Rogers	Auburn University (AL)	2005 1st Round Draft Pick
2005	Michael Huff	University of Texas (TX)	2005 First-Team All-American
2006	Aaron Ross	University of Texas (TX)	2006 All-American
2007	Antoine Cason	University of Arizona (AZ)	2007 First-Team All-American
2008	Malcolm Jenkins	Ohio State University (OH)	2008 First-Team All-American
2009	Eric Berry	University of Tennessee (TN)	2X Jack Tatum Trophy Winner
2010	Patrick Peterson	Louisiana State University (LA)	2010 Bednarik Award Winner

John Baronian Award

Since 1997, the John Baronian Award has been presented annually for a Lifetime Contribution to Football in the New England Area by the Gridiron Club of Greater Boston (9 Broadway, Unit 320, Saugus, MA 01906; Web site: http://www.gridclubofgreaterboston.com/). In 2002, the Award was renamed in honor of John Baronian (1950 Tufts University graduate [Medford, MA]), former president of the Gridiron Club, and 1982 winner of the National Football Foundation and Hall of Fame's Contribution to Amateur Football Award.

Year	*Winner*	*School*	*Note*
1997	Jack Grinold	Northeastern University (MA)	Won 2009 ECAC Commissioner's Award
1998	Jack Bicknell	Boston College (MA) / University of Maine (ME)	Won 1986 Hall of Fame Bowl
1999	Bill Bowes	University New Hampshire (NH)	Coached 27 Years at University of NH
2000	Jack Daly	Williams College (MA)	No Further Information
2001	Rocky Carzo	Tufts University (MA)	26 Seasons at Tufts
2002	Joe Yukica	University of New Hampshire (NH) / Boston College (MA) / Dartmouth College (NH)	Head Football Coach for 30+ Years
2003	Dan Allen	College of the Holy Cross (MA) / Boston University (MA)	Head Football Coach for 10+ Years
2004	Dick Farley	Williams College (MA)	2006 College Football Hall of Fame Inductee
2005	Bob Pickett	University of Massachusetts (MA)	Former UMASS Head Football Coach
2006	Barry Gallup	Boston College (MA) / Northeastern University (MA)	Head Football Coach for 20+ Years
2007	Harold Westerman	University of Maine (ME)	University of Maine Head Football Coach
2008	Ed Schluntz	Harvard University (MA)	No Further Information
2009	Robert "Bo" Lyons	Northeastern University (MA)	Northeastern University Football Coach
2010	Tom Austin	Colby College (ME)	Head Coach at Colby for 18 Years

John Mackey Award *see* NCAA Division I FBS

Johnny Unitas Golden Arm Award

The Johnny Unitas Golden Arm Award is presented annually to the nation's best senior quarterback in college football; was established in 1987 by the Johnny Unitas Foundation (he lived from 1933 to 2002); and is continued today by the non-profit Johnny Unitas Golden Arm Educational Foundation, Inc. (13812 Manor Glen Road, Baldwin, Maryland 21013; Telephone: 410-456-6785; Fax: 410-592-6538; Email: junitasjr@comcast.net; Web site: http://www.goldenarmfoundation.com/).

Johnny Unitas (John Constantine "Johnny" Unitas; born: May 7, 1933, in Pittsburgh, Pennsylvania; died: September 11, 2002, in Lutherville-Timonium, Maryland) played football at the University of Louisville (Kentucky, 1951–1954) and in the NFL (17 seasons) for the Baltimore Colts (1956–1972) and the San Diego Chargers (1973) and was often called "Johnny U." He won Super Bowl V (1971); was a two-time NFL Champion (1958–1959); named to the NFL 1960s All-Decade Team; selected to the NFL 75th Anniversary All-Time Team; a three-time NFL Most Valuable Player (1959, 1964, 1967); and was inducted into the Pro Football Hall of Fame in 1979. His record of throwing a touchdown pass in 47 consecutive games (1956–1960) still stands as of this writing and he was the first quarterback to throw for more than 40,000 (40,239) career yards.

As of this writing, no player has won this award twice.

Year	*Winner*	*School*	*Note*
1987	Don McPherson	Syracuse University (NY)	1987 Maxwell Award Winner
1988	Rodney Peete	University of Southern California (CA)	1988 First-Team All-American
1989	Tony Rice	University of Notre Dame (IN)	1989 All-American
1990	Craig Erickson	University of Miami (FL)	Won 1989 National Championship
1991	Casey Weldon	Florida State University (FL)	4th Round NFL Draft Pick
1992	Gino Torretta	University of Miami (FL)	1992 Heisman Trophy Winner
1993	Charlie Ward	Florida State University (FL)	1993 Heisman Trophy Winner
1994	Jay Barker	University of Alabama (AL)	Won 1992 National Championship
1995	Tommie Frazier	University of Nebraska (NE)	1995 Big Eight Offensive Player of the Year
1996	Danny Wuerffel	University of Florida (FL)	1996 Heisman Trophy Winner
1997	Peyton Manning	University of Tennessee (TN)	1997 Maxwell Award Winner
1998	Cade McNown	University of California, Los Angeles (CA)	1998 First-Team All-American
1999	Chris Redman	University of Louisville (KY)	Won Super Bowl XXXV (2001)
2000	Chris Weinke	Florida State University (FL)	2000 Heisman Trophy Winner
2001	David Carr	California State University, Fresno (CA)	2001 Sammy Baugh Trophy Winner
2002	Carson Palmer	University of Southern California (CA)	2002 Heisman Trophy Winner
2003	Eli Manning	University of Mississippi (MS)	2003 Maxwell Award Winner
2004	Jason White	University of Oklahoma (OK)	2004 Maxwell Award Winner
2005	Matt Leinart	University of Southern California (CA)	2005 Walter Camp Award Winner
2006	Brady Quinn	University of Notre Dame (IN)	2006 Maxwell Award Winner
2007	Matt Ryan	Boston College (MA)	2007 ACC Player of the Year
2008	Graham Harrell	Texas Tech University (TX)	2008 Gator Bowl MVP
2009	Colt McCoy	University of Texas (TX)	2009 Maxwell Award Winner
2010	Scott Tolzien	University of Wisconsin (WI)	Best Completion % in School History (.675)

Joseph P. McKenney Award

Since 1997, the Joseph P. McKenney Award (named in honor of Joe McKenney, former head coach of Boston College and college referee) has been presented annually by the Gridiron Club of Greater Boston (9 Broadway, Unit 320, Saugus, MA 01906; Web site: http://www.gridclubofgreaterboston.com/) to the best college official in New England.

Year	*Winner*	*Conference*
1997	Paul Tighe	Big East Conference
1998	Ron Abdow	Big East Conference
1999	John Collins	Eastern College Athletic Conference
2000	Steve McBride	Big East Conference
2001	John Salmon	Big East Conference
2002	Art Bellows	Eastern College Athletic College
2003	Brian Sullivan	Atlantic 10 Conference
2004	Bill Ward	Ivy & Patriot Leagues
2005	Paul King	Big East Conference
2006	David A. Carter	Eastern College Athletic Conference
2007	Bryan Platt	Big East Conference
2008	Mike Kelley	Atlantic Coast Conference
2009	Christopher Smith	Colonial Athletic Association
2010	Ronald Kumiega	Big East Conference

Joseph P. Zabilski Award *see* NCAA Division II and NCAA Division III

Joseph V. Paterno Award

Replacing the George Munger Award (which had been presented from 1989 to 2009), the Joseph V. Paterno Award was established in 2010 and is given annually to the college football head coach who best exemplifies Penn State head coach Joe Paterno's dedication to the development of student-athletes and the advancement of the university beyond athletics.

The award is presented by the Maxwell Football Club (P.O, Box 1225, Southampton, PA 18966; Telephone: 610-277-8900; Fax: 610-277-2239; Email: info@maxwellfootballclub.org; Web site: http://www.maxwellfootballclub.org) and nominees come from each of the FBS schools. In addition to on-field football excellence, winners of this award must also have a significant impact on players' graduation rates and be a force in their local community through philanthropic endeavors and volunteer work.

Year	*Coach*	*School*	*Note*
2010	Frank Beamer	Virginia Tech	2X ACC Coach of the Year (2004–2005)

Lambert Cup *see* NCAA Division I FCS, NCAA Division II, NCAA Division III

Lambert-Meadowlands Trophy *see* NCAA Division I FBS

Lombardi Award *see* Rotary Lombardi Award

Lott Trophy

Since 2004, the Lott Trophy (Ronnie Lott Award) has been sponsored by the Pacific Club IMPACT Foundation (4110 MacArthur Boulevard, Newport Beach, CA 92660; Telephone: 949-428-0042; Email: karen@pacificclub.org; Web site: http://lotttrophy.com/index.php) and has been presented annually to the college football Defensive IMPACT Player of the Year. IMPACT is an acronym for: *I*ntegrity, *M*aturity, *P*erformance, *A*cademics, *C*ommunity, and *T*enacity. The Trophy honors the personal character of the winning player as well as his athletic excellence.

Winners are voted on by members of the national media, previous finalists, the board of directors of the Pacific Club IMPACT Foundation, and The Master Coaches (a group of former college football head coaches) and is named for hall of famer Ronnie Lott.

Ronnie Lott (Ronald Mandel "Ronnie" Lott; born: May 8, 1959, in Albuquerque, New Mexico) played college football for the University of Southern California (Los Angeles, CA; 1977–1980; shared the national championship in 1978) and in the NFL for the San Francisco 49ers (1981–1990), Los Angeles Raiders (1991–1992), New York Jets (1993–1994), and the Kansas City Chiefs (1995). He helped San Francisco win four Super Bowls (XVI [1982], XIX [1985], XXIII [1989], XXIV [1990]); was named to the NFL 1980s All-Decade Team; to the NFL 1990s All-Decade Team; and was selected to the NFL 75th Anniversary All-Time Team.

Lott was inducted into the Pro Football Hall of Fame in 2000 and the College Football Hall of Fame in 2002.

Made of cast bronze on a marble base, the trophy's size is 13" × 14" × 9" and weighs 50 pounds.

Year	*Player*	*School*	*Note*
2004	David Pollack	University of Georgia (GA)	3X All-American (2002–2004)
2005	DeMeco Ryans	University of Alabama (AL)	2005 First-Team All-SEC
2006	Daymeion Hughes	University of California (CA)	2006 First Team All-American
2007	Glenn Dorsey	Louisiana State University (LA)	2007 Lombardi Award Winner
2008	James Laurinaitis	Ohio State University (OH)	3X All-American (2006–2008)
2009	Jerry Hughes	Texas Christian University (TX)	2X Consensus All-American
2010	J.J. Watt	University of Wisconsin (WI)	2010 Team Co-MVP

Lou Groza Award

Since 1992, the Lou Groza Award has been presented annually to the best NCAA Division I college football placekicker by the Palm Beach County Sports Commission (1555 Palm Beach Lakes Boulevard, Suite 1410, West Palm Beach, FL 33401; Telephone: 561-233-3124; Fax: 561-233-3125; Web site: http://www.lougrozaaward.com/).

The Award is named for Lou Groza (Louis Roy Groza; born: January 25, 1924, in Martins Ferry, Ohio; died: November 29, 2000, in Middleburg Heights, Ohio) who played college football for Ohio State University (Columbus, OH) for one season and for the Cleveland Browns (1946–1959, 1961–1967) in the NFL for 21 seasons. He won four championships in the AAFC (1946–1949) and four NFL Championship Games (1950, 1954–1955, 1964); selected to the NFL 1950s All-Decade Team; and was inducted into the Pro Football Hall of Fame in 1974.

As of this writing, only Sebastian Janikowski (Florida State University) has won this award more than once.

Year	*Winner*	*School*	*Note*
1992	Joe Allison	University of Memphis (TN)	1992 First-Team All-American
1993	Judd Davis	University of Florida (FL)	Leading Scorer in School History
1994	Steve McLaughlin	University of Arizona (AZ)	1994 All-American
1995	Michael Reeder	Texas Christian University (TX)	1995 All-American
1996	Marc Primanti	North Carolina State University (NC)	Made an ACC-Record 27 Straight Field Goals
1997	Martín Gramática	Kansas State University (KS)	School's All-Time Leading Scorer
1998	Sebastian Janikowski	Florida State University (FL)	Third-Leading Scorer in School History
1999	Sebastian Janikowski	Florida State University (FL)	Won 1999 National Championship
2000	Jonathan Ruffin	University of Cincinnati (OH)	All-Time Leading Scorer in School History
2001	Seth Marler	Tulane University (LA)	All-Time Leading Scorer in School History
2002	Nate Kaeding	University of Iowa (IA)	Most Single-Season Points in Big Ten History
2003	Jonathan Nichols	University of Mississippi (MS)	Set School Single-Season Scoring Record
2004	Mike Nugent	Ohio State University (OH)	30th Individual Award by a Team Player
2005	Alexis Serna	Oregon State University (OR)	NCAA 1A Kicking Leader in Points
2006	Art Carmody	University of Louisville (KY)	Helped School Win the FedEx Orange Bowl
2007	Thomas Weber	Arizona State University (AZ)	Set School Record with 17 Straight Field Goals
2008	Graham Gano	Florida State University (FL)	Made School Record 18 Straight Field Goals
2009	Kai Forbath	University of California, Los Angeles (CA)	2009 Consensus All-American
2010	Dan Bailey	Oklahoma State University (OK)	2010 Big 12 Special Teams Player of the Year

Lowe's Senior CLASS Award

Since 2001, the Lowe's Senior CLASS Award has been presented annually to the best senior (NCAA Division I) student-athlete by Lowe's and the NCAA in nine sports (Men's Basketball, Women's Basketball, Baseball, Football, Hockey, Lacrosse, Men's Soccer, Women's Soccer, Softball), with the award for football being established in 2009. The acronym CLASS stands for *C*elebrating *L*oyalty and *A*chievement for *S*taying in *S*chool and recognizes the loyalty of seniors that honor a four-year commitment to their university.

Award winners are voted on by NCAA Division I college coaches (in their respective sport), national media, and fans (who cast their ballots via text messaging and on the Lowe's Senior CLASS Award web site [http://www.seniorclassaward.com/]).

Sportscaster Dick Enberg first suggested a national award for seniors during the NCAA Men's Final Four (basketball) on CBS in 2001 when player Shane Battier avoided the lure of the NBA, returned to Duke University (Durham, North Carolina), and helped lead Duke to the 2001 championship (while earning his college degree). Premier Sports Management (7450 West 130th Street; Suite 360, Overland Park, KS 66213; Telephone: 913-681-6990; Fax: 913-681-8864; Web site: http://www.premiersportsonline.com/) created the Senior CLASS Award in 2001 during a trend of college basketball players leaving their schools early to enter the professional ranks. With Enberg as the program's honorary chair and CBS as a broadcast partner, Premier began presenting the award annually in men's and women's basketball. With the addition of Lowe's as a title sponsor in 2006, the program has expanded to include more sports.

To be eligible for the award, a student-athlete must be classified as an NCAA Division I senior and have notable achievements in four areas of excellence: community, classroom, character and competition.

Year	*Winner*	*School*	*Note*
2009	James Laurinitis	Ohio State University (OH)	3X All-American (2006–2008)
2010	Ricky Dobbs	U.S. Naval Academy	2009 Texas Bowl MVP

Manning Award

Since 2004, the Manning Award has been presented annually to the best college football quarterback (regardless of the NCAA level of play) and is sponsored by the AllState Sugar Bowl (Louisiana Superdome, 1500 Sugar Bowl Drive, New Orleans, LA 70112; Telephone: 504-828-2440; Fax: 504-828-2441; Email: info@sugarbowl.org; Web site: http://allstatesugarbowl.org/). It was created to honor the Manning family of quarterbacks (father Archie and his sons Peyton and Eli).

From the sponsor's original "Watch List" (which can include any number of quarterbacks), ten finalists are determined by a selected panel of national media covering college football, as well as each of the Mannings. From this list, a winner is announced.

Archie Manning (Elisha Archibald "Archie" Manning III; born: May 19, 1949, in Drew, Mississippi) played football at the University of Mississippi (University, MS) and in the NFL for 14 seasons with the New Orleans Saints (1971–1982), Houston Oilers (1982–1983), and the Minnesota Vikings (1983–1984). In 1969, he accumulated a total of 540 yards in a 33–32 loss to the University of Alabama, still a Southeastern Conference record for most yards in a single game. In 1978, he was named the National Football Conference Player of the Year and was inducted into the College Football Hall of Fame in 1989.

Peyton Manning (Peyton Williams Manning; born: March 24, 1976, in New Orleans, LA) played college football at the University of Tennessee (Knoxville) and has played in the NFL since 1998 with the Indianapolis Colts. Although his career is not yet over as of this writing, Manning has already been named NFL Most Valuable Player four times (2003–2004, 2008–2009; was named to the NFL 2000s All-Decade Team; and was named Super Bowl MVP in 2007 as he helped the team win Super Bowl XLI with a 29–19 win over the Chicago Bears.

Eli Manning (Elisha Nelson "Eli" Manning; born: January 3, 1981, in New Orleans, LA) played football at the University of Mississippi (University, MS) and has been playing in the NFL for the New York Giants since 2004. He was selected to the Pro Bowl in 2008 and was named Super Bowl MVP in 2008 as he helped the team win Super Bowl XLII with a 17–14 win over the New England Patriots.

Year	*Winner*	*School*	*Note*
2004	Matt Leinart	University of Southern California (CA)	2004 Heisman Trophy Winner
2005	Vince Young	University of Texas (TX)	2005 Davey O'Brien Award Winner
2006	JaMarcus Russell	Louisiana State University (LA)	2006 Davey O'Brien Award Winner
2007	Matt Ryan	Boston College (MA)	2007 ACC Player of the Year
2008	Tim Tebow	University of Florida (FL)	2007 Heisman Trophy Winner
2009	Colt McCoy	University of Texas (TX)	2009 Big 12 Offensive Player of the Year
2010	Cameron Newton	Auburn University (AL)	2010 AP College Football Player of the Year

Maxwell Award

Since 1937, the Maxwell Award has been presented annually to the best college football player in the country as voted on by a panel of sportscasters, sportswriters, NCAA head coaches, and the membership of the Maxwell Football Club (P.O. Box 1225, Southampton PA 18966; Telephone: 215-643-3833; Web site: http://www.maxwellfootballclub.org). The award is named in honor of Robert W. "Tiny" Maxwell (born: September 8, 1883, in Chicago, IL; died: June 30, 1922, in Norristown, PA), a college player, official, and sports columnist. He played football at the University of Chicago (IL, 1902); Swarthmore College (PA in 1904 and 1905); and was inducted into the College Football Hall of Fame in 1974.

He later played professional football for the Canton Bulldogs and Massillon Tigers (both of the Ohio League); was a sports editor for the *Philadelphia Public Ledger*; served as a football official; and was an assistant coach at both Swarthmore and the University of Pennsylvania (Philadelphia).

The Maxwell Football Club (originally called the Maxwell Football Club of Philadelphia) was established in 1935 in his honor to promote safety in the game of American football and is physically located in King of Prussia, Pennsylvania. In 1937, the Robert W. Maxwell Memorial Football Club was founded in Philadelphia (Pennsylvania) by Maxwell's friend, Bert Bell (future National Football League commissioner from 1946 to 1959).

As of this writing, only John Lattner (University of Notre Dame) and Tim Tebow (University of Florida) have won this award twice.

Year	*Winner*	*School*	*Note*
1937	Clinton E. Frank	Yale University (CT)	1937 Heisman Trophy Winner
1938	Davey O'Brien	Texas Christian University (TX)	1938 Heisman Trophy Winner
1939	Nile Kinnick	University of Iowa (IA)	1939 Heisman Trophy Winner
1940	Tom Harmon	University of Michigan (MI)	1940 Heisman Trophy Winner
1941	Bill Dudley	University of Virginia (VA)	1941 All-American
1942	Paul V. Governali	Columbia University (NY)	1986 College Football Hall of Fame Inductee
1943	Robert H. Odell	University of Pennsylvania (PA)	1992 College Football Hall of Fame Inductee
1944	Glenn Davis	U.S. Military Academy at West Point (NY)	1946 Heisman Trophy Winner
1945	Felix A. Blanchard	U.S. Military Academy at West Point (NY)	1945 Heisman Trophy Winner
1946	Charles Trippi	University of Georgia (GA)	1959 College Football Hall of Fame Inductee
1947	Doak Walker	Southern Methodist University (TX)	1948 Heisman Trophy Winner
1948	Charles Bednarik	University of Pennsylvania (PA)	1969 College Hall of Fame Inductee
1949	Leon Hart	University of Notre Dame (IN)	1949 Heisman Trophy Winner
1950	Reds Bagnell	University of Pennsylvania (PA)	1977 College Football Hall of Fame Inductee
1951	Dick Kazmaier	Princeton University (NJ)	1951 Heisman Trophy Winner
1952	John Lattner	University of Notre Dame (IN)	1952 College Football All-America Team
1953	John Lattner	University of Notre Dame (IN)	1953 Heisman Trophy Winner
1954	Ronald Beagle	U.S. Naval Academy (MD)	1986 College Football Hall of Fame Inductee
1955	Howard "Hopalong" Cassady	Ohio State University (OH)	1955 Heisman Trophy Winner
1956	Tommy McDonald	University of Oklahoma (OK)	1985 College Football Hall of Fame Inductee
1957	Robert H. Reifsnyder	U.S. Naval Academy (MD)	1997 College Football Hall of Fame Inductee
1958	Peter J. Dawkins	U.S. Military Academy at West Point (NY)	1958 Heisman Trophy Winner
1959	Richie Lucas	Pennsylvania State University (PA)	1986 College Football Hall of Fame Inductee
1960	Tia Nicholas	Rutgers University (NJ)	No Further Information
1961	Bob Ferguson	Ohio State University (OH)	1996 College Football Hall of Fame Inductee
1962	Terry Baker	Oregon State University (OR)	1962 Heisman Trophy Winner

Year	Winner	School	Note
1963	Roger Staubach	U.S. Navel Academy (MD)	1963 Heisman Trophy Winner
1964	Glenn Ressler	Pennsylvania State University (PA)	2001 College Football Hall of Fame Inductee
1965	Tommy Nobis	University of Texas (TX)	1981 College Football Hall of Fame Inductee
1966	Jim Lynch	University of Notre Dame (IN)	Won 1966 National Championship
1967	Gary Beban	University of California, Los Angeles (CA)	1967 Heisman Trophy Winner
1968	O.J. Simpson	University of Southern California (CA)	1968 Heisman Trophy Winner
1969	Mike Reid	Pennsylvania State University (PA)	1987 College Football Hall of Fame Inductee
1970	Jim Plunkett	Stanford University (CA)	1990 College Football Hall of Fame Inductee
1971	Ed Marinaro	Cornell University (NY)	1991 College Football Hall of Fame Inductee
1972	Brad Van Pelt	Michigan State University (MI)	2001 College Football Hall of Fame Inductee
1973	John Cappelletti	Pennsylvania State University (PA)	1973 Heisman Trophy Winner
1974	Steve Joachim	Temple University (PA)	7th Round NFL Draft Pick
1975	Archie Griffin	Ohio State University (OH)	2X Heisman Trophy Winner (1974–1975)
1976	Tony Dorsett	University of Pittsburgh (PA)	1976 Heisman Trophy Winner
1977	Ross Browner	University of Notre Dame (IN)	1999 College Football Hall of Fame Inductee
1978	Charles Fusina	Pennsylvania State University (PA)	1978 All-American
1979	Charles White	University of Southern California (CA)	1979 Heisman Trophy Winner
1980	Hugh Green	University of Pittsburgh (PA)	1996 College Football Hall of Fame Inductee
1981	Marcus Allen	University of Southern California (PA)	1981 Heisman Trophy Winner
1982	Herschel Walker	University of Georgia (GA)	1982 Heisman Trophy Winner
1983	Mike Rozier	University of Nebraska (NE)	1983 Heisman Trophy Winner
1984	Doug Flutie	Boston College (MA)	1984 Heisman Trophy Winner
1985	Chuck Long	University of Iowa (IA)	1999 College Football Hall of Fame Inductee
1986	Vinny Testaverde	University of Miami (FL)	1986 Heisman Trophy Winner
1987	Don McPherson	Syracuse University (NY)	1987 Davey O'Brien Award Winner
1988	Barry Sanders	Oklahoma State University (OK)	1988 Heisman Trophy Winner
1989	Anthony Thompson	Indiana University (IN)	2007 College Football Hall of Fame Inductee
1990	Ty Detmer	Brigham Young University (UT)	1990 Heisman Trophy Winner
1991	Desmond Howard	University of Michigan (MI)	1991 Heisman Trophy Winner
1992	Gino Torretta	University of Miami (FL)	1992 Heisman Trophy Winner
1993	Charlie Ward	Florida State University (FL)	1993 Heisman Trophy Winner
1994	Kerry Collins	Pennsylvania State University (PA)	1994 Sammy Baugh Award Winner
1995	Eddie George	Ohio State University (OH)	1995 Heisman Trophy Winner
1996	Danny Wuerffel	University of Florida (FL)	1996 Heisman Trophy Winner
1997	Peyton Manning	University of Tennessee (TN)	1997 Davey O'Brien Award Winner
1998	Ricky Williams	University of Texas (TX)	1998 Heisman Trophy Winner
1999	Ron Dayne	University of Wisconsin (WI)	1999 Heisman Trophy Winner
2000	Drew Brees	Purdue University (IN)	2000 Chicago Tribune Silver Football Winner
2001	Ken Dorsey	University of Miami (FL)	2X Archie Griffin Award Winner (2001–2002)
2002	Larry Johnson	Pennsylvania State University (PA)	2002 Jim Brown Trophy Winner
2003	Eli Manning	University of Mississippi (MS)	2003 Johnny Unitas Golden Arm Award Winner
2004	Jason White	University of Oklahoma (OK)	2003 Heisman Trophy Winner
2005	Vince Young	University of Texas (TX)	2005 Manning Award Winner
2006	Brady Quinn	University of Notre Dame (IN)	2006 Johnny Unitas Golden Arm Award Winner

Year	Winner	School	Note
2007	Tim Tebow	University of Florida (FL)	2007 Heisman Trophy Winner
2008	Tim Tebow	University of Florida (FL)	2008 Davey O'Brien Award Winner
2009	Colt McCoy	University of Texas (TX)	2009 Big 12 Offensive Player of the Year
2010	Cameron Newton	Auburn University (AL)	2010 Heisman Trophy Winner

Melberger Award *see* NCAA Division III

Mosi Tatupu Award

From 1997 to 2006, the Mosi Tatupu Award was presented annually to the college football Special Teams Player of the Year by the Maui Quarterback Club and the Hula Bowl.

Mosi Tatupu (Mosiula Faasuka Tatupu [born: April 26, 1955, in Pago Pago, American Samoa; died: February 23, 2010, in Attleboro, MA]) played football at the University of Southern California (Los Angeles, 1974–1978) and for 14 seasons in the NFL with the New England Patriots (1978–1990) and the Los Angeles Rams (1991). He was named to the NFL Pro Bowl in 1986.

Year	Winner	School	Note
1997	Brock Olivo	University of Missouri (MO)	Briefly Held School Rushing Record
1998	Chris McAlister	University of Arizona (AZ)	1st Round NFL Draft Pick
1999	Deltha O'Neal	University of California (CA)	1st Round NFL Draft Pick
2000	J. T. Thatcher	University of Oklahoma (OK)	2000 All-American
2001	Kahlil Hill	University of Iowa (IA)	Played in both the NFL and the CFL
2002	Glenn Pakulak	University of Kentucky (KY)	2002 First-Team All-SEC
2003	Wes Welker	Texas Tech University (TX)	Entered the NFL as an Undrafted Player
2004	Chad Owens	University of Hawaii (HI)	2X Hawaii Bowl Winner (2004–2005)
2005	Ryan Hoffman	Illinois State University (IL)	Ranked Number 3 in the Nation (43.87 Punting Yards Avg)
2006	A.J. Trapasso	Ohio State University (OH)	Entered the NFL as an Unsigned Free Agent

NAIA Football Player of the Year Award *see* NAIA

National Football Foundation Distinguished American Award

Each year since 1966, the National Football Foundation (433 East Las Colinas Boulevard, Suite 1130, Irving, TX, 75039; Telephone: 972-556-1000; Fax: 972-556-9032; Email: membership@footballfoundation.com; Web site: http://www.footballfoundation.org/distinguish.php) and the College Football Hall of Fame honor an individual for scholarship, citizenship, and leadership with the National Football Foundation Distinguished American Award. Additionally, the NFF also recognizes individuals for their support of the organization's mission to promote the game of amateur football. The recipient of the Award is not limited to a former college player or coach, but can be presented to any one who has maintained a lifetime interest in the game and who has made significant contribution to the betterment of amateur football in the United States.

Nominees are submitted by former recipients, NFF board members, selected corporate leaders, NFF chapter presidents, and others as directed to the NFF Chairman. The winner is selected by the NFF Awards Committee and ratified by its Board of Directors.

Year	Winner	Note
1966	William Carpenter	1960 West Point Graduate; 1959 First-Team All-American
1967	No Winner Selected	
1968	No Winner Selected	
1969	Archibald MacLeish	Librarian of Congress; 3X Pulitzer Prize Winner (1933, 1953, 1959)
1970	Vince Lombardi	Legendary Professional Football Coach; Won Super Bowl I and II
1971	Dr. Frank Boyden	Headmaster of Deerfield Academy (Massachusetts)
1972	Dr. Jerome H. Holland	College President; Former U.S. Ambassador to Sweden
1973	No Winner Selected	

Year	*Winner*	*Note*
1974	Bob Hope	Entertainer and Comedian
1975	The Rev. Theodore Hesburgh	University of Notre Dame (IN) President (1952–1987)
1976	James A. Van Fleet	Commanding General of U.S. Army During Korean War
1977	The Rev. Edmund P. Joyce	University of Notre Dame (IN) Executive Vice President (1952–1987)
1978	No Winner Selected	
1979	John W. Galbreath	Sportsman; Owner of MLB's Pittsburgh Pirates (1945–1985)
1980	Fred Russell	Sports Writer; Honors Court Chairman of the College Football Hall of Fame
1981	David Sonny Werblin	Entertainment Executive; One-Time Owner of the New York Jets
1982	Jim Brown	College Football (1995) and Pro Football Hall of Fame Inductee (1971)
1982	Willie Davis	1981 Pro Football Hall of Fame Inductee
1982	Jack Kemp	Played 12 Seasons in the NFL; Former Congressman
1982	Ron Kramer	1978 College Football Hall of Fame Inductee
1982	Jim Swink	1980 College Football Hall of Fame Inductee
1983	Leon Hess	Former Owner of the New York Jets
1983	Jimmy Stewart	Actor
1984	David Moir Nelson	NCAA Football Rules Committee Member; 1987 Hall of Fame Inductee
1985	Bill Flynn	President of the NCAA; Athletic Director at Boston College (MA)
1986	John L. Toner	NCAA President; Former Athletic Director University of Connecticut (CT)
1987	Ike Sewell	Pizzeria Uno Founder and Creator of the Deep-Dish Pizza
1988	Joe Rodgers	Former U.S. Ambassador to France; Emeritus NFF Board Member
1989	Edward "Moose" Krause	Former University of Notre Dame (IN) Player and College Coach
1990	Pete Rozelle	Former NFL Commissioner
1991	Joe Paterno	Football Coach at Pennsylvania State University (PA)
1992	Wellington Mara	Former Co-Owner of the NFL's New York Giants
1993	Dick Kazmaier	1951 Heisman Trophy Winner; 1966 College Football Hall of Fame Inductee
1994	Charles F. Bolden, Jr.	NASA Administrator; Marine Corp General
1995	Tom Osborne	Former College Coach (University of Nebraska) and Congressman
1996	J. Donald Monan S.J.	Boston College (MA) President and Chancellor
1997	No Winner Selected	
1998	Roy Kramer	Former Commissioner of the Southeastern Conference
1999	No Winner Selected	
2000	Arthur J. Decio	Chairman of Skyline Corporation for Five Decades
2001	Dr. James Frank	Athlete, Coach, College President, and SWAC Commissioner
2002	George B. Young	Senior Vice President for Football Operations for the NFL
2003	Dr. Robert C. Khayat	University of Mississippi (MS) Chancellor
2004	Robert F. Casciola	President of the NFF and College Football Hall of Fame
2005	Alan Page	MN Supreme Court Judge; College and Pro Football HOF Inductee
2006	Pat Tillman	AZ State Player and Soldier Killed in Afghanistan by "Friendly Fire"
2007	Rocky Bleier	Notre Dame Player; Served in Vietnam; Won Four Super Bowls
2008	T. Boone Pickens	Investor and Financier
2009	Billy Payne	Chairman of the Augusta National Golf Club
2010	Tom Brokaw	*NBC Nightly News* anchor

National Football Foundation Gold Medal

Since 1958, the National Football Foundation Gold Medal, the highest individual award presented by The National Football Foundation (433 East Las Colinas Boulevard, Suite 1130, Irving, TX, 75039; Telephone: 972-556-1000; Fax: 972-556-9032; Email: membership@footballfoundation.com; Web site: http://www.football foundation.org/gold.php) and College Football Hall of Fame, recognizes an outstanding American who has contributed significantly to the sport of college football and to the country. A recipient's life must reflect the values of those who have excelled in amateur sport, particularly football, and have achieved success in an industrial, business, financial, educational, professional, or related career. Additionally, he or she must have made significant contributions in public service to the welfare of the country and its citizens, either in a private role and/or as a government official.

Nominees are submitted by former recipients, NFF board members, selected corporate leaders, NFF chapter presidents, and others as directed to the NFF Chairman. The winner is selected by the NFF Awards Committee and ratified by its Board of Directors.

Year	*Winner*	*Note*
1958	Dwight D. Eisenhower	Former U.S. President
1959	Douglas MacArthur	Former Army General
1960	Herbert C. Hoover	Former U.S. President
1960	Amos Alonzo Stagg	College Football Coach
1961	John F. Kennedy	Former U.S. President
1962	Byron "Whizzer" White	U.S. Supreme Court Justice
1963	Roger Q. Blough	Former Chairman of U.S. Steel
1964	Donold B. Lourie	President of Quaker Oats; 1974 College Hall of Fame Inductee
1965	Juan T. Trippe	President of Pan American World Airways
1966	Earl H. "Red" Blaik	Army Football Coach; 1964 College Football Hall of Fame Inductee
1967	Frederick L. Hovde	President of Purdue University (IN)
1968	Chester J. LaRoche	Yale Quarterback (CT); Helped create the National Football Foundation
1969	Richard M. Nixon	Former U.S. President
1970	Thomas J. Hamilton	Naval Academy Head Coach; 1965 College Football Hall of Fame Inductee
1971	Ronald W. Reagan	Former U.S. President
1972	Gerald R. Ford	Former U.S. president
1973	John Wayne	Actor
1974	Gerald B. Zornow	President of Eastman Kodak
1975	David Packard	Co-Founder of Hewlett-Packard
1976	Edgar B. Speer	Former Chairman and CEO of U.S. Steel Corporation
1977	Louis H. Wilson	Congressional Medal of Honor Winner; Commandant of the Marine Corps
1978	Vincent dePaul Draddy	Longtime Chairman of the NFF's College Hall of Fame
1979	William P. Lawrence	Former POW; Superintendent of the Naval Academy (1978–1981)
1980	Walter J. Zable	Former Member of the College of William & Mary Board of Visitors
1981	Justin W. Dart	Medal of Freedom Recipient
1982	Jim Brown	College Football (1995) and Pro Football (1971) Hall of Fame Inductee
1982	Willie Davis	1981 Pro Football Hall of Fame Inductee
1982	Jack Kemp	Played 12 Seasons in the NFL; Former Congressman
1982	Ron Kramer	1978 College Football Hall of Fame Inductee
1982	Jim Swink	1980 College Football Hall of Fame Inductee
1983	Jack Kemp	Played 12 Seasons in the NFL; Former Congressman
1984	John F. McGillicuddy	Chairman of Manufacturers Hanover Corporation
1985	William I. Spencer	No. 2 Executive at Citibank
1986	William H. Morton	President of American Express
1987	Charles R. Meyer	1935 Heisman Trophy Candidate; Army Brigadier General
1988	Clinton E. Frank	1937 Heisman Trophy Winner; Advertising Executive
1989	Paul Brown	NFL Football Coach; Helped Form the NFL
1990	Thomas H. Moorer	Chairman of the Joint Chiefs of Staff
1991	George H. Bush	Former U.S. President
1992	Donald R. Keough	President and CEO of Coca-Cola Compnay
1993	Norman Schwarzkopf	Commander of the Coalition Forces in the 1991 Gulf War
1994	Thomas S. Murphy	CEO of Capital Cities / ABC
1995	Harold Alfond	Founded Dexter Shoe Company; Invented the Factory Outlet Store Idea
1996	Gene Corrigan	Athletic Director at the University of Notre Dame
1997	Jackie Robinson	1st African American to Break Major League Baseball's Color Line
1998	John H. McConnell	Founder and CEO of Worthington Industries
1999	Keith Jackson	ABC College Football Announcer
2000	Fred M. Kirby II	Co-Founder of F.W. Woolworth Company
2001	Billy Joe "Red" McCombs	Founder of Red McCombs Automotive Group
2002	George M. Steinbrenner III	Former Owner of Major League Baseball's New York Yankees
2003	General Tommy R. Franks	U.S. General Led the Attack Against the Taliban in Afghanistan
2004	William V. Campbell	Director at Apple; Intuit Chairman of the Board
2005	Jon F. Hanson	Business Leader; Chairman of the NFF and College Hall of Fame
2006	Joe Paterno	Longtime Football Coach at Pennsylvania State University

Year	Winner	Note
2006	Bobby Bowden	Longtime Football Coach at Florida State University
2007	Pete Dawkins	1958 Heisman Trophy Winner; Former Chairman of Citigroup
2007	Roger Staubach	1963 Heisman Trophy Winner; College Football Hall of Fame, 1981
2008	John Glenn	Former Astronaut and U.S. Senator
2009	Phil Knight	Co-founder and Chairman of Nike, Inc.
2009	Bill Bowerman	Co-founder of Nike
2010	Bill Cosby	Actor / Comedian

Nils V. "Swede" Nelson Award

Since 1946, the Nils V. "Swede" Nelson Award has been presented annually by the Gridiron Club of Greater Boston (9 Broadway, Unit 320, Saugus, MA 01906; Web site: http://www.gridclubofgreaterboston.com/) to the player whose on-field and off-field behavior exemplifies the football code and demonstrates sportsmanship. In 1982, the criteria was narrowed to the "very best and most academically talented college football player in New England."

Since 1989, the award has been given annually to two players (with the exception of a single winner in 1996 and three winners in 2007), one from a National Collegiate Athletic Association Division I football program, and one from a small college.

The award is named in honor of Nils Nelson, the founder of the Gridiron Club of Greater Boston; a former college player at Harvard University (Cambridge, Massachusetts); and Harvard coach who led his team to a 7–6 victory over the University of Oregon in the 1920 Rose Bowl.

Year	Winner	School	Note
1946	Perry Moss	University of Illinois (IL)	Won 1945 Orange Bowl and 1947 Rose Bowl
1947	Everett Dorr	Boston University (MA)	Also a 3X Baseball Letter Winner
1948	Gordon Long	University of Arkansas (AR)	Completed 57% of His Passes in 1948
1949	Doak Walker	Southern Methodist University (TX)	1959 College Football Hall of Fame Inductee
1950	Bob Williams	University of Arkansas (AR)	Arkansas State Hall of Honor, 1987
1951	Johnny Bright	Drake University (IA)	College Football Hall of Fame, 1984
1952	Joseph Mitinger	Yale University (CT)	1952 Team Captain
1953	Don King	Clemson University (SC)	Clemson Hall of Fame, 1992
1954	Arthur Luppino	University of Arizona (AZ)	1st Player to lead the NCAA Twice in Rushing
1955	Don Hollender	U.S. Military Academy at West Point (NY)	College Football Hall of Fame, 1985
1956	James Swink	Texas Christian University (TX)	College Football Hall of Fame, 1980
1957	Thomas Salvo	Boston University (MA)	Outside Linebacker at BU
1958	John W. Brodnax	Louisiana State University (LA)	Won 1958 National Championship
1959	George Roden	Colby College (ME)	1950 Team Co-Captain
1960	Alan Rozycki	Dartmouth College (NH)	Set Numerous Rushing & Scoring School Records
1961	Joseph Kowalski	Rutgers University (NJ)	3X Letter Winner (1959–1961)
1962	Pat Culpepper	University of Texas (TX)	2X SWC Champion (1961–1962)
1963	Bob Cappadona	Northeastern University (MA)	Played Three Seasons in the AFL
1964	Arthur Roberts	Columbia University (NY)	Also Lettered in Baseball and Basketball
1965	Thomas Clarke	Dartmouth College (NH)	2nd Team All-Dartmouth (50 Years)
1966	Floyd Little	Syracuse University (NY)	College Football Hall of Fame, 1983
1967	Brian Dowling	Yale University (CT)	Model for B.D. Character of *Doonesbury* Cartoon
1968	Vic Gatto	Harvard University (MA)	1968 Team Captain
1969	Steve Smear	Pennsylvania State University (PA)	1968 All-American
1970	Renso Perdoni	Georgia Tech University (GA)	1970 All-American
1971	Richard Jauron	Yale University (CT)	2001 AP NFL Coach of the Year
1972	Otis Armstrong	Purdue University (IN)	Purdue All-Time Team, 1987
1973	James Stoeckel	Harvard University (MA)	School's First-Ever Ivy League Player of the Year

Year	*Winner*	*School*	*Note*
1974	Peter Gorniewicz	Colby College (ME)	Scored 24 Points in a Game vs. Hobart in 1971
1975	George Niland	Trinity College (CT)	292 Total School Tackles (Rank: 10th)
1976	Peter Cronan	Boston College (MA)	Boston College Radio Color Commentator
1977	Roy Heffernan	Middlebury College (VT)	311 Rushing Yards in a Single Game (1975)
1978	Rich Leach	University of Michigan (MI)	Started 48 Games in College, a School Record
1979	Tom Bell	Brigham Young University (UT)	Helped Team to its first Undefeated Season (1979)
1980	Jerry Pierce	Dartmouth College (NH)	School-Record 385 Career Tackles
1981	Kenny Duckett	Wake Forest University (NC)	Played Four Seasons in the NFL
1982	John Loughery	Boston College (MA)	Succeeded at QB by Doug Flutie
1983	Matt Martin	College of the Holy Cross (MA)	Senior Co-Captain
1984	Steve Strachan	Boston College (MA)	1985 Cotton Bowl MVP
1985	Guy Carbone	University of Rhode Island (RI)	Had 109-Yard Interception for TD in 1985
1986	Stan Kaczorowski	University of Massachusetts (MA)	1986 First-Team All-Yankee Conference
1987	Gordie Lockbaum	College of the Holy Cross (MA)	College Football Hall of Fame, 2001
1988	Tom Waddle	Boston College (MA)	1989 Undrafted NFL Free Agent
1989	Ben Cowan	Boston University (MA)	1990 BU Scarlet Key Award
1989	Rich Schachner	U.S. Coast Guard Academy (CT)	1989 NFF Scholar-Athlete Award Winner
1990	Brad Preble	Dartmouth College (NH)	1990 All-Ivy First-Team Defense
1990	Mark Katz	Bowdoin College (ME)	Maine Sports Hall of Fame Inductee
1991	Paul Capriotti	University of Maine (ME)	Became a Coach After His Playing Days
1991	Paul Oliveira	Tufts University (MA)	Rushed for 1,550 Yards (1987–1991)
1992	Jay Fiedler	Dartmouth College (NH)	1992 Ivy League Player of the Year
1992	Roderick Tranum	Massachusetts Institute of Technology (MA)	1992 Academic All-American
1993	Keith Miller	Boston College (MA)	Caught 11 Touchdowns In His College Career
1993	Michael Turmelle	Bowdoin College (ME)	Academic All-American
1994	Andre Maksimow	Boston University (MA)	BU Athletics Hall of Fame, 2008
1994	Nate Sleeper	Williams College (MA)	1995 All-Conference
1995	Tim O'Brien	Boston College (MA)	No Further Information
1995	Mike Rymsha	Bentley College (MA)	No Further Information
1996	Joseph DeAngelis	Trinity College (CT)	1997 School Touchdowm Club Member
1997	Matt Hasselbeck	Boston College (MA)	6th Round NFL Draft Selection
1997	Daniel Lord	Tufts University (MA)	13 Tackle Assists in 1995 Against Colby College
1998	Matt Jordan	University of Massachusetts (MA)	Helped Team Win Division I-AA Championship
1998	Eric Trum	Tufts University (MA)	No Further Information
1999	Isaiah Kacyvenski	Harvard University (MA)	3X First-Team All-Ivy League (1997–1999)
1999	Nicholas Kozy	Massachusetts Institute of Technology (MA)	No Further Information
2000	Eric Johnson	Yale University (CT)	7th Round NFL Selection
2000	Tim McCarthy	Middlebury College (VT)	No Further Information
2001	John Richardson	Boston College (MA)	No Further Information
2001	Bob Montgomery	University of Massachusetts (MA)	No Further Information
2002	Kevin Noone	Dartmouth College (NH)	2002 Division I-AA All-American
2002	Chuck McGraw	Tufts University (MA)	No Further Information
2003	Steve Fox	College of the Holy Cross (MA)	No Further Information

Year	Winner	School	Note
2003	Greg Wood	Worcester State College (MA)	3,002 Rushing Yards in Three Years
2004	Keron Henry	University of Connecticut (CT)	No Further Information
2004	Fletcher Ladd	Amherst College (MA)	Team Co-Captain
2005	David Diamond	Bowdoin College (ME)	No Further Information
2005	Nick Hartigan	Brown University (RI)	Walter Camp First-Team All-American
2006	Ed McCarthy	Yale University (CT)	2006 First-Team All-American
2006	Brendan Fulmer	Williams College (MA)	No Further Information
2007	Dan Guariglia	Amherst College (MA)	Captain of the Team as a Senior
2007	Ryne Nutt	Central Connecticut State University (CT)	3X All-NEC Selection
2007	Steve Morgan	Brown University (RI)	2004 Ivy League Rookie of the Year
2008	Andrew Berry	Harvard University (MA)	No Further Information
2008	James Oleinik	Massachusetts Institute of Technology (MA)	No Further Information
2009	Alex Rubino	Massachusetts Institute of Technology (MA)	No Further Information
2009	Mark Herzlich	Boston College (MA)	No Further Information
2010	Anthony Castonzo	Boston College (MA)	NCAA Division I
2010	Ryan Schmid	Coast Guard Academy (CT)	NCAA Division II/III

Outland Trophy

Since 1946, the Outland Trophy has been awarded annually to the best college football interior lineman by the Football Writers Association of America (http://www.sportswriters.net/fwaa/awards/outland/).

It is named after John H. Outland (born: March 7, 1871, in Douglas County, Kansas; died: March 24, 1947, in Laguna Beach, CA), a college player and coach who was one of only a few players in college football history to be named All-American at two positions (University of Pennsylvania; 1898 at tackle and 1899 at halfback). After earning his medical degree, Outland was a surgeon during World War I, after serving as a football coach at Franklin & Marshall College (Lancaster, Pennsylvania in 1900), the University of Kansas (Lawrence, 1901), and Washburn University (Topeka, Kansas from 1904 to 1905). He was inducted into the College Football Hall of Fame in 2001.

As of this writing, Dave Rimington (University of Nebraska) is the only player to win this Trophy twice.

Year	Winner	School	Note
1946	George Connor	University of Notre Dame (IN)	1963 College Football Hall of Fame Inductee
1947	Joe Steffy	U.S. Military Academy at West Point (NY)	1987 College Football Hall of Fame Inductee
1948	Bill Fischer	University of Notre Dame (IN)	1983 College Football Hall of Fame Inductee
1949	Ed Bagdon	Michigan State University (MI)	1950 7th-Round Draft Pick
1950	Bob Gain	University of Kentucky (KY)	1980 College Hall of Fame Inductee
1951	Jim Weatherall	University of Oklahoma (OK)	1992 College Football Hall of Fame Inductee
1952	Dick Modzelewski	University of Maryland (MD)	1993 College Football Hall of Fame Inductee
1953	John Roberts	University of Oklahoma (OK)	1993 College Hall of Fame Inductee
1954	William "Bud" Brooks	University of Arkansas (AR)	1954 All-American
1955	Calvin Jones	University of Iowa (IA)	1980 College Football Hall of Fame Inductee
1956	Jim Parker	Ohio State University (OH)	1974 College Football Hall of Fame Inductee
1957	Alex Karras	University of Iowa (IA)	1991 College Football Hall of Fame Inductee
1958	Zeke Smith	Auburn University (AL)	1959 4th-Round NFL Draft Pick

Outland

Year	*Winner*	*School*	*Note*
1959	Mike McGee	Duke University (NC)	1990 College Football Hall of Fame Inductee
1960	Tom Brown	University of Minnesota (MN)	2003 College Football Hall of Fame Inductee
1961	Merlin Olsen	Utah State University (UT)	1980 College Football Hall of Fame Inductee
1962	Bobby Bell	University of Minnesota (MN)	1991 College Football Hall of Fame Inductee
1963	Scott Appleton	University of Texas (TX)	Won 1963 National Championship
1964	Steve DeLong	University of Tennessee (TN)	1993 College Football Hall of Fame Inductee
1965	Tommy Nobis	University of Texas (TX)	1981 College Football Hall of Fame Inductee
1966	Loyd Phillips	University of Arkansas (AR)	1992 College Football Hall of Fame Inductee
1967	Ron Yary	University of Southern California (CA)	1987 College Football Hall of Fame Inductee
1968	Bill Stanfill	University of Georgia (GA)	1998 College Football Hall of Fame Inductee
1969	Mike Reid	Pennsylvania State University (PA)	1987 College Football Hall of Fame Inductee
1970	Jim Stillwagon	Ohio State University (OH)	1991 College Football Hall of Fame Inductee
1971	Larry Jacobson	University of Nebraska (NE)	2X National Champions (1970–1971)
1972	Rich Glover	University of Nebraska (NE)	1972 All-American
1973	John Hicks	Ohio State University (OH)	2001 College Football Hall of Fame Inductee
1974	Randy White	University of Maryland (MD)	1994 College Football Hall of Fame Inductee
1975	Lee Roy Selmon	University of Oklahoma (OK)	1988 College Football Hall of Fame Inductee
1976	Ross Browner	University of Notre Dame (IN)	1999 College Football Hall of Fame Inductee
1977	Brad Shearer	University of Texas (TX)	Played Three NFL Seasons
1978	Greg Roberts	University of Oklahoma (OK)	No Further Information
1979	Jim Ritcher	North Carolina State (NC)	1998 College Football Hall of Fame Inductee
1980	Mark May	University of Pittsburgh (PA)	2005 College Football Hall of Fame Inductee
1981	Dave Rimington	University of Nebraska (NE)	2X Outland Trophy Winner (1981–1982)
1982	Dave Rimington	University of Nebraska (NE)	1997 College Football Hall of Fame Inductee
1983	Dean Steinkuhler	University of Nebraska (NE)	1983 Lombardi Award Winner
1984	Bruce Smith	Virginia Tech Institute (VA)	2006 College Football Hall of Fame Inductee
1985	Mike Ruth	Boston College (MA)	Only BC Player to Win Outland Trophy
1986	Jason Buck	Brigham Young University (UT)	No Further Information
1987	Chad Hennings	U.S. Air Force Academy (CO)	2006 College Football Hall of Fame Inductee
1988	Tracy Rocker	Auburn University (AL)	2004 College Football Hall of Fame Inductee
1989	Mohammed Elewonibi	Brigham Young University (UT)	No Further Information
1990	Russell Maryland	University of Miami (FL)	1990 UPI Lineman of the Year
1991	Steve Emtman	University of Washington (WA)	2006 College Football Hall of Fame Inductee
1992	Will Shields	University of Nebraska (NE)	1992 All-American
1993	Rob Waldrop	University of Arizona (AZ)	Three Year NFL Career
1994	Zach Wiegert	University of Nebraska (NE)	1994 UPI Lineman of the Year
1995	Jonathan Ogden	University of California, Los Angeles (CA)	1995 UPI Lineman of the Year

Year	*Winner*	*School*	*Note*
1996	Orlando Pace	Ohio State University (OH)	2X Lombardi Award Winner (1995–1996)
1997	Aaron Taylor	University of Nebraska (NE)	3X National Champion (1994–1995, 1997)
1998	Kris Farris	University of California, Los Angeles (CA)	3rd-Round NFL Draft Selection
1999	Chris Samuels	University of Alabama (AL)	2000 1st-Round NFL Draft Pick
2000	John Henderson	University of Tennessee (TN)	2004 & 2006 NFL Pro Bowl Selection
2001	Bryant McKinnie	University of Miami (FL)	2001 Jim Parker Award Winner
2002	Rien Long	Washington State University (WA)	2004 4th-Round NFL Selection
2003	Robert Gallery	University of Iowa (IA)	2003 First-Team All-American
2004	Jammal Brown	University of Oklahoma (OK)	2004 All-American
2005	Greg Eslinger	University of Minnesota (MN)	No Further Information
2006	Joe Thomas	University of Wisconsin (WI)	2006 All-American
2007	Glenn Dorsey	Louisiana State University (LA)	2007 Lott Trophy Winner
2008	Andre Smith	University of Alabama)AL)	2008 All-American
2009	Ndamukong Suh	University of Nebraska (NE)	2009 AP Player of the Year
2010	Gabe Carimi	University of Wisconsin (WI)	2010 Big Ten Offensive Lineman of the Year

Paul "Bear" Bryant Award (sponsored by the Marathon Oil Corporation and the American Heart Association)

The Paul "Bear" Bryant Award (Paul "Bear" Bryant Coach of the Year Award) has been presented annually since 1986 to the NCAA college football national coach of the year. It is voted on by members of the National Sportscasters & Sportswriters Association (P.O. Box 1545, Salisbury, NC 28145; Telephone: 704-633-4275; Web site: http://www.americanheart) and is sponsored by the Marathon Oil Corporation and the American Heart Association.

Paul "Bear" Bryant (Paul William "Bear" Bryant; born: September 11, 1913, in Moro Bottom, AR; died: January 26, 1983, in Tuscaloosa, AL) played college football at the University of Alabama (Tuscaloosa, 1932–1936); was most well known as the head coach at the University of Alabama (1958–1982); and ended his career with an overall record of 323–85–17 (.760). Before the University of Alabama, he also served as the head coach at the University of Maryland (College Park, 1945); the University of Kentucky (1946–1953); and Texas A&M University (College Station, 1954–1957).

He won seven national titles (1950, 1961, 1964–1965, 1973, 1978–1979); was a three-time American Football Coaches Association Coach of the Year (1961, 1971, 1973); and a 12-time SEC Coach of the Year (1950, 1959, 1961, 1964–1965, 1971, 1973–1974, 1977–1979, 1981).

The College Football Coach of the Year Award began in 1957 and was renamed for Bryant in 1986. He was inducted into the College Football Hall of Fame in 1986.

Year	*Winner*	*School*
1986	Joe Paterno	Pennsylvania State University (PA)
1987	Dick MacPherson	Syracuse University (NY)
1988	Lou Holtz	University of Notre Dame (IN)
1989	Bill McCartney	University of Colorado (CO)
1990	Bobby Ross	Georgia Tech (GA)
1991	Don James	University of Washington (WA)
1992	Gene Stallings	University of Alabama (AL)
1993	Terry Bowden	Auburn University (AL)
1994	Rich Brooks	University of Oregon (OR)
1995	Gary Barnett	Northwestern University (IL)
1996	Bruce Snyder	Arizona State University (AZ)
1997	Lloyd Carr	University of Michigan (MI)
1998	Bill Snyder	Kansas State University (KS)
1999	Frank Beamer	Virginia Tech (VA)
2000	Bob Stoops	University of Oklahoma (OK)
2001	Larry Coker	University of Miami (FL)

2002	Jim Tressel	Ohio State University (OH)
2003	Nick Saban	Louisiana State University (LA)
2004	Tommy Tuberville	Auburn University (AL)
2005	Mack Brown	University of Texas (TX)
2006	Chris Petersen	Boise State University (ID)
2007	Mark Mangino	University of Kansas (KS)
2008	Kyle Whittingham	University of Utah (UT)
2009	Chris Petersen	Boise State University (ID)
2010	Gene Chizik	Auburn University (AL)

Paul "Bear" Bryant Lifetime Achievement Award (sponsored by the American Heart Association)

The Paul "Bear" Bryant Lifetime Achievement Award has been presented annually since 2000 to the NCAA college football coach who has displayed excellence on and off the field over an entire career. It is voted on by members of the National Sportscasters & Sportswriters Association (P.O. Box 1545, Salisbury, NC 28145; Telephone: 704-633-4275; Web site: http://www.americanheartorg/bryantawards) and is sponsored by the American Heart Association.

Paul "Bear" Bryant (Paul William "Bear" Bryant; born: September 11, 1913 in Moro Bottom, AR; died: January 26, 1983 in Tuscaloosa, AL) played college football at the University of Alabama (Tuscaloosa, 1932–1936); was most well known as the head coach at the University of Alabama (1958–1982); and ended his career with an overall record of 323–85–17 (.760). Before the University of Alabama, he also served as the head coach at the University of Maryland (College Park, 1945); the University of Kentucky (1946–1953); and Texas A&M University (College Station, 1954–1957).

He won seven national titles (1950, 1961, 1964–1965, 1973, 1978–1979); was a three-time American Football Coaches Association Coach of the Year (1961, 1971, 1973); and a 12-time SEC Coach of the Year (1950, 1959, 1961, 1964–1965, 1971, 1973–1974, 1977–1979, 1981).

The College Football Coach of the Year Award began in 1957 and was renamed for Bryant in 1986. He was inducted into the College Football Hall of Fame in 1986.

Year	*Winner*	*Note*
2000	Darrell Royal	1983 College Football Hall of Fame Inductee
2001	Charles McClendon	1986 College Football Hall of Fame Inductee
2002	Bill Yeoman	2001 College Football Hall of Fame Inductee
2003	Frank Broyles	1983 College Football Hall of Fame Inductee
2004	Gene Stallings	1992 Walter Camp Coach of the Year
2005	Lou Holtz	2008 College Football Hall of Fame Inductee
2006	Jack Pardee	1986 College Football Hall of Fame Inductee
2007	Bo Schembechler	1993 College Football Hall of Fame Inductee
2008	Tom Osborne	1999 College Football Hall of Fame Inductee
2009	Barry Switzer	2002 College Football Hall of Fame Inductee
2010	Bobby Bowden	2006 College Football Hall of Fame Inductee

Paul Hornung Award

Beginning in 2010, the Paul Hornung Award is presented annually by the Louisville Sports Commission (One Riverfront Plaza, Suite 2200, 401 West Main Street, Louisville, KY 40202; Telephone: 866-587-7767, 502-587-7767; Fax: 502-587-6767; Web site: http://louisvillesports.org/) to the most versatile and high-level performers in major college football.

Hornung is a native son (born: December 23, 1935, in Louisville, KY); won the 1956 Heisman Trophy while at the University of Notre Dame (South Bend, IN); played for the NFL's Green Bay Packers and won four NFL championships (1961–1962, 1965, Super Bowl I); was the 1961 NFL Most Valuable Player; and was inducted into both the College Footbal Hall of Fame (1985) and the Pro Football Hall of Fame (1986).

In addition to starting or playing significant downs on offense or defense, award winners will be judged on playing multiple positions on offense/defense, as well as on special teams. Winners are selected by the Selection Committee, made up of sports journalists from across the country.

Year	Player	Position	School
2010	Owen Marecic	Fullback/Linebacker	Stanford University (CA)

Paul Warfield Trophy

Presented by the Touchdown Club of Columbus (Ohio, http:www.touchdownclubofcolumbus.com) since 1991, the Paul Warfield Trophy is given annually to the nation's best collegiate wide receiver.

Sam B. Nicola (who died in 1993) founded the Touchdown Club of Columbus in 1956 and was president of the Athletic Club of Columbus when the initial All-Sports Banquet was held in January 1956. Although a local organization, its range has always been national (not limited to the Columbus, Ohio, area) and athletes from all sports have been recognized. Honored athletes are selected by the appropriate Touchdown Club's committees, consisting of coaches, sportswriters, and former players.

Paul Dryden Warfield (born: November 28, 1942, in Warren, Ohio) played college football at Ohio State University (Columbus) and professional football for 14 years with the Cleveland Browns (NFL, 1964–1969), Miami Dolphins (NFL, 1970–1974), Memphis Southmen (World Football League, 1975), and the Cleveland Browns (NFL, 1976–1977). He won the NFL Championship in 1964; two Super Bowls (SB VII [1973] and SB VIII [1974]); and was selected to the NFL 1970s All-Decade Team. He was inducted into the Pro Football Hall of Fame in 1983.

As of this writing, Michael Crabtree (Texas Tech University) is the only player to win this award more than once.

Year	Winner	School	Note
1991	Desmond Howard	University of Michigan (MI)	1991 Heisman Trophy Winner
1992	O.J. McDuffie	Pennsylvania State University (PA)	1992 All-American
1993	David Palmer	University of Alabama (AL)	1992 All-American
1994	Michael Westbrook	University of Colorado (CO)	1995 1st-Round Draft Pick
1995	Keyshawn Johnson	University of Southern California (CA)	2X All-American
1996	Marcus Harris	University of Wyoming (WY)	1996 Fred Biletnikoff Award Winner
1997	Randy Moss	Marshall University (WV)	1997 Fred Biletnikoff Award Winner
1998	Troy Edwards	Louisiana Tech University (LA)	1998 Fred Biletnikoff Award Winner
1999	Peter Warrick	Florida State University (FL)	2X All-American (1998–1999)
2000	Santana Moss	University of Miami (FL)	2001 All-Big East Conference
2001	Jabar Gaffney	University of Florida (FL)	No Further Information
2002	Charles Rogers	Michigan State University (MI)	No Further Information
2003	Larry Fitzgerald	University of Pittsburgh (PA)	2003 First-Team All-American
2004	Braylon Edwards	University of Michigan (MI)	2004 Fred Biletnikoff Award Winner
2005	Dwayne Jarrett	University of Southern California (CA)	2X All-American (2005–2006)
2006	Calvin Johnson	Georgia Institute of Technology (GA)	2006 Fred Biletnikoff Award Winner
2007	Michael Crabtree	Texas Tech University (TX)	2X First-Team All-American (2007–2008)
2008	Michael Crabtree	Texas Tech University (TX)	2X Fred Biletnikoff Award Winner (2007–2008)
2009	Jordan Shipley	University of Texas (TX)	2008 All Big-12 Second Team Selection
2010	Justin Blackmon	Oklahoma State University (OK)	2010 Big 12 Offensive Player of the Year

President Gerald R. Ford Legendary Center Award *see* the Rimington Trophy

Quarterback of the Year

Not yet having received an official name, the Quarterback of the Year award is sponsored by the Touchdown Club of Columbus (Ohio, http://www.touchdownclubofcolumbus.com) and has been presented annually since 1991 to college football's top quarterback. This award differs from the Sammy Baugh Trophy in that it goes to college football's top quarterback, not the top passer.

Sam B. Nicola (who died in 1993) founded the Touchdown Club of Columbus in 1956 and was president of the Athletic Club of Columbus when the initial All-Sports Banquet was held in January 1956. Although a local organization, its range has always been national (not limited to the Columbus, Ohio area) and athletes from all sports have been recognized. Honored athletes are selected by the appropriate Touchdown Club's committees, consisting of coaches, sportswriters, and former players.

As of this writing, only Ken Dorsey (University of Miami) and Matt Leinart (University of Southern California) have won this award twice.

Year	*Winner*	*School*	*Note*
1991	Casey Weldon	Florida State University (FL)	1991 Johnny Unitas Golden Arm Award Winner
1992	Rick Mirer	University of Notre Dame (IN)	Won the 1993 Cotton Bowl Classic
1993	Charlie Ward	Florida State University (FL)	1993 Heisman Trophy Winner
1994	Kerry Collins	Pennsylvania State University (PA)	1994 Sammy Baugh Award Winner
1995	Tommie Frazier	University of Nebraska (NE)	1995 Orange Bowl MVP
1996	Danny Wuerffel	University of Florida (FL)	1996 Heisman Trophy Winner
1997	Peyton Manning	University of Tennessee (TN)	1997 Johnny Unitas Golden Arm Award Winner
1998	Tim Couch	University of Kentucky (KY)	1998 SEC Player of the Year
1999	Joe Hamilton	Georgia Institute of Technology (GA)	1999 Davey O'Brien Award Winner
2000	Josh Heupel	University of Oklahoma (OK)	2000 Walter Camp Award Winner
2001	Ken Dorsey	University of Miami (FL)	2001 National Champion
2002	Ken Dorsey	University of Miami (FL)	2X Archie Griffin Award Winner (2001–2002)
2003	Jason White	University of Oklahoma (OK)	2003 Heisman Trophy Winner
2004	Matt Leinart	University of Southern California (CA)	2004 Heisman Trophy Winner
2005	Matt Leinart	University of Southern California (CA)	2005 Walter Camp Award Winner
2006	Troy Smith	Ohio State University (OH)	2006 Heisman Trophy Winner
2007	Tim Tebow	University of Florida (FL)	2007 Heisman Trophy Winner
2008	Sam Bradford	University of Oklahoma (OK)	2008 Heisman Trophy Winner
2009	Colt McCoy	University of Texas (TX)	2009 *Sporting News* College Athlete of the Year
2010	Kellen Moore	Boise State University (ID)	2X WAC Offensive Player of the Year

Randy Moss Award (Randy Moss Return Man Award)

The Randy Moss Return Man Award was named after the former Marshall University (Huntington, West Virginia) wide receiver and kick/punt returner Randy Moss and was awarded only once (after the 2006 season) to DeSean Jackson from the University of California (Berkeley). The Award was created in 2006 by Gulf Coast Events and GameDay Consultants, operators of the 2007 North-South All-Star Classic.

Randall Gene Moss (born: February 13, 1977, in Rand, WV) played college football at Marshall University (Huntington, West Virginia) after being released by Florida State University (Tallahassee) and is currently active in the NFL (Minnesota Vikings (1998–2004); Oakland Raiders (2005–2006); New England Patriots (2007–present). He was a two-time collegiate All-American (1996–1997); NFL Offensive Rookie of the Year (1998); and was selected to the NFL 2000s All-Decade Team.

As of this writing, he holds several NCAA college records, including: most games with a touchdown reception in a season (11 in 1996) and most receiving yards gained by a freshman in a season (1,073 in 1996). Although still active, he holds several NFL records, including most touchdown receptions in a season (23 in 2007); most games in a season with at least two touchdown receptions (eight in 2007); only player to have 1,600 receiving yards and 16 receiving touchdowns in a season (2003); youngest player in NFL history to record his 100th receiving touchdown (29 years and 235 days); and fastest player to reach 5,000 career receiving yards (59 games).

Year	*Player*	*School*
2006	DeSean Jackson	University of California (CA)

Ray Guy Award *see* NCAA Division I FBS

Rimington Trophy

Since 2000, the Rimington Trophy (sometimes referred to as the Dave Rimington Trophy) has been sponsored by the Cystic Fibrosis Foundation-Nebraska (11917 Pierce Plaza, Omaha NE 68144; Telephone: 402-330-6164; Fax: 402-330-8458; Email: info@rimingtontrophy.com; Web site: http://www.rimingtontrophy.com) and is awarded annually to college football's best center by a vote of members from the American Football Coaches Association, the Walter Camp Foundation, *The Sporting News*, and the Football Writers Association of America.

The trophy is named in honor of the University of Nebraska's Dave Rimington (born on May 22, 1960, in Omaha, Nebraska), a two-time All-American center (1981–1982) who played at the school from 1979 to 1982. Often called the best center ever in the history of college football, Rimington (Dave Brian Rimington) won the Outland Trophy as college football's best offensive lineman twice (1981–1982), had his jersey number 50 retired by the team in 1982, and was inducted into the College Football Hall of Fame in 1997.

After college, he played in the NFL for seven seasons (five with the Cincinnati Bengals [1983–1987] and two with the Philadelphia Eagles [1988–1989]).

A member of the National College Football Awards Association, the Rimington Trophy also serves as a fundraiser for the Boomer Esiason Foundation's fight against cystic fibrosis. In addition to recognizing each season's most outstanding center in college football, the Rimington Trophy also recognizes legendary centers from the past with the President Gerald R. Ford Legendary Center Award, which is presented annually to a former collegiate or professional center.

Year	*Name*	*School*	*Note*
2000	Dominic Raiola	University of Nebraska (NE)	2000 All-American
2001	LeCharles Bentley	Ohio State University (OH)	2001 First-Team All-American
2002	Brett Romberg	University of Miami (FL)	2001 NCAA National Champion
2003	Jake Grove	Virginia Tech (VA)	2004 Consensus All-American
2004	David Baas	University of Michigan (MI)	2004 All-American
2004	Ben Wilkerson	Louisiana State University (LA)	2003 BCS National Champion
2005	Greg Eslinger	University of Minnesota (MN)	2X AP All-American
2006	Dan Mozes	West Virginia University (WV)	3X All-American
2007	Jonathan Luigs	University of Arkansas (AR)	2007 All-American
2008	A. Q. Shipley	Pennsylvania State University (PA)	2008 All-American
2009	Maurkice Pouncey	University of Florida (FL)	2009 First Team All-American
2010	Jake Kirkpatrick	Texas Christian University (TX)	2010 All American

Rotary Lombardi Award

Since 1970 (after the death of coach Vince Lombardi), the Rotary Lombardi Award has been presented annually to the best college football lineman or linebacker by Wachovia Bank. The Rotary Club of Houston (P. O. Box 690673, Houston, TX 77269; Telephone: 713-526-8100, 713-973-9936; Email: geraldine@rotaryhouston.org; Web site: http://www.rotaryhouston.org/), active since 1912, represents individuals and institutions, including Wachovia Bank.

Vincent Thomas Lombardi (born: June 11, 1913, in Brooklyn, NY; died: September 3, 1970, in Washington, D.C.) played college football at Fordham University (New York, New York) before embarking on a legendary coaching career with the NFL's New York Giants (1954–1958), Green Bay Packers (1959–1967), and the Washington Redskins (1969). He won the first two Super Bowls (SB I [1967] and SB II [1968]), five NFL Championships (1961–1962, 1965–1967), and was inducted into the Pro Football Hall of Fame in 1971.

This award is not the same as the Vince Lombardi Trophy, which is presented to the National Football League's Super Bowl winner. As of this writing, only Orlando Pace (Ohio State University) has won this award twice.

Year	*Name*	*School*	*Note*
1970	Jim Stillwagon	Ohio State University (OH)	1970 Outland Trophy Winner
1971	Walt Patulski	University of Notre Dame (IN)	1971 All-American
1972	Rich Glover	University of Nebraska (NE)	1995 College Football Hall of Fame
1973	John Hicks	Ohio State University (OH)	1973 Outland Trophy Winner
1974	Randy White	University of Maryland (MD)	1974 Outland Trophy Winner
1975	Lee Roy Selmon	University of Oklahoma (OK)	1975 Outland Trophy Winner
1976	Wilson Whitley	University of Houston (TX)	2007 College Football Hall of Fame Inductee
1977	Ross Browner	University of Notre Dame (IN)	1977 Maxwell Award Winner
1978	Bruce Clark	Pennsylvania State University (PA)	1st Junior to Win Lombardi Award
1979	Brad Budde	University of Southern California (CA)	1990 College Football Hall of Fame Inductee
1980	Hugh Green	University of Pittsburgh (PA)	1980 Walter Camp Award Winner
1981	Kenneth Sims	University of Texas (TX)	2X All-American (1980–1981)
1982	Dave Rimington	University of Nebraska (NE)	2X Outland Trophy Award Winner (1981–1982)
1983	Dean Steinkuhler	University of Nebraska (NE)	1983 Outland Trophy Winner
1984	Tony Degrate	University of Texas (TX)	1985 127th NFL Selection
1985	Tony Casillas	University of Oklahoma (OK)	Won 1985 National Championship
1986	Cornelius Bennett	University of Alabama (AL)	1986 SEC Player of the Year
1987	Chris Spielman	Ohio State University (OH)	2009 College Football Hall of Fame Inductee
1988	Tracy Rocker	Auburn University (AL)	1988 Outland Trophy Winner
1989	Percy Snow	Michigan State University (MI)	1989 Butkus Award Winner
1990	Chris Zorich	University of Notre Dame (IN)	2007 College Football Hall of Fame Inductee
1991	Steve Emtman	University of Washington (WA)	2007 College Football Hall of Fame Inductee
1992	Marvin Jones	Florida State University (FL)	1992 Butkus Award Winner
1993	Aaron Taylor	University of Notre Dame (IN)	2X All-American (1992–1993)
1994	Warren Sapp	University of Miami (FL)	1994 Bronko Nagurski Trophy Winner
1995	Orlando Pace	Ohio State University (OH)	1997 1st-Round NFL Pick
1996	Orlando Pace	Ohio State University (OH)	Outland Trophy Winner
1997	Grant Wistrom	University of Nebraska (NE)	1997 Bill Willis Award Winner
1998	Dat Nguyen	Texas A&M University (TX)	1998 Chuck Bednarik Award Winner
1999	Corey Moore	Virginia Tech Institute (VA)	1999 Bronko Nagurski Trophy Winner
2000	Jamal Reynolds	Florida State University (FL)	2000 Bill Willis Trophy Winner
2001	Julius Peppers	University of North Carolina (NC)	2001 Bill Willis Award Winner
2002	Terrell Suggs	Arizona State University (AZ)	2002 Ted Hendricks Award Winner
2003	Tommie Harris	University of Oklahoma (OK)	2003 Bill Willis Trophy Winner
2004	David Pollack	University of Georgia (GA)	2004 Lott Trophy Winner
2005	A. J. Hawk	Ohio State University (OH)	2005 Jack Lambert Trophy Winner
2006	LaMarr Woodley	University of Michigan (MI)	2006 Ted Hendricks Award Winner
2007	Glenn Dorsey	Louisiana State University (LA)	2007 SEC Defensive Player of the Year
2008	Brian Orakpo	University of Texas (TX)	2008 Bill Willis Award Winner
2009	Ndamukong Suh	University of Nebraska (NE)	2X First Team All Big-12 (2008–2009)
2010	Nick Fairley	Auburn University (AL)	2011 BCS National Championship MVP

The Rudy Awards (College Football)

Daniel "Rudy" Ruettiger launched The Rudy Awards in 2007 to honor Division I football players who brought that "something extra" to the team. This Award honors the most inspirational and motivational players in America who best defined what he refers to as "The Four C's": Character, Courage, Contribution, and Commitment.

During its first year, 26 coaches nominated the "Rudy" from their own team and the inaugural award was presented to Terry Clayton of the University of Kentucky, a senior linebacker who had lost his hearing at age five. He later persevered as a walk-on for the University of Kentucky team and twice was named to the Southeast Conference Academic Honor Roll.

Any Division I college football (freshman through senior) is eligible and does not have to be a walk-on. Only coaches can make nominations and winners are chosen by a national Selection Committee.

Year	*Player*	*School*	*Position*	*Note*
2007	Terry Clayton	University of Kentucky (KY)	Linebacker	Went Deaf at Age Five
2008	Drew Combs	Texas Christian University (TX)	Kickoff Specialist	Born with a Deformed Left Arm
2009	LeVon Morefield	University of Akron (OH)	Running Back	Born Addicted to Crack Cocaine
2010	Mark Herzlich	Boston College (MA)	Linebacker	Fought Bone Cancer in College

Sammy Baugh Trophy

Since 1959, the Sammy Baugh Trophy, sponsored by the Touchdown Club of Columbus (Ohio, http://www.touchdownclubofcolumbus.com) has been awarded annually to the nation's top college passer. The award is named after former Texas Christian University and Washington Redskins (National Football League) quarterback Sammy Baugh.

Sam B. Nicola (who died in 1993) founded the Touchdown Club of Columbus in 1956 and was president of the Athletic Club of Columbus when the initial All-Sports Banquet was held in January 1956. Although a local organization, its range has always been national (not limited to the Columbus, Ohio area) and athletes from all sports have been recognized. Honored athletes are selected by the appropriate Touchdown Club's committees, consisting of coaches, sportswriters, and former players.

Sammy Baugh (Samuel Adrian Baugh; born: March 17, 1914, in Temple, TX; died: December 17, 2008, in Rotan, Texas) played college football at Texas Christian University (Fort Worth); spent 16 seasons with the NFL's Washington Redskins (1937–1952); and coached both the New York Titans (American Football League, 1960–1961) and the Houston Oilers (AFL, 1964). He was a two-time All-American in college (1935–1936); a two-time NFL Player of the Year (1947–1948); named to the NFL's 1940s All-Decade Team; selected to the NFL 75th Anniversary All-Time Team; and was inducted into both the College Football Hall of Fame (1951) and the Pro Football Hall of Fame (1963).

As of this writing, only Baylor University's (Texas) Don Trull has won the award twice.

Year	*Winner*	*School*	*Note*
1959	Dick Norman	Stanford University (CA)	1961 Senior Bowl MVP
1960	Harold Stephens	Hardin-Simmons University (TX)	Played One NFL Season
1961	Ron Miller	University of Wisconsin (WI)	Played One NFL Season
1962	Don Trull	Baylor University (TX)	2X All-American
1963	Don Trull	Baylor University (TX)	No Further Information
1964	Jerry Rhome	University of Tulsa (OK)	College Football Hall of Fame, 1998
1965	Steve Sloan	University of Alabama (AL)	Won 1965 National Champion
1966	Bob Griese	Purdue University (IN)	1984 College Football Hall of Fame Inductee
1967	Terry Hanratty	University of Notre Dame (IN)	Won 1966 National Championship
1968	Chuck Hixson	Southern Methodist University (TX)	13th Round NFL Selection
1969	Mike Phipps	Purdue University (IN)	2006 College Football Hall of Fame Inductee
1970	Sonny Sixkiller	University of Washington (WA)	No Further Information
1971	John Reaves	University of Florida (FL)	Played 11 NFL Seasons
1972	Don Strock	Virginia Tech & State University (VA)	Led the Nation in Total Passing Yards, 1972
1973	Jesse Freitas	San Diego State University (CA)	Played Two Seasons in the NFL
1974	Gary Scheide	Brigham Young University (UT)	Won 1974 Western Athletic Conference
1975	Gene Swick	University of Toledo (OH)	1st College Player to Attain 8,000 Total Yards
1976	Tommy Kramer	Rice University (TX)	1976 All-American
1977	Guy Benjamin	Stanford University (CA)	Won the 1977 Sun Bowl
1978	Steve Dils	Stanford University (CA)	Won the 1978 Bluebonnet Bowl

Year	Winner	School	Note
1979	Marc Wilson	Brigham Young University (UT)	1996 College Football Hall of Fame Inductee
1980	Mark Herrmann	Purdue University (IN)	1980 First-Team All-American
1981	Jim McMahon	Brigham Young University (UT)	2X All-American (1980–1981)
1982	John Elway	Stanford University (CA)	2000 College Football Hall of Fame Inductee
1983	Steve Young	Brigham Young University (UT)	2001 College Football Hall of Fame Inductee
1984	Robbie Bosco	Brigham Young University (UT)	Won 1984 Holiday Bowl
1985	Brian McClure	Bowling Green State University (OH)	2X MAC MVP (1984–1985)
1986	Vinny Testaverde	University of Miami (FL)	1986 Heisman Trophy Winner
1987	Don McPherson	Syracuse University (NY)	1987 Davey O'Brien Award Winner
1988	Steve Walsh	University of Miami (FL)	Won 1987 National Championship
1989	Jeff George	University of Illinois (IL)	1990, 1st Pick in the NFL Draft
1990	David Klingler	University of Houston (TX)	Most Yards in a Single Game (1990, 716 Yards)
1991	Ty Detmer	Brigham Young University (UT)	1990 Heisman Trophy Winner
1992	Elvis Grbac	University of Michigan (MI)	8th Round NFL Selection
1993	Trent Dilfer	California State University, Fresno (CA)	1993 AP All-American
1994	Kerry Collins	Pennsylvania State University (PA)	1994 Davey O'Brien Award Winner
1995	Danny Wuerffel	University of Florida (FL)	1996 Heisman Trophy Winner
1996	Steve Sarkisian	Brigham Young University (UT)	2X WAC Champion (1995–1996)
1997	Ryan Leaf	Washington State University (WA)	Won 1997 Pac-10 Championship
1998	Daunte Culpepper	University of Central Florida (FL)	First-Round NFL Selection
1999	Chad Pennington	Marshall University (WV)	1999 Draddy Trophy Winner
2000	Chris Weinke	Florida State University (FL)	2000 Heisman Trophy Winner
2001	David Carr	California State University, Fresno (CA)	2001 Johnny Unitas Golden Arm Award Winner
2002	Kliff Kingsbury	Texas Tech University (TX)	6th Round NFL Draft Pick, 2003
2003	Brian Symons	Texas Tech University (TX)	No Further Information
2004	Stefan LeFors	University of Louisville (KY)	Won the 2004 Liberty Bowl
2005	Brady Quinn	University of Notre Dame (IN)	2005 AP All-American
2006	Colt Brennan	University of Hawaii (HI)	Won the 2006 Hawaii Bowl
2007	Graham Harrell	Texas Tech University (TX)	2007 Academic All-Big Ten
2008	Sam Bradford	University of Oklahoma (OK)	2008 Heisman Trophy Winner
2009	Case Keenum	University of Houston (TX)	C-USA Most Valuable Player
2010	Landry Jones	University of Oklahoma (OK)	Named After the NFL's Tom Landry

Sasser Cup *see* Big South Conference (NCAA Division I FCS)

Sporting News College Football Coach of the Year Award

The Sporting News College Football Coach of the Year Award has been presented annually since 1963.by *Sporting News* magazine (formerly known as *The Sporting News*) (http://www.sportingnews.com/).

Year	Coach	School
1963	Darrell Royal	University of Texas (TX)
1964	Frank Broyles	University of Arkansas (AR)
1965	Duffy Daugherty	Michigan State University (MI)
1966	Ara Parseghian	University of Notre Dame (IN)
1967	John Pont	University of Indiana (IN)
1968	Woody Hayes	Ohio State University (OH)
1969	Darrell Royal	University of Texas (TX)
1970	John Ralston	Stanford University (CA)
1971	Chuck Fairbanks	University of Oklahoma (OK)
1972	John McKay	University of Southern California (CA)

Year	*Coach*	*School*
1973	Barry Switzer	University of Oklahoma (OK)
1974	Jerry Claiborne	University of Maryland (MD)
1975	Emory Bellard	Texas A&M University (TX)
1976	Johnny Majors	University of Pittsburgh (PA)
1977	Lou Holtz	University of Arkansas (AR)
1978	Darryl Rogers	Michigan State University (MI)
1979	John Mackovic	Wake Forest University (NC)
1980	Vince Dooley	University of Georgia (GA)
1981	Hayden Fry	University of Iowa (IA)
1982	George MacIntyre	Vanderbilt University (TN)
1983	Mike White	University of Illinois (IL)
1984	Jim Wacker	Texas Christian University (TX)
1985	Bo Schembechler	University of Michigan (MI)
1986	John Cooper	Arizona State University (AZ)
1987	Dick MacPherson	Syracuse University (NY)
1988	Lou Holtz	University of Notre Dame (IN)
1989	No Selection	
1990	Bobby Ross	Georgia Institute of Technology (GA)
1991	Don James	University of Washington (WA)
1992	Dennis Erickson	University of Miami (FL)
1993	Terry Bowden	Auburn University (AL)
1994	Rich Brooks	University of Oregon (OR)
1995	Gary Barnett	Northwestern University (IL)
1996	Bruce Snyder	Arizona State University (AZ)
1997	Mike Price	Washington State University (WA)
1998	Phil Fulmer	University of Tennessee (TN)
1999	June Jones	University of Hawaii (HI)
2000	Dennis Erickson	Oregon State University (OR)
2001	Ralph Friedgen	University of Maryland (MD)
2002	Jim Tressel	Ohio State University (OH)
2003	Urban Meyer	University of Utah (UT)
2004	Tommy Tuberville	Auburn University (AL)
2005	Joe Paterno	Pennsylvania State University (PA)
2006	Jim Grobe	Wake Forest University (NC)
2007	Mark Mangino	University of Kansas (KS)
2008	Nick Saban	University of Alabama (AL)
2009	Gary Patterson	Texas Christian University (TX)
2010	Chip Kelly	University of Oregon

Sporting News College Football Player of the Year Award

Since 1942, the *Sporting News* College Football Player of the Year Award has been presented annually to the nation's best collegiate football player. It is presented by *Sporting News* (formerly known as *The Sporting News*) (http://www.sportingnews.com/).

As of this writing, three players have won this award twice, including Howard Cassady (Ohio State University), Billy Cannon (Louisiana State University), and Archie Griffin (Ohio State University),

Year	*Winner*	*School*	*Note*
1942	Frank Sinkwich	University of Georgia (GA)	1942 Heisman Trophy Winner
1943	Angelo Bertelli	University of Notre Dame (IN)	1943 Heisman Trophy Winner
1944	Les Horvath	Ohio State University (OH)	1944 Heisman Trophy Winner
1945	Felix Blanchard	U.S. Military Academy at West Point (NY)	1945 Heisman Trophy Winner
1946	Glenn Davis	U.S. Military Academy at West Point (NY)	1946 Heisman Trophy Winner
1947	John Lujack	University of Notre Dame (IN)	1947 Heisman Trophy Winner
1948	Doak Walker	Southern Methodist University (TX)	1948 Heisman Trophy Winner
1949	Leon Hart	University of Notre Dame (IN)	1949 Heisman Trophy Winner
1950	Vic Janowicz	Ohio State University (OH)	1950 Heisman Trophy Winner

Sporting News College Football Player of the Year

Year	*Winner*	*School*	*Note*
1951	Dick Kazmaier	Princeton University (NJ)	1951 Heisman Trophy Winner
1952	Billy Vessels	University of Oklahoma (OK)	1952 Heisman Trophy Winner
1953	John Lattner	University of Notre Dame (IN)	1953 Heisman Trophy Winner
1954	Howard Cassady	Ohio State University (OH)	Scored 37 Touchdowns in 36 Games
1955	Howard Cassady	Ohio State University (OH)	1979 College Football Hall of Fame Inductee
1956	Tommy McDonald	University of Oklahoma (OK)	1985 College Football Hall of Fame Inductee
1957	John David Crow	Texas A&M University (TX)	1957 Heisman Trophy Winner
1958	Billy Cannon	Louisiana State University (LA)	1958 UPI Player of the Year
1959	Billy Cannon	Louisiana State University (LA)	1959 Heisman Trophy Winner
1960	Joe Bellino	U.S. Naval Academy (MD)	1960 Heisman Trophy Winner
1961	Bob Ferguson	Ohio State University (OH)	1996 College Football Hall of Fame Inductee
1962	Terry Baker	Oregon State University (OR)	1962 Heisman Trophy Winner
1963	Roger Staubach	U.S. Naval Academy (MD)	1963 Heisman Trophy Winner
1964	Dick Butkus	University of Illinois (IL)	1983 College Football Hall of Fame Inductee
1965	Donny Anderson	Texas Tech University (TX)	1989 College Football Hall of Fame Inductee
1965	Jim Grabowski	University of Illinois (IL)	1995 College Football Hall of Fame Inductee
1966	Steve Spurrier	University of Florida (FL)	1966 Heisman Trophy Winner
1967	Gary Beban	University of California, Los Angeles (CA)	1967 Heisman Trophy Winner
1968	O.J. Simpson	University of Southern California (CA)	1968 Heisman Trophy Winner
1969	Steve Owens	University of Oklahoma (OK)	1191 College Football Hall of Fame Inductee
1970	Jim Plunkett	Stanford University (CA)	1970 Heisman Trophy Winner
1971	Ed Marinaro	Cornell University (NY)	1991 College Football Hall of Fame Inductee
1971	Pat Sullivan	Auburn University (AL)	1971 Heisman Trophy Winner
1972	Bert Jones	Louisiana State University (LA)	1972 All-American
1973	John Hicks	Ohio State University (OH)	2001 College Football Hall of Fame Inductee
1974	Archie Griffin	Ohio State University (OH)	1974 Heisman Trophy Winner
1975	Archie Griffin	Ohio State University (OH)	1975 Heisman Trophy Winner
1976	Tony Dorsett	University of Pittsburgh (PA)	1976 Heisman Trophy Winner
1977	Earl Campbell	University of Texas (TX)	1977 Heisman Trophy Winner
1978	Billy Sims	University of Oklahoma (OK)	1978 Heisman Trophy Winner
1979	Charles White	University of Southern California (CA)	1979 Heisman Trophy Winner
1980	Hugh Green	University of Pittsburgh (PA)	1980 Lombardi Award Winner
1981	Marcus Allen	University of Southern California (CA)	1981 Heisman Trophy Winner
1982	Herschel Walker	University of Georgia (GA)	1982 Heisman Trophy Winner
1983	Mike Rozier	University of Nebraska (NE)	1983 Heisman Trophy Winner
1984	Doug Flutie	Boston University (MA)	1984 Heisman Trophy Winner
1985	Bo Jackson	Auburn University (AL)	1985 Heisman Trophy Winner
1986	Vinny Testaverde	University of Miami (FL)	1986 Heisman Trophy Winner
1987	Tim Brown	University of Notre Dame (IN)	1987 Heisman Trophy Winner
1988	Barry Sanders	Oklahoma State University (OK)	1988 Heisman Trophy Winner
1989	Darian Hagan	University of Colorado (CO)	Threw 1000+ Yards & Ran 1000+ Yards, 1989
1990	Raghib Ismail	University of Notre Dame (IN)	2X All-American (1989–1990)
1991	Desmond Howard	University of Michigan (MI)	1991 Heisman Trophy Winner
1992	Marvin Jones	Florida State University (FL)	1992 Butkus Award Winner
1993	Charlie Ward	Florida State University (FL)	1993 Heisman Trophy Winner
1994	Rashaan Salaam	University of Colorado (CO)	1994 Heisman Trophy Winner
1995	Tommy Frazier	University of Nebraska (NE)	2X National Champion (1994–1995)
1996	Danny Wuerffel	University of Florida (FL)	1996 Heisman Trophy Winner

Year	*Winner*	*School*	*Note*
1997	Charles Woodson	University of Michigan (MI)	1997 Heisman Trophy Winner
1998	Ricky Williams	University of Texas (TX)	1998 Heisman Trophy Winner
1999	Ron Dayne	University of Wisconsin (WI)	1999 Heisman Trophy Winner
2000	Chris Weinke	Florida State University (FL)	2000 Heisman Trophy Winner
2001	Eric Crouch	University of Nebraska (NE)	2001 Heisman Trophy Winner
2002	Carson Palmer	University of Southern California (CA)	2002 Heisman Trophy Winner
2003	Jason White	University of Oklahoma (OK)	2003 Heisman Trophy Winner
2004	Alex Smith	University of Utah (UT)	2004 Mountain West Conference Player of the Year
2005	Reggie Bush	University of Southern California (CA)	2005 Heisman Trophy Winner
2006	Troy Smith	Ohio State University (OH)	2006 Heisman Trophy Winner
2007	Tim Tebow	University of Florida (FL)	2007 Heisman Trophy Winner
2008	Graham Harrell	Texas Tech University (TX)	2008 Johnny Unitas Golden Arm Winner
2008	Sam Bradford	University of Oklahoma (OK)	2008 Heisman Trophy Winner
2008	Colt McCoy	University of Texas (TX)	2008 Archie Griffin Award
2009	Mark Ingram	University of Alabama (AL)	2009 Heisman Trophy Winner
2010	Cameron Newton	Auburn University (AL)	2010 Heisman Trophy Winner

Ted Hendricks Award

Presented annually since 2002, the Ted Hendricks Award is given to the best defensive end in college football by the non-profit Ted Hendricks Foundation (Award: 2642 South Field Court, Lakewood, CO 80227; Email: Sam_Poulos@TedHendricks.com; Foundation: P.O. Box 7470, Buffalo Grove, IL 60089; Email: Linda_Babl@Ted Hendricks.com; Web site: http://tedhendricks.com/foundation.htm). Winners of this Award are voted on by college coaches, former players, media members, and selected football professionals.

Theodore "Ted" Paul Hendricks (born: November 1, 1947, in Guatemala City, Guatemala) played college football at the University of Miami (Coral Gables) and spent 15 years in the NFL with the Baltimore Colts (1969–1973), Green Bay Packers (1974), and the Oakland / Los Angeles Raiders (1975–1983). He was a three-time All-American (1966–1968); named United Press International Lineman of the Year (1968); won four Super Bowls (SB V [1971], SB XI [1977], SB XV [1981], and SB XVIII [1984]); selected to the NFL 1970s All-Decade Team; and was named to the NFL 75th Anniversary All-Time Team. He is the first player in NFL history to have four Super Bowl rings and never play for the San Francisco 49ers, Dallas Cowboys, or Pittsburgh Steelers.

He was inducted into both the College Football Hall of Fame (1987) and the Pro Football Hall of Fame (1990).

As of this writing, David Pollack (University of Georgia in Atlanta) is the only two-time winner (2003–2004).

Year	*Winner*	*School*	*Note*
2002	Terrell Suggs	Arizona State University (AZ)	Lombardi Award Winner
2003	David Pollack	University of Georgia (GA)	3X All-American (2002–2004)
2004	David Pollack	University of Georgia (GA)	2004 Lott Trophy Winner
2005	Elvis Dumervil	University of Louisville (KY)	2005 Big East Defensive Player of the Year
2006	LaMarr Woodley	University of Michigan (MI)	2006 First-Team All-American
2007	Chris Long	University of Virginia (VA)	2007 First-Team All-American
2008	Brian Orakpo	University of Texas (TX)	2008 First-Team All-American
2009	Jerry Hughes	Texas Christian University (TX)	2009 Lott Trophy Winner
2010	Da'Quan Bowers	Clemson University (SC)	2010 Bronko Nagurski Trophy Winner

Theodore Roosevelt Award

The Theodore Roosevelt Award is the highest honor the National Collegiate Athletic Association (700 West Washington Street, P.O. Box 6222, Indianapolis, IN 46206; Telephone: 317-917-6222; Fax:

317-917-6888; Web site: http://www.ncaa.org/) presents to an individual. It is given annually to a graduate of an NCAA member institution who earned a varsity letter in college for participation in intercollegiate athletics, and who ultimately became a distinguished citizen of national reputation based on outstanding life accomplishment.

The Award, nicknamed "The Teddy," is named after President Theodore Roosevelt, whose concern for the conduct of intercollegiate athletes and athletic programs led to the formation of the NCAA in 1906.

Theodore "Teddy" Roosevelt (born: October 27, 1858, in New York, NY; died: January 6, 1919, in Oyster Bay, NY) was a Republican; the 26th President of the United States (September 14, 1901–March 4, 1909); and the 33rd Governor of New York (January 1, 1899–December 31, 1900), among many of his political positions.

As of this writing, past winners include four former Presidents of the United States, Dwight D. Eisenhower (1967), Gerald R. Ford (1975), George H.W. Bush (1986) and Ronald Reagan (1990).

Year	*Winner*	*School*	*Note*
1967	Dwight D. Eisenhower	U.S. Military Academy (NY) (football)	34th President of the United States
1968	Leverett Saltonstall	Harvard University (MA) (rowing)	Governor of MA & Senator
1969	Byron "Whizzer" White	University of Colorado at Boulder (CO) (football)	U.S. Supreme Court Justice
1970	Frederick L. Hovde	University of Minnesota (MN) (football)	President of Purdue University
1971	Christopher C. Kraft Jr.	Virginia Polytechnic Institute (VA) (baseball)	NASA Mission Control Director
1972	Jerome H. Holland	Cornell University (NY) (football)	Ambassador to Sweden
1973	Omar Bradley	U.S. Military Academy (NY) (baseball)	U.S. General of the Army
1974	Jesse Owens	Ohio State University (OH) (track and field)	Won Gold Medal at 1936 Summer Olympics
1975	Gerald Ford	University of Michigan (MI) (football)	38th President of the United States
1976	Thomas J. Hamilton	U.S. Naval Academy (NY) (football / basketball / baseball)	21st Head Football Coach at the Naval Academy
1977	Tom Bradley	University of California, Los Angeles (CA)	5-Term Mayor of Los Angeles, CA
1978	Gerald B. Zornow	University of Rochester (NY) (football / basketball / baseball)	President and Chairman of the Eastman Kodak Company
1979	Otis Chandler	Stanford University (CA) (track and field)	Publisher of the *Los Angeles Times*
1980	Denton Cooley	University of Texas (TX) (basketball)	Performed 1st Heart Transplant in the U.S.
1981	Art Linkletter	San Diego State University (CA)	Radio and Television Star
1982	Bill Cosby	Temple University (PA) (football)	Television and Movie Star
1983	Arnold Palmer	Wake Forest University (NC) (golf)	Professional Golfer
1984	William P. Lawrence	U.S. Naval Academy (MD) (basketball / football / tennis)	Superintendent of the U.S. Naval Academy
1985	Robben Fleming	Beloit College (WI)	University of Michigan's Ninth President
1986	George H. W. Bush	Yale University (CT) (baseball)	41st President of the United States
1987	Walter J. Zable	College of William and Mary (VA) (football)	College of William & Mary Board Member
1988	No Award		
1989	Paul Ebert	Ohio State University (OH) (baseball / basketball)	American College of Surgeons Director
1990	Ronald Reagan	Eureka College (IL) (football)	40th President of the United States
1991	Althea Gibson	Florida A&M University (FL) (tennis)	1st African American Woman to win Tennis Grand Slam
1992	Jack Kemp	Occidental College (CA) (football)	Nine-Term Congressman
1993	Lamar Alexander	Vanderbilt University (TN) (track and field)	Tennessee U.S. Senator

Year	*Winner*	*School*	*Note*
1994	Rafer Johnson	University of California, Los Angeles (CA) (track and field)	1956 & 1960 Olympic Medal Winner
1995	Bob Mathias	Stanford University (CA) (track and field)	2X Olympic Decathlon Gold Medalist
1996	John Wooden	Purdue University (IN) (basketball)	Won 10 NCAA Basketball Championships
1997	William Porter Payne	University of Georgia (GA) (football)	Chairman, Augusta National Golf Club
1998	Bob Dole	Washburn University (KS) (basketball)	Kansas U.S. Senator
1999	Bill Richardson	Tufts University (MA) (baseball)	30th Governor of Mexico
2000	Roger Staubach	U.S. Naval Academy (MD) (football)	1963 Heisman Trophy Winner
2001	William Cohen	Bowdoin College (ME) (basketball)	Congressman & Senator
2002	Eunice Kennedy Shriver	Stanford University (CA) (swimming / track and field)	Founder of the Special Olympics
2003	Donna de Varona	University of California, Los Angeles (CA) (swimming)	Olympic Medal Winner
2004	Alan Page	University of Notre Dame (IN) (football)	Minnesota Supreme Court Associate Justice
2005	Sally Ride	Stanford University (CA) (tennis)	1st American Woman to Fly in Space (NASA)
2006	Robert Kraft	Columbia University (NY) (football)	Chairman of the Kraft Group
2007	Paul Tagliabue	Georgetown University (D.C.) (basketball)	National Football League Commissioner
2008	John Glenn	Muskingum College (OH)	1st American to Orbit the Earth (NASA)
2009	Madeleine Albright	Wellesley College (MA) (swimming / rowing / field hockey)	First Female United States Secretary of State
2010	George J. Mitchell	Bowdoin College (ME)	U.S. Senator from Maine
2011	Ann E. Dunwoody	SUNY Cortland (NY)	Commanding General, U.S. Army Materiel Command

Tight End of the Year

Since 2006, the Tight End of the Year Award has been presented annually by the Touchdown Club of Columbus (Ohio, http://www.touchdownclubofcolumbus.com) to college football's best tight end.

Sam B. Nicola (who died in 1993) founded the Touchdown Club of Columbus in 1956 and was president of the Athletic Club of Columbus when the initial All-Sports Banquet was held in January 1956. Although a local organization, its range has always been national (not limited to the Columbus, Ohio, area) and athletes from all sports have been recognized. Honored athletes are selected by the appropriate Touchdown Club's committees, consisting of coaches, sportswriters, and former players.

Year	*Name*	*School*	*Note*
2006	Matt Spaeth	University of Minnesota (MN)	2006 John Mackey Award Winner
2007	Travis Beckum	University of Wisconsin (WI)	2007 First-Team All-American
2008	Jermaine Gresham	University of Oklahoma (OK)	2008 First-Team All-American
2009	Aaron Hernandez	University of Florida (FL)	2009 John Mackey Award Winner
2010	Michael Egnew	University of Missouri (MO)	2010 College Football All-America Team

United Press International College Football Player of the Year

From 1950 until 1991, the United Press International College Football Player of the Year award was presented to the best college football player in the country (both offense and defense). Before the UPI ceased operations in 1997, the award had been discontinued. Like all UPI college awards, recipients were voted on by NCAA coaches.

Billy Cannon (Louisiana State University), O.J. Simpson (University of Southern California), and Archie Griffin (Ohio State University) were the only two-time winners.

Year	Player	School	Note
1950	Vic Janowicz	Ohio State University (OH)	1950 Heisman Trophy Winner
1951	Dick Kalmaler	Princeton University (NJ)	1951 Heisman Trophy Winner
1952	Bill Vessells	University of Oklahoma (OK)	1952 Heisman Trophy Winner
1953	Paul Giel	University of Minnesota (MN)	2X Big Ten Most Valuable Player
1954	Alan Ameche	University of Wisconsin (WI)	1954 Heisman Trophy Winner
1955	Howard Cassidy	Ohio State University (OH)	Scored 37 Touchdowns in 36 Games
1956	Johnny Majors	University of Tennessee (TN)	2X SEC Most Valuable Player
1957	John David Crow	Texas A&M University (TX)	1957 Heisman Trophy Winner
1958	Billy Cannon	Louisiana State University (LA)	1958 Chic Harley Award Winner
1959	Billy Cannon	Louisiana State University (LA)	1959 Heisman Trophy Winner
1960	Joe Bellino	United States Naval Academy (MD)	1960 Heisman Trophy Winner
1961	Bob Ferguson	Ohio State University (OH)	1961 Maxwell Award Winner
1962	Terry Baker	Oregon State University (OR)	1962 Heisman Trophy Winner
1963	Roger Staubach	United States Naval Academy (MD)	1963 Heisman Trophy Winner
1964	John Huarte	University of Notre Dame (IN)	1964 Heisman Trophy Winner
1965	Mike Garrett	University of Southern California (CA)	1965 Heisman Trophy Winner
1966	Steve Spurrier	University of Florida (FL)	1966 Heisman Trophy Winner
1967	O. J. Simpson	University of Southern California (CA)	1967 Walter Camp Award Winner
1968	O. J. Simpson	University of Southern California (CA)	1968 Heisman Trophy Winner
1969	Steve Owens	University of Oklahoma (OK)	1969 Heisman Trophy Winner
1970	Jim Plunkett	Stanford University (CA)	1970 Heisman Trophy Winner
1971	Ed Marinaro	Cornell University (NY)	1971 Maxwell Award Winner
1972	Johnny Rodgers	University of Nebraska (NE)	1972 Heisman Trophy Winner
1973	John Cappelletti	Pennsylvania State University (PA)	1973 Heisman Trophy Winner
1974	Archie Griffin	Ohio State University (OH)	1974 Heisman Trophy Winner
1975	Archie Griffin	Ohio State University (OH)	1975 Heisman Trophy Winner
1976	Tony Dorsett	University of Pittsburgh (PA)	1976 Heisman Trophy Winner
1977	Earl Campbell	University of Texas (TX)	1977 Heisman Trophy Winner
1978	Billy Sims	University of Oklahoma (OK)	1978 Heisman Trophy Winner
1979	Charles White	University of Southern California (CA)	1979 Heisman Trophy Winner
1980	Hugh Green	University of Pittsburgh (PA)	1980 Lombardi Award Winner
1981	Marcus Allen	University of Southern California (CA)	1981 Heisman Trophy Winner
1982	Herschel Walker	University of Georgia (GA)	1982 Heisman Trophy Winner
1983	Mike Rozier	University of Nebraska (NE)	1983 Heisman Trophy Winner
1984	Doug Flutie	Boston College (MA)	1984 Heisman Trophy Winner
1985	Bo Jackson	Auburn University (FL)	1985 Heisman Trophy Winner
1986	Vinny Testaverde	University of Miami (FL)	1986 Heisman Trophy Winner
1987	Tim Brown	University of Notre Dame (IN)	1987 Heisman Trophy Winner
1988	Barry Sanders	Oklahoma State University (OK)	1988 Heisman Trophy Winner
1989	Andre Ware	University of Houston (TX)	1989 Heisman Trophy Winner
1990	Ty Detmer	Brigham Young University (UT)	1990 Heisman Trophy Winner
1991	Desmond Howard	University of Michigan (MI)	1991 Heisman Trophy Winner

United Press International Lineman of the Year

From 1950 to 1996, United Press International presented this award to college football's best lineman (both offense and defense). Before the UPI ceased operations in 1997, the award had been discontinued. Like all UPI college awards, winners were voted on by NCAA coaches.

Ross Browner (University of Notre Dame) was the only two-time winner.

Year	Name	School	Note
1950	Les Richter	University of California, Berkeley (CA)	1982 College Football Hall of Fame Inductee
1951	Bill McColl	Stanford University (CA)	1973 College Football Hall of Fame Inductee
1952	Tom Catlin	University of Oklahoma (OK)	1952 All-American
1953	J.D. Roberts	University of Oklahoma (OK)	1993 College Football Hall of Fame Inductee

Year	*Name*	*School*	*Note*
1954	Jack Ellena	University of California, Los Angeles (CA)	1954 All-American
1955	Bob Pellegrini	University of Maryland (MD)	1955 ACC Player of the Year
1956	Jerry Tubbs	University of Oklahoma (OK)	1996 College Football Hall of Fame Inductee
1957	Alex Karras	University of Iowa (IA)	1991 College Football Hall of Fame Inductee
1958	Bob Harrison	University of Oklahoma (OK)	1958 All-American
1959	Roger Davis	Syracuse University (NY)	1960 1st-Round NFL Selection
1960	Tom Brown	University of Minnesota (MN)	1960 Outland Trophy Winner
1961	Joe Romig	University of Colorado (CO)	Two-Time First-Team All-American
1962	Bobby Bell	University of Minnesota (MN)	Two-Time All-American (1961–1962)
1963	Scott Appleton	University of Texas (TX)	1963 Outland Trophy Winner
1964	Dick Butkus	University of Illinois (IL)	1983 College Football Hall of Fame Inductee
1965	Howard Twilley	University of Tulsa (OK)	1992 College Football Hall of Fame Inductee
1966	Bubba Smith	Michigan State University (MI)	1988 College Football Hall of Fame Inductee
1967	Granville Liggins	University of Oklahoma (OK)	1967 All-American
1968	Ted Hendricks	University of Miami (FL)	1987 College Football Hall of Fame Inductee
1969	Mike McCoy	University of Notre Dame (IN)	1970 1st-Round NFL Pick
1970	Jim Stillwagon	Ohio State University (OH)	1991 College Football Hall of Fame Inductee
1971	Walt Patulski	University of Notre Dame (IN)	1971 All-American
1972	Rich Glover	University of Nebraska (NE)	1995 College Football Hall of Fame Inductee
1973	John Hicks	Ohio State University (OH)	2001 College Football Hall of Fame Inductee
1974	Randy White	University of Maryland (MD)	1974 Outland Trophy Winner
1975	Lee Roy Selmon	University of Oklahoma (OK)	1975 Lombardi Trophy Winner
1976	Ross Browner	University of Notre Dame (IN)	2X All-American (1976–1977)
1977	Ross Browner	University of Notre Dame (IN)	1999 College Football Hall of Fame Inductee
1978	Greg Roberts	University of Oklahoma (OK)	1978 All-American
1979	Brad Budde	University of Southern California (CA)	1990 College Football Hall of Fame Inductee
1980	Hugh Green	University of Pittsburgh (PA)	1980 Lombardi Award Winner
1981	Kenneth Sims	University of Texas (TX)	1981 Lombardi Award Winner
1982	Dave Rimington	University of Nebraska (NE)	1982 Outland Trophy Winner
1983	Dean Steinkuhler	University of Nebraska (NE)	1983 Outland Trophy Winner
1984	Bill Fralic	University of Pittsburgh (PA)	1999 College Hall of Fame Inductee
1985	Tony Casillas	University of Oklahoma (OK)	Won 1985 National Championship
1986	Jerome Brown	University of Miami (FL)	1987 1st-Round NFL Draft Pick
1987	Chad Hennings	U.S. Air Force Academy (CO)	1987 Outland Trophy Winner
1988	Tony Mandarich	Michigan State University (MI)	1988 First-Team All-American
1989	Chris Zorich	University of Notre Dame (IN)	2007 College Football Hall of Fame Inductee
1990	Russell Maryland	University of Miami (FL)	1990 Outland Trophy Winner
1991	Steve Emtman	University of Washington (WA)	2007 College Hall of Fame Inductee
1992	Eric Curry	University of Alabama (AL)	Won 1991 National Championship
1993	Rob Waldrop	University of Arizona (AZ)	1993 Outland Trophy Winner
1994	Zach Wiegert	University of Nebraska (NE)	1994 Outland Trophy Winner
1995	Jonathan Ogden	University of California, Los Angeles (CA)	1995 Outland Trophy Winner
1996	Orlando Pace	Ohio State University (OH)	1996 Outland Trophy Winner

United Press International National Champion

From 1950 to 1995, United Press International presented this award to college football's national champion. Before the UPI ceased operations in 1997, the award had been discontinued. Like all UPI college awards, winners were voted on by NCAA coaches.

Year	*School*
1950	University of Oklahoma (OK)
1951	University of Tennessee (TN)
1952	Michigan State University (MI)
1953	University of Maryland (MD)
1954	Ohio State University (OH)
1955	University of Oklahoma (OK)
1956	University of Oklahoma (OK)
1957	Ohio State University (OH)
1958	Louisiana State University (LA)
1959	Syracuse University (NY)
1960	University of Minnesota (MN)
1961	University of Alabama (AL)
1962	University of Southern California (CA)
1963	University of Texas (TX)
1964	University of Alabama (AL)
1965	Michigan State University (MI)
1966	University of Notre Dame (IN)
1967	University of Southern California (CA)
1968	Ohio State University (OH)
1969	University of Texas (TX)
1970	University of Texas (TX)
1971	University of Nebraska (NE)
1972	University of Southern California (CA)
1973	University of Alabama (AL)
1974	University of Southern California (CA)
1975	University of Oklahoma (OK)
1976	University of Pittsburgh (PA)
1977	University of Notre Dame (IN)
1978	University of Southern California (CA)
1979	University of Alabama (AL)
1980	University of Georgia (GA)
1981	Clemson University (SC)
1982	Pennsylvania State University (PA)
1983	University of Miami (FL)
1984	Brigham Young University (UT)
1985	University of Oklahoma (OK)
1986	Pennsylvania State University (PA)
1987	University of Miami (FL)
1988	University of Notre Dame (IN)
1989	University of Miami (FL)
1990	Georgia Tech University (GA)
1991	University of Washington (WA)
1992	University of Alabama (AL)
1993	Florida State University (FL)
1994	University of Nebraska (NE)
1995	University of Nebraska (NE)

Vince Lombardi Award *see* Rotary Lombardi Award

W.J. Voit Memorial Trophy

The W. J. Voit Memorial Trophy was awarded by the Helms Athletic Foundation from 1951 to 1978 to the best college football player on the Pacific Coast and winners were voted on by West Coast football writers and broadcasters. The Trophy was named after William J. Voit (1881–1946), founder of the W.J. Voit Rubber Company. Established in 1922, the company developed and patented the first full-molded, all-rubber inflatable ball and later became a leading manufacturer of both footballs and basketballs.

Unlike the Pop Warner Trophy (see Pacific-10 Conference), which was awarded from 1950 to 2004 to the top senior football player on the West Coast, the Voit Trophy was open to underclassmen and three players won the award twice (Jon Arnett [1955–1956, University of Southern California]; Jim Plunkett [1969–1970, Stanford University]; and Anthony Davis [1972 and 1975, University of Southern California]).

In 1975, the Pacific 10 Conference began awarding its own Player of the Year Awards for offense and defense and after the 1978 season, the Voit Trophy was discontinued.

Year	*Player*	*Position*	*School*
1951	Bill McColl	End	Stanford University (CA)
1952	Jim Sears	Halfback	University of Southern California (CA)
1953	Bobby Garrett	Quarterback	Stanford University (CA)
1954	Paul Larson	Running Back	University of California (Berkeley) (CA)
1955	Jon Arnett	Running Back	University of Southern California (CA)
1956	Jon Arnett	Running Back	University of Southern California (CA)
1957	Dick Wallen	End	University of California, Los Angeles (CA)

Year	*Player*	*Position*	*School*
1958	Joe Kapp	Quarterback	University of California (Berkeley) (CA)
1959	Bob Schloredt	Quarterback	University of Washington (WA)
1960	Bill Kilmer	Tailback	University of California, Los Angeles (CA)
1961	Hugh Campbell	Wide Receiver	Washington State University (WA)
1962	Terry Baker	Quarterback	Oregon State University (OR)
1963	Vern Burke	Split End	Oregon State University (OR)
1964	Craig Morton	Quarterback	University of California (Berkeley) (CA)
1965	Mike Garrett	Tailback	University of Southern California (CA)
1966	Pete Pifer	Fullback	Oregon State University (OR)
1967	Gary Beban	Quarterback	University of California, Los Angeles (CA)
1968	O.J. Simpson	Tailback	University of Southern California (CA)
1969	Jim Plunkett	Quarterback	Stanford University (CA)
1970	Jim Plunkett	Quarterback	Stanford University (CA)
1971	Don Bunce	Quarterback	Stanford University (CA)
1972	Anthony Davis	Tailback	University of Southern California (CA)
1973	No Award Presented		
1974	Anthony Davis	Tailback	University of Southern California (CA)
1975	Chuck Muncie	Halfback	University of California (Berkeley) (CA)
1976	Ricky Bell	Tailback	University of Southern California (CA)
1977	Guy Benjamin	Quarterback	Stanford University (CA)
1978	Charles White	Tailback	University of Southern California (CA)

Walter Camp Alumni of the Year Award

Sponsored by the Walter Camp Football Foundation, Inc. (P.O. Box 1663, New Haven, CT, 06507; Email: president@waltercamp.org; Web site: http://waltercamp.org), the Walter Camp Alumni of the Year Award has been presented since 1986 to individuals who have distinguished themselves as athletes, in their own personal career, and in doing good works for others.

Founded in 1967, the Walter Camp Football Foundation, Inc., continues the work of Walter Camp, which is to select and honor outstanding college football players. Winners of this award are selected by head coaches and sports information directors from ballots prepared by the Foundation.

Walter Chauncey Camp (born: April 7, 1859, in New Britain, CT; died: March 14, 1925, in New York, NY) was an early football pioneer; sports writer; played college football at Yale University (1887–1882); coached at Yale University (New Haven, 1888–1891) and Stanford University (CA, 1892, 1894–1895); inducted into the College Football Hall of Fame in 1951; and is often referred to as the "Father of American Football."

He served on numerous collegiate football rules committees that developed the American game from his time as a player at Yale University until his death (eliminating a lot of the brute force that was part of the early game). He is credited with innovations such as the snap-back from center, the system of downs, the points system, the introduction of the offensive formation (a seven-man offensive line and a four-man backfield of a quarterback, two halfbacks, and a fullback); and the awarding of a two-point safety to the defense for tackling a ball carrier in his own end zone (followed by a free kick by the offense from its own 20-yard line).

Camp also wrote more than 250 articles and almost 30 books on sports, including football (in various magazines and newspapers through the country); selected early All-Star college football teams; and helped establish the National Collegiate Athletic Association.

Year	*Name*	*School*	*Note*
1986	Joe Greene	North Texas State University (TX)	1984 College Football Hall of Fame Inductee
1987	Mike Reid	Pennsylvania State University (PA)	1987 College Football Hall of Fame Inductee
1988	Alan Page	University of Notre Dame (IN)	1993 College Football Hall of Fame Inductee
1989	Dr. Tommy Casanova	Louisiana State University (LA)	1995 College Football Hall of Fame Inductee

Year	*Name*	*School*	*Note*
1990	Tom Jackson	University of Louisville (KY)	2X MVC Player of the Year
1991	Steve Owens	University of Oklahoma (OK)	1969 Heisman Trophy Winner
1992	Kellen Winslow	University of Missouri (MO)	2002 College Football Hall of Fame Inductee
1993	Archie Griffin	Ohio State University (OH)	Only 2X Heisman Award Winner (1974–1975)
1994	Ed Marinaro	Cornell University (NY)	1991 College Football Hall of Fame Inductee
1995	Jim Covert	University of Pittsburgh (PA)	2003 College Football Hall of Fame Inductee
1996	Lee Roy Selmon	University of Oklahoma (OK)	1988 College Football Hall of Fame Inductee
1997	Jim Plunkett	Stanford University (CA)	1970 Heisman Trophy Winner
1998	Tony Dorsett	University of Pittsburgh (PA)	1976 Heisman Trophy Winner
1999	Bo Jackson	Auburn University (AL)	1985 Heisman Trophy Winner
2000	Don McPherson	Syracuse University (NY)	2008 College Football Hall of Fame Inductee
2001	Herschel Walker	University of Georgia (GA)	1982 Heisman Trophy Winner
2002	Dave Casper	University of Notre Dame (IN)	Won 1973 National Championship
2003	Mark May	University of Pittsburgh (PA)	2005 College Hall of Fame Inductee
2004	George Rogers	University of South Carolina (SC)	1980 Heisman Trophy Winner
2005	Cornelius Bennett	University of Alabama (AL)	2005 College Football Hall of Fame Inductee
2006	Mike Rozier	University of Nebraska (NE)	1983 Heisman Trophy Winner
2007	Ray Guy	University of Southern Mississippi (MS)	2004 College Football Hall of Fame Inductee
2008	Tim Brown	University of Notre Dame (IN)	1987 Heisman Trophy Winner
2009	David Fulcher	Arizona State University (AZ)	3X NFL Pro Bowl Selection (1988–1990)
2010	Tedy Bruschi	University of Arizona (AZ)	3X First Team All Pac-10

Walter Camp Coach of the Year *see* Football Bowl Subdivision

Walter Camp Distinguished American Award

Since 1978, the Walter Camp Distinguished American Award has been presented to individuals who have attained great success in business, private life, or public service and is given under the auspices of the Walter Camp Football Foundation, Inc. (P.O. Box 1663, New Haven, CT, 06507; Email: president@waltercamp.org; Web site: http://waltercamp.org). Each year's winner may or may not have participated in college and/or professional football.

Walter Chauncey Camp (born: April 7, 1859, in New Britain, CT; died: March 14, 1925, in New York, NY) was an early football pioneer; sports writer; played college football at Yale University (1887–1882); coached at Yale University (New Haven, 1888–1891) and Stanford University (1892, 1894–1895); inducted into the College Football Hall of Fame in 1951; and is often referred to as the "Father of American Football."

He served on numerous collegiate football rules committees that developed the American game from his time as a player at Yale University until his death (eliminating a lot of the brute force that was part of the early game). He is credited with innovations such as the snap-back from center, the system of downs, the points system, the introduction of the offensive formation (a seven-man offensive line and a four-man backfield of a quarterback, two halfbacks, and a fullback); and the awarding of a two-point safety to the defense for tackling a ball carrier in his own end zone (followed by a free kick by the offense from its own 20-yard line).

Camp also wrote more than 250 articles and almost 30 books on sports, including football (in various magazines and newspapers through the country); selected early All-Star college football teams; and helped establish the National Collegiate Athletic Association.

Walter Camp Distinguished American

Year	*Winner*	*School*	*Note*
1978	James Crowley	University of Notre Dame (IN)	1966 College Football Hall of Fame Inductee
1979	David "Sonny" Werblin	Rutgers University (NJ)	NFL's New York Jets Owner
1980	Alexander Haig	U.S. Military Academy (NY)	President Nixon's Chief of Staff
1980	George Halas	University of Illinois (IL)	1963 Pro Football Hall of Fame Inductee
1981	Harold "Red" Grange	University of Illinois (IL)	1951 College Football Hall of Fame Inductee
1982	Eddie Robinson	Grambling State University (LA)	1997 College Football Hall of Fame
1983	Tom Harmon	University of Michigan (MI)	1940 Heisman Trophy Winner
1984	General Bill Carpenter	U.S. Military Academy (NY)	1982 College Football Hall of Fame Inductee
1985	Bob Hope	N/A	Entertainer
1986	Tom Landry	University of Texas (TX)	1990 Pro Football Hall of Fame Inductee
1987	Weeb Ewbank	Miami University (OH)	1978 Pro Football Hall of Fame Inductee
1988	Sid Luckman	Columbia University (NY)	1960 College Football Hall of Fame Inductee
1988	Y.A. Tittle	Louisiana State University (LA)	1971 Pro Football Hall of Fame Inductee
1989	Dick Kazmaier	Princeton University (NJ)	1951 Heisman Trophy Winner
1989	Burt Reynolds	Florida State University (FL)	Actor
1990	Tex Schramm	University of Texas (TX)	President of the NFL's Dallas Cowboys
1991	Alexander Kroll	Rutgers University (NJ)	1997 College Football Hall of Fame Inductee
1992	Carmen Cozza	Yale University (CT)	2002 College Football Hall of Fame Inductee
1993	The Rev. Theodore Hesburgh	Catholic University of America (Washington, D.C.)	15th President of the University of Notre Dame
1994	Paul Tagliabue	Georgetown University (Washington, D.C.)	8th NFL Commissioner
1995	Keith Jackson	Washington State University (WA)	54-Year College Football Announcer
1996	Dick Ebersol	Yale University (CT)	Chairman of NBC
1997	Steve Largent	University of Tulsa (OK)	1995 Pro Football Hall of Fame Inductee
1998	Steve Young	Brigham Young University (UT)	2001 College Football Hall of Fame Inductee
1999	Bo Schembechler	Miami University (OH)	1993 College Football Hall of Fame Inductee
2000	Gene Upshaw	Texas A&I University (TX)	1987 Pro Football Hall of Fame
2001	NY Police / Fire / Emergency Medical Service Personnel	N/A	Heroes of 9/11/2001
2002	Regis Philbin	University of Notre Dame (IN)	Entertainer
2003	Bill Walsh	San Jose State University (CA)	1993 Pro Football Hall of Fame Inductee
2004	Pat Summerall	University of Arkansas (AR)	NFL Football Broadcaster
2005	Arthur Blank	Babson College (MA)	Owner of the NFL's Atlanta Falcons
2006	Dick Vermeil	San Jose State University (CA)	NFL Football Coach
2007	Frank Broyles	Georgia Institute of Technology (GA)	1983 College Football Hall of Fame Inductee
2008	Len Dawson	Purdue University (IN)	1987 Pro Football Hall of Fame Inductee
2009	Robin Roberts	Southeastern Louisiana University (LA)	Television Broadcaster

Walter Camp Man of the Year Award

Since 1967, the Walter Camp Man of the Year Award honors an individual who has been closely associated with college football as a player, coach, or contributor and is presented by the Walter Camp Football Foundation, Inc. (P.O. Box 1663, New Haven, CT, 06507; Email: president@waltercamp.org; Web site: http://waltercamp.org).

Walter Chauncey Camp (born: April 7, 1859, in New Britain, CT; died: March 14, 1925, in New York, NY) was an early football pioneer; sports writer; played college football at Yale University (1887–1882); coached at Yale University (New Haven, 1888–1891) and Stanford University (1892, 1894–1895); inducted into the College Football Hall of Fame in 1951; and is often referred to as the "Father of American Football."

He served on numerous collegiate football rules committees that developed the American game from his time as a player at Yale University until his death (eliminating a lot of the brute force that was part of the early game). He is credited with innovations such as the snap-back from center, the system of downs, the points system, the introduction of the offensive formation (a seven-man offensive line and a four-man backfield of a quarterback, two halfbacks, and a fullback); and the awarding of a two-point safety to the defense for tackling a ball carrier in his own end zone (followed by a free kick by the offense from its own 20-yard line).

Camp also wrote more than 250 articles and almost 30 books on sports, including football (in various magazines and newspapers through the country); selected early All-Star college football teams; and helped establish the National Collegiate Athletic Association.

Year	*Name*	*School*	*Note*
1967	Hamilton Fish III	Harvard University (MA)	Congressman; Creator of the Tomb of the Unknown Soldier
1968	Ted Blair	Yale University (CT)	Chairman of Yale Alumni Fund
1969	Pete Rozelle	University of San Francisco (CA)	7th NFL Commissioner
1970	Harry Kipke	University of Michigan (MI)	1958 College Football Hall of Fame Inductee
1971	Doc Blanchard	U.S. Military Academy (NY)	1945 Heisman Award Winner
1972	Clinton Frank	Yale University (CT)	1937 Heisman Award Winner
1973	Duffy Daugherty	Syracuse University (NY)	1984 College Hall of Fame Inductee
1974	Jake Gaither	Knoxville College (TN)	1975 College Football Hall of Fame Inductee
1975	Pete Dawkins	U.S. Military Academy (NY)	1958 Heisman Trophy Winner
1976	Edward Krause	University of Notre Dame (IN)	1st Basketball & Football Hall of Famer
1977	Fred Dunlap	Colgate University (NY)	23-Year Football Coach
1978	Floyd Little	Syracuse University (NY)	1983 College Football Hall of Fame Inductee
1979	Jack Kemp	Occidental College (CA)	Former College / Pro Football Player and Congressman
1980	Gale Sayers	University of Kansas (KS)	1977 College Football Hall of Fame Inductee
1981	Otto Graham	Northwestern University (IL)	2001 College Football Hall of Fame Inductee
1982	Merlin Olsen	Utah State University (UT)	1980 College Football Hall of Fame Inductee
1983	Roger Staubach	U.S. Naval Academy (MD)	1963 Heisman Trophy Winner
1984	Don Shula	John Carroll University (OH)	1997 Pro Football Hall of Fame Inductee
1985	Rocky Bleier	University of Notre Dame (IN)	Won Four Super Bowls (IX, X, XIII, XIV)
1986	Willie Davis	Grambling State University (LA)	1981 Pro Football Hall of Fame Inductee
1987	Levi Jackson	Yale University (CT)	1st African American to Play for Yale University
1988	Andy Robustelli	Arnold College (CT)	1971 Pro Football Hall of Fame Inductee

Year	*Name*	*School*	*Note*
1989	Paul Brown	Miami University (OH)	1967 Pro Football Hall of Fame Inductee
1990	Nick Buoniconti	University of Notre Dame (IN)	2001 Pro Football Hall of Fame Inductee
1991	Mel Blount	Southern University (LA)	1989 Pro Football Hall of Fame Inductee
1992	Bob Griese	Purdue University (IN)	1990 Pro Football Hall of Fame Inductee
1993	Warren Moon	University of Washington (WA)	2006 Pro Football Hall of Fame Inductee
1994	Dick Anderson	University of Colorado (CO)	1993 College Football Hall of Fame Inductee
1995	Reggie Williams	Dartmouth College (NH)	2007 College Football Hall of Fame Inductee
1996	Lynn Swann	University of Southern California (CA)	1991 College Football Hall of Fame Inductee
1997	Calvin Hill	Yale University (CT)	1969 NFL Offensive Rookie of the Year
1998	Lou Holtz	Kent State University (OH)	2008 College Football Hall of Fame Inductee
1999	Gil Brandt	University of Wisconsin (WI)	NFL Dallas Cowboys Executive
2000	Howie Long	Villanova University (PA)	2000 Pro Football Hall of Fame Inductee
2001	Mike Singletary	Baylor University (TX)	1995 College Football Hall of Fame
2002	Jim Kelly	University of Miami (FL)	2002 Pro Football Hall of Fame Inductee
2003	Ozzie Newsome	University of Alabama (AL)	1994 College Football Hall of Fame Inductee
2004	Anthony Muñoz	University of Southern California (CA)	1998 Pro Football Hall of Fame Inductee
2005	Dwight Stephenson	University of Alabama (AL)	1998 Pro Football Hall of Fame Inductee
2006	Mike Utley	Washington State University (WA)	Permanently Paralyzed in a Game on 11/17/91
2007	Dick Butkus	University of Illinois (IL)	1983 College Football Hall of Fame Inductee
2008	Morten Andersen	Michigan State University (MI)	2006 Danish American Football Federation Hall of Fame
2009	John Elway	Stanford University (CA)	2000 College Football Hall of Fame Inductee

Walter Camp Player of the Year Award

Since 1967, the Walter Camp Player of the Year Award has been presented annually to the College Player of the Year as determined by NCAA FBS head coaches and sports information directors and sponsored by the Walter Camp Football Foundation, Inc. (P.O. Box 1663, New Haven, CT, 06507; Email: president@waltercamp.org; Web site: http://waltercamp.org).

Walter Chauncey Camp (born: April 7, 1859, in New Britain, CT; died: March 14, 1925, in New York, NY) was an early football pioneer; sports writer; played college football at Yale University (1887–1882); coached at Yale University (New Haven, 1888–1891) and Stanford University (1892, 1894–1895); inducted into the College Football Hall of Fame in 1951; and is often referred to as the "Father of American Football."

He served on numerous collegiate football rules committees that developed the American game from his time as a player at Yale University until his death (eliminating a lot of the brute force that was part of the early game). He is credited with innovations such as the snap-back from center, the system of downs, the points system, the introduction of the offensive formation (a seven-man offensive line and a four-man backfield of a quarterback, two halfbacks, and a fullback); and the awarding of a two-point safety to the defense for tackling a ball carrier in his own end zone (followed by a free kick by the offense from its own 20-yard line).

Camp also wrote more than 250 articles and almost 30 books on sports, including football (in various magazines and newspapers through the country); selected early All-Star college football teams; and helped establish the National Collegiate Athletic Association.

As of this writing, only O.J. Simpson (University of Southern California), Archie Griffin (Ohio State University), and Colt McCoy (University of Texas) have won this award twice.

Year	*Name*	*School*	*Note*
1967	O.J. Simpson	University of Southern California (CA)	1967 UPI Player of the Year
1968	O.J. Simpson	University of Southern California (CA)	1968 Heisman Trophy Winner
1969	Steve Owens	University of Oklahoma (OK)	1969 Heisman Trophy Winner
1970	Jim Plunkett	Stanford University (CA)	1970 Heisman Trophy Winner
1971	Pat Sullivan	Auburn University (AL)	1971 Heisman Trophy Winner
1972	Johnny Rodgers	University of Nebraska (NE)	1972 Heisman Trophy Winner
1973	John Cappelletti	Pennsylvania State University (PA)	1973 Heisman Trophy Winner
1974	Archie Griffin	Ohio State University (OH)	1974 Heisman Trophy Winner
1975	Archie Griffin	Ohio State University (OH)	1975 Heisman Trophy Winner
1976	Tony Dorsett	University of Pittsburgh (PA)	1976 Heisman Trophy Winner
1977	Ken MacAfee	University of Notre Dame (IN)	1997 College Hall of Fame Inductee
1978	Billy Sims	University of Oklahoma (OK)	1978 Heisman Trophy Winner
1979	Charles White	University of Southern California (CA)	1979 Heisman Trophy Winner
1980	Hugh Green	University of Pittsburgh (PA)	3X All-American (1978–1980)
1981	Marcus Allen	University of Southern California (CA)	1981 Heisman Trophy Winner
1982	Herschel Walker	University of Georgia (GA)	1982 Heisman Trophy Winner
1983	Mike Rozier	University of Nebraska (NE)	1983 Heisman Trophy Winner
1984	Doug Flutie	Boston College (MA)	1984 Heisman Trophy Winner
1985	Bo Jackson	Auburn University (AL)	1985 Heisman Trophy Winner
1986	Vinny Testaverde	University of Miami (FL)	1986 Heisman Trophy Winner
1987	Tim Brown	University of Notre Dame (IN)	1987 Heisman Trophy Winner
1988	Barry Sanders	Oklahoma State University (OK)	1988 Heisman Trophy Winner
1989	Anthony Thompson	University of Indiana (IN)	2007 College Football Hall of Fame Inductee
1990	Raghib Ismail	University of Notre Dame (IN)	2X All-American (1989–1990)
1991	Desmond Howard	University of Michigan (MI)	1991 Heisman Trophy Winner
1992	Gino Torretta	University of Miami (FL)	1992 Heisman Trophy Winner
1993	Charlie Ward	Florida State University (FL)	1993 Heisman Trophy Winner
1994	Rashaan Salaam	University of Colorado (CO)	1994 Heisman Trophy Winner
1995	Eddie George	Ohio State University (OH)	1995 Heisman Trophy Winner
1996	Danny Wuerffel	University of Florida (FL)	1996 Heisman Trophy Winner
1997	Charles Woodson	University of Michigan (MI)	1997 Heisman Trophy Winner
1998	Ricky Williams	University of Texas (TX)	1998 Heisman Trophy Winner
1999	Ron Dayne	University of Wisconsin (WI)	1999 Heisman Trophy Winner
2000	Josh Heupel	University of Oklahoma (OK)	2000 Walter Camp Award Winner
2001	Eric Crouch	University of Nebraska (NE)	2001 Heisman Trophy Winner
2002	Larry Johnson	Pennsylvania State University (PA)	2002 Jim Brown Award Winner
2003	Larry Fitzgerald	University of Pittsburgh (PA)	2003 Paul Warfield Trophy Winner
2004	Matt Leinart	University of Southern California (CA)	2004 Heisman Trophy Winner
2005	Reggie Bush	University of Southern California (CA)	2005 Heisman Trophy Winner
2006	Troy Smith	Ohio State University (OH)	2006 Heisman Trophy Winner
2007	Darren McFadden	University of Arkansas (AR)	2X All-American (2006–2007)
2008	Colt McCoy	University of Texas (TX)	2008 Archie Griffin Award Winner
2009	Colt McCoy	University of Texas (TX)	No Further Information

Walter Payton Award *see* NCAA Division I FCS

William V. Campbell Trophy (formerly known as the Draddy Trophy or the Vincent dePaul Draddy Trophy)

The William V. Campbell Trophy (known as the Draddy Trophy from 1990 to 2009 and sometimes referred to as the Academic Heisman Trophy) is awarded annually (since 1990) by the HealthSouth Corporation (3660 Grandview Parkway, Suite 200, Birmingham, AL 35243; Telephone: 800-765-4772; Web site: http://www.healthsouth.com/) and the National Football Foundation (433 East Las Colinas Boulevard, Suite 1130, Irving, TX 75039; Telephone: 972-556-1000; Fax: 972-556-9032; Email: membership@footballfoundation.com; Web site: http://www.footballfoundation.org/Macarthurhist.php) to the college football player judged to have the best combination of academics, community service, and on-field performances (scholar-athlete).

Previously named in honor of Vincent dePaul Draddy (who served the National Football Foundation and its College Football Hall of Fame for 33 years), the Trophy was renamed in 2009 to honor William V. Campbell (former player and head coach at Columbia University (New York, New York) as well as the 2004 NFF Gold Medal recipient). He is now a well-known business executive who has worked with such companies as Apple, Google, and Intuit.

Winners of this Trophy are first nominated by their own school and must be a senior or graduate student in his final year of eligibility; maintain a grade point average of at least 3.2 on a 4.0 scale; have outstanding football ability as a first team player; and demonstrated leadership and citizenship. All finalists for this Trophy receive an $18,000 postgraduate scholarship as a member of the NFF National Scholar-Athlete Class and the person chosen to win the Trophy has his postgraduate scholarship increased to $25,000 and is presented the 25-pound bronze trophy.

The Trophy is sponsored by HealthSouth Corporation, and as such is officially named The William V. Campbell Trophy endowed by HealthSouth.

Year	*Player*	*School*	*Note*
1990	Chris Howard	U.S. Air Force Academy (CO)	First Team Academic All-American
1991	Brad Culpepper	University of Florida (FL)	Played Nine Years in the NFL
1992	Jim Hansen	University of Colorado (CO)	1993 GTE Academic All-American
1993	Thomas D. Burns	University of Virginia (VA)	Atlantic Coast Conference All-Academic
1994	Robert B. Zatechka	University of Nebraska (NE)	Played Three Years in the NFL
1995	Bobby Hoying	Ohio State University (OH)	2008 Ohio State Varsity O Hall of Fame
1996	Danny Wuerffel	University of Florida (FL)	1996 Heisman Trophy Winner
1997	Peyton Manning	University Tennessee (TN)	1997 NCAA Quarterback of the Year
1998	Matt Stinchcomb	University Georgia (GA)	2X All-American (1997 & 1998)
1999	Chad Pennington	Marshall University (WV)	1998 Motor City Bowl MVP
2000	Kyle Vanden Bosch	University of Nebraska (NE)	2000 First Team All-Big 12 Conference
2001	Joaquin Gonzalez	University of Miami (FL)	Won 2001 National Championship
2002	Brandon Roberts	Washington University in St. Louis (MO)	2001 Academic All-Conference First Team
2003	Craig Krenzel	Ohio State University (OH)	2X Fiesta Bowl MVP (2003 & 2004)
2004	Michael Muñoz	University of Tennessee (TN)	2003 All-Academic SEC Selection
2005	Rudy Niswanger	Louisiana State University (LA)	2005 Wuerffel Trophy Winner
2006	Brian Leonard	Rutgers University (NJ)	School Record All-Time Receptions (207)
2007	Dallas Griffin	University of Texas (TX)	2007 ESPN Academic All-American
2008	Alex Mack	University of California, Berkeley (CA)	2X Morris Trophy Winner (2007 & 2008)
2009	Tim Tebow	University of Florida (FL)	Heisman Trophy Winner

Woody Hayes Trophy

Since 1977, the Touchdown Club of Columbus (Ohio, http://www.touchdownclubofcolumbus.com) has annually selected the nation's top college football coach. The Trophy is named after the legendary coach at Ohio State University (Columbus, Ohio) who won three national championships (1954, 1957, 1968) and was inducted into the College Football Hall of Fame in 1983.

Sam B. Nicola (who died in 1993) founded the Touchdown Club of Columbus in 1956 and was president of the Athletic Club of Columbus when the initial All-Sports Banquet was held in January 1956. Although a local organization, its range has always been national (not limited to Columbus, Ohio) and athletes from all sports have been recognized. Honored athletes are selected by the appropriate Touchdown Club's committees, consisting of coaches, sportswriters, and former players.

Wayne Woodrow "Woody" Hayes (born: February 14, 1913, in Clifton, OH; died: March 12, 1987, in Upper Arlington, Ohio) was a college football coach most well-known for his tenure at Ohio State University and who compiled a career total (as a head coach) of 238–72–10 (.744) (205–61–10, .743). Hayes played football at Denison University (Granville, Ohio) from 1933 to 1935; served as an assistant football coach at two Ohio high schools; and joined the United States Navy during World War II. After the war, he embarked on a college football coaching career at Denison University (1946–1948), the University of Miami (OH, 1949–1950), and Ohio State University (1951–1978).

As of this writing, five coaches have won this award more than once and Joe Paterno (Pennsylvania State University) has received the honor four times.

Year	*Coach*	*School*	*Note*
1977	Lou Holtz	University of Arkansas (AR)	Played in 6 Bowl Games at Arkansas
1978	Joe Paterno	Pennsylvania State University (PA)	1978 Eddie Robinson Coach of the Year
1979	Earle Bruce	Ohio State University (OH)	2002 College Football Hall of Fame Inductee
1980	Vince Dooley	University of Georgia (GA)	Won 1980 National Championship
1981	Danny Ford	Clemson University (SC)	Won 1981 National Championship
1982	Joe Paterno	Pennsylvania State University (PA)	Won 1982 National Championship
1983	Tom Osborne	University of Nebraska (NE)	1999 College Football Hall of Fame Inductee
1984	Don James	University of Washington (WA)	1997 College Football Hall of Fame Inductee
1985	Bo Schembechler	University of Michigan (MI)	1993 College Football Hall of Fame Inductee
1986	Joe Paterno	Pennsylvania State University (PA)	Won 1986 National Championship
1987	Dick MacPherson	Syracuse University (NY)	2009 College Football Hall of Fame Inductee
1988	Lou Holtz	University of Notre Dame (IN)	Won 1988 National Championship
1989	Bobby Ross	Georgia Institute of Technology (GA)	Won 1990 National Championship
1990	No Selection		
1991	Don James	University of Washington (WA)	Won 1991 National Championship
1992	Dennis Erickson	University of Miami (FL)	Won Two National Championships (1989, 1991)
1993	Don Nehlan	University of West Virginia (WV)	2005 College Football Hall of Fame Inductee
1994	Tom Osborne	University of Nebraska (NE)	Won 1994 National Championship
1995	Gary Barnett	Northwestern University (IL)	Won 1995 Big Ten Championship
1996	Bruce Snyder	Arizona State University (AZ)	Won 1996 Pac-Ten Conference Championship
1997	Lloyd Carr	University of Michigan (MI)	Won 1997 National Championship
1998	Phil Fulmer	University of Tennessee (TN)	Won 1998 National Championship
1999	Frank Beamer	Virginia Polytechnic Institute and State University (VA)	1999 Paul "Bear" Bryant Award Winner
2000	Bob Stoops	University of Oklahoma (OK)	Won 2000 National Championship
2001	Ralph Friedgen	University of Maryland (MD)	Won 2001 ACC Title
2002	Jim Tressel	Ohio State University (OH)	Won 2002 National Championship
2003	Bob Stoops	University of Oklahoma (OK)	Won 2003 Big 12 South Conference
2004	Urban Meyer	University of Utah (UT)	2004 Eddie Robinson Coach of the Year Winner
2005	Joe Paterno	Pennsylvania State University (PA)	2005 Walter Camp Coach of the Year Winner
2006	Jim Tressel	Ohio State University (OH)	Won 2006 Big Ten Title
2007	Mark Mangino	University of Kansas (KS)	Won 10 "Coach of the Year" Awards in 2007

Year	Coach	School	Note
2008	Mike Leach	Texas Tech University (TX)	2008 Big 12 Coach of the Year Winner
2009	Gary Patterson	Texas Christian University (TX)	No Further Information

Wuerffel Trophy

Since 2005, the Wuerffel Trophy has been awarded annually by the All Sports Association of Fort Walton Beach (Florida), 1186 Eglin Parkway, (Pensacola) Shalimar, FL 32579; Telephone: 800-717-8120; Email: info@wuerffeltrophy.org; Web site: http://www.wuerffeltrophy.org/) to the college football player who combines outstanding community service with athletic and academic achievement. Winners must maintain at least a 3.0 Grade Point Average; be a first-team player; and consistently contribute to community service.

Daniel Carl "Danny" Wuerffel (born: May 27, 1974, in Fort Walton Beach, FL) won the Florida AAAA state football championship; won the 1996 Heisman Trophy; and (as the team's quarterback) led the University of Florida (Gainesville) to that year's college national championship. After college, he played professional football for the New Orleans Saints (NFL, 1997–2000); Rhein Fire (NFL Europe, 2000); Green Bay Packers (NFL, 2000); Chicago Bears (NFL, 2001), and the Washington Redskins (NFL, 2002).

Year	Player	School	Note
2005	Rudy Niswanger	Louisiana State University (LA)	2005 Draddy Trophy Winner
2006	Joel Penton	Ohio State University (OH)	No Further Information
2007	Paul Smith	University of Tulsa (OK)	Three-Year Letter Winner
2008	Tim Tebow	University of Florida (FL)	2007 Heisman Trophy Winner
2009	Tim Hilller	Western Michigan College (MI)	No Further Information

National Collegiate Athletic Association (NCAA) Division I — Football Bowl Subdivision (FBS)

National Collegiate Athletic Association

P.O. Box 6222, 700 West Washington Street, Indianapolis, IN 46202; Telephone: 317-917-6222; Fax: 317-917-6888; Web site: http://www.ncaa.org

According to National Collegiate Athletic Association rules, those colleges designated as Division I must sponsor at least seven sports for men and seven for women (or six for men and eight for women), which include two team sports for each gender. Focusing on schools that have football programs, in 2006 NCAA Division I institutions were further divided (by enrollment size) into either the Football Bowl Subdivision (FBS, formerly known as Division I-A since 1978) or the Football Championship Subdivision (FCS, formerly known as Division I-AA since 1978). FBS teams are the NCAA's largest and most well-known institutions.

As of this writing, FBS football is the only NCAA-sponsored sport without an organized tournament to determine its champion and schools in this category compete in post–season bowl games, one of which is designated as the "National Championship" game. FBS schools are limited to a total of 85 football players receiving financial assistance, except for the Service Academies (Army, Navy, and Air Force, which provide full financial scholarships to all of its students, including football players). Any conference that has at least 12 football teams (any NCAA level) may divide itself into two divisions and conduct a championship game between the division winners.

This section contains awards and trophies specifically related to the 11 Conferences (plus the Eastern College Athletic Conference) and the three Independent Teams (as of 2010) within the NCAA Division I Football Bowl Subdivision:

- Atlantic Coast Conference
- Big East Conference
- Big 10 Conference
- Big 12 Conference
- Conference USA
- Eastern College Athletic Conference (Division I, FBS, FCS)
- FBS Independent Teams (Army, Navy, University of Notre Dame)
- Mid-American Conference
- Mountain West Conference
- Pacific-10 Conference
- Southeastern Conference
- Sun Belt Conference
- Western Athletic Conference

Division I FBS National Champions

Since American college football began in the 1870s, there has been an effort to designate the nation's best football team and numerous groups have always waded in with their opinions and criteria. Since there is no national playoff system, and never has been, a mythical "national champion" has been designated for over a century with some teams having more credibility than others. In today's college football environment, the National Collegiate Athletic Association Division I Football Bowl Subdivision (formerly known as Division I-A) is the only NCAA sport in which a yearly champion is not determined by an NCAA-sanctioned championship playoff. Since a "national champion" is selected by several groups (such as the Associated Press, College Football Coach's poll, ESPN, Football Writers Association of America, Helms Athletic Foundation, National Football Foundation, United Press International [when the group was active], and *USA Today*), the validity of their choice has always been tied to the sponsoring group's prominence and stature, as determined by football schools, the media, and the general public. While the NCAA has never officially endorsed an annual championship team, the organization has recognized the majority choice(s) made each year by these selectors. As of this writing, the two most widely recognized and authoritative selectors are the Associated Press (which conducts a poll of football sportswriters) and the *USA Today* Coaches' Poll of the American Football Coaches Association.

In the early days of college football, a haphazard selection process for a mythical "national champion" was in place (which generated numerous champions) until the Associated Press began polling sportswriters in 1936. The AP poll was the most influential selector of the national champion until 1950. In the early days, the AP's main competition was United Press, which created the first-ever poll of football coaches in 1950. Starting in 1950 and continuing for the next three years, the AP and UP both named the same teams as the national champion, with the first disagreement between the two organizations coming in 1954, when the AP (and its writers) selected Ohio State University and the UP (and its coaches) chose the University of California in Los Angeles (UCLA). The two groups went on to disagree about the national champion six more years (1957, 1965, 1970, 1973–1974, and 1978), before both naming the same champion for the next 11 seasons. United Press went on to merge with the International News Service to form United Press International, until being acquired by *USA Today* and CNN (Cable News Network) in 1991. The coaches' poll was briefly the responsibility of ESPN (Entertainment and Sports Programming Network) from 1997 until 2005, when it was taken over exclusively by *USA Today*.

Year	*School*
1869	Princeton University (NJ)
1869	Rutgers (the State University of New Jersey) (NJ)
1870	Princeton University (NJ)
1871	None Selected
1872	Princeton University (NJ) / Yale University (CT)
1872	Yale University (CT)
1873	Princeton University (NJ)
1874	Harvard University (MA)
1874	Princeton University (NJ)
1874	Yale University (CT)
1875	Columbia University (NY)
1875	Harvard University (MA)
1875	Princeton University (NJ)
1876	Yale University (CT)
1877	Princeton University (NJ)
1877	Yale University (CT)
1878	Princeton University (NJ)
1879	Princeton University (NJ)
1879	Yale University (CT)
1880	Princeton University (NJ)
1880	Yale University (CT)
1881	Princeton University (NJ)
1881	Yale University (CT)
1882	Yale University (CT)
1883	Yale University (CT)
1884	Princeton University (NJ)
1884	Yale University (CT)
1885	Princeton University (NJ)
1886	Princeton University (NJ)
1886	Yale University (CT)
1887	Yale University (CT)
1888	Yale University (CT)
1889	Princeton University (NJ)
1890	Harvard University (MA)
1891	Yale University (CT)
1892	Yale University (CT)
1893	Princeton University (NJ)
1893	Yale University (CT)
1894	Princeton University (NJ)
1894	University of Pennsylvania (PA)
1894	Yale University (CT)
1895	University of Pennsylvania (PA)
1895	Yale University (CT)
1896	Lafayette College (PA)
1896	Princeton University (NJ)
1897	University of Pennsylvania (PA)
1897	Yale University (CT)
1898	Harvard University (MA)
1898	Princeton University (NJ)
1899	Harvard University (MA)
1899	Princeton University (NJ)
1900	Yale University (CT)
1901	Harvard University (MA)
1901	University of Michigan (MI)

Year	*School*
1901	Yale University (CT)
1902	University of Michigan (MI)
1902	Yale University (CT)
1903	Princeton University (NJ)
1903	University of Michigan (MI)
1904	University of Michigan (MI)
1904	University of Minnesota (MN)
1904	University of Pennsylvania (PA)
1905	University of Chicago (IL)
1905	Yale University (CT)
1906	Princeton University (NJ)
1906	Yale University (CT)
1907	Yale University (CT)
1908	Harvard University (MA)
1908	Louisiana State University LA)
1908	University of Pennsylvania (PA)
1909	Yale University (CT)
1910	Harvard University (MA)
1910	University of Pittsburgh (PA)
1911	Pennsylvania State University (PA)
1911	Princeton University (NJ)
1912	Harvard University (MA)
1912	Pennsylvania State University (PA)
1913	Auburn University (AL)
1913	Harvard University (MA)
1913	University of Chicago (IL)
1914	Army (U.S. Military Academy at West Point) (NY)
1914	University of Illinois (IL)
1914	University of Texas (TX)
1915	Cornell University (NY)
1915	University of Oklahoma (OK)
1915	University of Pittsburgh (PA)
1916	Army (U.S. Military Academy at West Point) (NY)
1916	University of Pittsburgh (PA)
1917	Georgia Institute of Technology (GA)
1918	University of Michigan (MI)
1918	University of Pittsburgh (PA)
1919	Centre College (KY)
1919	Harvard University (MA)
1919	Texas A&M University (TX)
1919	University of Illinois (IL)
1919	University of Notre Dame (IN)
1920	Harvard University (MA)
1920	Princeton University (NJ)
1920	University of California, Berkeley (CA)
1920	University of Notre Dame (IN)
1921	Cornell University (NY)
1921	Lafayette College (PA)
1921	University of California, Berkeley (CA)
1921	University of Iowa (IA)
1921	William and Jefferson College (PA)
1922	Cornell University (NY)
1922	Princeton University (NJ)
1922	University of California, Berkeley (CA)
1923	Cornell University (NY)
1923	University of California, Berkeley (CA)
1923	University of Illinois (IL)
1923	University of Michigan (MI)
1924	University of Notre Dame (IN)
1924	University of Pennsylvania (PA)
1925	Dartmouth University (NH)
1925	University of Alabama (AL)
1925	University of Michigan (MI)
1926	Lafayette College (PA)
1926	Navy (U.S. Naval Academy) (MD)
1926	Stanford University (CA)
1926	University of Alabama (AL)
1926	University of Michigan (MI)
1927	Texas A&M (TX)
1927	University of Georgia (GA)
1927	University of Illinois (IL)
1927	University of Notre Dame (IN)
1927	Yale University (CT)
1928	Georgia Institute of Technology (GA)
1928	University of Detroit (MI)
1928	University of Southern California (CA)
1929	University of Notre Dame (IN)
1929	University of Pittsburgh (PA)
1929	University of Southern California (CA)
1930	University of Alabama (AL)
1930	University of Notre Dame (IN)
1931	Purdue University (IN)
1931	University of Pittsburgh (PA)
1931	University of Southern California (CA)
1932	Colgate University (NY)
1932	University of Michigan (MI)
1932	University of Southern California (CA)
1933	Ohio State University (OH)
1933	Princeton University (NJ)
1933	University of Michigan (MI)
1933	University of Southern California (CA)
1934	University of Alabama (AL)
1934	University of Minnesota (MN)
1935	Louisiana State University (LA)
1935	University of Minnesota (MN)
1935	Princeton University (NJ)
1935	Southern Methodist University (TX)
1935	Texas Christian University (TX)
1936	Louisiana State University (LA)
1936	University of Minnesota (MN)
1936	University of Pittsburgh (PA)
1937	University of California, Berkeley (CA)
1937	University of Pittsburgh (PA)
1938	University of Notre Dame (IN)
1938	Texas Christian University (TX)
1938	University of Tennessee (TN)
1939	Cornell University (NY)
1939	Texas A&M University (TX)
1939	University of Southern California (CA)
1940	University of Minnesota (MN)
1940	Stanford University (CA)
1940	University of Tennessee (TN)
1941	University of Alabama (AL)
1941	University of Minnesota (MN)

Year	School
1941	University of Texas (TX)
1942	Ohio State University (OH)
1942	University of Georgia (GA)
1942	University of Wisconsin (WI)
1943	University of Notre Dame (IN)
1944	Army (U.S. Military Academy at West Point) (NY)
1944	Ohio State University (OH)
1945	Army (U.S. Military Academy at West Point) (NY)
1945	University of Alabama (AL)
1946	Army (U.S. Military Academy at West Point) (NY)
1946	University of Georgia (GA)
1946	University of Notre Dame (IN)
1947	University of Michigan (MI)
1947	University of Notre Dame (IN)
1948	University of Michigan (MI)
1949	University of Notre Dame (IN)
1949	University of Oklahoma (OK)
1950	Princeton University (NJ)
1950	University of Kentucky (KY)
1950	University of Oklahoma (OK)
1950	University of Tennessee (TN)
1951	Georgia Institute of Technology (GA)
1951	Michigan State University (MI)
1951	University of Illinois (IL)
1951	University of Maryland (MD)
1951	University of Tennessee (TN)
1952	Georgia Institute of Technology (GA)
1952	Michigan State University (MI)
1953	University of Maryland (MD)
1953	University of Notre Dame (IN)
1953	University of Oklahoma (OK)
1954	Ohio State University (OH)
1954	University of California at Los Angeles (CA)
1955	Michigan State University (MI)
1955	University of Oklahoma (OK)
1956	Georgia Institute of Technology (GA)
1956	University of Iowa (IA)
1956	University of Oklahoma (OK)
1956	University of Tennessee (TN)
1957	Auburn University (AL)
1957	Michigan State University (MI)
1957	Ohio State University (OH)
1957	University of Oklahoma (OK)
1958	Louisiana State University (LA)
1958	University of Iowa (IA)
1959	Syracuse University (NY)
1959	University of Mississippi (MS)
1960	University of Iowa (IA)
1960	University of Minnesota (MN)
1960	University of Mississippi (MS)
1960	University of Missouri (MO)
1960	University of Washington (WA)
1961	University of Alabama (AL)
1961	Ohio State University (OH)
1962	Louisiana State University (LA)

Year	School
1962	University of Mississippi (MS)
1962	University of Southern California (CA)
1963	University of Texas (TX)
1964	University of Alabama (AL)
1964	University of Arkansas (AR)
1964	University of Michigan (MI)
1964	University of Notre Dame (IN)
1965	Michigan State University (MI)
1965	University of Alabama (AL)
1966	Michigan State University (MI)
1966	University of Alabama (AL)
1966	University of Notre Dame (IN)
1967	University of Notre Dame (IN)
1967	University of Oklahoma (OK)
1967	University of Tennessee (TN)
1967	University of Southern California (CA)
1968	Ohio State University (OH)
1968	University of Georgia (GA)
1968	University of Texas (TX)
1969	Ohio State University (OH)
1969	Pennsylvania State University (PA)
1969	University of Texas (TX)
1970	Arizona State University (AZ)
1970	Ohio State University (OH)
1970	University of Nebraska (NE)
1970	University of Notre Dame (IN)
1970	University of Texas (TX)
1971	University of Nebraska (NE)
1972	University of Southern California (CA)
1973	Ohio State University (OH)
1973	University of Alabama (AL)
1973	University of Michigan (MI)
1973	University of Notre Dame (IN)
1973	University of Oklahoma (OK)
1974	Ohio State University (OH)
1974	University of Oklahoma (OK)
1974	University of Southern California (CA)
1975	Arizona State University (AZ)
1975	Ohio State University (OH)
1975	University of Alabama (AL)
1975	University of Oklahoma (OK)
1976	University of Pittsburgh (PA)
1976	University of Southern California (CA)
1977	University of Alabama (AL)
1977	University of Arkansas (AR)
1977	University of Notre Dame (IN)
1977	University of Texas (TX)
1978	University of Alabama (AL)
1978	University of Oklahoma (OK)
1978	University of Southern California (CA)
1979	University of Alabama (AL)
1979	University of Southern California (CA)
1980	Florida State University (FL)
1980	University of Georgia (GA)
1980	University of Nebraska (NE)
1980	University of Oklahoma (OK)
1980	University of Pittsburgh (PA)
1981	Clemson University (SC)

Year	*School*
1981	Pennsylvania State University (PA)
1981	Southern Methodist University (TX)
1981	University of Nebraska (NE)
1981	University of Pittsburgh (PA)
1981	University of Texas (TX)
1982	Pennsylvania State University (PA)
1982	Southern Methodist University (TX)
1982	University of Nebraska (NE)
1983	Auburn University (AL)
1983	University of Miami (FL)
1983	University of Nebraska (NE)
1984	Brigham Young University
1984	University of Florida (FL)
1984	University of Nebraska (NE)
1984	University of Washington (WA)
1985	University of Florida (FL)
1985	University of Michigan (MI)
1985	University of Oklahoma (OK)
1986	Pennsylvania State University (PA)
1986	University of Miami (FL)
1986	University of Oklahoma (OK)
1987	Florida State University (FL)
1987	University of Miami (FL)
1988	University of Miami (FL)
1988	University of Notre Dame (IN)
1989	University of Miami (FL)
1989	University of Notre Dame (IN)
1990	Georgia Institute of Technology (GA)
1990	University of Colorado (CO)
1990	University of Miami (FL)
1990	University of Washington (WA)
1991	University of Miami (FL)
1991	University of Washington (WA)
1992	Florida State University (FL)
1992	University of Alabama (AL)
1993	Auburn University (AL)
1993	Florida State University (FL)
1993	University of Nebraska (NE)
1993	University of Notre Dame (IN)
1994	Florida State University (FL)
1994	Pennsylvania State University (PA)
1994	University of Nebraska (NE)
1995	University of Nebraska (NE)
1996	Florida State University (FL)
1996	University of Florida (FL)
1997	University of Michigan (MI)
1997	University of Nebraska (NE)

As of this writing, the AP and Coaches' polls remain the major college football ranking organizations, in addition to the NCAA Bowl Championship Series, which is the successor of the Bowl Alliance (1995–1997). The national championship was determined by the winner of four, rotating Bowl Games (Sugar, Fiesta, Rose, and Orange from 1998 to 2005), which has since been replaced by the BCS National Championship Game from 2006 to the present. As of this writing, the winner of the BCS Championship Game is declared the national champion (through the Coaches' Poll), is awarded the AFCA (American Football Coaches Association) National Championship Trophy, and wins the MacArthur Trophy presented by the National Football Foundation.

The winners of the national championship (determined by the four rotating Bowl Games from 1998 to 2005) and the BCS Game (2006 to the present) include:

Season	*Date*	*Winner*	*Bowl Game*	*Site*
1998	1/4/99	University of Tennessee (SEC)	1999 Fiesta Bowl	Sun Devil Stadium (Tempe, AZ)
1999	1/4/00	Florida State University (ACC)	2000 Sugar Bowl	Louisiana Superdome (New Orleans, LA)
2000	1/3/01	University of Oklahoma (Big 12)	2001 Orange Bowl	Pro Player Stadium (Miami, FL)
2001	1/3/02	University of Miami (Florida Big East)	2002 Rose Bowl	Rose Bowl (Pasadena, CA)
2002	1/3/03	Ohio State University (Big Ten)	2003 Fiesta Bowl	Sun Devil Stadium (Tempe, AZ)
2003	1/4/04	Louisiana State University (SEC)	2004 Sugar Bowl	Louisiana Superdome (New Orleans, LA)
2004	1/4/05	University of Southern California (Pac-10)	2005 Orange Bowl	Pro Player Stadium (Miami Gardens, FL)
2005	1/4/06	University of Texas (Big 12)	2006 Rose Bowl	Rose Bowl (Pasadena, CA)
2006	1/8/07	University of Florida (SEC)	2007 BCS Title Game	University of Phoenix (Glendale, AZ)
2007	1/7/08	Louisiana State University (SEC)	2008 BCS Title Game	Louisiana Superdome (New Orleans, LA)
2008	1/8/09	University of Florida (SEC)	2009 BCS Title Game	Dolphin Stadiums (Miami Gardens, FL)
2009	1/7/10	University of Alabama (SEC)	2010 BCS Title Game	Rose Bowl (Pasadena, CA)
2010	1/10/11	Auburn University (SEC)	2011 BCS Title Game	University of Phoenix Stadium (Glendale, AZ)

American Football Coaches Association (AFCA) Coach of the Year

100 Legends Lane, Waco, TX 76706; Telephone: 254-754-9900; Fax: 254-754-7373; Email: email@afca.com; Web site: http://www.afca.com

The AFCA Coach of the Year Award is presented annually to each level of college football (NCAA FBS [and equivalent] since 1935, NCAA FCS since 1983, NCAA Division II since 1983, NCAA Division III since 1983, and NAIA since 2006). The Scripps-Howard newspaper chain conducted the balloting and presented the award from 1935 through 1959. In 1960, the AFCA itself began handling the voting and award presentation. Eastman Kodak Corporation sponsored the AFCA Coach of the Year program from 1960 until 1993, and from 1996 to 1999, the award was sponsored by GTE.

From 1960 through 1982, two national winners were selected (one from the University Division and one from the College Division). Beginning in 1983, four national winners were chosen, one from each school level (NCAA I-A, NCAA I-AA, NCAA Division II, and NCAA Division III) and in 2006, selection was expanded to five levels with the inclusion of the NAIA.

Currently, the AFCA selects 25 regional winners (five from each of the AFCA division levels), from which five national winners (one from each AFCA division level) are selected. All schools with eligible AFCA head coaches are listed on the national ballot and AFCA members are not limited to voting for regional winners. However, members are required to vote for coaches within their region for the AFCA Regional Coach of the Year and coaches within their division when voting for the AFCA National Coach of the Year.

The school of each AFCA National Coach of the Year winner receives $1,000 from the American Football Coaches Foundation for each full-time assistant football coach who was on staff the year the head coach was honored. If a school wins a national championship and the head coach wins the AFCA National Coach of the Year Award, the school then receives $1,500 for each full-time assistant who is an AFCA member.

As of this writing, Larry Kehres of Mount Union College (Ohio, NCAA Division III) is the only coach in AFCA history to win the National Coach of the Year Award nine times (1993, 1996–1998, 2000–2002, 2006, 2008) and Bob Reade of Augustana College (Illinois, NCAA Division III) is the only coach to win the award four consecutive years (1983–1986).

NCAA FBS AFCA Coach of the Year

Year	*Coach*	*School*
1935	Lynn Waldorf	Northwestern University (IL)
1936	Dick Harlow	Harvard University (MA)
1937	Edward E. Mylin	Lafayette College (PA)
1938	Bill Kern	Carnegie Institute of Technology (PA)
1939	Dr. Eddie Anderson	University of Iowa (IA)
1940	Clark Shaughnessy	Stanford University (CA)
1941	Frank Leahy	University of Notre Dame (IN)
1942	Bill Alexander	Georgia Institute of Technology (GA)
1943	Amos Alonzo Stagg	University of the Pacific (CA)
1944	Carroll Widdoes	Ohio State University (OH)
1945	Bo McMillin	Indiana University (IN)
1946	Red Blaik	United States Military Academy (Army) (NY)
1947	Fritz Crisler	University of Michigan (MI)
1948	Bennie Oosterbaan	University of Michigan (MI)
1949	Bud Wilkinson	University of Oklahoma (OK)
1950	Charles Caldwell	Princeton University (NJ)
1951	Charles Taylor	Stanford University (CA)
1952	Biggie Munn	Michigan State University (MI)
1953	James Tatum	University of Maryland (MD)
1954	Red Sanders	University of California, Los Angeles (CA)
1955	Duffy Daugherty	Michigan State University (MI)
1956	Bowden Wyatt	University of Tennessee (TN)
1957	Woody Hayes	Ohio State University (OH)

Year	*Coach*	*School*
1958	Paul Dietzel	Louisiana State University (LA)
1959	Ben Schwartzwalder	Syracuse University (NY)
1960	Murray Warmath	University of Minnesota (MN)
1961	Paul "Bear" Bryant	University of Alabama (AL)
1962	John McKay	University of Southern California (CA)
1963	Darrell Royal	University of Texas (TX)
1964	Frank Broyles	University of Arkansas (AR)
1964	Ara Parseghian	University of Notre Dame (IN)
1965	Tommy Prothro	University of California, Los Angeles (CA)
1966	Tom Cahill	United States Military Academy (Army) (NY)
1967	John Pont	Indiana University (IN)
1968	Joe Paterno	Pennsylvania State University (PA)
1969	Bo Schembechler	University of Michigan (MI)
1970	Charlie McClendon	Louisiana State University (LA)
1970	Darrell Royal	University of Texas (TX)
1971	Paul "Bear" Bryant	University of Alabama (AL)
1972	John McKay	University of Southern California (CA)
1973	Paul "Bear" Bryant	University of Alabama (AL)
1974	Grant Teaff	Baylor University (TX)
1975	Frank Kush	Arizona State University (AZ)
1976	Johnny Majors	University of Pittsburgh (PA)
1977	Don James	University of Washington (WA)
1978	Joe Paterno	Pennsylvania State University (PA)
1979	Earle Bruce	Ohio State University (OH)
1980	Vince Dooley	University of Georgia (GA)
1981	Danny Ford	Clemson University (SC)
1982	Joe Paterno	Pennsylvania State University (PA)
1983	Ken Hatfield	United States Air Force Academy (CO)
1984	LaVell Edwards	Brigham Young University (UT)
1985	Fisher DeBerry	United States Air Force Academy (CO)
1986	Joe Paterno	Pennsylvania State University (PA)
1987	Dick MacPherson	Syracuse University (NY)
1988	Don Nehlen	West Virginia University (WV)
1989	Bill McCartney	University of Colorado (CO)
1990	Bobby Ross	Georgia Institute of Technology (GA)
1991	Bill Lewis	East Carolina University (NC)
1992	Gene Stallings	University of Alabama (AL)
1993	Barry Alvarez	University of Wisconsin (WI)
1994	Tom Osborne	University of Nebraska (NE)
1995	Gary Barnett	Northwestern University (IL)
1996	Bruce Snyder	Arizona State University (AZ)
1997	Lloyd Carr	University of Michigan (MI)
1998	Phil Fulmer	University of Tennessee (TN)
1999	Frank Beamer	Virginia Polytechnic Institute and State University (VA)
2000	Bob Stoops	University of Oklahoma (OK)
2001	Larry Coker	University of Miami (FL)
2001	Ralph Friedgen	University of Maryland (MD)
2002	Jim Tressel	Ohio State University (OH)
2003	Pete Carroll	University of Southern California (CA)
2004	Tommy Tuberville	Auburn University (AL)
2005	Joe Paterno	Pennsylvania State University (PA)
2006	Jim Grobe	Wake Forest University (NC)
2007	Mark Mangino	University of Kansas (KS)
2008	Kyle Whittingham	University of Utah (UT)
2009	Gary Patterson	Texas Christian University (TX)
2010	Chip Kelly	University of Oregon (OR)

American Football Coaches Association (AFCA) Assistant Coach of the Year

100 Legends Lane, Waco, TX 76706; Telephone: 254-754-9900; Fax: 254-754-7373; http://www.afca.com

The AFCA Assistant Coach of the Year Award has been presented annually since 1997 to the best assistant coach in each of the five levels of college football (NCAA FBS, NCAA FCS, NCAA Division II, NCAA Division III, and the NAIA). For each of the five levels of college football, staff members from NCAA and NAIA football-playing schools nominate an assistant coach. From this list of nominees, a winner is then selected by the AFCA Public Relations Committee.

NCAA FBS Assistant Coach of the Year

Year	*Assistant Coach*	*School*
1997	Alan Gooch	University of Central Florida (FL)
1998	Richard Bell	United States Air Force Academy (CO)
1999	Jerry Sandusky	Pennsylvania State University (PA)
2000	John Gutekunst	University of South Carolina (SC)
2001	Fred Jackson	University of Michigan (MI)
2002	Ron Aiken	University of Iowa (IA)
2003	Chuck Petersen	United States Air Force Academy (CO)
2004	Brian White	University of Wisconsin (WI)
2005	Michael Haywood	University of Notre Dame (IN)
2006	John Chavis	University of Tennessee (TN)
2007	Calvin Magee	University of West Virginia (WV)
2008	Mac McWhorter	University of Texas TX)
2009	Mike MacIntyre	Duke University (NC)
2010	Luke Fickell	Ohio State University (OH)

College Football Performance Awards (CFPA)

Founded in 2008, the College Football Performance Awards (P.O. Box 4839, Davidson, NC 28036; Telephone: 570-854-1252; Email: smithefficiency@yahoo.com; Web site: http://collegefootballperformance.com) is an NCAA Division I FBS & FCS awards organization that recognizes weekly, annual, and career trophy recipients. For the purpose of this book, we focus only on the annual awards. For FCS awards, please refer to chapter three.

CPFA recipients are selected based exclusively on scientific rankings and mathematical algorithms based upon their individual performances and impact on the team's success. While the annual awards are generally based on the player's success in an individual season, the Elite Awards are based on multiple-season statistics and for those who break significant all-time records.

National Performer of the Year Trophy

Year	*Player*	*School*
2009	Ryan Mallett	University of Arkansas (AR)
2010	Cameron Newton	Auburn University (AL)

National Defensive Performer of the Year

Year	*Player*	*School*
2009	Adrian Clayborn	University of Iowa (IA)
2010	Da'Quan Bowers	Clemson University (SC)

National Freshman Performer of the Year

Year	*Player*	*School*
2009	LaMichael James	University of Oregon (OR)
2010	Marcus Lattimore	University of South Carolina (SC)

Quarterback Trophy

Year	*Player*	*School*
2009	Case Keenum	University of Houston (TX)
2010	Andrew Luck	Stanford University (CA)

Running Back Trophy

Year	*Player*	*School*
2009	Dexter McCluster	University of Mississippi (MS)
2010	Mikel LeShoure	University of Illinois (IL)

Tight End Trophy

Year	*Player*	*School*
2009	Dennis Morris	Louisiana Tech University (LA)
2010	Lance Kendricks	University of Wisconsin (WI)

Wide Receiver Trophy

Year	*Player*	*School*
2008	Dez Bryant	Oklahoma State University (OK)
2009	Danario Alexander	University of Missouri (MO)
2009	Golden Tate	University of Notre Dame (IN)
2010	Justin Blackmon	Oklahoma State University (OK)

Defensive Lineman Trophy

Year	*Player*	*School*
2009	Brandon Graham	University of Michigan (MI)
2010	Sam Acho	University of Texas (TX)

Defensive Back Trophy

Year	*Player*	*School*
2009	Earl Thomas	University of Texas (TX)
2010	Jayron Hosley	Virginia Tech (VA)

Linebacker Trophy

Year	*Player*	*School*
2009	Greg Jones	Michigan State University (MI)
2010	Justin Houston	University of Georgia

Punter Trophy

Year	*Player*	*School*
2009	Drew Butler	University of Georgia (GA)
2010	Chas Henry	University of Florida (FL)

Placekicker Trophy

Year	*Player*	*School*
2009	Blair Walsh	University of Georgia (GA)
2010	Alex Henry	University of Nebraska (NE)

Kickoff Returner Trophy

Year	*Player*	*Trophy*
2009	C.J. Spiller	Clemson University (SC)
2010	Eric Page	University of Toledo (OH)

Kickoff Specialist Trophy

Year	Player	School
2008	David Buehler	University of Southern California (CA)
2009	Quinn Sharp	Oklahoma State University (OK)
2010	Adi Kunalic	University of Nebraska (NE)

Punt Returner Trophy

Year	Player	School
2008	Javier Arenas	University of Alabama (AL)
2009	Damian Williams	University of Southern California (CA)
2010	Cliff Harris	University of Oregon (OR)

Elite Quarterback Trophy

Year	Player	School
2010	Colin Kaepernick	University of Nevada (NV)

Elite Running Back Trophy

Year	Player	School
2009	Jahvid Best	University of California-Berkeley (CA)

Elite Tight End Trophy

Year	Player	School
2009	Dennis Pitta	Brigham Young University (UT)
2009	Cody Slate	Marshall University (WV)

Elite Wide Receiver Trophy

Year	Player	School
2009	Freddie Barnes	Bowling Green State University (OH)
2010	Ryan Broyles	University of Oklahoma (OK)
2010	Leonard Hankerson	University of Miami (FL)

Elite Defensive Performer Trophy

Year	Player	School
2010	Von Miller	Texas A&M University (TX)

Elite Defensive Lineman Trophy

Year	Player	School
2010	Ryan Kerrigan	Purdue University (IN)

Elite Linebacker Trophy

Year	Player	School
2010	Nate Irving	North Carolina State University (NC)

Elite Kickoff Returner Trophy

Year	Player	School
2010	Andre Debose	University of Florida (FL)

Elite Punt Returner Trophy

Year	Player	School
2009	Greg Reid	Florida State University (FL)
2010	Patrick Peterson	Louisiana State University (LA)

Eddie Robinson Coach of the Year Award

The Eddie Robinson Coach of the Year Award has been presented annually (since 1957) to a Division I FBS college football coach voted on by the Football Writers Association of America (http://www.eddierobinson.com; http://www.sportswriters.net/fwaa/).

The Award is named for Eddie Robinson (Edward Gay Robinson; born: February 13, 1919 in Jackson, LA; died: April 3, 2007 in Ruston, LA), the 56-year (1941–1997) football coach at Grambling State University (Grambling, LA) who accumulated a career 408–165–15 (0.694) record (the winningest coach in FCS history). During his coaching career, Robinson had 45 winning seasons; won or shared the Southwestern Athletic Conference championship 17 times; and won nine black college football national championships. He was inducted into the College Football Hall of Fame in 1997.

As of this writing, Darrell Royal (University of Texas), Woody Hayes (Ohio State University), John McKay (University of Southern California), Johnny Majors (University of Pittsburgh), Joe Paterno (Pennsylvania State University), Lou Holtz (University of Arkansas, University of Notre Dame) and Nick Saban (Louisiana State University, University of Alabama) are the only multiple-time winners.

Year	*Winner*	*School*	*Note*
1957	Woody Hayes	Ohio State University (OH)	1957 NCAA I-A National Championship
1958	Paul Dietzel	Louisiana State University (LA)	1958 SEC Championship
1959	Ben Schwartzwalder	Syracuse University (NY)	1959 NCAA I-A National Championship
1960	Murray Warmath	University of Minnesota (MN)	1960 NCAA I-A National Championship
1961	Darrell Royal	University of Texas (TX)	Paul "Bear" Bryant Award Winner
1962	John McKay	University of Southern California (CA)	1962 NCAA I-A National Championship
1963	Darrell Royal	University of Texas (TX)	1963 NCAA I-A National Championship
1964	Ara Parseghian	University of Notre Dame (IN)	1980 College Football Hall of Fame Inductee
1965	Duffy Daugherty	Michigan State University (MI)	1965 UPI National Championship
1966	Tom Cahill	U.S. Military Academy (NY)	40–39–2 Record at Army
1967	John Pont	Indiana University (IN)	1984 Indiana Football Hall of Fame Inductee
1968	Woody Hayes	Ohio State University (OH)	1968 National Championship
1969	Bo Schembechler	University of Michigan (MI)	1969 Big 10 Championship
1970	Alex Agase	Northwestern University (IL)	1963 College Hall of Fame Inductee
1971	Bob Devaney	University of Nebraska (NE)	1971 NCAA I-A National Championship
1972	John McKay	University of Southern California (CA)	1972 NCAA I-A National Championship
1973	Johnny Majors	University of Pittsburgh (PA)	45–45–1 Record at Pittsburgh
1974	Grant Teaff	Baylor University (TX)	Paul "Bear" Bryant Award Winner
1975	Woody Hayes	Ohio State University (OH)	1975 Big Ten Championship
1976	Johnny Majors	University of Pittsburgh (PA)	1976 NCAA I-A National Championship
1977	Lou Holtz	University of Arkansas (AR)	60–21–2 in Seven Years at Arkansas
1978	Joe Paterno	Pennsylvania State University (PA)	2007 College Football Hall of Fame Inductee
1979	Earle Bruce	Ohio State University (OH)	1979 Big 10 Championship
1980	Vince Dooley	University of Georgia (GA)	1980 NCAA I-A National Championship
1981	Danny Ford	Clemson University (SC)	1981 NCAA I-A National Championship
1982	Joe Paterno	Pennsylvania State University (PA)	1982 NCAA I-A National Championship
1983	Howard Schnellen-berger	University of Miami (FL)	1983 NCAA I-A National Championship
1984	LaVell Edwards	Brigham Young University (UT)	1984 NCAA I-A National Championship
1985	Fisher DeBerry	U.S. Air Force Academy (CO)	1985 Walter Camp Coach of the Year
1986	Joe Paterno	Pennsylvania State University (PA)	1986 NCAA I-A National Championship
1987	Dick MacPherson	Syracuse University (NY)	11–0–1 Record in 1987
1988	Lou Holtz	University of Notre Dame (IN)	1988 NCAA I-A National Championship
1989	Bill McCartney	University of Colorado (CO)	3X Big Eight Coach of the Year
1990	Bobby Ross	Georgia Tech (GA)	1990 Paul "Bear" Bryant Award Winner
1991	Don James	University of Washington (WA)	1991 NCAA I-A National Championship
1992	Gene Stallings	University of Alabama (AL)	1992 NCAA I-A National Championship
1993	Terry Bowden	Auburn University (AL)	1993 Paul "Bear" Bryant Award Winner
1994	Rich Brooks	University of Oregon (OR)	1994 Pac-10 Championship

Year	Winner	School	Note
1995	Gary Barnett	Northwestern University (IL)	2X Big 10 Championship (1995 & 1996)
1996	Bruce Snyder	Arizona State University (AZ)	1996 Paul "Bear" Bryan Award Winner
1997	Mike Price	Washington State University (WA)	Coached 14 Years at WSU (1989–2002)
1998	Phillip Fulmer	University of Tennessee (TN)	1998 NCAA I-A National Championship
1999	Frank Beamer	Virginia Tech University (VA)	3X Big East Conference Championships
2000	Bob Stoops	University of Oklahoma (OK)	2000 NCAA I-A National Championship
2001	Ralph Friedgen	University of Maryland (MD)	2001 Walter Camp Coach of the Year
2002	Jim Tressel	Ohio State University (OH)	2002 NCAA I-A National Championship
2003	Nick Saban	Louisiana State University (LA)	2003 NCAA I-A National Championship
2004	Urban Meyer	University of Utah (UT)	2004 Home Depot Coach of the Year
2005	Charlie Weis	University of Notre Dame (IN)	Did Not Play College Football
2006	Greg Schiano	Rutgers University (NJ)	2006 Walter Camp Coach of the Year
2007	Mark Mangino	University of Kansas (KS)	2007 Walter Camp Coach of the Year
2008	Nick Saban	University of Alabama (AL)	2008 Walter Camp Coach of the Year
2009	Gary Patterson	Texas Christian University (TX)	Only School Coach to Have Six 10-Win Seasons
2010	Chip Kelly	University of Oregon (OR)	2010 Walter Camp Coach of the Year

Home Depot Coach of the Year

Since 1994, the Home Depot Coach of the Year Award has been presented annually to college football's FBS Division's best coach as voted on by both ESPN and ABC college football analysts. As of this writing, no coach has won the award twice.

Year	Winner	School	Note
1994	Bobby Bowden	Florida State University (FL)	2006 College Football Hall of Fame Inductee
1995	Gary Barnett	Northwestern University (IL)	1995 Big Ten Champion
1996	Rich Brooks	University of Oregon (OR)	1994 Pac 10 Champion
1997	Mike Price	Washington State University (WA)	Coached at WSU from 1989 to 2002
1998	Phillip Fulmer	University of Tennessee (TN)	1998 National Champion
1999	Tom Osborne	University of Nebraska (NE)	3X National Champion (1994–1995, 1997)
2000	Bob Stoops	University of Oklahoma (OK)	2000 National Champion
2001	Ralph Friedgen	University of Maryland)MD)	2001 Atlantic Coast Conference Champion
2002	Tyrone Willingham	University of Notre Dame (IN)	1999 Pacific 10 Conference Champion
2003	Pete Carroll	University of Southern California (CA)	2X National Champion (2003–2004)
2004	Urban Meyer III	University of Utah (UT)	2004 Eddie Robinson Coach of the Year
2005	Joe Paterno	Pennsylvania State University (PA)	2005 Walter Camp Coach of the Year
2006	Greg Schiano	Rutgers University (NJ)	2006 Big East Coach of the Year
2007	Mark Mangino	University of Kansas (KS)	2007 Woody Hayes Coach of the Year
2008	Nick Saban	University of Alabama (AL)	2008 Walter Camp Coach of the Year
2009	Brian Kelly	University of Cincinnati (OH)	2X NCAA Division II Champions (2002, 2003)
2010	Gene Chizik	Auburn University (AL)	2010 National Champions

John Mackey Award

Since 2000, the John Mackey Award has been presented annually to the best tight end in the FBS division. The award is voted on by the John Mackey Award Selection Committee, which is composed of media members and former NFL players and is named after NFL Hall of Fame member John Mackey, widely regarded as one of the NFL's all-time great tight ends. The non-profit Nassau County Sports Commission (800 Community Drive, Suite 306, Manhasset, NY 11030; Telephone: 516-365-9625; Fax: 516-365-3632; Web site: http://www.johnmackeyaward.org/) is responsible for administering both the John Mackey Award and the John Mackey Award Selection Committee.

John Mackey (born: September 24, 1941, in New York City, New York) played football at Syracuse

University (Syracuse, New York); for the NFL's Baltimore Colts (1963–1971) and San Diego Chargers (1972); named to the NFL 1960s All-Decade Team; helped the Colts win Super Bowl V (1971); and was inducted into the Pro Football Hall of Fame in 1992.

Year	*Winner*	*School*	*Note*
2000	Tim Stratton	Purdue University (IN)	2000 First-Team All–Big Ten
2001	Daniel Graham	University of Colorado (CO)	2001 All-American
2002	Dallas Clark	University of Iowa (IA)	2002 All–Big Ten
2003	Kellen Winslow II	University of Miami (FL)	2003 First-Team All-American
2004	Heath Miller	University of Virginia (VA)	1st ACC Player to win the Mackey Award
2005	Marcedes Lewis	University of California, Los Angeles (CA)	1st Round NFL Draft Pick
2006	Matt Spaeth	University of Minnesota (MN)	2006 First-Team All-American
2007	Fred Davis	University of Southern California (CA)	2007 First-Team All–Pac 10
2008	Chase Coffman	University of Missouri (MO)	3rd Round NFL Draft Pick
2009	Aaron Hernandez	University of Florida (FL)	2009 First Team All SEC
2010	D.J. Williams	University of Arkansas (AR)	2010 Disney Spirit Award Winner

Lambert-Meadowlands Trophy

The Lambert-Meadowlands Trophy is an annual award presented to the best team in the East (Division I FBS) college football and was established by brothers Victor and Henry Lambert in memory of their father, August. Established in 1936 as the "Lambert Trophy," it also recognizes (as the "Lambert Cup") the best college football team in the FCS (as of 1982), NCAA Division II (as of 1957), and Division III (as of 1966) levels.

The New Jersey Sports and Exposition Authority (Public Affairs Office, 50 State Route 120, East Rutherford, NJ 07073; Telephone: 201-935-8500; Email: publicaffairs@njsea.com; Web site: http://www.njsea.com/), operator of the Meadowlands Sports Complex, took over the administration of the Lambert Meadowlands Trophy in 1983.

To be eligible for this Trophy, a school must be located in the East or play half its schedule against eligible Lambert teams.

Year	*School*
1936	University of Pittsburgh (PA)
1937	University of Pittsburgh (PA)
1938	Carnegie Institute of Technology (PA)
1939	Cornell University (NY)
1940	Boston College (MA)
1941	Fordham College (NY)
1942	Boston College (MA)
1943	United States Naval Academy (MD)
1944	United States Military Academy at West Point (NY)
1945	United States Military Academy at West Point (NY)
1946	United States Military Academy at West Point (NY)
1947	Pennsylvania State University (PA)
1948	United States Military Academy at West Point (NY)
1949	United States Military Academy at West Point (NY)
1950	Princeton University (NJ)
1951	Princeton University (NJ)
1952	Syracuse University (NY)
1953	United States Military Academy at West Point (NY)
1954	United States Naval Academy (MD)
1955	University of Pittsburgh (PA)
1956	Syracuse University (NY)
1957	United States Naval Academy (MD)
1958	United States Military Academy at West Point (NY)
1959	Syracuse University (NY)
1960	U.S. Naval Academy (MD)
1960	Yale University (CT)
1961	Pennsylvania State University (PA)
1962	Pennsylvania State University (PA)
1963	U.S. Naval Academy (MD)
1964	Pennsylvania State University (PA)
1965	Dartmouth College (NH)
1966	Syracuse University (NY)
1967	Pennsylvania State University (PA)
1968	Pennsylvania State University (PA)
1969	Pennsylvania State University (PA)
1970	Dartmouth College (NH)
1971	Pennsylvania State University (PA)
1972	Pennsylvania State University (PA)
1973	Pennsylvania State University (PA)
1974	Pennsylvania State University (PA)
1975	Pennsylvania State University (PA)
1976	University of Pittsburgh (PA)
1977	Pennsylvania State University (PA)
1978	Pennsylvania State University (PA)

Year	School
1979	University of Pittsburgh (PA)
1980	University of Pittsburgh (PA)
1981	Pennsylvania State University (PA)
1982	Pennsylvania State University (PA)
1983	Boston College (MA)
1984	Boston College (MA)
1985	Pennsylvania State University (PA)
1986	Pennsylvania State University (PA)
1987	Syracuse University (NY)
1988	University of West Virginia (WV)
1989	Pennsylvania State University (PA)
1990	Pennsylvania State University (PA)
1991	Pennsylvania State University (PA)
1992	Syracuse University (NY)
1993	University of West Virginia (WV)
1994	Pennsylvania State University (PA)
1995	Virginia Polytechnic Institute and State University (VA)
1996	Pennsylvania State University (PA)
1997	Pennsylvania State University (PA)
1998	Pennsylvania State University (PA)
1999	Virginia Polytechnic Institute and State University (VA)
2000	University of Miami (FL)
2001	University of Miami (FL)
2002	University of Miami (FL)
2003	University of Miami (FL)
2004	Boston College (MA)
2005	Pennsylvania State University (PA)
2006	University of Louisville (KY)
2007	University of West Virginia (WV)
2008	Pennsylvania State University (PA)
2009	Pennsylvania State University (PA)
2010	University of Connecticut (CT)

Liberty Mutual Coach of the Year

Sponsored by the Liberty Mutual Insurance Company (175 Berkeley Street, Boston, MA 02116; Telephone: 800-837-5254; Web site: http://www.coachoftheyear.com/), the Liberty Mutual Coach of the Year is an annual college football award presented to the top head coach from each NCAA Division (FBS [as of 2006], FCS [as of 2007], NCAA Division II [as of 2007], and NCAA Division III [as of 2007]).

This award provides each coach with $50,000 to donate to the charity or charities of his choice, as well as a $20,000 grant to donate to his school's alumni association.

Year	Coach	School	Note
2006	Greg Schiano	Rutgers University (NJ)	2006 Big East Coach of the Year
2007	Ron Zook	University of Illinois (IL)	2007 Big Ten Coach of the Year
2008	Nick Saban	University of Alabama (AL)	2008 Walter Camp Coach of the Year
2009	Gary Patterson	Texas Christian University (TX)	2009 Woody Hayes Trophy Winner
2010	Gene Chizik	Auburn University (AL)	2010 Home Depot Coach of the Year

MacArthur Trophy

Sponsored and presented by the National Football Foundation since 1959 (433 East Las Colinas Boulevard, Suite 1130, Irving, TX, 75039; Telephone: 972-556-1000; Fax: 972-556-9032; Email: membership@footballfoundation.com; Web site: http://www.footballfoundation.org/Macarthurhist.php), the silver MacArthur Trophy has been awarded to the NCAA Division I (FBS) college football team (or teams) that have been selected national champion. There is only one physical trophy (much like professional hockey's Stanley Cup) and it is kept by the winning school for one year. The winning school's name is engraved on the Trophy.

The trophy weighs 400 ounces (of silver) and is in the shape of a football stadium 25 inches by 18 inches on its base and 10 inches tall. The trophy is one of many national championship awards presented to NCAA Division I (FBS) college football teams because the NCAA (as an organization) does not sanction a national championship tournament as it does in most other sports.

Occasionally since 1959, the MacArthur Trophy's winning team has differed from the Associated Press Poll winner and/or the United Press International Poll winner. Since the Bowl Championship Series began in 1998, the trophy has been awarded to the winner of the BCS National Championship Game. When not displayed by the winning school, the Trophy is housed at the College Football Hall of Fame in South Bend, Indiana.

Designed by Tiffany & Company, the Trophy was originally the gift of an anonymous donor in honor of General Douglas A. MacArthur, one of the founders of the National Football Foundation (and a chairman of the group's Advisory Board for several years) who had earlier served as student manager of the Army team (at West Point in New York) during his military cadet days.

Douglas MacArthur (born: January 26, 1880, in Little Rock, Arkansas; died: April 5, 1964, in Washington, D.C.) served in the United States Army from 1903 until 1951 and rose to the rank of General. He earned numerous awards, including the Medal of Honor; three Distinguished Service Crosses; five Army Distinguished Service Medals; seven Silver Stars; the Bronze Star; and two Purple Hearts.

He was the Field Marshal of the Philippine Army; Chief of Staff of the United States Army during the 1930s; and played a prominent role in the Pacific theater during World War II. He was one of only five men ever to rise to the rank of General of the Army and the only one to become a field marshal in the Philippine Army. He graduated from the United States Military Academy at West Point (New York) at the top of the class of 1903; became the Army's youngest major general in 1925; served as president of the United States Olympic Committee during the 1928 Summer Olympics in Amsterdam; became Chief of Staff of the United States Army in 1930; officially accepted Japan's surrender on September 2, 1945, ending World War II; led the United Nations Command in the Korean War (1950–1951); and was fired on April 11, 1951 by President Harry S Truman for disagreeing with Truman's policy on the Korean War.

Year	*Team*	*Coach*
1959	Syracuse University (NY)	Ben Schwartzwalder
1960	University of Minnesota (MN)	Murray Warmath
1961	University of Alabama (AL)	Paul "Bear" Bryant
1962	University of Southern California (CA)	John McKay
1963	University of Texas (TX)	Darrell Royal
1964	University of Notre Dame (IN)	Ara Parseghian
1965	Michigan State University (MI)	Duffy Daugherty
1966	Michigan State University (MI)	Duffy Daugherty
1966	University of Notre Dame (IN)	Ara Parseghian
1967	University of Southern California (CA)	John McKay
1968	Ohio State University (OH)	Woody Hayes
1969	University of Texas (TX)	Darrell Royal
1970	Ohio State University (OH)	Woody Hayes
1970	University of Texas (TX)	Darrell Royal
1971	University of Nebraska (NE)	Bob Devaney
1972	University of Southern California (CA)	John McKay
1973	University of Notre Dame (IN)	Ara Parseghian
1974	University of Southern California (CA)	John McKay
1975	University of Oklahoma (OK)	Barry Switzer
1976	University of Pittsburgh (PA)	Johnny Majors
1977	University of Notre Dame (IN)	Dan Devine
1978	University of Alabama (AL)	Paul "Bear" Bryant
1979	University of Alabama (AL)	Paul "Bear" Bryant
1980	University of Georgia (GA)	Vince Dooley
1981	Clemson University (SC)	Danny Ford
1982	Pennsylvania State University (PA)	Joe Paterno
1983	University of Miami (FL)	Howard Schnellenberger
1984	Brigham Young University (UT)	LaVell Edwards
1985	University of Oklahoma (OK)	Barry Switzer
1986	Pennsylvania State University (PA)	Joe Paterno
1987	University of Miami (FL)	Jimmy Johnson
1988	University of Notre Dame (IN)	Lou Holtz
1989	University of Miami (FL)	Dennis Erickson
1990	University of Colorado (CO)	Bill McCartney
1991	University of Washington (WA)	Don James
1992	University of Alabama (AL)	Gene Stallings
1993	Florida State University (FL)	Bobby Bowden
1994	University of Nebraska (NE)	Tom Osborne
1995	University of Nebraska (NE)	Tom Osborne

Year	*Team*	*Coach*
1996	University of Florida (FL)	Steve Spurrier
1997	University of Michigan (MI)	Lloyd Carr
1998	University of Tennessee (TN)	Phil Fulmer
1999	Florida State University (FL)	Bobby Bowden
2000	University of Oklahoma (OK)	Bob Stoops
2001	University of Miami (FL)	Larry Coker
2002	Ohio State University (OH)	Jim Tressel
2003	Louisiana State University (LA)	Nick Saban
2004	University of Southern California (CA)	Pete Carroll
2005	University of Texas (TX)	Mack Brown
2006	University of Florida (FL)	Urban Meyer
2007	Louisiana State University (LA)	Les Miles
2008	University of Florida (FL)	Urban Meyer
2009	University of Alabama (AL)	Nick Saban
2010	Auburn University (AL)	Gene Chizik

Ray Guy Award

Since 2000, the Ray Guy Award has been presented annually to college football's top punter by the Greater Augusta Sports Council (1450 Greene Street, Augusta, GA 30901; Telephone: 706-722-8326; Web site: http://www.augustasportscouncil.org). The Award is named after punter Ray Guy, a former All-American at the University of Southern Mississippi (Hattiesburg, Mississippi) and an All-Pro player for the National Football League's Oakland Raiders.

Winners are selected by votes from FBS coaches, sports information directors, national media, and former Ray Guy Award winners.

William Ray Guy (born: December 22, 1949, in Swainsboro, GA) played college football at the University of Southern Mississippi (Hattiesburg) and in the NFL for 14 seasons with the Oakland / Los Angeles Raiders (1973–1986). He won three Super Bowls (SB XI (1977), SB XV (1981), SB XVIII (1984); was selected to the NFL 1970s All-Decade Team; named to the NFL's 75th Anniversary Team; and was inducted into the Mississippi Sports Hall of Fame (1994), Georgia Sports Hall of Fame (1997), and the College Football Hall of Fame (2004).

He was the first pure punter to be drafted in the first round of the NFL (Oakland Raiders in 1973) and never had a punt returned for a touchdown.

As of this writing, only Daniel Sepulveda (Baylor University) has won this award twice.

Year	*Winner*	*School*	*Note*
2000	Kevin Stemke	University of Wisconsin (WI)	1999 First-Team Big Ten Conference
2001	Travis Dorsch	Purdue University (IN)	College Career Scoring Points Leader (355)
2002	Mark Mariscal	University of Colorado (CO)	No Further Information
2003	William Sander	Ohio State University (OH)	Started Only One Year at OSU
2004	Daniel Sepulveda	Baylor University (TX)	3X AP All-American (2004–2006)
2005	Ryan Plackemeier	Wake Forest University (NC)	2005 First-Team All-American
2006	Daniel Sepulveda	Baylor University (TX)	4X All–Big 12 (2003–2006)
2007	Durant Brooks	Georgia Institute of Technology (GA)	2X First-Team All-ACC (2006–2007)
2008	Matt Fodge	Oklahoma State University (OK)	Signed by the NFL's Dallas Cowboys (2009)
2009	Drew Butler	University of Georgia (GA)	2009 First Team All American
2010	Chas Henry	University of Florida	2010 BCS National Championship

Walter Camp Coach of the Year

Since 1967, the Walter Camp Coach of the Year award is presented annually to the top NCAA FBS college football coach and is voted on by NCAA head coaches and sports information directors, under the direction of the Walter Camp Football Foundation, Inc. (P.O. Box 1663, New Haven, CT, 06507; Email: president@waltercamp.org; Web site: http://waltercamp.org).

Walter Chauncey Camp (born: April 7, 1859, in New Britain, CT; died: March 14, 1925, in New York, NY) was an early football pioneer; sports writer; played college football at Yale University (1887–1882); coached at Yale University (New Haven, 1888–1891) and Stanford University (1892, 1894–1895); inducted into the College Football Hall of Fame in 1951; and is often referred to as the "Father of American Football."

He served on numerous collegiate football rules committees that developed the American game from his time as a player at Yale University until his death (eliminating a lot of the brute force that was part of the early game). He is credited with innovations such as the snap-back from center, the system of downs, the points system, the introduction of the offensive formation (a seven-man offensive line and a four-man backfield of a quarterback, two halfbacks, and a fullback); and the awarding of a two-point safety to the defense for tackling a ball carrier in his own end zone (followed by a free kick by the offense from its own 20-yard line).

Camp also wrote more than 250 articles and almost 30 books on sports, including football (in various magazines and newspapers through the country); selected early All-Star college football teams; and helped establish the National Collegiate Athletic Association.

As of this writing, only Joe Paterno (Pennsylvania State University) and Bob Stoops (University of Oklahoma) have won this award more than once.

Year	*Coach*	*School*	*Note*
1967	John Pont	University of Indiana (IN)	Only IU Coach to take a School Team to the Rose Bowl
1968	Woody Hayes	Ohio State University (OH)	Won 1968 National Championship
1969	Bo Schembechler	University of Michigan (MI)	1993 College Football Hall of Fame Inductee
1970	Bob Blackman	Dartmouth College (NH)	7–0 Record in 1970
1971	Bob Devaney	University of Nebraska (NE)	Won 1971 National Championship
1972	Joe Paterno	Pennsylvania State University (PA)	2007 College Football Hall of Fame Inductee
1973	Johnny Majors	University of Pittsburgh (PA)	1987 College Football Hall of Fame Inductee
1974	Barry Switzer	University of Oklahoma (OK)	Won 1974 National Championship
1975	Frank Kush	Arizona State University (AZ)	Won Seven WAC Conference Championships
1976	Frank R. Burns	Rutgers University (NJ)	Led School to its 1st Bowl Game—1978 Garden State Bowl
1977	Lou Holtz	University of Arkansas (AR)	2008 College Football Hall of Fame Inductee
1978	Warren Powers	University of Missouri (MO)	Appeared in 4 Straight Bowl Games (1978–1981)
1979	John Mackovic	Wake Forest University (NC)	14–20 W–L Record at Wake Forest
1980	Vince Dooley	University of Georgia (GA)	Won 1980 SEC Championship
1981	Jackie Sherrill	University of Pittsburgh (PA)	Won 4 Bowl Games at Pittsburgh
1982	Jerry Stovall	Louisiana State University (LA)	1982 Team Ranked #11 in the Final Polls
1983	Mike White	University of Illinois (IL)	Won 1983 Big Ten Championship
1984	Joe Morrison	University of South Carolina (SC)	Never Worked as an Assistant Coach
1985	Fisher DeBerry	U.S. Air Force Academy (CO)	South Carolina Sports Hall of Fame Inductee
1986	Jimmy Johnson	University of Miami (FL)	Won 1987 National Championship
1987	Dick MacPherson	Syracuse University (NY)	2009 College Football Hall of Fame Inductee
1988	Don Nehlen	West Virginia University (WV)	2005 College Football Hall of Fame Inductee
1989	Bill McCartney	University of Colorado (CO)	Won 1990 National Championship (AP)
1990	Bobby Ross	Georgia Institute of Technology (GA)	Won 1990 National Championship (Coaches Poll)
1991	Bobby Bowden	Florida State University (FL)	2006 College Football Hall of Fame Inductee
1992	Gene Stallings	University of Alabama (AL)	Won 1992 National Championship
1993	Terry Bowden	Auburn University (AL)	1993 Paul "Bear" Bryant Award Winner

Year	*Coach*	*School*	*Note*
1994	Joe Paterno	Pennsylvania State University (PA)	Won 1994 Big Ten Championship
1995	Gary Barnett	Northwestern University (IL)	Won 1995 Big Ten Championship
1996	Bruce Snyder	Arizona State University (AZ)	Won 1996 Pac-10 Conference Championship
1997	Lloyd Carr	University of Michigan (MI)	Won 1997 National Championship
1998	Bill Snyder	Kansas State University (KS)	Won 4 Big Twelve North Division Championships
1999	Frank Beamer	Virginia Polytechnic Institute and State University (VA)	Won 1999 Big East Conference
2000	Bob Stoops	University of Oklahoma (OK)	Won 2000 National Championship
2001	Ralph Friedgen	University of Maryland (MD)	Won 2001 ACC Championship
2002	Kirk Ferentz	University of Iowa (IA)	Won 2002 Big Ten Championship
2003	Bob Stoops	University of Oklahoma (OK)	Won 2004 Big Ten Championship
2004	Tommy Tuberville	Auburn University (AL)	Won 2004 SEC Championship
2005	Joe Paterno	Pennsylvania State University (PA)	Won 2005 Big Ten Championship
2006	Greg Schiano	Rutgers University (NJ)	School Finished 2006 Ranked #12
2007	Mark Mangino	University of Kansas (KS)	Won 2007 Big 12 Conference
2008	Nick Saban	University of Alabama (AL)	Won 2008 SEC Western Division Title
2009	Gary Patterson	Texas Christian University (TX)	Woody Hayes Trophy Winner
2010	Chip Kelly	University of Oregon	2X Pac-10 Champion (2009–2010)

Atlantic Coast Conference

P.O. Drawer ACC, Greensboro, NC 27417; Telephone: 336-854-8787; Web site: http://www.theacc.com

Founded on May 8, 1953 with seven charter schools (Clemson University, Duke University, North Carolina State University, University of Maryland, University of North Carolina, University of South Carolina, and Wake Forest University), the Atlantic Coast Conference currently consists of 12 schools. These schools came together after withdrawing from the Southern Conference and on June 14, 1953, the group adopted the name of the Atlantic Coast Conference.

As of this writing, the Atlantic Coast Conference currently consists of the following 12 schools:

- Boston College Eagles, Chestnut Hill, MA 02467; 800-294-0294; www.bc.edu
- Clemson University Tigers, Clemson, SC 29634; 864-656-3311; www.clemson.edu
- Duke University Blue Devils, Durham, NC 27708; 919-684-8111; www.duke.edu
- Florida State University Seminoles, Tallahassee, FL 32306; 850-644-2525; www.fsu.edu.
- Georgia Tech (Georgia Institute of Technology) Yellow Jackets, Atlanta, GA 30332; 404-894-2000; www.gatech.edu
- North Carolina State University Wolfpack, Raleigh, NC; 919-515-2011; www.ncsu.edu
- University of Maryland Terrapins, College Park, MD 20742; 301-405-1000; www.umd.edu
- University of Miami Hurricanes, Coral Gables, FL 33124; 305-284-2211; www.miami.edu
- University of North Carolina Tar Heels, Chapel Hill, NC 27599; 919-962-2211; www.unc.edu
- University of Virginia Cavaliers, Charlottesville, VA 22904; 434-924-0311; www.virginia.edu
- Virginia Tech (Virginia Polytechnic Institute and State University) Hokies, Blacksburg, VA 24061; 540-231-6267; www.vt.edu
- Wake Forest University Demon Deacons, Winston-Salem, NC 27106; 336-758-5000; www.wfu.edu

ACC Champions

Year	*Champion*
1953	Duke University (NC)
1953	University of Maryland (MD)
1954	Duke University (NC)
1955	Duke University (NC)
1955	University of Maryland (MD)
1956	Clemson University (SC)
1957	North Carolina State University (NC)
1958	Clemson University (SC)
1959	Clemson University (SC)
1960	Duke University (NC)

Year	Champion
1961	Duke University (NC)
1962	Duke University (NC)
1963	University of North Carolina (NC)
1963	North Carolina State University (NC)
1964	North Carolina State University (NC)
1965	Clemson University (SC)
1965	North Carolina State University (NC)
1966	Clemson University (SC)
1967	Clemson University (SC)
1968	North Carolina State University (NC)
1969	University of South Carolina (SC)
1970	Wake Forest University (NC)
1971	University of North Carolina (NC)
1972	University of North Carolina (NC)
1973	North Carolina State University (NC)
1974	University of Maryland (MD)
1975	University of Maryland (MD)
1976	University of Maryland (MD)
1977	University of North Carolina (NC)
1978	Clemson University (SC)
1979	North Carolina State University (NC)
1980	University of North Carolina (NC)
1981	Clemson University (SC)
1982	Clemson University (SC)
1983	University of Maryland (MD)
1984	University of Maryland (MD)
1985	University of Maryland (MD)
1986	Clemson University (SC)
1987	Clemson University (SC)
1988	Clemson University (SC)
1989	Duke University (NC)
1989	University of Virginia (VA)
1990	Georgia Tech (Georgia Institute of Technology) (GA)
1991	Clemson University (SC)
1992	Florida State University (FL)
1993	Florida State University (FL)
1994	Florida State University (FL)
1995	Florida State University (FL)
1995	University of Virginia (VA)
1996	Florida State University (FL)
1997	Florida State University (FL)
1998	Florida State University (FL)
1998	Georgia Tech (Georgia Institute of Technology) (GA)
1999	Florida State University (FL)
2000	Florida State University (FL)
2001	University of Maryland (MD)
2002	Florida State University (FL)
2003	Florida State University (FL)
2004	Virginia Tech (Virginia Polytechnic Institute and State University) (VA)
2005	Florida State University (FL)
2006	Wake Forest University (NC)
2007	Virginia Tech (Virginia Polytechnic Institute and State University) (VA)
2008	Virginia Tech (Virginia Polytechnic Institute and State University) (VA)
2009	Georgia Tech (Georgia Institute of Technology) (GA)
2010	Virginia Tech (Virginia Polytechnic Institute and State University) (VA)

ACC Coach of the Year

Voted on by members of the Atlantic Coast Sports Media Association.

Year	Coach	School
1953	Jim Tatum	University of Maryland (MD)
1954	Bill Murray	Duke University (NC)
1955	Jim Tatum	University of Maryland (MD)
1956	Paul Amen	Wake Forest University (NC)
1957	Earle Edwards	North Carolina State (NC)
1958	Frank Howard	Clemson University (SC)
1959	Paul Amen	Wake Forest University (NC)
1960	Bill Murray	Duke University (NC)
1961	Bill Elias	University of Virginia (VA)
1962	Bill Murray	Duke University (NC)
1963	Jim Hickey	University of North Carolina (NC)
1963	Earle Edwards	North Carolina State (NC)
1964	Bill Tate	Wake Forest University (NC)
1965	Earle Edwards	North Carolina State (NC)
1966	Frank Howard	Clemson University (SC)
1967	Earle Edwards	North Carolina State (NC)
1968	George Blackburn	University of Virginia (VA)
1969	Paul Dietzel	University of South Carolina (SC)
1970	Cal Stoll	Wake Forest University (NC)
1971	Bill Dooley	University of North Carolina (NC)

Year	Coach	School
1972	Lou Holtz	North Carolina State (NC)
1973	Jerry Claiborne	University of Maryland (MD)
1974	Red Parker	Clemson University (SC)
1975	Jerry Claiborne	University of Maryland (MD)
1976	Jerry Claiborne	University of Maryland (MD)
1977	Charley Pell	Clemson University (SC)
1978	Charley Pell	Clemson University (SC)
1979	John Mackovic	Wake Forest University (NC)
1980	Dick Crum	University of North Carolina (NC)
1981	Danny Ford	Clemson University (SC)
1982	Bobby Ross	University of Maryland (MD)
1983	George Welsh	University of Virginia (VA)
1984	George Welsh	University of Virginia (VA)
1985	Bill Curry	Georgia Tech (Georgia Institute of Technology) (GA)
1986	Dick Sheridan	North Carolina State (NC)
1987	Bill Dooley	Wake Forest University (NC)
1988	Steve Spurrier	Duke University (NC)
1989	Steve Spurrier	Duke University (NC)
1990	Bobby Ross	Georgia Tech (Georgia Institute of Technology) (GA)
1991	George Welsh	University of Virginia (VA)
1992	Bill Dooley	Wake Forest University (NC)
1993	Bobby Bowden	Florida State University (FL)
1994	Fred Goldsmith	Duke University (NC)
1995	George Welsh	University of Virginia (VA)
1996	Mack Brown	University of North Carolina (NC)
1997	Bobby Bowden	Florida State University (FL)
1998	George O'Leary	Georgia Tech (Georgia Institute of Technology) (GA)
1999	Tommy Bowden	Clemson University (SC)
2000	George O'Leary	Georgia Tech (Georgia Institute of Technology) (GA)
2001	Ralph Friedgen	University of Maryland (MD)
2002	Al Groh	University of Virginia (VA)
2003	Tommy Bowden	Clemson University (SC)
2004	Frank Beamer	Virginia Tech (Virginia Polytechnic Institute and State University) (VA)
2005	Frank Beamer	Virginia Tech (Virginia Polytechnic Institute and State University) (VA)
2006	Jim Grobe	Wake Forest University (NC)
2007	Al Groh	University of Virginia (VA)
2008	Paul Johnson	Georgia Tech (Georgia Institute of Technology) (GA)
2009	Paul Johnson	Georgia Tech (Georgia Institute of Technology) (GA)
2010	Ralph Friedgen	University of Maryland (MD)

ACC Player of the Year

Voted on by members of the Atlantic Coast Sports Media Association; beginning in 1993, the ACC Offensive Player of the Year Award and the ACC Defensive Player of the Year Award were established as different awards from the ACC Player of the Year Award.

Year	Player	Position	School
1953	Bernie Faloney	Quarterback	University of Maryland (MD)
1954	Jerry Barger	Quarterback	Duke University (NC)
1955	Bob Pellegrini	Center	University of Maryland (MD)
1956	Bill Barnes	Running Back	Wake Forest University (NC)
1957	Dick Christy	Halfback	North Carolina State University (NC)
1958	Alex Hawkins	Running Back	University of South Carolina (SC)
1959	Mike McGee	Guard	Duke University (NC)
1960	Roman Gabriel	Quarterback	North Carolina State University (NC)
1961	Roman Gabriel	Quarterback	North Carolina State University (NC)
1962	Billy Gambrell	Wide Receiver	University of South Carolina (SC)
1963	Jay Wilkinson	Halfback	Duke University (NC)

Year	*Player*	*Position*	*School*
1964	Brian Piccolo	Fullback	Wake Forest University (NC)
1965	Danny Talbott	Quarterback	University of North Carolina (NC)
1966	Bob Davis	Quarterback	University of Virginia (VA)
1967	Buddy Gore	Running Back	Clemson University (SC)
1968	Frank Quayl	Running Back	University of Virginia (VA)
1969	Don McCauley	Running Back	University of North Carolina (NC)
1970	Don McCauley	Running Back	University of North Carolina (NC)
1971	Ernie Jackson	Cornerback	Duke University (NC)
1972	Steve Jones	Running Back	Duke University (NC)
1973	Willie Burden	Running Back	North Carolina State University (NC)
1974	Randy White	Defensive Tackle	University of Maryland (MD)
1975	Mike Voight	Running Back	University of North Carolina (NC)
1976	Mike Voight	Running Back	University of North Carolina (NC)
1977	Steve Fuller	Quarterback	Clemson University (SC)
1978	Steve Fuller	Quarterback	Clemson University (SC)
1979	Jay Venuto	Quarterback	Wake Forest University (NC)
1980	Lawrence Taylor	Linebacker	University of North Carolina (NC)
1981	Jeff Davis	Linebacker	Clemson University (SC)
1982	Chris Castor	Wide Receiver	Duke University (NC)
1983	Ben Bennett	Quarterback	Duke University (NC)
1984	William Perry	Defensive Lineman	Clemson University (SC)
1985	Barry Word	Running Back	University of Virginia (VA)
1986	Erik Kramer	Quarterback	North Carolina State University (NC)
1987	Michael Perry	Defensive Tackle	Clemson University (SC)
1988	Anthony Dilweg	Quarterback	Duke University (NC)
1989	Clarkston Hines	Wide Receiver	Duke University (NC)
1990	Shawn Moore	Quarterback	University of Virginia (VA)
1991	Matt Blundin	Quarterback	University of Virginia (VA)
1992	Charlie Ward	Quarterback	Florida State University (FL)
1993	Charlie Ward	Quarterback	Florida State University (FL)
1994	Robert Baldwin	Running Back	Duke University (NC)
1995	Danny Kanell	Quarterback	Florida State University (FL)
1996	Tiki Barber	Running Back	University of Virginia (VA)
1997	Andre Wadsworth	Defensive End	Florida State University (FL)
1998	Torry Holt	Wide Receiver	North Carolina State University (NC)
1999	Joe Hamilton	Quarterback	Georgia Tech (Georgia Institute of Technology) (GA)
2000	Chris Weinke	Quarterback	Florida State University (FL)
2001	E.J. Henderson	Linebacker	University of Maryland (MD)
2002	Matt Schaub	Quarterback	University of Virginia (VA)
2003	Philip Rivers	Quarterback	North Carolina State University (NC)
2004	Bryan Randall	Quarterback	Virginia Tech (Virginia Polytechnic Institute and State University) (VA)
2005	Chris Barclay	Running Back	Wake Forest University (NC)
2006	Calvin Johnson	Wide Receiver	Georgia Tech (Georgia Institute of Technology) (GA)
2007	Matt Ryan	Quarterback	Boston College (MA)
2008	Jonathan Dwyer	Running Back	Georgia Tech (Georgia Institute of Technology) (GA)
2009	C.J. Spiller	Running Back	Clemson University (SC)
2010	Tyrod Taylor	Quarterback	Virginia Tech (Virginia Polytechnic Institute and State University) (VA)

ACC Offensive Player of the Year Award

Voted on by members of the Atlantic Coast Sports Media Association; established in 1993 as a separate award from the ACC Player of the Year Award.

Year	Player	Position	School
1993	Charlie Ward	Quarterback	Florida State University (FL)
1994	Robert Baldwin	Running Back	Duke University (NC)
1995	Danny Kanell	Quarterback	Florida State University (FL)
1996	Tiki Barber	Running Back	University of Virginia (VA)
1997	Thad Busby	Quarterback	Florida State University (FL)
1998	Torry Holt	Wide Receiver	North Carolina State University (NC)
1999	Joe Hamilton	Quarterback	Georgia Tech (Georgia Institute of Technology) (GA)
2000	Chris Weinke	Quarterback	Florida State University (FL)
2001	Bruce Perry	Running Back	University of Maryland (MD)
2002	Matt Schaub	Quarterback	University of Virginia (VA)
2003	Philip Rivers	Quarterback	North Carolina State University (NC)
2004	Bryan Randall	Quarterback	Virginia Tech (Virginia Polytechnic Institute and State University) (VA)
2005	Chris Barclay	Running Back	Wake Forest University (NC)
2006	Calvin Johnson	Wide Receiver	Georgia Tech (Georgia Institute of Technology) (GA)
2007	Matt Ryan	Quarterback	Boston College (MA)
2008	Jonathan Dwyer	Running Back	Georgia Tech (Georgia Institute of Technology) (GA)
2009	C.J. Spiller	Running Back	Clemson University (SC)
2010	Tyrod Taylor	Quarterback	Virginia Tech (Virginia Polytechnic Institute and State University) (VA)

ACC Defensive Player of the Year Award

Voted on by members of the Atlantic Coast Sports Media Association; established in 1993 as a separate award from the ACC Player of the Year Award.

Year	Player	Position	School
1993	Derrick Brooks	Linebacker	Florida State University (FL)
1994	Derrick Alexander	Defensive End	Florida State University (FL)
1995	Marcus Jones	Defensive End	University of North Carolina (NC)
1996	Peter Boulware	Linebacker	Florida State University (FL)
1997	Andre Wadsworth	Defensive End	Florida State University (FL)
1998	Anthony Poindexter	Defensive Back	University of Virginia (VA)
1999	Keith Adams	Linebacker	Clemson University (SC)
2000	Levar Fisher	Linebacker	North Carolina State University (NC)
2001	E.J. Henderson	Linebacker	University of Maryland (MD)
2002	E.J. Henderson	Linebacker	University of Maryland (MD)
2003	Darnell Dockett	Defensive Lineman	Florida State University (FL)
2004	Leroy Hill	Linebacker	Clemson University (SC)
2005	D'Qwell Jackson	Linebacker	University of Maryland (MD)
2006	Gaines Adams	Defensive End	Clemson University (SC)
2007	Chris Long	Defensive Long	University of Virginia (VA)
2008	Mark Herzlich	Linebacker	Boston College (MA)
2009	Derrick Morgan	Defensive End	Georgia Tech (Georgia Institute of Technology) (GA)
2010	Da'Quan Bowers	Defensive Back	Clemson University (SC)

ACC Offensive Rookie of the Year

Voted on by members of the Atlantic Coast Sports Media Association.

Year	Player	Position	School
1975	Ted Brown	Running Back	North Carolina State University (NC)
1976	James McDougald	Running Back	Wake Forest University (NC)
1977	Amos Lawrence	Running Back	University of North Carolina (NC)
1978	Darrell Nicholson	Linebacker	University of North Carolina (NC)
1979	Chuck McSwain	Running Back	Clemson University (SC)
1980	Ben Bennett	Quarterback	Duke University (NC)
1981	Joe McIntosh	Running Back	North Carolina State University (NC)
1982	Michael Ramseur	Running Back	Wake Forest University (NC)

Year	*Player*	*Position*	*School*
1983	Cory Collier	Running Back	Georgia Tech (Georgia Institute of Technology) (GA)
1984	John Ford	Wide Receiver	University of Virginia (VA)
1985	Jerry Mays	Running Back	Georgia Tech (Georgia Institute of Technology) (GA)
1986	Ray Agnew	Defensive Tackle	North Carolina State University (NC)
1987	Terry Allen	Running Back	Clemson University (SC)
1988	Jesse Campbell	Defensive Back	North Carolina State University (NC)
1989	Shawn Jones	Quarterback	Georgia Tech (Georgia Institute of Technology) (GA)
1990	Ronald Williams	Running Back	Clemson University (SC)
1991	Jimy Lincoln	Running Back	Georgia Tech (Georgia Institute of Technology) (GA)
1992	Tamarick Vanover	Wide Receiver	Florida State University (FL)
1993	Leon Johnson	Running Back	University of North Carolina (NC)
1994	Ronde Barber	Cornerback	University of Virginia (VA)
1995	Anthony Simmons	Linebacker	Clemson University (SC)
1996	Dre' Bly	Defensive Back	University of North Carolina (NC)
1997	Travis Minor	Running Back	Florida State University (FL)
1998	Ray Robinson	Running Back	North Carolina State University (NC)
1999	Koren Robinson	Wide Receiver	North Carolina State University (NC)
2000	Philip Rivers	Quarterback	North Carolina State University (NC)
2001	Chris Rix	Quarterback	Florida State University (FL)
2002	T.A. McLendon	Running Back	North Carolina State University (NC)
2003	Reggie Ball	Quarterback	Georgia Tech (Georgia Institute of Technology) (GA)
2004	Calvin Johnson	Wide Receiver	Georgia Tech (Georgia Institute of Technology) (GA)
2005	James Davis	Running Back	Clemson University (SC)
2006	Riley Skinner	Quarterback	Wake Forest University (NC)
2007	Josh Adams	Running Back	Wake Forest University (NC)
2008	Russell Wilson	Quarterback	North Carolina State University (NC)
2009	Ryan Williams	Running Back	Virginia Tech (Virginia Polytechnic Institute and State University) (VA)
2010	Danny O'Brien	Quarterback	University of Maryland (MD)

ACC Defensive Rookie of the Year

Voted on by members of the Atlantic Coast Sports Media Association.

Year	*Player*	*Position*	*School*
2007	Deunta Williams	Defensive Back	University of North Carolina (NC)
2008	Sean Spence	Linebacker	University of Miami (FL)
2009	Luke Kuechly	Linebacker	Boston College (MA)
2010	Xavier Rhodes	Cornerback	Florida State University (FL)

Brian Piccolo Award

One of Wake Forest University's (Winston-Salem, North Carolina) most famous athletes (1961–1964), Brian Piccolo (born: October 31, 1943, in Pittsfield, MA; died: June 16, 1970, in New York City, NY) was an All-American in 1964 after leading the nation in rushing and scoring. After finishing his college career, he played four seasons (1966–1969) in the National Football League for the Chicago Bears before his career came to a premature end after he was diagnosed with cancer in 1970 (made famous in the television movie *Brian's Song*). The Brian Piccolo Award was established that year by the conference's head coaches to honor the ACC's most courageous football player.

Year	*Player*	*Position*	*School*
1970	Paul Miller	Quarterback	University of North Carolina (NC)
1971	Jim Webster	Linebacker	University of North Carolina (NC)
1972	Mark Johnson	Quarterback	Duke University (NC)
1973	Al Neville	Quarterback	University of Maryland (MD)
1974	David Visaggio	Defensive Guard	University of Maryland (MD)
1975	Scott Gardner	Quarterback	University of Virginia (VA)
1976	Jeff Green	Defensive End	Duke University (NC)
1977	Ralph Stringer	Defensive Back	North Carolina State University (NC)

Year	Player	Position	School
1978	Rex Varn	Defensive Back	Clemson University (SC)
1979	No Winner Named		
1980	Jack Cain	Defensive Back	Clemson University (SC)
1981	Aaron Stewart	Defensive Back	Duke University (NC)
1982	Kenny Duckett	Wide Receiver	Wake Forest University (NC)
1983	John Piedmonte	Outside Linebacker	Wake Forest University (NC)
1984	J.D. Maarleveld	Tackle	University of Maryland (MD)
1985	Danny Burmeister	Defensive Back	University of North Carolina (NC)
1986	Ray Williams	Wide Receiver	Clemson University (SC)
1987	No Winner Named		
1988	Jerry Mays	Defensive Lineman	Georgia Tech (Georgia Institute of Technology) (GA)
1989	Michael Anderson	Running Back	University of Maryland (MD)
1990	Marc Mays	Wide Receiver	Duke University (NC)
1991	Scott Adell	Tackle	North Carolina State University (NC)
1992	Dan Footman	Defensive End	Florida State University (FL)
1992	Randy Cuthbert	Running Back	Duke University (NC)
1993	Scott Youmans	Defensive Lineman	Duke University (NC)
1994	Chris Harrison	Tackle	University of Virginia (VA)
1995	Warren Forney	Defensive Tackle	Clemson University (SC)
1996	John Lewis	Running Back	Wake Forest University (NC)
1997	Sam Cowart	Linebacker	Florida State University (FL)
1998	Anthony Poindexter	Defensive Back	University of Virginia (VA)
1998	Corey Simon	Defensive Tackle	Florida State University (FL)
1999	Chris Weinke	Quarterback	Florida State University (FL)
2000	Ed Wilder	Fullback	Georgia Tech (Georgia Institute of Technology) (GA)
2001	Matt Crawford	Tackle	University of Maryland (MD)
2002	Anquan Boldin	Wide Receiver	Florida State University (FL)
2003	Kevin Bailey	Outside Linebacker	University of Virginia (VA)
2004	Frank Gore	Running Back	University of Miami (FL)
2005	Ryan Best	Safety	University of Virginia (VA)
2006	Glenn Sharpe	Cornerback	University of Miami (FL)
2007	Matt Robinson	Defensive End	Wake Forest University (NC)
2008	Robert Quinn	Defensive End	University of North Carolina (NC)
2009	Toney Baker	Running Back	North Carolina State University (NC)
2010	Mark Herzlich	Linebacker	Boston College (MA)
2010	Nate Irving	Linebacker	North Carolina State University (NC)

Jacobs Blocking Trophy

Awarded by several football conferences (including the ACC since 1953), the Jacobs Blocking Trophy is presented to the ACC's best blocker as voted on by the conference's coaches. The Trophy is presented in honor of William Plumer Jacobs (born: March 15, 1842, in Yorkville [now known as York], SC; died: September 10, 1975, in Clinton, SC), founder and president of Presbyterian College (Clinton, South Carolina).

Year	Player	Position	School
1953	Bill Wohrman	Fullback	University of South Carolina (SC)
1954	Bill Wohrman	Fullback	University of South Carolina (SC)
1955	Bob Pellegrini	Center	University of Maryland (MD)
1956	Hal McElhaney	Fullback	Duke University (NC)
1957	Hal McElhaney	Fullback	Duke University (NC)
1958	John Saunders	Fullback	University of South Carolina (SC)
1959	Doug Cline	Fullback	Clemson University (SC)
1960	Dwight Bumgardner	Tackle	Duke University (NC)
1961	Art Gregory	Tackle	Duke University (NC)
1961	Jim LeCompte	Guard	University of North Carolina (NC)
1962	Art Gregory	Tackle	Duke University (NC)
1963	Chuck Walker	Tackle	Duke University (NC)

Year	*Player*	*Position*	*School*
1964	Eddie Kesler	Fullback	University of North Carolina (NC)
1965	John McNabb	Guard	Duke University (NC)
1966	Wayne Mass	Tackle	Clemson University (SC)
1967	Harry Olszewski	Guard	Clemson University (SC)
1968	Greg Shelly	Tackle	University of Virginia (VA)
1969	Ralph Sonntag	Tackle	University of Maryland (MD)
1970	Dan Ryczek	Center	University of Virginia (VA)
1971	Geof Hamlin	Fullback	University of North Carolina (NC)
1972	Ron Rusnak	Guard	University of North Carolina (NC)
1973	Bill Yoest	Guard	North Carolina State University (NC)
1974	Ken Huff	Guard	University of North Carolina (NC)
1975	Billy Bryan	Center	Duke University (NC)
1976	Billy Bryan	Center	Duke University (NC)
1977	Joe Bostic	Guard	Clemson University (SC)
1978	Jim Ritcher	Center	North Carolina State University (NC)
1979	Jim Ritcher	Center	North Carolina State University (NC)
1980	Ron Wooten	Guard	University of North Carolina (NC)
1981	Lee Nanney	Tackle	Clemson University (SC)
1982	Dave Pacella	Tackle	University of Maryland (MD)
1983	James Farr	Guard	Clemson University (SC)
1984	Jim Dombrowski	Tackle	University of Virginia (VA)
1985	Jim Dombrowski	Tackle	University of Virginia (VA)
1986	Paul Kiser	Guard	Wake Forest University (NC)
1987	John Phillips	Guard	Clemson University (SC)
1988	Jeff Garnica	Center	University of North Carolina (NC)
1989	Chris Port	Tackle	Duke University (NC)
1990	Ray Roberts	Tackle	University of Virginia (VA)
1991	Ray Roberts	Tackle	University of Virginia (VA)
1992	Ben Coleman	Tackle	Wake Forest University (NC)
1993	Mark Dixon	Guard	University of Virginia (VA)
1994	Clay Shiver	Center	Florida State University (FL)
1995	Clay Shiver	Center	Florida State University (FL)
1996	No Winner Named		
1997	Tra Thomas	Tackle	Florida State University (FL)
1998	Craig Page	Center	Georgia Tech (Georgia Institute of Technology) (GA)
1999	John St. Clair	Center	University of Virginia (VA)
2000	Tarlos Thomas	Tackle	Florida State University (FL)
2001	Brett Williams	Tackle	Florida State University (FL)
2002	Brett Williams	Tackle	Florida State University (FL)
2003	Elton Brown	Guard	University of Virginia (VA)
2004	Elton Brown	Guard	University of Virginia (VA)
2005	Eric Winston	Tackle	University of Miami (FL)
2006	Josh Beekman	Guard-Center	Boston College (MA)
2007	Steve Justice	Center	Wake Forest University (NC)
2008	Eugene Monroe	Tackle	University of Virginia (VA)
2009	Rodney Hudson	Guard	Florida State University (FL)
2010	Rodney Hudson	Guard	Florida State University (FL)

Big East Conference (Big East)

222 Richmond Street, Suite 110, Providence, RI 02903; Telephone: 401-272-9108; Fax: 401-274-5967; Web site: http://www.bigeast.org

The Big East (now the nation's largest Division I-A Conference as of 2005) was founded in May 1979 when Georgetown University, Providence College, St. John's University, and Syracuse University joined Boston College, Seton Hall University, and the University of Connecticut to form a conference primarily focused on basketball. About 10 years later, the Big East decided to become a football conference and began playing football in 1991.

Eight of the conference's teams play FBS football (Rutgers University, Syracuse University, University of Cincinnati, University of Connecticut, University of Louisville, University of Pittsburgh, University of South Florida, West Virginia University); two of its member schools play football in the FCS (Georgetown University is a football-only associate member of the Patriot League and Villanova University is a football-only associate member of the Colonial Athletic Association); and the University of Notre Dame maintains an independent football program.

As of this writing, the Big East Conference currently consists of the following 16 schools:

- DePaul University Blue Demons, Chicago, IL 60604; 312-362-8300; www.depaul.edu — no footbal program
- Georgetown University Hoyas, Washington D.C. 20057; 202-687-0100; www.georgetown.edu — plays football in the Patriot League (FCS)
- Marquette University Golden Eagles, Milwaukee, WI 53233; 414-288-7250; www.marquette.edu— no football program
- Providence College Friars, Providence RI 02918; 401-865-1000; www.providence.edu — no football program
- Rutgers University Scarlet Knights, New Brunswick, NJ 08901; 732-445-4636; www.rutgers.edu
- St. John's University Red Storm, Queens, NY 11439; 718-990-2000; www.stjohns.edu— no football program
- Seton Hall University Pirates, South Orange, NJ 07079; 973-761-9000; www.shu.com — no football program
- Syracuse University Orange, Syracuse, NY 13210; 315-443-1870; www.syr.edu
- University of Cincinnati Bearcats, Cincinnati OH 45221; 513-556-6000; www.uc.edu
- University of Connecticut Huskies, Storrs, CT 06269; 860-486-2000; www.uconn.edu
- University of Louisville Cardinals, Louisville, KY 40208; 502-852-5555; www.louisville.edu
- University of Notre Dame Fighting Irish, Notre Dame, Indiana 46556; 574-631-5000; www.nd.edu— plays Division I football as an independent school
- University of Pittsburgh Panthers, Pittsburgh, PA 15260; 412-624-4141; www.pitt.edu
- University of South Florida Bulls, Tampa, FL 33620; 813-974-2011; www.usf.edu
- Villanova University Wildcats, Villanova, PA 19085; 610-519-4500; www.villanova.edu — plays football in the Colonial Athletic Association (FCS)
- West Virginia University Mountaineers, Morgantown, WV 26501; 304-293-0111; www.wvu.edu

Big East Conference Champions

Year	*School*
1991	Syracuse University (NY)
1991	University of Miami (FL)
1992	University of Miami (FL)
1993	West Virginia University (WV)
1994	University of Miami (FL)
1995	University of Miami (FL)
1995	Virginia Tech (Virginia Polytechnic Institute and State University) (VA)
1996	Syracuse University (NY)
1996	University of Miami (FL)
1996	Virginia Tech (Virginia Polytechnic Insttute and State University) (VA)
1997	Syracuse University (NY)
1998	Syracuse University (NY)
1999	Virginia Tech (Virginia Polytechnic Institute and State University) (VA)
2000	University of Miami (FL)
2001	University of Miami (FL)
2002	University of Miami (FL)
2003	University of Miami (FL)
2003	West Virginia University (WV)
2004	Boston College (MA)
2004	Syracuse University (NY)
2004	University of Pittsburgh (PA)
2004	West Virginia University (WV)
2005	West Virginia University (WV)
2006	University of Louisville (KY)
2007	West Virginia University (WV)
2007	University of Connecticut (CT)
2008	University of Cincinnati (OH)
2009	University of Cincinnati (OH)
2010	University of Connecticut (CT)

Big East Coach of the Year

Voted on by the conference's head football coaches.

Year	*Coach*	*School*
1991	Dennis Erickson	University of Miami (FL)
1992	Dennis Erickson	University of Miami (FL)
1993	Don Nehlen	West Virginia University (WV)
1994	Dennis Erickson	University of Miami (FL)
1995	Frank Beamer	Virginia Tech University (Virginia Polytechnic Institute and State University) (VA)
1996	Frank Beamer	Virginia Tech University (Virginia Polytechnic Institute and State University) (VA)
1997	Walt Harris	University of Pittsburgh (PA)
1998	Terry Shea	Rutgers State University (NJ)
1999	Frank Beamer	Virginia Tech University (Virginia Polytechnic Institute and State University) (VA)
2000	Butch Davis	University of Miami (FL)
2001	Larry Coker	University of Miami (FL)
2002	Larry Coker	University of Miami (FL)
2003	Rich Rodriguez	West Virginia University (WV)
2004	Walt Harris	University of Pittsburgh (PA)
2005	Rich Rodriguez	West Virginia University (WV)
2006	Greg Schiano	Rutgers State University (NJ)
2007	Brian Kelly	University of Cincinnati (OH)
2008	Brian Kelly	University of Cincinnati (OH)
2009	Brian Kelly	University of Cincinnati (OH)
2010	Randy Edsall	University of Connecticut (CT)
2010	Charlie Strong	University of Louisville (KY)

Big East Offensive Player of the Year

Voted on by the conference's head football coaches.

Year	*Player*	*Position*	*School*	*Class*
1991	Gino Torretta	Quarterback	University of Miami (FL)	Junior
1992	Gino Torretta	Quarterback	University of Miami (FL)	Senior
1993	Glenn Foley	Quarterback	Boston College (MA)	Senior
1994	Billy West	Running Back	University of Pittsburgh (PA)	Sophomore
1995	Marco Battaglia	Tight End	Rutgers State University (NJ)	Senior
1996	Jim Druckenmiller	Quarterback	Virginia Tech University (VA)	Senior
1996	Donovan McNabb	Quarterback	Syracuse University (NY)	Sophomore
1997	Donovan McNabb	Quarterback	Syracuse University (NY)	Junior
1998	Donovan McNabb	Quarterback	Syracuse University (NY)	Senior
1999	Michael Vick	Quarterback	Virginia Tech University (VA)	Freshman
2000	Antonio Bryant	Wide Receiver	University of Pittsburgh (PA)	Sophomore
2000	Lee Suggs	Running Back	Virginia Tech University (VA)	Sophomore
2000	Santana Moss	Wide Receiver	University of Miami (FL)	Senior
2001	William Green	Running Back	Boston College (MA)	Junior
2001	Ken Dorsey	Quarterback	University of Miami (FL)	Junior
2002	Ken Dorsey	Quarterback	University of Miami (FL)	Senior
2002	Willis McGahee	Running Back	University of Miami (FL)	Sophomore
2003	Larry Fitzgerald	Wide Receiver	University of Pittsburgh (PA)	Sophomore
2004	Rasheed Marshall	Quarterback	West Virginia University (WV)	Senior
2005	Brian Brohm	Quarterback	University of Louisville (KY)	Sophomore
2006	Pat White	Quarterback	West Virginia University (WV)	Sophomore
2007	Pat White	Quarterback	West Virginia University (WV)	Junior
2008	Donald Brown	Running Back	University of Connecticut (CT)	Junior
2009	Dion Lewis	Running Back	University of Pittsburgh (PA)	Freshman
2010	Jordan Todman	Running Back	University of Connecticut (CT)	Junior

Big East Defensive Player of the Year

Voted on by the conference's head football coaches.

Year	*Player*	*Position*	*School*	*Class*
1991	Darrin Smith	Linebacker	University of Miami (FL)	Junior
1991	George Rooks	Defensive Tackle	Syracuse University (NY)	Senior
1992	Micheal Barrow	Linebacker	University of Miami (FL)	Senior
1993	Kevin Patrick	Defensive End	University of Miami (FL)	Senior
1994	Warren Sapp	Defensive Lineman	University of Miami (FL)	Junior
1995	Cornell Brown	Defensive End	Virginia Tech University (VA)	Junior
1996	Canute Curtis	Defensive Lineman	West Virginia University (WV)	Senior
1997	Donovin Darius	Safety	Syracuse University (NY)	Senior
1998	Corey Moore	Defensive End	Virginia Tech University (VA)	Junior
1999	Corey Moore	Defensive End	Virginia Tech University (VA)	Senior
2000	Dan Morgan	Linebacker	University of Miami (FL)	Senior
2001	Edward Reed	Strong Safety	University of Miami (FL)	Senior
2001	Dwight Freeney	Defensive End	Syracuse University (NY)	Senior
2002	Dan Klecko	Defensive Lineman	Temple University (PA)	Senior
2003	Sean Taylor	Free Safety	University of Miami (FL)	Junior
2004	Mathias Kiwanuka	Defensive End	Boston College (MA)	Junior
2005	Elvis Dumervil	Defensive End	University of Louisville (KY)	Senior
2006	H.B. Blades	Linebacker	University of Pittsburgh (PA)	Senior
2007	George Selvie	Defensive End	University of South Florida (FL)	Sophomore
2008	Scott McKillop	Linebacker	University of Pittsburgh (PA)	Senior
2009	Greg Romeus	Defensive End	University of Pittsburgh (PA)	Junior
2009	Mick Williams	Defensive Tackle	University of Pittsburgh ({PA)	Senior
2010	Jabaal Sheard	Defensive End	University of Pittsburgh (PA)	Senior

Big East Special Teams Player of the Year

Voted on by the conference's head football coaches.

Year	*Player*	*Position*	*School*	*Class*
1991	Kevin Williams	Return Specialist	University of Miami (FL)	Sophomore
1992	John Biskup	Place Kicker	Syracuse University (NY)	Senior
1993	Pat O'Neill	Punter / Place Kicker	Syracuse University (NY)	Senior
1994	Todd Sauerbrun	Punter	West Virginia University (WV)	Senior
1995	Marvin Harrison	Return Specialist	Syracuse University (NY)	Senior
1996	Tremain Mack	Return Specialist	University of Miami (FL)	Senior
1997	Quinton Spotwood	Kick Returner	Syracuse University (NY)	Sophomore
1998	Kevin Johnson	Kick Returner	Syracuse University (NY)	Senior
1999	Shayne Graham	Place Kicker	Virginia Tech University (VA)	Senior
2000	Santana Moss	Punt Returner	University of Miami (FL)	Senior
2001	Phillip Buchanon	Punt Returner / Kick Returner	University of Miami (FL)	Junior
2002	Andy Lee	Punter	University of Pittsburgh (PA)	Junior
2002	Nate Jones	Kick Returner	Rutgers State University (NJ)	Junior
2003	Andy Lee	Punter	University of Pittsburgh (PA)	Senior
2003	DeAngelo Hall	Punt Returner	Virginia Tech University (VA)	Junior
2004	Adam Jones	Return Specialist	West Virginia University (WV)	Junior
2005	Willie Foster	Return Specialist	Rutgers State University (NJ)	Junior
2006	Ean Randolph	Return Specialist	University of South Florida (FL)	Senior
2007	Kevin Huber	Punter	University of Cincinnati (OH)	Junior
2008	Mardy Gilyard	Wide Receiver	University of Cincinnati (OH)	Junior
2009	Mardy Gilyard	Wide Receiver	University of Cincinnati (OH)	Senior
2010	Lindsey Lamar	Wide Receiver	University of South Florida (FL)	Sophomore

Big East Rookie of the Year

Voted on by the conference's head football coaches.

Year	*Player*	*Position*	*School*
1991	Tom Tumulty	Linebacker	University of Pittsburgh (PA)
1992	Bruce Presley	Running Back	Rutgers State University (NJ)
1993	Terrell Willis	Running Back	Rutgers State University (NJ)
1994	Kenard Lang	Defensive End	University of Miami (FL)
1995	Donovan McNabb	Quarterback	Syracuse University (NY)
1996	Amos Zereoue	Running Back	West Virginia University (WV)
1997	Reggie Wayne	Wide Receiver	University of Miami (FL)
1998	Joaquin Gonzalez	Offensive Tackle	University of Miami (FL)
1999	Michael Vick	Quarterback	Virginia Tech University (VA)
2000	Grant Wiley	Linebacker	West Virginia University (WV)
2001	Kevin Jones	Running Back	Virginia Tech University (VA)
2002	Larry Fitzgerald	Wide Receiver	University of Pittsburgh (PA)
2003	Chris Henry	Wide Receiver	West Virginia University (WV)
2004	Brian Toal	Linebacker	Boston College (MA)
2005	Steve Slaton	Running Back	West Virginia University (WV)
2006	Matt Grothe	Quarterback	University of South Florida (FL)
2007	LeSean McCoy	Running Back	University of Pittsburgh (PA)
2008	Victor Anderson	Running Back	University of Louisville (KY)
2009	Dion Lewis	Running Back	University of Pittsburgh (PA)
2010	Hakeem Smith	Safety	University of Louisville (KY)

Big Ten Conference (Big Ten)

1500 West Higgins Road, Park Ridge, Illinois 60068; Telephone: 847-696-1010; Fax: 847-696-1150; Web site: www.bigten.org

From an initial meeting on January 11, 1895, in Chicago (Illinois), the Big Ten Conference (originally known as the Intercollegiate Conference of Faculty Representatives, the Western Conference, or the Big Nine) is now the oldest football conference in American college football. Originally, the conference included Northwestern University, Purdue University, the University of Chicago, University of Illinois, University of Michigan, University of Minnesota, and the University of Wisconsin. When Indiana University and the University of Iowa joined in 1900, the conference became known as the Big Nine. Later, the conference became known as the Big Ten when the University of Michigan rejoined in 1917.

Although commonly referred to as the Big Ten, the conference was officially known as the Intercollegiate Conference of Faculty Representatives until 1987, when the Big Ten became its official name. When Pennsylvania State University joined in 1990, the conference members decided to retain the name Big Ten, but modified its logo so that the number 11 (representing the number of schools in the conference) can be seen in the white areas of the traditionally blue "Big Ten" lettering.

As of this writing, the Big Ten Conference currently consists of the following 11 schools:

- Indiana University Hoosiers, Bloomington, IN 47405; 812-855-4848; www.indiana.edu
- Michigan State University Spartans, East Lansing, MI 48824; 517-355-1855; www.msu.edu
- Northwestern University Wildcats, Evanston, IL 60208; 847-491-3741; www.northwestern.edu
- Ohio State University Buckeyes, Columbus, Ohio 43210; 614-292-OHIO; www.osu.edu
- Pennsylvania State University Nittany Lions, University Park, PA 16802; 814-865-5471; www.psu.edu
- Purdue University Boilermakers, West Lafayette, IN 47907; 765-494-4600; www.purdue.com
- University of Illinois Fighting Illini, Champaign, IL 61820; 217-333-1000; www.illinois.edu
- University of Iowa Hawkeyes, Iowa City, IA 52242; 319-335-3500; www.uiowa.edu
- University of Michigan Wolverines, Ann Arbor, MI 48109; 734-764-1817; www.umich.edu
- University of Minnesota Golden Gophers, Minneapolis, MN 55455; 612-625-5000; www.umn.edu
- University of Wisconsin Badgers, Madison, WI 53706; 608-263-2400; www.wisc.edu

Big Ten Champions

Year	Team	Coach
1896	University of Wisconsin (WI)	Philip King
1897	University of Wisconsin (WI)	Philip King
1898	University of Michigan (MI)	Gustave Ferbert
1899	University of Chicago (IL)	Amos Alonzo Stagg
1900	University of Iowa (IA)	Alden Knipe
1900	University of Minnesota (MN)	Henry L. Williams
1901	University of Michigan (MI)	Fielding Yost
1901	University of Wisconsin (WI)	Philip King
1902	University of Michigan (MI)	Fielding Yost
1903	Northwestern University (IL)	Walter McCornack
1903	University of Michigan (MI)	Fielding Yost
1903	University of Minnesota (MN)	Henry L. Williams
1904	University of Michigan (MI)	Fielding Yost
1904	University of Minnesota (MN)	Henry L. Willians
1905	University of Chicago (IL)	Amos Alonzo Stagg
1906	University of Michigan (MI)	Fielding Yost
1906	University of Minnesota (MN)	Henry L. Williams
1906	University of Wisconsin (WI)	Charles P. Hutchins
1907	University of Chicago (IL)	Amos Alonzo Stagg
1908	University of Chicago (IL)	Amos Alonzo Stagg
1909	University of Minnesota (MN)	Henry L. Williams
1910	University of Illinois (IL)	Arthur Hall
1910	University of Minnesota (MN)	Henry L. Williams
1911	University of Minnesota (MN)	Henry L. Williams
1912	University of Wisconsin (WI)	William Juneau
1913	University of Chicago (IL)	Amos Alonzo Stagg
1914	University of Illinois (IL)	Robert Zuppke
1915	University of Illinois (IL)	Robert Zuppke
1915	University of Minnesota (MN)	Henry L. Williams
1916	Ohio State University (OH)	John Wilce
1917	Ohio State University (OH)	John Wilce
1918	Purdue University (IN)	A. G. Scanlon
1918	University of Illinois (IL)	Robert Zuppke
1918	University of Michigan (MI)	Fielding Yost
1919	University of Illinois (IL)	Robert Zuppke
1920	Ohio State University (OH)	John Wilce
1921	University of Iowa (IA)	Howard Jones
1922	University of Chicago (IL)	Amos Alonzo Stagg
1922	University of Iowa (IA)	Howard Jones
1922	University of Michigan (MI)	Fielding Yost
1923	University of Illinois (IL)	Robert Zuppke
1923	University of Michigan (MI)	Fielding Yost
1924	University of Chicago (IL)	Amos Alonzo Stagg
1925	University of Michigan (MI)	Fielding Yost
1926	Northwestern University (IL)	Glenn Thistlethwaite
1926	University of Michigan (MI)	Fielding Yost
1927	University of Illinois (IL)	Robert Zuppke
1927	University of Minnesota (MN)	Clarence Spears
1928	University of Illinois (IL)	Robert Zuppke
1929	Purdue University (IN)	James Phelan
1930	Northwestern University (IL)	Dick Hanley
1930	University of Michigan (MI)	Harry G. Kipke
1931	Northwestern University (IL)	Dick Hanley
1931	Purdue University (IN)	Noble Kizer
1931	University of Michigan (MI)	Harry G. Kipke
1932	Purdue University (IN)	Noble Kizer

Year	*Team*	*Coach*
1932	University of Michigan (MI)	Harry G. Kipke
1933	University of Michigan (MI)	Harry G. Kipke
1933	University of Minnesota (MN)	Bernie Bierman
1934	University of Minnesota (MN)	Bernie Bierman
1935	Ohio State University (OH)	Francis Schmidt
1935	University of Minnesota (MN)	Bernie Bierman
1936	Northwestern University (IL)	Pappy Waldorf
1937	University of Minnesota (MN)	Bernie Bierman
1938	University of Minnesota (MN)	Bernie Bierman
1939	Ohio State University (OH)	Francis Schmidt
1940	University of Minnesota (MN)	Bernie Bierman
1941	University of Minnesota (MN)	Bernie Bierman
1942	Ohio State University (OH)	Paul Brown
1943	Purdue University (IN)	Elmer Burnham
1943	University of Michigan (MI)	Fritz Crisler
1944	Ohio State University (OH)	Carroll Widdoes
1945	Indiana University (IN)	Bo McMillin
1946	University of Illinois (IL)	Ray Eliot
1947	University of Michigan (MI)	Fritz Crisler
1948	University of Michigan (MI)	Bennie Oosterbaan
1949	Ohio State University (OH)	Wes Fesler
1949	University of Michigan (MI)	Bennie Oosterbaan
1950	University of Michigan (MI)	Bennie Oosterbaan
1951	University of Illinois (IL)	Ray Eliot
1952	Purdue University (IN)	Stu Holcomb
1952	University of Wisconsin (WI)	Ivy Williamson
1953	Michigan State University (MI)	Clarence Munn
1953	University of Illinois (IL)	Ray Eliot
1954	Ohio State University (OH)	Woody Hayes
1955	Ohio State University (OH)	Woody Hayes
1956	University of Iowa (IA)	Forest Evashevski
1957	Ohio State University (OH)	Woody Hayes
1958	University of Iowa (IA)	Forest Evashevski
1959	University of Wisconsin (WI)	Milt Bruhn
1960	University of Iowa (IA)	Forest Evashevski
1960	University of Minnesota (MN)	Murray Warmath
1961	Ohio State University (OH)	Woody Hayes
1962	University of Wisconsin (WI)	Milt Bruhn
1963	University of Illinois (IL)	Pete Elliott
1964	University of Michigan (MI)	Bump Elliott
1965	Michigan State University (MI)	Duffy Daugherty
1966	Michigan State University (MI)	Duffy Daugherty
1967	Indiana University (IN)	John Pont
1967	Purdue University (IN)	Jack Mollenkopf
1967	University of Minnesota (MN)	Murray Warmath
1968	Ohio State University (OH)	Woody Hayes
1969	Ohio State University (OH)	Woody Hayes
1969	University of Michigan (MI)	Bo Schembechler
1970	Ohio State University (OH)	Woody Hayes
1971	University of Michigan (MI)	Bo Schembechler
1972	Ohio State University (OH)	Woody Hayes
1972	University of Michigan (MI)	Bo Schembechler
1973	Ohio State University (OH)	Woody Hayes
1973	University of Michigan (MI)	Bo Schembechler
1974	Ohio State University (OH)	Woody Hayes
1974	University of Michigan (MI)	Bo Schembechler
1975	Ohio State University (OH)	Woody Hayes

Year	*Team*	*Coach*
1976	Ohio State University (OH)	Woody Hayes
1976	University of Michigan (MI)	Bo Schembechler
1977	Ohio State University (OH)	Bo Schembechler
1977	University of Michigan (MI)	Bo Schembechler
1978	Michigan State University (MI)	Darryl Rogers
1978	University of Michigan (MI)	Bo Schembechler
1979	Ohio State University (OH)	Earle Bruce
1980	University of Michigan (MI)	Bo Schembechler
1981	Ohio State University (OH)	Earle Bruce
1981	University of Iowa (IA)	Hayden Fry
1982	University of Michigan (MI)	Bo Schembechler
1983	University of Illinois (IL)	Mike White
1984	Ohio State University (OH)	Earle Bruce
1985	University of Iowa (IA)	Hayden Fry
1986	Ohio State University (OH)	Earle Bruce
1986	University of Michigan (MI)	Bo Schembechler
1987	Michigan State University (MI)	George Perles
1988	University of Michigan (MI)	Bo Schembechler
1989	University of Michigan (MI)	Bo Schembechler
1990	Michigan State University (MI)	George Perles
1990	University of Illinois (IL)	John Mackovic
1990	University of Iowa (IA)	Hayden Fry
1990	University of Michigan (MI)	Gary Moeller
1991	University of Michigan (MI)	Gary Moeller
1992	University of Michigan (MI)	Gary Moeller
1993	Ohio State University (OH)	John Cooper
1993	University of Wisconsin (WI)	Barry Alvarez
1994	Pennsylvania State University (PA)	Joe Paterno
1995	Northwestern University (IL)	Gary Barnett
1996	Northwestern University (IL)	Gary Barnett
1996	Ohio State University (OH)	John Cooper
1997	University of Michigan (MI)	Lloyd Carr
1998	Ohio State University (OH)	John Cooper
1998	University of Michigan (MI)	Lloyd Carr
1998	University of Wisconsin (WI)	Barry Alvarez
1999	University of Wisconsin (WI)	Barry Alvarez
2000	Northwestern University (IL)	Randy Walker
2000	Purdue University (IN)	Joe Tiller
2000	University of Michigan (MI)	Lloyd Carr
2001	University of Illinois (IL)	Ron Turner
2002	Ohio State University (OH)	Jim Tressel
2002	University of Iowa (IA)	Kirk Ferentz
2003	University of Michigan (MI)	Lloyd Carr
2004	University of Iowa (IA)	Kirk Ferentz
2004	University of Michigan (MI)	Lloyd Carr
2005	Ohio State University (OH)	Jim Tressel
2005	Pennsylvania State University (PA)	Joe Paterno
2006	Ohio State University (OH)	Jim Tressel
2007	Ohio State University (OH)	Jim Tressel
2008	Ohio State University (OH)	Jim Tressel
2008	Pennsylvania State University (PA)	Joe Paterno
2009	Ohio State University (OH)	Jim Tressel

Big Ten Coach of the Year

Year	*Coach*	*School*
1982	Bo Schembechler	University of Michigan (MI)
1983	Mike White	University of Illinois (IL)
1984	Leon Burtnett	Purdue University (IN)
1985	Bo Schembechler	University of Michigan (MI)
1986	Bill Mallory	Indiana University (IN)
1987	George Perles	Michigan State University (MI)
1988	John Mackovic	University of Illinois (IL)
1989	Bo Schembechler	University of Michigan (MI)
1990	Hayden Fry	University of Iowa (IA)
1991	Hayden Fry	University of Iowa (IA)

Big Ten Dave McClain Coach of the Year

With the honoree selected by media representatives, this award has been presented since 1972, and beginning in 1986, has been dedicated in honor of Dave McClain (born: 1938 in Upper Sandusky, OH; died: April 28, 1986, in Madison, WI), who served as the University of Wisconsin head coach from 1978 to 1985. From 1982 until 1991, the coaches voted (in addition to the media) for the winner of this award.

Year	*Coach*	*School*
1972	Bo Schembechler	University of Michigan (MI)
1973	Woody Hayes	Ohio State University (OH)
1974	Denny Stolz	Michigan State University (MI)
1975	Woody Hayes	Ohio State University (OH)
1976	Bo Schembechler	University of Michigan (MI)
1977	Darryl Rogers	Michigan State University (MI)
1978	Jim Young	Purdue University (IN)
1979	Earle Bruce	Ohio State University (OH)
1980	Bo Schembechler	University of Michigan (MI)
1981	Hayden Fry	University of Iowa (IA)
1982	Dennis Green	Northwestern University (IL) (media)
1982	Bo Schembechler	University of Michigan (MI) (coaches)
1983	Mike White	University of Illinois (IL) (media and coaches)
1984	Leon Burtnett	Purdue University (IN) (media and coaches)
1985	Bo Schembechler	University of Michigan (MI) (media and coaches)
1986	Bill Mallory	Indiana University (IN) (media and coaches)
1987	Bill Mallory	Indiana University (IN) (media)
1987	George Perles	Michigan State University (MI) (coaches)
1988	John Mackovic	University of Illinois (IL) (media and coaches)
1989	John Mackovic	University of Illinois (IL) (media)
1989	Bo Schembechler	University of Michigan (MI) (coaches)
1990	Hayden Fry	University of Iowa (IA) (media and coaches)
1991	Hayden Fry	University of Iowa (IA) (coaches)
1991	Gary Moeller	University of Michigan (MI) (media)
1992	Gary Moeller	University of Michigan (MI)
1993	Barry Alvarez	University of Wisconsin (WI)
1994	Joe Paterno	Pennsylvania State University (PA)
1995	Gary Barnett	Northwestern University (IL)
1996	Gary Barnett	Northwestern University (IL)
1997	Joe Tiller	Purdue University (IN)
1998	Barry Alvarez	University of Wisconsin (WI)
1999	Glen Mason	University of Minnesota (MN)
2000	Randy Walker	Northwestern University (IL)
2001	Ron Turner	University of Illinois (IL)
2002	Kirk Ferentz	University of Iowa (IA)

Year	Coach	School
2003	John L. Smith	Michigan State University (MI)
2004	Kirk Ferentz	University of Iowa (IA)
2005	Joe Paterno	Pennsylvania State University (PA)
2006	Bret Bielema	University of Wisconsin (WI)
2007	Ron Zook	University of Illinois (IL)
2008	Joe Paterno	Pennsylvania State University (PA)
2009	Kirk Ferentz	University of Iowa (IA)
2010	Mark Dantonio	Michigan State University (MI)

Chicago Tribune Silver Football (Chicago Tribune Big Ten Most Valuable Player)

The Chicago Tribune Silver Football is awarded by the *Chicago Tribune* newspaper (Chicago, IL) to the college football player determined to be the Most Valuable Player of the Big Ten Conference. The award has been presented annually since 1924, when Red Grange of the University of Illinois was its first recipient. The winner of the Silver Football is determined by a vote of Big Ten coaches, the Big Ten Conference headquarters office, and the *Chicago Tribune* staff. Each school of the Big Ten submits the MVP from its team and members elect the award's winner from this list.

Year	Player	School	Note
1924	Harold "Red" Grange	University of Illinois (IL)	1951 College Football HOF Inductee
1925	Tim Lowry	Northwestern University (IL)	School's First All-American
1926	Benny Friedman	University of Michigan (MI)	1951 College Football HOF Inductee
1927	Ken Rouse	University of Chicago (IL)	One of Only Two School Players to Win MVP
1928	Chuck Bennett	Indiana University (IN)	Played Two NFL Seasons
1929	Bill Glassgow	Iowa University (IA)	Played Two NFL Seasons
1930	Wes Fesler	Ohio State University (OH)	1954 College Football HOF Inductee
1931	Clarence Munn	University of Minnesota (MN)	Longtime Michigan State Univ Coach
1932	Harry Newman	University of Michigan (MI)	1975 College Hall of Fame Inductee
1933	Joe Laws	University of Iowa (IA)	Green Bay Packers HOF Inductee
1934	Pug Lund	University of Minnesota (MN)	1958 College Football HOF Inductee
1935	Jay Berwanger	University of Chicago (IL)	1954 College Football HOF Inductee
1936	Vernon Huffman	Indiana University (IN)	1974 Indiana Football HOF Inductee
1937	Corbett Davis	University of Indiana (IN)	1938 #1 NFL Draft Pick—Cleveland
1938	Howard Weiss	University Wisconsin (WI)	1937 & 1938 School MVP
1939	Nile Kinnick	University of Iowa (IA)	1951 College Football HOF Inductee
1940	Tom Harmon	University of Michigan (MI)	1940 Heisman Trophy Winner
1941	Jack Graf	Ohio State University (OH)	1988 Ohio State Varsity O HOF
1942	Dave Schreiner	University of Wisconsin (WI)	1955 College Football HOF Inductee
1943	Otto Graham	Northwestern University (IL)	1956 College Football HOF Inductee
1944	Les Horvath	Ohio State University (OH)	1944 Heisman Trophy Winner
1945	Ollie Cline	Ohio State University (OH)	2000 Ohio State Varsity O HOF
1946	Alex Agase	University of Illinois (IL)	1963 College Football HOF Inductee
1947	Chalmers Elliott	University of Michigan (MI)	1989 College Football HOF Inductee
1948	Art Murakowski	Northwestern University (IL)	Played One Season in the NFL
1949	Red Wilson	University of Wisconsin (WI)	Played 10 Major League Baseball Seasons
1950	Vic Janowicz	Ohio State University (OH)	1976 College Football HOF Inductee
1951	Bill Reichardt	University of Iowa (IA)	1952 All-American
1952	Paul Giel	University of Minnesota (MN)	1975 College Football HOF Inductee
1953	Paul Giel	University of Minnesota (MN)	1953 UPI Player of the Year
1954	Alan Ameche	University of Wisconsin (WI)	1954 Heisman Trophy Winner
1955	Howard Cassady	Ohio State University (OH)	1955 Heisman Trophy Winner
1956	Ken Ploen	University of Iowa (IA)	Won the 1957 Rose Bowl Game
1957	Jim Pace	University of Michigan (MI)	1957 Team Most Valuable Player
1958	Randy Duncan	University of Iowa (IA)	1997 College Football HOF Inductee
1959	Bill Burrell	University of Illinois (IL)	1959 All-American
1960	Tom Brown	University of Minnesota (MN)	2003 College Football HOF Inductee

Year	*Player*	*School*	*Note*
1961	Sandy Stephens	University of Minnesota (MN)	First Black QB in School History
1962	Ron VanderKelen	University of Wisconsin (WI)	1963 Rose Bowl Most Valuable Player
1963	Dick Butkus	University of Illinois (IL)	1983 College Football HOF Inductee
1964	Bob Timberlake	University of Michigan (MI)	Won the 1965 Rose Bowl Game
1965	Jim Grabowski	University of Illinois (IL)	1995 College Football HOF Inductee
1966	Bob Griese	Purdue University (IN)	1984 College Football HOF Inductee
1967	Leroy Keyes	Purdue University (IN)	1st in School History to Rush for 1,000 Yards
1968	Ron Johnson	University of Michigan (MI)	1992 College Football HOF Inductee
1969	Mike Phipps	Purdue University (IN)	2006 College Football HOF Inductee
1970	Mike Adamle	Northwestern University (IL)	1970 All-American
1971	Eric Allen	Michigan State University (MI)	1972 Co-Captain
1972	Otis Armstrong	Purdue University (IN)	First Round NFL Draft Pick — Denver
1973	Archie Griffin	Ohio State University (OH)	1st Player to Start in Four Rose Bowl Games
1974	Archie Griffin	Ohio State University (OH)	2-Time Heisman Trophy Winner (1974/1975)
1975	Cornelius Greene	Ohio State University (OH)	1st Black Starting QB at Ohio State
1976	Rob Lytle	University of Michigan (MI)	1976 All-American
1977	Larry Bethea	Michigan State University (MI)	1st Round NFL Draft Pick — Dallas
1978	Rick Leach	University of Michigan (MI)	2008 Michigan Sports HOF Inductee
1979	Tim Clifford	Indiana University (IN)	1979 & 1980 School Most Valuable Player
1980	Mark Herrmann	Purdue University (IN)	1980 First-Team All-American
1981	Art Schlichter	Ohio State University (OH)	Last Starting QB for Legendary Woody Hayes
1982	Anthony Carter	University of Michigan (MI)	2001 College Football HOF Inductee
1983	Don Thorp	University of Illinois (IL)	Played Four NFL Seasons
1984	Keith Byars	Ohio State University (OH)	1st Round NFL Draft — Philadelphia
1985	Chuck Long	University of Iowa (IA)	1999 College Football HOF Inductee
1986	Jim Harbaugh	University of Michigan (MI)	Won the 1986 Fiesta Bowl
1987	Lorenzo White	Michigan State University (MI)	1st Big 10 RB to Accumulate 2,000 Yards
1988	Anthony Thompson	Indiana University (IN)	2007 College Football HOF Inductee
1989	Anthony Thompson	Indiana University (IN)	1989 Maxwell and Walter Camp Award Winner
1990	Nick Bell	University of Iowa (IA)	Played Three NFL Seasons
1991	Desmond Howard	University of Michigan (MI)	1991 Heisman Trophy Winner
1992	Lee Gissendaner	Northwestern University (IL)	Named to Big Ten's 100-Year Anniversary Team
1993	Brent Moss	University of Wisconsin (WI)	Won the 1994 Rose Bowl
1994	Kerry Collins	Pennsylvania State University (PA)	1994 College Quarterback of the Year
1995	Eddie George	Ohio State University (OH)	1995 Heisman Trophy Winner
1996	Orlando Pace	Ohio State University (OH)	1996 Outland Trophy Winner
1997	Charles Woodson	University of Michigan (MI)	1997 Heisman Trophy Winner
1998	Joe Germaine	Ohio State University (OH)	Helped Win the 1997 Rose Bowl Game
1999	Ron Dayne	University of Wisconsin (WI)	1999 Heisman Trophy Winner
2000	Drew Brees	Purdue University (IN)	2000 Maxwell Award Winner
2001	Antwaan Randle El	Indiana University (IN)	1st to Record 2,500 Yards Four Straight Seasons
2002	Brad Banks	University of Iowa (IA)	Won 2002 Davey O'Brien Award
2003	Chris Perry	University of Michigan (MI)	2003 Jim Brown Trophy Winner
2004	Braylon Edwards	University of Michigan (MI)	2004 Fred Biletnikoff Award Winner
2005	Michael Robinson	Pennsylvania State University (PA)	Won the 2005 Big Ten Conference
2006	Troy Smith	Ohio State University (OH)	2006 Heisman Trophy Winner
2007	Rashard Mendenhall	University of Illinois (IL)	2007 Big 10 Offensive Player of the Year
2008	Shonn Greene	University of Iowa (IA)	School Record 20 Rushing TDs in 2008
2009	Daryll Clark	Pennsylvania State University (PA)	2X All–Big Ten
2009	Brandon Graham	University of Michigan (MI)	2010 Senior Bowl MVP
2010	Denard Robinson	University of Michigan (MI)	Big Ten Rushing Leader

Big Ten Player of the Year Award

This Award has been presented since 1982; originally voted on by the Associated Press and United Press International; now voted on by selected media representatives and conference coaches; in 1990, this award was divided into the Big Ten Offensive Player of the Year Award and the Big Ten Defensive Player of the Year Award)

Year	*Player*	*Position*	*School*
1982	Anthony Carter	Wide Receiver	University of Michigan (MI)
1983	Don Thorp	Defensive Tackle	University of Illinois (IL)
1984	Keith Byars	Tail Back	Ohio State University (OH)
1985	Chuck Long	Quarterback	University of Iowa (IA)
1985	Lorenzo White	Tail Back	Michigan State University (MI)
1986	Jim Harbaugh	Quarterback	University of Michigan (MI)
1987	Lorenzo White	Tail Back	Michigan State University (MI)
1987	Ernie Jones	Wide Receiver	Indiana University (IN)
1988	Anthony Thompson	Tail Back	Indiana University (IN)
1989	Anthony Thompson	Tail Back	Indiana University (IN)

Big Ten Offensive Player of the Year Award

The Big Ten Player of the Year Award has been presented since 1982; originally voted on by the Associated Press and United Press International; now voted on by selected media representatives and conference coaches; in 1990, this award was divided into the Big Ten Offensive Player of the Year Award and the Big Ten Defensive Player of the Year Award)

Year	*Player*	*Position*	*School*
1990	Nick Bell	Running Back	University of Iowa (IA) (coaches)
1990	Matt Rodgers	Quarterback	University of Iowa (IA) (coaches)
1990	Jon Vaughn	Tail Back	University of Michigan (MI) (coaches)
1990	Tico Duckett	Running Back	Michigan State University (MI) (media)
1991	Desmond Howard	Wide Receiver	University of Michigan (MI) (coaches and media)
1992	Tyrone Wheatley	Running Back	University of Michigan (MI) (coaches and media)
1993	Brent Moss	Running Back	University of Wisconsin (WI) (coaches and media)
1994	Kerry Collins	Quarterback	Pennsylvania State University (PA) (coaches and media)
1995	Eddie George	Running Back	Ohio State University (OH) (coaches and media)
1996	Orlando Pace	Offensive Tackle	Ohio State University (OH) (coaches and media)
1997	Curtis Enis	Running Back	Pennsylvania State University (PA) (coaches)
1997	Tavian Banks	Running Back	University of Iowa (IA) (media)
1998	Joe Germaine	Quarterback	Ohio State University (OH) (coaches)
1998	Drew Brees	Quarterback	Purdue University (IN) (media)
1999	Ron Dayne	Running Back	University of Wisconsin (WI) (coaches and media)
2000	Drew Brees	Quarterback	Purdue University (IN) (coaches and media)
2001	Antwaan Randle El	Quarterback	Indiana University (IN) (coaches and media)
2002	Brad Banks	Quarterback	University of Iowa (IA) (coaches and media)
2003	Chris Perry	Running Back	University of Michigan (MI) (coaches and media)
2004	Braylon Edwards	Wide Receiver	University of Michigan (MI) (coaches and media)
2005	Michael Robinson	Quarterback	Pennsylvania State University (PA) (coaches)
2005	Brett Basanez	Quarterback	Northwestern University (IL) (media)
2006	Troy Smith	Quarterback	Ohio State University (OH) (coaches and media)
2007	Rashard Mendenhall	Running Back	University of Illinois (IL) (coaches and media)
2008	Shonn Greene	Running Back	University of Iowa (IA) (coaches and media)
2009	John Clay	Running Back	University of Wisconsin (WI) (coaches and media)
2010	Denard Robinson	Quarterback	University of Michigan (MI) (coaches and media)

Big Ten Defensive Player of the Year Award

The Big Ten Player of the Year Award has been presented since 1982; originally voted on by the Associated Press and United Press International; now voted on by selected media representatives and conference coaches; in 1990, this award was divided into the Big Ten Offensive Player of the Year Award and the Big Ten Defensive Player of the Year Award.

Year	*Player*	*Position*	*School*
1990	Moe Gardner	Nose Tackle	University of Illinois (IL) (coaches)
1990	Darrick Brownlow	Linebacker	University of Illinois (IL) (media)
1991	Leroy Smith	Defensive End	University of Iowa (IA) (coaches)
1991	Troy Vincent	Corner Back	University of Wisconsin (WI) (media)
1992	Steve Tovar	Linebacker	Ohio State University (OH) (coaches)
1992	Jeff Zgonina	Defensive Tackle	Purdue University (IN) (media)
1993	Dana Howard	Linebacker	University of Illinois (IL) (coaches and media)
1993	Dan Wilkinson	Defensive Tackle	Ohio State University (OH) (media)
1994	Dana Howard	Linebacker	University of Illinois (IL) (coaches and media)
1995	Pat Fitzgerald	Linebacker	Northwestern University (IL) (coaches and media)
1996	Shawn Springs	Corner Back	Ohio State University (OH) (coaches)
1996	Pat Fitzgerald	Linebacker	Northwestern University (IL) (media)
1997	Charles Woodson	Corner Back	University of Michigan (MI) (coaches and media)
1998	LaVar Arrington	Linebacker	Pennsylvania State University (PA) (coaches)
1998	Tom Burke	Defensive Lineman	University of Wisconsin (WI) (media)
1999	Courtney Brown	Defensive Lineman	Pennsylvania State University (PA) (coaches and media)
2000	Jamar Fletcher	Defensive Back	University of Wisconsin (WI) (coaches and media)
2001	Larry Foote	Linebacker	University of Michigan (MI) (coaches and media)
2002	Mike Doss	Defensive Back	Ohio State University (OH) (coaches)
2002	Michael Haynes	Defensive Lineman	Pennsylvania State University (PA) (media)
2003	Will Smith	Defensive End	Ohio State University (OH) (coaches and media)
2004	Erasmus James	Defensive Lineman	University of Wisconsin (WI) (coaches and media)
2005	A.J. Hawk	Linebacker	Ohio State University (OH) (coaches and media)
2006	LaMarr Woodley	Defensive End	University of Michigan (MI) (coaches and media)
2007	James Laurinaitis	Linebacker	Ohio State University (OH) (coaches and media)
2008	James Laurinaitis	Linebacker	Ohio State University (OH) (coaches and media)
2009	Jared Odrick	Defensive Tackle	Pennsylvania State University (PA) (coaches)
2009	Greg Jones	Linebacker	University of Michigan State (MI) (media)
2010	Ryan Kerrigan	Defensive End	Purdue University (IN) (coaches and media)

Big Ten Offensive Lineman of the Year Award

Beginning in 1984, this award was voted on by radio broadcasters until 1991, when conference coaches began voting on award winners.

Year	*Player*	*Position*	*School*
1984	Jeff Dellenbach	Guard	University of Wisconsin (WI)
1985	Mike Haight	Tackle	University of Iowa (IA)
1986	Dave Croston	Guard	University of Iowa (IA)
1987	Tony Mandarich	Tackle	Michigan State University (MI)
1988	Tony Mandarich	Tackle	Michigan State University (MI)
1989	Bob Kula	Tackle	Michigan State University (MI)
1990	No Award Given		
1991	Greg Skrepenak	Tackle	University of Michigan (MI)
1992	Mike Devlin	Center	University of Iowa (IA)
1993	Korey Stringer	Tackle	Ohio State University (OH)
1994	Korey Stringer	Tackle	Ohio State University (OH)
1995	Orlando Pace	Tackle	Ohio State University (OH)
1996	Orlando Pace	Tackle	Ohio State University (OH)
1997	Flozell Adams	Tackle	Michigan State University (MI)
1998	Jon Jansen	Tackle	University of Michigan (MI)
1999	Chris McIntosh	Tackle	University of Wisconsin (WI)
2000	Steve Hutchinson	Guard	University of Michigan (MI)
2001	LeCharles Bentley	Center	Ohio State University (OH)
2002	Eric Steinbach	Offensive Lineman	University of Iowa (IA)

Year	Player	Position	School
2003	Robert Gallery	Tackle	University of Iowa (IA)
2004	David Baas	Center	University of Michigan (MI)
2005	Greg Eslinger	Center	University of Minnesota (MN)
2006	Jake Long	Tackle	University of Michigan (MI)
2007	Jake Long	Tackle	University of Michigan (MI)
2008	A. Q. Shipley	Center	Pennsylvania State University (PA)
2009	Bryan Bulaga	Tackle	University of Iowa (IA)
2010	Gabe Carimi	Tackle	University of Wisconsin (WI)

Big Ten Defensive Lineman of the Year Award

Beginning in 1984, this award was voted on by radio broadcasters until 1991, when coaches began voting on award winners.

Year	Player	Position	School
1984	Paul Hufford	Tackle	University of Iowa (IA)
1985	Mike Hammerstein	Tackle	University of Michigan (MI)
1986	Eric Kumerow	Outside Linebacker	Ohio State University (OH)
1987	Dave Haight	Nose Guard	University of Iowa (IA)
1988	Mark Messner	Tackle	University of Michigan (MI)
1989	Moe Gardner	Nose Tackle	University of Illinois (IL)
1990	No Award Given		
1991	Leroy Smith	Defensive End	University of Iowa (IA)
1992	Chris Hutchinson	Defensive Lineman	University of Michigan (MI)
1993	Dan Wilkinson	Tackle	Ohio State University (OH)
1994	Simeon Rice	Defensive End	University of Illinois (IL)
1995	Mike Vrabel	Defensive End	Ohio State University (OH)
1996	Mike Vrabel	Defensive End	Ohio State University (OH)
1997	Jared DeVries	Defensive Lineman	University of Iowa (IA)
1998	Tom Burke	Defensive Lineman	University of Wisconsin (WI)
1999	Courtney Brown	Defensive End	Pennsylvania State University (PA)
2000	Wendell Bryant	Defensive Lineman	University of Wisconsin (WI)
2000	Karon Riley	Defensive End	University of Minnesota (MN)
2001	Wendell Bryant	Defensive Lineman	University of Wisconsin (WI)
2002	Jimmy Kennedy	Defensive Tackle	Pennsylvania State University (PA)
2003	Will Smith	Defensive End	Ohio State University (OH)
2004	Erasmus James	Defensive End	University of Wisconsin (WI)
2005	Tamba Hali	Defensive End	Pennsylvania State University (PA)
2006	LaMarr Woodley	Defensive End	University of Michigan (MI)
2007	Vernon Gholston	Defensive End	Ohio State University (OH)
2008	Mitch King	Defensive Tackle	University of Iowa (IA)
2009	Jared Odrick	Defensive Tackle	Pennsylvania State University (PA)
2010	Ryan Kerrigan	Defensive End	Purdue University (IN)

Big Ten Freshman of the Year Award

Winners of the award are selected by conference coaches and media representatives.

Year	Player	Position	School
1986	Darrell Thompson	Running Back	University of Minnesota (MN) (coaches)
1987	Tony Lowery	Quarterback	University of Wisconsin (WI) (coaches)
1988	Brian Fox	Quarterback	Purdue University (IN) (coaches)
1988	Ed Sutter	Linebacker	Northwestern University (IL) (media)
1989	Eric Hunter	Quarterback	Purdue University (IN) (coaches and media)
1990	Robert Smith	Running Back	Ohio State University (OH) (coaches and media)
1991	Corey Rogers	Running Back	Purdue University (IN) (coaches and media)
1992	Korey Stringer	Offensive Tackle	Ohio State University (OH) (coaches)
1992	Simeon Rice	Defensive Lineman	University of Illinois (IL) (media)
1993	Reggie Garnett	Middle Linebacker	Michigan State University (MI) (coaches and media)

Year	Player	Position	School
1994	Orlando Pace	Offensive Tackle	Ohio State University (OH) (coaches and media)
1995	Charles Woodson	Defensive Back	University of Michigan (MI) (coaches)
1995	Curtis Enis	Running Back	Pennsylvania State University (PA) (media)
1996	Andy Katzenmoyer	Linebacker	Ohio State University (OH) (coaches and media)
1996	Ron Dayne	Running Back	University of Wisconsin (WI) (coaches)
1997	Anthony Thomas	Running Back	University of Michigan (MI) (coaches and media)
1998	Antwaan Randle El	Quarterback	Indiana University (IN) (coaches and media)
1999	Brooks Bollinger	Quarterback	University of Wisconsin (WI) (coaches and media)
2000	Stuart Schweigert	Defensive Back	Purdue University (IN) (coaches and media)
2001	Anthony Davis	Running Back	University of Wisconsin (WI) (coaches and media)
2002	Maurice Clarett	Running Back	Ohio State University (OH) (coaches and media)
2003	Laurence Maroney	Running Back	University of Minnesota (MN) (coaches and media)
2003	Steve Breaston	Wide Receiver	University of Michigan (MI) (coaches)
2004	Mike Hart	Running Back	University of Michigan (MI) (coaches and media)
2005	Tyrell Sutton	Running Back	Northwestern University (IL) (coaches and media)
2006	P. J. Hill	Running Back	University of Wisconsin (WI) (coaches and media)
2007	Arrelious Benn	Wide Receiver	University of Illinois (IL) (coaches and media)
2008	Terrelle Pryor	Quarterback	Ohio State University (OH) (coaches and media)
2009	Chris Borland	Linebacker	University of Wisconsin (WI) (coaches and media)
2010	James White	Running Back	University of Wisconsin (WI) (coaches and media)

Within various Big Ten football programs, there have developed several rivalries and the winner of these annual "rivalry games" claim assorted trophies, each of which travel to the winning school.

- Floyd of Rosedale Trophy (University of Iowa–University of Minnesota)
- Governor's Victory Bell (University of Minnesota–Pennsylvania State University)
- Heartland Trophy (University of Iowa–University of Wisconsin)
- Illibuck (University of Illinois–Ohio State University)
- Land Grant Trophy (Michigan State University–Pennsylvania State University)
- Little Brown Jug (University of Michigan–University of Minnesota)
- Old Brass Spittoon (Indiana University–Michigan State University)
- Old Oaken Bucket (Indiana University–Purdue University)
- Paul Bunyan Trophy (University of Michigan–Michigan State University)
- Purdue Cannon (University of Illinois–Purdue University)
- Slab of Bacon / Paul Bunyan's Axe (University of Minnesota–University of Wisconsin)
- Sweet Sioux Tomahawk / Land of Lincoln Trophy (University of Illinois–Northwestern University)

Big 12 Conference (Big 12)

400 East John Carpenter Freeway, Irving, Texas 75062; Telephone: 469-524-1000; Fax: 469-524-1045; Web site: http://www.big12sports.com

The Big 12 Conference was officially formed on February 25, 1994, when the former Big Eight Conference (eight teams) joined with four Texas schools that had been members of the Southwest Conference, which had just disbanded. Athletic competition began in August 1996. As of this writing, for most sports (including football), the conference is divided into two divisions: South (the Oklahoma and Texas schools) and North (all other schools).

As of this writing, the Big 12 Conference currently consists of the following 12 schools:

- Baylor University Bears, Waco, TX 76706; 254-710-3435; www.baylor.edu
- Iowa State University Cyclones, Ames, Iowa 50011; 515-294-4111; www.iastate.edu
- Kansas State University Wildcats, Manhattan, KS 66506; 785-532-6011; www.k-state.edu
- Oklahoma State University Cowboys, Stillwater, OK 74078; 405-744-5000; www.okstate.edu
- Texas Agricultural and Mechanical University Aggies, College Station, TX 77843; 979-845-3211; www.tamu.edu
- Texas Technical University Red Raiders, Lubbock, TX 79409; 806-742-2011; www.ttu.edu
- University of Colorado Buffaloes, Boulder, CO 80309; 303-492-1411; www.colorado.edu
- University of Kansas Jayhawks, Lawrence, KS 66045; 785-864-2700; www.ku.edu

- University of Missouri Tigers, Columbia, MO 65211; 573-882-2121; www.missouri.edu
- University of Nebraska, Lincoln Cornhuskers, Lincoln, NE 68588; 402-472-2023; www.unl.edu
- University of Oklahoma Sooners, Norman, OK 73019; 405-325-0000; www.ou.edu
- University of Texas at Austin Longhorns, Austin, TX 78712; 512-471-3434; www.utexas.edu

Big-12 Champions

Year	School
1996	University of Texas (TX)
1997	University of Nebraska (NE)
1998	Texas A&M University (TX)
1999	University of Nebraska (NE)
2000	University of Oklahoma (OK)
2001	University of Colorado (CO)
2002	University of Oklahoma (OK)
2003	Kansas State University (KS)
2004	University of Oklahoma (OK)
2005	University of Texas (TX(
2006	University of Oklahoma (OK)
2007	University of Oklahoma (OK)
2008	University of Oklahoma (OK)
2009	University of Texas (TX)
2010	University of Oklahoma (OK)

Big-12 Coach of the Year

Selected by conference coaches.

Year	Coach	School
1996	Spike Dykes	Texas Tech University (TX)
1997	Bob Simmons	Oklahoma State University (OK)
1998	Bill Snyder	Kansas State University (KS)
1999	Frank Solich	University of Nebraska (NE)
2000	Bob Stoops	University of Oklahoma (OK)
2001	Frank Solich	University of Nebraska (NE)
2002	Bill Snyder	Kansas State University (KS)
2003	Bob Stoops	University of Oklahoma (OK)
2004	Dan McCarney	Iowa State University (IA)
2005	Mack Brown	University of Texas (TX)
2006	Bob Stoops	University of Oklahoma (OK)
2007	Mark Mangino	University of Kansas (KS)
2008	Bob Stoops	University of Oklahoma (OK)
2008	Mike Leach	Texas Tech University (TX)
2009	Mack Brown	University of Texas (TX)
2010	Mike Gundy	Oklahoma State University (OK)

Big-12 Offensive Player of the Year

Selected by the conference coaches.

Year	Player	School	Position	Class
1996	Troy Davis	Iowa State University (IA)	Running Back	Junior
1997	Ricky Williams	University of Texas (TX)	Running Back	Junior
1998	Ricky Williams	University of Texas (TX)	Running Back	Senior
1999	Major Applewhite	University of Texas (TX)	Quarterback	Sophomore
1999	Eric Crouch	University of Nebraska (NE)	Quarterback	Sophomore
2000	Josh Heupel	University of Oklahoma (OK)	Quarterback	Senior
2001	Eric Crouch	University of Nebraska (NE)	Quarterback	Senior
2002	Chris Brown	University of Colorado (CO)	Running Back	Junior
2003	Jason White	University of Oklahoma (OK)	Quarterback	Senior
2004	Jason White	University of Oklahoma (OK)	Quarterback	Senior
2005	Vince Young	University of Texas (TX)	Quarterback	Junior
2006	Zac Taylor	University of Nebraska (NE)	Quarterback	Senior
2007	Chase Daniel	University of Missouri (MO)	Quarterback	Junior
2008	Sam Bradford	University of Oklahoma (OK)	Quarterback	Sophomore
2009	Colt McCoy	University of Texas (TX)	Quarterback	Senior
2010	Justin Blackmon	Oklahoma State University (OK)	Wide Receiver	Sophomore

Big-12 Defensive Player of the Year

Selected by conference coaches.

Year	*Player*	*School*	*Position*	*Class*
1996	Grant Wistrom	University of Nebraska (NE)	Defensive End	Junior
1997	Grant Wistrom	University of Nebraska (NE)	Defensive End	Senior
1998	Dat Nguyen	Texas A&M University (TX)	Linebacker	Senior
1999	Mark Simoneau	Kansas State University (KS)	Linebacker	Senior
2000	Casey Hampton	University of Texas (TX)	Defensive Lineman	Senior
2001	Roy Williams	University of Oklahoma (OK)	Defensive Back	Junior
2002	Terence Newman	Kansas State University (KS)	Defensive Back	Junior
2003	Teddy Lehman	University of Oklahoma (OK)	Linebacker	Senior
2004	Derrick Johnson	University of Texas (TX)	Linebacker	Senior
2005	Nick Reid	University of Kansas (KS)	Linebacker	Senior
2006	Rufus Alexander	University of Oklahoma (OK)	Linebacker	Senior
2007	Jordan Dizon	University of Colorado (CO)	Linebacker	Senior
2008	Brian Orakpo	University of Texas (TX)	Defensive Lineman	Senior
2009	Ndamukong Suh	University of Nebraska (NE)	Defensive Tackle	Senior
2010	Prince Amukamara	University of Nebraska (NE)	Cornerback	Senior

Big-12 Offensive Lineman of the Year

Selected by conference coaches.

Year	*Player*	*School*	*Position*	*Class*
2006	Justin Blalock	University of Texas (TX)	Offensive Guard	Senior
2007	Adam Spieker	University of Missouri (MO)	Offensive Lineman	Senior
2007	Cody Wallace	Texas A&M University (TX)	Center	Senior
2008	Jon Cooper	University of Oklahoma (OK)	Offensive Lineman	Senior
2009	Russell Okung	Oklahoma State University (OK)	Offensive Tackle	Senior
2010	Nate Solder	University of Colorado (CO)	Offensive Tackle	Senior

Big-12 Defensive Lineman of the Year

Selected by conference coaches.

Year	*Player*	*School*	*Position*	*Class*
2006	Adam Carriker	University of Nebraska (NE)	Defensive End	Senior
2007	James McClinton	University of Kansas (KS)	Defensive Lineman	Senior
2008	Brian Orakpo	University of Texas (TX)	Outside Linebacker	Senior
2009	Ndamukong Suh	University of Nebraska (NE)	Defensive Tackle	Senior
2010	Jeremy Beal	University of Oklahoma (OK)	Defensive End	Senior

Big-12 Special Teams Player of the Year

Selected by conference coaches.

Year	*Player*	*School*	*Position*	*Class*
2005	Mason Crosby	University of Colorado (CO)	Place Kicker	Junior
2006	Daniel Sepulveda	Baylor University (TX)	Place Kicker	Senior
2007	Marcus Herford	University of Kansas (KX)	Kick Returner	Junior
2008	Dez Bryant	Oklahoma State University (OK)	Punt Returner / Kick Returner	Sophomore
2009	Brandon Banks	Kansas State University (KS)	Wide Receiver	Senior
2010	Dan Bailey	Oklahoma State University (OK)	Punter/Kicker	Senior

Big-12 Offensive Newcomer of the Year

Selected by conference coaches.

Year	*Player*	*School*	*Position*	*Class*
1996	Scott Frost	University of Nebraska (NE)	Quarterback	Junior
1997	Michael Bishop	Kansas State University (KS)	Quarterback	Junior

Year	Player	School	Position	Class
1998	Mike Moschetti	University of Colorado (CO)	Quarterback	Junior
1999	Josh Heupel	University of Oklahoma (OK)	Quarterback	Junior
2000	Robert Ferguson	Texas A&M University (TX)	Wide Receiver	Junior
2001	Seneca Wallace	Iowa State University (IA)	Quarterback	Junior
2002	Bill Whittemore	University of Kansas (KS)	Quarterback	Junior
2003	Joe Vaughn	University of Kansas (KS)	Center	Junior
2004	Adrian Peterson	University of Oklahoma (OK)	Running Back	Freshman
2005	Robert Johnson	Texas Tech University (TX)	Wide Receiver	Junior
2006	Adarius Bowman	Oklahoma State University (OK)	Wide Receiver	Junior
2007	Deon Murphy	Kansas State University (KS)	Wide Receiver	Junior
2008	Brandon Banks	Kansas State University (KS)	Wide Receiver	Junior
2009	Daniel Thomas	Kansas State University (KS)	Running Back	Junior
2010	No Selection Made			

Big-12 Defensive Newcomer of the Year

Selected by conference coaches.

Year	Player	School	Position	Class
1996	Gana Joseph	University of Oklahoma (OK)	Defensive Back	Sophomore
1997	Jeff Kelly	Kansas State University (KS)	Linebacker	Junior
1998	Jess Beckom	Iowa State University (IA)	Defensive Lineman	Junior
1999	Mario Fatafehi	Kansas State University (KS)	Defensive Lineman	Junior
2000	Derrick Yates	Kansas State University (KS)	Defensive Lineman	Junior
2001	Tank Reese	Kansas State University (KS)	Defensive Lineman	Junior
2002	Lance Mitchell	University of Oklahoma (OK)	Linebacker	Junior
2003	Donte Nicholson	University of Oklahoma (OK)	Defensive Back	Junior
2004	Tim Dobbins	Iowa State University (IA)	Linebacker	Junior
2005	C.J. Ah You	University of Oklahoma (OK)	Defensive Lineman	Junior
2006	Misi Tupe	Texas A&M University (TX)	Linebacker	Junior
2007	Gary Chandler	Kansas State University (KS)	Defensive Back	Junior
2008	McKinner Dixon	Texas Tech University (TX)	Defensive End	Junior
2009	David Sims	Iowa State University (IA)	Defensive Back	Junior
2010	Lavonte David	University of Nebraska (NE)	Linebacker	Junior

Big-12 Offensive Freshman of the Year

Selected by conference coaches.

Year	Player	School	Position
1996	De'Mond Parker	University of Oklahoma (OK)	Running Back
1997	Tony Lindsay	Oklahoma State University (OK)	Quarterback
1998	Major Applewhite	University of Texas (TX)	Quarterback
1999	Shaud Williams	Texas Tech University (TX)	Running Back
2000	Roy Williams	University of Texas (TX)	Wide Receiver
2001	Cedric Benson	University of Texas (TX)	Running Back
2002	Brad Smith	University of Missouri (MO)	Quarterback
2003	Vince Young	University of Texas (TX)	Quarterback
2004	Adrian Peterson	University of Oklahoma (OK)	Running Back
2005	Jamaal Charles	University of Texas (TX)	Running Back
2006	Colt McCoy	University of Texas (TX)	Quarterback
2007	Jeremy Maclin	University of Missouri (MO)	Wide Receiver
2007	Michael Crabtree	Texas Tech University (TX)	Wide Receiver
2008	Robert Griffin	Baylor University (TX)	Quarterback
2009	Christine Michael	Texas A&M University (TX)	Running Back
2010	Taylor Martinez	University of Nebraska (NE)	Quarterback

Big-12 Defensive Freshman of the Year

Selected by conference coaches.

Year	Player	School	Position
1996	Mark Simoneau	Kansas State University (KS)	Linebacker
1997	Ben Kelly	University of Colorado (CO)	Defensive Back
1998	Justin Smith	University of Missouri (MO)	Defensive End
1999	Cory Redding	University of Texas (TX)	Defensive Lineman
2000	Terry Pierce	Kansas State University (KS)	Linebacker
2001	Tommie Harris	University of Oklahoma (OK)	Defensive Lineman
2001	Derrick Johnson	University of Texas (TX)	Linebacker
2002	Rodrique Wright	University of Texas (TX)	Defensive Lineman
2003	Jason Berryman	Iowa State University (IA)	Defensive Lineman
2003	Brock Stratton	Texas Tech University (TX)	Linebacker
2004	Jordon Dizon	University of Colorado (CO)	Linebacker
2005	Brian Orakpo	University of Texas (YX)	Defensive Lineman
2006	Andre Sexton	Oklahoma State University (OK)	Safety
2007	Gerald McCoy	University of Oklahoma (OK)	Defensive Tackle
2008	Travis Lewis	University of Oklahoma (OK)	Linebacker
2009	Aldon Smith	University of Missouri (MO)	Defensive Lineman
2010	Tony Jefferson	University of Oklahoma (OK)	Defensive Back
2010	Shaun Lewis	Oklahoma State University (OK)	Linebacker

Conference USA (C-USA)

5201 North O'Connor Boulevard, Suite 300, Irving, TX 75039; Telephone: 214-774-1300; Web site: http://conferenceusa.cstv.com/

Conference USA (C-USA) was formed in April 1995 with the merger of the Metro Conference and Great Midwest Conference, two Division I conferences that did not sponsor football. Starting in 1996, the conference began competing in all sports, including football. The original 12 members included the DePaul University, Marquette University, St. Louis University, Tulane University, the University of Alabama at Birmingham, the University of Cincinnati, the University of Louisville, the University of North Carolina at Charlotte, the University of Houston, the University of Memphis, the University of South Florida, and the University of Southern Mississippi.

As of this writing, Conference USA currently consists of the following 12 schools:

- East Carolina University Pirates, Greenville, NC 27858; 252-328-6131; www.ecu.edu
- Marshall University Thundering Herd, Huntington, WV 25755; 800-642-3463; www.marshall.edu
- Rice University Owls, Houston, Texas 77251; 713-348-0000; www.rice.edu
- Southern Methodist University Mustangs, Dallas, TX 75205; 214-768-2000; www.smu.edu
- Tulane University Green Wave, New Orleans, LA 70118; 504-865-5000; www.tulane.edu
- University of Alabama, Birmingham Blazers, Birmingham, AL 35294; 205-934-4011; www.uab.edu
- University of Central Florida Golden Knights, Orlando, FL 32816; 407-823-2000; www.ucf.edu
- University of Houston Cougars, Houston, TX 77004; 713-743-2255; www.uh.edu
- University of Memphis Tigers, Memphis, TN 38152; 901-678-2370; www.memphis.edu
- University of Southern Mississippi Golden Eagles, Hattiesburg, MS 39406; 601-266-1000; www.usm.edu
- University of Texas at El Paso Miners, El Paso, Texas 79968; 915-747-5000; www.utep.edu
- University of Tulsa Golden Hurricane, Tulsa, OK 74104; 918-631-2000; www.utulsa.edu

Conference USA Champions

Year	School	Year	School
1996	University of Houston (TX)	1999	University of Southern Mississippi (MO)
1996	University of Southern Mississippi (MO)	2000	University of Louisville (KY)
1997	University of Southern Mississippi (MO)	2001	University of Louisville (KY)
1998	Tulane University (LA)	2002	Texas Christian University (TX)

Year	School
2002	University of Cincinnati (OH)
2003	University of Southern Mississippi (MO)
2004	University of Louisville (KY)
2005	University of Tulsa (OK)
2006	University of Houston (TX)
2007	University of Tulsa (OK)
2008	University of Tulsa (OK)
2009	East Carolina University (NC)
2010	University of Central Florida (FL)

Conference USA Coach of the Year

Year	Coach	School
1996	Kim Helton	University of Houston (TX)
1997	Jeff Bower	University of Southern Mississippi (MO)
1998	Tommy Bowden	Tulane University (LA)
1999	Jeff Bower	University of Southern Mississippi (MO)
2000	John L. Smith	University of Louisville (KY)
2001	John L. Smith	University of Louisville (KY)
2002	Gary Patterson	Texas Christian University (TX)
2003	Jeff Bower	University of Southern Mississippi (MO)
2004	Bobby Petrino	University of Louisville (KY)
2005	George O'Leary	University of Central Florida (FL)
2006	Art Briles	University of Houston (TX)
2006	Todd Graham	Rice University (TX)
2007	George O'Leary	University of Central Florida (FL)
2008	David Bailiff	Rice University (TX)
2009	Kevin Sumlin	University of Houston (TX)
2010	George O'Leary	University of Central Florida (FL)

Conference USA Most Valuable Player

Year	Player	Position	School
2008	Chase Clement	Quarterback	Rice University (TX)
2009	Case Keenum	Quarterback	University of Houston (TX)
2010	Dwayne Harris	Wide Receiver/Kick Returner/Punt Returner	East Carolina University (NC)

Conference USA Offensive Player of the Year

Year	Player	Position	School
1995	Robert Tate	Wide Receiver	University of Cincinnati (OH)
1996	Antowain Smith	Running Back	University of Houston (TX)
1997	Shaun King	Quarterback	Tulane University (LA)
1998	Shaun King	Quarterback	Tulane University (LA)
1999	Chris Redman	Quarterback	University of Louisville (KY)
2000	Dave Ragone	Quarterback	University of Louisville (KY)
2001	Dave Ragone	Quarterback	University of Louisville (KY)
2002	Dave Ragone	Quarterback	University of Louisville (KY)
2003	DeAngelo Williams	Running Back	University of Memphis (TN)
2004	Stefan LeFors	Quarterback	University of Louisville (KY)
2004	DeAngelo Williams	Running Back	University of Memphis (TN)
2005	DeAngelo Williams	Running Back	University of Memphis (TN)
2006	Kevin Kolb	Quarterback	University of Houston (TX)
2007	Kevin Smith	Running Back	University of Central Florida (FL)
2007	Paul Smith	Quarterback	University of Tulsa (OK)
2008	Case Keenum	Quarterback	University of Houston (TX)
2009	Joe Webb	Quarterback	University of Alabama, Birmingham (AL)
2010	G.J. Kinne	Quarterback	University of Tulsa (OK)

Conference USA Defensive Player of the Year

Year	Player	Position	School
1995	Tyrus McCloud	Linebacker	University of Louisville (KY)
1996	Tyrus McCloud	Linebacker	University of Louisville (KY)

Year	Player	Position	School
1997	Patrick Surtain	Cornerback	University of Southern Mississippi (MO)
1998	Adalius Thomas	Defensive End	University of Southern Mississippi (MO)
1999	Adalius Thomas	Defensive End	University of Southern Mississippi (MO)
2000	Wayne Rogers	Linebacker	University of Houston (TX)
2000	Cedric Scott	Defensive End	University of Southern Mississippi (MO)
2001	Dewayne White	Defensive End	University of Louisville (KY)
2002	LaMarcus McDonald	Linebacker	Texas Christian University (TX)
2003	Rod Davis	Linebacker	University of Southern Mississippi (MO)
2004	Michael Boley	Linebacker	University of Southern Mississippi (MO)
2005	Kevis Coley	Linebacker	University of Southern Mississippi (MO)
2006	Albert McClellan	Defensive End	Marshall University (WV)
2006	Nick Bunting	Linebacker	University of Tulsa (OK)
2007	Gerald McRath	Linebacker	University of Southern Mississippi (MO)
2008	Phillip Hunt	Linebacker	University of Houston (TX)
2009	Bruce Miller	Defensive End	University of Central Florida (FL)
2009	Bruce Miller	Defensive End	University of Central Florida (FL)

Conference USA Special Teams Player of the Year

Year	Player	Position	School
1995	Robert Tate	Kick Returner	University of Cincinnati (OH)
1996	Jeff Liggon	Kick Returner	Tulane University (LA)
1997	Tinker Keck	Punt Returner	University of Cincinnati (OH)
1998	Ryan White	Kicker	University of Memphis (TN)
1999	Rodregis Brooks	Punt Returner	University of Alabama, Birmingham (AL)
2000	Jonathan Ruffin	Kicker	University of Cincinnati (OH)
2001	Seth Marler	Kicker	Tulane University (LA)
2002	Broderick Clark	Kick Returner	University of Louisville (KY)
2003	Nick Browne	Kicker	Texas Christian University (TX)
2004	John Eubanks	Kick Returner	University of Southern Mississippi (MO)
2005	Stephen Gostkowski	Kicker	University of Memphis (TN)
2006	Johnnie Lee Higgins	Kick Returner / Punt Returner	University of Texas at El Paso (TX)
2007	Chris Johnson	Kick Returner	East Carolina University (NC)
2008	Joe Burnett	Kick Returner / Punt Returner	University of Central Florida (FL)
2009	Dwayne Harris	Kick Returner	East Carolina University (NC)
2010	Damaris Johnson	Kick Returner/Punt Returner	University of Tulsa (OK)

Conference USA Freshman of the Year

Year	Player	Position	School
1996	Ketric Sanford	Running Back / Kick Returner	University of Houston (TX)
1997	Jason McKinley	Quarterback	University of Houston (TX)
1998	Derrick Nix	Running Back	University of Southern Mississippi (MO)
1999	LaDaris Vann	Wide Receiver	University of Cincinnati (OH)
1999	Travis Anglin	Quarterback	University of Memphis (TN)
2000	Mewelde Moore	Running Back	Tulane University (LA)
2001	Gino Guidugli	Quarterback	University of Cincinnati (OH)
2002	Lonta Hobbs	Running Back	Texas Christian University (TX)
2003	Kevin Kolb	Quarterback	University of Houston (TX)
2004	Brian Brohm	Quarterback	University of Louisville (KY)
2005	Kevin Smith	Running Back	University of Central Florida (FL)
2006	Justin Willis	Quarterback	Southern Methodist University (TX)
2007	Case Keenum	Quarterback	University of Houston (TX)
2008	Bryce Beall	Running Back	University of Houston (TX)
2009	Charles Sims	Running Back	University of Houston (TX)
2010	Jeff Godfrey	Quarterback	University of Central Florida (FL)

Conference USA Newcomer of the Year

Year	*Player*	*Position*	*School*
2007	Brennan Marion	Wide Receiver	University of Tulsa (OK)
2008	Curtis Steele	Running Back	University of Memphis (TN)
2009	James Cleveland	Wide Receiver	University of Houston (TX)
2010	Dominique Davis	Quarterback	East Carolina University (NC)

Eastern College Athletic Conference

1311 Craigville Beach Road, Centerville, MA 02632; Telephone: 508-771-5060; Fax: 508-771-9486; Web site: http://www.ecac.org; http://www.ecacsports.com

Established in 1938 as the Central Office for Eastern Intercollegiate Athletics with 58 charter members, the Eastern College Athletic Conference has grown to become the nation's largest (and only multi-divisional) athletic conference in the United States with 304 members (as of this writing) (Division I—90 members, Division II—23 members, and Division III—191 members). Member schools of the ECAC also compete in at least one other conference (or as independent schools) and play in the ECAC postseason, when eligible. See NCAA Division II and NCAA Division III for a complete schools list within each division.

Football Alignments (Division I)—Members of the ECAC

- Atlantic Coast Conference (Boston College, Duke University, University of Maryland, University of Virginia)
- Big East Conference (Rutgers University, Syracuse University, University of Connecticut, University of Pittsburgh, West Virginia University)
- Big South Conference (Liberty University, Stony Brook University, Virginia Military Institute)
- Colonial Athletic Association (College of William & Mary, Hofstra University, James Madison University, Northeastern University, Towson University, University of Delaware, University of Maine, University of Massachusetts, University of New Hampshire, University of Rhode Island, Villanova University)
- Independent Schools (Davidson College, East Carolina University, Marist College, Pennsylvania State University, U.S. Military Academy, U.S. Naval Academy)
- Ivy League (Brown University, Columbia University, Cornell University, Dartmouth College, Harvard University, Princeton University, University of Pennsylvania, Yale University)
- Mid-American Conference (Temple University, University at Buffalo)
- Mid-Eastern Athletic Conference (Delaware State University, Hampton University, Morgan State University)
- Northeast Conference (Bryant University, Central Connecticut State University, Duquesne University, Monmouth University, Robert Morris University, Sacred Heart University, Saint Francis University (PA), University at Albany, Wagner College)
- Patriot League (Bucknell University, Colgate University, College of the Holy Cross, Fordham University, Georgetown University, Lafayette College, Lehigh University)

Division I Members (90)

- American University Eagles (Patriot League) (Washington, D.C.)
- Binghamton University Bearcats (America East Conference) (Binghamton, NY)
- Boston College Eagles (Atlantic Coast Conference) (Chestnut Hill, MA)
- Boston University Terriers (America East Conference) (Boston, MA)
- Brown University Brown Bears (Ivy League) (Providence, RI)
- Bryant University Bulldogs (Northeast Conference) (Smithfield, RI)
- Bucknell University Bison (Patriot League) (Lewisburg, PA)
- Canisius College Golden Griffins (Metro Atlantic Athletic Conference) (Buffalo, NY)
- Central Connecticut State University Blue Devils (Northeast Conference) (New Britain, CT)
- Colgate University Raiders (Patriot League) (Hamilton, NY)
- College of the Holy Cross Crusaders (Patriot League) (Worcester, MA)

- College of William & Mary Tribe (Colonial Athletic Association) (Williamsburg, VA)
- Columbia University Lions (Ivy League) (New York, NY)
- Coppin State College Eagles (Mid-Eastern Athletic Conference) (Baltimore, MD)
- Cornell University Big Red (Ivy League) (Ithaca, NY)
- Dartmouth College Big Green (Ivy League) (Hanover, NH)
- Davidson College Wildcats (Pioneer Conference) (Davidson, NC)
- Delaware State University Hornets (Mid-Eastern Athletic Conference) (Dover, DE)
- Duke University Blue Devils (Atlantic Coast Conference) (Durham, NC)
- Duquesne University Dukes (Atlantic 10 Conference) (Pittsburgh, PA)
- East Carolina University Pirates (Conference USA) (Greenville, NC)
- Fairfield University Stags (Metro Atlantic Athletic Conference) (Fairfield, CT)
- Fairleigh Dickinson University Knights (Northeast Conference) (Teaneck, NJ)
- Fordham University Rams (Atlantic 10 Conference) (Bronx, NY)
- George Mason University Patriots (Colonial Athletic Association) (Fairfax, VA)
- George Washington University Colonials (Atlantic 10 Conference) (Washington, D.C.)
- Georgetown University Hoyas (Big East Conference) (Washington, D.C.)
- Hampton University Pirates (Mid-Eastern Athletic Conference) (Hampton, VA)
- Harvard University Crimson (Ivy League) (Boston, MA)
- Hofstra University Pride (Colonial Athletic Association (Hempstead, NY)
- Iona College Gaels (Metro Atlantic Athletic Conference) (New Rochelle, NY)
- James Madison University Dukes (Colonial Athletic Association) (Harrisonburg, VA)
- La Salle University Explorers (Atlantic 10 Conference) (Philadelphia, PA)
- Lafayette College Leopards (Patriot League) (Easton, PA)
- Lehigh University Mountain Hawks (Patriot League) (Bethlehem, PA)
- Liberty University Flames (Big South Conference) (Lynchburg, VA)
- Long Island University, Brooklyn Campus Blackbirds (Northeast Conference) (Brooklyn, NY)
- Longwood University Lancers (Independent) (Farmville, VA)
- Loyola University Maryland Greyhounds (Metro Atlantic Athletic Conference) (Baltimore, MD)
- Manhattan College Jaspers (Metro Atlantic Athletic Conference) (Riverdale, NY)
- Marist College Red Foxes (Metro Atlantic Athletic Conference) (Poughkeepsie, NY)
- Monmouth University Hawks (Northeast Conference) (West Long Branch, NJ)
- Morgan State University Bears (Mid-Eastern Athletic Conference) (Baltimore, MD)
- Mount St. Mary's University The Mount (Northeast Conference) (Emmitsburg, MD)
- New Jersey Institute of Technology Highlanders (Independent) (Newark, NJ)
- Niagara University Purple Eagles (Metro Atlantic Athletic Conference) (Niagara University, NY)
- Northeastern University Huskies (Colonial Athletic Association) (Boston, MA)
- Pennsylvania State University Nittany Lions (Big Ten Conference) (University Park, PA)
- Princeton University Tigers (Ivy League) (Princeton, NJ)
- Providence College Friars (Big East Conference) (Providence, RI)
- Quinnipiac University Bobcats (Northeast Conference) (Hamden, CT)
- Rider University Broncs (Metro Atlantic Athletic Conference) (Lawrenceville, NJ)
- Robert Morris University Colonials (Northeast Conference) (Moon Township, PA)
- Rutgers University Scarlet Knights (Big East Conference) (Piscataway, NJ)
- Sacred Heart University Pioneers (Northeast Conference) (Fairfield, CT)
- Saint Francis University Red Flash (Northeast Conference) (Loretto, PA)

FBS Independent Teams (Army, Navy, University of Notre Dame)

United States Military Academy at West Point Black Knights, West Point, NY 10996; Telephone: 845-938-3701; Fax: 845-446-1322; Web site: http://www.usma.edu

While the U.S. Army football team plays as an independent entity, it competes in the Patriot League for all other sports. Since its football team started play in 1890, it has won three national championships (1914, 1944–1945); acted as an independent entity from 1890 to 1997; played in Conference-USA from 1998 to 2004; and returned as an independent team from 2005 to the present.

Currently, Army competes with both Navy and Air Force for the Commander-in-Chief's Trophy.

United States Naval Academy Midshipmen, Annapolis, MD 21402; Telephone: 410-293-8775; Web site: http://www.usna.edu; http://www.navysports.com

University of Notre Dame Fighting Irish, Notre Dame, IN; Telephone: 574-631-6107; Web site: http://www.und.com/sports/m-footbl/nd-m-footbl-body.html; the only individual school to have its own national television contract and is the only independent school to be part of the BCS coalition.

Mid-American Conference (MAC)

24 Public Square, 15th Floor, Cleveland, OH 44113; Telephone: 216-566-4622; Fax: 216-696-2622; Web site: http://www.mac-sports.com

The Mid-American Conference was founded as a five-school league in February 1946 in Columbus, Ohio with charter members being Butler University, (Case) Western Reserve University, Ohio University, University of Cincinnati, and Wayne State University. As currently configured, the conference consists of 12 schools and Temple University for football only.

As of this writing, the Mid-American Conference currently consists of the following 13 schools:

- Ball State University Cardinals, Muncie, IN 47306; 765-289-1241; www.bsu.edu
- Bowling Green State University Falcons, Bowling Green, OH 43403; 419-372-2531; www.bgsu.edu
- Central Michigan University Chippewas, Mount Pleasant, MI 48859; 989-774-4000; www.cmich.edu
- Eastern Michigan University Eagles, Ypsilanti, MI, 48197; 734-487-1849; www.emich.edu
- Kent State University Golden Flashes, Kent, OH 44242; 330-672-3000; www.kent.edu
- Miami University RedHawks, Oxford, OH 45056; 513-529-1809; www.muohio.edu
- Northern Illinois University Huskies, DeKalb, IL 60115; 815-753-1000; www.niu.edu
- Ohio University Bobcats, Athens, OH 45701; 740-593-1000; www.ohio.edu
- Temple University Owls, Philadelphia, PA 19122; 215-204-7000; www.temple.edu
- University at Buffalo Bulls, Buffalo, NY 14260; 716-645-2000; www.buffalo.edu
- University of Akron Zips, Akron, OH 44325; 330-972-7111; www.uakron.edu
- University of Toledo Rockets, Toledo, OH 43606; 800-586-5336; www.utoledo.com
- Western Michigan University Broncos, Kalamazoo MI 49008; 269-387-1000; www.wmich.edu

MAC Champions

Year	*Team*
1947	University of Cincinnati (OH)
1948	Miami University (OH)
1949	University of Cincinnati (OH)
1950	Miami University (OH)
1951	University of Cincinnati (OH)
1952	University of Cincinnati (OH)
1953	Ohio University (OH)
1954	Miami University (OH)
1955	Miami University (OH)
1956	Bowling Green State University (OH)
1957	Miami University (OH)
1958	Miami University (OH)
1959	Bowling Green State University (OH)
1960	Ohio University (OH)
1961	Bowling Green State University (OH)
1962	Bowling Green State University (OH)
1963	Ohio University (OH)
1964	Bowling Green State University (OH)
1965	Bowling Green State University (OH)
1965	Miami University (OH)
1966	Miami University (OH)
1966	Western Michigan University (MI)
1967	Ohio University (OH)
1967	University of Toledo (OH)
1968	Ohio University (OH)
1969	University of Toledo (OH)
1970	University of Toledo (OH)
1971	University of Toledo (OH)
1972	Kent State University (OH)
1973	Miami University (OH)
1974	Miami University (OH)
1975	Miami University (OH)
1976	Ball State University (IN)
1977	Miami University (OH)
1978	Ball State University (IN)
1979	Central Michigan University (MI)
1980	Central Michigan University (MI)
1981	University of Toledo (OH)
1982	Bowling Green State University (OH)
1983	Northern Illinois University (IL)
1984	University of Toledo (OH)
1985	Bowling Green State University (OH)
1986	Miami University (OH)
1987	Eastern Michigan University (MI)
1988	Western Michigan University (MI)
1989	Ball State University (IN)
1990	Central Michigan University (MI)
1990	University of Toledo (OH)

Year	*Team*
1991	Bowling Green State University (OH)
1992	Bowling Green State University (OH)
1993	Ball State University (IN)
1994	Central Michigan University (MI)
1995	University of Toledo (OH)
1996	Ball State University (IN)
1997	Marshall University (WV)
1998	Marshall University (WV)
1999	Marshall University (WV)
2000	Marshall University (WV)
2001	University of Toledo (OH)
2002	Marshall University (WV)
2003	Miami University (OH)
2004	University of Toledo (OH)
2005	University of Akron (OH)
2006	Central Michigan University (MI)
2007	Central Michigan University (MI)
2008	University at Buffalo (NY)
2009	Central Michigan University (MI)
2010	Miami University (OH)

MAC Coach of the Year

First awarded in 1965, only Frank Lauterbur (University of Toledo) has won the award more than twice, and only one coach, Bill Mallory, has won the award coaching for two separate teams (1973 with Ohio University and in 1983 with Northern Illinois University). The winners of this award are chosen by the members of the MAC News Media Association.

Year	*Coach*	*School*
1965	Bo Schembechler	Miami University (OH)
1966	Bill Doolittle	Western Michigan University (MI)
1967	Frank Lauterbur	University of Toledo (OH)
1968	Bill Hess	Ohio University (OH)
1969	Frank Lauterbur	University of Toledo (OH)
1970	Frank Lauterbur	University of Toledo (OH)
1971	Jack Murphy	University of Toledo (OH)
1972	Don James	Kent State University (OH)
1973	Bill Mallory	Miami University (OH)
1974	Dick Crum	Miami University (OH)
1975	Dave McClain	Ball State University (IN)
1976	Elliot Uzelac	Western Michigan University (MI)
1977	Ed Schlebek	Eastern Michigan University (MI)
1978	Dwight Wallace	Ball State University (IN)
1979	Chuck Stobart	University of Toledo (OH)
1980	Herb Deromedi	Central Michigan University (MI)
1981	Chuck Stobart	University of Toledo (OH)
1982	Denny Stolz	Bowling Green State University (OH)
1983	Bill Mallory	Northern Illinois University (IL)
1984	Dan Simrell	University of Toledo (OH)
1985	Denny Stolz	Bowling Green State University (OH)
1986	Glen Mason	Kent State University (OH)
1987	Jim Harkema	Eastern Michigan University (MI)
1988	Al Molde	Western Michigan University (MI)
1989	Paul Schudel	Ball State University (IN)
1990	Herb Deromedi	Central Michigan University (MI)
1991	Gary Blackney	Bowling Green State University (OH)
1992	Gary Blackney	Bowling Green State University (OH)
1993	Paul Schudel	Ball State University (IN)
1994	Dick Flynn	Central Michigan University (MI)
1995	Gary Pinkel	University of Toledo (OH)
1996	Jim Grobe	Ohio University (OH)
1997	Gary Pinkel	University of Toledo (OH)
1998	Bob Pruett	Marshall University (WV)
1999	Bob Pruett	Marshall University (WV)
2000	Gary Darnell	Western Michigan University (MI)
2001	Urban Meyer	Bowling Green State University (OH)
2002	Joe Novak	Northern Illinois University (IL)
2003	Terry Hoeppner	Miami University (OH)

Year	Coach	School
2004	J.D. Brookhart	University of Akron (OH)
2005	Bill Cubit	Western Michigan University (MI)
2006	Frank Solich	Ohio University (OH)
2007	Turner Gill	University at Buffalo (NY)
2008	Brady Hoke	Ball State University (IN)
2009	Al Golden	Temple University (PA)
2010	Mike Haywood	Miami University (OH)

Vern Smith Leadership Award (MAC Player of the Year)

Presented to the top football player in the conference, the Vern Smith Leadership Award (originally known as the Jefferson Award) was started in 1982 by the Downtown Toledo (Ohio) Athletic Club and was renamed in 1987 to honor University of Toledo Athletic Director Vern Smith. Annual winners are selected by conference coaches.

As of this writing, four players have won the award more than once; Larry English (Northern Illinois University) is the only defensive player to win (2007–2008); and Brad Maynard (1996, Ball State University) is the only Special Teams player winner.

Year	Player	School	Position
1982	Ray Bentley	Central Michigan University (MI)	Linebacker
1983	Tim Tyrrell	Northern Illinois University (IL)	Quarterback
1984	Brian McClure	Bowling Green State University (OH)	Quarterback
1985	Brian McClure	Bowling Green State University (OH)	Quarterback
1986	Terry Morris	Miami University (OH)	Quarterback
1987	Eric Wilkerson	Kent State University (OH)	Running Back
1988	Tony Kimbrough	Western Michigan University (MI)	Quarterback
1989	David Riley	Ball State University (IN)	Quarterback
1990	Jeff Bender	Central Michigan University (MI)	Quarterback
1991	Erik White	Bowling Green State University (OH)	Quarterback
1992	Erik White	Bowling Green State University (OH)	Quarterback
1993	Mike Neu	Ball State University (IN)	Quarterback
1994	Brian Pruitt	Central Michigan University (MI)	Running Back
1995	Wasean Tait	University of Toledo (OH)	Running Back
1996	Brad Maynard	Ball State University (IN)	Punter
1997	Randy Moss	Marshall University (WV)	Wide Receiver
1998	Travis Prentice	Miami University (OH)	Running Back
1999	Chad Pennington	Marshall University (WV)	Quarterback
2000	Robert Sanford	Western Michigan University (MI)	Running Back
2001	Byron Leftwich	Marshall University (WV)	Quarterback
2002	Byron Leftwich	Marshall University (WV)	Quarterback
2003	Ben Roethlisberger	Miami University (OH)	Quarterback
2004	Charlie Frye	University of Akron (OH)	Quarterback
2005	Bruce Gradkowski	University of Toledo (OH)	Quarterback
2005	Greg Jennings	Western Michigan University (MI)	Wide Receiver
2006	Garrett Wolfe	Northern Illinois University (IL)	Running Back
2007	Larry English	Northern Illinois University (IL)	Defensive End
2008	Larry English	Northern Illinois University (IL)	Defensive End
2009	Dan LeFevour	Central Michigan University (MI)	Quarterback
2010	Chad Spann	Northern Illinois University (IL)	Running Back

MAC Offensive Player of the Year

Voted on by the members of the MAC News Media Association.

Year	Player	School	Position
1965	Willie Asbury	Kent State University (OH)	Running Back
1966	Bruce Matte	Miami University (OH)	Quarterback
1967	John Schneider	University of Toledo (OH)	Quarterback
1968	Cleve Bryant	Ohio University (OH)	Quarterback

Year	*Player*	*School*	*Position*
1969	Chuck Ealey	University of Toledo (OH)	Quarterback
1970	Chuck Ealey	University of Toledo (OH)	Quarterback
1971	Chuck Ealey	University of Toledo (OH)	Quarterback
1971	Phil Villapiano	Bowling Green State University (OH)	Linebacker
1972	Bob Hitchens	Miami University (OH)	Running Back
1973	Paul Miles	Bowling Green State University (OH)	Running Back
1974	Gene Swick	University of Toledo (OH)	Quarterback
1975	Gene Swick	University of Toledo (OH)	Quarterback
1976	Jerome Persell	Western Michigan University (MI)	Tailback
1977	Jerome Persell	Western Michigan University (MI)	Tailback
1978	Jerome Persell	Western Michigan University (MI)	Tailback
1978	Dave Petzke	Northern Illinois University (IL)	Split End
1979	Gary Hogeboom	Central Michigan University (MI)	Quarterback
1980	Mark O'Connell	Ball State University (IN)	Punter
1981	Sam Shon	Ohio University (OH)	Quarterback
1982	Curtis Adams	Central Michigan University (MI)	Running Back
1983	Brian McClure	Bowling Green State University (OH)	Quarterback
1984	Brian McClure	Bowling Green State University (OH)	Quarterback
1985	Brian McClure	Bowling Green State University (OH)	Quarterback
1986	Terry Morris	Miami University (OH)	Quarterback
1987	Erik Wilkerson	Kent State University (OH)	Running Back
1988	Tony Kimbrough	Western Michigan University (MI)	Quarterback
1989	David Riley	Ball State University (IN)	Quarterback
1990	Jeff Bender	Central Michigan University (MI)	Quarterback
1991	Erik White	Bowling Green State University (OH)	Quarterback
1992	Erik White	Bowling Green State University (OH)	Quarterback
1993	Mike Neu	Ball State University (IN)	Quarterback
1994	Brian Pruitt	Central Michigan University (MI)	Running Back
1995	Wasean Tait	University of Toledo (OH)	Running Back
1996	Kareem Wilson	Ohio University (OH)	Quarterback
1997	Randy Moss	Marshall University (WV)	Wide Receiver
1998	Travis Prentice	Miami University (OH)	Running Back
1999	Chad Pennington	Marshall University (WV)	Quarterback
2000	Robert Sanford	Western Michigan University (MI)	Halfback
2001	Byron Leftwich	Marshall University (WV)	Quarterback
2002	Byron Leftwich	Marshall University (WV)	Quarterback
2003	Ben Roethlisberger	Miami University (OH)	Quarterback
2004	Omar Jacobs	Bowling Green State University (OH)	Quarterback
2005	Greg Jennings	Western Michigan University (MI)	Wide Receiver
2006	Garrett Wolfe	Northern Illinois University (IL)	Running Back
2007	Dan LeFevour	Central Michigan University (MI)	Quarterback
2008	Nate Davis	Ball State University (IN)	Quarterback
2009	Dan LeFevour	Central Michigan University (MI)	Quarterback
2010	Chad Spann	Northern Illinois University (IL)	Running Back

MAC Defensive Player of the Year

Voted on by the members of the MAC News Media Association.

Year	*Player*	*School*	*Position*
1965	Bob Rowe	Western Michigan University (MI)	Defensive End
1966	Bob Rowe	Western Michigan University (MI)	Defensive End
1967	Tom Beutler	University of Toledo (OH)	Linebacker
1968	Bob Babich	Miami University (OH)	Linebacker
1969	Joe Green	Bowling Green State University (OH)	Cornerback / Safety
1970	Dick Adams	Miami University (OH)	Punt Returner
1971	Mel Long	University of Toledo (OH)	Defensive Tackle
1972	Jack Lambert	Kent State University (OH)	Linebacker

Year	*Player*	*School*	*Position*
1973	Brad Cousino	Miami University (OH)	Linebacker
1974	Brad Cousino	Miami University (OH)	Linebacker
1975	Shafer Suggs	Ball State University (IN)	Safety
1976	Aaron Bivins	University of Toledo (OH)	Linebacker
1977	Jack Glowik	Miami University (OH)	Defensive Guard
1978	Ken Kremer	Ball State University (IN)	Nose Tackle–Defensive End
1979	Frank Lewandowski	Northern Illinois University (IL)	Linebacker
1980	Kent McCormick	Miami University (OH)	Linebacker
1980	Mike Terra	Northern Illinois University (IL)	No Further Information
1981	John Zupancic	Miami University (OH)	No Further Information
1982	Ray Bentley	Central Michigan University (MI)	Linebacker
1983	Brian Pillman	Miami University (OH)	Defensive Tackle
1984	Mark Brandon	University of Toledo (OH)	Cornerback
1985	John Offerdahl	Western Michigan University (MI)	Linebacker
1986	Mark Garalczyk	Western Michigan University (MI)	Defensive Tackle–Defensive End
1987	Greg Garnica	Ball State University (IN)	Linebacker
1988	Greg Garnica	Ball State University (IN)	Linebacker
1989	Greg Garnica	Ball State University (IN)	Linebacker
1990	Sean Mulhearn	Western Michigan University (MI)	Linebacker
1991	Curt McMillan	Miami University (OH)	Linebacker
1992	Curt McMillan	Miami University (OH)	Linebacker
1993	Vince Palko	Bowling Green State University (OH)	Linebacker
1994	Vince Palko	Bowling Green State University (OH)	Linebacker
1995	Johhnie Williams	Miami University (OH)	No Further Information
1996	Brad Maynard	Ball State University (IN)	Punter
1997	JoJuan Armour	Miami University (OH)	Linebacker / Safety
1998	JoJuan Armour	Miami University (OH)	Linebacker / Safety
1999	Dustin Cohen	Miami University (OH)	Linebacker
2000	Dwight Smith	University of Akron (OH)	Defensive Back
2001	Max Yates	Marshall University (WV)	Linebacker
2002	Jason Babin	Western Michigan University (MI)	Defensive End
2003	Jason Babin	Western Michigan University (MI)	Defensive End
2004	Johnathan Goddard	Marshall University (WV)	Defensive End–Linebacker
2005	Dan Bazuin	Central Michigan University (MI)	Defensive End
2006	Ameer Ismail	Western Michigan University (MI)	Linebacker
2007	Clayton Mullins	Miami University (OH)	Linebacker
2008	Larry English	Northern Illinois University (IL)	Defensive End
2009	Adrian Robinson	Temple University (PA)	Defensive End
2010	Roosevelt Nix	Kent State University (OH)	Defensive Tackle

MAC Special Teams Player of the Year

Voted on by the members of the MAC News Media Association.

Year	*Player*	*School*	*Position*
1998	Brad Selent	Western Michigan University (MI)	Kicker
1999	Dave Zastudil	Ohio University (OH)	Punter
2000	Justin McCareins	Northern Illinois University (IL)	Wide Receiver
2001	Dave Zastudil	Ohio University (OH)	Punter
2001	Steve Azar	Northern Illinois University (IL)	Place Kicker
2002	Dan Sheldon	Northern Illinois University (IL)	Wide Receiver
2003	Steve Azar	Northern Illinois University (IL)	Place Kicker
2004	Ryne Robinson	Miami University (OH)	Wide Receiver
2005	Jason Robbins	University of Toledo (OH)	Kicker
2006	Brian Jackson	Ball State University (IN)	Kicker
2007	Brett Kern	University of Toledo (OH)	Punter
2008	Antonio Brown	Central Michigan University (MI)	Wide Receiver
2009	Antonio Brown	Central Michigan University (MI)	Wide Receiver
2010	Eric Page	University of Toledo (OH)	Kick Returner

MAC Freshman of the Year

Voted on by the members of the MAC News Media Association.

Year	*Player*	*School*	*Position*
1982	Brian McClure	Bowling Green State University (OH)	Quarterback
1983	Kelly Spielmaker	Western Michigan University (MI)	Tight End
1984	Pete Genatempo	Northern Illinois University (IL)	Quarterback
1985	Marshall Taylor	Northern Illinois University (IL)	Quarterback
1986	Patrick Young	Kent State University (OH)	Quarterback
1987	Bernie Parmalee	Ball State University (IN)	Running Back
1988	Jeff Bender	Central Michigan University (MI)	Quarterback
1989	Brad Tayles	Western Michigan University (MI)	Quarterback
1990	Troy Parker	University of Toledo (OH)	No Further Information
1991	Morrey Norris	Kent State University (OH)	Linebacker
1992	Deland McCullough	Miami University (OH)	Running Back
1993	Michael Blair	Ball State University (IN)	Running Back
1994	Astron Whatley	Kent State University (OH)	Running Back
1995	Silas Massey III	Central Michigan University (MI)	Tailback
1996	Walt Church	Eastern Michigan University (MI)	Quarterback
1996	Tim Lester	Western Michigan University (MI)	Quarterback
1997	Robert Sanford	Western Michigan University (MI)	Halfback
1998	Kurt Gerling	Bowling Green State University (OH)	Wide Receiver
1999	Brandon Payne	University of Akron (OH)	Running Back
2000	Talmadge Hill	Ball State University (IN)	Quarterback
2001	Ben Roethlisberger	Miami University (OH)	Quarterback
2002	Aaron Leeper	University at Buffalo (NY)	Running Back
2003	Jerry Seymour	Central Michigan University (MI)	Tailback
2004	Adell Givens	Ball State University (IN)	Tailback
2005	Tim Hiller	Western Michigan University (MI)	Quarterback
2006	Dan LeFevour	Central Michigan University (MI)	Quarterback
2007	Antonio Brown	Central Michigan University (MI)	Wide Receiver
2008	Sean Baker	Ball State University (IN)	Strong Safety
2009	Bernard Pierce	Temple University (PA)	Running Back
2010	Roosevelt Nix	Kent State University (OH)	Defensive Tackle

Mountain West Conference (MWC)

15455 Gleneagle Drive, Suite 200, Colorado Springs, CO 80921; Telephone: 719-488-4040; Fax: 719-487-7240; Web site: http://www.themwc.com

The Mountain West Conference was established in 1999 and was the first to establish a sports television network dedicated solely to an intercollegiate athletic conference. Charter members included Brigham Young University, Colorado State University, San Diego State University, the United States Air Force Academy, the University of Nevada at Las Vegas, the University of New Mexico, the University of Utah, and the University of Wyoming.

As of this writing, the Mountain West Conference currently consists of the following nine schools:

- Brigham Young University Cougars, Provo, UT 84602; 801-422-4636; http://home.byu.edu
- Colorado State University Rams, Fort Collins, CO 80523; 970-491-1101; www.colostate.edu
- San Diego State University Aztecs, San Diego, CA 92182; 619-594-5200; www.sdsu.com
- Texas Christian University Horned Frogs, Fort Worth, TX 76129; 817-257-7000; www.tcu.edu
- United States Air Force Academy Falcons, Colorado Springs, CO 80840; 719-333-2025; www.usafa.af.mil
- University of Nevada, Las Vegas Rebels, Las Vegas, NV 89154; 702-895-3011; www.unlv.edu
- University of New Mexico Lobos, Albuquerque, NM 87131; 505-277-0111; www.unm.edu
- University of Utah Utes, Salt Lake City, UT 84112; 801-581-7200; www.utah.edu
- University of Wyoming Cowboys, Laramie, WY 82071; 307-766-1121; www.uwyo.edu

MWC Champions

Year	School
1999	Brigham Young University (UT)
1999	Colorado State University (CO)
1999	University of Utah (UT)
2000	Colorado State University (CO)
2001	Brigham Young University (UT)
2002	Colorado State University (CO)
2003	University of Utah (UT)
2004	University of Utah (UT)
2005	Texas Christian University (TX)
2006	Brigham Young University (UT)
2007	Brigham Young University (UT)
2008	University of Utah (UT)
2009	Texas Christian University (TX)
2010	Texas Christian University (TX)

MWC Coach of the Year

Year	Coach	School
1999	Sonny Lubick	Colorado State University (CO)
2000	Sonny Lubick	Colorado State University (CO)
2000	John Robinson	University of Nevada, Las Vegas (NV)
2001	Gary Crowton	Brigham Young University (UT)
2002	Rocky Long	University of New Mexico (NM)
2003	Urban Meyer	University of Utah (UT)
2004	Urban Meyer	University of Utah (UT)
2005	Gary Patterson	Texas Christian University (TX)
2006	Bronco Mendenhall	Brigham Young University (UT)
2007	Troy Calhoun	United States Air Force Academy (CO)
2008	Kyle Whittingham	University of Utah (UT)
2009	Gary Patterson	Texas Christian University (TX)
2010	Brady Hoke	San Diego State University (CA)

MWC Player of the Year

Superseded by the MWC Offensive Player of the Year Award and the MWC Defensive Player of the Year Award.

Year	Player	Class	Position	School
1999	Brian Urlacher	Senior	Linebacker	University of New Mexico (NM)

MWC Offensive Player of the Year

Year	Player	Class	Position	School
1999	Kevin McDougal	Senior	Running Back	Colorado State University (CO)
2000	Matt Newton	Senior	Quarterback	Colorado State University (CO)
2000	Mike Thiessen	Senior	Quarterback	United States Air Force Academy (CO)
2001	Luke Staley	Junior	Running Back	Brigham Young University (UT)
2002	Bradlee Van Pelt	Junior	Quarterback	Colorado State University (CO)
2003	Bradlee Van Pelt	Senior	Quarterback	Colorado State University (CO)
2004	Alex Smith	Junior	Quarterback	University of Utah (UT)
2005	DonTrell Moore	Senior	Running Back	University of New Mexico (NM)
2006	John Beck	Senior	Quarterback	Brigham Young University (UT)
2007	Chad Hall	Senior	Running Back / Wide Receiver	United States Air Force Academy (CO)
2008	Brian Johnson	Senior	Quarterback	University of Utah (UT)
2009	Andy Dalton	Junior	Quarterback	Texas Christian University (TX)
2010	Andy Dalton	Senior	Quarterback	Texas Christian University (TX)

MWC Defensive Player of the Year

Year	Player	Class	Position	School
1999	John Frank	Senior	Defensive End	University of Utah (UT)
2000	Rick Crowell	Senior	Linebacker	Colorado State University (CO)
2001	Kevin Thomas	Senior	Defensive Back	University of Nevada, Las Vegas (NV)
2002	Jamaal Brimmer	Sophomore	Defensive Back	University of Nevada, Las Vegas (NV)
2003	Kirk Morrison	Junior	Linebacker	San Diego State University (CA)

Year	Player	Class	Position	School
2004	Kirk Morrison	Senior	Linebacker	San Diego State University (CA)
2004	Morgan Scalley	Senior	Defensive Back	University of Utah (UT)
2005	Eric Weddle	Junior	Defensive Back	University of Utah (UT)
2006	Eric Weddle	Senior	Defensive Back	University of Utah (UT)
2007	Beau Bell	Senior	Linebacker	University of Nevada, Las Vegas (NV)
2008	Jerry Hughes	Junior	Defensive End	Texas Christian University (TX)
2009	Jerry Hughes	Senior	Defensive End	Texas Christian University (TX)
2010	Tank Carder	Junior	Linebacker	Texas Christian University (TX)

MWC Special Teams Player of the Year

Established in 2006.

Year	Player	Class	Position	School
2006	Kenny Byrd	Senior	Place Kicker	University of New Mexico (NM)
2006	Louie Sakoda	Sophomore	Place Kicker–Punter	University of Utah (UT)
2007	Louie Sakoda	Junior	Place Kicker–Punter	University of Utah (UT)
2008	Louie Sakoda	Junior	Place Kicker–Punter	University of Utah (UT)
2009	Jeremy Kerley	Junior	Kick Returner	Texas Christian University (TX)
2010	Jeremy Kerley	Senior	Kick Returner–Punt Returner	Texas Christian University (TX)

MWC Freshman of the Year

Year	Player	Position	School
1999	Luke Staley	Running Back	Brigham Young University (UT)
2000	Jason Kaufusi	Defensive Lineman	University of Utah (UT)
2000	Brandon Ratcliff	Defensive Back	University of New Mexico (NM)
2001	Dominique Dorsey	Running Back–Kick Returner	University of Nevada, Las Vegas (NV)
2002	DonTrell Moore	Running Back	University of New Mexico (NM)
2003	Lynell Hamilton	Running Back	San Diego State University (CA)
2004	Austin Collie	Wide Receiver	Brigham Young University (UT)
2005	Aaron Brown	Running Back	Texas Christian University (TX)
2006	Ryan Wolfe	Wide Receiver	University of Nevada, Las Vegas (NV)
2007	Harvey Unga	Running Back	Brigham Young University (UT)
2008	Tim Jefferson	Quarterback	United States Air Force Academy (CO)
2009	Austyn Carta-Samuels	Quarterback	University of Wyoming (WY)
2010	Ronnie Hillman	Running Back	San Diego State University (CA)

Pacific-10 Conference (Pac-10)

1350 Treat Boulevard, Suite 500, Walnut Creek, CA 94597; Telephone: 925-932-4411; Fax: 925-932-4601; Web site: http://www.pac-10.org

The Pacific-10 Conference (originally known as the Pacific Coast Conference) began operations in 1916 with four schools: Oregon State College (now known as Oregon State University), the University of California at Berkeley, the University of Oregon, and the University of Washington. The PCC competed as a 10-member league until 1950, when the University of Montana left the conference, leaving it with nine teams, which the conference maintained until 1958. In 1959, the PCC was dissolved and the Athletic Associates of Western Universities was formed with charter members Stanford University, the University of California, Berkeley, the University of California at Los Angeles, the University of Southern California; and the University of Washington. While the conference was known as the Pac-8 (Pacific-8) in 1968, in 1978, both the University of Arizona and Arizona State University joined, and the conference became known as the Pac-10 Conference (Pacific-10).

As of this writing, the Pacific-10 Conference currently consists of the following 10 schools:

- Arizona State University Sun Devils, Tempe, AZ 85287; 480-965-9011; www.asu.edu
- Oregon State University Beavers, Corvallis, OR 97331; 541-737-1000; http://oregonstate.edu/
- Stanford University Cardinal, Stanford, CA 94305; 650-723-2300; www.stanford.edu

- University of Arizona Wildcats, Tucson, AZ 85721; 520-621-2211; www.arizona.edu
- University of California, Berkeley Golden Bears, Berkeley, CA 94720; 510-642-6000; http://berkeley.edu/
- University of California, Los Angeles Bruins, Los Angeles, CA 90095; 310-825-4321; www.ucla.edu
- University of Oregon Ducks, Eugene, OR 97403; 541-346-1000; www.www.uoregon.edu
- University of Southern California Trojans, Los Angeles, CA 90089; 213-740-2311; www.usc.edu
- University of Washington Huskies, Seattle, WA 98195; 206-543-2100; www.washington.edu
- Washington State University Cougars, Pullman, WA 99164; 509-335-3564; www.wsu.edu

Pac-10 Champions

Year	*School*
1916	University of Washington (WA)
1917	Washington State University (WA)
1918	University of California, Berkeley (CA)
1919	University of Oregon (OR)
1919	University of Washington (WA)
1920	University of California, Berkeley (CA)
1921	University of California, Berkeley (CA)
1922	University of California, Berkeley (CA)
1923	University of California, Berkeley (CA)
1924	Stanford University (CA)
1925	University of Washington (WA)
1926	Stanford University (CA)
1927	Stanford University (CA)
1927	University of Southern California (CA)
1928	University of Southern California (CA)
1929	University of Southern California (CA)
1930	Washington State University (WA)
1931	University of Southern California (CA)
1932	University of Southern California (CA)
1933	University of Oregon (OR)
1933	Stanford University (CA)
1934	Stanford University (CA)
1935	University of California, Berkeley (CA)
1935	Stanford University (CA)
1935	University of California, Los Angeles (CA)
1936	University of Washington (WA)
1937	University of California, Berkeley (CA)
1938	University of California, Berkeley (CA)
1939	University of Southern California (CA)
1939	University of Southern California (CA)
1940	Stanford University (CA)
1941	Oregon State University (OR)
1942	University of California, Los Angeles (CA)
1943	University of Southern California (CA)
1944	University of Southern California (CA)
1945	University of Southern California (CA)
1946	University of California, Los Angeles (CA)
1947	University of Southern California (CA)
1948	University of California, Berkeley(CA)
1948	University of Oregon (OR)
1949	University of California, Berkeley (CA)
1950	University of California, Berkeley (CA)
1951	Stanford University (CA)
1952	University of Southern California (CA)
1953	University of California, Los Angeles (CA)
1954	University of California, Los Angeles (CA)
1955	University of California, Los Angeles (CA)
1956	Oregon State University (OR)
1957	University of Oregon (OR)
1957	Oregon State University (OR)
1958	University of California, Berkeley (CA)
1959	University of California, Los Angeles (CA)
1959	University of Southern California (CA)
1959	University of Washington (WA)
1960	University of Washington (WA)
1961	University of California, Los Angeles (CA)
1962	University of Southern California (CA)
1963	University of Washington (WA)
1964	Oregon State University (OR)
1964	University of Southern California (CA)
1965	University of California, Los Angeles (CA)
1966	University of Southern California (CA)
1967	University of Southern California (CA)
1968	University of Southern California (CA)
1969	University of Southern California (CA)
1970	Stanford University (CA)
1971	Stanford University (CA)
1972	University of Southern California (CA)
1973	University of Southern California (CA)
1974	University of Southern California (CA)
1975	University of California, Berkeley (CA)
1975	University of California, Los Angeles (CA)
1976	University of Southern California (CA)
1977	University of Washington (WA)
1978	University of Southern California (CA)
1979	University of Southern California (CA)
1980	University of Washington (WA)
1981	University of Washington (WA)
1982	University of California, Los Angeles (CA)
1983	University of California, Los Angeles (CA)
1984	University of Southern California (CA)
1985	University of California, Los Angeles (CA)
1986	Arizona State University (AZ)
1987	University of California, Los Angeles (CA)
1987	University of Southern California (CA)
1988	University of Southern California (CA)
1989	University of Southern California (CA)
1990	University of Washington (WA)
1991	University of Washington (WA)
1992	Stanford University (CA)
1992	University of Washington (WA)
1993	University of Arizona (AZ)
1993	University of California, Los Angeles (CA)
1993	University of Southern California (CA)

Year	School
1994	University of Oregon (OR)
1995	University of Southern California (CA)
1995	University of Washington (WA)
1996	Arizona State University (AZ)
1997	University of California, Los Angeles (CA)
1997	Washington State University (WA)
1998	University of California, Los Angeles (CA)
1999	Stanford University (CA)
2000	University of Oregon (OR)
2000	Oregon State University (OR)
2000	University of Washington (WA)
2001	University of Oregon (OR)
2002	University of Southern California (CA)
2002	Washington State University (WA)
2003	University of Southern California (CA)
2004	University of Southern California (CA)
2005	University of Southern California (CA)
2006	University of California, Berkeley (CA)
2006	University of Southern California (CA)
2007	Arizona State University (AZ)
2007	University of Southern California (CA)
2008	University of Southern California (CA)
2009	University of Oregon (OR)
2010	University of Oregon (OR)

Pac-10 Coach of the Year

Voted on by conference coaches.

Year	Coach	School
1975	Dick Vermeil	University of California, Los Angeles (CA)
1976	John Robinson	University of Southern California (CA)
1977	Bill Walsh	Stanford University (CA)
1978	John Robinson	University of Southern California (CA)
1979	Rich Brooks	University of Oregon (OR)
1980	Don James	University of Washington (WA)
1981	Jim Walden	Washington State University (WA)
1982	Joe Kapp	University of California, Berkeley (CA)
1983	Jim Walden	Washington State University (WA)
1984	Ted Tollner	University of Southern California (CA)
1985	Terry Donahue	University of California, Los Angeles (CA)
1986	John Cooper	Arizona State University (AZ)
1987	Larry Smith	University of Southern California (CA)
1988	Dennis Erickson	Washington State University (WA)
1988	Larry Smith	University of Southern California (CA)
1989	Dave Kragthorpe	Oregon State University (OR)
1990	Don James	University of Washington (WA)
1990	Bruce Snyder	University of California, Berkeley (CA)
1991	Don James	University of Washington (WA)
1992	Dick Tomey	University of Arizona (AZ)
1993	Terry Donahue	University of California, Los Angeles (CA)
1994	Rich Brooks	University of Oregon (OR)
1995	Tyrone Willingham	Stanford University (CA)
1996	Bruce Snyder	Arizona State University (AZ)
1997	Mike Price	Washington State University (WA)
1998	Bob Toledo	University of California, Los Angeles (CA)
1999	Tyrone Willingham	Stanford University (CA)
2000	Dennis Erickson	Oregon State University (OR)
2001	Mike Price	Washington State University (WA)
2002	Jeff Tedford	University of California, Berkeley (CA)
2003	Pete Carroll	University of Southern California (CA)
2003	Bill Doba	Washington State University (WA)
2004	Jeff Tedford	University of California, Berkeley (CA)
2005	Pete Carroll	University of Southern California (CA)
2005	Karl Dorrell	University of California, Los Angeles (CA)
2006	Pete Carroll	University of Southern California (CA)
2007	Dennis Erickson	Arizona State University (AZ)
2008	Mike Riley	Oregon State University (OR)
2009	Chip Kelly	University of Oregon (OR)
2010	Chip Kelly	University of Oregon (OR)

Pac-10 Offensive Player of the Year

Voted on by conference coaches.

Year	*Player*	*Position*	*School*
1975	Chuck Muncie	Running Back	University of California, Berkeley (CA)
1976	Ricky Bell	Running Back	University of Southern California (CA)
1977	Guy Benjamin	Quarterback	Stanford University (CA)
1977	Warren Moon	Quarterback	University of Washington (WA)
1978	Charles White	Running Back	University of Southern California (CA)
1979	Charles White	Running Back	University of Southern California (CA)
1980	John Elway	Quarterback	Stanford University (CA)
1981	Marcus Allen	Running Back	University of Southern California (CA)
1982	John Elway	Quarterback	Stanford University (CA)
1982	Tom Ramsey	Quarterback	University of California, Los Angeles (CA)
1983	Steve Pelluer	Quarterback	University of Washington (WA)
1984	Rueben Mayes	Running Back	Washington State University (WA)
1985	Rueben Mayes	Running Back	Washington State University (WA)
1986	Brad Muster	Tail Back	Stanford University (CA)
1987	Troy Aikman	Quarterback	University of California, Los Angeles (CA)
1988	Rodney Peete	Quarterback	University of Southern California (CA)
1989	Steve Broussard	Running Back	Washington State University (WA)
1990	Greg Lewis	Running Back	University of Washington (WA)
1991	Mike Pawlawski	Quarterback	University of California, Berkeley (CA)
1991	Mario Bailey	Wide Receiver	University of Washington (WA)
1992	Drew Bledsoe	Quarterback	Washington State University (WA)
1993	J.J. Stokes	Split End	University of California, Los Angeles (CA)
1994	Napoleon Kaufman	Tail Back	University of Washington (WA)
1995	Keyshawn Johnson	Wide Receiver	University of Southern California (CA)
1996	Jake Plummer	Quarterback	Arizona State University (AZ)
1997	Ryan Leaf	Quarterback	Washington State University (WA)
1998	Cade McNown	Quarterback	University of California, Los Angeles (CA)
1998	Akili Smith	Quarterback	University of Oregon (OR)
1999	Troy Walters	Flanker	Stanford University (CA)
2000	Marques Tuiasosopo	Quarterback	University of Washington (WA)
2001	Joey Harrington	Quarterback	University of Oregon (OR)
2002	Jason Gesser	Quarterback	Washington State University (WA)
2002	Carson Palmer	Quarterback	University of Southern California (CA)
2003	Matt Leinart	Quarterback	University of Southern California (CA)
2004	Reggie Bush	Tail Back	University of Southern California (CA)
2004	Matt Leinart	Quarterback	University of Southern California (CA)
2005	Reggie Bush	Tail Back	University of Southern California (CA)
2006	Marshawn Lynch	Running Back	University of California, Berkeley (CA)
2007	Dennis Dixon	Quarterback	University of Oregon (OR)
2008	Jacquizz Rodgers	Tail Back	Oregon State University (OR)
2009	Toby Gerhart	Tail Back	Stanford University (CA)
2010	Andrew Luck	Quarterback	Stanford University (CA)

Pac-10 Pat Tillman Defensive Player of the Year

Tillman was a college and professional football player who gave up his sporting career to enter the Army after the September 2001 terrorist attack on the Twin Towers in New York City, NY; he served multiple tours before being killed by "friendly fire" in Afghanistan; this Award is voted on by conference coaches.

Year	*Player*	*Position*	*School*
1983	Ricky Hunley	Linebacker	University of Arizona (AZ)
1983	Ron Rivera	Linebacker	University of California, Berkeley (CA)
1984	Duane Bickett	Linebacker	University of Southern California (CA)
1985	Mark Walen	Tackle	University of California, Los Angeles (CA)

Year	Player	Position	School
1986	Byron Evans	Inside Linebacker	University of Arizona (AZ)
1987	Chuck Cecil	Free Safety	University of Arizona (AZ)
1988	Dana Wells	Nose Guard	University of Arizona (AZ)
1989	Junior Seau	Outside Linebacker	University of Southern California (CA)
1990	Steve Emtman	Tackle	University of Washington (WA)
1990	Darryl Lewis	Cornerback	University of Arizona (AZ)
1991	Steve Emtman	Tackle	University of Washington (WA)
1992	Dave Hoffmann	Inside Linebacker	University of Washington (WA)
1993	Rob Waldrop	Nose Guard	University of Arizona (AZ)
1994	Mark Fields	Middle Linebacker	Washington State University (WA)
1995	Tedy Bruschi	End	University of Arizona (AZ)
1996	Jason Chorak	Outside Linebacker	University of Washington (WA)
1997	Pat Tillman	Outside Linebacker	Arizona State University (AZ)
1998	Chris Claiborne	Inside Linebacker	University of Southern California (CA)
1999	Deltha O'Neal	Corner Back	University of California, Berkeley (CA)
2000	Adam Archuleta	Outside Linebacker	Arizona State University (AZ)
2001	Robert Thomas	Middle Linebacker	University of California, Los Angeles (CA)
2002	Terrell Suggs	End	Arizona State University (AZ)
2003	Dave Ball	End	University of California, Los Angeles (CA)
2004	Shaun Cody	Linebacker	University of Southern California (CA)
2004	Bill Swancutt	End	Oregon State University (OR)
2005	Haloti Ngata	Tackle	University of Oregon (OR)
2005	Dale Robinson	Middle Linebacker	Arizona State University (AZ)
2006	Daymeion Hughes	Corner Back	University of California, Berkeley (CA)
2007	Sedrick Ellis	Nose Tackle	University of Southern California (CA)
2008	Rey Maualuga	Linebacker	University of Southern California (CA)
2009	Brian Price	Tackle	University of California, Los Angeles (CA)
2010	Stephen Paea	Defensive Tackle	Oregon State University (OR)

Morris Trophy — Offense

An annual award presented to the top offensive lineman in the Pacific-10 Conference; the Award is voted on by conference coaches.

Year	Player	School
1980	Roy Foster	University of Southern California (CA)
1981	Roy Foster	University of Southern California (CA)
1982	Bruce Matthews	University of Southern California (CA)
1983	Gary Zimmerman	University of Oregon (OR)
1984	Dan Lynch	Washington State University (WA)
1985	Jeff Bregel	University of Southern California (CA)
1986	Danny Villa	Arizona State University (AZ)
1987	Randall McDaniel	Arizona State University (AZ)
1988	Joe Tofflemire	University of Arizona (AZ)
1989	Bern Brostek	University of Washington (WA)
1990	Pat Harlow	University of Southern California (CA)
1991	Lincoln Kennedy	University of Washington (WA)
1992	Lincoln Kennedy	University of Washington (WA)
1993	Todd Steussie	University of California, Berkeley (CA)
1994	Tony Boselli	University of Southern California (CA)
1995	Jonathan Ogden	University of California, Los Angeles (CA)
1996	Bob Sapp	University of Washington (WA)
1997	Olin Kreutz	University of Washington (WA)
1998	Yusuf Scott	University of Arizona (AZ)
1999	Travis Claridge	University of Southern California (CA)
2000	Chad Ward	University of Washington (WA)
2001	Levi Jones	Arizona State University (AZ)
2002	Kwame Harris	Stanford University (CA)

Year	Player	School
2003	Jacob Rogers	University of Southern California (CA)
2004	Adam Snyder	University of Oregon (OR)
2005	Ryan O'Callaghan	University of California, Berkeley (CA)
2006	Ryan Kalil	University of Southern California (CA)
2007	Alex Mack	University of California, Berkeley (CA)
2008	Alex Mack	University of California, Berkeley (CA)
2009	Charles Brown	University of Southern California (CA)
2010	Tyron Smith	University of Southern California (CA)

Morris Trophy — Defense

An annual award presented to the top defensive lineman in the Pacific-10 Conference; the Award is voted on by conference coaches.

Year	Player	School
1980	Vince Goldsmith	University of Oregon (OR)
1981	Fletcher Jenkins	University of Washington (WA)
1982	George Achica	University of Southern California (CA)
1983	Keith Millard	Washington State University (WA)
1984	Ron Holmes	University of Washington (WA)
1985	Erik Howard	Washington State University (WA)
1986	Reggie Rogers	University of Washington (WA)
1987	Dana Wells	University of Arizona (AZ)
1988	Dana Wells	University of Arizona (AZ)
1989	Esera Tuaolo	Oregon State University (OR)
1990	Steve Emtman	University of Washington (WA)
1991	Steve Emtman	University of Washington (WA)
1992	Rob Waldrop	University of Arizona (AZ)
1993	D'Marco Farr	University of Washington (WA)
1994	Chad Eaton	Washington State University (WA)
1995	Tedy Bruschi	University of Arizona (AZ)
1996	Darrell Russell	University of Southern California (CA)
1997	Jeremy Staat	Arizona State University (AZ)
1998	Inoke Brecterfield	Oregon State University (OR)
1999	Willie Howard	Stanford University (CA)
2000	Andre Carter	University of California, Berkeley (CA)
2001	Kenyon Coleman	University of California, Los Angeles (CA)
2002	Terrell Suggs	Arizona State University (AZ)
2003	Dave Ball	University of California, Los Angeles (CA)
2004	Bill Swancutt	Oregon State University (OR)
2005	Haloti Ngata	University of Oregon (OR)
2006	Sedrick Ellis	University of Southern California (CA)
2007	Sedrick Ellis	University of Southern California (CA)
2008	Nick Reed	University of Oregon (OR)
2009	Stephen Paea	Oregon State University (OR)
2010	Stephen Paea	Oregon State University (OR)

Pac-10 Freshman of the Year

Voted on by conference coaches.

Year	Player	Position	School
1999	Kareem Kelly	Split End	University of Southern California (CA)
2000	Terrell Suggs	Defensive End	Arizona State University (AZ)
2001	Teyo Johnson	Wide Receiver	Stanford University (CA)
2001	Reggie Williams	Wide Receiver	University of Washington (WA)
2002	Mike Williams	Wide Receiver	University of Southern California (CA)
2003	Brandon Browner	Corner Back	Oregon State University (OR)
2004	Zach Miller	Tight End	Arizona State University (AZ)

Year	Player	Position	School
2005	Jeremy Perry	Offensive Guard	Oregon State University (OR)
2005	Mike Thomas	Wide Receiver	University of Arizona (AZ)
2006	Jairus Byrd	Corner Back	University of Oregon (OR)
2006	Taylor Mays	Free Safety	University of Southern California (CA)
2006	Alterraun Verner	Corner Back	University of California, Los Angeles (CA)
2007	Jake Locker	Quarterback	University of Washington (WA)
2008	Jacquizz Rodgers	Tail Back	Oregon State University (OR)
2009	LaMichael James	Running Back (Offense)	University of Oregon (OR)
2009	Vontaze Burfict	Middle Line Backer (Defense)	Arizona State University (AZ)
2010	Robert Woods	Wide Receiver (Offense)	University of Southern California (CA)
2010	Junior Onyeali	Defensive Tackle (Defense)	Arizona State University (AZ)

Glenn "Pop" Warner Memorial Trophy

Top Senior Football Player on the West Coast (an annual award voted on by offensive and defensive coordinators from all West Coast NCAA 1-A schools from 1949 to 2004 and presented by the Palo Club (Palo Alto, CA); the award was established in 1949 by then–San Jose State football coach Bob Bronzan to honor the legendary coach "Pop" Warner)

Year	Player	School
1949	Eddie LeBaron	College of the Pacific (CA)
1950	Russ Pomeroy	Stanford University (CA)
1952	Jim Sears	University of Southern California (CA)
1953	Bob Garrett	Stanford University (CA)
1954	George Shaw	University of Oregon (OR)
1955	Bob Davenport	University of California, Los Angeles (CA)
1956	Jon Arnett	University of Southern California
1957	Joe Francis	Oregon State University (OR)
1958	Joe Kapp	University of California, Berkeley (CA)
1959	Chris Burford	Stanford University (CA)
1960	Bill Kilmer	University of California, Los Angeles (CA)
1962	Terry Baker	Oregon State University (OR)
1963	Vern Burke	Oregon State University (OR)
1964	Craig Morton	University of California, Berkeley (CA)
1965	Mike Garrett	University of Southern California (CA)
1966	Pete Pifer	Oregon State University (OR)
1967	Gary Beban	University of California, Los Angeles (CA)
1968	O.J. Simpson	University of Southern California (CA)
1969	Don Parish	Stanford University (CA)
1970	Jim Plunkett	Stanford University (CA)
1971	Jeff Siemon	Stanford University (CA)
1972	Mike Rae	University of Southern California (CA)
1973	Lynn Swann	University of Southern California (CA)
1974	Anthony Davis	University of Southern California (CA)
1975	Chuck Muncie	University of California, Berkeley (CA)
1976	Ricky Bell	University of Southern California (CA)
1977	Guy Benjamin	Stanford University (CA)
1978	Jerry Robinson	University of California, Los Angeles (CA)
1979	Charles White	University of Southern California (CA)
1980	Ken Margerum	Stanford University (CA)
1981	Marcus Allen	University of Southern California (CA)
1982	John Elway	Stanford University (CA)
1983	Ron Rivera	University of California, Berkeley (CA)
1984	Jack Del Rio	University of Southern California (CA)
1985	Rueben Mayes	Washington State University (WA)
1986	Dave Wyman	Stanford University (CA)
1988	Rodney Peete	University of Southern California (CA)
1989	Tim Ryan	University of Southern California (CA)

Year	Player	School
1990	Greg Lewis	University of Washington (WA)
1991	Tommy Vardell	Stanford University (CA)
1992	Glyn Milburn	Stanford University (CA)
1993	Johnnie Morton	University of Southern California (CA)
1994	Steve Stenstrom	Stanford University (CA)
1995	Keyshawn Johnson	University of Southern California (CA)
1996	Jake Plummer	Arizona State University (AZ)
1997	Skip Hicks	University of California, Los Angeles (CA)
1998	Cade McNown	University of California, Los Angeles (CA)
1999	Deltha O'Neal	University of California, Berkeley (CA)
2000	Marques Tuiasosopo	University of Washington (WA)
2002	Carson Palmer	University of Southern California (CA)
2003	Dave Ball	University of California, Los Angeles (CA)
2004	J.J. Arrington	University of California, Berkeley (CA)

Southeastern Conference (SEC)

2201 Richard Arrington Boulevard North, Birmingham, AL 35203; Telephone: 205-458-3000; Fax: 205-458-3031; Web site: http://www.secsports.com

The Southeastern Conference was formed in December 1932 (and began athletic competition in 1933) with 13 charter member schools: Auburn University, Georgia Institute of Technology, Louisiana State University, Mississippi State University, Tulane University, the University of Alabama, the University of Florida, the University of Georgia, the University of Kentucky, the University of Mississippi, the University of Tennessee, University of the South (Sewanee), and Vanderbilt University.

In 1991, the SEC aligned itself into two divisions (Eastern Division and Western Division) and in 1992, became the first conference to receive permission from the NCAA to sponsor an annual football championship game (between the winners of each division).

As of this writing, the Southeastern Conference currently consists of the following 12 schools:

- Auburn University Tigers, Auburn, AL 36849; 334-844-4000; www.auburn.edu
- Louisiana State University Tigers, Baton Rouge, LA 70803; 225-578-1686; www.lsu.edu
- Mississippi State University Bulldogs, Starkville, MS 39762; 662-325-2323; www.msstate.edu
- University of Alabama Crimson Tide, Tuscaloosa, AL 35487; 205-348-6010; www.ua.edu
- University of Arkansas Razorbacks, Fayetteville, AR 72701; 800-377-8632; www.uark.edu
- University of Florida Gators, Gainesville, FL 32611; 352-392-3261; www.ufl.edu
- University of Georgia Bulldogs, Athens, GA 30602; 706-542-3000; www.uga.edu
- University of Kentucky Wildcats, Lexington, KY 40506; 859-257-9000; www.uky.edu
- University of Mississippi Rebels, Oxford, MS 38677; 662-915-7226; www.olemiss.edu
- University of South Carolina Gamecocks, Columbia, SC 29208; 803-777-7000; www.sc.edu
- University of Tennessee Volunteers, Knoxville, TN 37996; 865-974-1000; www.utk.edu
- Vanderbilt University Commodores, Nashville, TN 37240; 615-322-7311; www.vanderbilt.edu

SEC Champions

Year	Team
1933	University of Alabama (AL)
1934	University of Alabama (AL)
1934	Tulane University (LA)
1935	Louisiana State University (LA)
1936	Louisiana State University (LA)
1937	University of Alabama (AL)
1938	University of Tennessee (TN)
1939	Georgia Tech University (Georgia Institute of Technology) (GA)
1939	University of Tennessee (TN)
1939	Tulane University (LA)
1940	University of Tennessee (TN)
1941	Mississippi State University (MS)
1942	University of Georgia (GA)
1943	Georgia Tech University (Georgia Institute of Technology) (GA)
1944	Georgia Tech University (Georgia Institute of Technology) (GA)
1945	University of Alabama (AL)
1946	University of Georgia (GA)
1946	University of Tennessee (TN)
1947	University of Mississippi (MS)
1948	University of Georgia (GA)
1949	Tulane University (LA)

Year	Team
1950	University of Kentucky (KY)
1951	Georgia Tech University (Georgia Institute of Technology) (GA)
1951	University of Tennessee (TN)
1952	Georgia Tech University (Georgia Institute of Technology) (GA)
1953	University of Alabama (AL)
1954	University of Mississippi (MS)
1955	University of Mississippi (MS)
1956	University of Tennessee (TN)
1957	Auburn University (AL)
1958	Louisiana State University (LA)
1959	University of Georgia (GA)
1960	University of Mississippi (MS)
1961	University of Alabama (AL)
1961	Louisiana State University (LA)
1962	University of Mississippi (MS)
1963	University of Mississippi (MS)
1964	University of Alabama (AL)
1965	University of Alabama (AL)
1966	University of Alabama (AL)
1966	University of Georgia (GA)
1967	University of Tennessee (TN)
1968	University of Georgia (GA)
1969	University of Tennessee (TN)
1970	Louisiana State University (LA)
1971	University of Alabama (AL)
1972	University of Alabama (AL)
1973	University of Alabama (AL)
1974	University of Alabama (AL)
1975	University of Alabama (AL)
1976	University of Georgia (GA)
1976	University of Kentucky (KY)
1977	University of Alabama (AL)
1978	University of Alabama (AL)
1979	University of Alabama (AL)
1980	University of Georgia (GA)
1981	University of Alabama (AL)
1982	University of Georgia (GA)
1983	Auburn University (AL)
1984	(Championship forfeited by the University of Florida)
1985	University of Tennessee (TN)
1986	Louisiana State University (LA)
1987	Auburn University (AL)
1988	Auburn University (AL)
1988	Louisiana State University (LA)
1989	University of Alabama (AL)
1989	University of Tennessee (TN)
1990	University of Tennessee (TN)
1991	University of Florida (FL)
1992	University of Alabama (AL)
1993	University of Florida (FL)
1994	University of Florida (FL)
1995	University of Florida (FL)
1996	University of Florida (FL)
1997	University of Tennessee (TN)
1998	University of Tennessee (TN)
1999	University of Alabama (AL)
2000	University of Florida (FL)
2001	Louisiana State University (LA)
2002	University of Georgia (GA)
2003	Louisiana State University (LA)
2004	Auburn University (AL)
2005	University of Georgia (GA)
2006	University of Florida (FL)
2007	Louisiana State University (LA)
2008	University of Florida (FL)
2009	University of Alabama (AL)
2010	Auburn University (AL)

SEC Coach of the Year

Voted on by conference coaches and media; the Associated Press has voted since 1946 and United Press International voted from 1960 to 1990.

Year	Coach	School
1935	Jack Meagher	Auburn University (AL)
1936	Robert Neyland	University of Tennessee (TN)
1937	Ray Morrison	Vanderbilt University (TN)
1938	Robert Neyland	University of Tennessee (TN)
1939	Bill Alexander	Georgia Tech University (Georgia Institute of Technology) (GA)
1940	Allyn McKeen	Mississippi State University (MS)
1941	Henry Russell Sanders	Vanderbilt University (TN)
1942	Wally Butts	University of Georgia (GA)
1943	No Selection	
1944	John Barnhill	University of Tennessee (TN)
1945	Frank Thomas	University of Alabama (AL)
1946	Wally Butts	University of Georgia (GA) (coaches and AP)
1947	Johnny Vaught	University of Mississippi (MS) (coaches and AP)
1948	Henry Frnka	Tulane University (LA) (coaches)
1948	Johnny Vaught	University of Mississippi (MS) (AP)
1949	Gaynell Tinsley	Louisiana State University (LA) (coaches and AP)

Year	*Coach*	*School*
1950	Robert Neyland	University of Tennessee (TN) (coaches)
1950	Bear Bryant	University of Kentucky (KY) (AP)
1951	Bobby Dodd	Georgia Tech University (Georgia Institute of Technology) (GA) (coaches)
1951	Robert Neyland	University of Tennessee (TN) (AP)
1952	Harold Drew	University of Alabama (AL) (coaches)
1952	Bobby Dodd	Georgia Tech University (Georgia Institute of Technology) (GA) (AP)
1953	Ralph Jordan	Auburn University (AL) (coaches and AP)
1954	Blanton Collier	University of Kentucky (KY) (coaches)
1954	Johnny Vaught	University of Mississippi (MS) (AP)
1955	Arthur Guepe	Vanderbilt University (TN) (coaches)
1955	Johnny Vaught	University of Mississippi (MS) (AP)
1956	Bowden Wyatt	University of Tennessee (TN) (coaches and AP)
1957	Wade Walker	Mississippi State University (MS) (coaches)
1957	Ralph Jordan	Auburn University (AP)
1958	Paul Dietzel	Louisiana State University (LA) (coaches and AP)
1959	Wally Butts	University of Georgia (GA) (coaches)
1959	Bear Bryant	University of Alabama (AL) (AP)
1960	Ray Graves	University of Florida (FL) (coaches)
1960	Johnny Vaught	University of Mississippi (MS) (AP and UPI)
1961	Bear Bryant	University of Alabama (AL) (coaches, AP, and UPI)
1962	Johnny Vaught	University of Mississippi (MS) (coaches, AP, and UPI)
1963	Ralph Jordan	Auburn University (AL) (coaches and UPI)
1963	Paul E. Davis	Mississippi State University (MS) (AP)
1964	Bear Bryant	University of Alabama (AL) (coaches, AP, and UPI)
1965	Doug Dickey	University of Tennessee (TN) (coaches)
1965	Bear Bryant	University of Alabama (AL) (AP and UPI)
1966	Vince Dooley	University of Georgia (GA) (coaches, AP, and UPI)
1967	Doug Dickey	University of Tennessee (TN) (coaches, AP, and UPI)
1968	Vince Dooley	University of Georgia (GA) (coaches, AP, and UPI)
1969	Charles McClendon	Louisiana State University (LA) (coaches, AP, and UPI)
1970	Charles McClendon	Louisiana State University (LA) (coaches and UPI)
1970	Charley Shira	Mississippi State University (MS) (AP)
1971	Bear Bryant	University of Alabama (AL) (coaches, AP, and UPI)
1972	Ralph Jordan	Auburn University (AL) (coaches, AP, and UPI)
1973	Bear Bryant	University of Alabama (AL) (coaches, AP, and UPI)
1974	Bear Bryant	University of Alabama (AL) (coaches and UPI)
1974	Steve Sloan	Vanderbilt University (TN) (AP)
1975	Ken Cooper	University of Mississippi (MS) (coaches, AP, and UPI)
1976	Vince Dooley	University of Georgia (GA) (coaches, AP, and UPI)
1977	Bear Bryant	University of Alabama (AL) (coaches and UPI)
1977	Fran Curci	University of Kentucky (KY) (AP)
1978	Vince Dooley	University of Georgia (GA) (coaches)
1978	Bear Bryant	University of Alabama (AL) (AP and UPI)
1979	Bear Bryant	University of Alabama (AL) (coaches, AP, and UPI)
1980	Vince Dooley	University of Georgia (GA) (coaches and AP)
1980	Charley Pell	University of Florida (FL) (UPI)
1981	Bear Bryant	University of Alabama (AL) (coaches, AP, and UPI)
1982	George MacIntyre	Vanderbilt University (TN) (coaches and UPI)
1982	Jerry Stovall	Louisiana State University (LA) (AP)
1983	Pat Dye	Auburn University (AL) (coaches and UPI)
1983	Billy Brewer	University of Mississippi (MS) (AP)
1983	Jerry Claiborne	University of Kentucky (KY) (AP)
1984	Bill Arnsparger	Louisiana State University (LA) (coaches)
1984	Galen Hall	University of Florida (FL) (AP and UPI)
1985	Johnny Majors	University of Tennessee (TN) (coaches, AP, and UPI)
1986	Bill Arnsparger	Louisiana State University (LA) (coaches and AP)
1986	Billy Brewer	University of Mississippi (MS) (UPI)

Year	*Coach*	*School*
1987	Pat Dye	Auburn University (AL) (coaches and AP)
1987	Bill Curry	University of Alabama (UPI)
1988	Pat Dye	Auburn University (AL) (coaches, AP, and UPI)
1989	Bill Curry	University of Alabama (AL) (coaches, AP, and UPI)
1990	Billy Brewer	University of Mississippi (MS) (coaches)
1990	Steve Spurrier	University of Florida (FL) (AP and UPI)
1991	Steve Spurrier	University of Florida (FL) (coaches)
1991	Gerry DiNardo	Vanderbilt University (TN) (AP)
1992	Gene Stallings	University of Alabama (AL) (coaches and AP)
1993	Terry Bowden	Auburn (University (AL) (coaches and AP)
1994	Steve Spurrier	University of Florida (FL) (coaches)
1994	Gene Stallings	University of Alabama (AL) (AP)
1995	Steve Spurrier	University of Florida (FL) (coaches and AP)
1996	Steve Spurrier	University of Florida (FL) (coaches and AP)
1997	Jim Donnan	University of Georgia (GA) (coaches)
1997	Tommy Tuberville	University of Mississippi (MS) (AP)
1998	Phillip Fulmer	University of Tennessee (TN) (coaches and AP)
1999	Mike DuBose	University of Alabama (AL) (coaches and AP)
2000	Lou Holtz	University of South Carolina (SC) (coaches and AP)
2001	Houston Nutt	University of Arkansas (AR) (coaches and AP)
2002	Mark Richt	University of Georgia (GA) (coaches and AP)
2003	David Cutcliffe	University of Mississippi (MS) (coaches and AP)
2003	Nick Saban	Louisiana State University (LA) (AP)
2004	Tommy Tuberville	Auburn University (AL) (coaches and AP)
2005	Mark Richt	University of Georgia (GA) (coaches)
2005	Steve Spurrier	University of South Carolina (SC) (AP)
2006	Houston Nutt	University of Arkansas (AR) (coaches and AP)
2007	Sylvester Croom	Mississippi State University (MS) (coaches and AP)
2008	Nick Saban	University of Alabama (AL) (coaches and AP)
2008	Bobby Johnson	Vanderbilt University (TN) (coaches)
2008	Houston Nutt	University of Mississippi (MS) (coaches)
2009	Nick Saban	University of Alabama (AL) (AP)
2010	Steve Spurrier	University of South Carolina (SC)

SEC Most Valuable Player

Voted on by conference coaches and media; beginning in 2003, this award was split up into the SEC Offensive Player of the Year, the SEC Defensive Player of the Year, and in 2004, the SEC Special Teams Player of the Year Award was created.

Year	*Player*	*Position*	*School*
1933	Beattie Feathers	Half Back	University of Tennessee (TN)
1934	Dixie Howell	Tail Back	University of Alabama (AL)
1935	Willie Geny	End	Vanderbilt University (TN)
1936	Walter Gilbert	Center	Auburn University (AL)
1937	Carl Hinkle	Center	Vanderbilt University (TN)
1938	George Cafego	Half Back	University of Tennessee (TN)
1939	Ken Kavanaugh	End	Louisiana State University (LA)
1939	Bob Foxx	Wing Back	University of Tennessee (TN)
1940	Erwin Elrod	End	Mississippi State University (MS)
1941	Jack Jenkins	Fulback	Vanderbilt University (TN)
1942	Frank Sinkwich	Tail Back	University of Georgia (GA)
1943	No Selection Made		
1944	Tom McWilliams	Halfback	Mississippi State University (MS)
1945	Harry Gilmer	Tail Back	University of Alabama (AL)
1946	Charley Trippi	Halfback	University of Georgia (GA)
1947	Charlie Conerly	Tail Back	University of Mississippi (MS)
1948	John Rauch	Quarterback	University of Georgia (GA)

Year	*Player*	*Position*	*School*
1949	Travis Tidwell	Quarterback	Auburn University (AL)
1950	Babe Parilli	Quarterback	University of Kentucky (KY)
1951	Bill Wade	Quarterback	Vanderbilt University (TN)
1952	Jackie Parker	Quarterback	Mississippi State University (MS)
1953	Jackie Parker	Quarterback	Mississippi State University (MS)
1954	Art Davis	Halfback	Mississippi State University (MS)
1955	John Majors	Tailback	University of Tennessee (TN)
1956	John Majors	Tailback	University of Tennessee (TN)
1957	Lou Michaels	Tackle	University of Kentucky (KY)
1958	Billy Cannon	Halfback	Louisiana State University (LA)
1959	Billy Cannon	Halfback	Louisiana State University (LA)
1960	Jake Gibbs	Quarterback	University of Mississippi (MS)
1961	Pat Trammell	Quarterback	University of Alabama (AL)
1962	Jerry Stovall	Halfback	Louisiana State University (LA)
1963	Jimmy Sidle	Quarterback	Auburn University (AL)
1964	Tucker Frederickson	Fullback	Auburn University (AL)
1965	Steve Sloan	Quarterback	University of Alabama (AL)
1966	Steve Spurrier	Quarterback	University of Florida (FL)
1967	Bob Goodridge	End	Vanderbilt University (TN)
1968	Jake Scott	Safety	University of Georgia (GA)
1969	Archie Manning	Quarterback	University of Mississippi (MS)
1970	Pat Sullivan	Quarterback	Auburn University (AL)
1971	Johnny Musso	Tailback	University of Alabama (AL)
1972	Terry Davis	Quarterback	University of Alabama (AL)
1973	Sonny Collins	Tailback	University of Kentucky (KY)
1974	Rockey Felker	Quarterback	Mississippi State University (MS)
1975	Jimmy DuBose	Fullback	University of Florida (FL)
1976	Ray Goff	Quarterback	University of Georgia (GA)
1977	Charles Alexander	Tailback	Louisiana State University (LA)
1978	Willie McClendon	Tailback	University of Georgia (GA)
1979	Joe Cribbs	Running Back	Auburn University (AL)
1980	Herschel Walker	Running Back	University of Georgia (GA)
1981	Herschel Walker	Running Back	University of Georgia (GA)
1982	Herschel Walker	Running Back	University of Georgia (GA)
1983	Reggie White	Defensive Tackle	University of Tennessee (TN)
1984	Kerwin Bell	Quarterback	University of Florida (FL)
1985	Bo Jackson	Running Back	Auburn University (AL)
1986	Cornelius Bennett	Linebacker	University of Alabama (AL)
1987	Wendell Davis	Wide Receiver	Louisiana State University (LA)
1988	Tracy Rocker	Defensive Tackle	Auburn University (AL)
1989	Emmitt Smith	Running Back	University of Florida (FL)
1990	Shane Matthews	Quarterback	University of Florida (FL)
1991	Shane Matthews	Quarterback	University of Florida (FL)
1992	Garrison Hearst	Running Back	University of Georgia (GA)
1993	Heath Shuler	Quarterback	University of Tennessee (TN)
1994	Jay Barker	Quarterback	University of Alabama (AL)
1995	Danny Wuerffel	Quarterback	University of Florida (FL)
1996	Danny Wuerffel	Quarterback	University of Florida (FL)
1997	Peyton Manning	Quarterback	University of Tennessee (TN)
1998	Tim Couch	Quarterback	University of Kentucky (KY)
1999	Shaun Alexander	Running Back	University of Alabama (AL)
2000	Rudi Johnson	Running Back	Auburn University (AL)
2001	Rex Grossman	Quarterback	University of Florida (FL)
2002	David Pollack	Defensive End	University of Georgia (GA)

SEC Offensive Player of the Year

Voted on by conference coaches and media.

Year	*Player*	*Position*	*School*
2003	Eli Manning	Quarterback	University of Mississippi (MS)
2004	Jason Campbell	Quarterback	Auburn University (AL)
2005	Jay Cutler	Quarterback	Vanderbilt University (TN)
2006	Darren McFadden	Running Back	University of Arkansas (AR)
2007	Darren McFadden	Running Back	University of Arkansas (AR)
2008	Tim Tebow	Quarterback	University of Florida (FL)
2009	Mark Ingram	Running Back	University of Alabama (AL)
2010	Cameron Newton	Quarterback	Auburn University (AL)

SEC Defensive Player of the Year

Voted on by conference coaches and media.

Year	*Player*	*Position*	*School*
2003	Chad Lavalais	Defensive Tackle	Louisiana State University (LA)
2004	David Pollack	Defensive End	University of Georgia (GA)
2005	DeMeco Ryans	Linebacker	University of Alabama (AL)
2006	Patrick Willis	Linebacker	University of Mississippi (MS)
2007	Glenn Dorsey	Defensive Tackle	Louisiana State University (LA)
2008	Eric Berry	Defensive Back	University of Tennessee (TN)
2009	Rolando McClain	Linebacker	University of Alabama (AL)
2010	Patrick Peterson	Defensive Back	Louisiana State University (LA)

SEC Special Teams Player of the Year

Voted on by conference coaches and media.

Year	*Player*	*Position*	*School*
2004	Carnell Williams	Running Back–Special Teams	Auburn University (AL)
2005	Skyler Green	Wide Receiver–Return Specialist	Louisiana State University (LA)
2006	John Vaughn	Placekicker	Auburn University (AL)
2007	Felix Jones	Tailback–Special Teams	University of Arkansas (AR)
2008	Brandon James	Wide Receiver–Return Specialist	University of Florida
2009	Javier Arenas	Cornerback–Return Specialist	University of Alabama (AL)
2010	Patrick Peterson	Return Specialist	Louisiana State University (LA)

SEC Freshman of the Year

Voted on by SEC coaches and media.

Year	*Player*	*Position*	*School*
1986	Tommy Hodson	Quarterback	Louisiana State University (LA)
1987	Emmitt Smith	Running Back	University of Florida (FL)
1988	No Selection Made		
1989	No Selection Made		
1990	Garrison Hearst	Running Back	University of Georgia (GA) (offense)
1990	James Willis	Linebacker	Auburn University (AL) (defense)
1991	Eric Zeier	Quarterback	University of Georgia (GA)
1992	Steve Taneyhill	Quarterback	University of South Carolina (SC) (offense)
1992	Randall Godfrey	Inside Linebacker	University of Georgia (GA) (defense)
1993	Danny Wuerffel	Quarterback	University of Florida (FL)
1994	Peyton Manning	Quarterback	University of Tennessee (TN)
1995	Kevin Faulk	Running Back	Louisiana State University (LA)
1995	Anthony McFarland	Defensive Lineman	Louisiana State University (LA)
1996	Derick Logan	Running Back	University of Kentucky (KY)
1997	Jamal Lewis	Running Back	University of Tennessee (TN)
1998	Quincy Carter	Quarterback	University of Georgia (GA)

Year	Player	Position	School
1999	Ronney Daniels	Wide Receiver	Auburn University (AL)
2000	Jabar Gaffney	Wide Receiver	University of Florida (FL)
2001	David Greene	Quarterback	University of Georgia (GA)
2002	Kwane Doster	Running Back	Vanderbilt University (TN)
2003	Chris Leak	Quarterback	University of Florida (FL)
2004	Brandon Siler	Linebacker	University of Florida (FL)
2005	Darren McFadden	Running Back	University of Arkansas (AR)
2006	Percy Harvin	Wide Receiver	University of Florida (FL)
2007	Knowshon Moreno	Running Back	University of Georgia (GA)
2008	A.J. Green	Wide Receiver	University of Georgia (GA)
2009	Warren Norman	Running Back	Vanderbilt University (TN)
2010	Marcus Lattimore	Running Back	University of South Carolina (SC)

Jacobs Blocking Trophy (Outstanding SEC Blocker)

Awarded by several football conferences (including the SEC since 1935), the Jacobs Blocking Trophy is presented to the SEC's best blocker as voted on by the conference's coaches. The trophy is presented in honor of William Plumer Jacobs (born: March 15, 1842, in Yorkville [now known as York], SC; died: September 10, 1975, in Clinton, SC), founder and president of Presbyterian College (Clinton, South Carolina).

Year	Player	School
1935	Riley Smith	University of Alabama (AL)
1936	Billy May	Louisiana State University (LA)
1937	Leroy Monsky	University of Alabama (AL)
1938	Sam Bartholomew	University of Tennessee (TN)
1939	Sam Bartholomew	University of Tennessee (TN)
1940	Lloyd Cheatham	Auburn University (AL)
1941	Jack Jenkins	Vanderbilt University (TN)
1942	Jack Jenkins	Vanderbilt University (TN)
1943	John Steber	Georgia Tech University (Georgia Institute of Technology) (GA)
1944	Billy Bevis	University of Tennessee (TN)
1945	Billy Bevis	University of Tennessee (TN)
1946	Hal Self	University of Alabama (AL)
1947	Buddy Bowen	University of Mississippi (MS)
1948	Truitt Smith	Mississippi State University (MS)
1949	Butch Avinger	University of Alabama (AL)
1950	Butch Avinger	University of Alabama (AL)
1951	Jimmy Hahn	University of Tennessee (TN)
1952	John Michels	University of Tennessee (TN)
1953	Crawford Mims	University of Mississippi (MS)
1954	Charles Evans	Mississippi State University (MS)
1955	Paige Cothren	University of Mississippi (MS)
1956	Stockton Adkins	University of Tennessee (TN)
1957	Stockton Adkins	University of Tennessee (TN)
1958	J. W. Brodnax	Louisiana State University (LA)
1959	Jim Cartwright	University of Tennessee (TN)
1960	Jim Cartwright	University of Tennessee (TN)
1961	Billy Neighbors	University of Alabama (AL)
1962	Butch Wilson	University of Alabama (AL)
1963	Tucker Frederickson	Auburn University (AL)
1964	Tucker Frederickson	Auburn University (AL)
1965	Hal Wantland	University of Tennessee (TN)
1966	Cecil Dowdy	University of Alabama (AL)
1967	Bob Johnson	University of Tennessee (TN)
1968	Brad Johnson	University of Georgia (GA)
1969	Chip Kell	University of Tennessee (TN)
1970	Chip Kell	University of Tennessee (TN)

Year	*Player*	*School*
1971	Royce Smith	University of Georgia (GA)
1972	John Hannah	University of Alabama (AL)
1973	Buddy Brown	University of Alabama (AL)
1974	Sylvester Croom	University of Alabama (AL)
1975	Randy Johnson	University of Georgia (GA)
1976	Warren Bryant	University of Kentucky (KY)
1977	Bob Cryder	University of Alabama (AL)
1978	Robert Dugas	Louisiana State University (LA)
1979	Dwight Stephenson	University of Alabama (AL)
1980	Nat Hudson	University of Georgia (GA)
1981	Wayne Harris	Mississippi State University (MS)
1982	Wayne Harris	Mississippi State University (MS)
1983	Guy McIntyre	University of Georgia (GA)
1984	Lomas Brown	University of Florida (FL)
1985	Peter Anderson	University of Georgia (GA)
1986	Wes Neighbors	University of Alabama (AL)
1987	Harry Galbreath	University of Tennessee (TN)
1988	Howard Cross	University of Alabama (AL)
1989	Eric Still	University of Tennessee (TN)
1990	Antone Davis	University of Tennessee (TN)
1991	Cal Dixon	University of Florida (FL)
1992	Everett Lindsay	University of Mississippi (MS)
1993	Tobie Sheils	University of Alabama (AL)
1994	Jason Odom	University of Florida (FL)
1995	Jason Odom	University of Florida (FL)
1996	Donnie Young	University of Florida (FL)
1997	Alan Faneca	Louisiana State University (LA)
1998	Matt Stinchcomb	University of Georgia (GA)
1999	Chris Samuels	University of Alabama (AL)
2000	Kenyatta Walker	University of Florida (FL)
2001	Kendall Simmons	Auburn University (AL)
2002	Shawn Andrews	University of Arkansas (AR)
2003	Shawn Andrews	University of Arkansas (AR)
2004	Wesley Britt	University of Alabama (AL)
2005	Marcus McNeill	Auburn University (AL)
2006	Arron Sears	University of Tennessee (TN)
2007	Andre Smith	University of Alabama (AL)
2007	Jonathan Luigs	University of Arkansas (AR)
2008	Michael Oher	University of Mississippi (MS)
2009	Warren Norman	Vanderbilt University (TN)
2010	Lee Ziemba	Auburn University (AL)

Okefenokee Oar

The Okefenokee Oar is presented to the winning team of the annual University of Florida vs. the University of Georgia football game. Although the Oar was first introduced for the 2009 game (won by Florida), the football rivalry between the two schools began in 1915. The Oar was made from a 1,000-year-old cypress tree that grew in the Okefenokee Swamp that straddles the Florida-Georgia border.

Sun Belt Conference (Sun Belt)

601 Poydras Street, Suite 2355, New Orleans, LA 70130; Telephone: 504-299-9066; Web page: http://www.sunbeltsports.org

The Sun Belt Conference was founded in August 4, 1976, with six charter members: Georgia State University, Jacksonville University, the University of New Orleans, the University of North Carolina at Charlotte, the University of South Alabama, and the University of South Florida. In 1991, the Sun

Belt Conference merged with the American South Conference and the newly-formed conference did not sponsor football until 2001.

As of this writing, the Sun Belt Conference currently consists of the following 13 schools:

- Arkansas State University Red Wolves, Jonesboro, AR 72401; 870-972-2100; www.astate.edu
- Florida Atlantic University Owls, Boca Raton, FL 33431; 561-297-3000; www.fau.edu
- Florida International University Golden Panthers, Miami, FL 33199; 305-348-2000; www.fiu.edu
- Middle Tennessee State University Blue Raiders, Murfreesboro, TN 37132; 615-898-2300; www.mtsu.edu
- Troy University Trojans, Troy, AL 36082; 800-414-5756; www.troy.edu
- University of Arkansas at Little Rock Trojans, Little Rock, AR 72204; 501-569-3000; http://ualr.edu; no football program
- University of Denver Pioneers, Denver, CO 80208; 303-871-2000; www.du.edu; no football program
- University of Louisiana at Lafayette Ragin' Cajuns, Lafayette, LA 70504; 337-482-1000; www.louisiana.edu
- University of Louisiana at Monroe Warhawks, Monroe, LA 71209; 318-342-1000; www.ulm.edu
- University of New Orleans Privateers, New Orleans, LA 70148; 504-280-6000; www.uno.edu; no football program
- University of North Texas Mean Green, Denton, TX 76203; 940-565-2000; www.unt.edu
- University of South Alabama Jaguars, Mobile, AL 36688; 251-460-6101; www.southalabama.edu
- Western Kentucky University Hilltoppers, Bowling Green, KY 42101; 270-745-0111; www.wku.edu

Sun Belt Champions

Year	*Team*
2001	University of North Texas (TX)
2001	Middle Tennessee State University (TN)
2002	University of North Texas (TX)
2003	University of North Texas (TX)
2004	University of North Texas (TX)
2005	Arkansas State University (AR)
2005	University of Louisiana, Lafayette (LA)
2005	University of Louisiana, Monroe (LA)
2006	Troy University (AL)
2006	Middle Tennessee State University (TN)
2007	Florida Atlantic University (FL)
2007	Troy University (AL)
2008	Troy University (AL)
2009	Troy University (AL)
2010	Florida International University (FL)
2010	Troy University (AL)

Sun Belt Coach of the Year

Selected by conference coaches.

Year	*Coach*	*School*
2001	Darrell Dickey	University of North Texas (TX)
2002	Darrell Dickey	University of North Texas (TX)
2003	Darrell Dickey	University of North Texas (TX)
2004	Darrell Dickey	University of North Texas (TX)
2005	Steve Roberts	Arkansas State University (AR)
2006	Rick Stockstill	Middle Tennessee State University (TN)
2007	Howard Schnellenberger	Florida Atlantic University (FL)
2008	Larry Blakeney	Troy University (AL)
2009	Rick Stockstill	Middle Tennessee State University (TN)
2009	Larry Blakeney	Troy University (AL)
2010	Mario Cristobal	Florida International University (FL)

Sun Belt Player of the Year

Selected by conference coaches.

Year	*Player*	*School*
2001	Wes Counts	Middle Tennessee State University (TN)
2002	Brandon Kennedy	University of North Texas (TX)

Year	Player	School
2003	Brandon Kennedy	University of North Texas (TX)
2004	Jamario Thomas	University of North Texas (TX)
2005	Steven Jyles	University of Louisiana, Monroe (LA)
2006	Omar Haugabook	Troy University (AL)
2007	Rusty Smith	Florida Atlantic University (FL)
2008	Tyrell Fenroy	University of Louisiana, Lafayette (LA)
2009	Levi Brown	Troy University (AL)
2010	T.Y. Hilton	Florida International University (FL)

Sun Belt Offensive Player of the Year

Selected by conference coaches.

Year	Player	School
2001	Dwone Hicks	Middle Tennessee State University (TN)
2002	Danny Smith	Arkansas State University (AR)
2003	Patrick Cobbs	University of North Texas (TX)
2004	Jamario Thomas	University of North Texas (TX)
2005	Steven Jyles	University of Louisiana, Monroe (LA)
2006	Omar Haugabook	Troy University (AL)
2007	Omar Haugabook	Troy University (AL)
2008	Michael Desormeaux	University of Louisiana, Lafayette (LA)
2009	Levi Brown	Troy University (AL)
2010	Bobby Rainey	Western Kentucky University (KY)

Sun Belt Defensive Player of the Year

Selected by conference coaches.

Year	Player	School
2001	Brad Kassell	University of North Texas (TX)
2002	Brandon Kennedy	University of North Texas (TX)
2003	Chris Hurd	University of North Texas (TX)
2004	Demarcus Ware	Troy University (AL)
2005	Jeff Littlejohn	Middle Tennessee State University (TN)
2006	Keyonvis Bouie	Florida International University (FL)
2007	Tyrell Johnson	Arkansas State University (AR)
2008	Alex Carrington	Arkansas State University (AR)
2009	Cardia Jackson	University of Louisiana, Monroe (LA)
2009	Chris McCoy	Middle Tennessee State University (TN)
2010	Jamari Lattimore	Middle Tennessee State University (TN)

Sun Belt Freshman of the Year

Selected by conference coaches.

Year	Player	School
2001	Ja'Mel Branch	University of North Texas (TX)
2002	Paul Dombrowski	New Mexico State University (NM)
2003	Kevin Payne	University of Louisiana, Monroe (LA)
2004	Jamario Thomas	University of North Texas (TX)
2005	Tyrell Fenroy	University of Louisiana, Lafayette (LA)
2006	Reggie Arnold	Arkansas State University (AR)
2007	Giovanni Vizza	University of North Texas (TX)
2008	T.Y. Hilton	Florida International University (FL)
2009	Shawn Southward	Troy University (AL)
2010	Corey Robinson	Troy University (AL)

Sun Belt Newcomer of the Year

Selected by conference coaches.

Year	*Player*	*School*
2001	Kevin Galbreath	University of North Texas (TX)
2002	Jonathan Burke	Arkansas State University (AR)
2003	Aubrey Dorisme	New Mexico State University (NM)
2004	Dylan Lineberry	University of North Texas (TX)
2005	Aaron Weathers	University of North Texas (TX)
2006	Omar Haugabook	Troy University (AL)
2007	Chris Bradwell	Troy University (AL)
2008	Levi Brown	Troy University (AL)

Western Athletic Conference (WAC)

9250 East Costilla Avenue, Suite 300, Englewood, CO 80112; Telephone: 303-799-9221; 303-799-3888 (FAX); Web site: http://www.wacsports.com

The Western Athletic Conference was formed in July 1962 and is considered a "mid-major" conference, since it is not a member of the Bowl Championship Series selection system. The six charter schools included Arizona State University, Brigham Young University, the University of Arizona, the University of New Mexico, the University of Utah, and the University of Wyoming.

Ty Detmer won the 1990 Heisman Trophy while attending Brigham Young University, the first for any WAC football athlete and in 1996, the WAC was the nation's largest NCAA Division I-A conference with 16 members.

As of this writing, the Western Athletic Conference currently consists of the following nine schools:

- Boise State University Broncos, Boise, ID 83725; 208-426-1000; www.boisestate.edu
- California State University, Fresno Bulldogs, Fresno, CA 93740; 559-278-4240; www.csufresno.edu
- Louisiana Technical University Bulldogs, Ruston, LA 71272; 318-257-2000; www.latech.edu
- New Mexico State University Aggies, Las Cruces, NM 88003; 575-646-0111; www.nmsu.edu
- San Jose State University Spartans, San Jose, CA 95192; 408-924-1000; www.sjsu.edu
- University of Hawai'i at Mānoa Warriors, Honolulu, HI 96822; 808-956-8111; www.uhm.hawaii.edu
- University of Idaho Vandals, Moscow, ID 83844; 208-885-6111; www.uidaho.edu
- University of Nevada at Reno Wolf Pack, Reno, NV 89557; 775-784-4700; www.unr.edu
- Utah State University Aggies, Logan, UT 84322; 435-797-1000; www.usu.edu

WAC Champions

Year	*School*
1962	New Mexico State University (NM)
1963	New Mexico State University (NM)
1964	University of Arizona (AZ)
1964	University of Utah (UT)
1964	University of New Mexico (NM)
1965	Brigham Young University (UT)
1966	University of Wyoming (WY)
1967	University of Wyoming (WY)
1968	University of Wyoming (WY)
1969	Arizona State University (AZ)
1970	Arizona State University (AZ)
1971	Arizona State University (AZ)
1972	Arizona State University (AZ)
1973	University of Arizona (AZ)
1973	Arizona State University (AZ)
1974	Brigham Young University (UT)
1975	Arizona State University (AZ)
1976	Brigham Young University (UT)
1976	University of Wyoming (WY)
1977	Arizona State University (AZ)
1977	Brigham Young University (UT)
1978	Brigham Young University (UT)
1979	Brigham Young University (UT)
1980	Brigham Young University (UT)
1981	Brigham Young University (UT)
1982	Brigham Young University (UT)
1983	Brigham Young University (UT)
1984	Brigham Young University (UT)
1985	U.S. Air Force Academy (CO)
1985	Brigham Young University (UT)
1986	San Diego State University (CA)
1987	University of Wyoming (WY)
1988	University of Wyoming (WY)
1989	Brigham Young University (UT)
1990	Brigham Young University (UT)
1991	Brigham Young University (UT)
1992	University of Hawai'i (HI)
1992	California State University, Fresno (CA)

1Year	School
992	Brigham Young University (UT)
1993	Brigham Young University (UT)
1993	California State University, Fresno (CA)
1993	University of Wyoming (WY)
1994	Colorado State University (CO)
1995	Colorado State University (CO)
1995	Brigham Young University (UT)
1995	University of Utah (UT)
1995	U.S. Air Force Academy (CO)
1996	University of Wyoming (WY)
1996	Brigham Young University (UT)
1997	Colorado State University (CO)
1997	University of New Mexico (NM)
1998	Brigham Young University (UT)
1998	U.S. Air Force Academy (CO)
1999	University of Hawai'i (HI)
1999	Texas Christian University (TX)

Year	School
1999	California State University, Fresno (CA)
2000	Texas Christian University (TX(
2000	University of Texas, El Paso (TX)
2001	Louisiana Tech University (LA)
2002	Boise State University (ID)
2003	Boise State University (ID)
2004	Boise State University (ID)
2005	University of Nevada (NV)
2005	Boise State University (ID)
2006	Boise State University (ID)
2007	University of Hawai'i (HI)
2008	Boise State University (ID)
2009	Boise State University (ID)
2010	Boise State University (ID)
2010	University of Hawai'i (HI)
2010	University of Nevada at Reno (NV)

WAC Coach of the Year

Selected by conference coaches.

Year	Coach	School
1962	Hal Mitchell	Brigham Young University (UT)
1963	Frank Kush	Arizona State University (AZ)
1964	Ray Nagel	University of Utah (UT)
1965	Tommy Hudspeth	Brigham Young University (UT)
1966	Lloyd Eaton	University of Wyoming (WY)
1967	Lloyd Eaton	University of Wyoming (WY)
1968	Darrell Mudra	University of Arizona (AZ)
1969	Bill Meek	University of Utah (UT)
1970	Frank Kush	Arizona State University (AZ)
1971	Frank Kush	Arizona State University (AZ)
1972	LaVell Edwards	Brigham Young University (UT)
1973	Jim Young	University of Arizona (AZ)
1974	Gil Bartosh	University of Texas, El Paso (TX)
1975	Frank Kush	Arizona State University (AZ)
1976	Fred Akers	University of Wyoming (WY)
1977	Frank Kush	Arizona State University (AZ)
1978	Wayne Howard	University of Utah (UT)
1979	LaVell Edwards	Brigham Young University (UT)
1980	LaVell Edwards	Brigham Young University (UT)
1981	Dick Tomey	University of Hawai'i (HI)
1982	Ken Hatfi eld	U.S. Air Force Academy (CO)
1983	LaVell Edwards	Brigham Young University (UT)
1984	LaVell Edwards	Brigham Young University (UT)
1985	Fisher DeBerry	U.S. Air Force Academy (CO)
1986	Denny Stolz	San Diego State University (CA)
1987	Paul Roach	University of Wyoming (WY)
1988	Paul Roach	University of Wyoming (WY)
1989	Bob Wagner	University of Hawai'i (HI)
1990	LaVell Edwards	Brigham Young University (UT)
1991	Al Luginbill	San Diego State University (CA)
1992	Bob Wagner	University of Hawai'i (HI)
1993	Dennis Franchione	University of New Mexico (NM)
1994	Sonny Lubick	Colorado State University (CO)
1995	Fisher DeBerry	U.S. Air Force Academy (CO)
1996	Joe Tiller	University of Wyoming (WY)

1996	LaVell Edwards	Brigham Young University (UT)
1997	Sonny Lubick	Colorado State University (CO)
1997	Dennis Franchione	University of New Mexico (NM)
1998	Ted Tollner	San Diego State University (CA)
1998	Fisher DeBerry	U.S. Air Force Academy (CO)
1999	June Jones	University of Hawai'i (HI)
2000	Gary Nord	University of Texas, El Paso (TX)
2001	Jack Bicknell	Louisiana Technical University (LA)
2002	Dan Hawkins	Boise State University (ID)
2003	Steve Kragthorpe	University of Tulsa (OK)
2004	Dan Hawkins	Boise State University (ID)
2005	Chris Ault	University of Nevada (NV)
2006	June Jones	University of Hawai'i (HI)
2007	June Jones	University of Hawai'i (HI)
2008	Chris Petersen	Boise State University (ID)
2009	Chris Petersen	Boise State University (ID)
2010	Chris Ault	University of Nevada (NV)

WAC Offensive Player of the Year

Selected by conference coaches.

Year	*Player*	*Position*	*School*
1962	Eldon Fortie	Halfback	Brigham Young University (UT)
1963	Tony Lorick	Fullback	Arizona State University (AZ)
1964	Stan Quintana	Quarterback	University of New Mexico (NM)
1965	Virgil Carter	Quarterback	Brigham Young University (UT)
1966	Virgil Carter	Quarterback	Brigham Young University (UT)
1967	Paul Toscano	Quarterback	University of Wyoming (WY)
1968	Art Malone	Fullback	Arizona State University (ZA)
1969	Dave Buchanan	Running Back	Arizona State University (AZ)
1970	Joe Spagnola	Quarterback	Arizona State University (AZ)
1971	Rocky Long	Quarterback	University of New Mexico (NM)
1972	Woody Green	Running Back	Arizona State University (AZ)
1973	Danny White	Quarterback	Arizona State University (AZ)
1974	Gary Sheide	Quarterback	Brigham Young University (UT)
1975	Bruce Hill	Quarterback	University of Arizona (AZ)
1976	Gifford Nielson	Quarterback	Brigham Young University (UT)
1977	Marc Wilson	Quarterback	Brigham Young University (UT)
1978	Jim McMahon	Quarterback	Brigham Young University (UT)
1978	Mike Williams	Running Back	University of New Mexico (NM)
1979	Marc Wilson	Quarterback	Brigham Young University
1980	Jim McMahon	Quarterback	Brigham Young University (UT)
1981	Jim McMahon	Quarterback	Brigham Young University (UT)
1982	Steve Young	Quarterback	Brigham Young University (UT)
1983	Steve Young	Quarterback	Brigham Young University (UT)
1984	Robbie Bosco	Quarterback	Brigham Young University (UT)
1985	Bart Weiss	Quarterback	U.S. Air Force Academy (CO)
1986	Steve Bartalo	Running Back	Colorado State University (CO)
1987	Todd Santos	Quarterback	San Diego State University (CA)
1988	Randy Welniak	Quarterback	University of Wyoming (WY)
1989	Dee Dowis	Quarterback	U.S. Air Force Academy (CO)
1990	Ty Detmer	Quarterback	Brigham Young University (UT)
1991	Ty Detmer	Quarterback	Brigham Young University (UT)
1992	Marshall Faulk	Running Back	San Diego State University (CA)
1993	Trent Dilfer	Quarterback	California State University, Fresno (CA)
1994	Stoney Case	Quarterback	University of New Mexico (NM)
1995	George Jones	Running Back	San Diego State University (CA)
1996	Beau Morgan	Quarterback	U.S. Air Force Academy (Pacific) (CO)
1996	Marcus Harris	Wide Receiver	University of Wyoming (Pacific) (WY)

Year	Player	Position	School
1996	Steve Sarkisian	Quarterback	Brigham Young University (Mountain) (UT)
1997	Moses Moreno	Quarterback	Colorado State University (Pacific) (CO)
1997	Graham Leigh	Quarterback	University of New Mexico (Mountain) (NM)
1998	Jaime Kimbrough	Tailback	California State University, Fresno (CA)
1998	Blane Morgan	Quarterback	U.S. Air Force Academy (Mountain) (CO)
1999	LaDainian Tomlinson	Running Back	Texas Christian University (TX)
2000	LaDainian Tomlinson	Running Back	Texas Christian University (TX)
2001	David Carr	Quarterback	California State University, Fresno (CA)
2002	Brock Forsey	Running Back	Boise State University (ID)
2003	Ryan Dinwiddie	Quarterback	Boise State University (ID)
2004	Ryan Moats	Running Back	Louisiana Technical University (LA)
2005	B.J. Mitchell	Running Back	University of Nevada (NV)
2006	Colt Brennan	Quarterback	University of Hawai'i (HI)
2007	Colt Brennan	Quarterback	University of Hawai'i (HI)
2008	Colin Kaepernick	Quarterback	University of Nevada (NV)
2009	Kellen Moore	Quarterback	Boise State University (ID)
2010	Colin Kaepernick	Quarterback	University of Nevada (NV)
2010	Kellen Moore	Quarterback	Boise State University (ID)

WAC Defensive Player of the Year

Selected by conference coaches.

Year	Player	Position	School
1981	Steve Clark	Defensive Lineman	University of Utah (UT)
1981	Kyle Whittington	Linebacker	Brigham Young University (UT)
1982	Johnny Jackson	Linebacker	University of New Mexico (NM)
1983	Raymond Morris	Linebacker	University of Texas, El Paso (TX)
1984	Chris Funk	Defensive Lineman	U.S. Air Force Academy (CO)
1984	Kyle Morrell	Defensive Back	Brigham Young University (UT)
1984	Filipo Mokofisi	Defensive Lineman	University of Utah (UT)
1985	Jason Buck	Defensive Tackle	Brigham Young University (UT)
1986	Al Noga	Defensive Tackle	Universiyt of Hawai'i (HI)
1987	Chad Hennings	Defensive Tackle	U.S. Air Force Academy (CO)
1988	Pat Rabold	Defensive Tackle	University of Wyoming (WY)
1989	Mitch Donahue	Defensive End	University of Wyoming (WY)
1990	Mitch Donahue	Defensive End	University of Wyoming (WY)
1991	Carlton McDonald	Defensive Back	U.S. Air Force Academy (CO)
1992	Carlton McDonald	Defensive Back	U.S. Air Force Academy (CO)
1993	Barron Wortham	Linebacker	University of Texas, El Paso (TX)
1994	Luther Elliss	Defensive Tackle	University of Utah (UT)
1995	Brady Smith	Defensive End	Colorado State University (CO)
1996	Chris Gizzi	Linebacker	U.S. Air Force Academy (Pacific) (CO)
1996	Shay Muirbrook	Linebacker	Brigham Young University (Mountain) (UT)
1997	Chris Gizzi	Linebacker	U.S. Air Force Academy (Pacific) (CO)
1997	Chris Bordano	Linebacker	Southern Methodist University (Mountain) (TX)
1998	Rob Morris	Linebacker	Brigham Young University (Pacific) (UT)
1998	Bryce Fisher	Defensive Tackle	U.S. Air Force Academy (Mountain) (CO)
1999	Brian Young	Defensive End	University of Texas, El Paso (TX)
2000	Aaron Schobel	Defensive End	Texas Christian University (TX)
2001	Alan Harper	Defensive Tackle	California State University, Fresno (CA)
2002	Quintin Mikell	Defensive Back	Boise State University (ID)
2003	Travis LaBoy	Defensive End	University of Hawai'i (HI)
2004	Robert Rodriguez	Linebacker	University of Texas, El Paso (TX)
2005	Garrett McIntyre	Defensive Lineman	California State University, Fresno (CA)
2006	Korey Hall	Linebacker	Boise State University (ID)
2007	Marcus Riley	Linebacker	California State University, Fresno (CA)
2008	Solomon Elimimian	Linebacker	University of Hawai'i (HI)

Year	Player	Position	School
2008	Jarron Gilbert	Defensive Tackle	San Jose State University (CA)
2009	Dontay Moch	Defensive End	University of Nevada (NV)
2010	Chris Carter	Defensive Lineman	California State University, Fresno (CA)

WAC Lineman of the Year

Selected by conference coaches.

Year	Player	Position	School
1962	Dave Costa	Offensive Tackle	University of Utah (UT)
1963	Eddie Stokes	Center	University of New Mexico (NM)
1964	John Briscoe	Center	University of Arizona (AZ)
1965	Phil Odle	Split End	Brigham Young University (UT)
1966	John Stipech	Defensive Tackle	University of Utah (UT)
1967	Curley Culp	Middle Guard	Arizona State University (AZ)
1968	Tom Nelson	Defensive Tackle	University of Arizona (AZ)
1969	Jeff Slipp	Defensive End	Brigham Young University (UT)
1970	Bill McKinley	Defensive End	University of Arizona (AZ)
1971	Gordon Gravelle	Offensive Guard / Tackle	Brigham Young University (UT)
1972	John Urban	Offensive Tackle	University of New Mexico (NM)
1973	Ron Rydalch	Defensive Tackle	University of Utah (UT)
1974	Bob Bruenig	Linebacker	University of Arizona (AZ)
1975	Mike Dawson	Defensive Lineman	University of Arizona (AZ)
1976	Robin Cole	Defensive Lineman	University of New Mexico (NM)
1977	Mike Bell	Defensive Lineman / End	Colorado State University (CO)
1978	Ken Fantetti	Linebacker	University of Wyoming (WY)
1979	Tom Bell	Defensive Lineman	Brigham Young University (UT)
1980	Nick Eyre	Defensive Lineman	Brigham Young University (UT)

WAC Newcomer of the Year

Voted on by conference coaches.

Year	Player	Position	School
1971	Woody Green	Running Back	Arizona State University (AZ)
1972	Paul Linford	Defensive Tackle	Brigham Young University (UT)
1973	Bruce Hill	Quarterback	University of Arizona (AZ)
1974	Bobby McKinley	Quarterback	University of Texas, El Paso (TX)
1975	Willie Scroggins	Defensive Lineman	Arizona State University (AZ)
1976	Jack Steptoe	Right Safety / Wide Receiver	University of Utah (UT)
1977	Myron Hardeman	Running Back	University of Wyoming (WY)
1978	Jeff Lyall	Defensive End	University of Utah (UT)
1979	Tom Tuinei	Defensive Lineman	University of Hawai'i (HI)
1980	Falanko Noga	Defensive Lineman	University of Hawai'i (HI)
1981	Johnny Jackson	Linebacker	University of New Mexico (NM)
1982	Jay Haynes	Outside Linebacker	University of Wyoming (WY)
1983	Steve Bartalo	Running Back	Colorado State University (CO)
1984	Eddie Johnson	Running Back	University of Utah (UT)
1984	Galand Thaxton	Linebacker	University of Wyoming (WY)
1985	Larry Egger	Quarterback	University of Utah (UT)
1986	Anthony Sargent	Wide Receiver	University of Wyoming (WY)
1987	Pat Hegarty	Quarterback	University of Texas, El Paso (TX)
1988	Dabby Dawson	Running Back	University of Wyoming (WY)

WAC Freshman of the Year

Voted on by conference coaches.

Year	Player	Position	School
1989	Jamal Farmer	Running Back	University of Hawai'i (HI)
1990	Barron Wortham	Linebacker	University of Texas, El Paso (TX)

Year	*Player*	*Position*	*School*
1991	Marshall Faulk	Running Back	San Diego State University (CA)
1992	Winslow Oliver	Running Back	University of New Mexico (NM)
1993	Steve Scrifes	Offensive Tackle	University of Wyoming (WY)
1994	Will Blackwell	Wide Receiver	San Diego State University (CA)
1995	Chris Fuamatu-Ma'afala	Running Back	University of Utah (UT)
1996	Jon Denton	Quarterback	University of Nevada, Las Vegas (Pacific) (NV)
1996	Ronney Jenkins	Running Back	Brigham Young University (Mountain) (UT)
1997	Charles Tharp	Running Back	University of Hawai'i (HI)
1997	Jaron Dabney	Right Safety	Brigham Young University (Mountain) (UT)
1998	Jerome Haywood	Defensive Tackle	San Diego State University (Pacific) (CA)
1998	James Sunia	Linebacker	University of Nevada, Las Vegas (Mountain) (NV)
1999	Josh Blankenship	Quarterback	University of Tulsa (OK)
2000	Timmy Chang	Quarterback	University of Hawai'i (HI)
2001	Chance Kretschmer	Running Back	University of Nevada (NV)
2002	Paul Pinegar	Quarterback	California State University, Fresno (CA)
2003	Nick Bunting	Linebacker	University of Tulsa (OK)
2004	Ryan Wendell	Guard / Center	California State University, Fresno (CA)
2004	Quintin Demps	Free Safety	University of Texas, El Paso (TX)
2005	Davone Bess	Wide Receiver	University of Hawai'i (HI)
2006	Paul Igboeli	Linebacker	Utah State University (UY)
2007	Colin Kaepernick	Quarterback	University of Nevada (NV)
2008	Kellen Moore	Quarterback	Boise State University (ID)
2009	Brandon Wimberly	Wide Receiver	University of Nevada (NV)
2010	Keith Smith	Linebacker	San Jose State University (CA)

WAC Special Teams Player of the Year

Voted on by conference coaches.

Year	*Player*	*School*
1991	Robert Rivers	University of Wyoming (WY)
1992	Jason Elam	University of Hawai'i (HI)
1993	Chris MacInnis	U.S. Air Force Academy (CO)
1994	David Dunn	California State University, Fresno (Fresno State University) (CA)
1995	James Dye	Brigham Young University (UT)

National Collegiate Athletic Association (NCAA) Division I — Football Championship Subdivision (FCS)

P.O. Box 6222, 700 West Washington Street, Indianapolis, IN 46202; Telephone: 317-917-6222; Fax: 317-917-6888; Web site: http://www.ncaa.org

According to National Collegiate Athletic Association rules, those colleges designated as Division I must sponsor at least seven sports for men and seven for women (or six for men and eight for women), which include two team sports for each gender. Focusing on schools that have football programs, in 2006 NCAA Division I institutions were further divided (by enrollment size) into either the Football Bowl Subdivision (FBS, formerly known as Division I-A since 1978) or the Football Championship Subdivision (FCS, formerly known as Division I-AA since 1978). FBS teams are the NCAA's largest and most well-known institutions.

Any conference that has at least 12 football teams (any NCAA level) may divide itself into two divisions and conduct a championship game between the division winners.

While FBS teams must attract an average of 15,000 fans per home game, there is no such requirement for FCS institutions. As of this writing, FCS schools are restricted to giving financial assistance amounting to 63 football players. However, unlike FBS institutions, FCS schools may divide their financial allotment into partial scholarships, but covering no more than 85 players.

As of this writing, the Ivy League, the Patriot League (no football scholarships), and the Pioneer Football League provide no scholarships at all.

Unlike the FBS, where "national champions" are determined through the result of post-season football Bowl Games (known as the Bowl Championship Series), FCS champions are determined in a 20-team, single-elimination tournament (as of 2010). The 20 teams are made up of 10 conference champions (not all conferences participate in the post-season tournament) and 10 "at-large" selections (teams must have at least seven wins to be eligible for an "at-large" spot). The tournament usually begins during the Thanksgiving weekend (late November) and runs into mid to late December, with the championship game in early January.

This section contains awards and trophies specifically related to the 14 conferences (plus the Eastern College Athletic Conference) and five Independent Teams within the NCAA Division I Football Championship Subdivision:

- Big Sky Conference (Big Sky)
- Big South (Big South)
- Colonial Athletic Association (CAA)
- Eastern College Athletic Conference
- FCS Independent Teams
- Great West Football Conference (Great West)
- Ivy League (Ivy)
- Mid-Eastern Athletic Conference (MEAC)
- Missouri Football Conference (MVC)
- Northeast Conference (NEC)

- Ohio Valley Conference (OVC)
- Patriot League (Patriot)
- Pioneer Football League (Pioneer)
- Southern Conference (Southern)
- Southland Conference (Southland)
- Southwestern Athletic Conference (SWAC)

DIVISION I FCS NATIONAL CHAMPIONS

Year	*School*	*Conference*	*Coach*
1978	Florida A&M University (FL)	Mid-East Athletic Conference	Rudy Hubbard
1979	Eastern Kentucky University (KY)	Ohio Valley Conference	Roy Kidd
1980	Boise State University (ID)	Big Sky Conference	Jim Criner
1981	Idaho State University (ID)	Big Sky Conference	Dave Kragthorpe
1982	Eastern Kentucky University (KY)	Ohio Valley Conference	Roy Kidd
1983	Southern Illinois University (IL)	Missouri Valley Football Conference	Rey Dempsey
1984	Montana State University (MT)	Big Sky Conference	Dave Arnold
1985	Georgia Southern University (GA)	Southern Conference	Erk Russell
1986	Georgia Southern University (GA)	Southern Conference	Erk Russell
1987	Northeast Louisiana University (LA)	Southland Conference	Pat Collins
1988	Furman University (SC)	Southern Conference	Jimmy Satterfield
1989	Georgia Southern University (GA)	Southern Conference	Erk Russell
1990	Georgia Southern University (GA)	Southern Conference	Tim Stowers
1991	Youngstown State University (OH)	Missouri Valley Football Conference	Jim Tressel
1992	Marshall University (WV)	Southern Conference	Jim Donnan
1993	Youngstown State University (OH)	Missouri Valley Football Conference	Jim Tressel
1994	Youngstown State University (OH)	Missouri Valley Football Conference	Jim Tressel
1995	University of Montana (MT)	Big Sky Conference	Don Read
1996	Marshall University (WV)	Southern Conference	Bob Pruett
1997	Youngstown State University (OH)	Missouri Valley Football Conference	Jim Tressel
1998	University of Massachusetts (MA)	Colonial Athletic Conference	Mark Whipple
1999	Georgia Southern University (GA)	Southern Conference	Paul Johnson
2000	Georgia Southern University (GA)	Southern Conference	Paul Johnson
2001	University of Montana (MT)	Big Sky Conference	Joe Glenn
2002	Western Kentucky University (KY)	Gateway Conference	Jack Harbaugh
2003	University of Delaware (DE)	Colonial Athletic Association	K. C. Keeler
2004	James Madison University (VA)	Colonial Athletic Association	Mickey Matthews
2005	Appalachian State University (NC)	Southern Conference	Jerry Moore
2006	Appalachian State University (NC)	Southern Conference	Jerry Moore
2007	Appalachian State University (NC)	Southern Conference	Jerry Moore
2008	University of Richmond (VA)	Colonial Athletic Association	Mike London
2009	Villanova University (PA)	Colonial Athletic Association	Andy Talley
2010	Eastern Washington University (WA)	Big Sky Conference	Beau Baldwin

American Football Coaches Association (AFCA) Coach of the Year

100 Legends Lane, Waco, TX 76706; Telephone: 254-754-9900; Fax: 254-754-7373; http://www.afca.com

The AFCA Coach of the Year Award is presented annually to each level of college football (NCAA FBS (and equivalent) since 1935, NCAA FCS since 1983, NCAA Division II since 1983, NCAA Division III since 1983, and NAIA since 2006). The Scripps-Howard newspaper chain conducted the balloting and presented the award from 1935 through 1959. In 1960, the AFCA itself began handling the voting and award presentation. Eastman Kodak Corporation sponsored the AFCA Coach of the Year program from 1960 until 1993, and from 1996 to 1999, the award was sponsored by GTE.

From 1960 through 1982, two national winners were selected (one from the University Division and one from the College Division). Beginning in 1983, four national winners were chosen, one from each school level (NCAA I-A, NCAA I-AA, NCAA Division II, and NCAA Division III) and in 2006, selection was expanded to five levels with the inclusion of the NAIA.

Currently, the AFCA selects 25 regional winners (five from each of the AFCA division levels), from which five national winners (one from each AFCA division level) are selected. All schools with eligible AFCA head coaches are listed on the national ballot and AFCA members are not limited to voting for regional winners. However, members are required to vote for coaches within their region for the AFCA Regional Coach of the Year and coaches within their division when voting for the AFCA National Coach of the Year.

The school of each AFCA National Coach of the Year winner receives $1,000 from the American Football Coaches Foundation for each full-time assistant football coach who was on staff the year the head coach was honored. If a school wins a national championship and the head coach wins the AFCA National Coach of the Year Award, the school then receives $1,500 for each full-time assistant who is an AFCA member.

As of this writing, Larry Kehres of Mount Union College (Ohio, (NCAA Division III) is the only coach in AFCA history to win the National Coach of the Year Award nine times (1993, 1996–1998, 2000–2002, 2006, 2008) and Bob Reade of Augustana College (Illinois, NCAA Division III) is the only coach to win the award four consecutive years (1983–1986).

NCAA FCS AFCA Coach of the Year

Year	*Coach*	*School*
1983	Rey Dempsey	Southern Illinois University (IL)
1984	Dave Arnold	Montana State University (MT)
1985	Dick Sheridan	Furman University (SC)
1986	Erk Russell	Georgia Southern University (GA)
1987	Mark Duffner	College of the Holy Cross (MA)
1988	Jimmy Satterfield	Furman University (SC)
1989	Erk Russell	Georgia Southern University (GA)
1990	Tim Stowers	Georgia Southern University (GA)
1991	Jim Tressel	Youngstown State University (OH)
1992	Charlie Taaffe	The Citadel—The Military College of South Carolina (SC)
1993	Dan Allen	Boston University (MA)
1994	Jim Tressel	Youngstown State University (OH)
1995	Don Read	University of Montana (MT)
1996	Ray Tellier	Columbia University (NY)
1997	Andy Talley	Villanova University (PA)
1998	Mark Whipple	University of Massachusetts (MA)
1999	Paul Johnson	Georgia Southern University (GA)
2000	Paul Johnson	Georgia Southern University (GA)
2001	Bobby Johnson	Furman University (SC)
2002	Jack Harbaugh	Western Kentucky University (KY)
2003	Dick Biddle	Colgate University (NY)
2004	Mickey Matthews	James Madison University (VA)
2005	Jerry Moore	Appalachian State University (NC)
2006	Jerry Moore	Appalachian State University (NC)
2007	Jerry Moore	Appalachian State University (NC)
2008	Mike London	University of Richmond (VA)
2009	Andy Talley	Villanova University (PA)
2010	K.C. Keeler	University of Delaware (DE)

American Football Coaches Association (AFCA) Assistant Coach of the Year

100 Legends Lane, Waco, TX 76706; Telephone: 254-754-9900; Fax: 254-754-7373; http://www.afca.com

The AFCA Assistant Coach of the Year Award has been presented annually since 1997 to the best assistant coach in each of the five levels of college football (NCAA FBS, NCAA FCS, NCAA Division II, NCAA Division III, and the NAIA).

For each of the five levels of college football, staff members from NCAA and NAIA football-playing schools nominate an assistant coach. From this list of nominees, a winner is then selected by the AFCA Public Relations Committee.

NCAA FCS Assistant Coach of the Year

Year	*Assistant Coach*	*School*
1997	Alonzo Lee	Hampton University (VA)
1998	John Wright	Hampton University (VA)
1999	David Bailiff	Southwest Texas State University (TX)
2000	John Shannon	Jackson State University (MS)
2001	Tom Gilmore	Lehigh University (PA)
2002	Roy Wittke	Eastern Illinois University (IL)
2003	Donovan Rose	Hampton University (VA)
2004	Tony Pierce	Alabama State University (AL)
2005	Galen Scott	Illinois State University (IL)
2006	Sam Eddy	Youngstown State University (OH)
2007	Tom Matukewicz	Southern Illinois University (IL)
2008	John Loose	Lafayette College (PA)
2009	Mark Speir	Appalachian State University (NC)
2010	Rick Fox	Drake University (IA)

Buck Buchanan Award

Since 1995, the Buck Buchanan Award has been presented annually by The Sports Network (http://www.sportsnetwork.com) to the most outstanding defensive player in the NCAA FCS division. It was first presented in 1995 after the Walter Payton Award (which was initially awarded to both offensive and defensive players) was designated solely for offensive players.

The award is named for Junious "Buck" Buchanan (6'7", 287 pounds, born: September 10, 1940, in Gainesville, Alabama; died: July 16, 1992, in Kansas City, Missouri), who was a college football star at Grambling State University (Grambling, Louisiana, 1959–1962); played 13 seasons with the AFL/NFL Kansas City Chiefs; helped the team win Super Bowl IV (1970) over the Minnesota Vikings; inducted into the Pro Football Hall of Fame in 1990; and was inducted into the College Football Hall of Fame in 1996.

As of this writing, Dexter Coakley (Appalachian State University, North Carolina) is the only two-time winner.

Year	*Winner*	*School*	*Note*
1995	Dexter Coakley	Appalachian State University (NC)	Played 10 Seasons in the NFL
1996	Dexter Coakley	Appalachian State University (NC)	Two-Time Athlete of the Year
1997	Chris McNeil	North Carolina A&T (NC)	Defensive Player of the Year
1998	James Milton	Western Illinois University (IL)	Gateway Football Conference
1999	Al Lucas	Troy State University (AL)	Played in NFL & NFL Europe
2000	Edgerton Hartwell	Western Illinois University (IL)	Played in the NFL
2001	Derrick Lloyd	James Madison University (VA)	Won Award on a Losing Team
2002	Rashean Mathis	Bethune-Cookman University (FL)	Plays in the NFL
2003	Jared Allen	Idaho State University (ID)	Plays in the NFL
2004	Jordan Beck	Cal Poly State University (CA)	Plays in the NFL
2005	Chris Gocong	Cal Poly State University (CA)	Two-Time Little All-American
2006	Kyle Shotwell	Cal Poly State University (CA)	Drafted into the NFL
2007	Kroy Biermann	University of Montana (MT)	Two-Time All Big Sky
2008	Greg Peach	Eastern Washington (WA)	Plays in the CFL
2009	Arthur Moats	James Madison University (VA)	2009 CAA Defensive Player of the Year
2010	J.C. Sherritt	Eastern Washington University (WA)	2010 Big Sky Conference Defensive Player of the Year

College Football Performance Awards (CFPA)

Founded in 2008, the College Football Performance Awards (P.O. Box 4839, Davidson, NC 28036; Telephone: 570-854-1252; Email: smithefficiency@yahoo.com; Web site: http://collegefootball performance.com) is an NCAA Division I FBS & FCS awards organization that recognizes weekly, annual, and career trophy recipients. For the purpose of this book, we focus only on the annual awards. For FBS awards, please refer to the National Collegiate Athletic Association (NCAA) Division I — Football Bowl Subdivision (FBS) chapter.

CPFA recipients are selected based exclusively on scientific rankings and mathematical algorithms based upon their individual performances and impact on the team's success. While the annual awards are generally based on the player's success in an individual season, the Elite Awards are based on multiple-season statistics and for those who break significant all-time records.

National Performer of the Year

Year	*Player*	*School*
2010	Pat Devlin	University of Delaware (DE)

Defensive Performer of the Year

Year	*Player*	*School*
2010	Tyler Holmes	University of Massachusetts (MA)

Freshman Performer of the Year

Year	*Player*	*School*
2010	Denarius McGhee	Montana State University (MT)

Quarterback Award

Year	*Player*	*School*
2010	DeAndre Presley	Appalachian State University (NC)

Running Back Award

Year	*Player*	*School*
2010	Taiwan Jones	Eastern Washington University (WA)

Tight End Award

Year	*Player*	*School*
2010	Andrew Kennedy	Columbia University (NY)

Wide Receiver Award

Year	*Player*	*School*
2010	Chris Summers	Liberty University (VA)

Defensive End Award

Year	*Player*	*School*
2010	Ameet Pall	Wofford College (SC)

Linebacker Award

Year	*Player*	*School*
2010	Tyler Holmes	University of Massachusetts (MA)

Defensive Back Award

Year	*Player*	*School*
2010	Moses Ellis	Prairie View A&M University (TX)
2010	Anthony Walters	University of Delaware (DE)

Defensive Tackle Award

Year	Player	School
2010	Kenrick Ellis	Hampton University (VA)

Placekicker Award

Year	Player	School
2010	Adrian Mora	Georgia Southern University (GA)

Punter Award

Year	Player	School
2010	John Prelvitz	North Dakota State University (ND)

Punt Returner Award

Year	Player	School
2010	Shawn Abuhoff	Dartmouth College (NH)

Kickoff Returner Award

Year	Player	School
2010	Gerald Stevenson	Charleston Southern University (SC)

Elite Quarterback Award

Year	Player	School
2010	Jeremy Moses	Stephen F. Austin State University (TX)
2010	Scott Riddle	Elon University (NC)

Elite Running Back Award

Year	Player	School
2010	Nate Eachus	Colgate University (NY)

Elite Wide Receiver Award

Year	Player	School
2010	Tysson Poots	Southern Utah University (UT)
2010	Lito Senatus	Western Illinois University (IL)

Elite Tight End Award

Year	Player	School
2010	Stephen Skelton	Fordham University (NY)

Elite Linebacker Award

Year	Player	School
2010	Keith Pough	Howard University (Washington, D.C.)

Elite Defensive Back Award

Year	Player	School
2010	Mark LeGree	Appalachian State University (NC)
2010	Korey Lindsey	Southern Illinois University (IL)

Elite Defensive Tackle Award

Year	Player	School
2010	Martin Parker	University of Richmond (VA)

ELITE KICKOFF RETURNER AWARD

Year	*Player*	*School*
2010	Matt Szczur	Villanova University (PA)
2010	Terrence Holt	Austin Peay State University (TN)

ELLITE PUNT RETURNER AWARD

Year	*Player*	*School*
2010	Dontrell Johnson	Murray State University (KY)

Eddie Robinson Award

The Eddie Robinson Award is presented annually to college football's top head coach in the NCAA FCS Division. The Award was established by The Sports Network in 1987 (http://www.sportsnetwork.com/merge/tsnform.aspx?c=sportsnetwork&page=cfoot2/misc/robinson.htm) and winners are voted on by FCS sports information directors and selected sports writers.

The award is named for Eddie Robinson (Edward Gay Robinson; born: February 13, 1919, in Jackson, LA; died: April 3, 2007, in Ruston, LA), the 56-year (1941–1997) football coach at Grambling State University (Grambling, LA) who accumulated a career 408–165–15 (0.694) record (the winningest football coach in FCS history). During his coaching career, Robinson had 45 winning seasons; won or shared the Southwestern Athletic Conference championship 17 times; and won nine black college football national championships. He was inducted into the College Football Hall of Fame in 1997.

As of this writing, only James Madison University's Mickey Matthews has won the award more than once.

Year	*Winner*	*School*	*Note*
1987	Mark Duffner	College of the Holy Cross (MA)	Led 1987 Team to 11–0 Record
1988	Bill Russo	Lafayette College (PA)	Won Three Patriot League Titles
1989	Erk Russell	Georgia Southern University (GA)	Had a Final Year 11–0 Record
1990	Gene McDowell	University of Central Florida (FL)	87–61 School Record (.588)
1991	Chris Ault	University of Nevada (NE)	6X Conference Coach of the Year
1992	Charlie Taaffe	The Citadel (SC)	Coached at The Citadel for 10 Years
1993	Dan Allen	Boston University (MA)	Coached to a 11–0 Record in 1993
1994	Jim Tressel	Youngstown State University (OH)	4X Division I-AA Championships
1995	Houston Nutt	Murray State University (KY)	3X SEC Coach of the Year
1996	Darren Barbier	Nicholls State University (LA)	17–28 (.486) Record at Nicholls
1997	Andy Talley	Villanova University (PA)	1997 Atlantic-10 Champions
1998	Paul Johnson	Georgia Southern University (GA)	2X Southern Conference Coach of the Year
1999	Mickey Matthews	James Madison University (VA)	2004 National Champions
2000	Joe Glenn	University of Montana (MT)	2001 Division I-AA National Champions
2001	Pete Lembo	Lehigh University (PA)	44–14 Record at Lehigh
2002	Tommy Tate	McNeese State University (LA)	Won 2002 Southland Conference Title
2003	Mike Ayers	Wofford College (SC)	4X Southern Conference Coach of the Year
2004	Jerry Kill	Southern Illinois University (IL)	2X Division I-AA Coach of the Year
2005	Sean McDonnell	University of New Hampshire (NH)	1997 College Assistant Coach of the Year
2006	Jerry Moore	Appalachian State University (NC)	6X Southern Conference Coach of the Year
2007	Mark Farley	University of Northern Iowa (IA)	2007 11–0 Record
2008	Mickey Matthews	James Madison University (VA)	2X Eddie Robinson Award Winner
2009	Henry Frazier III	Prairie View A&M University (TX)	Fourth Winningest Coach in School History
2010	Tony Samuel	Southeast Missouri State University (MO)	2010 Ohio Valley Conference Championship

Lambert-Meadowlands Cup

The Lambert-Meadowlands Trophy is an annual award given to the best team in the East in Division I FBS college football. Established in 1936 as the "Lambert Trophy," it also recognizes (as the "Lambert Cup") the best college football team in the FCS (as of 1982), NCAA Division II (as of 1957), and Division III (as of 1966) levels.

The Lambert Trophy was established by brothers Victor and Henry Lambert (owners of a jewelry store) in memory of their father, August.

The New Jersey Sports and Exposition Authority (Public Affairs Office, 50 State Route 120, East Rutherford, NJ 07073; Telephone: 201-935-8500; Email: publicaffairs@njsea.com; Web site: http://www.njsea.com/), operator of the Meadowlands Sports Complex, took over the administration of the Lambert Meadowlands Awards in 1983.

To be eligible for this award, a school must be located in the East or play half its schedule against eligible Lambert teams.

Year	*School*
1982	University of Delaware (DE)
1983	College of the Holy Cross (MA)
1984	University of Rhode Island (RI)
1985	University of Rhode Island (RI)
1986	College of the Holy Cross (MA)
1987	College of the Holy Cross (MA)
1988	College of the Holy Cross (MA)
1989	College of the Holy Cross (MA)
1990	College of William & Mary (VA)
1991	University of Delaware (DE)
1992	Villanova University (PA)
1993	Boston University (MA)
1994	James Madison University (VA)
1995	University of Delaware (DE)
1996	College of William & Mary (VA)
1997	University of Delaware (DE)
1998	University of Massachusetts (MA)
1999	Hofstra University (NY)
2000	University of Delaware (DE)
2001	Lehigh University (PA)
2002	Villanova University (PA)
2003	University of Delaware (DE)
2004	James Madison University (VA)
2005	University of New Hampshire (NH)
2006	University of Massachusetts (MA)
2007	University of Delaware (DE)
2008	James Madison University (VA)
2009	Villanova University (PA)
2010	University of Delaware (DE)

Liberty Mutual Coach of the Year

Sponsored by the Liberty Mutual Insurance Company (175 Berkeley Street, Boston, MA 02116; Telephone: 800-837-5254; Web site: http://www.coachoftheyear.com/), the Liberty Mutual Coach of the Year Award is an annual college football presentation given to the head coach from each NCAA Division (FBS [as of 2006], FCS [as of 2007], NCAA Division II [as of 2007], NCAA Division III [as of 2007]).

This award provides each coach with $50,000 to donate to the charity or charities of his choice, as well as a $20,000 grant to donate to his school's alumni association.

Year	*Coach*	*School*	*Note*
2007	Jerry Kill	Southern Illinois University (IL)	2004 Eddie Robinson Coach of the Year Winner
2008	Mickey Matthews	James Madison University (VA)	2004 FCS National Championship
2009	Jerry Moore	Appalachian State University (NC)	2006 Eddie Robinson Award Winner
2010	K.C. Keeler	University of Delaware (DE)	2010 Colonial Athletic Association Champions

Walter Payton Award

Since 1987, the Walter Payton Award has been presented annually to the most outstanding offensive player in the FCS College Football Division as chosen by a nationwide panel of media and college sports information directors. From its inception, the award was presented to the Division's top offensive or defensive player, but in 1995, its focus changed to only offensive players, and the Buck Buchanan Award for defensive players was then created.

The award is named in honor of the late National Football League's Walter Payton, who starred at Jackson State University (Jackson, Mississippi) and later with the NFL's Chicago Bears. He was inducted into both the College Football Hall of Fame (1996) and the Pro Football Hall of Fame (1993). As of this writing, only Armanti Edwards of Appalachian State University (NC) has won this award more than once.

Year	*Player*	*School*	*Note*
1987	Kenny Gamble	Colgate University (NY)	2002 College Football Hall of Fame Inductee
1988	Dave Meggett	Towson University (MD)	Won Super Bowl XXV Championship
1989	John Friesz	University of Idaho (ID)	2006 College Football Hall of Fame Inductee
1990	Walter Dean	Grambling State University (LA)	Nation's Top Rusher—1990
1991	Jamie Martin	Weber State University (UT)	Led NCAA Division I-AA in Passing (1991)
1992	Michael Payton	Marshall University (WV)	Won 1992 I-AA National Championship
1993	Doug Nussmeier	University of Idaho (ID)	1 of Only 32 Left-Handed QB to Play in NFL
1994	Steve McNair	Alcorn State University (MS)	3X First-Team All-SWAC
1995	Dave Dickenson	University of Montana (MT)	Won 1995 NCAA I-AA Championship
1996	Archie Amerson	Northern Arizona University (AZ)	Won CFL's 87th Grey Cup (1999)
1997	Brian Finneran	Villanova University (PA)	1997 All-American (AP)
1998	Jerry Azumah	University of New Hampshire (NH)	1999 5th-Round NFL Draft Pick
1999	Adrian Peterson	Georgia Southern University (GA)	1st Sophomore to Win This Award
2000	Louis Ivory	Furman University (SC)	No Further Information
2001	Brian Westbrook	Villanova University (PA)	All-Time NCAA Record—Total Yards (9,512)
2002	Tony Romo	Eastern Illinois University (IL)	3X All-American (2000–2002)
2003	Jamaal Branch	Colgate University (NY)	Led Division I—Rushing Yards Per Game—168.8
2004	Lang Campbell	College of William & Mary (VA)	Threw 54 College Touchdowns
2005	Erik Meyer	Eastern Washington University (WA)	Threw 84 College Touchdowns
2006	Ricky Santos	University of New Hampshire (NH)	3X All-American (2005–2007)
2007	Jayson Foster	Georgia Southern University (GA)	SoCon Freshman of the Year (2004)
2008	Armanti Edwards	Appalachian State University (NC)	4X All-Southern Conference (2006–2009)
2009	Armanti Edwards	Appalachian State University (NC)	2X Southern Conference Off Player of the Year
2010	Jeremy Moses	Stephen F. Austin (TX)	2009 Southland Conference Player of the Year

Big Sky Conference (Big Sky)

2491 Washington Boulevard, Suite 201, Ogden, UT 84401; Telephone: 801-392-1978; Fax Number: 801-392-5568; Web site: http://www.bigskyconf.com

The Big Sky Conference was founded in February 1963 with six charter members: Gonzaga University, Idaho State University, Montana State University, the University of Idaho, the University of Montana, and Weber State University.

As of this writing, the Big Sky Conference currently consists of the following nine schools:

- California State University, Sacramento Hornets, Sacramento, CA 95819; 916-278-6011; www.csus.edu
- Eastern Washington University Eagles, Cheney, WA 99004; 509-359-6200; www.ewu.edu
- Idaho State University Bengals, Pocatello, ID 83209; 208-282-0211; www.isu.edu
- Montana State University Bobcats, Bozeman, MT 59717; 406-994-0211; www.montana.edu
- Northern Arizona University Lumberjacks, Flagstaff, AZ 86011; 928-523-9011; http://home.nau.edu
- Portland State University Vikings, Portland, OR 97207; 503-725-3000; www.pdx.edu
- University of Montana Grizzlies, Missoula, MT 59812; 406-243-0211; www.umt.edu

- University of Northern Colorado Bears, Greeley, CO 80639; 970-351-1890; www.unco.edu
- Weber State University Wildcats, Ogden, UT 84408; 801-626-6000; www.weber.edu

Big Sky Champions

Year	*School*	*Year*	*School*
1963	Idaho State University (ID)	1991	University of Nevada, Reno (NV)
1964	Montana State University (MT)	1992	Eastern Washington University (WA)
1965	University of Idaho (ID)	1992	University of Idaho (ID)
1965	Weber State University (UT)	1993	University of Montana (MT)
1966	Montana State University (MT)	1994	Boise State University (ID)
1967	Montana State University (MT)	1995	University of Montana (MT)
1968	Montana State University (MT)	1996	University of Montana (MT)
1968	University of Idaho (ID)	1997	Eastern Washington University (WA)
1968	Weber State University (UT)	1998	University of Montana (MT)
1969	University of Montana (MT)	1999	University of Montana (MT)
1970	University of Montana (MT)	2000	University of Montana (MT)
1971	University of Idaho (ID)	2001	University of Montana (MT)
1972	Montana State University (MT)	2002	Idaho State University (ID)
1973	Boise State University (ID)	2002	Montana State University (MT)
1974	Boise State University (ID)	2002	University of Montana (MT)
1975	Boise State University (ID)	2003	Montana State University (MT)
1976	Montana State University (MT)	2003	Northern Arizona University (AZ)
1977	Boise State University (ID)	2003	University of Montana (MT)
1978	Northern Arizona University (AZ)	2004	Eastern Washington University (WA)
1979	Montana State University (MT)	2004	University of Montana (MT)
1980	Boise State University (ID)	2005	Eastern Washington University (WA)
1981	Idaho State University (ID)	2005	Montana State University (MT)
1982	University of Montana (MT)	2005	University of Montana (MT)
1983	University of Nevada, Reno (NV)	2006	University of Montana (MT)
1984	Montana State University (MT)	2007	University of Montana (MT)
1985	University of Idaho (ID)	2008	University of Montana (MT)
1986	University of Nevada, Reno (NV)	2008	Weber State University (UT)
1987	University of Idaho (ID)	2009	University of Montana (MT)
1988	University of Idaho (ID)	2010	Eastern Washington University (WA)
1989	University of Idaho (ID)	2010	Montana State University (MT)
1990	University of Nevada, Reno (NV)		

Big Sky Coach of the Year (selected by conference coaches)

Year	*Coach*	*School*
1963	Babe Caccia	Idaho State University (ID)
1964	Jim Sweeney	Montana State University (MT)
1965	Sark Arslanian	Weber State University (UT)
1966	Jim Sweeney	Montana State University (MT)
1967	Jim Sweeney	Montana State University (MT)
1968	Tom Parac	Montana State University (MT)
1969	Jack Swarthout	University of Montana (MT)
1970	Jack Swarthout	University of Montana (MT)
1971	Tony Knap	Boise State University (ID)
1972	Sonny Holland	Montana State University (MT)
1973	Tony Knap	Boise State University (ID)
1974	Tony Knap	Boise State University (ID)
1975	Tony Knap	Boise State University (ID)
1976	Sonny Holland	Montana State University (MT)
1977	Joe Salem	Northern Arizona University (AZ)
1978	Joe Salem	Northern Arizona University (AZ)
1979	Sonny Lubick	Montana State University (MT)

Year	Coach	School
1980	Jim Criner	Boise State University (ID)
1981	Dave Kragthorpe	Idaho State University (ID)
1982	Dennis Erickson	University of Idaho (ID)
1983	Chris Ault	University of Nevada, Reno (NV)
1984	Dave Arnold	Montana State University (MT)
1985	Dennis Erickson	University of Idaho (ID)
1986	Chris Ault	University of Nevada, Reno (NV)
1987	Mike Price	Weber State University (UT)
1988	Keith Gilbertson	University of Idaho (ID)
1989	Don Read	University of Montana (MT)
1990	Chris Ault	University of Nevada, Reno (NV)
1991	Chris Ault	University of Nevada, Reno NV)
1992	Dick Zornes	Eastern Washington University (WA)
1993	Don Read	University of Montana (MT)
1994	Pokey Allen	Boise State University (ID)
1995	Don Read	University of Montana (MT)
1996	Mick Dennehy	University of Montana (MT)
1997	Mike Kramer	Eastern Washington University (WA)
1998	Ron Ponciano	California State University, Northridge (CA)
1999	Jerome Souers	Northern Arizona University (AZ)
2000	Joe Glenn	University of Montana (MT)
2001	Joe Glenn	University of Montana (MT)
2001	Paul Wulff	Eastern Washington University (WA)
2002	Joe Glenn	University of Montana (MT)
2002	Mike Kramer	Montana State University (MT)
2003	Jerry Graybeal	Weber State University (UT)
2004	Paul Wulff	Eastern Washington University (WA)
2005	Paul Wulff	Eastern Washington University (WA)
2005	Mike Kramer	Montana State University (MT)
2006	Bobby Hauck	University of Montana (MT)
2007	Bobby Hauck	University of Montana (MT)
2008	Ron McBride	Weber State University (UT)
2009	Bobby Hauck	University of Montana (MT)
2010	Rob Ash	Montana State University (MT)

Big Sky Offensive Player of the Year

Selected by conference media, coaches, and sports information directors.

Year	Player	Position	School
1974	Jim McMillan	Quarterback	Boise State University (ID)
1975	John Smith	Running Back	Boise State University (ID)
1976	John Yarno	Center	University of Idaho (ID)
1977	Tom Jurich	Place Kicker	Northern Arizona University (AZ)
1978	Allan Clark	Running Back	Northern Arizona University (AZ)
1979	Joe Aliotti	Quarterback	Boise State University (ID)
1980	Frank Hawkins	Running Back	University of Nevada, Reno (NV)
1981	Mike Machurek	Quarterback	Idaho State University (ID)
1982	Ken Hobart	Quarterback	University of Idaho (ID)
1983	Ken Hobart	Quarterback	University of Idaho (ID)
1984	Kelly Bradley	Quarterback	Montana State University (MT)
1985	Eric Yarber	Wide Receiver	University of Idaho (ID)
1986	Eric Beavers	Quarterback	University of Nevada, Reno (NV)
1987	John Friesz	Quarterback	University of Idaho (ID)
1988	John Friesz	Quarterback	University of Idaho (ID)
1989	John Friesz	Quarterback	University of Idaho (ID)
1990	Jamie Martin	Quarterback	Weber State University (UT)
1990	Devon Pearce	Running Back	University of Idaho (ID)

Year	Player	Position	School
1991	Jamie Martin	Quarterback	Weber State University (UT)
1992	Doug Nussmeier	Quarterback	University of Idaho (ID)
1993	Dave Dickenson	Quarterback	University of Montana (MT)
1994	Dave Dickenson	Quarterback	University of Montana MT)
1995	Dave Dickenson	Quarterback	University of Montana (MT)
1996	Archie Amerson	Running Back	Northern Arizona University (AZ)
1996	Brian Ah Yat	Quarterback	University of Montana (MT)
1997	Harry Leons	Quarterback	Eastern Washington University (WA)
1998	Brian Ah Yat	Quarterback	University of Montana (MT)
1999	Charles Roberts	Running Back	California State University, Sacramento State (CA)
2000	Charles Roberts	Running Back	California State University, Sacramento State (CA)
2000	Charles Dunn	Running Back	Portland State University (OR)
2001	Jesse Chatman	Running Back	Eastern Washington University (WA)
2002	Josh Blankenship	Quarterback	Eastern Washington University (WA)
2002	John Edwards	Quarterback	University of Montana (MT)
2003	Jason Murrietta	Quarterback	Northern Arizona University (AZ)
2004	Erik Meyer	Quarterback	Eastern Washington University (WA)
2005	Erik Meyer	Quarterback	Eastern Washington University (WA)
2006	Jason Murrietta	Quarterback	Northern Arizona University (AZ)
2007	Matt Nichols	Quarterback	Eastern Washington University (WA)
2008	Cameron Higgins	Quarterback	Weber State University (UT)
2009	Matt Nichols	Quarterback	Eastern Washington University (WA)
2010	Taiwan Jones	Running Back	Eastern Washington University (WA)
2010	Denarius McGhee	Quarterback	Montana State University (MT)

Big Sky Defensive Player of the Year

Selected by conference media, coaches, and sports information directors.

Year	Player	Position	School
1974	Ron Rosenberg	Linebacker	University of Montana (MT)
1975	Rick Noel	Linebacker	Idaho State University (ID)
1976	Greg Anderson	Defensive Back	University of Montana (MT)
1977	Chris Malmgren	Defensive Tackle	Boise State University (ID)
1978	Bob Macauley	Linebacker	Boise State University (ID)
1978	Jerry Lumpkin	Linebacker	Northern Arizona University (AZ)
1979	Doug Scott	Defensive Tackle	Boise State University (ID)
1980	Mike Humiston	Linebacker	Weber State University (UT)
1981	Randy Trautman	Defensive Tackle	Boise State University (ID)
1982	John Rade	Linebacker	Boise State University (ID)
1983	Tony Shaw	Defensive Back	University of Nevada, Reno (NV)
1984	Mark Fellows	Linebacker	Montana State University (MT)
1985	Tom Hennessey	Linebacker	University of Idaho (ID)
1986	Henry Rolling	Defensive End	University of Nevada, Reno (NV)
1987	Pete Kwiatkowski	Defensive End	Boise State University (ID)
1988	Tim Hauck	Defensive Back	University of Montana (MT)
1989	Tim Hauck	Defensive Back	University of Montana (MT)
1990	Corey Widmer	Defensive Tackle	Montana State University (MT)
1991	Jeff Robinson	Defensive End	University of Idaho (ID)
1992	Jeff Robinson	Defensive End	University of Idaho (ID)
1993	Jason Marsh	Linebacker	Eastern Washington University (WA)
1994	Joe O'Brien	Defensive End	Boise State University (ID)
1995	Ryan Phillips	Defensive End	University of Idaho (ID)
1996	Jason Crebo	Linebacker	University of Montana (MT)
1997	Chris Scott	Defensive Tackle	Eastern Washington University (WA)
1998	Scott Shields	Strong Safety	Weber State University (UT)
1999	Vince Huntsberger	Strong Safety	University of Montana (MT)
2000	Andy Petek	Defensive End	University of Montana (MT)

Year	Player	Position	School
2001	Vince Huntsberger	Strong Safety	University of Montana (MT)
2002	Trey Young	Free Safety	University of Montana (MT)
2003	Kane Ioane	Strong Safety	Montana State University (MT)
2004	Roger Cooper	Linebacker	Montana State University (MT)
2004	Brady Fosmark	Defensive End	Weber State University (UT)
2005	Joey Cwik	Linebacker	Eastern Washington University (WA)
2005	Jeff Charleston	Defensive End	Idaho State University (ID)
2005	Matt Logue	Linebacker	California State University, Sacramento State (CA)
2006	Adam Hayward	Linebacker	Portland State University (OR)
2007	Kroy Biermann	Defensive End	University of Montana (MT)
2008	Greg Peach	Defensive End	Eastern Washington University (WA)
2009	Dane Fletcher	Defensive End	Montana State University (MT)
2010	J.C. Sherritt	Linebacker	Eastern Washington University (WA)

Big Sky Newcomer of the Year

Selected by conference media, coaches, and sports information directors.

Year	Player	Position	School
1983	Mike Mendoza	Quarterback	Northern Arizona University (AZ)
1984	Jon Francis	Running Back	Boise State University (ID)
1985	Charvez Foger	Running Back	University of Nevada, Reno (NV)
1986	Greg Wyatt	Quarterback	Northern Arizona University (AZ)
1987	Fine Unga	Running Back	Weber State University (UT)
1988	Lavon Worley	Running Back	Northern Arizona University (AZ)
1989	Fred Gatlin	Quarterback	University of Nevada, Reno (NV)
1990	Hendricks Johnson	Wide Receiver	Northern Arizona University (AZ)
1991	Bryan Reeves	Wide Receiver	University of Nevada, Reno (NV)
1992	Beau Smith	Linebacker	Northern Arizona University (AZ)
1993	Alfredo Anderson	Running Back	Idaho State University (ID)
1994	K.C. Adams	Running Back	Boise State University (ID)
1995	Archie Amerson	Running Back	Northern Arizona University (AZ)
1996	Aaron Flowers	Quarterback	California State University, Northridge (CA)
1997	Charles Dunn	Running Back	Portland State University (OR)
1998	Marcus Brady	Quarterback	California State University, Northridge (CA)
1999	Drew Miller	Quarterback	University of Montana (MT)
2000	Kane Ioane	Safety	Montana State University (MT)
2001	Ryan Fuqua	Running Back	Portland State University (OR)
2002	Josh Blankenship	Quarterback	Eastern Washington University (WA)
2002	Travis Lulay	Quarterback	Montana State University (MT)
2003	Justin Green	Running Back	University of Montana (MT)
2004	Ryan Mole	Running Back	California State University, Sacramento State (CA)
2004	Rocky Hanni	Offensive Guard	Eastern Washington University (WA)
2004	Rick Gatewood	Wide Receiver	Montana State University (MT)
2005	Jeff Charleston	Defensive End	Idaho State University (ID)
2006	Alex Henderson	Running Back	Northern Arizona University (AZ)
2007	Cameron Higgins	Quarterback	Weber State University (UT)
2008	Deonte Williams	Running Back	Northern Arizona University (AZ)
2009	Zach Schrader	Defensive Back	California State University, Sacramento State (CA)
2010	Denarius McGhee	Quarterback	Montana State University (MT)

Big South Conference (Big South)

7233 Pineville-Matthews Road, Suite 100, Charlotte, NC 28226; Telephone: 704-341-7990; Fax: 704-341-7991; Web site: http://www.bigsouthsports.com

The Big South Conference was founded in August 1983 (sports competition began in 1984) with charter members Armstrong Atlantic State University, Augusta State University, Campbell University,

Charleston Southern University (then known as Baptist College), Coastal Carolina University, Radford University, University of North Carolina, Asheville, and Winthrop University. As of 2010, the Big South Conference champion receives an automatic bid for the FCS football championship tournament.

As of this writing, the Big South Conference currently consists of the following 10 schools and one associate member (football):

- Charleston Southern University Buccaneers, North Charleston, SC 29406; 843-863-7000; www.csuniv.edu
- Coastal Carolina University Chanticleers, Conway, SC 29528; 843-347-3161; www.coastal.edu
- Gardner-Webb University Runnin' Bulldogs, Boiling Springs, NC 28017; 704-406-4000; http://gardner-webb.edu
- High Point University Panthers, High Point, NC 27262; 336-841-9000; www.highpoint.edu; no football program
- Liberty University Flames, Lynchburg, VA 24502; 434-582-2000; www.liberty.edu
- Presbyterian College Blue Hose, Clinton, SC 29325; 864-833-2820; www.presby.edu
- Radford University Highlanders, Radford, VA 24142; 540-831-5000; www.radford.edu; no football program
- Stony Brook University SeaWolves (Stony Brook, NY 11794; 631-632-6000; www.stonybrook.edu; associate member (football only) from the America East Conference
- University of North Carolina, Asheville, Asheville, NC 28804; 828-251-6600; www.unca.edu; no football program
- Virginia Military Institute Keydets, Lexington, VA 24450; 540-464-7207; www.vmi.edu
- Winthrop University Eagles, Rock Hill, SC 29733; 803-323-2133; www.winthrop.edu; no football program

Big South Champions

Season	*School*	*Season*	*School*
2002	Gardner-Webb University (NC)	2008	Liberty University (VA)
2003	Gardner-Webb University (NC)	2009	Stony Brook University (NY)
2004	Coastal Carolina University (SC)	2009	Liberty University (VA)
2005	Charleston Southern University (SC)	2010	Coastal Carolina University (SC)
2005	Coastal Carolina University (SC)	2010	Liberty University (VA)
2006	Coastal Carolina University (SC)	2010	Stony Brook University (NY)
2007	Liberty University (VA)		

Big South Coach of the Year

Year	*Coach*	*School*
2002	Steve Patton	Gardner-Webb University (NC)
2003	Steve Patton	Gardner-Webb University (NC)
2004	David Bennett	Coastal Carolina University (SC)
2005	Jay Mills	Charleston Southern University (SC)
2006	Danny Rocco	Liberty University (VA)
2007	Danny Rocco	Liberty University (VA)
2008	Danny Rocco	Liberty University (VA)
2009	Chuck Priore	Stony Brook University (NY)
2010	David Bennett	Coastal Carolina University (SC)

Big South Offensive Player of the Year

Year	*Player*	*Class*	*Position*	*School*
2002	Jeremy Martin	Senior	Quarterback	Gardner-Webb University (NC)
2003	Dre Barnes	Junior	Running Back	Liberty University (VA)
2004	Patrick Hall	Junior	Running Back	Coastal Carolina University (SC)
2005	Collin Drafts	Junior	Quarterback	Charleston Southern University (SC)
2006	Tyler Thigpen	Senior	Quarterback	Coastal Carolina University (SC)
2007	Rashad Jennings	Junior	Running Back	Liberty University (VA)
2008	Rashad Jennings	Senior	Running Back	Liberty University (VA)

Year	Player	Class	Position	School
2009	Mike Brown	Sophomore	Quarterback–Wide Receiver	Liberty University (VA)
2010	Mike Brown	Junior	Quarterback	Liberty University (VA)

Big South Defensive Player of the Year

Year	Player	Class	Position	School
2002	Mario Williams	Sophomore	Free Safety	Gardner-Webb University (NC)
2003	Mario Williams	Junior	Free Safety	Gardner-Webb University (NC)
2004	Harold Wells	Senior	Defensive Tackle	Gardner-Webb University (NC)
2005	Jada Ross	Sophomore	Linebacker	Charleston Southern University (SC)
2006	Brian Johnston	Junior	Defensive End	Gardner-Webb University (NC)
2007	Brian Johnston	Senior	Defensive End	Gardner-Webb University (NC)
2008	Jeffery Williams	Sophomore	Linebacker	Gardner-Webb University (NC)
2009	Tyler Santucci	Senior	Linebacker	Stony Brook University (NY)
2010	Andrae Jacobs	Sophomore	Linebacker	Coastal Carolina University (SC)

Big South Freshman of the Year

Year	Player	Position	School
2002	Keppy Baucom	Linebacker	Gardner-Webb University (NC)
2003	Jonna Lee	Linebacker	Charleston Southern University (SC)
2004	Jerome Simpson	Wide Receiver	Coastal Carolina University (SC)
2005	Zach Terrell	Running Back	Liberty University (VA)
2006	Tim Maypray	Quarterback	Virginia Military Institute (VA)
2007	Jeffery Williams	Linebacker	Gardner-Webb University (NC)
2008	Edwin Gowins	Running Back	Stony Brook University (NY)
2009	Matt Goods	Defensive Lineman	Gardner-Webb University (NC)
2010	Preston Pemasa	Defensive Lineman	Gardner-Webb University (NC)

Colonial Athletic Association (CAA)

8625 Patterson Avenue, Richmond, VA 23229; Telephone: 804-754-1616; Fax: 804-754-1830; Web site: http://www.CAASports.com

The Colonial Athletic Association (non-football teams) was founded in 1983 with seven charter schools: The College of William & Mary, East Carolina University, George Mason University, James Madison University, the United States Naval Academy, the University of North Carolina, Wilmington, and the University of Richmond. Originally called the Eastern College Athletic Conference South Basketball League, it was renamed the Colonial Athletic Association in 1985 when it added championships in other sports. The CAA Football Conference was formed in 2005, although it did not start playing football until 2007.

Even though CAA Football (in its present name) did not start play until 2007, its roots and history can be directly traced back to the Yankee Conference (1946), which then became the Atlantic 10 Conference in 1997. The Yankee Conference consisted of the following schools: Boston University (1973–1997), College of William & Mary (1993), James Madison University (1993), Northeastern University (1993), University of Connecticut (1946), University of Delaware (1986), University of Maine (1946), University of Massachusetts (1946), University of New Hampshire (1946), University of Rhode Island (1946), University of Richmond (1986), University of Vermont (which left in 1974), and Villanova University (1988).

In 1997, the Yankee Conference (and its 11 teams) transformed itself into the Atlantic 10 Conference. While the University of Connecticut left in 1999, in 2004 both Hofstra University and Towson University joined, bringing the conference to 12 members. When the Atlantic 10 Conference changed its name to CAA Football in 2007, the teams stayed the same.

As of this writing, the CAA currently consists of the following 12 schools (six of which have football programs) and six football-playing associate members:

- College of William & Mary Tribe, Williamsburg, VA 23187; 757-221-4000; www.wm.edu
- Drexel University Dragons, Philadelphia, PA 19104; 215-895-2000; www.drexel.edu; no football program

- George Mason University Patriots, Fairfax, VA 22030; 703-993-1000; www.gmu.edu; no football program
- Georgia State University Panthers, Atlanta, GA 30303; 404-413-2000; www.gsu.edu
- Hofstra University Pride, Hempstead, NY 11549; 516-463-6600; www.hofstra.edu; no football program
- James Madison University Dukes, Harrisonburg, VA 22807; 540-568-6211; www.jmu.edu
- Northeastern University Huskies, Boston, MA 02115; 617-373-2000; www.northeastern.edu; no football program
- Old Dominion University Monarchs, Norfolk, VA 23529; 757-683-3000; www.odu.edu
- Towson University Tigers, Towson, MD 21252; 410-704-2000; www.towson.edu
- University of Delaware Fightin' Blue Hens, Newark, DE 19716; 302-831-2792; www.udel.edu
- University of Maine Black Bears, Orono, ME 04469; 207-581-1110; www.umaine.edu; associate member from the America East Conference
- University of Massachusetts Minutemen, Amherst, MA 01003; 413-545-0111; www.umass.edu; associate member from the America East Conference
- University of New Hampshire Wildcats, Durham, NH 03824; 603-862-1234; www.unh.edu; associate member from the America East Conference
- University of North Carolina, Wilmington Sea Hawks, Wilmington, NC 28403; 910-962-3000; http://uncw.edu; no football program
- University of Rhode Island Rams, Kingston, RI 02881; 401-874-1000; www.uri.edu; associate member from the Atlantic 10 Conference
- University of Richmond Spiders, Richmond, VA 23173; 804-289-8000; www.richmond.edu; associate member from the Atlantic 10 Conference
- Villanova University Wildcats, Villanova, PA 19085; 610-519-4500; www.villanova.edu; associate member from the Big East Conference
- Virginia Commonwealth University Rams, Richmond, VA 23284; 804-828-0100; www.vcu.edu; no football program

CAA Champions

Year	*School*	*Coach*
1947	University of New Hampshire (NH)	Bill Glassford
1948	University of New Hampshire (NH)	Bill Glassford
1949	University of Connecticut (CT)	J.O. Christian
1949	University of Maine (ME)	David Nelson
1950	University of New Hampshire (NH)	Chief Boston
1951	University of Maine (ME)	Harold Westerman
1952	University of Connecticut (CT)	Bob Ingalls
1952	University of Maine (ME)	Harold Westerman
1952	University of Rhode Island (RI)	Hal Kopp
1953	University of New Hampshire (NH)	Chief Boston
1953	University of Rhode Island (RI)	Hal Kopp
1954	University of New Hampshire (NH)	Chief Boston
1955	University of Rhode Island (RI)	Hal Kopp
1956	University of Connecticut (CT)	Bob Ingalls
1957	University of Connecticut (CT)	Bob Ingalls
1957	University of Rhode Island (RI)	Herb Maack
1958	University of Connecticut (CT)	Bob Ingalls
1959	University of Connecticut (CT)	Bob Ingalls
1960	University of Connecticut (CT)	Bob Ingalls
1960	University of Massachusetts (MA)	Charles Studley
1961	University of Maine (ME)	Harold Westerman
1962	University of New Hampshire (NH)	Chief Boston
1963	University of Massachusetts (MA)	Victor Fusia
1964	University of Massachusetts (MA)	Victor Fusia
1965	University of Maine (ME)	Harold Westerman
1966	University of Massachusetts (MA)	Victor Fusia
1967	University of Massachusetts (MA)	Victor Fusia

Year	School	Coach
1968	University of Connecticut (CT)	John Toner
1968	University of New Hampshire (NH)	Jim Root
1969	University of Massachusetts (MA)	Victor Fusia
1970	University of Connecticut (CT)	John Toner
1971	University of Connecticut (CT)	Bob Casciola
1971	University of Massachusetts (MA)	Dick MacPherson
1972	University of Massachusetts (MA)	Dick MacPherson
1973	University of Connecticut (CT)	Larry Naviaux
1974	University of Maine (ME)	Walter Abbott
1974	University of Massachusetts (MA)	Dick MacPherson
1975	University of New Hampshire (NH)	Bill Bowes
1976	University of New Hampshire (NH)	Bill Bowes
1977	University of Massachusetts (MA)	Dick MacPherson
1978	University of Massachusetts (MA)	Bob Pickett
1979	Boston University (MA)	Rick Taylor
1979	University of Massachusetts (MA)	Bob Pickett
1980	Boston University (MA)	Rick Taylor
1981	University of Massachusetts (MA)	Bob Pickett
1981	University of Rhode Island (RI)	Bob Griffin
1982	Boston University (MA)	Rick Taylor
1982	University of Connecticut (CT)	Walt Nadzak
1982	University of Maine (ME)	Ronald Rogerson
1982	University of Massachusetts (MA)	Bob Pickett
1983	Boston University (MA)	Rick Taylor
1983	University of Connecticut (CT)	Tom Jackson
1984	Boston University (MA)	Rick Taylor
1984	University of Rhode Island (RI)	Bob Griffin
1985	University of Rhode Island (RI)	Bob Griffin
1986	University of Connecticut (CT)	Tom Jackson
1986	University of Delaware (DE)	Tubby Raymond
1986	University of Massachusetts (MA)	Jim Reid
1987	University of Maine (ME)	Tim Murphy
1987	University of Richmond (VA)	Dal Shealy
1988	University of Delaware (DE)	Tubby Raymond
1988	University of Massachusetts (MA)	Jim Reid
1989	University of Connecticut (CT)	Tom Jackson
1989	University of Maine (ME)	Tom Lichtenberg
1989	Villanova University (PA)	Andy Talley
1990	University of Massachusetts (MA)	Jim Reid
1991	University of Delaware (DE)	Tubby Raymond
1991	University of New Hampshire (NH)	Bill Bowes
1991	Villanova University (PA)	Andy Talley
1992	University of Delaware (DE)	Tubby Raymond
1993	Boston University (MA)	Dan Allen
1994	University of New Hampshire (NH)	Bill Bowes
1995	University of Delaware (DE)	Tubby Raymond
1996	College of William & Mary (VA)	Jimmye Laycock
1997	Villanova University (PA)	Andy Talley
1998	University of Richmond (VA)	Jim Reid
1999	James Madison University (VA)	Mickey Matthews
1999	University of Massachusetts (MA)	Mark Whipple
2000	University of Delaware (DE)	Tubby Raymond
2000	University of Richmond (VA)	Jim Reid
2001	Hofstra University (NY)	Joe Gardi
2001	University of Maine (ME)	Jack Cosgrove
2001	Villanova University (PA)	Andy Talley
2001	College of William & Mary (VA)	Jimmye Laycock

Year	School	Coach
2002	University of Maine (ME)	Jack Cosgrove
2002	Northeastern University (MA)	Don Brown
2003	University of Delaware (DE)	K.C. Keeler
2003	University of Massachusetts (MA)	Mark Whipple
2004	University of Delaware (DE)	K.C. Keeler
2004	James Madison University (VA)	Mickey Matthews
2004	College of William & Mary (VA)	Jimmye Laycock
2005	University of New Hampshire (NH)	Sean McDonnell
2005	University of Richmond (VA)	Dave Clawson
2006	University of Massachusetts (MA)	Don Brown
2007	University of Massachusetts (MA)	Don Brown
2007	University of Richmond (VA)	Dave Clawson
2008	James Madison University (VA)	Mickey Matthews
2009	University of Richmond (VA)	Mike London
2009	Villanova University (PA)	Andy Talley
2010	College of William & Mary (VA)	Jimmye Laycock
2010	University of Delaware (DE)	K.C. Keeler

CAA Coach of the Year

Year	Coach	School
1982	Ron Rogerson	University of Maine (ME)
1983	Rick Taylor	Boston University (MA)
1984	Bob Griffin	University of Rhode Island (RI)
1985	Bob Griffin	University of Rhode Island (RI)
1986	Tom Jackson	University of Connecticut (CT)
1987	Dal Shealy	University of Richmond (VA)
1988	Jim Reid	University of Massachusetts (MA)
1989	Tom Lichtenberg	University of Maine (ME)
1989	Bill Bowes	University of New Hampshire (NH)
1990	Jim Reid	University of Massachusetts (MA)
1991	Tubby Raymond	University of Delaware (DE)
1992	Jim Marshall	University of Richmond (VA)
1993	Dan Allen	Boston University (MA)
1994	Bill Bowes	University of New Hampshire (NH)
1995	Floyd Keith	University of Rhode Island (RI)
1995	Jim Reid	University of Richmond (VA)
1996	Jack Cosgrove	University of Maine (ME)
1997	Andy Talley	Villanova University (PA)
1998	Jim Reid	University of Richmond (VA)
1999	Mickey Matthews	James Madison University (VA)
2000	Jim Reid	University of Richmond (VA)
2001	Jack Cosgrove	University of Maine (ME)
2001	Tim Stowers	University of Rhode Island (RI)
2002	Don Brown	Northeastern University (MA)
2003	Mark Whipple	University of Massachusetts (MA)
2004	Sean McDonnell	University of New Hampshire (NH)
2005	Dave Clawson	University of Richmond (VA)
2006	Don Brown	University of Massachusetts (MA)
2007	Dave Clawson	University of Richmond (VA)
2008	Mickey Matthews	James Madison University (VA)
2009	Andy Talley	Villanova University (PA)
2010	Joe Trainer	University of Rhode Island (RI)

CAA Offensive Player of the Year

Year	Player	School
1980	Jim Jensen	Boston University (MA)
1981	Ken Sweitzer	University of Connecticut (CT)

Year	*Player*	*School*
1982	Rich LaBonte	University of Maine (ME)
1983	Paul Lewis	Boston University (MA)
1984	Tom Ehrhardt	University of Rhode Island (RI)
1985	Tom Ehrhardt	University of Rhode Island (RI)
1986	Rich Gannon	University of Delaware (DE)
1987	Mike Buck	University of Maine (ME)
1988	Matt DeGennaro	University of Connecticut (CT)
1989	Mike Buck	University of Maine (ME)
1990	Stan Greene	Boston University (MA)
1990	Gary Wilkos	University of Massachusetts (MA)
1991	Barry Bourassa	University of New Hampshire (NH)
1992	Greg Lilly	University of Richmond (VA)
1993	Robert Dougherty	Boston University (MA)
1994	Robert Dougherty	Boston University (MA)
1995	Leo Hamlett	University of Delaware (DE)
1996	Jerry Azumah	University of New Hampshire (NH)
1997	Brian Finneran	Villanova University (PA)
1998	Jerry Azumah	University of New Hampshire (NH)
1999	Curtis Keaton	James Madison University (VA)
2000	Brian Westbrook	Villanova University (PA)
2001	Brian Westbrook	Villanova University (PA)
2002	Brett Gordon	Villanova University (PA)
2003	Andy Hall	University of Delaware (DE)
2004	Lang Campbell	College of William & Mary (VA)
2005	Ricky Santos	University of New Hampshire (NH)
2006	Ricky Santos	University of New Hampshire (NH)
2006	Steve Baylark	University of Massachusetts (MA)
2007	Joe Flacco	University of Delaware (DE)
2007	Ricky Santos	University of New Hampshire (NH)
2008	Rodney Landers	James Madison University (VA)
2009	Matt Szczur	Villanova University (PA)
2010	Pat Devlin	University of Delaware (DE)

CAA Defensive Player of the Year

Year	*Player*	*School*
1980	Mike Kelleher	Boston University (MA)
1981	Steve Doig	University of New Hampshire (NH)
1982	John Dorsey	University of Connecticut (CT)
1983	John Dorsey	University of Connecticut (CT)
1984	Tim Teevens	University of New Hampshire (NH)
1985	Neal Zonfrelli	University of New Hampshire (NH)
1985	Mark Michaels	University of Connecticut (CT)
1986	Kevin Murphy	Boston University (MA)
1987	Paul Boulay	University of New Hampshire (NH)
1988	John McKeown	University of Massachusetts (MA)
1989	Troy Ashley	University of Connecticut (CT)
1990	James Smith	University of Richmond (VA)
1991	Curtis Eller	Villanova University (PA)
1992	Curtis Eller	Villanova University (PA)
1993	Craig Staub	College of William & Mary (VA)
1994	Brian Corcoran	University of Massachusetts (MA)
1995	Jason Miller	College of William & Mary (VA)
1996	Darren Sharper	College of William & Mary (VA)
1997	Shawn Barber	University of Richmond (VA)
1998	Marc Megna	University of Richmond (VA)
1999	Chris Morant	James Madison University (VA)
2000	Brian McKenna	University of Delaware (DE)

Year	*Player*	*School*
2001	Stephen Cooper	University of Maine (ME)
2001	Derrick Lloyd	James Madison University (VA)
2002	Stephen Cooper	University of Maine (ME)
2003	Shawn Johnson	University of Delaware (DE)
2004	Shannon James	University of Massachusetts (MA)
2005	Tony LeZotte	James Madison University (VA)
2006	Akeem Jordan	James Madison University (VA)
2007	Tony LeZotte	James Madison University (VA)
2008	Jovan Belcher	University of Maine (ME)
2009	Arthur Moats	James Madison University (VA)
2010	Tyler Holmes	University of Massachusetts (MA)
2010	Eric McBride	University of Richmond (VA)

CAA Rookie of the Year

Year	*Player*	*School*
1980	Curt Collins	University of New Hampshire (NH)
1981	Rich LaBonte	University of Maine (ME)
1982	Bill Brooks	Boston University (MA)
1983	Dameon Reilly	University of Rhode Island (RI)
1984	Pat Mancini	Boston University (MA)
1985	Dave Palazzi	University of Massachusetts (MA)
1986	Tim Bryant	University of Massachusetts (MA)
1987	Matt DeGennaro	University of Connecticut (CT)
1988	Carl Smith	University of Maine (ME)
1989	Bill Vergantino	University of Delaware (DE)
1990	John Johnson	University of Massachusetts (MA)
1991	Daryl Brown	University of Delaware (DE)
1992	Rene Ingoglia	University of Massachusetts (MA)
1993	Chris Hixson	University of Rhode Island (RI)
1994	Julien Dale	Boston University (MA)
1995	Tory Taylor	University of Connecticut (CT)
1996	Dave Conklin	College of William & Mary (VA)
1997	Recolon Jumpp	University of Connecticut (CT)
1998	Adrian Zullo	University of Massachusetts (MA)
1999	Dave Corley Jr.	College of William & Mary (VA)
2000	Rich Musinski	College of William & Mary (VA)
2001	Sidney Haugabrook	University of Delaware (DE)
2002	R.J. Cobbs	University of Massachusetts (MA)
2003	Ron Whitcomb	University of Maine (ME)
2004	Tony LeZotte	James Madison University (VA)
2004	Ricky Santos	University of New Hampshire (NH)
2005	Offense: Joe Casey	University of Rhode Island (RI)
2005	Defense: Sherman Logan	University of Richmond (VA)
2006	Offense: Eric Ward	University of Richmond (VA)
2006	Defense: Luke Bonus	Hofstra University (NY)
2007	Offense: Kevin Grayson	University of Richmond (VA)
2007	Defense: Eric McBride	University of Richmond (VA)
2008	Offense: Jonathan Grimes	College of William & Mary (VA)
2008	Defense: Brian McNally	University of New Hampshire (NH)
2008	Defense: Pat Williams	James Madison University (VA)
2009	Offense: Justin Thorpe	James Madison University (VA)
2009	Defense: B.W. Webb	College of William & Mary (VA)
2010	Offense: Andrew Pierce	University of Delaware (DE)
2010	Defense: Stephon Robertson	James Madison University (VA)

CAA Special Teams Player of the Year

Year	*Player*	*School*
2003	Wendall Williams	University of Rhode Island (RI)
2004	Greg Kuehn	College of William & Mary (VA)
2005	Christian Koegel	University of Massachusetts (MA)
2006	Rob Zarrilli	Hofstra University (NY)
2007	Justin Rogers	University of Richmond (VA)
2008	Scotty McGee	James Madison University (VA)
2009	Matt Szczur	Villanova University (PA)
2010	Jonathan Grimes	College of William & Mary (VA)

Eastern College Athletic Conference

1311 Craigville Beach Road, Centerville, MA 02632; Telephone: 508-771-5060; Fax: 508-771-9486; Web site: http://www.ecac.org; http://www.ecacsports.com

Established in 1938 as the Central Office for Eastern Intercollegiate Athletics with 58 charter members, the Eastern College Athletic Conference has grown to become the nation's largest (and only multi-divisional) athletic conference in the United States with 304 members (as of this writing) (Division I — 90 members, Division II — 23 members, and Division III — 191 members). Member schools of the ECAC also compete in at least one other conference (or as independent schools) and play in the ECAC postseason, when eligible. Please see NCAA Division II and NCAA Division III for a complete schools list within each division.

Football Alignments (Division I)

Members of the ECAC:

- Atlantic Coast Conference (Boston College, Duke University, University of Maryland, University of Virginia)
- Big East Conference (Rutgers University, Syracuse University, University of Connecticut, University of Pittsburgh, West Virginia University)
- Big South Conference (Liberty University, Stony Brook University, Virginia Military Institute)
- Colonial Athletic Association (College of William & Mary, Hofstra University, James Madison University, Northeastern University, Towson University, University of Delaware, University of Maine, University of Massachusetts, University of New Hampshire, University of Rhode Island, Villanova University)
- Independent Schools (Davidson College, East Carolina University, Marist College, Pennsylvania State University, U.S. Military Academy, U.S. Naval Academy)
- Ivy League (Brown University, Columbia University, Cornell University, Dartmouth College, Harvard University, Princeton University, University of Pennsylvania, Yale University)
- Mid-American Conference (Temple University, University at Buffalo)
- Mid-Eastern Athletic Conference (Delaware State University, Hampton University, Morgan State University)
- Northeast Conference (Bryant University, Central Connecticut State University, Duquesne University, Monmouth University, Robert Morris University, Sacred Heart University, Saint Francis University (PA), University at Albany, Wagner College)
- Patriot League (Bucknell University, Colgate University, College of the Holy Cross, Fordham University, Georgetown University, Lafayette College, Lehigh University)

Division I Members (90)

- American University Eagles (Patriot League) (Washington, D.C.)
- Binghamton University Bearcats (America East Conference) (Binghamton, NY)
- Boston College Eagles (Atlantic Coast Conference) (Chestnut Hill, MA)
- Boston University Terriers (America East Conference) (Boston, MA)
- Brown University Brown Bears (Ivy League) (Providence, RI)
- Bryant University Bulldogs (Northeast Conference) (Smithfield, RI)

- Bucknell University Bison (Patriot League) (Lewisburg, PA)
- Canisius College Golden Griffins (Metro Atlantic Athletic Conference) (Buffalo, NY)
- Central Connecticut State University Blue Devils (Northeast Conference) (New Britain, CT)
- Colgate University Raiders (Patriot League) (Hamilton, NY)
- College of the Holy Cross Crusaders (Patriot League) (Worcester, MA)
- College of William & Mary Tribe (Colonial Athletic Association) (Williamsburg, VA)
- Columbia University Lions (Ivy League) (New York, NY)
- Coppin State College Eagles (Mid-Eastern Athletic Conference) (Baltimore, MD)
- Cornell University Big Red (Ivy League) (Ithaca, NY)
- Dartmouth College Big Green (Ivy League) (Hanover, NH)
- Davidson College Wildcats (Pioneer Conference) (Davidson, NC)
- Delaware State University Hornets (Mid-Eastern Athletic Conference) (Dover, DE)
- Duke University Blue Devils (Atlantic Coast Conference) (Durham, NC)
- Duquesne University Dukes (Atlantic 10 Conference) (Pittsburgh, PA)
- East Carolina University Pirates (Conference USA) (Greenville, NC)
- Fairfield University Stags (Metro Atlantic Athletic Conference) (Fairfield, CT)
- Fairleigh Dickinson University Knights (Northeast Conference) (Teaneck, NJ)
- Fordham University Rams (Atlantic 10 Conference) (Bronx, NY)
- George Mason University Patriots (Colonial Athletic Association) (Fairfax, VA)
- George Washington University Colonials (Atlantic 10 Conference) (Washington, D.C.)
- Georgetown University Hoyas (Big East Conference) (Washington, D.C.)
- Hampton University Pirates (Mid-Eastern Athletic Conference) (Hampton, VA)
- Harvard University Crimson (Ivy League) (Boston, MA)
- Hofstra University Pride (Colonial Athletic Association (Hempstead, NY)
- Iona College Gaels (Metro Atlantic Athletic Conference) (New Rochelle, NY)
- James Madison University Dukes (Colonial Athletic Association) (Harrisonburg, VA)
- La Salle University Explorers (Atlantic 10 Conference) (Philadelphia, PA)
- Lafayette College Leopards (Patriot League) (Easton, PA)
- Lehigh University Mountain Hawks (Patriot League) (Bethlehem, PA)
- Liberty University Flames (Big South Conference) (Lynchburg, VA)
- Long Island University, Brooklyn Campus Blackbirds (Northeast Conference) (Brooklyn, NY)
- Longwood University Lancers (Independent) (Farmville, VA)
- Loyola University Maryland Greyhounds (Metro Atlantic Athletic Conference) (Baltimore, MD)
- Manhattan College Jaspers (Metro Atlantic Athletic Conference) (Riverdale, NY)
- Marist College Red Foxes (Metro Atlantic Athletic Conference) (Poughkeepsie, NY)
- Monmouth University Hawks (Northeast Conference) (West Long Branch, NJ)
- Morgan State University Bears (Mid-Eastern Athletic Conference) (Baltimore, MD)
- Mount St. Mary's University The Mount (Northeast Conference) (Emmitsburg, MD)
- New Jersey Institute of Technology Highlanders (Independent) (Newark, NJ)
- Niagara University Purple Eagles (Metro Atlantic Athletic Conference) (Niagara University, NY)
- Northeastern University Huskies (Colonial Athletic Association) (Boston, MA)
- Pennsylvania State University Nittany Lions (Big Ten Conference) (University Park, PA)
- Princeton University Tigers (Ivy League) (Princeton, NJ)
- Providence College Friars (Big East Conference) (Providence, RI)
- Quinnipiac University Bobcats (Northeast Conference) (Hamden, CT)
- Rider University Broncs (Metro Atlantic Athletic Conference) (Lawrenceville, NJ)
- Robert Morris University Colonials (Northeast Conference) (Moon Township, PA)
- Rutgers University Scarlet Knights (Big East Conference) (Piscataway, NJ)
- Sacred Heart University Pioneers (Northeast Conference) (Fairfield, CT)
- Saint Francis University Red Flash (Northeast Conference) (Loretto, PA)

Great West Conference (Great West)

P.O. Box 9344, Naperville, IL 60567; Telephone: 630-428-4492; Fax: 630-548-0705; http://www.greatwestconference.org

The Great West Football Conference was formed in February 2004 (play started in September 2004) as a football-only league with six charter member schools: the California Polytechnic State University; North Dakota State University, South Dakota State University, Southern Utah University, the University of California, Davis; and the University of Northern Colorado.

Although started as a football-only entity, the Great West Conference has expanded (as of the 2009–2010 school year) to include other sports, including cross country (men and women), indoor and outdoor track and field (men and women), golf (men and women), baseball, basketball, soccer, softball, tennis, and volleyball.

As of this writing, the Great West Conference currently consists of the following 10 schools:

- California Polytechnic State University Mustangs, San Luis Obispo, CA 93407; 805-756-2311; www.calpoly.edu; affiliate member from the Big West Conference
- Chicago State University Cougars, Chicago, IL 60628; 773-995-2000; www.csu.edu; no football program
- Houston Baptist University Huskies, Houston, TX 77074; 281-649-3000; www.hbu.edu; no football program
- New Jersey Institute of Technology Highlanders, Newark, NJ 07102; 973-596-3000; www.njit.edu; no football program
- Southern Utah University Thunderbirds, Cedar City, UT 84720; 435-586-7700; www.suu.edu; associate member from The Summit League
- University of California, Davis Aggies (Davis, CA); associate member from the Big West Conference
- University of North Dakota Fighting Sioux, Grand Forks, ND 58202; 701-777-3000; www.und.edu
- University of South Dakota Coyotes, Vermillion, SD 57069; 877-269-6837; www.usd.edu
- University of Texas, Pan American Broncos, Edinburg, TX 78539; 866-441-8872; www.utpa.edu; no football program
- Utah Valley University Wolverines, Orem, UT 84058; 801-863-4636; www.uvu.edu; no football program

Great West Champions

Year	*School*
2004	California Polytechnic State University (CA)
2005	California Polytechnic State University (CA)
2005	University of California, Davis (CA)
2006	University of North Dakota (ND)
2007	University of South Dakota (SD)
2008	California Polytechnic State University (CA)
2009	University of California, Davis (CA)
2010	Southern Utah University (UT)

Great West Coach of the Year

Year	*Coach*	*School*
2004	Rich Ellerson	California Polytechnic State University (CA)
2005	Rich Ellerson	California Polytechnic State University (CA)
2006	Craig Bohl	North Dakota State University (ND)
2007	John Stiegelmeier	South Dakota State University (SD)
2008	Rich Ellerson	California Polytechnic State University (CA)
2009	Bob Biggs	University of California, Davis (CA)
2010	Ed Lamb	Southern Utah University (UT)

Great West Offensive Player of the Year

Year	*Player*	*Position*	*School*
2004	Vincent Jackson	Wide Receiver	University of Northern Colorado (CO)
2005	Jon Grant	Quarterback	University of California, Davis (CA)
2005	James Noble	Running Back	California Polytechnic State University (CA)
2006	Steve Walker	Quarterback	North Dakota State University (ND)
2007	Ramses Barden	Wide Receiver	California Polytechnic State University (CA)
2007	Steve Walker	Quarterback	North Dakota State University (ND)

Year	Player	Position	School
2008	Ramses Barden	Wide Receiver	California Polytechnic State University (CA)
2009	Chris Carter	Wide Receiver	University of California, Davis (CA)
2010	Tysson Poots	Wide Receiver	Southern Utah University (UT)

GREAT WEST DEFENSIVE PLAYER OF THE YEAR

Year	Player	Position	School
2004	Jordan Beck	Linebacker	California Polytechnic State University (CA)
2005	Chris Gocong	Linebacker	California Polytechnic State University (CA)
2005	Kyle Shotwell	Linebacker	California Polytechnic State University (CA)
2006	Kyle Shotwell	Linebacker	California Polytechnic State University (CA)
2007	Joe Mays	Linebacker	North Dakota State University (ND)
2008	John Faletoese	Defensive Lineman	University of California, Davis (CA)
2009	Mike Morales	Linebacker	University of California, Davis (CA)
2010	Marty Mohamed	Linebacker	California Polytechnic State University (CA)

GREAT WEST SPECIAL TEAMS PLAYER OF THE YEAR

Year	Player	School
2004	Jesse Oliva	University of California, Davis (CA)
2005	Parker Douglass	South Dakota State University (SD)
2006	Parker Douglass	South Dakota State University (SD)
2007	Shamen Washington	North Dakota State University (ND)
2008	Nick Miller	Southern Utah University (UT)
2009	Trevor Ward	Southern Utah University (UT)
2010	Cole Zwiefelhofer	University of South Dakota (SD)

GREAT WEST ROOKIE OF THE YEAR

Year	Player	School
2004	Bradon Godfrey	Southern Utah University (UT)
2005	James Noble	California Polytechnic State University (CA)
2006	Chris Carter	University of California, Davis (CA)
2007	Jason Cox	California Polytechnic State University (CA)
2008	Asa Jackson	California Polytechnic State University (CA)
2009	Mitch Sutton	University of North Dakota (ND)
2010	Randy Wright	University of California, Davis (CA)

Independents

Currently, there are no FCS Independent football teams.

Ivy League (Ivy)

228 Alexander Street, Second Floor, Princeton, NJ 08540; Telephone: 609-258-6426; Fax: 609-258-1690; Web site: http://www.ivyleaguesports.com

Containing some of the oldest colleges and universities in the United States, the start of the Ivy League Conference football program is generally traced to when the NCAA Division I was formed in 1954 (and the term "Ivy League" was first used officially). In 1945, the first "Ivy Group Agreement" was signed (applying only to football) which outlined academic standards, eligibility requirements, and need-based financial aid, with no athletic scholarships. In February 1954, the "Ivy Group Agreement" was extended to all conference sports and in May 1974, the Agreement extended to women's sports. In December 1981, the NCAA created the "I-AA" football division and Ivy League members begin play in that division in September 1982.

The eight schools in the Ivy League are:

- Brown University Bears, Providence, RI 02912; 401-863-1000; www.brown.edu; established in 1764 as the College in the English Colony of Rhode Island and Providence Plantations

- Columbia University Lions, New York, NY 10027; 212-854-1754; www.columbia.edu; established in 1754 as King's College
- Cornell University Big Red, Ithaca, NY 14853; 607-254-4636; www.cornell.edu; established in 1865
- Dartmouth College Big Green, Hanover, NH 03755; 603-646-1110; established in 1769
- Harvard University Crimson, Cambridge, MA 02138; 617-495-1000; www.harvard.edu; established in 1636 as New College
- Princeton University Tigers, Princeton, NJ 08544; 609-258-3000; www.princeton.edu; established in 1746 as the College of New Jersey
- University of Pennsylvania Quakers, Philadelphia, PA 19104; 215-898-5000; www.upenn.edu; established in 1740 as the Church and Charity School of Philadelphia
- Yale University Bulldogs, New Haven, CT 06520; 203-432-1333; www.yale.edu; established in 1701 as the Collegiate School

Schools in the Ivy League (even before the conference had that name) have been competing in college sports as long as events have existed in the United States. Boat clubs from Harvard and Yale met in the first sporting event held between students of two U.S. colleges (at Lake Winnipesaukee, New Hampshire in 1852). As an informal football league, the Ivy League dates from 1900 when Yale took the conference championship with a 5–0 record. For many years, the United States Military Academy and the United States Naval Academy were considered members, but dropped out before the Ivy League became a formal league.

Ivy League Champions

Year	*School*	*Coach*
1956	Yale University (CT)	Jordan Olivar
1957	Princeton University (NJ)	Dick Colman
1958	Dartmouth College (NH)	Bob Blackman
1959	University of Pennsylvania (PA)	Steve Sebo
1960	Yale University (CT)	Jordan Olivar
1961	Columbia University (NY)	Buff Donelli
1961	Harvard University (MA)	John Yovicisin
1962	Dartmouth College (NH)	Bob Blackman
1963	Dartmouth College (NH)	Bob Blackman
1963	Princeton University (NJ)	Dick Colman
1964	Princeton University (NJ)	Dick Colman
1965	Dartmouth College (NH)	Bob Blackman
1966	Dartmouth College (NH)	Bob Blackman
1966	Harvard University (MA)	John Yovicisin
1966	Princeton University (NJ)	Dick Colman
1967	Yale University (CT)	Carm Cozza
1968	Harvard University (MA)	John Yovicisin
1968	Yale University (CT)	Carm Cozza
1969	Dartmouth College (NH)	Bob Blackman
1969	Princeton University (NJ)	Jake McCandless
1969	Yale University (CT)	Carm Cozza
1970	Dartmouth College (NH)	Bob Blackman
1971	Cornell University (NY)	Jack Musick
1971	Dartmouth College (NH)	Jake Crouthamel
1972	Dartmouth College (NH)	Jake Crouthamel
1973	Dartmouth College (NH)	Jake Crouthamel
1974	Harvard University (MA)	Joe Restic
1974	Yale University (CT)	Carm Cozza
1975	Harvard University (MA)	Joe Restic
1976	Brown University (RI)	John Anderson
1976	Yale University (CT)	Carm Cozza
1977	Yale University (CT)	Carm Cozza
1978	Dartmouth College (NH)	Joe Yukica
1979	Yale University (CT)	Carm Cozza

Year	School	Coach
1980	Yale University (CT)	Carm Cozza
1981	Dartmouth College (NH)	Joe Yukica
1981	Yale University (CT)	Carm Cozza
1982	Dartmouth College (NH)	Joe Yukica
1982	Harvard University (MA)	Joe Restic
1982	University of Pennsylvania (PA)	Jerry Berndt
1983	Harvard University (MA)	Joe Restic
1983	University of Pennsylvania (PA)	Jerry Berndt
1984	University of Pennsylvania (PA)	Jerry Berndt
1985	University of Pennsylvania (PA)	Jerry Berndt
1986	University of Pennsylvania (PA)	Ed Zubrow
1987	Harvard University (MA)	Joe Restic
1988	Cornell University (NY)	Maxie Baughan
1988	University of Pennsylvania (PA)	Ed Zubrow
1989	Princeton University (NJ)	Steve Tosches
1989	Yale University (CT)	Carm Cozza
1990	Cornell University (NY)	Jim Hofher
1990	Dartmouth College (NH)	Buddy Teevens
1991	Dartmouth College (NH)	Buddy Teevens
1992	Dartmouth College (NH)	John Lyons
1992	Princeton University (NJ)	Steve Tosches
1993	University of Pennsylvania (PA)	Al Bagnoli
1994	University of Pennsylvania (PA)	Al Bagnoli
1995	Princeton University (NJ)	Steve Tosches
1996	Dartmouth College (NH)	John Lyons
1997	Harvard University (MA)	Tim Murphy
1998	University of Pennsylvania (PA)	Al Bagnoli
1999	Brown University (RI)	Phil Estes
1999	Yale University (CT)	Jack Siedlecki
2000	University of Pennsylvania (PA)	Al Bagnoli
2001	Harvard University (MA)	Tim Murphy
2002	University of Pennsylvania (PA)	Al Bagnoli
2003	University of Pennsylvania (PA)	Al Bagnoli
2004	Harvard University (MA)	Tim Murphy
2005	Brown University (RI)	Phil Estes
2006	Princeton University (NJ)	Roger Hughes
2006	Yale University (CT)	Jack Siedlecki
2007	Harvard University (MA)	Tim Murphy
2008	Brown University (RI)	Phil Estes
2008	Harvard University (MA)	Tim Murphy
2009	University of Pennsylvania (PA)	Al Bagnoli
2010	University of Pennsylvania (PA)	Al Bagnoli

Ivy League Player of the Year (the Asa S. Bushnell Cup)

Since 1970, the Asa S. Bushnell Cup has been presented annually to the Ivy League's Player of the Year. Bushnell graduated from Princeton University (New Jersey) in 1921 and was the long-time Commissioner of the Eastern College Athletic Conference (1938–1970). Winners are selected by conference head coaches.

Year	Player	Position	School
1970	Jim Chasey	Quarterback	Dartmouth College (NH)
1970	Ed Marinaro	Running Back	Cornell University (NY)
1971	Ed Marinaro	Running Back	Cornell University (NY)
1972	Dick Jauron	Running Back	Yale University (CT)
1973	Jim Stoeckel	Quarterback	Harvard University (MA)
1974	Walt Snickenberger	Running Back	Princeton University (NJ)
1975	Doug Jackson	Running Back	Columbia University (NY)

Year	*Player*	*Position*	*School*
1976	John Pagliaro	Running Back	Yale University (CT)
1977	John Pagliaro	Running Back	Yale University (CT)
1978	Buddy Teevens	Quarterback	Dartmouth College (NH)
1979	Tim Tumpane	Linebacker	Yale University (CT)
1980	Kevin Czinger	Middle Guard	Yale University (CT)
1981	Rich Diana	Running Back	Yale University (CT)
1982	John Witkowski	Quarterback	Columbia University (NY)
1983	Derrick Harmon	Running Back	Cornell University (NY)
1984	Tim Chambers	Defensive Back	University of Pennsylvania (PA)
1985	Tom Gilmore	Defensive Tackle	University of Pennsylvania (PA)
1986	Rich Comizio	Running Back	University of Pennsylvania (PA)
1987	Kelly Ryan	Quarterback	Yale University (CT)
1988	Jason Garrett	Quarterback	Princeton University (NJ)
1989	Judd Garrett	Running Back	Princeton University (NJ)
1990	Shon Page	Running Back	Dartmouth College (NH)
1991	Al Rosier	Running Back	Dartmouth College (NH)
1992	Jay Fiedler	Quarterback	Dartmouth College (NH)
1993	Keith Elias	Running Back	Princeton University (NJ)
1994	Pat Goodwillie	Linebacker	University of Pennsylvania (PA)
1995	Dave Patterson	Linebacker	Princeton University (NJ)
1996	Chad Levitt	Running Back	Cornell University (NY)
1997	Sean Morey	Wide Receiver	Brown University (RI)
1998	Jim Finn	Running Back	University of Pennsylvania (PA)
1999	James Perry	Quarterback	Brown University (RI)
2000	Gavin Hoffman	Quarterback	University of Pennsylvania (PA)
2001	Carl Morris	Wide Receiver	Harvard University (MA)
2002	Carl Morris	Wide Receiver	Harvard University (MA)
2003	Mike Mitchell	Quarterback	University of Pennsylvania (PA)
2004	Ryan Fitzpatrick	Quarterback	Harvard University (MA)
2005	Nick Hartigan	Running Back	Brown University (RI)
2006	Jeff Terrell	Quarterback	Princeton University (NJ)
2007	Mike McLeod	Running Back	Yale University (CT)
2008	Chris Pizzotti	Quarterback	Harvard University (MA)
2009	Buddy Farnham	Wide Receiver	Brown University (RI)
2009	Jake Lewko	Linebacker	University of Pennsylvania (PA)
2010	Gino Gordon	Running Back	Harvard University (MA)
2010	Nick Schwieger	Tailback	Dartmouth College (NH)

Ivy League Rookie of the Year

Initially called the Sophomore of the Year in 1981 when it was first presented, this award's name was changed to Rookie of the Year in 1993 to reflect freshman eligibility.

Year	*Player*	*Position*	*School*
1981	Derrick Harmon	Running Back	Cornell University (NY)
1982	Mike Caraviello	Quarterback	Dartmouth College (NH)
1983	Doug Butler	Quarterback	Princeton University (NJ)
1984	Rich Comizio	Running Back	University of Pennsylvania (PA)
1985	Chris Flynn	Running Back	University of Pennsylvania (PA)
1986	Craig Morton	Wide Receiver	Dartmouth College (NH)
1987	Bryan Keys	Running Back	University of Pennsylvania (PA)
1988	Solomon Johnson	Running Back	Columbia University (NY)
1989	John McNiff	Running Back	Cornell University (NY)
1990	Matt Brzica	Quarterback	Dartmouth College (NH)
1991	Jay Fiedler	Quarterback	Dartmouth College (NH)
1992	Pat Goodwillie	Linebacker	University of Pennsylvania (PA)
1993	Miles Macik	Wide Receiver	University of Pennsylvania (PA)
1994	Eion Hu	Running Back	Harvard University (MA)

Year	Player	Position	School
1995	Sean Morey	Wide Receiver	Brown University (RI)
1996	Isaiah Kacyvenski	Linebacker	Harvard University (MA)
1997	Todd Tomich	Defensive Back	Yale University (CT)
1998	Johnathan Reese	Running Back	Columbia University (NY)
1999	Chas Gessner	Wide Receiver	Brown University (RI)
2000	Dante Balestracci	Linebacker	Harvard University (MA)
2001	Steve Jensen	Defensive Back	Dartmouth College (NH)
2002	Josh Dooley	Linebacker	Dartmouth College (NH)
2003	Ed McCarthy	Offensive Lineman	Yale University (CT)
2004	Steve Morgan	Kicker / Punter	Brown University (RI)
2005	Mike McLeod	Running Back	Yale University (CT)
2006	Austin Knowlin	Wide Receiver	Columbia University (NY)
2007	Alex Gross	Linebacker	Columbia University (NY)
2008	Matthew Hanson	Defensive Back	Harvard University (MA)
2009	Treavor Scales	Running Back	Harvard University (MA)
2010	Jeff Mathews	Quarterback	Cornell University (NY)

Mid-Eastern Athletic Conference (MEAC)

P.O. Box 62547, Virginia Beach, VA 23466; 222 Central Park Avenue, Suite 1150, Virginia Beach, VA 23462; Telephone: 757-416-7100; Fax: 757-416-7103; http://www.meac sports.com

The Mid-Eastern Athletic Conference was formed in 1970 (and began playing football in 1971) with seven charter schools: Delaware State College, Howard University, Morgan State University, North Carolina A&T State University, North Carolina Central University, South Carolina State College, and the University of Maryland, Eastern Shore. Operating as an NCAA Division II conference, in June 1980, the MEAC was re-classified as a Division I conference, which is how it operates today (with the exception of the Winston-Salem State University Rams, which plays football in the NCAA Division II Central Intercollegiate Athletic Division).

As of this writing, the Mid-Eastern Athletic Conference currently consists of the following 13 schools:

- Bethune-Cookman University Wildcats, Daytona Beach, FL 32114; 386-481-2000; www.cookman.edu
- Coppin State University Eagles, Baltimore, MD 21216; 410-951-3000; www.coppin.edu; no football program
- Delaware State University Hornets, Dover, DE 19901; 302-857-6060; www.desu.edu
- Florida Agricultural and Mechanical University Rattlers, Tallahassee, FL 32307; 850-599-3000; www.famu.edu
- Hampton University Pirates, Hampton, VA 23668; 757-727-5000; www.hampton.edu
- Howard University Bison, Washington, D.C. 20059; 202-806-6100; www.howard.edu
- Morgan State University Bears, Baltimore, MD 21251; 443-885-3333; www.morgan.edu
- Norfolk State University Spartans, Norfolk, VA 23504; 757-823-8600; www.nsu.edu
- North Carolina Agricultural and Technical State University Aggies, Greensboro, NC 27411; 336-334-7500; www.ncat.edu
- North Carolina Central University Eagles, Durham, NC 27707; 919-530-6100; www.nccu.edu
- Savannah State University Tigers, Savannah, GA 31404; 912-358-4778; www.savannahstate.edu
- South Carolina State University Bulldogs, Orangeburg, SC 29117; 803-536-7000; www.scsu.edu
- University of Maryland, Eastern Shore Hawks, Princess Anne, MD 21853; 410-651-2200; www.umes.edu; no football program

MEAC Champions

Year	School	Year	School
1971	Morgan State University (MD)	1975	South Carolina State University (SC)
1972	North Carolina Central University (NC)	1976	South Carolina State University (SC)
1973	North Carolina Central University (NC)	1977	South Carolina State University (SC)
1974	South Carolina State University (SC)	1978	South Carolina State University (SC)

Year	School
1979	Morgan State University (MD)
1980	South Carolina State University (SC)
1981	South Carolina State University (SC)
1982	South Carolina State University (SC)
1983	South Carolina State University (SC)
1984	Bethune Cookman University (FL)
1985	Delaware State University (DE)
1986	North Carolina Agricultural and Technical State University (NC)
1987	Howard University (Washington, D.C.)
1988	Bethune Cookman University (FL)
1988	Delaware State University (DE)
1988	Florida Agricultural and Mechanical University (FL)
1989	Delaware State University (DE)
1990	Florida Agricultural and Mechanical University (FL)
1991	North Carolina Agricultural and Technical State University (NC)
1992	North Carolina Agricultural and Technical State University (NC)
1993	Howard University (Washington, D.C.)
1994	South Carolina State University (SC)
1995	Florida Agricultural and Mechanical University (FL)
1996	Florida Agricultural and Mechanical University (FL)
1997	Hampton University (VA)
1998	Florida Agricultural and Mechanical University (FL)
1998	Hampton University (VA)
1999	North Carolina Agricultural and Technical State University (NC)
2000	Florida Agricultural and Mechanical University (FL)
2001	Florida Agricultural and Mechanical University (FL)
2002	Bethune Cookman University (FL)
2003	North Carolina Agricultural and Technical State University (NC)
2004	Hampton University (VA)
2004	South Carolina State University (SC)
2005	Hampton University (VA)
2006	Hampton University (VA)
2007	Delaware State University (DE)
2008	South Carolina State University (SC)
2009	South Carolina State University (SC)
2010	Bethune-Cookman University (FL)
2010	Florida A&M University (FL)
2010	South Carolina State University (SC)

MEAC Coach of the Year

Selected by conference head football coaches and sports information directors.

Year	Coach	School
1971	George Quiett	North Carolina Central University (NC)
1972	Tillman Sease	Howard University (Washington, D.C.)
1973	Willie Jeffries	South Carolina State University (SC)
1974	Willie Jeffries	South Carolina State University (SC)
1974	Hornsby Howell	North Carolina Agricultural and Technical State University (NC)
1974	Douglas Porter	Howard University (Washington, D.C.)
1975	Hornsby Howell	North Carolina Agricultural and Technical State University (NC)
1976	Willie Jeffries	South Carolina State University (SC)
1976	Henry Lattimore	Morgan State University (MD)
1977	Edmund Wyche	Delaware State University (DE)
1978	Willie Jeffries	South Carolina State University (SC)
1979	Clarence Thomas	Morgan State University (MD)
1980	Jim McKinley	North Carolina Agricultural and Technical State University (NC)
1981	Bill Davis	South Carolina State University (SC)
1982	Bill Davis	South Carolina State University (SC)
1983	Joe Purzycki	Delaware State University (DE)
1984	Larry Little	Bethune-Cookman University (FL)
1985	William Collick	Delaware State University (DE)
1986	Mo Forte	North Carolina Agricultural and Technical State University (NC)
1987	Willie Jeffries	South Carolina State University (SC)
1988	Ken Riley	Florida Agricultural and Mechanical University (FL)
1989	Steve Wilson	Howard University (Washington, D.C.)
1990	Ken Riley	Florida Agricultural and Mechanical University (FL)
1991	Bill Hayes	North Carolina Agricultural and Technical State University (NC)
1992	Willie Jeffries	South Carolina State University (SC)
1993	Steve Wilson	Howard University (Washington, D.C.)
1994	Cy McClairen	Bethune-Cookman University (FL)
1995	Billy Joe	Florida Agricultural and Mechanical University (FL)

Year	Coach	School
1996	Billy Joe	Florida Agricultural and Mechanical University (FL)
1997	Joe Taylor	Hampton University (VA)
1998	Alvin Wyatt	Bethune-Cookman University (FL)
1999	Bill Hayes	North Carolina Agricultural and Technical State University (NC)
2000	Ben Blacknall	Delaware State University (DE)
2001	Billy Joe	Florida Agricultural and Mechanical University (FL)
2002	Donald Hill-Eley	Morgan State University (MD)
2003	George Small	North Carolina Agricultural and Technical State University (NC)
2004	Joseph Taylor	Hampton University (VA)
2005	Joseph Taylor	Hampton University (VA)
2006	Joseph Taylor	Hampton University (VA)
2007	Pete Adrian	Norfolk State University (VA)
2008	Buddy Pough	South Carolina State University (SC)
2009	Buddy Pough	South Carolina State University (SC)
2010	Brian Jenkins	Bethune-Cookman University (FL)

MEAC Offensive Player of the Year

Selected by conference head football coaches and sports information directors.

Year	Player	School
1971	Willie Wright	North Carolina Agricultural and Technical State University (NC)
1972	Jefferson Inman	North Carolina Central University (NC)
1973	Eddie Richardson	Howard University (Washington, D.C.)
1974	Michael Banks	Howard University (Washington, D.C.)
1975	George Ragsdale	North Carolina Agricultural and Technical State University (NC)
1976	Elsworth Turner	North Carolina Agricultural and Technical State University (NC)
1977	Ricky Anderson	South Carolina State University (SC)
1978	Nate Rivers	South Carolina State University (SC)
1979	Darrell Coulter	Morgan State University (MD)
1980	Ron Wilson	Howard University (Washington, D.C.)
1981	Tracy Singleton	Howard University (Washington, D.C.)
1982	Tracy Singleton	Howard University (Washington, D.C.)
1983	Ray Alexander	Florida Agricultural and Mechanical University (FL)
1984	Gene Lake	Delaware State University (DE)
1985	John Taylor	Delaware State University (DE)
1986	Alan Hooker	North Carolina Agricultural and Technical State University (NC)
1987	Harvey Reed	Howard University (Washington, D.C.)
1988	Lee DeBose	Howard University (Washington, D.C.)
1989	Amir Rasul	Florida Agricultural and Mechanical University (FL)
1990	Connell Maynor	North Carolina Agricultural and Technical State University (NC)
1991	Connell Maynor	North Carolina Agricultural and Technical State University (NC)
1992	Terry Mickens	Florida Agricultural and Mechanical University (FL)
1993	Jay Walker	Howard University (Washington, D.C.)
1994	Marvin Marshall	South Carolina State University (SC)
1995	Michael Hicks	South Carolina State University (SC)
1996	Ted White	Howard University (Washington, D.C.)
1997	Oteman Sampson	Florida Agricultural and Mechanical University (FL)
1998	Patrick Bonner	Florida Agricultural and Mechanical University (FL)
1999	Jajuan Seider	Florida Agricultural and Mechanical University (FL)
2000	Rahsaan Matthews	Delaware State University (DE)
2001	Maurice Hicks	North Carolina Agricultural and Technical State University (NC)
2002	Allen Suber	Bethune-Cookman University (FL)
2003	Allen Suber	Bethune-Cookman University (FL)
2004	Bradshaw Littlejohn	Morgan State University (MD)
2005	Alonzo Coleman	Hampton University (VA)
2006	Deshawn Baker	South Carolina State University (SC)
2007	Chad Simpson	Morgan State University (MD)

Year	*Player*	*School*
2008	Will Ford	South Carolina State University (SC)
2009	Curtis Pulley	Florida Agricultural and Mechanical University (FL)
2010	Matthew Johnson	Bethune-Cookman University (FL)

MEAC Defensive Player of the Year

Selected by conference head football coaches and sports information directors.

Year	*Player*	*School*
1971	Ben Blacknall	North Carolina Agricultural and Technical State University (NC)
1972	Alexander Jones	North Carolina Central University (NC)
1973	Eugene Simms	Morgan State University (MD)
1974	Harry Carson	South Carolina State University (SC)
1975	Harry Carson	South Carolina State University (SC)
1976	Robert Sims	South Carolina State University (SC)
1977	Dwaine Board	North Carolina Agricultural and Technical State University (NC)
1978	Bobby Moore	South Carolina State University (SC)
1979	Phil Murphy	South Carolina State University (SC)
1980	John Alford	South Carolina State University (SC)
1981	Booker Reese	Bethune-Cookman University (FL)
1982	John Courtney	South Carolina State University (SC)
1983	Barney Bussey	South Carolina State University (SC)
1984	John Bostic	Bethune-Cookman University (FL)
1985	Dan Cadeloro	Delaware State University (DE)
1986	Joe Burton	Delaware State University (DE)
1987	Robert Presbury	Delaware State University (DE)
1988	Demetrius Harrison	North Carolina Agricultural and Technical State University (NC)
1989	Demetrius Harrison	North Carolina Agricultural and Technical State University (NC)
1990	James Dozier	Morgan State University (MD)
1991	Robert Porcher	South Carolina State University (SC)
1992	Rodney Edwards	North Carolina Agricultural and Technical State University (NC)
1993	Joe Montford	South Carolina State University (SC)
1994	Jose' White	Howard University (Washington, D.C.)
1995	Earl Holmes	Florida Agricultural and Mechanical University (FL)
1996	Darrell Flythe	Hampton University (VA)
1997	Chris McNeil	North Carolina Agricultural and Technical State University (NC)
1998	Jermaine Derricott	South Carolina State University (SC)
1999	Deon Hunt	Hampton University (VA)
2000	Tracy White	Howard University (Washington, D.C.)
2001	No Selection	
2002	RaShean Mathis	Bethune-Cookman University (FL)
2003	Steve Baggs	Bethune-Cookman University (FL)
2004	Justin Durant	Hampton University (VA)
2005	Justin Durant	Hampton University (VA)
2006	Justin Durant	Hampton University (VA)
2007	Ronnie McCullough	Bethune-Cookman University (FL)
2008	Jarrell Guyton	Morgan State University (MD)
2009	George Howard	Morgan State University (MD)
2010	David Erby	South Carolina State University (SC)

MEAC Offensive Lineman of the Year

Selected by conference head football coaches and sports information directors.

Year	*Player*	*School*
1996	Jamie Nails	Florida Agricultural and Mechanical University (FL)
1997	Lamont Turner	Hampton University (VA)
1998	Russell Mills	Hampton University (VA)
1999	Mpumi Masimini	Howard University (Washington, D.C.)

Year	*Player*	*School*
2000	Freddie Moore	Florida Agricultural and Mechanical University (FL)
2001	No Selection	
2002	Erik Steiner	Hampton University (VA)
2003	Patrick Cheatham	Hampton University (VA)
2004	Jelani Clement	Hampton University (VA)
2005	Gerrell Golightly	Hampton University (VA)
2006	Clyde Reed	South Carolina State University (SC)
2007	James Lee	South Carolina State University (SC)
2008	Raymond Harrison	South Carolina State University (SC)
2009	Johnny Culbreath	South Carolina State University (SC)
2010	Josh Harrison	South Carolina State University (SC)

MEAC Rookie of the Year

Selected by conference head football coaches and sports information directors.

Year	*Player*	*School*
1996	Antoine Flowers	Florida Agricultural and Mechanical University (FL)
1997	Jacquay Nunnally	Florida Agricultural and Mechanical University (FL)
1998	Pa'Tell Troutman	Bethune-Cookman University (FL)
1999	Vontre Long	Howard University (Washington, D.C.)
2000	Juan Vasquez	Florida Agricultural and Mechanical University (FL)
2001	Deon Rheubottom	Delaware State University (DE)
2002	Bradshaw Littlejohn	Morgan State University (MD)
2003	Alonzo Coleman	Hampton University (VA)
2004	Shaheer McBride	Delaware State University (DE)
2005	Vashon Winton	Delaware State University (DE)
2006	William Ford	South Carolina State University (SC)
2007	Phillip Sylvester	Florida Agricultural and Mechanical University (FL)
2008	Willie Carter	Howard University (Washington, D.C.)
2009	Mike Mayhew	North Carolina Agricultural and Technical State University (NC)
2010	Antwon Chisholm	Hampton University (VA)

Missouri Valley Conference (MVC)

1818 Chouteau Avenue, St. Louis, MO 63103; Telephone: 314-421-0339; Fax: 314-421-3505; http://www.mvc-sports.com

Founded as a women's athletic organization in August 1982 (originally called The Gateway Conference), the Missouri Valley Conference football program was created in August 1985; was originally called the Gateway Football Conference; and competed under that name until 2007. In June 2008, the nine-member Gateway Football Conference and the 10-member Missouri Valley Conference (which was originally formed in 1907) realigned their women's and men's sports programs and adopted the name of the Missouri Valley Conference for all athletic activities. Although the schools adopted the Missouri Valley Conference name, the football-playing institutions compete as a separate administrative entity, which is known as the Missouri Valley Football Conference.

Originally founded in 1907 as the Missouri Valley Intercollegiate Athletic Association, the MVC is technically the second oldest Division I collegiate athletic conference in America. It has not sponsored football since 1985 (when it was classified as a I-A (now FBS) conference), but five schools (Illinois State University, Indiana State University, Missouri State University, Northern Iowa University, and Southern Illinois University) have football programs that participate in the Missouri Valley Football Conference (known as the Gateway Conference from 1985 to 2008) in Division I FCS (formerly I-AA), and a sixth school (Drake University) plays football in the Pioneer Football League (another FCS conference). Although both the Missouri Valley Conference and the Missouri Valley Football Conference operate from the same headquarters in St. Louis, the two entities have separate administrative structures.

The original MVC was founded in January 1907 as the MVIAA with charter members University of Iowa, University, University of Kansas, University of Missouri, University of Nebraska, and Washington University in St. Louis (Missouri).

As of this writing, the following member schools compete in the Missouri Valley Conference (Missouri Valley Football Conference):

- Bradley University Braves, Peoria, IL 61625; 309-676-7611; www.bradley.edu; no football program
- Creighton University Blue Jays, Omaha, NE 68178; 402-280-2700; www.creighton.edu; no football program
- Drake University Bulldogs, Des Moines, IA 50311; 515-271-2011; www.drake.edu; plays football in the Pioneer Football League (FCS)
- Illinois State University Redbirds, Normal, IL 61790; 309-438-2111; http://illinoisstate.edu
- Indiana State University Sycamores, Terre Haute, IN 47809; 812-237-6311; www.indstate.edu
- Missouri State University Bears, Springfield, MO 65897; 417-836-5000; www.missouristate.edu
- North Dakota State University Bison, Fargo, ND 58102; 701-231-8011; www.ndsu.nodak.edu; associate football member from The Summit League
- South Dakota State University Jackrabbits, Brookings, SD 57007; 800-952-3541; www.sdstate.edu; associate football member from The Summit League
- Southern Illinois University Salukis, Carbondale, IL 62901; 618-453-2121; www.siuc.edu
- University of Evansville Purple Aces, Evansville, IN 47722; 800-423-8633; www.evansville.edu; no football program
- University of Northern Iowa Panthers, Cedar Falls, IA 50614; 319-273-2311; www.uni.edu
- Western Illinois University Leathernecks, Macomb, IL 61455; 309-298-1414; www.wiu.edu; associate football member from The Summit League
- Wichita State University Shockers, Wichita, KS 67260; 316-978-3456; www.wichita.edu; no football program
- Youngstown State University Penguins, Youngstown OH 44555; 330-941-3000; http://web.wsu.edu; associate football member from the Horizon League

MVC Champions

Year	*School*
1985	University of Northern Iowa (IA)
1986	Eastern Illinois University (IL)
1987	University of Northern Iowa (IA)
1988	Western Illinois University (IL)
1989	Missouri State University (MO)
1990	Missouri State University (MO)
1990	University of Northern Iowa (IA)
1991	University of Northern Iowa (IA)
1992	University of Northern Iowa (IA)
1993	University of Northern Iowa (IA)
1994	University of Northern Iowa (IA)
1995	Eastern Illinois University (IL)
1995	University of Northern Iowa (IA)
1996	University of Northern Iowa (IA)
1997	Western Illinois University (IL)
1998	Western Illinois University (IL)
1999	Illinois State University (IL)
2000	Western Illinois University (IL)
2001	University of Northern Iowa (IA)
2002	Western Illinois University (IL)
2002	Western Kentucky University (KY)
2003	University of Northern Iowa (IA)
2003	Southern Illinois University (IL)
2004	Southern Illinois University (IL)
2005	University of Northern Iowa (IA)
2005	Southern Illinois University (IL)
2005	Youngstown State University (OH)
2006	Youngstown State University (OH)
2007	University of Northern Iowa (IA)
2008	Southern Illinois University (IL)
2008	University of Northern Iowa (IA)
2009	Southern Illinois University (IL)
2010	University of Northern Iowa (IA)

MVC "Bruce Craddock" Coach of the Year

Voted on conference coaches, media, and sports information directors.

Year	*Coach*	*School*
1985	Darrell Mudra	University of Northern Iowa (IA)
1986	Al Molde	Eastern Illinois University (IL)
1987	Darrell Mudra	University of Northern Iowa (IA)
1987	Bruce Craddock	Western Illinois University (IL)

Year	Coach	School
1988	Bruce Craddock	Western Illinois University (IL)
1989	Jesse Branch	Missouri State University (MO)
1990	Jesse Branch	Missouri State University (MO)
1991	Terry Allen	University of Northern Iowa (IA)
1992	Terry Allen	University of Northern Iowa (IA)
1993	Terry Allen	University of Northern Iowa (IA)
1994	Terry Allen	University of Northern Iowa (IA)
1995	Bob Spoo	Eastern Illinois University (IL)
1996	Terry Allen	University of Northern Iowa (IA)
1997	Randy Ball	Western Illinois University (IL)
1998	Todd Berry	Illinois State University (IL)
1999	Todd Berry	Illinois State University (IL)
2000	Don Patterson	Western Illinois University (IL)
2001	Mark Farley	University of Northern Iowa (IA)
2002	Don Patterson	Western Illinois University (IL)
2003	Jerry Kill	Southern Illinois University (IL)
2004	Jerry Kill	Southern Illinois University (IL)
2005	Jon Heacock	Youngstown State University (OH)
2006	Jon Heacock	Youngstown State University (OH)
2007	Mark Farley	University of Northern Iowa (IA)
2008	Dale Lennon	Southern Illinois University (IL)
2009	Dale Lennon	Southern Illinois University (IL)
2010	Trent Miles	Indiana State University (IN)

MVC Offensive Player of the Year

Voted on conference coaches, media, and sports information directors.

Year	Player	Position	School
1985	Mike Smith	Quarterback	University of Northern Iowa (IA)
1986	Sean Payton	Quarterback	Eastern Illinois University (IL)
1987	Carl Boyd	Running Back	University of Northern Iowa (IA)
1988	Paul Singer	Quarterback	Western Illinois University (IL)
1989	DeAndre Smith	Quarterback	Missouri State University (MO)
1990	DeAndre Smith	Quarterback	Missouri State University (MO)
1991	Derrick Franklin	Running Back	Indiana State University (IN)
1992	Toby Davis	Running Back	Illinois State University (IL)
1993	Kurt Warner	Quarterback	University of Northern Iowa (IA)
1994	Rob St. Sauver	Quarterback	Western Illinois University (IL)
1995	Dedric Ward	Wide Receiver	University of Northern Iowa (IA)
1996	Dedric Ward	Wide Receiver	University of Northern Iowa (IA)
1997	Aaron Stecker	Running Back	Western Illinois University (IL)
1998	Karlton Carpenter	Running Back	Southern Illinois University (IL)
1999	Cornell Craig	Wide Receiver	Southern Illinois University (IL)
2000	Charles Tharp	Running Back	Western Illinois University (IL)
2001	P.J. Mays	Running Back	Youngstown State University (OH)
2002	Russ Michna	Quarterback	Western Illinois University (IL)
2003	Russ Michna	Quarterback	Western Illinois University (IL)
2004	Joel Sambursky	Quarterback	Southern Illinois University (IL)
2005	Laurént Robinson	Wide Receiver	Illinois State University (IL)
2006	Marcus Mason	Running Back	Youngstown State University (OH)
2007	Eric Sanders	Quarterback	University of Northern Iowa (IA)
2008	Herb Donaldson	Running Back	Western Illinois University (IL)
2009	Deji Karim	Running Back	Southern Illinois University (IL)
2010	Matt Barr	Quarterback	Western Illinois University (IL)

MVC Defensive Player of the Year

Voted on conference coaches, media, and sports information directors.

Year	*Player*	*Position*	*School*
1985	James Houston	Linebacker	Missouri State University (MO)
1985	Mark Farley	Linebacker	University of Northern Iowa (IA)
1986	Brian Gant	Linebacker	Illinois State University (IL)
1987	Matt Soraghan	Linebacker	Missouri State University (MO)
1988	John Jurkovic	Defensive Tackle	Eastern Illinois University (IL)
1989	John Jurkovic	Defensive Tackle	Eastern Illinois University (IL)
1990	Tim Lance	Defensive Back	Eastern Illinois University (IL)
1991	William Freeney	Linebacker	University of Northern Iowa (IA)
1992	William Freeney	Linebacker	University of Northern Iowa (IA)
1993	Andre Allen	Linebacker	University of Northern Iowa (IA)
1994	Andre Allen	Linebacker	University of Northern Iowa (IA)
1995	Tim Carver	Linebacker	Eastern Illinois University (IL)
1996	Mike Miano	Defensive Lineman	Missouri State University (MO)
1997	Harry Deligianis	Defensive Tackle	Youngstown State University (OH)
1998	James Milton	Linebacker	Western Illinois University (IL)
1999	Edgerton Hartwell	Linebacker	Western Illinois University (IL)
2000	Edgerton Hartwell	Linebacker	Western Illinois University (IL)
2001	Adam Vogt	Linebacker	University of Northern Iowa (IA)
2002	Boomer Grigsby	Linebacker	Illinois State University (IL)
2003	Boomer Grigsby	Linebacker	Illinois State University (IL)
2004	Boomer Grigsby	Linebacker	Illinois State University (IL)
2005	Brent Hawkins	Defensive End	Illinois State University (IL)
2006	Cameron Siskowic	Linebacker	Illinois State University (IL)
2007	Brannon Carter	Linebacker	University of Northern Iowa (IA)
2008	James Ruffin	Defensive Lineman	University of Northern Iowa (IA)
2009	Danny Batten	Defensive End	South Dakota State University (SD)
2009	James Ruffin	Defensive End	University of Northern Iowa (IA)
2010	Kyle Glazier	Linebacker	Western Illinois University (IL)

MVC Newcomer of the Year

Voted on conference coaches, media, and sports information directors.

Year	*Player*	*Position*	*School*
1994	Buck Phillips	Corner Back	Western Illinois University (IL)
1995	Jason Cannon	Wide Receiver	Missouri State University (MO)
1996	Vince Bruno	Linebacker	Western Illinois University (IL)
1997	Aaron Stecker	Running Back	Western Illinois University (IL)
1998	David Bowens	Defensive End	Western Illinois University (IL)
1999	Charles Tharp	Running Back	Western Illinois University (IL)
2000	Teddy Sims	Linebacker	Southern Illinois University (IL)
2001	Julian Reese	Quarterback	Indiana State University (IN)
2002	Muhammad Abdulqaadir	Running Back	Southern Illinois University (IL)
2003	Terrance Freeney	Running Back	University of Northern Iowa (IA)
2004	Brandon Jacobs	Running Back	Southern Illinois University (IL)
2005	Marcus Mason	Running Back	Youngstown State University (OH)
2006	Darian Williams	Running Back	University of Northern Iowa (IA)
2007	Ferlando Williams	Wide Receiver	Youngstown State University (OH)
2008	Brandon Summers	Quarterback	Youngstown State University (OH)
2009	Antoine Wilkinson	Linebacker	Missouri State University (MO)
2010	Tirrell Rennie	Quarterback	University of Northern Iowa (IA)

MVC Freshman of the Year

Voted on conference coaches, media, and sports information directors.

Year	Player	Position	School
1999	Dusty Burk	Quarterback	Illinois State University (IL)
2000	Lee Russell	Linebacker	Western Illinois University (IL)
2001	Tom Petrie	Quarterback	University of Northern Iowa (IA)
2002	Joel Sambursky	Quarterback	Southern Illinois University (IL)
2003	Justin Haddix	Quarterback	Western Kentucky University (KY)
2004	Eric Sanders	Quarterback	University of Northern Iowa (IA)
2005	Tom Nelson	Defensive Back	Illinois State University (IL)
2006	Brandin Jordan	Linebacker	Southern Illinois University (IL)
2007	Cody Kirby	Quarterback	Missouri State University (MO)
2008	Kamryn Keys	Running Back	Youngstown State University (OH)
2009	Matt Brown	Quarterback	Illinois State University (IL)
2010	Kurt Hess	Quarterback	Youngstown State University (OH)

Northeast Conference (NEC)

399 Campus Drive, Somerset, NJ 08873; Telephone: 732-469-0440; Fax: 732-469-0744; Web site: http://www.northeastconference.org

Formed in 1981 as the men's basketball-only Eastern College Athletic Conference (Metro Conference), the Northeast Conference has since become a 12-school, 22-sport organization. The conference began to expand its sports offerings in 1985 and in 1988, changed its name to the Northeast Conference. The 10 charter members included Fairleigh-Dickinson University, Long Island University, Loyola College, Marist College, Robert Morris University, Saint Francis College (NY), Saint Francis University (PA), Siena College, Towson University, and Wagner College.

As of this writing, the Northeast Conference consists of the following schools:

- Bryant University Bulldogs, Smithfield, RI 02917; 401-232-6000; www.bryant.edu
- Central Connecticut State University Blue Devils, New Britain, CT 06050; 860-832-2278; www.ccsu.edu
- Duquesne University Dukes, Pittsburgh, PA 15282; 412-396-6000; www.duq.edu; associate football member from the Atlantic 10 Conference
- Fairleigh-Dickinson University Knights, Teaneck, NJ 07666; 201-692-2000; www.fdu.edu; no football program
- Long Island University Blackbirds, Brooklyn, NY 11201; 718-488-1011; www.liunet.edu
- Monmouth University Hawks, West Long Branch, NJ 07764; 732-571-3400; www.monmouth.edu
- Mount Saint Mary's University Mountaineers, Emmitsburg, MD 21727; 301-447-6122; www.msmary.edu; no football program
- Quinnipiac University Bobcats, Hamden, CT 06518; 203-582-8200; www.quinnipiac.edu; no football program
- Robert Morris University Colonials, Moon Township, PA 15108; 800-762-0097; www.rmu.edu
- Sacred Heart University Pioneers, Fairfield, CT 06825; 203-371-7999; www.sacredheart.edu
- Saint Francis College (NY) Terriers, Brooklyn, NY 11201; 718-522-2300; www.stfranciscollege.edu; no football program
- Saint Francis University (PA) Red Flash, Loretto, PA 15940; 814-472-3000; www.francis.edu
- University at Albany (State University of New York) Great Danes, Albany, NY 12222; 518-442-3300; www.albany.edu; associate football member from the America East Conference
- Wagner College Seahawks, Staten Island, NY 10301; 718-390-3100; www.wagner.edu

NEC Champions

Year	School
1996	Robert Morris University (PA)
1997	Robert Morris University (PA)
1998	Monmouth University (NJ)
1998	Robert Morris University (PA)

Year	School
1999	Robert Morris University (PA)
2000	Robert Morris University (PA)
2001	Sacred Heart University (CT)
2002	University at Albany (NY)
2003	Monmouth University (NJ)
2003	University at Albany (NY)
2004	Central Connecticut State University (CT)
2004	Monmouth University (NJ)
2005	Central Connecticut State University (CT)
2005	Stony Brook University (NY)
2006	Monmouth University (NJ)
2007	University at Albany (NY)
2008	University at Albany (NY)
2009	Central Connecticut State University (CT)
2010	Central Connecticut State University (CT)
2010	Robert Morris University (PA)

NEC Coach of the Year

Year	Coach	School
1996	Joe Walton	Robert Morris University (PA)
1997	Joe Walton	Robert Morris University (PA)
1998	Kevin Callahan	Monmouth University (NJ)
1999	Joe Walton	Robert Morris University (PA)
2000	Jim Fleming	Sacred Heart University (CT)
2001	Jim Fleming	Sacred Heart University (CT)
2002	Bob Ford	University at Albany (NY)
2003	Kevin Callahan	Monmouth University (NJ)
2004	Tom Masella	Central Connecticut State University (CT)
2005	Sam Kornhauser	Stony Brook University (NY)
2006	Kevin Callahan	Monmouth University (NJ)
2007	Bob Ford	University at Albany (NY)
2008	Bob Ford	University at Albany (NY)
2009	Jeff McInerney	Central Connecticut State University (CT)
2010	Joe Walton	Robert Morris University (PA)

NEC Offensive Player of the Year

Year	Player	School
1996	Rick Sarille	Wagner College (NY)
1997	Dan Sabella	Monmouth University (NJ)
1998	Chris Reed	Monmouth University (NJ)
1999	Rick Sarille	Wagner College (NY)
2000	Tim Levcik	Robert Morris University (PA)
2001	Tim Levcik	Robert Morris University (PA)
2002	Gary Jones	University at Albany (NY)
2003	Gary Jones	University at Albany (NY)
2004	Cory Harge	Central Connecticut State University (CT)
2005	Anthony Doria	Saint Francis University (PA)
2006	Justise Hairston	Central Connecticut State University (CT)
2007	Jason Butler	Wagner College (NY)
2008	Dave Sinisi	Monmouth University (NJ)
2009	James Mallory	Central Connecticut State University (CT)
2010	Myles Russ	Robert Morris University (PA)

NEC Defensive Player of the Year

Year	Player	School
1996	Bill Sommers	Wagner College (NY)
1997	Jason Gmitter	Monmouth University (NJ)
1998	Steve Konopka	Central Connecticut State University (CT)
1999	Mike Grever	University at Albany (NY)
2000	Kayode Mayowa	Sacred Heart University (CT)
2001	Kayode Mayowa	Sacred Heart University (CT)
2002	Joe Sentipal	Monmouth University (NJ)
2003	Joe Sentipal	Monmouth University (NJ)
2004	James Noel	Robert Morris University (PA)

Year	Player	School
2005	Colin Disch	University at Albany (NY)
2006	Colin Disch	University at Albany (NY)
2007	Chad Wengert	Robert Morris University (PA)
2008	Kevin Walsh	Monmouth University (NJ)
2009	Jose Gumbs	Monmouth University (NJ)
2010	Alex DiMichele	Robert Morris University (PA)

NEC Offensive Rookie of the Year

Year	Player	School
1996	Archie Wannamaker	Robert Morris University (PA)
1997	Jeremy Swords	Saint Francis University (PA)
1998	Tim Levcik	Robert Morris University (PA)
1999	Wes Clemons	Saint Francis University (PA)
2000	Brent Hockenberry	Robert Morris University (PA)
2001	Londre Blocker	Stony Brook University (NY)
2002	Joe Migliore	Monmouth University (NJ)
2003	Cory Harge	Central Connecticut State University (CT)
2004	Andre Smith	Central Connecticut State University (CT)
2005	Aubrey Norris	Central Connecticut State University (CT)
2006	David Sinisi	Monmouth University (NJ)
2007	Dale Fink	Sacred Heart University (CT)
2008	James O'Quinn	Robert Morris University (PA)
2009	Nick Doscher	Wagner College (NY)
2010	Dillon Romain	University at Albany (NY)

NEC Defensive Rookie of the Year

Year	Player	School
1996	Murray Poole	Robert Morris University (PA)
1996	Samm Taranto	Saint Francis University (PA)
1997	Daryn Plummer	Wagner College (NY)
1998	Brad Miller	Robert Morris University (PA)
1999	Mike Steed	Wagner College (NY)
2000	Brian Pawlowski	Sacred Heart University (CT)
2001	Orion Sykes	St. John's University (NY)
2002	James Noel	Robert Morris University (PA)
2003	Mike Niklos	Robert Morris University (PA)
2004	Colin Disch	University at Albany (NY)
2005	Anthony Wilson	Central Connecticut State University (CT)
2006	Cory Giddings	Stony Brook University (NY)
2007	Scott Lewis	Saint Francis University (PA)
2008	Jose Gumbs	Monmouth University (NJ)
2009	Lawton Arnold	Central Connecticut State University (CT)
2010	Max Machado	Bryant University (RI)

Ohio Valley Conference (OVC)

215 Centerview Drive, Suite 115, Brentwood, TN 37027; Telephone: 615-371-1698; Fax: 615-371-1788; Web site: http://www.ovcsports.com

The country's eighth-oldest NCAA Division I organization, the Ohio Valley Conference was officially formed in 1948 with charter members Eastern Kentucky University, Morehead State University, Murray State University, University of Evansville, University of Louisville, and Western Kentucky University.

As of this writing, the following schools play in the Ohio Valley Conference:

- Austin Peay State University Governors, Clarksville, TN 37044; 931-221-7011; www.apsu.edu
- Eastern Illinois University Panthers, Charleston, IL 61920; 217-581-5000; www.eiu.edu

- Eastern Kentucky University Colonels, Richmond, KY 40475; 859-622-1000; www.eku.edu
- Jacksonville State University Gamecocks, Jacksonville, AL 36265; 256-782-5781; www.jsu.edu
- Morehead State University Eagles, Morehead, KY 40351; 800-585-6781; www.moreheadstate.edu; plays football in the Pioneer Football League
- Murray State University Racers, Murray, KY 42071; 800-272-4678; www.murraystate.edu
- Southeast Missouri State University Redhawks, Cape Girardeau, MO 63701; 573-651-2000; www.semo.edu
- Southern Illinois University, Edwardsville Cougars, Edwardsville, IL 62026; 888-328-5168; www.siue.edu; no football program
- Tennessee State University Tigers, Nashville, TN 37209; 615-963-5000; www.tnstate.edu
- Tennessee Tech University Golden Eagles, Cookeville, TN 38505; 931-372-3888; www.tntech.edu
- University of Tennessee, Martin, Skyhawks, Martin, TN 38238; 731-881-7000; www.utm.edu

OVC Champions

Year	*School*
1948	Murray State University (KY)
1948	University of Evansville (IN)
1949	University of Evansville (IN)
1950	Murray State University (KY)
1951	Murray State University (KY)
1952	Tennessee Technological University (TN)
1952	Western Kentucky University (KY)
1953	Tennessee Technological University (TN)
1954	Eastern Kentucky University (KY)
1955	Tennessee Technological University (TN)
1956	Middle Tennessee State University (TN)
1957	Middle Tennessee State University (TN)
1958	Middle Tennessee State University (TN)
1958	Tennessee Technological University (TN)
1959	Middle Tennessee State University (TN)
1959	Tennessee Technological University (TN)
1960	Tennessee Technological University (TN)
1961	Tennessee Technological University (TN)
1962	Eastern Kentucky University (KY)
1962	East Tennessee State University (TN)
1962	Middle Tennessee State University (TN)
1962	Morehead State University (KY)
1963	Western Kentucky University (KY)
1964	Middle Tennessee State University (TN)
1965	Middle Tennessee State University (TN)
1966	Morehead State University (KY)
1967	Eastern Kentucky University (KY)
1968	Eastern Kentucky University (KY)
1969	East Tennessee State University (TN)
1970	Western Kentucky University (KY)
1971	Western Kentucky University (KY)
1972	Tennessee Technological University (TN)
1973	Western Kentucky University (KY)
1974	Eastern Kentucky University (KY)
1975	Tennessee Technological University (TN)
1976	Eastern Kentucky University (KY)
1977	Austin Peay State University (TN)
1978	Western Kentucky University (KY)

Year	*School*
1979	Murray State University (KY)
1980	Western Kentucky University (KY)
1981	Eastern Kentucky University (KY)
1982	Eastern Kentucky University (KY)
1983	Eastern Kentucky University (KY)
1984	Eastern Kentucky University (KY)
1985	Middle Tennessee State University (TN)
1986	Eastern Kentucky University (KY)
1986	Murray State University (KY)
1987	Eastern Kentucky University (KY)
1987	Youngstown State University (OH)
1988	Eastern Kentucky University (KY)
1989	Middle Tennessee State University (TN)
1990	Eastern Kentucky University (KY)
1990	Middle Tennessee State University (TN)
1991	Eastern Kentucky University (KY)
1992	Middle Tennessee State University (TN)
1993	Eastern Kentucky University (KY)
1994	Eastern Kentucky University (KY)
1995	Murray State University (KY)
1996	Murray State University (KY)
1997	Eastern Kentucky University (KY)
1998	Tennessee State University (TN)
1999	Tennessee State University (TN)
2000	Western Kentucky University (KY)
2001	Eastern Illinois University (IL)
2002	Eastern Illinois University (IL)
2002	Murray State University (KY)
2003	Jacksonville State University (AL)
2004	Jacksonville State University (AL)
2005	Eastern Illinois University (IL)
2006	Eastern Illinois University (IL)
2006	University of Tennessee, Martin (TN)
2007	Eastern Kentucky University (KY)
2008	Eastern Kentucky University (KY)
2009	Eastern Illinois University (IL)
2010	Southeast Missouri State University (MO)

OVC Coach of the Year

In 2003, the OVC's Coach of the Year award was renamed the Roy Kidd Coach of the Year Award after the Eastern Kentucky coach who won the award 10 times during his career.

Year	*Coach*	*School*
1963	Nick Denes	Western Kentucky University (KY)
1964	Bill Dupes	Austin Peay State University (TN)
1965	Charles Murphy	Middle Tennessee State University (TN)
1966	Guy Penny	Morehead State University (KY)
1967	Roy Kidd	Eastern Kentucky University (KY)
1968	Bill Furgerson	Murray State University (KY)
1969	John Bell	East Tennessee State University (TN)
1970	Bill Peck	Middle Tennessee State University (TN)
1971	Don Wade	Tennessee Technological University (TN)
1972	Don Wade	Tennessee Technological University (TN)
1973	Jimmy Feix	Western Kentucky University (KY)
1974	Roy Kidd	Eastern Kentucky University (KY)
1975	Don Wade	Tennessee Technological University (TN)
1976	Roy Kidd	Eastern Kentucky University (KY)
1977	Boots Donnelly	Austin Peay State University (TN)
1978	Jimmy Feix	Western Kentucky University (KY)
1979	Mike Gottfried	Murray State University (KY)
1980	Jimmy Feix	Western Kentucky University (KY)
1981	Roy Kidd	Eastern Kentucky University (KY)
1982	Roy Kidd	Eastern Kentucky University (KY)
1982	Jim Dennison	University of Akron (OH)
1983	Roy Kidd	Eastern Kentucky University (KY)
1983	Boots Donnelly	Middle Tennessee State University (TN)
1984	Bill Narduzzi	Youngstown State University (OH)
1985	Boots Donnelly	Middle Tennessee State University (TN)
1986	Bill Baldridge	Morehead State University (KY)
1987	Jim Tressel	Youngstown State University (OH)
1988	Roy Kidd	Eastern Kentucky University (KY)
1989	Boots Donnelly	Middle Tennessee State University (TN)
1990	Roy Kidd	Eastern Kentucky University (KY)
1990	Cole Proctor	Morehead State University (KY)
1990	Joe Gilliam	Tennessee State University (TN)
1991	Roy Kidd	Eastern Kentucky University (KY)
1992	Jim Ragland	Tennessee Technological University (TN)
1993	Jim Ragland	Tennessee Technological University (TN)
1994	John Mumford	Southeast Missouri State University (MO)
1995	Houston Nutt	Murray State University (KY)
1996	Houston Nutt	Murray State University (KY)
1997	Roy Kidd	Eastern Kentucky University (KY)
1998	L.C. Cole	Tennessee State University (TN)
1999	L.C. Cole	Tennessee State University (TN)
2000	Jack Harbaugh	Western Kentucky University (KY)
2001	Bob Spoo	Eastern Illinois University (IL)
2002	Tim Billings	Southeast Missouri State University (MO)
2003	Bill Gray	Samford University (AL)
2004	Jack Crowe	Jacksonville State University (AL)
2005	Bob Spoo	Eastern Illinois University (IL)
2006	Jason Simpson	University of Tennessee, Martin (TN)
2007	Danny Hope	Eastern Kentucky University (KY)
2008	Dean Hood	Eastern Kentucky University (KY)
2009	Bob Spoo	Eastern Illinois University (IL)
2010	Tony Samuel	Southeast Missouri State University (MO)

OVC Offensive Player of the Year

Year	*Player*	*Position*	*School*
1963	Jim Baker	Quarterback	East Tennessee State University (TN)
1964	Carlton Flatt	Quarterback	Austin Peay State University (TN)
1965	Teddy Morris	Quarterback	Middle Tennessee State University (TN)
1966	Tommie Gray	Halfback	Morehead State University (KY)
1967	Dickie Moore	Halfback	Western Kentucky University (KY)
1968	Larry Tillman	Quarterback	Murray State University (KY)
1969	Larry Schreiber	Halfback	Tennessee Technological University (TN)
1970	Larry Graham	Quarterback	East Tennessee State University (TN)
1971	Rick Fisher	Tailback	Murray State University (KY)
1972	George Greenfield	Running Back	Murray State University (KY)
1973	Alan Chadwick	Quarterback	East Tennessee State University (TN)
1974	Everett Talbert	Running Back	Eastern Kentucky University (KY)
1975	Mike Moore	Running Back	Middle Tennessee State University (TN)
1976	Ernie House	Quarterback	Eastern Kentucky University (KY)
1976	Everett Talbert	Running Back	Eastern Kentucky University (KY)
1977	Phil Simms	Quarterback	Morehead State University (KY)
1978	Danny Johnson	Running Back	Murray State University (KY)
1979	John Hall	Quarterback	Western Kentucky University (KY)
1980	Sonny Defilippis	Quarterback	Austin Peay State University (TN)
1981	Gino Gibbs	Quarterback	Murray State University (KY)
1982	Steve Bird	Wide Receiver	Eastern Kentucky University (KY)
1983	James Black	Running Back	University of Akron (OH)
1984	Vince Hall	Tailback	Middle Tennessee State University (TN)
1985	Marvin Collier	Quarterback	Middle Tennessee State University (TN)
1986	Mike Clark	Tailback	University of Akron (OH)
1987	Trenton Lykes	Quarterback	Youngstown State University (OH)
1988	Elroy Harris	Tailback	Eastern Kentucky University (KY)
1989	Michael Proctor	Quarterback	Murray State University (KY)
1990	Joe Campbell	Tailback	Middle Tennessee State University (TN)
1991	Markus Thomas	Tailback	Eastern Kentucky University (KY)
1992	Markus Thomas	Tailback	Eastern Kentucky University (KY)
1993	Kippy Bayless	Tailback	Middle Tennessee State University (TN)
1994	Kippy Bayless	Tailback	Middle Tennessee State University (TN)
1995	Derrick Cullors	Tailback	Murray State University (KY)
1996	Mike Cherry	Quarterback	Murray State University (KY)
1997	Tyrone Butterfield	Wide Receiver	Tennessee State University (TN)
1997	Simon Fuentes	Quarterback	Eastern Kentucky University (KY)
1998	Leon Murray	Quarterback	Tennessee State University (TN)
1999	Justin Fuente	Quarterback	Murray State University (KY)
2000	Tony Romo	Quarterback	Eastern Illinois University (IL)
2001	Tony Romo	Quarterback	Eastern Illinois University (IL)
2002	Tony Romo	Quarterback	Eastern Illinois University (IL)
2003	Efrem Hill	Wide Receiver	Samford University (AL)
2004	Charles Anthony	Running Back	Tennessee State University (TN)
2005	Josh Greco	Quarterback	Eastern Kentucky University (KY)
2006	Vincent Webb	Running Back	Eastern Illinois University (IL)
2006	Don Chapman	Running Back	University of Tennessee, Martin (TN)
2007	Allan Holland	Quarterback	Eastern Kentucky University (KY)
2008	Javarris Williams	Running Back	Tennessee State University (TN)
2009	Ryan Perrilloux	Quarterback	Jacksonville State University (AL)
2010	Henry Harris	Running Back	Southeast Missouri State University (MO)

OVC Defensive Player of the Year

Year	*Player*	*Position*	*School*
1963	John Mutchler	Defensive End	Western Kentucky University (KY)
1964	John Wheeler	Nose Guard	Murray State University (KY)

Year	Player	Position	School
1965	Keith Atchley	Nose Guard	Middle Tennessee State University (TN)
1966	Buddy Pfaadt	Defensive Back	Eastern Kentucky University (KY)
1967	Ron Overbay	Defensive Back	East Tennessee State University (TN)
1968	Ron Overbay	Defensive Back	East Tennessee State University (TN)
1969	Lawrence Brame	Defensive End	Western Kentucky University (KY)
1970	Lawrence Brame	Defensive End	Western Kentucky University (KY)
1971	Jim Youngblood	Linebacker	Tennessee Technological University (TN)
1972	Jim Youngblood	Linebacker	Tennessee Technological University (TN)
1973	Lonnie Schuster	Defensive Tackle	Western Kentucky University (KY)
1974	Virgil Livers	Defensive Back	Western Kentucky University (KY)
1975	Rick Green	Linebacker	Western Kentucky University (KY)
1976	Biff Madon	Linebacker	Western Kentucky University (KY)
1977	Bob Bible	Linebacker	Austin Peay State University (TN)
1978	Mike Betts	Defensive Back	Austin Peay State University (TN)
1979	Terry Love	Defensive Back	Murray State University (KY)
1980	George Floyd	Defensive Back	Eastern Kentucky University (KY)
1981	George Floyd	Defensive Back	Eastern Kentucky University (KY)
1982	Dennis Mix	Defensive End	Middle Tennessee State University (TN)
1983	Dave Arango	Defensive Lineman	University of Akron (OH)
1984	Fred Harvey	Linebacker	Eastern Kentucky University (KY)
1985	Don Griffin	Defensive Back	Middle Tennessee State University (TN)
1986	Fred Harvey	Linebacker	Eastern Kentucky University (KY)
1987	Aaron Jones	Defensive Lineman	Eastern Kentucky University (KY)
1987	Paul Solis	Linebacker	Youngstown State University (OH)
1988	Don Thomas	Linebacker	Middle Tennessee State University (TN)
1989	Anthony Coleman	Linebacker	Middle Tennessee State University (TN)
1990	Marty Carter	Defensive Back	Middle Tennessee State University (TN)
1991	David Wilkins	Defensive End	Eastern Kentucky University (KY)
1992	Mike Caldwell	Linebacker	Middle Tennessee State University (TN)
1993	Chad Bratzke	Defensive End	Eastern Kentucky University (KY)
1994	Doug Berg	Defensive Lineman	Southeast Missouri State University (MO)
1995	William Hampton	Defensive Back	Murray State University (KY)
1996	Tony McCombs	Linebacker	Eastern Kentucky University (KY)
1997	Angel Rubio	Defensive Lineman	Southeast Missouri State University (MO)
1998	Branon Vaughn	Defensive End	Tennessee Technological University (TN)
1999	Lamar Carter	Defensive End	Tennessee State University (TN)
2000	Chad Evitts	Linebacker	Tennessee Technological University (TN)
2001	Yeremiah Bell	Defensive Back	Eastern Kentucky University (KY)
2002	Nick Ricks	Linebacker	Eastern Illinois University (IL)
2003	Cortland Finnegan	Defensive Back	Samford University (AL)
2004	Justen Rivers	Linebacker	Eastern Kentucky University (KY)
2005	Clint Sellers	Linebacker	Eastern Illinois University (IL)
2006	Donald Thomas	Linebacker	Eastern Illinois University (IL)
2007	Derrick Huff	Defensive Back	Eastern Kentucky University (KY)
2008	Nathan Williams	Linebacker	Murray State University (KY)
2009	Austen Lane	Defensive Lineman	Murray State University (KY)
2010	Andrew Soucy	Defensive Lineman	Eastern Kentucky University (KY)

OVC Freshman of the Year

Year	Player	Position	School
2004	Don Chapman	Running Back	University of Tennessee, Martin (TN)
2005	Javarris Williams	Running Back	Tennessee State University (TN)
2006	Lee Sweeney	Quarterback	Tennessee Technological University (TN)
2007	Jeff Ehrhardt	Quarterback	Murray State University (KY)
2008	Tim Benford	Wide Receiver	Tennessee Technological University (TN)
2009	T.J. Pryor	Quarterback	Eastern Kentucky University (KY)
2010	Coty Blanchard	Punter-Quarterback	Jacksonville State University (AL)

Patriot League (Patriot)

3773 Corporate Parkway, Suite 190, Center Valley, PA 18034; Telephone: 610-289-1950; Fax: 610-289-1951; Web site: http://www.patriotleague.org; http://www.patriotleague.com

The Patriot League (formerly known as the Colonial League) began as a Division I-AA (FCS) football conference in 1986 with five charter member schools (Bucknell University, Colgate University, College of the Holy Cross, Lafayette College, and Lehigh University) and adopted its current name in 1990.

As of this writing, the Patriot League consists of the following schools:

- American University Eagles, Washington, D.C.; 20016; 202-885-1000; www.american.edu; no football program
- Bucknell University Bison, Lewisburg, PA 17837; 570-577-2000; www.bucknell.edu
- Colgate University Raiders, Hamilton, NY 13346; 315-228-1000; www.colgate.edu
- College of the Holy Cross Crusaders, Worcester, MA 01610; 508-793-2011; www.holycross.edu
- Fordham University Rams, Bronx, NY 10458; 718-817-1000; www.fordham.edu; associate football member from the Atlantic 10 Conference
- Georgetown University Hoyas, Washington, D.C. 20057; 202-687-0100; www.georgetown.edu; associate football member from the Big East Conference
- Lafayette College Leopards, Easton, PA 18042; 610-330-5000; www.lafayette.edu
- Lehigh University Mountain Hawks, Bethlehem, PA 18015; 610-758-3000; www4.lehigh.edu
- United States Military Academy Black Knights, West Point, NY 10996; 845-938-4041; www.usma.edu; plays football as an independent team
- United States Naval Academy Midshipmen, Annapolis, MD 21402; 410-293-1000; www.usna.edu; plays football as an independent team

Patriot League Champions

Year	*School*
1986	College of the Holy Cross (MA)
1987	College of the Holy Cross (MA)
1988	Lafayette College (PA)
1989	College of the Holy Cross (MA)
1990	College of the Holy Cross (MA)
1991	College of the Holy Cross (MA)
1992	Lafayette College (PA)
1993	Lehigh University (PA)
1994	Lafayette College (PA)
1995	Lehigh University (PA)
1996	Bucknell University (PA)
1997	Colgate University (NY)
1998	Lehigh University (PA)
1999	Colgate University (NY)
1999	Lehigh University (PA)
2000	Lehigh University (PA)
2001	Lehigh University (PA)
2002	Colgate University (NY)
2002	Fordham University (NY)
2003	Colgate University (NY)
2004	Lafayette College (PA)
2004	Lehigh University (PA)
2005	Colgate University (NY)
2005	Lafayette College (PA)
2006	Lafayette College (PA)
2006	Lehigh University (PA)
2007	Fordham University (NY)
2008	Colgate University (NY)
2009	College of the Holy Cross (MA)
2010	Lehigh University (PA)

Patriot League Coach of the Year

Year	*Coach*	*School*
1986	Mark Duffner	College of the Holy Cross (MA)
1987	Mark Duffner	College of the Holy Cross (MA)
1988	Bill Russo	Lafayette College (PA)
1989	Mark Duffner	College of the Holy Cross (MA)
1990	Lou Maranzana	Bucknell University (PA)
1991	Mark Duffner	College of the Holy Cross (MA)
1992	Bill Russo	Lafayette College (PA)
1993	Hank Small	Lehigh University (PA)
1994	Bill Russo	Lafayette College (PA)
1995	Kevin Higgins	Lehigh University (PA)
1996	Dick Biddle	Colgate University (NY)

Year	Coach	School
1997	Tom Gadd	Bucknell University (PA)
1998	Kevin Higgins	Lehigh University (PA)
1999	Gordy Combs	Towson University (MD)
2000	Kevin Higgins	Lehigh University (PA)
2001	Dave Clawson	Fordham University (NY)
2001	Pete Lembo	Lehigh University (PA)
2002	Dave Clawson	Fordham University (NY)
2003	Dick Biddle	Colgate University (NY)
2004	Frank Tavani	Lafayette College (PA)
2005	Dick Biddle	Colgate University (NY)
2006	Tom Gilmore	College of the Holy Cross (MA)
2007	Tom Masella	Fordham University (NY)
2008	Dick Biddle	Colgate University (NY)
2009	Tom Gilmore	College of the Holy Cross (MA)
2010	Andy Coen	Lehigh University (PA)

Patriot League Player of the Year

Awarded from 1986 to 2000.

Year	Player	Position	School
1986	Gordie Lockbaum	Running Back / Defensive Back	College of the Holy Cross (MA)
1987	Gordie Lockbaum	Running Back	College of the Holy Cross (MA)
1988	Frank Bauer	Quarterback	Lafayette College (PA)
1989	Scott Auchenbach	Quarterback	Bucknell University (PA)
1990	Joe Segreti	Fullback	College of the Holy Cross (MA)
1991	Tom Ciaccio	Quarterback	College of the Holy Cross (MA)
1992	Tom Kirchhoff	Quarterback	Lehigh University (PA)
1993	Scott Semptimphelter	Quarterback	Lehigh University (PA)
1994	Rich Lemon	Tailback	Bucknell University (PA)
1994	Erik Marsh	Tailback	Lafayette College (PA)
1995	Bob Aylsworth	Quarterback	Lehigh University (PA)
1996	Ryan Vena	Quarterback	Colgate University (NY)
1997	Ryan Vena	Quarterback	Colgate University (NY)
1998	Phil Stambaugh	Quarterback	Lehigh University (PA)
1999	Ryan Vena	Quarterback	Colgate University (NY)
2000	Andrew Hollingsworth	Defensive End	Towson University (MD)

Patriot League Offensive Player of the Year

Year	Player	Position	School
1986	Kenny Gamble	Running Back	Colgate University (NY)
1987	Jeff Wiley	Quarterback	College of the Holy Cross (MA)
1988	Frank Bauer	Quarterback	Lafayette College (PA)
1989	Tom Costello	Running Back	Lafayette College (PA)
1990	Tom Ciaccio	Quarterback	College of the Holy Cross (MA)
1991	Horace Hamm	Wide Receiver	Lehigh University (PA)
1992	Erik Marsh	Tailback	Lafayette College (PA)
1993	Erik Marsh	Tailback	Lafayette College (PA)
1994	Rich Lemon	Tailback	Bucknell University (PA)
1995	Brian Klingerman	Wide Receiver	Lehigh University (PA)
1996	Anthony Caravetta	Running Back	Colgate University (NY)
1997	Daymon Smith	Running Back	Colgate University (NY)
1998	Corey Hill	Wide Receiver	Colgate University (NY)
1999	Ronald Jean	Running Back	Lehigh University (PA)
2000	Phil Yarberough	Wide Receiver	Lafayette College (PA)
2001	Josh Snyder	Wide Receiver	Lehigh University (PA)
2002	Kirwin Watson	Running Back	Fordham University (NY)
2003	Jamaal Branch	Running Back	Colgate University (NY)

Year	Player	Position	School
2004	Joe McCourt	Running Back	Lafayette College (PA)
2005	Steve Silva	Running Back	College of the Holy Cross (MA)
2006	Jonathan Hurt	Running Back	Lafayette College (PA)
2007	Dominic Randolph	Quarterback	College of the Holy Cross (MA)
2008	Dominic Randolph	Quarterback	College of the Holy Cross (MA)
2009	Dominic Randolph	Quarterback	College of the Holy Cross (MA)
2010	Nate Eachus	Running Back	Colgate University (NY)

Patriot League Defensive Player of the Year

Year	Player	Position	School
1986	Jerry McCabe	Linebacker	College of the Holy Cross (MA)
1987	Greg Manusky	Linebacker	Colgate University (NY)
1988	Rob McGovern	Linebacker	College of the Holy Cross (MA)
1989	Dave Murphy	Cornerback	College of the Holy Cross (MA)
1990	Craig Callahan	Linebacker	College of the Holy Cross (MA)
1991	Corey Vincent	Defensive Lineman	College of the Holy Cross (MA)
1992	Mark Blazejewski	Linebacker	Fordham University (NY)
1992	Tom McDonald	Defensive Lineman	College of the Holy Cross (MA)
1993	Aaron Dougherty	Linebacker	Fordham University (NY)
1994	Pat Smith	Free Safety	College of the Holy Cross (MA)
1995	Ed Burman	Defensive End	Bucknell University (PA)
1996	B.J. Gallis	Strong Safety	Lafayette College (PA)
1997	Dan Bengele	Linebacker	Lafayette College (PA)
1998	Nick Martucci	Defensive Lineman	Lehigh University (PA)
1999	Ian Eason	Linebacker	Lehigh University (PA)
2000	Andrew Hollingsworth	Defensive End	Towson University (MD)
2001	Abdul Byron	Defensive Back	Lehigh University (PA)
2002	Adam Lord	Defensive Lineman	Bucknell University (PA)
2002	Tem Lukabu	Linebacker	Colgate University (NY)
2003	Tem Lukabu	Linebacker	Colgate University (NY)
2004	Sean Conover	Defensive Lineman	Bucknell University)PA)
2005	Jared Nepa	Linebacker	Colgate University)NY)
2006	Marcus Taylor	Linebacker	Fordham University (NY)
2007	Andy Romans	Linebacker	Lafayette College (PA)
2008	Andy Romans	Linebacker	Lafayette College (PA)
2009	Matt Cohen	Linebacker	Lehigh University (PA)
2010	Zach Smith	Defensive End	Colgate University (NY)

Patriot League Rookie of the Year

Year	Player	Position	School
1986	Mark McGowan	Quarterback	Lehigh University (PA)
1987	Mike Guerrini	Wide Receiver	Bucknell University (PA)
1988	Tom Costello	Tailback	Lafayette College (PA)
1989	Jim Tierney	Tailback	Colgate University (NY)
1990	Art Dennis	Running Back	Lafayette College (PA)
1991	Erik Marsh	Tailback	Lafayette College (PA)
1992	Andy Fitzpatrick	Quarterback	College of the Holy Cross (MA)
1993	Rich Lemon	Tailback	Bucknell University (PA)
1994	Shawn McHale	Quarterback	Lafayette College (PA)
1994	J.R. Walz	Tailback	College of the Holy Cross (MA)
1995	Leonard Moore	Tailback	Lafayette College (PA)
1996	Ryan Vena	Quarterback	Colgate University (NY)
1997	Ed Weiss	Tailback	Colgate University (NY)
1998	Kenya Allen	Defensive Back	Lafayette College (PA)
1999	Brian Hall	Quarterback	College of the Holy Cross (MA)
2000	Marko Glavic	Quarterback	Lafayette College (PA)
2001	Joe McCourt	Running Back	Lafayette College (PA)

Year	Player	Position	School
2002	Gideon Akande	Running Back	College of the Holy Cross (MA)
2003	Micah Clukey	Punter / Kicker	Fordham University (NY)
2004	Jonte Coven	Running Back	Fordham University (NY)
2005	Jordan Scott	Running Back	Colgate University (NY)
2006	Charlie Houghton	Running Back	Georgetown University (Washington, D.C.)
2007	Xavier Martin	Running Back	Fordham University (NY)
2008	Nate Eachus	Running Back	Colgate University (NY)
2009	Demitri Diamond	Defensive Back	Colgate University (NY)
2010	Brandon Wesley	Quarterback	Bucknell University (PA)

PATRIOT LEAGUE SPECIAL TEAMS PLAYER OF THE YEAR

Year	Player	Position	School
2004	Dante Ross	Kickoff Returner	Bucknell University (PA)
2005	Steve Silva	Kickoff Returner	College of the Holy Cross (MA)
2006	Jason Leo	Kicker	Lehigh University (PA)

Pioneer Football League (Pioneer)

1818 Chouteau Avenue, St. Louis, MO 63103; Telephone: 314-421-2286; Fax: 314-421-3505; Web site: http://www.pioneer-football.org

The Pioneer Football League is the nation's only non-scholarship NCAA Football Championship Subdivision conference that offers football as its only sport, while it is one of only two conferences that sponsor football as its only sport (the Missouri Valley Football Conference being the other). Beginning football play in 1993, the PFL's five charter schools included Butler University, Drake University, the University of Dayton, the University of Evansville (which dropped football in 1997), and Valparaiso University.

As of this writing, the following schools play in the Pioneer Football League:

- Butler University Bulldogs, Indianapolis, IN 46208; 800-368-6852; www.butler.edu; associate member from the Horizon League
- Campbell University Fighting Camels, Buies Creek, NC 27506; 800-334-4111; www.campbell.edu; associate member from the Atlantic Sun Conference
- Davidson College Wildcats, Davidson, NC 28035; 704-894-2000; www3.davidson.edu; associate member from the Southern Conference
- Drake University Bulldogs, Des Moines, IA 50311; 515-271-2011; www.drake.edu; associate member from the Missouri Valley Conference
- Jacksonville University Dolphins, Jacksonville, FL 32211; 800-225-2027; www.ju.edu; associate member from the Atlantic Sun Conference
- Marist College Red Foxes, Poughkeepsie, NY 12601; 845-575-3000; www.marist.edu; associate member from the Metro Atlantic Athletic Conference
- Morehead State University Eagles, Morehead, KY 40351; 800-585-6781; www.moreheadstate.edu; associate member from the Ohio Valley Conference
- University of Dayton Flyers, Dayton, OH 45469; 937-229-1000; www.udayton.edu; associate member from the Atlantic 10 Conference
- University of San Diego Toreros, San Diego, CA 92110; 619-260-4600; www.sandiego.edu; associate member from the West Coast Conference
- Valparaiso University Crusaders, Valparaiso, IN 46383; 219-464-5096; www.valpo.edu; associate member from the Horizon League

PIONEER FOOTBALL LEAGUE CHAMPIONS

Year	School
1993	University of Dayton (OH)
1994	Butler University (IN)
1994	University of Dayton (OH)
1995	Drake University (IA)
1996	University of Dayton (OH)
1997	University of Dayton (OH)

Year	School
1998	Drake University (IA)
1999	University of Dayton (OH)
2000	University of Dayton (OH)
2000	Drake University (IA)
2000	Valparaiso University (IN)
2001	University of Dayton (OH)
2002	University of Dayton (OH)
2003	Valparaiso University (IN)
2004	Drake University (IA)
2005	University of San Diego (CA)
2006	University of San Diego (CA)
2007	University of San Diego (CA)
2007	University of Dayton (OH)
2008	Jacksonville University (FL)
2009	Butler University (IN)
2009	University of Dayton (OH)
2010	University of Dayton (OH)
2010	Jacksonville University (FL)

Pioneer Football League Coach of the Year

Year	Coach	School
1993	Mike Kelly	University of Dayton (OH)
1994	Mike Kelly	University of Dayton (OH)
1995	Rob Ash	Drake University (IA)
1996	Mike Kelly	University of Dayton (OH)
1997	Mike Kelly	University of Dayton (OH)
1998	Rob Ash	Drake University (IA)
1999	Tom Horne	Valparaiso University (IN)
2000	Mike Kelly	University of Dayton (OH)
2001	Mike Kelly	University of Dayton (OH)
2002	Kevin McGarry	University of San Diego (CA)
2002	Matt Ballard	Morehead State University (KY)
2003	Tom Home	Valparaiso University (IN)
2004	Rob Ash	Drake University (IA)
2004	Matt Ballard	Morehead State University (KY)
2005	Jim Harbaugh	University of San Diego (CA)
2006	Jim Harbaugh	University of San Diego (CA)
2006	Tripp Merritt	Davidson College (NC)
2007	Mike Kelly	University of Dayton (OH)
2008	Kerwin Bell	Jacksonville University (FL)
2009	Jeff Voris	Butler University (IN)
2010	Rick Chamberlin	University of Dayton (OH)

Pioneer Football League Offensive Player of the Year

Year	Player	School
2001	Jermaine Bailey	University of Dayton (OH)
2002	Kelly Spiker	University of Dayton (OH)
2002	Jay Bailey	Austin Peay State College (TN)
2003	Eric Rasmussen	University of San Diego (CA)
2003	David Caudill	Morehead State University (KY)
2004	Scott Phaydavong	Drake University (IA)
2004	Todd Mortensen	University of San Diego (CA)
2004	John Leverett	Davidson College (NC)
2005	Josh Johnson	University of San Diego (CA)
2006	Josh Johnson	University of San Diego (CA)
2007	Kevin Hoyng	University of Dayton (OH)
2008	John Matthews	University of San Diego (CA)
2009	Steve Valentino	University of Dayton (OH)
2010	Steve Valentino	University of Dayton (OH)

Pioneer Football League Defensive Player of the Year

Year	Player	School
2001	Mark Kasmer	University of Dayton (OH)
2001	Tyrone Wright	Jacksonville University (FL)
2002	Mark Kasmer	University of Dayton (OH)

Year	Player	School
2002	Jim Carney	Davidson College (NC)
2003	Brandon Wright	Butler University (IN)
2003	Craig Unger	Morehead State University (KY)
2003	Darryl Childers	Davidson College (NC)
2004	Doug Jones	University of Dayton (OH)
2004	Brendan Dete	Davidson College (NC)
2004	Craig Unger	Morehead State University (KY)
2005	John Hoppe	University of Dayton (OH)
2006	James Adams	Drake University (IA)
2006	Eric Bakhtiari	University of San Diego (CA)
2007	Eric Bakhtiari	University of San Diego (CA)
2008	Scott Vossley	University of Dayton (OH)
2009	Wes McDermott	Morehead State University (KY)
2010	Dain Taylor	Drake University (IA)

Pioneer Football League Freshman of the Year

Year	Player	School
2006	Gabe Derricks	University of San Diego (CA)
2007	Joe Castaneda	University of Dayton (OH)

Pioneer Football League Offensive Freshman of the Year

Year	Player	School
2008	John McGregor	Jacksonville University (FL)
2009	Kyle Warren	University of San Diego (CA)
2010	Jonathan Carkhuff	Davidson College (NC)

Pioneer Football League Defensive Freshman of the Year

Year	Player	School
2008	Al-Rilwan Adeyemi	University of San Diego (CA)
2009	Tyler Moorehead	Drake University (IA)
2010	Mike Klein	Jacksonville University (FL)

Southern Conference (Southern)

702 North Pine Street, Spartanburg, SC 29303; Telephone: 864-591-5100; Fax: 864-591-4282; Web site: http://www.soconsports.com

The fifth-oldest NCAA Division I college organization (after the Big Ten (1896), Missouri Valley (1907), and Southwestern Athletic (1920)), the Southern Conference was formed in February 1921 from 14 charter schools that left the Southern Intercollegiate Athletic Association: Alabama Polytechnic Institute (now known as Auburn University), Clemson University, Georgia School of Technology (now known as Georgia Institute of Technology), Mississippi A&M University (now known as Mississippi State University), North Carolina State University, University of Alabama, University of Georgia, University of Kentucky, University of Maryland, University of North Carolina, University of Tennessee, University of Virginia, Virginia Polytechnic Institute (now known as Virginia Polytechnic Institute) and State University), and Washington & Lee University.

As of this writing, the 12 schools that make up the Southern Conference include:

- Appalachian State University Mountaineers, Boone, NC 28608; 828-262-2000; www.appstate.edu
- The Citadel (The Military College of South Carolina) Bulldogs, Charleston, SC 29409; 843-225-3294; www.citadel.edu
- College of Charleston Cougars, Charleston, SC 29424; 843-805-5507; www.cofc.edu; no football program
- Davidson College Wildcats, Davidson, NC 28035; 704-894-2000; www3.davidson.edu; plays football in the Pioneer Football League
- Elon University Phoenix, Elon, NC 27244; 336-278-2000; www.elon.edu

- Furman University Paladins, Greenville, SC 29613; 864-294-2000; www2.furman.edu
- Georgia Southern University Eagles, Statesboro, GA 30458; 912-478-4636; www.georgiasouthern.edu
- Samford University Bulldogs, Birmingham, AL 35229; 205-726-2011; www.samford.edu
- University of North Carolina, Greensboro, Spartans, Greensboro, NC 27412; 336-334-5000; www.uncg.edu; no football program
- University of Tennessee, Chattanooga Mocs, Chattanooga, TN 37403; 423-425-4111; www.utc.edu
- Western Carolina University Catamounts, Cullowhee, NC 28723; 828-227-7317; www.wcu.edu
- Wofford College Terriers, Spartanburg, SC 29303; 864-597-4000; www.wofford.edu

Southern Conference Champions

Year	*School*
1933	Duke University (NC)
1934	Washington & Lee University (VA)
1935	Duke University (NC)
1936	Duke University (NC)
1937	University of Maryland (MD)
1938	Duke University (NC)
1939	Duke University (NC)
1940	Clemson University (SC)
1941	Duke University (NC)
1942	College of William & Mary (VA)
1943	Duke University (NC)
1944	Duke University (NC)
1945	Duke University (NC)
1946	University of North Carolina (NC)
1947	College of William & Mary (VA)
1948	Clemson University (SC)
1949	University of North Carolina (NC)
1950	Washington & Lee University (VA)
1951	University of Maryland (MD)
1951	Virginia Military Institute (VA)
1952	Duke University (NC)
1953	West Virginia University (WV)
1954	West Virginia University (WV)
1955	West Virginia University (WV)
1956	West Virginia University (WV)
1957	Virginia Military Institute (VA)
1958	West Virginia University (WV)
1959	Virginia Military Institute (VA)
1960	Virginia Military Institute (VA)
1961	The Citadel (The Military College of South Carolina) (SC)
1962	Virginia Military Institute (VA)
1963	Virginia Polytechnic Institute and State University (VA)
1964	West Virginia University (WV)
1965	West Virginia University (WV)
1966	East Carolina University (NC)
1966	College of William & Mary (VA)
1967	West Virginia University (WV)
1968	University of Richmond (VA)
1969	Davidson College (NC)
1969	University of Richmond (VA)
1970	College of William & Mary (VA)
1971	University of Richmond (VA)
1972	East Carolina University (NC)
1973	East Carolina University (NC)
1974	Virginia Military Institute (VA)
1975	University of Richmond (VA)
1976	East Carolina University (NC)
1977	University of Tennessee, Chattanooga (TN)
1977	Virginia Military Institute (VA)
1978	Furman University (SC)
1978	University of Tennessee, Chattanooga (TN)
1979	University of Tennessee, Chattanooga (TN)
1980	Furman University (SC)
1981	Furman University (SC)
1982	Furman University (SC)
1983	Furman University (SC)
1984	University of Tennessee, Chattanooga (TN)
1985	Furman University (SC)
1986	Appalachian State University (NC)
1987	Appalachian State University (NC)
1988	Furman University (SC)
1988	Marshall University (WV)
1989	Furman University (SC)
1990	Furman University (SC)
1991	Appalachian State University (NC)
1992	The Citadel (The Military College of South Carolina) (SC)
1993	Georgia Southern University (GA)
1994	Marshall University (WV)
1995	Appalachian State University (NC)
1996	Marshall University (WV)
1997	Georgia Southern University (GA)
1998	Georgia Southern University (GA)
1999	Furman University (SC)
1999	Georgia Southern University (GA)
1999	Appalachian State University (NC)
2000	Georgia Southern University (GA)
2001	Georgia Southern University (GA)
2001	Furman University (SC)
2002	Georgia Southern University (GA)
2003	Wofford College (SC)
2004	Furman University (SC)
2004	Georgia Southern University (GA)
2005	Appalachian State University (NC)
2006	Appalachian State University (NC)
2007	Appalachian State University (NC)
2007	Wofford College (SC)
2008	Appalachian State University (NC)
2009	Appalachian State University (NC)
2010	Appalachian State University (NC)
2010	Wofford College (SC)

Southern Conference Media Coach of the Year

This award is named in honor of Wallace Wade, the first commissioner of the Southern Conference (1951–1960). He won three national titles (1925–1926, 1930) as the head football coach at the University of Alabama (Tuscaloosa); was the head football coach at Duke University (Durham, NC) for 16 seasons (1931–1941, 1946–1950); and was inducted into the College Football Hall of Fame in 1955.

Year	*Coach*	*School*
1948	Frank Howard	Clemson University (SC)
1949	Wallace Wade	Duke University (NC)
1950	George Barclay	Washington & Lee University (VA)
1951	Jim Tatum	University of Maryland (MD)
1952	Bill Murray	Duke University (NC)
1953	Art Lewis	West Virginia University (WV)
1954	Art Lewis	West Virginia University (WV)
1955	Eugene Sherman	George Washington University (Washington, D.C.)
1956	Frank Moseley	Virginia Polytechnic Institute and State University (VA)
1957	John McKenna	Virginia Military Institute (VA)
1958	Ed Merrick	University of Richmond (VA)
1959	John McKenna	Virginia Military Institute (VA)
1960	Bill Elias	George Washington University (Washington, D.C.)
1961	Eddie Teague	The Citadel (The Military College of South Carolina) (SC)
1962	John McKenna	Virginia Military Institute (VA)
1963	Jerry Claiborne	Virginia Polytechnic Institute and State University (VA)
1964	Marv Levy	College of William & Mary (VA)
1965	Marv Levy	College of William & Mary (VA)
1966	Jim Camp	George Washington University (Washington, D.C.)
1967	Frank Jones	University of Richmond (VA)
1968	Frank Jones	University of Richmond (VA)
1969	Homer Smith	Davidson College (NC)
1970	Bob King	Furman University (SC)
1971	Frank Jones	University of Richmond (VA)
1972	Sonny Randle	East Carolina University (NC)
1973	Sonny Randle	East Carolina University (NC)
1974	Bob Thalman	Virginia Military Institute (VA)
1975	Jim Tait	University of Richmond (VA)
1976	Jim Root	College of William & Mary (VA)
1977	Joe Morrison	University of Tennessee, Chattanooga (TN)
1978	Dick Sheridan	Furman University (SC)
1979	Joe Morrison	University of Tennessee, Chattanooga (TN)
1980	Dick Sheridan	Furman University (SC)
1981	Bob Thalman	Virginia Military Institute (VA)
1982	Dick Sheridan	Furman University (SC)
1983	Bob Waters	Western Carolina University (NC)
1984	Tom Moore	The Citadel (The Military College of South Carolina)
1985	Sparky Woods	Appalachian State University (NC)
1986	Sparky Woods	Appalachian State University (NC)
1987	Sparky Woods	Appalachian State University (NC)
1988	Charlie Taaffe	The Citadel (The Military College of South Carolina) (SC)
1989	Jimmy Satterfield	Furman University (SC)
1990	Charlie Taaffe	The Citadel (The Military College of South Carolina) (SC)
1991	Jerry Moore	Appalachian State University (NC)
1992	Steve Hodgin	Western Carolina University (NC)
1993	Tim Stowers	Georgia Southern University (GA)
1994	Jerry Moore	Appalachian State University (NC)
1995	Jerry Moore	Appalachian State University (NC)
1996	Mike Cavan	Eastern Tennessee State University (TN)
1997	Paul Johnson	Georgia Southern University (GA)
1998	Paul Johnson	Georgia Southern University (GA)

Year	Coach	School
1999	Bobby Johnson	Furman University (SC)
2000	Mike Ayers	Wofford College (SC)
2001	Bill Bleil	Western Carolina University (NC)
2002	Mike Ayers	Wofford College (SC)
2003	Mike Ayers	Wofford College (SC)
2004	Bobby Lamb	Furman University (SC)
2005	Jerry Moore	Appalachian State University (NC)
2006	Jerry Moore	Appalachian State University (NC)
2007	Pete Lembo	Elon University (NC)
2008	Jerry Moore	Appalachian State University (NC)
2009	Russ Huesman	University of Tennessee, Chattanooga (TN)
2010	Mike Ayers	Wofford College (SC)

Southern Conference Coach of the Year

Selected by the conference's coaches since 1989.

Year	Coach	School
1989	Jimmy Satterfield	Furman University (SC)
1990	Buddy Nix	University of Tennessee, Chattanooga (TN)
1991	Jerry Moore	Appalachian State University (NC)
1992	Steve Hodgin	Western Carolina University (NC)
1993	Tim Stowers	Georgia Southern University (GA)
1994	Jerry Moore	Appalachian State University (NC)
1995	Jerry Moore	Appalachian State University (NC)
1996	Mike Cavan	Eastern Tennessee State University (TN)
1997	Paul Johnson	Georgia Southern University (GA)
1998	Paul Johnson	Georgia Southern University (GA)
1999	Bobby Johnson	Furman University (SC)
2000	Mike Ayers	Wofford College (SC)
2001	Bill Bleil	Western Carolina University (NC)
2002	Cal McCombs	Virginia Military Institute (VA)
2003	Mike Ayers	Wofford College (SC)
2004	Mike Sewak	Georgia Southern University (GA)
2005	Jerry Moore	Appalachian State University (NC)
2006	Jerry Moore	Appalachian State University (NC)
2007	Mike Ayers	Wofford College (SC)
2007	Pete Lembo	Elon University (NC)
2008	Jerry Moore	Appalachian State University (NC)
2009	Russ Huesman	University of Tennessee, Chattanooga (TN)
2009	Jerry Moore	Appalachian State University (NC)
2010	Jerry Moore	Appalachian State University (NC)

Southern Conference Player of the Year (Media Player of the Year)

The Media Player of the Year award is named after Roy M. "Legs" Hawley, director of athletics at West Virginia University (1938–1954) and was inducted into the National Association of Collegiate Directors of Athletics Hall of Fame in 1974.

Year	Player	Position	School
1948	Charlie Justice	Running Back	University of North Carolina, Chapel Hill (NC)
1949	Charlie Justice	Running Back	University of North Carolina (NC)
1950	Steve Wadiak	Running Back	University of South Carolina (SC)
1951	Bob Ward	Guard	University of Maryland (MD)
1952	Jack Scarbath	Quarterback	University of Maryland (MD)
1953	Steve Korcheck	Center	George Washington University (Washington, D.C.)
1954	Freddy Wyant	Quarterback	West Virginia University (WV)
1955	Bruce Bosley	Tackle	West Virginia University (WV)

Year	*Player*	*Position*	*School*
1956	Walt Brodie	End	College of William & Mary (VA)
1957	Bobby Jordan	Running Back	Virginia Military Institute (VA)
1958	Carroll Dale	End	Virginia Polytechnic Institute (VA)
1959	Paul Maguire	End	The Citadel (The Military College of South Carolina) (SC)
1960	Howard Dyer	Quarterback	Virginia Military Institute (VA)
1961	Earl Stoudt	Running Back	University of Richmond (VA)
1962	Bob Soleau	Guard	College of William & Mary (VA)
1963	Bob Schweickert	Quarterback	Virginia Polytechnic Institute (VA)
1964	Bob Schweickert	Quarterback	Virginia Polytechnic Institute (VA)
1965	George Pearce	End	College of William & Mary (VA)
1966	Garrett Ford	Running Back	West Virginia University (WV)
1966	Jimmy Poole	Quarterback	Davidson College (NC)
1967	Butch Colson	Running Back	East Carolina University (NC)
1968	Buster O'Brien	Quarterback	University of Richmond (VA)
1969	Gordon Slade	Quarterback	Davidson College (NC)
1970	Phil Mosser	Running Back	College of William & Mary (VA)
1971	Brian Baima	End	The Citadel (The Military College of South Carolina) (SC)
1972	Carlester Crumpler	Running Back	East Carolina University (NC)
1973	Carl Summerell	Quarterback	East Carolina University (NC)
1974	Andrew Johnson	Running Back	The Citadel (The Military College of South Carolina) (SC)
1975	Brian Ruff	Linebacker	The Citadel (The Military College of South Carolina) (SC)
1976	Brian Ruff	Linebacker	The Citadel (The Military College of South Carolina) (SC)
1977	Darrell Lipford	Running Back	Western Carolina University (NC)
1978	Gerald Harp	Wide Receiver	Western Carolina University (NC)
1978	David Henderson	Quarterback	Furman University (SC)
1979	Rick Beasley	Wide Receiver	Appalachian State University (NC)
1980	Stump Mitchell	Running Back	The Citadel (The Military College of South Carolina) (SC)
1981	Stanford Jennings	Running Back	Furman University (SC)
1982	Stanford Jennings	Running Back	Furman University (SC)
1983	Stanford Jennings	Running Back	Furman University (SC)
1984	Jeff Gilbert	Quarterback	Western Carolina University (NC)
1985	Bobby Lamb	Quarterback	Furman University (SC)
1986	Offense: John Settle	Running Back	Appalachian State University (NC)
1986	Defense: Scott Thompson	Tackle	The Citadel (The Military College of South Carolina) (SC)
1987	Offense: Tony Petersen	Quarterback	Marshall University (WV)
1987	Defense: Anthony Downs	Defensive Lineman	Appalachian State University (NC)
1988	Offense: Gene Brown	Quarterback	The Citadel (The Military College of South Carolina) (SC)
1988	Defense: Jeff Blankenship	Linebacker	Furman University (SC)
1989	Offense: George Searcy	Running Back	Eastern Tennessee State University (TN)
1989	Defense: Kelly Fletcher	Defensive End	Furman University (SC)
1990	Offense: Frankie DeBusk	Quarterback	Furman University (SC)
1990	Defense: Kevin Kendrick	Linebacker	Furman University (SC)
1991	Offense: Michael Payton	Quarterback	Marshall University (WV)
1991	Defense: Rico Mack	Linebacker	Appalachian State University (NC)
1992	Offense: Michael Payton	Quarterback	Marshall University (WV)
1992	Defense: Avery Hall	Defensive Lineman	Appalachian State University (NC)
1993	Offense: Chris Parker	Running Back	Marshall University (WV)
1993	Defense: William King	Linebacker	Marshall University (WV)
1994	Offense: Todd Donnan	Quarterback	Marshall University (WV)
1994	Defense: Dexter Coakley	Linebacker	Appalachian State University (NC)

Year	*Player*	*Position*	*School*
1995	Offense: Chris Parker	Running Back	Marshall University (WV)
1995	Defense: Dexter Coakley	Linebacker	Appalachian State University (NC)
1996	Offense: Thomas Haskins	Running Back	Virginia Military Institute (VA)
1996	Defense: Dexter Coakley	Linebacker	Appalachian State University (NC)
1997	Offense: B.J. Adigun	Wide Receiver	Eastern Tennessee State University (TN)
1997	Defense: Bryan Dailer	Defensive End	Furman University (SC)
1998	Offense: Adrian Peterson	Fullback	Georgia Southern University (GA)
1998	Defense: Eric Johnson	Free Safety	Western Carolina University (NC)
1999	Offense: Greg Hill	Quarterback	Georgia Southern University
1999	Defense: John Keith	Defensive Back	Furman University (SC)
2000	Offense: Louis Ivory	Tailback	Furman University (SC)
2000	Defense: Will Bouton	Linebacker	Furman University (SC)
2001	Offense: Louis Ivory	Tailback	Furman University (SC)
2001	Defense: Will Bouton	Linebacker	Furman University (SC)
2002	Offense: Chaz Williams	Quarterback	Georgia Southern University (GA)
2002	Defense: Josh Jeffries	Defensive End	Appalachian State University (NC)
2003	Offense: Jermaine Austin	Fullback	Georgia Southern University (GA)
2003	Defense: Matt Nelson	Defensive Back	Wofford College (SC)
2004	Offense: DaVon Fowlkes	Wide Receiver	Appalachian State University (NC)
2004	Defense: William Freeman	Linebacker	Furman University (SC)
2005	Offense: Richie Williams	Quarterback	Appalachian State University (NC)
2005	Defense: Chad Nkang	Linebacker	Elon University (NC)
2006	Offense: Kevin Richardson	Running Back	Appalachian State University (NC)
2006	Defense: Chad Nkang	Linebacker	Elon University (NC)
2007	Offense: Jayson Foster	Quarterback	Georgia Southern University (GA)
2007	Defense: Corey Lynch	Defensive Back	Appalachian State University (NC)
2008	Offense: Armanti Edwards	Quarterback	Appalachian State University (NC)
2008	Defense: Chris Covington	Linebacker	Georgia Southern University (GA)
2009	Offense: Armanti Edwards	Quarterback	Appalachian State University (NC)
2009	Defense: Josh Beard	Defensive End	University of Tennessee, Chattanooga (TN)
2010	Offense: DeAndre Presley	Quarterback	Appalachian State University (NC)
2010	Defense: Ameet Pall	Defensive Lineman	Wofford College (SC)

Southern Conference Coaches Player of the Year

Presented annually since 1989 to the top offensive and defensive players in the league and winners are selected by a vote of the conference coaches.

Year	*Player*	*Position*	*School*
1989	Offense: George Searcy	Running Back	Eastern Tennessee State University (TN)
1989	Defense: Junior Jackson	Linebacker	University of Tennessee, Chattanooga (TN)
1990	Offense: Frankie DeBusk	Quarterback	Furman University (SC)
1990	Defense: Troy Boeck	Defensive Lineman	University of Tennessee, Chattanooga (TN)
1990	Defense: Kevin Kendrick	Linebacker	Furman University (SC)
1991	Offense: Michael Payton	Quarterback	Marshall University (WV)
1991	Defense: Allen Edwards	Defensive Lineman	Furman University (SC)
1992	Offense: Michael Payton	Quarterback	Marshall University (WV)
1992	Defense: Avery Hall	Defensive Lineman	Appalachian State University (NC)
1993	Offense: Chris Parker	Running Back	Marshall University (WV)
1993	Defense: Alex Mash	Defensive Lineman	Georgia Southern University (GA)
1994	Offense: Todd Donnan	Quarterback	Marshall University (WV)
1994	Defense: Dexter Coakley	Linebacker	Appalachian State University (NC)
1995	Offense: Thomas Haskins	Running Back	Virginia Military Institute (VA)
1995	Defense: Dexter Coakley	Linebacker	Appalachian State University (NC)
1996	Offense: Thomas Haskins	Running Back	Virginia Military Institute (VA)
1996	Defense: Dexter Coakley	Linebacker	Appalachian State University (NC)
1997	Offense: B.J. Adigun	Wide Receiver	Eastern Tennessee State University (TN)
1997	Defense: Mario Hankerson	Linebacker	Eastern Tennessee State University (TN)

Year	Player	Position	School
1998	Offense: Adrian Peterson	Fullback	Georgia Southern University (GA)
1998	Defense: Eric Johnson	Free Safety	Western Carolina University (NC)
1999	Offense: Greg Hill	Quarterback	Georgia Southern University (GA)
1999	Defense: John Keith	Defensive Back	Furman University (SC)
2000	Offense: Louis Ivory	Tailback	Furman University (SC)
2000	Defense: Will Bouton	Linebacker	Furman University (SC)
2001	Offense: Adrian Peterson	Running Back	Georgia Southern University (GA)
2001	Defense: Freddy Pesqueira	Defensive Tackle	Georgia Southern University (GA)
2002	Offense: Chaz Williams	Quarterback	Georgia Southern University (GA)
2002	Defense: Josh Jeffries	Defensive End	Appalachian State University (NC)
2003	Offense: Jermaine Austin	Fullback	Georgia Southern University (GA)
2003	Defense: K.T. Stovall	Defensive Tackle	Appalachian State University (NC)
2004	Offense: DaVon Fowlkes	Wide Receiver	Appalachian State University (NC)
2004	Defense: William Freeman	Linebacker	Furman University (SC)
2005	Offense: Richie Williams	Quarterback	Appalachian State University (NC)
2005	Defense: Chad Nkang	Linebacker	Elon University (NC)
2005	Defense: Katon Bethay	Nose Tackle	Wofford College (SC)
2006	Offense: Kevin Richardson	Running Back	Appalachian State University (NC)
2006	Defense: Marques Murrell	Defensive Lineman	Appalachian State University (NC)
2007	Offense: Jayson Foster	Quarterback	Georgia Southern University (GA)
2007	Defense: Corey Lynch	Defensive Back	Appalachian State University (NC)
2008	Offense: Armanti Edwards	Quarterback	Appalachian State University (NC)
2008	Defense: Jacque Roman	Linebacker	Appalachian State University (NC)
2009	Offense: Armanti Edwards	Quarterback	Appalachian State University (NC)
2009	Defense: Josh Beard	Defensive End	University of Tennessee, Chattanooga (TN)
2010	Offense: DeAndre Presley	Quarterback	Appalachian State University (NC)
2010	Defense: Ameet Pall	Defensive Lineman	Wofford College (SC)

Southern Conference Freshman of the Year (Media Freshman of the Year)

Year	Player	Position	School
1979	Ron Lear	Running Back	Marshall University (WV)
1980	Barry Childers	Kicker	Marshall University (WV)
1981	Stanford Jennings	Running Back	Furman University (SC)
1982	Victor Frazier	Wide Receiver	The Citadel (The Military College of South Carolina) (SC)
1982	Stanford Glenn	Running Back	The Citadel (The Military College of South Carolina) (SC)
1983	John Settle	Running Back	Appalachian State University (NC)
1984	Kirk Roach	Kicker	Western Carolina University (NC)
1985	Tim Sanders	Running Back	Appalachian State University (NC)
1986	Ron Darby	Running Back	Marshall University (WV)
1987	Stan Nix	Quarterback	University of Tennessee, Chattanooga (TN)
1988	Dewey Klein	Kicker	Marshall University (WV)
1989	James Roberts	Running Back	University of Tennessee, Chattanooga (TN)
1990	Derrick Hollins	Running Back	Eastern Tennessee State University (TN)
1991	Chip Hooks	Running Back	Appalachian State University (NC)
1992	Alandus Sims	Defensive Back	Marshall University (WV)
1993	Dexter Coakley	Linebacker	Appalachian State University (NC)
1994	Kenny Robinson	Quarterback	Georgia Southern University (GA)
1995	Chad Pennington	Quarterback	Marshall University (WV)
1996	Randy Moss	Wide Receiver / Kick Returner	Marshall University (WV)
1997	Todd Wells	Quarterback	Eastern Tennessee State University (TN)
1998	Adrian Peterson	Fullback	Georgia Southern University (GA)
1999	Jesse McCoy	Running Back	Wofford College (SC)
2000	Lamont Seward	Wide Receiver	Western Carolina University (NC)
2001	Brian Bratton	Return Specialist	Furman University (SC)

Year	Player	Position	School
2002	Jermaine Austin	Fullback	Georgia Southern University (GA)
2003	Kevious Johnson	Running Back	Wofford College (SC)
2004	Andrew Thacker	Free Safety	Furman University (SC)
2005	Dedrick Bynam	Defensive Back	Georgia Southern University (GA)
2006	Armanti Edwards	Quarterback	Appalachian State University (NC)
2007	Scott Riddle	Quarterback	Elon University (NC)
2008	Dustin Taliaferro	Quarterback	Samford University (AL)
2009	Michael Johnson	Running Back	Western Carolina University (NC)
2010	Kadeem Wise	Defensive Back	University of Tennessee, Chattanooga (TN)

Southern Conference Freshman of the Year (Conference Coaches' selection)

Year	Player	Position	School
1989	James Roberts	Running Back	University of Tennessee, Chattanooga (TN)
1990	Derrick Hollins	Running Back	Eastern Tennessee State University (TN)
1991	Offense: Chip Hooks	Running Back	Appalachian State University (NC)
1991	Defense: Roger Johnson	Defensive Back	Marshall University (WV)
1992	Marlon Anderson	Wide Receiver	Virginia Military Institute (VA)
1993	Dexter Coakley	Linebacker	Appalachian State University (NC)
1994	Kenny Robinson	Quarterback	Georgia Southern University (GA)
1995	Chad Pennington	Quarterback	Marshall University (WV)
1996	Brandon Walker	Running Back	Eastern Tennessee State University (TN)
1997	Todd Wells	Quarterback	Eastern Tennessee State University (TN)
1998	Adrian Peterson	Fullback	Georgia Southern University (GA)
1999	Jesse McCoy	Running Back	Wofford College (SC)
2000	Lamont Seward	Wide Receiver	Western Carolina University (NC)
2001	Titus Green	Return Specialist	Virginia Military Institute (VA)
2002	Jermaine Austin	Running Back	Georgia Southern University (GA)
2003	Kevious Johnson	Running Back	Wofford College (SC)
2004	Jayson Foster	Quarterback	Georgia Southern University (GA)
2005	Dedrick Bynam	Defensive Back	Georgia Southern University (GA)
2006	Armanti Edwards	Quarterback	Appalachian State University (NC)
2007	Scott Riddle	Quarterback	Elon University (NC)
2008	Dustin Taliaferro	Quarterback	Samford University (AL)
2009	Michael Johnson	Running Back	Western Carolina University (NC)
2010	Kadeem Wise	Defensive Back	University of Tennessee, Chattanooga (TN)

Jacobs Blocking Trophy

The Jacobs Blocking Trophy is the name of several annual college football awards presented by different conferences to its best blocker. The awards are named in honor of William P. Jacobs, the founder and president of Presbyterian College (Clinton, South Carolina) from 1935 to 1945 and are presented by his sons, Hugh and William Jacobs, based upon voting of the coaches within each conference. The Southeastern Conference (FBS) began the award in 1935; the Atlantic Coast Conference (FBS) established its own award in 1953; and both the Division I FCS Southern Conference and the Division II South Atlantic Conference also have a version of this award.

Year	Player	School
1933	George Smith	Virginia Polytechnic Institute (VA)
1934	George Smith	Virginia Polytechnic Institute (VA)
1935	Herman Snyder	University of North Carolina (NC)
1936	John Gormley	University of Maryland (MD)
1937	George Watson	University of North Carolina (NC)
1938	Andy Trzeciak	Virginia Military Institute (VA)
1939	James Ringgold	Wake Forest University (NC)
1940	Billy Walker	Virginia Military Institute (VA)
1941	Tommy Prothro	Duke University (NC)

Year	Player	School
1942	Mike Cooke	University of North Carolina (NC)
1943	Elmer Barbour	Wake Forest University (NC)
1944	Tom Davis	Duke University (NC)
1945	Nick Ognovich	Wake Forest University (NC)
1946	Nick Ognovich	Wake Forest University (NC)
1947	Nick Ognovich	Wake Forest University (NC)
1948	Robert Bowlby	North Carolina State University (NC)
1949	Robert Bowlby	North Carolina State University (NC)
1950	Dick Hendley	Clemson University (SC)
1951	Jack Kistler	Duke University (NC)
1952	Louis Tepe	Duke University (NC)
1953	Tommy Allman	West Virginia University (WV)
1954	Gene Lamone	West Virginia University (WV)
1955	Bruce Bosley	West Virginia University (WV)
1956	John Hall	Virginia Polytechnic Institute (VA)
1957	Chuck Howley	West Virginia University (WV)
1958	Carroll Dale	Virginia Polytechnic Institute (VA)
1959	John Boggs	University of Richmond (VA)
1960	Lou Shuba	Virginia Military Institute (VA)
1961	Don Christman	University of Richmond (VA)
1962	Bob Soleau	College of William & Mary (VA)
1963	Bob Soleau	College of William & Mary (VA)
1964	Sonny Utz	Virginia Polytechnic Institute (VA)
1965	Norman Swindell	East Carolina University (NC)
1966	Brad Cashman	George Washington University (Washington, D.C.)
1967	Kevin Moran	East Carolina University (NC)
1968	Wayne Fowler	University of Richmond (VA)
1969	Wayne Fowler	University of Richmond (VA)
1970	Bob Herb	College of William & Mary (VA)
1971	Jackson Neal	College of William & Mary (VA)
1972	Barty Smith	University of Richmond (VA)
1973	Barty Smith	University of Richmond (VA)
1974	Andy Dearman	Virginia Military Institute (VA)
1975	Rodney Elam	University of Richmond (VA)
1976	Gill Beck	Appalachian State University (NC)
1977	Gill Beck	Appalachian State University (NC)
1978	Brette Simmons	Furman University (SC)
1979	John Shuman	Virginia Military Institute (VA)
1980	Charlie Anderson	Furman University (SC)
1981	Charlie Anderson	Furman University (SC)
1982	Mike Coleman	Furman University (SC)
1983	Mike Nease	University of Tennessee, Chattanooga (TN)
1984	Dinky Williams	Furman University (SC)
1985	Gene Reeder	Furman University (SC)
1986	Mike Callaway	Appalachian State University (NC)
1987	James Hardman	Appalachian State University (NC)
1988	Kennet Goldsmith	Furman University (SC)
1989	Derrick Graham	Appalachian State University (NC)
1990	Steve Duggan	Furman University (SC)
1991	Lorenzo Carpenter	Virginia Military Institute (VA)
1992	Phil Ratliff	Marshall University (WV)
1993	Chris Deaton	Marshall University (WV)
1994	Franklin Stephens	Georgia Southern University (GA)
1995	William Pannell	Marshall University (WV)
1996	Aaron Ferguson	Marshall University (WV)
1997	Mark Williams	Georgia Southern University (GA)
1998	Mark Williams	Georgia Southern University (GA)

Year	Player	School
1999	Ben Hall	Furman University (SC)
2000	Josh Moore	Furman University (SC)
2001	Donnie Littlejohn	Furman University (SC)
2002	Charles Clarke	Georgia Southern University (GA)
2003	Eric Deutsch	Wofford College (SC)
2004	Ben Bainbridge	Furman University (SC)
2005	Matt Isenhour	Appalachian State University (NC)
2006	Kerry Brown	Appalachian State University (NC)
2007	Kerry Brown	Appalachian State University (NC)
2008	Joel Bell	Furman University (SC)
2009	Kerry Brown	Appalachian State University (NC)
2010	Pat Illig	Wofford College (SC)

Southland Conference (Southland)

2600 Network Boulevard, Suite 150, Frisco, Texas 75034; Telephone: 972-422-9500; Fax: 972-422-9225; Web site: http://www.southland.org

The Southland Conference was formed in March 1963 with five charter schools: Abilene Christian University, Arkansas State University, Lamar University, Trinity University, and the University of Texas, Arlington (still in the conference). Originally an NAIA conference, Southland joined the NCAA College Division in 1968, which was renamed NCAA Division II in 1973. After two seasons, the conference became an NCAA Division I league (1975–1981), before joining the FCS in 1982.

As of this writing, the Southland Conference consists of the following 12 schools:

- Lamar University Cardinals, Beaumont, TX 77710; 409-880-7011; www.lamar.edu
- McNeese State University Cowboys, Lake Charles, LA 70609; 337-475-5000; www.mcneese.edu
- Nicholls State University Colonels, Thibodaux, LA 70310; 877-642-4655; www.nicholls.edu
- Northwestern State University Demons, Natchitoches, LA 71497; 318-357-6011; www.nsula.edu
- Sam Houston State University Bearkats, Huntsville, TX 77341; 936-294-1111
- Southeastern Louisiana University Lions, Hammond, LA 70402; 800-222-7358; www.selu.edu
- Stephen F. Austin State University Lumberjacks, Nacogdoches, TX 75962; 936-468-3401; www.sfasu.edu
- Texas A&M University, Corpus Christi Islanders, Corpus Christi, TX 78412; 361-825-5700; www.tamucc.edu; no football program
- Texas State University Bobcats, San Marcos, TX 78666; 512-245-2111; www.txstate.edu
- University of Central Arkansas Bears, Conway, AR 72035; 501-450-5000; www.uca.edu
- University of Texas, Arlington Mavericks, Arlington, TX 76019; 817-272-2011; www.uta.edu; no football program
- University of Texas, San Antonio Roadrunners, San Antonio, TX 78249; 210-458-4011; http://utsa.edu

Southland Conference Champions

Year	School
1964	Lamar University (TX)
1965	Lamar University (TX)
1966	Lamar University (TX)
1966	University of Texas, Arlington (TX)
1967	University of Texas, Arlington (TX)
1968	Arkansas State University (AR)
1969	Arkansas State University (AR)
1970	Arkansas State University (AR)
1971	Lamar University (TX)
1971	Louisiana Tech University (LA)
1971	Trinity University (TX)
1972	Louisiana Tech University (LA)
1973	Louisiana Tech University (LA)
1974	Louisiana Tech University (LA)
1975	Arkansas State University (AR)
1976	McNeese State University (LA)
1977	Louisiana Tech University (LA)
1978	Arkansas State University (AR)
1978	Louisiana Tech University (LA)
1979	McNeese State University (LA)
1980	McNeese State University (LA)
1981	University of Texas, Arlington (TX)
1982	Louisiana Tech University (LA)
1983	University of Louisiana, Monroe (LA)
1983	University of North Texas (TX)
1984	Louisiana Tech University (LA)

Year	School
1985	Arkansas State University (AR)
1986	Arkansas State University (AR)
1987	University of Louisiana, Monroe (LA)
1988	Northwestern State University (LA)
1989	Stephen F. Austin State University (TX)
1990	University of Louisiana, Monroe (LA)
1991	McNeese State University (LA)
1991	Sam Houston State University (TX)
1992	University of Louisiana, Monroe (LA)
1993	McNeese State University (LA)
1994	University of North Texas (TX)
1995	McNeese State University (LA)
1996	Troy University (Troy State University) (AL)
1997	McNeese State University (LA)
1997	Northwestern State University (LA)
1998	Northwestern State University (LA)
1999	Stephen F. Austin State University (TX)
1999	Troy University (Troy State University) (AL)
2000	Troy University (Troy State University) (AL)
2001	McNeese State University (LA)
2001	Sam Houston State University (TX)
2002	McNeese State University (LA)
2003	McNeese State University (LA)
2004	Northwestern State University (LA)
2004	Sam Houston State University (TX)
2005	Nicholls State University (LA)
2005	Texas State University (TX)
2006	McNeese State University (LA)
2007	McNeese State University (LA)
2008	Texas State University (TX)
2009	McNeese State University (LA)
2009	Stephen F. Austin State University (TX)
2010	Stephen F. Austin State University (TX)

Southland Conference Coach of the Year

Year	Coach	School
1964	Bennie Ellender	Arkansas State University (AR)
1965	Chena Gilstrap	University of Texas, Arlington (TX)
1966	Burley Bearden	University of Texas, Arlington (TX)
1967	Burley Bearden	University of Texas, Arlington (TX)
1968	Bennie Ellender	Arkansas State University (AR)
1969	Bennie Ellender	Arkansas State University (AR)
1970	Bennie Ellender	Arkansas State University (AR)
1970	Vernon Glass	Lamar University (TX)
1971	Maxie Lambright	Louisiana Tech University (LA)
1972	Maxie Lambright	Louisiana Tech University (LA)
1973	Maxie Lambright	Louisiana Tech University (LA)
1974	Vernon Glass	Lamar University (TX)
1975	Bill Davidson	Arkansas State University (AR)
1976	Jack Doland	McNeese State University (LA)
1977	Maxie Lambright	Louisiana Tech University (LA)
1978	Bill Davidson	Arkansas State University (AR)
1979	Ernie Duplechin	McNeese State University (LA)
1980	Sam Robertson	University of Louisiana, Lafayette (LA)
1981	Bud Elliott	University of Texas, Arlington (TX)
1982	Billy Brewer	Louisiana Tech University (LA)
1983	Corky Nelson	University of North Texas (TX)
1984	A.L. Williams	Louisiana Tech University (LA)
1985	Larry Lacewell	Arkansas State University (AR)
1986	Larry Lacewell	Arkansas State University (AR)
1987	Pat Collins	University of Louisiana, Monroe (LA)
1988	Sam Goodwin	Northwestern State University (LA)
1989	Lynn Graves	Stephen F. Austin State University (TX)
1990	Bobby Keasler	McNeese State University (LA)
1991	Bobby Keasler	McNeese State University (LA)
1991	Ron Randleman	Sam Houston State University (TX)
1992	Dave Roberts	University of Louisiana, Monroe (LA)
1993	Bobby Keasler	McNeese State University (LA)
1994	Matt Simon	University of North Texas (TX)
1995	Bobby Keasler	McNeese State University (LA)
1996	Darren Barbier	Nicholls State University (LA)
1997	Sam Goodwin	Northwestern State University (LA)

Year	Coach	School
1997	Bobby Keasler	McNeese State University (LA)
1998	Sam Goodwin	Northwestern State University (LA)
1999	Larry Blakeney	Troy University (Troy State University) (AL)
2000	Larry Blakeney	Troy University (Troy State University) (AL)
2001	Ron Randleman	Sam Houston State University (TX)
2002	Daryl Daye	Nicholls State University (LA)
2003	Tommy Tate	McNeese State University (LA)
2004	Scott Stoker	Northwestern State University (LA)
2005	Jay Thomas	Nicholls State University (LA)
2006	Matt Viator	McNeese State University (LA)
2007	Matt Viator	McNeese State University (LA)
2008	Clint Conque	University of Central Arkansas (AR)
2009	J.C. Harper	Stephen F. Austin State University (TX)
2010	J.C. Harper	Stephen F. Austin State University (TX)

Southland Conference Player of the Year

Year	Player	School
1964–1993		None Selected
1994	Mitch Maher	University of North Texas (TX)
1995	Kerry Joseph	McNeese State University (LA)
1996	Claude Mathis	Texas State University (TX)
1997	Claude Mathis	Texas State University (TX)
1998	Jermaine Jones	Northwestern State University (LA)
1999	Chris Chaloupka	Sam Houston State University (TX)
2000	C.J. Carroll	Texas State University (TX)
2001	Josh McCown	Sam Houston State University (TX)
2002	Hadley Prince	McNeese State University (LA)
2003	B.J. Sams	McNeese State University (LA)
2004	Dustin Long	Sam Houston State University (TX)
2005	Barrick Nealy	Texas State University (TX)
2006	Steven Whitehead	McNeese State University (LA)
2007	Bryan Smith	McNeese State University (LA)
2008	Nathan Brown	University of Central Arkansas (AR)
2009	Derrick Fourroux	McNeese State University (LA)
2010	Jeremy Moses	Stephen F. Austin State University (TX)

Southland Conference Offensive Player of the Year

Year	Player	School
1964	None Selected	
1965	Jackie Hall	Trinity University (TX)
1966	Phil Primm	Trinity University (TX)
1967	Mike Baylor	University of Texas, Arlington (TX)
1968	Frank McGuigan	Arkansas State University (AR)
1969	Jim Lindsey	Abilene Christian University (TX)
1970	Jim Lindsey	Abilene Christian University (TX)
1971	Kenny Lantrip	Louisiana Tech University (LA)
1972	Roger Carr	Louisiana Tech University (LA)
1973	Denny Duron	Louisiana Tech University (LA)
1974	Charles McDaniel	Louisiana Tech University (LA)
1975	David Hines	Arkansas State University (AR)
1976	Derrick Jensen	University of Texas, Arlington (TX)
1976	John Henry White	Louisiana Tech University (LA)
1977	Derrick Jensen	University of Texas, Arlington (TX)
1978	Roy Dewalt	University of Texas, Arlington (TX)
1979	Roy Dewalt	University of Texas, Arlington (TX)
1980	Stephen Starring	McNeese State University (LA)
1981	Buford Jordan	McNeese State University (LA)

Year	*Player*	*School*
1982	Matt Dunigan	Louisiana Tech University (LA)
1983	Greg Carter	University of North Texas (TX)
1984	Scotty Caldwell	University of Texas, Arlington (TX)
1985	Burton Murchison	Lamar University (TX)
1986	Dwane Brown	Arkansas State University (AR)
1987	Stan Humphries	University of Louisiana, Monroe (LA)
1988	Scott Davis	University of North Texas (TX)
1989	Todd Hammel	Stephen F. Austin State University (TX)
1990	Cisco Richard	University of Louisiana, Monroe (LA)
1991	Gilbert Price	Texas State University (TX)
1992	Roosevelt Potts	University of Louisiana, Monroe (LA)
1993	Robert Cobb	University of Louisiana, Monroe (LA)
1994	Donald Wilkerson	Texas State University (TX)
1995	Clarence Matthews	Northwestern State University (LA)
1996	Patrick Palmer	Northwestern State University (LA)
1997	Mikhael Ricks	Stephen F. Austin State University (TX)
1998	Montressa Kirby	Jacksonville State University (AL)
1999	Chris Chaloupka	Sam Houston State University (TX)
2000	Tony Taylor	Northwestern State University (LA)
2001	Wes Pate	Stephen F. Austin State University (TX)
2002	Vick King	McNeese State University (LA)
2003	Vick King	McNeese State University (LA)
2004	Derrick Johnese	Northwestern State University (LA)
2005	Yale Vannoy	Nicholls State University (LA)
2006	D.D. Terry	Sam Houston State University (TX)
2007	Nathan Brown	University of Central Arkansas (AR)
2008	Toddrick Pendland	McNeese State University (LA)
2009	Bradley George	Texas State University (TX)
2010	Jeremy Moses	Stephen F. Austin State University (TX)

Southland Conference Defensive Player of the Year

Year	*Player*	*School*
1964	None Selected	
1965	Vernon McManus	Lamar University (TX)
1966	Ken Ozee	University of Texas, Arlington (TX)
1967	Marvin Upshaw	Trinity University (TX)
1968	Clovis Swinney	Arkansas State University (AR)
1969	Clovis Swinney	Arkansas State University (AR)
1970	Dennis Meyer	Arkansas State University (AR)
1971	Dennis Meyer	Arkansas State University (AR)
1972	Fred Dean	Louisiana Tech University (LA)
1973	Joe McNeely	Louisiana Tech University (LA)
1974	Fred Dean	Louisiana Tech University (LA)
1975	Jerry Muckenstrum	Arkansas State University (AR)
1976	Roy Painter	Arkansas State University (AR)
1977	Larry Anderson	Louisiana Tech University (LA)
1977	Wesley Williams	Arkansas State University (AR)
1978	Ardis McCann	Louisiana Tech University (LA)
1979	Johnny Robinson	Louisiana Tech University (LA)
1980	Daryl Burckel	McNeese State University (LA)
1981	Rusty Guilbeau	McNeese State University (LA)
1982	Bruce Daigle	University of Louisiana, Monroe (LA)
1983	Eugene Seale	Lamar University (TX)
1984	Doug Landry	Louisiana Tech University (LA)
1985	Doug Landry	Louisiana Tech University (LA)
1986	Ed Fleming	University of North Texas (TX)
1986	Walter Johnson	Louisiana Tech University (LA)

Year	Player	School
1987	John Kulakowski	Northwestern State University (LA)
1988	Eric Lokey	Stephen F. Austin State University (TX)
1989	David Whitmore	Stephen F. Austin State University (TX)
1990	Mike Pierce	McNeese State University (LA)
1991	Andre Carron	Northwestern State University (LA)
1992	Terry Irving	McNeese State University (LA)
1993	Terry Irving	McNeese State University (LA)
1994	Vincent Landrum	McNeese State University (LA)
1995	Kavika Pittman	McNeese State University (LA)
1996	Pratt Lyons	Troy University (Troy State University) (AL)
1997	Tony Maranto	Northwestern State University (LA)
1998	Charles Ayro	McNeese State University (LA)
1999	Anthony Rabb	Troy University (Troy State University) (AL)
2000	Keith Davis	Sam Houston State University (TX)
2001	Joe Judge	McNeese State University (LA)
2002	Roy Locks	Northwestern State University (LA)
2003	Brent Hafford	Stephen F. Austin State University (TX)
2004	Jamall Johnson	Northwestern State University (LA)
2005	Fred Evans	Texas State University (TX)
2006	Bryan Smith	McNeese State University (LA)
2007	Kareem Moore	Nicholls State University (LA)
2008	Larry Hart	University of Central Arkansas (AR)
2009	Larry Hart	University of Central Arkansas (AR)
2009	Tim Knicky	Stephen F. Austin State University (TX)
2010	Jabara Williams	Stephen F. Austin State University (TX)

Southland Conference Freshman of the Year

Year	Player	School
1964–1977		None Selected
1978	Jessie Clark	Louisiana Tech University (LA)
1979	Lee Charles Wright	Arkansas State University (AR)
1980	Joey Granger	McNeese State University (LA)
1980	Buford Jordan	McNeese State University (LA)
1981	Willie Wiggins	University of Texas, Arlington (TX)
1982	Doug Landry	Louisiana Tech University (LA)
1983	Walter Johnson	Louisiana Tech University (LA)
1984	Dwane Brown	Arkansas State University (AR)
1985	Brian McZeal	McNeese State University (LA)
1986	Matt Stover	Louisiana Tech University (LA)
1987	Scott Davis	University of North Texas (TX)
1988	Chuck Rawlinson	Stephen F. Austin State University (TX)
1989	Ken Naquin	McNeese State University (LA)
1990	Cedric Walker	Stephen F. Austin State University (TX)
1991	Eric Acheson	McNeese State University (LA)
1991	Darryl Pounds	Nicholls State University (LA)
1992	Kerry Joseph	McNeese State University (LA)
1993	Zach Bronson	McNeese State University (LA)
1994	Claude Mathis	Texas State University (TX)
1995	Jeremiah Trotter	Stephen F. Austin State University (TX)
1996	Victor McKnight	Sam Houston State University (TX)
1997	Matt Dominguez	Sam Houston State University (TX)
1998	Jessie Burton	McNeese State University (LA)
1999	Reggie Stancil	Jacksonville State University (AL)
2000	Josh Son	Nicholls State University (LA)
2001	LeJuan Walker	Nicholls State University (LA)
2002	Tony Tompkins	Stephen F. Austin State University (TX)
2003	Chance Dennis	Stephen F. Austin State University (TX)

Year	Player	School
2004	Broderick Cole	Nicholls State University (LA)
2005	Blake Bercegeay	McNeese State University (LA)
2006	Derrick Fourroux	McNeese State University (LA)
2007	Karrington Bush	Texas State University (TX)
2008	Simmie Yarborough	Southeaster Louisiana University (LA)
2009	Malcolm Bronson	McNeese State University (LA)
2010	Tim Flanders	Sam Houston State University (TX)
2010	Jestin Love	University of Central Arkansas (AR)

Southland Conference Newcomer of the Year

Year	Player	School
1964–1990		None Selected
1991	Wendal Lowrey	University of Louisiana, Monroe (LA)
1992	Terrance Brown	University of North Texas (TX)
1993	Irving Spikes	University of Louisiana, Monroe (LA)
1994	Chad Reeves	McNeese State University (LA)
1995	Tim Denton	Sam Houston State University (TX)
1996	John Emery	Nicholls State University (LA)
1997	Ronnie Powell	Northwestern State University (LA)
1998	Spergon Wynn	Texas State University (TX)
1999	Chris Chaloupka	Sam Houston State University (TX)
2000	Demontray Carter	Troy University (Troy State University) (AL)
2001	Craig Nall	Northwestern State University (LA)
2002	Roderick Royal	McNeese State University (LA)
2003	Jamall Johnson	Northwestern State University (LA)
2004	Fred Evans	Texas State University (TX)
2005	Joseph Tobias	Nicholls State University (LA)
2006	Kareem Moore	Nicholls State University (LA)
2007	Lardarius Webb	Nicholls State University (LA)
2008	Duane Brooks	Stephen F. Austin State University (TX)
2009	Andre Banks	Stephen F. Austin State University (TX)
2010	Andre Anderson	McNeese State University (LA)

Southwestern Athletic Conference (SWAC)

2101 6th Avenue North, Suite 700, Birmingham, AL 35203; Telephone: 205-251-7573; Fax: 205-297-9820; Web site: http://www.swac.org

The Southwestern Athletic Conference was formed in 1920 with six charter schools: Bishop College, Paul Quinn College, Prairie View University (now known as Prairie View A&M (Agricultural & Mechanical)) University), Sam Huston University (now known as Huston-Tillotson University), Texas College, and Wiley College.

The SWAC is one of two conferences (in addition to the Ivy League) that does not participate in postseason play (FCS football tournament), and is the only one of the two whose member schools offer full football scholarships.

As of this writing, the Southwestern Athletic Conference consists of the following 10 schools:

- Alabama A&M (Agricultural & Mechanical) University Bulldogs, Normal, AL 35762; 256-372-5000; www.aamu.edu
- Alabama State University Hornets, Montgomery, AL 36104; 334-229-4100; www.alasu.edu
- Alcorn State University Braves, Alcorn State, MS 39096; 601-877-6100; www.alcord.edu
- Grambling State University Tigers, Grambling, LA 71245; 318-247-3811; www.gram.edu
- Jackson State University Tigers, Jackson, MS 39217; 601-979-2121; www.jsums.edu
- Mississippi Valley State University Delta Devils, Itta Bena, MS 38941; 662-254-9041; www.mvsu.edu
- Prairie View A&M (Agricultural & Mechanical) University Panthers, Prairie View, TX 77446; 936-261-3311; www.pvamu.edu

- Southern University and A&M College Jaguars, Baton Rouge, LA 70813; 225-771-4500; http://web.subr.edu
- Texas Southern University Tigers, Houston, TX 77004; 713-313-7011; www.tsu.edu
- University of Arkansas, Pine Bluff, Golden Lions, Pine Bluff, AR 71601; 870-575-8000; www.uapb.edu

SWAC Champions

Year	*School*
1921	Wiley College (TX)
1922	Paul Quinn College (TX)
1923	Wiley College (TX)
1924	Paul Quinn College (TX)
1925	Bishop College (TX)
1926	Sam Houston State University (TX)
1927	Wiley College (TX)
1928	Wiley College (TX)
1929	Wiley College (TX)
1930	Wiley College (TX)
1931	Prairie View University (TX)
1932	Wiley College (TX)
1933	Langston University (OK)
1933	Prairie View University (TX)
1934	Texas College (TX)
1935	Texas College (TX)
1936	Texas College (TX)
1936	Langston University (OK)
1937	Langston University (OK)
1937	Southern University (LA)
1938	Langston University (OK)
1938	Southern University (LA)
1939	Langston University (OK)
1940	Langston University (OK)
1940	Southern University (LA)
1941	No Champion
1942	Texas College (TX)
1943	No Champion
1944	Langston University (OK)
1944	Texas College (TX)
1944	Wiley College (TX)
1945	Wiley College (TX)
1946	Southern University (LA)
1947	Southern University (LA)
1948	Southern University (LA)
1949	Langston University (OK)
1949	Southern University (LA)
1950	Southern University (LA)
1951	Prairie View University (TX)
1952	Prairie View University (TX)
1953	Prairie View University (TX)
1954	Prairie View University (TX)
1955	Southern University (LA)
1956	Langston University (OK)
1956	Texas Southern University (TX)
1957	Wiley College (TX)
1958	Prairie View University (TX)
1959	Southern University (LA)
1960	Grambling State University (LA)
1960	Prairie View University (TX)
1960	Southern University (LA)
1961	Jackson State University (MS)
1962	Jackson State University (MS)
1963	Prairie View University (TX)
1964	Prairie View University (TX)
1965	Grambling State University (LA)
1966	Grambling State University (LA)
1966	Southern University (LA)
1966	Texas Southern University (TX)
1966	University of Arkansas, Pine Bluff (AR)
1967	Grambling State University (LA)
1968	Alcorn State University (MS)
1968	Grambling State University (LA)
1968	Texas Southern University (TX)
1969	Alcorn State University (MS)
1970	Alcorn State University (MS)
1971	Grambling State University (LA)
1972	Grambling State University (LA)
1972	Jackson State University (MS)
1973	Grambling State University (LA)
1973	Jackson State University (MS)
1974	Alcorn State University (MS)
1974	Grambling State University (LA)
1975	Grambling State University (LA)
1975	Southern University (LA)
1976	Alcorn State University (MS)
1977	Grambling State University (LA)
1978	Grambling State University (LA)
1979	Alcorn State University (MS)
1979	Grambling State University (LA)
1980	Grambling State University (LA)
1980	Jackson State University (MS)
1981	Jackson State University (MS)
1982	Jackson State University (MS)
1983	Grambling State University (LA)
1984	Alcorn State University (MS)
1985	Grambling State University (LA)
1985	Jackson State University (MS)
1986	Jackson State University (MS)
1987	Jackson State University (MS)
1988	Jackson State University (MS)
1989	Grambling State University (LA)
1990	Jackson State University (MS)
1991	Alabama State University (AL)
1992	Alcorn State University (MS)
1993	Southern University (LA)
1994	Alcorn State University (MS)
1994	Grambling State University (LA)
1995	Jackson State University (MS)
1996	Jackson State University (MS)
1997	Southern University (LA)
1998	Southern University (LA)

Year	School
1999	Southern University (LA)
2000	Grambling State University (LA)
2001	Grambling State University (LA)
2002	Grambling State University (LA)
2003	Southern University (LA)
2004	Alabama State University (AL)
2005	Grambling State University (LA)
2006	Alabama A&M University (AL)
2007	Jackson State University (MS)
2008	Grambling State University (LA)
2009	Prairie View A&M (Agricultural and Mechanical) University (TX)
2010	Texas Southern University (TX)

SWAC Coach of the Year

Year	Coach	School
1984	Marino Casem	Alcorn State University (MS)
1985	W.C. Gorden	Jackson State University (MS)
1986	W.C. Gorden	Jackson State University (MS)
1987	W.C. Gorden	Jackson State University (MS)
1988	W.C. Gorden	Jackson State University (MS)
1989	Eddie Robinson	Grambling State University (LA)
1990	Houston Markham	Alabama State University (AL)
1991	Houston Markham	Alabama State University (AL)
1992	Cardell Jones	Alcorn State University (MS)
1993	Pete Richardson	Southern University (LA)
1994	Eddie Robinson	Grambling State University (LA)
1995	James Carson	Jackson State University (MS)
1996	Larry Dorsey	Mississippi Valley State University (MS)
1997	Pete Richardson	Southern University (LA)
1998	Pete Richardson	Southern University (LA)
1999	Pete Richardson	Southern University (LA)
2000	Doug Williams	Grambling State University (LA)
2001	Doug Williams	Grambling State University (LA)
2002	Doug Williams	Grambling State University (LA)
2003	Pete Richardson	Southern University (LA)
2004	Charles Coe	Alabama State University (AL)
2005	Melvin Spears	Grambling State University (LA)
2006	Anthony Jones	Alabama A&M (Agricultural and Mechanical) University (AL)
2007	Rick Comegy	Jackson State University (MS)
2008	Rod Broadway	Grambling State University (LA)
2009	Henry Frazier	Prairie View A&M (Agricultural and Mechanical) University (TX)
2010	Johnnie Cole	Texas Southern University (TX)

SWAC Offensive Player of the Year

Year	Player	School
1984	Willie Totten	Mississippi Valley State University (MS)
1985	Willie Totten	Mississippi Valley State University (MS)
1986	Brad Baxter	Alabama State University (AL)
1987	Lewis Tillman	Jackson State University (MS)
1988	Lewis Tillman	Jackson State University (MS)
1989	Clemente Gordon	Grambling State University (LA)
1990	Walter Dean	Grambling State University (LA)
1991	Steve McNair	Alcorn State University (MS)
1992	Steve McNair	Alcorn State University (MS)
1993	Steve McNair	Alcorn State University (MS)
1994	Steve McNair	Alcorn State University (MS)
1995	Melvin Williams	Southern University (LA)
1996	Graylin Pratt	Jackson State University (MS)
1997	Steve Wofford	Southern University (LA)
1998	Sylvester Morris	Jackson State University (MS)
1999	Corey Holmes	Mississippi Valley State University (MS)

Year	Player	School
2000	Corey Holmes	Mississippi Valley State University (MS)
2001	Darnell Kennedy	Alabama State University (AL)
2002	Bruce Eugene	Grambling State University (LA)
2003	Quincy Richard	Southern University (LA)
2004	Thomas Ricks	Southern University (LA)
2005	Bruce Eugene	Grambling State University (LA)
2006	Chris Wallace	University of Arkansas, Pine Bluff (AR)
2007	Jay Peck	Alabama State University (AL)
2008	Bryant Lee	Southern University (LA)
2009	K.J. Black	Prairie View A&M (Agricultural and Mechanical) University (TX)
2010	Frank Warren	Grambling State University (LA)

SWAC Defensive Player of the Year

Year	Player	School
1984	Bruce Green	Texas Southern University (TX)
1985	Jackie Walker	Jackson State University (MS)
1986	Kevin Dent	Jackson State University (MS)
1987	Andre Lloyd	Jackson State University (MS)
1988	Kevin Dent	Jackson State University (MS)
1989	Darion Conner	Jackson State University (MS)
1990	Eddie Robinson, Jr.	Alabama State University (AL)
1991	Eddie Robinson, Jr.	Alabama State University (AL)
1992	Michael Strahan	Texas Southern University (TX)
1993	Sean Wallace	Southern University (LA)
1994	Keifer Phillips	Grambling State University (LA)
1995	Picasso Nelson	Jackson State University (MS)
1996	Sean Woodson	Jackson State University (MS)
1997	Terry Houzah	Mississippi Valley State University (MS)
1998	Terry Houzah	Mississippi Valley State University (MS)
1999	Tommy Head	Jackson State University (MS)
2000	Lernard Mack	Texas Southern University (TX)
2001	Bobby Perry	Prairie View A&M (Agricultural and Mechanical) University (TX)
2002	Robert Mathis	Alabama A&M University (AL)
2003	Lenny Williams	Southern University (LA)
2004	Ronald "Rock" Dillon	Alabama State University (AL)
2005	Tyler Knight	Mississippi Valley State University (MS)
2006	Stacey Thomas	Texas Southern University (TX)
2007	Zach East	Prairie View A&M (Agricultural and Mechanical) University (TX)
2008	Marcellus Speaks	Jackson State University (MS)
2009	Christian Anthony	Grambling State University (LA)
2010	Dejuan Fulghum	Texas Southern University (TX)

SWAC Newcomer of the Year

Year	Player	School
1984	Milton Barney	Alcorn State University (MS)
1985	Timothy Lemons	Alabama State University (AL)
1985	Daryl Jones	Jackson State University (MS)
1985	Chris Scott	Southern University (LA)
1986	No selection	
1987	No selection	
1988	No selection	
1989	Ike Ayozie	Jackson State University (MS)
1990	Rico White	Alabama State University (AL)
1991	No selection	
1992	Marcus Hinton	Alcorn State University (MS)
1993	Kendrick Nord	Grambling State University (LA)
1994	Melvin Williams	Southern University (LA)

Year	Player	School
1995	Ahndre Patterson	Alcorn State University (MS)
1996	Steve Wofford	Southern University (LA)
1997	Corey Bradford	Jackson State University (MS)
1998	Damon Ford	Alcorn State University (MS)
1999	No selection	
2000	Robert Kent	Jackson State University (MS)
2001	Donald Carrie	Alcorn State University (MS)
2002	Kenneth Peoples	Southern University (LA)
2003	Keldrick Williams	Alabama State University (AL)
2004	Aries Nelson	Mississippi Valley State University (MS)
2005	Hakeem Muhammad	Prairie View A&M (Agricultural and Mechanical) University (TX)
2006	Dedrick Poole	University of Arkansas, Pine Bluff (AR)
2007	Bruce Peters	University of Arkansas, Pine Bluff (AR)
2008	Greg Dillon	Grambling State University (LA)
2009	Arvell Nelson	Texas Southern University (TX)
2010	Casey Therriault	Jackson State University (MS)

SWAC Freshman of the Year

Year	Player	School
1986	Victor Pegram	Prairie View A&M (Agricultural and Mechanical) University (TX)
1987	Dexter Blackmon	Southern University (LA)
1988	Ronald Humphrey	Mississippi Valley State University (MS)
1989	Shawn Lawson	Prairie View A&M (Agricultural and Mechanical) University (TX)
1990	Marlo Perry	Jackson State University (MS)
1991	Steve McNair	Alcorn State University (MS)
1992	Eric Randall	Southern University (LA)
1993	Goree White	Alcorn State University (MS)
1994	Jerry Myers	Grambling State University (LA)
1995	Samuel Dickerson	Mississippi Valley State University (MS)
1996	Matt Bushart	Southern University (LA)
1997	Darnell Kennedy	Alabama State University (AL)
1998	Deontay Wilson	Prairie View A&M (Agricultural and Mechanical) University (TX)
1999	No selection	
2000	Santino Hall	Texas Southern University (TX)
2001	Brian Morgan	Grambling State University (LA)
2002	Terry Ross	Jackson State University (MS)
2003	Jarmaul George	Southern University (LA)
2004	Brandon Landers	Grambling State University (LA)
2005	Mickey Dean	University of Arkansas, Pine Bluff (AR)
2006	Ulysses Banks	Alabama A&M University (AL)
2007	Frank Warren	Grambling State University (LA)
2008	De'Markus Washington	Texas Southern University (TX)
2009	Ari Johnson	Grambling State University (LA)
2010	Jer-Ryan Harris	University of Arkansas, Pine Bluff (AR)

SWAC Return Specialist of the Year

Year	Player	School
1993	Goree White	Alcorn State University (MS)
1994	Cornelius Turner	Mississippi Valley State University (MS)
1995	Goree White	Alcorn State University (MS)
1996	Goree White	Alcorn State University (MS)
1997	Joey Jamison	Texas Southern University (TX)
1998	Joey Jamison	Texas Southern University (TX)
1999	Joey Jamison	Texas Southern University (TX)

National Collegiate Athletic Association (NCAA) Division II

P.O. Box 6222, 700 West Washington Street, Indianapolis, IN 46202; Telephone: 317-917-6222; Fax: 317-917-6888; Web site: http://www.ncaa.org

NCAA Division II (formerly called the NCAA College Division) institutions must sponsor at least five sports for men and five for women (or four for men and six for women). Within NCAA Division II, not all conferences support football programs and not all schools within each conference field football teams. As to football schedules, at least 50 percent of Division II games must be against FBS, FCS, or Division II teams. However, there is no NCAA rule preventing Division II schools from playing FBS, FCS, Division II, Division III, or NAIA schools. Unlike Division I football institutions, Division II programs do not have per-game attendance requirements.

Athletic scholarships are offered in most sponsored sports at most institutions, but with more severe limits than at the NCAA Division I level. Each Division II school can provide up to 36 football scholarships (compared to the 85 that are allowed in Division I), although some institutions offer less. Also, unlike Division I, transferring students at the Division II level do not have to sit out one year before participating in sports.

In addition to independent schools, as of this writing, NCAA Division II consists of the following 23 conferences (plus the Eastern College Athletic Conference):

- California Collegiate Athletic Association
- Central Atlantic Collegiate Conference
- Central Intercollegiate Athletic Association
- Conference Carolinas
- East Coast Conference
- Eastern College Athletic Conference
- Great Lakes Football Conference
- Great Lakes Intercollegiate Athletic Conference
- Great Lakes Valley Conference
- Great Northwest Athletic Conference
- Gulf South Conference
- Heartland Conference
- Independent Teams
- Lone Star Conference
- Mid-America Intercollegiate Athletics Association
- Northeast Ten Conference
- Northern Sun Intercollegiate Conference
- Pacific West Conference
- Peach Belt Conference
- Pennsylvania State Athletic Conference
- Rocky Mountain Athletic Conference
- South Atlantic Conference
- Southern Intercollegiate Athletic Conference

- Sunshine State Conference
- West Virginia Intercollegiate Athletic Conference

Division II Champions

The NCAA Division II National Football Championship began in 1973. Prior to that (1964–1972), four regional bowl games were played to determine local winners and a poll determined the final champion (not necessarily from the four winners). While previously played in different locations, since 1986, the Division II championship game has been played annually at Braly Municipal Stadium near the campus of the University of North Alabama (Florence, Alabama).

Winner of Regional Bowl games

1964

West: Montana State University (MT)
Midwest: University of Northern Iowa (IA)
Mideast: Middle Tennessee State University (TN)
East: East Carolina University (NC)

1965

West: California State University, Los Angeles (CA)
Midwest: North Dakota State University (ND)
Mideast: Ball State University (IN)
East: East Carolina University (NC)

1966

West: San Diego State University (CA)
Midwest: University of North Dakota (ND)
Mideast: Tennessee State University (TN)
East: Morgan State University (MD)

1967

West: San Diego State University (CA)
Midwest: University of Texas, Arlington (TX)
Mideast: Eastern Kentucky University (KY)
East: University of Tennessee, Martin (TN)

1968

West: Humboldt State University (CA)
Midwest: North Dakota State University (ND)

1968

Mideast: Louisiana Tech University (LA)
East: University of Delaware (DE)

1969

West: North Dakota State University (ND)
Midwest: Arkansas State University (AR)
Mideast: East Tennessee State University (TN)
East: University of Delaware (DE)

1970

West: North Dakota State University (ND)
Midwest: Arkansas State University (AR)
Mideast: Tennessee State University (TN)
East: University of Delaware (DE)

1971

West: Boise State University (ID)
Midwest: Louisiana Tech University (LA)
Mideast: Tennessee State University (TN)
East: University of Delaware (DE)

1972

West: University of North Dakota (ND)
Midwest: Tennessee State University (TN)
Mideast: Louisiana Tech University (LA)
East: University of Massachusetts (MA)

NCAA Division II National Champions (by polling)

Year	*School*
1958	University of Southern Mississippi (MS)
1959	Bowling Green State University (OH)
1960	University of Ohio (OH)
1961	Pittsburg State University (KS)
1962	University of Southern Mississippi (UPI) (MS)
1962	Florida A&M University (FL)
1963	University of Delaware (UPI) (DE)
1963	Northern Illinois University (AP) (IL)
1964	California State University, Los Angeles (UPI) (CA)
1964	Wittenberg University (AP) (OH)
1965	North Dakota State University (ND)
1966	San Diego State University (CA)
1967	San Diego State University (CA)
1968	San Diego State University (UPI) (CA)
1968	North Dakota State University (AP) (ND)
1969	North Dakota State University (ND)
1970	Arkansas State University (AR)
1971	University of Delaware (DE)
1972	University of Delaware (DE)
1973	Tennessee State University (TN)
1974	Louisiana Tech University (UPI) (LA)
1974	Central Michigan University (AP) (MI)

Beginning in 1973, a playoff series determined the Division II champion

Year	*Champion*
1973	Louisiana Tech University (LA)
1974	Central Michigan University (MI)
1975	Northern Michigan University (MI)
1976	Montana State University (MT)
1977	Lehigh University (PA)
1978	Eastern Illinois University (IL)
1979	University of Delaware (DE)
1980	California Polytechnic State University, San Luis Obispo (CA)
1981	Southwest Texas State University (TX)
1982	Southwest Texas State University (TX)
1983	North Dakota State University (ND)
1984	Troy State University (AL)
1985	North Dakota State University (ND)
1986	North Dakota State University (ND)
1987	Troy State University (AL)
1988	North Dakota State University (ND)
1989	Mississippi College (MS)
1990	North Dakota State University (ND)
1991	Pittsburg State University (KS)

Year	*Champion*
1992	Jacksonville State University (AL)
1993	University of North Alabama (AL)
1994	University of North Alabama (AL)
1995	University of North Alabama (AL)
1996	University of Northern Colorado (CO)
1997	University of Northern Colorado (CO)
1998	Northwest Missouri State University (MO)
1999	Northwest Missouri State University (MO)
2000	Delta State University (MS)
2001	University of North Dakota (ND)
2002	Grand Valley State University (MI)
2003	Grand Valley State University (MI)
2004	Valdosta State University (GA)
2005	Grand Valley State University (MI)
2006	Grand Valley State University (MI)
2007	Valdosta State University (GA)
2008	University of Minnesota, Duluth (MN)
2009	Northwest Missouri State University (MO)
2010	University of Minnesota, Duluth (MN)

Alonso S. "Jake" Gaither Award

Often referred to as the "Black Heisman" and sponsored by the 100% Wrong Club (http://www.100percentwrong.com), this award recognizes the most outstanding football player from a historically black college or university (the winner usually comes from an NCAA Division II or III school).

Alonso Smith Gaither (born: April 11, 1903, in Dayton, Tennessee and died on February 18, 1994, in Tallahassee, Florida) was the head football coach at Florida A&M University (Tallahassee, FL 32307) for 25 years (and its head basketball coach for six years), finishing with a football coaching record of 203–36–4 (.835). During his career, Gaither won 23 Southern Intercollegiate Athletic Conference titles and six national championships.

The 100% Wrong Club was established in 1934 in Atlanta, Georgia, to recognize and honor college athletes in the 1930s and 1940s. Today, the club maintains its historical link to the past and has expanded its scope by recognizing college and high school athletes, local community leaders, and national pioneers in the field of sports and social justice.

After college, he became an assistant to head coach William "Big Bill" Bell at Florida A&M College for Negroes in 1938, and went on that season to win the school's first Black College National Championship. After Bell entered the military during World War II, Gaither was hired as the head football coach in 1945. He later began annual coaching clinics and recruited some of the most well-known white coaches of his time, including Paul "Bear" Bryant, Frank Broyles, Darrell Royal, Woody Hayes and Adolph Rupp.

Gaither also coached basketball and track in his early years as football coach and later became the school's Director of Athletics. He continued to hold both positions until 1973 (after retiring as a coach in 1969).

In 1969, FAMU defeated the University of Tampa (Florida) 34–28 in the South's first football game between a white college and a predominately black college. His teams would eventually win six Black College National Championships(1950, 1952, 1954, 1957, 1959, 1961).

Gaither was later named Southern Intercollegiate Athletic Conference Coach of the Decade and inducted into the College Football Hall of Fame in 1975.

The Jake Gaither Trophy has been awarded to the best Black collegiate football player each year since 1978.

Year	*Player*	*School*
1978	Jeffery Moore	Jackson State University (MS)
1979	Joe Adams, Jr.	Tennessee State University (TN)

Year	Player	School
1980	Robert Parham	Grambling University (LA)
1981	James "Sugar Bear" Hamilton	Mississippi Valley State University (MS)
1982	Richard Dent	Tennessee State University (TN)
1983	Jerry Rice	Mississippi Valley State University (MS)
1984	Jerry Rice	Mississippi Valley State University (MS)
1985	Mark Corbin	Central State University (OH)
1986	Brad Baxter	Alabama State University (AL)
1987	Terry Morrow	Central State University (OH)
1988	Micheal Basnight	North Carolina A&T (University (NC)
1988	Louis Tillman	Jackson State University (MS)
1989	Clemente Gordon	Grambling State University (LA)
1990	Walter Dean	Grambling State University (LA)
1991	Carl Donnie Wright	Virginia Union University (VA)
1992	Douglas Grant	Savannah State College (GA)
1993	Jay "Sky" Walker	Howard University (Washington, D.C.)
1994	No Winner Named	
1995	Earl Holmes	Florida A&M University (FL)
1996	Antonio Leroy	Alabama State University (AL)
1997	Telly Priester	Virginia State University (VA)
1999	JaJuan Seider	Florida A&M University (FL)
2000	Andrew Braxton	Virginia Union University (VA)
2001	John Grant	Morehouse College (GA)
2002	Bruce Eugene	Grambling State University (LA)
2003	Quincy Richard	Southern University (LA)
2004	Derrick Winbush	Fort Valley State University (GA)
2005	Bruce Eugene	Grambling State University (LA)
2006	Justin Durant	Hampton University (VA)
2007	Curtis Johnson	Clark Atlanta University (GA)
2008	Jacary Atkinson	Tuskegee University (AL)

American Football Coaches Association (AFCA) Coach of the Year

100 Legends Lane, Waco, TX 76706; Telephone: 254-754-9900; Fax: 254-754-7373; http://www.afca.com

The AFCA Coach of the Year Award is presented annually to each level of college football (NCAA FBS (and equivalent) since 1935, NCAA FCS since 1983, NCAA Division II since 1983, NCAA Division III since 1983, and NAIA since 2006). The Scripps-Howard newspaper chain conducted the balloting and presented the award from 1935 through 1959. In 1960, the AFCA itself began handling the voting and award presentation. Eastman Kodak Corporation sponsored the AFCA Coach of the Year program from 1960 until 1993, and from 1996 to 1999, the award was sponsored by GTE.

From 1960 through 1982, two national winners were selected (one from the University Division and one from the College Division). Beginning in 1983, four national winners were chosen, one from each school level (NCAA I-A, NCAA I-AA, NCAA Division II, and NCAA Division III) and in 2006, selection was expanded to five levels with the inclusion of the NAIA.

Currently, the AFCA selects 25 regional winners (five from each of the AFCA division levels), from which five national winners (one from each AFCA division level) are selected. All schools with eligible AFCA head coaches are listed on the national ballot and AFCA members are not limited to voting for regional winners. However, members are required to vote for coaches within their region for the AFCA Regional Coach of the Year and coaches within their division when voting for the AFCA National Coach of the Year.

The school of each AFCA National Coach of the Year winner receives $1,000 from The American Football Coaches Foundation for each full-time assistant football coach who was on staff the year the head coach was honored. If a school wins a national championship and the head coach wins the AFCA National Coach of the Year Award, the school then receives $1,500 for each full-time assistant who is an AFCA member.

As of this writing, Larry Kehres of Mount Union College (Ohio, NCAA Division III) is the only coach in AFCA history to win the National Coach of the Year Award nine times (1993, 1996–1998, 2000–2002, 2006, 2008) and Bob Reade of Augustana College (Illinois, NCAA Division III) is the only coach to win the award four consecutive years (1983–1986).

NCAA DIVISION II AFCA COACH OF THE YEAR

Year	*Coach*	*School*
1983	Don Morton	North Dakota State University (ND)
1984	Chan Gailey	Troy State University (AL)
1985	George Landis	Bloomsburg University (PA)
1986	Earle Solomonson	North Dakota State University (ND)
1987	Rick Rhoades	Troy State University (AL)
1988	Rocky Hager	North Dakota State University (ND)
1989	John Williams	Mississippi College (MS)
1990	Rocky Hager	North Dakota State University (ND)
1991	Chuck Broyles	Pittsburg State University (KS)
1992	Bill Burgess	Jacksonville State University (AL)
1993	Bobby Wallace	University of North Alabama (AL)
1994	Bobby Wallace	University of North Alabama (AL)
1995	Bobby Wallace	University of North Alabama (AL)
1996	Joe Glenn	University of Northern Colorado (CO)
1997	Joe Glenn	University of Northern Colorado (CO)
1998	Mel Tjeerdsma	Northwest Missouri State University (MO)
1999	Mel Tjeerdsma	Northwest Missouri State University (MO)
2000	Danny Hale	Bloomsburg University (PA)
2001	Dale Lennon	University of North Dakota (ND)
2002	Brian Kelly	Grand Valley State University (MI)
2003	Brian Kelly	Grand Valley State University (MI)
2003	Mike Van Diest	Carroll College (MT)
2004	Chris Hatcher	Valdosta State University (GA)
2005	Chuck Martin	Grand Valley State University (MI)
2006	Chuck Martin	Grand Valley State University (MI)
2007	David Dean	Valdosta State University (GA)
2008	Mel Tjeerdsma	Northwest Missouri State University (MO)
2009	Mel Tjeerdsma	Northwest Missouri State University (MO)
2010	Bob Nielson	University of Minnesota, Duluth (MN)

American Football Coaches Association (AFCA) Assistant Coach of the Year

100 Legends Lane, Waco, TX 76706; Telephone: 254-754-9900; Fax: 254-754-7373; http://www.afca.com

The AFCA Assistant Coach of the Year Award has been presented annually since 1997 to the best assistant coach in each of the five levels of college football (NCAA FBS, NCAA FCS, NCAA Division II, NCAA Division III, and the NAIA).

For each of the five levels of college football, staff members from NCAA and NAIA football-playing schools nominate an assistant coach. From this list of nominees, a winner is then selected by the AFCA Public Relations Committee.

NCAA DIVISION II ASSISTANT COACH OF THE YEAR

Year	*Assistant Coach*	*School*
1997	Richard Cundiff	Texas A&M University, Kingsville (TX)
1998	Wesley McGriff	Kentucky State University (KY)
1999	Mike Moroski	University of California, Davis (CA)
2000	Kyle Schweigert	University of North Dakota (ND)
2001	Bart Tatum	Northwest Missouri State University (MO)

Year	Assistant Coach	School
2002	Tony Ierulli	Shippensburg University (PA)
2003	Mike Turner	Carson-Newman College (TN)
2004	Brian Hughes	Long Island University, C.W. Post Campus (NY)
2005	Cary Fowler	Midwestern State University (TX)
2006	Mike Terwilliger	East Stroudsburg University (PA)
2007	Scott Bostwick	Northwest Missouri State University (MO)
2008	Matt Entz	Winona State University (MN)
2009	David Needs	Carson-Newman College (TN)
2010	Joe Lorig	Central Washington University (WA)

Gene Upshaw Award (Gene Upshaw Division II Lineman of the Year Award)

The Gene Upshaw Award (presented since 2004) is presented annually to the best college football lineman (offensive or defensive) in Division II by the non-profit Manheim Touchdown Club (P.O. Box 361, Manheim, PA 17545; Web site: http://manheimtouchdownclub.com/). The award is named after former National Football League's Gene Upshaw (born: August 15, 1945, in Robstown, TX; died: August 20, 2008, in Lake Tahoe, CA), who played college football at Texas A&I University (Texas A&M University, Kingsville) and later for the Oakland Raiders in the NFL (1967–1981).

He won two Super Bowl titles (SB XI in 1977 and SB XV in 1981); named to the NFL 1970s All-Decade Team; selected to the NFL 75th Anniversary All-Time Team; inducted into the Pro Football Hall of Fame in 1987; and served, until his death, as Executive Director of the National Football League Players' Association.

To win this award, a player must be a junior or senior and have played in at least 70 percent of the team's regular season games. As of this writing, only Mike McFadden (Grand Valley State University) has won this award more than once.

Year	Player	School	Note
2004	Nathan Baker	Pittsburg State University (KS)	First Team MIAA All-American
2005	Mike McFadden	Grand Valley State University (MI)	School record 19 Quarterback sacks
2006	Mike McFadden	Grand Valley State University (MI)	AFCA First-Team All-American
2007	Brandon Barnes	Grand Valley State University (MI)	2X Division II All-American (2006 / 2007)
2008	Sam Collins	Abilene Christian University (TX)	2nd Team AP Little All-American
2009	Ben Staggs	West Liberty University (WV)	2009 All-American
2010	Brandon Fusco	Slippery Rock University of Pennsylvania (PA)	First in school history to play in the Senior Bowl

Harlon Hill Trophy

Since 1986, the Harlon Hill Trophy has been awarded annually to the NCAA Division II college football player of the year. Hill played offensive end at Florence State Teachers College (now known as the University of North Alabama, Florence, AL) and was an NAIA All-American in his senior year (1953). After college, he played in the National Football League for the Chicago Bears (1954–1961), Pittsburgh Steelers (1962), and Detroit Lions (1962). He was the NFL Rookie of the Year in 1954 and the league's Most Valuable Player in 1955.

The trophy is 30 inches tall; weighs 63 pounds; and is a replica of a football resting on a solid walnut base. As of this writing, only three players have won the award more than once: Johnny Bailey (Texas A&I University), Dusty Bonner (Valdosta State University), and Danny Woodhead (Chadron State College).

Year	Player	Position	School
1986	Jeff Bentrim	Quarterback	North Dakota State University (ND)
1987	Johnny Bailey	Running Back	Texas A&I University (TX)
1988	Johnny Bailey	Running Back	Texas A&I University (TX)

Year	*Player*	*Position*	*School*
1989	Johnny Bailey	Running Back	Texas A&I University (TX)
1990	Chris Simdorn	Quarterback	North Dakota State University (ND)
1991	Ronnie West	Wide Receiver	Pittsburg State University (KS)
1992	Ronald Moore	Running Back	Pittsburg State University (KS)
1993	Roger Graham	Running Back	University of New Haven (CT)
1994	Chris Hatcher	Quarterback	Valdosta State University (GA)
1995	Ronald McKinnon	Linebacker	University of North Alabama (AL)
1996	Jarrett Anderson	Running Back	Truman State University (MO)
1997	Irvin Sigler	Running Back	Bloomsburg University (PA)
1998	Brian Shay	Running Back	Emporia State University (KS)
1999	Corte McGuffey	Quarterback	University of Northern Colorado (CO)
2000	Dusty Bonner	Quarterback	Valdosta State University (GA)
2001	Dusty Bonner	Quarterback	Valdosta State University (GA)
2002	Curt Anes	Quarterback	Grand Valley State University (MI)
2003	Will Hall	Quarterback	University of North Alabama (AL)
2004	Chad Friehauf	Quarterback	Colorado School of Mines (CO)
2005	Jimmy Terwilliger	Quarterback	East Stroudsburg University (PA)
2006	Danny Woodhead	Running Back	Chadron State College (NE)
2007	Danny Woodhead	Running Back	Chadron State College (NE)
2008	Bernard Scott	Running Back	Abilene Christian University (TX)
2009	Joique Bell	Running Back	Wayne State University (MI)
2010	Eric Czerniewski	Quarterback	University of Central Missouri (MO)

Joseph P. Zabilski Award

Presented by the Gridiron Club of Greater Boston (9 Broadway, Unit 320, Saugus, MA 01906; Web site: http://www.gridclubofgreaterboston.com/) since 1996, the Joseph P. Zabilski Award is presented to the best New England player in both NCAA Division II and III. The award is named in honor of Joe Zabilski, who graduated from Boston College (MA) in 1943; coached Northeastern University (MA) from 1948 to 1971; and served as a former president of the Gridiron Club.

Year	*Player*	*School*
1996	Alex Bernstein	Amherst College (MA)
1996	Raymond Jones	Trinity College (CT)
1997	Ben Nassar	Bentley University (MA)
1997	Richard Willard	Amherst College (MA)
1998	Ben Nassar	Bentley University (MA)
1998	Sean Keenan	Williams College (MA)
1999	Christos Arsoniadis	Bridgewater State College (MA)
1999	Kavin Gailliard	American International College (MA)
2000	Brian Sanchez	Middlebury College (VT)
2000	Steven Cedor	University of New Haven (CT)
2001	Joseph Reardon	Williams College (MA)
2001	Josue Zamora	Westfield State College (MA)
2002	Marc Eddy	Bentley University (MA)
2002	Scott Farley	Williams College (MA)
2003	Mark Tilki	Tufts University (MA)
2003	Tom Pierandri	Trinity College (CT)
2004	Brian Robitaille	Curry College (MA)
2004	Marc Eddy	Bentley University (MA)
2005	Don Thibodeau	Maine Maritime Academy (ME)
2005	Mike Blair	Trinity College (CT)
2006	Chris Sharpe	Springfield College (MA)
2006	Sean Crowley	Curry College (MA)
2007	Patrick Lucey	Williams College (MA)
2007	Paul Tetzel	Bentley University (MA)
2008	Cody Andrews	Maine Maritime Academy (ME)

Year	Player	School
2008	Jeff Mack	Plymouth State University (NH)
2009	Jim Bower	Maine Maritime Academy (ME)
2009	Josh Mathieu	Westfield State College (MA)
2010	James McCarthy-Offense	Framingham State University (MA)
2010	Shawn Loiseau-Defense	Merrimack College (MA)

Lambert-Meadowlands Cup

The Lambert-Meadowlands Trophy is an annual award given to the best team in the East in Division I FBS college football and was established by brothers Victor and Henry Lambert in memory of their father, August. Established in 1936 as the "Lambert Trophy," it also recognizes (as the "Lambert Cup") the best college football team in the FCS (as of 1982), NCAA Division II (as of 1957), and Division III (as of 1966) levels.

The New Jersey Sports and Exposition Authority (Public Affairs Office, 50 State Route 120, East Rutherford, NJ 07073; Telephone: 201-935-8500; Email: publicaffairs@njsea.com; Web site: http://www.njsea.com/), operator of the Meadowlands Sports Complex, took over the administration of the Lambert Meadowlands Awards in 1983.

To be eligible for the Lambert Meadowlands Award, a school must be located in the East or play half its schedule against eligible Lambert teams.

Lambert-Meadowlands Trophy (NCAA Division II)

Year	School
1957	Lehigh University (PA)
1958	University of Buffalo (NY)
1959	University of Delaware (DE)
1960	Bucknell University (PA)
1961	Lehigh University (PA)
1962	University of Delaware (DE)
1963	University of Delaware (DE)
1964	Bucknell University (PA)
1965	University of Maine (ME)
1966	Gettysburg College (PA)
1967	West Chester University of Pennsylvania (PA)
1968	University of Delaware (DE)
1969	University of Delaware (DE)
1960	Wesleyan University (CT)
1970	University of Delaware (DE)
1971	University of Delaware (DE)
1972	University of Delaware (DE)
1973	University of Delaware(DE)
1973	Lehigh University (PA)
1974	University of Delaware (DE)
1975	Lehigh University (PA)
1976	University of Delaware (DE)
1977	Lehigh University (PA)
1978	University of Massachusetts (MA)
1979	University of Delaware (DE)
1980	Lehigh University (PA)
1981	Shippensburg University of Pennsylvania (PA)
1982	East Stroudsburg University of Pennsylvania (PA)
1983	Towson State University (Towson University) (MD)
1984	Towson State University (Towson University) (MD)
1985	Bloomsburg University of Pennsylvania (PA)
1986	Towson State University (Towson University) (MD)
1987	Indiana University of Pennsylvania (PA)
1988	Millersville University of Pennsylvania (PA)
1989	Indiana University of Pennsylvania (PA)
1990	Indiana University of Pennsylvania (PA)
1991	Indiana University of Pennsylvania (PA)
1992	University of New Haven (CT)
1993	Indiana University of Pennsylvania (PA)
1994	Indiana University of Pennsylvania (PA)
1995	University of New Haven (CT)
1996	Clarion University of Pennsylvania (PA)
1997	University of New Haven (CT)
1998	Slippery Rock University of Pennsylvania (PA)
1999	Indiana University of Pennsylvania (PA)
2000	Bloomsburg University of Pennsylvania (PA)
2001	Indiana University of Pennsylvania (PA)
2002	Indiana University of Pennsylvania (PA)
2003	Indiana University of Pennsylvania (PA)
2004	West Chester University of Pennsylvania (PA)
2005	East Stroudsburg University of Pennsylvania (PA)
2006	West Chester University of Pennsylvania (PA)
2007	California University of Pennsylvania (PA)
2008	West Chester University of Pennsylvania (PA)
2009	University of California (PA)
2010	Mercyhurst College (PA)

Liberty Mutual Coach of the Year

Sponsored by the Liberty Mutual Insurance Company (175 Berkeley Street, Boston, MA 02116; Telephone: 800-837-5254; Web site: http://www.coachoftheyear.com/), the Liberty Mutual Coach of the Year Award is an annual college football presentation given to the head coach from each NCAA Division (FBS (as of 2006), FCS (as of 2007), NCAA Division II (as of 2007), and the NCAA Division III (as of 2007)).

This award provides each coach with $50,000 to donate to the charity or charities of his choice, as well as a $20,000 grant to donate to his school's alumni association.

Year	*Coach*	*School*	*Note*
2007	Bill O'Boyle	Chadron State College (NE)	3X Rocky Mountain Athletic Conference Champions (2007–2009)
2008	Chuck Broyles	Pittsburg State University (KS)	2008 Division II Liberty Mutual Coach of the Year
2009	Mel Tjeerdsma	Northwest Missouri State University (MO)	3X Division II Champion (1998–1999, 2009)
2010	Bob Nielson	University of Minnesota, Duluth (MN)	2X Division II Champion (2008, 2010)

California Collegiate Athletic Association (CCAA)

1350 Treat Boulevard, Suite 500, Walnut Creek, CA 94597; Telephone: 925-472-8299; Fax: 925-472-8887; Web site: http://www.goccaa.org

Established in December 1938 with four charter schools (Fresno State University (now plays in the Western Athletic Conference); San Diego State University (now plays in the Mountain West Conference); San Jose State University (now plays in the Western Athletic Conference); and the University of California, Santa Barbara (now plays in the Big West Conference)), the 12-member (current alignment) California Collegiate Athletic Association does not sponsor a football program and only one of its schools, Humboldt State University, plays football (as an associate member in the Great Northwest Athletic Conference). All of its current members are public universities and all of its schools, except for the University of California at San Diego, are members of the California State University system.

The current 12 members of the CCAA include:

- California State Polytechnic University, Pomona, Broncos, Pomona, CA 91768; 909-869-7659; www.csupomona.edu; no football program
- California State University, Chico, Wildcats, Chico, CA 95929; 530-898-4636; www.csuchico.edu; no football program
- California State University, Dominguez Hills, Toros, Carson, CA 90747; 310-243-3696; www.csudh.edu; no football program
- California State University, East Bay, Pioneers, Hayward, CA 94542; 510-885-3000; www20.csueastbay.edu; no football program
- California State University, Los Angeles, Golden Eagles, Los Angeles, CA 90032; 323-343-3000; www.calstatela.edu; no football program
- California State University, Monterey Bay, Otters, Seaside, CA 93955; 831-582-3000; http://csumb.edu; no football program
- California State University, San Bernardino, Coyotes, San Bernardino, CA 92407; 909-537-5000; www. csusb.edu; no football program
- California State University, Stanislaus, Warriors, Turlock, CA 95382; 209-667-3122; www.csustan.edu; no football program
- Humboldt State University Lumberjacks, Arcata, CA 95521; 707-826-3011; www.humboldt.edu; plays football in the Great Northwest Athletic Conference and also as an independent team
- San Francisco State University Gators, San Francisco, CA 94132; 415-338-1111; www.sfsu.edu; no football program
- Sonoma State University Seawolves, Rohnert Park, CA 94928; 707-664-2880; www.sonoma.edu; no football program
- University of California, San Diego, Tritons, La Jolla, CA 92093; 858-534-2230; www.ucsd.edu; no football program

Central Atlantic Collegiate Conference (CACC)

P.O. Box 3575, New Haven, CT 06525; 111 Water Street, New Haven CT 06511; Telephone: 203-298-4806; Email: kreed@caccathletics.org; Web site: http://www.caccathletics.org/

Founded in 1965, the Central Atlantic Collegiate Conference does not sponsor football, while only one of its teams, Post University, plays football in the Collegiate Sprint Football League.

As of this writing, the Central Atlantic Collegiate Conference consists of the following 14 schools:

- Bloomfield College Deacons, Bloomfield, NJ 07003; 973-748-9000; www.bloomfield.edu; no football program
- Caldwell College Cougars, Caldwell, NJ 07006; 973-618-3000; www.caldwell.edu; no football program
- Chestnut Hill College Griffins, Philadelphia, PA 19118; 215-248-7001; www.chc.edu; no football program
- Concordia College Clippers, Bronxville, NY 10708; 914-337-9300; www.concordia-ny.edu; no football program
- Dominican College Chargers, Orangeburg, NY 10962; 845-359-7800; www.dc.edu; no football program
- Felician College Golden Falcons, Rutherford, NJ 07070; 201-559-6000; www.felician.edu; no football program
- Georgian Court University Lions, Lakewood, NJ 08701; 800-458-8422; www.georgian.edu; no football program
- Goldey-Beacom College Lightning, Wilmington, DE 19808; 302-998-8814; www.gbc.edu; no football program
- Holy Family University Tigers, Philadelphia, PA 19114; 215-637-7700; www.hfc.edu; no football program
- Nyack College Warriors, Nyack, NY 10960; 845-358-1710; www.nyackcollege.edu; no football program
- Philadelphia University Rams, Philadelphia, PA 19144; 215-951-2700; www.philau.edu; no football program
- Post University Eagles, Waterbury, CT 06723; 203-596-4500; www.post.edu; plays football in the Collegiate Sprint Football League
- University of the Sciences in Philadelphia Devils, Philadelphia, PA 19104; 215-596-8800; www.usciences.edu; no football program
- Wilmington University Wildcats, New Castle, DE 19720; 877-967-5464; www.wilmu.edu; no football program

Central Intercollegiate Athletic Association (CIAA)

P.O. Box 7349, 22 Enterprise Parkway, Suite 210, Hampton, VA 23666; Telephone: 757-865-0071; Fax: 757-865-8436; Email: TheCIAA@aol.com; http://www.theciaa.com

Consisting of 11 historically African American institutions (and Chowan University), the Central Intercollegiate Athletic Association was established in 1912 and is the nation's oldest black athletic conference. As of this writing, the conference is divided into Eastern and Western Divisions in all sports except baseball.

Originally known as the Colored Intercollegiate Athletic Association, the conference's eight charter members included Bowie State College, Elizabeth City College, Fayetteville State College, St. Augustine's College, St. Paul's College, Shaw University, Virginia Normal and Industrial Institute, and Virginia Union University.

As of this writing, the 13 current members of the CIAA include:

- Bowie State University Bulldogs, Bowie, MD 20715; 301-860-4000; www.bowiestate.edu
- Chowan University Hawks, Murfreesboro, NC 27855; 252-398-6500; www.chowan.edu
- Elizabeth City State University Vikings, Elizabeth City, NC 27909; 252-335-3400; www.ecsu.edu
- Fayetteville State University Broncos, Fayetteville, NC 28301; 910-672-1111; www.uncfsu.edu
- Johnson C. Smith University Golden Bulls, Charlotte, NC 28216; 704-378-1000; www.jcsu.edu

- Lincoln University of Pennsylvania Lions, Lincoln University, PA 19352; 484-365-8000; www.lincoln.edu
- Livingstone College Blue Bears, Salisbury, NC 28144; 800-835-3435; www.livingstone.edu
- St. Augustine's College Falcons, Raleigh, NC 27610; 919-516-4000; http://st-aug1.com
- St. Paul's College Tigers, Lawrenceville, VA 23868; 434-848-3111; www.saintpauls.edu
- Shaw University Bears, Raleigh, NC 27601; 919-546-8200; www.shawuniversity.edu
- Virginia State University Trojans, Petersburg, VA 23806; 804-524-5000; www.vsu.edu
- Virginia Union University Panthers, Richmond, VA 23220; 804-257-5600; www.vuu.edu
- Winston-Salem State University Rams, Winston-Salem, NC 27110; 336-750-2000; www.wssu.edu

CIAA Champions

Year	*School*
1912	Howard University (Washington, D.C.)
1913	Hampton University (VA)
1914	Hampton University (VA)
1915	Hampton University (VA)
1916	Hampton University (VA)
1917	Virginia Union University (VA)
1918	No Champion (World War I)
1919	No Champion (World War I)
1920	No Champion (World War I)
1921	Virginia Union University (VA)
1922	Hampton University (VA)
1923	Virginia Union University (VA)
1924	Lincoln University (PA)
1925	Hampton University (VA)
1926	Hampton University (VA)
1927	North Carolina Agricultural and Technical State University (NC)
1928	Hampton University (VA)
1929	Virginia State University (VA)
1930	Morgan State University (MD)
1931	Hampton University (VA)
1932	Morgan State University (MD)
1933	Morgan State University (MD)
1934	Morgan State University (MD)
1935	Morgan State University (MD)
1936	Virginia State University (VA)
1937	Morgan State University (MD)
1938	Virginia State University (VA)
1939	Virginia State University (VA)
1940	Morgan State University (MD)
1941	Morgan State University (MD)
1942	Morgan State University (MD)
1943	Morgan State University (MD)
1944	Morgan State University (MD)
1945	Virginia State University (VA)
1946	Morgan State University (MD)
1947	Shaw University (NC)
1948	West Virginia State University (WV)
1949	Morgan State University (MD)
1950	North Carolina Agricultural and Technical State University (NC)
1951	West Virginia State University (WV)
1952	Virginia State University (VA)
1953	North Carolina State University (NC)
1954	North Carolina State University (NC)
1955	Maryland State University (MD)
1956	North Carolina College (NC)
1956	Morgan State University (MD)
1956	Delaware State University (DE)
1957	Maryland State University (MD)
1958	North Carolina Agricultural and Technology University (NC)
1959	North Carolina Agricultural and Technology University (NC)
1960	Maryland State University (MD)
1961	North Carolina College (NC)
1962	Morgan State University (MD)
1963	North Carolina College (NC)
1964	North Carolina Agricultural and Technology University (NC)
1965	Morgan State University (MD)
1966	Morgan State University (MD)
1967	Morgan State University (MD)
1968	Morgan State University (MD)
1969	Johnson C. Smith University (NC)
1970	Virginia State University (VA)
1971	Elizabeth City State University (NC)
1972	Virginia State University (VA)
1973	Virginia Union University (VA)
1974	Norfolk State University (VA)
1975	Norfolk State University (VA)
1976	Norfolk State University (VA)
1977	Winston-Salem State University (NC)
1978	Winston-Salem State University (NC)
1979	Virginia Union University (VA)
1980	North Carolina Central University (NC)
1981	Virginia Union University (VA)
1982	Virginia Union University (VA)
1983	Virginia Union University (VA)
1984	Norfolk State University (VA)
1985	Hampton University (VA)
1986	Virginia Union University (VA)
1987	Winston-Salem State University (NC)
1988	Winston-Salem State University (NC)
1989	Bowie State University (MD)
1990	Winston-Salem State University (NC)
1991	Winston-Salem State University (NC)
1992	Hampton University (VA)
1993	Hampton University (VA)
1994	Hampton University (VA)
1995	Virginia State University (VA)
1996	Virginia State University (VA)

Year	School
1997	Livingstone College (NC)
1998	Livingstone College (NC)
1999	Winston-Salem State University (NC)
2000	Winston-Salem State University (NC)
2001	Virginia Union University (VA)
2002	Fayetteville State University (NC)
2003	Fayetteville State University (NC)
2004	Shaw University (NC)
2005	North Carolina Central University (NC)
2006	North Carolina Central University (NC)
2007	Shaw University (NC)
2008	Shaw University (NC)
2009	Fayetteville State University (NC)
2010	Shaw University (NC)

CIAA Coach of the Year

Year	Coach	School
2000	Kermit Blount	Winston-Salem State University (NC)
2001	Henry Frazier III	Bowie State University (MD)
2002	Kenny Phillips	Fayetteville State University (NC)
2003	Michael Costa	St. Augustine's College (NC)
2004	Deondri Clark	Shaw University (NC)
2005	Michael Costa	St. Augustine's College (NC)
2006	Waverly Tillar	Elizabeth City State University (NC)
2007	Arrington Jones III	Virginia Union University (VA)
2008	Waverly Tillar	Elizabeth City State University (NC)
2009	Kenny Phillips	Fayetteville State University (NC)
2010	Darrell Asberry	Shaw University (NC)

CIAA Offensive Player of the Year

Year	Player	School
2000	Andre Braxton	Virginia Union University (VA)
2001	Jimmy Bell	Johnson C. Smith University (NC)
2002	Kevin Jones	Virginia State University (VA)
2003	Kevin Jones	Virginia State University (VA)
2004	Adrian Warren	North Carolina Central University (NC)
2005	Martin Hicks	North Carolina Central University (NC)
2006	Stadford Brown	North Carolina Central University (NC)
2007	Lamar Little	Virginia Union University (VA)
2008	Curtis Rich, Jr.	Elizabeth City State University (NC)
2009	C.J. Westler	Chowan University (NC)
2010	Walter Sanders	St. Augustine's College (NC)

CIAA Defensive Player of the year

Year	Player	School
2000	Alvin Wilson	Elizabeth City State University (NC)
2001	Stephon Kelly	Winston-Salem State University (NC)
2002	Brian Holliday	Fayetteville State University (NC)
2003	Jason Ocean	Livingstone College (NC)
2004	Charles Roberts	Fayetteville State University (NC)
2005	Tyrone Pettaway	St. Augustine's College (NC)
2006	Kevin Jones	St. Augustine's College (NC)
2007	Louis Ellis	Shaw University (NC)
2008	Louis Ellis	Shaw University (NC)
2009	Quintez Smith	Shaw University (NC)
2010	Malcolm Jenkins	Elizabeth City State University (NC)

Conference Carolinas

1723 Country Club Drive, High Point, NC 27262; Telephone: 336-884-0482; Fax: 336-884-0489; Email: conferencecarolinas@triad.rr.com; Web site: http://www.conferencecarolinas.com

Formerly known as the Carolinas-Virginia Athletic Conference, Conference Carolinas was established in 1994. The conference does not support football; one of its teams plays football in the South Atlantic Conference; and its 13 member schools include:

- Barton College Bulldogs, Wilson, NC 27893; 252-399-6300; www.barton.edu; no football program
- Belmont Abbey College Crusaders, Belmont, NC 28012; 888-222-0110; www.belmontabbeycollege.edu; no football program
- Coker College Cobras, Hartsville, SC 29550; 843-383-8000; www.coker.edu; no football program
- Converse College Valkyries, Spartanburg, SC 29302; 864-596-9000; www.converse.edu; no football program
- Erskine College Flying Fleet, Due West, SC 29639; 864-379-2131; www.erskine.edu; no football program
- King College Tornado, Bristol TN 37620; 423-652-4861; www.king.edu; no football program
- Lees-McRae College Bobcats, Banner Elk, NC 28604; 828-898-5241; www.lmc.edu; no football program
- Limestone College Saints, Gaffney, SC 29340; 864-489-7151; www.limestone.edu; no football program
- Mount Olive College Trojans, Mount Olive, NC 28365; 800-653-0854; www.moc.edu; no football program
- North Greenville University Crusaders, Tigerville, SC 29688; 864-977-7000; www.ngu.edu; plays football in the South Atlantic Conference
- Pfeiffer University Falcons, Misenheimer, NC 28109; 704-463-1360; www.pfeiffer.edu; no football program
- Queens University of Charlotte Royals, Charlotte, NC 28274; 704-337-2200; www.queens.edu; no football program
- St. Andrews Presbyterian College Knights, Laurinburg, NC 28352; 910-277-5555; www.sapc.edu; no football program

Division II Independents

While these schools each belong to specific conferences, the squads play football as independent teams.

- Black Hills State University Yellow Jackets, Spearfish, SD 57799; 605-642-6343; www.bhsu.edu; plays football in the Dakota Athletic Conference
- Central State University Marauders, Wilberforce, OH 45384; 937-376-6011; www.centralstate.edu; plays football in the Great Lakes Valley Conference
- Lindenwood University Lions, Saint Charles, MO 63301; 636-949-2000; www.lindenwood.edu; beginning in 2012, will play football in the Mid-America Intercollegiate Athletics Association
- Malone University Pioneers, Canton OH 44709; 800-521-1146; www.malone.edu; plays football in the Mid-States Football Association
- McKendree University Bearcats, Lebanon, IL 62254; 618-537-4481; www.mckendree.edu; plays football in the Great Lakes Valley Conference
- Minot State University Beavers, Minot, ND 58707; 800-777-0750; www.minotstate.edu; as of 2012, will begin playing football in the Northern Sun Intercollegiate Conference
- North Greenville University Crusaders, Tigerville, SC 29688; 864-977-7000; www.ngu.edu; plays football in the South Atlantic Conference
- Notre Dame College Falcons, South Euclid, OH 44121; 877-632-6446; www.notredamecollege.edu; plays football as an independent team
- Oklahoma Panhandle State University Aggies, Goodwell, OK 73939; 580-349-2611; www.opsu.edu; plays football in the Independent Football Alliance (NCAA Division II) and the Central States Football League (NAIA)
- South Dakota School of Mines and Technology Hardrockers, Rapid City, SD 57701; 605-394-2511; http://sdmines.sdsmt.edu; plays football in the Dakota Athletic Conference
- Southwest Baptist University Bearcats, Bolivar, MO 65613; 417-328-5281; www.sbuniv.edu; plays football as an in dependent team

- University of North Carolina at Pembroke Braves, Pembroke, NC 28372; 910-521-6000; www.uncp.edu; plays football in the Peach Belt Conference
- University of Sioux Falls Cougars, Sioux Falls, SD 57105; 800-888-1047; www.usiouxfalls.edu/; plays football in the Great Plains Athletic Conference and will join the Northern Sun Intercollegiate Conference in 2012
- Urbana University Blue Knights, Urbana, OH 43078; 937-484-1400; www.urbana.edu; plays football in the Great Lakes Valley Conference
- Walsh University Cavaliers, North Canton, OH 44720; 330-490-7090; www.walsh.edu; plays football in the Mid-States Football Association

East Coast Conference

300 Carleton Avenue, NYIT SAC210, Central Islip, NY 11722; Telephone: 631-348-3453; Fax: 631-348-3455; Email: rdranoff@eccsports.org; Web site: http://www.eccsports.org

Founded in 1989 as the New York Collegiate Athletic Conference, the East Coast Conference's 11 charter members included Adelphi University, Concordia College, C.W. Post College, Dowling College, Mercy College, Molloy College, New York Institute of Technology, Queens College, University of Bridgeport, University of New Haven, and St. Thomas Aquinas College. The conference does not support a football program while one of its schools, C.W. Post, plays football in the Division II Pennsylvania State Athletic Conference.

As of this writing, the conference consists of the following eight schools:

- C.W. Post Campus / Long Island University Pioneers, Brookville, NY 11548; 516-299-2000; http://liu.edu/CWPost.aspx; plays football in the Pennsylvania State Athletic Conference
- Dowling College Golden Lions, Oakdale, NY 11769; 800-369-5464; www.dowling.edu; no football program
- Mercy College Mavericks, Dobbs Ferry NY 10522; 877-637-2946; www.mercy.edu; no football program
- Molloy College Lions, Rockville Centre, New York 11571; 888-466-5569; www.molloy.edu; no football program
- New York Institute of Technology Bears, Old Westbury, NY 11568; 516-686-1000; www.nyit.edu; no football program
- Queens College Knights, Flushing, NY 11367; 718-997-5000; http://www.qc.cuny.edu; no football program
- St. Thomas Aquinas College Spartans, Sparkill, NY 10976; 845-398-4100; www.stac.edu; no football program
- University of Bridgeport Purple Knights, Bridgeport, CT 06604; 800-392-3582; www.bridgeport.edu; no football program

Eastern College Athletic Conference

1311 Craigville Beach Road, Centerville, MA 02632; Telephone: 508-771-5060; Fax: 508-771-9486; Web site: http://www.ecac.org; http://www.ecacsports.com

Established in 1938 as the Central Office for Eastern Intercollegiate Athletics with 58 charter members, the Eastern College Athletic Conference has grown to become the nation's largest (and only multi-divisional) athletic conference in the United States with 304 members (as of this writing) (Division I—90 members, Division II—23 members, and Division III—191 members). Member schools of the ECAC also compete in at least one other conference (or as independent schools) and play in the ECAC postseason, when eligible. See NCAA Division I (FBS & FCS) and NCAA Division III for a complete schools list within each division.

Football Alignments (Division II)

Members of the ECAC:

- Independents School (Lake Erie College)
- Northeast-10 Conference (American International College, Assumption College, Bentley University,

Merrimack College, Pace University, Saint Anselm College, Southern Connecticut State University, Stonehill College)
- Pennsylvania State Athletic Conference (Long Island University—C.W. Post, Mercyhurst College, West Chester University)

Division II Members (23)

- Adelphi University Panthers (Northeast-10 Conference) (Garden City, NY)
- American International College Yellowjackets (Springfield, MA)
- Assumption College Greyhounds (Worcester, MA)
- Bentley University Falcons (Waltham, MA)
- C.W. Post Campus, Long Island University Pioneers (East Coast Conference) (Brookville, NY)
- Caldwell College Cougars (Central Atlantic Collegiate Conference) (Caldwell, NJ)
- Dominican College Chargers (Central Atlantic Collegiate Conference) (Orangeburg, NY)
- Dowling College Golden Lions (East Coast Conference) (Oakdale, NY)
- Lake Erie College Storm (Independent) (Painesville, OH)
- Le Moyne College Dolphins (Northeast-10 Conference) (Syracuse, NY)
- Lincoln University Lions (Independent) (Lincoln University, PA)
- Mansfield University of Pennsylvania Mountaineers (Pennsylvania State Athletic Conference) (Mansfield, PA)
- Mercyhurst College Lakers (Pennsylvania State Athletic Conference) (Erie, PA)
- Merrimack College Warriors (North Andover, MA)
- Pace University Setters (New York, NY)
- Post University Eagles (Central Atlantic Collegiate Conference) (Waterbury, CT)
- Saint Anselm College Hawks (Northeast-10 Conference) (Manchester, NH)
- Saint Michael's College Purple Knights (Northeast-10 Conference) (Colchester, VT)
- Salem International University Fighting Tigers (West Virginia Intercollegiate Athletic Conference) (Salem, WV)
- Southern Connecticut State University Owls (Northeast-10 Conference) (New Haven, CT)
- Stonehill College Skyhawks (Easton, MA)
- University of Bridgeport Purple Knights (East Coast Conference) (Bridgeport, CT)
- West Chester University Golden Rams (Pennsylvania State Athletic Conference) (West Chester, PA)

Great Lakes Football Conference

The four team of the conference will be absorbed by the Great Lakes Valley Conference in 2012.

- Kentucky Wesleyan College Panthers, Owensboro, KY 42301; 800-999-0592; www.kwc.edu
- Missouri University of Science and Technology Miners, Rolla, MO 65409; 573-341-4111; www.mst.edu;
- Saint Joseph's College Pumas, Rensselaer, IN 47978; 219-866-6000; www.saintjoe.edu;
- Urbana University Blue Knights, Urbana, OH 43078; 937-484-1400; www.urbana.edu

GREAT LAKES FOOTBALL CONFERENCE CHAMPIONS

Year	*School*
2006	Saint Joseph's College (IN)
2007	Tiffin University (OH)
2008	Missouri University of Science & Technology (MO)
2009	Saint Joseph's College (IN)
2010	Saint Joseph's College (IN)

Great Lakes Intercollegiate Athletic Conference (GLIAC)

1110 Washington Avenue, Bay City, MI 48708; Telephone: 989-894-2529; Fax: 989-894-2825; Web site: http://www.gliac.org

The Great Lakes Intercollegiate Athletic Conference was founded in June 1972 with four charter schools: Grand Valley State University, Lake Superior State University, Northwood University, and

Saginaw Valley State University. Football was dropped by the conference after the 1989 season and GLIAC schools joined with football-playing members of the Heartland Conference to form the Midwest Intercollegiate Football Conference, which began play in 1990. The MIFC then merged with the GLIAC in July 1999 and the GLIAC resumed sponsoring football that fall.

As of this writing, the following 16 schools compete in the GLIAC:

- Ashland University Eagles, Ashland, OH 44805; 419-289-4142; www.ashland.edu;
- Ferris State University Bulldogs, Big Rapids, MI 49307; 231-591-2000; www.ferris.edu
- Grand Valley State University Lakers, Allendale, MI 49401; 616-331-5000; www.gvsu.edu
- Hillsdale College Chargers, Hillsdale, MI 49242; 517-437-7341; www.hillsdale.edu
- Lake Erie College Storm, Painesville, OH 44077; 440-296-1856; www.lakeerie.edu
- Lake Superior State University Lakers, Sault Ste. Marie, MI 49783; 906-632-6841; www.lssu.edu; no football program
- Lewis University Flyers, Romeoville, IL; 815-838-0500; www.lewisu.edu; associate member — no football program
- Michigan Technical University Huskies, Houghton, MI 49931; 906-487-1885; www.mtu.edu
- Northern Michigan University Wildcats, Marquette, MI 49855; 906-227-1000; www.nmu.edu
- Northwood University Timberwolves, Midland, MI 48640; 800-622-9000; www.northwood.edu
- Old Dominion University Panthers, Columbus, Ohio 43219; 614-251-4500; www.ohiodominican.edu
- Saginaw Valley State University Cardinals, University Center, MI 48710; 989-964-4000; www.svsu.edu
- Tiffin University Dragons, Tiffin, OH 44883; 800-968-6446; www.tiffin.edu
- University of Findlay Oilers, Findlay, OH 45840; 419-422-8313; www.findlay.edu
- University of Indianapolis Greyhounds, Indianapolis, IN 46227; 317-788-3368; www.uindy.edu; associate member from the Great Lakes Valley Conference
- Wayne State University Warriors, Detroit, MI 48202; 877-978-4636; http://wayne.edu

GLIAC Champions

While playing as the Midwest Intercollegiate Football Conference.

Year	*School*
1990	Grand Valley State University (MI)
1991	Butler University (IN)
1992	Butler University (IN)
1992	Ferris State University (MI)
1992	Grand Valley State University (MI)
1992	Hillsdale College (MI)
1993	Ferris State University (MI)
1994	Ferris State University (MI)
1995	Ferris State University (MI)
1996	Ferris State University (MI)
1997	Ashland University (OH)
1997	Grand Valley State University (MI)
1998	Grand Valley State University (MI)

GLIAC Champions

Year	*School*
1999	Ferris State University (MI)
1999	Northwood University (MI)
2000	Northwood University (MI)
2000	Saginaw Valley State University (MI)
2001	Grand Valley State University (MI)
2002	Grand Valley State University (MI)
2003	Saginaw Valley State University (MI)
2004	Northwood University (MI)
2004	Michigan Technical University (MI)
2005	Grand Valley State University (MI)
2006	Grand Valley State University (MI)
2007	Grand Valley State University (MI)
2008	Grand Valley State University (MI)
2009	Grand Valley State University (MI)
2010	Grand Valley State University (MI)

GLIAC Coach of the Year

Selected by conference coaches.

Year	*Coach*	*School*
1990	Tom Beck	Grand Valley State University (MI)
1991	Bob Bartolomeo	Butler University (IN)

Year	Coach	School
1992	Keith Otterbein	Ferris State University (MI)
1993	Dr. Fred Martinelli	Ashland University (OH)
1994	Keith Otterbein	Ferris State University (MI)
1995	Jeff Pierce	Ferris State University (MI)
1996	Pat Riepma	Northwood University (MI)
1997	Gary Keller	Ashland University (OH)
1998	Pat Riepma	Northwood University (MI)
1999	Pat Riepma	Northwood University (MI)
1999	Pat Riepma	Northwood University (MI)
2000	Pat Riepma	Northwood University (MI)
2001	Brian Kelly	Grand Valley State University (MI)
2002	Dan Simrell	University of Findlay (OH)
2003	Randy Awrey	Saginaw Valley State University (MI)
2004	Bernie Anderson	Michigan Technical University (MI)
2005	Lee Owens	Ashland University (OH)
2006	Paul Winters	Wayne State University (MI)
2007	Chuck Martin	Grand Valley State University (MI)
2008	Paul Winters	Wayne State University (MI)
2009	Keith Otterbein	Hillsdale College (MI)
2010	Tom Kearly	Michigan Technical University (MI)

GLIAC Player of the Year

Selected by conference coaches.

Year	Player	School
1990	Eric Lynch	Grand Valley State University (MI)
1991	Paul Romanowski	Butler University (IN)
1992	Monty Brown	Ferris State University (MI)
1992	Scott Schulte	Hillsdale College (MI)
1993	Bill Royce	Ashland University (OH)
1994	Tyree Dye	Ferris State University (MI)
1995	Bill Love	Ferris State University (MI)
1996	Matt Hoard	Northern Michigan University
1997	Paul Spicer	Saginaw Valley State University (MI)
1998	Jeff Fox	Grand Valley State University (MI)
1999	Matt McCarthy	Ferris State University (MI)
2000	Brian Dolph	Saginaw Valley State University (MI)
2001	Curt Anes	Grand Valley State University (MI)
2002	Curt Anes	Grand Valley State University (MI)
2003	Mark Radlinski	Saginaw Valley State University (MI)
2004	Dan Mattlach	Michigan Technical University (MI)
2005	John DiGiorgio	Saginaw Valley State University (MI)
2006	Cullen Finnerty	Grand Valley State University (MI)
2007	Mark Nicolet	Hillsdale College (MI)
2008	Bill Cundiff	Ashland University (OH)
2009	Joique Bell	Wayne State University (MI)
2010	Troy Weatherhead	Hillsdale College (MI)

GLIAC Offensive Back of the Year

Selected by conference coaches.

Year	Player	School
1990	Eric Lynch	Grand Valley State University (MI)
1991	Paul Romanowski	Butler University (IN)
1992	Scott Schulte	Hillsdale College (MI)
1993	Scott Schulte	Hillsdale College (MI)
1994	Tyree Dye	Ferris State University (MI)

Year	Player	School
1995	Bill Love	Ferris State University (MI)
1996	Matt Hoard	Northern Michigan University (MI)
1997	Jeff Fox	Grand Valley State University (MI)
1997	Jeff Klopf	Saginaw Valley State University (MI)
1998	Donald Church	Ashland University (OH)
1998	Jeff Fox	Grand Valley State University (MI)
1999	Mo Harris	Ferris State University (MI)
2000	Alex Kowalski	Michigan Technical University (MI)
2001	Clarence Coleman	Ferris State University (MI)
2001	David Kircus	Grand Valley State University (MI)
2002	Robert Campbell	University of Findlay (OH)
2002	David Kircus	Grand Valley State University (MI)
2003	Matt Kohn	University of Indianapolis (IN)
2004	Lee Marana	Michigan Technical University (MI)
2005	Cullen Finnerty	Grand Valley State University (MI)
2006	Joique Bell	Wayne State University (MI)
2007	Joique Bell	Wayne State University (MI)
2008	James Berezik	Grand Valley State University (MI)
2009	Brad Iciek	Grand Valley State University (MI)
2010	Phil Milbrath	Michigan Technical University (MI)

GLIAC Defensive Back of the Year

Selected by conference coaches.

Year	Player	School
1990	Mark Maddox	Northern Michigan University (MI)
1991	Ron Greer	Ashland University (OH)
1992	Monty Brown	Ferris State University (MI)
1993	Rich Eash	Ferris State University (MI)
1994	Scott Elwer	Hillsdale College (MI)
1995	Scott Elwerhc	Hillsdale College (MI)
1996	Jovan Dewitt	Northern Michigan University (MI)
1997	Scott Duncan	Hillsdale College (MI)
1998	Ted Liette	University of Indianapolis (IN)
1999	Josh Gentry	University of Indianapolis (IN)
2000	Tim Mustapha	Hillsdale College (MI)
2001	Chris Volz	University of Indianapolis (IN)
2002	Scott Mackey	Grand Valley State University (MI)
2003	Scott Mackey	Grand Valley State University (MI)
2004	Martell Foster	Northwood University (MI)
2004	Lucius Hawkins	Grand Valley State University (MI)
2005	Devin Conwell	Ashland University (OH)
2006	Charleston Hughes	Northwood University (MI)
2007	Brandon Carr	Grand Valley State University (MI)
2008	Dante Dunn	Wayne State University (MI)
2009	John Jacobs	Saginaw Valley State University (MI)
2010	Craig Ray	University of Indianapolis (IN)

GLIAC Offensive Lineman of the Year

Selected by conference coaches.

Year	Player	School
1990	Chris Tiede	Grand Valley State University (MI)
1991	Chris Tiede	Grand Valley State University (MI)
1992	Ruben DeLuna	Butler University (IN)
1993	Larry Pearce	Ferris State University (MI)
1994	Mike Sheldon	Grand Valley State University (MI)

Year	Player	School
1995	Joe Gilbert	Saginaw Valley State University (MI)
1996	Brad Affholter	Hillsdale College (MI)
1997	Kent Kraatz	Saginaw Valley State University (MI)
1998	Tyrone Nelson	Northwood University (MI)
1999	Dennis Strey	Ferris State University (MI)
2000	Marc Dugas	Northern Michigan University (MI)
2001	Kent Cramer	Ashland University (OH)
2002	Dale Westrick	Grand Valley State University (MI)
2003	Joe Berger	Michigan Technical University (MI)
2004	Joe Berger	Michigan Technical University (MI)
2004	Todd Herremans	Saginaw Valley State University (MI)
2005	Josh Bourke	Grand Valley State University (MI)
2006	Brandon Barnes	Grand Valley State University (MI)
2007	Brandon Barnes	Grand Valley State University (MI)
2008	Billy Eisenhardt	Grand Valley State University (MI)
2009	Nick McDonald	Grand Valley State University (MI)
2010	Cameron Bradfield	Grand Valley State University (MI)

GLIAC Defensive Lineman of the Year

Selected by conference coaches.

Year	Player	School
1990	Morris Furman	Ashland University (OH)
1991	Greg Matheis	University of Indianapolis (IN)
1992	Bill Royce	Ashland University (OH)
1993	Bill Royce	Ashland University (OH)
1994	Sam Hohler	Ashland University (OH)
1995	Mike Brooks	Ferris State University (MI)
1996	Kelly Chisholm	Ferris State University (MI)
1997	Matthew "Bubba" Harris	Ashland University (OH)
1998	Lamar King	Saginaw Valley State University (MI)
1999	Dan Gibbons	Grand Valley State University (MI)
2000	Todd DeVree	Hillsdale College (MI)
2001	Neal Blank	University of Indianapolis (IN)
2002	Keyonta Marshall	Grand Valley State University (MI)
2003	Keyonta Marshall	Grand Valley State University (MI)
2004	Keyonta Marshall	Grand Valley State University (MI)
2005	Michael McFadden	Grand Valley State University (MI)
2006	Michael McFadden	Grand Valley State University (MI)
2007	Jake Visser	Ferris State University (MI)
2008	Dan Skuta	Grand Valley State University (MI)
2008	Jake Visser	Ferris State University (MI)
2009	Danny Richard	Grand Valley State University (MI)
2010	Todd Storm	Michigan Technical University (MI)

GLIAC Freshman of the Year

Selected by conference coaches.

Year	Player	School
2000	Derek Fudge	Ferris State University (MI)
2001	Harry Garland	University of Findlay (OH)
2002	Jon Horn	Northwood University (MI)
2003	Cullen Finnerty	Grand Valley State University (MI)
2004	Demonte Collins	Grand Valley State University (MI)
2005	Luke Krombach	Northwood University (MI)
2006	Joique Bell	Wayne State University (MI)
2007	Jimmy Berezik	Grand Valley State University (MI)

Year	*Player*	*School*
2008	Kevin Smith	Wayne State University (MI)
2009	Monerae Williams	University of Findlay (OH)
2010	Jamie Meder	Ashland University (OH)

Great Lakes Valley Conference (GLVC)

201 South Capitol Avenue, Pan Am Plaza, Suite 560, Indianapolis, IN 46225; Telephone: 317-237-2106; Fax: 317-237-5632; Web site: http://www.glvcsports.com

The Great Lakes Valley Conference will begin sponsoring football in 2012. As of this writing, five schools within the conference play football in other conferences. Beginning in 2012, all the football-playing schools will return and compete in the Great Lakes Valley Conference.

The GLVC currently consists of 16 schools:

- Bellarmine University Knights, Louisville, KY 40205; 502-272-8131; www.bellarmine.edu; no football program
- Drury University Panthers, Springfield, MO 65802; 417-873-7879; www.drury.edu; no football program
- Kentucky Wesleyan College Panthers, Owensboro, KY 42301; 800-999-0592; www.kwc.edu; plays football in the Great Lakes Football Conference
- Lewis University Flyers, Romeoville, IL 60446; 815-838-0500; www.lewisu.edu; no football program
- Maryville University Saints, St. Louis, MO 63141; 314-529-9300; www.maryville.edu; no football program
- Missouri University of Science and Technology Miners, Rolla, MO 65409; 573-341-4111; www.mst.edu; plays football in the Great Lakes Football Conference
- Northern Kentucky University Norse, Highland Heights, KY 41099; 859-572-5100; www.nku.edu; no football program
- Quincy University Hawks, Quincy, IL 62301; 217-222-8020; www.quincy.edu; plays football in the Mid-States Football Association (Mideast League)
- Rockhurst University Hawks, Kansas City, MO 64110; 816-501-4000; www.rockhurst.edu; no football program
- Saint Joseph's College Pumas, Rensselaer, IN 47978; 219-866-6000; http://saintjoe,edu; plays football in the Great Lakes Football Conference
- University of Illinois, Springfield, Prairie Stars, Springfield, IL 62703; 217-206-6600; www.uis.edu; no football program
- University of Indianapolis Greyhounds, Indianapolis, IN 46227; 317-788-3368; www.uindy.edu; plays football in the Great Lakes Intercollegiate Athletic Conference
- University of Missouri, St. Louis, Tritons, St. Louis, MO 63121; 314-516-5000; www.umsl.edu; no football program
- University of Southern Indiana Screaming Eagles, Evansville, IN 47712; 812-464-8600; www.usi.edu; no football program
- University of Wisconsin, Parkside, Rangers, Kenosha, WI 53141; 262-595-2345; www.uwp.edu; no football program
- William Jewell College Cardinals, Liberty, MO 64068; 816-781-7700; www.jewell.edu; before moving to the GLVC, played football in the Heart of America Athletic Conference

Great Northwest Athletic Conference (GNAC)

P.O. Box 9262, Spokane, WA 99209; 4305 East Trent Avenue., Suite 275, Spokane, WA 99202; Telephone: 509-535-5291; Fax: 509-535-5293; Web site: http://www.gnacsports.com

The Great Northwest Athletic Conference is the only NCAA division with a Canadian university as a member and was formed in 2001 when its original ten members left the Pacific West Conference.

As of this writing, the following 12 schools compete in the Great Northwest Athletic Conference:

- Central Washington University Wildcats, Ellensburg, WA 98926; 509-963-1111; www.cwu.edu
- Dixie State College of Utah Red Storm, St. George, UT 84770; 435-652-7500; www.dixie.edu; an associate football member from the Pacific West Conference

- Humboldt State University Lumberjacks, Arcata, CA 95521; 707-826-3011; www.humboldt.edu; associate football member from the California Collegiate Athletic Association
- Montana State University, Billings, Yellow Jackets, Billings, MT 59101; 406-657-2011; www.msubillings.edu; no football program
- Northwest Nazarene University Crusaders, Nampa, ID 83686; 208-467-8011; www.nnu.edu; no football program
- Saint Martin's University Saints, Lacey, WA 98503; 360-491-4700; www.stmartin.edu; no football program
- Seattle Pacific University Falcons, Seattle, WA 98119; 206-281-2000; www.spu.edu; no football program
- Simon Fraser University Clan, Burnaby, British Columbia, Canada V5A 1S6; 778-782-3111; www.sfu.ca
- University of Alaska, Anchorage, Seawolves, Anchorage, Alaska 99508; 907-786-1800; www.uaa.alaska.edu; no football program
- University of Alaska, Fairbanks, Nanooks, Fairbanks, AK 99775; 907-474-7205; www.uaf.edu; no football program
- Western Oregon University Wolves, Monmouth, OR 97361; 503-838-8000; www.wou.edu
- Western Washington University Vikings, Bellingham, WA 98225; 360-650-3000; www.wwu.edu; no football program

GNAC Champions

Year	*School*
2001	Western Washington University (WA)
2002	Central Washington University (WA)
2003	Western Washington University (WA)
2004	Central Washington University (WA)
2005	Central Washington University (WA)
2006	No Champion
2007	No Champion
2008	Central Washington University (WA)
2009	Central Washington University (WA)
2010	Central Washington University (WA)

GNAC Coach of the Year

Year	*Coach*	*School*
2001	Rob Smith	Western Washington University (WA)
2002	John Zamberlin	Central Washington University (WA)
2003	Rob Smith	Western Washington University (WA)
2004	John Zamberlin	Central Washington University (WA)
2005	John Zamberlin	Central Washington University (WA)
2006	No Selection	
2007	No Selection	
2008	Blaine Bennett	Central Washington University (WA)
2009	Blaine Bennett	Central Washington University (WA)
2010	Rob Smith	Humboldt State University (CA)

GNAC Offensive Player of the Year

Year	*Player*	*School*
2001	Scott Mitchell	Western Washington University (WA)
2002	Brian Potucek	Central Washington University (WA)
2003	Brad Satran	Western Oregon University (OR)
2004	Dustin Creager	Humboldt State University (CA)
2005	Brian Potucek	Central Washington University (WA)
2006	No Selection	
2007	No Selection	
2008	Mike Reilly	Central Washington University (WA)
2009	Johnny Spevak	Central Washington University (WA)
2010	Lyndon Rowells	Humboldt State University (CA)

GNAC Offensive Lineman of the Year

Year	*Player*	*School*
2010	Taylor Boggs	Humboldt State University (CA)

GNAC Defensive Player of the Year

Year	*Player*	*School*
2001	Jason Patterson	Central Washington University (WA)
2002	Lance Gibson	Central Washington University (WA)
2003	Levi Teasley	Central Washington University (WA)
2004	Jacob Galloway	Central Washington University (WA)
2005	Kyle Killingsworth	Humboldt State University (CA)
2005	Jon Apgar	Western Oregon University (OR)
2006	No Selection	
2007	No Selection	
2008	Matt Cox	Western Oregon University (OR)
2009	Buddy Wood	Central Washington University (WA)
2010	Adam Bighill	Central Washington University (WA)
2010	Caleb Singleton	Western Oregon University (OR)

GNAC Newcomer of the Year

Year	*Player*	*School*
2001	Anthony Dalton	Western Washington University (WA)
2002	Willie Johnson	Central Washington University (WA)
2003	Duval Seamster	Humboldt State University (CA)
2004	Christian Hodges	Humboldt State University (CA)
2005	Eliot Vinzant	Western Oregon University (OR)
2006	No Selection	
2007	No Selection	
2008	Randall Eldridge	Western Washington University (WA)
2009	Prince Hall	Central Washington University (WA)
2010	Lyndon Rowells	Humboldt State University (CA)

GNAC Freshman of the Year

Year	*Player*	*School*
2001	Dustin Creager	Humboldt State University (CA)
2002	Duncan Sherrard	Western Washington University (WA)
2002	Ron Kelly	Western Oregon University (OR)
2003	Ryan Andrews	Central Washington University (WA)
2004	Chris Robinson	Western Washington University (WA)
2005	Mike Reilly	Central Washington University (WA)
2006	No Selection	
2007	No Selection	
2008	Andrew Oney	Central Washington University (WA)
2009	Ryan Robertson	Central Washington University (WA)
2010	Stan Langlow	Central Washington University (WA)
2010	Cody Stevenson	Dixie State College of Utah (UT)

Gulf South Conference

2101 Providence Park; Suite 200, Birmingham, AL 35242; Telephone: 205-991-9880; Fax: 205-437-0505; Web site: http://www.gulfsouthconference.org

Founded in 1970 as the Mid-South Conference, the six charter schools of the Gulf South Conference were Delta State University, Florence State College (now known as the University of North Alabama), Jacksonville State University, Livingston State College (now known as the University of West Alabama), the University of Tennessee, Martin, and Troy State University. The conference adopted its current name in 1971.

As of this writing, the conference consists of the following 14 schools, three of which do not play football:

- Arkansas Technical University Wonder Boys, Russellville, AR 72801; 479-968-0389; www.atu.edu
- Christian Brothers University Buccaneers, Memphis, TN 38104; 901-321-3000; www.cbu.edu; no football program
- Delta State University Statesmen, Cleveland, MS 38733; 662-846-3000; www.deltastate.edu
- Harding University Bison, Searcy, AR 72149; 501-279-4000; www.harding.edu
- Henderson State University Reddies, Arkadelphia, AR 71999; 870-230-5000; www.hsu.edu
- Ouachita Baptist University Tigers, Arkadelphia, AR 71998; 870-245-5000; www.obu.edu
- Southern Arkansas University Muleriders, Magnolia, AR 71753; 870-235-4000; http://web.saumag.edu
- University of Alabama, Huntsville, Chargers, Huntsville, AL 35899; 256-824-1000; www.uah.edu; no football program
- University of Arkansas, Monticello Boll Weevils (Monticello, AR)
- University of North Alabama Lions, Florence, AL 35632; 800-825-5862; www.una.edu
- University of West Alabama Tigers, Livingston, AL 35470; 800-621-8044; www.uwa.edu
- University of West Florida Argonauts, Pensacola, FL 32514; 850-474-2000; www.uwf.edu; no football program
- University of West Georgia Wolves, Carrollton, GA 30118; 678-839-5000; www.westga.edu
- Valdosta State University Blazers, Valdosta, GA 31698; 229-333-5800; www.valdosta.edu

Gulf South Conference Champions

Year	*School*
1971	Troy State University (AL)
1971	University of West Alabama (AL)
1972	Northwestern Louisiana University (LA)
1973	Troy State University (AL)
1974	Jacksonville State University (AL)
1975	Nicholls State University (LA)
1976	Troy State University (AL)
1977	Jacksonville State University (AL)
1978	Jacksonville State University (AL)
1979	Mississippi College (MS)
1980	University of North Alabama (AL)
1981	Jacksonville State University (AL)
1982	Jacksonville State University (AL)
1983	University of North Alabama (AL)
1984	Troy State University (AL)
1985	University of North Alabama (AL)
1986	Troy State University (AL)
1987	Troy State University (AL)
1988	Jacksonville State University (AL)
1988	Mississippi College (MS)
1988	University of Tennessee, Martin (TN)
1989	Jacksonville State University (AL)
1990	Mississippi College (MO)
1991	Jacksonville State University (AL)
1992	Jacksonville State University (AL)
1993	University of North Alabama (AL)
1994	University of North Alabama (AL)
1995	University of North Alabama (AL)
1996	Valdosta State University (GA)
1997	Southern Arkansas University (AR)
1997	University of West Georgia (GA)
1998	Delta State University (MS)
1998	University of West Georgia (GA)
1999	Arkansas Tech University (AR)
2000	Delta State University (MS)
2000	University of West Georgia (GA)
2000	Valdosta State University (GA)
2001	Valdosta State University (GA)
2002	Valdosta State University (GA)
2003	University of North Alabama (AL)
2004	Valdosta State University (GA)
2005	University of Central Arkansas (AR)
2006	University of North Alabama (AL)
2007	Delta State University (MS)
2008	Delta State University (MS)
2009	University of North Alabama (AL)
2010	Delta State University (MS)
2010	Valdosta State University (GA)

Gulf South Conference Coach of the Year

Year	*Coach*	*School*
1971	Mickey Andrews	University of West Alabama (AL)
1972	George Doherty	Northwestern State University (LA)
1973	Tom Jones	Troy State University (AL)
1974	Jim King	University of West Alabama (AL)
1975	Jim King	University of West Alabama (AL)
1976	Charlie Bradshaw	Troy State University (AL)

Year	*Coach*	*School*
1977	Jim Fuller	Jacksonville State University (AL)
1978	Jim Fuller	Jacksonville State University (AL)
1979	John Williams	Mississippi College (MS)
1980	Wayne Grubb	University of North Alabama (AL)
1981	Jim Fuller	Jacksonville State University (AL)
1982	Jim Fuller	Jacksonville State University (AL)
1983	Wayne Grubb	University of North Alabama (AL)
1984	Chan Gailey	Troy State University (AL)
1985	Wayne Grubb	University of North Alabama (AL)
1986	Rick Rhoades	Troy State University (AL)
1987	Rick Rhoades	Troy State University (AL)
1988	Don McLeary	University of Tennessee, Martin (TN)
1989	Bill Burgess	Jacksonville State University (AL)
1990	John Williams	Mississippi College (MS)
1991	Bill Burgess	Jacksonville State University (AL)
1992	Bill Burgess	Jacksonville State University (AL)
1993	Bobby Wallace	University of North Alabama (AL)
1994	Bobby Wallace	University of North Alabama (AL)
1995	Bobby Wallace	University of North Alabama (AL)
1996	Hal Mumme	Valdosta State University (GA)
1997	Steve Roberts	Southern Arkansas University (AR)
1998	Todd Knight	Delta State University (MS)
1999	Steve Mullins	Arkansas Tech University (AR)
2000	Chris Hatcher	Valdosta State University (GA)
2001	Chris Hatcher	Valdosta State University (GA)
2002	Chris Hatcher	Valdosta State University (GA)
2003	Mark Hudspeth	University of North Alabama (AL)
2004	Steve Mullins	Arkansas Tech University (AR)
2005	Clint Conque	University of Central Arkansas (AR)
2006	Mark Hudspeth	University of North Alabama (AL)
2007	Ron Roberts	Delta State University (MS)
2008	Ron Roberts	Delta State University (MS)
2009	Terry Bowden	University of North Alabama (AL)
2009	Steve Mullins	Arkansas Tech University (AR)
2010	David Dean	Valdosta State University (GA)
2010	Ronnie Huckeba	Harding University (AR)
2010	Scott Maxfield	Henderson State University (AR)

Gulf South Conference Offensive Player of the Year

Year	*Player*	*Position*	*School*
1971	Clemit Spruiell	Quarterback	University of West Alabama (AL)
1972	Donald Johnson	Running Back	Northwestern State Louisiana (LA)
1973	David Bradberry	Quarterback	Delta State University (MS)
1974	Perry Griggs	Split End	Troy State University (AL)
1975	Roger Ralph	Split End	University of North Alabama (AL)
1976	Don Griffin	Quarterback	Southeastern Louisiana University (LA)
1977	Alvin Smalls	Quarterback	University of Tennessee, Martin (TN)
1978	Bobby Ray Green	Quarterback	Jacksonville State University (AL)
1979	Calvin Howard	Running Back	Mississippi College (MS)
1980	Willie Tullis	Quarterback	Troy State University (AL)
1981	Ed Lett	Quarterback	Jacksonville State University (AL)
1982	Ed Lett	Quarterback	Jacksonville State University (AL)
1983	Scott Butler	Quarterback	Delta State University (MS)
1984	Scott Butler	Quarterback	Delta State University (MS)
1985	Clarence Johnson	Running Back	University of North Alabama (AL)
1986	Mike Turk	Quarterback	Troy State University (AL)
1987	Mike Turk	Quarterback	Troy State University (AL)

Year	Player	Position	School
1988	Leon Reed	Quarterback	University of Tennessee, Martin (TN)
1989	David Gulledge	Quarterback	Jacksonville State University (AL)
1990	Fred McAfee	Running Back	Mississippi College (MS)
1991	Nickey Edmondson	Quarterback	Jacksonville State University (AL)
1992	Tyrone Rush	Running Back	University of North Alabama (AL)
1993	Tyrone Rush	Running Back	University of North Alabama (AL)
1994	Chris Hatcher	Quarterback	Valdosta State University (GA)
1995	Cody Gross	Quarterback	University of North Alabama (AL)
1996	Lance Funderburk	Quarterback	Valdosta State University (GA)
1997	Toby Strange	Quarterback	University of West Georgia (GA)
1998	Jeremy Clements	Quarterback	University of West Georgia (GA)
1999	Ed Duncan	Running Back	Arkansas Tech University (AR)
1999	Josh Price	Quarterback	Arkansas Tech University (AR)
2000	Dusty Bonner	Quarterback	Valdosta State University (GA)
2000	Josh Bright	Quarterback	Delta State University (MS)
2001	Dusty Bonner	Quarterback	Valdosta State University (GA)
2002	Aaron Jenkins	Running Back	Valdosta State University (GA)
2003	Cory Allred	Quarterback	University of Arkansas, Monticello (AR)
2004	Cory Allred	Quarterback	University of Arkansas, Monticello (AR)
2005	Scott Eyster	Quarterback	Delta State University (MS)
2006	Scott Eyster	Quarterback	Delta State University (MS)
2007	David Knighton	Quarterback	Harding University (AR)
2008	Scott Buisson	Quarterback	University of Arkansas, Monticello (AR)
2009	Nick Graziano	Quarterback	Arkansas Tech University (AR)
2010	Nick Hardesty	Quarterback	Henderson State University (AR)

Gulf South Conference Defensive Player of the Year

Year	Player	Position	School
1971	Greg Wright	Linebacker	Troy State University (AL)
1972	Ken Hutcherson	Linebacker	University of West Alabama (AL)
1973	Adrian Gant	Defensive End	University of West Alabama (AL)
1974	Alan Klein	Nose Guard	Southeastern Louisiana University (LA)
1975	Stanley King	Defensive Back	University of West Alabama (AL)
1976	Danny Watkins	Linebacker	University of Tennessee, Martin (TN)
1977	Rusty Rebowe	Linebacker	Nicholls State University (LA)
1978	Tim Tucker	Linebacker	Troy State University (AL)
1979	Greg Robinson	Linebacker	Jacksonville State University (AL)
1979	Ralph Ashley	Linebacker	Mississippi College (MS)
1980	Sherman Wilkinson	Defensive Back	Troy State University (AL)
1980	Willie Cameron	Nose Guard	University of West Alabama (AL)
1981	Alvin Wright	Nose Guard	Jacksonville State University (AL)
1982	Charles Martin	Defensive Tackle	University of West Alabama (AL)
1983	Leonard Jackson	Nose Guard	University of West Alabama (AL)
1984	Earl Conway	Defensive Tackle	Mississippi College (MS)
1985	Earl Conway	Defensive Tackle	Mississippi College (MS)
1986	Jessie Tuggle	Linebacker	Valdosta State University (GA)
1987	Freddie Thomas	Defensive Back	Troy State University (AL)
1988	Emanuel McNeil	Defensive Tackle	University of Tennessee, Martin (TN)
1989	Terry Fleming	Nose Guard	Mississippi College (MS)
1990	James Davis	Linebacker	University of North Alabama (AL)
1991	Roderick Magee	Linebacker	Mississippi College (MS)
1992	Antonio Edwards	Defensive End	Valdosta State University (GA)
1993	Jeff Redcross	Defensive End	University of North Alabama (AL)
1994	Ronald McKinnon	Linebacker	University of North Alabama (AL)
1995	Ronald McKinnon	Linebacker	University of North Alabama (AL)
1996	No Selection Chosen		
1997	Fred Perry	Linebacker	Southern Arkansas University (AR)

Year	Player	Position	School
1998	Antonio Speed	Linebacker	Valdosta State University (GA)
1999	Antonio Speed	Linebacker	Valdosta State University (GA)
2000	Danielle Rollins	Linebacker	University of Arkansas, Monticello (AR)
2001	Nate Coggins	Safety	University of West Georgia (GA)
2002	Dewayne Smith	Defensive End	Valdosta State University (GA)
2003	Anthony Maddox	Defensive Tackle	Delta State University (MS)
2004	Cedric Cursh	Defensive End	Arkansas Tech University (AR)
2005	Kelvin Morris	Linebacker	University of West Georgia (GA)
2006	Michael Eubanks	Linebacker	Delta State University (MS)
2007	Michael Eubanks	Linebacker	Delta State University (MS)
2008	Lardester Hicks-Green	Linebacker	Delta State University (MS)
2009	Michael Johnson	Linebacker	University of North Alabama (AL)
2010	Larry Dean	Linebacker	Valdosta State University (GA)

Gulf South Conference Freshman of the Year

Year	Player	Position	School
1980	Alvin Wright	Nose Guard	Jacksonville State University (AL)
1981	Doug Brown	Quarterback	Troy State University (AL)
1982	Anthony Henton	Nose Guard	Troy State University (AL)
1983	Bryan Watts	Punter	University of West Georgia (GA)
1984	Mike Turk	Quarterback	Troy State University (AL)
1985	Terry Fleming	Nose Guard	Mississippi College (MS)
1986	Randy Fisher	Wide Receiver	Valdosta State University (GA)
1987	Fred McAfee	Running Back	Mississippi College (MS)
1988	Ramon Allen	Running Back	Valdosta State University (GA)
1989	Ollie Thigpen	Running Back	Delta State University (MS)
1990	O.J. Patrick	Defensive Tackle	University of North Alabama (AL)
1991	Marcus Hunter	Defensive End	University of North Alabama (AL)
1992	Ronald McKinnon	Linebacker	University of North Alabama (AL)
1993	Gerald Smith	Defensive Back	University of North Alabama (AL)
1993	Marty Hammond	Wide Receiver	University of West Alabama (AL)
1994	Reginald Ruffin	Defensive End	University of North Alabama (AL)
1995	Chad Moran	Quarterback / Running Back / Wide Receiver / Punt Returner	University of Central Arkansas (AR)
1996	Tregnel Thomas	Running Back	Delta State University (MS)
1997	Kevin McCarn	Quarterback	University of Arkansas, Monticello (AR)
1998	Channing Williams	Defensive Tackle	University of West Georgia (GA)
1999	Conelius Alvin	Guard	University of West Georgia (GA)
2000	Chris Reil	Quarterback	Henderson State University (AR)
2000	Montoya Brown	Running Back	Ouachita Baptist University (AR)
2001	Michael Norvell	Wide Receiver	University of Central Arkansas (AR)
2002	DeMarcus Blount	Running Black	University of North Alabama (AL)
2003	Scott Eyster	Quarterback	Delta State University (MS)
2004	Bernard Scott	Running Back	University of Central Arkansas (AR)
2005	Nathan Brown	Quarterback	University of Central Arkansas (AR)
2006	Cedric Jones	Wide Receiver	Valdosta State University (GA)
2007	Scott Buisson	Quarterback	University of Arkansas, Monticello (AR)
2008	Offense: Chris Hart	Quarterback	Valdosta State University (GA)
2008	Offense: Mark Johnson	Running Back	Southern Arkansas University (AR)
2008	Defense: Dominique Davenport	Defensive Back	Delta State University (MS)
2009	Offense: Gerald Ford	Wide Receiver	Valdosta State University (GA)
2009	Defense: Shontral Ford	Defensive Back	University of West Alabama (AL)
2010	Offense: Brandon White	Offensive Lineman	University of West Georgia (GA)
2010	Defense: Xavier Triplett	Linebacker	Delta State University (MS)

Gulf South Conference Commissioner's Trophy

Since 1975, the Gulf South Conference has presented its Commissioner's Trophy annually to the student-athlete who best combines outstanding performance as both a player and a student. The football-playing winners of this trophy include:

Year	*Player*	*School*
1975	Mark King	Troy State University (AL)
1976	Billy Hood	Delta State University (MS)
1976	Anthony Saway	Mississippi College (MS)
1980	Stevie Johnson	Mississippi College (MS)
1981	Jimmy Price	Mississippi College (MS)
1982	Jimmy Clarke	Mississippi College (MS)
1984	Wayne Frazier	Mississippi College (MS)
1985	Scott Butler	Delta State University (MS)
1986	Earl Conway	Mississippi College (MS)
1991	James Davis	University of North Alabama (AL)
1994	Chris Hatcher	Valdosta State University (GA)
1995	Chris Hatcher	Valdosta State University (GA)
1996	Cody Gross	University of North Alabama (AL)
1997	Lance Funderburk	Valdosta State University (GA)
1999	Lee Daily	Henderson State University (AR)
2001	Paul Peletz	Arkansas Tech University (AR)
2002	Eddie Key	Southern Arkansas University (AR)
2005	Jonathan Hayes	Arkansas Tech University (AR)
2006	Cory Cangelosi	University of Central Arkansas (AR)
2007	Scott Eyster	Delta State University (MS)
2008	Michael Eubanks	Delta State University (MS)

Heartland Conference

100 North Sixth Street, Suite 406, Waco, TX 76701; Telephone: 800-287-6070, 254-714-0907; Fax: 254-662-6627; Email: conferenceoffice@heartlandsports.org; Web site: http://www.heartlandsports.org

Founded in 1999 (the newest of the NCAA Division II conferences), the Heartland Conference does not sponsor a football program, while three of its member schools play football in other conferences. As of this writing, the conference consists of the following nine schools:

- Dallas Baptist University Patriots, Dallas, TX 75211; 214-333-5360; www.dbu.edu; no football program
- Lincoln University of Missouri Blue Tigers, Jefferson City, MO 65101; 573-681-5000; www.lincolnu.edu; plays football in the Mid-America Intercollegiate Athletics Association
- Newman University Jets, Wichita, KS 67213; 316-942-4291; www.newmanu.edu; no football program
- Oklahoma Panhandle State University Aggies, Goodwell, OK 73939; 580-349-2611; www.opsu.edu; plays football in the Central States Football League
- St. Edwards University Hilltoppers, Austin, TX 78704; 512-448-8400; www.stedwards.edu; no football program
- St. Mary's University Rattlers, San Antonio, TX 78228; 210-436-3011; www.stmarytx.edu; no football program
- Texas A&M International University Dust Devils, Laredo, TX 78041; 956-326-2001; www.tamiu.edu; no football program
- University of Arkansas, Fort Smith Lions, Fort Smith, AR 72913; 479-788-7000; www.uafortsmith.edu; no football program
- University of Texas of the Permian Basin Falcons, Odessa, TX 79762; 432-552-2020; www.utpb.edu; no football program

Lone Star Conference

1221 West Campbell Road, Suite 171, Richardson, TX 75080; Telephone: 972-234-0033; Fax: 972-234-4110; Web site: http://www.lonestarconference.org

Founded in April 1931, the Lone Star Conference was started with five charter schools: East Texas State College (now known as Texas A&M University, Commerce), North Texas State College, Sam Houston State University, Southwest Texas State College (now known as Texas State University, San Marcos), and Stephen F. Austin State University.

As of this writing, the conference consists of the following 16 schools:

- Abilene Christian University Wildcats, Abilene, TX 79699; 325-674-2000; www.acu.edu
- Angelo State University Rams, San Angelo, TX 76909; 800-946-8627; www.angelo.edu
- Cameron University Aggies, Lawton, OK 73505; 580-581-2200; www.cameron.edu; no football program
- East Central University Tigers, Ada, OK 74820; 580-332-8000; www.ecok.edu
- Eastern New Mexico University Greyhounds, Portales, NM 88130; 575-562-1011; www.enmu.edu
- Midwestern State University Mustangs, Wichita Falls, TX 76308; 940-397-4000; www.mwsu.edu
- Northeastern State University RiverHawks, Tahlequah, OK 74464; 918-456-5511; www.nsuok.edu
- Southeastern Oklahoma State University Savage Storm, Durant, OK 74701; 580-745-2000; www.se.edu
- Southwestern Oklahoma State University Bulldogs, Weatherford, OK 73096; 580-772-6611; www.swosu.edu
- Tarleton State University Texans, Stephenville, TX 76402; 254-968-9000; www.tarleton.edu
- Texas A&M University, Commerce, Lions, Commerce, TX 75428; 903-886-5102; http://web.tamu-commerce.edu
- Texas A&M University, Kingsville, Javelinas, Kingsville, TX 78363; 361-593-2111; www.tamuk.edu
- Texas Woman's University Pioneers, Denton, TX 76204; 940-898-2000; www.twu.edu; no football program
- University of Central Oklahoma Bronchos, Edmond, OK 73034; 405-974-2000; www.uco.edu
- University of the Incarnate Word Cardinals, San Antonio, TX 78209; 210-829-6000; www.uiw.edu
- West Texas A&M University Buffaloes, Canyon, TX 79016; 806-651-0000; www.wtamu.edu

Lone Star Conference Football Champions

Year	*School*
1932	North Texas State University (TX)
1933	East Texas State University (TX)
1934	East Texas State University (TX)
1935	East Texas State University (TX)
1935	North Texas State University (TX)
1935	Stephen F. Austin State University (TX)
1936	North Texas State University (TX)
1937	East Texas State University (TX)
1938	East Texas State University (TX)
1939	North Texas State University (TX)
1940	North Texas State University (TX)
1941	North Texas State University (TX)
1942	East Texas State University (TX)
1946	North Texas State University (TX)
1947	North Texas State University (TX)
1948	Southwest Texas State Teachers College (TX)
1949	East Texas State University (TX)
1950	Sul Ross State University (TX)
1951	East Texas State University (TX)
1952	East Texas State University (TX)
1953	East Texas State University (TX)
1954	East Texas State University (TX)
1954	Southwest Texas State Teachers College (TX)
1955	East Texas State University (TX)
1955	Sam Houston State University (TX)
1955	Southwest Texas State Teachers College (TX)
1956	Sam Houston State University (TX)
1957	East Texas State University (TX)
1957	Lamar University (TX)
1958	East Texas State University (TX)
1959	East Texas State University (TX)
1959	Texas A&I University (TX)
1960	Texas A&I University (TX)
1961	Sam Houston State University (TX)
1962	Texas A&I University (TX)
1963	Southwest Texas State Teachers College (TX)
1964	Sam Houston State University (TX)
1965	Sul Ross State University (TX)
1966	East Texas State University (TX)
1967	Texas A&I University (TX)
1968	Texas A&I University (TX)
1969	East Texas State University (TX)

Year	School
1969	Texas A&I University (TX)
1970	Texas A&I University (TX)
1971	Howard Payne University (TX)
1971	Southwest Texas State Teachers College (TX)
1972	East Texas State University (TX)
1973	Abilene Christian University (TX)
1974	Texas A&I University (TX)
1975	Texas A&I University (TX)
1976	Texas A&I University (TX)
1977	Abilene Christian University (TX)
1977	Texas A&I University (TX)
1978	Angelo State University (TX)
1979	Texas A&I University (TX)
1980	Southwest Texas State University (TX)
1981	Southwest Texas State University (TX)
1982	Southwest Texas State University (TX)
1983	East Texas State University (TX)
1983	Southwest Texas State University (TX)
1984	Angelo State University (TX)
1985	Texas A&I University (TX)
1986	West Texas State University (TX)
1987	Angelo State University (TX)
1987	Texas A&I University (TX)
1988	Texas A&I University (TX)
1989	Texas A&I University (TX)
1990	East Texas State University (TX)
1991	Eastern New Mexico University (NM)
1992	Texas A&I University (TX)
1993	Texas A&M University, Kingsville (TX)
1994	Texas A&M University, Kingsville (TX)
1995	Texas A&M University, Kingsville (TX)
1996	Texas A&M University, Kingsville (TX)
1997	Texas A&M University, Kingsville (TX)
1998	University of Central Oklahoma (OK)
1999	University of Central Oklahoma (OK)
1999	Northeastern State University (OK)
1999	Southeastern Oklahoma State University (OK)
2000	Northeastern State University (OK)
2001	Tarleton State University (TX)
2001	Texas A&M University-Kingsville (TX)
2002	Texas A&M University-Kingsville (TX)
2003	Texas A&M University-Kingsville (TX)
2004	Texas A&M University-Kingsville (TX)
2005	West Texas A&M University (TX)
2006	West Texas A&M University (TX)
2007	West Texas A&M University (TX)
2008	Abilene Christian University (TX)
2009	Midwestern State University (TX)
2009	Tarleton State University (TX)
2009	Texas A&M University-Kingsville (TX)
2010	Abilene Christian University (TX)

Lone Star Conference Coach of the Year

Year	Coach	School
1984–2000	North: No Information	
1984–2000	South: No Information	
2001	North: Todd Whitten	Tarleton State University (TX) **Verify 2001**
2001	South: No Information	**Verify for 2001**
2002	North: Todd Whitten	Tarleton State University (TX)
2002	South: Bud Elliott	Eastern New Mexico University (NM)
2003	North: No Information	
2003	South: No Information	
2004	North: Keith Baxter	Southwestern Oklahoma State University (OK)
2004	South: Richard Cundiff	Texas A&M University, Kingsville (TX)
2005	North: Ray Richards	Southwestern Oklahoma State University (OK)
2005	South: No Information	
2006	North: Ryan Held	Southwestern Oklahoma State University (OK)
2006	South: Don Carthel	West Texas A&M University (TX)
2006	South: Chris Thomsen	Abilene Christian University (TX)
2007	North: John Horner	Northeastern State University (OK)
2007	South: Don Carthel	West Texas A&M University (TX)
2007	South: Chris Thomsen	Abilene Christian University (TX)
2008	North: Tracy Holland	University of Central Oklahoma (OK)
2008	South: Chris Thomsen	Abilene Christian University (TX)
2009	North: Guy Morriss	Texas A&M University, Commerce (TX)
2009	South: Bill Maskill	Midwestern State University (TX)
2010	North: Tim McCarty	East Central University (OK)
2010	South: Chris Thomsen	Abilene Christian University (TX)

Lone Star Conference Offensive Back of the Year

Year	*Player*	*School*
1984–2000	North: No Information	
1984–2000	South: No Information	
2001	North: Brett Manning	University of Central Oklahoma (OK)
2001	South: Steve Kelly	Tarleton State University (TX) (North or South)
2002	North: Gerome Castleberry	East Central University (OK)
2002	South: Abel Gonzales	Texas A&M University, Kingsville (TX)
2003	North: No Information	
2003	South: No Information	
2004	North: Drew Beard	Southeastern Oklahoma State University (OK)
2004	South: Pat McCoy	West Texas A&M University (TX)
2004	South: Daniel Taylor	Texas A&M University, Kingsville (TX)
2005	North: Cliff Edwards	Texas A&M University, Commerce (TX)
2005	South: Derrick Ross	Tarleton State University (TX) (North or South)
2006	North: Cliff Edwards	Texas A&M University, Commerce (TX)
2006	North: Justin Pitrucha	Southeastern Oklahoma State University (OK)
2006	South: Michael Sampson	Tarleton State University (TX) (North or South)
2007	North: Marcus Johnson	East Central University (OK)
2007	South: Bernard Scott	Abilene Christian University (TX)
2008	North: Marcus Johnson	East Central University (OK)
2008	South: Bernard Scott	Abilene Christian University (TX)
2009	North: Jason Palmer	University of Central Oklahoma (OK)
2009	South: Zack Eskridge	Midwestern State University (TX)
2009	South: Keithon Flemming	West Texas A&M University (TX)
2010	North: Baylen Laury	Southeastern Oklahoma State University (OK)
2010	North: Wes Wood	Eastern New Mexico University (NM)
2010	South: Mitchell Gale	Abilene Christian University (TX)

Lone Star Conference Offensive Lineman of the Year

Year	*Player*	*School*
1984–2000	North: No Information	
1984–2000	South: No Information	
2001	North: Micah Lomas	Northeastern State University (OK)
2001	South: Ryan Seward	Tarleton State University (TX) (North or South)
2002	North: Micah Lomas	Northeastern State University (OK)
2002	South: Walter Wigfall	Texas A&M University, Kingsville (TX)
2003	North: No Information	
2003	South: No Information	
2004	North: Sam Skidmore	Tarleton State University (TX)
2004	South: No Information	
2005	North: Ryan Graves	Texas A&M University, Commerce (TX)
2005	South: Sam Skidmore	Tarleton State University (TX) (North or South)
2006	North: Rayshaun Hollings	Southeastern Oklahoma State University (OK)
2006	South: Nathan Young	Abilene Christian University (TX)
2007	North: Austin Ellis	Southwestern Oklahoma State University (OK)
2007	North: Darron Sheppard	Texas A&M University, Commerce (TX)
2007	South: Nathan Young	Abilene Christian University (TX)
2008	North: R.J. Brisbon	Texas A&M University, Commerce (TX)
2008	North: Dustin Finn	University of Central Oklahoma (OK)
2008	South: Tony Washington	Abilene Christian University (TX)
2009	North: R.J. Brisbon	Texas A&M University, Commerce (TX)
2009	North: Luke Sapolu	University of Central Oklahoma (OK)
2009	South: Tony Washington	Abilene Christian University (TX)
2010	North: Carlos Savala	East Central University (OK)
2010	South: Amini Silatolu	Midwestern State University (TX)
2010	South: Royland Tubbs	Abilene Christian University (TX)

Lone Star Conference Receiver of the Year

Year	Player	School
1984–2000	North: No Information	
1984–2000	South: No Information	
2001	North: Dee Dee Carter	University of Central Oklahoma (OK)
2001	South: Eric Spencer	Texas A&M University, Kingsville (TX)
2002	North: Dee Dee Carter	University of Central Oklahoma (OK)
2002	South: Gary Lusk	Texas A&M University, Kingsville (TX)
2003	North: No Information	
2003	South: No Information	
2004	North: Zach Edwards	University of Central Oklahoma (OK)
2004	South: Maurice Washington	Texas A&M University, Kingsville (TX)
2005	North: Jeremie Berry	Southeastern Oklahoma State University (OK)
2005	North: Danny Howard	Southwestern Oklahoma State University (OK)
2005	South: Tonae Martin	West Texas A&M University (TX)
2006	North: Jarrett Byers	Northeastern State University (OK)
2006	South: Jerale Badon	Abilene Christian University (TX)
2007	North: JaMichael Palmer	Texas A&M University, Commerce (TX)
2007	South: Johnny Knox	Abilene Christian University (TX)
2008	North: Willie Thornton	Texas A&M University, Commerce (TX)
2008	South: Charly Martin	West Texas A&M University (TX)
2009	North: Daniel Nichols	Southeastern Oklahoma State University (OK)
2009	South: Andy Tanner	Midwestern State University (TX)
2010	North: Trey McVey	Northeastern State University (OK)
2010	South: Edmund Gates	Abilene Christian University (TX)

Lone Star Conference Defensive Back of the Year

Year	Player	School
1984–2000	North: No Information	
1984–2000	South: No Information	
2001	North: Germont Jackson	Midwestern State University (TX)
2001	South: Charles Davis	Tarleton State University (TX) (North or South)
2002	North: Brandon Young	Tarleton State University (TX) (North or South)
2002	South: Nicholas Davis	Texas A&M University, Kingsville (TX)
2003	North: No Information	
2003	South: No Information	
2004	North: Courtenay Sanders	Tarleton State University (TX) (North or South)
2004	South: Danieal Manning	Abilene Christian University (TX)
2005	North: Norman Dawson	Southeastern Oklahoma State University (OK)
2005	South: Renardrick Phillips	Tarleton State University (TX) (North or South)
2006	North: Darvin Peterson	Texas A&M University, Commerce (TX)
2006	South: Renardrick Phillips	Tarleton State University (TX) (North or South)
2007	North: Broderick Mondy	Northeastern State University (OK)
2007	South: Renardrick Phillips	Tarleton State University (TX) (North or South)
2008	North: Broderick Mondy	Northeastern State University (OK)
2008	South: Jabir Perkins	Texas A&M University, Kingsville (TX)
2009	North: Giorgio Durham	University of Central Oklahoma (OK)
2009	South: Tony Harp	Abilene Christian University (TX)
2009	South: Micah Hill	Midwestern State University (TX)
2010	North: Tillman Stevens	Eastern New Mexico University (NM)
2010	South: Tae Evans	West Texas A&M University (TX)

Lone Star Conference Linebacker of the Year

Year	Player	School
1984–2000	North: No Information	
1984–2000	South: No Information	
2001	North: Columbus Wooley	Midwestern State University (TX)

Year	Player	School
2001	South: Kiah Johnson	Texas A&M University, Kingsville (TX)
2002	North: Kwame Ferguson	East Central University (OK)
2002	South: Chaun Thompson	West Texas A&M University (TX)
2003	North: No Information	
2003	South: No Information	
2004	North: Ken Jones	Tarleton State University (TX) (North or South)
2004	North: Chris Sawyer	Southeastern Oklahoma State University (OK)
2004	South: Deandrae Fillmore	Texas A&M University, Kingsville (TX)
2004	South: James Williamson	Angelo State University (TX)
2005	North: J.D. Hearn	Texas A&M University, Commerce (TX)
2005	South: Deandrae Fillmore	Texas A&M University, Kingsville (TX)
2006	North: Will Clewis	University of Central Oklahoma (OK)
2006	South: Erick Smith	Tarleton State University (TX) (North or South)
2007	North: Will Clewis	University of Central Oklahoma (OK)
2007	South: Jared Brock	West Texas A&M University (TX)
2008	North: K.C. Asiodu	University of Central Oklahoma (OK)
2008	North: Ruzell McCoy	Southwestern Oklahoma State University (OK)
2008	South: Jared Brock	West Texas A&M University (TX)
2009	North: Cory Whitfield	Texas A&M University, Commerce (TX)
2009	South: Marcus Phillips	Tarleton State University (TX) (North or South)
2010	North: Johnny Evans	Northeastern State University (OK)
2010	South: Tressor Baptiste	Texas A&M University, Kingsville (TX)

Lone Star Conference Defensive Lineman of the Year

Year	Player	School
1984–2000	North: No Information	
1984–2000	South: No Information	
2001	North: Michael Matthew	Northeastern State University (OK)
2001	South: Mike Clay	Texas A&M University, Kingsville (TX)
2002	North: Kevin Mohr	Tarleton State University (TX) (North or South)
2002	South: Mike Clay	Texas A&M University, Kingsville (TX)
2003	North: No Information	
2003	South: No Information	
2004	North: Justin Brown	East Central University (OK)
2004	South: Clayton Farrell	Abilene Christian University (TX)
2004	South: Wilbert Martin	Texas A&M University, Kingsville (TX)
2005	North: Terrance Smith	Texas A&M University, Commerce (TX)
2005	South: Clayton Farrell	Abilene Christian University (TX)
2006	North: Brad Hill	Southeastern Oklahoma State University (OK)
2006	North: Sean McKinney	Texas A&M University, Commerce (TX)
2006	South: Tywain Myles	Tarleton State University (TX) (North or South)
2007	North: Marcus Smith	Texas A&M University, Commerce (TX)
2007	South: Brandon Swain	West Texas A&M University (TX)
2008	North: Ricky Hope	Texas A&M University, Commerce (TX)
2008	South: Aston Whiteside	Abilene Christian University (TX)
2008	South: Jimmy Saddler-McQueen	Texas A&M University, Kingsville (TX)
2008	South: Eugene Sims	West Texas A&M University (TX)
2009	North: William Green	Texas A&M University, Commerce (TX)
2009	South: Eugene Sims	West Texas A&M University (TX)
2010	North: Armonty Bryant	East Central University (OK)
2010	South: Aston Whiteside	Abilene Christian University (TX)

Lone Star Conference Freshman of the Year

Year	Player	School
1984–2000	North: No Information	
1984–2000	South: No Information	
2001	North: Jim Jenkins	Southwestern Oklahoma State University (OK)

Year	*Player*	*School*
2001	South: Kyle Masters	Tarleton State University (TX) (North or South)
2002	North: No Information	
2002	South: No Information	
2003	North: No Information	
2003	South: No Information	
2004	North: Tywain Myles	Tarleton State University (TX) (North or South)
2004	North: Drew Rigsby	Southwestern Oklahoma State University (OK)
2004	South: Daniel Polk	Midwestern State University (TX)
2005	North: Justin Pitrucha	Southeastern Oklahoma State University (OK)
2005	South: Kyle Fox	Angelo State University (TX)
2006	North: Daniel Nichols	Southeastern Oklahoma State University (OK)
2006	South: Tony Harp	Abilene Christian University (TX)
2006	South: Roderick Smith	Tarleton State University (TX) (North or South)
2007	North: Jim Evans	Northeastern State University (OK)
2007	North: Jake Olivarez	Southwestern Oklahoma State University (OK)
2007	South: Keithon Flemming	West Texas A&M University (TX)
2008	North: Luke Lundy	Southwestern Oklahoma State University (OK)
2008	South: Aston Whiteside	Abilene Christian University (TX)
2009	North: Michael Yoder	Northeastern State University (OK)
2009	South: Dakarai Pecikonis	Angelo State University (TX)
2010	North: Josh Birmingham	University of Central Oklahoma (OK)
2010	South: Daryl Cantu-Harkless	Abilene Christian University (TX)

Mid-America Intercollegiate Athletic Association (MIAA)

114 West. 11th Street, Suite 105, Kansas City, MO 64105; Telephone: 816-421-MIAA (6422); Fax: 816-421-6423; Web site: http://www.themiaa.com

Originally called the Missouri Intercollegiate Athletic Association, the MIAA was founded in 1912 with 14 charter schools: Cape Girardeau State Teachers College (now known as Southeast Missouri State University), Central College (now known as Central Methodist University), Central Wesleyan College, Culver Stockton College, Drury University, Kirksville State Teachers College (now known as Truman State University), Maryville State Teachers College (now known as Northwest Missouri State University), Missouri Valley College, Missouri Wesleyan College, Springfield State Teachers College (now know as Missouri State University), Tarkio College, Warrensburg Teachers College (now known as University of Central Missouri), Westminster College, and William Jewell College. In 1924, the conference adopted its current name.

As of this writing, the following schools belong to the MIAA:

- Emporia State University Hornets, Emporia, KS 66801; 620-341-1200; www.emporia.edu
- Fort Hays State University Tigers, Hays, KS 67601; 785-628-3478; www.fhsu.edu
- Lincoln University of Missouri Blue Tigers, Jefferson City, MO 65101; 573-681-5000; www.lincolnu.edu
- Missouri Southern State University Lions, Joplin, MO 64801; 417-625-9300; www.mssu.edu
- Missouri Western State University Griffons, St. Joseph, MO 64507; 816-271-4200; www.missouriwestern.edu
- Northwest Missouri State University Bearcats, Maryville, MO 64468; 660-562-1212; www.nwmissouri.edu
- Pittsburg State University Gorillas, Pittsburg, KS 66762; 620-231-7000; www.pittstate.edu
- Southwest Baptist University Bearcats, Bolivar, MO 65613; 417-328-5281; www.sbuniv.edu; plays football as an independent team
- Truman State University Bulldogs, Kirksville, MO 63501; 660-785-4000; www.truman.edu
- University of Central Missouri Mules, Warrensburg, MO 64093; 660-543-4111; www.ucmo.edu
- Washburn University Ichabods, Topeka, KS 66621; 785-670-1010; www.washburn.edu

MIAA Champions

Year	*School*
1924	Truman State University (MO)
1925	Northwest Missouri State University (MO)
1926	University of Central Missouri (MO)
1927	Truman State University (MO)
1928	Missouri State University (MO)
1928	Truman State University (MO)
1929	Truman State University (MO)
1930	Truman State University (MO)
1931	Northwest Missouri State University (MO)
1932	Truman State University (MO)
1933	Truman State University (MO)
1934	Truman State University (MO)
1935	Truman State University (MO)
1936	Truman State University (MO)
1937	Southeast Missouri State University (MO)
1938	Northwest Missouri State University (MO)
1939	Northwest Missouri State University (MO)
1940	Missouri State University (MO)
1941	Northwest Missouri State University (MO)
1941	University of Missouri, Rolla (MO)
1942	Northwest Missouri State University (MO)
1942	Southeast Missouri State University (MO)
1943	No Champion during World War II
1944	No Champion during World War II
1945	No Champion during World War II
1946	Southeast Missouri State University (MO)
1947	University of Missouri, Rolla (MO)
1948	Missouri State University (MO)
1948	Northwest Missouri State University (MO)
1949	University of Missouri, Rolla (MO)
1950	University of Missouri, Rolla (MO)
1951	Missouri State University (MO)
1951	Truman State University (MO)
1952	Northwest Missouri State University (MO)
1952	Truman State University (MO)
1953	Truman State University (MO)
1954	Truman State University (MO)
1956	University of Central Missouri (MO)
1957	Southeast Missouri State University (MO)
1957	University of Missouri, Rolla (MO)
1958	Southeast Missouri State University (MO)
1959	Southeast Missouri State University (MO)
1960	Truman State University (MO)
1961	Truman State University (MO)
1962	Southeast Missouri State University (MO)
1963	Missouri State University (MO)
1964	Truman State University (MO)
1965	Truman State University (MO)
1966	Missouri State University (MO)
1967	Southeast Missouri State University (MO)
1968	Southeast Missouri State University (MO)
1969	Southeast Missouri State University (MO)
1969	Truman State University (MO)
1970	Truman State University (MO)
1970	University of Central Missouri (MO)
1971	Truman State University (MO)
1972	Lincoln University of Missouri (MO)
1972	Northwest Missouri State University (MO)
1973	Southeast Missouri State University (MO)
1974	Northwest Missouri State University (MO)
1975	Southeast Missouri State University (MO)
1976	Southeast Missouri State University (MO)
1976	Truman State University (MO)
1977	Southeast Missouri State University (MO)
1977	University of Missouri, Rolla (MO)
1978	Missouri State University (MO)
1979	Northwest Missouri State University (MO)
1980	University of Missouri, Rolla (MO)
1981	Truman State University (MO)
1982	Truman State University (MO)
1983	University of Central Missouri (MO)
1983	University of Missouri, Rolla (MO)
1984	Northwest Missouri State University (MO)
1985	Truman State University (MO)
1986	University of Central Missouri (MO)
1987	Southeast Missouri State University (MO)
1987	University of Central Missouri (MO)
1988	Truman State University (MO)
1988	University of Central Missouri (MO)
1989	Pittsburg State University (KS)
1990	Pittsburg State University (KS)
1991	Pittsburg State University (KS)
1992	Pittsburg State University (KS)
1993	Missouri Southern State University (MO)
1994	Pittsburg State University (KS)
1995	Pittsburg State University (KS)
1996	Northwest Missouri State University (MO)
1996	Pittsburg State University (KS)
1997	Northwest Missouri State University (MO)
1998	Northwest Missouri State University (MO)
1999	Northwest Missouri State University (MO)
2000	Northwest Missouri State University (MO)
2001	Pittsburg State University (KS)
2002	Northwest Missouri State University (MO)
2003	Emporia State University (KS)
2003	Missouri Western State University (MO)
2003	Northwest Missouri State University (MO)
2003	Pittsburg State University (KS)
2003	University of Central Missouri (MO)
2004	Pittsburg State University (KS)
2005	Washburn University (KS)
2006	Northwest Missouri State University (MO)
2007	Northwest Missouri State University (MO)
2008	Northwest Missouri State University (MO)
2009	Northwest Missouri State University (MO)
2010	Northwest Missouri State University (MO)

MIAA Coach of the Year

Year	Coach	School
1981	Bruce Craddock	Truman State University (MO)
1982	Bruce Craddock	Truman State University (MO)
1983	Charlie Finley	University of Missouri, Rolla (MO)
1984	Vern Thomsen	Northwest Missouri State University (MO)
1985	Jack Ball	Truman State University (MO)
1986	Terry Noland	University of Central Missouri (MO)
1987	Bob Smith	Southeast Missouri State University (MO)
1988	Jack Ball	Truman State University (MO)
1989	Dennis Franchione	Pittsburg State University (KS)
1990	Chuck Broyles	Pittsburg State University (KS)
1990	Eric Holm	Truman State University (MO)
1991	Charlie Finley	University of Missouri, Rolla (MO)
1992	Chuck Broyles	Pittsburg State University (KS)
1993	Jon Lantz	Missouri Southern State University (MO)
1994	Chuck Broyles	Pittsburg State University (KS)
1995	Mel Tjeerdsma	Northwest Missouri State University (MO)
1996	Mel Tjeerdsma	Northwest Missouri State University (MO)
1997	Mel Tjeerdsma	Northwest Missouri State University (MO)
1998	Mel Tjeerdsma	Northwest Missouri State University (MO)
1999	Chuck Broyles	Pittsburg State University (KS)
1999	Tony DeMeo	Washburn University (KS)
1999	Mel Tjeerdsma	Northwest Missouri State University (MO)
2000	Jerry Partridge	Missouri Western State University (MO)
2000	Mel Tjeerdsma	Northwest Missouri State University (MO)
2001	Ray Richards	Southwest Baptist University (MO)
2002	Mel Tjeerdsma	Northwest Missouri State University (MO)
2003	Dave Wiemers	Emporia State University (KS)
2004	Chuck Broyles	Pittsburg State University (KS)
2005	Craig Schurig	Washburn University (KS)
2006	Mel Tjeerdsma	Northwest Missouri State University (MO)
2007	Mel Tjeerdsma	Northwest Missouri State University (MO)
2008	Mel Tjeerdsma	Northwest Missouri State University (MO)
2009	Mel Tjeerdsma	Northwest Missouri State University (MO)
2010	Mel Tjeerdsma	Northwest Missouri State University (MO)

MIAA Offensive Player of the Year

Year	Player	Position	School
1966	Chuck Koemer	Wide Receiver	Southeast Missouri State University (MO)
1967	Ken Brumley	Quarterback	University of Central Missouri (MO)
1968	Walt Smallwood	Running Back	Southeast Missouri State University (MO)
1969	Bruce Hoffman	Running Back	Southeast Missouri State University (MO)
1970	Steve Eckinger	Quarterback	University of Central Missouri (MO)
1971	Tom Geredine	Wide Receiver	Truman State University (MO)
1972	Walter Rhone	Running Back	University of Central Missouri (MO)
1973	Lance Brune	Quarterback	Southeast Missouri State University (MO)
1974	No Selection		
1975	Rick Wieser	Quarterback	Southeast Missouri State University (MO)
1976	Mike Wood	Kicker	Southeast Missouri State University (MO)
1977	Steve Powell	Running Back	Truman State University (MO)
1978	Mike Harris	Running Back	Truman State University (MO)
1979	Mitch Ware	Quarterback	Southeast Missouri State University (MO)
1980	Bill Vining	Quarterback	University of Central Missouri (MO)
1981	Tom Hayes	Quarterback	Truman State University (MO)
1982	Tom Hayes	Quarterback	Truman State University (MO)
1983	Tom Hayes	Quarterback	Truman State University (MO)
1984	Scott Loveland	Quarterback	University of Central Missouri (MO)

Year	*Player*	*Position*	*School*
1985	Chris Hegg	Quarterback	Truman State University (MO)
1986	Jeff Phillips	Quarterback	University of Central Missouri (MO)
1987	Jeff Phillips	Quarterback	University of Central Missouri (MO)
1988	Steve Bohlken	Quarterback / Punter	Lincoln University (MO)
1988	Elliott Eley	Running Back	University of Central Missouri (MO)
1989	Lester Baker	Running Back	Southwest Baptist University (MO)
1990	Jeff Frost	Quarterback	Truman State University (MO)
1991	Rod Smith	Wide Receiver	Missouri Southern State University (MO)
1992	Ronald Moore	Running Back	Pittsburg State University (KS)
1993	Matt Cook	Quarterback	Missouri Southern State University (MO)
1994	Steven Thompson	Quarterback	Truman State University (MO)
1995	Jarrett Anderson	Running Back	Truman State University (MO)
1996	Jarrett Anderson	Running Back	Truman State University (MO)
1997	Brian Shay	Running Back	Emporia State University (KS)
1998	Chris Greisen	Quarterback	Northwest Missouri State University (MO)
1999	Lester McCoy	Wide Receiver	Emporia State University (KS)
2000	Tony Miles	Wide Receiver / Kick Return	Northwest Missouri State University (MO)
2001	Jerris Evans	Wide Receiver / Kick Return	Missouri Western State University (MO)
2002	Josh Chapman	Quarterback	Missouri Southern State University (MO)
2003	Neal Philpot	Quarterback	Pittsburg State University (KS)
2004	Neal Philpot	Quarterback	Pittsburg State University (KS)
2005	Germaine Race	Running Back	Pittsburg State University (KS)
2006	Germaine Race	Running Back	Pittsburg State University (KS)
2007	Xavier Omon	Running Back	Northwest Missouri State University (MO)
2008	Joel Osborn	Quarterback	Northwest Missouri State University (MO)
2009	LaRon Council	Running Back	Northwest Missouri State University (MO)
2010	Eric Czerniewski	Quarterback	University of Central Missouri (MO)

MIAA Defensive Player of the Year

Year	*Player*	*Position*	*School*
1987	Jeff Wright	Nose Guard	University of Central Missouri (MO)
1988	Mark Peoples	Defensive Back	University of Central Missouri (MO)
1989	John Roderique	Linebacker	Pittsburg State University (KS)
1990	Mike Glass	Defensive Lineman	University of Central Missouri (MO)
1991	Shane Tafoya	Linebacker	Pittsburg State University (KS)
1992	Bart Woods	Defensive Lineman	University of Central Missouri (MO)
1993	Bart Woods	Defensive Lineman	University of Central Missouri (MO)
1994	Andy Sweet	Linebacker	Pittsburg State University (KS)
1995	Richard Jordan	Defensive End / Linebacker	Missouri Southern State University (MO)
1995	B.J. McGivern	Linebacker	Pittsburg State University (KS)
1996	Richard Jordan	Linebacker	Missouri Southern State University (MO)
1997	Chad Webb	Defensive Tackle	Pittsburg State University (KS)
1998	Ben Peterson	Defensive End	Pittsburg State University (KS)
1999	Colston Weatherington	Defensive End	University of Central Missouri (MO)
2000	Brian Williams	Linebacker	Northwest Missouri State University (MO)
2001	Earl Henry	Linebacker	Pittsburg State University (KS)
2002	Dontaye McCoy	Strong Safety	Emporia State University (KS)
2003	Aaron McConnell	Defensive Tackle	Pittsburg State University (KS)
2004	Adam Long	Linebacker	Northwest Missouri State University (MO)
2005	Dave Tollefson	Defensive Lineman	Northwest Missouri State University (MO)
2006	Trey Lewis	Defensive Lineman	Washburn University (KS)
2007	Jared Erspamer	Linebacker	Northwest Missouri State University (MO)
2008	Myles Burnsides	Defensive Back	Northwest Missouri State University (MO)
2009	Zach Watkins	Linebacker	Washburn University (KS)
2010	Ryan Jones	Defensive Back	Northwest Missouri State University (MO)

MIAA Special Teams Player of the Year

Year	Player	Position	School
2010	Steve Ivanisevic	Kicker	Washburn University (KS)

MIAA Freshman of the Year

Year	Player	Position	School
1993	Jarrett Anderson	Running Back	Truman State University (MO)
1994	Jason Politte	Quarterback	University of Missouri, Rolla (MO)
1995	Jarett Vito	Wide Receiver	Emporia State University (KS)
1996	Andrew Poling	Free Safety	Pittsburg State University (KS)
1997	Charles Spencer	Running Back	Missouri Western State University (MO)
1998	Joey Ballard	Running Back	Missouri Southern State University (MO)
1998	Kevin Nickerson	Wide Receiver / Kick Returner	University of Central Missouri (MO)
1998	Kasey Waterman	Quarterback	Missouri Western State University (MO)
1999	Andrew Blakley	Wide Receiver	Truman State University (MO)
2000	Tyler Schuerman	Quarterback	Washburn University (KS)
2001	Jamaica Rector	Wide Receiver / Kick Returner	Northwest Missouri State University (MO)
2002	Sam Sissom	Wide Receiver	Washburn University (KS)
2003	Trent Hearn	Running Back	Washburn University (KS)
2003	Germaine Race	Running Back	Pittsburg State University (KS)
2004	Nathan Emert	Quarterback	Missouri Southern State University (MO)
2005	Roger Allen	Offensive Lineman	Missouri Western State University (MO)
2005	Adam Hinspeter	Quarterback	Missouri Southern State University (MO)
2006	C.J. Lovett	Defensive Back / Kick Returner	Fort Hays State University (KS)
2006	Zach Watkins	Linebacker	Washburn University (KS)
2007	Drew Newhart	Quarterback	Missouri Western State University (MO)
2008	Josh Lorenson	Defensive Lineman	Northwest Missouri State University (MO)
2009	Levi Terrell	Running Back	University of Nebraska, Omaha (NE)
2010	Nate Dreiling	Linebacker	Pittsburg State University (KS)

MIAA Newcomer of the Year

Awarded from 1987 to 1992.

Year	Player	Position	School
1987	Chris Cannon	DT	Truman State University (MO)
1988	Jeremy Wilson	QB	Northwest Missouri State University (MO)
1989	Chris Brooks	RB	University of Central Missouri (MO)
1990	Ronnie West	WR/KR	Pittsburg State University (KS)
1991	Terren Adams	WR	Missouri Western State University (MO)
1992	Maurice Zander	DL	University of Central Missouri (MO)

MIAA Sportsmanship Award

Awarded from 1952 to 1962.

Year	Player	School
1952	LaVerne "Horse" Dabney	Truman State University (MO)
1953	Parker Bennett	University of Missouri, Rolla (MO)
1954	Charles Weitzel	University of Missouri, Rolla (MO)
1955	Darrell Walker	Northwest Missouri State University (MO)
1956	James Toler	Southeast Missouri State University (MO)
1957	William Varga	University of Missouri, Rolla (MO)
1958	Frank Freeman	University of Central Missouri (MO)
1959	Louis Meisenheimer	University of Missouri, Rolla (MO)
1960	Dale Mills	Truman State University (MO)
1961	Patrick O'Mealy	University of Missouri, Rolla (MO)
1962	Harry Lane	Southeast Missouri State University (MO)

Northeast-10 Conference

16 Belmont Street, South Easton, MA 02375; Fax: 508-230-9845; Web site: http://www.northeast10.org

The Northeast-10 Conference was established in 1979; started athletic play in 1980 (and had its first football game in August 2001); and was initially known as the Northeast-7 because of its seven charter members: American International College, Assumption College, Bentley University, Bryant University, Springfield College, Stonehill College, and the University of Hartford. In June 1981, the conference became known as the Northeast-8 with the addition of Saint Anselm College, and changed its name to the Northeast-10 Conference in July 1987 with the addition of Quinnipiac College and Saint Michael's College.

Although the conference would later expand to 16 teams, it retained its current name. As of this writing, nine of the 16 member schools play football in the conference:

- Adelphi University Panthers, Garden City, NY 11530; 800-233-5744; www.adelphi.edu; no football program
- American International College Yellow Jackets, Springfield, MA 01109; 800-242-3142; www.aic.edu
- Assumption College Greyhounds, Worcester, MA 01609; 508-767-7000; www.assumption.edu
- Bentley University Falcons, Waltham, MA 02452; 781-891-2000; www.bentley.edu
- Franklin Pierce University Ravens, Rindge, NH 03461; 603-899-4000; www.franklinpierce.edu; no football program
- Le Moyne College Dolphins, Syracuse, NY 13214; 315-445-4100; www.lemoyne.edu; no football program
- Merrimack College Warriors, North Andover, MA 01845; 978-837-5000; www.merrimack.edu
- Pace University Setters, Pleasantville, NY 10570; 866-722-3338; www.pace.edu
- Saint Anselm College Hawks, Manchester, NH 03102; 603-641-7000; www.anselm.edu
- Saint Michael's College Purple Knights, Colchester, VT 05439; 802-654-2000; www.smcvt.edu; no football program
- Southern Connecticut State University Owls, New Haven, CT 06515; 203-392-5200; www.southernct.edu
- Southern New Hampshire University Penmen, Manchester, NH 03106; 800-668-1249; www.snhu.edu; no football program
- Stonehill College Skyhawks, Easton, MA 02357; 508-565-1000; www.stonehill.edu
- The College of Saint Rose Golden Knights, Albany, NY 12203; 800-637-8556; www.strose.edu; no football program
- University of Massachusetts-Lowell River Hawks, Lowell, MA 01854; 978-934-4000; www.uml.edu; no football program
- University of New Haven Chargers, West Haven, CT 06516; 800-342-5864; www.newhaven.edu

Northeast-10 Conference Champions

Year	*School*
2001	C.W. Post College of Long Island University (NY)
2002	C.W. Post College of Long Island University (NY)
2003	Bentley University (MA)
2004	Bentley University (MA)
2004	C.W. Post College of Long Island University (NY)
2005	C.W. Post College of Long Island University (NY)
2006	Bryant University (RI)
2006	C.W. Post College of Long Island University (NY)
2006	Merrimack College (MA)
2006	Southern Connecticut State University (CT)
2007	Bryant University (RI)
2008	American International College (MA)
2009	Bentley University (MA)
2009	Merrimack College (MA)
2009	Southern Connecticut State University (CT)
2010	University of New Haven (CT)

Northeast-10 Conference Coach of the Year

Selected by team coaches.

Year	*Coach*	*School*
1997	Bob Ford	University of Albany (NY)
1998	Bob Ford	University of Albany (NY)
1999	Bryan Collins	C.W. Post College of Long Island University (NY)
2000	Bryan Collins	C.W. Post College of Long Island University (NY)
2001	Peter Yetten	Bentley University (MA)
2002	Bryan Collins	C.W. Post College of Long Island University (NY)
2003	Peter Yetten	Bentley University (MA)
2004	Peter Yetten	Bentley University (MA)
2005	Bryan Collins	C.W. Post College of Long Island University (NY)
2006	Jim Murphy	Merrimack College (MA)
2007	Marty Fine	Bryant University (RI)
2008	Rich Cavanaugh	Southern Connecticut State University (CT)
2008	Art Wilkins	American International College (MA)
2009	Thom Boerman	Bentley University (MA)
2010	Peter Rossomando	University of New Haven (CT)

Northeast-10 Conference Most Valuable Player of the Year

Selected by team coaches.

Year	*Player*	*School*
1997	Joe Savino	University of Albany (NY)
1998	Kavin Gailliard	American International College (MA)
1998	Rashaan Dumas	Southern Connecticut State University (CT)
1999	Mark DeBrito	Bentley University (MA)
1999	Rick Hebert	American International College (MA)
2000	William Yarocki	C.W. Post College of Long Island University (NY)
2001	Ian Smart	C.W. Post College of Long Island University (NY)
2002	Ian Smart	C.W. Post College of Long Island University (NY)
2003	Marc Eddy	Bentley University (MA)
2004	Marc Eddy	Bentley University (MA)
2005	Rob Blount	C.W. Post College of Long Island University (NY)
2006	Lorenzo Perry	Bryant University (RI)
2007	Steve Armstrong	Southern Connecticut State University (CT)
2008	Travis Poole	American International College (MA)
2009	James Suozzo	Merrimack College (MA)
2010	Bryant Johnson	Bentley University (MA)

Northeast-10 Conference Offensive Player of the Year

Selected by team coaches.

Year	*Player*	*School*
1997	Matt Rapoza	Bentley University (MA)
1998	None Selected	
1999	Kavin Gailliard	American International College (MA)
2000	Ian Smart	C.W. Post College of Long Island University (NY)
2001	Dallas Mall	Bentley University (MA)
2002	Marc Eddy	Bentley University (MA)
2003	Jeremiah Pope	C.W. Post College of Long Island University (NY)
2004	Dallas Mall	Bentley University (MA)
2005	Jim Lukowiak	Southern Connecticut State University (CT)
2006	Marlon Beckles	American International College (MA)
2007	Charlie Granatell	Bryant University (RI)
2008	John Wiechman	Southern Connecticut State University (CT)
2009	Herbert Woodard	Assumption College (MA)
2010	David Canney	Assumption College (MA)

Northeast-10 Conference Defensive Player of the Year

Selected by team coaches.

Year	*Player*	*School*
1997	Ben Nassar	Bentley University (MA)
1998	Ben Nassar	Bentley University (MA)
1999	Jimmy Festa	Merrimack College (MA)
2000	William Yarocki	C.W. Post College of Long Island University (NY)
2001	Charlie Cook	C.W. Post College of Long Island University (NY)
2002	Isiah Williams	C.W. Post College of Long Island University (NY)
2003	Joe Gangemi	C.W. Post College of Long Island University (NY)
2004	Joe Gangemi	C.W. Post College of Long Island University (NY)
2005	David Ihedigbo	American International College (MA)
2006	Chris Anzano	Pace University (NY)
2007	Paul Tetzel	Bentley University (MA)
2008	Jerome Pinckney	Southern Connecticut State University (CT)
2009	Matt Zahoruiko	Bentley University (MA)
2009	Dustin Zitzmann	Assumption College (MA)
2010	Shawn Loiseau	Merrimack College (MA)

Northeast-10 Conference Offensive Lineman of the Year

Selected by team coaches.

Year	*Player*	*School*
1997	Loren Baker	University of Albany (NY)
1998	Ray Shuster	American International College (MA)
1999	Ryan McLaughlin	American International College (MA)
2000	Angelo Troiano	C.W. Post College of Long Island University (NY)
2001	Dan Porter	American International College (MA)
2002	Jon Isopo	C.W. Post College of Long Island University (NY)
2003	Mike Schunder	Bentley University (MA)
2004	Taibika Hickson	C.W. Post College of Long Island University (NY)
2005	Steven Broecker	C.W. Post College of Long Island University (NY)
2006	Mackenzy Bernadeau	Bentley University (MA)
2007	Mackenzy Bernadeau	Bentley University (MA)
2008	Ed Peters	Southern Connecticut State University (CT)
2009	Greg Tuba	Southern Connecticut State University (CT)
2010	Matt Sidebottom	Assumption College (MA)

Northeast-10 Conference Defensive Lineman of the Year

Selected by team coaches.

Year	*Player*	*School*
1997	Steve Baptiste	American International College (MA)
1998	Robert Slattery	Merrimack College (MA)
1999	Robert Slattery	Merrimack College (MA)
2000	William Yarocki	C.W. Post College of Long Island University (NY)
2001	Charlie Cook	C.W. Post College of Long Island University (NY)
2002	Jacques Cesaire	Southern Connecticut State University (CT)
2003	Pater Lazare	C.W. Post College of Long Island University (NY)
2004	Peter Lazare	C.W. Post College of Long Island University (NY)
2005	Rashard Howard	Southern Connecticut State University (CT)
2006	Andrew Ruggiero	Bentley University (MA)
2006	Casey Larson	Saint Anselm College (NH)
2007	Scott Miller	Bentley University (MA)
2008	Jean Simeon	American International College (MA)
2009	Jashawn Williams	American International College (MA)
2010	Tony Johnson	Merrimack College (MA)

NORTHEAST-10 CONFERENCE FRESHMAN/ROOKIE OF THE YEAR

Selected by team coaches.

Year	*Player*	*School*
1997	Charles Thomas	Southern Connecticut State University (CT)
1998	Eric Williams	C.W. Post College of Long Island University (NY)
1999	Kevin Clive	Assumption College (MA)
2000	Tom Gy	American International College (MA)
2001	Marc Eddy	Bentley University (MA)
2002	Jeff Molesso	Bentley University (MA)
2003	Marlon Beckles	American International College (MA)
2004	Elfren Quiles	Merrimack College (MA)
2005	Austin Davis	Assumption College (MA)
2006	Terrence Holley	American International College (MA)
2007	Herbert Woodard	Assumption College (MA)
2007	Rob Parent	American International College (MA)
2008	Marc Wilson	Saint Anselm College (NH)
2009	Jareed Gaines	Stonehill College (MA)
2009	Ethan Sylvain	Saint Anselm College (NH)
2010	Justin Tervo	American International College (MA)

Northern Sun Intercollegiate Conference (NSIC)

161 St. Anthony Avenue, Suite 920, St. Paul, MN 55103; Telephone: 651-288-4015; Fax: 651-224-8583; Web site: http://www.northernsun.org

Originally called the Northern Teachers Athletic Conference, the Northern Sun Intercollegiate Conference was founded in 1932 with charter members Bemidji State University, Duluth State (now known as the University of Minnesota, Duluth), Mankato State University (now known as Minnesota State University, Mankato), Moorhead State University (now known as Minnesota State University, Moorhead), St. Cloud State University, and Winona State University. In 1942, the conference changed its name to the State Teacher's College Conference of Minnesota; to the Northern Intercollegiate Conference in 1962; and to its current name in 1992 with the merger of the NIC (men's conference) and the Northern Sun Conference (women's conference).

As of this writing, the following 14 schools belong to the NSIC, all of which play football within the conference:

- Augustana College Vikings, Sioux Falls, SD 57197; 605-274-0770; www.augie.edu
- Bemidji State University Beavers, Bemidji, MN 56601; 218-755-2001; www.bemidjistate.edu
- Concordia University, St. Paul, Golden Bears, Saint Paul, MN 55104; 651-641-8230; www.csp.edu
- Minnesota State University, Mankato, Mavericks, Mankato, MN 56001; 800-722-0544; www.mnsu.edu
- Minnesota State University, Moorhead, Dragons, Moorhead, MN 56563; 800-593-7246; www.mnstate.edu
- Northern State University Wolves, Aberdeen, SD 57401; 800-678-5330; www.northern.edu
- St. Cloud State University Huskies, St. Cloud, MN 56301; 320-308-0121; www.stcloudstate.edu
- Southwest Minnesota State University Mustangs, Marshall, MN 56258; 800-642-0684; www.smsu.edu
- University of Mary Marauders, Bismarck, ND 58504; 701-355-8030; www.umary.edu
- University of Minnesota, Crookston, Golden Eagles, Crookston, MN 56716; 800-862-6466; http://www1.crk.umn.edu/
- University of Minnesota, Duluth, Bulldogs, Duluth, MN 55812; 218-726-8000; www.d.umn.edu
- Upper Iowa University Peacocks, Fayette, IA 52142; 800-553-4150; www.uiu.edu
- Wayne State College Wildcats, Wayne, NE 68787; 800-228-9972; www.wsc.edu
- Winona State University Warriors, Winona, MN 55987; 507-457-5000; www.winona.edu

Northern Sun Intercollegiate Conference Champions

Year	*School*
1932	Mankato State University (MN)
1932	Minnesota State University, Moorhead (MN)
1932	St. Cloud State University (MN)
1932	University of Minnesota, Duluth (MN)
1933	St. Cloud State University (MN)
1934	University of Minnesota, Duluth (MN)
1935	Mankato State University (MN)
1935	Minnesota State University, Moorhead (MN)
1936	St. Cloud State University (MN)
1937	University of Minnesota, Duluth (MN)
1938	Mankato State University (MN)
1938	University of Minnesota, Duluth (MN)
1939	Winona State University (MN)
1940	St. Cloud State University (MN)
1941	St. Cloud State University (MN)
1942	Mankato State University (MN)
1942	St. Cloud State University (MN)
1943	No Champion during World War II
1945	No Champion during World War II
1946	Mankato State University (MN)
1946	University of Minnesota, Duluth (MN)
1947	Bemidji State University (MN)
1947	Winona State University (MN)
1948	Mankato State University (MN)
1948	St. Cloud State University (MN)
1948	University of Minnesota, Duluth (MN)
1949	Mankato State University (MN)
1950	Bemidji State University (MN)
1950	Mankato State University (MN)
1951	St. Cloud State University (MN)
1952	Minnesota State University, Moorhead (MN)
1952	Mankato State University (MN)
1952	St. Cloud State University (MN)
1953	St. Cloud State University (MN)
1954	St. Cloud State University (MN)
1955	St. Cloud State University (MN)
1956	Winona State University (MN)
1957	Bemidji State University (MN)
1957	Winona State University (MN)
1958	Mankato State University (MN)
1959	Bemidji State University (MN)
1959	Mankato State University (MN)
1959	Michigan Technological University (MI)
1960	Mankato State University (MN)
1961	Mankato State University (MN)
1962	Winona State University (MN)
1963	Michigan Technological University (MI)
1964	Winona State University (MN)
1965	Michigan Technological University (MI)
1966	Minnesota State University, Moorhead (MN)
1967	St. Cloud State University (MN)
1968	Mankato State University (MN)
1968	Winona State University (MN)
1969	Michigan Technological University (MI)
1970	Michigan Technological University (MI)
1970	St. Cloud State University (MN)
1970	University of Minnesota, Morris (MN)
1971	Minnesota State University, Moorhead (MN)
1972	Michigan Technological University (MI)
1973	Minnesota State University, Moorhead (MN)
1974	Michigan Technological University (MI)
1975	University of Minnesota, Morris (MN)
1976	University of Minnesota, Morris (MN)
1977	University of Minnesota, Morris (MN)
1978	University of Minnesota, Morris (MN)
1979	Minnesota State University, Moorhead (MN)
1979	University of Minnesota, Duluth (MN)
1980	University of Minnesota, Duluth (MN)
1981	Minnesota State University, Moorhead (MN)
1982	Minnesota State University, Moorhead (MN)
1983	Winona State University (MN)
1984	Minnesota State University, Moorhead (MN)
1984	University of Minnesota, Morris (MN)
1985	University of Minnesota, Duluth (MN)
1986	University of Minnesota, Morris (MN)
1987	University of Minnesota, Morris (MN)
1988	Minnesota State University, Moorhead (MN)
1989	Minnesota State University, Moorhead (MN)
1990	Northern State University (SD)
1990	Southwest Minnesota State University (MN)
1990	University of Minnesota, Duluth (MN)
1991	Minnesota State University, Moorhead (MN)
1992	Northern State University (SD)
1993	Winona State University (MN)
1994	Winona State University (MN)
1995	Minnesota State University, Moorhead (MN)
1995	University of Minnesota, Duluth (MN)
1996	University of Minnesota, Duluth (MN)
1997	Winona State University (MN)
1998	Winona State University (MN)
1999	Northern State University (SD)
2000	Winona State University (MN)
2001	Winona State University (MN)
2002	University of Minnesota, Duluth (MN)
2003	Concordia University, St. Paul (MN)
2003	Winona State University (MN)
2004	Winona State University (MN)
2005	Concordia University, St. Pau (MN)1

Year	School
2005	Winona State University (MN)
2006	Bemidji State University (MN)
2007	Winona State University (MN)
2008	University of Minnesota, Duluth (MN)
2009	University of Minnesota, Duluth (MN)
2010	University of Minnesota, Duluth (MN)

Northern Sun Intercollegiate Conference Coach of the Year

Year	Coach	School
1985	Jim Malosky	University of Minnesota, Duluth (MN)
1986	Dennis Miller	Northern State University (SD)
1987	Gary Buer	Southwest Minnesota State University (MN)
1988	Ross Fortier	Minnesota State University, Moorhead (MN)
1989	Kris Diaz	Bemidji State University (MN)
1990	Dennis Miller	Northern State University (SD)
1991	Ross Fortier	Minnesota State University, Moorhead (MN)
1992	Dennis Miller	Northern State University (SD)
1993	Tom Hosier	Winona State University (MN)
1994	Brent Jeffers	Southwest Minnesota State University (MN)
1994	Ralph Micheli	Minnesota State University, Moorhead (MN)
1995	Kris Diaz	Bemidji State University (MN)
1996	Jim Malosky	University of Minnesota, Duluth (MN)
1997	Tom Sawyer	Winona State University (MN)
1998	Jeff Tesch	Bemidji State University (MN)
1999	Ken Heupel	Northern State University (SD)
2000	Tom Sawyer	Winona State University (MN)
2001	Tom Sawyer	Winona State University (MN)
2002	Bob Nielson	University of Minnesota, Duluth (MN)
2003	Shannon Currier	Concordia University, St. Paul (MN)
2004	Tom Sawyer	Winona State University (MN)
2005	Mark Mauer	Concordia University, St. Paul (MN)
2006	Jeff Tesch	Bemidji State University (MN)
2007	Dan McLaughlin	Wayne State College (NE)
2008	Bob Nielson	University of Minnesota, Duluth (MN)
2009	Todd Hoffner	Minnesota State, Mankato (MN)
2010	Bob Nielson	University of Minnesota, Duluth (MN)

Northern Sun Intercollegiate Conference Offensive Player of the Year

Year	Player	Position	School
1967	Gary Bahr	Running Back	St. Cloud State University (MN)
1968	Bernie Maczuga	Running Back	Mankato State University (MN)
1969	Leo Jacobson	Running Back	University of Minnesota, Moorhead (MN)
1970	Mike Bah	Split End	University of Minnesota, Morris (MN)
1971	Larry Ras	Running Back	Michigan Technological University (MI)
1972	Mike Scally	Quarterback	Michigan Technological University (MI)
1973	George Spanish	Running Back	Minnesota State University, Moorhead (MN)
1974	Chuck Wilson	Quarterback	St. Cloud State University (MN)
1975	Dick Sagehorn	(Linebacker)	Minnesota State University, Moorhead (MN)
1976	Chuck Senkyr	Quarterback	University of Minnesota, Morris (MN)
1977	Jeff Arnold	Unknown	University of Minnesota, Morris (MN)
1977	Ed Schultz	Quarterback	Minnesota State University, Moorhead (MN)
1978	Jack Siljendahl	Split Back	University of Minnesota, Morris (MN)
1979	Al Kreb	Quarterback	University of Minnesota, Morris (MN)
1980	Amory Bodin	Running Back	University of Minnesota, Duluth (MN)
1981	Curt Strasheim	Quarterback	Southwest Minnesota State University (MN)
1982	Dennis Eastman	Quarterback	Minnesota State University, Moorhead (MN)
1983	Lief Nelson	Wide Receiver	Winona State University (MN)
1984	Dale Mehr	Quarterback	University of Minnesota, Morris (MN)
1984	Randy Sullivan	Running Back	Minnesota State University, Moorhead (MN)

Year	Player	Position	School
1985	Steve Peterson	Unknown	University of Minnesota, Duluth (MN)
1985	Troy Hendricks	Running Back	Minnesota State University, Moorhead (MN)
1986	Jim Williamson	Unknown	University of Minnesota, Morris (MN)
1987	James Ashley	Wide Receiver	Southwest Minnesota State University (MN)
1988	Terry Fergen	Quarterback	Minnesota State University, Moorhead (MN)
1989	Jason Landmark	Quarterback	Northern State University (SD)
1990	Jeff Loots	Quarterback	Southwest Minnesota State University (MN)
1991	Bob Jones	Quarterback	Minnesota State University, Moorhead (MN)
1992	Jeff Loots	Quarterback	Southwest Minnesota State University (MN)
1993	Dave Ludy	Running Back	Winona State University (MN)
1994	Dave Ludy	Running Back	Winona State University (MN)
1995	Brett Rechtenbaugh	Running Back	Northern State University (SD)
1995	Scott Schmaltz	Wide Receiver	Winona State University (MN)
1996	Matt Brandt	Running Back	Winona State University (MN)
1997	Travis Walch	Running Back	Winona State University (MN)
1998	Jake Goettl	Quarterback	Winona State University (MN)
1999	Tyrone Morgan	Running Back	Northern State University (SD)
2000	Tyrone Morgan	Running Back	Northern State University (SD)
2001	Eddie Acosta	Running Back	Bemidji State University (MN)
2002	Rick Fritz	Quarterback	University of Minnesota, Duluth (MN)
2003	James McNear	Quarterback	Concordia University, St. Paul (MN)
2004	Chris Samp	Wide Receiver	Winona State University (MN)
2005	James McNear	Quarterback	Concordia University, St. Paul (MN)
2006	Zach Molacek	Running Back	Wayne State College (NE)
2007	Dustin Long	Quarterback	Minnesota State University, Moorhead (MN)
2008	Ted Shalfke	Quarterback	University of Minnesota, Duluth (MN)
2009	Isaac Odim	Running Back	University of Minnesota, Duluth (MN)
2010	Isaac Odim	Running Back	University of Minnesota, Duluth (MN)

Northern Sun Intercollegiate Conference Defensive Player of the Year

Year	Player	Position	School
1995	Scott Graunke	Defensive Lineman	University of Minnesota, Duluth (MN)
1996	Mike Meier	Linebacker	Southwest Minnesota State University (MN)
1997	Evile Puna	Linebacker	Northern State University (SD)
1998	Jason Jacobs	Defensive Tackle	Southwest Minnesota State University (MN)
1999	Naki Angilau	Linebacker	Northern State University (SD)
2000	Jim Mages	Defensive Tackle	University of Minnesota, Crookston (MN)
2001	Kevin Westbrock	Strong Safety	University of Minnesota, Duluth (MN)
2002	Deric Sieck	Linebacker	Winona State University (MN)
2003	Deric Sieck	Linebacker	Winona State University (MN)
2004	Jim Stanek	Defensive Tackle	Winona State University (MN)
2005	John Tackmann	Strong Safety	Winona State University (MN)
2006	John Tackmann	Strong Safety	Winona State University (MN)
2007	Zach Stafford	Defensive Lineman	Bemidji State University (MN)
2008	Cale Pulczinski	Defensive Lineman	St. Cloud State University (MN)
2009	Robbie Aurich	Linebacker	University of Minnesota, Duluth (MN)
2010	Kiel Fechtelkotter	Linebacker	University of Minnesota, Duluth (MN)

Northern Sun Intercollegiate Conference Offensive Newcomer of the Year

Year	Player	Position	School
2001	Joseph Mapson	Wide Receiver	Concordia University, St. Paul (MN)
2002	James McNear	Quarterback	Concordia University, St. Paul (MN)
2003	Toby Korrodi	Quarterback	Northern State University (SD)
2004	Adrian Headen	Quarterback	Southwest Minnesota State University (MN)

Year	Player	Position	School
2005	Tyrone Ruffin	Wide Receiver	Concordia University, St. Paul (MN)
2006	Dustin Long	Quarterback	Minnesota State University, Moorhead (MN)
2007	Frederick Bruno	Wide Receiver	Wayne State College (NE)
2008	DJ Winfield	Wide Receiver	University of Minnesota, Duluth (MN)
2009	Ryan Ratekin	Quarterback	Southwest Minnesota State University (MN)
2010	Phillip Klaphake	Quarterback	St. Cloud State University (MN)

Northern Sun Intercollegiate Conference Defensive Newcomer of the Year

Year	Player	Position	School
2001	Adam Long	Unknown	Wayne State College (NE)
2002	Jason Carson	Linebacker	Northern State University (SD)
2003	Steve Espinoza	Linebacker	Northern State University (SD)
2004	Roy Kratt	Defensive Tackle	Winona State University (MN)
2005	Una Latu	Free Safety	Northern State University (SD)
2006	Brad Wolf	Defensive Tackle	Southwest Minnesota State University (MN)
2007	Darius Davis	Defensive Lineman	Wayne State College (NE)
2008	Bryan Schmid	Defensive Lineman	Minnesota State University, Mankato (MN)
2009	Junior Aumavae	Defensive Tackle	Minnesota State University, Mankato (MN)
2010	Denzell Blackmon	Defensive Back	Concordia University, St. Paul (MN)

Northern Sun Intercollegiate Conference Glen Galligan Award

Since 1948, the Glen Galligan Award has been presented to a senior who has played four years of college football; made significant contributions to his school; and maintained high academic grades. The award is named after the former football coach and athletic director at Winona State University (MN).

Year	Player	Position	School
1948	John "Otto" Klug	Running Back	Minnesota State University, Moorhead (MN)
1949	Jim Richmire	Running Back	Bemidji State University (MN)
1949	John "Otto" Klug	Running Back	Minnesota State Moorhead, Moorhead (MN)
1950	Bill Campbell	End	St. Cloud State University (MN)
1951	Jack Buckley	Running Back	Bemidji State University (MN)
1952	Manny Beckman	Quarterback	St. Cloud State University (MN)
1953	Mel Fischer	Guard	St. Cloud State University (MN)
1954	Jerry Grebin	Running Back	Winona State University (MN)
1955	Bob Kosel	Quarterback	St. Cloud State University (MN)
1956	Harold Drescher	Tackle	Bemidji State University (MN)
1957	Dave Mertes	Center	Winona State University (MN)
1958	Lowell Glynn		Mankato State University (MN)
1959	No Award Presented		
1960	Andrew Jackson	Center	St. Cloud State University (MN)
1961	Gale Sprute	Linebacker	Winona State University (MN)
1962	Roger Meyer	Offensive Tackle	Mankato State University (MN)
1963	Bruce Bausman	End	Minnesota State University, Moorhead (MN)
1964	Don Thompson	Halfback	Bemidji State University (MN)
1965	Ray Walsh	Defensive Back	Winona State University (MN)
1966	Tom Csmarich	Running Back	Michigan Technological University (MI)
1967	Jim Leitzke	Linebacker	Mankato State University (MN)
1968	Bill McNary	Defensive Tackle	Winona State University (MN)
1969	Alex Pociask	Center	Michigan Technological University (MI)
1970	Jerry LaJeunesse	Defensive Back	Michigan Technological University (MI)
1971	Larry Ras	Running Back	Michigan Technological University (MI)
1972	Tom Bergner	Quarterback	University of Minnesota, Morris (MN)
1973	Tim Mullaney	Offensive Guard	Winona State University (MN)
1974	Dan Rhude	Offensive Guard	Michigan Technological University (MI)
1975	Tom Van Wagner	Offensive Guard	Michigan Technological University (MI)

Year	*Player*	*Position*	*School*
1976	Jim Van Wagner	Running Back	Michigan Technological University (MI)
1977	Mark Williamson	Offensive Guard	University of Minnesota, Morris (MN)
1978	Keith Nord	Defensive Back	St. Cloud State University (MN)
1979	Bob Stouffer	Linebacker	Winona State University (MN)
1980	Mark Reed	Quarterback	Minnesota State University, Moorhead (MN)
1981	Dave Tuomi	Defensive Tackle	Minnesota State University, Moorhead (MN)
1982	Pat Cox	Offensive Guard	Minnesota State University, Moorhead (MN)
1982	Todd Roden	Offensive Guard	University of Minnesota, Morris (MN)
1983	Reggie Johnson	Running Back	Winona State University (MN)
1984	Dan Koster	Quarterback	Southwest Minnesota State University (MN)
1984	Mike Kraetsch	Defensive Tackle	University of Minnesota, Morris (MN)
1985	Dale Mehr	Quarterback	University of Minnesota, Morris (MN)
1986	Matt Wellumson	Defensive Tackle	Bemidji State University (MN)
1986	Mike Ross	Running Back	University of Minnesota, Morris (MN)
1987	Randy Knecht	Tight End	Northern State University (SD)
1988	Bruce Saugstad	Free Safety	Southwest Minnesota State University (MN)
1988	Mike Peterson	Quarterback	University of Minnesota, Morris (MN)
1989	Brad Shamla	Defensive End	Minnesota State Universal, Moorhead (MN)
1990	Rod Leman	Quarterback	University of Minnesota, Morris (MN)
1991	Wayne Wicka	Defensive End	Winona State University (MN)
1992	Marty Follis	Quarterback	Bemidji State University (MN)
1993	Ed May	Offensive Tackle	Northern State University (SD)
1993	Matt Juhl	Linebacker	Bemidji State University (MN)
1994	Nate Gruber	Strong Safety	Winona State University (MN)
1995	Preston Cunningham	Wide Receiver	Southwest Minnesota State University (MN)
1996	Eric Lee	Defensive End	Southwest Minnesota State University (MN)
1997	John Porisch	Offensive Lineman	Northern State University (SD)
1998	Bart Johnson	Defensive Tackle	Minnesota State Universal, Moorhead (MN)
1999	Jason Jacobs	Defensive Tackle	Southwest Minnesota State University (MN)
2000	Andrew Fleischman	Offensive Guard	Concordia University, St. Paul (MN)
2001	Steven Brandt	Cornerback	University of Minnesota, Crookston (MN)
2002	Bruce Carpenter	Quarterback	Winona State University (MN)
2003	Tim Battaglia	Wide Receiver	University of Minnesota, Duluth (MN)
2004	Blaine Thomas	Offensive Tackle	Bemidji State University (MN)
2005	Nathan Sannes	Quarterback	Bemidji State University (MN)
2006	John Tackmann	Linebacker	Winona State University (MN)
2007	Tyler Fischer	Linebacker	Southwest Minnesota State University (MN)
2008	Tyler Reed	Safety	Southwest Minnesota State University (MN)
2009	Marcus Greatens	Offensive Tackle	Winona State University (MN)
2009	Silas Fluellen	Quarterback	Wayne State University (NE)
2010	Dan Schoen	Offensive Lineman	Augustana College (SD)

Pacific West Conference

(Commissioner): P.O. Box 23124, Honolulu, HI 96823; Telephone: 808-285-5537; Fax: 808-922-4225; Email: senatorbobhogue@yahoo.com; (Assistant Commissioner, Media Relations Tom Di Camillo): 5235 East Silverbell Road, Queen Creek, AZ 85143; Telephone: 480-983-6605; Fax: 480-983-6605; Email: pacificwestconference@msn.com; Web site: http://www.pacificwestsports.org

The Pacific West Conference (also known as the PacWest and the largest geographic conference in Division II) was formed in 1992 when the Great Northwest Conference (a men's conference) merged with the Continental Divide Conference (a women's conference). At one time, it had 16 member schools, but has now settled on a total of nine. Although the conference does not support football, one of its teams (Dixie State College) plays football in the Great Northwest Athletic Conference.

- Academy of Art University Urban Knights, San Francisco, CA 94105; 415-274-2200; www.academy art.edu; no football program

- Brigham Young University, Hawaii, Seasiders, Laie, HI 96762; 808-675-3211; www.byuh.edu; no football program
- Chaminade University of Honolulu Silverswords, Honolulu, HI 96816; 808-735-4711; www.chaminade.edu; no football program
- Dixie State College of Utah Red Storm, St. George, UT 84770; 435-652-7500; www.dixie.edu; plays football in the Great Northwest Athletic Conference
- Dominican University of California Penguins, San Rafael, CA 94901; 415-457-4440; www.dominican.edu; no football program
- Grand Canyon University Antelopes, Phoenix, AZ 85017; 602-639-7500; www.gcu.edu; no football program
- Hawaii Pacific University Sea Warriors, Honolulu, HI 96813; 808-544-0200; www.hpu.edu; no football program
- Notre Dame de Namur University Argonauts, Belmont, CA 94002; 650-508-3500; www.ndnu.edu; no football program
- University of Hawaii-Hilo Vulcans, Hilo, HI 96720; 808-974-7414; http://hilo.hawaii.edu; no football program

Peach Belt Conference

503 Blackburn Drive, Martinez, GA 30907; Telephone: 706-860-8499; Fax: 706-650-8113; Web site: http://www.peachbelt.com

The Peach Belt Conference was founded in December 1989 (and began athletic play in 1990) with seven charter members: Armstrong Atlantic State University, Columbus State University, Francis Marion University, Georgia College & State University, Lander University, University of South Carolina, Aiken, and University of South Carolina, Upstate. Initially called the Peach Belt Athletic Conference, it took its present name in May 2000.

While the conference does not support football, one of its schools (University of North Carolina, Pembroke), plays football as an independent team. The 13-member Peach Belt Conference includes:

- Armstrong Atlantic State University Pirates, Savannah, GA 31419; 912-344-2576; www.armstrong.edu; no football program
- Augusta State University Jaguars, Augusta, GA 30904; 706-737-1405; www.aug.edu; no football program
- Clayton State University Lakers, Morrow, GA 30260; 678-466-4000; www.clayton.edu; no football program
- Columbus State University Cougars, Columbus, GA 31907; 706-507-8800; www.columbusstate.edu; no football program
- Flagler College Saints, St. Augustine, FL 32084; 904-829-6481; www.flagler.edu; no football program
- Francis Marion University Patriots, Florence, SC 29502; 800-368-7551; www.fmarion.edu; no football program
- Georgia College and State University Bobcats, Milledgeville, GA 31061; 478-445-5004; www.gcsu.edu; no football program
- Georgia Southwestern State University Hurricanes, Americus, GA 31709; 877-871-4594; http://gsw.edu/main/; no football program
- Lander University Bearcats, Greenwood, SC 29649; 864-388-8000; www.lander.edu; no football program
- North Georgia College & State University Saints, Dahlonega, GA; 30597; 706-864-1400; www.northgeorgia.edu; no football program
- University of Montevallo Falcons, Montevallo, AL 35115; 205-665-6000; www.montevallo.edu; no football program
- University of North Carolina, Pembroke, Braves, Pembroke, NC 28372; 910-521-6000; www.uncp.edu; plays football as an independent team
- University of South Carolina, Aiken, Pacers, Aiken, SC 29801; 803-648-6851; http://web.usca.edu/; no football program

Pennsylvania State Athletic Conference (PSAC)

206 Annex Building, Lock Haven, PA 17745, Telephone: 570-484-2512; Web site: http://www.psac-sports.org

Founded in 1951, the Pennsylvania State Athletic Conference began offering women's sports in 1977 and became an NCAA Division II Conference in 1980. Its charter schools in 1951 included Bloomsburg University of Pennsylvania, California University of Pennsylvania, Cheney University, Clarion University, East Stroudsburg University, Edinboro University, Indiana University of Pennsylvania, Kutztown University, Lock Haven University, Mansfield University, Millersville University, Shippensburg University, Slippery Rock University, and West Chester University.

The PSAC is the largest one-state conference in the NCAA (only associate member C.W. Post is not located in the state); the largest Division II conference; and the NCAA's largest football conference. As of this writing, the PSAC consists of 16 full-time members and one associate member (C.W. Post). All of its schools except Mansfield University play conference football.

- Bloomsburg University of Pennsylvania Huskies, Bloomsburg, PA 17815; 570-389-4000; www.bloomu.edu
- C.W. Post Campus at Long Island University Pioneers, Brookville, NY 11548; 516-299-2000; http://liu.edu/CWPost.aspx; associate member for football from the East Coast Conference
- California University of Pennsylvania Vulcans, California, PA 15419; 724-938-4000; www.calu.edu
- Cheyney University Wolves, Cheyney, PA 19319; 610-399-2275; www.cheyney.edu
- Clarion University Golden Eagles, Clarion, PA 16214; 814-393-2000; www.clarion.edu
- East Stroudsburg University Warriors, East Stroudsburg, PA 18301; 570-422-3211; www4.esu.edu
- Edinboro University Fighting Scots, Edinboro, PA 16444; 814-732-2000; www.edinboro.edu
- Gannon University Golden Knights, Erie, PA 16541; 814-871-7000; www.gannon.edu
- Indiana University of Pennsylvania Crimson Hawks, Indiana, PA 15705; 724-357-2100; www.iup.edu
- Kutztown University Golden Bears, Kutztown, PA 19530; 610-683-4000; www.kutztown.edu
- Lock Haven University of Pennsylvania Bald Eagles, Lock Haven, PA 17745; 570-484-2011; www.lhup.edu
- Mansfield University Mountaineers, Mansfield, PA 16933; 570-662-4000; http://mansfield.edu; plays football in the Collegiate Sprint Football League
- Mercyhurst College Lakers, Erie, PA 16546; 814-824-2000; www.mercyhurst.edu
- Millersville University Marauders, Millersville, PA 17551; 717-872-3011; www.millersville.edu
- Shippensburg University Raiders, Shippensburg, PA 17257; 717-477-7447; www.ship.edu
- Slippery Rock University The Rock, Slippery Rock, PA 16057; 724-738-9000; www.sru.edu
- West Chester University Golden Rams, West Chester, PA 19383; 610-436-1000; www.wcupa.edu

Pennsylvania State Athletic Conference Champions

As voted on by sports writers.

Year	*School*
1934	Indiana University of Pennsylvania (PA)
1935	Shippensburg University (PA)
1936	Lock Haven University (PA)
1937	Lock Haven University (PA)
1938	Mansfield College (PA)
1939	Slippery Rock University (PA)
1940	Indiana University of Pennsylvania (PA)
1940	Millersville University (PA)
1941	Millersville University (PA)
1942	East Stroudsburg University (PA)
1943	No Selection during World War II
1944	No Selection during World War II
1945	No Selection during World War II
1946	California University of Pennsylvania (PA)
1947	Mansfield College (PA)
1948	Bloomsburg University of Pennsylvania (PA)
1949	Bloomsburg University of Pennsylvania (PA)

Pennsylvania State Athletic Conference Champions

As determined by the Saylor Points System.

Year	School
1950	West Chester University (PA)
1951	Bloomsburg University of Pennsylvania (PA)
1952	West Chester University (PA)
1953	West Chester University (PA)
1954	Bloomsburg University of Pennsylvania (PA)
1954	East Stroudsburg University (PA)
1954	West Chester University (PA)
1955	Bloomsburg University of Pennsylvania (PA)
1956	West Chester University (PA)
1957	Lock Haven University (PA)
1957	Shippensburg University (PA)
1958	California University of Pennsylvania (PA)
1959	West Chester University (PA)

Pennsylvania State Athletic Conference Champions

As determined by a championship game between the winners of each division (East and West).

Year	Winning School
1960	West Chester University (PA)
1961	West Chester University (PA)
1962	Slippery Rock University (PA)
1963	West Chester University (PA)
1964	East Stroudsburg University (PA)
1965	East Stroudsburg University (PA)
1966	Clarion University (PA)
1967	West Chester University (PA)
1968	California University of Pennsylvania (PA)
1969	West Chester University (PA)
1970	Edinboro University (PA)
1971	West Chester University (PA)
1972	Slippery Rock University (PA)
1973	Slippery Rock University (PA)
1974	Slippery Rock University (PA)
1975	East Stroudsburg University (PA)
1976	East Stroudsburg University (PA)
1977	Clarion University (PA)
1978	East Stroudsburg University (PA)
1979	Lock Haven University (PA)
1980	Clarion University (PA)
1981	Shippensburg University (PA)
1982	East Stroudsburg University (PA)
1983	Clarion University (PA)
1984	California University of Pennsylvania (PA)
1985	Bloomsburg University of Pennsylvania (PA)
1986	Indiana University of Pennsylvania (PA)
1987	Indiana University of Pennsylvania (PA)

Pennsylvania State Athletic Conference Champions

As determined by the winner of each division (East and West).

Year	School
1988	East: Millersville University (PA)
1988	West: Shippensburg University (PA)
1989	East: West Chester University (PA)
1989	West: Edinboro University (PA)
1990	East: Millersville University (PA)
1990	West: Indiana University of Pennsylvania (PA)
1991	East: East Stroudsburg University (PA)
1991	West: Indiana University of Pennsylvania (PA)
1992	East: West Chester University (PA)
1992	West: Indiana University of Pennsylvania (PA)
1993	East: Millersville University (PA)
1993	West: Indiana University of Pennsylvania (PA)
1994	East: Bloomsburg University of Pennsylvania (PA)
1994	East: West Chester University (PA)
1994	West: Indiana University of Pennsylvania (PA)
1995	East: Bloomsburg University of Pennsylvania (PA)
1995	East: Millersville University (PA)
1995	West: Edinboro University (PA)
1996	East: Bloomsburg University of Pennsylvania (PA)
1996	West: Clarion University (PA)
1996	West: Indiana University of Pennsylvania (PA)
1997	East: Bloomsburg University of Pennsylvania (PA)
1997	West: Slippery Rock University (PA)
1998	East: Millersville College (PA)
1998	West: Slippery Rock University (PA)
1999	East: West Chester University (PA)

Year	School
1999	West: Slippery Rock University (PA)
2000	East: Bloomsburg University of Pennsylvania (PA)
2000	West: Clarion University (PA)
2000	West: Indiana University of Pennsylvania (PA)
2000	West: Slippery Rock University (PA)
2001	East: Bloomsburg University of Pennsylvania (PA)
2001	West: Indiana University of Pennsylvania (PA)
2002	East: Bloomsburg University of Pennsylvania (PA)
2002	East: East Stroudsburg University (PA)
2002	West: Indiana University of Pennsylvania (PA)
2003	East: Bloomsburg University of Pennsylvania (PA)
2003	East: East Stroudsburg University (PA)
2003	West: Edinboro University (PA)
2003	West: Indiana University of Pennsylvania (PA)
2004	East: West Chester University (PA)
2004	West: Edinboro University (PA)
2004	West: Shippensburg University (PA)
2004	West: Indiana University of Pennsylvania (PA)
2005	East: Bloomsburg University of Pennsylvania (PA)
2005	West: California University of Pennsylvania (PA)
2005	West: Edinboro University (PA)
2006	East: Bloomsburg University of Pennsylvania (PA)
2006	West: Indiana University of Pennsylvania (PA)
2007	East: West Chester University (PA)
2007	West: California University of Pennsylvania (PA)

In 2008, the Pennsylvania State Athletic Conference Champion was again determined by a championship game between the winners of each division (East and West)

Year	School
2008	California University of Pennsylvania (PA)
2009	Shippensburg University (PA)
2010	Mercyhurst College (PA)

Pennsylvania State Athletic Conference Coach of the Year

Year	Coach	School
1985	East: George Landis	Bloomsburg University of Pennsylvania (PA)
1985	West: George Landis	Bloomsburg University of Pennsylvania (PA)
1986	East: Danny Hale	West Chester University (PA)
1986	West: Frank Cignetti	Indiana University of Pennsylvania (PA)
1987	East: Danny Hale	West Chester University (PA)
1987	West: Frank Cignetti	Indiana University of Pennsylvania (PA)
1988	East: Gene Carpenter	Millersville University (PA)
1988	West: Joe Bottiglieri	Shippensburg University (PA)
1989	East: Rick Daniels	West Chester University (PA)
1989	West: Tom Hollman	Edinboro University (PA)
1990	East: Tom Elsasser	Mansfield University (PA)
1990	West: Frank Cignetti	Indiana University of Pennsylvania (PA)
1991	East: Barry Fetterman	Kutztown University (PA)
1991	West: Rocky Rees	Shippensburg University (PA)
1992	East: Rick Daniels	West Chester University (PA)
1992	West: Gene Sobolewski	Clarion University (PA)
1993	East: Chris Roulhac	Cheyney University (PA)
1993	West: Frank Cignetti	Indiana University of Pennsylvania (PA)
1994	East: Danny Hale	Bloomsburg University of Pennsylvania (PA)
1994	West: Frank Cignetti	Indiana University of Pennsylvania (PA)
1995	East: Danny Hale	Bloomsburg University of Pennsylvania (PA)
1995	West: Tom Hollman	Edinboro University (PA)
1996	East: Danny Hale	Bloomsburg University of Pennsylvania (PA)
1996	West: Malen Luke	Clarion University (PA)
1997	East: Danny Hale	Bloomsburg University of Pennsylvania (PA)
1997	West: George Mihalik	Slippery Rock University (PA)
1998	East: Rick Daniels	West Chester University (PA)

Year	Coach	School
1998	West: George Mihalik	Slippery Rock University (PA)
1999	East: Rich Daniels	West Chester University (PA)
1999	West: George Mihalik	Slippery Rock University (PA)
2000	East: Danny Hale	Bloomsburg University of Pennsylvania (PA)
2000	West: Malen Luke	Clarion University (PA)
2001	East: Danny Hale	Bloomsburg University of Pennsylvania (PA)
2001	West: Rocky Rees	Shippensburg University (PA)
2002	East: Denny Douds	East Stroudsburg University (PA)
2002	West: Mark Luther	Lock Haven University (PA)
2003	East: Chris Woods	Mansfield University (PA)
2003	West: Lou Tepper	Edinboro University (PA)
2004	East: Bill Zwaan	West Chester University (PA)
2004	West: Rocky Rees	Shippensburg University (PA)
2005	East: Danny Hale	Bloomsburg University of Pennsylvania (PA)
2005	West: Lou Tepper	Edinboro University (PA)
2006	East: Danny Hale	Bloomsburg University of Pennsylvania (PA)
2006	West: Lou Tepper	Indiana University of Pennsylvania (PA)
2007	East: Bill Zwaan	West Chester University (PA)
2007	West: John Luckhardt	California University of Pennsylvania (PA)
2008	East: Bill Zwaan	West Chester University (PA)
2008	West: Marty Schaetzle	Mercyhurst College (PA)
2009	East: Rocky Rees	Shippensburg University (PA)
2009	West: Jay Foster	Clarion University (PA)
2010	East: Raymond Monica	Kutztown University (PA)
2010	West: Marty Schaetzle	Mercyhurst College (PA)

Pennsylvania State Athletic Conference Player of the Year

Year	Player	School
1985	East: Paul Magistro	Kutztown University (PA)
1985	West: Rich Ingold	Indiana University of Pennsylvania (PA)
1986	East: Al Niemela	West Chester University (PA)
1986	West: Scott Dodds	Edinboro University (PA)
1987	East: Al Niemela	West Chester University (PA)
1987	West: Doug Emminger	Clarion University (PA)
1988	East: Bill Hess	West Chester University (PA)
1988	West: Greg Paterra	Slippery Rock University (PA)
1989	East: Desi Washington	Millersville University (PA)
1989	West: Elbert Cole	Edinboro University (PA)
1990	East: Andy Breault	Kutztown University (PA)
1990	East: Stef Kern	Bloomsburg University of Pennsylvania (PA)
1990	West: Ernest Priester	Edinboro University (PA)
1990	West: Sam Mannery	California University of Pennsylvania (PA)
1991	East: Andy Breault	Kutztown University (PA)
1991	West: Michael Mann	Indiana University of Pennsylvania (PA)
1992	East: Dave MacDonald	West Chester University (PA)
1992	West: Larry Jackson	Edinboro University (PA)
1993	East: Keith Higdon	Cheyney University (PA)
1993	West: Michael Mann	Indiana University of Pennsylvania (PA)
1994	East: Dave MacDonald	West Chester University (PA)
1994	West: Larry Jackson	Edinboro University (PA)
1995	East: John Mobley	Kutztown University (PA)
1995	West: Pat Schuster	Edinboro University (PA)

Pennsylvania State Athletic Conference Offensive Player of the Year

Year	*Player*	*School*
1996	East: Irv Sigler	Bloomsburg University of Pennsylvania (PA)
1996	West: Steve Witte	Clarion University (PA)
1997	East: Irv Sigler	Bloomsburg University of Pennsylvania (PA)
1997	West: Randy McKavish	Slippery Rock University (PA)
1998	East: Mike McFetridge	Millersville University (PA)
1998	West: Randy McKavish	Slippery Rock University (PA)
1999	East: Kevin Ingram	West Chester University (PA)
1999	West: Chris Gickling	Shippensburg University (PA)
2000	East: Mike DeMarteleire	Kutztown University (PA)
2000	West: Randy McKavish	Slippery Rock University (PA)
2001	East: Marques Glaze	Bloomsburg University of Pennsylvania (PA)
2001	West: Wesley Cates	California University of Pennsylvania (PA)
2002	East: Mike Eckmeyer	West Chester University (PA)
2002	West: Brian Everman	Indiana University of Pennsylvania (PA)
2003	East: Jim Terwilliger	East Stroudsburg University (PA)
2003	West: John Kuhn	Shippensburg University (PA)
2004	East: Jim Terwilliger	East Stroudsburg University (PA)
2004	West: Antoine Bagwell	California University of Pennsylvania (PA)
2005	East: Jamar Brittingham	Bloomsburg University of Pennsylvania (PA)
2005	West: Antoine Bagwell	California University of Pennsylvania (PA)
2006	East: Jim Terwilliger	East Stroudsburg University (PA)
2006	West: Chris Morgan	Indiana University of Pennsylvania (PA)
2007	East: Jamar Brittingham	Bloomsburg University of Pennsylvania (PA)
2007	West: Trevor Harris	Edinboro University (PA)
2008	East: Mike Washington	West Chester University (PA)
2008	West: Trevor Harris	Edinboro University (PA)
2009	East: Mike Harris	Shippensburg University (PA)
2009	West: Alfonso Hoggard	Clarion University (PA)
2010	East: Kevin Morton	Kutztown University (PA)
2010	West: Trevor Kennedy	Mercyhurst College (PA)

Pennsylvania State Athletic Conference Defensive Player of the Year

Year	*Player*	*School*
1996	East: Ben Tonon	West Chester University (PA)
1996	West: Mike Sims	Edinboro University (PA)
1997	East: Ben Tonon	West Chester University (PA)
1997	West: Brian Decker	Edinboro University (PA)
1998	East: Kevin Nagle	East Stroudsburg University (PA)
1998	West: Brian Polk	Slippery Rock University (PA)
1999	East: Terrence Miles	Kutztown University (PA)
1999	West: Mike Borisenko	Indiana University of Pennsylvania (PA)
2000	East: Kevin Nagle	East Stroudsburg University (PA)
2000	West: Mike Borisenko	Indiana University of Pennsylvania (PA)
2001	East: Pete Mendez	Kutztown University (PA)
2001	West: Joey Flora	Indiana University of Pennsylvania (PA)
2002	East: Dan Holland	Mansfield University (PA)
2002	West: Troy Bowers	Clarion University (PA)
2003	East: Dan Holland	Mansfield University (PA)
2003	West: Troy Bowers	Clarion University (PA)
2004	East: Joe Hollister	Millersville University (PA)
2004	West: Seth Fragale	Edinboro University (PA)
2005	East: Michael Baldwin	Kutztown University (PA)
2005	West: Chris Amico	Edinboro University (PA)

Year	Player	School
2006	East: Lateef Ferguson	West Chester University (PA)
2006	West: Ben Stroup	Edinboro University (PA)
2007	East: Lateef Ferguson	West Chester University (PA)
2007	West: Gary Butler	California University of Pennsylvania (PA)
2008	East: Mike Dell	West Chester University (PA)
2008	West: Terrence Jackson	Indiana University of Pennsylvania (PA)
2009	East: Anthony Smith	Bloomsburg University of Pennsylvania (PA)
2009	West: Willie Walker	California University of Pennsylvania (PA)
2010	East: Mike Varanavage	Bloomsburg University of Pennsylvania (PA)
2010	West: Bryan Boyce	Mercyhyrst College (PA)

Pennsylvania State Athletic Conference Rookie of the Year

Year	Player	School
1985	West: Gene Sobolewski	Clarion University (PA)
1986	East: Craig Jobes	Mansfield University (PA)
1986	West: Greg Paterra	Slippery Rock University (PA)
1986	West: Paul Palamara	Indiana University of Pennsylvania (PA)
1987	East: James Williams	Cheyney University (PA)
1987	West: Sam Mannery	California University of Pennsylvania (PA)
1988	East: Mark Steinmeyer	Kutztown University (PA)
1988	West: Andrew Hill	Indiana University of Pennsylvania (PA)
1989	East: Dean Stewart	Mansfield University (PA)
1989	West: Aaron Spears	Clarion University (PA)
1990	East: Scott Frick	Mansfield University (PA)
1990	West: Mario Houston	Edinboro University (PA)
1991	East: Marc DeBellis	Millersville University (PA)
1991	West: Jody Dickerson	Edinboro University (PA)
1992	East: Jarmin Culbreath	West Chester University (PA)
1992	West: Bob McLaughlin	Lock Haven University (PA)
1993	East: Nick Hanych	Kutztown University (PA)
1993	East: Scott Mack	Millersville University (PA)
1993	East: Brian Woodworth	Mansfield University (PA)
1993	West: Eric Carter	California University of Pennsylvania (PA)
1993	West: Harold Brister	Indiana University of Pennsylvania (PA)
1994	East: Kevin Mobley	Kutztown University (PA)
1994	West: Mike Carver	Shippensburg University (PA)
1995	East: Kevin Wimberly	Kutztown University (PA)
1995	West: Gerald Thompson	Edinboro University (PA)
1996	East: Mike Mitros	West Chester University (PA)
1996	West: Tyson Cook	Edinboro University (PA)
1997	East: Drew Folmar	Millersville University (PA)
1997	West: Randy McKavish	Slippery Rock University (PA)
1998	East: Mike DeMarteleire	Kutztown University (PA)
1998	West: D.J. Flick	Slippery Rock University (PA)
1999	East: Pete Mendez	Kutztown University (PA)
1999	West: Tony Johnson	Shippensburg University (PA)
2000	East: Dan Holland	Mansfield University (PA)
2000	West: Marcus Burkley	Lock Haven University (PA)
2001	East: Bob Findora	West Chester University (PA)
2001	West: Maurice Walker	Lock Haven University (PA)
2002	East: Stephen Gammage	Kutztown University (PA)
2002	West: Brent Grimes	Shippensburg University (PA)
2003	East: Earnest McNeal	Mansfield University (PA)
2003	West: Raji El-Amin	Edinboro University (PA)
2004	East: Jamar Brittingham	Bloomsburg University of Pennsylvania (PA)
2004	West: Kirby Griffin	Indiana University of Pennsylvania (PA)
2005	East: Dominique Curry	Cheyney University (PA)

Year	Player	School
2005	West: Terrence Jackson	Indiana University of Pennsylvania (PA)
2006	East: Dan Latorre	Bloomsburg University of Pennsylvania (PA)
2006	West: Trevor Harris	Edinboro University (PA)
2007	East: Jamal Smith	Millersville University (PA)
2007	West: Alfonso Hoggard	Clarion University (PA)

PENNSYLVANIA STATE ATHLETIC CONFERENCE FRESHMAN OF THE YEAR

Year	Player	School
2008	East: Derrick Price	Bloomsburg University of Pennsylvania (PA)
2008	West: Branden Williams	Edinboro University (PA)
2009	East: Thomas Beverly	C.W. Post College at Long Island University (NY)
2009	West: Rontez Miles	California University of Pennsylvania (PA)
2010	East: Franklyn Quiteh	Bloomsburg University of Pennsylvania (PA)
2010	West: Darnell Harding	California University of Pennsylvania (PA)

Rocky Mountain Athletic Conference (RMAC)

1867 Austin Bluffs Parkway, Suite 101, Colorado Springs, CO 80918; Telephone: 719-471-0066; Fax: 719-471-0088; Web site: http:www.rmacsports.org

Originally called the Colorado Faculty Athletic Conference, the Rocky Mountain Athletic Conference was formed in March 1909 with four charter schools: Colorado A&M (now known as Colorado State University), Colorado College, Colorado School of Mines, and the University of Colorado. In 1910, its name was changed to the Rocky Mountain Faculty Athletic Conference; renamed the Rocky Mountain Athletic Conference in 1967; and became an NCAA Division II conference in 1992.

As of this writing, the RMAC contains 14 member schools, 10 of which play football in the conference:

- Adams State College Grizzlies, Alamosa, CO 81102; 719-587-7011; www.adams.edu
- Chadron State College Eagles, Chadron, NE 69337; 800-242-3766; www.csc.edu
- Colorado Christian University Cougars, Lakewood, CO 80226; 303-963-3000; www.ccu.edu; no football program
- Colorado School of Mines Orediggers, Golden, CO 80401; 303-273-3000; www.mines.edu
- Colorado State University, Pueblo, Thunderwolves, Pueblo, CO 81001; 719-549-2100; www.colostate-pueblo.edu
- Fort Lewis College Skyhawks, Durango, CO 81301; 877-352-2656; http://explore.fortlewis.edu
- Mesa State College Mavericks, Grand Junction, CO 81501; 970-248-1020; www.mesastate.edu
- Metropolitan State College of Denver Roadrunners, Denver, CO 80217; 303-556-2400; www.mscd.edu; no football program
- New Mexico Highlands University Cowboys, Las Vegas, NM 87701; 877-850-9064; www.nmhu.edu
- Regis University Rangers, Denver, CO 80221; 800-388-2366; www.regis.edu; no football program
- University of Colorado, Colorado Springs, Mountain Lions, Colorado Springs, CO 80918; 719-255-8227; www.uccs.edu; no football program
- University of Nebraska, Kearney, Lopers, Kearney, NE 68849; 308-865-8441; www.unk.edu
- Western New Mexico University Mustangs, Silver City, NM 88062; 800-872-9668; www.wnmu.edu
- Western State College of Colorado Mountaineers, Gunnison, CO 81231; 800-876-5309; www.western.edu

ROCKY MOUNTAIN ATHLETIC CONFERENCE CHAMPIONS

Year	School
1909	University of Colorado (CO)
1909	University of Denver (CO)
1910	Colorado College (CO)
1910	University of Colorado (CO)
1911	University of Colorado (CO)
1912	Colorado School of Mines (CO)
1913	University of Colorado (CO)
1914	Colorado School of Mines (CO)
1915	Colorado State University (CO)
1916	Colorado State University (CO)
1917	University of Denver (CO)
1918	Colorado School of Mines (CO)

Year	School
1919	Colorado College (CO)
1920	Colorado State University (CO)
1921	University of Colorado (CO)
1922	University of Utah (UT)
1923	University of Colorado (CO)
1924	University of Colorado (CO)
1925	Colorado State University (CO)
1926	University of Utah (UT)
1927	Colorado State University (CO)
1928	University of Utah (UT)
1929	University of Utah (UT)
1930	University of Utah (UT)
1931	University of Utah (UT)
1932	University of Utah (UT)
1933	University of Utah (UT)
1934	University of Colorado (CO)
1935	University of Colorado (CO)
1936	Utah State University (UT)
1937	University of Colorado (CO)
1938	Montana State College (MT)
1939	Colorado School of Mines (CO)
1940	Colorado College (CO)
1941	Colorado College (CO)
1942	Colorado School of Mines (CO)
1943	Football Not Played during World War II
1945	Colorado College (CO)
1946	Montana State College (MT)
1947	Montana State College (MT)
1948	University of Northern Colorado (CO)
1949	Colorado College (CO)
1950	Colorado College (CO)
1951	Colorado School of Mines (CO)
1952	Idaho State University (ID)
1953	Idaho State University (ID)
1954	Montana State College (MT)
1955	Idaho State University (ID)
1956	Montana State College (MT)
1957	Idaho State University (ID)
1958	Colorado College (CO)
1958	Colorado School of Mines (CO)
1959	Idaho State University (ID)
1960	Adams State College (CO)
1961	Adams State College (CO)
1962	Adams State College (CO)
1963	Western State College of Colorado (CO)
1964	Western State College of Colorado (CO)
1965	Western State College of Colorado (CO)
1966	Western State College of Colorado (CO)
1967	Adams State College (CO)
1968	Adams State College (CO)
1969	University of Northern Colorado (CO)
1970	Pittsburg State University (KS)
1971	University of Northern Colorado (CO)
1972	Adams State College (CO)
1973	Western State College of Colorado (CO)
1974	Western State College of Colorado (CO)
1975	Western State College of Colorado (CO)
1976	Western State College of Colorado (CO)
1977	Western State College of Colorado (CO)
1978	Western State College of Colorado (CO)
1979	Western State College of Colorado (CO)
1980	Adams State College (CO)
1980	University of Southern Colorado (CO)
1981	New Mexico Highlands University (NM)
1982	Mesa State College (CO)
1983	Mesa State College (CO)
1984	Fort Lewis College (CO)
1985	Mesa State College (CO)
1986	Mesa State College (CO)
1987	Mesa State College (CO)
1988	Mesa State College (CO)
1989	Adams State College (CO)
1990	Mesa State College (CO)
1991	Western State College of Colorado (CO)
1992	Western State College of Colorado (CO)
1993	Fort Hays State University (KS)
1994	Western State College of Colorado (CO)
1995	Fort Hays State University (KS)
1995	Western State College of Colorado (CO)
1996	Chadron State College (NE)
1997	Western State College of Colorado (CO)
1998	Chadron State College (NE)
1998	Western State College of Colorado (CO)
1999	Chadron State College (NE)
1999	New Mexico Highlands University (NM)
2000	Mesa State College (CO)
2001	Chadron State College (NE)
2002	Chadron State College (NE)
2002	University of Nebraska-Kearney (NE)
2003	Mesa State College (CO)
2004	Colorado School of Mines (CO)
2005	University of Nebraska, Kearney (NE)
2006	Chadron State College (NE)
2007	Chadron State College (NE)
2008	Chadron State College (NE)
2009	University of Nebraska, Kearney (NE)
2010	Colorado School of Mines (CO)
2010	University of Nebraska, Kearney (NE)

Rocky Mountain Athletic Conference Coach of the Year

Year	Coach	School
1996	Brad Smith	Chadron State College (NE)
1997	Duke Iverson	Western State College of Colorado (CO)
1998	Duke Iverson	Western State College of Colorado (CO)
1999	Brad Smith	Chadron State College (NE)
1999	Ed Rifilato	New Mexico Highlands University (NM)

Year	Coach	School
2000	Joe Ramunno	Mesa State College (CO)
2001	Brad Smith	Chadron State College (NE)
2002	Darrell Morris	University of Nebraska, Kearney (NE)
2003	Joe Ramunno	Mesa State College (CO)
2004	Bob Stitt	Colorado School of Mines (CO)
2005	Darrell Morris	University of Nebraska, Kearney (NE)
2006	Bill O'Boyle	Chadron State College (NE)
2007	Bill O'Boyle	Chadron State College (NE)
2008	Bill O'Boyle	Chadron State College (NE)
2009	Darrell Morris	University of Nebraska, Kearney (NE)
2010	Bob Stitt	Colorado School of Mines (CO)

Rocky Mountain Athletic Conference Player of the Year

Year	Player	School
1996	Shane Carwin	Western State College of Colorado (CO)
1997	Conan Smith	New Mexico Highlands University (NM)
1998	Eric Hannah	Western State College of Colorado (CO)
1999	Justin Coleman	University of Nebraska, Kearney (NE)
2000	Andy Coryell	Mesa State College (CO)

Rocky Mountain Athletic Conference Offensive Player of the Year

Year	Player	School
2001	Matt Strand	Chadron State College (NE)
2002	Mike Miller	University of Nebraska, Kearney (NE)
2003	Richie Ross	University of Nebraska, Kearney (NE)
2004	Chad Friehauf	Colorado School of Mines (CO)
2005	Danny Woodhead	Chadron State College (NE)
2006	Danny Woodhead	Chadron State College (NE)
2007	Danny Woodhead	Chadron State College (NE)
2008	Joe McLain	Chadron State College (NE)
2009	Rustin Dring	University of Nebraska, Kearney (NE)
2010	Clay Garcia	Colorado School of Mines (CO)

Rocky Mountain Athletic Conference Defensive Player of the Year

Year	Player	School
1999	Casey Beran	Chadron State College (NE)
2000	Josh Hotchkiss	Western State College of Colorado (CO)
2001	Josh Hotchkiss	Western State College of Colorado (CO)
2002	Marvin Jackson	Chadron State College (NE)
2003	Adam McGurk	Adams State College (CO)
2004	Adam McGurk	Adams State College (CO)
2005	Reed Duvall	Fort Lewis College (CO)
2006	Christian Serena	Western New Mexico University (NM)
2007	Kurt Kissner	Mesa State College (CO)
2008	Mark Meng	Fort Lewis College (CO)
2009	Marc Schiechl	Colorado School of Mines (CO)
2010	Marc Schiechl	Colorado School of Mines (CO)

Rocky Mountain Athletic Conference Special Teams Player of the Year

Year	Player	School
1999	Ryan Bedlan	University of Nebraska, Kearney (NE)
2000	Adam Ryan	Fort Hays State University (KS)
2001	Brian Sump	Colorado School of Mines (CO)
2002	Brian Sump	Colorado School of Mines (CO)
2003	Travis Snyder	Western State College of Colorado (CO)

Year	Player	School
2004	Garth Mins	University of Nebraska, Kearney (NE)
2005	Justin Gallas	Colorado School of Mines (CO)
2006	Kirk Peterson	University of Nebraska, Kearney (NE)
2007	Jared Keating	Mesa State College (CO)
2008	Jared Keating	Mesa State College (CO)
2009	Travis Atter	Chadron State College (NE)
2010	Kevin Berg	Chadron State College (NE)

Rocky Mountain Athletic Conference Freshman of the Year

Year	Player	School
1996	Mike Fackrell	Chadron State College (NE)
1997	Justin Coleman	University of Nebraska, Kearney (NE)
1998	Zach Mader	University of Nebraska, Kearney (NE)
1999	DeMeco Moore	Fort Lewis College (CO)
2000	Joe Moore	Fort Lewis College (CO)
2001	Mike Miller	University of Nebraska, Kearney (NE)
2002	Chris Brewer	Fort Lewis College (CO)
2003	Cody Assman	Chadron State College (NE)

Rocky Mountain Athletic Conference Offensive Freshman of the Year

Year	Player	School
2004	Danny Woodhead	Chadron State College (NE)
2005	Bobby Coy	Mesa State College (CO)
2006	Jack Hiatt	University of Nebraska, Kearney (NE)
2007	Bobby Washington	Adams State College (CO)
2008	Jake Spitzleberger	University of Nebraska, Kearney (NE)
2009	Tim Jenkins	Fort Lewis College (CO)
2009	Trevor Eggleston	Adams State College (CO)
2010	Glen Clinton	Chadron State College (NE)

Rocky Mountain Athletic Conference Defensive Freshman of the Year

Year	Player	School
2004	Marin Richardson	Colorado School of Mines (CO)
2005	Trevor Wikre	Mesa State College (CO)
2006	Josh Knouse	Chadron State College (NE)
2007	Marc Schiechl	Colorado School of Mines (CO)
2008	Grant Jansen	Colorado State University, Pueblo (CO)
2009	James Ackel	Adams State College (CO)
2010	Beau Martin	Colorado State University, Pueblo (CO)

South Atlantic Conference (SAC)

226 North Park Drive, Gateway Plaza, Suite 130, Rock Hill, SC 29730; Telephone: 803-981-5240; Fax: 803-981-9444; Web site: http://www.thesac.com

Founded in 1930 and originally called the North State Atlantic Conference (or more commonly, the "Little Six"), the conference changed its name to the Carolinas Intercollegiate Athletic Conference in May 1961; adopted its current name in 1975 (as a football-only conference); and in 1981, the South Atlantic Conference became an all-sports conference by sponsoring 10 sports.

The "Little Six" was created when six charter schools left the North Carolina Intercollegiate Athletic Conference: Lenoir-Rhyne College, Atlantic Christian College, Catawba College, Guilford College, Elon College, and High Point University.

As of this writing, the SAC consists of the following 10 schools, eight of which play football in the conference:

- Anderson University Trojans, Anderson SC 29621; 864-231-2000; www.andersonuniversity.edu; no football program
- Brevard College Tornados, Brevard, NC 28712; 828-883-8292; www.brevard.edu
- Carson-Newman College Eagles, Jefferson City, TN 37760; 865-471-2000; www.cn.edu
- Catawba College Indians, Salisbury, NC 28144; 800-228-2922; www.catawba.edu
- Lenoir-Rhyne University Bears, Hickory, NC 28601; 828-328-7300; www.lr.edu
- Lincoln Memorial University Railsplitters, Harrogate, TN 37752; 423-869-3611; www.lmunet.edu; no football program
- Mars Hill College Lions, Mars Hill, NC 28754; 866-642-4968; www.mhc.edu
- Newberry College Rowdy Reds, Newberry, SC 29108; 800-845-4955; www.newberry.edu
- Tusculum College Pioneers, Greeneville, TN 37743; 423-636-7300; www.tusculum.edu
- Wingate University Bulldogs, Wingate, NC 28174; 704-233-8000; www.wingate.edu

South Atlantic Conference Champions

Year	*School*
1975	Lenoir-Rhyne University (NC)
1976	Elon College (NC)
1977	Elon College (NC)
1978	Elon College (NC)
1978	Presbyterian College (SC)
1979	Presbyterian College (SC)
1980	Elon College (NC)
1980	Mars Hill College (NC)
1981	Elon College (NC)
1982	Carson-Newman College (TN)
1983	Carson-Newman College (TN)
1984	Carson-Newman College (TN)
1985	Mars Hill College (NC)
1986	Carson-Newman College (TN)
1987	Gardner-Webb University (NC)
1988	Carson-Newman College (TN)
1988	Catawba College (NC)
1988	Lenoir-Rhyne University (NC)
1989	Carson-Newman College (TN)
1990	Carson-Newman College (TN)
1991	Carson-Newman College (TN)
1992	Gardner-Webb University (NC)
1993	Carson-Newman College (TN)
1994	Carson-Newman College (TN)
1994	Lenoir-Rhyne University (NC)
1995	Carson-Newman College (TN)
1996	Carson-Newman College (TN)
1996	Catawba College (NC)
1997	Carson-Newman College (TN)
1998	Carson-Newman College (TN)
1999	Carson-Newman College (TN)
2000	Catawba College (NC)
2001	Catawba College (NC)
2002	Carson-Newman College (TN)
2003	Carson-Newman College (TN)
2003	Catawba College (NC)
2003	Tusculum College (TN)
2004	Carson-Newman College (TN)
2005	Presbyterian College (SC)
2006	Newberry College (SC)
2007	Carson-Newman College (TN)
2007	Catawba College (NC)
2008	Carson-Newman College (TN)
2008	Newberry College (SC)
2008	Tusculum College (TN)
2009	Carson-Newman College (TN)
2010	Wingate University (NC)

South Atlantic Conference Coach of the Year

Year	*Coach*	*School*
1975	Fred Herren	Newberry College (SC)
1976	Warren Klawiter	Catawba College (NC)
1977	Cally Gault	Presbyterian College (SC)
1978	Reed Charpia	Newberry College (SC)
1979	Cally Gault	Presbyterian College (SC)
1980	Charles Gibson	Mars Hill College (NC)
1980	Jerry Tolley	Elon College (NC)
1981	Jerry Tolley	Elon College (NC)
1982	Ken Sparks	Carson-Newman College (TN)
1983	Ken Sparks	Carson-Newman College (TN)
1984	Cally Gault	Presbyterian College (SC)
1985	Steve Patton	Mars Hill College (NC)
1986	Ken Sparks	Carson-Newman College (TN)
1987	Woody Fish	Gardner-Webb University (NC)

Year	Coach	School
1988	John Perry	Lenoir-Rhyne University (NC)
1989	Ken Sparks	Carson-Newman College (TN)
1990	Ken Sparks	Carson-Newman College (TN)
1991	Ken Sparks	Carson-Newman College (TN)
1992	Leon Hart	Elon College (NC)
1993	Ken Sparks	Carson-Newman College (TN)
1994	Charles Forbes	Lenoir-Rhyne University (NC)
1995	David Bennett	Catawba College (NC)
1996	Ken Sparks	Carson-Newman College (TN)
1997	Ken Sparks	Carson-Newman College (TN)
1998	Daryl Dickey	Presbyterian College (SC)
1999	David Bennett	Catawba College (NC)
2000	David Bennett	Catawba College (NC)
2001	David Bennett	Catawba College (NC)
2002	Ken Sparks	Carson-Newman College (TN)
2003	Ken Sparks	Carson-Newman College (TN)
2004	Joe Reich	Wingate University (NC)
2005	Tommy Spangler	Presbyterian College (SC)
2006	Zak Willis	Newberry College (SC)
2007	Chip Hester	Catawba College (NC)
2008	Frankie DeBusk	Tusculum College (TN)
2009	Ken Sparks	Carson-Newman College (TN)
2010	Joe Reich	Wingate University (NC)

South Atlantic Conference Offensive Player of the Year

Year	Player	School
1975	Scott Crawford	Lenoir-Rhyne University (NC)
1976	Howard Ferguson	Elon College (NC)
1977	Johnny Walker	Gardner-Webb University (NC)
1978	Jimmy Spence	Presbyterian College (SC)
1979	Clayto Burke	Presbyterian College (SC)
1980	Bobby Hedrick	Elon College (NC)
1981	John Bangley	Elon College (NC)
1982	Chip Stuart	Gardner-Webb University (NC)
1983	Cameron Brooks	Gardner-Webb University (NC)
1984	Kenneth Tyson	Carson-Newman College (TN)
1985	Joe Pizzo	Mars Hill College (NC)
1986	Dwayne Clark	Elon College (NC)
1987	Kenneth Tyson	Carson-Newman College (TN)
1988	Tommy Laurendine	Lenoir-Rhyne University (NC)
1989	Tommy Laurendine	Lenoir-Rhyne University (NC)
1990	Robert Hardy	Carson-Newman College (TN)
1991	Robert Thomas	Carson-Newman College (TN)
1992	Rodney Robinson	Gardner-Webb University (NC)
1993	Ken Avent	Catawba College (NC)
1994	Leonard Davis	Lenoir-Rhyne University (NC)
1995	Matt Penland	Carson-Newman College (TN)
1996	Kevin Brown	Catawba College (NC)
1997	Ty Westmoreland	Carson-Newman College (TN)
1997	Tracy Bowen	Wingate University (NC)
1998	Heath Hawkins	Carson-Newman College (TN)
1999	Todd Cunningham	Presbyterian College (SC)
2000	Todd Cunningham	Presbyterian College (SC)
2000	Terrance Stokes	Mars Hill College (NC)
2001	Todd Cunningham	Presbyterian College (SC)
2002	Leonard Guyton	Carson-Newman College (TN)
2003	Luke Samples	Catawba College (NC)

Year	Player	School
2004	Shane Kelley	Carson-Newman College (TN)
2005	Zach Ellis	Presbyterian College (SC)
2006	Josh Stepp	Newberry College (SC)
2007	Brad Roach	Catawba College (NC)
2008	Corey Russell	Tusculum College (TN)
2009	Alex Good	Carson-Newman College (TN)
2009	Jonas Randolph	Mars Hill College (NC)
2010	Bo Cordell	Tusculum College (TN)

South Atlantic Conference Defensive Player of the Year

Year	Player	School
1975	Sanders Shiver	Carson-Newman College (TN)
1976	Ricky Locklear	Elon College (NC)
1977	Wes McLaughlin	Elon College (NC)
1978	Charlie Coles	Newberry College (SC)
1979	Steve Campbell	Mars Hill College (NC)
1980	John Gulledge	Mars Hill College (NC)
1980	Steve Campbell	Mars Hill College (NC)
1981	Stanley Tootoo	Elon College (NC)
1982	Stanley Tootoo	Elon College (NC)
1983	Butch Gunter	Lenoir-Rhyne University (NC)
1984	Charlie Huff	Presbyterian College (SC)
1985	Darryl Perry	Gardner-Webb University (NC)
1986	Lee Marchman	Mars Hill College (NC)
1987	Sam Pinkney	Presbyterian College (SC)
1988	Mike Schlechter	Carson-Newman College (TN)
1989	Joe Fishback	Carson-Newman College (TN)
1990	LeRoy Mincey	Carson-Newman College (TN)
1991	Clayton Holmes	Carson-Newman College (TN)
1992	Lamar Adams	Elon College (NC)
1993	Robert Burnett	Elon College (NC)
1994	Steve Mellon	Carson-Newman College (TN)
1995	Mike Belk	Mars Hill College (NC)
1996	Mike Clowney	Carson-Newman College (TN)
1997	Maurice Miller	Catawba College (NC)
1998	Michael Robinson	Catawba College (NC)
1999	DeVonte Peterson	Catawba College (NC)
2000	Radell Lockhart	Catawba College (NC)
2001	Shawn Sanders	Catawba College (NC)
2002	Khalid Abdullah	Mars Hill College (NC)
2003	Ricardo Colclough	Tusculum College (TN)
2004	Tim Clarke	Lenoir-Rhyne University (NC)
2005	Anthony Robinson	Carson-Newman College (TN)
2006	Ron Ellington	Catawba College (NC)
2007	Eric Rice	Carson-Newman College (TN)
2008	Will Newell	Newberry College (SC)
2009	Ron Parker	Newberry College (SC)
2010	Marcus Shuford	Lenoir-Rhyne University (NC)

South Atlantic Conference Freshman of the Year

Year	Player	School
1984	Brian Bryson	Lenoir-Rhyne University (NC)
1985	Steve Riggins	Presbyterian College (SC)
1986	Edwin Lowery	Carson-Newman College (TN)
1987	Mike Warren	Catawba College (NC)
1988	Robert Thomas	Carson-Newman College (TN)
1989	Chuck Proffitt	Carson-Newman College (TN)

Year	*Player*	*School*
1990	Derrick Sharpe	Mars Hill College (NC)
1991	Vernon Buck	Wingate University (NC)
1992	Maurice Blakeney	Elon College (NC)
1993	Offense: Randy Sullivan	Presbyterian College (SC)
1993	Defense: Corey Hardy	Gardner-Webb University (NC)
1994	Offense: Michael Byrley	Mars Hill College (NC)
1994	Defense: Steve Fox	Lenoir-Rhyne University (NC)
1995	Offense: Shawn Gannaway	Elon College (NC)
1995	Defense: Duane Thompson	Presbyterian College (SC)
1996	Offense: Clint Conner	Gardner-Webb University (NC)
1996	Defense: Cedric Killings	Carson-Newman College (TN)
1997	Offense: Vic Gilmore	Newberry College (SC)
1997	Defense: Darryl Henderson	Gardner-Webb University (NC)
1998	Offense: Todd Cunningham	Presbyterian College (SC)
1998	Defense: Shawn Sanders	Catawba College (NC)
1999	Offense: Jameil Surratt	Lenoir-Rhyne University (NC)
1999	Offense: Rodney Williams	Wingate University (NC)
1999	Defense: Khalid Abdullah	Mars Hill College (NC)
2000	Offense: Kennard France	Lenoir-Rhyne University (NC)
2000	Defense: Craig Pritchett	Tusculum College (TN)
2001	Offense: Rodney Wallace	Catawba College (NC)
2001	Offense: Shane Kelley	Carson-Newman College (TN)
2001	Defense: Maurice Jackson	Mars Hill College (NC)
2002	Offense: Chris Winford	Lenoir-Rhyne University (NC)
2002	Defense: Samario Houston	Catawba College (NC)
2003	Offense: Brandon Sims	Mars Hill College (NC)
2003	Defense: Marcus Huntley	Catawba College (NC)
2004	Offense: George Washington	Mars Hill College (NC)
2004	Defense: Sherman Burnett	Presbyterian College (SC)
2005	Offense: Alex Rouse	Carson-Newman College (TN)
2005	Defense: Antwan Thomas	Presbyterian College (SC)
2006	Offense: Justin Sanders	Lenoir-Rhyne University (NC)
2006	Defense: Brian Brown	Carson-Newman College (TN)
2007	Offense: Nelson Woods	Wingate University (NC)
2007	Defense: Revel Coffey	Carson-Newman College (TN)
2008	Offense: John Brown	Mars Hill College (NC)
2008	Defense: Lakeem Perry	Catawba College (NC)
2009	Offense: Bo Cordell	Tusculum College (TN)
2009	Defense: Qua Jackson	Carson-Newman College (TN)
2010	Offense: Kelvin Jeter	Brevard College (NC)
2010	Defense: Damein Lee	Catawba College (NC)

Jacobs Blocking Trophy

The Jacobs Blocking Trophy is the name of several annual college football awards presented by different conferences to its best blocker. The award is named in honor of William P. Jacobs, the founder and president of Presbyterian College (Clinton, South Carolina) from 1935 to 1945 and is presented by his sons, Hugh and William Jacobs, based upon voting of the coaches within each conference.

The Southeastern Conference began the award in 1935; the Atlantic Coast Conference established its own award in 1953; while the Division I FCS Southern Conference and the Division II South Atlantic Conference (1990) also have a version of this award.

Year	*Player*	*School*
1990	Paige Belcher	Carson-Newman College (TN)
1991	Kevin Sims	Carson-Newman College (TN)
1992	Kevin Sims	Carson-Newman College (TN)
1993	Bill Clarke	Elon College (NC)

Year	Player	School
1994	Hugo Ieremia	Carson-Newman College (TN)
1995	Jason Self	Wingate University (NC)
1996	Brian Estes	Presbyterian College (SC)
1997	Ryan Keese	Presbyterian College (SC)
1998	Alan Collis	Carson-Newman College (TN)
1999	Brian Hinson	Catawba College (NC)
2000	Clay Clevenger	Carson-Newman College (TN)
2001	David Cassell	Mars Hill College (NC)
2002	Alan Dunn	Tusculum College (TN)
2003	Alan Dunn	Tusculum College (TN)
2004	Reggie Perkins	Carson-Newman College (TN)
2005	Marcus Brisbone	Presbyterian College (SC)
2006	Heath Benedict	Newberry College (SC)
2007	Heath Benedict	Newberry College (SC)
2008	Thomas Battle	Carson-Newman College (TN)
2009	Michael Tribue	Carson-Newman College (TN)
2010	Chandler Rearden	Lenoir-Rhyne University (NC)

Southern Intercollegiate Athletic Conference (SIAC)

3469 Lawrenceville Highway, Tucker, GA 30084; Telephone: 770-908-0482; Web site: http://www.thesiac.com

The Southern Intercollegiate Athletic Conference was founded in December 1913 as the Southeastern Intercollegiate Athletic Conference with nine charter schools: Alabama State University, Atlanta University, Clark College (now known as Clark Atlanta University), Fisk University, Jackson College, Morehouse College, Morris Brown College, Talladega College, and Tuskegee Institute. The conference adopted its current name in 1929.

As of this writing, the following schools belong to the SIAC:

- Albany State University Golden Rams, Albany, GA 31705; 229-430-4600; www.asurams.edu
- Benedict College Tigers, Columbia, SC 29204; 803-253-5000; www.benedict.edu
- Claflin University Panthers, Orangeburg, SC 29115; 803-535-5000; www.claflin.edu; no football program
- Clark Atlanta University Panthers, Atlanta, GA 30314; 404-880-8000; www.cau.edu
- Fort Valley State University Wildcats, Fort Valley, GA 31030; 478-825-6211; www.fvsu.edu
- Kentucky State University Thorobreds, Frankfort, KY 40601; 502-597-6000; www.kysu.edu
- Lane College Dragons, Jackson, TN 38301; 731-426-7500; www.lanecollege.edu
- LeMoyne-Owen College Magicians, Memphis, TN 38126; 901-435-1000; www.loc.edu; no football program
- Miles College Golden Bears, Fairfield, AL 35064; 205-929-1000; www.miles.edu
- Morehouse College Maroon Tigers, Atlanta, GA 30314; 404-681-2800; www.morehouse.edu
- Paine College Lions, Augusta, GA 30901; 706-821-8200; www.paine.edu; no football program
- Stillman College Tigers, Tuscaloosa, AL 35403; 800-841-5722; www.stillman.edu
- Tuskegee University Golden Tigers, Tuskegee, AL 36088; 334-727-8011; www.tuskegee.edu

Southern Intercollegiate Athletic Conference Champions

Year	School
1913	Fisk University (TN)
1914	Talladega College (AL)
1915	Fisk University (TN)
1916	Morehouse College (GA)
1917	Tuskegee University (AL)
1918	Talladega College (AL)
1919	Fisk University (TN)
1920	Morehouse College (GA)
1921	Morehouse College (GA)
1922	Morehouse College (GA)
1923	Fisk University (TN)
1923	Morehouse College (GA)
1924	Tuskegee University (AL)
1925	Tuskegee University (AL)
1926	Tuskegee University (AL)
1927	Tuskegee University (AL)
1928	Tuskegee University (AL)
1928	Clark Atlanta University (GA)

Year	School
1929	Tuskegee University (AL)
1930	Tuskegee University (AL)
1931	Tuskegee University (AL)
1931	Clark Atlanta University (GA)
1932	Tuskegee University (AL)
1933	Tuskegee University (AL)
1934	Morris Brown College (GA)
1935	Alabama State University (AL)
1936	Tuskegee University (AL)
1937	Florida A&M (Agricultural & Mechanical) University (FL)
1938	Florida A&M (Agricultural & Mechanical) University (FL)
1939	Alabama State University (AL)
1940	Morris Brown College (GA)
1941	Morris Brown College (GA)
1942	Florida A&M (Agricultural & Mechanical) University (FL)
1943	Florida A&M (Agricultural & Mechanical) University (FL)
1944	Tuskegee University (AL)
1945	Florida A&M (Agricultural & Mechanical) University (FL)
1946	Florida A&M (Agricultural & Mechanical) University (FL)
1947	Florida A&M (Agricultural & Mechanical) University (FL)
1948	Florida A&M (Agricultural & Mechanical) University (FL)
1949	Florida A&M (Agricultural & Mechanical) University (FL)
1950	Florida A&M (Agricultural & Mechanical) University (FL)
1951	Morris Brown College (GA)
1952	Florida A&M (Agricultural & Mechanical) University (FL)
1953	Florida A&M (Agricultural & Mechanical) University (FL)
1954	Florida A&M (Agricultural & Mechanical) University (FL)
1955	Florida A&M (Agricultural & Mechanical) University (FL)
1956	Florida A&M (Agricultural & Mechanical) University (FL)
1957	Florida A&M (Agricultural & Mechanical) University (FL)
1958	Florida A&M (Agricultural & Mechanical) University (FL)
1959	Florida A&M (Agricultural & Mechanical) University (FL)
1960	Florida A&M (Agricultural & Mechanical) University (FL)
1961	Florida A&M (Agricultural & Mechanical) University (FL)
1962	Alabama A&M (Agricultural & Mechanical University (AL)
1963	Florida A&M (Agricultural & Mechanical) University (FL)
1964	Florida A&M (Agricultural & Mechanical) University (FL)
1965	Florida A&M (Agricultural & Mechanical) University (FL)
1966	Alabama A&M (Agricultural & Mechanical) University (AL)
1967	Florida A&M (Agricultural & Mechanical) University (FL)
1968	Florida A&M (Agricultural & Mechanical) University (FL)
1969	Florida A&M (Agricultural & Mechanical) University (FL)
1970	Tuskegee University (AL)
1971	Alabama A&M (Agricultural & Mechanical) University (AL)
1972	Alabama A&M (Agricultural & Mechanical) University (AL)
1973	Bethune-Cookman College (FL)
1974	Tuskegee University (AL)
1975	Bethune-Cookman College (FL)
1976	Bethune-Cookman College (FL)
1977	Florida A&M (Agricultural & Mechanical) University (FL)
1978	Florida A&M (Agricultural & Mechanical) University (FL)
1979	Alabama A&M (Agricultural & Mechanical) University (AL)
1980	Alabama A&M (Agricultural & Mechanical) University (AL)
1981	Alabama A&M (Agricultural & Mechanical) University (AL)
1982	Fort Valley State University (GA)
1983	Fort Valley State University (GA)
1984	Albany State University (GA)
1985	Albany State University (GA)
1985	Fort Valley State University (GA)
1986	Albany State University (GA)
1987	Alabama A&M (Agricultural & Mechanical) University (AL)
1987	Tuskegee University (AL)
1988	Albany State University (GA)
1989	Alabama A&M (Agricultural & Mechanical) University (AL)
1990	Alabama A&M (Agricultural & Mechanical) University (AL)
1991	Alabama A&M (Agricultural & Mechanical) University (AL)
1991	Clark Atlanta University (GA)
1991	Fort Valley State University (GA)
1991	Morehouse College (GA)
1991	Tuskegee University (AL)
1992	Fort Valley State University (GA)
1993	Albany State University (GA)
1994	Albany State University (GA)
1995	Albany State University (GA)
1996	Albany State University (GA)
1997	Albany State University (GA)
1998	Tuskegee University (AL)
1999	Fort Valley State University (GA)
2000	Tuskegee University (AL)
2001	Tuskegee University (AL)

Year	School
2002	Tuskegee University (AL)
2003	Albany State University (GA)
2004	Albany State University (GA)
2005	Albany State University (GA)
2006	Albany State University (GA)
2006	Tuskegee University (AL)
2007	Tuskegee University (AL)
2008	Tuskegee University (AL)
2009	Tuskegee University (AL)
2010	Albany State University (GA)

Southern Intercollegiate Athletic Conference Coach of the Year

Selected by conference football coaches.

Year	Coach	School
2003	James "Mike" White	Albany State University (GA)
2004	No Information	
2005	James "Mike" White	Albany State University (GA)
2006	Johnny Cole	Lane College (TN)
2007	Willie Slater	Tuskegee University (AL)
2008	Willie Slater	Tuskegee University (AL)
2009	Willie Slater	Tuskegee University (AL)
2010	James "Mike" White	Albany State University (GA)

Southern Intercollegiate Athletic Conference Most Valuable Player of the Year

Selected by conference football coaches.

Year	Coach	School
2004	No Information	
2005	Kevin Huff	Tuskegee University (AL)
2006	Jacoby Jones	Lane College (TN)
2007	Jacary Atkinson	Tuskegee University (AL)
2008	Jacary Atkinson	Tuskegee University (AL)
2009	A.J. McKenna	Albany State University (GA)
2010	Stanley Jennings	Albany State University (GA)

Southern Intercollegiate Athletic Conference Offensive Player of the Year

Selected by conference football coaches.

Year	Player	School
2003	Derrick Wimbush	Fort Valley State University (GA)
2004	No Information	
2005	Kevin Huff	Tuskegee University (AL)
2006	Jacoby Jones	Lane College (TN)
2007	Jacary Atkinson	Tuskegee University (AL)
2008	Jacary Atkinson	Tuskegee University (AL)
2009	AJ McKenna	Albany State University (GA)
2010	Stanley Jennings	Albany State University (GA)

Southern Intercollegiate Athletic Conference Defensive Player of the Year

Selected by conference football coaches.

Year	Player	School
2003	Walter Curry	Albany State University (GA)
2004	No Information	
2005	Alton Pettway	Albany State University (GA)
2006	Alton Pettway	Albany State University (GA)
2007	Curtis Johnson	Clark Atlanta University (GA)
2008	Jeffrey Cargile	Morehouse College (GA)

Year	Player	School
2009	Justin Hannah	Tuskegee University (AL)
2009	Zimier McCloud	Clark Atlanta University (GA)
2010	Derrin Nettles	Morehouse College (GA)

Southern Intercollegiate Athletic Conference Freshman of the Year

Selected by conference football coaches.

Year	Player	School
2004	No Information	
2005	Sherard Ellis	Lane College (TN)
2006	Nathaniel Samas	Fort Valley State University (GA)
2007	Andrew Ramsey	Kentucky State University (KY)
2008	Tyren Futch	Lane College (TN)
2009	Dejuan Williams	Fort Valley State University (GA)
2010	Tahj Dent	Lane College (TN)

Sunshine State Conference

7061 Grand National Drive, Suite 140, Orlando, FL 32819; Telephone: 407-248-8460; Fax: 407-248-8325; Web site: http://www.sunshinestateconference.com

The Sunshine State Conference was founded in March 1975 with six charter schools: Biscayne College (now known as Saint Thomas University), Eckerd College, Florida Southern College, Florida Technological University (now known as the University of Central Florida), Rollins College, and Saint Leo College. The conference has since grown to nine members and does not support football.

- Barry College Buccaneers, Miami Shores, FL 33161; 305-899-3000; www.barry.edu; no football program
- Eckerd College Tritons, St. Petersburg, FL 33711; 727-867-1166; www.eckerd.edu; no football program
- Florida Southern College Mocs, Lakeland, FL 33801; 863-680-4111; www.flsouthern.edu; no football program
- Florida Institute of Technology Panthers, Melbourne, FL 32901; 321-674-8000; www.fit.edu; no football program but plans to start playing in 2013
- Lynn University Fighting Knights, Boca Raton, FL 33431; 561-237-7000; www.lynn.edu; no football program
- Nova Southeastern University Sharks, Fort Lauderdale-Davie, FL 33314; 800-541-6682; www.nova.edu; no football program
- Rollins College Tars, Winter Park, FL 32789; 407-646-2000; www.rollins.edu; no football program
- Saint Leo University Lions, Saint Leo, FL 33574; 352-588-8200; www.saintleo.edu; no football program
- University of Tampa Spartans, Tampa, FL 33606; 813-253-3333; www.ut.edu; no football program

West Virginia Intercollegiate Athletic Conference (WVIAC)

1422 East Main Street, Princeton, WV 24740; Telephone: 304-487-6298; Fax: 304-487-6299; Web site: http://www.wviac.org

The 16-member West Virginia Intercollegiate Athletic Conference was founded in 1924 with charter schools Alderson Academy, Bethany College, Broaddus College, Concord University, Davis & Elkins College, Fairmont State University, Glenville State College, Marshall University, Morris Harvey College (now known as the University of Charleston), New River State (now known as West Virginia University Institute of Technology), Potomac State College, Salem International University, Shepherd University, West Liberty State University, West Virginia University, and West Virginia Wesleyan College.

It is the largest NCAA Division II conference. After playing in the NAIA for many years, the WVIAC moved to the NCAA Division II in 1994. As of this writing, the 15 member schools (nine of which play football within the conference) of the WVIAC include:

- Alderson-Broaddus College Battlers, Philippi, WV 26416; 304-457-1700; www.ab.edu; no football program
- Bluefield State College Big Blues, Bluefield, WV 24701; 304-327-4000; www.bluefieldstate.edu; no football program
- Concord University Lions, Athens, WV 24712; 800-344-6679; www.concord.edu
- Davis & Elkins College Senators, Elkins, WV 26241; 304-637-1900; www.dewv.edu; no football program
- Fairmont State University Fighting Falcons, Fairmont, WV 26554; 304-367-4892; www.fairmontstate.edu
- Glenville State College Pioneers, Glenville, WV 26351; 304-462-7361; www.glenville.edu
- Ohio Valley University Fighting Scots, Vienna, WV 26105; 877-446-8668; www.ovu.edu; no football program
- Seton Hill University Griffins, Greensburg, PA 15601; 724-834-2200; www.setonhill.edu
- Shepherd University Rams, Shepherdstown, WV 25443; 304-876-5000; www.shepherd.edu
- University of Charleston Golden Eagles, Charleston, WV 25304; 304-357-4800; www.ucwv.edu
- University of Pittsburgh at Johnstown Mountain Cats, Johnstown, PA 15904; 814-269-7000; www.upj.pitt.edu; no football program
- West Liberty University Hilltoppers, West Liberty, WV 26074; 304-336-8025; http://westliberty.edu
- West Virginia State University Yellow Jackets, Institute, WV 25112; 800-987-2112; www.wvstateu.edu
- West Virginia Wesleyan College Bobcats, Buckhannon, WV 26201; 304-473-8000; www.wvwc.edu
- Wheeling Jesuit University Cardinals, Wheeling, WV 26003; 800-624-6992; www.wju.edu; no football program

West Virginia Intercollegiate Athletic Conference Champions

Year	*School*
1925	Marshall University (WV)
1926	West Virginia Wesleyan College (WV)
1927	West Liberty University (WV)
1928	Marshall University (WV)
1928	Potomac State College (WV)
1929	West Liberty University (WV)
1929	West Virginia University Institute of Technology (WV)
1930	Marshall University (WV)
1930	West Liberty University (WV)
1930	West Virginia Wesleyan College (WV)
1931	Marshall University (WV)
1932	Fairmont State University (WV)
1933	Davis & Elkins College (WV)
1934	Fairmont State University (WV)
1934	West Virginia Wesleyan College (WV)
1935	West Virginia Wesleyan College (WV)
1936	West Liberty University (WV)
1936	West Virginia Wesleyan College (WV)
1937	Glenville State College (WV)
1937	Potomac State College (WV)
1938	Concord University (WV)
1938	Morris Harvey College (WV)
1939	West Liberty University (WV)
1940	West Liberty University (WV)
1941	West Liberty University (WV)
1942	Morris Harvey College (WV)
1943	No Champion during World War II
1944	No Champion during World War II
1945	No Champion during World War II
1946	West Liberty University (WV)
1947	Potomac State College (WV)
1947	West Liberty University (WV)
1948	Morris Harvey College (WV)
1949	West Liberty University (WV)
1949	West Virginia University Institute of Technology (WV)
1950	Morris Harvey College (WV)
1950	Potomac State College (WV)
1950	West Liberty University (WV)
1951	Morris Harvey College (WV)
1952	Fairmont State University (WV)
1952	Morris Harvey College (WV)
1953	Morris Harvey College (WV)
1954	Morris Harvey College (WV)
1955	Shepherd University (WV)
1956	West Liberty University (WV)
1957	Fairmont State University (WV)
1958	Glenville State College (WV)
1958	Shepherd University (WV)
1959	Fairmont State University (WV)
1960	Fairmont State University (WV)
1961	Eastern: Salem International University (WV)
1961	Western: West Virginia Wesleyan College (WV)
1962	Eastern: West Liberty University (WV)
1962	Western: Concord University (WV)
1963	Eastern: West Liberty University (WV)
1963	Western: Glenville State College (WV)
1964	Fairmont State University (WV)
1965	Fairmont State University (WV)
1966	Concord University (WV)
1967	Fairmont State University (WV)

Year	School
1968	West Virginia State University (WV)
1969	Fairmont State University (WV)
1970	West Liberty University (WV)
1971	West Liberty University (WV)
1972	Shepherd University (WV)
1973	Northern: Fairmont State University (WV)
1973	Southern: Glenville State College (WV)
1974	Northern: Fairmont State University (WV)
1974	Southern: Bluefield State College (WV)
1974	Southern: Concord University (WV)
1974	Southern: Glenville State College (WV)
1975	Northern: Salem International University (WV)
1975	Southern: Concord University (WV)
1976	Northern: Shepherd University (WV)
1976	Southern: Concord University (WV)
1977	Northern: Salem International University (WV)
1977	Northern: Shepherd University (WV)
1977	Northern: West Virginia Wesleyan College (WV)
1977	Southern: Concord University (WV)
1978	Northern: Shepherd University (WV)
1978	Northern: West Virginia Wesleyan College (WV)
1978	Southern: Concord University (WV)
1979	Northern: Fairmont State University (WV)
1979	Northern: West Liberty University (WV)
1979	Southern: West Virginia State University (WV)
1980	Northern: Fairmont State University (WV)
1980	Northern: Shepherd University (WV)
1980	Southern: Concord University (WV)
1981	Concord University (WV)
1981	Fairmont State University (WV)
1982	Shepherd University (WV)
1983	Shepherd University (WV)
1984	Concord University (WV)
1984	Salem International University (WV)
1985	Salem International University (WV)
1986	Shepherd University (WV)
1987	Concord University (WV)
1988	Fairmont State University (WV)
1989	Concord University (WV)
1989	West Virginia University Institute of Technology (WV)
1990	Concord University (WV)
1991	Shepherd University (WV)
1992	Shepherd University (WV)
1993	Glenville State College (WV)
1994	Glenville State College (WV)
1994	Shepherd University (WV)
1995	Glenville State College (WV)
1995	West Virginia Wesleyan College (WV)
1996	Fairmont State University (WV)
1996	Glenville State College (WV)
1997	Glenville State College (WV)
1997	Shepherd University (WV)
1998	Shepherd University (WV)
1999	Shepherd University (WV)
2000	Fairmont State University (WV)
2000	West Liberty University (WV)
2001	Glenville State College (WV)
2002	West Virginia Wesleyan College (WV)
2003	West Virginia Wesleyan College (WV)
2004	Shepherd University (WV)
2005	Shepherd University (WV)
2006	Shepherd University (WV)
2007	Shepherd University (WV)
2008	Glenville State College (WV)
2009	West Liberty University (WV)
2010	Shepherd University (WV)

West Virginia Intercollegiate Athletic Conference Coach of the Year

Year	Coach	School
1976	Tony Colobro	Concord University (WV)
1977	Tony Colobro	Concord University (WV)
1978	Tony Colobro	Concord University (WV)
1979	David Ritchie	Fairmont State University (WV)
1980	Tony Colobro	Concord University (WV)
1981	Roy Lucas	West Virginia University Institute of Technology (WV)
1982	Walter Barr	Shepherd University (WV)
1983	Walter Barr	Shepherd University (WV)
1984	Marvin Williams	Concord University (WV)
1985	Terry Bowden	Salem International University (WV)
1986	Mike Jacobs	Shepherd University (WV)
1987	Marvin Williams	Concord University (WV)
1988	Wally Hood	Fairmont State University (WV)
1989	Bob Gobel	West Virginia University Institute of Technology (WV)
1990	Bob Mullett	Concord University (WV)
1991	Monte Cater	Shepherd University (WV)
1992	Monte Cater	Shepherd University (WV)
1993	Rich Rodriguez	Glenville State College (WV)

Year	Coach	School
1994	Rich Rodriguez	Glenville State College (WV)
1995	Bill Struble	West Virginia Wesleyan College (WV)
1996	Doug Sams	Fairmont State University (WV)
1997	Monte Cater	Shepherd University (WV)
1998	Monte Cater	Shepherd University (WV)
1999	Monte Cater	Shepherd University (WV)
2000	Bob Eaton	West Liberty University (WV)
2001	Paul Shaffner	Glenville State College (WV)
2002	Bill Struble	West Virginia Wesleyan College (WV)
2003	Bill Struble	West Virginia Wesleyan College (WV)
2004	Monte Cater	Shepherd University (WV)
2005	Monte Cater	Shepherd University (WV)
2006	Monte Cater	Shepherd University (WV)
2007	Monte Cater	Shepherd University (WV)
2008	Alan Fiddler	Glenville State College (WV)
2009	Roger Waialae	West Liberty University (WV)
2010	Dennis Creehan	West Virginia Wesleyan College (WV)

West Virginia Intercollegiate Athletic Conference Offensive Player of the Year

Year	Player	School
1974	Jack Deloplaine	Salem International University (WV)
1974	Randy Little	West Liberty University (WV)
1975	Jack Deloplaine	Salem International University (WV)
1976	Larry Riley	Salem International University (WV)
1977	Jeff Boyles	Concord University (WV)
1978	Carlos Lee	Concord University (WV)
1979	Frank Zebrasky	West Liberty University (WV)
1980	Dave Renner	Concord University (WV)
1981	Luc Tousignant	Fairmont State University (WV)
1982	Mike Coyle	Shepherd University (WV)
1983	Mike Coyle	Shepherd University (WV)
1984	Mike Coyle	Shepherd University (WV)
1985	Jimbo Fisher	Salem International University (WV)
1985	John Fotta	Shepherd University (WV)
1986	Jimbo Fisher	Salem International University (WV)
1987	Keith Franklin	West Virginia State University (WV)
1988	Keith Franklin	West Virginia State University (WV)
1989	Lee Holder	West Virginia University Institute of Technology (WV)
1990	Bryan Hamm	Concord University (WV)
1991	Chris Hairston	Concord University (WV)
1992	Jed Drenning	Glenville State College (WV)
1993	Jed Drenning	Glenville State College (WV)
1994	Chris George	Glenville State College (WV)
1995	Scott Otis	Glenville State College (WV)
1996	Mike Joseph	Fairmont State University (WV)
1997	Wilkie Perez	Glenville State College (WV)
1998	Damian Beane	Shepherd University (WV)
1999	Damian Beane	Shepherd University (WV)
2000	Bryan Harman	Fairmont State University (WV)
2001	Bryan Harman	Fairmont State University (WV)
2002	Duriel Cobb	West Virginia Wesleyan College (WV)
2003	Luke Struble	West Virginia Wesleyan College (WV)
2003	Joey Conrad	Glenville State College (WV)
2004	Antonio Carter	Glenville State College (WV)
2005	Joey Conrad	Glenville State College (WV)
2006	Dervon Wallace	Shepherd University (WV)

Year	Player	School
2007	Dervon Wallace	Shepherd University (WV)
2008	Jerry Seymour	Glenville State College (WV)
2009	Zach Amedro	West Liberty University (WV)
2010	Zach Amedro	West Liberty University (WV)

West Virginia Intercollegiate Athletic Conference Defensive Player of the Year

Year	Player	School
1974	Ed Evans	West Liberty University (WV)
1975	Jim Meeker	Salem International University (WV)
1976	Rocky Martin	Salem International University (WV)
1977	Jim Calhoun	West Liberty University (WV)
1978	Bob Pauley	Concord University (WV)
1979	Steve Brinkley	Concord University (WV)
1980	Milton Spradley	West Virginia State University (WV)
1981	Randy Jones	Fairmont State University (WV)
1982	Gene Lugat	Shepherd University (WV)
1983	Mark Brower	Shepherd University (WV)
1984	Mike Payne	Glenville State College (WV)
1985	Jeff Shaw	Salem International University (WV)
1985	Kevin Johnson	Concord University (WV)
1986	Kevin Johnson	Concord University (WV)
1987	Craig Plymal	Concord University (WV)
1988	Steve Borlie	Shepherd University (WV)
1989	Tracy Gravely	Concord University (WV)
1990	Mike Spradling	Concord University (WV)
1991	Brooks Bennett	Shepherd University (WV)
1992	Brooks Bennett	Shepherd University (WV)
1993	Henry Newby	Fairmont State University (WV)
1994	Freddie Ford	Concord University (WV)
1995	Quinton Barnes	West Virginia University Institute of Technology (WV)
1995	Dave Peterson	West Liberty University (WV)
1996	Greg Stup	Shepherd University (WV)
1997	Charles Smith	West Virginia State University (WV)
1998	Andre Jones	West Virginia State University (WV)
1999	E.J. Burt	West Liberty University (WV)
2000	E.J. Burt	West Liberty University (WV)
2001	Davon Deveaux	West Virginia University Institute of Technology (WV)
2002	Mike Mayer	West Virginia State University (WV)
2003	Jadae McGuire	West Virginia University Institute of Technology (WV)
2004	Alan Krutulis	West Virginia Wesleyan College (WV)
2005	Dan Peters	Shepherd University (WV)
2006	Dan Peters	Shepherd University (WV)
2007	Vince Black	Fairmont State University (WV)
2008	Darren Banks	West Liberty University (WV)
2009	Andrew Eggleton	West Virginia State University (WV)
2010	Clay Beeler	West Liberty University (WV)

West Virginia Intercollegiate Athletic Conference Offensive Freshman of the Year

Year	Player	School
2010	Logan Moore	Fairmont State University (WV)

West Virginia Intercollegiate Athletic Conference Defensive Freshman of the Year

Year	Player	School
2010	Alec Wood	West Liberty University (WV)

National Collegiate Athletic Association (NCAA) Division III

P.O. Box 6222, 700 West Washington Street, Indianapolis, IN 46202; Telephone: 317-917-6222; Fax: 317-917-6888; Web site: http://www.ncaa.org

National Collegiate Athletic Association Division III member schools must sponsor at least five sports for men and five for women (six for men and six for women as of 2012 for schools with an attendance of more than 1,000). With attendance ranging from 500 to 10,000 students, Division III schools compete in athletics as a non-revenue generating, extracurricular activity for students, and thus players receive no financial aid related to their athletic ability and athletic departments are staffed and funded like any other department in the university. Not all Division III conferences support football programs (although some of their schools may play football) and not all schools within each conference play football. Division III has the most member schools of the three sanctioned NCAA Divisions (I, II, III).

As of this writing, the NCAA Division III consists of the following 68 conferences (which includes Independent Teams, the Eastern College Athletic Conference, and those dedicated to specific sports):

- Allegheny Mountain Collegiate Conference
- American Southwest Conference
- Atlantic Central Football Conference
- Atlantic Women's College Conference
- Capital Athletic Conference
- Centennial Conference
- City University of New York Athletic Conference
- College Conference of Illinois and Wisconsin
- Colonial States Athletic Conference
- Commonwealth Coast Conference
- Commonwealth Conference
- Eastern College Athletic Conference
- Eastern College Athletic Conference Division III Men's East Hockey League
- Eastern College Athletic Conference Division III Men's West Hockey League
- Eastern College Athletic Conference Division III Northeast Hockey League
- Eastern College Athletic Conference Division III Women's East Hockey League
- Eastern College Athletic Conference Division III Women's West Hockey League
- Eastern Collegiate Football Conference
- Empire 8 Athletic Conference
- Empire Collegiate Wrestling Conference
- Freedom Conference
- Great Northeast Atlantic Conference
- Great South Athletic Conference
- Heartland Collegiate Athletic Conference
- Independent Teams
- Iowa Intercollegiate Athletic Conference
- Landmark Conference

- Liberty League
- Little East Conference
- Massachusetts State Collegiate Athletic Conference
- Michigan Intercollegiate Athletic Association
- Mid-Atlantic Rowing Conference
- Middle Atlantic Corporation (Conference)
- Midwest Collegiate Hockey Association
- Midwest Conference
- Midwest Lacrosse Conference
- Midwest Women's Lacrosse Conference
- Minnesota Intercollegiate Athletic Conference
- New England College Wrestling Association
- New England Collegiate Conference
- New England Football Conference
- New England Small College Athletic Conference
- New England Women's and Men's Athletic Conference
- New England Women's Lacrosse Alliance
- New Jersey Athletic Conference
- North Atlantic Conference
- North Coast Athletic Conference
- North East Collegiate Volleyball Association
- North Eastern Athletic Conference
- Northern Athletics Conference
- Northern Collegiate Hockey Association
- Northern Illinois–Iowa Conference
- Northwest Conference
- Ohio Athletic Conference
- Old Dominion Athletic Conference
- Pennsylvania Athletic Conference
- Pilgrim Lacrosse League
- Presidents' Athletic Conference
- St. Louis Intercollegiate Athletic Conference
- Skyline Conference
- Southern California Intercollegiate Athletic Conference
- Southern Collegiate Athletic Conference
- State University of New York Athletic Conference
- United Volleyball Conference
- University Athletic Association
- Upper Midwest Athletic Conference
- USA South Athletic Conference
- Western Water Polo Association
- Wisconsin Intercollegiate Athletic Conference

NCAA Division III Champions

The NCAA Division III football championship game, known as the Stagg Bowl, has been played annually in Salem, Virginia (at Salem Football Stadium) since 1993. It was previously played in Phenix City, Alabama (1973–1982, 1985–1989), at the College Football Hall of Fame, when the Hall was located in Kings Island, Ohio (1983–1984) and Bradenton, Florida (1990–1992).

Year	*School*
1973	Wittenberg University (OH)
1974	Central College (IA)
1975	Wittenberg University (OH)
1976	St. John's University (MN)
1977	Widener University (PA)
1978	Baldwin-Wallace College (OH)
1979	Ithaca College (NY)
1980	University of Dayton (OH)
1981	Widener University (PA)
1982	University of West Georgia (GA)

Year	School
1983	Augustana College (IL)
1984	Augustana College (IL)
1985	Augustana College (IL)
1986	Augustana College (IL)
1987	Wagner College (NY)
1988	Ithaca College (NY)
1989	University of Dayton (OH)
1990	Allegheny College (PA)
1991	Ithaca College (NY)
1992	University of Wisconsin, La Crosse (WI)
1993	Mount Union College (OH)
1994	Albion College (MI)
1995	University of Wisconsin, La Crosse (WI)
1996	Mount Union College (OH)
1997	Mount Union College (OH)
1998	Mount Union College (OH)
1999	Pacific Lutheran University (WA)
2000	Mount Union College (OH)
2001	Mount Union College (OH)
2002	Mount Union College (OH)
2003	St. John's University (MN)
2004	Linfield College (OR)
2005	Mount Union College (OH)
2006	Mount Union College (OH)
2007	University of Wisconsin, Whitewater (WI)
2008	Mount Union College (OH)
2009	University of Wisconsin, Whitewater (WI)
2010	University of Wisconsin, Whitewater (WI)

American Football Coaches Association (AFCA) Coach of the Year

100 Legends Lane, Waco, TX 76706; Telephone: 254-754-9900; Fax: 254-754-7373; http://www.afca.com

The AFCA Coach of the Year Award is presented annually to each level of college football (NCAA FBS (and equivalent) since 1935, NCAA FCS since 1983, NCAA Division II since 1983, NCAA Division III since 1983, and NAIA since 2006). The Scripps-Howard newspaper chain conducted the balloting and presented the award from 1935 through 1959. In 1960, the AFCA itself began handling the voting and award presentation. Eastman Kodak Corporation sponsored the AFCA Coach of the Year program from 1960 until 1993, and from 1996 to 1999, the award was sponsored by GTE.

From 1960 through 1982, two national winners were selected (one from the University Division and one from the College Division). Beginning in 1983, four national winners were chosen, one from each school level (NCAA I-A, NCAA I-AA, NCAA Division II, and NCAA Division III) and in 2006, selection was expanded to five levels with the inclusion of the NAIA.

Currently, the AFCA selects 25 regional winners (five from each of the AFCA division levels), from which five national winners (one from each AFCA division level) are selected. All schools with eligible AFCA head coaches are listed on the national ballot and AFCA members are not limited to voting for regional winners. However, members are required to vote for coaches within their region for the AFCA Regional Coach of the Year and coaches within their division when voting for the AFCA National Coach of the Year.

The school of each AFCA National Coach of the Year winner receives $1,000 from The American Football Coaches Foundation for each full-time assistant football coach who was on staff the year the head coach was honored. If a school wins a national championship and the head coach wins the AFCA National Coach of the Year Award, the school then receives $1,500 for each full-time assistant who is an AFCA member.

As of this writing, Larry Kehres of Mount Union College (Ohio, (NCAA Division III) is the only coach in AFCA history to win the National Coach of the Year Award nine times (1993, 1996–1998, 2000–2002, 2006, 2008) and Bob Reade of Augustana College (Illinois, NCAA Division III) is the only coach to win the award four consecutive years (1983–1986).

NCAA Division III AFCA Coach of the Year

Year	Coach	School
1983	Bob Reade	Augustana College (IL)
1984	Bob Reade	Augustana College (IL)
1985	Bob Reade	Augustana College (IL)
1986	Bob Reade	Augustana College (IL)
1987	Walt Hameline	Wagner College (NY)
1988	Jim Butterfield	Ithaca College (NY)

Year	*Coach*	*School*
1989	Mike Kelly	University of Dayton (OH)
1990	Ken O'Keefe	Allegheny College (PA)
1991	Jim Butterfield	Ithaca College (NY)
1992	John Luckhardt	Washington & Jefferson College (PA)
1993	Larry Kehres	Mount Union College (OH)
1994	Pete Schmidt	Albion College (MI)
1995	Roger Harring	University of Wisconsin, La Crosse (WI)
1996	Larry Kehres	Mount Union College (OH)
1997	Larry Kehres	Mount Union College (OH)
1998	Larry Kehres	Mount Union College (OH)
1999	Frosty Westering	Pacific Lutheran University (WA)
2000	Larry Kehres	Mount Union College (OH)
2001	Larry Kehres	Mount Union College (OH)
2002	Larry Kehres	Mount Union College (OH)
2003	John Gagliardi	St. John's University (MN)
2004	Jay Locey	Linfield College (OR)
2005	Bob Berezowitz	University of Wisconsin, Whitewater (WI)
2006	Larry Kehres	Mount Union College (OH)
2007	Lance Leipold	University of Wisconsin, Whitewater (WI)
2008	Larry Kehres	Mount Union College (OH)
2009	Lance Leipold	University of Wisconsin, Whitewater (WI)
2010	Lance Leipold	University of Wisconsin, Whitewater (WI)

American Football Coaches Association (AFCA) Assistant Coach of the Year

100 Legends Lane, Waco, TX 76706; Telephone: 254-754-9900; Fax: 254-754-7373; http://www.afca.com

The AFCA Assistant Coach of the Year Award has been presented annually since 1997 to the best assistant coach in each of the five levels of college football (NCAA FBS, NCAA FCS, NCAA Division II, NCAA Division III, and the NAIA).

For each of the five levels of college football, staff members from NCAA and NAIA football-playing schools nominate an assistant coach. From this list of nominees, a winner is then selected by the AFCA Public Relations Committee.

NCAA Division III AFCA Assistant Coach of the Year

Year	*Assistant Coach*	*School*
1997	Roland Christensen	University of Wisconsin, La Crosse (WI)
1998	Mike Plinske	Bethel College (MN)
1999	Don Montgomery	Mount Union College (OH)
2000	Don DeWaard	Central College (IA)
2001	Chris Meidt	Bethel College (MN)
2002	Brian Ward	Wabash College (IN)
2003	Pedro Arruza	Washington University (MO)
2004	Keith Emery	Johns Hopkins University (MD)
2005	Dan Garrett	Kean University (NJ)
2006	Jeff Wojtowicz	Mount Union College (OH)
2007	Neal Neathery	Wabash College (IN)
2008	Dick Bowzer	Central College (IA)
2009	Jeff Thomas	University of Redlands (CA)
2010	Chris Rusiewicz	Ursinus College (PA)

Gagliardi Trophy

The Gagliardi Trophy (first presented in 1993) is awarded to the Outstanding Division III college football player of the year by the Jostens Company (3601 Minnesota Drive, Minneapolis, MN 55435; Telephone: 952-830-3300; Fax: 952-830-3293; Web site: http://www.jostens.com; a leading producer of school yearbooks and class rings) and the J-Club of Saint John's University in Minnesota (P.O. Box 2000, Collegeville, MN 56321; Telephone: 320-363-2011; Web site: http://www.csbsju.edu/).

The award honors excellence in athletics, academics, and community service and is named for John Gagliardi, head football coach of St. John's University in Minnesota (born: November 1, 1926, in Trinidad, Colorado); head football coach at Saint John's University in Collegeville, MN since 1953; with 471, as of this writing, he has the most wins of any coach in college football history; his Saint John's teams have won four national titles (the NAIA National Football Championship in 1963 and 1965, and the NCAA Division III National Football Championship in 1976 and 2003); and he was inducted into the College Football Hall of Fame in 2006. Currently, the trophy is presented by the Salem Rotary Club each year in Salem, Virginia (Rotary Club Of Salem, P.O. Box 608, Salem, MA 01970; Email: salem_rotary@yahoo.com; Web site: http://www.salemrotary.com).

Nominations for the award are made by the college president with supporting materials provided by each school's head football coach. After reviewing each nomination, the SJU J-Club Board of Directors narrows the field to 10 finalists, including at least one from each of the four NCAA regions. The 35-member Gagliardi Trophy National Selection Committee reviews each candidate and casts their votes. Beginning in 2007, fans were given one collective vote.

Year	*Player*	*School*	*Note*
1993	Jim Ballard	Mount Union College (OH)	2008 College Football Hall of Fame Inductee
1994	Carey Bender	Coe College (IA)	Established 18 NCAA Division III Records
1995	Chris Palmer	St. John's University (MN)	1,195 receiving yards in 1995
1996	Lon Erickson	Illinois Wesleyan University (IL)	Threw for 392 yards (1996) against Millikin
1997	Bill Borchert	Mount Union College (OH)	2009 Greater Cleveland Sports Hall of Fame Inductee
1998	Scott Hvistendahl	Augsburg College (MN)	4,696 career receiving yards in college
1999	Danny Ragsdale	University of Redlands (CA)	380 passing attempts in 1999
2000	Chad Johnson	Pacific Lutheran University (WA)	Threw TD passes in 22 consecutive games
2001	Chuck Moore	Mount Union College (OH)	432 college career points
2002	Dan Pugh	Mount Union College (OH)	School Record 1,467 rushing yards in 2002
2003	Blake Elliott	St. John's University (MN)	Scored 78 touchdowns in his college career
2004	Rocky Myers	Wesley College (DE)	124 tackles in 2004
2005	Brett Elliott	Linfield College (OR)	2005 All-American
2006	Josh Brehm	Alma College (MI)	MIAA 2006 Offensive MVP
2007	Justin Beaver	University of Wisconsin, Whitewater (WI)	Won 2007 Championship Game (Stagg Bowl)
2008	Greg Micheli	Mount Union College (OH)	Threw for 3,743 yards in 2008
2009	Blaine Westermeyer	Augustana College (IL)	No Further Information
2010	Eric Watt	Trine University (IN)	No Further Information

Joseph P. Zabilski Award (Division II and Division III Best College Player in New England)

Presented annually since 1996 by the Gridiron Club of Greater Boston (Web site: http://www.gridclubofgreaterboston.com), the Joseph P. Zabilski Award is named in honor of Joe Zabilski (1943 graduate of Boston College [MA]); former coach at Northeastern University (Boston, MA); and former Gridiron

Club president. This award is presented to New England's best collegiate football players in NCAA Divisions II and III.

Year	*Player*	*School*
1996	Raymond Jones	Trinity College (CT)
1996	Alex Bernstein	Amherst College (MA)
1997	Ben Nassar	Bentley University (MA)
1997	Richard Willard	Amherst College (MA)
1998	Ben Nassar	Bentley University (MA)
1998	Sean Keenan	Williams College (MA)
1999	Kavin Gailliard	American International College (MA)
1999	Christos Arsoniadis	Bridgewater State College (MA)
2000	Steven Cedor	University of New Haven (CT)
2000	Brian Sanchez	Middlebury College (VT)
2001	Josue Zamora	Westfield State College (MA)
2001	Joseph Reardon	Williams College (MA)
2002	Scott Farley	Williams College (MA)
2002	Marc Eddy	Bentley University (MA)
2003	Mark Tilki	Tufts University (MA)
2003	Tom Pierandri	Trinity College (CT)
2004	Brian Robitaille	Curry College (MA)
2004	Marc Eddy	Bentley University (MA)
2005	Mike Blair	Trinity College (CT)
2005	Don Thibodeau	Maine Maritime Academy (ME)
2006	Chris Sharpe	Springfield College (MA)
2006	Sean Crowley	Curry College (MA)
2007	Paul Tetzel	Bentley University (MA)
2007	Patrick Lucey	Williams College (MA)
2008	Cody Andrews	Maine Maritime Academy (ME)
2008	Jeff Mack	Plymouth State University (NH)
2009	Josh Mathieu	Westfield State College (MA)
2009	Jim Bower	Maine Maritime Academy (ME)
2010	James McCarthy	Framingham State University (MA)

Lambert-Meadowlands Trophy

The Lambert-Meadowlands Trophy is an annual award given to the best team in the East in Division I FBS college football and was established by brothers Victor and Henry Lambert in memory of their father, August. Established in 1936 as the "Lambert Trophy," it also recognizes (as the "Lambert Cup") the best college football team in the FCS (as of 1982), NCAA Division II (as of 1957), and Division III (as of 1966) levels.

The New Jersey Sports and Exposition Authority (Public Affairs Office, 50 State Route 120, East Rutherford, NJ 07073; Telephone: 201-935-8500; Email: publicaffairs@njsea.com; Web site: http://www.njsea.com/), operator of the Meadowlands Sports Complex, took over the administration of the Lambert Meadowlands Awards in 1983.

To be eligible for the Lambert Meadowlands Award, a school must be located in the East or play half its schedule against eligible Lambert teams.

Year	*School*
1966	Wilkes University (PA)
1967	Wagner College (NY)
1968	Wilkes University (PA)
1969	United States Merchant Marine Academy (NY)
1970	Edinboro University of Pennsylvania (PA)
1971	Alfred University (NY)
1972	Franklin & Marshall College (PA)
1973	Long Island University C.W. Post Campus (NY)
1974	Ithaca College (NY)
1975	Ithaca College (NY)
1976	Long Island University C.W. Post Campus (NY)
1977	Westminster College (MO)
1978	Ithaca College (NY)
1979	Carnegie Mellon University (PA)

Year	School
1980	Ithaca College (NY)
1981	Widener University (PA)
1982	Plymouth State University (NH)
1983	Hofstra University (NY)
1984	Union College (NY)
1984	Ithaca College (NY)
1985	Ithaca College (NY)
1986	Salisbury State (Salisbury State University) (MD)
1987	Wagner College (NY)
1988	Ithaca College (NY)
1989	Union College (NY)
1990	Allegheny College (PA)
1991	Ithaca College (NY)
1992	Washington & Jefferson College (PA)
1993	Rowan University (NJ)
1994	Washington & Jefferson College (PA)
1995	Rowan University (NJ)
1996	Rowan University (NJ)
1997	Lycoming College (PA)
1998	Rowan University (NJ)
1999	Rowan University (NJ)
2000	Widener University (PA)
2001	Rowan University (NJ)
2002	State University of New York at Brockport (NY)
2003	Rensselaer Polytechnic Institute (NY)
2004	Rowan University (NJ)
2005	Rowan University (NJ)
2006	St. John Fisher College
2007	Wesley College (DE)
2008	State University of New York at Cortland (NY)
2009	Wesley College (DE)
2010	Wesley College (DE)

Liberty Mutual Coach of the Year

Sponsored by the Liberty Mutual Insurance Company (175 Berkeley Street, Boston, MA 02116; Telephone: 800-837-5254; Web site: http://www.coachoftheyear.com/), the Liberty Mutual Coach of the Year Award is an annual college football presentation given to the head coach from each NCAA Division (FBS (as of 2006), FCS (as of 2007), NCAA Division II (as of 2007), and NCAA Division III (as of 2007)).

This award provides each coach with $50,000 to donate to the charity or charities of his choice, as well as a $20,000 grant to donate to his school's alumni association.

Year	Coach	School	Note
2007	John Gagliardi	St. John's University (MN)	Career Coaching Leader with 471 Victories
2008	Larry Kehres	Mount Union College (OH)	2008 Division III Liberty Mutual Coach of the Year
2009	Steve Staker	Coe College (IA)	No Further Information
2010	Glen Caruso	University of St. Thomas (MN)	No Further Information

Melberger Award

Since 1993, the Melberger Award has been presented annually to the most outstanding Division III college football player and is named after Clifford Melberger, president of Diversified Information Technologies (which sponsors the award).

Year	Player	School
1993	Jim Ballard	Mount Union College (OH)
1994	Carey Bender	Coe College (IA)
1995	Craig Kusick, Jr.	University of Wisconsin, La Crosse (WI)
1996	Bill Borchert	Mount Union College (OH)
1997	Bill Borchert	Mount Union College (OH)
1998	Mike Burton	Trinity University (TX)
1999	Scott Pingel	Westminster College (MO)
2000	R.J. Bowers	Grove City College (PA)
2001	Chuck Moore	Mount Union College (OH)
2002	Daniel Pincelli	Hartwick College (NY)
2003	Brett Trichilo	Wilkes University (PA)
2004	Brett Trichilo	Wilkes University (PA)
2005	Brett Elliott	Linfield College (OR)
2006	Chris Sharpe	Springfield College (MA)

Year	*Player*	*School*
2007	Jason Boltus	Hartwick College (NY)
2008	Nate Kmic	Mount Union College (OH)
2009	Alex Tanney	Monmouth College (IL)
2010	Ben McLaughlin	Louisiana College (LA)

Allegheny Mountain Collegiate Conference (AMCC)

508 Lacebark Court, Gibsonia, PA 15044; Telephone: 724-934-1978; Fax: 724-934-1979; Web site: http://www.amcconf.org

The non-profit Allegheny Mountain Collegiate Conference was formed in 1997 with charter members Frostburg State University, Lake Erie College, La Roche College, Pennsylvania State University at Erie, University of Pittsburgh at Bradford, and the University of Pittsburgh at Greensburg. This conference does not support football and consists of the following 10 members:

- D'Youville College Spartans, Buffalo, NY 14201; 716-829-8000; www.dyc.edu; no football program
- Franciscan University of Steubenville Barons, Steubenville, OH 43952; 740-283-3771; www.franciscan.edu; no football program
- Hilbert College Hawks, Hamburg, NY 14075; 716-649-7900; www.hilbert.edu; no football program
- La Roche College Redhawks, Pittsburgh, PA 15237; 412-367-9300; www.laroche.edu; no football program
- Medaille College Mavericks, Buffalo, NY 14214; 716-880-2000; www.medaille.edu; no football program
- Mount Aloysius College Mounties, Cresson, PA 16630; 814-886-4131; www.mtaloy.edu; no football program
- Penn State, Altoona, Lions, Altoona, PA 16601; 814-949-5000; www.aa.psu.edu; no football program
- Penn State, Erie, The Behrend College Lions, Erie, PA 16563; 814-898-6000; http://psbehrend.psu.edu; no football program
- University of Pittsburgh, Bradford, Panthers, Bradford, PA 16701; 814-362-7500; www.upb.pitt.edu; no football program
- University of Pittsburgh, Greensburg, Bobcats, Greensburg, PA 15601; 724-837-7040; www.greensburg.pitt.edu; no football program

American Southwest Conference

Office of the Commissioner, 1221 West Campbell Road, Suite 171, Richardson, TX 75080; Telephone: 972-234-0033; Web site: http://www.ascsports.org

The American Southwest Conference was founded in May 1996 and includes former members of the Texas Intercollegiate Athletic Association and other schools from outside Texas. Starting with eight founding members, the conference has grown to its current lineup of 16 schools, nine of which play football in the conference:

- Centenary College Gents, Shreveport, LA 71104; 318-869-5011; www.centenary.edu; no football program
- Concordia University Texas Tornados, Austin, TX 78726; 512-313-3000; www.concordia.edu; no football program
- East Texas Baptist University Tigers, Marshall, TX 75670; 903-923-2000; www.etbu.edu
- Hardin-Simmons University Cowboys, Abilene, TX 79698; 325-670-1000; www.hsutx.edu
- Howard Payne University Yellow Jackets, Brownwood, TX 76801; 325-649-8020; www.hputx.edu
- LeTourneau University Yellow Jackets, Longview, TX 75607; 800-759-8811; www.letu.edu; no football program
- Louisiana College Wildcats, Pineville, LA 71360; 318-487-7011; www.lacollege.edu
- McMurry University War Hawks, Abilene, TX 79697; 325-793-3800; www.mcm.edu; in 2012, the school will join the Heartland Conference in NCAA Division II
- Mississippi College Choctaws, Clinton, MS 39058; 601-925-3000; www.mc.edu

- Schreiner University Mountaineers, Kerrville, TX 78028; 830-896-5411; www.schreiner.edu; no football program
- Sul Ross State University Lobos, Alpine, TX 79832; 432-837-8011; www.sulross.edu
- Texas Lutheran University Bulldogs, Seguin, TX 78155; 830-372-8000; www.tlu.edu
- University of Mary Hardin, Baylor, Crusaders, Belton, TX 76513; 254-295-8642; www.umhb.edu
- University of Texas at Dallas Comets, Richardson, TX 75080; 972-883-2111; www.utdallas.edu; no football program
- University of Texas at Tyler Patriots, Tyler, TX 75799; 903-566-7202; www.uttyler.edu; no football program
- University of the Ozarks Eagles, Clarksville, AR 72830; 800-264-8636; www.ozarks.edu; no football program

American Southwest Conference Champions

When the conference was known as the Texas Intercollegiate Athletic Association.

Year	*School*
1976	Trinity College (TX)
1977	Tarleton State University (TX)
1978	Tarleton State University (TX)
1979	Austin College College (TX)
1980	McMurry University (TX)
1981	Austin College (TX)
1981	Sul Ross State University (TX)
1982	Sul Ross State University (TX)
1983	McMurry University (TX)
1983	Sul Ross State University (TX)
1984	Austin College (TX(
1985	Austin College (TX)
1985	Sul Ross State University (TX)
1986	Tarleton State University (TX)
1987	Tarleton State University (TX)
1988	Austin College (TX)
1989	Tarleton State University (TX)
1989	Howard Payne University (TX)
1990	Tarleton State University (TX)
1991	Midwestern State University (TX)
1992	Howard Payne University (TX)
1993	Hardin-Simmons University (TX)
1994	Hardin-Simmons University (TX)
1994	Midwestern State University (TX)
1994	Howard Payne University (TX)
1995	Hardin-Simmons University (TX)
1995	Howard Payne University (TX)

American Southwest Conference Champions

Year	*School*
1996	Hardin-Simmons University (TX)
1996	Sul Ross State University (TX)
1997	Mississippi College (MS)
1998	Hardin-Simmons University (TX)
1999	Hardin-Simmons University (TX)
2000	Hardin-Simmons University (TX)
2001	Hardin-Simmons University (TX)
2002	University of Mary Hardin, Baylor (TX)
2003	East Texas Baptist University (TX)
2003	Hardin-Simmons University (TX)
2003	University of Mary Hardin, Baylor (TX)
2004	Hardin-Simmons University (TX)
2005	University of Mary Hardin, Baylor (TX)
2006	University of Mary Hardin, Baylor (TX)
2007	University of Mary Hardin, Baylor (TX)
2008	University of Mary Hardin, Baylor (TX)
2009	Mississippi College (MS)
2009	University of Mary Hardin, Baylor (TX)
2010	University of Mary Hardin, Baylor (TX)

American Southwest Conference Athlete of the Year Award

Presented to an athlete (not necessarily a football player) since 2000 on the basis of athletic accomplishment, participation in a specific sport, and a contribution to the school's athletic program. This list includes only football players who have received the Award.

Year	*Player*	*School*
2001	Aaron Kernek	Austin College (TX)
2003	Preston Meyer	University of Mary Hardin, Baylor (TX)
2004	Cody Fredenburg	University of Mary Hardin, Baylor (TX)
2007	Josh Kubiak	University of Mary Hardin, Baylor (TX)
2008	Jerrell Freeman	University of Mary Hardin, Baylor (TX)
2009	Jake Mullin	McMurry University (TX)
2010	Ben McLaughlin	Louisiana College (LA)

American Southwest Conference Coach of the Year

Year	*Coach*	*School*
2001	Jimmie Keeling	Hardin-Simmons University (TX)
2002	Pete Fredenburg	University of Mary Hardin, Baylor (TX)
2003	Ralph Harris	East Texas Baptist University (TX)
2004	Tom Mueller	Texas Lutheran University (TX)
2005	Mike Redwine	Howard Payne University (TX)
2006	Pete Fredenburg	University of Mary Hardin, Baylor (TX)
2006	Steve Wright	Sul Ross State University (TX)
2007	Pete Fredenburg	University of Mary Hardin, Baylor (TX)
2008	Pete Fredenburg	University of Mary Hardin, Baylor (TX)
2008	Jimmie Keeling	Hardin-Simmons University (TX)
2009	Norman Joseph	Mississippi College (MS)
2010	Pete Fredenburg	University of Mary Hardin, Baylor (TX)

American Southwest Conference Offensive Player of the Year

Year	*Player*	*Position*	*School*
2001	Dustin Proctor	Quarterback	Hardin-Simmons University (TX)
2002	Adam King	Quarterback	Howard Payne University (TX)
2003	Cody Fredenburg	Quarterback	University of Mary Hardin, Baylor (TX)
2004	Lance Moore	Running Back	Hardin-Simmons University (TX)
2005	Ty Sellers	Quarterback	McMurry University (TX)
2006	Jordan Neal	Quarterback	Hardin-Simmons University (TX)
2007	Jake Allen	Wide Receiver	Mississippi College (MS)
2008	Justin Feaster	Quarterback	Hardin-Simmons University (TX)
2009	Adam Shaffer	Quarterback	Mississippi College (MS)
2010	Ben McLaughlin	Quarterback	Louisiana College (LA)

American Southwest Conference Defensive Player of the Year

Year	*Player*	*Position*	*School*
2001	Jared Sanderson	Linebacker	Hardin-Simmons University (TX)
2002	Preston Meyer	Linebacker	University of Mary Hardin, Baylor (TX)
2003	Tony Salazar	Free Safety	University of Mary Hardin, Baylor (TX)
2004	Brent Gailey	Linebacker	Hardin-Simmons University (TX)
2005	Josh Kubiak	Free Safety	University of Mary Hardin, Baylor (TX)
2006	Josh Kubiak	Free Safety	University of Mary Hardin, Baylor (TX)
2007	Jerrell Freeman	Linebacker	University of Mary Hardin, Baylor (TX)
2008	Eric Henri	Linebacker	University of Mary Hardin, Baylor (TX)
2009	Quartez Ashmore	Linebacker	Mississippi College (MS)
2010	Hank Hornsby	End	Hardin-Simmons University (TX)
2010	Will Morris	Back	McMurry University (TX)

American Southwest Conference Special Teams Player of the Year

Year	*Player*	*Position*	*School*
2004	Jared May	Returner	Hardin-Simmons University (TX)
2005	P.J. Williams	Returner	University of Mary Hardin, Baylor (TX)
2006	Will Galusha	Kick & Punt Returner	Hardin-Simmons University (TX)
2007	Joel Munoz	Kicker & Punter	University of Mary Hardin, Baylor (TX)
2008	Jordan Rideaux	Kick Returner	Louisiana College (LA)
2009	Jordan Rideaux	Kick Returner	Louisiana College (LA)
2010	Jordan Rideaux	Kick Returner	Louisiana College (LA)

American Southwest Conference Offensive Lineman of the Year

Year	*Player*	*Position*	*School*
2001	Matt Morris	Tackle	Hardin-Simmons University (TX)
2002	Ryan Harris	Guard	University of Mary Hardin, Baylor (TX)

Year	Player	Position	School
2003	Adam Hernandez	Guard	Hardin-Simmons University (TX)
2003	Matt Miller	Tackle	Louisiana College (LA)
2003	Jeff Oliver	Tackle	University of Mary Hardin, Baylor (TX)
2004	Adam Hernandez	Guard	Hardin-Simmons University (TX)
2005	Jeremy Pawelek	Guard	Texas Lutheran University (TX)
2006	Josh Knox	Center	Hardin-Simmons University (TX)
2007	Caleb Woodall	Tackle	University of Mary Hardin, Baylor (TX)
2008	Josh Littlejohn	Guard	University of Mary Hardin, Baylor (TX)
2009	Josh Lankford	Guard	Mississippi College (MS)
2010	Max Taylor	Tackle	University of Mary Hardin, Baylor (TX)

American Southwest Conference Defensive Lineman of the Year

Year	Player	Position	School
2001	Keith Browning	Tackle	Howard Payne University (TX)
2002	D'Andre Wilson	Tackle	Howard Payne University (TX)
2003	Keith Zunker	End	University of Mary Hardin, Baylor (TX)
2004	Reggie Robinson	End	Hardin-Simmons University (TX)
2005	Chad Glover	End	East Texas Baptist University (TX)
2005	Elex Reed	Tackle	University of Mary Hardin, Baylor (TX)
2006	Terrance Carroll	Tackle	University of Mary Hardin, Baylor (TX)
2007	William Dewease	End	University of Mary Hardin, Baylor (TX)
2008	Brannon Willisson	End	Mississippi College (MS)
2009	Marco Coppola	End	University of Mary Hardin, Baylor (TX)
2010	Hank Hornsby	End	Hardin-Simmons University (TX)

American Southwest Conference Freshman of the Year

Year	Player	Position	School
2001	Adam King	Quarterback	Howard Payne University (TX)
2002	RoShawn Johnson	Running Back	East Texas Baptist University (TX)
2003	A.J. Edwards	Running Back	Howard Payne University (TX)
2004	T.J. Barber	Running Back	Sul Ross State University (TX)
2005	Sylvester Walker	Defensive Back	Howard Payne University (TX)
2006	Ben McLaughlin	Quarterback	Louisiana College (LA)
2007	Carlo Dominguez	Quarterback & Wide Receiver	Sul Ross State University (TX)
2008	Tre Mason	Wide Receiver	Howard Payne University (TX)
2008	Tommy Reyer	Quarterback	Mississippi College (MS)
2009	LiDarral Bailey	Quarterback	University of Mary Hardin, Baylor (TX)
2010	Peter Ford	Defensive Lineman	Louisiana College (LA)

Atlantic Central Football Conference (ACFC)

Apprentice School, Newport News, VA; Telephone: 757-688-4935; Email: james.heath@ngc.com; Web site: http://www.acfcfootball.com

The Atlantic Central Football Conference, a football-only league, was formed in 1997 and began play in 1998. The conference's charter membership included six previous football-independent schools: Chowan College, Ferrum College, Frostburg State University, Methodist College, Salisbury University, and Wesley College. The teams in the ACFC have schedules that allow each team to play games outside the conference.

As of this writing, the following four team play in the ACFC:

- Apprentice School Builders, Newport News, VA 23607; 757-380-3809; www.apprenticeschool.com; this is a vocational school that does not grant degrees (is not affiliated with the NCAA or NAIA); all other sports (except wrestling) participate in the United States Collegiate Athletic Association
- Frostburg State University Bobcats, Frostburg, MD 21532; 301-687-4000; www.frostburg.edu;

plays football in the Empire 8 Athletic Conference and in the Capital Athletic Conference for all other sports

- Salisbury University Sea Gulls, Salisbury, MD 21801; 410-543-6000; www.salisbury.edu; plays football in the Empire 8 Athletic Conference and in the Capital Athletic Conference for all other sports
- Wesley College Wolverines, Dover, DE 19901; 302-736-2300; www.wesley.edu; plays football as an independent team

Atlantic Central Football Conference Champions

Year	*School*
1998	No Champion Declared
1999	Frostburg State University (MD)
2000	Wesley College (DE)
2001	Wesley College (DE)
2002	Frostburg State University (MD)
2003	Frostburg State University (MD)
2004	Frostburg State University (MD)
2005	Salisbury University (MD)
2005	SUNY, Brockport (NY)
2005	Wesley College (DE)
2006	Wesley College (DE)
2007	Wesley College (DE)
2008	Wesley College (DE)
2009	Wesley College (DE)
2010	Wesley College (DE)

Atlantic Central Football Conference Coach of the Year

Year	*Coach*	*School*
1998	Mike Drass	Wesley College (DE)
1999	Ed Sweeney	Frostburg State University (MD)
2000	Mike Drass	Wesley College (DE)
2001	Mike Drass	Wesley College (DE)
2002	Rubin Stevenson	Frostburg State University (MD)
2003	Rubin Stevenson	Frostburg State University (MD)
2003	Sherman Wood	Salisbury University (MD)
2004	Sherman Wood	Salisbury University (MD)
2005	Mike Drass	Wesley College (DE)
2006	Phil Janaro	Apprentice School (VA)
2007	Mike Drass	Wesley College (DE)
2008	Mike Drass	Wesley College (DE)
2009	Mike Drass	Wesley College (DE)
2010	Mike Drass	Wesley College (DE)

Atlantic Central Football Conference Offensive Player of the Year

Year	*Player*	*School*
1998	Brandon Walker	Frostburg State University (MD)
1999	Greg Cooper	Frostburg State University (MD)
1999	Myron Dent	Salisbury University (MD)
2000	Jason Visconti	Wesley College (DE)
2001	Jason Visconti	Wesley College (DE)
2002	Grant Burrough	Frostburg State University (MD)
2003	Grant Burrough	Frostburg State University (MD)
2004	Leroy Satchell	Salisbury University (MD)
2005	Chris Warrick	Wesley College (DE)
2006	Chris Warrick	Wesley College (DE)
2007	Travis Reid	Apprentice School (VA)
2008	Shane McSweeny	Wesley College (DE)
2009	Shane McSweeny	Wesley College (DE)
2010	Bryan Cain	Apprentice School (VA)
2010	Justin Sottilare	Wesley College (DE)

Atlantic Central Football Conference Defensive Player of the Year

Year	Player	School
1998	J.C. Harmon	Ferrum College (VA)
1999	Andre Summers	Wesley College (DE)
2000	Andre Summers	Wesley College (DE)
2000	Tone' Dancy	Ferrum College (VA)
2001	George O'Brien	Frostburg State University (MD)
2002	Mike Simpson	Wesley College (DE)
2003	Brad DeHaven	Salisbury University (MD)
2003	Kevin Culbert	Frostburg State University (MD)
2004	Brad DeHaven	Salisbury University (MD)
2005	Kevin Culbert	Frostburg State University (MD)
2006	Bryan Robinson	Wesley College (DE)
2007	Bryan Robinson	Wesley College (DE)
2008	Sean Matthews	Wesley College (DE)
2009	Mike Ward	Wesley College (DE)
2010	Chris Mayes	Wesley College (DE)

Atlantic Central Football Conference Special Teams Player of the Year

Year	Player	School
2003	Rick Nistler	Salisbury University (MD)
2004	Brock Boland	Salisbury University (MD)
2004	Ricky Doles	Apprentice School (VA)
2005	Brock Boland	Salisbury University (MD)
2006	Christian Cattanea	Wesley College (DE)
2007	Larry Beavers	Wesley College (DE)
2008	Larry Beavers	Wesley College (DE)
2009	Avery Willie	Frostburg State University (MD)
2010	Jonathan Briscoe	Salisbury University (MD)

Atlantic Central Football Conference Rookie of the Year

Year	Player	School
1998	Tony Ellis	Salisbury University (MD)
1999	Phil Hairston	Ferrum College (VA)
2000	John Boyter	Chowan College (NC)
2000	Mac Mollett	Salisbury University (MD)
2001	Milo Austin	Salisbury University (MD)
2002	Dustin Johnson	Salisbury University (MD)
2003	Omar Muhammad	Wesley College (DE)
2004	Jon Lanouette	Wesley College (DE)
2005	Zack Luke	SUNY, Brockport (NY)
2006	Aaron Jackson	Wesley College (DE)
2007	Collin Blugis	Wesley College (DE)
2008	Mana Ohia	Apprentice School (VA)
2009	Louis Norwood	Apprentice School (VA)
2010	Byron Eaton	Wesley College (DE)

Atlantic Women's College Conference (Women's Sports Only)

Capital Athletic Conference

Commissioner, 115 Grantley Hall, York College of Pennsylvania, York, PA 17405; Telephone: 717-815-6817; Fax: 717-849-1676; Web site: http://www.cacsports.com

The Capital Athletic Conference was founded in 1989 with charter schools Catholic University of America, Gallaudet University, Mary Washington College, Marymount University, St. Mary's College of Maryland, and York College of Pennsylvania. The conference currently consists of nine member schools and does not support football, although four of its schools play football in other conferences.

- Frostburg State University Bobcats, Frostburg, MD 21532; 301-687-4000; www.frostburg.edu; plays football in the Empire 8 Athletic Conference
- Hood College Blazers, Frederick, MD 21701; 301-663-3131; www.hood.edu; no football program
- Marymount University Saints, Arlington, VA 22207; 703-522-5600; www.marymount.edu; no football program
- St. Mary's College of Maryland Sea Hawks, St. Mary's City, MD 20686; 240-895-2000; www.smcm.edu; no football program
- Salisbury University Sea Gulls, Salisbury, MD 21801; 410-543-6000; www.salisbury.edu; plays football in the Empire 8 Athletic Conference
- Stevenson University Mustangs, Stevenson, MD 21153; 877-468-6852; www.stevenson.edu; plays football as an independent team
- University of Mary-Washington Eagles, Fredericksburg, VA 22401; 540-654-1000; www.umw.edu; no football program
- Wesley College Wolverines, Dover, DE 19901; 302-736-2300; www.wesley.edu; plays football as an independent team
- York College of Pennsylvania Spartans, York, PA 17403; 717-846-7788; www.ycp.edu; no football program

Centennial Conference

563 College Avenue, B-101, Lancaster, PA 17603; Telephone: 717-358-4463; Fax: 717-358-4480; Web site: http://www.centennial.org

The Centennial Conference was founded in June 1981, originally as a football-only league (called the Centennial Football Conference) with eight charter members: Dickinson College, Franklin & Marshall College, Gettysburg College, Johns Hopkins University, Muhlenberg College, Swarthmore College, Ursinus College, and Western Maryland (now McDaniel) College. In 1992, the conference began accepting other schools and expanded its sporting activity beyond football, while changing to its current name that same year.

As of this writing, the conference consists of 11 member schools, seven of which play football in the conference. Its football program also sponsors three associate members outside the conference.

- Bryn Mawr College Owls, Bryn Mawr, PA 19010; 610-526-5000; www.brynmawr.edu; no football program
- Dickinson College Red Devils, Carlisle, PA 17013; 717-243-5121; www.dickinson.edu
- Franklin & Marshall College Diplomats, Lancaster, PA 17604; 717-291-3911; www.fandm.edu
- Gettysburg College Bullets, Gettysburg, PA 17325; 717-337-6300; www.gettysburg.edu
- Haverford College Fords, Haverford, PA 19041; 610-896-1000; www.haverford.edu; no football program
- Johns Hopkins University Blue Jays, Baltimore, MD 21218; 410-516-8000; www.jhu.edu
- Juniata College Eagles, Huntingdon, PA 16652; 877-586-4282; plays football as an associate member from the Landmark Conference
- McDaniel College Green Terror, Westminster, MD 21157; 410-848-7000; www.mcdaniel.edu
- Moravian College Greyhounds, Bethlehem, PA 18018; 610-861-1300; www.moravian.edu; plays football as an associate member from the Landmark Conference
- Muhlenberg College Mules, Allentown, PA 18104; 484-664-3100; www.muhlenberg.edu
- Susquehanna University Crusaders, Selinsgrove, PA 17870; 570-374-0101; www.susqu.edu; plays football as an associate member from the Landmark Conference
- Swarthmore College Garnet, Swarthmore, PA 19081; 610-328-8000; www.swarthmore.edu; no football program
- Ursinus College Bears, Collegeville, PA 19426; 610-409-3000; www.ursinus.edu
- Washington College Shoremen, Chestertown, MD 21620; 410-778-2800; www.washcoll.edu; no football program

Centennial Conference Champions

Year	School
1983	Gettysburg College (PA)
1983	Muhlenberg College (PA)
1983	Swarthmore College (PA)
1984	Gettysburg College (PA)
1984	Swarthmore College (PA)
1985	Gettysburg College (PA)
1986	Franklin & Marshall College (PA)
1986	Muhlenberg College (PA)
1987	Franklin & Marshall College (PA)
1988	Dickinson College (PA)
1988	Franklin & Marshall College (PA)
1989	Dickinson College (PA)
1990	Dickinson College (PA)
1991	Dickinson College (PA)
1992	Dickinson College (PA)
1993	Dickinson College (PA)
1993	Franklin & Marshall College (PA)
1994	Dickinson College (PA)
1995	Franklin & Marshall College (PA)
1996	Ursinus College (PA)
1997	Western Maryland (McDaniel) College (MD)
1998	Western Maryland (McDaniel) College (MD)
1999	Western Maryland (McDaniel) College (MD)
2000	Western Maryland (McDaniel) College (MD)
2001	Muhlenberg College (PA)
2001	Western Maryland (McDaniel) College (MD)
2002	Johns Hopkins University (MD)
2002	Muhlenberg College (PA)
2002	Western Maryland (McDaniel) College (MD)
2003	Johns Hopkins University (MD)
2003	Muhlenberg College (PA)
2004	Dickinson College (PA)
2004	Franklin & Marshall College (PA)
2004	Johns Hopkins University (MD)
2004	McDaniel College (MD)
2004	Muhlenberg College (PA)
2005	Johns Hopkins University (MD)
2006	Dickinson College (PA)
2007	Muhlenberg College (PA)
2008	Muhlenberg College (PA)
2009	Johns Hopkins University (MD)
2010	Johns Hopkins University (MD)
2010	Muhlenberg College (PA)
2010	Ursinus College (PA)

Centennial Conference Coach of the Year Award

Year	Coach	School
2008	Mike Donnelly	Muhlenberg College (PA)
2009	John Troxell	Franklin & Marshall College (PA)
2010	Mike Donnelly	Muhlenberg College (PA)

Centennial Conference Player of the Year

Year	Player	Position	Class	School
1983	Rick Conner	Defensive Back	Senior	Western Maryland (McDaniel) College (MD)
1984	Glenn Bennett	Quarterback	Junior	Swarthmore College (PA)
1985	Mark Campbell	Quarterback	Senior	Johns Hopkins University (MD)
1986	John Travagline	Quarterback	Senior	Franklin & Marshall College (PA)
1987	Dale Amos	Wide Receiver	Sophomore	Franklin & Marshall College (PA)
1988	Jack Savage	Defensive Tackle	Senior	Franklin & Marshall College (PA)
1989	Dale Amos	Wide Receiver	Senior	Franklin & Marshall College (PA)
1989	Mike Birosak	Running Back	Senior	Dickinson College (PA)
1990	John Bernatavitz	Running Back	Senior	Dickinson College (PA)
1991	Eric Frees	Running Back	Senior	Western Maryland (McDaniel) College (MD)
1992	Chip Chevalier	Quarterback	Senior	Swarthmore College (PA)

Centennial Conference Offensive Player of the Year

Year	Player	Position	Class	School
1993	Bill Sedgwick	Running Back	Senior	Ursinus College (PA)
1994	Chris Adams	Quarterback	Senior	Gettysburg College (PA)
1995	Beau Eckert	Quarterback	Junior	Franklin & Marshall College (PA)

Year	Player	Position	Class	School
1996	Beau Eckert	Quarterback	Senior	Franklin & Marshall College (PA)
1997	Ron Sermarini	Quarterback	Sophomore	Western Maryland (McDaniel) College (MD)
1998	Ron Sermarini	Quarterback	Junior	Western Maryland (McDaniel) College (MD)
1999	Paul Smith	Running Back	Senior	Gettysburg College (PA)
1999	Ron Sermarini	Quarterback	Senior	Western Maryland (McDaniel) College (MD)
2000	Jamie "Boo" Harris	Quarterback	Junior	Western Maryland (McDaniel) College (MD)
2000	Joshua Carter	Wide Receiver	Junior	Muhlenberg College (PA)
2001	Jamie "Boo" Harris	Quarterback	Senior	Western Maryland (McDaniel) College (MD)
2002	Justin Jones	Quarterback	Senior	Muhlenberg College (PA)
2003	Kodi Shay	Wide Receiver	Senior	Muhlenberg College (PA)
2004	Broderick Maybank	Running Back	Junior	McDaniel College (MD)
2005	Anthony Triplin	Wide Receiver	Senior	Johns Hopkins University (MD)
2006	Matt Torchia	Quarterback	Senior	Dickinson College (PA)
2007	Tom Sturges	Running Back	Senior	Gettysburg College (PA)
2008	John DeLuca	Running Back	Senior	Muhlenberg College (PA)
2009	Andrew Kase	Running Back	Senior	Johns Hopkins University (MD)
2010	Sam Wernick	Wide Receiver	Junior	Johns Hopkins University (MD)

Centennial Conference Defensive Player of the Year

Year	Player	Position	Class	School
1993	Frank Fosko	Defensive End	Senior	Dickinson College (PA)
1994	Jason Fox	Linebacker	Senior	Dickinson College (PA)
1995	Matt Bixler	Linebacker	Junior	Dickinson College (PA)
1996	Jim Wilson	Defensive Lineman	Senior	Johns Hopkins University (MD)
1997	Harrison Bernstein	Defensive Back	Sophomore	Johns Hopkins University (MD)
1998	Jason Shoff	Defensive Lineman	Senior	Dickinson College (PA)
1999	Tommy Selecky	Linebacker	Senior	Western Maryland (McDaniel) College (MD)
2000	Aaron Bartolain	Linebacker	Senior	Western Maryland (McDaniel) College (MD)
2001	Jason Wingeart	Defensive Back	Senior	Western Maryland (McDaniel) College (MD)
2002	Matt Wilchinski	Linebacker	Senior	McDaniel College (MD)
2003	Matt Campbell	Defensive Back	Junior	Johns Hopkins University (MD)
2004	Ryan Peer	Linebacker	Senior	Muhlenberg College (PA)
2005	Dan McCall	Linebacker	Senior	Muhlenberg College (PA)
2006	Eric Dube	Linebacker	Junior	Dickinson College (PA)
2007	Eric Dube	Linebacker	Senior	Dickinson College (PA)
2008	Matt Rathbun	Linebacker	Senior	Muhlenberg College (PA)
2009	Colin Wixted	Linebacker	Senior	Johns Hopkins University (MD)
2010	Pat McDonough	Linebacker	Senior	Muhlenberg College (PA)

City University of New York (CUNY) Athletic Conference

CUNY Athletic Conference, 6530 Kissena Boulevard, Flushing, NY 11367; Web site: http://www.cunyathletics.com

The City University of New York Athletic Conference consists of 10 member schools in its senior college division and five member schools in its community college division. It was formed in 1978 with 10 charter schools: Baruch College, Brooklyn College, City College of New York, College of Staten Island, Hunter College, John Jay College of Criminal Justice, Lehman College, Medgar Evers College, Queens College, and York College. The conference does not support football and none of its schools field football teams.

- Baruch College Bearcats (Senior College), New York, NY 10010; 646-312-1000; www.baruch.cuny.edu; no football program
- Borough of Manhattan Community College Panthers (Community College), New York, NY 10007; 212-220-8000; www.bmcc.cuny.edu; no football program
- Bronx Community College Broncos (Community College), Bronx, NY 10453; 718-289-5100; www.bcc.cuny.edu; no football program
- Brooklyn College Bulldogs (Senior College), Brooklyn, NY 11210; 718-951-5000; www.brooklyn.cuny.edu;no football program
- City College of New York Beavers (Senior College), New York, NY 10031; 212-650-7000; wwwl.ccny.cuny.edu; no football program
- College of Staten Island Dolphins (Senior College), Staten Island, NY 10314; 718-982-2000; www.csi.cuny.edu; no football program
- Hostos Community College Caimans (Community College), Bronx, NY 10451; 718-518-4444; www.hostos.cumy.edu; no football program
- Hunter College Hawks (Senior College), New York, NY 10065; 212-772-4000; www.hunter.cuny.edu; no football program
- John Jay College of Criminal Justice Bloodhounds (Senior College), New York, NY 10019; 212-237-8000; www.jjay.cuny.edu; no football program
- Kingsborough Community College Wave (Community College), Brooklyn, NY 11235; 718-265-5343; www.kbcc.cuny.edu; no football program
- Lehman College Lightning (Senior College), Bronx, NY 10468; 718-960-8000; www.lehman.cuny.edu; no football program
- Medgar Evers College Cougars (Senior College), Brooklyn, NY 11225; 718-270-4900; www.mec.cuny.edu; no football program
- New York City College of Technology Yellow Jackets (Senior College), Brooklyn, NY 11201; 718-260-5500; www.citytech.cuny.edu; no football program
- Queensborough Community College Tigers (Community College), Bayside, NY Bayside, NY 11364; 718-631-6262; www.qcc.cuny.edu; no football program
- York College Cardinals (Senior College), Jamaica, NY 11451; 718-262-2000; www.york.cuny.edu; no football program

College Conference of Illinois and Wisconsin

30 North Brainard Street, Naperville, IL 60540; Telephone: 630-637-5693; Fax: 630-637-5694; Web site: http://www.cciw.org

The College Conference of Illinois and Wisconsin was formed in April 1946 (as the College Conference of Illinois) with nine charter members: Augustana College, Carthage College, Elmhurst Conference, Illinois College, Illinois Wesleyan University, Lake Forest College, Millikin University, North Central College, and Wheaton College. The conference adopted its current name in 1967.

As of this writing, the CCIW consists of eight schools, all of which play football within the conference:

- Augustana College Vikings, Rock Island, IL 61201; 309-794-7000; www.augustana.edu
- Carthage College Red Men, Kenosha, WI 53140; 262-551-8500; www.carthage.edu
- Elmhurst College Bluejays, Elmhurst, IL 60126; 630-279-4100; www.elmhurst.edu
- Illinois Wesleyan University Titans, Bloomington, IL 61701; 309-556-1000; www.iwu.edu
- Millikin University Big Blue, Decatur, IL 62522; 800-373-7733; www.milikin.edu
- North Central College Cardinals, Naperville, IL 60540; 630-637-5100; http://northcentralcollege.edu/home
- North Park University Vikings, Chicago, IL 60625; 773-244-6200; www.northpark.edu
- Wheaton College Thunder, Wheaton, IL 60187; 630-752-5000; www.wheaton.edu

College Conference of Illinois and Wisconsin Champions

Year	*School*
1946	North Central College (IL)
1947	North Central College (IL)
1948	Illinois Wesleyan University (IL)
1949	Augustana College (IL)

Year	School
1949	Wheaton College (IL)
1950	Wheaton College (IL)
1951	Illinois Wesleyan University (IL)
1952	Lake Forest College (IL)
1952	Millikin University (IL)
1953	Wheaton College (IL)
1954	Millikin University (IL)
1954	Wheaton College (IL)
1955	Wheaton College (IL)
1956	Wheaton College (IL)
1957	Lake Forest College (IL)
1957	Wheaton College (IL)
1958	Wheaton College (IL)
1959	Wheaton College (IL)
1960	North Central College (IL)
1961	Millikin University (IL)
1962	Carthage College (WI)
1963	Carthage College (WI)
1964	Illinois Wesleyan University (IL)
1965	Illinois Wesleyan University (IL)
1966	Augustana College (IL)
1967	Carthage College (WI)
1968	Augustana College (IL)
1969	Carthage College (WI)
1970	Carthage College (WI)
1971	Carthage College (WI)
1972	Carthage College (WI)
1973	Carthage College (WI)
1974	Illinois Wesleyan University (IL)
1974	Millikin University (IL)
1975	Augustana College (IL)
1976	Carroll University (WI)
1977	Illinois Wesleyan University (IL)
1977	Millikin University (IL)
1978	Elmhurst College (IL)
1978	Millikin University (IL)
1979	Millikin University (IL)
1980	Elmhurst College (IL)
1980	Illinois Wesleyan University (IL)
1981	Augustana College (IL)
1982	Augustana College (IL)
1983	Augustana College (IL)
1984	Augustana College (IL)
1985	Augustana College (IL)
1986	Augustana College (IL)
1987	Augustana College (IL)
1988	Augustana College (IL)
1988	Carroll University (WI)
1989	Millikin University (IL)
1990	Augustana College (IL)
1990	Millikin University (IL)
1991	Augustana College (IL)
1992	Illinois Wesleyan University (IL)
1993	Augustana College (IL)
1994	Augustana College (IL)
1994	Illinois Wesleyan University (IL)
1995	Wheaton College (IL)
1996	Illinois Wesleyan University (IL)
1997	Augustana College (IL)
1998	Millikin University (IL)
1999	Augustana College (IL)
2000	Illinois Wesleyan University (IL)
2000	Millikin University (IL)
2000	Wheaton College (IL)
2001	Augustana College (IL)
2001	Illinois Wesleyan University (IL)
2002	Wheaton College (IL)
2003	Wheaton College (IL)
2004	Carthage College (WI)
2004	Wheaton College (IL)
2005	Augustana College (IL)
2006	Augustana College (IL)
2006	North Central College (IL)
2006	Wheaton College (IL)
2007	Illinois Wesleyan University (IL)
2007	North Central College (IL)
2008	North Central College (IL)
2009	Illinois Wesleyan University (IL)
2009	North Central College (IL)
2010	North Central College (IL)

College Conference of Illinois and Wisconsin — Bob Reade Coach of the Year

Born on July 22, 1932, in Monticello, Iowa, Bob Reade was the head football coach at Augustana College (Rock Island, IL) from 1979 to 1994, accumulating a record of 146–23–1 (.859); he went to five consecutive NCAA Division III national championship games (1982–1986) and won four national championships in a row (1983–1986). Augustana was unbeaten for 60 straight games (59 wins and one tie, from the beginning of the 1983 season until the second round of the 1987 Division III playoffs, still a record in Division III football history). His teams won or shared 12 CCIW championships; he was named Conference Coach of the Year nine times (1981, 1983–1987, 1990, 1993–1994); and was inducted into the College Football Hall of Fame in 1998. Winners are selected by conference coaches.

Year	Coach	School
1978	Tom Beck	Elmhurst College (IL)
1979	Merle Chapman	Millikin University (IL)
1980	Don Larson	Illinois Wesleyan University (IL)
1981	Bob Reade	Augustana College (IL)

Year	Coach	School
1982	Lloyd Krumlauf	North Central College (IL)
1983	Bob Reade	Augustana College (IL)
1984	Bob Reade	Augustana College (IL)
1984	Carl Poelker	Millikin University (IL)
1985	Bob Reade	Augustana College (IL)
1986	Bob Reade	Augustana College (IL)
1987	Bob Reade	Augustana College (IL)
1988	Merle Masonholder	Carroll University (WI)
1989	Carl Poekler	Millikin University (IL)
1990	Bob Reade	Augustana College (IL)
1991	J.R. Bishop	Wheaton College (IL)
1992	Norm Eash	Illinois Wesleyan University (IL)
1993	Bob Reade	Augustana College (IL)
1994	Bob Reade	Augustana College (IL)
1995	J.R. Bishop	Wheaton College (IL)
1996	Norm Eash	Illinois Wesleyan University (IL)
1997	Tom Schmulbach	Augustana College (IL)
1998	Doug Neibuhr	Millikin University (IL)
1999	Tom Schmulbach	Augustana College (IL)
2000	Mike Swider	Wheaton College (IL)
2001	Norm Eash	Illinois Wesleyan University (IL)
2002	Mike Swider	Wheaton College (IL)
2003	Mike Swider	Wheaton College (IL)
2003	Paul Krohn	Elmhurst College (IL)
2004	Tim Rucks	Carthage College (WI)
2005	Jim Barnes	Augustana College (IL)
2006	Mike Swider	Wheaton College (IL)
2007	Norm Eash	Illinois Wesleyan University (IL)
2008	John Thorne	North Central College (IL)
2009	Norm Eash	Illinois Wesleyan University (IL)
2010	John Thorne	North Central College (IL)

College Conference of Illinois and Wisconsin— Art Keller Offensive Player of the Year

Selected by conference coaches; Keller was a 31-year head football coach at Carthage College (Kenosha, WI, 1952–1982) who accumulated a record of 177–87–7 (.666); he won eight conference titles (1962–1963, 1967, 1969–1973); and was a four-time NAIA District Coach of the Year.

Year	Player	School
1962	Erv Olson	Carthage College (WI)
1963	Vic Armstron	Illinois Wesleyan University (IL)
1966	Steve Laub	Illinois Wesleyan University (IL)
1970	Ken Anderson	Augustana College (IL)
1971	Craig Deaton	Carthage College (WI)
1975	Jim Jodat	Carthage College (WI)
1976	Joe Thompson	Augustana College (IL)
1977	John Boettcher	Augustana College (IL)
1978	Pete Thompson	Carthage College (WI)
1979	Mike Jakovich	North Central College (IL)
1980	George Donald	Elmhurst College (IL)
1981	Steve Finch	Elmhurst College (IL)
1982	Lance Hofer	Augustana College (IL)
1983	Steve Thonn	Wheaton College (IL)
1984	Greg King	Augustana College (IL)
1984	John Rooney	Illinois Wesleyan University (IL)
1984	Keith Bishop	Wheaton College (IL)
1985	Keith Bishop	Wheaton College (IL)

Year	*Player*	*School*
1986	Brad Price	Augustana College (IL)
1987	Dave Weber	Carroll University (WI)
1988	John Bothe	Augustana College (IL)
1989	John Arlis	Millikin University (IL)
1990	John Love	North Park University (IL)
1991	Chris Bisaillon	Illinois Wesleyan University (IL)
1992	Tom Monken	Illinois Wesleyan University (IL)
1993	Scott Tumility	Augustana College (IL)
1994	Scott Tumility	Augustana College (IL)
1995	Scott Tumility	Augustana College (IL)
1996	Lon Erickson	Illinois Wesleyan University (IL)
1997	Eric Larsen	Illinois Wesleyan University (IL)
1998	Tim Hardy	Wheaton College (IL)
1999	Joe Schmulbach	Augustana College (IL)
2000	Tim Brylka	Millikin University (IL)
2001	Dave Chorney	Augustana College (IL)
2002	Randall Baker	Carthage College (WI)
2003	Chad Bradley	Wheaton College (IL)
2004	Dante Washington	Carthage College (WI)
2005	Kam Kniss	North Central College (IL)
2006	Kam Kniss	North Central College (IL)
2007	Aaron Fanthorpe	North Central College (IL)
2008	Aaron Fanthorpe	North Central College (IL)
2009	Aaron Fanthorpe	North Central College (IL)
2010	Evan Jones	Carthage College (WI)

College Conference of Illinois and Wisconsin — Don Larson Defensive Player of the Year

Voted on by conference coaches; Don "Swede" Larson was a head football coach at Illinois Wesleyan University (Bloomington, IL) from 1954 to 1986; accumulated an overall record of 166–121–6 (.567); and won five conference championships (1964–1965, 1974, 1977, 1980).

Year	*Player*	*School*
1977	Earl Wilcek	Elmhurst College (IL)
1978	Jerome Brown	Millikin University (IL)
1979	Keith Cornwell	Illinois Wesleyan University (IL)
1980	Rick Hanna	Illinois Wesleyan University (IL)
1981	Fred Battaglia	North Park University (IL)
1981	Jim Perryman	Millikin University (IL)
1981	Jon Kuperus	Augustana College (IL)
1982	Jim Perryman	Millikin University (IL)
1983	Pete Kasap	Augustana College (IL)
1984	Joe Wheeler	Augustana College (IL)
1985	Mark Long	Augustana College (IL)
1986	Lynn Thomsen	Augustana College (IL)
1987	Jim Bentz	Carthage College (WI)
1988	Chad Thorson	Wheaton College (IL)
1989	Chad Thorson	Wheaton College (IL)
1990	Tim Funk	Millikin University (IL)
1991	Shawn Feuker	Carthage College (WI)
1992	George Annang	Augustana College (IL)
1993	Kermit Ellison	Wheaton College (IL)
1994	Rusty VanWetzinga	Augustana College (IL)
1995	Rusy Vanwetzinga	Augustana College (IL)
1996	Chip Parrish	Wheaton College (IL)
1996	John Munch	Illinois Wesleyan University (IL)
1997	John Munch	Illinois Wesleyan University (IL)

Year	Player	School
1998	Carlos Burns	Millikin University (IL)
1999	Bob Meyer	Millikin University (IL)
1999	Norm Robinson	North Central College (IL)
2000	J.D. Leman	Wheaton College (IL)
2001	Mike Lindsey	Millikin University (IL)
2002	Justin Knapp	Wheaton College (IL)
2003	Mike Hansen	Augustana College (IL)
2004	Lenny Radtke	North Central College (IL)
2005	Tom Anthony	Augustana College (IL)
2006	Andy Studebaker	Wheaton College (IL)
2007	Pete Ittersagen	Wheaton College (IL)
2008	Matt Wenger	North Central College (IL)
2009	Nick Nikolich	Illinois Wesleyan University (IL)
2010	Matt Wenger	North Central College (IL)

Colonial States Athletic Conference (CSAC)

C/o Neumann University, One Neumann Drive, Aston, PA 19014; Telephone: 610-361-5344; Fax: 610-361-5262; Web site: http://www.csacsports.org/

Originally known as the Pennsylvania Athletic Conference, the Colonial States Athletic Commission was created in November 1991 (athletic competition began in 1992) with 10 charter member schools: Alvernia College, Beaver College (now known as Arcadia University), Cabrini College, Cedar Crest College, Eastern University, Gwynedd-Mercy College, Immaculata University, Marywood University, Misericordia University, and Rosemont College. The conference adopted its current name in July 2008.

As of this writing, the CSAC consists of 12 schools and does not support a football program.

- Baptist Bible College Defenders, Clarks Summit, PA 18411; 570-586-2400; www.bbc.edu; no football program
- Cabrini College Cavaliers, Radnor, PA 19087; 610-902-8100; www.cabrini.edu; no football program
- Cedar Crest College Falcons, Allentown, PA 18104; 800-360-1222; www.cedarcrest.edu; no football program
- Centenary College Cyclones, Hackettstown, NJ 07840; 908-852-1400; www.centenarycollege.edu; no football program
- College of Notre Dame of Maryland Gators, Baltimore, MD 21210; 410-435-0100; www.ndm.edu; no football program
- Gwynedd-Mercy College Griffins, Gwynedd Valley, PA 19437; 215-646-7300; www.gmc.edu; no football program
- Immaculata University Mighty Macs, Immaculata, PA 19345; 610-647-4400; www.immaculata.edu; no football program
- Keystone College Giants, La Plume, PA 18440; 570-945-8000; www.keystone.edu; no football program
- Marywood University Pacers, Scranton, PA 18509; 570-348-6211; www.marywood.edu; no football program
- Neumann University Knights, Aston, PA 19014; 610-459-0905; www.neumann.edu; no football program
- Philadelphia Biblical University Crimson Eagles, Langhorne, PA 19047; 215-752-5800; http://pbu.edu; no football program
- Rosemont College Ravens, Rosemont, PA 19010; 610-527-0200; www.rosemont.edu; no football program

Commonwealth Coast Conference

C/o Western New England College, 1215 Wilbraham Road, Springfield, MA 01119; Telephone: 413-796-2329; Fax: 413-796-2338; Web site: http://www.thecommonwealthcoastconference. .com

Established in 1984, the Commonwealth Coast Conference consists of 14 member schools and does not support a football program, although six of its member schools play football outside the conference.

- Anna Maria College AmCats, Paxton, MA 01612; 800-344-4586; www.annamaria.edu; plays football in the Eastern Collegiate Football Conference
- Colby-Sawyer College Chargers, New London, NH 03257; 603-526-3000; www.colby-sawyer.edu; no football program
- Curry College Colonels, Milton, MA 02186; 617-333-0500; www.curry.edu; plays football in the New England Football Conference
- Eastern Nazarene College Lions, Quincy, MA 02170; 617-745-3000; www.enc.edu; no football program
- Endicott College Gulls, Beverly, MA 01915; 978-927-0585; www.endicott.edu; plays football in the New England Football Conference
- Gordon College Fighting Scots, Wenham, MA 01984; 978-927-2300; www.gordon.edu; no football program
- New England College Pilgrims, Henniker, NH 03242; 603-428-2000; www.nec.edu; no football program
- Nichols College Bison, Dudley, MA 01571; 508-213-1560; www.nichols.edu; plays football in the New England Football Conference
- Regis College Pride, Weston, MA 02493; 781-768-7000; www.regiscollege.edu;; no football program
- Roger Williams University Hawks, Bristol, RI 02809; 401-253-1040; www.rwu.edu; no football program
- Salve Regina University Seahawks, Newport, RI 02840; 401-847-6650; www.salve.edu; plays football in the New England Football Conference
- University of New England Nor'easters, Biddeford, ME 04005; 207-283-0171; www.une.edu; no football program
- Wentworth Institute of Technology Leopards, Boston, MA 02115; 617.989.4590; www.wit.edu; no football program
- Western New England University Golden Bears, Springfield, MA 01119; 413-782-3111; www.wne.edu; plays football in the New England Football Conference

Commonwealth Conference *see* Middle Atlantic Corporation

Eastern College Athletic Conference (ECAC)

1311 Craigville Beach Road, Centerville, MA 02632; Telephone: 508-771-5060; Fax: 508-771-9486; Web site: http://www.ecac.org; http://www.ecacsports.com

Established in 1938 as the Central Office for Eastern Intercollegiate Athletics with 58 charter members, the Eastern College Athletic Conference has grown to become the nation's largest (and only multi-divisional) athletic conference in the United States with 304 members (as of this writing) (Division I—90 members, Division II—23 members, and Division III—191 members). Member schools of the ECAC also compete in at least one other conference (or as independent schools) and play in the ECAC postseason, when eligible. See NCAA Division I (FBS & FCS) and NCAA Division II for a complete schools list within each division.

Football Alignments (Division III)

Members of the ECAC:

Northeast Region

- Eastern Collegiate Football Conference (Anna Maria College, Becker College, Castleton State College, Gallaudet University, Husson College, Mount Ida College, Norwich University, State University of New York Maritime College)
- New England Football Conference (Bridgewater State College, Curry College, Endicott College, Fitchburg State College, Framingham State College, Maine Maritime Academy, Massachusetts Institute of Technology, Massachusetts Maritime Academy, Nichols College, Plymouth State University, Salve

Regina University, U.S. Coast Guard Academy, University of Massachusetts, Dartmouth, Western New England College, Westfield State College, Worcester State College)
- New England Small College Athletic Conference (Amherst College, Bates College, Bowdoin College, Colby College, Hamilton College, Middlebury College, Trinity College, Tufts University, Wesleyan University, Williams College)

Northwest Region

- Empire 8 Athletic Conference (Alfred University, Hartwick College, Ithaca College, Springfield College, St. John Fisher College, Utica College)
- Liberty League (Hobart College, Rensselaer Polytechnic Institute, St. Lawrence University, U.S. Merchant Marine Academy, Union College, University of Rochester, Worcester Polytechnic Institute)

Southeast Region

- Middle Atlantic States Collegiate Athletic Corporation (Albright College, Delaware Valley College, Fairleigh Dickinson University, Florham, King's College, Lebanon Valley College, Widener University, Wilkes University)
- New Jersey Athletic Conference (Buffalo State College, Kean University, Montclair State University, Morrisville State College, Rowan University, State University of New York at Brockport, State University of New York at Cortland, The College of New Jersey, Western Connecticut State University, William Paterson University)

Southwest Region

- Atlantic Central Football Conference (Frostburg State University, Salisbury University, Wesley College)
- Centennial Conference (Dickinson College, Franklin & Marshall College, Gettysburg College, Johns Hopkins University, Juniata College, McDaniel College, Moravian College, Muhlenberg College, Ursinus College)
- Independents Schools (Carnegie Mellon University, Catholic University)
- Presidents' Athletic Conference (Bethany College, Chatham University, Geneva College, Grove City College, Saint Vincent College, Washington & Jefferson College, Waynesburg University, Westminster College)

Division III Members (191)

- Albertus Magnus College Falcons (Great Northeast Athletic Conference) (New Haven, CT)
- Albright College Lions (Middle Atlantic States Collegiate Athletic Corporation) (Reading, PA)
- Alfred University Saxons (Empire 8 Athletic Conference) (Alfred, NY)
- Alvernia University Crusaders (Middle Atlantic States Collegiate Athletic Corporation) (Reading, PA)
- Amherst College Lord Jeffs (New England Small College Athletic Conference) (Amherst, MA)
- Anna Maria College Amcats (The Commonwealth Coast Conference) (Paxton, MA)
- Babson College Beavers (New England Women's and Men's Athletic Conference) (Babson Park, MA)
- Bard College Raptors (Skyline Conference) (Annandale-on-Hudson, NY)
- Baruch College Bearcats (City University of New York Athletic Conference) (New York, NY)
- Bates College Bobcats (New England Small College Athletic Conference) (Lewiston, ME)
- Becker College Hawks (New England Collegiate Conference) (Leicester, MA)
- Bethany College Bison (Presidents' Athletic Conference) (Bethany, WV)
- Bowdoin College Polar Bears (New England Small College Athletic Conference) (Brunswick, ME)
- Brandeis University Judges (University Athletic Association) (Waltham, MA)
- Bridgewater State College Bears (Massachusetts State Collegiate Athletic Conference) (Bridgewater, MA)
- Brooklyn College Bridges (City University of New York Athletic Conference) (Brooklyn, NY)
- Buffalo State College Bengals (State University of New York Athletic Conference) (Buffalo, NY)
- Cabrini College Cavaliers (Colonial States Athletic Conference) (Radnor, PA)
- Carnegie Mellon University Tartans (University Athletic Association) (Pittsburgh, PA)
- Castleton State College Spartans (North Atlantic Conference) (Castleton, VT)
- Catholic University of America Cardinals (Landmark Conference) (Washington, D.C.)

- Cazenovia College Wildcats (North Eastern Athletic Conference) (Cazenovia, NY)
- Centenary College Cyclones (Colonial States Athletic Conference) (Hackettstown, NJ)
- Chatham University Cougars (Presidents' Athletic Conference) (Pittsburgh, PA)
- City College of New York Beavers (City University of New York Athletic Conference) (New York, NY)
- Clark University Cougars (New England Women's and Men's Athletic Conference) (Worcester, MA)
- Clarkson University Golden Knights (Liberty League) (Potsdam, NY)
- Colby College Mules (New England Small College Athletic Conference) (Waterville, ME)
- Colby-Sawyer College Chargers (The Commonwealth Coast Conference) (New London, NH)
- College of Mount Saint Vincent Dolphins (Skyline Conference) (Riverdale, NY)
- College of Saint Elizabeth Eagles (Independent) (Morristown, NJ)
- College of Staten Island Dolphins (City University of New York Athletic Conference) (Staten Island, NY)
- Connecticut College Camels (New England Small College Athletic Conference) (New London, CT)
- Curry College Colonels (The Commonwealth Coast Conference) (Milton, MA)
- D'Youville College Spartans (Allegheny Mountain Collegiate Conference) (Buffalo, NY)
- Daniel Webster College Eagles (New England Collegiate Conference) (Nashua, NH)
- Delaware Valley College Aggies (Middle Atlantic States Collegiate Athletic Corporation) (Doylestown, PA)
- DeSales University Bulldogs (Middle Atlantic States Collegiate Athletic Corporation) (Center Valley, PA)
- Dickinson College Red Devils (Centennial Conference (Carlisle, PA)
- Drew University Rangers (Landmark Conference) (Madison, NJ)
- Eastern Connecticut State University Warriors (Little East Conference) (Willimantic, CT)
- Eastern Nazarene College Crusaders (The Commonwealth Coast Conference) (Quincy, MA)
- Elmira College Soaring Eagles (Empire 8 Athletic Conference) (Elmira, NY)
- Elms College Blazers (New England Collegiate Conference) (Chicopee, MA)
- Emerson College Lions (Great Northeast Athletic Conference) (Boston, MA)
- Emmanuel College Saints (Great Northeast Athletic Conference) (Boston, MA)
- Endicott College Gulls (The Commonwealth Coast Conference) (Beverly, MA)
- Fairleigh Dickinson University, College at Florham Devils (Middle Atlantic States Collegiate Athletic Corporation) (Madison NJ)
- Farmingdale State College Rams (Skyline Conference) (Farmingdale, NY)
- Fitchburg State College Falcons (Massachusetts State Collegiate Athletic Conference) (Fitchburg, MA)
- Framingham State College Rams (Massachusetts State Collegiate Athletic Conference) (Framingham, MA)
- Franklin & Marshall College Diplomats (Centennial Conference) (Lancaster, PA)
- Frostburg State University Bobcats (Allegheny Mountain Collegiate Conference) (Frostburg, MD)
- Gallaudet University Bison (Capital Athletic Conference) (Washington, D.C.)
- Geneva College Golden Tornadoes (Presidents' Athletic Conference) (Beaver Falls, PA)
- Gettysburg College Bullets (Centennial Conference) (Gettysburg, PA)
- Gordon College Fighting Scots (The Commonwealth Coast Conference) (Wenham, MA)
- Grove City College Wolverines (Presidents' Athletic Conference) (Grove City, PA)
- Gwynedd-Mercy College Griffins (Colonial States Athletic Conference) (Gwynedd Valley, PA)
- Hamilton College Continentals (New England Small College Athletic Conference) (Clinton, NY)
- Hartwick College Hawks (Empire 8 Athletic Conference) (Oneonta, NY)
- Hilbert College Hawks (Allegheny Mountain Collegiate Conference) (Hamburg, NY)
- Hobart College Statesmen (Liberty League) (Geneva, NY)
- Hunter College Hawks (City University of New York Athletic Conference) (New York, NY)
- Husson University Eagles (North Atlantic Conference) (Bangor, ME)
- Ithaca College Bombers (Empire 8 Conference) (Ithaca, NY)
- John Jay College Bloodhounds (City University of New York Athletic Conference) (New York, NY)
- Johns Hopkins University Blue Jays (Centennial Conference) (Baltimore, MD)
- Johnson & Wales University Wildcats (Great Northeast Athletic Conference) (Providence, RI)
- Juniata College Eagles (Landmark Conference) (Huntingdon, PA)

- Kean University Cougars (New Jersey Athletic Conference) (Union, NJ)
- Keene State College Owls (Little East Conference) (Keene, NH)
- Keuka College Storm (North Eastern Athletic Conference) (Keuka Park, NY)
- King's College Monarchs (Middle Atlantic Conference) (Wilkes-Barre, PA)
- La Roche College Redhawks (Allegheny Mountain Collegiate Conference) (Pittsburgh, PA)
- Lasell College Lasers (Great Northeast Athletic Conference) (Newton, MA)
- Lebanon Valley College Flying Dutchmen (Middle Atlantic States Collegiate Athletic Corporation) (Annville, PA)
- Lehman College Lightning (City University of New York Athletic Conference) (Bronx, NY)
- Lesley University Lynx (New England Collegiate Conference) (Cambridge, MA)
- Lyndon State College Hornets (North Atlantic Conference) (Lyndonville, VT)
- Maine Maritime Academy Mariners (North Atlantic Conference) (Castine, ME)
- Manhattanville College Valiants (Middle Atlantic States Collegiate Athletic Corporation) (Purchase, NY)
- Massachusetts College of Liberal Arts Trailblazers (Massachusetts State Collegiate Athletic Conference) (North Adams, MA)
- Massachusetts Institute of Technology Engineers (New England Women's and Men's Athletic Conference) (Cambridge, MA)
- Massachusetts Maritime Academy Buccaneers (Massachusetts State Collegiate Athletic Conference) (Buzzards Bay, MA)
- McDaniel College Green Terror (Centennial Conference) (Westminster, MD)
- Medaille College Mavericks (Allegheny Mountain Collegiate Conference) (Buffalo, NY)
- Medgar Evers College Cougars (City University of New York Athletic Conference) (Brooklyn, NY)
- Middlebury College Panthers (New England Small College Athletic Conference) (Middlebury, VT)
- Misericordia University Cougars (Middle Atlantic States Collegiate Athletic Corporation) (Dallas, PA)
- Mitchell College Pequots (New England Collegiate Conference) (New London, CT)
- Montclair State University Red Hawks (New Jersey Athletic Conference) (Montclair, NJ)
- Moravian College Greyhounds (Landmark Conference) (Bethlehem, PA)
- Morrisville State College Mustangs (North Eastern Athletic Conference) (Morrisville, NY)
- Mount Holyoke College Lyons (New England Women's and Men's Athletic Conference) (South Hadley, MA)
- Mount Ida College Mustangs (Great Northeast Athletic Conference) (Newton, MA)
- Mount Saint Mary College Knights (Skyline Conference) (Newburgh, NY)
- Muhlenberg College Mules (Centennial Conference) (Allentown, PA)
- Neumann University Knights (Colonial States Athletic Conference) (Aston, PA)
- New England College Pilgrims (The Commonwealth Coast Conference) (Henniker, NH)
- New Jersey City University Gothic Knights (New Jersey Athletic Conference) (Jersey City, NJ)
- New York City College of Technology Yellow Jackets (City University of New York Athletic Conference) (Brooklyn NY)
- New York University Violets (University Athletic Association) (New York, NY)
- Newbury College Nighthawks (New England Collegiate Conference) (Brookline, MA)
- Nichols College Bison (The Commonwealth Coast Conference) (Dudley, MA)
- Norwich University Cadets (Great Northeast Athletic Conference) (Northfield, VT)
- Pennsylvania State University, Abington, Lions (North Eastern Athletic Conference) (Abington, PA)
- Pennsylvania State University, Altoona, Lions (Allegheny Mountain Collegiate Conference) (Altoona, PA)
- Pennsylvania State University, Erie, The Behrend College Lions (Allegheny Mountain Collegiate Conference) (Erie, PA)
- Plymouth State University Panthers (Little East Conference) (Plymouth, NH)
- Ramapo College Roadrunners (New Jersey Athletic Conference) (Mahwah, NJ)
- Regis College Pride (The Commonwealth Coast Conference) (Weston, MA)
- Rensselaer Polytechnic Institute Reds (Liberty League) (Troy, NY)
- Rhode Island College Anchormen (Little East Conference) (Providence, RI)
- Richard Stockton College of New Jersey Ospreys (New Jersey Athletic Conference) (Pomona, NJ)

- Rivier College Raiders (Great Northeast Athletic Conference) (Nashua, NH)
- Rochester Institute of Technology Tigers (Empire 8 Athletic Conference) (Rochester, NY)
- Roger Williams University Hawks (The Commonwealth Coast Conference) (Bristol, RI)
- Rowan University Owls (New Jersey Athletic Conference) (Glassboro, NJ)
- Rutgers University, Camden, Scarlet Raptors (New Jersey Athletic Conference) (Camden, NJ)
- Rutgers University, Newark, Scarlet Raiders (New Jersey Athletic Conference) (Newark, NJ)
- St. John Fisher College Cardinals (Empire 8 Athletic Conference) (Rochester, NY)
- Saint Joseph College Blue Jays (Great Northeast Athletic Conference) (West Hartford, CT)
- St. Joseph's College Bears (Skyline Conference) (Patchogue NY)
- Saint Joseph's College Monks (Great Northeast Athletic Conference) (Standish, ME)
- St. Lawrence University Saints (Liberty League) (Canton, NY)
- Saint Vincent College Bearcats (Presidents' Athletic Conference) (Latrobe, PA)
- Salem State College Vikings (Massachusetts State Collegiate Athletic Conference) (Salem, MA)
- Salisbury University Sea Gulls (Capital Athletic Conference) (Salisbury, MD)
- Salve Regina University Seahawks (The Commonweath Coast Conference) (Newport, RI)
- Simmons College Sharks (Great Northeast Athletic Conference) (Boston, MA)
- Skidmore College Thouroughbreds (Liberty League) (Saratoga, NY)
- Smith College Pioneers (New England Women's and Men's Athletic Conference) (Northampton, MA)
- Southern Vermont College Mountaineers (New England Collegiate Conference) (Bennington, VT)
- Springfield College Pride (New England Women's and Men's Athletic Conference) (Springfield, MA)
- State University of New York at Brockport Golden Eagles (State University of New York Athletic Conference) Brockport NY
- State University of New York at Cobleskill Fighting Tigers (Northeast Athletic Conference) (Cobleskill, NY)
- State University of New York at Cortland Red Dragons (State University of New York Athletic Conference) (Cortland, NY)
- State University of New York at Fredonia Blue Devils (State University of New York Athletic Conference) (Fredonia, NY)
- State University of New York at Geneseo Blue Knights (State University of New York Athletic Conference) (Geneseo, NY)
- State University of New York at New Paltz Hawks (State University of New York Athletic Conference) (New Paltz, NY)
- State University of New York at Oneonta Red Dragons (State University of New York Athletic Conference) (Oneonta, NY)
- State University of New York at Oswego Lakers (State University of New York Athletic Conference) (Oswego, NY)
- State University of New York at Plattsburgh Cardinals (State University of New York Athletic Conference) (Plattsburgh, NY)
- State University of New York at Potsdam Bears (State University of New York Athletic Conference) (Potsdam, NY)
- State University of New York College at Old Westbury Panthers (Skyline Conference) (Old Westbury, NY)
- State University of New York Institute of Technology Wildcats (North Eastern Athletic Conference) (Utica, NY)
- State University of New York Maritime College (Independent) (New York, NY)
- State University of New York Purchase College Panthers (Skyline Conference) (Purchase, NY)
- Stevens Institute of Technology Ducks (Empire 8 Athletic Conference) (Hoboken, NJ)
- Stevenson University Mustangs (Capital Athletic Conference) (Stevenson, MD)
- Suffolk University Rams (Great Northeast Athletic Conference) (Boston, MA)
- Swarthmore College Garnet (Centennial Conference) (Swarthmore, PA)
- The College of New Jersey Lions (New Jersey Athletic Conference) (Ewing, NJ)
- The Sage Colleges Gators (Skyline Conference) (Troy, NY)
- Trinity College Bantams (New England Small College Athletic Conference) (Hartford, CT)
- Tufts University Jumbos (New England Small College Athletic Conference) (Medford, MA)

- U.S. Coast Guard Academy Bears (New England Women's and Men's Athletic Conference) (New London, CT)
- U.S. Merchant Marine Academy Mariners (Landmark Conference) (Kings Point, NY)
- Union College Dutchmen (Liberty League) (Schenectady, NY)
- University of Massachusetts, Boston, Beacons (Little East Conference) (Boston, MA)
- University of Massachusetts, Dartmouth, Corsairs (Little East Conference) (North Dartmouth, MA)
- University of New England Nor'easters (The Commonwealth Coast Conference) (Biddeford, ME)
- University of Pittsburgh at Bradford Panthers (Allegheny Mountain Collegiate Conference) (Bradford, PA)
- University of Pittsburgh at Greensburg Bobcats (Allegheny Mountain Collegiate Conference) (Greensburg, PA)
- University of Rochester Yellowjackets (Liberty League) (Rochester, NY)
- University of Southern Maine Huskies (Little East Conference) (Gorham, ME)
- Ursinus College Bears (Centennial Conference) (Collegeville, PA)
- Utica College Pioneers (Empire 8 Athletic Conference) (Utica, NY)
- Vassar College Brewers (Liberty League) (Poughkeepsie, NY)
- Washington & Jefferson College Presidents (Presidents' Athletic Conference) (Washington, PA)
- Waynesburg University Yellow Jackets (Presidents' Athletic Conference) (Waynesburg, PA)
- Wellesley College Blue Pride (New England Women's and Men's Athletic Conference) (Wellesley, MA)
- Wentworth Institute of Technology Leopards (The Commonwealth Coast Conference) (Boston, MA)
- Wesley College Wolverines (Capital Athletic Conference) (Dover, DE)
- Wesleyan University Cardinals (New England Small College Athletic Conference) (Middletown, CT)
- Western Connecticut State University Colonials (Little East Conference) (Danbury, CT)
- Western New England College Golden Bears (The Commonwealth Coast Conference) (Springfield, MA)
- Westfield State College Owls (Massachusetts State Collegiate Athletic Conference) (Westfield, MA)
- Westminster College Titans (Presidents' Athletic Conference) (New Wilmington, PA)
- Wheaton College Lyons (New England Women's and Men's Athletic Conference) (Norton, MA)
- Widener University Pioneers (Middle Atlantic States Collegiate Athletic Corporation) (Chester, PA)
- Wilkes University Colonels (Middle Atlantic States Collegiate Athletic Corporation) (Wilkes Barre, PA)
- William Paterson University Pioneers (New Jersey Athletic Conference) (Wayne, NJ)
- William Smith College Herons (New York State Women's Collegiate Athletic Association) (Geneva, NY)
- Williams College Ephs (New England Small College Athletic Conference) (Williamstown, MA)
- Wilson College Phoenix (North Eastern Athletic Conference) (Chambersburg, PA)
- Worcester Polytechnic Institute Engineers (New England Women's and Men's Athletic Conference) (Worcester, MA)
- Worcester State College Lancers (Massachusetts State Collegiate Athletic Conference) (Worcester, MA)
- Yeshiva University Maccabees (Skyline Conference) (New York, NY)
- York College Cardinals (City University of New York Athletic Conference) (Jamaica Queens, NY)

Eastern College Athletic Conference (ECAC) Division III Men's East Hockey League

Non-football conference

Eastern College Athletic Conference (ECAC) Division III Men's West Hockey League

Non-football conference

Eastern College Athletic Conference (ECAC) Division III Northeast Hockey League

Non-football conference

Eastern College Athletic Conference Division III Women's East Hockey League

Non-football conference

Eastern College Athletic Conference Division III Women's West Hockey League

Non-football conference

Eastern Collegiate Football Conference (ECFC)

Wilmington, VT; Email: info@easterncollegiatefootball.com; Web site: http://www.easterncollegiatefootball.com

The Eastern Collegiate Football Conference was founded in the spring of 2009 as a football-only entity. While all of its schools play football in this conference, each member institution belongs to other conferences for other sports. As of this writing, the eight ECFC members include:

- Anna Maria College AmCats, Paxton, MA 01612; 800-344-4586; www.annamaria.edu; member from the Commonwealth Coast Conference
- Becker College Hawks, Leicester, MA 01524; 774-354-0481; www.becker.edu; member from the New England Collegiate Conference
- Castleton State College Spartans, Castleton, VT 05735; 802-468-5611; www.castleton.edu; member from the North Atlantic Conference
- Gallaudet University Bison, Washington, D.C. 20002; 202-651-5000; www.gallaudet.edu; member from the North Eastern Athletic Conference
- Husson University Eagles, Bangor, ME 04401; 800-448-7766; www.husson.edu; member from the North Atlantic Conference
- Mount Ida College Mustangs, Newton, MA 02459; 617-928-4500; www.mountida.edu; member from the Great Northeast Athletic Conference
- Norwich University Cadets, Northfield, VT 05663; 802-485-2000; www.norwich.edu; member from the Great Northeast Athletic Conference
- State University of New York Maritime College Privateers, Throggs Neck, NY 10465; 718-409-7200; www.sunymaritime.edu; member from the Skyline Conference

Eastern Collegiate Football Conference Champions

Year	*School*
2009	Norwich University (VT)
2010	State University of New York Maritime College (NY)

Eastern Collegiate Football Conference Coach of the Year

Selected by conference coaches.

Year	*Coach*	*School*
2009	Ed Hottle	Gallaudet University (Washington, D.C.)
2010	Clayton Kendrick-Holmes	State University of New York Maritime College (NY)

Eastern Collegiate Football Conference Offensive Player of the Year

Selected by conference coaches.

Year	*Player*	*Position*	*School*
2009	Johrone Bunch	Running Back	Mount Ida College (MA)
2010	Shane Brozowski	Quarterback	Castleton State College (VT)
2010	Kris Sabourin	Quarterback	Norwich University (VT)

Eastern Collegiate Football Conference Defensive Player of the Year

Selected by conference coaches.

Year	*Player*	*Position*	*School*
2009	Reza Afsarmanesh	Defensive End	Norwich University (VT)
2010	Keith Barnes	Linebacker	State University of New York Maritime College (NY)

Eastern Collegiate Football Conference Special Teams Player of the Year

Selected by conference coaches.

Year	*Player*	*Position*	*School*
2009	Kyle Watkins	Kick Return Specialist	Mount Ida College (MA)
2010	Long Ding	Kicker	Norwich University (VT)

Eastern Collegiate Football Conference Rookie of the Year

Selected by conference coaches.

Year	*Player*	*Position*	*School*
2009	Tom Pangia	Middle Linebacker	Norwich University (VT)
2009	Kris Sabourin	Quarterback	Gallaudet University (Washington, D.C.)
2010	Tony Tatum	Cornerback	Gallaudet University (Washington, D.C.)

Empire 8 Athletic Conference

Commissioner Chuck Mitrano; Rochester, NY; Telephone: 585-329-2234; Email: cmitrano@empire8.com; Web site: http://www.empire8.com/

The Empire 8 Athletic Conference was created in 1964 as the Independent College Athletic Conference with six member schools: Alfred University, Clarkson University, Hobart College, Rensselaer Polytechnic Institute, St. Lawrence University, and Union College. In 1991, the conference changed its name to the Empire Athletic Association; since 1993, the EAA served as a single-sport conference (men and women's basketball); and in 1999, it adopted its current name and has since evolved into a multi-sport conference.

As of this writing, the Empire 8 Athletic Conference consists of eight members (five of which play football within the conference) and an associate member for football:

- Alfred University Saxons, Alfred, NY 14802; 607-871-2175; www.alfred.edu
- Elmira College Soaring Eagles, Elmira, NY 14901; 607-735-1800; www.elmira.edu; no football program
- Hartwick College Hawks, Oneonta, NY 13820; 607-431-4000; www.hartwick.edu
- Ithaca College Bombers, Ithaca, NY 14850; 607-274-3011; www.ithaca.edu

- Nazareth College Golden Flyers, Rochester, NY 14618; 585-389-2525; www.naz.edu; no football program
- St. John Fisher College Cardinals, Rochester, NY 14618; 585-385-8000; www.sjfc.edu
- Springfield College Pride, Springfield, MA 01109; 413-748-3000; www.spfldcol.edu; associate football member from the New England Women's & Men's Athletic Conference
- Stevens Institute of Technology Ducks, Hoboken, NJ 07030; 201-216-5000; www.stevens.edu; no football program
- Utica College Pioneers, Utica, NY 13502; 315-792-3006; www.utica.edu

Empire 8 Athletic Conference Champions

Year	*School*
2002	Ithaca College (NY)
2003	Ithaca College (NY)
2004	Ithaca College (NY)
2004	St. John Fisher College (NY)
2005	Ithaca College (MY)
2006	Springfield College (MA)
2006	St. John Fisher College (NY)
2007	Hartwick College (NY)
2007	St. John Fisher College (NY)
2008	Ithaca College (NY)
2009	Alfred University (NY)
2009	St. John Fisher College (NY)
2010	Alfred University (NY)

Empire 8 Athletic Conference Coach of the Year

Year	*Coach*	*School*
2002	Paul Vosburgh	St. John Fisher College (NY)
2003	Mike Welch	Ithaca College (NY)
2004	Paul Vosburgh	St. John Fisher College (NY)
2005	Dave Murray	Alfred University (NY)
2006	Mike DeLong	Springfield College (MA)
2007	Mark Carr	Hartwick College (NY)
2008	Mike Welch	Ithaca College (NY)
2009	Dave Murray	Alfred University (NY)
2010	Dave Murray	Alfred University (NY)

Empire 8 Athletic Conference Player of the Year

Year	*Player*	*School*
2002	Dan Pincelli	Hartwick College (NY)
2003	Jesse Raynor	Alfred University (NY)
2004	Brenton Brady	Alfred University (NY)
2005	Josh Felicetti	Ithaca College (NY)

Empire 8 Athletic Conference Offensive Player of the Year

Year	*Player*	*School*
2006	Chris Sharpe	Springfield College (MA)
2007	Jason Boltus	Hartwick College (NY)
2008	Jason Boltus	Hartwick College (NY)
2009	Jared Manzer	Alfred University (NY)
2010	Tim Bailey	St. John Fisher College (NY)

Empire 8 Athletic Conference Defensive Player of the Year

Year	*Player*	*School*
2006	Gene Lang	St. John Fisher College (NY)
2007	Steve Stepnick	St. John Fisher College (NY)
2008	Matt Scalice	Ithaca College (NY)
2009	Andy Episcopo	St. John Fisher College (NY)
2010	Nick Clark	Alfred University (NY)

EMPIRE 8 ATHLETIC CONFERENCE SPECIAL TEAMS PLAYER OF THE YEAR

Year	*Player*	*School*
2010	Andrew Rogowski	Ithaca College (NY)

EMPIRE 8 ATHLETIC CONFERENCE ROOKIE OF THE YEAR

Year	*Player*	*School*
2002	Josh Fellicetti	Ithaca College (NY)
2003	Aaron Meyers	Alfred University (NY)
2004	Jamie Donovan	Ithaca College (NY)
2005	Jason Boltus	Hartwick College (NY)
2006	Jared Manzer	Alfred University (NY)
2007	Jason Springer	Norwich University (VT)
2008	Tom Secky	Alfred University (NY)
2009	Andrew Benkwitt	Utica College (NY)
2010	Austin Dwyer	Alfred University (NY)

Empire Collegiate Wrestling Conference

Non-football conference

Freedom Conference *see* Middle Atlantic Corporation

Great Northeast Athletic Conference (GNAC)

P.O. Box 15671, Boston, MA 02215; Web site: http://www.thegnac.com

Founded in 1995, the Great Northeast Athletic Conference does not support football, although three of its schools play football in other conferences. As of this writing, 13 member schools belong to the GNAC:

- Albertus Magnus College Falcons, New Haven, CT 06511; 800-578-9160; www.albertus.edu; no football program
- Anna Maria College AmCats, Paxton, MA 01612; 800-344-4586; www.annamaria.edu; plays football in the Eastern Collegiate Football Conference
- Emerson College Lions, Boston, MA 02116; 617-824-8500; www.emerson.edu; no football program
- Emmanuel College Saints, Boston, MA 02115; 617-735-9715; www.emmanuel.edu; no football program
- Johnson & Wales University Wildcats, Providence, RI 02903; 401-598-1000; www.jwu.edu; no football program
- Lasell College Lasers, Newton, MA 02466; 617-243-2000; www.lasell.edu; no football program
- Mount Ida College Mustangs, Newton, MA 02459; 617-928-4500; www.mountida.edu; plays football in the Eastern Collegiate Football Conference
- Norwich University Cadets, Northfield, VT 05663; 802-485-2000; www.norwich.edu; plays football in the Eastern Collegiate Football Conference
- Pine Manor College Gators, Chestnut Hill, MA 02467; 617-731-7000; www.pmc.edu; no football program
- Rivier College Raiders, Nashua, NH 03060; 603-888-1311; www.rivier.edu; no football program
- Saint Joseph College of Connecticut Blue Jays, West Hartford, CT 06117; 860-232-4571; www.sjc.edu; no football program
- Saint Joseph's College of Maine Monks, Standish, ME 04084; 207-893-7512; www.sjcme.edu; no football program
- Simmons College Sharks, Boston, MA 02115; 617-521-2000; www.simmons.edu; no football program
- Suffolk University Rams, Boston, MA 02108; 617-573-8000; www.suffolk.edu; no football program

Great South Athletic Conference (GSAC)

601 Broad Street, LaGrange, GA 30240; Telephone: 706-880-8330; Web site: http://www.greatsouth.org/

The Great South Athletic Conference was founded in 1999 with charter members Fisk University, LaGrange College, Maryville College, Piedmont College, and Stillman College. This conference does not support football, although three of its members play football outside the conference. As of this writing, the nine members of the GSAC include:

- Agnes Scott College Scotties, Decatur, GA 30030; 404-471-6000; www.agnesscott.edu; no football program
- Covenant College Scots, Lookout Mountain, GA 30750; 706-820-1560; www.covenant.edu; no football program
- Huntingdon College Hawks, Montgomery, AL 36106; 334-833-4497; www.huntingdon.edu; plays football as an independent team
- LaGrange College Panthers, LaGrange, GA 30240; 706-880-8000; www.lagrange.edu; plays football as an independent team
- Maryville College Scots, Maryville, TN 37804; 800-597-2687; www.maryvillecollege.edu; plays football in the USA South Athletic Conference
- Piedmont College Lions, Demorest, GA 30535; 706-778-3000; www.piedmont.edu; no football program
- Salem College Spirits, Winston-Salem, NC 27101; 336-721-2600; www.salem.edu; no football program
- Spelman College Jaguars, Atlanta, GA 30314; 404-681-3643; www.spelman.edu; no football program
- Wesleyan College Pioneers, Macon, GA 31210; 800-447-6610; www.wesleyancollege.edu; no football program

Heartland Collegiate Athletic Conference

P.O. Box 425, 205 South Madison Avenue, Greenwood, IN 46142; Web site: http://www.heartlandconf.org/landing/index

The Heartland Collegiate Athletic Conference was founded in June 1987 as the Indiana Collegiate Athletic Conference with six charter members: Anderson College, DePauw University, Franklin College, Hanover College, Manchester College, and Wabash College. The conference adopted its current name in 1998. As of this writing, it consists of 10 member schools, nine of which play football within the conference.

- Anderson University Ravens, Anderson, IN 46012; 800-428-6414; www.anderson.edu
- Bluffton University Beavers, Bluffton, OH 45817; 419-358-3000; www.bluffton.edu
- College of Mount St. Joseph Lions, Cincinnati, OH 45233; 513-244-4200; www.msj.edu
- Defiance College Yellow Jackets, Defiance, OH 43512; 800-520-4632; www.defiance.edu
- Earlham College Quakers, Richmond, IN 47374; 800-327-5426; www.earlham.edu
- Franklin College Grizzlies, Franklin, IN 46131; 800-852-0232; www.franklincollege.edu
- Hanover College Panthers, Hanover, IN 47243; 812-866-7000; www.hanover.edu
- Manchester College Spartans, North Manchester, IN 46962; 260-982-5000; www.manchester.edu
- Rose-Hulman Institute of Technology Fightin' Engineers, Terre Haute, IN 47803; 812-877-1511; www.rose-hulman.edu
- Transylvania University Pioneers, Lexington, KY 40508; 859-233-8300; www.transy.edu; no football program

Heartland Collegiate Athletic Conference Champions

Year	*School*	*Year*	*School*
1989	Hanover College (IN)	1993	Anderson University (IN)
1990	DePauw University (IN)	1994	Hanover College (IN)
1991	Wabash College (IN)	1994	Wabash College (IN)
1992	Wabash College (IN)	1995	Hanover College (IN)

Year	*School*
1996	DePauw University (IN)
1997	Hanover College (IN)
1998	Wabash College (IN)
1999	Hanover College (IN)
2000	Bluffton College (University) (OH)
2000	Hanover College (IN)
2001	Anderson University (IN)
2001	Defiance College (OH)
2002	Hanover College (IN)
2003	Hanover College (IN)
2004	College of Mount St. Joseph (OH)
2005	College of Mount St. Joseph (OH)
2006	College of Mount St. Joseph (OH)
2007	Franklin College (IN)
2008	Franklin College (IN)
2009	College of Mount St. Joseph (OH)
2010	Franklin College (IN)

Heartland Collegiate Athletic Conference Coach of the Year

Year	*Coach*	*School*
1989	Wayne Perry	Hanover College (IN)
1990	Nick Mourouzis	DePauw University (IN)
1991	Greg Carlson	Wabash College (IN)
1992	Greg Carlson	Wabash College (IN)
1993	Mike Manley	Anderson University (IN)
1994	Scott Duncan	Rose-Hulman Institute of Technology (IN)
1994	Wayne Perry	Hanover College (IN)
1995	Wayne Perry	Hanover College (IN)
1996	Nick Mourouzis	DePauw University (IN)
1997	Wayne Perry	Hanover College (IN)
1998	Greg Carlson	Wabash College (IN)
1999	Wayne Perry	Hanover College (IN)
2000	Carlin Carpenter	Bluffton University (OH)
2000	Greg Psconda	Defiance College (OH)
2001	Greg Psconda	Defiance College (OH)
2002	Rod Huber	College of Mount Saint Joseph (OH)
2003	Wayne Perry	Hanover College (IN)
2004	Rod Huber	College of Mount Saint Joseph (OH)
2005	Robert Taylor	Defiance College (OH)
2006	Mike Leonard	Franklin College (IN)
2007	Mike Leonard	Franklin College (IN)
2008	Mike Leonard	Franklin College (IN)
2009	Rod Huber	College of Mount Saint Joseph (OH)
2010	Mike Leonard	Franklin College (IN)

Heartland Collegiate Athletic Conference Player of the Year

Year	*Player*	*Position*	*School*
1989	Mike Funk	Wide Receiver	Wabash College (IN)

Heartland Collegiate Athletic Conference Offensive Player of the Year

Year	*Player*	*Position*	*School*
1990	Steve Kunselman	Running Back	Hanover College (IN)
1991	Paul Gray	Quarterback	Hanover College (IN)
1992	Brian Glesing	Wing Back	Hanover College (IN)
1993	Thomas Lee	Tail Back	Anderson University (IN)
1994	Terry Peebles	Quarterback	Hanover College (IN)
1995	Terry Peebles	Quarterback	Hanover College (IN)
1996	Rick Etienne	Tail Back	Franklin College (IN)
1997	Chris Stormer	Quarterback	Hanover College (IN)
1998	Chris Stormer	Quarterback	Hanover College (IN)
1999	Adam Ryan	Quarterback	Wilmington College (OH)
2000	Tyson Goings	Running Back	Bluffton University (OH)
2001	Joel Steele	Quarterback	Anderson University (IN)
2002	Joel Steele	Quarterback	Anderson University (IN)

Year	Player	Position	School
2003	Joel Steele	Quarterback	Anderson University (IN)
2004	Andy Wellendorf	Wide Receiver	College of Mount Saint Joseph (OH)
2005	Mike Lovell	Running Back	College of Mount Saint Joseph (OH)
2006	Mike Lovell	Running Back	College of Mount Saint Joseph (OH)
2007	Chad Rupp	Quarterback	Franklin College (IN)
2007	Luke Dillon	Wide Receiver	Defiance College (OH)
2008	Chad Rupp	Quarterback	Franklin College (IN)
2009	Derek Eitel	Quarterback	Rose-Hulman Institute of Technology (IN)
2010	Kyle Ray	Quarterback	Franklin College (IN)

Heartland Collegiate Athletic Conference Defensive Player of the Year

Year	Player	Position	School
1990	Dion Anglin	Corner Back	Manchester College (IN)
1991	Jason Gallman	Middle Linebacker	Wabash College (IN)
1992	Eric Schoettle	Outside Linebacker	Wabash College (IN)
1993	Phil Tyler	Free Safety	Anderson University (IN)
1994	Tracey Smith	Defensive Tackle	Wabash College (IN)
1995	Kevin O'Donohue	Linebacker	Hanover College (IN)
1995	Mike Brouwer	Defensive Back	Franklin College (IN)
1996	Kevin O'Donohue	Linebacker	Hanover College (IN)
1997	Michael Wilhelm	Linebacker	Wabash College (IN)
1998	Matthew Rose	Linebacker	Wabash College (IN)
1999	Jason Welty	Nose Guard	Hanover College (IN)
2000	Mickey White	Linebacker	Anderson University (IN)
2001	Nate Schaublin	Linebacker	Defiance College (OH)
2002	Pat McAtee	Defensive Lineman	College of Mount Saint Joseph (OH)
2003	Eric Johnson	Defensive Lineman	College of Mount Saint Joseph (OH)
2004	Matt Lawless	Defensive Lineman	College of Mount Saint Joseph (OH)
2005	Kris Zajac	Linebacker	Defiance College (OH)
2006	Jason Allen	Linebacker	Hanover College (IN)
2006	Matt Lawless	Linebacker	College of Mount Saint Joseph (OH)
2007	Paul Spreen	Defensive Lineman	Rose-Hulman Institute of Technology (IN)
2008	Dan McManus	Defensive Lineman	Franklin College (IN)
2009	Erik Prosser	Linebacker	College of Mount Saint Joseph (OH)
2010	Kyle Longsdorf	Defensive Back	Defiance College (OH)

Heartland Collegiate Athletic Conference Special Teams Player of the Year

Year	Player	Position	School
1996	Justin Shively	Punter	Anderson University (IN)
1997	Justin Shively	Punter	Anderson University (IN)
1998	Tarrik Wilson	Wing Back	Hanover College (IN)
1999	Jim Larkin	Wide Receiver	Franklin College (IN)
2000	Dustin Winkler	Kick Returner	Defiance College (OH)
2001	Dustin Winkler	Kick Returner	Defiance College (OH)
2002	Drew Starck	Kicker	Hanover College (IN)
2003	Nathan Littlefield	Kicker	Hanover College (IN)
2004	Danny Sears	Kick Returner	Franklin College (IN)
2005	Kevin Koch	Kicker	College of Mount Saint Joseph (OH)
2006	Danny Sears	Wing Back / Returner	Franklin College (IN)
2007	Denny Kimmel	Running Back / Kick Returner	Anderson University (IN)
2007	Machy Magdalinos	Kicker	Franklin College (IN)
2008	Tyler Thiems	Wide Receiver / Returner	Hanover College (IN)
2009	Chris Cecil	Returner	Manchester College (IN)
2010	Tom Foos	Kicker	Defiance College (OH)

Heartland Collegiate Athletic Conference Freshman of the Year

Year	Player	School
1999	Nathan Boulais	Wabash College (IN)
2000	Brad Huff	Franklin College (IN)
2001	David Vance	Anderson University (IN)
2002	Andy Wellendorf	College of Mount Saint Joseph (OH)
2003	Denny Kimmel	Anderson University (IN)
2004	Ryan Christy	Bluffton University (OH)
2005	Hans Vetter	Defiance College (OH)
2006	Teddy Henkle	Franklin College (IN)
2007	Reed Eason	Rose-Hulman Institute of Technology (IN)
2008	Nick Sharp	Hanover College (IN)
2009	Kyle Kovach	Rose-Hulman Institute of Technology (IN)
2010	Zack Corpe	Franklin College (IN)

Independent Teams

For the purpose of this book, NCAA Division III independent schools are four-year institutions that compete at this level, but do so independently of an established college athletic conference. These same institutions often compete as members of an intercollegiate athletic conference in other sports. The reason for independent status in football varies among institutions, but is frequently because the primary athletic conference to which the institution belongs does not sponsor football.

- Chapman University Panthers, Orange, CA 92866; 714-997-6815; www.chapman.edu; belongs in the Southern California Intercollegiate Athletic Conference but plays football as an independent team
- Huntingdon College Hawks, Montgomery, AL 36106; 334-833-4497; www.huntingdon.edu; belongs in the Great South Athletic Conference but plays football as an independent team
- Husson University Eagles, Bangor, ME 04401; 800-448-7766; www.husson.edu; belongs to the North Atlantic Conference but plays football in the Eastern Collegiate Football Conference
- LaGrange College Panthers, LaGrange, GA 30240; 706-880-8000; www.lagrange.edu; belongs to the Great South Athletic Conference but plays football as an independent team
- Macalester College Scots, St. Paul, MN 55105; 651-696-6000; www.macalester.edu; belongs to the Minnesota Intercollegiate Athletic Conference but plays football as an independent team
- Menlo College Oaks, Atherton, CA 94027; 800-556-3656; www.menlo.edu; belongs to the California Pacific Conference (NAIA) but plays football as an independent team
- Mount Ida College Mustangs, Newton, MA 02459; 617-928-4500; www.mountida.edu; belongs to the Great Northeast Athletic Conference but plays football in the Eastern Collegiate Football Conference
- SUNY Maritime College Privateers, Throggs Neck, NY 10465; 718-409-7200; www.sunymaritime.edu; belongs to the Skyline Conference but plays football in the Eastern Collegiate Football Conference

Iowa Intercollegiate Athletic Conference (IIAC)

222 Third Street Southeast, Suite 423, Cedar Rapids, IA 52401; Telephone: 319-366-4845; Fax: 319-366-4911; Web site: http://www.iowaconference.com/

The Iowa Intercollegiate Athletic Conference was formed in December 1922 as the Iowa Intercollegiate Athletic Association (with athletic competition beginning in 1923) with 12 charter schools: Buena Vista University, Central College, Ellsworth College, Iowa Wesleyan College, Luther College, Morningside College, Parsons College, St. Ambrose University, Simpson College, Upper Iowa University, Westmar College, and William Penn University. The conference adopted its current name in 1953. As of this writing, the IIAC consists of nine members, all of which play football in the conference.

- Buena Vista University Beavers, Storm Lake, IA 50588; 800-383-9600; www.bvu.edu
- Central College Dutch, Pella, IA 50219; 877-462-3687; www.central.edu

- Coe College Kohawks, Cedar Rapids, IA 52402; 319-399-8500; www.coe.edu
- Cornell College Rams, Mount Vernon, IA 52314; 319-895-4000; www.cornellcollege.edu
- Loras College DuHawks, Dubuque, IA 52001; 800-245-6727; www.lorass.edu
- Luther College Norse, Decorah, IA 52101; 563-387-2000; www.luther.edu
- Simpson College Storm, Indianola, IA 50125; 515-961-6251; www.simpson.edu
- University of Dubuque Spartans, Dubuque, IA 52001; 563-589-3000; www.dbq.edu
- Wartburg College Knights, Waverly, IA 50677; 800-772-2085; www.wartburg.edu

Iowa Intercollegiate Athletic Conference Champions

Year	*School*
1923	Simpson College (IA)
1924	Simpson College (IA(
1925	Simpson College (IA)
1925	Upper Iowa University (IA)
1926	Parsons College (IA)
1927	Iowa State Teachers College (IA)
1928	Iowa State Teachers College (IA)
1929	Iowa Wesleyan College (IA)
1930	Iowa Wesleyan College (IA)
1931	Simpson College (IA)
1931	William Penn University (IA)
1932	Luther College (IA)
1933	Simpson College (IA)
1934	Simpson College (IA)
1935	Luther College (IA)
1936	Parsons College (IA)
1937	Upper Iowa University (IA)
1938	Luther College (IA)
1939	Central College (IA)
1939	Upper Iowa University (IA)
1940	University of Dubuque (IA)
1941	Luther College (IA)
1942	University of Dubuque (IA)
1943	No Champion During World War II
1944	No Champion During World War II
1945	Central College (IA)
1946	Central College (IA)
1946	Upper Iowa University (IA)
1947	Upper Iowa University (IA)
1948	University of Dubuque (IA)
1949	Simpson College (IA)
1950	St. Ambrose University (IA)
1951	St. Ambrose University (IA)
1952	Buena Vista University (IA)
1953	Iowa Wesleyan College (IA)
1954	Luther College (IA)
1955	Parsons College (IA)
1956	Central College (IA)
1957	Luther College (IA)
1958	Wartburg College (IA)
1959	Wartburg College (IA)
1960	Luther College (IA)
1960	Parsons College (IA)
1961	Parsons College (IA)
1962	Parsons College (IA)
1963	Luther College (IA)
1964	Central College (IA)
1964	Upper Iowa University (IA)
1965	Central College (IA)
1966	Central College (IA)
1967	Central College (IA)
1968	Wartburg College (IA)
1969	Simpson College (IA)
1970	Luther College (IA)
1971	Luther College (IA)
1972	Buena Vista University (IA)
1972	William Penn University (IA)
1973	Buena Vista University (IA)
1974	Central College (IA)
1975	William Penn University (IA)
1976	William Penn University (IA)
1977	Central College (IA)
1978	Buena Vista University (IA)
1978	Central College (IA)
1978	Luther College (IA)
1978	University of Dubuque (IA)
1979	University of Dubuque (IA)
1980	University of Dubuque (IA)
1981	Central College (IA)
1982	Wartburg College (IA)
1983	Central College (IA)
1983	Wartburg College (IA)
1984	Central College (IA)
1985	Central College (IA)
1986	Central College (IA)
1987	Central College (IA)
1988	Simpson College (IA)
1989	Central College (IA)
1990	Central College (IA)
1991	Simpson College (IA)
1992	Central College (IA)
1993	Wartburg College (IA)
1994	Central College (IA)
1995	Central College (IA)
1996	Simpson College (IA)
1997	Simpson College (IA)
1998	Central College (IA)
1999	Wartburg College (IA)
2000	Central College (IA)
2001	Central College (IA)
2002	Central College (IA)
2002	Coe College (IA)
2002	Wartburg College (IA)
2003	Wartburg College (IA)
2004	Coe College (IA)
2004	Wartburg College (IA)

Year	School
2005	Central College (IA)
2005	Coe College (IA)
2006	Central College (IA)
2007	Central College (IA)
2008	Wartburg College (IA)
2009	Central College (IA)
2010	Wartburg College (IA)

Iowa Intercollegiate Athletic Conference Coach of the Year

Year	Coach	School
1968	Lee Bondhus	Wartburg College (IA)
1969	John Sullivan	Simpson College (IA)
1970	Edsel Schweizer	Luther College (IA)
1971	Edsel Schweizer	Luther College (IA)
1971	Jim Hershberger	Buena Vista University (IA)
1972	Maury Waugh	University of Dubuque (IA)
1973	Jim Hershberger	Buena Vista University (IA)
1974	Ron Schipper	Central College (IA)
1975	Ron Randleman	William Penn University (IA)
1976	Jim Hershberger	Buena Vista University (IA)
1977	Ron Schipper	Central College (IA)
1978	Bob Naslund	Luther College (IA)
1978	Ron Schipper	Central College (IA)
1979	Don Birmingham	University of Dubuque (IA)
1980	Don Birmingham	University of Dubuque (IA)
1981	Ron Schipper	Central College (IA)
1982	Don Canfield	Wartburg College (IA)
1983	Don Canfield	Wartburg College (IA)
1983	Jim Hershberger	Buena Vista University (IA)
1983	Ron Schipper	Central College (IA)
1984	Ron Schipper	Central College (IA)
1985	Ron Schipper	Central College (IA)
1986	Jim Hershberger	Buena Vista University (IA)
1987	Don Turner	University of Dubuque (IA)
1988	Jim Williams	Simpson College (IA)
1989	Ron Schipper	Central College (IA)
1990	Ron Schipper	Central College (IA)
1991	Jim Williams	Simpson College (IA)
1992	Paul Rudolph	Upper Iowa University (IA)
1993	Bob Nielson	Wartburg College (IA)
1994	Ron Schipper	Central College (IA)
1995	Ron Schipper	Central College (IA)
1996	Jim Williams	Simpson College (IA)
1997	Jim Williams	Simpson College (IA)
1998	Rich Kacmarynski	Central College (IA)
1999	Rick Willis	Wartburg College (IA)
2000	Rich Kacmarynski	Central College (IA)
2001	Steve Miller	Cornell College (IA)
2002	Erik Raeburn	Coe College (IA)
2003	Jay Niemann	Simpson College (IA)
2004	Steve Osterberger	Buena Vista University (IA)
2005	Jeff McMartin	Central College (IA)
2006	Jeff McMartin	Central College (IA)
2007	Jeff McMartin	Central College (IA)
2008	Jay Anderson	Buena Vista University (IA)
2009	Steve Staker	Coe College (IA)
2010	Rick Willis	Wartburg College (IA)

Iowa Intercollegiate Athletic Conference Most Valuable Player

Year	Player	Position	School
1968	Murray McMurray	Offensive Guard / Linebacker	Wartburg College (IA)
1969	Connie Hellerich	Linebacker	Wartburg College (IA)
1970	Vern Den Herder	Defensive End	Central College (IA)
1971	Bernie Peeters	Fullback	Luther College (IA)
1972	Dave Dolan	Unknown	Buena Vista University (IA)
1973	Charlie Mulligan	Unknown	Buena Vista University (IA)
1974	Al Dorenkamp	Linebacker	Central College (IA)
1975	Jeff Parsons	Quarterback	William Penn University (IA)
1976	Mike Mitchell	Linebacker	William Penn University (IA)
1977	Don Taylor	Running Back	Central College (IA)
1978	Rollie Wiebers	Quarterback	Buena Vista University (IA)
1979	Rick Steil	Quarterback	University of Dubuque (IA)
1980	Mike Woodhouse	Quarterback	Luther College (IA)
1981	Bruce Wendt	Offensive Lineman	Central College (IA)
1982	Mike Ward	Running Back	Wartburg College (IA)
1983	Scott Fritz	Unknown	Wartburg College (IA)
1984	Gary Walljasper	Quarterback	Wartburg College (IA)
1985	Rich Thomas	Defensive Lineman	Central College (IA)
1986	Darryl Kosut	Quarterback	William Penn University (IA)
1986	Paul Hefty	Quarterback	Luther College (IA)
1987	Jim Higley	Strong Safety	Buena Vista University (IA)
1988	Mike Stumberg	Defensive Lineman	Central College (IA)
1989	Ricky Gales	Running Back	Simpson College (IA)
1990	Ron Saak	Linebacker	Central College (IA)
1991	Rich Kacmarynski	Fullback	Central College (IA)
1992	Jeff Roth	Quarterback	Upper Iowa University (IA)
1993	Kendall Griffin	Wide Receiver	Loras College (IA)
1994	Mark Kacmarynski	Running Back	Central College (IA)
1995	Vince Penningroth	Defensive Lineman	Wartburg College (IA)
1996	Brad Jorgensen	Unknown	Simpson College (IA)
1997	Brad Jorgensen	Unknown	Simpson College (IA)
1998	Guy Leman	Running Back	Simpson College (IA)
1999	Matt Wheeler	Quarterback	Wartburg College (IA)
2000	Jeff Sanger	Linebacker	Central College (IA)
2001	Fredrick Jackson	Running Back	Coe College (IA)
2002	Fredrick Jackson	Running Back	Coe College (IA)
2003	Mike Donnenwerth	Quarterback	Simpson College (IA)
2004	Joe Brannen	Quarterback	Coe College (IA)
2005	Vance Schuring	Running Back	Central College (IA)
2006	Vance Schuring	Running Back	Central College (IA)
2007	Tim Connell	Quarterback	Central College (IA)
2008	Alex McGrew	Running Back	Loras College (IA)
2009	Brad Boyle	Quarterback	Coe College (IA)

Iowa Intercollegiate Athletic Conference Offensive Player of the Year

Year	Player	Position	School
2010	Brad Boyle	Quarterback	Coe College (IA)

Iowa Intercollegiate Athletic Conference Defensive Player of the Year

Year	Player	Position	School
2010	Shane Wong	Defensive Lineman	Central College (IA)

Landmark Conference

Drew University, President's House Annex, 36 Madison Avenue, Madison, NJ 07940; Telephone: 973-805-8836; Fax: 973-805-8838; Web site: http://www.landmarkconference.org/landing/index#

The Landmark Conference (tentatively called the "Conference of 8" during its early planning stages) was created in June 2006 (with its first athletic contest on September 15, 2007) with charter schools Drew University, Goucher College, Juniata College, Moravian College, Stevens Institute of Technology, Susquehanna University, The Catholic University of America, and the U.S. Merchant Marine Academy.

The Landmark Conference does not support football, although five of its members play football outside the conference. As of this writing, the Landmark Conference consists of eight members:

- Drew University Rangers, Madison, NJ 07940; 973-408-3000; www.drew.edu; no football program
- Goucher College Gophers, Baltimore, MD 21204; 410-337-6000; www.goucher.edu; no football program
- Juniata College Eagles, Huntingdon, PA 16652; 877-586-4282; www.juniata.edu; plays football in the Centennial Conference
- Moravian College Greyhounds, Bethlehem, PA 18018; 610-861-1300; www.moravian.edu; plays football in the Centennial Conference
- Susquehanna University Crusaders, Selinsgrove, PA 17870; 570-374-0101; www.susqu.edu; plays football in the Centennial Conference
- The Catholic University of America Cardinals, Washington, D.C. 20064; 202-319-5000; www.cua.edu; plays football in the Old Dominion Athletic Conference
- U.S. Merchant Marine Academy Mariners, Kings Point, NY 11024; 516-726-5800; www.usmma.edu; plays football in the Liberty League
- University of Scranton Royals, Scranton, PA 18510; 570-941-7400; http://matrix.scranton.edu; no football program

Liberty League

Canton, NY; Web site: http://www.libertyleaguesports.org/

Originally founded in 1995 as the Upstate Collegiate Athletic Association, the Liberty League adopted its current name in 2004 and all of its permanent members are located in the state of New York. The League has 11 full-time members (six play football in the Liberty League, five do not have a football program) and two associate members for football only.

- Bard College Raptors, Annandale-on-Hudson, NY 12504; 845-758-6822; www.bard.edu; no football program
- Clarkson University Golden Knights, Potsdam, NY 13699; 315-268-6400; www.clarkson.edu; no football program
- Hobart and William Smith Colleges Statesmen, Geneva, NY 14456; 315-781-3000; www.hws.edu
- Rensselaer Polytechnic Institute Engineers, Troy, NY 12180; 518-276-6000; http://rpi.edu
- Rochester Institute of Technology Tigers, Rochester, NY 14623; 585-475-2229; www.rit.edu; no football program
- St. Lawrence University Saints, Canton, NY 13617; 315-229-5011; www.stlawu.edu
- Skidmore College Thoroughbreds, Saratoga Springs, NY 12866; 518-580-5000; http://cms.skidmore.edu/index.cfm; no football program
- Union College Dutchmen, Schenectady, NY 12308; 518-388-6000; www.union.edu
- U.S. Merchant Marine Academy Mariners, Kings Point, NY 11024; 516-726-5800; www.usmma.edu; associate member from the Landmark Conference
- University of Rochester Yellowjackets, Rochester, NY 14627; 585-275-2121; www.rochester.edu; plays football in both the Liberty League and the University Athletic Association
- Vassar College Brewers, Poughkeepsie, NY 12604; 845-437-7000; www.vassar.edu; no football program
- William Smith College Herons, Geneva, NY 14456; 315-781-3000; no football program

- Worcester Polytechnic Institute Engineers, Worcester, MA 01609; 508-831-5000; www.wpi.edu; associate member from the New England Women's and Men's Athletic Conference

Liberty League (UCAA) Champions

Year	School	Year	School
2003	Hobart College (NY)	2007	Hobart College (NY)
2003	Rensselaer Polytechnic Institute (NY)	2007	Rensselaer Polytechnic Institute (NY)
2004	Hobart College (NY)	2008	Hobart College (NY)
2005	Union College (NY)	2009	Susquehanna University (PA)
2006	Hobart College (NY)	2009	Union College (NY)
2006	Union College (NY)	2010	St. Lawrence University (NY)

Liberty League (UCAA) Coaching Staff of the Year

Year	Head Coach	School
2003	Mike Cragg	Hobart College (NY)
2003	Joe King	Rensselaer Polytechnic Institute (NY)
2004	Mike Cragg	Hobart College (NY)
2005	John Audino	Union College (NY)
2006	John Audino	Union College (NY)
2007	Joe King	Rensselaer Polytechnic Institute (NY)
2008	Mike Cragg	Hobart College (NY)
2009	Steve Briggs	Susquehanna University (PA)
2010	Mark Raymond	St. Lawrence University (NY)

Liberty League (UCAA) Offensive Player of the Year

Year	Player	Position	Class	School
2003	Dan Cole	Quarterback	Senior	Rensselaer Polytechnic Institute (NY)
2004	Jason Hardwick	Tailback	Junior	U.S. Merchant Marine Academy (NY)
2005	Tom Arcidiacono	Running Back	Junior	Union College (NY)
2006	Tom Arcidiacono	Running Back	Senior	Union College (NY)
2007	Andrew Strom	Quarterback	Senior	Hobart College (NY)
2008	Jimmy Robertson	Quarterback	Senior	Rensselaer Polytechnic Institute (NY)
2009	Dave Paveletz	Running Back	Senior	Susquehanna University (PA)
2010	Chris Coney	Running Back	Senior	Union College (NY)

Liberty League (UCCA) Defensive Player of the Year

Year	Player	Position	Class	School
2003	Tony Clemente	Linebacker	Sophomore	Hobart College (NY)
2003	Mike Defilippi	Defensive Back	Senior	Rensselaer Polytechnic Institute (NY)
2004	Chris Purtell	Defensive End	Senior	Hobart College (NY)
2005	Tony Clemente	Linebacker	Senior	Hobart College (NY)
2006	Matt Boudreau	Linebacker	Sophomore	Worcester Polytechnic Institute (MA)
2007	James Alexander	Cornerback	Senior	Hobart College (NY)
2008	Justin Hager	Linebacker	Senior	Hobart College (NY)
2009	Gerard Bryant	Defensive Tackle	Senior	St. Lawrence University (NY)
2010	Brendan Pidgeon	Linebacker	Sophomore	University of Rochester (NY)

Liberty League (UCCA) Special Teams Player of the Year

Year	Player	Position	Class	School
2003	Cliff Eisenhut	Kicker	Senior	Union College (NY)
2004	Miguel Concepcion	Kick Returner	Senior	Worcester Polytechnic Institute (MA)
2005	Geoff Troy	Kicker / Punter	Freshman	U.S. Merchant Marine Academy (NY)
2006	Adam LoGiudice	Kick Returner	Senior	Rensselaer Polytechnic Institute (NY)
2007	Dominick Ancona	Kicker / Punter	Senior	Hobart College (NY)
2008	Geoff Troy	Kicker / Punter	Senior	U.S. Merchant Marine Academy (NY)

Year	Player	Position	Class	School
2009	Bobby Eppleman	Kicker / Punter	Junior	Susquehanna University (PA)
2010	Peter Nilson	Kicker	Senior	Rensselaer Polytechnic Institute (NY)

Liberty League (UCCA) Rookie of the Year

Year	Player	Position	School
2003	Nolan Robinson	Linebacker	Hobart College (NY)
2004	Brett Young	Tight End	St. Lawrence University (NY)
2005	Jimmy Robertson	Quarterback	Rensselaer Polytechnic Institute (NY)
2006	Grant Wright	Wide Receiver	U.S. Merchant Marine Academy (NY)
2007	Clarence Onyiruika	Running Back	University of Rochester (NY)
2008	Drake Woodard	Corner Back	Hobart College (NY)
2009	Jalon Scott	Defensive Back	Susquehanna University (PA)
2010	Devin Worthington	Strong Safety	Hobart College (NY)

Little East Conference

North Dartmouth, MA; Web site: http://www.littleeast.com/

The Little East Conference began in April 1986 as a playing conference for men's and women's basketball among six New England–based schools: Eastern Connecticut State University, Plymouth State University, Rhode Island College, the University of Massachusetts, Boston, the University of Massachusetts, Dartmouth, and the University of Southern Maine. The conference has since added more sports and more schools.

The Little East Conference does not support football, although three of its members play football outside the conference. The eight members of the LEC include:

- Eastern Connecticut State University Warriors, Willimantic, CT 06226; 860-465-5000; www.easternct.edu; no football program
- Keene State College Owls, Keene, NH 03435; 800-572-1909; www.keene.edu; no football program
- Plymouth State University Panthers, Plymouth, NH 03264; 603-535-5000; www.plymouth.edu; plays football in the New England Football Conference
- Rhode Island College Anchormen, Providence, RI 02908; 401-456-8000; www.ric.edu; no football program
- University of Massachusetts, Boston, Deacons, Boston, MA 02125; 617-287-5000; www.umb.edu; no football program
- University of Massachusetts, Dartmouth, Corsairs, North Dartmouth, MA 02747; 508-999-8000; www.umass.d.edu; plays football in the New England Football Conference
- University of Southern Maine Huskies, Portland, ME 04104; 800-800-4876; http://usm.maine.edu; no football program
- Western Connecticut State University Colonials, Danbury, CT 06810; 203-837-8200; www.wcsu.edu; plays football in the New Jersey Athletic Conference

Massachusetts State Collegiate Athletic Conference (MASCAC)

577 Western Avenue, Westfield, MA 01086; Telephone: 508-830-5054; Email: mascacinfo@wsc.ma.edu; Web site: http://www.mascac.com

The Massachusetts State Collegiate Athletic Conference was founded in 1971 and its members are all located in the state of Massachusetts. As of this writing, the MASCAC has eight members, six of which play football in the conference (and also in the New England Football Conference—Bogan Division)

- Bridgewater State College Bears, Bridgewater, MA 02325; 508-531-1000; www.bridgew.edu
- Fitchburg State College Falcons, Fitchburg, MA 01420; 978-345-2151; www.fitchburgstste.edu
- Framingham State College Rams, Framingham, MA 01701; 508-620-1220; www.framingham.edu
- Massachusetts College of Liberal Arts Trailblazers, North Adams, MA 01247; 413-662-5000; www.mcla.edu; no football program

- Massachusetts Maritime Academy Buccaneers, Buzzards Bay, MA 02532; 508-830-5000; www.maritime.edu
- Salem State College (University) Vikings, Salem, MA 01970; 978-542-6000; www.salemstate.edu; no football program
- Westfield State College (University) Owls, Westfield, MA 01086; 413-572-5300; www.westfield.ma.edu
- Worcester State College (University) Lancers, Worcester, MA 01602; 508-929-8000; www.worcester.edu

Massachusetts State Collegiate Athletic Conference Champions

The Massachusetts State Collegiate Athletic Conference provides only weekly awards.

Year	*School*
1986	Bridgewater State College (MA)
1987	Worcester State College (MA)
1988	Worcester State College (MA)
1989	Bridgewater State College (MA)
1990	Bridgewater State College (MA)
1991	Bridgewater State College (MA)
1992	Bridgewater State College (MA)
1993	Bridgewater State College (MA)
1993	Westfield State College (MA)
1993	Worcester State College (MA)
1994	Bridgewater State College (MA)
1995	Worcester State College (MA)
1996	Worcester State College (MA)
1997	Bridgewater State College (MA)
1997	Worcester State College (MA)
1998	Bridgewater State College (MA)
1999	Bridgewater State College (MA)
2000	Bridgewater State College (MA)
2000	Worcester State College (MA)
2001	Westfield State College (MA)
2002	Westfield State College (MA)
2003	Westfield State College (MA)
2004	Fitchburg State College (MA)
2005	Fitchburg State College (MA)
2006	None
2007	None
2008	None
2009	Westfield State College (MA)
2010	Framingham State College (MA)

Michigan Intercollegiate Athletic Association (MIAA)

29488 Woodward Avenue, Suite 308, Royal Oak, MI 48073; Telephone: 248-336-1677; Fax: 248-547-3445; Web site: http://www.miaa.org

Originally founded in March 1888, the Michigan Intercollegiate Athletic Association is the nation's oldest collegiate conference and was created with four charter schools: Agricultural College of the State of Michigan (now known as Michigan State University), Albion College, Hillsdale College, and Olivet College. The first intercollegiate football game in the MIAA was in 1891, with Albion College beating Hillside College (36–4), although the game would not become an official conference sport until 1894.

As of this writing, the MIAA consists of nine members, seven of which play football in the conference:

- Adrian College Bulldogs, Adrian, MI 49221; 517-265-5161; www.adrian.edu
- Albion College Britons, Albion, MI 49224; 517-629-1000; www.albion.edu
- Alma College Scots, Alma, MI 48801; 989-463-7111; www.alma.edu
- Calvin College Knights, Grand Rapids, MI 49546; 616-526-6000; www.calvin.edu; no football program
- Hope College Flying Dutchmen, Holland, MI 49423; 616-395-7000; www.hope.edu
- Kalamazoo College Hornets, Kalamazoo, MI 49006; 269-337-7000; www.kzoo.edu
- Olivet College Comets, Olivet, MI 49076; 800-456-7189; www.olivetcollege.edu
- Saint Mary's College Belles, Notre Dame, IN 46556; 574-284-4000; http://www3.saintmarys.edu; no football program
- Trine University Thunder, Angola, IN 46703; 260-665-4100; www.trine.edu

Michigan Intercollegiate Athletic Association Champions

Year	*School*
1894	Albion College (MI)
1895	Olivet College (MI)
1896	Eastern Michigan University (MI)
1897	Kalamazoo College (MI)

MIAA

Year	School
1898	Kalamazoo College (MI)
1899	Kalamazoo College (MI)
1900	Albion College (MI)
1901	Olivet College (MI)
1902	Alma College (MI)
1903	Albion College (MI)
1903	Michigan State University (MI)
1904	Albion College (MI)
1905	Michigan State University (MI)
1906	Olivet College (MI)
1907	Olivet College (MI)
1908	Albion College (MI)
1909	Olivet College (MI)
1910	Alma College (MI)
1911	Adrian College (MI)
1911	Olivet College (MI)
1912	Alma College (MI)
1913	Olivet College (MI)
1914	Hillsdale College (MI)
1914	Olivet College (MI)
1915	Albion College (MI)
1915	Alma College (MI)
1916	Kalamazoo College (MI)
1917	Alma College (MI)
1918	No Champion
1919	Kalamazoo College (MI)
1920	Albion College (MI)
1921	No Champion
1922	Albion College (MI)
1923	Alma College (MI)
1924	Hillsdale College (MI)
1925	Eastern Michigan University (MI)
1926	Alma College (MI)
1927	Alma College (MI)
1928	Albion College (MI)
1929	Alma College (MI)
1930	Alma College (MI)
1930	Kalamazoo College (MI)
1931	Hillsdale College (MI)
1932	Hillsdale College (MI)
1933	Hillsdale College (MI)
1934	Hope College (MI)
1934	Kalamazoo College (MI)
1935	Alma College (MI)
1936	Kalamazoo College (MI)
1937	Kalamazoo College (MI)
1938	Hillsdale College (MI)
1939	Albion College (MI)
1940	Albion College (MI)
1941	Alma College (MI)
1942	Alma College (MI)
1946	Hillside College (MI)
1946	Kalamazoo College (MI)
1947	Hillside College (MI)
1947	Kalamazoo College (MI)
1948	Alma College (MI)
1949	Hillsdale College (MI)

Year	School
1950	Alma College (MI)
1951	Alma College (MI)
1951	Hope College (MI)
1952	Albion College (MI)
1953	Hope College (MI)
1954	Hillsdale College (MI)
1955	Hillsdale College (MI)
1956	Hillsdale College (MI)
1957	Hillsdale College (MI)
1958	Albion College (MI)
1958	Hillsdale College (MI)
1958	Hope College (MI)
1959	Hillsdale College (MI)
1960	No Champion
1961	Albion College (MI)
1962	Kalamazoo College (MI)
1963	Hope College (MI)
1963	Kalamazoo College (MI)
1964	Albion College (MI)
1965	Albion College (MI)
1966	Albion College (MI)
1967	Alma College (MI)
1968	Alma College (MI)
1969	Albion College (MI)
1970	Adrian College (MI)
1970	Alma College (MI)
1971	Adrian College (MI)
1971	Alma College (MI)
1972	Adrian College (MI)
1972	Alma College (MI)
1973	Hope College (MI)
1974	Olivet College (MI)
1975	Hope College (MI)
1976	Albion College (MI)
1977	Albion College (MI)
1978	Hope College (MI)
1979	Hope College (MI)
1980	Adrian College (MI)
1981	Hope College (MI)
1982	Hope College (MI)
1983	Adrian College (MI)
1984	Hope College (MI)
1985	Albion College (MI)
1986	Hope College (MI)
1987	Hope College (MI)
1988	Adrian College (MI)
1988	Alma College (MI)
1989	Adrian College (MI)
1989	Albion College (MI)
1990	Albion College (MI)
1991	Albion College (MI)
1992	Albion College (MI)
1993	Albion College (MI)
1994	Albion College (MI)
1995	Albion College (MI)
1996	Albion College (MI)
1997	Adrian College (MI)

Year	School
1997	Hope College (MI)
1998	Albion College (MI)
1999	Albion College (MI)
1999	Alma College (MI)
1999	Hope College (MI)
2000	Hope College (MI)
2001	Albion College (MI)
2002	Alma College (MI)
2003	Hope College (MI)
2004	Alma College (MI)
2005	Albion College (MI)
2006	Hope College (MI)
2007	Hope College (MI)
2007	Olivet College (MI)
2008	Trine University (IN)
2009	Trine University (IN)
2010	Trine University (IN)

Michigan Intercollegiate Athletic Association Player of the Year

Year	Player	Position	School
1938	Ordell McElhaney	End	Albion College (MI)
1939	Bob Powers	Center	Hope College (MI)
1939	Dan Wood	Back	Kalamazoo College (MI)
1940	Dick Thompson	Tackle	Adrian College (MI)
1941	Bob Kirby	Back	Alma College (MI)
1942	Burt Manby	Back	Hillsdale College (MI)
1943	No Selection During World War II		
1944	No Selection During World War II		
1945	No Selection During World War II		
1946	William Young	Back	Hillsdale College (MI)
1947	Tom Ward	Back	Hillsdale College (MI)
1948	Rex Roseman	Guard	Alma College (MI)
1949	Nick Yonker	Quarterback	Hope College (MI)
1950	Tom Van Wingen	Fullback	Hope College (MI)
1951	Frank Joranko	Defensive Back	Albion College (MI)
1952	Bob Wikstrom	Running Back	Albion College (MI)
1953	Fritz Shurmur	Center	Albion College (MI)
1954	Marv Frankel	Back	Hillsdale College (MI)
1955	Marv Raab	Back	Alma College (MI)
1956	Bob Urschalitz	Back	Kalamazoo College (MI)
1957	Doug Maison	Back	Hillsdale College (MI)
1958	Larry TerMolen	Tackle	Hope College (MI)
1958	Tom Taylor	End	Albion College (MI)
1959	Jim Northrup	Offensive Back	Alma College (MI)
1960	Duke Davis	Center	Hillsdale College (MI)
1961	Joe Shurmur	Offensive Guard–Linebacker	Albion College (MI)
1961	Sherwood VanderWoude	Linebacker	Hope College (MI)
1962	Bryce Fauble	Offensive Back	Adrian College (MI)
1963	J.B. Elzy	Offensive Back	Albion College (MI)
1964	Irv Sigler	Offensive Back	Olivet College (MI)
1965	Jim Gray	Linebacker	Alma College (MI)
1965	Ron Springer	Offensive Tackle	Albion College (MI)
1966	Barry Siler	Defensive End	Albion College (MI)
1967	Bob Harple	Running Back	Olivet College (MI)
1967	Gordon Hetrick	Defensive Back	Alma College (MI)
1968	Tom Jakovac	Quarterback	Alma College (MI)
1969	Chris Clark	Running Back	Alma College (MI)
1970	Dave Egnatuk	Running Back	Albion College (MI)
1971	Ted Rycenga	Inside Linebacker	Hope College (MI)
1972	Rick Johnson	Defensive Back–End	Alma College (MI)
1973	Ed Sanders	Running Back	Hope College (MI)
1974	Tim Baker	Running Back	Olivet College (MI)
1975	Tim Van Heest	Quarterback	Hope College (MI)
1976	Steve Robb	Quarterback	Albion College (MI)

Year	*Player*	*Position*	*School*
1977	Steve Spencer	Defensive Tackle	Albion College (MI)
1978	Joe Bacani	Wide Receiver	Adrian College (MI)
1978	Tim Lont	Linebacker	Hope College (MI)
1979	Fletcher Williams	Linebacker	Adrian College (MI)
1980	Ray Moran	Middle Guard	Adrian College (MI)
1981	Tom Koenigsknecht	Linebacker	Adrian College (MI)
1982	Todd Holstege	Running Back	Hope College (MI)
1983	Steve Motte	Fullback	Adrian College (MI)
1983	John Iafolla	Linebacker	Adrian College (MI)
1984	Offense: Greg Heeres	Quarterback	Hope College (MI)
1984	Defense: Dan Korson	Linebacker	Albion College (MI)
1985	Offense: Bob Smedley	Tight End	Adrian College (MI)
1985	Offense: Lance Brown	Running Back	Albion College (MI)
1985	Defense: Dirk VerMeulen	Defensive Tackle	Hope College (MI)
1986	Offense: Chris Mendels	Quarterback	Hope College (MI)
1986	Defense: Mike Grant	Defensive Back	Albion College (MI)
1987	Offense: Todd Ackermann	Tight End	Hope College (MI)
1987	Offense: Bill Vanderbilt	Tight End	Hope College (MI)
1987	Defense: Don Dahlquist	Linebacker	Hope College (MI)
1988	Offense: Bill Badour	Fullback	Adrian College (MI)
1988	Defense: Tim Doty	Linebacker	Adrian College (MI)
1989	Offense: Bill Barker	Running Back	Albion College (MI)
1989	Defense: Scott Ammons	Tackle	Albion College (MI)
1990	Offense: Ken Kubiak	Quarterback	Olivet College (MI)
1990	Defense: Jeff Veronie	Linebacker	Olivet College (MI)
1991	Offense: Hank Wineman	Running Back	Albion College (MI)
1991	Defense: Mike Sherrill	Linebacker	Olivet College (MI)
1992	Offense: Mike Montico	Quarterback	Albion College (MI)
1992	Defense: Kris Knobloch	Tackle	Albion College (MI)
1993	Offense: Jeff Robinson	Running Back	Albion College (MI)
1993	Defense: Chad Ackermann	Defensive End	Hope College (MI)
1994	Offense: Jeff Robinson	Running Back	Albion College (MI)
1994	Offense: Todd Morris	Running Back	Albion College (MI)
1994	Defense: Jim Davis	Linebacker	Albion College (MI)
1995	Offense: Jason Falk	Quarterback	Alma College (MI)
1995	Defense: Robert Taylor	Defensive Lineman	Albion College (MI)
1996	Offense: Kyle Klein	Quarterback	Albion College (MI)
1996	Defense: Jason Beglin	Defensive Lineman	Albion College (MI)
1997	Offense: Brandon Graham	Running Back	Hope College (MI)
1997	Defense: Landon Casey	Defensive Back	Olivet College (MI)
1998	Offense: Jason Van Der Maas	Quarterback	Alma College (MI)
1998	Defense: Pat Slone	Defensive Tackle	Albion College (MI)
1999	Offense: J.D. Graves	Quarterback	Hope College (MI)
1999	Defense: Eric Gerwin	Linebacker	Kalamazoo College (MI)
2000	Offense: J.D. Graves	Quarterback	Hope College (MI)
2000	Defense: Ben Gitler	Linebacker	Albion College (MI)
2001	Offense: Brian Adloff	Wide Receiver	Hope College (MI)
2001	Defense: Brant Haverdink	Linebacker	Kalamazoo College (MI)
2002	Offense: Steve Slowke	Quarterback	Alma College (MI)
2002	Defense: Travis Lehman	Defensive Back	Olivet College (MI)
2003	Offense: Phil Butler	Quarterback	Hope College (MI)
2003	Defense: Glen Brittich	Linebacker	Albion College (MI)
2004	Offense: Dustin Louwaert	Running Back	Albion College (MI)
2004	Defense: Jeremy Vanisacker	Linebacker	Kalamazoo College (MI)
2005	Offense: Steve Wasil	Quarterback	Albion College (MI)
2005	Defense: Mike Lewis	Defensive Lineman	Adrian College (MI)
2006	Offense: Josh Brehm	Quarterback	Alma College (MI)

Year	Player	Position	School
2006	Defense: Matt Rugenstein	Defensive Lineman	Hope College (MI)
2007	Offense: Doug Van Eerden	Wide Receiver	Hope College (MI)
2007	Offense: Troy Niblock	Quarterback	Adrian College (MI)
2007	Defense: Courtney Pearson	Linebacker	Trine University (IN)
2007	Defense: Marc Miller	Defensive Lineman	Olivet College (MI)
2008	Offense: Troy Niblock	Quarterback–Running Back	Adrian College (MI)
2008	Defense: Courtney Pearson	Linebacker	Trine University (IN)
2009	Offense: Eric Watt	Quarterback	Trine University (IN)
2009	Defense: Gino Panza	Defensive Lineman	Adrian College (IN)
2010	Offense: Eric Watt	Quarterback	Trine University (IN)
2010	Defense: Aaron Selking	Defensive Back	Trine University (IN)

Mid-Atlantic Rowing Conference

Non-football conference.

Middle Atlantic Corporation (Conference) (MAC)

Lebanon Valley College, 101 North College Avenue, Annville, PA 17003; Telephone: 717-867-6395; Fax: 717-867-6399; Web site: http://gomacsports.com/

The Middle Atlantic Corporation (Conference) was organized in December 1912 as a loose confederation of colleges, with the first sporting event (a track meet) taking place in May 1913. In 1952, the conference unified and recognized competition in all sports, but many of the universities left the conference in 1974 when the NCAA created Divisions I, II, and III. In 1978, the MAC added women's sports; in 1993, ten schools left to form their own association, leaving the MAC with 16 schools; and in 1999, the MAC restructured itself as an umbrella organization for three separate conferences (Commonwealth, Freedom, and Middle Atlantic) that compete at the NCAA Division III level. The main conferences are the Freedom and the Commonwealth, while the Middle Atlantic Conference combines members from the other two conferences and is used for certain sports to which only a smaller number of members participate, including football.

The original 13 charter schools of the MAC (1922) included Bucknell University, Drexel University, Franklin & Marshall College, Gettysburg College, Haverford College, Muhlenberg College, New York University, Princeton University, Rutgers University, Stevens Institute of Technology, Susquehanna University, Swarthmore College, and the University of Delaware. Five other schools were not present at the meeting, but had approved of the plan for reorganization, including Columbia University, Johns Hopkins University, Lehigh University, Ursinus College, and Widener University.

As of this writing, the MAC is organized as follows:

Commonwealth Conference

- Albright College Lions, Reading, PA 19612; 610-921-2381; www.albright.edu
- Alvernia University Crusaders, Reading, PA 19607; 888-258-3764; www.alvernia.edu; no football program
- Arcadia University Knights, Glenside, PA 19038; 215-572-2900; www.arcadia.edu; no football program
- Elizabethtown College Blue Jays, Elizabethtown, PA 17022; 717-361-1000; www.etown.edu; mo football program
- Lebanon Valley College Flying Dutchmen, Annville, PA 17003; 866-582-4236; www.lvc.edu
- Lycoming College Warriors, WilliamSport, PA 17701; 570-321-4000; www.lycoming.edu
- Messiah College Falcons, Grantham, PA 17027; 717-766-2511; www.messiah.edu; no football program
- Widener University Pride, Chester, PA 19013; 888-943-3637; www.widener.edu

Freedom Conference

- Delaware Valley College Aggies, Doylestown, PA 18901; 800-233-5825; www.delval.edu
- DeSales University Bulldogs, Center Valley, PA 18034; 610-282-1100; www.desales.edu; no football program

- Eastern University Eagles, St. Davids, PA 19087; 610-341-5800; www.eastern.edu; no football program
- Fairleigh Dickinson University, Florham, Devils, Madison, NJ 07940; 973-443-8500; www.fdu.edu
- King's College Monarchs, Wilkes-Barre, PA 18711; 888-546-4772; www.kings.edu
- Manhattanville College Valiants, Purchase, NY 10577; 914-694-2200; www.manhattanville.edu; no football program
- Misericordia University Cougars, Dallas, PA 18612; 570-674-6400; www.misericordia.edu; will begin playing football in 2012
- Wilkes University Colonels, Wilkes-Barre, PA 18766; 800-945-5378; www.wilkes.edu

Middle Atlantic Conference

- Albright College Lions (Reading, PA) (Commonwealth Conference)
- Delaware Valley College Aggies (Doylestown, PA) (Freedom Conference)
- Fairleigh Dickinson University, Florham, Devils (Madison, NJ) (Freedom Conference)
- King's College Monarchs (Wilkes-Barre, PA) (Freedom Conference)
- Lebanon Valley College Flying Dutchmen (Annville, PA) (Commonwealth Conference)
- Lycoming College Warriors (Williamsport, PA) (Commonwealth Conference)
- Misericordia University Cougars, Dallas, PA 18612; 570-674-6400; www.misericordia.edu; to begin playing football in 2012 (Freedom Conference)
- Stevenson University Mustangs, Stevenson, MD, 21153; 877-468-6852; www.stevenson.edu; an associate member for football from the Capital Athletic Conference
- Widener University Pride (Chester, PA) (Commonwealth Conference)
- Wilkes University Colonials (Wilkes-Barre, PA) (Freedom Conference)

Middle Atlantic Corporation (Conference) Champions

Year	*School*
2000	Commonwealth: Widener University (PA)
2000	Freedom: Lycoming College (PA)
2001	Widener University (PA)
2002	No Title
2003	Lycoming College (PA)
2004	Delaware Valley College (PA)
2005	Delaware Valley College (PA)
2006	Wilkes University (PA)
2007	Widener University (PA)
2008	Albright College (PA)
2008	Delaware Valley College (PA)
2008	Lycoming College (PA)
2009	Delaware Valley College (PA)
2010	Delaware Valley College (PA)

Middle Atlantic Corporation (Conference) Coach of the Year

Year	*Coach*	*School*
2000	Bill Zwaan	Widener University (PA)
2001	Bill Zwann	Widener University (PA)
2002	Rich Mannello	King's College (PA)
2003	G.A. Mangus	Delaware Valley College (PA)
2004	G.A. Mangus	Delaware Valley College (PA)
2005	Frank Sheptock	Wilkes University (PA)
2006	Frank Sheptock	Wilkes University (PA)
2007	David Wood	Widener University (PA)
2008	Mike Clark	Lycoming College (PA)
2009	Jim Clements	Delaware Valley College (PA)
2010	Jim Clements	Delaware Valley College (PA)

Middle Atlantic Corporation (Conference) Most Valuable Player

Year	*Player*	*Position*	*School*
2000	Mike Granato	Quarterback	Widener University (PA)
2001	Jim Jones	Wide Receiver	Widener University (PA)
2001	Mike Coleman	Wide Receiver	Widener University (PA)

Middle Atlantic Corporation (Conference) Offensive Player of the Year

Year	Player	Position	School
2002	Mark Bartosic	Wide Receiver	Susquehanna University (PA)
2003	Brett Trichilo	Running Back	Wilkes University (PA)
2004	Brett Trichilo	Running Back	Wilkes University (PA)
2005	Adam Knoblauch	Quarterback	Delaware Valley College (PA)
2006	Jim Jordan	Wide Receiver	Wilkes University (PA)
2007	Tanner Kelly	Quarterback	Albright College (PA)
2008	Mike Isgro	Quarterback	Delaware Valley College (PA)
2009	Tanner Kelly	Quarterback	Albright College (PA)
2010	Matt Cook	Running Back	Delaware Valley College (PA)

Middle Atlantic Corporation (Conference) Defensive Player of the Year

Year	Player	Position	School
2002	Steven Wilson	Defensive Lineman	King's College (PA)
2003	Thomas DeMoss	Defensive Lineman	Widener University (PA)
2004	Andrew Erby	Linebacker	Delaware Valley College (PA)
2005	Kyle Follweiler	Linebacker	Wilkes University (PA)
2006	Kyle Follweiler	Linebacker	Wilkes University (PA)
2007	Kyle Follweiler	Linebacker	Wilkes University (PA)
2008	Brian Cottone	Linebacker	Lebanon Valley College (PA)
2009	Kyle Gesswein	Linebacker	Delaware Valley College (PA)
2010	Kyle Gesswein	Linebacker	Delaware Valley College (PA)

Middle Atlantic Corporation (Conference) Rookie of the Year

Year	Player	Position	School
2000	Mark Bartosic	Wide Receiver	Susquehanna University (PA)
2001	Greg Troutman	Quarterback	Juniata College (PA)
2002	Adam Knoblauch	Quarterback	Delaware Valley College (PA)
2003	Chris Jacoubs	Running Back	Moravian College (PA)
2004	Kyle Follweiler	Linebacker	Wilkes University (PA)
2005	Khalee Prothro	Running Back	Widener University (PA)
2006	Tanner Kelly	Quarterback	Albright College (PA)
2007	Joe Favinger	Linebacker	Widener University (PA)
2008	Josan Holmes	Tailback	Albright College (PA)
2009	Andrew Yacina	Linebacker	Wilkes University (PA)
2009	John Lavelle	Outside Linebacker	Delaware Valley College (PA)
2010	Laquan Robinson	Strong Safety	Widener University (PA)

Midwest Collegiate Hockey Association

Non-football conference.

Midwest Conference

Ripon College, 300 Seward Street, Ripon, WI 54971; Telephone: 920-748-8157; Fax: 920-748-8158; Web site: http://www.midwestconference.org

The modern-era Midwest Conference was created in 1994 with the merger of the Midwest Collegiate Athletic Conference (which had been active since 1921) and the Midwest Athletic Conference for Women (which had been formed in 1977). Charter members of the MCAC (May 1921) were Beloit College, Carleton College Coe College, Cornell College, Knox College, and Lawrence University. Athletic competition began in December 1921 with a track and field meet between Hamline University and Millikin University.

As of this writing, the Midwest Conference consists of 10 schools, all of which play football in the conference:

- Beloit College Buccaneers, Beloit, WI 53511; 608-363-2000; www.beloit.edu
- Carroll University Pioneers, Waukesha, WI 53186; 262-547-1211; www.carrollu.edu
- Grinnell College Pioneers, Grinnell, IA 50112; 641-269-4000; www.grinnell.edu
- Illinois College Blueboys, Jacksonville, IL 62650; 217-245-3000; www.ic.edu
- Knox College Prairie Fire, Galesburg, IL 61401; 309-341-7000; www.knox.edu
- Lake Forest College Foresters, Lake Forest, IL 60045; 847-234-3100; www.lakeforest.edu
- Lawrence University Vikings, Appleton, WI 54911; 920-832-7000; www.lawrence.edu
- Monmouth College Scots, Monmouth, IL 61462; 800-747-2687; www.monmouthcollege.edu
- Ripon College Red Hawks, Ripon, WI 54971; 800-947-4766; www.ripon.edu
- St. Norbert College Green Knights, De Pere, WI 54115; 920-337-3181; www.snc.edu

Midwest Conference Champions

Year	*School*
1922	Coe College (IA)
1922	Lawrence University (WI)
1922	Millikin University (IL)
1923	Beloit College (WI)
1923	Carleton College (MN)
1924	Cornell College (IA)
1924	Knox College (IL)
1924	Lawrence University (WI)
1925	Beloit College (WI)
1925	Carleton College (MN)
1925	Cornell College (IA)
1926	Carleton College (MN)
1927	Cornell College (IA)
1927	Monmouth College (IL)
1928	Coe College (IA)
1928	Hamline University (MN)
1929	Coe College (IA)
1929	Lawrence University (WI)
1929	Ripon College (WI)
1930	Coe College (IA)
1931	Carleton College (MN)
1931	Monmouth College (IL)
1931	Ripon College (WI)
1932	Carleton College (MN)
1932	Monmouth College (IL)
1932	Ripon College (WI)
1933	Coe College (IA)
1934	Coe College (IA)
1934	Monmouth College (IL)
1935	Ripon College (WI)
1936	Coe College (IA)
1936	Carleton College (MN)
1937	Cornell College (IA)
1938	Lawrence University (WI)
1939	Knox College (IL)
1939	Ripon College (WI)
1940	Beloit College (WI)
1940	Carleton College (MN)
1941	Ripon College (WI)
1942	Lawrence University (WI)
1943	No Champion during World War II
1944	No Champion during World War II
1945	No Champion during World War II
1946	Lawrence University (WI)
1947	Lawrence University (WI)
1948	Ripon College (WI)
1949	Lawrence University (WI)
1950	Coe College (IA)
1950	Knox College (IL)
1950	Ripon College (WI)
1951	Lawrence University (WI)
1952	Coe College (IA)
1953	St. Olaf College (MN)
1954	Carleton College (MN)
1955	Coe College (IA)
1956	Carleton College (MN)
1956	Knox College (IL)
1956	St. Olaf College (MN)
1957	Ripon College (WI)
1958	Coe College (IA)
1959	Coe College (IA)
1960	St. Olaf College (MN)
1961	Cornell College (IA)
1961	Grinnell College (IA)
1961	St. Olaf College (MN)
1962	Grinnell College (IA)
1963	Ripon College (WI)
1964	Coe College (IA)
1964	Cornell College (IA)
1964	Ripon College (WI)
1965	Ripon College (WI)
1966	Lawrence University (WI)
1966	Ripon College (WI)
1966	St. Olaf College (MN)
1967	Lawrence University (WI)
1968	Ripon College (WI)
1969	St. Olaf College (MN)
1970	St. Olaf College (MN)
1971	Monmouth College (IL)
1971	St. Olaf College (MN)
1972	Monmouth College (IL)
1973	Coe College (IA)
1974	Coe College (IA)
1975	Lawrence University (WI)
1976	Cornell College (IA)
1976	Knox College (IL)
1976	Monmouth College (IL)
1977	Ripon College (WI)

Year	School
1978	Cornell College (IA)
1978	Ripon College (WI)
1979	Lawrence University (WI)
1980	Cornell College (IA)
1980	Lawrence University (WI)
1981	Lawrence University (WI)
1982	Ripon College (WI)
1983	Lake Forest College (IL)
1984	Coe College (IA)
1984	Cornell College (IA)
1985	Coe College (IA)
1985	St. Norbert College (WI)
1986	Lawrence University (WI)
1987	St. Norbert College (WI)
1988	St. Norbert College (WI)
1989	St. Norbert College (WI)
1990	Coe College (IA)
1991	Coe College (IA)
1992	Cornell College (IA)
1993	Coe College (IA)
1994	Coe College (IA)
1995	Cornell College (IA)
1996	Ripon College (WI)
1997	Carroll University (IA)
1998	Grinnell College (IA)
1999	St. Norbert College (WI)
2000	St. Norbert College (WI)
2001	Ripon College (WI)
2001	St. Norbert College (WI)
2002	Lake Forest College (IL)
2002	St. Norbert College (WI)
2003	St. Norbert College (WI)
2004	St. Norbert College (WI)
2005	Monmouth College (IL)
2006	St. Norbert College (WI)
2007	St. Norbert College (WI)
2008	Monmouth College (IL)
2009	Monmouth College (IL)
2010	St. Norbert College (WI)

Midwest Conference Coach of the Year

Year	Coach	School
1995	Steve Miller	Cornell College (IA)
1996	Ron Ernst	Ripon College (WI)
1997	Greg Wallace	Grinnell College (IA)
1998	Greg Wallace	Grinnell College (IA)
1999	Jim Purtill	St. Norbert College (WI)
2000	Tom Rowland	Illinois College (IL)
2001	Steve Bell	Monmouth College (IL)
2002	Chad Eisele	Lake Forest College (IL)
2003	Jim Purtill	St. Norbert College (WI)
2004	Steve Bell	Monmouth College (IL)
2005	Ed DeGeorge	Beloit College (WI)
2006	Jim Purtill	St. Norbert College (WI)
2007	Jim Purtill	St. Norbert College (WI)
2008	Steve Bell	Monmouth College (IL)
2009	Steve Bell	Monmouth College (IL)
2010	Jeff Pederson	Grinnell College (IA)

Midwest Conference Offensive Player of the Year

Year	Player	Position	School
1993	Steve Dixon	Running Back	Beloit College (WI)
1993	Carey Bender	Running Back	Coe College (IA)
1994	Steve Harris	Running Back	Carroll University (WI)
1994	Carey Bender	Running Back	Coe College (IA)
1995	Jeff Kiniger	Quarterback	Lawrence University (WI)
1995	Andy Ehresman	Running Back	Cornell College (IA)
1996	Corey Honore	Running Back	Lake Forest College (IL)
1996	Tim Hinton	Running Back	Cornell College (IA)
1997	Brad Olson	Running Back	Lawrence University (WI)
1997	Troy Daugherty	Quarterback	Grinnell College (IA)
1998	Troy Daugherty	Quarterback	Grinnell College (IA)
1999	Tim Pierret	Quarterback	St. Norbert College (WI)
2000	Matt O'Grady	Running Back	St. Norbert College (WI)
2001	Jason Augustynowicz	Running Back	St. Norbert College (WI)

Year	Player	Position	School
2002	Luke Hagel	Running Back	Ripon College (WI)
2003	Rob Purlee	Quarterback	Monmouth College (IL)
2004	Ryan Hartman	Quarterback	St. Norbert College (WI)
2005	Mitch Tanney	Quarterback	Monmouth College (IL)
2006	Dante Daniels	Running Back	Monmouth College (IL)
2007	Cody Craig	Quarterback	St. Norbert College (WI)
2008	Alex Tanney	Quarterback	Monmouth College (IL)
2009	Alex Tanney	Quarterback	Monmouth College (IL)
2010	Rob Berger	Suqrterback	St. Norbert College (WI)

MIDWEST CONFERENCE DEFENSIVE PLAYER OF THE YEAR

Year	Player	Position	School
1993	Mike Sikma	Defensive Back	Carroll University (WI)
1993	Tim Smyth	Linebacker	Coe College (IA)
1994	Maurice Redd	Defensive Back	Beloit College (WI)
1994	Brian Lenz	Linebacker	Coe College (IA)
1995	Jim Wallace	Defensive Back	Ripon College (WI)
1995	Brian Lenz	Defensive End	Coe College (IA)
1996	Brock Goehler	Linebacker	Ripon College (WI)
1996	Heath Allard	Defensive Back	Cornell College (IA)
1997	Jeff Lueck	Defensive Back	Carroll University (WI)
1997	Josh Fourdyce	Defensive End	Knox College (IL)
1998	Josh Fourdyce	Defensive End	Knox College (IL)
1999	Matt Krill	Defensive Lineman	Beloit College (WI)
2000	Jerimiah Janssen	Linebacker	St. Norbert College (WI)
2001	Jerimiah Janssen	Linebacker	St. Norbert College (WI)
2002	Casey Urlacher	Linebacker	Lake Forest College (IL)
2003	David Bleitner	Defensive Lineman	Lake Forest College (IL)
2004	David Bleitner	Defensive Lineman	Lake Forest College (IL)
2005	Justin Zigler	Linebacker	Monmouth College (IL)
2006	Brendan O'Malley	Linebacker	St. Norbert College (WI)
2007	Jay Arndt	Defensive Lineman	St. Norbert College (WI)
2008	Jeremy Winter	Linebacker	Carroll University (WI)
2009	Anthony Goranson	Defensive End	Monmouth College (IL)
2010	Tony Baratti	Linebacker	Beloit College (WI)
2010	Ricky Padilla	Linebacker	Illinois College (IL)

Midwest Lacrosse Conference

Non-football conference.

Midwest Women's Lacrosse Conference

Non-football conference.

Minnesota Intercollegiate Athletic Conference (MIAC)

475 Cleveland Avenue North, Suite 307, St. Paul, MN 55104; Telephone: 651-644-3964; Fax: 651-647-6422; Web site: http://www.miac-online.org

The Minnesota Intercollegiate Athletic Conference was founded in March 1920 with charter schools Carleton College, Gustavus Adolphus College, Hamline University, Macalester College, St. John's University, St. Olaf College, and the University of St. Thomas.

As of this writing, the MIAC consists of 13 members (nine of which play football in the conference, one school plays football as an independent team, and three schools do not sponsor a football program):

- Augsburg College Auggies, Minneapolis, MN 55454; 612-330-1000; www.augsburg.edu
- Bethel University Royals, St. Paul, MN 55112; 651-638-6400; www.bethel.edu
- Carleton College Knights, Northfield, MN 55057; 507-222-4000; www.carleton.edu
- College of Saint Benedict Blazers, St. Joseph, MN 56374; 320-363-5011; www.csbsju.edu; no football program
- Concordia College Cobbers, Moorhead, MN 56562; 218-299-4000; www.cord.edu
- Gustavus Adolphus College Gusties, St. Peter, MN 56082; 507-933-8000; https://gustavus.edu
- Hamline University Pipers, St. Paul, MN 55104; 651-523-2800; www.hamline.edu
- Macalester College Scots, St. Paul, MN 55105; 651-696-6000; www.macalester.edu; plays football as an independent team
- St. Catherine University Wildcats, St. Paul, MN 55105; 651-690-6000; www.stkate.edu; no football program
- Saint John's University Johnnies, Collegeville, MN 56321; 320-363-2011; www.csbsju.edu
- Saint Mary's University Cardinals, Winona, MN 55987; 800-635-5987; www.smumn.edu; no football program
- St. Olaf College Oles, Northfield, MN 55057; 507-786-2222; www.stolaf.edu
- University of St. Thomas Tommies, St. Paul, MN 55105; 651-962-5000; www.stthomas.edu

Minnesota Intercollegiate Athletic Conference Champions

Year	*School*
1920	Hamline University (MN)
1921	Hamline University (MN)
1922	St. Olaf College (MN)
1922	University of St. Thomas (MN)
1923	St. Olaf College (MN)
1924	Carleton College (MN)
1925	Macalester College (MN)
1926	Gustavus Adolphus College (MN)
1927	Gustavus Adolphus College (MN)
1928	Augsburg College (MN)
1928	Saint Mary's University (MN)
1929	University of St. Thomas (MN)
1930	St. Olaf College (MN)
1930	University of St. Thomas (MN)
1931	Concordia College (MN)
1932	Saint John's University (MN)
1933	Gustavus Adolphus College (MN)
1934	Concordia College (MN)
1935	Gustavus Adolphus College (MN)
1935	Saint John's University (MN)
1935	St. Olaf College (MN)
1936	Gustavus Adolphus College (MN)
1936	Saint John's University (MN)
1937	Gustavus Adolphus College (MN)
1938	Saint John's University (MN)
1939	University of St. Thomas (MN)
1940	Gustavus Adolphus College (MN)
1941	University of St. Thomas (MN)
1942	Concordia College (MN)
1942	University of St. Thomas (MN)
1943	No Champion
1944	No Champion
1945	Gustavus Adolphus College (MN)
1946	Gustavus Adolphus College (MN)
1947	Macalester College (MN)
1947	University of St. Thomas (MN)
1948	University of St. Thomas (MN)
1949	University of St. Thomas (MN)
1950	Gustavus Adolphus College (MN)
1951	Gustavus Adolphus College (MN)
1952	Concordia College (MN)
1952	Gustavus Adolphus College (MN)
1953	Gustavus Adolphus College (MN)
1953	Saint John's University (MN)
1954	Gustavus Adolphus College (MN)
1955	Gustavus Adolphus College (MN)
1956	University of St. Thomas (MN)
1957	Concordia College (MN)
1958	Gustavus Adolphus College (MN)
1959	Gustavus Adolphus College (MN)
1960	University of Minnesota, Duluth (MN)
1961	University of Minnesota, Duluth (MN)
1962	Saint John's University (MN)
1963	Saint John's University (MN)
1964	Concordia College (MN)
1965	Saint John's University (MN)
1966	Hamline University (MN)
1967	Gustavus Adolphus College (MN)
1968	Gustavus Adolphus College (MN)
1969	Concordia College (MN)
1970	Concordia College (MN)
1971	Gustavus Adolphus College (MN)
1971	Saint John's University (MN)
1972	Gustavus Adolphus College (MN)
1973	University of Minnesota (MN)
1973	University of St. Thomas (MN)
1974	Concordia College (MN)
1974	Saint John's University (MN)
1975	Saint John's University (MN)
1976	Saint John's University (MN)
1977	Saint John's University (MN)
1978	Concordia College (MN)
1978	St. Olaf College (MN)
1979	Concordia College (MN)

Year	School
1979	Saint John's University (MN)
1979	St. Olaf College (MN)
1979	University of St. Thomas (MN)
1980	Concordia College (MN)
1981	Concordia College (MN)
1982	Saint John's University (MN)
1983	University of St. Thomas (MN)
1984	Hamline University (MN)
1985	Saint John's University (MN)
1986	Concordia College (MN)
1987	Gustavus Adolphus College (MN)
1988	Concordia College (MN)
1988	Hamline University (MN)
1989	Saint John's University (MN)
1990	Concordia College (MN)
1990	University of St. Thomas (MN)
1991	Saint John's University (MN)
1992	Carleton College (MN)
1993	Saint John's University (MN)
1994	Saint John's University (MN)

Year	School
1995	Concordia College (MN)
1995	Saint John's University (MN)
1996	Saint John's University (MN)
1997	Augsburg College (MN)
1998	Saint John's University (MN)
1999	Saint John's University (MN)
2000	Bethel University (MN)
2001	Bethel University (MN)
2001	Saint John's University (MN)
2002	Saint John's University (MN)
2003	Saint John's University (MN)
2004	Concordia College (MN)
2005	Saint John's University (MN)
2006	Bethel University (MN)
2006	Saint John's University (MN)
2007	Bethel University (MN)
2008	Saint John's University (MN)
2009	Saint John's University (MN)
2010	University of St. Thomas (MN)

Minnesota Intercollegiate Athletic Conference Coach of the Year

Year	Coach	School
1920–1971	No Information	
1972	Dennis Raarup	Gustavus Adolphus College (MN)
1973–1976	No Information	
1977	Dennis Raarup	Gustavus Adolphus College (MN)
1977	Al Kloppen	Augustana College (IL)
1978	Tom Porter	St. Olaf College (MN)
1979	No Information	
1980	Jim Christopherson	Concordia College (MN)
1981	Jim Christopherson	Concordia College (MN)
1982	John Gagliardi	Saint John's University (MN)
1983	Mark Dienhart	University of St. Thomas (MN)
1984	Dick Tressel	Hamline University (MN)
1985	John Gagliardi	Saint John's University (MN)
1986	Jim Christopherson	Concordia College (MN)
1987	Dennis Raarup	Gustavus Adolphus College (MN)
1988	No Information	
1989	Steve Johnson	Bethel College (MN)
1990	Vic Wallace	University of St. Thomas (MN)
1991	No Information	
1992	Bob Sullivan	Carleton College (MN)
1993	Mal Scanlan	University of St. Thomas (MN)
1994	John Gagliardi	Saint John's University (MN)
1995	Jim Christopherson	Concordia College (MN)
1996	Jack Osberg	Augsburg College (MN)
1997	Jack Osberg	Augsburg College (MN)
1998	John Gagliardi	Saint John's University (MN)
1999	John Gagliardi	Saint John's University (MN)
2000	Steve Johnson	Bethel College (MN)
2001	John Gagliardi	Saint John's University (MN)
2002	Terry Horan	Concordia College (MN)
2003	John Gagliardi	Saint John's University (MN)
2004	Terry Horan	Concordia College (MN)
2005	John Gagliardi	Saint John's University (MN)
2006	Steve Johnson	Bethel University (MN)

Year	Coach	School
2007	Steve Johnson	Bethel University (MN)
2008	Kurt Ramler	Carleton College (MN)
2009	John Gagliardi	Saint John's University (MN)
2010	Glenn Caruso	University of St. Thomas (MN)

Minnesota Intercollegiate Athletic Conference Jim Christopherson Most Valuable Player of the Year

Former Concordia College coach.

Year	Player	School
1995	Chris Palmer	Saint John's University (MN)
1996	Derrin Lamker	Augsburg College (MN)
1997	Derrin Lamker	Augsburg College (MN)
1998	Scott Hvistendahl	Augsburg College (MN)
1999	Brandon Novak	St. John's University (MN)
2000	Steve Ryan	St. Olaf College (MN)
2001	Mike Johnson	Bethel College (MN)
2002	Blake Elliott	Saint John's University (MN)
2003	Blake Elliott	Saint John's University (MN)
2004	Brian Schumacher	Concordia College (MN)
2005	Brian Schumacher	Concordia College (MN)
2006	Kirby Carr	Bethel University (MN)
2007	Ben Wetzell	Bethel University (MN)
2008	Royce Winford	Augsburg College (MN)
2009	Fritz Waldvogel	University of St. Thomas (MN)
2010	Logan Flannery	Bethel University (MN)

Mike Stam Award (Interior Lineman of the Year)

Year	Player	School
1989	Scott Bunnell	Carleton College (MN)
1990	Mike Bindorff	Concordia College (MN)
1991	No Information Available	
1992	Burh Chamberlin	Saint John's University (MN)
1993	Jam Wagner	Saint John's University (MN)
1994	Brian Kohorst	Saint John's University (MN)
1995	No Information Available	
1996	Matt Griffith	Saint John's University (MN)
1997	Matt Briffith	Saint John's University (MN)
1998	Brent Staples	Gustavus Adolphus College (MN)
1999	Chico Rowland	Bethel University (MN)
2000	Mark Hankel	Concordia College (MN)
2001	Matt Chappius	Augsburg College (MN)
2002	Derek Flann	Concordia College (MN)
2003	Ryan Weinandt	Saint John's University (MN)
2004	Nick Didier	Concordia College (MN)
2005	Damien Dumonceaux	Saint John's University (MN)
2006	Zach Danielson	Bethel University (MN)
2007	Grant Weller	Concordia College (MN)
2008	Travis Aufderheide	Concordia College (MN)
2009	C.J. Tabasky	St. Olaf College (MN)
2010	Kyle Schroeder	Saint John's University (MN)

New England College Wrestling Association

Non-football conference.

New England Collegiate Conference (NECC)

14 Gerri Drive, Attleboro, MA 02703; Web site: http://www.neccathletics.com/landing/index

The New England Collegiate Conference was established in May 2007; does not support football; and consists of 10 schools, one of which plays football outside the conference.

- Bay Path College Wildcats, Longmeadow, MA 01106; 800-782-7284; www.baypath.edu; no football program
- Becker College Hawks, Worcester, MA 01609; 508-791-9241; www.becker.edu; plays football in the Eastern Collegiate Football Conference
- Daniel Webster College Eagles, Nashua, NH 03063; 800-325-6876; www.dwc.edu; no football program
- Elms College Blazers, Chicopee, MA 01013; 413-594-2761; www.elms.edu; no football program
- Lesley University Lynx, Cambridge, MA 02138; 617-868-9600; www.lesley.edu; no football program
- Mitchell College Mariners, New London, CT 06320; 860-701-5000; www.mitchell.edu; no football program
- Newbury College Nighthawks, Brookline, MA 02445; 617-730-7000; www.newbury.edu; no football program
- Regis College Pride, Weston, MA 02493; 781-768-7000; www.regiscollege.edu; no football program
- Southern Vermont College Mountaineers, Bennington, VT 05201; 802-447-4000; www.svc.edu; no football program
- Wheelock College Wildcats, Boston, MA 02215; 617-879-2000; www.wheelock.edu; no football program

New England Football Conference (NEFC)

Commissioner: Sue Lauder, Fitchburg State College; Telephone: 978-665-3313; Fax: 978-665-3710; Email: slauder@fsc.edu; Web site: http://www.newenglandfootballconference.com

The New England Football Conference was founded in 1965 with only three charter schools: Bridgewater State College, Curry College, and the Maine Maritime Academy. In its present form, the NEFC is a football-only conference with 16 teams, all of which belong to other conferences for other sports. Currently, the sixteen teams are divided into two divisions (Bogan and Boyd) with eight schools in each.

- Bridgewater State College Bears, Bridgewater, MA 02325; 508-531-1000; www.bridgew.edu; plays football in the Bogan Division; associate member from the Massachusetts State Collegiate Athletic Conference
- Curry College Colonels, Milton, MA 02186; 617-333-0500; www.curry.edu; plays football in the Boyd Division; associate member from the Commonwealth Coast Conference
- Endicott College Gulls, Beverly, MA 01915; 978-927-0585; www.endicott.edu; plays football in the Boyd Division; associate member from the Commonwealth Coast Conference
- Fitchburg State College Falcons, Fitchburg, MA 01420; 978-345-2151; www.fitchburgstste.edu; plays football in the Bogan Division; associate member from the Massachusetts State Collegiate Athletic Conference
- Framingham State College (University) Rams, Framingham, MA 01701; 508-620-1220; www.framingham.edu; plays football in the Bogan Division; associate member from the Massachusetts State Collegiate Athletic Conference
- Maine Maritime Academy Mariners, Castine, ME 04420; 800-464-6565; www.mainemaritime.edu; plays football in the Bogan Division; associate member from the North Atlantic Conference
- Massachusetts Institute of Technology Engineers, Cambridge, MA 02139; 617-253-1000; http://web.mit.edu; plays football in the Boyd Division; associate member from the New England Women's and Men's Athletic Conference
- Massachusetts Maritime Academy Buccaneers, Buzzards Bay, MA 02532; 508-830-5000; www.maritime.edu; plays football in the Bogan Division; associate member from the Massachusetts State Collegiate Athletic Conference

- Nichols College Bison, Dudley, MA 01571; 508-213-1560; www.nichols.edu; plays football in the Boyd Division; associate member from the Commonwealth Coast Conference
- Plymouth State University Panthers, Plymouth, NH 03264; 603-535-5000; www.plymouth.edu; plays football in the Boyd Division; associate member from the Little East Conference
- Salve Regina University Seahawks, Newport, RI 02840; 401-847-6650; www.salve.edu; plays football in the Boyd Division; associate member from the Commonwealth Coast Conference
- United States Coast Guard Academy Bears, New London, CT 06320; 800-883-8724; www.cga.edu; plays Football in the Bogan Division; associate member from the New England Women's and Men's Athletic Conference
- University of Massachusetts, Dartmouth, Corsairs, North Dartmouth, MA 02747; 508-999-8000; www.umass.d.edu; plays football in the Boyd Division; associate member from the Little East Conference
- Western New England College Golden Bears, Springfield, MA 01119; 413-782-3111; www.wne.edu; plays football in the Boyd Division; associate member from the Commonwealth Coast Conference
- Westfield State College (University) Owls, Westfield, MA 01086; 413-572-5300; www.westfield.ma.edu; plays football in the Bogan Division; associate member from the Massachusetts State Collegiate Athletic Conference
- Worcester State College (University) Lancers, Worcester, MA 01602; 508-929-8000; www.worcester.edu; plays football in the Bogan Division; associate member from the Massachusetts State Collegiate Athletic Conference

New England Football Conference Champions

Year	*School*
1965	Maine Maritime Academy (ME)
1966	Bridgewater State College (MA)
1967	Maine Maritime Academy (ME)
1968	Maine Maritime Academy (ME)
1969	Bridgewater State College (MA)
1970	Curry College (MA)
1971	Curry College (MA)
1972	Maine Maritime Academy (ME)
1973	Nichols College (MA)
1974	Boston State College (MA)
1974	Nichols College (MA)
1975	Nichols College (MA)
1976	Nichols College (MA)
1977	Massachusetts Maritime Academy (MA)
1978	Nichols College (MA)
1978	University of Massachusetts, Boston (MA)
1979	University of New Haven (CT)
1980	Maine Maritime Academy (ME)
1981	Plymouth State University (NH)
1982	Plymouth State University (NH)
1983	Massachusetts Maritime Academy (MA)
1983	Plymouth State University (NH)
1984	Plymouth State University (NH)
1985	Plymouth State University (NH)
1985	Western Connecticut State University (CT)
1986	Plymouth State University (NH)
1987	Plymouth State University (NH)
1988	Plymouth State University (NH)
1989	Bridgewater State College (MA)
1990	Plymouth State University (NH)
1991	University of Massachusetts, Lowell (MA)
1992	Bridgewater State College (MA)
1993	Maine Maritime Academy (ME)
1994	Maine Maritime Academy (ME)
1994	University of Massachusetts, Dartmouth (MA)
1995	Worcester State College (MA)
1996	Worcester State College (MA)
1997	Bridgewater State College (MA)
1997	Worcester State College (MA)
1998	Bridgewater State College (Bogan Division) (MA)
1998	Maine Maritime Academy (Bogan Division) (ME)
1998	Salve Regina University (Boyd Division) (RI)
1999	Bridgewater State College (Bogan Division) (MA)
1999	Salve Regina University (Boyd Division) (RI)
2000	Bridgewater State College (MA)
2001	Westfield State College (MA)
2002	University of Massachusetts, Dartmouth (MA)
2003	Curry College (MA)
2004	Curry College (MA)
2005	Curry College (MA)
2006	Curry College (MA)
2007	Curry College (MA)
2008	Plymouth State University (NH)
2009	Maine Maritime Academy (ME)
2010	Endicott College (MA)
2010	Western New England College (MA)

New England Football Conference Coach of the Year

Year	Coach	School
2000	Brien Cullen	Worcester State College (MA)
2000	Dave Flynn	Fitchburg State College (MA)
2001	Steve Marino	Westfield State College (MA)
2002	Bill Kavanaugh	University of Massachusetts, Dartmouth (MA)
2003	Steve Nelson	Curry College (MA)
2004	Steve Nelson	Curry College (MA)
2005	Chris McKenney	Maine Maritime Academy (ME)
2006	Bogan: Chris McKenney	Maine Maritime Academy (ME)
2006	Boyd: Skip Bandini	Curry College (MA)
2007	Bogan: Bill George	United States Coast Guard Academy (CT)
2007	Boyd: Paul Castonia	Plymouth State University (NH)
2008	Bogan: Chris McKenney	Maine Maritime Academy (ME)
2008	Boyd: Dwight Smith	Massachusetts Institute of Technology (MA)
2009	Bogan: Jeremy Cameron	Massachusetts Maritime Academy (ME)
2009	Boyd: Skip Bandini	Curry College (MA)
2010	Bogan: Tom Kelley	Framingham State College (University) (MA)
2010	Boyd: Keith Emery	Western New England College (MA)

New England Football Conference Offensive Player of the Year

Year	Player	Position	Class	School
2000	Matt Fox		Senior	Nichols College (MA)
2000	Marvin Langley		Junior	Western New England College (MA)
2001	Jarrod Rouanzion	Quarterback	Senior	Nichols College (MA)
2002	Raphael Zammit	Running Back	Junior	Curry College (MA)
2003	Raphael Zammit	Running Back	Senior	Curry College (MA)
2004	Brenden Kavey	Running Back	Junior	Bridgewater State College (MA)
2005	Don Thibodeau	Running Back	Senior	Maine Maritime Academy (ME)
2006	Bogan: Christian George		Junior	United States Coast Guard Academy (CT)
2006	Boyd: Michael Carven		Senior	Nichols College (MA)
2007	Bogan: Christian George		Senior	United States Coast Guard Academy (CT)
2007	Boyd: Ryan Van De Geisen		Junior	Curry College (MA)
2008	Bogan: Bruce Burley		Senior	Bridgewater State College (MA)
2008	Boyd: DeRon Brown	Running Back	Junior	Massachusetts Institute of Technology (MA)
2009	Bogan: Jim Bower	Running Back	Senior	Maine Maritime Academy (ME)
2009	Boyd: DeRon Brown	Running Back	Senior	Massachusetts Institute of Technology (MA)
2010	Bogan: Jim Bower	Running Back	Senior	Maine Maritime Academy (ME)
2010	Boyd: Bryce Brown	Quarterback	Junior	Western New England College (MA)

New England Football Conference Defensive Player of the Year

Year	Player	Position	Class	School
2000	Jason Smith		Senior	Fitchburg State College (MA)
2001	Josue Zamora	Linebacker	Junior	Westfield State College (MA)
2002	Josue Zamora	Linebacker	Senior	Westfield State College (MA)
2003	Brian Robitialle	Linebacker	Junior	Curry College (MA)
2004	Brian Robitialle	Linebacker	Senior	Curry College (MA)
2005	Charlie Gibbs	Defensive Back	Senior	Curry College (MA)
2006	Bogan: Mike Sirignano		Senior	Bridgewater State College (MA)
2006	Boyd: Sean Crowley		Senior	Curry College (MA)
2007	Bogan: Chris Tracy		Senior	Maine Maritime Academy (ME)
2007	Boyd: Tom Pinto		Senior	Curry College (MA)
2008	Bogan: Jay Fielding		Senior	Westfield State College (MA)

Year	Player	Position	Class	School
2008	Boyd: Scott Driscoll		Senior	Curry College (MA)
2009	Bogan: Josh Mathieu	Defensive Back	Senior	Westfield State College (MA)
2009	Boyd: Scott Driscoll	Linebacker	Senior	Curry College (MA)
2010	Bogan: Anthony Pappagallo	Defensive Back	Senior	Framingham State College (University) (MA)
2010	Bogan: Tyler Russell	Linebacker	Senior	Worcester State College (MA)
2010	Boyd: Kevin Eagan	Defensive Lineman	Junior	Endicott College (MA)

New England Football Conference Offensive Rookie of the Year

Year	Player	Position	Class	School
2000	Cean Oksanish	Quarterback	Freshman	Worcester State College (MA)
2001	Don Thibodeau	Running Back	Freshman	Maine Maritime Academy (ME)
2002	Dave McDonnell	Running Back	Freshman	Fitchburg State College (MA)
2003	Kevin Holleran	Quarterback	Freshman	Curry College (MA)
2004	Corey Williams	Wide Receiver	Freshman	University of Massachusetts, Dartmouth (MA)
2005	Rick Mancuso	Quarterback	Freshman	Massachusetts Institute of Technology (MA)
2006	Bogan: Stefan Stauber		Freshman	Massachusetts Maritime Academy (MA)
2006	Boyd: Anthony Pillari		Freshman	Nichols College (MA)
2007	Bogan: C.J. Franklin		Freshman	Westfield State College (MA)
2007	Boyd: Robert Morris		Freshman	Nichols College (MA)
2008	Bogan: Jessy Resende	Quarterback	Freshman	Bridgewater State College (MA)
2008	Boyd: Norman Landry	Wide Receiver	Freshman	Curry College (MA)
2008	Boyd: Mike Lane	Running Back	Freshman	Endicott College (MA)
2009	Bogan: Jonathan Emond	Wide Receiver	Freshman	Massachusetts Maritime Academy (MA)
2009	Boyd: Tyler Long	Wide Receiver	Freshman	Plymouth State University (NH)
2010	Bogan: Melikke Van Alstyne	Running Back	Freshman	Framingham State College (University) (MA)
2010	Boyd: Jaron Hargrove	Running Back	Freshman	University of Massachusetts, Dartmouth (MA)

New England Football Conference Defensive Rookie of the Year

Year	Player	Position	Class	School
2000	Jason Faessler	Linebacker	Freshman	University of Massachusetts, Boston (MA)
2001	Alfonzo Dixon	Defensive Back	Freshman	Curry College (MA)
2002	Farnk Famularo	Linebacker	Sophomore	Fitchburg State College (MA)
2003	Dan Harris	Defensive Back	Freshman	Worcester State College (MA)
2004	Chris Tracy	Linebacker	Freshman	Maine Maritime Academy (ME)
2005	Kyle Audette	Linebacker	Freshman	Massachusetts Maritime Academy (MA)
2006	Bogan: Steve Arguelles		Freshman	United States Coast Guard Academy (CT)
2006	Boyd: Chris Ciesluk		Freshman	University of Massachusetts, Dartmouth (MA)
2006	Boyd: Bill Hassett		Freshman	Nichols College (MA)
2007	Bogan: Ryan Howley		Freshman	Massachusetts Maritime Academy (MA)
2007	Boyd: Curtis Smith		Freshman	Nichols College (MA)
2008	Bogan: Andrew Fodera	Linebacker	Freshman	Westfield State College (MA)
2008	Boyd: Kevin Eagan		Freshman	Endicott College (MA)
2009	Bogan: Carlito Weaver	Defensive Back	Freshman	Framingham State College (MA)
2009	Boyd: Max Shubert	Defensive Back	Freshman	Salve Regina University (RI)

Year	Player	Position	Class	School
2010	Bogan: Stefan Gustafson	Defensive Back	Freshman	Massachusetts Maritime Academy (MA)
2010	Boyd: Dan McLaughlin	Linebacker	Sophomore	Curry College (MA)

New England Football Conference Offensive Lineman of the Year

Year	Player	Class	School
2006	Bogan: Ryan Sifflard	Senior	United States Coast Guard Academy (CT)
2006	Boyd: Joe Fellini	Senior	Plymouth State University (NH)
2007	Bogan: Nick Hartmann	Senior	United States Coast Guard Academy (CT)
2007	Boyd: James Oleinik	Junior	Massachusetts Institute of Technology (MA)
2008	Bogan: Chris Mitchell	Senior	Maine Maritime Academy (ME)
2008	Boyd: James Oleinik	Senior	Massachusetts Institute of Technology (MA)
2009	Bogan: Jeff Smith	Senior	Bridgewater State College (MA)
2009	Boyd: Zac Duval	Senior	Plymouth State University (NH)
2010	Bogan: Dan Wearner	Senior	Maine Maritime Academy (ME)
2010	Boyd: None		

New England Small College Athletic Conference (NESCAC)

100 Venture Way, 3rd Floor, Hadley, MA 01035; Telephone: 413-587-2105; Fax: 413-587-2167; Web site: http://www.nescac.com

Created in 1971, the New England Small College Athletic Conference started with charter schools Amherst College, Bates College, Bowdoin College, Colby College, Hamilton College, Middlebury College, Trinity College, Tufts University, Wesleyan University, and Williams College. Connecticut College joined in 1982, bringing the conference's membership to its current total of 11 schools, 10 of which play football within the conference.

- Amherst College Lord Jeffs, Amherst, MA 01002; 413-542-2000; www.amherst.edu
- Bates College Bobcats, Lewiston, ME 04240; 207-786-6255; www.bates.edu
- Bowdoin College Polar Bears, Brunswick, ME 04011; 207-725-3000; www.bowdoin.edu
- Colby College White Mules, Waterville, ME 04901; 207-859-4000; www.colby.edu
- Connecticut College Camels, New London, CT 06320; 860-447-1911; www.conncoll.edu; no football program
- Hamilton College Continentals, Clinton, NY 13323; 315-859-4011; www.hamilton.edu
- Middlebury College Panthers, Middlebury, VT 05753; 802-443-5000; www.middlebury.edu
- Trinity College Bantams, Hartford, CT 06106; 860-297-2000; www.trincoll.edu
- Tufts University Jumbos, Medford, MA 02155; 617-628-5000; www.tufts.edu
- Wesleyan University Cardinals, Middletown, CT 06459; 860-685-2000; www.wesleyan.edu
- Williams College Ephs, Williamstown, MA 01267; 413-597-3131; www.williams.edu

New England Small College Athletic Conference Champions

Year	School	Year	School
2000	Amherst College (MA)	2004	Trinity College (CT)
2000	Colby College (ME)	2005	Trinity College (CT)
2000	Middlebury College (VT)	2006	Williams College (MA)
2001	Williams College (MA)	2007	Middlebury College (VT)
2002	Trinity College (CT)	2008	Trinity College (CT)
2002	Williams College (MA)	2009	Amherst College (MA)
2003	Trinity College (CT)	2010	Williams College (MA)

New England Small College Athletic Conference Coach of the Year

Year	Coach	School
2000	Tom Austin	Colby College (ME)
2001	Richard Farley	Williams College (MA)
2002	Richard Farley	Williams College (MA)

Year	Coach	School
2003	Chuck Priore	Trinity College (CT)
2004	Chuck Priore	Trinity College (CT)
2005	Chuck Priore	Trinity College (CT)
2006	Mike Whalen	Williams College (MA)
2007	Bob Ritter	Middlebury College (VT)
2008	Jeff Devanney	Trinity College (CT)
2009	E.J. Mills	Amherst College (MA)
2010	Aaron Kelton	Williams College (MA)

New England Small College Athletic Conference Offensive Player of the Year

Year	Player	Position	Class	School
2000	Bryan Sanchez	Running Back	Senior	Middlebury College (VT)
2001	Joe Reardon	Quarterback	Sophomore	Williams College (MA)
2002	Joe Reardon	Quarterback	Junior	Williams College (MA)
2003	Tom Pierandri	Running Back	Senior	Trinity College (CT)
2004	Fletcher Ladd	Running Back	Senior	Amherst College (MA)
2005	Mark Hannon	Wide Receiver	Junior	Amherst College (MA)
2006	Patrick Lucey	Quarterback	Junior	Williams College (MA)
2007	Patrick Lucey	Quarterback	Senior	Williams College (MA)
2008	Eric McGrath	Quarterback	Senior	Trinity College (CT)
2009	Donald McKillop	Quarterback	Junior	Middlebury College (VT)
2010	Patrick Moffitt	Quarterback	Senior	Williams College (MA)

New England Small College Athletic Conference Defensive Player of the Year

Year	Player	Position	Class	School
2000	Andy Steele	Linebacker	Senior	Middlebury College (VT)
2001	Pat McGee	Defensive Lineman	Senior	Amherst College (MA)
2002	Scott Farley	Safety	Senior	Williams College (MA)
2003	Graham Goldwasser	Linebacker	Senior	Williams College (MA)
2004	Aaron Goldstein	Defensive Back	Senior	Trinity College (CT)
2005	Michael Blair	Defensive Lineman	Senior	Trinity College (CT)
2006	Mike Soules	Defensive Back	Senior	Trinity College (CT)
2007	Erik Woodring	Linebacker	Senior	Middlebury College (VT)
2008	Tyler Berry	Linebacker	Senior	Trinity College (CT)
2009	Michael Taylor	Linebacker	Senior	Amherst College (MA)
2010	Walter Fallas	Linebacker	Junior	Trinity College (CT)

New England Small College Athletic Conference Offensive Rookie of the Year

Year	Player	Position	Class	School
2000	Brennan Carney	Quarterback	Freshman	Wesleyan University (CT)
2001	Aaron Stepka	Running Back	Freshman	Colby College (ME)
2002	Pat Curran	Running Back	Freshman	Wesleyan University (CT)
2003	Ken Adams	Running Back	Freshman	Bates College (ME)
2004	Brandon Colon	Quarterback	Freshman	Bates College (ME)

New England Small College Athletic Conference Defensive Rookie of the Year

Year	Player	Position	Class	School
2000	Pat Foley	Linebacker	Freshman	Bates College (ME)
2001	Peter Simon	Defensive Back	Freshman	Hamilton College (NY)
2002	Michael Blair	Defensive Lineman	Freshman	Trinity College (CT)
2003	Scott Secor	Defensive Back	Freshman	Middlebury College (VT)
2004	Adam Arsenault	Linebacker	Freshman	Tufts University (MA)

New England Small College Athletic Conference
Rookie of the Year

Year	*Player*	*Position*	*Class*	*School*
2006	John Lawrence	Running Back–Linebacker	Freshman	Hamilton College (NY)
2007	Donald McKillop	Quarterback	Freshman	Middlebury College (VT)
2008	Donnie Simmons	Defensive Lineman	Freshman	Tufts University (MA)
2009	Chris Cameron	Linebacker	Freshman	Williams College (MA)
2010	Even Bunker	Running Back	Freshman	Trinity College (CT)

New England Women's and Men's Athletic Conference (NEWMAC)

Babson College, Webster Center, 231 Forest Street, Babson Park, MA 02457; Fax Number: 866-550-0685; Wellesley, MA; Web site: http://www.newmacsports.com/landing/index

The New England Women's and Men's Athletic Conference was created in 1998 when the former New England Women's 8 Conference (NEW 8) voted to begin sponsoring conference play and championships for men. At the same time, the conference expanded its membership to include Springfield College and the United States Coast Guard Academy. Originally called the New England Women's 6 Conference and beginning play in 1985, charter schools included: Babson College, Brandeis University, Massachusetts Institute of Technology, Smith College, Wellesley College, and Wheaton College.

As of this writing, the NEWMAC consists of 10 schools and does not support football, although four of its members play football in other conferences:

- Babson College Beavers, Babson Park, MA 02457; 781-235-1200; www.babson.edu; no football program
- Clark University Cougars, Worcester, MA 01610; 508-793-7711; www.clarku.edu; no football program
- Massachusetts Institute of Technology Engineers, Cambridge, MA 02139; 617-253-1000; http://web.mit.edu; plays football in the New England Football Conference
- Mount Holyoke College Lyons, South Hadley, MA 01075; 413-538-2000; www.mtholyoke.edu; no football program
- Smith College Pioneers, Northampton, MA 01063; 413-584-2700; www.smith.edu; no football program
- Springfield College Pride, Springfield, MA 01109; 413-748-3000; www.spfldcol.edu; plays football in the Empire 8 Athletic Conference
- United States Coast Guard Academy Bears, New London, CT 06320; 800-883-8724; www.cga.edu; plays football in the New England Football Conference
- Wellesley College Blue, Wellesley, MA 02481; 781-283-1000; www.wellesley.edu; no football program
- Wheaton College Lyons, Norton, MA 02766; 508-286-8200; http://wheatoncollege.edu; no football program
- Worcester Polytechnic Institute Engineers, Worcester, MA 01609; 508-831-5000; www.wpi.edu; plays football in the Liberty League

New England Women's Lacrosse Alliance

Non-football conference.

New Jersey Athletic Conference (NJAC)

Commissioner Terry Small: 528 Alcyon Boulevard, Pitman, NJ 08071; Telephone: 856-582-3679; Fax: 856-582-5877; Email: tsmall@njac.net; Web site: http://www.njacsports.com

The New Jersey Athletic Conference was founded in 1985 when the New Jersey State Athletic Conference (a men's sports organization) merged with corresponding institutions in the Jersey Athletic Conference (a women's sports organization) with 10 charter members: Glassboro State College (now known as Rowan University), Jersey City State College (now University), Kean College (now University), Montclair State College (now University), Ramapo College, Rutgers University, Camden, Rutgers University, Newark, Stockton State College (now known as Richard Stockton College), Trenton State College (now known as The College of New Jersey), and William Paterson College (now University).

As of this writing, the NJAC consists of 10 members, five of which play football in the conference, and five associate members (for football).

- Buffalo State College Bengals (State University of New York College at Buffalo), Buffalo, NY 14222; 716-878-4000; www.buffalostate.edu; associate member from the State University of New York Athletic Conference
- Kean University Cougars, Union Township, NJ 07083; 908-737-5326; www.kean.edu
- Montclair State University Red Hawks, Upper Montclair, NJ 07043; 973-655-4000; www.montclair.edu
- New Jersey City University Gothic Knights, Jersey City, NJ 07305; 201-200-2000; www.njcu.edu; no football program
- Ramapo College Roadrunners, Mahwah, NJ 07430; 201-684-7500; www.ramapo.edu; no football program
- Richard Stockton College of New Jersey Ospreys, Galloway, NJ 08205; 609-652-1776; www.stockton.edu; no football program
- Rowan University Profs, Glassboro, NJ 08028; 856-256-4000; www.rowan.edu
- Rutgers University, Camden, Scarlet Raptors, Camden, NJ 08102; 856-225-1766; www.camden.rutgers.edu; no football program
- Rutgers University, Newark, Scarlet Raiders, Newark, NJ 07102; 973-353-5581; www.newark.rutgers.edu; no football program
- State University of New York at Brockport (The College at Brockport) Golden Eagles, Brockport, NY 14420; 585-395-2211; www.brockport.edu; associate member from the State University of New York Athletic Conference
- State University of New York at Cortland (State University of New York College at Cortland) Red Dragons, Cortland, NY 13045; 607-753-2011; http://www2.cortland.edu/home; associate member from the State University of New York Athletic Conference
- State University of New York at Morrisville (Morrisville State College) Mustangs, Morrisville, NY 13408; 800-258-0111; www.morrisville.edu
- The College of New Jersey Lions, Ewing, NJ 08628; 609-771-1855; www.tcnj.edu
- Western Connecticut State University Colonials, Danbury, CT 06810; 203-837-8200; www.wcsu.edu; associate member from the Little East Conference
- William Paterson University Pioneers, Wayne, NJ 07470; 973-720-2000; www.wpunj.edu

New Jersey Athletic Conference Champions

As the New Jersey State Athletic Conference.

Year	*School*	*Year*	*School*
1969	Montclair State College (NJ)	1977	Glassboro State College (NJ)
1970	Montclair State College (NJ)	1978	Montclair State College (NJ)
1971	Montclair State College (NJ)	1979	Montclair State College (NJ)
1972	Glassboro State College (NJ)	1980	Trenton State College (NJ)
1972	Jersey City State College (NJ)	1981	Montclair State College (NJ)
1972	Montclair State College (NJ)	1982	Montclair State College (NJ)
1973	Montclair State University (NJ)	1983	Glassboro State College (NJ)
1974	Glassboro State College (NJ)	1983	Montclair State College (NJ)
1975	Glassboro State College (NJ)	1983	Trenton State College (NJ)
1976	Glassboro State College (NJ)	1984	Montclair State College (NJ)

New Jersey Athletic Conference Champions

Year	*School*	*Year*	*School*
1985	Montclair State College (NJ)	1988	Trenton State College (NJ)
1986	Montclair State College (NJ)	1989	Montclair State College (NJ)
1987	Kean College (NJ)	1990	Trenton State College (NJ)

NJAC

Year	School
1991	Glassboro State College (NJ)
1992	Rowan College (NJ)
1993	Rowan College (NJ)
1994	Kean College (University) (NJ)
1994	Trenton State College (NJ)
1995	Rowan College (NJ)
1996	The College of New Jersey (NJ)
1997	Rowan University (NJ)
1998	The College of New Jersey (NJ)
1999	Montclair State University (NJ)
2000	Montclair State University (NJ)
2001	Rowan University (NJ)
2002	Rowan University (NJ)
2003	Montclair State University (NJ)
2004	Rowan University (NJ)
2005	Rowan University (NJ)
2006	Rowan University (NJ)
2007	State University of New York at Cortland (NY)
2007	The College of New Jersey (NJ)
2008	Montclair State University (NJ)
2008	State University of New York at Cortland (NY)
2009	Montclair State University (NJ)
2010	Montclair State University (NJ)
2010	Rowan University (NJ)
2010	State University of New York at Cortland (NY)

New Jersey Athletic Conference Coach of the Year

Year	Coach	School
2000	Rick Giancola	Montclair State University (NJ)
2001	K.C. Keeler	Rowan University (NJ)
2002	Jay Accorsi	Rowan University (NJ)
2003	Rick Giancola	Montclair State University (NJ)
2004	Jay Accorsi	Rowan University (NJ)
2005	Jay Accorsi	Rowan University (NJ)
2006	Dan Garrett	Kean University (NJ)
2007	Eric Hamilton	The College of New Jersey (NJ)
2008	Dan MacNeill	State University of New York at Cortland (NY)
2009	Rick Giancola	Montclair State University (NJ)
2010	Rick Giancola	Montclair State University (NJ)

New Jersey Athletic Conference Offensive Player of the Year

Year	Player	School
2000	Ed Collins	Montclair State University (NJ)
2001	Tony Racioppi	Rowan University (NJ)
2002	Tony Racioppi	Rowan University (NJ)
2003	John DiGirolamo	Montclair State University (NJ)
2004	Mike Orihel	Rowan University (NJ)
2005	Phil Silva	Rowan University (NJ)
2006	A.J. Roque	Kean University (NJ)
2007	A.J. Roque	Kean University (NJ)
2008	Jared Chunn	Kean University (NJ)
2009	Jared Chunn	Kean University (NJ)
2010	Justin Autera	State University of New York at Cortland (NY)
2010	Tom Fischer	Montclair State University (NJ)

New Jersey Athletic Conference Defensive Player of the Year

Year	Player	School
2000	Kevin Kelly	Montclair State University (NJ)
2001	Omar Lucas	Montclair State University (NJ)
2002	Gerrit Tosh	Rowan University (NJ)
2003	Domenic Tomeo	Rowan University (NJ)
2004	Steve Skakum	Kean University (NJ)
2005	Adam Haas	State University of New York at Cortland (NY)
2006	Keith Heimerl	Rowan University (NJ)
2007	Joseph King	The College of New Jersey (NJ)
2008	Cornell Hunt	Montclair State University (NJ)

Year	Player	School
2009	Bryan Wiley	State University of New York at Cortland (NY)
2010	Matt Hoffman	Rowan University (NJ)

New Jersey Athletic Conference Offensive Rookie of the Year

Year	*Player*	*School*
2000	Ryshaun Conover	New Jersey City University (NJ)
2001	Steven Davis	State University of New York at Cortland (NY)
2002	John DiGirolamo	Montclair State University (NJ)
2003	Mike Orihel	Rowan University (NJ)
2004	A.J. Roque	Kean University (NJ)
2005	Chase Long	Kean University (NJ)
2006	James Williams	Western Connecticut State University (CT)
2007	Wayne Neal	Western Connecticut State University (CT)
2008	Thomas D'Ambrisi	Kean University (NJ)
2009	Tyler DeRosa	Western Connecticut State University (CT)
2010	Jake Spalik	State University of New York at Brockport (NY)

New Jersey Athletic Conference Defensive Rookie of the Year

Year	*Player*	*School*
2000	Shane Smith	New Jersey City University (NJ)
2001	Amir Womack	New Jersey City University (NJ)
2002	Kelvin Bellamy	Rowan University (NJ)
2003	Chuck Eich	State University of New York at Cortland (NY)
2004	Sal Fama	Montclair State University (NJ)
2005	Zach Garren	Rowan University (NJ)
2006	Stephon Anderson	William Paterson University (NJ)
2007	Brian Haas	State University of New York at Cortland (NY)
2008	Doug Dudek	William Paterson University (NJ)
2009	Eddie Weiser	Buffalo State College (NY)
2010	Dan Avento	Montclair State University (NJ)

New Jersey Athletic Conference Special Teams Player of the Year

Year	*Player*	*School*
2008	Durell Dukes	Kean University (NJ)
2009	Marco Capozzoli	Montclair State University (NJ)
2010	Dan Keegan	Montclair State University (NJ)

North Atlantic Conference (NAC)

P.O. Box 195, Whitingham, VT 05361; Telephone: 802-368-0050; Fax: 802-368-2641; Web site: http://www.nacathletics.com/landing/index

The North Atlantic Conference was originally founded in 1996 as the North Atlantic Women's Conference and adopted its current name in 1999. The six charter schools included Bay Path College, Lasell College, Lesley University, Marine Maritime Academy, Massachusetts College of Pharmacy, and Wheelock College.

The NAC currently has 10 members and does not support football, although three of its members play football outside the conference.

- Castleton State College Spartans, Castleton, VT 05735; 802-468-1365; www.csc.vsc.edu; plays football in the Eastern Collegiate Football Conference
- Colby-Sawyer College Chargers, New London, NH 03257; 603-526-3000; www.colby-sawyer.edu; no football program
- Green Mountain College Eagles, Poultney, VT 05764; 800-776-6675; www.greenmtn.edu; no football program
- Husson University Eagles, Bangor, ME 04401; 800-448-7766; www.husson.edu; plays football in the Eastern Collegiate Football Conference

- Johnson State College Badgers, Johnson, VT 05656; 802-635-1485; www.jsc.edu; no football program
- Lyndon State College Hornets, Lyndonville, VT 05851; 802-626-6224; www.lsc.vsc.edu; no football program
- Maine Maritime Academy Mariners, Castine, ME 04420; 800-464-6565; www.mma.edu; plays football in the New England Football Conference
- New England College Pilgrims; Henniker, NH 03242; 603-428-2335; www.nec.edu; no football program
- Thomas College Terriers, Waterville, ME 04901; 207-859-1111; www.thomas.edu; no football program
- University of Maine, Farmington, Beavers, Farmington, ME 04938; 207-778-7000; www.umf.maine.edu; no football program

North Coast Athletic Conference (NCAC)

P. O. Box 16679, Cleveland, OH 44116; 815 Crocker Road, Suite 5, Westlake, OH 44145; Telephone: 440-871-8100; Fax: 440-871-4221; Email: ncac@northcoast.org; Web site: http://www.northcoast.org

The North Coast Athletic Conference was founded in 1983 and consists of 10 schools, all of which play football in the conference.

- Allegheny College Gators, Meadville, PA 16335; 814-332-3100; www.allegheny.edu
- College of Wooster Fighting Scots, Wooster, OH 44691; 330-263-2000; www.wooster.edu
- Denison University Big Red, Granville, OH 43023; 800-336-4766; www.denison.edu
- DePauw University Tigers, Greencastle, IN 46135; 765-658-4800; www.depauw.edu
- Hiram College Terriers, Hiram, OH 44234; 330-569-3211; www.hiram.edu
- Kenyon College Lords, Gambier, OH 43022; 740-427-5000; www.kenyon.edu/index.xml
- Oberlin College and Conservatory Yeomen, Oberlin, OH 44074; 440-775-8121; http://new.oberlin.edu
- Ohio Wesleyan University Battling Bishops, Delaware, OH 43015; 740-368-2000; www.owu.edu
- Wabash College Little Giants, Crawfordsville, IN 47933; 765-361-6100; www.wabash.edu
- Wittenberg University Tigers, Springfield, OH 45501; 800-677-7558; www.wittenberg.edu

North Coast Athletic Conference Champions

Year	*School*
1984	Case Western Reserve University (OH)
1985	Denison University (OH)
1986	Denison University (OH)
1987	Allegheny College (PA)
1988	Allegheny College (PA)
1989	Kenyon College (OH)
1989	Ohio Wesleyan University (OH)
1990	Allegheny College (PA)
1991	Allegheny College (PA)
1992	Wittenberg University (OH)
1993	Allegheny College (PA)
1994	Allegheny College (PA)
1995	Wittenberg University (OH)
1996	Allegheny College (PA)
1997	Allegheny College (PA)
1997	College of Wooster (OH)
1997	Wittenberg University (OH)
1998	Wittenberg University (OH)
1999	Wittenberg University (OH)
2000	Wittenberg University (OH)
2001	Wittenberg University (OH)
2002	Wabash College (IN)
2003	Allegheny College (PA)
2004	College of Wooster (OH)
2005	Wabash College (IN)
2006	Wabash College (IN)
2006	Wittenberg University (OH)
2007	Wabash College (IN)
2008	Wabash College (IN)
2009	Wabash College (IN)
2010	Wittenberg University (OH)

North Coast Athletic Conference Coach of the Year

Selected by the vote of NCAC football coaches.

Year	*Coach*	*School*
1984	Jim Chapman	Case Western Reserve University (OH)
1985	Keith Piper	Denison University (OH)

Year	Coach	School
1986	Keith Piper	Denison University (OH)
1987	Peter Vaas	Allegheny College (PA)
1988	Peter Vaas	Allegheny College (PA)
1989	Mike Hollway	Ohio Wesleyan University (OH)
1989	Jim Meyer	Kenyon College (OH)
1990	Ken O'Keefe	Allegheny College (PA)
1991	Ken O'Keefe	Allegheny College (PA)
1992	Doug Neibuhr	Wittenberg University (OH)
1993	Ken O'Keefe	Allegheny College (PA)
1994	Frank Carr	Earlham College (IN)
1995	Doug Neibuhr	Wittenberg University (OH)
1996	Ken O'Keefe	Allegheny College (PA)
1997	Jim Barnes	College of Wooster (OH)
1998	Joe Fincham	Wittenberg University (OH)
1999	Joe Fincham	Wittenberg University (OH)
2000	Joe Fincham	Wittenberg University (OH)
2001	Joe Fincham	Wittenberg University (OH)
2002	Chris Creighton	Wabash College (IN)
2003	Mark Matlak	Allegheny College (PA)
2004	Mike Schmitz	College of Wooster (OH)
2005	Chris Creighton	Wabash College (IN)
2006	Joe Fincham	Wittenberg University (OH)
2007	Chris Creighton	Wabash College (IN)
2008	Mike Schmitz	College of Wooster (OH)
2009	Joe Fincham	Wittenberg University (OH)
2010	Joe Fincham	Wittenberg University (OH)

North Coast Athletic Conference Mike Gregory Award (Offensive Player of the Year)

Year	Player	Position	School
1984	Fred DiSanto	Quarterback	Case Western Reserve University (OH)
1985	Chris Spriggs	Tailback	Denison University (OH)
1986	Chris Spriggs	Tailback	Denison University (OH)
1987	Eric Dahlquist	Quarterback	Kenyon College (OH)
1988	Paul Washlock	Quarterback	Case Western Reserve University (OH)
1989	Chris Creighton	Quarterback	Kenyon College (OH)
1990	Jon Warga	Tailback	Wittenberg University (OH)
1991	Brian Grandison	Tailback	College of Wooster (OH)
1992	Stanley Drayton	Tailback	Allegheny College (PA)
1993	Marlon Perryman	Tailback	Wittenberg University (OH)
1994	Paul Bell	Quarterback	Allegheny College (PA)
1995	Marcus Booker	Fullback	Wittenberg University (OH)
1996	Marcus Booker	Fullback	Wittenberg University (OH)
1997	Jim Mormino	Tailback	Allegheny College (PA)
1998	Casey Donaldson	Tailback	Wittenberg University (OH)
1999	Casey Donaldson	Tailback	Wittenberg University (OH)
2000	Casey Donaldson	Tailback	Wittenberg University (OH)
2001	Jake Knott	Quarterback	Wabash College (IN)
2002	Jake Knott	Quarterback	Wabash College (IN)
2003	Tony Sutton	Running Back	College of Wooster (OH)
2004	Tony Sutton	Running Back	College of Wooster (OH)
2005	Russ Harbaugh	Quarterback	Wabash College (IN)
2006	Tristan Murray	Running Back	Wittenberg University (OH)
2007	R.V. Carroll	Running Back	Oberlin College (OH)
2008	Matt Hudson	Quarterback	Wabash College (IN)
2009	Matt Hudson	Quarterback	Wabash College (IN)
2010	Ben Zoeller	Quarterback	Wittenberg University (OH)

North Coast Athletic Conference Hank Critchfield Award (Defensive Player of the Year)

Year	*Player*	*Position*	*School*
1984	Bob Nau	Linebacker	Oberlin College (OH)
1985	Jay Todd	Linebacker	Case Western Reserve University (OH)
1986	Dan Holland	Nose Guard	Denison University (OH)
1987	Mike Parker	Nose Guard	Allegheny College (PA)
1988	Mike Parker	Nose Guard	Allegheny College (PA)
1989	Neil Ringers	Defensive End	Ohio Wesleyan University (OH)
1990	Neil Ringers	Defensive End	Ohio Wesleyan University (OH)
1991	Keith Rucker	Nose Guard	Ohio Wesleyan University (OH)
1992	Taver Johnson	Linebacker	Wittenberg University (OH)
1993	Taver Johnson	Linebacker	Wittenberg University (OH)
1993	Rich Zdrojewski	Defensive Tackle	Case Western Reserve University (OH)
1994	Mike Sanders	Defensive End	Wittenberg University (OH)
1995	Tim Altman	Defensive Tackle	Wittenberg University (OH)
1996	Nick Reiser	Defensive End	Allegheny College (PA)
1997	Kent Rafey	Linebacker	Wittenberg University (OH)
1998	Ken Pope	Cornerback	Wittenberg University (OH)
1999	Seth Duerr	Inside Linebacker	College of Wooster (OH)
2000	Seth Duerr	Inside Linebacker	College of Wooster (OH)
2001	Juan Howard	Defensive Lineman	Wittenberg University (OH)
2002	Nate Boulais	Linebacker	Wabash College (IN)
2003	Blair Hammer	Defensive Lineman	Wabash College (IN)
2004	Joe Kearney	Defensive Lineman	College of Wooster (OH)
2005	Cisco Clervoix	Defensive Lineman	Ohio Wesleyan University (OH)
2006	Adrian Pynenberg	Inside Linebacker	Wabash College (IN)
2007	Adrian Pynenberg	Inside Linebacker	Wabash College (IN)
2008	Darryl Kennon	Defensive Lineman	Wabash College (IN)
2009	Eddie Vallery	Defensive Lineman	Wittenberg University (OH)
2010	C.J. Gum	Inside Linebacker	Wabash College (IN)

North Coast Athletic Conference Newcomer of the Year

Selected by vote of the NCAC football coaches.

Year	*Player*	*School*
1995	Ken Pope	Wittenberg University (OH)
1996	Brock Wanless	College of Wooster (OH)
1997	Casey Donaldson	Wittenberg University (OH)
1998	Dustin Goldsbury	Wittenberg University (OH)
1999	Elio Harmon	Wittenberg University (OH)
2000	Sam Hobi	Oberlin College (OH)
2001	Ricky Valenzuela	Oberlin College (OH)
2002	Tony Sutton	College of Wooster (OH)
2003	Aaron Lafitte	Wabash College (IN)
2004	Tristan Murray	Wittenberg University (OH)
2005	Dustin Sheppard	College of Wooster (OH)
2006	Aaron Huffman	Wittenberg University (OH)
2007	Brad McKinley	Wittenberg University (OH)
2008	Jon Hull	Hiram College (OH)
2009	James Huddleston	Ohio Wesleyan University (OH)
2010	Richard Barnes	College of Wooster (OH)

North East Collegiate Volleyball Association

Non-football conference.

North Eastern Athletic Conference (NEAC)

8 Heather Drive, Gansevoort, NY 12831; Telephone: 518-320-7354; Fax: 518-320-7356; Email: info@neacsports.com; Web site: http://www.neacsports.com

The North Eastern Athletic Conference was formed in 2004; currently has 13 members; and does not support football, although two of its members play football outside the conference.

- Cazenovia College Wildcats, Cazenovia, NY 13035; 800-654-3210; www.cazenovia.edu; no football program
- College of St. Elizabeth Screaming Eagles, Morristown, NJ 07960; 973-290-4000; www.cse.edu; no football program
- Gallaudet University Bison, Washington, D.C. 20002; 202-651-5000; www.gallaudet.edu; plays football in the Eastern Collegiate Football Conference
- Keuka College Storm, Keuka Park, NY 14478; 315-279-5000; http://keuka.edu; no football program
- Lancaster Bible College Chargers, Lancaster, PA 17601; 717-569-7071; www.lbc.edu; no football program
- Pennsylvania State University, Abington, Nittnay Lions, Abington, PA 19001; 215-881-7300; www.abington.psu.edu; no football program
- Pennsylvania State University, Berks, Nittany Lions, Reading, PA 19610; 610-396-6000; www.bk.psu.edu; no football program
- Pennsylvania State University, Harrisburg, Nittany Lions, Middletown, PA 17057; 717-948-6250; http://hbg.psu.edu; no football program
- State University of New York at Cobleskill Fighting Tigers, Cobleskill, NY 12043; 518-255-5700; www.cobleshill.edu; no football program
- State University of New York at Morrisville Mustangs (also known as Morrisville State College), Morrisville, NY 13408; 800-258-0111; www.morrisville.edu; plays football in the New Jersey Athletic Conference
- State University of New York Institute of Technology Wildcats, Utica, NY 13502; 315-792-7500; www.suny.it; no football program
- Wells College Express, Aurora, NY 13026; 315-364-3266; www.wells.edu; no football program
- Wilson College Phoenix, Chambersburg, PA 17201; 717-264-4141; www.wilson.edu; no football program

Northern Athletics Conference

P.O. Box 1536, Waukesha, WI 53187; Telephone: 262-993-8884; Fax: 262-349-9517; Web site: http://northernac.org/

Formed in the fall of 2006, the Northern Athletics Conference was created when the Lake Michigan Conference and the Northern Illinois–Iowa Conference merged. Charter members included: Alverno College, Aurora University, Benedictine University, Concordia University Chicago, Concordia University Wisconsin, Dominican University, Edgewood College, Lakeland College, Maranatha Baptist Bible College, Marian University, Rockford College, and Wisconsin Lutheran College. The Milwaukee School of Engineering joined the NAC in the fall of 2007.

As of this writing, the NAC has 13 members, eight of which play football in the conference.

- Alverno College Inferno, Milwaukee, WI 53234; 414-382-6000; www.alverno.edu; no football program
- Aurora University Spartans, Aurora, IL 60506; 630-892-6431; www.aurora.edu
- Benedictine University Eagles, Lisle, IL 60532; 630-829-6000; www.ben.edu
- Concordia University, Chicago, Cougars, River Forest, IL 60305; 708-771-8300; www.cuchicago.edu
- Concordia University, Wisconsin, Falcons, Mequon, WI 53097; 262-243-5700; www.cuw.edu
- Dominican University Stars, River Forest, IL 60305; 708-366-2490; www.dom.edu; no football program
- Edgewood College Eagles, Madison, WI 53711; 800-444-4861; www.edgewood.edu; no football program
- Lakeland College Muskies, Sheboygan, WI 53073; 800-569-2166; http://lakeland.edu

- Maranatha Baptist Bible College Crusaders, Watertown, WI 53094; 920-261-9300; www.mbbc.edu
- Marian University Sabres, Fond du Lac, WI 54935; 800-262-7426; www.marianuniversity.edu; no football program
- Milwaukee School of Engineering Raiders, Milwaukee, WI 53202; 800-332-6763; www.msoe.edu; no football program
- Rockford College Regents, Rockford, IL 61108; 815-226-4000; www.rockford.edu
- Wisconsin Lutheran College Warriors, Milwaukee, WI 53226; 414-443-8800; www.wlc.edu

Northern Athletics Conference Champions

Year	*School*
2008	Aurora University (IL)
2009	Lakeland College (WI)
2010	Benedictine University (IL)

Northern Athletics Conference Coach of the Year

Year	*Coach*	*School*
2008	Rich Duncan	Aurora University (IL)
2009	Kevin Doherty	Lakeland College (WI)
2009	Lonnie Pries	Concordia University, Chicago (IL)
2010	Jon Cooper	Benedictine University (IL)

Northern Athletics Conference Offensive Player of the Year

Year	*Player*	*School*
2008	Matt Pawlyk	Lakeland College (WI)
2009	Jacob Heinemeyer	Lakeland College (WI)
2009	Mike Marotta	Concordia University, Chicago (IL)
2010	Khyree Copeland	Concordia University, Chicago (IL)

Northern Athletics Conference Defensive Player of the Year

Year	*Player*	*School*
2008	John Wagner	Lakeland College (WI)
2009	Mike Budzinski	Aurora University (IL)
2010	Kaylan Gaines	Wisconsin Lutheran College (WI)

Northern Athletics Conference Freshman of the Year

Year	*Player*	*School*
2009	John Alessi	Benedictine University (IL)
2009	Zach Shaw	Wisconsin Lutheran College (WI)
2010	Josiah Brendemuehl	Maranatha Baptist Bible College (WI)

Northern Collegiate Hockey Association

Non-football conference.

Northwest Conference

P.O. Box 22865, Seattle, WA 98122; Telephone: 206-325-5096; Fax: 206-932-4149; Email: information@nwcsports.com; Web site: http://www.nwcsports.com/landing/index

The Northwest Conference was originally formed in 1926 exclusively for men's sports, but in 1984 it combined with the Women's Conference of Independent Colleges to become the Northwest Conference of Independent Colleges. It changed its name to Northwest Conference in 1996 when it joined the NCAA as a Division III conference. Charter members included: College of Puget Sound (now known as the University of Puget Sound), the College of Idaho, Linfield College, Pacific University, and Willamette University.

As of this writing, the Northwest Conference consists of nine full-time members, seven of which play football in the conference.

- George Fox University Bruins, Newberg, OR 97132; 503-538-8383; www.georgefox.edu; will have a football program in 2013
- Lewis & Clark College Pioneers, Portland, OR 97219; 503-768-7000; www.lclark.edu
- Linfield College Wildcats, McMinnville, OR 97128; 503-883-2200; www.linfield.edu
- Pacific University Boxers, Forest Grove, OR 97116; 503-352-6151; www.pacificu.edu
- Pacific Lutheran University Lutes, Tacoma, WA 98447; 253-531-6900; www.plu.edu
- University of Puget Sound Loggers, Tacoma, WA 98416; 253-879-3211; www.pugetsound.edu
- Whitman College Missionairies, Walla Walla, WA 99362; 509-527-5111; www.whitman.edu; no football program
- Whitworth University Pirates, Spokane, WA 99251; 509-777-1000; www.whitworth.edu
- Willamette University Bearcats, Salem, OR 97301; 503-370-6300; www.willamette.edu

Northwest Conference Champions (1926–1984)

Year	*School*
1926	College of Idaho (ID)
1927	College of Idaho (ID)
1928	Whitman College (WA)
1929	Willamette University (OR)
1930	Whitman College (WA)
1931	Whitman College (WA)
1932	University of Puget Sound (WA)
1933	University of Puget Sound (WA)
1934	Willamette University (OR)
1935	Willamette University (OR)
1936	Willamette University (OR)
1937	Willamette University (OR)
1938	Pacific University (OR)
1938	Willamette University (OR)
1939	Pacific University (OR)
1940	Willamette University (OR)
1941	Willamette University (OR)
1942	Willamette University (OR)
1943	No Champion During World War II
1944	No Champion During World War II
1945	No Champion During World War II
1946	Willamette University (OR)
1947	Willamette University (OR)
1948	College of Idaho (ID)
1949	Lewis & Clark College (OR)
1949	Pacific University (OR)
1950	Lewis & Clark College (OR)
1951	Lewis & Clark College (OR)
1951	Pacific University (OR)
1952	College of Idaho (ID)
1952	Pacific University (OR)
1953	College of Idaho (ID)
1954	College of Idaho (ID)
1954	Lewis & Clark College (OR)
1954	Willamette University (OR)
1955	College of Idaho (ID)
1955	Lewis & Clark College (OR)
1956	Linfield College (OR)
1957	Linfield College (OR)
1958	Willamette University (OR)
1959	Willamette University (OR)
1960	Willamette University (OR)
1961	Linfield College (OR)
1962	Linfield College (OR)
1963	Lewis & Clark College (OR)
1964	Linfield College (OR)
1965	Linfield College (OR)
1966	Lewis & Clark College (OR)
1967	Lewis & Clark College (OR)
1967	Willamette University (OR)
1968	Willamette University (OR)
1969	Lewis & Clark College (OR)
1969	Linfield College (OR)
1969	Pacific Lutheran University (WA)
1969	Whitman College (WA)
1970	Linfield College (OR)
1971	Linfield College (OR)
1971	Pacific Lutheran University (WA)
1971	Willamette University (OR)
1972	Linfield College (OR)
1973	Pacific Lutheran University (WA)
1974	Linfield College (OR)
1975	Linfield College (OR)
1975	Pacific Lutheran University (WA)
1975	Whitworth University (WA)
1976	Linfield College (OR)
1977	Linfield College (OR)
1978	Linfield College (OR)
1979	Pacific Lutheran University (WA)
1980	Linfield College (OR)
1981	Pacific Lutheran University (WA)
1982	Linfield College (OR)
1983	Pacific Lutheran University (WA)
1984	Linfield College (OR)
1985–1995	No Champion

Northwest Conference Champions (1996–Present)

Year	School	Year	School
1996	Willamette University (OR)	2003	Linfield College (OR)
1997	Willamette University (OR)	2004	Linfield College (OR)
1998	Pacific Lutheran University (WA)	2005	Linfield College (OR)
1999	Willamette University (OR)	2006	Whitworth University (WA)
2000	Linfield College (OR)	2007	Whitworth University (WA)
2001	Linfield College (OR)	2008	Willamette University (OR)
2001	Pacific Lutheran University (WA)	2009	Linfield College (OR)
2001	Whitworth University (WA)	2010	Linfield College (OR)
2002	Linfield College (OR)		

Northwest Conference Coach of the Year

Year	Coach	School
1996	Dan Hawkins	Willamette University (WA)
1997	Dan Hawkins	Willamette University (WA)
1998	Frosty Westering	Pacific Lutheran University (WA)
1999	Mark Speckman	Willamette University (WA)
2000	Jay Locey	Linfield College (OR)
2001	John Tully	Whitworth University (WA)
2002	Jay Locey	Linfield College (OR)
2003	Jay Locey	Linfield College (OR)
2004	Jay Locey	Linfield College (OR)
2005	Jay Locey	Linfield College (OR)
2006	John Tully	Whitworth University (WA)
2007	John Tully	Whitworth University (WA)
2008	Mark Speckman	Willamette University (WA)
2009	Joseph Smith	Linfield College (OR)
2010	Joseph Smith	Linfield College (OR)

Northwest Conference Offensive Player of the Year

Year	Player	School
1996	Chuck Pinkerton	Willamette University (WA)
1997	Rich Rideout	Willamette University (WA)
1998	Anthony Hicks	Pacific Lutheran University (WA)
1999	Chad Johnson	Pacific Lutheran University (WA)
1999	Anthony Hicks	Pacific Lutheran University (WA)
2000	Chad Johnson	Pacific Lutheran University (WA)
2001	Scott Biglin	Whitworth University (WA)
2002	David Russell	Linfield College (OR)
2003	Tyler Matthews	Linfield College (OR)
2003	Aaron Binger	Pacific Lutheran University (WA)
2003	Greg Reed	Willamette University (WA)
2004	Brett Elliott	Linfield College (OR)
2005	Brett Elliott	Linfield College (OR)
2006	Joel Clark	Whitworth University (WA)
2007	Adam Anderson	Whitworth University (WA)
2008	Adam Anderson	Whitworth University (WA)
2008	Merben Woo	Willamette University (WA)
2009	Aaron Boehme	Linfield College (OR)
2010	Aaron Boehme	Linfield College (OR)

Northwest Conference Defensive Player of the Year

Year	Player	School
1996	Branden Hughes	Linfield College (OR)
1997	Brandon Folkert	Willamette University (WA)

Year	Player	School
1998	Brandon Woods	Pacific Lutheran University (WA)
1998	Brandon Folkert	Willamette University (WA)
1999	Bruce Assily	Linfield College (OR)
1999	Aaron Lawson	Willamette University (WA)
2000	Sky Blake	Whitworth University (WA)
2000	Alex Rix	Linfield College (OR)
2001	Doug Edmonson	Whitworth University (WA)
2002	Ray Lions	Linfield College (OR)
2003	Harrison Bertsch	Linfield College (OR)
2003	Casey Carlson	Pacific Lutheran University (WA)
2003	Nate Matlock	Willamette University (WA)
2004	Logan Lord	Willamette University (WA)
2005	Brandon Olson	Linfield College (OR)
2005	Josh Ort	Linfield College (OR)
2006	Casey Clifton	Whitworth University (WA)
2007	Jay Tully	Whitworth University (WA)
2007	Ander Eisentrout	Pacific Lutheran University (WA)
2008	Taylor Summers	Linfield College (OR)
2008	Tommy Grove	Willamette University (WA)
2009	Ralph Pineda	Willamette University (WA)
2010	Eric Hedin	Linfield College (OR)

Ohio Athletic Conference (OAC)

P.O. Box 4656, 4990 Mahoning Avenue, Suite C, Austintown, OH 44515; Telephone: 330-259-9090; Fax: 330-259-9091; Web site: www.oac.org

The Ohio Athletic Conference was created in 1902 and is the third oldest conference in college athletics (behind the Michigan Intercollegiate Athletic Association (1888) and the Big Ten (1895)). The six charter members were Case Institute of Technology (now in the University Athletic Association), Kenyon College (now in the North Coast Athletic Conference), Oberlin College (now in the North Coast Athletic Conference), Ohio State University (now in the Big Ten Conference), Ohio Wesleyan University (now in the North Coast Athletic Conference), and Wesleyan Reserve University (now in the University Athletic Association).

The OAC currently consists of 10 schools, all of which play football in the conference.

- Baldwin-Wallace College Yellow Jackets, Berea, OH 44017; 440-826-2900; www.bw.edu
- Capital University Crusaders, Columbus, OH 43209; 614-236-6011; www.capital.edu
- Heidelberg University Student Princes, Tiffin, OH 44883; 800-434-3352; www.heidelberg.edu
- John Carroll University Blue Streaks, University Heights, OH 44118; 216-397-1886; www.jcu.edu
- Marietta College Pioneers, Marietta, OH 45750; 800-331-7896; www.marietta.edu
- Mount Union College (University of Mount Union) Purple Raiders, Alliance, OH 44601; 800-992-6682; www.mountunion.edu
- Muskingum University Fighting Muskies, New Concord, OH 43762; 740-826-8211; www.muskingum.edu
- Ohio Northern University Polar Bears, Ada, OH 45810; 419-772-2000; www.onu.edu
- Otterbein College (University) Cardinals, Westerville, OH 43081; 614-890-3000; www.otterbein.edu
- Wilmington College Quakers, Wilmington, OH 45177; 800-341-9318; www.wilmington.edu

Ohio Athletic Conference Champions

Year	School
1902	Case Institute of Technology (OH)
1903	Case Institute of Technology (OH)
1904	Case Institute of Technology (OH)
1905	Case Institute of Technology (OH)
1906	Ohio State University (OH)
1907	Western Reserve University (OH)
1908	Western Reserve University (OH)
1909	Oberlin College (OH)
1910	Oberlin College (OH)
1911	Oberlin College (OH)
1912	Ohio State University (OH)
1913	Oberlin College (OH)

Year	School
1914	Denison University (OH)
1915	Western Reserve University (OH)
1916	Miami University (OH)
1917	Miami University (OH)
1918	Wittenberg University (OH)
1919	College of Wooster (OH)
1920	College of Wooster (OH)
1921	Miami University (OH)
1922	Ohio Wesleyan University (OH)
1923	College of Wooster (OH)
1924	Oberlin College (OH)
1925	Ohio Wesleyan University (OH)
1926	Muskingum University (OH)
1927	Miami University (OH)
1927	Muskingum University (OH)
1928	Heidelberg University (OH)
1929	Muskingum University (OH)
1930	Muskingum University (OH)
1931	Muskingum University (OH)
1932	Case Institute of Technology (OH)
1933	University of Dayton (OH)
1934	College of Wooster (OH)
1935	Baldwin-Wallace College (OH)
1936	Marietta College (OH)
1937	Baldwin-Wallace College (OH)
1938	John Carroll University (OH)
1939	Muskingum University (OH)
1940	Wittenberg University (OH)
1941	Case Institute of Technology (OH)
1942	Ohio Northern University (OH)
1943	No Champion During World War II
1944	No Champion During World War II
1945	Oberlin College (OH)
1946	Otterbein College (OH)
1947	Denison University (OH)
1948	Heidelberg University (OH)
1949	Muskingum University (OH)
1950	Muskingum University (OH)
1951	Ohio Wesleyan University (OH)
1952	Heidelberg University (OH)
1953	Ohio Wesleyan University (OH)
1954	Heidelberg University (OH)
1955	Muskingum University (OH)
1956	Heidelberg University (OH)
1957	Denison University (OH)
1957	Wittenberg University (OH)
1958	Wittenberg University (OH)
1959	Heidelberg University (OH)
1959	College of Wooster (OH)
1960	Muskingum University (OH)
1961	Wittenberg University (OH)
1962	Wittenberg University (OH)
1963	Wittenberg University (OH)
1964	Wittenberg University (OH)
1965	Muskingum University (OH)
1966	Muskingum University (OH)
1966	Wittenberg University (OH)
1967	Ohio Wesleyan University (OH)
1968	Baldwin-Wallace College (OH)
1969	Wittenberg University (OH)
1970	No Champion
1971	Ohio Wesleyan University (OH)
1972–1983	No Champion
1984	Baldwin-Wallace College (OH)
1985	Mount Union College (OH)
1986	Mount Union College (OH)
1987	Capital University (OH)
1988	Baldwin-Wallace College (OH)
1988	Wittenberg University (OH)
1989	John Carroll University (OH)
1990	Mount Union College (OH)
1991	Baldwin-Wallace College (OH)
1992	Mount Union College (OH)
1993	Mount Union College (OH)
1994	Baldwin-Wallace College (OH)
1994	John Carroll University (OH)
1994	Mount Union College (OH)
1995	Mount Union College (OH)
1996	Mount Union College (OH)
1997	Mount Union College (OH)
1998	Mount Union College (OH)
1999	Mount Union College (OH)
2000	Mount Union College (OH)
2001	Mount Union College (OH)
2002	Mount Union College (OH)
2003	Mount Union College (OH)
2004	Mount Union College (OH)
2005	Mount Union College (OH)
2006	Mount Union College (OH)
2007	Mount Union College (OH)
2008	Mount Union College (OH)
2009	Mount Union College (OH)
2010	Mount Union College (OH)

Ohio Athletic Conference Coach of the Year

Year	College	School
1968	Lee Tressel	Baldwin-Wallace College (OH)
1969	Dave Maurer	Wittenberg University (OH)
1970	Gene Slaughter	Capital University (OH)
1971	Jack Fouts	Ohio Wesleyan University (OH)
1972	Pete Riesen	Heidelberg University (OH)
1973	Dave Maurer	Wittenberg University (OH)
1974	Lee Tressel	Baldwin-Wallace College (OH)

Year	*College*	*School*
1975	Al Christopher	Muskingum University (OH)
1976	Dave Maurer	Wittenberg University (OH)
1977	Lee Tressel	Baldwin-Wallace College (OH)
1978	Lee Tressel	Baldwin-Wallace College (OH)
1978	Dave Maurer	Wittenberg University (OH)
1979	Dave Maurer	Wittenberg University (OH)
1980	Lee Tressel	Baldwin-Wallace College (OH)
1981	Tom McHugh	Kenyon College (OH)
1982	Ken Wable	Mount Union College (OH)
1982	Wally Hood	Ohio Northern University (OH)
1983	Jeff Heacock	Muskingum University (OH)
1984	Bob Packard	Baldwin-Wallace College (OH)
1985	Ken Wable	Mount Union College (OH)
1986	Larry Kehres	Mount Union College (OH)
1987	Roger Welsh	Capital University (OH)
1988	Dick West	Heidelberg University (OH)
1989	Jeff Heacock	Muskingum University (OH)
1989	Larry Van Dusen	Baldwin-Wallace College (OH)
1990	Larry Kehres	Mount Union College (OH)
1991	Bob Packard	Baldwin-Wallace College (OH)
1992	Larry Kehres	Mount Union College (OH)
1993	Dick West	Heidelberg University (OH)
1994	Tony DeCarlo	John Carroll University (OH)
1994	Larry Kehres	Mount Union College (OH)
1995	Gene Epley	Marietta College (OH)
1996	Larry Kehres	Mount Union College (OH)
1997	Tony DeCarlo	John Carroll University (OH)
1997	Larry Kehres	Mount Union College (OH)
1998	Bob Packard	Baldwin-Wallace College (OH)
1999	Tom Kaczkowski	Ohio Northern University (OH)
2000	Wally Hood	Otterbein College (OH)
2001	Jim Collins	Capital University (OH)
2002	John Snell	Baldwin-Wallace College (OH)
2002	Regis Scafe	John Carroll University (OH)
2003	Jim Collins	Capital University (OH)
2004	Todd Glaser	Marietta College (OH)
2005	Joe Loth	Otterbein College (OH)
2006	Jim Collins	Capital University (OH)
2006	John Snell	Baldwin-Wallace College (OH)
2007	Mike Hallett	Heidelberg University (OH)
2008	Joe Loth	Otterbein College (OH)
2009	Al Logan	Muskingum University (OH)
2010	Dean Paul	Ohio Northern University (OH)

Ohio Athletic Conference Assistant Coach of the Year

Year	*Assistant Coach*	*School*
2001	Don Montgomery	Mount Union College (OH)
2002	Jim Bickel	Capital University (OH)
2003	Adam Howard	Baldwin-Wallace College (OH)
2004	Ron Bendekovic	Ohio Northern University (OH)
2004	Jeff Wojtowicz	Mount Union College (OH)
2005	Ron Bendekovic	Ohio Northern University (OH)
2006	Vince Kehres	Mount Union College (OH)
2007	Jeff Filkovski	Heidelberg University (OH)
2007	Jim Bickel	Capital University (OH)
2008	Tim Doup	Otterbein College (OH)
2009	Troy Rothenbuhler	Ohio Northern (OH)

Year	Assistant Coach	School
2009	Henry Standford	Capital University (OH)
2010	Jason Bendekovic	Heidelberg University (OH)

Mike Gregory Awards (Offensive Back of the Year and Offensive Lineman of the Year)

These awards were established in 1956 and are named in honor of Mike Gregory, one of the great all-around athletes in conference history. He was a multi-sport standout at Denison University (Granville, OH) in the 1920s.

Ohio Athletic Conference Offensive Back of the Year

Year	Player	Position	School
1956	Tom Dingle	Halfback	College of Wooster (OH)
1956	Walt Livingston	Halfback	Heidelberg University (OH)
1957	Bill Cooper	Fullback	Muskingum University (OH)
1958	Bill Cooper	Fullback	Muskingum University (OH)
1959	Bill Cooper	Fullback	Muskingum University (OH)
1960	Gary Tranquill	Quarterback	Wittenberg University (OH)
1961	Tony Hall	Halfback	Denison University (OH)
1962	Charlie Green	Quarterback	Wittenberg University (OH)
1963	Charlie Green	Quarterback	Wittenberg University (OH)
1964	Rod Dingle	Halfback	College of Wooster (OH)
1965	Rick Harbold	Halfback	Muskingum University (OH)
1966	Rick Harbold	Halfback	Muskingum University (OH)
1967	Dick Cromwell	Quarterback	Ohio Wesleyan University (OH)
1968	Mike Blake	Quarterback	Baldwin-Wallace College (OH)
1969	Rocky Alt	Quarterback	Wittenberg University (OH)
1970	No Selection		
1971	Ed Exler	Halfback	Denison University (OH)
1971	Steve Chase	Quarterback	Ohio Wesleyan University (OH)
1972	Bob Hunt	Fullback	Heidelberg University (OH)
1973	Glenn Hendrix	Halfback	Wittenberg University (OH)
1974	Gary Frost	Quarterback	Mount Union College (OH)
1975	Dave Caldwell	Tailback	Muskingum University (OH)
1976	Dave Merritt	Halfback	Wittenberg University (OH)
1977	Dave Merritt	Halfback	Wittenberg University (OH)
1978	Roger Andrachik	Fullback	Baldwin-Wallace College (OH)
1979	Clay Sampson	Tailback	Denison University (OH)
1980	Clay Sampson	Tailback	Denison University (OH)
1981	Mike Wallace	Quarterback	Oho Wesleyan University (OH)
1982	Dave McLaughlin	Tailback	Mount Union College (OH)
1983	Tony Colao	Quarterback	Mount Union College (OH)
1984	Brian Moore	Quarterback	Baldwin-Wallace College (OH)
1985	Scott Woolf	Quarterback	Mount Union College (OH)
1986	Scott Gindlesberger	Quarterback	Mount Union College (OH)
1987	Russ Kring	Fullback	Mount Union College (OH)
1988	Bryce Tuohy	Tailback	Heidelberg University (OH)
1989	Mike Garn	Halfback	Mount Union College (OH)
1990	Brad Petro	Quarterback	Mount Union College (OH)
1991	John Koz	Quarterback	Baldwin-Wallace College (OH)
1992	Jim Ballard	Quarterback	Mount Union College (OH)
1993	Jim Ballard	Quarterback	Mount Union College (OH)
1994	P.J. Insana	Quarterback	John Carroll University (OH)
1995	Curt Weikart	Tailback	Marietta College (OH)
1996	Bill Borchert	Quarterback	Mount Union College (OH)
1997	Bill Borchert	Quarterback	Mount Union College (OH)
1998	Geoff Helmlinger	Quarterback	Baldwin-Wallace College (OH)

Year	Player	Position	School
1999	Matt D'Orazio	Quarterback	Otterbein College (OH)
2000	Jamal Robertson	Running Back	Ohio Northern University (OH)
2000	Gary Smeck	Quarterback	Mount Union College (OH)
2001	Chuck Moore	Running Back	Mount Union College (OH)
2002	Dan Pugh	Running Back	Mount Union College (OH)
2003	Mark Anders	Running Back	Baldwin-Wallace College (OH)
2004	Zac Bruney	Quarterback	Mount Union College (OH)
2005	Doug Phillips	Quarterback	John Carroll University (OH)
2006	Rocky Pentello	Quarterback	Capital University (OH)
2007	Greg Micheli	Quarterback	Mount Union College (OH)

Bob Packard Award (Offensive Back of the Year)

This award has been presented annually since 2008 by Baldwin-Wallace College (Berea, OH) in honor of Bob Packard, who served as head coach of the Yellow Jackets from 1981 to 2001. He led the school to six OAC championships and a 156–54–2 (.736) overall record.

Year	Player	School
2008	Nate Kmic	Mount Union College (OH)
2009	Kyle Simmons	Ohio Northern University (OH)
2010	Andrew Miller	Heidelberg University (OH)

Ohio Athletic Conference Ed Sherman Award (Receiver of the Year)

This award has been presented annually since 1988 by Muskingum College/University (New Concord, OH) in honor of the winningest coach in school history. Sherman served as the team's coach from 1945 to 1966 and compiled an overall record of 141–43–8 (.734), the second most wins in conference history (behind Bob Packard).

Year	Player	Position	School
1988	Ed Hogya	Wide Receiver	Mount Union College (OH)
1989	Bob Aleksandrovic	Wide Receiver	Heidelberg University (OH)
1990	Ron Severance	Wide Receiver	Otterbein College (OH)
1991	Ron Severance	Wide Receiver	Otterbein College (OH)
1992	Rob Atwood	Tight End	Mount Union College (OH)
1993	Ed Bubonics	Wide Receiver	Mount Union College (OH)
1994	Sean Williams	Wide Receiver	John Carroll University (OH)
1995	LaVant King	Wide Receiver	Ohio Northern University (OH)
1996	Kevin Knestrick	Wide Receiver	Mount Union College (OH)
1997	Kevin Knestrick	Wide Receiver	Mount Union College (OH)
1998	Steve Vagedes	Wide Receiver	Ohio Northern University (OH)
1999	Adam Marino	Wide Receiver	Mount Union College (OH)
2000	Adam Marino	Wide Receiver	Mount Union College (OH)
2001	Jeff Gibbs	Tight End	Otterbein College (OH)
2002	Jeff Lerner	Wide Receiver	John Carroll University (OH)
2003	Randell Knapp	Wide Receiver	Mount Union College (OH)
2004	Greg Evilsizor	Wide Receiver	Ohio Northern University (OH)
2005	Scott Casto	Wide Receiver	Mount Union College (OH)
2006	Pierre Garcon	Wide Receiver	Mount Union College (OH)
2007	Pierre Garcon	Wide Receiver	Mount Union College (OH)
2008	Cecil Shorts	Wide Receiver	Mount Union College (OH)
2009	Cecil Shorts	Wide Receiver	Mount Union College (OH)
2010	Mike Preston	Wide Receiver	Heidelberg University (OH)

Mike Gregory Awards (Offensive Back of the Year and Offensive Lineman of the Year)

These awards were established in 1956 and are named in honor of Mike Gregory, one of the great all-around athletes in conference history. He was a multi-sport standout at Denison University (Granville, OH) in the 1920s.

Ohio Athletic Conference Offensive Lineman of the Year

Year	*Player*	*Position*	*School*
1956	Tom Zesiger	End	Ohio Wesleyan University (OH)
1957	Ken Pleger	Tackle	Capital University (OH)
1958	Dave Adolph	Guard	University of Akron (OH)
1959	Max Urich	Center	Ohio Wesleyan University (OH)
1960	Max Urich	Center	Ohio Wesleyan University (OH)
1961	Don Gerosa	End	Ohio Wesleyan University (OH)
1962	Tom Goosby	Guard	Baldwin-Wallace College (OH)
1963	Bob Cherry	End	Wittenberg University (OH)
1964	Jerry Roberts	End	Baldwin-Wallace College (OH)
1965	Mark DeVilling	Tackle	Muskingum University (OH)
1966	Mark DeVilling	Tackle	Muskingum University (OH)
1967	Rod Miller	End	Wittenberg University (OH)
1968	Bob Quackenbush	Tackle	Baldwin-Wallace College (OH)
1969	Fred Minnear	Center	Oberlin College (OH)
1970	Chris Myers	End	Kenyon College (OH)
1971	John Grof	Tackle	Baldwin-Wallace College (OH)
1971	Tom Hattersley	Center	Denison University (OH)
1972	John Yezerski	Guard	Baldwin-Wallace College (OH)
1973	Steve Drongowski	Tackle	Wittenberg University (OH)
1974	Greg Arnold	Tackle	Capital University (OH)
1975	Sam Crumpton	End	Baldwin-Wallace College (OH)
1976	Bob Gerhardstein	Tackle	Muskingum University (OH)
1977	Rick Colvin	Guard	Muskingum University (OH)
1978	Blake Moore	Center	College of Wooster (OH)
1979	Blake Moore	Center	College of Wooster (OH)
1980	Steve Wigton	Center	Capital University (OH)
1981	Tom Dolder	Guard	Otterbein College (OH)
1981	Chuck Krajacic	Guard	Baldwin-Wallace College (OH)
1982	Scott Brinkerhoff	Tight End	Ohio Northern University (OH)
1983	Steve Harter	Tacklle	Mount Union College (OH)
1984	Dave Miller	End	Baldwin-Wallace College (OH)
1985	Chuck Longnecker	End	Heidelberg University (OH)
1986	Mike Groff	Tackle	Mount Union College (OH)
1987	Keith Willike	End	Capital University (OH)
1988	Eric Horstman	Tackle	Wittenberg University (OH)
1989	Doug Morgan	Tackle	Muskingum University (OH)
1990	John Bouloubasis	Center	Mount Union College (OH)
1991	Shaun Martin	Tackle	Heidelberg University (OH)
1992	Mike Elder	Tackle	Mount Union College (OH)
1993	Tom Trace	Tackle	Capital University (OH)
1994	Matt Johnson	Tackle	Mount Union College (OH)
1995	Mike Wenderfer	Guard	Mount Union College (OH)
1996	Josh Weber	Tackle	Mount Union College (OH)
1997	Joe Weimer	Tackle	Mount Union College (OH)
1998	J.W. Wearley	Tackle	Mount Union College (OH)
1999	Tom Bauer	Center	Mount Union College (OH)
2000	Jason Gerber	Tackle	Mount Union College (OH)
2001	Ed Malone	Center	Mount Union College (OH)
2002	Matt Payne	Tackle	John Carroll University (OH)
2003	Larry Kinnard	Tackle	Mount Union College (OH)
2004	Victor DeBoer	Tackle	John Carroll University (OH)
2005	Jason Lewis	Tackle	Mount Union College (OH)
2006	Jason Lewis	Tackle	Mount Union College (OH)
2007	Derek Blanchard	Guard	Mount Union College (OH)

Ken Wable Award (Offensive Lineman of the Year)

This award has been presented since 2008 by Mount Union College (Alliance, OH) in honor of Ken Wable, who spent 24 years (1962–1985) leading the school's football program. He led the Purple Raiders to 123 victories and one OAC championship.

Year	*Player*	*School*
2008	Andy Fries	Otterbein College (OH)
2009	Cory Dutcher	Capital University (OH)
2010	Nathan Kater	Heidelberg University (OH)

Ohio Athletic Conference Defensive Player of the Year

Year	*Player*	*Position*	*School*
1971	Bob Baun	Linebacker	Wittenberg University (OH)
1972	Lynn Sherman	Tackle	Capital University (OH)
1973	Tom Coffman	End	Heidelberg University (OH)
1974	Brian Burby	End	Ohio Wesleyan University (OH)
1974	Antone Strothers	Tackle	Wittenberg University (OH)
1975	Dennis Thorne	Middle Guard	Denison University (OH)
1976	Dean Caven	End	Wittenberg University (OH)
1977	Bob Foster	Linebacker	Wittenberg University (OH)
1978	Paul Petrella	Tackle	Baldwin-Wallace College (OH)
1979	Joe Govern	Tackle	Wittenberg University (OH)
1980	Dan Delfino	Tackle	Baldwin-Wallace College (OH)
1981	Pete Primeau	Tackle	Baldwin-Wallace College (OH)
1982	Pete Primeau	Tackle	Baldwin-Wallace College (OH)
1983	Bryant Lemon	Tackle	Wittenberg University (OH)
1983	Gary Curren	End	Ohio Northern University (OH)
1984	Tim Swanger	Nose Tackle	Muskingum University (OH)

Ohio Athletic Conference Lee Tressel Award (Defensive Back of the Year)

This award has been presented annually since 1985 and is named in honor of Lee Tressel, who played football (fullback) for Baldwin-Wallace College (Berea, OH; 1943–1944, 1946–1947) and later coached the team from 1958 to 1980. He compiled an overall school record of 155–52–6 (.728); won an NCAA Division III championship in 1978; selected Kodak National Coach of the Year three times by the American Football Coaches Association; and was inducted into the College Football Hall of Fame in 1996.

Year	*Player*	*Position*	*School*
1985	Kert Boedicker	Linebacker	Baldwin-Wallace College (OH)
1986	Scott Watters	Linebacker	Wittenberg University (OH)
1987	Keith Szanto	Cornerback	Capital University (OH)
1988	Sean Kelly	Safety	Capital University (OH)
1989	Corey Harper	Safety	Muskingum University (OH)
1990	Corey Harper	Safety	Muskingum University (OH)
1991	Bill Kaikis	Safety	Capital University (OH)
1992	Scott Reifschneider	Safety	Ohio Northern University (OH)
1993	Bryan Bown	Safety	Marietta College (OH)
1993	Bill Linder	Safety	Baldwin-Wallace College (OH)
1994	Adam Smith	Safety	Heidelberg University (OH)
1995	Connon Thompson	Safety	Muskingum University (OH)
1996	Sean Moore	Defensive Back	Mount Union College (OH)
1997	Mark Black	Defensive Back	Mount Union College (OH)
1998	Kris Bugara	Defensive Back	Mount Union College (OH)
1999	Tom Rini	Safety	John Carroll University (OH)
2000	Antonio Broadnax	Defensive Back	Wilmington College (OH)
2001	Chris Kern	Defensive Back	Mount Union College (OH)

Year	*Player*	*Position*	*School*
2002	Chris Kern	Defensive Back	Mount Union College (OH)
2003	Greg Koch	Defensive Back	Baldwin-Wallace College (OH)
2004	Jesse Clum	Defensive Back	Mount Union College (OH)
2005	Kyle Hausler	Defensive Back	Capital University (OH)
2006	Chad Otte	Defensive Back	Wilmington College (OH)
2007	James Starks	Defensive Back	Capital University (OH)
2008	Daryl Ely	Defensive Back	Mount Union College (OH)
2008	Carlo Melaragno	Defensive Back	John Carroll University (OH)
2009	Drew McClain	Defensive Back	Mount Union (OH)
2010	Dominic Jones	Defensive Back	Otterbein College (OH)

Bill Edwards Award (Linebacker of the Year)

This award has been presented annually since 1988 and is named after Edwards, a long-time coach at Case Western Reserve University (Cleveland, OH; 1936–1940), Detroit Lions in the National Football League (1941–1942), Vanderbilt University (Nashville, TN; 1949–1952), and Wittenberg University (Springfield, OH; 1955–1968)). He compiled a 168–45–8 (.760) college record; won five OAC championships (1958, 1961–1964); and was inducted into the College Football Hall of Fame in 1986.

Year	*Player*	*School*
1988	Phil Medvetz	Baldwin-Wallace College (OH)
1989	Dave Rastoka	John Carroll University (OH)
1990	Dave Lasecki	Mount Union College (OH)
1991	Jim Clardy	Baldwin-Wallace College (OH)
1992	Jim Clardy	Baldwin-Wallace College (OH)
1993	Rob Rodgers	Mount Union College (OH)
1994	Rob Rodgers	Mount Union College (OH)
1995	Chris Anderson	John Carroll University (OH)
1996	Chris Anderson	John Carroll University (OH)
1997	London Fletcher	John Carroll University (OH)
1998	Jason Hall	Mount Union College (OH)
1999	Roger Ailiff	Otterbein College (OH)
2000	Jesse Pearson	Mount Union College (OH)
2001	Jason Perkins	Mount Union College (OH)
2002	Chris Cubero	John Carroll University (OH)
2003	Ron Swearingin	Capital University (OH)
2004	Shaun Spisak	Mount Union College (OH)
2005	Mike Gibbons	Mount Union College (OH)
2006	Jack Junker	Muskingum University (OH)
2007	Lenny Trusnik	Ohio Northern University (OH)

Gene Slaughter Award (Linebacker of the Year)

This award has been presented annually since 2008 by Capital University (Columbus, OH) in honor of Slaughter, who spent 25 years (1961–1985) in charge of the school's football program. He compiled a 120–94–3 record (.553); won the Stagg Bowl in 1970; and served as the school's Athletic Director from 1981 to 1987.

Year	*Player*	*School*
2008	Pete Ankrom	Capital University (OH)
2008	Mike Nettling	John Carroll University (OH)
2009	Sam Kershaw	Mount Union College (OH)
2010	Sam Jacobs	Capital University (OH)

Ohio Athletic Conference Paul Hoernemann Award (Defensive Lineman of the Year)

This award has been presented annually since 1985 and is named after Hoernemann, the long-time coach at Heidelberg College/University (Tiffin, OH), where he compiled a school record of 102–

18–4 (.823); won five OAC championships; and was inducted into the College Football Hall of Fame in 1997.

Year	*Player*	*Position*	*School*
1985	John Heather	Tackle	Mount Union College (OH)
1985	Phil Schmucker		Marietta College (OH)
1986	Kevin Woods	Tackle	Muskingum University (OH)
1987	Mike Eberhardt		Capital University (OH)
1988	Mike Kauffeld	Tackle	Capital University (OH)
1989	Doug Haubert	End	Baldwin-Wallace College (OH)
1990	Mike Rodak	Tackle	Baldwin-Wallace College (OH)
1991	Patrick Engle	End	Otterbein College (OH)
1992	Mike Hallett	Tackle	Mount Union College (OH)
1993	Mike Hallett	Tackle	Mount Union College (OH)
1994	Phil Sahley	End	Baldwin-Wallace College (OH)
1995	Jason Olivea	Tackle	Marietta College (OH)
1996	Scott O'Donnell	End	John Carroll University (OH)
1997	Jim Eismon	Tackle	Mount Union College (OH)
1998	Jeremy Yoder	End	Mount Union College (OH)
1999	Len VanDeVelde	End	Ohio Northern University (OH)
2000	Joe Dobies	Tackle	Baldwin-Wallace College (OH)
2001	Matt Campbell	End	Mount Union College (OH)
2002	Matt Campbell	End	Mount Union College (OH)
2003	Nate Mitchell	End	Baldwin-Wallace College (OH)
2004	Jason Trusnik	End	Ohio Northern University (OH)
2005	Ryan Lewis	End	Baldwin-Wallace College (OH)
2006	Jason Trusnik	End	Ohio Northern University (OH)
2007	Pat McCullough	Tackle	Mount Union College (OH)
2008	James Herbert	Lineman	Mount Union College (OH)
2009	Joe Millings	End	Mount Union College (OH)
2010	Keith Darbut	Lineman	Baldwin-Wallace College (OH)

Old Dominion Athletic Conference (ODAC)

P.O. Box 971, 402B Idaho Street, Salem, VA 24153; Telephone: 540-387-9073; Fax: 540-389-6196; Web site: http://www.odaconline.com

The 14-member (including one associate member) Old Dominion Athletic Conference is the second-largest, multi-sport NCAA Division III conference in the country. It was formed in May 1975 as the Virginia College Conference and began operations in September 1976. Before the conference even began operations, it had changed its name to the Old Dominion Athletic Conference (in January 1976). Charter schools included Bridgewater College, Eastern Mennonite College, Emory & Henry College, Hampden-Sydney College, Lynchburg College, Randolph-Macon College, Roanoke College, and Washington & Lee University.

As of this writing, the conference consists of 13 members (and two associate members), seven of which play football in the ODAC and one plays football outside the conference:

- Bridgewater College Eagles, Bridgewater, VA 22812; 540-828-8000; www.bridgewater.edu
- Eastern Mennonite University Royals, Harrisonburg, VA 22802; 540-432-4000; www.emu.edu; no football program
- Emory & Henry College Wasps, Emory, VA 24327; 276-944-4121; www.ehc.edu
- Guilford College Quakers, Greensboro, NC 27410; 336-316-2000; www.guilford.edu
- Hampden-Sydney College Tigers, Hampden Sydney, VA 23943; 434-223-6000; www.hsc.edu
- Hollins University (no sports nickname), Roanoke, VA 24020; 800-456-9595; www.hollins.edu; no football program
- Lynchburg College Hornets, Lynchburg, VA 24501; 434-544-8100; www.lynchburg.edu; no football program
- Randolph College Wildcats, Lynchburg, VA 24503; 434-947-8000; www.randolphcollege.edu; no football program

- Randolph-Macon College Yellow Jackets, Ashland, VA 23005; 804-752-7200; www.rmc.edu
- Roanoke College Maroons, Salem, VA 24153; 540-375-2500; http://roanoke.edu; no football program
- Shenandoah University Hornets, Winchester, VA 22601; 800-432-2266; www.su.edu; plays football in the USA South Athletic Conference
- Sweet Briar College Vixens, Sweet Briar, VA 24595; 434-381-6100; www.sbc.edu; no football program
- The Catholic University of America Cardinals, Washington, D.C. 20064; 202-319-5000; www.cua.edu; plays football in the conference and is an associate member from the Landmark Conference
- Virginia Wesleyan College Marlins, Norfolk, VA 23502; 757-455-3200; http://ww2.vwc.edu; no football program
- Washington & Lee University Generals, Lexington, VA 24450; 540-458-8400; www.wlu.edu

Old Dominion Athletic Conference Champions

Year	*School*
1976	Randolph-Macon College (VA)
1977	Hampden-Sydney College (VA)
1978	Randolph-Macon College (VA)
1979	Randolph-Macon College (VA)
1980	Bridgewater College (VA)
1981	Washington & Lee University (VA)
1982	Hampden-Sydney College (VA)
1983	Hampden-Sydney College (VA)
1984	Randolph-Macon College (VA)
1985	Emory & Henry College (VA)
1985	Randolph-Macon College (VA)
1985	Washington & Lee University (VA)
1986	Emory & Henry College (VA)
1987	Hampden-Sydney College (VA)
1988	Emory & Henry College (VA)
1989	Randolph-Macon College (VA)
1990	Emory & Henry College (VA)
1991	Guilford College (NC)
1992	Emory & Henry College (VA)
1993	Randolph-Macon College (VA)
1994	Emory & Henry College (VA)
1995	Emory & Henry College (VA)
1996	Emory & Henry College (VA)
1997	Emory & Henry College (VA)
1997	Guilford College (NC)
1997	Randolph-Macon College (VA)
1998	Emory & Henry College (VA)
1999	Catholic University of America (Washington, D.C.)
2000	Emory & Henry College (VA)
2001	Bridgewater College (VA)
2002	Bridgewater College (VA)
2003	Bridgewater College (VA)
2004	Bridgewater College (VA)
2005	Bridgewater College (VA)
2006	Washington & Lee University (VA)
2007	Hampden-Sydney College (VA)
2008	Randolph-Macon College (VA)
2009	Hampden-Sydney College (VA)
2010	Washington & Lee University (VA)

Old Dominion Athletic Conference Coach of the Year

Year	*Coach*	*School*
1976	Ted Keller	Randolph-Macon College (VA)
1977	Stokeley Fulton	Hampden-Sydney College (VA)
1978	Ted Keller	Randolph-Macon College (VA)
1979	Ted Keller	Randolph-Macon College (VA)
1980	John Spencer	Bridgewater College (VA)
1981	Gary Fallon	Washington & Lee University (VA)
1982	Stokeley Fulton	Hampden-Sydney College (VA)
1983	Stokeley Fulton	Hampden-Sydney College (VA)
1984	Jim Blackburn	Randolph-Macon College (VA)
1985	Lou Wacker	Emory & Henry College (VA)
1986	Lou Wacker	Emory & Henry College (VA)
1987	Joe Bush	Hampden-Sydney College (VA)
1988	Gary Fallon	Washington & Lee University (VA)
1989	Jim Blackburn	Randolph-Macon College (VA)
1990	Joe Bush	Hampden-Sydney College (VA)
1991	Mike Ketchum	Guilford College (NC)
1992	Gary Fallon	Washington & Lee University (VA)
1993	Joe Riccio	Randolph-Macon College (VA)

Year	Coach	School
1994	Lou Wacker	Emory & Henry College (VA)
1995	Lou Wacker	Emory & Henry College (VA)
1996	Frank Miriello	Washington & Lee University (VA)
1997	Mike Ketchum	Guilford College (NC)
1998	Lou Wacker	Emory & Henry College (VA)
1999	Tom Clark	Catholic University of America (Washington, D.C.)
2000	Mike Clark	Bridgewater College (VA)
2001	Frank Miriello	Washington & Lee University (VA)
2001	Mike Clark	Bridgewater College (VA)
2002	Mike Clark	Bridgewater College (VA)
2003	Marty Favret	Hampden-Sydney College (VA)
2004	Frank Miriello	Washington & Lee University (VA)
2005	Mike Clark	Bridgewater College (VA)
2006	Frank Miriello	Washington & Lee University (VA)
2007	Marty Favret	Hampden-Sydney College (VA)
2008	Pedro Arruza	Randolph-Macon College (VA)
2009	Marty Favret	Hampden-Sydney College (VA)
2010	Frank Miriello	Washington & Lee University (VA)

Old Dominion Athletic Conference Player of the Year (Stokeley Fulton Award — Offensive Player of the Year) (Lou Wacker Award — Defensive Player of the Year)

Year	Player	Position	School
1976	Tony Perry	Wide Receiver	Washington & Lee University (VA)
1977	Jim Ferguson	Running Back	Hampden-Sydney College (VA)
1978	Carl Folcik	Linebacker	Washington & Lee University (VA)
1979	Ricky Eades	Defensive Tackle	Randolph-Macon College (VA)
1979	Tim Smith	Defensive Tackle	Hampden-Sydney College (VA)
1980	Ricky Eades	Defensive Lineman	Randolph-Macon College (VA)
1981	Chris Cavalline	Running Back	Washington & Lee University (VA)
1982	Hiter Harris	Kicker	Hampden-Sydney College (VA)
1983	Ralph Fucillo	Defensive Lineman	Catholic University of America (Washington, D.C.)
1984	Cody Dearing	Quarterback	Randolph-Macon College (VA)
1985	Kevin Weaver	Running Back	Washington & Lee University (VA)
1986	Sandy Rogers	Running Back	Emory & Henry College (VA)
1987	Gary Collier	Quarterback	Emory & Henry College (VA)
1988	Anthony Lawrence	Running Back	Bridgewater College (VA)
1989	Jody Kane	Defensive End	Randolph-Macon College (VA)
1990	B. I. Salyers	Offensive Lineman	Emory & Henry College (VA)
1991	Calvin Hunter	Quarterback	Guilford College (NC)
1992	Cary Perkins	Quarterback	Emory & Henry College (VA)
1993	Ronnie Howard	Running Back	Bridgewater College (VA)
1994	David Heggie	Running Back	Guilford College (NC)
1995	Robert Hull	Defensive Tackle	Washington & Lee University (VA)
1996	Tim Armoska	Linebacker	Randolph-Macon College (VA)
1997	Sidney Chappell	Quarterback	Randolph-Macon College (VA)
1998	Oliver Jordan	Running Back	Emory & Henry College (VA)
1999	A. Notarfrancesco	Running Back	Catholic University of America (Washington, D.C.)
2000	Marc Watson	Running Back	Washington & Lee University (VA)
2001	Jason Lutz	Quarterback	Bridgewater College (VA)
2002	Jermaine Taylor	Linebacker	Bridgewater College (VA)
2003	Conrad Singh	Wide Receiver	Hampden-Sydney College (VA)
2003	Jermaine Taylor	Linebacker	Bridgewater College (VA)
2004	Offense: CW Clemmons	Running Back	Hampden-Sydney College (VA)

Year	Player	Position	School
2004	Defense: Lawrence Frierson	Defensive Linebacker	Bridgewater College (VA)
2005	Offense: JD Ricca	Quarterback	Hampden-Sydney College (VA)
2005	Defense: Bobby Stutz	Linebacker	Catholic University of America (Washington, D.C.)
2006	Offense: Chris Barnette	Wide Receiver	Guilford College (NC)
2006	Defense: Marshall Doss	Linebacker	Emory & Henry College (VA)
2007	Offense: Drew Smith	Wide Receiver	Hampden-Sydney College (VA)
2007	Defense: Kyle Luby	Defensive Back	Washington & Lee University (VA)
2008	Offense: Keith Ricca	Quarterback	Catholic University of America (Washington, D.C.)
2008	Defense: Nick Olivero	Defensive Back	Catholic University of America (Washington, D.C.)
2009	Offense: Caleb Jennings	Running Back	Emory & Henry College (VA)
2009	Defense: Will Riggenbach	Defensive Lineman	Hampden-Sydney College (VA)
2010	Offense: Tyler Beiler	Wide Receiver	Bridgewater College (VA)
2010	Defense: Trevor Ikwild	Linebacker	Hampden-Sydney College (VA)

Old Dominion Athletic Conference Rookie of the Year

Year	Player	Position	School
2002	Clay Muench	Wide Receiver	Randolph-Macon College (VA)
2003	Todd Woods	Quarterback	Emory & Henry College (VA)
2004	Drew Smith	Wide Receiver	Hampden-Sydney College (VA)
2005	Josh Vogelbach	Quarterback	Guilford College (NC)
2006	R.J. Varner	Quarterback	Washington & Lee University (VA)
2007	Greg Kurkis	Offensive Lineman	Washington & Lee University (VA)
2008	Charlie Westfal	Quarterback	Washington & Lee University (VA)
2009	Daniel Biggerstaff	Outside Linebacker	Guilford College (NC)
2010	Mike Pitsenberger	Running Back	Catholic University of America (Washington, D.C.)

Pilgrim Lacrosse League

Non-football conference.

Presidents' Athletic Conference (PAC)

8500 Brooktree Road, Suite 130, Wexford, PA 15090; Telephone: 724-933-4630; Fax: 724-933-4635; Web site: http://www.pacathletics.org

The Presidents' Athletic Conference was founded in 1955 with charter schools Case Institute of Technology, John Carroll University, Wayne State University, and Western Reserve University. Currently, the PAC consists of 10 schools, nine of which play football within the conference.

- Bethany College Bison, Bethany, WV 26032; 304-829-7000; www.bethanywv.edu
- Chatham University Cougars, Pittsburgh, PA 15232; 412-365-1100; www.chatham.edu; no football program
- Geneva College Golden Tornadoes, Beaver Falls, PA 15010; 800-847-8255; www.geneva.edu
- Grove City College Wolverines, Grove City, PA 16127; 724-458-2000; www.gcc.edu
- Saint Vincent College Bearcats, Latrobe, PA 15650; 724-532-6600; www.stvincent.edu
- Thiel College Tomcats, Greenville, PA 16125; 800-248-4435; www.thiel.edu
- Thomas More College Saints, Crestview Hills, KY 41017; 859-341-5800; www.thomasmore.edu
- Washington & Jefferson College Presidents, Washington, PA 15301; 888-W26-3529; www.washjeff.edu
- Waynesburg University Yellow Jackets, Waynesburg, PA 15370; 724-627-8191; www.waynesburg.edu
- Westminster College Titans, New Wilmington, PA 16172; 800-942-8033; www.westminster.edu

Presidents' Athletic Conference Champions

Year	School
1955	Western Reserve University (OH)
1956	Wayne State University (MI)
1957	John Carroll University (OH)
1958	Western Reserve University (OH)
1959	John Carroll University (OH)
1960	Western Reserve University (OH)
1961	Allegheny College (PA)
1962	John Carroll University (OH)
1963	John Carroll University (OH)
1964	Wayne State University (MI)
1965	Bethany College (WV)
1966	Bethany College (WV)
1967	Thiel College (PA)
1968	Allegheny College (PA)
1969	John Carroll University (OH)
1970	Washington & Jefferson College (PA)
1971	John Carroll University (OH)
1972	Thiel College (PA)
1973	John Carroll University (OH)
1974	Allegheny College (PA)
1974	John Carroll University (OH)
1975	Bethany College (WV)
1976	Allegheny College (PA)
1977	Carnegie Mellon University (PA)
1978	Carnegie Mellon University (PA)
1979	Carnegie Mellon University (PA)
1980	Bethany College (WV)
1981	Carnegie Mellon University (PA)
1982	Hiram College (OH)
1983	Carnegie Mellon University (PA)
1984	Washington & Jefferson College (PA)
1985	Carnegie Mellon University (PA)
1986	Washington & Jefferson College (PA)
1987	Washington & Jefferson College (PA)
1988	Washington & Jefferson College (PA)
1989	Carnegie Mellon University (PA)
1989	Washington & Jefferson College (PA)
1990	Washington & Jefferson College (PA)
1991	Washington & Jefferson College (PA)
1992	Washington & Jefferson College (PA)
1993	Washington & Jefferson College (PA)
1994	Washington & Jefferson College (PA)
1995	Washington & Jefferson College (PA)
1996	Washington & Jefferson College (PA)
1997	Grove City College (PA)
1998	Grove City College (PA)
1998	Washington & Jefferson College (PA)
1999	Washington & Jefferson College (PA)
2000	Washington & Jefferson College (PA)
2001	Washington & Jefferson College (PA)
2002	Washington & Jefferson College (PA)
2003	Waynesburg University (PA)
2004	Washington & Jefferson College (PA)
2005	Thiel College (PA)
2006	Washington & Jefferson College (PA)
2007	Washington & Jefferson College (PA)
2008	Thomas More College (KY)
2009	Thomas More College (KY)
2010	Thomas More College (KY)

Presidents' Athletic Conference Coach of the Year

Year	Coach	School
2006	Mike Sirianni	Washington & Jefferson College (PA)
2007	Mike Sirianni	Washington & Jefferson College (PA)
2008	Jim Hilvert	Thomas More College (KY)
2009	Jim Hilvert	Thomas More College (KY)
2010	Jim Hilvert	Thomas More College (KY)

Presidents' Athletic Conference Player of the Year

Year	Player	Class	Position	School
2006	Mark Carlisle	Senior	Linebacker	Thomas More College (KY)
2007	Mike Czerwien	Senior	Defensive End	Waynesburg University (PA)
2008	Bobby Swallow	Senior	Quarterback	Washington & Jefferson College (PA)
2009	Brad Steinmetz	Senior	Linebacker	Thomas More College (KY)
2010	Tyler Owens	Senior	Defensive Lineman	Thomas More College (KY)

Skyline Conference

New York, NY; Commissioner Tracy King: 4 Spice Mill Boulevard, Clifton Park, NY 12065–2638; Email: tking@skylineconference.org; Web site: http://www.skylineconference.org/

The Skyline Conference currently consists of 11 members and does not support football, although one of its members plays football outside the conference.

- Bard College Raptors, Annandale-on-Hudson, NY 12504; 845-758-6822; www.bard.edu; no football program
- College of Mount Saint Vincent Dolphins, Riverdale, NY 10471; 718-405-3267; www.mountsaintvincent.edu; no football program
- Farmingdale State College Rams, Farmingdale, NY 11735; 631-420-2000; www.farmingdale.edu; no college program
- Mount Saint Mary College Knights, Newburgh, NY 12550; 845-561-0800; www.msmc.edu; no football program
- Polytechnic Institute of New York University Fighting Blue Jays, Brooklyn, NY 11201; 718-260-3600; www.poly.edu; no football program
- Purchase College Panthers–State University of New York, Purchase, NY 10577; 914-251-6000; www.purchase.edu; no football program
- St. Joseph's College Golden Eagles, Patchogue, NY 11772; 631-687-5100; www.sjcny.edu; no football program
- State University of New York–College at Old Westbury Panthers, Old Westbury, NY 11568; 516-876-3000; www.oldwestbury.edu; no football program
- State University of New York Maritime College Privateers, Throggs Neck, NY 10465; 718-409-7200; www.sunymaritime.edu; plays football in the Eastern Collegiate Football Conference
- The Sage Colleges Gators, Troy, NY 12180; 518-244-2000; www.sage.edu; no football program
- Yeshiva University Maccabees, New York, NY 10033; 212-960-5400; www.yu.edu; no football program

Southern California Intercollegiate Athletic Conference (SCIAC)

1330 North Gardner Street #208, Los Angeles, CA 90046 (7119 West Sunset Boulevard #258, Los Angeles, CA 90046); Telephone: 323-851-4740; Fax: 323-544-2233; Web site: http://www.thesciac.org

The Southern California Intercollegiate Athletic Conference was formed in 1915 with five charter members, all of which still belong to the conference: California Institute of Technology, Occidental College, Pomona College, University of Redlands, and Whittier College. As of this writing, the SCIAC consists of eight members, seven of which play football in the conference:

- California Institute of Technology Beavers, Pasadena, CA 91125; 626-395-6811; www.caltech.edu; no football program
- California Lutheran University Kingsmen, Thousand Oaks, CA 91360; 805-493-3135; www.callutheran.edu
- Claremont McKenna College, Harvey Mudd College, Scripps College Stags, Claremont, CA 91711; 909-621-8088; www.cmc.edu
- Occidental College Tigers, Los Angeles, CA 90041; 323-259-2500; www.oxy.edu
- Pomona-Pitzer Colleges Sagehens, Claremont, CA 91711; 909-621-8000; www.pomona.edu
- University of La Verne Leopards, La Verne, CA 91750; 909-593-3511; http://laverne.edu
- University of Redlands Bulldogs, Redlands, CA 92373; 909-793-2121; www.redlands.edu
- Whittier College Poets, Whittier, CA 90608; 562-907-4200; www.whittier.edu

Southern California Intercollegiate Athletic Conference Champions

Year	*School*
2006	Occidental College (CA)
2007	California Lutheran University (CA)
2007	University of Redlands (CA)
2008	Occidental College (CA)
2009	California Lutheran University (CA)
2010	California Lutheran University (CA)

Southern California Intercollegiate Athletic Conference Offensive Player of the Year

Year	*Player*	*Position*	*Class*	*School*
2008	Justin Goltz		Senior	Occidental College (CA)
2009	Brian Stuart	Running Back	Senior	California Lutheran University (CA)
2010	Jacob Caron		Senior	Pomona-Pitzer College (CA)

Southern California Intercollegiate Athletic Conference Defensive Player of the Year

Year	Player	Position	Class	School
2008	Jacob Calderon		Senior	California Lutheran University (CA)
2009	Alex Wertheimer	Defensive Lineman	Junior	Occidental College (CA)
2010	Michael Nicolini		Senior	University of Redlands (CA)

Southern California Intercollegiate Athletic Conference Newcomer of the Year Award

Year	Player	Position	Class	School
2008	Jordan Washington		Freshman	Occidental College (CA)
2009	Cedric Ho	Wide Receiver	Junior	University of La Verne (CA)
2010	Taylor Irwin		Freshman	University of Redlands (CA)

Southern Collegiate Athletic Conference (SCAC)

2940 Horizon Park Drive, Suite D, Sewanee, GA 30024; Telephone: 678-546-3470; Fax: 678-546-3471; Web site: http://www.scacsports.com

The Southern Collegiate Athletic Conference began operations on September 1, 1962 as the College Athletic Conference with four charter schools: Centre College of Danville, Southwestern at Memphis (now known as Rhodes College); Sewanee–The University of the South, and Washington and Lee University. The conference adopted its current name in 1991.

As of this writing, the SCAC consists of 12 schools, seven of which play football in the conference.

- Austin College Kangaroos, Sherman, TX 75090; 903-813-2000; www.austincollege.edu
- Birmingham-Southern College Panthers, Birmingham, AL 35254; 800-523-5793; www.bsc.edu
- Centre College Colonels, Danville, KY 40422; 859-238-5200; www.centre.edu
- Colorado College Tigers, Colorado Springs, CO 80903; 719-389-6000; www.coloradocollege.edu; no football program
- Hendrix College Warriors, Conway, AR 72032; 800-277-9017; www.hendrix.edu; no football program
- Millsaps College Majors, Jackson, MS 39210; 601-974-1000; www.millsaps.edu
- Oglethorpe University Stormy Petrels, Atlanta, GA 30319; 404-261-1441; www.oglethorpe.edu; no football program
- Rhodes College Lynx, Memphis, TN 38112; 901-843-3000; www.rhodes.edu.
- Sewanee–The University of the South Tigers, Sewanee, TN 37383; 931-598-1000; www.sewanee.edu
- Southwestern University Pirates, Georgetown, TX 78626; 512-863-6511; www.southwestern.edu; no football program
- Trinity University Tigers, San Antonio, TX 78212; 800-874-6489; www.trinity.edu
- University of Dallas Crusaders, Irving, TX 75062; 972-721-5000; www.udallas.edu; no football program

Southern Collegiate Athletic Conference Champions

Year	School
1962	Washington & Lee University (VA)
1963	Sewanee–University of the South (TN)
1964	Sewanee–University of the South (TN)
1964	Washington University of St. Louis (MO)
1965	Sewanee–University of the South (TN)
1966	Washington University of St. Louis (MO)
1967	Sewanee–University of the South (TN)
1968	Centre College (KY)
1968	Southwestern at Memphis (TN)
1969	Centre College (KY)
1970	Southwestern at Memphis (TN)
1970	Washington University of St. Louis (MO)
1971	Centre College (KY)
1971	Southwestern at Memphis (TN)
1972	Centre College (KY)
1973	Southwestern at Memphis (TN)
1974	Rose-Hulman Institute of Technology (IN)
1975	Rose-Hulman Institute of Technology (IN)
1975	Sewanee–University of the South (TN)

Year	School
1976	Sewanee–University of the South (TN)
1977	Southwestern at Memphis (TN)
1978	Sewanee–University of the South (TN)
1978	Southwestern at Memphis (TN)
1979	Rose-Hulman Institute of Technology (IN)
1979	Sewanee–University of the South (TN)
1979	Southwestern at Memphis (TN)
1980	Centre College (KY)
1981	Rose-Hulman Institute of Technology (IN)
1982	Sewanee–University of the South (TN)
1983	Centre College (KY)
1983	Rose-Hulman Institute of Technology (IN)
1984	Centre College (KY)
1985	Centre College (KY)
1985	Rhodes College (TN)
1986	Rose-Hulman Institute of Technology (IN)
1987	Rhodes College (TN)
1988	Rose-Hulman Institute of Technology (IN)
1989	Centre College (KY)
1990	Centre College (KY)
1990	Sewanee–University of the South (TN)
1991	Millsaps College (MI)
1992	Sewanee–University of the South (TN)
1993	Trinity University (TX)
1994	Trinity University (TX)
1995	Centre College (KY)
1995	Rhodes College (TN)
1995	Trinity University (TX)
1996	Millsaps College (MI)
1996	Trinity University (TX)
1997	Trinity University (TX)
1998	Trinity University (TX)
1999	Trinity University (TX)
2000	DePauw University (IN)
2000	Sewanee–University of the South (TN)
2000	Trinity University (TX)
2001	Trinity University (TX)
2002	Trinity University (TX)
2003	Centre College (KY)
2003	Trinity University (TX)
2004	Trinity University (TX)
2005	DePauw University (IN)
2005	Trinity University (TX)
2006	Millsaps College (MI)
2007	Millsaps College (MI)
2007	Trinity University (TX)
2008	Millsaps College (MI)
2009	DePauw University (IN)
2009	Millsaps College (MI)
2010	DePauw University (IN)

Southern Collegiate Athletic Conference Coach of the Year

Selected by conference football coaches.

Year	Coach	School
1987	Frank Carr	Earlham College (IN)
1987	Mike Clary	Rhodes College (TN)
1988	No Information Available	
1989	Joe McDaniel	Centre College (KY)
1990	Bill Samko	Sewanee–University of the South (TN)
1990	Joe McDaniel	Centre College (KY)
1991	Tommy Ranager	Millsaps College (MI)
1992	Bill Samko	Sewanee–University of the South (TN)
1993	Steve Mohr	Trinity University (TX)
1994	Steve Mohr	Trinity University (TX)
1995	Joe McDaniel	Centre College (KY)
1995	Steve Mohr	Trinity University (TX)
1996	Ron Jurney	Millsaps College (MI)
1997	Steve Mohr	Trinity University (TX)
1998	Steve Mohr	Trinity University (TX)
1999	Steve Mohr	Trinity University (TX)
2000	Nick Mourouzis	DePauw University (IN)
2001	Steve Mohr	Trinity University (TX)
2002	Steve Mohr	Trinity University (TX)
2003	Joe White	Rhodes College (TN)
2004	Bill Lynch	DePauw University (IN)
2004	Steve Mohr	Trinity University (TX)
2005	John Windham	Sewanee–University of the South (TN)
2006	Mike Dubose	Millsaps College (MI)
2007	Steve Mohr	Trinity University (TX)

Year	Coach	School
2008	Mike Dubose	Millsaps College (MI)
2009	Robby Long	DePauw University (IN)
2010	Robby Long	DePauw University (IN)

Southern Collegiate Athletic Conference Offensive Player of the Year

Selected by conference football coaches.

Year	Player	Position	Class	School
1987	Bobby Morales		Senior	Sewanee–University of the South (TN)
1988	No Information Available			
1989	Tim McDaniel		Sophomore	Centre College (KY)
1990	Tim McDaniel	Running Back	Senior	Centre College (KY)
1991	Carl Cravens	Running Back	Sophomore	Sewanee–University of the South (TN)
1992	Drew Robison	Quarterback	Senior	Rhodes College (TN)
1993	Brian Vandegrift	Wide Receiver	Senior	Rhodes College (TN)
1993	Kelvin Gladney	Running Back	Junior	Millsaps College (MI)
1994	Kelvin Gladney	Running Back	Senior	Millsaps College (MI)
1995	Kris Garrett	Running Back	Senior	Centre College (KY)
1996	Brad Madden	Running Back	Senior	Millsaps College (MI)
1997	Mark Byarlay	Running Back	Senior	Trinity University (TX)
1998	Michael Burton	Quarterback	Junior	Trinity University (TX)
1999	Michael Burton	Quarterback	Senior	Trinity University (TX)
2000	Jason Lee	Quarterback	Junior	DePauw University (IN)
2001	Roy Hampton	Quarterback	Junior	Trinity University (TX)
2002	Roy Hampton	Quarterback	Senior	Trinity University (TX)
2003	Daniel Swanstrom	Quarterback	Junior	Rhodes College (TN)
2003	Lorenzo Engleman	Running Back	Senior	Centre College (KY)
2004	Dan DesPlaines	Quarterback	Senior	Trinity University (TX)
2005	Adam Clark	Wide Receiver	Junior	Centre College (KY)
2005	Robert Kelner	Wide Receiver	Senior	Trinity University (TX)
2005	Wesley Satterfield	Quarterback	Junior	Sewanee–University of the South (TN)
2006	Juan Joseph	Quarterback	Sophomore	Millsaps College (MI)
2007	Juan Joseph	Quarterback	Junior	Millsaps College (MI)
2008	Juan Joseph	Quarterback	Senior	Millsaps College (MI)
2009	Alex Koors	Wide Receiver	Junior	DePauw University (IN)
2010	Alex Koors	Wide Receiver	Senior	DePauw University (IN)

Southern Collegiate Athletic Conference Defensive Player of the Year

Selected by conference football coaches.

Year	Name	Position	Class	School
1987	Pat Thomas		Junior	Rose-Hulman Institute of Technology (IN)
1988	No Information Available			
1989	Jeff Bezold		Senior	Centre College (KY)
1990	Ray McGowan	Defensive Lineman	Senior	Sewanee–University of the South (TN)
1991	Sean Brewer	Defensive Tackle	Junior	Millsaps College (MI)
1992	Sean Brewer	Defensive Tackle	Senior	Millsaps College (MI)
1993	John Tobola	Defensive End	Senior	Trinity University (TX)
1994	James Vallerie	Linebacker	Senior	Trinity University (TX)
1995	Zach Woods	Defensive Tackle	Senior	Centre College (KY)
1996	John Beckwith	Linebacker	Senior	Trinity University (TX)
1997	Clay Curry	Strong Safety	Senior	Centre College (KY)
1998	Alex Doran	Free Safety	Senior	Trinity University (TX)
1999	Ryan Deck	Linebacker	Senior	Trinity University (TX)

Year	Name	Position	Class	School
2000	John-Paul Visosky	Linebacker	Senior	Trinity University (TX)
2001	Matt O'Bryant	Linebacker	Junior	Millsaps College (MI)
2002	Matt O'Bryant	Linebacker	Senior	Millsaps College (MI)
2003	Jarrod Smith	Defensive Lineman	Senior	Trinity University (TX)
2004	Jake Vieck	Nose Guard	Senior	Rose-Hulman Institute of Technology (IN)
2005	Tyrell Elston	Defensive Lineman	Senior	Sewanee–University of the South (TN)
2006	Dustin Hertel	Defensive End	Senior	DePauw University (IN)
2007	Casey Younger	Defensive Tackle	Senior	Millsaps College (MI)
2007	Desmond Hendricks	Linebacker	Junior	Rhodes College (TN)
2008	Mason Mosby	Linebacker	Senior	Rhodes College (TN)
2009	Will Hawkins	Linebacker	Junior	Millsaps College (MI)
2010	Will Hawkins	Linebacker	Senior	Millsaps College (MI)

Southern Collegiate Athletic Conference Special Teams Player of the Year

Selected by conference football coaches.

Year	Player	Position	Class	School
1999	Brian Britt	Punt Returner	Sophomore	Centre College (KY)
2000	Brian Britt	Punt Returner	Junior	Centre College (KY)
2001	Brian Britt	Punt Returner	Senior	Centre College (KY)
2002	Ely Santos	Kick Returner	Senior	Centre College (KY)
2002	Jason Hunt	Punt Returner	Senior	Trinity University (TX)
2003	Jamarcus Shephard	Kick Returner	Junior	DePauw University (IN)
2004	Jamarcus Shephard	Kick Returner	Senior	DePauw University (IN)
2004	Robin Kelner	Punt Returner	Junior	Trinity University (TX)
2005	Kelly Altman	Place Kicker	Senior	Trinity University (TX)
2006	Chris Jackson	Punt Returner / Kick Returner	Senior	Millsaps College (MI)
2007	John Milazzo	Punt Returner / Kick Returner	Sophomore	Millsaps College (MI)
2008	Michael Galatas	Kick Returner	Sophomore	Millsaps College (MI)
2009	Michael Galatas	Kick Returner	Junior	Millsaps College (MI)
2010	Michael Galatas	Kick Returner	Senior	Millsaps College (MI)

Southern Collegiate Athletic Conference Newcomer of the Year

Selected by conference football coaches.

Year	Player	Position	Class	School
2007	Walter Arrington	Wide Receiver	Freshman	Birmingham-Southern College (AL)
2008	Shane Bowser	Running Back	Freshman	Millsaps College (MI)
2008	Tyler Osterman	Quarterback	Freshman	Centre College (KY)
2009	Kyle Trella	Punter	Freshman	Trinity University (TX)
2010	Jordan Gay	Punter / Place Kicker	Sophomore	Centre College (KY)

St. Louis Intercollegiate Athletic Conference (SLIAC)

964 South Highway Drive, Fenton, MO 63026; Telephone: 314-529-9586; Fax: 636-349-8976; Web site: http://www.sliac.org/

The St. Louis Intercollegiate Athletic Conference was created in September 1989 with five charter schools: Blackburn College, Fontbonne University, Parks College, Principia College, and Webster University. Currently the SLIAC has nine members and does not support football, although four of its members play football in the Upper Midwest Athletic Conference.

- Blackburn College Beavers, Carlinville, IL 62626; 217-854-3231; www.blackburn.edu; no football program

- Eureka College Red Devils, Eureka, IL 61530; 888-438-7352; www.eureka.edu; plays football in the Upper Midwest Athletic Conference
- Fontbonne University Griffins, St. Louis, MO 63105; 314-862-3456; www.fontbonne.edu; no football program
- Greenville College Panthers, Greenville, IL 62246; 618-664-2800; www.greenville.edu; plays football in the Upper Midwest Athletic Conference
- MacMurray College Highlanders, Jacksonville, IL 62650; 217-479-7000; www.mac.edu; plays football in the Upper Midwest Athletic Conference
- Principia College Panthers, Elsah, IL 62028; 618-374-2131; www.principiacollege.edu; no football program
- Spalding University Golden Eagles, Louisville, KY 40203; 502-585-9911; www.spalding.edu; no football program
- Webster University Gorloks, St. Louis, MO 63119; 800-981-9801; www.webster.edu; no football program
- Westminster College Blue Jays, Fulton, MO 65251; 573-642-3361; www.wesminster-mo.edu; plays football in the Upper Midwest Athletic Conference

State University of New York Athletic Conference

SUNY Fredonia, Jewett Hall #118, Fredonia, NY 14063; Telephone: 866-578-2950, 716-673-3105; Fax: 716-673-3135; Email: sunyac@fredonia.edu; Web site: http://www.sunyac.com

In September 1958, the New York State Intercollegiate Athletic Conference was formed (and later adopted its current name in 1963) with nine charter schools: Buffalo State College, SUNY at Brockport, SUNY at Potsdam, SUNY Cortland, SUNY New Paltz, SUNY Oneonta, SUNY Oswego, SUNY Plattsburgh, and University at Albany.

Currently, the SUNYAC consists of 10 members and does not support football, although three of its schools play football in the New Jersey Athletic Conference.

- College of Brockport (State University of New York at Brockport) Golden Bears, Brockport, NY 14420; 585-395-2211; www.brockport.edu; plays football in the New Jersey Athletic Conference
- Buffalo State College (State University of New York College at Buffalo) Bengals, Buffalo, NY 14222; 716-878-4000; www.buffalostate.edu; plays football in the New Jersey Athletic Conference
- Cortland State (State University of New York at Cortland) Red Dragons, Cortland, NY 13045; 607-753-2011; www2.cortland.edu; plays football in the New Jersey Athletic Conference
- Fredonia State University (State University College at Fredonia) Blue Devils, Fredonia, NY 14063; 716-673-3111; www.fredonia.edu; no football program
- Geneseo State (State University of New York at Geneseo) Blue Knights, Geneseo, NY 14454; 585-245-5000; www.geneseo.edu; no football program
- Oneonta State (State University of New York at Oneonta) Red Dragons, Oneonta, NY 13820; 607-436-3500; no football program
- Oswego State (State University College at Oswego) Lakers, Oswego, NY 13126; 315-312-2500; www.oswego.edu; no football program
- Plattsburgh State (State University of New York at Plattsburgh) Cardinals, Plattsburgh, NY 12901; 518-564-2000; www.plattsburgh.edu; no football program
- State University of New York at New Paltz (SUNY New Paltz) Hawks, New Paltz, NY 12561; 845-257-7869; www.newpaltz.com; no football program
- State University of New York at Potsdam (SUNY Potsdam) Bears, Potsdam, NY 13676; 315-267-2000; www.potsdam.edu; no football program

United Volleyball Conference

Non-football conference.

University Athletic Association

151 Sully's Trail, Suite 4, Pittsford, NY 14534; Telephone: 585-419-0575; Fax: 585-218-0951; Web site: http://www.uaa.rochester.edu/

The University Athletic Association was formed in June 1986 with charter members Carnegie Mellon University, Case Western Reserve University, Emory University, Johns Hopkins University, New York University, the University of Chicago, the University of Rochester, and Washington University in St. Louis. As of this writing, the UAA consists of eight members, four of which play football within the Association and one school plays football in the Liberty League.

- Brandeis University Judges, Waltham, MA 02453; 781-736-2000; www.brandeis.edu; no football program
- Carnegie Mellon University Tartans, Pittsburgh, PA 15213; 412-268-2000; www.cmu.edu
- Case Western Reserve University Spartans, Cleveland, OH 44106; 216-368-2000; www.case.edu
- Emory University Eagles, Atlanta, GA 30322; 404-727-6123; www.emory.edu
- New York University Violets, New York, NY 10012; 212-998-1212; www.nyu.edu; no football program
- University of Chicago Maroons, Chicago, IL 60637; 773-702-1234; www.uchicago.edu
- University of Rochester Yellowjackets, Rochester, NY 14627; 585-275-2121; www.rochester.edu; plays football in the Liberty League
- Washington University in St. Louis Bears, St. Louis, MO 63130; 314-935-5000; www.wustl.edu.

University Athletic Association Champion

Year	*School*
1988	Case Western Reserve University (OH)
1988	University of Rochester (NY)
1989	University of Rochester (NY)
1990	Carnegie Mellon University (PA)
1991	Carnegie Mellon University (PA)
1992	University of Rochester (NY)
1993	Carnegie Mellon University (PA)
1994	Carnegie Mellon University (PA)
1994	Washington University in St. Louis (MO)
1995	Carnegie Mellon University (PA)
1995	Washington University in St. Louis (MO)
1996	Carnegie Mellon University (PA)
1996	Case Western Reserve University (OH)
1996	Washington University in St. Louis (MO)
1997	Carnegie Mellon University (PA)
1998	University of Chicago (IL)
1999	Washington University in St. Louis (MO)
2000	University of Chicago (IL)
2001	Washington University in St. Louis (MO)
2002	Washington University in St. Louis (MO)
2003	Washington University in St. Louis (MO)
2004	Washington University in St. Louis (MO)
2005	University of Chicago (IL)
2006	Carnegie Mellon University (PA)
2007	Case Western Reserve University (OH)
2008	Case Western Reserve University (OH)
2009	Case Western Reserve University (OH)
2010	University of Chicago (IL)

University Athletic Association Coach of the Year

Year	*Coach*	*School*
1990	Rich Lackner	Carnegie Mellon University (PA)
1991	Rich Lackner	Carnegie Mellon University (PA)
1992	Rich Parrinello	University of Rochester (NY)
1993	Rich Lackner	Carnegie Mellon University (PA)
1994	Dick Maloney	University of Chicago (IL)
1995	Larry Kindbom	Washington University in St. Louis (MO)
1996	Regis Scafe	Case Western Reserve University (OH)
1997	Rich Lackner	Carnegie Mellon University (PA)
1998	Dick Maloney	University of Chicago (IL)
1999	Larry Kindbom	Washington University in St. Louis (MO)
2000	Dick Maloney	University of Chicago (IL)
2001	Larry Kindbom	Washington University in St. Louis (MO)

Year	*Coach*	*School*
2002	Larry Kindbom	Washington University in St. Louis (MO)
2003	Larry Kindbom	Washington University in St. Louis (MO)
2004	Greg Debeljak	Case Western Reserve University (OH)
2005	Dick Maloney	University of Chicago (IL)
2005	Larry Kindbom	Washington University in St. Louis (MO)
2006	Rich Lackner	Carnegie Mellon University (PA)
2007	Greg Debeljak	Case Western Reserve University (OH)
2008	Not Available	Not Available
2009	Greg Debeljak	Case Western Reserve University (OH)
2010	Dick Maloney	University of Chicago (IL)

University Athletic Association Offensive Player of the Year

Year	*Player*	*School*
1990	Scott Barnyak	Carnegie Mellon University (PA)
1991	Greg Marmol	Carnegie Mellon University (PA)
1992	Isaac Collins	University of Rochester (NY)
1992	Jeremy Hurd	University of Rochester (NY)
1993	Frank Baker	University of Chicago (IL)
1994	Derrick Brooms	University of Chicago (IL)
1995	Derrick Brooms	University of Chicago (IL)
1996	Brandon Way	University of Chicago (IL)
1996	Joe El-Etr	Washington University in St. Louis (MO)
1997	Vernon Butler	Washington University in St. Louis (MO)
1998	Brandon Way	University of Chicago (IL)
1999	Mike Campie	Washington University in St. Louis (MO)
2000	Josh Dunn	University of Chicago (IL)
2001	Bobby Collins Jr	Washington University In St. Louis (MO)
2002	Brandon McDowell	Case Western Reserve University (OH)
2003	Brad Stanley	Carnegie Mellon University (PA)
2004	Brad Duesing	Washington University in St. Louis (MO)
2004	David Kallevig	Case Western Reserve University (OH)
2005	Brad Duesing	Washington University in St. Louis (MO)
2006	Travis Sivek	Carnegie Mellon University (PA)
2007	Dan Whalen	Case Western Reserve University (OH)
2007	Travis Sivek	Carnegie Mellon University (PA)
2008	Not Available	Not Available
2009	Dan Whalen	Case Western Reserve University (OH)
2010	Dee Brizzolara	University of Chicago (IL)

University Athletic Association Defensive Player of the Year

Year	*Player*	*School*
1990	Dennis Braniecki	University of Rochester (NY)
1991	Ed Trebets	Case Western Reserve University (OH)
1992	Brian Laudadio	University of Rochester (NY)
1993	Chad Wilson	Carnegie Mellon University (PA)
1993	Geoffrey Long	University of Rochester (NY)
1993	Rich Zdrojewski	Case Western Reserve University (OH)
1994	Matt Gomric	Washington University in St. Louis (MO)
1995	Ray Ardire	Carnegie Mellon University (PA)
1996	Aaron Boehm	Washington University in St. Louis (MO)
1997	Brad Klein	Washington University in St. Louis (MO)
1998	Tom Courtad	Case Western Reserve University (OH)
1999	Tim Runnalls	Washington University in St. Louis (MO)
2000	Dan Phillips	University of Chicago (IL)
2001	James Molnar	Washington University in St. Louis (MO)
2002	John Woock	Washington University in St. Louis (MO)
2003	Rick Schmitz	Washington University in St. Louis (MO)

Year	Player	School
2004	Matt Armbruster	University of Chicago (IL)
2005	Rob Tamillow	University of Chicago (IL)
2006	Drew Wethington	Washington University in St. Louis (MO)
2006	Tom Brew	Case Western Reserve University (OH)
2007	Not Available	Not Available
2008	Not Available	Not Available
2009	Jess Brown	Case Western Reserve University (OH)
2010	Brandon Brown	Washington University in St. Louis (MO)

University Athletic Association Special Teams Player of the Year

Year	Player	School
2010	Austin Morman	Washington University in St. Louis (MO)
2010	Jeff Sauer	University of Chicago (IL)

University Athletic Association Rookie of the Year

Year	Player	School
2000	John Savage	University of Rochester (NY)
2000	Jonathan Feig	Washington University in St. Louis (MO)
2001	Dave Kallevig	Case Western Reserve University (OH)
2002	Jason Cellura	Case Western Reserve University (OH)
2003	Aaron Lewis	Carnegie Mellon University (PA)
2004	Gabriel Fernandez	University of Chicago (IL)
2004	Travis Sivek	Carnegie Mellon University (PA)
2005	Todd Young	University of Chicago (IL)
2006	Bobby Bott	Case Western Reserve University (OH)
2007	Jim O'Brien	Washington University in St. Louis (MO)
2007	Justin Kaderabek	University of Chicago (IL)
2007	Shaun Nicely	Case Western Reserve University (OH)
2008	Not Available	Not Available
2009	Dee Brizzolara	University of Chicago (IL)
2010	Joshua Burandt	University of Chicago (IL)

Upper Midwest Athletic Conference (UMAC)

Administration & Sports Information Offices, Northwestern College, 3003 Snelling Avenue North, St. Paul, MN 55113; Telephone: 651-631-5363; Fax: 651-628-3350; Web site: http://www.umacathletics.com

The Upper Midwest Athletic Conference began in 1972 as the Twin Rivers Conference and adopted its current name in 1983. As of this writing, the conference has eight full-time members (five of which play football in the UMAC) and four associate (football-only) members.

- Bethany Lutheran College Vikings, Mankato, MN 56001; 507-344-7000; www.blc.edu; no football program
- College of St. Scholastica Saints, Duluth, MN 55811; 218-723-6000; www.css.edu
- Crown College Storm, St. Bonifacius, MN 55375; 952-446-4100; www.crown.edu
- Eureka College Red Devils, Eureka, IL 61530; 888-438-7352; www.eureka.edu; an associate member from the St. Louis Intercollegiate Athletic Conference
- Greenville College Panthers, Greenville, IL 62246; 618-664-2800; www.greenville.edu; an associate member from the St. Louis Intercollegiate Athletic Conference
- MacMurray College Highlanders, Jacksonville, IL 62650; 217-479-7000; www.mac.edu; an associate member from the St. Louis Intercollegiate Athletic Conference
- Martin Luther College Knights, New Ulm, MN 56073; 507-354-8221; www.mlc-wels.edu
- Northland College LumberJacks, Ashland, WI 54806; 715-682-1699; www.northland.edu; no football program
- Northwestern College Eagles, St. Paul, MN 55113; 651-631-5100; www.nwc.edu

- Presentation College Saints, Aberdeen, SD 57401; 800-437-6060; www.presentation.edu
- University of Minnesota, Morris, Cougars, Morris, MN 56267; 320-589-6035; http://morris.umn.edu
- Westminster College Blue Jays, Fulton, MO 65251; 573-592-5251; www.westminster-mo.edu; an associate member from the St. Louis Intercollegiate Athletic Conference

Upper Midwest Athletic Conference Champions

Year	School
1974	Northwestern College (MN)
1975	Northwestern College (MN)
1976	Concordia University, St. Paul (MN)
1976	Loras College (IA)
1976	Maranatha Baptist Bible College (WI)
1976	Northwestern College (MN)
1976	Northwestern College (WI)
1977	Concordia University, St. Paul (MN)
1977	Martin Luther College (MN)
1978	Northwestern College (WI)
1979	Northwestern College (MN)
1980	Mount Senario College (WI)
1981	Concordia University, St. Paul (MN)
1981	Northwestern College (MN)
1982	Concordia University, St. Paul (MN)
1982	Mount Senario College (WI)
1982	Northwestern College (MN)
1983	Mount Scenario College (WI)
1983	Northwestern College (WI)
1984	Northwestern College (MN)
1985	Mount Senario College (WI)
1986	Northwestern College (WI)
1987	Mount Senario College (WI)
1988	Concordia University, St. Paul (MN)
1989	Mount Senario College (WI)
1990	Marantha Baptist Bible College (WI)
1990	Northwestern College (MN)
1991	Concordia University, St. Paul (MN)
1992	Mount Senario College (WI)
1993	Mount Senario College (WI)
1994	Mount Senario College (WI)
1995	Martin Luther College (MN)
1996	Northwestern College (MN)
1997	Mount Senario College (WI)
1998	Marantha Baptist Bible College (WI)
1998	Martin Luther College (MN)
1998	Mount Senario College (WI)
1999	Mount Senario College (WI)
2000	Mount Senario College (WI)
2001	Northwestern College (MN)
2002	Northwestern College (MN)
2003	Westminster College (MO)
2004	Westminster College (MO)
2005	Northwestern College (MN)
2006	University of Minnesota, Morris (MN)
2007	Northwestern College (MN)
2008	Northwestern College (MN)
2009	North: Martin Luther College (MN)
2009	South: Greenville College (IL)
2010	Greenville College (IL)

Upper Midwest Athletic Conference Coach of the Year

Year	Coach	School
2007	North: Eric Slivoskey	Trinity Bible College (ND)
2007	South: Randy Schrader	Rockford College (IL)
2007	Overall: Eric Slivoskey	Trinity Bible College (ND)
2008	Kirk Talley	Northwestern College (MN)
2009	North: Doug Lange	Martin Luther College (MN)
2009	South: Eric Hehman	Greenville College (IL)
2010	Ordell Walker	Greenville College (IL)

Upper Midwest Athletic Conference Offensive Player of the Year

Year	Player	Position	School
2007	North: Zack Tarter	Quarterback	Northwestern College (MN)
2007	South: Tony LaGrone	Running Back	Blackburn College (IL)
2007	Overall: Tony LaGrone	Running Back	Blackburn College (IL)
2007	Overall: Zack Tarter	Quarterback	Northwestern College (MN)
2008	Zach Tarter	Quarterback	Northwestern College (MN)
2009	North: Christopher Henagin		College of St. Scholastica (MN)
2009	North: Zach Tarter	Quarterback	Northwestern College (MN)
2009	South: Anthony Ambers		Greenville College (IL)
2009	South: Nick Lindsey		Eureka College (IL)
2010	Anthony Ambers		Greenville College (IL)

Upper Midwest Athletic Conference Defensive Player of the Year

Year	*Player*	*Position*	*School*
2007	North: Seth Scheuerlein	Defensive Tackle	Martin Luther College (MN)
2007	South: Patrick Clark	Defensive End	Westminster College (MO)
2007	Overall: Seth Scheuerlein	Defensive Tackle	Martin Luther College (MN)
2008	Kyle Nash		Northwestern College (MN)
2009	North: Chuqee Fletcher		Martin Luther College (MN)
2009	South: Garrett Young		Greenville College (IL)
2010	Joel Deayon		Greenville College (IL)

Upper Midwest Athletic Conference Lineman of the Year

Year	*Player*	*Position*	*School*
2007	North: Nate Fehr	Defensive End	Northwestern College (MN)
2007	South: Jeff Cihlar	Offensive Lineman	Rockford College (IL)
2007	Overall: Jeff Cihlar	Offensive Lineman	Rockford College (IL)
2008	Josh Prokosch		Crown College (MN)
2009	North: Chuqee Fletcher		Martin Luther College (MN)
2009	South: Tim Burroughs		Greenville College (IL)
2010	David Butler		Greenville College (IL)

Upper Midwest Athletic Conference Special Teams Player of the Year

Year	*Player*	*Position*	*School*
2009	North: Cody Crum		Northwestern College (MN)
2009	South: Daniel Eidson		Westminster College (MO)
2010	Luis Diaz		Greenville College (IL)

USA South Athletic Conference

5400 Ramsey Street, Fayetteville, NC 28311; Telephone: 910-630-7282; Email: commish@usasouth.net; Web site: http://www.usasouth.net

The USA South Athletic Conference was initially formed as the Dixie Intercollegiate Athletic Conference in 1963 with six charter schools: Charlotte College (now known as the University of North Carolina, Charlotte), College of Charleston (SC), Lynchburg College, Methodist College (now known as Methodist University), North Carolina Wesleyan College, and St. Andrews Presbyterian College. The conference adopted its current name in July 2003. It was initially affiliated with the National Association of Intercollegiate Athletics (NAIA), where it stayed until 1973, when the NCAA divided itself into three levels (I, II, III) and USA South joined the NCAA Division III level. USA South sponsored its first year of football in 2001.

As of this writing, USA South consists of 13 schools, eight of which play football in the conference and one school plays an independent football schedule.

- Agnes Scott College Scotties, Decatur, GA 30030; 404-471-6000; www.agnesscott.edu; no football program
- Averett University Cougars, Danville, VA 24541; 434-791-5600; www.averett.edu
- Christopher Newport University Captains, Newport News, VA 23606; 757-594-7000; www.cnu.edu
- Ferrum College Panthers, Ferrum, VA 24088; 540-365-2121; www.ferrum.edu
- Greensboro College Pride, Greensboro, NC 27401; 336-272-7102; www.greensborocollege.edu
- LaGrange College Panthers, LaGrange, GA 30240; 706-880-8000; www.lagrange.edu; plays an independent football schedule
- Mary Baldwin College Fighting Squirrels, Staunton, VA 24402; 800-468-2262; www.mbc.edu; no football program
- Maryville College Fighting Scots, Maryville, TN 37804; 800-597-2687; www.maryvillecollege.edu; an associate member (for football) from the Great South Athletic Conference
- Meredith College Avenging Angels, Raleigh, NC 27607; 919-760-8600; www.meredith.edu; no football program
- Methodist University Monarchs, Fayetteville, NC 28311; 910-630-7000; www.methodist.edu

- North Carolina Wesleyan College Battling Bishops, Rocky Mount, NC 27804; 252-985-5100; www.ncwc.edu
- Peace College Pacers, Raleigh, NC 27604; 800-732-2347; www.peace.edu; no football program
- Shenandoah University Hornets, Winchester, VA 22601; 800-432-2266; www.su.edu

USA South Athletic Conference Champions

Year	School
2001	Christopher Newport University (VA)
2001	Ferrum College (VA)
2002	Christopher Newport University (VA)
2002	Ferrum College (VA)
2003	Christopher Newport University (VA)
2003	Shenandoah University (VA)
2004	Christopher Newport University (VA)
2004	Shenandoah University (VA)
2005	Ferrum College (VA)
2005	Methodist University (NC)
2006	Averett University (VA)
2006	Christopher Newport University (VA)
2007	North Carolina Wesleyan College (NC)
2008	Christopher Newport University (VA)
2009	North Carolina Wesleyan College (NC)
2010	Christopher Newport University (VA)
2010	North Carolina Wesleyan College (NC)

USA South Athletic Conference Coach of the Year

Year	Coach	School
2001	Matt Kelchner	Christopher Newport University (VA)
2002	Matt Kelchner	Christopher Newport University (VA)
2003	Mike Dunlevy	Averett University (VA)
2004	Paul Barnes	Shenandoah University (VA)
2005	Dave Davis	Ferrum College (VA)
2006	Matt Kelchner	Christopher Newport University (VA)
2007	Jack Ginn	North Carolina Wesleyan College (NC)
2008	Matt Kelchner	Christopher Newport University (VA)
2009	Mark Henninger	North Carolina Wesleyan College (NC)
2010	Matt Kelchner	Christopher Newport University (VA)

USA South Athletic Conference Offensive Player of the Year

Year	Player	School
2001	Phil Hairston	Ferrum College (VA)
2002	Jawarren Cowles	Chowan College (NC)
2003	Moncrief Holmes	Ferrum College (VA)
2004	Roland Hilliard	Christopher Newport University (VA)
2005	Chris Roncketti	Methodist University (NC)
2006	Cedric Townsend	North Carolina Wesleyan College (NC)
2007	Cedric Townsend	North Carolina Wesleyan College (NC)
2008	Tunde Ogun	Christopher Newport University (VA)
2009	Bo Jordan	North Carolina Wesleyan College (NC)
2010	Marcus Mayo	Ferrum College (VA)

USA South Athletic Conference Defensive Player of the Year

Year	Player	School
2001	Quincy Malloy	Methodist University (NC)
2002	Darren Venable	Ferrum College (VA)
2003	Darren Venable	Ferrum College (VA)
2004	Darren Venable	Ferrum College (VA)
2005	Rob Rodriguez	Christopher Newport University (VA)
2006	Jermaine Moore	Averett University (VA)
2007	Daryl Lawrence	Methodist University (NC)
2008	Kyle Chewning	Maryville College (TN)
2009	LeeRon Boykin	North Carolina Wesleyan College (NC)
2010	James Carter	North Carolina Wesleyan College (NC)

USA SOUTH ATHLETIC CONFERENCE ROOKIE OF THE YEAR

Year	*Player*	*School*
2001	Offense: Kaveh Conaway	Christopher Newport University (VA)
2001	Defense: Olando Holmes	Christopher Newport University (VA)
2002	Offense: Chris Roncketti	Methodist University (NC)
2002	Defense: Jermaine Moore	Averett University (VA)
2003	Offense: George Jones	Christopher Newport University (VA)
2003	Defense: Ronnie Fields	Chowan College (NC)
2004	Offense: Javon Williams	North Carolina Wesleyan College (NC)
2004	Defense: Andrew Quigley	North Carolina Wesleyan College (NC)
2005	Offense: Torrey Lowe	Greensboro College (NC)
2005	Defense: Quinderra Spellman	North Carolina Wesleyan College (NC)
2006	Offense: Teron Bush	North Carolina Wesleyan College (NC)
2006	Defense: Brick Crowder	Greensboro College (NC)
2007	Offense: Mike Vann	Ferrum College (VA)
2007	Defense: Adrin Diggs	Christopher Newport University (VA)
2008	Offense: Stedman Mathis	North Carolina Wesleyan College (NC)
2008	Defense: Mario Huffman	Averett University (VA)
2009	Offense: Antwan Thorpe	Greensboro College (NC)
2009	Defense: James Wallace	North Carolina Wesleyan College (NC)
2010	Offense: Jordan Vann	North Carolina Wesleyan College (NC)
2010	Defense: Tazmon Foster	North Carolina Wesleyan College (NC)

Western Water Polo Association

Non-football conference.

Wisconsin Intercollegiate Athletic Conference (WIAC)

780 Regent Street, Madison, WI 53715; Fax: 608-265-3176; Web site: http://www.wiacsports.com

The Wisconsin Intercollegiate Athletic Conference was founded in July 1913 as the Wisconsin State University Athletic Conference (known at the time as the State Normal Conference) with charter schools (all in Wisconsin): University of Wisconsin, La Crosse, University of Wisconsin, River Falls, University of Wisconsin, Stevens Point, and the University of Wisconsin, Superior.

As of this writing, the WIAC consists of nine member institutions, eight of which play football in the conference:

- University of Wisconsin, Eau Claire, Blugolds, Eau Claire, WI 54702; 715-836-4636; www.uwec.edu
- University of Wisconsin, La Crosse, Eagles, La Crosse, WI 54601; 608-785-8000; www.uwlax.edu
- University of Wisconsin, Oshkosh, Titans, Oshkosh, WI 54901; 920-424-1234; www.uwosh.edu
- University of Wisconsin, Platteville, Pioneers, Platteville, WI 53818; 800-362-5515; www.uwplatt.edu
- University of Wisconsin, River Falls, Falcons, River Falls, WI 54022; 715-425-3911; www.uwrf.edu
- University of Wisconsin, Stevens Point, Pointers, Stevens Point, WI 54481; 715-346-0123; www.uwsp.edu
- University of Wisconsin, Stout, Blue Devils, Menomonie, WI 54751; 715-232-1122; www.uwstout.edu
- University of Wisconsin, Superior, Yellowjackets, Superior, WI 54880; 715-394-8101; www.uwsuper.edu; no football program
- University of Wisconsin, Whitewater, Warhawks, Whitewater, WI 53190; 262-472-1170; www.uww.edu

WISCONSIN INTERCOLLEGIATE ATHLETIC CONFERENCE CHAMPIONS

Year	*School*
1913	University of Wisconsin, Superior (WI)
1913	University of Wisconsin, Whitewater (WI)
1914	University of Wisconsin, Whitewater (WI)
1915	University of Wisconsin, River Falls (WI)
1916	University of Wisconsin, River Falls (WI)
1917	University of Wisconsin, La Crosse (WI)
1918	No Champion
1919	University of Wisconsin, La Crosse (WI)

Year	School
1920	University of Wisconsin, Oshkosh (WI)
1921	University of Wisconsin, Stout (WI)
1922	University of Wisconsin, Eau Claire (WI)
1922	University of Wisconsin, Whitewater (WI)
1923	University of Wisconsin, Oshkosh (WI)
1924	University of Wisconsin, River Falls (WI)
1925	University of Wisconsin, River Falls (WI)
1926	University of Wisconsin, River Falls (WI)
1927	University of Wisconsin, La Crosse (WI)
1928	University of Wisconsin, Oshkosh (WI)
1928	University of Wisconsin, Stevens Point (WI)
1928	University of Wisconsin, Superior (WI)
1929	University of Wisconsin, Milwaukee (WI)
1930	University of Wisconsin, Milwaukee (WI)
1931	University of Wisconsin, Milwaukee (WI)
1932	University of Wisconsin, Whitewater (WI)
1933	University of Wisconsin, La Crosse (WI)
1933	University of Wisconsin, River Falls (WI)
1933	University of Wisconsin, Stevens Point (WI)
1934	University of Wisconsin, La Crosse (WI)
1934	University of Wisconsin, Stevens Point (WI)
1935	University of Wisconsin, Oshkosh (WI)
1935	University of Wisconsin, Superior (WI)
1936	University of Wisconsin, Stevens Point (WI)
1936	University of Wisconsin, Superior (WI)
1937	University of Wisconsin, Superior (WI)
1937	University of Wisconsin, Whitewater (WI)
1938	University of Wisconsin, Milwaukee (WI)
1938	University of Wisconsin, Platteville (WI)
1938	University of Wisconsin, River Falls (WI)
1939	University of Wisconsin, La Crosse (WI)
1939	University of Wisconsin, Milwaukee (WI)
1940	University of Wisconsin, La Crosse (WI)
1940	University of Wisconsin, Whitewater (WI)
1941	University of Wisconsin, La Crosse (WI)
1941	University of Wisconsin, Platteville (WI)
1941	University of Wisconsin, Stout (WI)
1941	University of Wisconsin, Whitewater (WI)
1942	University of Wisconsin, La Crosse (WI)
1942	University of Wisconsin, Milwaukee (WI)
1942	University of Wisconsin, Platteville (WI)
1943	No Champion During World War II
1944	No Champion During World War II
1945	No Champion During World War II
1946	University of Wisconsin, Milwaukee (WI)
1946	University of Wisconsin, Stevens Point (WI)
1946	University of Wisconsin, Superior (WI)
1947	University of Wisconsin, Milwaukee (WI)
1947	University of Wisconsin, River Falls (WI)
1948	University of Wisconsin, Eau Claire (WI)
1949	University of Wisconsin, La Crosse (WI)
1949	University of Wisconsin, Stevens Point (WI)
1949	University of Wisconsin, Stout (WI)
1950	University of Wisconsin, La Crosse (WI)
1950	University of Wisconsin, Whitewater (WI)
1951	University of Wisconsin, La Crosse (WI)
1952	University of Wisconsin, La Crosse (WI)
1952	University of Wisconsin, Platteville (WI)
1953	University of Wisconsin, La Crosse (WI)
1953	University of Wisconsin, Platteville (WI)
1954	University of Wisconsin, La Crosse (WI)
1955	University of Wisconsin, Stevens Point (WI)
1956	University of Wisconsin, Eau Claire (WI)
1956	University of Wisconsin, Platteville (WI)
1957	University of Wisconsin, Platteville (WI)
1958	University of Wisconsin, River Falls (WI)
1959	University of Wisconsin, Whitewater (WI)
1960	University of Wisconsin, Whitewater (WI)
1961	University of Wisconsin, Stevens Point (WI)
1962	University of Wisconsin, Whitewater (WI)
1963	University of Wisconsin, Eau Claire (WI)
1964	University of Wisconsin, Eau Claire (WI)
1965	University of Wisconsin, Stout (WI)
1966	University of Wisconsin, Whitewater (WI)
1967	University of Wisconsin, Whitewater (WI)
1968	University of Wisconsin, Oshkosh (WI)
1968	University of Wisconsin, Platteville (WI)
1969	University of Wisconsin, Platteville (WI)
1969	University of Wisconsin, Whitewater (WI)
1970	University of Wisconsin, Platteville (WI)
1971	University of Wisconsin, La Crosse (WI)
1971	University of Wisconsin, Platteville (WI)
1972	University of Wisconsin, Oshkosh (WI)
1973	University of Wisconsin, La Crosse (WI)
1974	University of Wisconsin, La Crosse (WI)
1974	University of Wisconsin, Platteville (WI)
1974	University of Wisconsin, Whitewater (WI)
1975	University of Wisconsin, La Crosse (WI)
1975	University of Wisconsin, River Falls (WI)
1975	University of Wisconsin, Whitewater (WI)
1976	University of Wisconsin, Oshkosh (WI)
1976	University of Wisconsin, Platteville (WI)
1976	University of Wisconsin, River Falls (WI)
1977	University of Wisconsin, Stevens Point (WI)
1978	University of Wisconsin, La Crosse (WI)
1978	University of Wisconsin, Whitewater (WI)
1979	University of Wisconsin, River Falls (WI)
1980	University of Wisconsin, La Crosse (WI)
1980	University of Wisconsin, Platteville (WI)
1980	University of Wisconsin, River Falls (WI)
1980	University of Wisconsin, Whitewater (WI)
1981	University of Wisconsin, Eau Claire (WI)
1982	University of Wisconsin, La Crosse (WI)
1983	University of Wisconsin, Eau Claire (WI)
1984	University of Wisconsin, River Falls (WI)
1984	University of Wisconsin, Whitewater (WI)
1985	University of Wisconsin, River Falls (WI)

Year	School
1986	University of Wisconsin, La Crosse (WI)
1986	University of Wisconsin, River Falls (WI)
1986	University of Wisconsin, Stevens Point (WI)
1987	University of Wisconsin, River Falls (WI)
1987	University of Wisconsin, Whitewater (WI)
1988	University of Wisconsin, Whitewater (WI)
1989	University of Wisconsin, La Crosse (WI)
1990	University of Wisconsin, Whitewater (WI)
1991	University of Wisconsin, La Crosse (WI)
1992	University of Wisconsin, La Crosse (WI)
1993	University of Wisconsin, La Crosse (WI)
1994	University of Wisconsin, Whitewater (WI)
1995	University of Wisconsin, La Crosse (WI)
1996	University of Wisconsin, La Crosse (WI)
1997	University of Wisconsin, Whitewater (WI)
1998	University of Wisconsin, Eau Claire (WI)
1998	University of Wisconsin, River Falls (WI)
1998	University of Wisconsin, Stevens Point (WI)
1998	University of Wisconsin, Whitewater (WI)
1999	University of Wisconsin, La Crosse (WI)
1999	University of Wisconsin, Stevens Point (WI)
2000	University of Wisconsin, Stout (WI)
2001	University of Wisconsin, Eau Claire (WI)
2001	University of Wisconsin, Stevens Point (WI)
2002	University of Wisconsin, La Crosse (WI)
2003	University of Wisconsin, La Crosse (WI)
2004	University of Wisconsin, La Crosse (WI)
2005	University of Wisconsin, Whitewater (WI)
2006	University of Wisconsin, Whitewater (WI)
2007	University of Wisconsin, Whitewater (WI)
2008	University of Wisconsin, Stevens Point (WI)
2008	University of Wisconsin, Whitewater (WI)
2009	University of Wisconsin, Whitewater (WI)
2010	University of Wisconsin, Whitewater (WI)

Wisconsin Intercollegiate Athletic Conference George Chryst Coach of the Year

Selected by conference coaches.

Year	Coach	School
1981	George Chryst	University of Wisconsin, Platteville
1982	Link Walker	University of Wisconsin, Eau Claire
1983	Roger Harring	University of Wisconsin, La Crosse
1984	Link Walker	University of Wisconsin, Eau Claire
1985	Forrest Perkins	University of Wisconsin, Whitewater
1986	Mike Farley	University of Wisconsin, River Falls
1987	D.J. LeRoy	University of Wisconsin, Stevens Point
1988	No Winner	
1989	Bob Berezowitz	University of Wisconsin, Whitewater
1990	Roger Harring	University of Wisconsin, La Crosse
1991	Bob Berezowitz	University of Wisconsin, Whitewater
1992	Roger Harring	University of Wisconsin, La Crosse
1993	Roger Harring	University of Wisconsin, La Crosse
1993	Roland Christensen	University of Wisconsin, La Crosse
1994	Roger Harring	University of Wisconsin, La Crosse
1995	Bob Berezowitz	University of Wisconsin, Whitewater
1996	John O'Grady	University of Wisconsin, River Falls
1997	Roger Harring	University of Wisconsin, La Crosse
1998	John Miech	University of Wisconsin, Stevens Point
1999	Roger Harring	University of Wisconsin, La Crosse
2000	Ed Meierkort	University of Wisconsin, Stout
2001	John Miech	University of Wisconsin, Stevens Point
2002	Larry Terry	University of Wisconsin, La Crosse
2003	Larry Terry	University of Wisconsin, La Crosse
2004	Mike Emendorfer	University of Wisconsin, Platteville
2004	Larry Terry	University of Wisconsin, La Crosse
2005	Bob Berezowitz	University of Wisconsin, Whitewater
2006	Bob Berezowitz	University of Wisconsin, Whitewater
2007	Todd Glaser	University of Wisconsin, Eau Claire
2008	John Miech	University of Wisconsin, Stevens Point

Year	Coach	School
2009	Lance Leipold	University of Wisconsin, Whitewater
2010	Lance Leipold	University of Wisconsin, Whitewater

Wisconsin Intercollegiate Athletic Conference Most Valuable Player

Selected by conference coaches.

Year	Player	School
1998	Clint Kriewaldt	University of Wisconsin, Stevens Point
1999	Jared Arn	University of Wisconsin, La Crosse
2000	Jeff Hazuga	University of Wisconsin, Stout
2001	Paul Schmitt	University of Wisconsin, Stevens Point
2001	Darrell Souhrada	University of Wisconsin, Eau Claire
2002	Thaddeus Rego	University of Wisconsin, La Crosse
2003	Scott Krause	University of Wisconsin, Stevens Point
2004	Scott Burnoski	University of Wisconsin, La Crosse
2005	Justin Jacobs	University of Wisconsin, Whitewater
2006	Justin Jacobs	University of Wisconsin, Whitewater
2007	Justin Beaver	University of Wisconsin, Whitewater
2008	Brad Vickroy	University of Wisconsin, Stevens Point
2009	Jeff Donovan	University of Wisconsin, Whitewater
2010	Levell Coppage	University of Wisconsin, Whitewater

National Association of Intercollegiate Athletics (NAIA)

National Association of Intercollegiate Athletics

1200 Grand Boulevard, Kansas City, MO 64106; Telephone: 816-595-8000; Fax: 816-595-8200; Web site: http://www.naia.org

Formed in 1937, the National Association of Intercollegiate Athletics is a non–NCAA college association that provides basically the same opportunities for student-athletes, but at a lower and less well-known level. Small colleges and universities participate in the NAIA, which also accepts educational institutions from outside the United States (as of this writing, there are five Canadian members). Currently, the NAIA consists of 23 conferences and 291 member institutions; sponsors 23 national championships in 13 sports (12 for men and 11 for women); and has the CBS College Sports Network as its national media outlet. Once focused solely on basketball and originally called the National Association of Intercollegiate Basketball (whose formation was helped by basketball inventor Dr. James Naismith), the NAIA adopted its current name in 1952 when it began offering an extended sports program.

Some of the NAIA's most historic moments include: coach John Wooden's Indiana State team brings the first African American student-athletes to the NAIB tournament (1948); the association invites historically black institutions into membership (1953); Tennessee State University (Nashville, TN) becomes the first historically black institution to win a collegiate basketball national championship (in 1957 against Southeastern Oklahoma State University (Durant, OK)); and in 1980, the NAIA becomes the first collegiate athletics association to sponsor both men's and women's championships. In 1970, the NAIA's football program was divided into Division I and Division II, based on school enrollment, but converted back into a single division in 1997.

Currently, the NAIA consists of 23 conferences (270 schools, some of which sponsor football and some do not), the Association of Independent Institutions, the Central States Football League, independent football teams, and the Mid-States Football Association.

- American Mideast Conference
- American Midwest Conference
- Appalachian Athletic Conference
- Association of Independent Institutions
- California Pacific Conference
- Cascade Collegiate Conference
- Central States Football League
- Chicagoland Collegiate Athletic Conference
- Dakota Athletic Conference
- Frontier Conference
- Golden State Athletic Conference
- Great Plains Athletic Conference
- Gulf Coast Athletic Conference
- Heart of America Athletic Conference
- Independent football teams
- Kansas Collegiate Athletic Conference
- Kentucky Intercollegiate Athletic Conference
- Mid-Central College Conference

- Mid-South Conference
- Mid-States Football Association
- Midlands Collegiate Athletic Conference
- Midwest Collegiate Conference
- Red River Athletic Conference
- Sooner Athletic Conference
- Southern States Athletic Conference
- Sunrise Conference
- The Sun Conference
- TranSouth Athletic Conference
- Wolverine-Hoosier Athletic Conference

Since 1956, the NAIA National Football Championship has been decided by a post-season playoff system. In 1970, NAIA football was divided into two divisions (Division I and Division II) and a championship game was played in each division. In 1997, all NAIA football programs were again consolidated into one division.

NAIA Champions

Year	*School*
1956	Montana State University, Bozeman (Bozeman, MT)
1956	Saint Joseph's College (Rensselaer, IN)
1957	Pittsburg State University (Pittsburg, KS)
1958	Northeastern State University (Tahlequah, OK)
1959	Texas A&I University, Kingsville (now known as Texas A&M University, Kingsville) (Kingsville, TX)
1960	Lenoir-Rhyne College (Hickory, NC)
1961	Pittsburg State University (Pittsburg, KS)
1962	Central State University (University of Central Oklahoma) (Edmond, OK)
1963	St. John's University (Collegeville, MN)
1964	Concordia College, Moorhead (Moorhead, MN)
1964	Sam Houston State University (Huntsville, TX)
1965	St. John's University (Collegeville, MN)
1966	Waynesburg College (now known as Waynesburg University) (Waynesburg, PA)
1967	Fairmont State College (now known as Fairmont State University) (Fairmont, WV)
1968	Troy State University (now known as Troy University) (Troy, AL)
1969	Texas A&I University, Kingsville (now known as Texas A&M University, Kingsville) (Kingsville, TX)
1970	Division I: Texas A&I University, Kingsville
1970	Division II: Westminster College (New Wilmington, PA)
1971	Division I: University of West Alabama (Livingston, AL)
1971	Division II: California Lutheran University (Thousand Oaks, CA)
1972	Division I: East Texas State University (now known as Texas A&M University, Commerce) (Commerce, TX)
1972	Division II: Missouri Southern State University (Joplin, MO)
1973	Division I: Abilene Christian University (Abilene, TX)
1973	Division II: Northwestern College (Orange City, IA)
1974	Division I: Texas A&I University, Kingsville (now known as Texas A&M University, Kingsville (Kingsville, TX)
1974	Division II: Texas Lutheran University (Seguin, TX)
1975	Division I: Texas A&I University, Kingsville (now known as Texas A&M University, Kingsville (Kingsville, TX)
1975	Division II: Texas Lutheran University (Seguin, TX)
1976	Division I: Texas A&I University, Kingsville (now known as Texas A&M University, Kingsville (Kingsville, TX)
1976	Division II: Westminster College (New Wilmington, PA)
1977	Division I: Abilene Christian University (Abilene, TX)
1977	Division II: Westminster College (New Wilmington, PA)
1978	Division I: Angelo State University (San Angelo, TX)
1978	Division II: Concordia College, Moorhead (Moorhead, MN)
1979	Division I: Texas A&I University, Kingsville (now known as Texas A&M University, Kingsville (Kingsville, TX)
1979	Division II: University of Findlay (Findlay, OH)
1980	Division I: Elon University (Elon, NC)
1980	Division II: Pacific Lutheran University (Parkland, WA)
1981	Division I: Elon University (Elon, NC)

Year	School
1981	Division II: Austin College (Sherman, TX)
1981	Division II: Concordia College, Moorhead (Moorhead, MN)
1982	Division I: Central State (now known as the University of Central Oklahoma) (Edmond, OK)
1982	Division II: Linfield College (McMinnville, OR)
1983	Division I: Carson-Newman College (Jefferson City, TN)
1983	Division II: Northwestern College (Orange City, IA)
1984	Division I: Carson-Newman College (Jefferson City, TN)
1984	Division I: University of Central Arkansas (Conway, AR)
1984	Division II: Linfield College (McMinnville, OR)
1985	Division I: Hillsdale College (Hillside, MI)
1985	Division I: University of Central Arkansas (Conway, AR)
1985	Division II: University of Wisconsin, La Crosse (La Crosse, WI)
1986	Division I: Carson-Newman College (Jefferson City, TN)
1986	Division II: Linfield College (McMinnville, OR)
1987	Division I: Cameron University (Lawton, OK)
1987	Division II: Pacific Lutheran University (Parkland, WA)
1988	Division I: Carson-Newman College (Jefferson City, TN)
1988	Division II: Westminster College (New Wilmington, PA)
1989	Division I: Carson-Newman College (Jefferson City, TN)
1989	Division II: Westminster College (New Wilmington, PA)
1990	Division I: Central State University (Wilberforce, OH)
1990	Division II: Peru State College (Peru, NE)
1991	Division I: University of Central Arkansas (Conway, AR)
1991	Division II: Georgetown College (Georgetown, KY)
1992	Division I: Central State University (Wilberforce, OH)
1992	Division II: University of (Findlay, OH)
1993	Division I: East Central University (Ada, OK)
1993	Division II: Pacific Lutheran University (Parkland, WA)
1994	Division I: Northeastern State University (Tahlequah, OK)
1994	Division II: Westminster College (New Wilmington, PA)
1995	Division I: Central State University (Wilberforce, OH)
1995	Division II: Central Washington University (Ellensburg, WA)
1995	Division II: University of (Findlay, OH)
1996	Division I: Southwestern Oklahoma State University (Weatherford, OK)
1996	Division II: University of Sioux Falls (Sioux Falls, SD)
1997	University of Findlay (Findlay, OH)
1998	Azusa Pacific University (Azusa, CA)
1999	Northwestern Oklahoma State University (Alva, OK)
2000	Georgetown College (Georgetown, KY)
2001	Georgetown College (Georgetown, KY)
2002	Carroll College (Helena, MT)
2003	Carroll College (Helena, MT)
2004	Carroll College (Helena, MT)
2005	Carroll College (Helena, MT)
2006	University of Sioux Falls (Sioux Falls, SD)
2007	Carroll College (Helena, MT)
2008	University of Sioux Falls (Sioux Falls, SD)
2009	University of Sioux Falls (Sioux Falls, SD)
2010	Carroll College (Helena, MT)

NAIA Coach of the Year

Year	Coach	School
1956	Dewey Halford	Morningside College (Sioux City, IA)
1957	Frank Waters	Hillsdale College (Hillsdale, MI)
1958	Volney Ashford	Missouri Valley College (Marshall, MO)
1959	Clarence Stasavich	Lenoir-Rhyne University (Hickory, NC)
1960	Phil Sarboe	Humboldt State University (Arcata, CA)
1961	Carnie Smith	Pittsburg State University (Pittsburg, KS)
1962	Paul Durham	Linfield College (McMinnville, OR)
1963	Billy Nicks	Prairie View A&M University (Prairie View, TX)
1964	Jake Christiansen	Concordia College (Moorhead, MN)
1965	John Gagliardi	St. John's University (Collegeville, MN)
1966	Forrest Perkins	University of Wisconsin-Whitewater (Whitewater, WI)
1967	Deacon Duvall	Fairmont State University (Fairmont, WV)
1968	Bill Atkins	Troy State University (Troy, AL)
1969	Jake Gaither	Florida A&M University (Tallahassee, FL)

Year	*Coach*	*School*
1970	Gil Steinke	Texas A&I University, Kingsville (now known as Texas A&M University, Kingsville) (Kingsville, TX)
1971	Robert Shoup	California Lutheran University (Thousand Oaks, CA)
1972	Jim Frazier	Missouri Southern State University (Joplin, MO)
1973	Larry Korver	Northwestern College (Orange City, IA)
1974	Gil Steinke	Texas A&I University, Kingsville (now known as Texas A&M University, Kingsville) (Kingsville, TX)
1975	Gil Steinke	Texas A&I University, Kingsville (now known as Texas A&M University, Kingsville) (Kingsville, TX)
1976	Gil Steinke	Texas A&I University, Kingsville (now known as Texas A&M University, Kingsville) (Kingsville, TX)
1977	DeWitt Jones	Abilene Christian University (Abilene, TX)
1978	Jim Hess	Angelo State University (San Angelo, TX)
1979	Division I: Ron Harms	Texas A&I, Kingsville (now known as Texas A&M University, Kingsville) (Kingsville, TX)
1979	Division II: Richard Strahm	University of Findlay (Findlay, OH)
1980	Division I: Jerry Tolley	Elon University (Elon, NC)
1980	Division II: -II Stan McGarvey	William Jewell College (Liberty, MO)
1981	Division I: Ron Randleman	Pittsburg State University (Pittsburg, KS)
1981	Division II: Jim Christopherson	Concordia College, Moorhead (Moorhead, MN)
1982	Division I: Dick Lowry	Hillsdale College (Hillsdale, MI)
1982	Division II: Ad Rutschman	Linfield College (McMinnville, OR)
1983	Division I: Harold Horton	University of Central Arkansas (Conway, AR)
1983	Division II: Frosty Westering	Pacific Lutheran University (Parkland, WA)
1984	Division I: Ken Sparks	Carson-Newman College (Jefferson City, TN)
1984	Division II: Ad Rutschman	Linfield College (McMinnville, OR)
1985	Division I: Ralph Carpenter	Henderson State University (Arkadelphia, AR)
1985	Division II: Larry Korver	Northwestern College (Orange City, IA)
1986	Division I: Dennis Franchione	Pittsburg State University (Pittsburg, KS)
1986	Division II: Ad Rutschman	Linfield College (McMinnville, OR)
1987	Division I: Dennis Franchione	Pittsburg State University (Pittsburg, KS)
1987	Division II: No Selection	
1988	Division I: Jon Lantz	Southeastern Oklahoma State University (Durant, OK)
1988	Division II: Joe Fusco	Westminster College (New Wilmington, PA)
1989	Division I: Jeff Geiser	Adams State College (Alamosa, CO)
1989	Division II: Joe Fusco	Westminster College (New Wilmington, PA)
1990	Division I: Mike Isom	University of Central Arkansas (Conway, AR)
1990	Division II: Tom Shea	Peru State College (Peru, NE)
1991	Division I: Carl "Duke" Iverson	Western State College (Gunnison, CO)
1991	Division II: Kevin Donley	Georgetown College (Georgetown, KY)
1992	Division I: Billy Joe	Central State University (Wilberforce, OH)
1992	Division II: Dick Strahm	University of Findlay (Findlay, OH)
1993	Division I: Rich Rodriguez	Glenville State College (Glenville, WV)
1993	Division II: Frosty Westering	Pacific Lutheran University (Parkland, WA)
1994	Division I: Tom Eckert	Northeastern State University (Tahlequah, OK)
1994	Division II: Gene Nicholson	Westminster College (New Wilmington, PA)
1995	Division I: Rick Comegy	Central State University (Wilberforce, OH)
1995	Division II: Dick Strahm	University of Findlay (Findlay, OH)
1996	Division I: Paul Sharp	Southwestern Oklahoma State University (Weatherford, OK)
1996	Division II: Bob Young	University of Sioux Falls (Sioux Falls, SD)
1997	Dick Strahm	University of Findlay (Findlay, OH)
1998	Vic Shealy	Azusa Pacific University (Azusa, CA)
1999	Tim Albin	Northwestern Oklahoma State University (Alva, OK)
2000	Bill Cronin	Georgetown College (Georgetown, KY)
2001	Bill Cronin	Georgetown College (Georgetown, KY)
2002	Carl Poelker	McKendree University (Lebanon, IL)
2003	Mike Van Diest	Carroll College (Helena, MT)
2004	Kevin Donley	University of St. Francis (Fort Wayne, IN)

Year	Coach	School
2005	Mike Van Diest	Carroll College (Helena, MT)
2006	Kalen DeBoer	University of Sioux Falls (Sioux Falls, SD)
2007	Mike Van Diest	Carroll College (Helena, MT)
2008	Kalen DeBoer	University of Sioux Falls (Sioux Falls, SD)
2009	Kalen DeBoer	University of Sioux Falls (Sioux Falls, SD)
2010	Mike Van Diest	Carroll College (Helena, MT)

American Football Coaches Association (AFCA) Coach of the Year

100 Legends Lane, Waco, TX 76706; Telephone: 254-754-9900; Fax: 254-754-7373; http://www.afca.com

The AFCA Coach of the Year Award is presented annually to each level of college football (NCAA FBS (and equivalent) since 1935, NCAA FCS since 1983, NCAA Division II since 1983, NCAA Division III since 1983, and NAIA since 2006). The Scripps-Howard newspaper chain conducted the balloting and presented the award from 1935 through 1959. In 1960, the AFCA itself began handling the voting and award presentation. Eastman Kodak Corporation sponsored the AFCA Coach of the Year program from 1960 until 1993, and from 1996 to 1999, the award was sponsored by GTE.

From 1960 through 1982, two national winners were selected (one from the University Division and one from the College Division). Beginning in 1983, four national winners were chosen, one from each school level (NCAA I-A, NCAA I-AA, NCAA Division II, and NCAA Division III) and in 2006, selection was expanded to five levels with the inclusion of the NAIA.

Currently, the AFCA selects 25 regional winners (five from each of the AFCA division levels), from which five national winners (one from each AFCA division level) are selected. All schools with eligible AFCA head coaches are listed on the national ballot and AFCA members are not limited to voting for regional winners. However, members are required to vote for coaches within their region for the AFCA Regional Coach of the Year and coaches within their division when voting for the AFCA National Coach of the Year.

The school of each AFCA National Coach of the Year winner receives $1,000 from the American Football Coaches Foundation for each full-time assistant football coach who was on staff the year the head coach was honored. If a school wins a national championship and the head coach wins the AFCA National Coach of the Year Award, the school then receives $1,500 for each full-time assistant who is an AFCA member.

As of this writing, Larry Kehres of Mount Union College (Ohio, (NCAA Division III) is the only coach in AFCA history to win the National Coach of the Year Award nine times (1993, 1996–1998, 2000–2002, 2006, 2008) and Bob Reade of Augustana College (Illinois, NCAA Division III) is the only coach to win the award four consecutive years (1983–1986).

NAIA AFCA Coach of the Year

Year	Coach	School
2006	Kalen DeBoer	University of Sioux Falls (SD)
2007	Mike Van Diest	Carroll College (MT)
2008	Kalen DeBoer	University of Sioux Falls (SD)
2009	Kalen DeBoer	University of Sioux Falls (SD)
2010	Mike Van Diest	Carroll College (Helena, MT)

American Football Coaches Association (AFCA) Assistant Coach of the Year

100 Legends Lane, Waco, TX 76706; Telephone: 254-754-9900; Fax: 254-754-7373; http://www.afca.com

The AFCA Assistant Coach of the Year Award has been presented annually since 1997 to the best assistant coach in each of the five levels of college football (NCAA FBS, NCAA FCS, NCAA Division II, NCAA Division III, and the NAIA).

For each of the five levels, staff members from NCAA and NAIA football-playing schools nominate an assistant coach. From this list of nominees, a winner is then selected by the AFCA Public Relations Committee.

NAIA AFCA Assistant Coach of the Year

Year	*Assistant Coach*	*School*
1997	Samuel Wickliffe	Campbellsville University (KY)
1998	Eric Graves	Campbellsville University (KY)
1999	Haywood Riner	Campbellsville University (KY)
2000	Bill O'Boyle	Hastings College (NE)
2001	Roger VanDeZande	Southern Oregon University (OR)
2002	Charles Gartenmayer	Benedictine College (KS)
2003	Mike Gardner	Tabor College (KS)
2004	Nick Howlett	Carroll College (MT)
2005	Allen Friesen	Dana College (NE)
2006	Colby Hensley	Kansas Wesleyan University (KS)
2007	Ryan Nourse	Morningside College (IA)
2008	Dennis Murphy	Benedictine College (KS)
2009	Josh Gehring	Morningside College (IA)
2010	Doug Schleeman	Montana Tech (The University of Montana) (MT)

Rawlings-NAIA Football Player of the Year

Presented annually since 1997 by the Rawlings sport equipment manufacturer (St. Louis, MO).

Year	*Player*	*School*
1997	Bo Hurley	University of Findlay (Findlay, OH)
1998	Jack Williams	Azusa Pacific University (Azusa, CA)
1999	Eddie Eviston	Georgetown College (Georgetown, KY)
2000	Eddie Eviston	Georgetown College (Georgetown, KY)
2001	Eddie Eviston	Georgetown College (Georgetown, KY)
2002	Nick Kortan	University of Sioux Falls (Sioux Falls, SD)
2003	Tyler Emmert	Carroll College (Helena, MT)
2004	Cory Jacquay	University of St. Francis (Fort Wayne, IN)
2005	Tyler Emmert	Carroll College (Helena, MT)
2006	Brian Kurtz	University of St. Francis (Fort Wayne, IN)
2007	Chad Cavender	University of Sioux Falls (Sioux Falls, SD)
2008	Owen Koeppen	Carroll College (Helena, MT)
2009	Lorenzo Brown	University of Sioux Falls (Sioux Falls, SD)
2010	Jon Ryan	University of Sioux Falls (Sioux Falls, SD)

American Mideast Conference

Dr. James Houdeshell, AMC Commissioner, University of Findlay, 1000 North Main Street, Findlay, OH 45840; Telephone: 419-434-4551; Fax: 419-434-6974; Web site: http://www.amcsports.org/

The American Mideast Conference was founded in 1949 as the Mid-Ohio League with charter schools Ashland University, Bluffton College, Cedarville University, Defiance College, and the University of Findlay. The conference adopted its current name in 1998. As of this writing, the AMC consists of eight member schools and does not support football, although one of its members play football outside the conference.

- Carlow University Celtics, Pittsburgh, PA 15213; 800-333-2275; www.carlow.edu; no football program
- Daemen College Wildcats, Amherst, NY 14226; 800-462-7652; www.daemwn.edu; no football program

- Fisher College Falcons, Boston, MA 02116; 617-236-8800; www.fisher.edu; no football program
- Houghton College Highlanders, Houghton, NY 14744; 800-777-2556; www.houghton.edu; no football program
- Point Park University Pioneers, Pittsburgh, PA 15222; 412-391-4100; www.pointpark.edu; no football program
- Roberts Wesleyan College Raiders, Rochester, NY 14624; 800-777-4792; www.roberts.edu; no football program
- Walsh University Cavaliers, North Canton, OH 44720; 330-490-7090; www.walsh.edu; plays football in the Mid-States Football Association (Mideast League)
- Wilberforce University Bulldogs, Wilberforce, OH 45384; 937-376-2911; www.wilberforce.edu; no football program

American Midwest Conference

AMC Commissioner, Missouri Baptist University, One College Park Drive, St. Louis, Mo. 63141; Telephone: 314-392-2317; Fax: 314-392-2390; Web site: http://www.amcsportsonline.com/ index.php

The American Midwest Conference consists of nine schools and does not support football.

- Benedictine University Bulldogs, Springfield, IL 62702; 217-525-1420; www.ben.edu; no football program
- Columbia College Cougars, Columbia, MO 65216; 573-875-8700; www.ccis.edi; no football program
- Hannibal-LaGrange College Trojans, Hannibal, MO 63401; 573-221-3675; www.hlg.edu; no football program
- Harris-Stowe State University Hornets, St. Louis, MO 63103; 314-340-3300; www.hssu.edu; no football program
- Missouri Baptist University Spartans, St. Louis, MO 63141; 314-434-1115; www.mobap.edu; no football program
- Park University Pirates, Parkville, MO 64152; 816-741-2000; www.park.edu; no football program
- Stephens College Stars, Columbia, MO 65215; 800-876-7207; www.stephens.edu; no football program
- William Woods University Owls, Fulton, MO 65251; 573-642-2251; www.williamwoods.edu; no football program
- Williams Baptist College Eagles, Walnut Ridge, AR 72476; 870-886-6741; www.wbcoll.edu; no football program

Appalachian Athletic Conference

P.O. Box 19371, Asheville, NC 28815; Telephone: 828-298-8822; Fax: 828-298-1398; Web site: http://www.aacsports.com/

The Appalachian Athletic Conference was originally named the Volunteer State Athletic Conference, which was formed in the early 1940s and lasted until the 1980s when several of its schools left and formed the Tennessee Valley Athletic Conference. In the 1990s, the conference changed its name to the Tennessee-Virginia Athletic Conference when Bluefield College joined in the early 1990s. The conference adopted its current name in 2001 after the addition of Montreat College (NC), Alice Lloyd College (KY), and Union College (KY).

As of this writing, the AAC consists of eight members and does not support football, although one of its members plays football outside the conference and two schools are starting football programs.

- Bluefield College Rams, Bluefield, VA 24605; 800-872-0176; www.bluefield.edu; starting a football program
- Bryan College Lions, Dayton, TN 37321; 423-775-2041; www.bryan.edu; no football program
- Columbia College Fighting Koalas, Columbia, SC 29203; 800-277-1301; www.columbiacollege.edu; no football program

- Milligan College Buffaloes, Milligan College, TN 37682; 423-461-8700; www.milligan.edu; no football program
- Montreat College Cavaliers, Montreat, NC 28757; 828-669-8012; www.montreat.edu; no football program
- Point University Skyhawks, East Point, GA 30344; 404-761-8861; http://point.edu; plays football as an independent team
- Reinhardt College Eagles, Waleska, GA 30183; 770-720-5600; www.reinhardt.edu; starting a football program
- Tennessee Wesleyan College Bulldogs, Athens, TN 37303; 800-742-5892; www.twcnet.edu; no football program
- Union College Bulldogs, Barbourville, KY 40906; 800-489-8646; www.unionky.edu; plays football in the Mid-South Conference
- Virginia Intermont College Cobras, Bristol, VA 24201; 800-451-1842; www.vic.edu; no football program

Association of Independent Institutions

Sports Association Management, Inc., 12742 England Street, Overland Park, KS 66213; Telephone: 913-645-4623; Email (Ted Breidenthal, Commissioner): ted@SAMIsports.com; Web site: http://www.aiisports.com

As of this writing, the Association of Independent Institutions consists of 34 independent NAIA teams, eight of which sponsor football programs.

- Allen University Yellow Jackets, Columbia, SC 29204; 803-376-5700; www.allenuniversity.edu; no football program
- Arizona Christian University Firestorm, Phoenix, AZ 85032; 602-489-5300; http://arizonachristian.edu; no football program
- California State University, San Marcos, Cougars, San Marcos, CA 92096; 760-750-4000; www.csusm.edu; no football program
- Dakota State University Trojans, Madison SD 57042; 605-256-5111; www.dsu.edu; plays football as an independent team
- Dickinson State University Blue Hawks, Dickinson, ND 58601; 701-483-2507; www.dsu.nodak.edu; plays football in the Dakota Athletic Conference
- Embry-Riddle Aeronautical University Eagles, Prescott, AZ 86301; 928-777-3728; www.erau.edu; no football program
- Indiana University Northwest Redhawks, Gary, IN 46408; 888-968-7486; www.iun.edu; no football program
- Jamestown College Jimmies, Jamestown, ND 58405; 701-252-3467; www.jc.edu; plays football in the Dakota Athletic Conference
- Johnson & Wales University-Colorado Wildcats, Denver, CO 80220; www.jwu.edu/denver; no football program
- Kentucky Christian University Knights, Grayson, KY 41143; 800-522-3181; www.kcu.edu; Associate Member; plays football in the Mid-South Conference
- La Sierra University Golden Eagles, Riverside, CA 92515; 800-874-5587; www.lasierra.edu; no football program
- Lawrence Technological University Blue Devils, Southfield, MI 48075; 800-225-5588; www.ltu.edu; Associate Member; no football program
- Life University Running Eagles, Marietta, GA 30060; 770-426-2600; www.life.edu; no football program
- Louisiana State University-Alexandria Generals, Alexandria, LA 71302; 888-473-6417; www.lsua.edu; no football program
- Marygrove College Mustangs, Detroit, MI 48221; 313-927-1200; www.marygrove.edu; no football program
- Marymount College Mariners, Rancho Palos Verdes, CA 90275; 310-377-5501; www.marymountpv.edu; no football program

- Mayville State University Comets, Mayville, ND 58257; 800-437-4104; www.mayvillestate.edu; plays football in the Dakota Athletic Conference
- Morris College Hornets, Sumter, SC 29150; 803-934-3200; www.morris.edu; no football program
- Mountain State University Cougars, Beckley, WV 25801; 866-367-6781; www.mountainstate.edu; no football program
- Northern New Mexico College Eagles, Española, NM 87532; 505-747-2100; http://nnmc.edu; no football program
- Patten University Lions, Oakland, CA 94601; 510-534-4344; www.patten.edu; no football program
- Rochester College Warriors, Rochester Hills, MI 48307; 248-218-2031; Associate Member; www.rc.edu; no football program
- Savannah College of Art and Design Bees, Atlanta, GA 30309; 404-253-2700; www.scad.edu; no football program
- Soka University of America Lions, Aliso Viejo, CA 92656; 949-480-4000; www.soka.edu; no football program
- Southern Virginia University Knights, Buena Vista, VA 24416; 800-229-8420; http://svu.edu; Associate Member; plays football as an independent team
- State University of New York at Delhi (SUNY Delhi) Broncos, Delhi, NY 13753; 800-963-3544; www.delhi.edu; no football program
- Thomas University NightHawks, Thomasville, GA 31792; 800-538-9784; www.thomas.edu; no football program
- University of British Columbia Thunderbirds, Vancouver, British Columbia, Canada V6T 1Z4; 604-822-2211; www.ubc.ca; plays football in the Canada West Universities Athletic Association
- University of Houston-Victoria Jaguars, Victoria, TX 77901; 361-570-4848; www.uhv.edu; no football program
- University of Victoria Vikes, Victoria, British Columbia, Canada V8P 5C2; 250-721-7211; www.uvic.ca; no football program
- Valley City State University Vikings, Valley City ND 58072; 800-532-8641; www.vcsu.edu; plays football in the Dakota Athletic Conference
- Voorhees College Tigers, Denmark, SC 29042; 803-780-1234; http://voorhees.edu; no football program
- Walla Walla University Wolves, College Place, WA 99324; 800-541-8900; www.wallawalla.edu; no football program
- Warren Wilson College Owls, Swannanoa, NC 28778; 828-298-3325; www.warren-wilson.edu; no football program

California Pacific Conference

Commissioner Don Ott: 18550 Redwood Road, Castro Valley CA, 94546; Telephone: 510-432-7699; Email: donott@calpacathletics.com; Web site: http://www.calpac athletics.com/

The California Pacific Conference (NAIA, Division II) was created in May 1995 with seven charter schools: Bethany University, California State University, Maritime, Dominican College, Holy Names University, Pacific Union College, Patten College, and Simpson University. Currently, the CPC consists of eight members and does not support football, although one of its schools sponsors a football program.

- California State University-Maritime (California Maritime Academy) Keelhaulers, Vallejo, CA 94590; 707-654-1000; www.csum.edu; no football program
- Holy Names University Hawks, Oakland, CA 94619; 510-436-1000; www.hnu.edu; no football program
- Menlo College Oaks, Atherton, CA 94027; 800-556-3656; www.menlo.edu; plays football as an independent team
- Pacific Union College Pioneers, Angwin, CA 94508; 707-965-6311; www.puc.edu; no football program
- Simpson University Red Hawks, Redding, CA 96003; 530-224-5600; www.simpsonu.edu; no football program

- University of California-Merced Bobcats, Merced, CA 95343; 209-228-4400; www.ucmerced.edu; no football program
- William Jessup University Warriors, Rocklin, CA 95765; 916-577-2200; www.jessup.edu; no football program

Cascade Collegiate Conference

13668 Southeast Sierra Drive, Clackamas, OR 97015; Telephone: 503-855-3169; Fax: 509-855-3169; Web site: http://www.cascadeconference.org/

Originally formed in 1978 as a scheduling alliance for volleyball, the charter members of the Cascade Collegiate Conference were Concordia University, Eastern Oregon University, George Fox University, Northwest Nazarene University, Oregon Institute of Technology, Southern Oregon University, The College of Idaho, Western Baptist College (now known as Corban College), and Western Oregon University. As of this writing, the CCC consists of 10 members, two of which sponsor football.

- College of Idaho Coyotes, Caldwell, ID 83605; 208-459-5011; www.collegeofidaho.edu; no football program
- Concordia University Cavaliers, Portland, OR 97211; 503-288-9371; www.cu-portland.edu; no football program
- Corban College Warriors, Salem, OR 97317; 503-581-8600; www.corban.edu; no football program
- Eastern Oregon University Mountaineers, La Grande, OR 97850; 541-962-3672; www.eou.edu; plays football in the Frontier Conference
- Evergreen State College Geoducks, Olympia, WA 98505; 360-867-6000; www.evergreen.edu; no football program
- Northwest Christian University Beacons, Eugene, OR 97401; 541-343-1641; www.nwcu.edu; no football program
- Northwest University Eagles, Kirkland, WA 98033; 425-822-8266; www.northwestu.edu; no football program
- Oregon Institute of Technology Owls, Klamath Falls, OR 97601; 541-885-1000; www.oit.edu; no football program
- Southern Oregon University Raiders, Ashland, OR 97520; 541-552-7672; www.sou.edu; plays football as an independent team
- Warner Pacific College Knights, Portland, OR 97215; 503-517-1020; www.warnerpacific.edu; no football program

Central States Football League

100 North 6th Street, Suite 201, Waco, TX 76710; Telephone: 254-744-8542; Fax: 254-662-6627; Web site: http://www.centralstatesfootball.com

The Central States Football League was established in 1999 with charter schools Haskell Indian Nations University, Langston University, Northwestern Oklahoma State University, Southwestern Assemblies of God University, and Peru State College. As of this writing, the CSFL is affiliated with the NAIA and consists of six schools and one associate member, all of which play football in the conference and all of which come from other conferences.

- Bacone College Warriors, Muskogee, OK 74403; 918-683-4581; www.bacone.edu; member from the Red River Athletic Conference
- Langston University Lions, Langston, OK 73050; 877-466-2231; www.langston.edu; member from the Red River Athletic Conference
- Northwestern Oklahoma State University Rangers, Alva, OK 73717; 580-327-1700; www.nmosu.edu; member from the Sooner Athletic Conference
- Oklahoma Panhandle State University Aggies, Goodwell, OK 73939; 580-349-2611; www.opsu.edu; alliance member from the Heartland Conference, not eligible for conference championship
- Southern Nazarene University Crimson Storm, Bethany, OK 73008; 405-789-6400; http://snu.edu; member from the Sooner Athletic Conference

- Southwestern Assemblies of God University Lions, Waxahachie, TX 75165; 888-937-7248; www.sagu.edu; member from the National Christian College Athletic Association (Division I)
- Texas College Steers, Tyler, TX 75702; 800-306-6299; www.texascollege.edu; member from the Red River Athletic Conference

Central States Football League Champions

Year	School
1999	Northwestern Oklahoma State University (OK)
2000	Northwestern Oklahoma State University (OK)
2001	Northwestern Oklahoma State University (OK)
2002	Northwestern Oklahoma State University (OK)
2003	Northwestern Oklahoma State University (OK)
2004	Northwestern Oklahoma State University (OK)
2005	Langston University (OK)
2005	Texas College (TX)
2006	Southern Nazarene University (OK)
2006	Texas College (TX(
2007	Northwestern Oklahoma State University (OK)
2008	Langston University (OK)
2009	Langston University (OK)
2010	Northwestern Oklahoma State University (OK)

Central States Football League Coach of the Year

Year	Coach	School
2000	Garin Higgins	Northwestern Oklahoma State University (OK)
2001	Garin Higgins	Northwestern Oklahoma State University (OK)
2002	Garin Higgins	Northwestern Oklahoma State University (OK)
2003	Garin Higgins	Northwestern Oklahoma State University (OK)
2004	Garin Higgins	Northwestern Oklahoma State University (OK)
2005	Greg Johnson	Langston University (OK)
2005	Jay Brown	Texas College (TX(
2006	Fred Slaughter	Northwestern Oklahoma State University (OK)
2007	Keith Barefield	Northwestern Oklahoma State University (OK)
2008	Greg Johnson	Langston University (OK)
2009	Greg Johnson	Langston University (OK)
2010	Mike Cochran	Southern Nazarene University (OK)

Central States Football League Offensive Player of the Year

Year	Player	Class	Position	School
1999	Al Hunt	Junior	Quarterback	Northwestern Oklahoma State University (OK)
2000	Al Hunt	Senior	Quarterback	Northwestern Oklahoma State University (OK)
2001	Issac Hall	Junior	Quarterback	Northwestern Oklahoma State University (OK)
2002	Issac Hall	Senior	Quarterback	Northwestern Oklahoma State University (OK)
2002	Scott Beveridge	Sophomore	Wide Receiver	Peru State College (NE)
2003	Patrick Crayton	Senior	Quarterback	Northwestern Oklahoma State University (OK)
2004	Clay Waggle	Senior	Quarterback	Bacone College (OK)
2005	Kendrick Dozier	Junior	Quarterback	Langston University (OK)
2006	Thez Robinson	Junior	Running Back	Northwestern Oklahoma State University (OK)
2007	Thez Robinson	Senior	Running Back	Northwestern Oklahoma State University (OK)
2008	Billy Barefield			Northwestern Oklahoma State University (OK)
2009	Nate Guillory			Northwestern Oklahoma State University (OK)
2010	Brady Wardlaw	Junior	Quarterback	Southern Nazarene University (OK)
2010	Korey Williams	Wide Receiver	Senior	Northwestern Oklahoma State University (OK)

Central States Football League Defensive Player of the Year

Year	Player	Class	Position	School
1999	Dustin Loveless	Senior	Defensive Lineman	Northwestern Oklahoma State University (OK)

Year	Player	Class	Position	School
2000	Lynn Scott	Senior	Free Safety	Northwestern Oklahoma State University (OK)
2001	James Keys	Senior	Defensive Lineman	Northwestern Oklahoma State University (OK)
2002	Paul Heusinkvelt	Senior	Linebacker	Peru State College (NE)
2002	Sedric Fuller	Senior	Defensive Back	Northwestern Oklahoma State University (OK)
2003	Travares Osley	Junior	Linebacker	Northwestern Oklahoma State University (OK)
2004	Walter Taylor	Senior	Defensive Lineman	Northwestern Oklahoma State University (OK)
2005	Dathan Brown	Sophomore	Defensive Back	Texas College (TX)
2006	Ryan Miles	Sophomore	Defensive Lineman	Texas College (TX(
2007	Frits Remedor			Southern Nazarene University (OK)
2008	Brandon Kennard			Langston University (OK)
2009	Lantz Mathers			Northwestern Oklahoma State University (OK)
2010	Rocky Lee	Senior	Linebacker	Northwestern Oklahoma State University (OK)

Central States Football League Special Teams Player of the Year

Year	Player	Class	Position	School
2007	Aaron Vermillion			Northwestern Oklahoma State University (OK)
2008	Peter Orth			Southern Nazarene University (OK)
2009	Aaron Thomas			Bacone College (OK)
2010	Nate Guillory	Senior	Kick Returner	Northwestern Oklahoma State University (OK)

Chicagoland Collegiate Athletic Conference (CCAC)

University of Saint Francis, 500 Wilcox Street, Joliet IL, 60435; Telephone: 815-740-3842; Fax: 815-740-3841; Web site:http://www.ccacsports.com/

The Chicagoland Collegiate Athletic Conference began in 1949 (with a meeting of baseball coaches and the first sporting event, a baseball tournament, was in 1950) with charter schools Chicago Teachers College (now known as Northeastern Illinois University), Illinois Institute of Technology, University of Chicago, and the University of Illinois, Chicago Navy Pier.

Currently, the CCAC consists of 15 members and does not support football, although six of its member schools support football programs.

- Calumet College of St. Joseph Crimson Wave, Whiting, IN 46394; 219-473-4215; www.ccsj.edu; no football program
- Cardinal Stritch University Wolves, Milwaukee, WI 53217; 414-410-4000; www.stritch.edu; no football program
- Holy Cross College Saints, Notre Dame, IN 46556; 574-239-8377; www.hcc-nd.edu; no football program
- Illinois Institute of Technology Scarlet Hawks, Chicago, IL 60616; 312-567-3000; www.iit.edu; no football program
- Indiana University-South Bend Titans, South Bend, IN 46634; 574-520-4872; www.iusb.edu; no football program
- Judson University Eagles, Elgin, IL 60123; 847-628-2500; www.judsonu.edu; no football program
- Olivet Nazarene University Tigers, Bourbonnais, IL 60914; 815-939-5011; www.olivet.edu; plays football in the Mid-States Football Association (Midwest League)
- Purdue University, Calumet, Peregrines, Hammond, IN 46323; 219-989-2400; www.purduecal.edu; no football program
- Purdue University, North Central, Panthers, Westville, IN 46391; 219-785-5200; www.pnc.edu; no football program

- Robert Morris University Eagles, Chicago, IL 60605; 800-762-5960; www.robertmorris.edu; plays football as an independent team
- Roosevelt University Lakers, Chicago, IL 60605; 312-341-3500; www.roosevelt.edu; no football program
- Saint Xavier University Cougars, Chicago, IL 60655; 773-298-3000; www.sxu.edu; plays football in the Mid-States Football Association (Mideast Division)
- Trinity Christian College Trolls, Palos Heights, IL 60463; 866-874-6463; www.trinity.edu; no football program
- Trinity International University Trojans, Deerfield, IL 60015; 800-822-3225; www.tiu.edu; plays football in the Mid-States Football Association (Midwest League)
- University of St. Francis Fighting Saints, Joliet, IL 60435; 800-735-7500; www.stfrancis.edu; plays football in the Mid-States Football Association (Midwest League)

Dakota Athletic Conference (DAC)

Dickinson State, DSU Mail Box 9, 291 Campus Drive, Dickinson, ND 58601; Telephone (Commissioner): 701-483-2023; Web site: http://www.dakotaac.org

The Dakota Athletic Conference was formed in 2000 by teams from the South Dakota Athletic Conference and the North Dakota Athletic Conference. As of this writing, the DAC is affiliated with the NAIA (although it is slowly losing member schools), and has four members, all of which play football in the conference.

- Dickinson State University Blue Hawks, Dickinson, ND 58601; 701-483-2507; www.dsu.nodak.edu; from the Frontier Conference
- Jamestown College Jimmies, Jamestown, ND 58405; 701-252-3467; www.jc.edu
- Mayville State University Comets, Mayville, ND 58257; 800-437-4104; www.mayvillestate.edu
- Valley City State University Vikings, Valley City, ND 58072; 800-532-8641; www.vcsu.edu

Dakota Athletic Conference Champions

Year	*School*
2000	Valley City State University (ND)
2001	University of Mary (ND)
2002	Dickinson State University (ND)
2002	Minot State University (ND)
2002	University of Mary (ND)
2003	Dickinson State University (ND)
2004	Dickinson State University (ND)
2004	University of Mary (ND)
2005	Dickinson State University (ND)
2005	Valley City State University (ND)
2006	Black Hills State University (SD)
2007	Black Hills State University (SD)
2007	Jamestown College (ND)
2007	Minot State University (ND)
2008	Dickinson State University (ND)
2009	Dickinson State University (ND)
2009	Minot State University (ND)
2010	Dickinson State University (ND)

All post-season awards are selected by the coaches of each sport.

Dakota Athletic Conference Coach of the Year

Year	*Coach*	*School*
2000	Dennis McCulloch	Valley City State University (ND)
2001	Myron Schultz	University of Mary (ND)
2002	Hank Biesiot	Dickinson State University (ND)
2003	Hank Biesiot	Dickinson State University (ND)
2004	Myron Schulz	University of Mary (ND)
2005	Dennis McCulloch	Valley City State University (ND)
2006	John Scott	Black Hills State University (SD)
2007	Pau Rudolph	Minot State University (ND)
2008	Hank Biesiot	Dickinson State University (ND)
2009	Hank Biesiot	Dickinson State University (ND)
2010	Hank Biesiot	Dickinson State University (ND)

Dakota Athletic Conference Most Valuable Player

Year	*Player*	*School*
2000	Jeremy Peschel	Valley City State University (ND)
2001	Jeremy Peschel	Valley City State University (ND)
2002	Kenny Smith	Minot State University (ND)
2002	Nick Walker	Dickinson State University (ND)
2003	Tim Garcia	University of Mary (ND)
2004	Jake Pfau	University of Mary (ND)
2005	Tommy Hofer	Dakota State University (SD)
2006	Tanner Tetrault	Black Hills State University (SD)
2007	Josh Kittell	Jamestown College (ND)
2007	Nick Banks	Minot State University (ND)
2008	Nick Banks	Minot State University (ND)
2009	Wacey Coleman	Black Hills State University (SD)
2010	Johnny Lester	Minot State University (ND)

Dakota State Conference Most Valuable Senior

Year	*Player*	*School*
2000	Jeremy Auch	Minot State University (ND)
2001	Brian Fettig	University of Mary (ND)
2001	Jeremy Peschel	Valley City State University (ND)
2002	Steve Battle	Valley City State University (ND)
2003	Harry Mills	Minot State University (ND)
2004	Jace Schillinger	Dickinson State University (ND)
2005	Kylan Klauzer	Dickinson State University (ND)
2006	Eric Dirk	Jamestown College (ND)
2007	Lukas Munsell	South Dakota School of Mines & Technology (SD)
2008	Chauncey Calhoun	Valley City State University (ND)
2009	Brian Rohles	Minot State University (ND)
2010	Cody Holland	Dickinson State University (ND)

Frontier Conference

966 Colorado Avenue, Whitefish, MT 59937; Telephone: 406-253-5374; Fax: 406-862-5376; Email: frontierconference@gmail.com; Web Site: http://www.frontierconference.com

The Frontier Conference was founded in 1952 with charter schools Carroll College, Montana State University, Northern, Montana Tech of the University of Montana, Rocky Mountain College, and the University of Montana, Western. Teams play each other twice during the season and the conference champion qualifies for the NAIA Championship Series if the champion is ranked in the Top 20 in the final regular-season poll. Currently, the conference consists of eight member schools, five of which play football and one football-only associate member.

- Carroll College Fighting Saints, Helena, MT 59625; 406-447-4300; www.carroll.edu
- Dickinson State University Blue Hawks, Dickinson, ND 58601; 701-483-2507; www.dsu.nodak.edu; plays football in the Dakota Athletic Conference
- Eastern Oregon University Mountaineers, La Grande, OR 97850; 541-962-3672; www.eou.edu; associate member from the Cascade Collegiate Conference
- Lewis-Clark State College Warriors, Lewiston, ID 83501; 208-792-5272; www.lcsc.edu; no football program
- Montana State University-Northern Lights, Havre, MT 59501; 800-662-6132; www.msum.edu
- Montana Tech of The University of Montana Orediggers, Butte, MT 59701; 406-496-4102; www.mtech.edu
- Rocky Mountain College Battlin' Bears, Billings, MT 59102; 406-657-1000; www.rocky.edu
- University of Great Falls Argos, Great Falls, MT 59405; 800-856-9544; www.ugf.edu; no football program

- University of Montana Western Bulldogs, Dillon, MT 59725; 406-683-7331; www.umwestern.edu
- Westminster College Griffins, Salt Lake City, UT 84105; 801-484-7651; www.westminstercollege.edu; no football program

Frontier Conference Champions

Year	*School*
1997	Montana Tech, The University of Montana (MT)
1998	Rocky Mountain College (MT)
1999	Rocky Mountain College (MT)
2000	Carroll College (MT)
2001	Carroll College (MT)
2002	Carroll College (MT)
2002	University of Montana, Western (MT)
2003	Carroll College (MT)
2004	Carroll College (MT)
2004	Montana Tech, The University of Montana (MT)
2004	University of Montana, Western (MT)
2005	Carroll College (MT)
2006	Carroll College (MT)
2007	Carroll College (MT)
2008	Carroll College (MT)
2009	Carroll College (MT)
2010	Carroll College (MT)

Frontier Conference Coach of the Year

Year	*Coach*	*School*
2006	Mark Samson	Montana State University, Northern (MT)
2006	Mike Van Diest	Carroll College (MT)
2007	Mike Van Diest	Carroll College (MT)
2008	Mike Van Diest	Carroll College (MT)
2009	Mike Van Diest	Carroll College (MT)
2010	Brian Armstrong	Rocky Mountain College (MT)

Frontier Conference Offensive Player of the Year

Year	*Player*	*Position*	*School*
2006	Kyle Samson	Quarterback	Montana State University, Northern (MT)
2007	John Barnett	Quarterback	Carroll College (MT)
2008	Justin Moe		Montana State University, Northern (MT)
2009	Kasey Peters	Quarterback	Rocky Mountain College (MT)
2009	Chris Ware	Quarterback	Eastern Oregon University (OR)
2010	Kasey Peters	Quarterback	Rocky Mountain College (MT)
2010	Gary Wagner	Quarterback	Carroll College (MT)

Frontier Conference Defensive Player of the Year

Year	*Player*	*Position*	*School*
2006	J. Perino	Outside Linebacker	Montana Tech, The University of Montana (MT)
2007	Owen Koeppen	Linebacker	Carroll College (MT)
2008	Owen Koeppen	Linebacker	Carroll College (MT)
2009	Thomas Dolan	Linebacker	Carroll College (MT)
2009	Chad Schira	Linebacker	University of Montana, Western (MT)
2010	Thomas Dolan	Linebacker	Carroll College (MT)

Golden State Athletic Conference

Commissioner Azusa Pacific University, 901 East Alosta Avenue, Azusa, CA 91702; Telephone: 626-812-3097; Fax: 626-812-3068; Web site: http://gsacsports.org/

The Golden State Athletic Conference was established in 1986 and its members are all Christian colleges. The conference contains 10 schools and does not support football, although one of its members plays football as an independent team.

- Azusa Pacific University Cougars, Azusa, CA 91702; 626-969-3434; www.apu.edu; plays football as an independent team

- Biola University Eagles, La Mirada, CA 90639; 562-903-6000; www.biola.edu; no football program
- Concordia University Eagles, Irvine, CA 92612; 949-854-8002; www.cui.edu; no football program
- Fresno Pacific University Sunbirds, Fresno, CA 93702; 559-453-2000; www.fresno.edu; no football program
- Hope International University Royals, Fullerton, CA 92831; 714-879-3901; www.hiu.edu; no football program
- Point Loma Nazarene University Sea Lions, San Diego, CA 92106; 619-849-2200; www.pointloma.edu; no football program
- San Diego Christian College Hawks, El Cajon, CA 92019; 619-201-8700; http://sdcc.edu; no football program
- The Master's College Mustangs, Santa Clarita, CA 91321; 800-568-6248; www.masters.edu; no football program
- Vanguard University Lions, Costa Mesa, CA 92626; 714-556-3610; www.vanguard.edu; no football program
- Westmont College Warriors, Santa Barbara, CA 93108; 805-565-6000; www.westmont.edu; no football program

Great Plains Athletic Conference

Commissioner: 4728 Birch Way, Sioux City, IA 51106; Telephone: 712-226-4722; Fax: 303-374-5868; Web site: http://www.gpacsports.com

Founded in 1969 as the Nebraska Intercollegiate Athletic Conference, the Great Plains Athletic Conference currently consists of 13 private, faith-based colleges and universities. All six of its charter members are still in the conference: Concordia University, Dana College, Doane College, Hastings College, Midland Lutheran College, and Nebraska Wesleyan University. In 1992, the NIAC became known as the Nebraska-Iowa Athletic Conference and adopted its current name in 2000. Of the GPAC's 12 members, 11 play football in the conference.

- Briar Cliff University Chargers, Sioux City, IA 51104; 800-662-3303; www.briarcliff.edu
- Concordia University Bulldogs, Seward, NE 68434; 402-643-3651; www.cune.edu
- Dakota Wesleyan University Tigers, Mitchell, SD 57301; 800-333-8506; www.dwu.edu
- Doane College Tigers, Crete, NE 68333; 800-333-6263; www.doane.edu
- Dordt College Defenders, Sioux Center, IA 51250; 800-343-6738; www.dordt.edu
- Hastings College Bronocs, Hastings, NE 68901; 800-532-7642; www.hastings.edu
- Midland University Warriors, Fremont, NE 68025; 800-642-8382; www.midlandu.edu
- Morningside College Mustangs, Sioux City, IA 51106; 800-831-0806; www.morningside.edu
- Mount Marty College Lancers, Yanktown, SD 57078; 605-668-1545; www.mtmc.edu; no football program
- Nebraska Wesleyan University Prairie Wolves, Lincoln, NE 68504; 800-541-3818; www.nebraskawesleyan.edu
- Northwestern College Red Raiders, Orange City, IA 51041; 712-707-7000; www.nwciowa.edu

Great Plains Athletic Conference Champions

Year	*School*
2000	Nebraska Wesleyan University (NE)
2000	Northwestern College (IA)
2001	Concordia University (NE)
2001	University of Sioux Falls (SD)
2002	University of Sioux Falls (SD)
2003	University of Sioux Falls (SD)
2004	University of Sioux Falls (SD)
2005	Morningside College (IA)
2006	University of Sioux Falls (SD)
2007	University of Sioux Falls (SD)
2008	University of Sioux Falls (SD)
2009	University of Sioux Falls (SD)
2010	University of Sioux Falls (SD)

GREAT PLAINS ATHLETIC CONFERENCE COACH OF THE YEAR

Year	*Coach*	*School*
2000	Brian Keller	Nebraska Wesleyan University (NE)
2000	Orv Otten	Northwestern College (IA)
2001	Courtney Meyer	Concordia University (NE)
2002	Bob Young	University of Sioux Falls (SD)
2003	Bob Young	University of Sioux Falls (SD)
2004	Steve Ryan	Morningside College (IA)
2005	Steve Ryan	Morningside College (IA)
2006	Kalen De Boer	University of Sioux Falls (SD)
2007	Kalen De Boer	University of Sioux Falls (SD)
2008	Brad Pole	Dakota Wesleyan University (SD)
2009	Kalen De Boer	University of Sioux Falls (SD)
2010	Casey Thiele	Midland University (NE)

GREAT PLAINS ATHLETIC CONFERENCE PLAYER OF THE YEAR

Year	*Player*	*Position*	*School*
2000	David Perrigo	Running Back	Northwestern College (IA)
2001	Dax Michelena	Quarterback	University of Sioux Falls (SD)
2002	Nick Kortan	Running Back	University of Sioux Falls (SD)
2003	Jon Burckhardt	Quarterback	University of Sioux Falls (SD)
2004	Craig Fobbe	Quarterback	Morningside College (IA)
2004	Eric Moody	Running Back	Hastings College (NE)
2005	Craig Fobbe	Quarterback	Morningside College (IA)
2006	Austin Janssen	Linebacker	Northwestern College (IA)
2007	Offense: Chad Cavender	Quarterback	University of Sioux Falls (SD)
2007	Defense: Chad Hustedt	Defensive Back	Morningside College (IA)
2008	Offense: Ian Gilworth	Quarterback	Morningside College (IA)
2008	Defense: Nathan Jansen	Linebacker	Northwestern College (IA)
2009	Offense: Lorenzo Brown	Quarterback	University of Sioux Falls (SD)
2009	Defense: Trevor Holleman	Defensive Back	University of Sioux Falls (SD)
2010	Offense: Jon Ryan	Wide Receiver	University of Sioux Falls (SD)
2010	Defense: Marshal Tuttle	Linebacker	Morningside College (IA)

Gulf Coast Athletic Conference

Commissioner: Department of History, William Jewell College, 500 College Hill, Liberty MO 64068; Telephone: 318-792-6368, 816-415-7617; Fax: 816-415-6994; Web site: http://www.gcaconf. com/

The Gulf Coast Athletic Conference was formed in May 1981 with charter members Belhaven College, Dillard University, Louisiana College, Spring Hill College, Tougaloo College, William Carey University, and Xavier University of Louisiana. As of this writing, the GCAC has eight members and does not support football, although one of its schools plays football outside the conference.

- Dillard University Blue Devils, New Orleans, LA 70122; 504-283-8822; www.dillard.edu; no football program
- Edward Waters College Tigers, Jacksonville, FL 32209; 904-470-8000; www.ewc.edu; plays football as an independent team
- Fisk University Bulldogs, Nashville, TN 37208; 615-329-8500; www.fisk.edu; no football program
- Philander Smith College Panthers, Little Rock, AR 72202; 501-370-5221; www.philander.edu; no football program
- Southern University at New Orleans Knights, New Orleans, LA 70126; 504-286-5000; www.suno.edu; no football program
- Talladega College Tornadoes, Talladega, AL 35160; 256-362-0206; www.talladega.edu; no football program
- Tougaloo College Bulldogs, Tougaloo, MS 39174; 601-977-7700; www.tougaloo.edu; no football program

- Xavier University of Louisiana Gold Rush, New Orleans, LA 70125; 504-486-7411; www.xula.edu; no football program

Heart of America Athletic Conference (HAAC)

15221 Midland Drive, Shawnee KS, 66217; Telephone: 913-631-5579; Web site: http://www.haac-sports.com

The Heart of America Athletic Conference was founded in 1971 with charter schools Baker University, Central Methodist University, College of Emporia (Kansas), Graceland University, Missouri Valley College, Ottawa University (Kansas), Tarkio College (Missouri), and William Jewell College.

Conference football teams play each other once during the season with the conference champion qualifying for the Football Championship Series if the team is ranked at No. 20 or higher in the final poll. As of this writing, the HAAC consists of 10 members, all of which play football in the conference.

- Avila University Eagles, Kansas City, MO 64145; 816-942-8400; www.avila.edu
- Baker University Wildcats, Baldwin City, KS 66006; 785-594-6451; www.bakeru.edu
- Benedictine College Ravens, Atchison, KS 66002; 800-467-5340; www.benedictine.edu
- Central Methodist University Eagles, Fayette, MO 65248; 877-268-1854; www.centralmethodist.edu
- Culver-Stockton College Wildcats, Canton, MO 63435; 800-537-1883; www.culver.edu
- Evangel University Crusaders, Springfield, MO 65802; 417-865-2815; www.evangel.edu
- Graceland University Yellowjackets, Lamoni, IA 50140; 641-784-5000; www.graceland.edu
- MidAmerica Nazarene University Pioneers, Olathe, KS 66062; 913-782-3750; www.mnu.edu
- Missouri Valley College Vikings, Marshall, MO 65340; 660-831-4000; www.moval.edu
- Peru State College Bobcats, Peru, NE 68421; 800-742-4412; www.peru.edu

HAAC Conference Champions

Year	*School*
1971	Missouri Valley College (MO)
1972	Ottawa University (KS)
1973	William Jewell College (MO)
1974	Missouri Valley College (MO)
1975	Central Methodist University (MO)
1975	Graceland University (IA)
1975	Missouri Valley College (MO)
1976	Missouri Valley College (MO)
1977	Missouri Valley College (MO)
1978	Missouri Valley College (MO)
1979	Baker University (KS)
1979	William Jewell College (MO)
1980	Baker University (KS)
1980	William Jewell College (MO)
1981	William Jewell College (MO)
1982	William Jewell College (MO)
1983	Baker University (KS)
1984	Baker University (KS)
1985	Baker University (KS)
1985	MidAmerica Nazarene University (KS)
1985	William Jewell College (MO)
1986	Baker University (KS)
1987	Baker University (KS)
1988	Baker University (KS)
1989	Missouri Valley College (MO)
1990	Baker University (KS)

Year	*School*
1990	William Jewell College (MO)
1991	Baker University (KS)
1991	William Jewell College (MO)
1992	Baker University (KS)
1992	Benedictine College (KS)
1993	Baker University (KS)
1993	Evangel University (MO)
1994	Missouri Valley College (MO)
1995	Benedictine College (KS)
1996	Evangel University (MO)
1997	Benedictine College (KS)
1997	Evangel University (MO)
1998	Benedictine College (KS)
1999	Missouri Valley College (MO)
2000	Benedictine College (KS)
2001	Evangel University (MO)
2002	MidAmerica Nazarene University (KS)
2003	MidAmerica Nazarene University (KS)
2004	Lindenwood University (MO)
2005	Evangel University (MO)
2006	Missouri Valley College (MO)
2007	Lindenwood University (MO)
2008	MidAmerica Nazarene University (KS)
2009	Lindenwood University (MO)
2010	MidAmerica Nazarene University (KS)

HAAC Coach of the Year

Year	*Coach*	*School*
2007	Patrick Ross	Lindenwood University (MO)
2008	Jed Stugart	MidAmerica Nazarene University (KS)
2009	No Information	
2010	No Information	

HAAC Player of the Year

Year	*Player*	*School*
2007	Conference: Derek Doerfler	Baker University (KS)
2007	Offense: Matt Schneider	MidAmerica Nazarene University (KS)
2007	Defense: Reggie Singletary	Missouri Valley College (MO)
2008	Conference: Pat Ealy	MidAmerica Nazarene University (KS)
2008	Offense: Richie Bryant	Baker University (KS)
2008	Defense: Robbie Schultz	Benedictine College (KS)
2009	No Information	
2010	No Information	

Independent Schools

NAIA independent schools are four-year institutional members of the NAIA that play a football schedule independent of any formal conference affiliation.

- Ave Maria University Gyrenes, Ave Maria, FL 34142; 877-283-8648; www.avemaria.edu; belongs to The Sun Conference, but plays football as an independent team
- Azusa Pacific University Cougars, Azusa, CA 91702; 626-969-3434; www.apu.edu; belongs to the Golden State Athletic Conference, but plays football as an independent team
- Dakota State University Trojans, Madison, SD 57042; 605-256-5111; www.dsu.edu; belongs to the Association of Independent Institutions
- Edward Waters College Tigers, Jacksonville, FL 32209; 904-470-8000; www.ewc.edu; belongs to the Gulf Coast Athletic Conference, but plays football as an independent team
- Haskell Indian Nations University Indians, Lawrence, KS 66046; 785-749-8404; www.haskell.edu; belongs to the Midlands Collegiate Athletic Conference, but plays football as an independent team
- Southern Virginia University Knights, Buena Vista, VA 24416; 540-261-8400; www.svu.edu; belongs to the United States Collegiate Athletic Association, but plays football as an independent team
- Webber International University Warriors, Babson Park, FL 33827; 800-741-1844; www.webber.edu; belongs to The Sun Conference, but plays football as an independent team

Kansas Collegiate Athletic Conference (KCAC)

Garvey Center Offices at Friends University, 2100 West University Avenue, Wichita, KS 67213; Telephone: 316-425-3460; Web site: http://www.kcacsports.com (3460 North Ridge Road Suite 50, Wichita, KS 67205; Telephone: 316-425-3460; Fax: 316-425-3461; Web site: http://www.kcacsports.com

The Kansas Collegiate Athletic Conference was formed in 1928 with six charter schools: Baker University, Bethany College, Kansas Wesleyan University, McPherson College, Ottawa University, and St. Mary's College. All of its members are from Kansas; conference members play each other once during the season; and the conference football champion receives an automatic berth into the championship series if that team is ranked in the Top 20 of the national poll. The KCAC consists of 10 teams, all of which play football within the conference.

- Bethany College Swedes, Lindsborg, KS 67456; 785-227-3380; www.bethanylb.edu
- Bethel College Threshers, North Newton, KS 67117; 316-283-2500; www.bethelks.edu
- Friends University Falcons, Wichita, KS 67213; 316-295-5000; www.friends.edu
- Kansas Wesleyan University Coyotes, Salina, KS 67401; 785-827-5541; www.kwu.edu
- McPherson College Bulldogs, McPherson, KS 67460; 620-242-0400; www.mcpherson.edu

- Ottawa University Braves, Ottawa, KS 66067; 800-755-5200; www.ottawa.edu
- Southwestern College Moundbuilders, Winfield, KS 67156; 800-846-1543; www.sckans.edu
- Sterling College Warriors, Sterling, KS 67579; 620-278-2173; www.sterling.edu
- Tabor College Blue Jays, Hillsboro, KS 67063; 800-822-6799; www.tabor.edu
- University of Saint Mary Spires, Leavenworth, KS 66048; 913-682-5151; www.stmary.edu

Kansas Collegiate Athletic Conference Champions

Year	School
1997	Ottawa University (KS)
1998	Southwestern College (KS)
1999	Bethany College (KS)
1999	Southwestern College (KS)
2000	Ottawa University (KS)
2001	Bethany College (KS)
2001	Kansas Wesleyan University (KS)
2002	Kansas Wesleyan University (KS)
2003	Ottawa University (KS)
2004	Tabor College (KS)
2005	Tabor College (KS)
2006	Bethel College (KS)
2006	Friends University (KS)
2007	Bethel College (KS)
2007	Friends University (KS)
2008	Friends University (KS)
2009	Ottawa University (KS)
2010	McPherson College (KS)

Kansas Collegiate Athletic Conference Coach of the Year

Year	Name	School
2009	Kent Kessinger	Ottawa University (KS)
2010	Joe Bettasso	McPherson College (KS)

Kansas Collegiate Athletic Conference Assistant Coach of the Year

Year	Name	School
2009	Matt Welch	Friends University (KS)
2010	Chuck Lambert	Sterling College (KS)

Kansas Collegiate Athletic Conference Player of the Year

Year	Player	Class	Position	School
2009	Ethan Haller	Freshman	Quarterback	Ottawa University (KS)
2010	Shane Mascarenas	Senior	Quarterback	McPherson College (KS)

Kansas Collegiate Athletic Conference Offensive Player of the Year

Year	Player	Class	Position	School
2009	Ethan Haller	Freshman	Quarterback	Ottawa University (KS)
2010	Doug Webster	Senior	Quarterback	Kansas Wesleyan University (KS)

Kansas Collegiate Athletic Conference Defensive Player of the Year

Year	Player	Class	Position	School
2009	James McCartney	Senior	Defensive Lineman	Bethel College (KS)
2010	Scott Jones	Senior	Defensive Lineman	McPherson College (KS)

Kansas Collegiate Athletic Conference Special Teams Player of the Year

Year	Player	Class	Position	School
2009	Stephen Harrison	Senior	Wide Receiver	McPherson College (KS)
2010	No Information			

Kentucky Intercollegiate Athletic Conference (KIAC)

2008 Balfour Drive, Louisville, KY 40242; Telephone: 502-327-1307; Web site: http://www.kiacsports.com/ (313 Bocote Drive, Berea, KY 40403; Telephone: 859-200-3510)

The Kentucky Intercollegiate Athletic Conference was founded in 1917; currently has 10 member schools; and does not support football.

- Alice Lloyd College Eagles, Pippa Passes, KY 41844; 606-368-6000; www.alc.edu; no football program
- Asbury University Eagles, Wilmore, KY 40390; 859-858-3511; www.asbury.edu; no football program
- Berea College Mountaineers, Berea, KY 40404; 859-985-3000; www.berea.edu; no football program
- Brescia University Bearcats, Owensboro, KY 42301; 877-273-7242; www.brescia.edu; no football program
- Cincinnati Christian University Eagles, Cincinnati, OH 45204; 513-244-8100; www.ccuniversity.edu; no football program
- Indiana University East Red Wolves, Richmond, IN 47374; 765-973-8200; www.iue.edu; no football program
- Indiana University-Southeast Grenadiers, New Albany, IN 47150; 812-941-2333; www.ius.edu; no football program
- Midway College Eagles, Midway, KY 40347; 859-846-4421; www.midway.edu; no football program
- Mountain State University Cougars, Beckley, WV 25801; 866-367-6781; www.mountainstate.edu; no football program
- St. Louis College of Pharmacy Eutectics, St. Louis, MO 63110; 314-367-8700; www.stlcop.edu; no football program

Mid-Central College Conference (MCCC)

2277 South Angling Pike, Harford City, IN 47348; Telephone: 765-748-1776; Web site: http://www.mid-centralconf.org/

The Mid-Central College Conference is made up of private Christian colleges in Indiana and Michigan. The MCCC consists of 10 members and does not support football, although three of its schools play football outside the conference.

- Bethel College Pilots, Mishawaka, IN 46545; 574-807-7000; www.bethelcollege.edu; no football program
- Goshen College Maple Leafs, Goshen, IN 46526; 574-535-7000; www.goshen.edu; no football program
- Grace College & Theological Seminary Lancers, Winona Lake, IN 46590; 574-372-5100; www.grace.edu; no football program
- Huntington University Foresters, Huntington, IN 46750; 260-356-6000; www.huntington.edu; no football program
- Indiana Wesleyan University Wildcats, Marion, IN 46953; 765-674-6901; www.indwes.edu; no football program
- Marian University Knights, Indianapolis, IN 46222; 317-955-6000; www.marian.edu; plays football in the Mid-States Football Association (Mideast League)
- Mount Vernon Nazarene University Cougars, Mount Vernon, Ohio, 43050; 740-392-6868; www.mvnu.edu; nofootball program
- Spring Arbor University Cougars, Spring Arbor, MI 49283; 800-968-9103; www.arbor.edu; no football program
- Taylor University Trojans, Upland, IN 46989; 800-882-3456; www.taylor.edu; plays football in the Mid-States Football Association (Mideast Division)
- University of Saint Francis Cougars, Fort Wayne, IN 46808; 260-399-7999; www.sf.edu; plays football in the Mid-States Football Association (Mideast League)

Mid-South Conference

401 West Main Street # 2200, Louisville, KY 40202; Telephone: 502-587-7767; Fax: 502-587-6767; Web site: http://www.mid-southconference.org

The Mid-South Conference was formed in April 1995 and consists of 17 member institutions, 14 of which play football within the conference.

- Belhaven College Blazers, Jackson, MS 39202; 601-968-5940; www.bellhaven.edu; associate member from the Southern States Athletic Conference
- Bethel University: The Cumberland Presbyterian University Wildcats, McKenzie, TN 38201; 731-352-4000; www.bethelu.edu; associate member from the TranSouth Athletic Conference
- Campbellsville University Tigers, Campbellsville, KY 42718; 270-789-5000; www.campbellsville.edu
- Cumberland University Bulldogs, Lebanon, TN 37087; 800-467-0562; www.cumberland.edu; associate member from the TranSouth Athletic Conference
- Faulkner University Eagles, Montgomery, AL 36109; 334-272-5820; www.faulkner.edu; associate member from the Southern States Athletic Conference
- Georgetown College Tigers, Georgetown, KY 40324; 502-863-8000; www.georgetowncollege.edu
- Kentucky Christian University Knights, Grayson, KY 41143; 800-522-3181; www.kcu.edu; associate member from the Association of Independent Institutions
- Lindsey Wilson College Blue Raiders, Columbia, KY 42728; 270-384-2126; www.lindsey.edu
- St. Catharine College Patriots, St. Catharine, KY 40061; 859-336-5082; www.sccky.edu; no football program
- Shawnee State University Bears, Portsmouth, OH 45662; 740-351-4778; www.shawnee.edu; no football program
- Shorter University Hawks, Rome, GA 30165; 800-868-6980; www.shorter.edu; associate member from the Southern States Athletic Conference
- Union College Bulldogs, Barbourville, KY 40906; 800-489-8646; www.unionky.edu; associate member from the Appalachian Athletic Conference
- University of Rio Grande RedStorm, Rio Grande, OH 45674; 800-282-7201; www.rio.edu; no football program
- University of Pikeville Bears, Pikeville, KY 41501; 606-218-5250; www.upike.edu
- University of the Cumberlands Patriots, Williamsburg, KY 40769; 606-539-4241; www.ucumberlands.edu
- University of Virginia's College at Wise Highland Cavaliers, Wise, VA 24293; 276-328-0100; www.wise.virginia.edu
- West Virginia University Institute of Technology Golden Bears, Montgomery, WV 25136; 304-442-1000; www.wvutech.edu

Mid-South Conference Champions

Year	School
2005	Georgetown College (KY)
2006	Georgetown College (KY)
2007	University of the Cumberlands (KY)
2007	University of Virginia's College at Wise (VA)
2008	University of the Cumberlands (KY)
2009	Lambuth University (TN)
2010	Georgetown College (KY)

Mid-South Conference Coach of the Year

Year	Coach	School
2006	Dino Kaklis	Bethel College (TN)
2006	Bruce Wasem	University of Virginia's College at Wise (VA)
2007	No Information	
2008	East: John Bland	University of the Cumberlands (KY)
2008	West: Phil Jones	Shorter College (GA)
2009	East: John Bland	University of the Cumberlands (KY)
2009	West: Hugh Freeze	Lambuth University (TN)

Year	Coach	School
2010	East: Bill Cronin	Georgetown College (KY)
2010	West: John Bland	Cumberland University (TN)

Mid-South Conference Offensive Player of the Year

Year	Player	Class	Position	School
2006	No Information			
2007	Ni Information			
2008	East: Randy Hippeard	Senior	Quarterback	University of Virginia's College at Wise (VA)
2008	West: A.J. Cooley	Junior	Fullback	Shorter College (GA)
2009	No Information			
2010	East: Kaelin Ammons	Junior	Quarterback	Georgetown College (KY)
2010	West: Armond Smith	Senior	Running Back	Union College (KY)

Mid-South Conference Defensive Player of the Year

Year	Player	Class	Position	School
2006	No Information			
2007	No Information			
2008	East: Travis Thurmond	Senior	Linebacker	University of the Cumberlands (KY)
2008	West: Logan Lollis	Junior		Shorter College (GA)
2009	No Information			
2010	East: Kyle Anderson	Senior	Defensive Lineman	Georgetown College (KY)
2010	West: Ricky Wadlington	Junior	Linebacker	Bellhaven University (MS)

Mid-South Conference Offensive Freshman of the Year

Year	Player	Position	School
2006	No Information		
2007	No Information		
2008	East: Maurice Berryhill	(Defensive Back)	University of the Cumberlands (KY)
2008	West: Edward Robinson	Running Back	Lambuth University (TN)
2009	No Information		
2010	East: Gerwan Brewer	Running Back	Campbellsville University (KY)
2010	West: Terrance Cobb	Running Back	University of the Cumberlands (KY)

Mid-South Conference Defensive Freshman of the Year

Year	Player	Position	School
2006	No Information		
2007	No Information		
2008	East: Chris Thomas	(Wide Receiver)	Union College (KY)
2008	West: Ladarruis Madden	Defensive Back	Lambuth University (TN)
2009	No Information		
2010	East: Sam Wilson	Linebacker	Lindsey Wilson College (KY)
2010	West: Weston Hazelhurst	Linebacker	University of the Cumberlands (KY)

Mid-States Football Association (Mideast League / Midwest League) (MSFA)

Commissioner: University of Findlay

1000 North Main Street, Findlay, OH 45840; Telephone: 419-434-4551; Fax: 419-434-6974; Web site: http://www.midstatesfootball.org

Formed in 1993 (first season of competition was 1994) with charter schools Geneva College, Lindenwood University, Malone College, Olivet Nazarene University, Saint Xavier University, Taylor University, Tiffin University, Trinity International University, University of Findlay, Urbana University, and Westminster College, teams in the Mid-States Football Association play each other within the league and the champions of the two leagues receive automatic berths into the NAIA playoffs if they both are ranked in the Top 20 of the final regular-season poll.

The MSFA sponsors teams only in football. For other sports, member schools play in a variety of other conferences. As of this writing, the MSFA's 17 teams are divided into the Mideast League and the Midwest League.

- Concordia University Cardinals, Ann Arbor, MI 48105; 877-995-7520; www.cuaa.edu; plays football in the Mideast League, associate member from the Wolverine-Hoosier Athletic Conference
- Grand View University Vikings, Des Moines, IA 50316; 515-263-2800; www.grandview.edu; plays football in the Midwest League; associate member from the Midwest Collegiate Conference
- Iowa Wesleyan College Tigers, Mount Pleasant, IA 52641; 800-582-2383; www.iwc.edu; plays football in the Midwest League; associate member from the Midwest Collegiate Conference
- Malone University Pioneers, Canton, OH 44709; 800-521-1146; www.malone.edu; plays football in the Great Lakes Intercollegiate Athletic Conference
- Marian University Knights, Indianapolis, IN 46222; 317-955-6000; www.marian.edu; plays football in the Mideast League; associate member from the Mid-Central College Conference
- McKendree University Bearcats, Lebanon, IL 62254; 618-537-4481; www.mckendree.edu; plays football in the Midwest League; transitioning to the Great Lakes Valley Conference in Division II of the NCAA
- Olivet Nazarene University Tigers, Bourbonnais, IL 60914; 815-939-5011; www.olivet.edu; plays football in the Midwest League; associate member from the Chicagoland Collegiate Athletic Conference
- Quincy University Hawks, Quincy, IL 62301; 217-222-8020; www.quincy.edu; plays football in the Mideast League; associate member from the Great Lakes Valley Conference
- St. Ambrose University Fighting Bees, Davenport, IA 52803; 563-333-6000; www.sau.edu; plays football in the Midwest League; associate member from the Midwest Collegiate Conference
- Saint Xavier University Cougars, Chicago, IL 60655; 773-298-3000; www.sxu.edu; plays football in the Mideast League; associate member from the Chicagoland Collegiate Athletic Conference
- Siena Heights University Saints, Adrian, MI 49221; 517-263-0731; www.sienaheights.edu; will join the MSFA in 2012
- Taylor University Trojans, Upland, IN 46989; 800-882-3456; www.taylor.edu; plays football in the Mideast League; associate member from the Mid-Central College Conference
- Trinity International University Trojans, Deerfield, IL 60015; 800-822-3225; www.tiu.edu; plays football in the Midwest League; associate member from the Chicagoland Collegiate Athletic Conference
- University of Saint Francis Cougars, Fort Wayne, IN 46808; 260-399-7999; www.sf.edu; plays football in the Mideast League; associate member from the Mid-Central College Conference
- University of St. Francis Fighting Saints, Joliet, IL 60435; 800-735-7500; www.stfrancis.edu; plays football in the Midwest League; associate member from the Chicagoland Collegiate Athletic Conference
- Waldorf College Warriors, Forest City, IA 50436; 800-292-1903; www.waldorf.edu; plays football in the Midwest League; associate member from the Midwest Collegiate Conference
- Walsh University Cavaliers, North Canton, OH 44720; 330-490-7090; www.walsh.edu; plays football in the Mideast League; associate member from the American Mideast Conference
- William Penn University Statesmen, Oskaloosa, IA 52577; 641-673-1001; www.wmpenn.edu; plays football in the Midwest League; associate member from the Midwest Collegiate Conference

Mid-States Football Association Champions

Year	*School*
1997	Mideast: Geneva College (PA)
1997	Midwest: McKendree University (IL)
1998	Mideast: Malone University (OH)
1998	Midwest: Taylor University (IN)
1999	Mideast: University of Saint Francis (IL or IN)
1999	Midwest: McKendree University (IL)
1999	Midwest: Olivet Nazarene University (IL)
1999	Midwest: Taylor University (IN)
2000	Mideast: University of Saint Francis (IL or IN)
2000	Midwest: St. Ambrose University (IA)
2001	Mideast: Tri-State University (IN)
2001	Mideast: University of Saint Francis (IL or IN)
2001	Mideast: Walsh University (OH)

Year	School
2001	Midwest: St. Ambrose University (IA)
2002	Mideast: University of Saint Francis (IL or IN)
2002	Midwest: McKendree University (IL)
2002	Midwest: Saint Xavier University (IL)
2002	Midwest: St. Ambrose University (IA)
2003	Mideast: University of Saint Francis (IL or IN)
2003	Midwest: McKendree University (IL)
2003	Midwest: Olivet Nazarene University (IL)
2003	Midwest: Saint Xavier University (IL)
2003	Midwest: St. Ambrose University (IA)
2003	Midwest: Trinity International University (IL)
2004	Mideast: University of Saint Francis (IL or IN)
2004	Midwest: McKendree University (IL)
2005	Mideast: No Information
2005	Midwest: McKendree University (IL)
2005	Midwest: Saint Xavier University (IL)
2006	Mideast: University of Saint Francis (IL or IN)
2006	Midwest: St. Ambrose University (IA)
2007	Mideast: Ohio Dominican University (OH)
2007	Midwest: St. Ambrose University (IA)
2008	Mideast: University of Saint Francis (IL or IN)
2008	Midwest: St. Ambrose University (IA)
2009	Mideast: Saint Xavier University (IL)
2010	Mideast: Saint Xavier University (IL)
2010	Midwest: McKendree University (IL)

Mid-States Football Association Coach of the Year

Year	Coach	School
2002	Mideast: Kevin Dunley	University of Saint Francis (IL or IN)
2003	Mideast: Kevin Donley	University of Saint Francis (IL or IN)
2003	Midwest: Andy Lambert	Trinity International University (IL)
2004	Mideast: Kevin Donley	University of Saint Francis (IL or IN)
2004	Midwest: Derek DeWitt	Trinity International University (IL)
2005	Mideast: Gene DeMarco	Geneva College (PA)
2005	Midwest: Mike Feminis	Saint Xavier University (IL)
2006	Mideast: Kevin Donley	University of Saint Francis (IL or IN)
2006	Midwest: Todd Sturdy	St. Ambrose University (IA)
2007	Mideast: Dale Carlson	Ohio Dominican University (OH)
2007	Midwest: Gary Newsome	Olivet Nazarene University (IL)
2007	Midwest: Mike Magistrelli	St. Ambrose University (IA)
2008	Mideast: Kevin Donley	University of Saint Francis (IL or IN)
2008	Midwest: Todd Hafner	William Penn University (IA)
2009	Mideast: Mike Feminis	Saint Xavier University (IL)
2009	Midwest: Mike Woodley	Grand View University (IL)
2010	Mideast: Mike Feminis	Saint Xavier University (IL)
2010	Midwest: Todd Hafner	William Penn University (IA)

Mid-States Football Association Assistant Coach of the Year

Year	Coach	School
2010	Mideast: Mike Slovick	Saint Xavier University (IL)
2010	Midwest: Aaron Hafner	William Penn University (IA)

Mid-States Football Association Player of the Year

Year	Player	Class	Position	School
2002	Mideast: Derek Besgrove			Walsh University (OH)
2003	Mideast: Derek Besgrove			Walsh University (OH)
2003	Midwest: Joe Schimmel			St. Ambrose University (IA)
2004	Mideast: Cory Jaquay	Junior	Running Back	University of Saint Francis (IL or IN)
2004	Midwest: Kevin Oberlander	Senior	Quarterback	Trinity International University (IL)
2005	Mideast: Chris Bramell	Senior	Quarterback	University of Saint Francis (IL or IN)
2005	Midwest: Jarrod Nowman	Senior	Wide Receiver	Saint Xavier University (IL)
2006	Mideast: Brian Kurtz	Senior	Inside Line Backer	University of Saint Francis (IL or IN)
2006	Midwest: Andy Ricca	Sophomore	Wide Receiver	Saint Xavier University (IL)
2007	Mideast: Cris Reisert	Junior	Quarterback	Ohio Dominican University (OH)
2007	Midwest: Jim DuPage	Senior	Quarterback	St. Ambrose University (IA)

Year	*Player*	*Class*	*Position*	*School*
2008	Mideast: Daniel Carter	Junior	Running Back	University of Saint Francis (IL or IN)
2008	Midwest: Michael Hayward	Sophomore	Quarterback	St. Ambrose University (IA)
2009	Mideast: Mike Lally	Senior	Linebacker	Saint Xavier University (IL)
2009	Midwest: Byron Gettis	Junior	Tight End	McKendree University (IL)
2009	Midwest: Dale Woods	Junior	Defensive End	William Penn University (IA)
2010	Mideast: Mike Maher	Senior	Wide Receiver	Saint Xavier University (IL)
2010	Midwest: Michael Hayward	Senior	Wide Receiver	St. Ambrose University (IA)
2010	Midwest: E.J. Peterson	Senior	Linebacker	Grand View University (IL)

Midlands Collegiate Athletic Conference

P.O. Box 17, Point Lookout, MO 65726; Telephone: 417-690-2568; Fax: 417-348-1432; Web site: http://www.mcac-naia.org/

The Midlands Collegiate Athletic Conference was formed in 1994; consists of nine members; and does not sponsor football, although one of its members supports a football program.

- Bellevue University Bruins, Bellevue, NE 68005; 402-293-2000; www.bellevue.edu; no football program
- Central Baptist College Mustangs, Conway, AR 72034; 501-329-6872; www.cbc.edu; no football program
- Central Christian College Tigers, McPherson, KS 67460; 620-241-0723; www.centralchristian.edu; no football program
- College of Saint Mary Flames, Omaha, NE 68106; 402-399-2400; www.csm.edu; no football program
- College of the Ozarks Bobcats, Point Lookout, MO 65726; 800-222-0525; www.cofo.edu; no football program
- Haskell Indian Nations University Indians, Lawrence, KS 66046; 785-749-8404; www.haskell.edu; plays football as an independent team
- Oklahoma Wesleyan University Eagles, Bartlesville, OK 74006; 918-335-6200; www.okwu.edu; no football program
- Southwestern Christian University Eagles, Bethany, OK 73008; 405-789-7661; www.swcu.edu; no football program
- York College Panthers, York, NE 68467; 800-950-9675; www.york.edu; no football program

Midwest Collegiate Conference

3133 Sycamore Road, Ames, IA 50014; Telephone: 888-430-7705; Web site: Web site: http://www.midwestcollegiateconference.com/

The Midwest Collegiate Conference (originally referred to as the Midwest Catholic Conference) was founded in 1988 with six charter member Catholic schools: Clarke College, Edgewood College, Marycrest University, Mount Mercy College, Mount St. Clare College, and Viterbo College. In 1989, it became known as the Midwest Classic Conference and adopted its current name in 2007. The MCC currently consists of 10 member schools and does not support football, although five of its members play football in the Mid-States Football Association.

- AIB College of Business Eagles, Des Moines, IA 50321; 515-244-4221; www.aib.edu; no football program
- Ashford University Saints, Clinton, IA 52732; 866-711-1700; www.ashford.edu; no football program
- Clarke University Crusaders, Dubuque, IA 52001; 888-825-2753; www.clarke.edu; no football program
- Grand View University Vikings, Des Moines, IA 50316; 515-263-2800; www.grandview.edu; plays football in the Mid-States Football Association (Midwest League)
- Iowa Wesleyan College Tigers, Mount Pleasant, IA 52641; 800-582-2383; www.iwc.edu; plays football in the Mid-States Football Association (Midwest League)
- Mount Mercy University Mustangs, Cedar Rapids, IA 52402; 319-363-8213; www.mtmercy.edu; no football program

- Saint Ambrose University Fighting Bees (Davenport, IA); plays football in the Mid-States Football Association (Midwest League)
- Viterbo University V-Hawks, La Crosse, WI 54601; 608-796-3000; www.viterbo.edu; no football program
- Waldorf College Warriors, Forest City, IA 50436; 800-292-1903; www.waldorf.edu; plays football in the Mid-States Football Association (Midwest League)
- William Penn University Statesmen, Oskaloosa, IA 52577; 641-672-9653; www.wmpenn.edu; plays football in the Mid-States Football Association (Midwest League)

Red River Athletic Conference

100 North 6th Street, Suite 406, Waco TX, 76710; Telephone: 254-744-8542 Fax: 254-662-6627; Web site: http://www.redriverconference.com/

The Red River Athletic Conference consists of 15 members and does not support football, although four of its schools play football in the Central States Football League.

- Bacone College Warriors, Muskogee, OK 74403; 918-683-4581; www.bacone.edu; plays football in the Central States Football League
- Huston-Tillotson University Rams, Austin, TX 78702; 512-505-3000; www.htu.edu; no football program
- Jarvis Christian College Bulldogs, Hawkins, TX 75765; 903-769-6100; www.jarvis.edu; no football program
- Langston University Lions, Langston, OK 73050; 877-466-2231; www.langston.edu; plays football in the Central States Football League
- Louisiana State University-Shreveport Pilots, Shreveport, LA 71115; 318-797-5000; www.lsus.edu; no football program
- Northwood University Knights, Cedar Hill, TX 75104; 800-622-9000; www.northwood.edu; no football program
- Our Lady of the Lake University Saints, San Antonio, TX 78207; 210-434-6711; www.ollusa.edu; no football program
- Paul Quinn College Tigers, Dallas, TX 75241; 214-379-5500; www.pqc.edu; no football program
- Southwestern Assemblies of God University Lions, Waxahachie, TX 75165; 888-937-7248; www.sagu.edu; plays football in the Central States Football League
- Texas College Steers, Tyler, TX 75702; 800-306-6299; www.texascollege.edu; plays football in the Central States Football League
- Texas Wesleyan University Rams, Fort Worth, TX 76105; 817-531-4444; www.txwes.edu; no football program
- University of St. Thomas Celts, Houston, TX 77006; 713-522-7911; www.stthom.edu; no football program
- University of Texas-Brownsville Scorpions, Brownsville, TX 78520; 956-882-8200; www.utb.edu; no football program
- University of the Southwest Mustangs, Hobbs, NM 88240; 575-392-6561; www.usw.edu; no football program
- Wiley College Wildcats, Marshall, TX 75670; 903-927-3300; www.wileyc.edu; no football program

Sooner Athletic Conference (SAC)

Commissioner: 5400 North Classen Boulevard, Oklahoma City, OK 73118; Telephone: 405-848-1581; 405-840-4671; Web site: http://www.soonerathletic.org/

The Sooner Athletic Conference was founded in 1978 with five charter schools: Oklahoma Baptist University, Oklahoma Christian University, Phillips University, Southern Nazarene University, and the University of Science and Arts of Oklahoma. The SAC has 12 members and does not support football, although four of its members either do or will stat sponsoring football programs.

- John Brown University Golden Eagles, Siloam Springs, AR 72761; 479-524-9500; www.jbu.edu; no football program

- Lubbock Christian University Chapparals, Lubbock, TX 79407; 800-933-7601; www.lcu.edu; no football program
- Mid-America Christian University Evangels, Oklahoma City, OK 73170; 405-691-3800; www.macu.edu; no football program
- Northwestern Oklahoma State University Rangers, Alva, OK 73717; 580-327-1700; www.nwosu.edu; plays football in the Central States Football League
- Oklahoma Baptist University Bison, Shawnee, OK 74804; 405-275-2850; www.okbu.edu; will start a football program in 2013
- Oklahoma Christian University Eagles, Edmond, OK 73013; 405-425-5000; www.oc.edu; no football program
- Oklahoma City University Stars, Oklahoma City, OK 73106; 405-208-5000; www.okcu.edu; no football program
- Rogers State University Hillcats, Claremore, OK 74017; 918-343-7777; www.rsu.edu; no football program
- St. Gregory's University Cavaliers, Shawnee, OK 74804; 405-878-5100; www.stgregorys.edu; no football program
- Southern Nazarene University Crimson Storm, Bethany, OK 73008; 405-789-6400; www.snu.edu; plays football in the Central States Football League
- University of Science and Arts of Oklahoma Drovers, Chickasha, OK 73018; 405-224-3140; www.usao.edu; no football program
- Wayland Baptist University Pioneers, Plainview, TX 79072; 806-291-1000; www.wbu.edu; will play football in the Central States Football League in 2012

Southern States Athletic Conference (SSAC)

3139 Campus Drive, c/o Brenau University, Norcross GA, 30071;

Telephone: 770-447-5700; Email: commissioner@ssacsports.com; Web site: http://www.ssacsports.com/

The Southern States Athletic Conference was founded in March 1999 as the Georgia Alabama Carolina Conference with charter schools Auburn University, Montgomery, Brenau University, Brewton-Parker College, Emmanuel College, Faulkner University, Georgia Southwestern State University, North Georgia College & State University, Reinhardt College, Shorter College, Southern Polytechnic State University, and Southern Wesleyan University.

In June 2005, the conference adopted its current name. The SSAC has 15 members and does not support football, although three of its members have football programs.

- Auburn University at Montgomery Warhawks, Montgomery, AL 36124; 334-244-3000; www.aum.edu; no football program
- Belhaven University Blazers, Jackson, MS 39202; 601-968-5940; www.belhaven.edu; plays football in the Mid-South Conference
- Brenau University Golden Tigers, Gainesville, GA 30501; 770-534-6100; www2009.brenau.edu; no football program
- Brewton-Parker College Barons, Mt. Vernon, GA 30445; 912-583-2241; www.bpc.edu; no football program
- Emmanuel College Lions, Franklin Springs, GA 30639; 800-860-8800; www.ec.edu; no football program
- Faulkner University Eagles, Montgomery, AL 36109; 334-272-5820; www.faulkner.edu; plays football in the Mid-South Conference
- Lee University Flames, Cleveland, TN 37320; 800-533-9930; www.leeuniversity.edu; no football program
- Loyola University,New Orleans, Wolfpack, New Orleans, LA 70118; 504-865-3240; www.loyno.edu; no football program
- Shorter University Hawks, Rome, GA 30165; 800-868-6980; www.shorter.edu; plays football in the Mid-South Conference
- Southern Polytechnic State University Runnin' Hornets, Marietta, GA 30060; 678-915-7778; www.spsu.edu; no football program

- Southern Wesleyan University Warriors, Central, SC 29630; 864-644-5000; www.swu.edu; no football program
- Spring Hill College Badgers, Mobile, AL 36608; 251-380-4000; www.shc.edu; no football program
- Truett-McConnell College Bears, Cleveland, GA 30528; 706-865-2134; www.truett.edu; no football program
- University of Mobile Rams, Mobile, AL 36613; 251-675-5990; www.umobile.edu; no football program
- William Carey University Crusaders, Hattiesburg, MS 39401; 601-318-6051; www.wmcarey.edu; no football program

The Sun Conference (TSC)

616 Northpoint Avenue, Liberty MO, 64068; Telephone: 913-449-3356; Web site: http:// www.thesunconference.com/

The Sun Conference was formed in March 1990 as the Florida International Athletic Conference, renamed itself the Florida Sun Conference in 1992, and adopted its current name in August 2008. Original charter members included Embry-Riddle University, Flagler College, Florida Memorial University, Nova Southeastern University, Palm Beach Atlantic University, St. Thomas University, Warner Southern University, and Webber International University.

Currently, TSC consists of 11 schools and does not support football, although two of its schools play football as independent teams.

- Ave Maria University Gyrenes, Ave Maria, FL 34142; 877-283-8648; www.avemaria.edu; plays football as an independent team
- Embry-Riddle Aeronautical University Eagles, Daytona Beach, FL 32114; 386-226-6000; www.erau.edu; no football program
- Florida Memorial University Lions, Miami Gardens, FL 33054; 305-626-3600; www.fmuniv.edu; no football program
- Johnson & Wales University Wildcats, North Miami, FL 33181; 800-342-5598; www.jwu.edu/northmiami; no football program
- Northwood University Seahawks, West Palm Beach, FL 33409; 800-622-9000; www.northwood.edu/fl; no football program
- St. Thomas University Bobcats, Miami Gardens, FL 33054; 305-628-6546; www.stu.edu; no football program
- Savannah College of Art and Design Bees (SCAD Savannah), Savannah, GA 31415; 912-525-5100; www.scad.edu; no football program
- Southeastern University Fire, Lakeland, FL 33801; 863-667-5000; www.seu.edu;; no football program
- University of South Carolina-Beaufort Sand Sharks, Beaufort, SC 29902; 843-521-4100; www.uscb.edu; no football program
- Warner University Royals, Lake Wales, FL 33859; 863-638-1426; www.warner.edu;; no football program
- Webber International University Warriors, Babson Park, FL 33827; 800-741-1844; plays football as an independent team

TranSouth Athletic Conference

506 Melody Lane, Memphis, TN 38120; Telephone: 901-767-6194; Web site: http://www.transouth.org/

The TranSouth Athletic Conference was founded in 1996; consists of nine members; and does not support football, although two of its schools play football in the Mid-South Conference.

- Bethel University (the Cumberland Presbyterian University) Wildcats, McKenzie, TN 38201; 731-352-4000; www.bethelu.edu; plays football in the Mid-South Conference
- Blue Mountain College Toppers, Blue Mountain, MS 38610; 662-685-4771; www.bmc.edu; no football program

- Cumberland University Bulldogs, Lebanon, TN 37087; 800-467-0562; www.cumberland.edu; plays football in the Mid-South Conference
- Freed-Hardeman University Lions, Henderson, TN 38340; 800-348-3481; www.fhu.edu; no football program
- Lyon College Scots, Batesville, AR 72503; 870-307-7000; www.lyon.edu; no football program
- Martin Methodist College Redhawks, Pulaski, TN 38478; 800-467-1273; www.martinmethodist.edu; no football program
- Mid-Continent University Cougars, Mayfield, KY 42066; 270-247-8521; www.midcontinent.edu; no football program
- Trevecca Nazarene University Trojans, Nashville, TN 37210; 615-248-1200; www.trevecca.edu; no football program
- Union University Bulldogs, Jackson, TN 38305; 731-668-1818; www.uu.edu; no football program

Wolverine-Hoosier Athletic Conference (WHAC)

38793 Windmill Pointe North, Clinton Township, MI 48038 (36600 Schoolcraft Road, Livonia, MI 48150; Telephone: 734-432-5604; Fax: 734-432-5611); Web site: http://www whac.net/

The Wolverine-Hoosier Athletic Conference was formed in 1992 with charter schools Aquinas College, Concordia College, Cornerstone University, Siena Heights University, Spring Arbor College, and Tri-State University. The WHAC has 10 members and does not support football, although one of its schools plays football as an independent team and one member will play football in the Mid-States Football Association starting in 2010.

- Aquinas College Saints, Grand Rapids, MI 49506; 616-632-8900; www.aquinas.edu; no football program
- Concordia University Cardinals, Ann Arbor, MI 48105; 877-995-7520; www.cuaa.edu; plays football in the Mid-States Football Association (Mideast League)
- Cornerstone University Golden Eagles, Grand Rapids, MI Grand Rapids, MI 49525; 616-949-5300; no football program
- Davenport University Panthers, Grand Rapids, MI 49512; 800-686-1600; www.davenport.edu; no football program
- Indiana Institute of Technology Warriors, Fort Wayne, IN 46803; 800-937-2448; www.indianatech.edu; no football program
- Lourdes University Gray Wolves, Sylvania, OH 43580; 800-878-3210; www.lourdes.edu; no football program
- Madonna University Crusaders, Livonia, MI 48150; 800-852-4951; www.madonna.edu; no football program
- Siena Heights University Saints, Adrian, MI 49221; 517-263-0731; www.sienaheights.edu; scheduled to begin playing football in the Mid-States Football Association in 2010
- University of Michigan-Dearborn Wolves, Dearborn, MI 48128; 313-593-5000; www.umd.umich.edu; no football program
- University of Northwestern Ohio Racers, Lima, OH 45805; 419-998-3120; www.unoh.edu; no football program

National Christian College Athletic Association (NCCAA)

National Christian College Athletic Association

302 West Washington Street, Greenville, SC 29601; 864-250-1199; Fax: 864-250-1141; Email: info@thenccaa.org; Web site: http://www.thenccaa.org; http://www.nccaa.org

The National Christian College Athletic Association (NCCAA) is an association of Christian universities, colleges, and Bible colleges in the United States and Canada. As of this writing, the schools are divided into Division I (seven regions [Central, East, Mid-East, Midwest, North-Central, South, and West] with a total of 64 schools) and Division II (eight regions [Central, East, Mid-East, Midwest, North-Central, South, Southwest, and West] with a total of 40 schools). Some of the schools play football, while others do not.

Division I is made up predominantly four-year Christian liberal arts universities and colleges, while Division II is made up predominantly of Bible colleges and smaller four-year Christian colleges.

The NCCAA was formed in 1968 in Canton, Ohio, during a meeting at Malone College to provide a place for athletic competition for Christian Colleges around the nation. While originally in Chattanooga, Tennessee, the headquarters has moved several times as its membership list of schools grew. Membership into the NCCAA is not exclusive and many schools belong to other conference also compete athletically in the National Christian College Athletic Association, the National Association of Intercollegiate Athletics, and/or the National Collegiate Athletic Association.

In order to be accepted by the NCCAA, a school has to be a Christian-based learning institution and must offer Christian degrees for its students.

The NCCAA, itself, does not sponsor a football program, although many of its schools do play football in other conferences.

Division I Schools

- Arizona Christian University Firestorm (formerly known as Southwestern College) (West Region), Phoenix, AZ 85032; 602-489-5300; www.arizonachristian.edu; no football program
- Asbury University Eagles (Mid-East Region), Wilmore, KY 40390; 859-858-3511; www.asbury. edu; no football program
- Azusa Pacific University Cougars (West Region), Azusa, CA 91702; 626-969-3434; www.apu. edu; plays football as an independent team
- Baptist College of Florida Eagles (South Region), Graceville, FL 32440; 800-328-2660; www. baptistcollege.edu; no football program
- Bethel College Pilots (Midwest Region), Mishawaka, IN 46545; 574-807-7000; www.bethelcollege.edu; no football program
- Bethesda Christian University Flames (West Region), Anaheim, CA 92801; 714-517-1945; www.bcu. edu; no football program
- Bluefield College Rams (Mid-East Region), Bluefield, VA 24605; 800-872-0176; www.bluefield.edu; plays football in the Mid-South Conference (NAIA)
- California Baptist University Lancers (West Region), Riverside, CA 925041; 877-228; www. calbaptist. edu; no football program
- Campbellsville University Tigers (Mid-East Region), Campbellsville, KY 42718; 270-789-5000; www.campbellsville.edu; plays football in the Mid-South Conference (NAIA)

- Carver (Bible) College Cougars (South Region), Atlanta, GA 30331; 404-527-4520; www.carver.edu; no football program
- Cedarville University Yellow Jackets (Midwest Region), Cedarville, OH 45314; 937-766-7700; www.cedarville.edu; no football program
- Central Baptist College Mustangs (Central Region), Conway, AR 72034; 501-329-6872; www.cbc.edu; no football program
- Central Christian College of Kansas Tigers (Central Region), McPherson, KS 67460; 620-241-0723; www.centralchristian.edu; no football program
- Chowan University Hawks (South Region), Murfreesboro, NC 27855; 252-398-6500; www.chowan.edu; plays football in the Central Intercollegiate Athletic Association (NCAA Division II)
- Cincinnati Christian University Eagles (Midwest Region), Cincinnati, OH 45204; 513-244-8100; www.ccuniversity.edu; no football program
- Colorado Christian University Cougars (Central Region), Lakewood, CO 80226; 303-963-3000; www.ccu.edu; no football program
- Corban University Warriors (West Region), Salem, OR 97317; 503-581-8600; www.corban.edui; no football program
- Covenant College Scots (Mid-East Region), Lookout Mountain, GA 30750; 706-820-1560; www.covenant.edu; no football program
- Crowley's Ridge College Pioneers (Central Region), Paragould, AR 72450; 870-236-6901; www.crc.edu; no football program
- Dallas Baptist University Patriots (Central Region), Dallas, TX 75211; 214-333-5360; www.dbu.edu; no football program
- Ecclesia College Royals (Central Region) Royals, Springdale, AR, 72762; 479-248-7236; www.ecollege.edu; no football program
- Emmanuel College Lions South Region), Franklin Springs, GA 30639; 800-860-8800; www.ec.edu; no football program
- Geneva College Golden Tornadoes (East Region), Beaver Falls, PA 15010; 800-847-8255; www.geneva.edu; plays football in the Presidents' Athletic Conference (NCAA Division III)
- Grace College & Theological Seminary Lancers (Midwest Region), Winona Lake, IN 46590; 574-372-5100; www.grace.edu; no football program
- Greenville College Panthers (North-Central Region), Greenville, IL 62246; 618-664-2800; www.greenville.edu; plays football in the Upper Midwest Athletic Conference (NCAA Division III)
- Hiwassee College Tigers (Mid-East Region), Madisonville, TN 37354; 800-356-2187; www.hiwassee.edu; no football program
- Hope International University Royals (West Region), Fullerton, CA 92831; 714-879-3901; www.hiu.edu; no football program
- Houghton College Highlanders (East Region), Houghton, NY 14744; 800-777-2556; www.houghton.edu; no football program
- Huntington University Foresters (Midwest Region, Associate Member), Huntington, IN 46750; 260-356-6000; www.huntington.edu; no football program
- Indiana Wesleyan University Wildcats (Midwest Region), Marion, IN 46953; 765-674-6901; www.indwes.edu; no football program
- Judson University Eagles (North-Central Region), Elgin, IL 60123; 847-628-2500; www.judsonu.edu; no football program
- Malone University Pioneers (East Region), Canton OH 44709; 800-521-1146; www.malone.edu; plays football in the Mid-States Football Association (Mideast League) (NAIA)
- Mid-America Christian University Evangels (Central Region), Oklahoma City, OK 73170; 405-691-3800; www.macu.edu; no football program
- Mid-Continent University (Mid-East Region), Mayfield, KY 42066; 270-247-8521; www.midcontinent.edu; no football program
- Mount Vernon Nazarene Cougars University (East Region), Mount Vernon, Ohio, 43050; 740-392-6868; www.mvnu.edu; no football program
- New Hope Christian College Deacons (West Region), Eugene, OR 97405; 541-485-1780; www.newhope.edu; no football program

- North Greenville University Crusaders (South Region), Tigerville, SC 29688; 864-977-7000; www.ngu.edu; plays football as an independent team
- Northwestern College Eagles (North-Central Region), St. Paul, MN 55113; 651-631-5100; www.nwc.edu; plays football in the Upper Midwest Athletic Conference (NCAA Division III)
- Nyack College and Alliance Theological Seminary Warriors (East Region), Nyack, NY 10960; 845-358-1710; www.nyack.edu; no football program
- Oakland City University Oaks (Mid-East Region), Oakland City, IN 47660; 800-737-5125; www.oak.edu; mo football program
- Oklahoma Wesleyan University Eagles (Central Region), Bartlesville, OK 74006; 918-335-6200; www.okwu.edu; no football program
- Olivet Nazarene University Tigers (North-Central Region), Bourbonnais, IL 60914; 815-939-5011; www.olivet.edu; plays football in the Mid-States Football Association (Midwest League) (NAIA)
- Palm Beach Atlantic University Sailfish (South Region), West Palm Beach, FL 33401; 888-468-6722; www.pba.edu; no football program
- Pensacola Christian College Eagles (South Region), Pensacola, FL 32523; 850-478-8496; www.pcci.edu; no football program
- Point Loma Nazarene University Sea Lions (West Region, Associate Member), San Diego, CA 92106; 619-849-2200; www.pointloma.edu; no football program
- Point University Chargers (South Region), East Point, GA 30344; 404-761-8861; http://point.edu; plays football as an independent team
- Roberts Wesleyan College Raiders (East Region), Rochester, NY 14624; 800-777-4792; www.roberts.edu; no football program
- San Diego Christian College Hawks (West Region), El Cajon, CA 92019; 619-201-8700; http://sdcc.edu; no football program
- Simpson University Red Hawks (West Region), Redding, CA 96003; 530-224-5600; www.simpson.edu; no football program
- Southeastern University Fire (South Region), Lakeland, FL 33801; 863-667-5000; www.seu.edu; no football program
- Southern Wesleyan University Warriors (South Region), Central, SC 29630; 864-644-5000; www.swu.edu; no football program
- Southwestern Assemblies of God University Lions (Central Region), Waxahachie, TX 75165; 888-937-7248; www.sagu.edu; plays football in the Central States Football League (NAIA)
- Southwestern Christian University Eagles (Central Region), Bethany, OK 73008; 405-789-7661; www.swcu.edu; no football program
- Spring Arbor University Cougars (Midwest Region), Spring Arbor, MI 49283; 800-968-9103; www.arbor.edu; no football program
- Taylor University Trojans (Midwest Region, Associate Member), Upland, IN 46989; 800-882-3456; www.taylor.edu; plays football in the Mid-States Football Association (Mideast League) (NAIA)
- Tennessee Temple University Crusaders (Mid-East Region), Chattanooga, TN 37404; 800-553-4050; www.tntemple.edu; no football program
- The Master's College for Christ and Scripture Mustangs (West Region), Santa Clarita, California 91321; 800-568-6248; www.masters.edu; no football program
- Trevecca Nazarene University Trojans (Mid-East Region), Nashville, TN 37210; 615-248-1200; www.trevecca.edu; no football program
- Trinity Christian College Trolls (North-Central Region), Palos Heights, IL 60463; 866-874-6463; www.trinity.edu; no football program
- Trinity International University Trojans (North-Central Region), Deerfield, IL 60015; 800-822-3225; www.tiu.edu; plays football in the Mid-States Football Association (Midwest League) (NAIA)
- Trinity Lutheran College Eagles (West Region), Everett, WA 98201; 800-843-5659; www.tlc.edu; no football program
- Truett-McConnell College Bears (South Region), Cleveland, GA 30528; 706-865-2134; www.truett.edu; no football program
- Victory University Eagles (Mid-East Region), Memphis, TN 38111; 800-960-9777; www.victory.edu; no football program

- York College Panthers (Central Region), York, NE 68467; 800-950-9675; www.york.edu; no football program

Division II Schools

- Appalachian Bible College Warriors (Mid-East Region), Mount Hope WV 25880; 304-877-6428; www.abc.edu; no football program
- Arlington Baptist College Patriots (Southwest Region), Arlington, TX 76012; 817-461-8741; www.abconline.edu; no football program
- Baptist Bible College Patriots (MO) (Central Region), Springfield, MO 65803; 800-228-5754; www.gobbc.edu; no football program
- Baptist Bible College & Seminary Defenders (PA) (East Region), Clarks Summit, PA 18411; 570-586-2400; www.bbc.edu; no football program
- Boyce College Bulldogs (Mid-East Region), Louisville, KY 40280; 800-626-5525; www.boycecollege.com; no football program
- Central Bible College Spartans (Central Region), Springfield, MO 65803; 800-831-4222; www.cbcag.edu; no football program
- Central Christian College of the Bible Saints (Central Region, Associate Member), Moberly, MO 65270; 660-263-3900; www.cccb.edu; no football program
- Clearwater Christian College Cougars (South Region), Clearwater, FL 33759; 727-726-1153; www.clearwater.edu; no football program
- Dallas Christian College Crusaders (Southwest Region), Dallas, TX 75234; 972-241-3371; www.dallas.edu; no football program
- Emmaus Bible College Eagles (Midwest Region), Dubuque, IA 52001; 563-588-8000; www.emmaus.edu; no football program
- Faith Baptist Bible College Eagles (North-Central Region), Ankeny, IA 50023; 515-964-0601; www.faith.edu; no football program
- Florida Christian College Suns (South Region), Kissimmee FL 34744; 407-847-8966; www.fcc.edu; no football program
- Free Will Baptist Bible College Flames (Mid-East Region), Nashville, TN 37205; 615-844-5000; www.fwbbc.edu; no football program
- Grace Bible College Tigers (Midwest Region), Grand Rapids, MI 49509; 616-538-2330; www.gbcol.edu; no football program
- Grace University Royals (Central Region), Omaha NE 68108; 402-449-2800; www.graceuniversity.edu; no football program
- Great Lakes Christian College Crusaders (Midwest Region), Lansing, MI 48917; 517-321-0242; www.glcc.edu; no football program
- Hillsdale Free Will Baptist College Saints (Southwest Region), Moore, OK 73160; 405-912-9000; www.hc.edu; no football program
- Johnson University Preachers (Mid-East Region), Knoxville, TN 37998; 865-573-4517; www.johnsonu.edu; no football program
- Kentucky Christian University Knights (Mid-East Region), Grayson, KY 41143; 800-522-3181; www.kcu.edu; plays football in the Mid-South Conference (NAIA)
- Kuyper College Cougars (Midwest Region), Grand Rapids, MI 49525; 616-222-3000; www.kuyper.edu; no football program
- Lancaster Bible College Chargers (East Region), Lancaster, PA 17601; 717-569-7071; www.lbc.edu; no football program
- Lincoln Christian University Red Lions (Midwest Region), Lincoln IL 62656; 888-522-5228; www.lincolnchristian.edu; no football program
- Manhattan Christian College Crusdaers (Central Region), Manhattan, KS 66502; 785-539-3571; www.mccks.edu; no football program
- Maranatha Baptist Bible College Crusaders (Midwest Region), Watertown, WI 53094; 920-261-9300; www.mbbc.edu; plays football in the Northern Athletics Conference (NCAA Division III)
- Moody Bible Institute Archers (Midwest Region), Chicago, IL 60610; 800-967-4624; www.moody.edu; no football program

- Multnomah University Lions (West Region), Portland, OR 97220; 503-255-0332; www.multnomah.edu; no football program
- North Central University Rams (North-Central Region), Minneapolis MN 55404; 612-343-4400; www.northcentral.edu; no football program
- Northland International University Pioneers (Midwest Region), Dunbar, WI 54119; 715-324-6900; www.ni.edu; no football program
- Ohio Christian University Trailblazers (Mid-East Region), Circleville, OH 43113; 877-762-8669; www.ohiochristian.edu; no football program
- Ozark Christian College Ambassadors (Southwest Region), Joplin, MO 64801; 417-626-1234; www.occ.edu; no football program
- Philadelphia Biblical University Crimson Eagles (East Region), Langhorne, PA 19047; 215-752-5800; http://pbu.edu; no football program
- Piedmont Baptist College Conquerors (South Region), Winston-Salem, NC 27101; 336-725-8344; www.pbc.edu; no football program
- Portland Bible College Wildcats (West Region), Portland, OR 97220; 503-255-3540; www.portlandbiblecollege.org; no college program
- Providence University College Freemen (North-Central Region), Otterburne, Manitoba, Canada, R0A 1G0; 204-433-7488; www.providencecollege.ca; no football program
- The Crown College of the Bible Royal Crusaders (TN) (Mid-East Region), Powell, TN 37849; 865-938-8186; www.thecrowncollege.com; no football program
- Toccoa Falls College Eagles (South Region), Toccoa Falls, GA 30598; 706-886-6831; www.tfc.edu; no football program
- Trinity Bible College Lions (North-Central Region), Ellendale, ND 58436; 800-523-1603; www.trinitibiblecollege.edu; plays football as an independent team
- Trinity College of Florida Tigers (South Region), Trinity, FL 34655; 727-376-6911; www.trinitycollege.edu; no football program
- Valley Forge Christian College Patriots (East Region), Phoenixville, PA 19460; 610-935-0450; www.vfcc.edu; no football program
- West Coast Baptist College Eagles (West Region), Lancaster, CA 93535; 888-694-9222; www.wcbc.edu; no football program

Community College/Junior College Football Conferences

This section contains a comprehensive listing of community colleges and junior colleges. There is no single-source national "football" authority for these schools and no single "national champion." There are three main organizations listed in this section (California Community College Athletic Association, National Junior College Athletic Association, and the Northwest Athletic Association of Community Colleges) and a group of other non-affiliated collegiate sports organizations. The largest, by far, of the community college and junior college groups is the National Junior College Athletic Association, which consists of 24 separate regions, representing 512 schools.

The conferences listed in this section include:

- California Community College Athletic Association
- National Junior College Athletic Association
- Northwest Athletic Association of Community Colleges

California Community College Athletic Association (CCCAA)

(Commission on Athletics): 2017 O Street, Sacramento, CA 95814; Telephone: 916-444-1600; Fax: 916-444-2616; Web site: http://www.coasports. org

The California Community College Athletic Association consists of 10 conferences and one Wrestling Alliance (which covers both Northern California and Southern California). The Commission on Athletics, authorized by the California State Legislature, regulates and administers the CCCAA's conferences and athletes. The COA was founded in 1929 as the California Junior College Federation and united the Southern California, Northern California Junior College, and Central California Athletic Association.

While the CCCAA has 10 conferences (and the non-football Wrestling Alliance), its football program is divided into 12 conferences (six each in northern and southern California, further divided into three Divisions [North, Central, South] for northern California and [National, American, Central] for southern California. Thus, while a school may belong to one conference for all other sports, it may play in another conference completely for football. The teams in northern California play in the Northern California Football Association, while the teams in southern California play in the Southern California Football Association. Additionally, individual schools may play difference sports in more than one conference.

California Community College Athletic Association Football State Champions

Year	*School*
1946	Compton Community College (Compton)
1947	Chaffey College (Glendora)
1948	Compton Community College (Compton)
1949	Santa Ana College (Santa Ana)
1950	Long Beach City College (Long Beach)
1951	Pasadena City College (Pasadena)
1952	Hartnell College (Salinas)
1953	Bakersfield College (Bakersfield)
1954	El Camino College (Torrance)
1955	Compton Community College (Compton)
1956	Compton Community College (Compton)
1957	Cerritos College (Norwalk)
1958	Santa Monica College (Santa Monica)
1959	Bakersfield College (Bakersfield)
1960	Long Beach City College (Long Beach)
1961	Bakersfield College (Bakersfield)

Year	School
1962	Santa Ana College (Santa Ana)
1963	Orange Coast College (Costa Mesa)
1964	Long Beach City College (Long Beach)
1965	Fullerton College (Fullerton)
1966	Pasadena City College (Pasadena)
1967	Fullerton College (Fullerton)
1968	Fresno City College (Fresno)
1969	Fresno City College (Fresno)
1970	College of the Sequoias (Visalia)
1971	El Camino College (Torrance)
1972	Fresno City College (Fresno)
1973	Fresno City College (Fresno)
1973	Los Angeles City College (Los Angeles)
1974	East Los Angeles College (Monterey Park)
1975	Orange Coast College (Costa Mesa)
1976	Bakersfield College (Bakersfield)
1977	Pasadena City College (Pasadena)
1978	Santa Rosa Junior College (Santa Rosa)
1979	De Anza College (Cupertino)
1980	Modesto Junior College (Modesto)
1981	Sacramento City College (Sacramento)
1982	Taft College (Taft)
1983	Fullerton College (Fullerton)
1984	Taft College (Taft)
1985	Saddleback College (Mission Viejo)
1986	San Jose City College (San Jose)
1987	El Camino College (Torrance)
1988	Bakersfield College (Bakersfield)
1989	Riverside Community College (Riverside)
1990	Taft College (Taft)
1991	Palomar College (San Marcos)
1992	Saddleback College (Mission Viejo)
1993	Palomar College (San Marcos)
1994	City College of San Francisco (San Francisco)
1995	Long Beach City College (Long Beach)
1996	Saddleback College (Mission Viejo)
1997	Mount San Antonio College (Walnut)
1998	Palomar College (San Marcos)
1999	City College of San Francisco (San Francisco)
2000	City College of San Francisco (San Francisco)
2001	City College of San Francisco (San Francisco)
2002	Reedley College (Reedley)
2003	City College of San Francisco (San Francisco)
2004	College of the Canyons (Santa Clarita)
2005	Grossmont College (El Cajon)
2006	El Camino College (Torrance)
2007	City College of San Francisco (San Francisco)
2008	Butte College (Oroville)
2009	Mount San Antonio College (Walnut)
2010	Mount San Antonio College (Walnut)

California Community College Athletic Association Football Coach of the Year (Statewide & by Region)

Year	Region	Coach	School
2000	Statewide	George Rush	City College of San Francisco (San Francisco)
2000	Region I	Dave Banducci	College of the Redwoods (Eureka)
2000	Region II	Tony Caviglia	Fresno Junior College (Fresno)
2000	Region III	Dave Jordan	Grossmont College (El Cajon)
2000	Region IV	No Information	
2001	No Information		
2002	Statewide	Michael White	Reedley College (Reedley)
2002	Region I	Craig Rigsbee	Butte College (Oroville)
2002	Region II	Michael White	Reedley College (Reedley)
2002	Region III	Jim Bittner	Moorpark College (Moorpark)
2002	Region IV	Larry Reisbig	Long Beach City College (Long Beach)
2003	Statewide	George Rush	City College of San Francisco (San Francisco)
2003	Region I	George Rush	City College of San Francisco (San Francisco)
2003	Region I	Keith Simmons	Santa Rosa Junior College (Santa Rosa)
2003	Region I	Jeff Tisdel	Sierra College (Rocklin)
2003	Region II	Michael White	Reedley College (Reedley)
2003	Region III	Dave Jordan	Grossmont College (El Cajon)
2003	Region IV	Gene Murphy	Fullerton College (Fullerton)
2004	No Information		
2005	Statewide	Dave Jordan	Grossmont College (El Cajon)
2005	Region I	Don Dillon	American River College (Sacramento)
2005	Region I	George Rush	City College of San Francisco (San Francisco)
2005	Region II	Stan Peters	Laney College (Oakland)
2005	Region III	John Cicuto	Glendale Community College (Glendale)

Year	Region	Coach	School
2005	Region IV	John Featherstone	El Camino College (Torrance)
2006	Statewide	John Featherstone	El Camino College (Torrance)
2006	Region I	Marshall Sperbeck	Foothill College (Los Altos Hills)
2006	Region II	Ralph De Pew	Diablo Valley College (Pleasant Hill)
2006	Region III	Jeff Chudy	Bakersfield College (Bakersfield)
2006	Region IV	Mark McElroy	Saddleback College (Mission Viejo)
2007	Statewide	George Rush	City College of San Francisco (San Francisco)
2007	Region I	Jay Uchiumi	Laney College (Oakland)
2007	Region II	Jeff Tisdel	Sierra College (Rocklin)
2007	Region III	Jeff Chudy	Bakersfield College (Bakersfield)
2007	Region IV	John Featherstone	El Camino College (Torrance)
2008	Statewide	Jeff Jordan	Butte College (Oroville)
2008	Region I	Jeff Jordan	Butte College (Oroville)
2008	Region II	Mike Rasmussen	Monterey Peninsula College (Monterey)
2008	Region III	Bob Jastrab	Mount San Antonio College (Walnut)
2008	Region IV	Matt Koffler	San Diego Mesa College (San Diego)
2009	Statewide	Bob Jastrab	Mount San Antonio College (Walnut)
2009	Region I	Bret Pollack	College of San Mateo (San Mateo)
2009	Region II	Dan Atencio	De Anza College (Cupertino)
2009	Region III	Bob Jastrab	Mount San Antonio College (Walnut)
2009	Region IV	George Swade	Los Angeles Harbor College (Wilmington)
2010	Statewide	Bob Jastrah	Mount San Antonio College (Walnut)
2010	Region I	George Rush	City College of San Francisco (San Francisco)
2010	Region II	Jerry Haflich	American River College (Sacramento)
2010	Region III	Floyd Burnsed	Solano Community College (Fairfield)
2010	Region IV	Bob Jastrah	Mount San Antonio College (Walnut)
2010	Region V	Tom Craft	Riverside Community College (Riverside)
2010	Region VI	Kevin Emerson	San Bernardino Valley College (San Bernardino)

California Community College Athletic Association Offensive Player of the Year (Statewide & by Region)

Year	Region	Player	Position	Class	School
2000	Statewide	Robert Hodge	Quarterback	Sophomore	El Camino College (Torrance)
2000	Region I	Marty Johnson	Running Back	Sophomore	Butte College (Oroville)
2000	Region II	Grant Mattos	Wide Receiver	Sophomore	Foothill College (Los Altos Hills)
2000	Region III	Clint Womack	Quarterback	Sophomore	Grossmont College (El Cajon)
2000	Region IV	Robert Hodge	Quarterback	Sophomore	El Camino College (Torrance)
2001	No Information				
2002	Statewide	Kyle Bauer	Quarterback	Sophomore	College of the Canyons (Santa Clarita)
2002	Region I	Aaron Rodgers	Quarterback	Sophomore	Butte College (Oroville)
2002	Region II	Robert Johnson	Quarterback	Freshman	Reedley College (Reedley)
2002	Region III	Kyle Bauer	Quarterback	Sophomore	College of the Canyons (Santa Clarita)
2002	Region IV	Craig Richardson	Running Back	Sophomore	Long Beach City College (Long Beach)
2003		Tim Brown	Running Back		City College of San Francisco (San Francisco)
2003	Region I	Tim Brown	Running Back		City College of San Francisco (San Francisco)
2003	Region II	Robert Johnson			Reedley College (Reedley)
2003	Region III	Todd Watkins			Grossmont College (El Cajon)
2003	Region IV	Delanie Walker			Mount San Antonio College (Walnut)
2004	No Information				
2005		Derrell Hutsona	Kick Returner	Freshman	Grossmont College (El Cajon)

Year	*Region*	*Player*	*Position*	*Class*	*School*
2005		Brent Schaeffer	Quarterback	Sophomore	College of the Sequoias (Visalia)
2005	Region I	Julian Edelman	Quarterback	Freshman	College of San Mateo (San Mateo)
2005	Region II	Brent Schaeffer	Quarterback	Sophomore	College of the Sequoias (Visalia)
2005	Region III	Derrell Hutsona	Kick Returner	Freshman	Grossmont College (El Cajon)
2005	Region IV	Brian Flowers	Running Back	Sophomore	El Camino College (Torrance)
2006		Schneider Julien	Wide Receiver	Sophomore	Foothill College (Los Altos Hills)
2006		Tyler Lorensen	Quarterback	Sophomore	Palomar College (San Marcos)
2006	Region I	Schneider Julien	Wide Receiver	Sophomore	Foothill College (Los Altos Hills)
2006	Region II	Tavares Pressley	Running Back	Freshman	Monterey Peninsula College (Monterey)
2006	Region III	Terence Scott	Wide Receiver	Sophomore	College of the Canyons (Santa Clarita)
2006	Region IV	Tyler Lorenzen	Quarterback	Sophomore	Palomar College (San Marcos)
2007		Kevin Craft	Quarterback	Sophomore	Mount San Antonio College (Walnut)
2007	Region I	Jeremiah Masoli	Quarterback	Freshman	City College of San Francisco (San Francisco)
2007	Region II	Lamon Muldrow	Running Back	Freshman	Sierra College (Rocklin)
2007	Region III	Jacob Bower	Quarterback	Freshman	Bakersfield College (Bakersfield)
2007	Region IV	Kevin Craft	Quarterback	Sophomore	Mount San Antonio College (Walnut)
2008		Adam Froman	Quarterback	Sophomore	Santa Rosa Junior College (Santa Rosa)
2008	Region I	Adam Froman	Quarterback	Sophomore	Santa Rosa Junior College (Santa Rosa)
2008	Region II	Lamon Muldrow	Running Back	Sophomore	Sierra College (Rocklin)
2008	Region III	Nick Lamaison	Quarterback	Freshman	Mount San Antonio College (Walnut)
2008	Region IV	Dominic Blood	Running Back	Sophomore	Antelope Valley College (Lancaster)
2008	Region IV	Bret Visciglia	Quarterback	Freshman	Los Angeles Valley College (Valley Glen)
2009		Dominique Blackman	Quarterback	Freshman	Los Angeles Harbor College (Wilmington)
2009	Region I	Darius Bell	Quarterback	Freshman	City College of San Francisco (San Francisco)
2009	Region II	Thomas Hampton	Running Back	Sophomore	Los Medanos College (Pittsburg)
2009	Region III	Matt Faulkner	Quarterback	Sophomore	Mount San Antonio College (Walnut)
2009	Region IV	Dominque Blackman	Quarterback	Freshman	Los Angeles Harbor College (Wilmington)
2010		Steele Jantz	Quarterback	Sophomore	City College of San Francisco (San Francisco)
2010		Nick Lamaison	Quarterback	Sophomore	Mount San Antonio College (Walnut)
2010	Region I	Steele Jantz	Quarterback	Sophomore	City College of San Francisco (San Francisco)
2010	Region II	Jeremiah Oates	Wide Receiver	Sophomore	Sacramento City College (Sacramento)
2010	Region III	Boy Humphrey	Quarterback	Sophomore	Solano Community College (Fairfield)
2010	Region IV	Nick Lamaison	Quarterback	Sophomore	Mount San Antonio College (Walnut)

Year	Region	Player	Position	Class	School
2010	Region V	Dalton Livingston	Quarterback	Freshman	Riverside Community College (Riverside)
2010	Region VI	Kristin James			San Bernardino Valley College (San Bernardino)

California Community College Athletic Association Defensive Player of the Year (Statewide & by Region)

Year	Region	Player	Position	Class	School
2000		Kai Ellis	Linebacker	Sophomore	City College of San Francisco (San Francisco)
2000	Region I	Ricky Sailor	Defensive Back	Sophomore	Butte College (Oroville)
2000	Region II	Kai Ellis	Linebacker	Sophomore	City College of San Francisco (San Francisco)
2000	Region III	Isaac Sopoaga	Defensive Lineman	Sophomore	College of the Canyons (Santa Clarita)
2000	Region IV	No Information			
2001	No Information				
2002		Donyell Booker	Defensive Lineman	Sophomore	Reedley College (Reedley)
2002	Region I	Joe Maningo	Linebacker	Sophomore	Foothill College (Los Altos Hills)
2002	Region II	Donyell Booker	Defensive Lineman	Sophomore	Reedley College (Reedley)
2002	Region III	Will Poole	Defensive Back	Sophomore	Ventura College (Ventura)
2002	Region IV	Andrew PaoPao	Defensive Lineman	Sophomore	Palomar College (San Marcos)
2003		Scott Ware	Safety		Santa Rosa Junior College (Santa Rosa)
2003	Region I	Scott Ware	Safety		Santa Rosa Junior College (Santa Rosa)
2003	Region II	Matt Swan			Laney College (Oakland)
2003	Region III	Dan Catalano			Grossmont College (El Cajon)
2003	Region IV	Josh Hargis			Palomar College (San Marcos)
2004	No Information				
2005		Larry Grant	Linebacker	Sophomore	City College of San Francisco (San Francisco)
2005	Region I	Larry Grant	Linebacker	Sophomore	City College of San Francisco (San Francisco)
2005	Region II	Ervin Baldwin	Defensive Lineman	Sophomore	Reedley College (Reedley)
2005	Region III	David Tahi	Linebacker	Sophomore	Chaffey College (Rancho Cucamonga)
2005	Region IV	Jeff Benjamin	Defensive Lineman	Sophomore	Riverside Community College (Riverside)
2006		Devin Bishop	Linebacker	Sophomore	City College of San Francisco (San Francisco)
2006		Woodney Turrene	Defensive Back	Sophomore	College of the Sequoias (Visalia)
2006	Region I	Devin Bishop	Linebacker	Sophomore	City College of San Francisco (San Francisco)
2006	Region II	Woodney Turrene	Defensive Back	Sophomore	College of the Sequoias (Visalia)
2006	Region III	Justin Halas	Linebacker	Sophomore	Victor Valley College (Victorville)
2006	Region IV	Vuna Tuihalamaka	Linebacker	Sophomore	El Camino College (Torrance)
2007		Grant Valentine	Defensive Lineman	Sophomore	Glendale Community College (Glendale)
2007	Region I	Albertson Alexandre	Defensive Lineman	Freshman	Foothill College (Los Altos Hills)

Year	*Region*	*Player*	*Position*	*Class*	*School*
2007	Region II	Caleb Hale	Linebacker	Sophomore	Fresno City College (Fresno)
2007	Region III	Grant Valentine	Defensive Lineman	Sophomore	Bakersfield College (Bakersfield)
2007	Region IV	Bernard Afutitti	Defensive Lineman	Sophomore	Mount San Antonio College (Walnut)
2008		Brandon Rankin	Defensive Lineman	Sophomore	Butte College (Oroville)
2008	Region I	Brandon Rankin	Defensive Lineman	Sophomore	Butte College (Oroville)
2008	Region II	Bryson Littlejohn	Linebacker	Sophomore	Sierra College (Rocklin)
2008	Region III	Marquise Jackson	Defensive Lineman	Freshman	College of the Canyons (Santa Clarita)
2008	Region IV	Troy Butler	Defensive Back	Sophomore	Antelope Valley College (Lancaster)
2009		Eddie Elder	Defensive Back	Sophomore	College of San Mateo (San Mateo)
2009	Region I	Eddie Elder	Defensive Back	Sophomore	College of San Mateo (San Mateo)
2009	Region II	Dontea Smith	Defensive Back	Sophomore	Reedley College (Reedley)
2009	Region III	Bruce Irvin	Linebacker	Sophomore	Mount San Antonio College (Walnut)
2009	Region IV	Clarence Laster	Defensive Back	Sophomore	Mt. San Jacinto College (San Jacinto)
2010		Bojay Fillimoeaeu	Defensive Lineman	Sophomore	Mount San Antonio College (Walnut)
2010	Region I	Sua Tuala	Linebacker	Sophomore	City College of San Francisco (San Francisco)
2010	Region II	Colton Russi	Linebacker	Sophomore	American River College (Sacramento)
2010	Region III	Kiero Small	Linebacker	Sophomore	Hartnell College (Salinas)
2010	Region IV	Bojay Fillimoeaeu	Defensive Lineman	Sophomore	Mount San Antonio College (Walnut)
2010	Region V	Ryan Hofmeister	Linebacker	Freshman	Riverside Community College (Riverside)
2010	Region VI	Josh Fely	Linebacker	Sophomore	San Diego Mesa College (San Diego)

As of this writing, the conferences within the CCCAA include:

- Bay Valley Conference
- Big Eight Conference
- Central Valley Conference
- Coast Conference
- Foothill Athletic Conference
- Golden Valley Conference
- Orange Empire Conference
- Pacific Coast Athletic Conference
- South Coast Conference
- Western State Conference
- Wrestling Alliance (non-football conference)

Bay Valley Conference

(Shirley Baskin, Commissioner); Los Medanos College, 2700 East Leland Road, Pittsburg, CA 94565; Telephone: 925-439-2181 x3211; Fax: 925-439-4613; Email: sbaskin@losmedanos.edu. The Big Valley Conference currently has 17 schools, 12 of which support football programs.

- American River College Beavers, Sacramento, CA 95841; 916-484-8011; www.arc.losrios.edu; plays football in the Northern California Football Association (Central Division–Mid-Empire Conference)

- College of Alameda Cougars, Alameda, CA 94501; 510-522-7221; http://alameda.peralta.edu; no football program
- College of Marin Mariners, Kentfield, CA 94904; 415-457-8811; www.marin.edu; no football program
- Cosumnes River College Hawks, Sacramento, CA 95823; 916-691-7344; www.crc.losrios.edu; no football program
- Contra Costa College Comets, San Pablo, CA 510-235-7800; www.contracosta.edu; plays football in the Norhtern California Football Association (South Division–Bay Valley Conference)
- Diablo Valley College Vikings, Pleasant Hill, CA 94523; 925-685-1230; www.dvc.edu; plays football in the Northern California Football Association (Central Division–Golden Gate Conference)
- Laney College Eagles, Oakland, CA 94607; 510-834-5740; www.laney.edu; plays football in the Northern California Football Association (North Division–NorCal Conference)
- Los Medanos College Mustangs, Pittsburg, CA 94565; 925-439-2181; www.losmedanos.edu; plays football in the Northern California Football Association (Central Division–Golden Gate Conference)
- Mendocino College Eagles, Ukiah, CA 95482; 707-468-3000; www.mendocino.edu; plays football in the Northern California Football Association (Central Division–Mid-Empire Conference)
- Merritt College Thunderbirds, Oakland, CA 94619; 510-531-4911; no football program
- Napa Valley College Storm, Napa, CA 94558; 707-253-3000; www.napavalley.edu; no football program
- Sacramento City College Panthers, Sacramento, CA 95822; 916-558-2111; www.scc.losrios.edu; plays football in the Northern California Football Association (Central Division–Mid-Empire Conference)
- San Joaquin Delta College Mustangs, Stockton, CA 95207; 209-954-5151; www.deltacollege.edu; plays football in the Northern California Football Association (North Division–Central Valley Conference)
- Santa Rosa Junior College Bear Cubs, Santa Rosa, CA 95401; 707-527-4011; www.santarosa.edu; plays football in the Northern California Football Association (North Division–NorCal Conference)
- Sierra College Wolverines, Rocklin, CA 95677; 916-624-3333; www.sierracollege.edu; plays football in the Northern California Football Association (North Division–Central Valley Conference)
- Solano Community College Falcons, Fairfield, CA 94534; 707-864-7000; www.solano.edu; plays football in the Northern California Football Association (South Division–Bay Valley Conference)
- Yuba College 49ers, Marysville, CA 95901; 530-741-6700; http://yc.yccd.edu; plays football in the Northern California Football Association (South Division–Bay Valley Conference)

Big Eight Conference

(Mike Liddell, Commissioner); Chico, CA; Telephone: 530-321-0198; Fax: 530-343-7842; Email: liddellm@sbcglobal.net. The Big Eight Conference currently has eight schools, seven of which support football programs.

- American River College Beavers, Sacramento, CA 95841; 916-484-8011; www.arc.losrios.edu; plays football in the Northern California Football Association (Central Division–Mid-Empire Conference)
- Cosumnes River College Hawks, Sacramento, CA 95823; 916-691-7344; www.crc.losrios.edu; no football program
- Diablo Valley College Vikings, Pleasant Hill, CA 94523; 925-685-1230; www.dvc.edu; plays football in the Northern California Football Association (Central Division–Golden Gate Conference)
- Modesto Junior College Pirates, Modesto, CA 95350; 209-575-6550; www.mjc.edu; plays football in the Northern California Football Association (North Division–Central Valley Conference)
- Sacramento City College Panthers, Sacramento, CA 95822; 916-558-2111; www.scc.losrios.edu; plays football in the Northern California Football Association (Central Division–Mid-Empire Conference)
- San Joaquin Delta College Mustangs, Stockton, CA 95207; 209-954-5151; www.deltacollege.edu; plays football in the Northern California Football Association (North Division–Central Valley Conference)
- Santa Rosa Junior College Bear Cubs, Santa Rosa, CA 95401; 707-527-4011; www.santarosa.edu; plays football in the Northern California Football Association (North Division–NorCal Conference)
- Sierra College Wolverines, Rocklin, CA 95677; 916-624-3333; www.sierracollege.edu; plays football in the Northern California Football Association (North Division–Central Valley Conference)

Central Valley Conference

(Logan McKechnie, Commissioner); Merced, CA; Telephone: 209-722-9911; Fax: 209-722-8822; Email: lmckech@aol.com. The Central Valley Conference currently has 10 schools, six of which support football programs.

- College of the Sequoias Giants, Visalia, CA 93277; 559-730-3700; www.cos.edu; plays football in the • Northern California Football Association (North Division–Central Valley Conference)
- Columbia College Claim Jumpers, Sonora, CA 95370; 209-588-5100; http://columbia.yosemite.cc.ca.us; no football program
- Fresno City College Rams, Fresno, CA 93741; 559-442-4600; www.fresnocitycollege.edu; plays football in the Northern California Football Association (North Division–Central Valley Conference)
- Merced College Blue Devils, Merced, CA 95348; 209-384-6000; www.mccd.edu; plays football in the Northern California Football Association (Central Division–Golden Gate Conference)
- Modesto Junior College Pirates, Modesto, CA 95350; 209-575-6550; www.mjc.edu; plays football in the Northern California Football Association (North Division–Central Valley Conference)
- Porterville College Pirates, Porterville, CA 93257; 559-791-2200; www.portervillecollege.edu; no football program
- Reedley College Tigers, Reedley, CA 93654; 559-638-3641; www.reedleycollege.edu; plays football in the Northern California Football Association (North Division–Central Valley Conference)
- Taft College Cougars, Taft, CA 93268; 661-763-7700; http://web.taftcollege.edu; no football program
- West Hills College, Coalinga, Falcons, Coalinga, CA 93210; 559-934-2000; www.westhillscollege.com/coalinga; plays football in the Northern California Football Association (Central Division–Golden Gate Conference)
- West Hills College Golden Eagles, Lemoore, CA 93245; 559-925-3000; www.westhillscollege.com/lemoore; no football program

Coast Conference

(Dale Murray, Commissioner), Cabrillo College, 6500 Soquel Drive, Aptos, CA 95003; Telephone: 831-479-6149; Fax: 831-479-6580; Email: damurray@cabrillo.edu; Web site: http://www.cabrillo.edu. The Coast Conference currently has 17 schools, 11 of which support football programs.

- Cabrillo College Seahawks, Aptos, CA 95003; 831-479-6100; www.cabrillo.edu; plays football in the Northern California Football Association (South Division–Coast Conference)
- Cañada College Colts, Redwood City, CA 94061; 650-306-3100; http://canadacollege.net; no football program
- Chabot College Gladiators, Hayward, CA 94545; 510-723-6600; www.chabotcollege.edu; plays football in the Northern California Football Association (Central Division–Golden Gate Conference)
- City College of San Francisco Rams, San Francisco, CA 94112; 415-239-3000; www.ccsf.edu; plays football in the Northern California Football Association (North Division–Nor Cal Conference)
- College of San Mateo Bulldogs, San Mateo, CA 94402; 650-574-6161; www.collegeofsanmateo.edu; plays football in the Northern California Football Association (North Division–NorCal Conference)
- De Anza College Dons, Cupertino, CA 95014; 408-864-5678; www.deanza.edu; plays football in the Northern California Football Association (Central Division–Golden Gate Conference)
- Evergreen Valley College Hawks, San Jose, CA 95135; 408-274-7900; www.evc.edu; no football program
- Foothill College Owls, Los Altos Hills, CA 94022; 650-949-7777; www.foothill.edu; plays football in the Northern California Football Association (North Division–NorCal Conference)
- Gavilan College Rams, Gilroy, CA 95020; 408-848-4800; www.gavilan.edu; plays football in the Northern California Football Association (South Division–Coast Conference)
- Hartnell College Panthers, Salinas, CA 93901; 831-755-6700; www.hartnell.edu; plays football in the Northern California Football Association (South Division–Coast Conference)
- Las Positas College Hawks, Livermore, CA 94551; 925-424-1000; www.laspositascollege.edu; no foot-

ball program
- Mission College Saints, Santa Clara, CA 95054; 408-988-2200; www.missioncollege.org; no football program
- Monterey Peninsula College Lobos, Monterey, CA 93940; 831-646-4000; www.mpc.edu; plays football in the Northern California Football Association (South Division–Coast Conference)
- Ohlone College Renegades, Fremont, CA 94539; 510-659-6000; www.ohlone.edu; no football program
- San Jose City College Jaguars, San Jose, CA 95128; 408-298-2181; www.sjcc.edu; plays football in the Northern California Football Association (South Division–Coast Conference)
- Skyline College Trojans, San Bruno, CA 94066; 650-738-4100; www.skylinecollege.edu; no football program
- West Valley College Vikings, Saratoga, CA 95070; 408-867-2200; www.westvalley.edu; plays football in the Northern California Football Association (South Division–Coast Conference)

Foothill Athletic Conference

(Dean Crowley , Commissioner); 13605 Terrace Place, Whittier, CA. 90601; Telephone: 562-698-1265; Fax: 562-698-1093; Email: FoothillCommish@msn.com. The Foothill Athletic Conference currently has nine schools, six of which support football programs.

- Antelope Valley College Marauders, Lancaster, CA 93536; 661-722-6300; www.avc.edu; plays football in the Southern California Football Association (Central Division–West Conference)
- Barstow Community College Vikings, Barstow, CA 92311; 760-252-2411; www.barstow.edu; no football program
- Cerro Coso Community College Coyotes, Ridgecrest, CA 93555; 760-384-6100; www.cc.cc.ca.us; no football program
- Chaffey College Panthers, Rancho Cucamonga, CA 91737; 909-652-6000; www.chaffey.edu; plays football in the Southern California Football Association (Central Division–West Conference)
- College of the Desert Roadrunners, Palm Desert, CA 92260; 760-346-8041; www.collegeofthe desert.edu; plays football in the Southern California Football Association (Central Division–East Conference)
- Mt. San Jacinto College Eagles, San Jacinto, CA 92583; 951-487-6752; www.msjc.edu; plays football in the Southern California Football Association (American Division–Mountain Conference)
- Rio Hondo College Roadrunners, Whittier, CA 90601; 562-692-0921; www.riohondo.edu; no football program
- San Bernardino Valley College Wolverines, San Bernardino, CA 92410; 909-384-4400; www.valley-college.edu; plays football in the Southern California Football Association (American Division–Mountain Conference)
- Victor Valley College Rams, Victorville, CA 92395; 760-245-4271; www.vvc.edu; plays football in the Southern California Football Association(American Division–Mountain Conference)

Golden Valley Conference

(Phil Alan Maas, Interim Commissioner); P.O. Box 916, Weed, CA 96094; Telephone: 530-938-3669; Fax: 530-938-1642; Email: maasgvc@yahoo.com. The Golden Valley Conference currently has seven schools, five of which support football programs.

- Butte College Roadrunners, Oroville, CA 95965; 530-895-2511;www.butte.edu; plays football in the Northern California Football Association (North Division–NorCal Conference)
- College of the Redwoods Corsairs, Eureka, CA 95501; 707-476-4100; www.redwoods.edu; plays football in the Northern California Football Association (South Division–Bay Valley Conference)
- College of the Siskiyous Eagles, Weed, CA 96094; 530-938-5555; www.sikiyous.edu; plays football in the Northern California Football Association (Central Division–Mid-Empire Conference)
- Feather River College Golden Eagles, Quincy, CA 95971; 530-283-0202; www.frc.edu; plays football in the Northern California Football Association (Central Division–Mid-Empire Conference)
- Lake Tahoe Community College Kokanees, South Lake Tahoe, CA 96150; 530-541-4660; www.ltcc.

edu; no football program
- Lassen Community College Cougars, Susanville, CA 96130; 530-257-6181; www.lassencollege.edu; no football program
- Shasta College Knights, Redding, CA 96049; 530-242-7500; www.shastacollege.edu; plays football in the Northern California Football Association (South Division–Bay Valley Conference)

Orange Empire Conference

(John Keever, Commissioner); 978 Amber Drive, Camarillo, CA 93010; Telephone & Fax: 805-482-1523; Email: oec.keever@gmail.com. The conference currently has nine schools, six of which support football.

- Cypress College Chargers, Cypress, CA 90630; 714-484-7000; www.cypresscollege.edu; no football program
- Fullerton College Hornets, Fullerton, CA 92832; 714-992-7000; www.fullcoll.edu; plays football in the Southern California Football Association (National Division–Southern Conference)
- Golden West College Rustlers, Huntington Beach, CA 92647; 714-892-7711; www.goldenwestcollege.edu; plays football in the Southern California Football Association (Central Division–East Conference)
- Irvine Valley College lasers, Irvine, CA 92618; 949-451-5100; www.ivc.edu; no football program
- Orange Coast College Pirates, Costa Mesa, CA 92626; 714-432-5072; www.orangecoastcollege.edu; plays football in the Southern California Football Association (Central Division–East Conference)
- Riverside Community College Tigers, Riverside, CA 92506; 951-222-8000; www.rcc.edu; plays football in the Southern California Football Association (Central Division–East Conference)
- Saddleback College Gauchos, Mission Viejo, CA 92692; 949-582-4500; www.saddleback.edu; plays football in the Southern California Football Association (National Division–Southern Conference)
- Santa Ana College Dons, Santa Ana, CA 92706; 714-564-6000; www.sac.edu; plays football in the Southern California Football Association (Central Division–East Conference)
- Santiago Canyon College Hawks, Orange, CA 92869; 714-628-4900; www.sccollege.edu; no football program

Pacific Coast Athletic Conference

(John Woods, Commissioner); 1464 Oak Knoll Lane, Valley Center, CA 92082; Telephone & Fax: 760-749-2065; Email: jwoodspcc@gmail.com. The Pacific Coast Athletic Conference currently has nine schools, five of which support football.

- Cuyamaca College Coyotes, El Cajon, CA 92019; 619-660-4000; www.cuyamaca.edu; no football program
- Grossmont College Griffins, El Cajon, CA 92020; 619-644-7000; www.grossmont.edu; plays football in the Southern California Football Association (National Division–Southern Conference)
- Imperial Valley College Arabs, Imperial, CA 92251; 760-352-8320; www.imperial.edu; no football program
- MiraCosta College Spartans, Oceanside, CA 92056; 760-757-2121; www.miracosta.edu; no football program
- Miramar College Jets, San Diego, CA 92126; 619-388-7800; www.sdmiramar.edu; no football program
- Palomar College Comets, San Marcos, CA 92069; 760-744-1150; www.palomar.edu; plays football in the Southern California Football Association (National Division–Southern Conference)
- San Diego City College Knights, San Diego, CA 92101; 619-388-3400; www.sdcity.edu; no football program
- San Diego Mesa College Olympians, San Diego, CA 92111; 619-388-2600; www.sdmesa.edu; plays football in the Southern California Football Association (American Division–Mountain Conference)
- Southwestern College Jaguars, Chula Vista, CA 91910; 619-421-6700; www.swccd.edu; plays football in the Southern California Football Association (Central Division–East Conference)

South Coast Conference

(Rich Kollen, Commissioner) (Southern California Football Association); Telephone: 562-239-2001; Fax: 562-926-3837; Email: dayofgame@aol.com. The South Coast Conference currently has 11 schools, nine of which support football programs.

- Cerritos College Falcons, Norwalk, CA 90650; 562-860-2451; www.cerritos.edu; plays football in the Southern California Football Association (National Division–Northern Conference)
- East Los Angeles College Huskies, Monterey Park, CA 91754; 323-265-8650; www.elac.edu; plays football in the Southern California Football Association (American Division–Mountain Conference)
- El Camino College, Compton, Community Educational Center Tartars, Compton, CA 90221; 310-9001600; www.compton.edu; plays football in the Southern California Football Association (American Division, Mountain Conference)
- El Camino College Warriors, Torrance, CA 90506; 310-532-3670; www.elcamino.edu; plays football in the Southern California Football Association (National Division–Northern Conference)
- Long Beach City College Vikings, Long Beach, CA 90808; 562-938-4111; www.lbcc.edu; plays in the Southern California Football Association (Central Division–West Conference)
- Los Angeles City College Cubs, Los Angeles, CA 90029; 323-953-4000; www.lacitycollege.edu; no football program
- Los Angeles Harbor College Seahawks, Wilmington, CA 90744; 310-233-4000; www.lahc.edu; plays football in the Southern California Football Association (Central Division–West Conference)
- Los Angeles Southwest College Cougars, Los Angeles, CA 90047; 323-241-5321; www.lasc.edu; plays football in the Southern California Football Association (American Division–Pacific Conference)
- Los Angeles Trade-Technical College Techsters, , Los Angeles, CA 90015; 213-763-7000; http://college.lattc.edu; no football program
- Mount San Antonio College Mounties, Walnut, CA 91789; 909-274-7500; www.mtsac.edu; plays football in the Southern California Football Association (National Division–Southern Conference)
- Pasadena City College Lancers, Pasadena, CA 91106; 626-585-7123; www.pasadena.edu; plays football in the Southern California Football Association (National Division–Southern Conference)

Western State Conference

(Jerry White, Commissioner), 5351 Butterfield Street, Camarillo, CA 93012; Telephone: 805-482-7097; Fax: 805-482-7097; Email: wscjerry@yahoo.com. The Western State Conference currently has 14 schools, 12 of which support football programs.

- Allan Hancock College Bulldogs, Santa Maria, CA 93454; 805-922-6966; www.hancockcollege.edu; plays football in the Southern California Football Association (National Division–Northern Conference)
- Bakersfield College Gades, Bakersfield, CA 93305; 661-395-4011; www.bakersfieldcollege.edu; plays football in the Southern California Football Association (National Division–Northern Conference)
- Citrus College Fighting Owls, Glendora, CA 91741; 626-963-0323; www.citruscollege.edu; plays football in the Southern California Football Association (Central Division–West Conference)
- College of the Canyons Cougars, Santa Clarita, CA 91355; 661-259-7800; www.canyons.edu; plays football in the Southern California Football Association (National Division–Northern Conference)
- Cuesta College Cougars, San Luis Obispo, CA 93403; 805-546-3100; www.cuesta.edu; no football program
- Glendale Community College Vaqueros, Glendale, CA 91208; 818-240-1000; www.glendale.edu; plays football in the Southern California Football Association (American Division–Pacific Conference)
- Los Angeles Valley College Monarchs, Valley Glen, CA 91401; 818-947-2600; www.lavc.edu; plays football in the Southern California Football Association (American Division–Pacific Conference)
- Moorpark College Raiders, Moorpark, CA 93021; 805-378-1400; www.moorparkcollege.edu; plays football in the Southern California Football Association (Central Division–West Conference)
- Oxnard College Condors, Oxnard, CA 93033; 805-986-5800; www.oxnardcollege.edu; no football program
- Pierce College (Los Angeles Pierce College) Brahmas, Woodland Hills, CA 91371; 818-719-6401;

www.piercecollege.edu; plays football in the Southern California Football Association (American Division, Pacific Conference)

- Santa Barbara City College Vaqueros, Santa Barbara, CA 93109; 805-965-0581; www.sbcc.edu; plays football in the Southern California Football Association (American Division–Pacific Conference)
- Santa Monica College Corsairs, Santa Monica, CA 90405; 310-434-4000; www.smc.edu; plays football in the Southern California Football Association (American Division–Pacific Conference)
- Ventura College Pirates, Ventura, CA 93003; 805-654-6400; www.venturacollege.edu; plays football in the Southern California Football Association (National Division–Northern Conference)
- West Los Angeles College Wildcats, Culver City, CA 90230; 310-287-4200; www.wlac.edu; plays football in the Southern California Football Association (American Division–Pacific Conference)

Wrestling Alliance

Non-football alliance.

Northern California Football Association

(Gary Kollenborn, Commissioner), 827 Westmont Drive, Chico, CA 95926; 530-345-1451

Central Division

Golden Gate Conference

- Chabot College Gladiators, Hayward, CA 94545; 510-723-6600; www.chabotcollege.edu
- De Anza College Dons, Cupertino, CA 95014; 408-864-5300; www.deanza.edu
- Diablo Valley College Vikings, Pleasant Hill, CA 94523; 925-685-1230; www.dvc.edu
- Los Medanos College Mustangs, Pittsburg, CA 94565; 925-439-2181; www.losmedanos.edu
- Merced College Blue Devils, Merced, CA 95348; 209-384-6000; www.mccd.edu
- West Hills College Falcons, Coalinga, CA 93210; 800-266-1114; www.westhillscollege.com

Golden Gate Conference Coach of the Year

Year	*Coach*	*School*
2008	Sam C Young	Modesto Junior College (Modesto)
2009	Jay Uchiumi	Laney College (Oakland)
2010	Dan Atencio	De Anza College (Cupertino)

Golden Gate Conference Offensive Player of the Year

Year	*Player*	*Class*	*Position*	*School*
2008	Marcus Allen	Sophomore	Receiver	Modesto Junior College (Modesto)
2009	Tyler Mason	Sophomore	Running Back	Chabot College (Hayward)
2010	Joey Bradley	Freshman	Quarterback	Diablo Valley College (Pleasant Hill)

Golden Gate Conference Defensive Player of the Year

Year	*Player*	*Class*	*Position*	*School*
2008	Scott Cozart	Sophomore	Linebacker	Modesto Junior College (Modesto)
2009	Keith Yamamoto	Sophomore	Linebacker	Modesto Junior College (Modesto)
2010	Ty Powell	Sophomore	Defensive Back	De Anza College (Cupertino)

Golden Gate Conference All-Purpose Player of the Year

Year	*Player*	*Class*	*Position*	*School*
2008	Troy Evans	Sophomore		Laney College (Oakland)
2009	Tyler Mason	Sophomore	Running Back	Chabot College (Hayward)
2010	Jerry Slota	Freshman	Quarterback	De Anza College (Cupertino)

Golden Gate Conference Return Specialist of the Year

Year	Player	Class	School
2008	Kevin Williams	Sophomore	Los Medanos College (Pittsburg)
2009	No Selection		
2010	Chris Mamon	Freshman	Diablo Valley College (Pleasant Hill)

Golden Gate Conference Place Kicker of the Year

Year	Player	Class	School
2008	Jason Burgos	Sophomore	Laney College (Oakland)
2009	Ernie Collins	Freshman	Laney College (Oakland)
2010	Blaze Vela	Freshman	De Anza College (Cupertino)

Golden Gate Conference Punter of the Year

Year	Player	Class	School
2008	Daniel Ayers	Sophomore	Laney College (Oakland)
2009	Fabian Miramontes	Sophomore	Merced College (Merced)
2010	Aaron Godwin		De Anza College (Cupertino)

Mid-Empire Conference

- American River College Beavers, Foothill Farms / Sacramento, CA 95841; 916-484-8011; www.arc.losrios.edu
- College of the Siskiyous Eagles, Weed, CA 96094; 530-938-5555; www.siskiyous.edu
- Feather River College Golden Eagles, Quincy, CA 95971; 530-283-0202; www.frc.edu
- Mendocino College Eagles, Ukiah, CA 95482; 707-468-3000; www.mendocino.edu
- Sacramento City College Panthers, Sacramento, CA 95822; 916-558-2111; www.scc.losrios.edu

Mid-Empire Conference Coach of the Year

Year	Coach	School
2008	Mike Clemons	Sacramento City College
2009	Tom Gang	Mendocino College (Ukiah)
2009	Danny Walker	Sacramento City College (Sacramento)
2010	Jerry Haflich	American River College (Sacramento)

Mid-Empire Conference Offensive Player of the Year

Year	Player	Class	Position	School
2008	Neville Bryce		Running Back	Feather River College
2009	Jake Strickler	Sophomore	Quarterback	Mendocino College (Ukiah)
2009	Cody Allen	Freshman	Quarterback	Sacramento City College (Sacramento)
2010	Cody Allen	Sophomore	Quarterback	Sacramento City College (Sacramento)

Mid-Empire Conference Defensive Player of the Year

Year	Player	Class	Position	School
2008	Lincoln Togiai		Linebacker	Sacramento City College (Sacramento)
2009	Russell Merritt	Freshman	Linebacker	Sacramento City College (Sacramento)
2010	Colton Russi	Sophomore	Linebacker	American River College (Sacramento)

Mid-Empire Conference All-Purpose Player of the Year

Year	Player	Class	Position	School
2008	Stefon Ceaser			American River College (Sacramento)
2009	Rico Pendergrass	Freshman		American River College (Sacramento)
2010	Ricky Mitchell	Sophomore		Feather River College (Quincy)

Mid-Empire Conference Return Specialist of the Year

Year	Player	Class	School
2008	Darius Davis		College of the Siskiyous (Weed)
2009	Alex Hines	Sophomore	American River College (Sacramento)
2010	Michael Lindsay	Freshman	American River College (Sacramento)

Mid-Empire Conference Place Kicker of the Year

Year	Player	Class	School
2008	Derrick Caruthers		Sacramento City College (Sacramento)
2009	Bryan Folsom	Freshman	American River College (Sacramento)
2010	Jose Amezcua	Sophomore	Sacramento City College (Sacramento)

Mid-Empire Conference Punter of the Year

Year	Player	Class	School
2008	D Ransdol		College of the Siskiyous (Weed)
2009	Donavan Ramsdal	Freshman	College of the Siskiyous (Weed)
2010	Zack Tapia	Freshman	American River College (Sacramento)

North Division

Central Valley Conference

- College of the Sequoias Giants, Visalia, CA 93277; 559-730-3700; www.cos.edu
- Fresno City College Rams, Fresno, CA 93741; 559-442-4600; www.fresnocitycollege.edu
- Modesto Junior College Pirates, Modesto, CA 95350; 209-575-6550; www.mjc.edu
- Reedley College Tigers, Reedley, CA 93654; 559-638-3641; www.reedleycollege.edu
- San Joaquin Delta College Mustangs, Stockton, CA 95207; 209-954-5151; www.deltacollege.edu
- Sierra College Wolverines, Rocklin, CA 95677; 916-624-3333; www.sierracollege.edu

Central Valley Conference Coach of the Year

Year	Coach	School
2008	Michael White	Reedley College (Reedley)
2009	Randy Whited	Reedley College (Reedley)
2010	Tony Caviglia	Fresno City Collge (Fresno)

Central Valley Conference Offensive Player of the Year

Year	Player	Class	Position	School
2008	Lamon Muldrow	Sophomore	Running Back	Sierra College (Rocklin)
2009	Brandon Michalkiewicz	Sophomore	Wide Receiver	Sierra College (Rocklin)
2010	Devin Combs	Freshman	Quarterback	Modesto Junior College (Modesto)

Central Valley Conference Defensive Player of the Year

Year	Player	Class	Position	School
2008	Bryson Littlejohn	Sophomore	Linebacker	Sierra College (Rocklin)
2009	Dontea Smith	Sophomore	Defensive Back	Reedley College (Reedley)
2010	Louvan Green	Sophomore	Defensive Tackle	College of the Sequoias (Visalia)

Central Valley Conference All-Purpose Player of the Year

Year	Player	Class	Position	School
2008	Eric Johnson	Freshman	Running Back	Reedley College (Reedley)
2009	Keontric Reynolds	Sophomore	Wide Receiver	College of the Sequoias (Visalia)
2010	Eric Johnson	Sophomore	Running Back	College of the Sequoias (Visalia)

Central Valley Conference Return Specialist of the Year

Year	*Player*	*Class*	*School*
2008	Billy Foster	Sophomore	College of the Sequoias (Visalia)
2009	Dontea Smith	Sophomore	Reedley College (Reedley)
2010	None Selected		

Central Valley Conference Place Kicker of the Year

Year	*Player*	*Class*	*School*
2008	AJ Forestire	Sophomore	Reedley College (Reedley)
2009	Curtis O'Neil		Reedley College (Reedley)
2010	Irvin Gonzales	Sophomore	College of the Sequoias (Visalia)
2010	Donovan Wallace	Sophomore	Modesto Junior College (Modesto)

Central Valley Conference Punter of the Year

Year	*Player*	*Class*	*School*
2008	Tim Cowdrey	Sophomore	Reedley College (Reedley)
2009	John Lessary		Fresno City College (Fresno)
2010	Joe O'Gorman	Sophomore	Sierra College (Rocklin)

NorCal Conference

- Butte College Roadrunners, Oroville, CA 95965; 530-895-2511; www.butte.edu
- City College of San Francisco Rams, San Francisco, 94112; 415-239-3000; www.ccsf.edu
- College of San Mateo Bulldogs, San Mateo, CA 94402; 650-574-6161; www.collegeofsanmateo.edu
- Foothill College Owls, Los Altos Hills, CA 94022; 650-949-7777; www.foothill.edu
- Laney College Eagles, Oakland CA 94607; 510-834-5740; www.laney.edu
- Santa Rosa Junior College Bear Cubs, Santa Rosa, CA 95401; 707-527-4011; www.santarosa.edu

NorCal Conference Coach of the Year

Year	*Coach*	*School*
2008	Jeff Jordan	Butte College (Oroville)
2009	Brett Pollack	College of San Mateo (San Mateo)
2010	George Rush	City College of San Francisco (San Francisco)

NorCal Conference Offensive Player of the Year

Year	*Player*	*Class*	*Position*	*School*
2008	Adam Froman	Sophomore	Quarterback	Santa Rosa Junior College (Santa Rosa)
2009	Darius Bell	Freshman	Quarterback	City College of San Francisco (San Francisco)
2010	Steel Jants	Sophomore	Quarterback	City College of San Francisco (San Francisco)

NorCal Conference Defensive Player of the Year

Year	*Player*	*Class*	*Position*	*School*
2008	Brandon Rankin	Sophomore	Defensive Lineman	Butte College (Oroville)
2009	Jeff Thomas	Sophomore	Linebacker	Foothill College (Los Altos Hills)
2010	Sua Tuala	Sophomore	Linebacker	City College of San Francisco (San Francisco)

NorCal Conference All-Purpose Player of the Year

Year	*Player*	*Class*	*Position*	*School*
2008	John Henderschott	Sophomore	Receiver	Diablo Valley College (Pleasant Hill)
2009	Ricky Barr	Freshman	Running Back	Butte College (Oroville)
2010	Ross Rashad	Sophomore	Return Specialist	Butte College (Oroville)

NorCal Conference Return Specialist of the Year

Year	Player	Class	School
2008	Eric Roberson	Freshman	College of San Mateo (San Mateo)
2009	Ross Rashad	Freshman	Butte College (Oroville)
2010	Ross Rashad	Sophomore	Butte College (Oroville)

NorCal Conference Place Kicker of the Year

Year	Player	Class	School
2008	Ian Mullen	Sophomore	Santa Rosa Junior College (Santa Rosa)
2009	Jens Alnervik	Sophomore	City College of San Francisco (San Francisco)
2010	Andrew Amezquita	Freshman	Foothill College (Los Altos Hills)

NorCal Conference Punter of the Year

Year	Player	Class	School
2008	Ian Mullen	Sophomore	Santa Rosa Junior College (Santa Rosa)
2009	Jens Alnervik	Sophomore	City College of San Francisco (San Francisco)
2010	Ernie Collins	Sophomore	Laney College (Oakland)

South Division

Bay Valley Conference

- College of the Redwoods Corsairs, Eureka, CA 95501; 707-476-4100; www.redwoods.edu
- Contra Costa College Comets, San Pablo, CA 94806; 510-235-7800; www.contracosta.edu
- Shasta College Knights, Redding, CA 96049; 530-242-7500; www.shastacollege.edu
- Solano Community College Falcons, Fairfield, CA 94534; 707-864-7000; www.solano.edu
- Yuba College 49ers, Marysville CA 95901; 530-741-6700; http://yc.yccd.edu

Bay Valley Conference Coach of the Year

Year	Coach	School
2008	Craig Thompson	Shasta College (Redding)
2009	Dave Banducci	College of the Redwoods (Eureka)
2010	Floyd Burnsed	Solano Community College (Fairfield)

Bay Valley Conference Offensive Player of the Year

Year	Player	Class	Position	School
2008	Lyndon Rowells	Sophomore	Running Back	College of the Redwoods (Eureka)
2009	Kenonte Howard	Sophomore	Wide Receiver	Solano Community College (Fairfield)
2010	Boy Humphrey	Sophomore	Quarterback	Solano Community College (Fairfield)

Bay Valley Conference Defensive Player of the Year

Year	Player	Class	Position	School
2008	Zack Gibbons	Freshman	Linebacker	Shasta College (Redding)
2009	Rony Nelson	Sophomore	Defensive Lineman	Yuba College (Marysville)
2010	Niko Aumua	Sophomore	Defensive Lineman	Contra Costa College (San Pablo)

Bay Valley Conference All-Purpose Player of the Year

Year	Player	Class	Position	School
2008	Lyndon Rowells	Sophomore	Running Back	College of the Redwoods (Eureka)
2009	Colton Johnson	Sophomore	Quarterback	Shasta College (Redding)
2010	Manuel Barragan	Sophomore	Running Back	Shasta College (Redding)

Bay Valley Conference Return Specialist of the Year

Year	Player	Class	Position	School
2008	Lyndon Rowells	Sophomore	Running Back	College of the Redwoods (Eureka)
2009	Manuel Barragan	Freshman		Shasta College (Redding)
2010	Davel Brumfield	Freshman	Wide Receiver	Solano Community College (Fairfield)

Bay Valley Conference Place Kicker of the Year

Year	Player	Class	School
2008	Ryan Martin	Sophomore	Yuba College (Marysville)
2009	Kelly Crowley	Freshman	Shasta College (Redding)
2010	Keith Leenders	Freshman	Solano Community College (Fairfield)

Bay Valley Conference Punter of the Year

Year	Player	Class	School
2008	Tyler Bales	Freshman	Solano Community College (Fairfield)
2009	Justin Naterman	Sophomore	Contra Costs College (San Pablo)
2010	Brad Winters	Sophomore	Shasta College (Redding)

Coast Conference

- Cabrillo College Seahawks, Aptos, CA 95003; 831-479-6100; www.cabrillo.edu
- Gavilan College Rams, Gilroy, CA 95020; 408-848-4800; www.gavilan.edu
- Hartnell College Panthers, Salinas, CA 93901; 831-755-6700
- Monterey Peninsula College Lobos, Monterey, CA 93940; 831-646-4000; www.mpc.edu
- San Jose City College Jaguars, San Jose, CA 95128; 408-298-2181; www.sjcc.edu
- West Valley College Vikings, Saratoga, CA 95070; 408-867-2200; www.westvalley.edu

Coast Conference Coach of the Year

Year	Coach	School
2008	Mike Rasmussen	Monterey Peninsula College (Monterey)
2009	Dan Atencio	De Anza College (Cupertino)
2010	Carlton Connor	San Jose City College (San Jose)

Coast Conference Offensive Player of the Year

Year	Player	Class	Position	School
2008	Brian Reader	Freshman	Quarterback	Monterey Peninsula College (Monterey)
2009	Kevin Vye	Sophomore	Quarterback	De Anza College (Cupertino)
2010	Alvin Jelks	Freshman	Running Back	Hartnel College (Salinas)

Coast Conference Defensive Player of the Year

Year	Player	Class	Position	School
2008	Obed Lologo	Sophomore	Linebacker	Monterey Peninsula College (Monterey)
2009	Russ Jenkins	Sophomore	Linebacker	De Anza College (Cupertino)
2010	Kiero Small	Sophomore	Linebacker	Hartnell College (Salinas)

Coast Conference All-Purpose Player of the Year

Year	Player	Class	Position	School
2008	Josh Uribe			West Valley College (Saratoga)
2009	Zachkary Heager			Monterey Peninsula College (Monterey)
2010	Alvin Jelks	Freshman	Running Back	Hartnel College (Salinas)
2010	Doug Stewart			Gavilan College (Gilroy)

Coast Conference Return Specialist of the Year

Year	Player	Class	Position	School
2008	Chris Jones	Sophomore	Defensive Back	San Jose City College (San Jose)
2008	Brett Taylor	Sophomore	Wide Receiver	Monterey Peninsula College (Monterey)
2009	Zachkary Heager			Monterey Peninsula College (Monterey)
2010	Kenny Pope	Sophomore	Wide Receiver	San Jose City College (San Jose)

Coast Conference Place Kicker of the Year

Year	Player	Class	School
2008	Chris Pinto		Monterey Peninsula College (Monterey)
2009	Victor Aguirre		De Anza College (Cupertino)
2010	Eduardo Ochoa		Monterey Peninsula College (Monterey)

Coast Conference Punter of the Year

Year	Player	Class	School
2008	Chris Pinto		Monterey Peninsula College (Monterey)
2009	Nathan Kanlecek		San Jose City College (San Jose)
2010	Nathan Kadleck		San Jose City College (San Jose)

Southern California Football Association

(Jim Sartoris, Commissioner), Telephone: 818-841-0446; Fax: 818-861-7955; Email: sartoris.scfa@gmail.com. Prior to 2010, the SCFA was divided into only two Divisions: National (Northern Conference, Central Conference, Southern Conference) and American (Mountain Conference, Pacific Conference).

American Division

Mountain Conference

- East Los Angeles College Huskies, Monterey Park, CA 91754; 323-265-8650; www.elac.edu
- El Camino College, Compton Center (Compton Community College) Tartars, Compton, CA 90221; 310-900-1600; www.compton.edu
- Mt. San Jacinto College Eagles, San Jacinto, CA 92583; 951-487-6752; www.msjc.edu
- San Bernardino Valley College Wolverines, San Bernardino, CA 92410; 909-384-4400; www.valleycollege.edu
- San Diego Mesa College Olympians, San Diego, CA 92111; 619-388-2600; www.sdmesa.edu
- Victor Valley College Rams, Victorville, CA 92395; 760-245-4271; www.vvc.edu

Mountain Conference Coach of the Year

Year	Coach	School
2008	Matt Kofler	San Diego Mesa (San Diego)
2009	George Swade	Los Angeles Harbor College (Wilmington)
2010	Kevin Emerson	San Bernardino Valley College (San Bernardino)

Mountain Conference Offensive Player of the Year

Year	Player	Class	Position	School
2008	Phil Staback	Sophomore		San Diego Mesa (San Diego)
2009	Dominique Blackman	Freshman	Quarterback	Los Angeles Harbor College (Wilmington)
2010	Kristin James	Sophomore	Running Back	San Bernardino Valley College (San Bernardino)

Mountain Conference Defensive Player of the Year

Year	Player	Class	Position	School
2008	Mychal Conel	Freshman		Golden West College (Huntington Beach)
2009	Clarence Laster	Sophomore	Safety	Mt. San Jacnito College (San Jacinto)
2010	Ricky Pesquera	Sophomore	Linebacker	San Bernardino Valley College (San Bernardino)

Mountain Conference All-Purpose Player of the Year

Year	Player	Class	Position	School
2008	Brandon Grissom	Freshman		Golden West College (Huntington Beach)
2009	Jon White	Freshman		Los Angeles Harbor College.(Wilmington)
2010	Jeremy Edwards	Sophomore		El Camino College, Compton Center (Compton)

Mountain Conference Return Specialist of the Year

Year	Player	Class	School
2008	Donyae Coleman	Freshman	El Camino College, Compton Center (Compton)
2009	Brandon Grissom	Sophomore	Golden West College (Huntington Beach)
2010	Emanuel Hamilton	Freshman	Mt. San Jacinto College (San Jacinto)

Mountain Conference Place Kicker of the Year

Year	Player	Class	School
2008	Stan Shurson	Sophomore	San Diego Mesa College (San Diego)
2009	Abel Perez	Sophomore	Southwestern College (Chula Vista)
2010	Andre Owens	Freshman	San Bernardino Valley College (San Bernardino)

Mountain Conference Punter of the Year

Year	Player	Class	School
2008	Mike Langston	Sophomore	San Bernardino Valley College (San Bernardino)
2009	Zoltan Riazzo	Sophomore	Mt. San Jacinto College (San Jacinto)
2010	Dylan Schul	Freshman	San Bernardino Valley College (San Bernardino)

Pacific Conference

- Glendale Community College Vaqueros, Glendale, CA 91208; 818-240-1000; www.glendale.edu
- Los Angeles Southwest College Cougars, Los Angeles, CA 90047; 323-241-5321; www.lasc.edu
- Los Angeles Valley College Monarchs, Valley Glen, CA 91401; 818-947-2600; www.lavc.edu
- Pierce College (Los Angeles Pierce College) Brahma Bulls, Woodland Hills, CA 91371; 818-719-6401; www.piercecollege.edu
- Santa Barbara City College Vaqueros, Santa Barbara, CA 93109; 805-965-0581; www.sbcc.edu
- Santa Monica College Corsairs, Santa Monica, CA 90405; 310-434-4000; www.smc.edu
- West Los Angeles College Wildcats, Culver City, CA 90230; 310-287-4200; www.wlac.edu

Pacific Conference Coach of the Year

Year	Coach	School
2008	Perry Jehlicka	Antelope Valley College (Lancaster)
2009	Efrain Martinez	Pierce College (Woodland Hills)
2010	Efrain Martinez	Pierce College (Woodland Hils)

Pacific Conference Offensive Player of the Year

Year	Player	Class	Position	School
2008	Dominic Blood	Sophomore	Running Back	Antelope Valley College (Lancaster)
2008	Bret Visciglia	Freshman	Quarterback	Los Angeles Valley College (Valley Glen)
2009	Coleman Edmond	Sophomore	Wide Receiver	Pierce College (Woodland Hills)
2010	John Uribe	Sophomore	Quarterback	Santa Barbara City College (Santa Barbara)

Pacific Conference Defensive Player of the Year

Year	Player	Class	Position	School
2008	Troy Butler	Sophomore	Defensive Back	Antelope Valley College (Lancaster)
2009	Chris Whitney	Sophomore	Linebacker	Antelope Valley College (Lancaster)
2010	Aaron Morgan	Sophomore	Linebacker	Los Angeles Southwest College (Los Angeles)

Pacific Conference All-Purpose Player of the Year

Year	Player	Class	School
2008	Antoine Smithson	Sophomore	East Los Angeles College (Monterey Park)
2009	Brandon Mims	Freshman	Antelope Valley College (Lancaster)
2010	Jon McNeal	Freshman	Santa Monica College (Santa Monica)

Pacific Conference Return Specialist of the Year

Year	Player	Class	School
2008	Eddie Russ	Sophomore	Antelope Valley College (Lancaster)
2009	Jakharie Murphy	Sophomore	Santa Barbara City College (Santa Barbara)
2010	Deshawn Stewart	Freshman	Santa Monica College (Santa Monica)

Pacific Conference Place Kicker of the Year

Year	Player	Class	School
2008	Wilmer Segura	Freshman	Los Angeles Valley College (Valley Glen)
2009	Wilmer Segura	Sophomore	Los Angeles Valley College (Valley Glen)
2010	Eduardo Montoya	Freshman	West Los Angeles College (Culver City)

Pacific Conference Punter of the Year

Year	Player	Class	School
2008	Brandon Reid	Sophomore	Los Angeles Southwest College (Los Angeles)
2009	Armando Quintero	Freshman	Antelope Valley College (Lancaster)
2010	Manny Hernandez	Freshman	Santa Barbara College (Santa Barbara)

Central Division

The Central Division with the East and West conferences began operations in 2010.

East Conference

- College of the Desert Roadrunners, Palm Desert, CA 92260; 760-346-8041; www.collegeofthedesert.edu
- Golden West College Rustlers, Huntington Beach, CA 92647; 714-892-7711; www.goldenwestcollege.edu
- Orange Coast College Pirates, Costa Mesa, CA 92626; 714-432-5072; www.orangecoastcollege.edu
- Riverside Community College Tigers, Riverside, CA 92506; 951-222-8000; www.rcc.edu
- Santa Ana College Dons, Santa Ana, CA 92706; 714-564-6000; www.sac.edu
- Southwestern College Jaguars, Chula Vista, CA 91910; 619-421-6700; www.swccd.edu

East Conference Coach of the Year

Year	Coach	School
2010	Tom Craft	Riverside Community College (Riverside)

East Conference Offensive Player of the Year

Year	Player	Class	Position	School
2010	Dalton Livingston	Freshman	Quarterback	Riverside Community College (Riverside)

East Conference Defensive Player of the Year

Year	Player	Class	Position	School
2010	Ryan Hofrmeister	Freshman	Linebacker	Riverside Community College (Riverside)

East Conference All-Purpose Player of the Year

Year	Player	Class	School
2010	Akeelie Mustafa	Freshman	Santa Ana College (Santa Ana)

East Conference Return Specialist of the Year

Year	Player	Class	School
2010	Sadale Foster	Freshman	Riverside Community College (Riverside)

East Conference Place Kicker of the Year

Year	Player	Class	School
2010	Chris Navarro	Freshman	Southwestern College (Chula Vista)

East Conference Punter of the Year

Year	Player	Class	School
2010	Chase Lansford	Sophomore	Santa Ana College (Santa Ana)

West Conference

- Antelope Valley College Marauders, Lancaster, CA 93536; 661-722-6300; www.avc.edu
- Chaffey College Panthers, Rancho Cucamonga, CA 91737; 909-652-6000; www.chaffey.edu
- Citrus College Fighting Owls, Glendora, CA 91741; 626-963-0323; www.citruscollege.edu
- Long Beach City College Vikings, Long Beach, CA 90808; 562-938-4111; www.lbcc.edu
- Los Angeles Harbor College Seahawks, Wilmington, CA 90744; 310-233-4000; www.lahc.edu
- Moorpark College Raiders, Moorpark, CA 93021; 805-378-1400; www.moorparkcollege.edu

West Conference Coach of the Year

Year	Coach	School
2010	Brett Peabody	Los Angeles Harbor College (Wilmington)

West Conference Offensive Player of the Year

Year	Player	Class	Position	School
2010	John White	Sophomore	Running Back	Los Angeles Harbor College (Wilmington)

West Conference Defensive Player of the Year

Year	Player	Class	Position	School
2010	Byron Moore	Freshman	Defensive Back	Los Angeles Harbor College (Wilmington)

West Conference All-Purpose Player of the Year

Year	Player	Class	School
2010	Brandon Mims	Sophomore	Antelope Valley College (Lancaster)

West Conference Return Specialist of the Year

Year	Player	Class	School
2010	Dominick McMarkam	Freshman	Moorpark College (Moorpark)

West Conference Place Kicker of the Year

Year	Player	Class	School
2010	Trevor Layne	Sophomore	Chaffey College (Cucamonga)

West Conference Punter of the Year

Year	Player	Class	School
2010	Justin Doerner	Sophomore	Los Angeles Harbor College (Wilmington)

National Division

Northern Conference

- Allan Hancock College Bulldogs, Santa Maria, CA 93454; 805-922-6966; www.hancockcollege.edu
- Bakersfield College Renegades, Bakersfield, CA 93305; 661-395-4011; www.bakersfieldcollege.edu
- Cerritos College Falcons, Norwalk, CA 90650; 562-860-2451; www.cerritos.edu
- College of the Canyons Cougars, Santa Clarita, CA 91355; 661-259-7800; www.canyons.edu
- El Camino College Warriors, Torrance, CA 90506; 310-532-3670; www.elcamino.edu
- Ventura College Pirates, Ventura, CA 93003; 805-654-6400; www.venturacollege.edu

Northern Conference Coach of the Year

Year	Coach	School
2008	Garett Tujague	College of the Canyons (Santa Clarita)
2009	Jeff Chudy	Bakersfield College (Bakersfield)
2010	Jeff Chudy	Bakersfield College (Bakersfield)
2010	Frank Mazotta	Cerritos College (Norwalk)

Northern Conference Offensive Player of the Year

Year	Player	Class	Position	School
2008	Hayo Carpenter			College of Canyons (Santa Clarita)
2009	Logan Kilgore	Freshman	Quarterback	Bakersfield College (Bakersfield)
2010	Daveon Barner	Sophomore	Running Back	Cerritos College (Norwalk)

Northern Conference Defensive Player of the Year

Year	Player	Class	Position	School
2008	Marquis Jackson			College of the Canyons (Santa Clarita)
2009	Tyrone Crawford	Sophomore	Defensive End	Bakersfield College (Bakersfield)
2010	Keith McGill	Sophomore	Safety	Cerritos College (Norwalk)

Northern Conference All-Purpose Player of the Year

Year	Player	Class	School
2008	Diondre Bryant	Sophomore	Allan Hancock College (Santa Maria)
2009	Rishard Matthews	Freshman	Bakersfield College (Bakersfield)
2010	Mike Davis	Sophomore	Ventura College (Ventura)

Northern Conference Return Specialist of the Year

Year	Player	Class	School
2008	Chuckie Covington	Freshman	Bakersfield College (Bakersfield)
2009	Gabe Bostic	Sophomore	Ventura College (Ventura)
2010	Andre Buford	Sophomore	El Camino College (Torrance)

Northern Conference Place Kicker of the Year

Year	Player	Class	School
2008	Ricky Drake	Freshman	College of the Canyons (Santa Clarita)
2009	Josh Gallington	Sophomore	Bakersfield College (Bakersfield)
2010	Josh Gallington	Sophomore	Bakersfield College (Bakersfield)

Northern Conference Punter of the Year

Year	Player	Class	School
2008	Will Mahan	Sophomore	Bakersfield College (Bakersfield)
2009	Mike Trujillo	Sophomore	Allan Hancock College (Santa Marita)
2010	Kyle Dugandzic	Sophomore	Ventura College (Ventura)

Central Conference (2008 & 2009 Only)

Central Conference Coach of the Year

Year	Coach	School
2008	Robert Jastrah	Mount San Antonio College (Walnut)
2009	Robert Jastrab	Mount San Antonio College (Walnut)

Central Conference Offensive Player of the Year

Year	Player	Class	Position	School
2008	Nick Lamaison		Quarterback	Mount San Antonio College (Walnut)
2009	Matt Faulkner	Sophomore	Quarterback	Mount San Antonio College (Walnut)

Central Conference Defensive Player of the Year

Year	Player	Class	Position	School
2008	Daniel Stewart		Defensive End	El Camino College (Torrance)
2009	Bruce Irvin	Sophomore	Linebacker	Mount San Antonio College (Walnut)

Central Conference All-Purpose Player of the Year

Year	Player	Class	Position	School
2008	James Calhoun	Freshman		Riverside Community College (Riverside)
2009	Eric Russell	Sophomore		Cerritos College (Norwalk)

Central Conference Return Specialist of the Year

Year	Player	Class	School
2008	Eric Russell		Cerritos College (Norwalk)
2009	Tavoy Moore	Sophomore	Cerritos College (Norwalk)

Central Conference Place Kicker of the Year

Year	Player	Class	School
2008	Jacob Harfman	Sophomore	Mount San Antonio College (Walnut)
2009	Stephen Locke	Sophomore	El Camino College (Torrance)

Central Conference Punter of the Year

Year	Player	Class	School
2008	Jeramey Cutler	Freshman	Cerritos College (Norwalk)
2009	Alex Alvarez	Freshman	Riverside Community College (Riverside)

Southern Conference

- Fullerton College Hornets, Fullerton, CA 92832; 714-992-7000; www.fullcoll.edu
- Grossmont College Griffins, El Cajon, CA 92020; 619-644-7000; www.grossmont.edu
- Mount San Antonio College Mounties, Walnut, CA 91789; 909-274-7500; www.mtsac.edu
- Palomar College Comets, San Marcos, CA 92069; 760-744-1150; www.palomar.edu
- Pasadena City College Lancers, Pasadena, CA 91106; 626-585-7123; www.pasadena.edu
- Saddleback College Gauchos, Mission Viejo, CA 92692; 949-582-4500; www.saddleback.edu

Southern Conference Coach of the Year

Year	*Coach*	*School*
2008	Tim Byrnes	Fullerton College (Fullerton)
2009	Tim Byrnes	Fullerton College (Fullerton)
2010	Bob Jastrab	Mount San Antonio College (Walnut)

Southern Conference Offensive Player of the Year

Year	*Player*	*Class*	*Position*	*School*
2008	Jeff Fleming	Freshman	Quarterback	Fullerton College (Fullerton)
2008	Jai Morris	Freshman	Running Back	Saddleback College (Mission Viejo)
2009	Kenny Turner	Freshman	Running Back	Fullerton College (Fullerton)
2010	Kelvin York	Freshman	Running Back	Fullerton College (Fullerton)

Southern Conference Defensive Player of the Year

Year	*Player*	*Class*	*Position*	*School*
2008	Dean DeLeone	Sophomore	Defensive End	Orange Coast College (Costa Mesa)
2009	Genesis Fonoimoana	Sophomore	Defensive Back	Long Beach City College (Long Beach)
2010	Bojay Filimoeatu	Sophomore	Defensive Lineman	Mount San Antonio College (Walnut)

Southern Conference All-Purpose Player of the Year

Year	*Player*	*Class*	*School*
2008	Phil Van Holland	Sophomore	Santa Ana College (Santa Ana)
2009	Jai Morris	Sophomore	Saddleback College (Mission Viejo)
2010	Tyrese Jones	Sophomore	Palomar College (San Marcos)

Southern Conference Return Specialist of the Year

Year	*Player*	*Class*	*School*
2008	Xavier Martin	Freshman	Grossmont College (El Cajon)
2009	Richard Crawford	Sophomore	Saddleback College (Mission Viejo)
2009	Mikey Head	Freshman	Palomar College (San Marcos)
2010	George Whigham	Sophomore	Fullerton College (Fullerton)

Southern Conference Place Kicker of the Year

Year	*Player*	*Class*	*School*
2008	Brandon Bogotay	Freshman	Grossmont College (El Cajon)
2009	Kevin Ditch	Sophomore	Palomar College (San Marcos)
2010	Mike Frisina	Sophomore	Saddleback College (Mission Viejo)

Southern Conference Punter of the Year

Year	*Player*	*Class*	*School*
2008	Sean Wren	Freshman	Fullerton College (Fullerton)
2009	Morris Keseloff	Sophomore	Saddleback College (Mission Viejo)
2010	Brendan Rowland	Freshman	Saddleback College (Mission Viejo)

National Junior College Athletic Association

1755 Telstar Drive, Suite 103, Colorado Springs, CO 80920; Telephone: 719-590-9788; Fax: 719-590-7324; Web site: http://www.njcaa.org

The National Junior College Athletic Association was founded in May 1938 and is an association of community college and junior college athletic departments throughout the United States. After initially dividing the nation into 16 Divisions, the NJCAA is currently divided into 24 Regions (aligned geographically) with a total of 512 member institutions. The NJCAA supports 15 men's sports and 13 women's sports, many of which are divided into one, two, or three Divisions. Selected teams play in one of eight postseason bowls (Citizen's Bank Bowl, North Star Bowl, Graphic Edge Bowl, Valley of the Sun Bowl, C.H.A.M.P.S. Heart of Texas Bowl, Zion's Bank Top of the Mountains Bowl, Central Bank Salt City Bowl, and Mississippi Bowl), from which the NJCAA national champion is selected.

National Junior College Athletic Association Champions

Year	*School*
1956	Coffeyville Community College (KS)
1957	Texarkana College (TX)
1958	Boise Junior College (ID)
1959	Northeastern Oklahoma A&M College (OK)
1960	Cameron State College (OK)
1960	Tyler Junior College (TX)
1961	No champion
1962	No champion
1963	No champion
1964	Phoenix College (AZ)
1965	Ferrum Junior College (VA)
1966	Kilgore College (TX)
1967	Northeastern Oklahoma A&M College (OK)
1968	Ferrum Junior College (VA)
1969	Northeastern Oklahoma A&M College (OK)
1970	Fort Scott Community College (KS)
1971	Mississippi Gulf Coast Community College (MS)
1972	Arizona Western College (AZ)
1973	Mesa Community College (AZ)
1974	Ferrum Junior College (VA)
1975	Mesa Community College (AZ)
1976	Ellsworth Community College (IA)
1977	Ferrum College (VA)
1978	Iowa Central Community College (IA)
1979	Ranger Junior College (TX)
1980	Northeastern Oklahoma A&M College (OK)
1981	Butler County Community College (KS)
1982	Northwest Mississippi Community College (MS)
1983	Coffeyville Community College (KS)
1984	Mississippi Gulf Coast Community (Junior) College (MS)
1985	Snow College (UT)
1986	Northeastern Oklahoma A&M College (OK)
1987	Ellsworth Community College (IA)
1988	Glendale Community College (AZ)
1989	Navarro College (TX)
1990	Coffeyville Community College (KS)
1991	Northeastern Oklahoma A&M College (OK)
1992	Northwest Mississippi Community College (MO)
1993	Mississippi Delta Community College (MS)
1994	Trinity Valley Community College (TX)
1995	Blinn College (TX)
1996	Blinn College (TX)
1997	Trinity Valley Community College (TX)
1998	Butler Community College (KS)
1999	Butler Community College (KS)
2000	Glendale Community College (AZ)
2001	Georgia Military College (GA)
2002	Joliet Junior College (IL)
2003	Butler Community College (KS)
2004	Pearl River Community College (MS)
2005	Glendale Community College (AZ)
2006	Blinn College (TX)
2007	Butler Community College (KS)
2007	Mississippi Gulf Coast Community College (MS)
2008	Butler Community College (KS)
2009	Blinn College (TX)
2010	Navarro College (TX)

National Junior College Athletic Association Player of the Year

Year	*Player*	*Position*	*School*
1990	John Kaleo	Quarterback	Montgomery College (MD)
1991	Kalin Hall	Running Back	Dixie State College of Utah (UT)
1992	Russell Evans	Quarterback	Northwest Mississippi Community College (MS)
1993	Roger Cook	Quarterback	Dixie State College of Utah (UT)
1994	Chris Windsor	Quarterback	Garden City Community College (KS)
1995	Fred Taylor	Quarterback	Hinds Community College (MS)
1996	Rodrick Johnson	Running Back	Dixie State College of Utah (UT)
1997	Frank Murphy	Running Back	Garden City Community College (KS)
1998	Terrance Williams	Running Back	Hinds Community College (MS)
1999	Rudi Johnson	Running Back	Butler County Community College (KS)

National Junior College Athletic Association Offensive Player of the Year

Year	*Player*	*Position*	*School*
2000	Marc Dunn	Quarterback	Ricks College (ID)
2001	Rashad Armstrong	Running Back	Mesa Community College (AZ)
2002	Kelvin Hayden	Wide Receiver	Joliet Junior College (IL)
2003	Emmanuel Marc	Running Back	Hudson Valley Community College (NY)
2004	Jimmy Oliver	Quarterback	Pearl River Community College (MS)
2005	Jimmy Oliver	Quarterback	Pearl River Community College (MS)
2006	Cade Cooper	Quarterback	Snow College (UT)
2007	Jocques Crawford	Running Back	Cisco Junior College (TX)
2008	Terrence Cain	Quarterback	Blinn Cllege (TX)
2009	Jasmin Hopkins	Running Back	Fort Scott Community College (KS)
2010	Reggie Bullock	Running Back	Arizona Western College (AZ)

National Junior College Athletic Association Defensive Player of the Year

Year	*Player*	*Position*	*School*
2000	Dustin Looman	Defensive Lineman	Rochester Community & Technical College (MN)
2001	Randy Jackson	Defensive End	Georgia Military College (GA)
2002	Jamaal Jackson	Defensive Back	Northwest Mississippi Community College (MS)
2003	Larry Kendrick	Defensive Back	Pearl River Community College (MS)
2004	Mickey Pimental	Linebacker	Pima Community College (AZ)
2005	Jonathon Batson	Free Safety	Cisco Junior College (TX)
2006	Austin Panter	Linebacker	Butler Community College (KS)
2007	Markus White	Defensive End	Butler Community College (KS)
2008	Eugene Kinlaw	Defensive Lineman	Hutchinson Community College (KS)
2009	Brad Graham	Linebacker	Navarro College (TX)
2010	Cornelios Carradine	Defensive End	Butler Community College (KS)

There are 516 different schools in the NJCAA, some of which play in numerous Divisions (I, II, or III) simultaneously, depending on the sport.

NJCAA Division I Schools

There are 263 Division I teams in the NJCAA that play in 24 different regions.

- Abraham Baldwin Agricultural College Golden Stallions (Georgia Collegiate Athletic Association and NJCAA Region 17); Tifton, GA 31793; 229-391-5001; www.abac.edu; no football program
- Aiken Technical College Knights (NJCAA Region 10), Graniteville, SC 29829; 803-593-9231; www.atc.edu; no football program
- Alabama Southern Community College Eagles (NJCAA Region 22), Monroeville, AL 36461; 251-575-3156; www.ascc.edu; no football program
- Albany Technical College Titans (Georgia Collegiate Athletic Association and NJCAA Region 17), Albany, GA 31701; 229-430-3500; www.albanytech.edu; no football program
- Allegany College of Maryland Trojans (Maryland Junior College Athletic Conference and NJCAA Region 20), Cumberland, MD 21502; 301-784-5000; www.allegany.edu; no football program
- Allen County Community College Red Devils (Kansas Jayhawk Community College Conference and NJCAA Region 6), Iola, KS 66749; 620-365-5116; www.allencc.edu; no football program
- Alvin Community College Dolphins (NJCAA Region 14), Alvin, TX 77511; 281-756-3500; www.alvincollege.edu; no football program
- Andrew College Fighting Tigers (NJCAA Region 17), Cuthbert, GA 39840; 229-209-5270; www.andrewcollege.edu; no football program
- Angelina College Roadrunners (NJCAA Region 14), Lufkin, TX 75904; 936-639-1301; www.angelina.edu; no football program
- Arizona Western College Matadors (Arizona Community College Athletic Conference and NJCAA

Region 1), Yuma, AZ 85366; 928-317-6000; www.azwestern.edu; plays football in the Western States Football League

- Arkansas Baptist College Buffaloes (Bi-State Conference and NJCAA Region 2), Little Rock, AR 72202; 501-370-4000; http://arkansasbaptist.edu; plays football as an independent team
- ASA College Avengers (NJCAA Region 15), Brooklyn, NY 11201; 718-522-2547; www.asa.edu; plays football in the Northeast Football Conference
- Atlanta Metropolitan College Red-Eyed Panthers (NJCAA Region 17), Atlanta, GA 30310; 404-756-4000; www.atlm.edu; no football program
- Barton Community College Cougars (Kansas Jayhawk Community College Conference and NJCAA Region 6), Great Bend, KS 67530; 620-792-2701; www.bartonccc.edu; no football program
- Baton Rouge Community College Bears (MISS-Lou Junior College Conference and NJCAA Region 23), Baton Rouge, LA 70806; 225-216-8000; www.mybrcc.edu; no football program
- Bishop State Community College Wildcats (NJCAA Region 22), Mobile, AL 36603; 251-405-7000; http://www.bscc.cc.al.us; no football program
- Black Hawk College, East, Warriors (Arrowhead Conference and NJCAA Region 4), Galva, IL 61434; 309-854-1700; Kewanee, IL 61443; 309-854-1875; www.bhc.edu; no football program
- Blinn College Buccaneers (NJCAA Region 14), Brenham, TX 77833; 979-830-4000; www.blinn.edu; plays football in the Southwest Junior College Football Conference
- Bossier Parish Community College Cavaliers (NJCAA Region 14), Bossier City, LA 71111; 318-678-6000; www.bpcc.edu; no football program
- Brevard Community College Titans (Florida Community College Activities Association, Suncoast Conference, and NJCAA Region 8), Cocoa, FL 32922; 321-632-1111; www.brevard.cc.fl.us; no football program
- Broward College (Broward Community College) Seahawks (Florida Community College Activities Association, Suncoast Conference, and NJCAA Region 8), Fort Lauderdale, FL 33301; 954-201-7350; www.broward.edu; no football program
- Brunswick Community College Dolphins (NJCAA Region 10), Bolivia, NC 28422; 910-755-7300; www.brunswickcc.edu; no football program
- Bryant & Stratton College Bobcats (Western New York Athletic Conference and NJCAA Region 3), Syracuse, NY 13203; 315-472-6603; www.bryantstratton.edu/Locations/New-York/Syracuse.aspx; no football program
- Butler Community College Grizzly Bears (Grizzlies) (Kansas Jayhawk Community College Conference and NJCAA Region 6), El Dorado, KS 67042; 316-321-2222; www.butlercc.edu; plays football in the KJCCC
- Calhoun Community College Warhawks (Alabama Community College Conference and NJCAA Region 22), Decatur, AL 35609; 256-306-2500; www.calhoun.edu; no football program
- Cape Fear Community College Sea Devils (NJCAA Region 10), Wilmington, NC 28401; 910-362-7000; http://cfcc.edu; no football program
- Carl Albert State College Vikings (Oklahoma Collegiate Athletic Conference, Bi-State Conference and NJCAA Region 2), Poteau, OK 74953; 918-647-1200; www.carlalbert.edu; no football program
- Casper College Thunderbirds (NJCAA Region 9), Casper, WY 82601; 307-268-2100; www.caspercol lege.edu; no football program
- Central Alabama Community College Trojans (Alabama Community College Conference and NJCAA Region 22), Alexander City, AL 35010; 256-234-6346; www.cacc.edu; no football program
- Central Arizona College Vaqueros (Arizona Community College Athletic Conference and NJCAA Region 1), Coolidge, AZ 85128; 800-237-9814; www.centralaz.edu; no football program
- Central Georgia Technical College Cougars (Georgia Collegiate Athletic Association and NJCAA Region 17), Macon, GA 31206; 478-757-3400; www.centralgatech.edu; no football program
- Central Wyoming College Rustlers (NJCAA Region 9), Riverton, WY 82501; 307-855-2000; www.cwc.edu; no football program
- Chattahoochie Technical College Golden Eagles (Georgia Collegiate Athletic Association and NJCAA Region 17), Marietta, GA 30060; 770-528-4545; www.chattahoocheetech.edu; plays Club Football in the National Club Football Association
- Chattahoochee Valley Community College Pirates (Alabama Community College Conference and NJCAA Region 22), Phenix City, AL 36869; 334-291-4900; www.cv.edu; no football program

- Chattanooga State Community College Tigers (Tennessee Junior and Community College Athletic Association and NJCAA Region 7), Chattanooga, TN 37406; 423-697-4404; www.chattanoogastate.edu; no football program
- Chesapeake College Skipjacks (Maryland Junior College Athletic Conference and NJCAA Region 20), Wye Mills, MD 21679; 410-822-5400; www.chesapeake.edu; no football program
- Chipola College Indians (Florida Community College Activities Association, Suncoast Conference, and NJCAA Region 8), Marianna, FL 32446; 850-526-2761; www.chipola.edu; no football program
- Cisco College Wranglers (North Texas Junior College Athletic Conference and NJCAA Region 5), Cisco, TX 76437; 254-442-5000; www.cisco.edu; plays football in the Southwest Junior College Football Conference
- Clackamas Community College Cougars (Northwest Athletic Association of Community Colleges and NJCAA Region 18), Oregon City, OR 97045; 503-594-6000; www.clackamas.edu; no football program
- Clarendon College Bulldogs (Western Junior College Athletic Conference and NJCAA Region 5), Clarendon, TX 79226; 806-874-3571; www.clarendoncollege.edu; no football program
- Cleveland State Community College Cougars (Tennessee Junior and Community College Athletic Association and NJCAA Region 7), Cleveland, TN 37320; 423-472-7141; www.clevelandstatecc.edu; no football program
- Clinton Junior College Golden Bears (NJCAA Region 10), Rock Hill, SC 29730; 803-327-7402; www.clintonjuniorcollege.edu; no football program
- Cloud County Community College Thunderbirds (Kansas Jayhawk Community College Conference and NJCAA Region 6), Concordia, KS 66901; 800-729-5101; www.cloud.edu; no football program
- Coahoma Community College Tigers (Mississippi Association of Community & Junior Colleges and NJCAA Region 23), Clarksdale, MS 38614; 662-627-2571; www.ccc.cc.ms.us; plays football in the MACJC
- Cochise College Apaches (Arizona Community College Athletic Conference and NJCAA Region 1), Douglas, AZ 85607; 520-364-7943; www.cochise.edu; no football program
- Coffeyville Community College Ravens (Kansas Jayhawk Community College Conference and NJCAA Region 6), Coffeyville, KS 67337; 620-251-7700; www.coffeycille.edu; plays football in the KJCCC
- Colby Community College Trojans (Kansas Jayhawk Community College Conference and NJCAA Region 6), Colby, KS 67701; 785-462-3984; www.colbycc.edu; no football program
- College of Central Florida (Central Florida Community College) Patriots (Florida Community College Activities Association, Suncoast Conference, and NJCAA Region 8), Ocala, FL 34474; 352-873-5800; www.cf.edu; no football program
- College of Southern Idaho Eagles (Scenic West Athletic Conference and NJCAA Region 18), Twin Falls, ID 83303; 208-733-9554; www.csi.edu; no football program
- College of Southern Nevada Coyotes (Scenic West Athletic Conference and NJCAA Region 18), Henderson, NV 89002; 702-651-3000; www.csn.edu/about/locations/henderson.asp; no football program
- Collin College (formerly known as Collin County Community College) Cougars (North Texas Junior College Athletic Conference and NJCAA Region 5), McKinney, TX 75071; 972-548-6790; www.collin.edu; no football program
- Colorado Northwestern Community College Spartans (Scenic West Athletic Conference and NJCAA Region 18), Rangely, CO 81648; 800-562-1105; www.cncc.edu; no football program
- Columbia State Community College Chargers (Tennessee Junior and Community College Athletic Association and NJCAA Region 7), Columbia, TN 38401; 931-540-2722; www.columbiastate.edu; no football program
- Connors State College Cowboys (Oklahoma Collegiate Athletic Conference, Bi-State Conference and NJCAA Region 2), Warner, OK 74469; 918-463-2931; http://connorsstate.edu; no football program
- Copiah-Lincoln Community College Wolfpack (Wolves) (Mississippi Association of Community & Junior Colleges and NJCAA Region 23), Wesson, MS 39191; 601-643-5101; www.colin.edu; plays football in the MACJC
- Cowley County Community College Tigers (Kansas Jayhawk Community College Conference and NJCAA Region 6), Arkansas City, KS 67005; 620-442-0430; www.cowley.edu; no football program
- Crowder College Roughriders (NJCAA Region 16), Neosho MO 64850; 417-451-3223; www.crowder.edu; no football program

- Dakota County Technical College Blue Knights (Minnesota College Athletic Conference and NJCAA Region 13), Rosemount, MN 55068; 651-423-8301; www..dctc.edu; no football program
- Darton College Cavaliers (Georgia Collegiate Athletic Association and NJCAA Region 17), Albany, GA 31707; 229-317-6000; www.darton.edu; no football program
- Dawson Community College Buccaneers (NJCAA Region 9), Glendive, MT 59330; 406-377-3396; www.dawson.edu; no football program
- Daytona State College (Daytona Beach Community College) Falcons (Mid-Florida Conference, Florida Community College Activities Association, Suncoast Conference, and NJCAA Region 8), Daytona Beach, FL 32114; 386-506-3000; www.daytonastate.edu; no football program
- Delaware Technical and Community College, Terry, Hawks (NJCAA Region 19), Dover, DE 19904; 302-857-1100; ww.dtcc.edu/terry; no football program
- Delgado Community College Dolphins (MISS-Lou Junior College Conference and NJCAA Region 23), New Orleans, LA 70119; 504-671-5000; www.dcc.edu; no football program
- Denmark Technical College Panthers (NJCAA Region 10), Denmark, SC 29042; 803-793-5176; www.denmarktech.edu; no football program
- Dodge City Community College Conquistadors (Kansas Jayhawk Community College Conference and NJCAA Region 6), Dodge City, KS 67801; 620-227-9310; www.dc3.edu; plays football in the KJCCC
- Dyersburg State Community College Eagles (Tennessee Junior and Community College Athletic Association and NJCAA Region 7), Dyersburg, TN 38024; 731-286-3200; www.dscc.edu; no football program
- East Central College Falcons (Midwest Community College Athletic Conference and NJCAA Region 16), Union, MO 63084; 636-584-6500; www.eastcentral.edu; no football program
- East Central Community College Warriors (Mississippi Association of Community & Junior Colleges and NJCAA Region 23), Decatur, MS 39327; 601-635-2111; www.eccc.edu; plays football in the MACJC
- East Georgia College Bobcats (Georgia Collegiate Athletic Association and NJCAA Region 17), Swainsboro, GA 30401; 478-289-2017; www.ega.edu; no football program
- East Mississippi Community College Lions (Mississippi Association of Community & Junior Colleges and NJCAA Region 23), Scooba, MS 39358; 662-476-5000; www.eastms.edu; plays football in the MACJC
- Eastern Arizona College Gila Monsters (Arizona Community College Athletic Conference and NJCAA Region 1), Thatcher, AZ 85552; 800-678-3808; www.eac.edu; plays football in the Western States Football League
- Eastern Iowa Community College (Scott Community College) Cougars (Iowa Junior College Athletic Association and NJCAA Region 11), Bettendorf, IA 52722; 563-441-4001; www.eicc.edu/general/scott/index.html; no football program
- Eastern Oklahoma State College Mountaineers (Oklahoma Collegiate Athletic Conference, Bi-State Conference and NJCAA Region 2), Wilburton, OK 74578; 918-465-2361; www.eosc.edu; no football program
- Eastern Wyoming College Lancers (NJCAA Region 9), Torrington, WY 82240; 866-327-8996; http://ewc.wy.edu; no football program
- El Paso Community College Tejanos (Western Junior College Athletic Conference and NJCAA Region 5), El Paso, TX 79925; 915-831-3722; www.epcc.edu; no football program
- Enterprise State Community College Boll Weevils (Enterprise-Ozark Community College) (NJCAA Region 22), Enterprise, AL 36330; 334-347-2623; www.escc.edu; no football program
- Estrella Mountain Community College Mountain Lions (Arizona Community College Athletic Conference and NJCAA Region 1), Avondale, AZ 85392; 623-935-8000; www.estrellamountain.edu; no football program
- Faulkner State Community College Sun Chiefs (Alabama Community College Conference and NJCAA Region 22); Bay Minette, AL 36507; 251-580-2100; www.faulknerstate.edu; no football program
- Florence-Darlington Technical College Stingers (NJCAA Region 10), Florence, SC 29502; 843-661-8324; www.fdtc.edu; no football program
- Florida State College at Jacksonville Stars (Mid-Florida Conference, Suncoast Conference, and NJCAA Region 8), Jacksonville, FL 32246; 904-646-2205; www.fscj.edu; no football program
- Fort Scott Community College Greyhounds (Kansas Jayhawk Community College Conference and

NJCAA Region 6), Fort Scott, KS 66701; 800-874-3722; www.fortscott.edu; plays football in the KJCCC

- Frank Phillips College Plainsman (Western Junior College Athletic Conference and NJCAA Region 5), Borger, TX 79008; 806-457-4200; www.fpctx.edu; no football program
- Gadsden State Community College Cardinals (Alabama Community College Conference and NJCAA Region 22), Gadsden, AL 35903; 256-549-8200; www.gadsdenstate.edu; no football program
- Galveston College Whitecaps (NJCAA Region 14), Galveston, TX 77550; 409-944-4242; www.gc.edu; no football program
- Garden City Community College Broncbusters (Kansas Jayhawk Community College Conference and NJCAA Region 6), Garden City, KS 67846; 620-276-7611; www.gcccks.edu; plays football in the KJCCC
- Garrett College Lakers (Maryland Junior College Athletic Conference and NJCCAA Region 20), McHenry, MD 21541; 301-387-3000; www.garrettcollege.edu; no football program
- GateWay Community College Geckos (Arizona Community College Athletic Conference and NJCAA Region 1), Phoenix, AZ 85034; 602-286-8000; www.gatewaycc.edu; no football program
- Georgia Military College Bulldogs (NJCAA Region 17), Milledgeville, GA 31061; 478-387-4900; www.gmc.cc.ga.us; plays football as an independent team
- Georgia Perimeter College Jaguars (NJCAA Region 17), Clarkston, GA 30021; 678-891-3200; http://jobs.gpc.edu; no football program
- Gillette College Pronghorns (NJCAA Region 9), Gillette, WY 82718; 307-686-0254; www.sheridan.edu/site/gc; no football program
- Globe Institute of Technology Knights (NJCAA Region 15), New York, NY 10018; 212-349-4330; www.globeinstitute.org; plays football as an independent team
- Gordon College Highlanders (NJCAA Region 17), Barnesville, GA 30204; 678-359-5555; www.gdn.edu; no football program
- Grayson County College Vikings (Western Junior College Athletic Conference and NJCAA Region 5), Denison, TX 75020; 903-465-6030; www.grayson.edu; no football program
- Guilford Technical Community College Titans (NJCAA Region 10), Jamestown, NC 27282; 336-334-4822; www.gtcc.edu; no football program
- Gulf Coast State College (Gulf Coast Community College) Commondores (Florida Community College Activities Association, Suncoast Conference, and NCAA Region 8), Panama City, FL 32401; 850-769-1551; www.gulfcoast.edu; no football program
- Hagerstown Community College Hawks (Maryland Junior College Athletic Conference and NJCAA Region 20), Hagerstown, MD 21742; 240-500-2000; www.hagerstowncc.edu; no football program
- Harford Community College Fighting Owls (Maryland Junior College Athletic Conference and NJCAA Region 20), Bel Air, MD 21015; 443-412-2000; www.harford.edu; no football program
- Harry S Truman College (Truman College) (one of the City Colleges of Chicago) Falcons (Arrowhead Conference and NJCAA Region 4), Chicago IL 60640; 773-907-4000; www.trumancollege.edu; no football program
- Highland Community College Cougars (Arrowhead Conference and NJCAA Region 4), Freeport, IL 61032; 815-235-6121; www.highland.edu; no football program
- Highline Community College Thunderbirds (Northwest Athletic Association of Community Colleges and NJCAA Region 18), Des Moines, WA 98198; 206-878-3710; www.highline.edu; no football program
- Hill College Rebels (North Texas Junior College Athletic Conference and NJCAA Region 5), Hillsboro, TX 76645; 254-659-7500; www.hillcollege.edu; no football program
- Hillsborough Community College Hawks (Florida Community College Activities Association, Suncoast Conference, and NJCAA Region 8), Tampa, FL 33614; 813-253-7000; www.hccfl.edu; no football program
- Hinds Community College Eagles (Mississippi Association of Community & Junior Colleges and NJCAA Region 23), Raymond, MS 39154; 601-857-5261; www.hindscc.edu; plays football in the MACJC
- Holmes Community College Bulldogs (Mississippi Association of Community & Junior Colleges and NJCAA Region 23); Goodman, MS 39079; 662-472-2312; www.holmes.cc.ms.us; plays football in the MACJC

- Howard College Hawks (Western Junior College Athletic Conference and NJCAA Region 5), Big Spring, TX 79720; 432-264-5000; www.howardcollege.edu; no football program
- Hutchinson Community College Blue Dragons (Kansas Jayhawk Community College Conference and NJCAA Region 6), Hutchinson, KS 67501; 620-665-3500; www.hutchcc.edu; plays football in the KJCCC
- Independence Community College Pirates (Kansas Jayhawk Community College Conference and NJCAA Region 6), Independence, KS 67301; 620-331-4100; www.indycc.edu; plays football in the KJCCC
- Indian Hills Community College, Centerville, Falcons (Iowa Community College Athletic Conference and NJCAA Region 11), Centerville, IA 52544; 800-726-2585; www.ihcc.cc.ia.us/about/locations/centerville.html; no football program
- Indian Hills Community College, Ottumwa, Warriors (Iowa Community College Athletic Conference and NJCAA Region 11), Ottumwa, IA 52501; 800-726-2585; http://www.ihcc.cc.ia.us/about/locations/ottumwa.html; no football program
- Indian River State College (Indian River Community College) Pioneers (Florida Community College Activities Association, Suncoast Conference, and NJCAA Region 8), Fort Pierce, FL.34981; 772-462-4772; www.irsc.edu; no football program
- Iowa Western Community College Reivers (Iowa Community College Athletic Conference and NJCAA Region 11), Council Bluffs, IA 51503; 712-325-3200; www.iwcc.edu; plays football in the Midwest Football Conference
- Itawamba Community College Indians (Mississippi Association of Community & Junior Colleges and NJCAA Region 23), Fulton, MS 38843; 662-862-8000; www.iccms.edu; plays football in the MACJC
- Jackson State Community College Generals (Tennessee Junior and Community College Athletic Association and NJCAA Region 7), Jackson, TN 38301; 731-424-3520; www.jscc.edu; no football program
- Jacksonville College Jaguars (NJCAA Region 14), Jacksonville, TX 75766; 903-586-2518; www.jacksonville-college.edu; no football program
- Jefferson College Vikings (Midwest Community College Athletic Conference and NJCAA Region 16), Hillsboro, MO 63050; 636-797-3000; www.jeffco.edu; no football program
- Jefferson Davis Community College Warhawks (NJCAA Region 22), Brewton, AL 36427; 251-867-4832; www.jdcc.edu; no football program
- John A. Logan College Volunteers (Great Rivers Athletic Conference and NJCAA Region 24), Carterville, IL 62918; 618-985-3741; www.jalc.edu; no football program
- Jones County Junior College Bobcats (Mississippi Association of Community & Junior Colleges and NJCAA Region 23), Ellisville, MS 39437; 601-477-4000; www.jcjc.edu; plays football in the MACJC
- Kankakee Community College Cavaliers (North Central Community College Conference and NJCAA Region 4), Kankakee, IL 60901; 815-802-8100; www.kcc.edu; no football program
- Kansas City Kansas Community College Blue Devils (Kansas Jayhawk Community College Conference and NJCAA Region 6), Kansas City, KS 66112; 913-334-1100; www.kckcc.edu; no football program
- Kaskaskia College Blue Devils (Great Rivers Athletic Conference and NJCAA Region 24), Centralia, IL 62801; 618-545-3000; www.kaskaskia.edu; no football program
- Kennedy-King College (one of the City Colleges of Chicago) Statesmen (North Central Community College Conference and NJCAA Region 4), Chicago, IL 60621; 773-602-5000; http://kennedyking.ccc.edu; no football program
- Kilgore College Rangers (NJCAA Region 14), Kilgore, TX 75662; 903-984-8531; www.kilgore.edu; plays football in the Southwest Junior College Football Conference
- Labette Community College Cardinals (Kansas Jayhawk Community College Conference and NJCAA Region 6), Parsons, KS 67357; 620-421-6700; www.labette.edu; no football program
- Lake Land College Lakers (Great Rivers Athletic Conference and NJCAA Region 24), Mattoon, IL 61938; 217-234-5253; www.lakeland.cc.il.us; no football program
- Lake Region State College Royals (Mon-Dak Athletic Conference and NJCAA Region 13), Devils Lake, ND 58301; 701-662-1600; www.lrsc.edu; no football program
- Lake Sumter Community College (Florida Community College Activities Association, Suncoast Conference, and NJCAA Region 8), Leesburg, FL 34788; 352-787-3747; www.lscc.edu; no football program

- Lamar Community College Runnin' Lopes (NJCAA Region 9), Lamar, CO 81052; 719-336-2248; www.lamarcc.edu; no football program
- Laramie County Community College Golden Eagles (NJCAA Region 9), Cheyenne, WY 82007; 800-522-2993; www.lccc.wy.edu; no football program
- Laredo Community College Palominos (NJCAA Region 14), Laredo, TX 78046; 956-794-4000; www.laredo.edu; no football program
- Lawson State Community College Cougars (Alabama Community College Conference and NJCAA Region 22), Birmingham, AL 35221; 205-925-2515; www.ls.cc.al.us; no football program
- Lee College Runnin' Rebels (NJCAA Region 14), Baytown, TX 77522; 281-427-5611; www.lee.edu; no football program
- Lenoir Community College Lancers (NJCAA Region 10), Kinston, NC 28502; 252-527-6223; www.lenoircc.edu; no football program
- Lincoln Trail College Statesman (NJCAA Region 24), Robinson, IL 62454; 618-544-8657; www.iecc.edu/LTC; no football program
- Little Big Horn College Rams (NJCAA Region 9), Crow Agency, MT 59022; 406-638-3100; www.lbhc.edu; no football program
- Lon Morris College Bearcats (NJCAA Region 14), Jacksonville, TX 75766; 903-589-4000; www.lonmorris.edu; no football program
- Louisburg College Hurricanes (NJCAA Region 10), Louisburg, NC 27549; 919-496-2521; www.louisburg.edu; plays football in the Northeast Football Conference
- Lurleen B. Wallace Community College Saints (Alabama Community College Conference and NJCAA Region 22), Andalusia AL 36420; 334-222-6591; www.lbwcc.edu; no football program
- Malcolm X College Hawks (North Central Community College Conference and NJCAA Region 4), Chicago, IL 60612; 312-850-7000; http://malcolmx.ccc.edu; no football program
- Marion Military Institute Tigers (Alabama Community College Conference and NJCAA Region 22), Marion, AL 36756; 800-664-1842; www.marionmilitary.edu; no football program
- Marshalltown Community College Tigers (Iowa Community College Athletic Conference and NJCAA Region 11), Marshalltown, Iowa 50158; 641-752-7106; www.iavalley.edu/mcc; no football program
- McCook Community College Indians (Nebraska Community College Athletic Conference and NJCAA Region 9), McCook, NE 69001; 308-345-8100; www.mpcc.edu/mccook_college.html; no football program
- McLennan Community College Highlanders (Western Junior College Athletic Conference and NJCAA Region 5), Waco, TX 76708; 254-299-8000; www.mclennan.edu; no football program
- Mercyhurst North East Saints (Western New York Athletic Conference and NJCAA Region 3), North East, PA 16428; 814-725-6100; 866-846-6042; http://northeast.mercyhurst.edu; no football program
- Meridian Community College Eagles (NJCAA Region 23), Meridian, MS 39307; 601-483-8241; www.mcc.cc.ms.us; no football program
- Mesa Community College Thuderbird (Arizona Community College Athletic Conference and NJCAA Region 1), Mesa, AZ 85202; 480-461-7000; www.mesacc.edu; plays football in the Western States Football League
- Metropolitan Community College, Blue River, Trail Blazers (NJCAA Region 16), Independence, MO 64057; 816-604-6500; mcckc.edu/explore/campuses/blueriver/welcome.asp; no football program
- Metropolitan Community College, Longview, Lakers (NJCAA Region 16), Lee's Summit, MO 64081; 816-604-2000; mcckc.edu/explore/campuses/longview/welcome.asp; no football program
- Metropolitan Community College, Maple Woods, Monarchs (NJCAA Region 16), Kansas City, MO 64156; 816-604-3000; mcckc.edu/explore/campuses/maplewoods/welcome.asp; no football program
- Miami Dade College Sharks (Florida Community College Activities Association, Suncoast Conference, and NJCAA Region 8), Miami, FL 33132; 305-237-8888; www.mdc.edu; no football program
- Middle Georgia College Warriors (NJCAA Region 17), Cochran, GA 31014; 478-934-6221; www.mgc.edu; no football program
- Midland College Chaparrals (Western Junior College Athletic Conference and NJCAA Region 5), Midland, TX 79705; 432-685-4500; www.midland.edu; no football program
- Miles Community College Pioneers (Mon-Dak Athletic Conference and NJCAA Region 9), Miles City, MT 59301; 406-874-6100; www.milescc.edu; no football program

- Mineral Area College Cardinals (Midwest Community College Athletic Conference and NJCAA Region 16), Park Hills, MO 63601; 573-431-4593; www.mineralarea.edu; no football program
- Mississippi Delta Community College Trojans (Mississippi Association of Community & Junior Colleges and NJCAA Region 23), Moorhead, MS 38761; 662-246-6322; www.msdelta.edu; plays football in the MACJC
- Mississippi Gulf Coast Community College Bulldogs (Mississippi Association of Community & Junior Colleges and NJCAA Region 23), Perkinston, MS 39573; 601-928-5211; www.mgccc.edu; plays football in the MACJC
- Missouri State University, West Plains, Grizzles (NJCAA Region 16), West Plains, MO 65775; 417-255-7255; http://wp.missouristate.edu; no football program
- Moberly Area Community College Greyhounds (NJCAA Region 16), Moberly, MO 65270; 660-263-4110; www.macc.edu; no football program
- Monroe College Mustangs (NJCAA Region 15), Bronx, NY 10468; 718-933-6700; www.monroecollege.edu; no football program
- Motlow State Community College Bucks (Tennessee Junior and Community College Athletic Association and NJCAA Region 7), Lynchburg, TN 37352; 931-393-1500; www.mscc.edu; no football program
- Murray State College Aggies (Oklahoma Collegiate Athletic Conference, Bi-State Conference and NJCAA Region 2), Tishomingo, OK 73460; 580-371-2371; www.mscok.edu; no football program
- Navarro College Bulldogs (NJCAA Region 14), Corsicana, TX 75110; 800-628-2776; www.navarrocollege.edu; plays football in the Southwest Junior College Football Conference
- Neosho County Community College Panthers (Kansas Jayhawk Community College Conference and NJCAA Region 6), Chanute, KS 66720; 620-431-2820; www.neosho.edu; no football program
- New Mexico Junior College Thunderbirds (Western Junior College Athletic Conference and NJCAA Region 5), Hobbs, NM 88240; 575-392-4510; www.nmjc.edu; no football program
- New Mexico Military Institute Broncos (Western Junior College Athletic Conference and NJCAA Region 5), Roswell, NM 88201; 800-421-5376; www.nmmi.edu; plays football in the Western States Football League)
- North Central Texas College Lions (North Texas Junior College Athletic Conference and NJCAA Region 5), Gainesville, TX 76240; 940-668-7731; www.nctc.edu; no football program
- North Dakota State College of Science Wildcats (NJCAA Region 13), Wahpeton, ND 58076; 701-671-2401; www.ndscs.nodak.edu; plays football in the Midwest Football Conference
- North Georgia Technical College Eagles (NJCAA Region 17), Clarkesville, GA 30523; 706-754-7700; www.northgatech.edu/pages/visitors_alumni/campuses/clarkesville.aspx; no football program
- North Idaho College Cardinals (Scenic West Athletic Conference and NJCAA Region 18), Coeur d'Alene, ID 83814; 208-769-3300; www.nic.edu; no football program
- North Platte Community College Knights (NJCAA Region 9), North Platte, NE 69101; 308-535-3600; www.mpcc.edy/North_Platte_Community_College.cfm; no football program
- Northeast Community College Hawks (NJCAA Region 9), Norfolk, NE 68701; 402-371-2020; www.northeast.edu; no football program
- Northeast Mississippi Community College Tigers (Mississippi Association of Community & Junior Colleges and NJCAA Region 23), Booneville, MS 38829; 800-555-2154; www.nemcc.edu; plays football in the MACJC
- Northeast Texas Community College Eagles (NJCAA Region 14), Mt. Pleasant, TX 75456; 903-434-8100; www.ntcc.edu; no football program
- Northeastern Junior College Plainsman (NJCAA Region 9), Sterling, CO 80751; 800-626-4637; www.njc.edu; no football program
- Northeastern Oklahoma A&M College Golden Norseman (Oklahoma Collegiate Athletic Conference, Bi-State Conference and NJCAA Region 2), Miami, OK 74354; 918-542-8441; www.Neo.edu; plays football as an independent team
- Northern Oklahoma College Jets (Oklahoma Collegiate Athletic Conference, Bi-State Conference and NJCAA Region 2), Enid, OK 73702; 580-242-6300; www.north-ok.edu; no football program
- Northern Oklahoma College, Tonkawa, Mavericks (Oklahoma Collegiate Athletic Conference, Bi-State Conference and NJCAA Region 2), Tonkawa, OK 74653; 580-628-6200; www.north-ok.edu/Tonkawa; no football program

- Northwest College Trappers (Wyoming Community College Athletic Conference and NJCAA Region 9), Powell, WY 82435; 800-560-4692; www.nwc.cc.wy.us; no football program
- Northwest Florida State College Raiders (Florida Community College Activities Association, Suncoast Conference, and NJCAA Region 8), Niceville, FL 32578; 850-678-5111; www.nwfsc.edu/Niceville; no football program
- Northwest Kansas Technical College Mavericks (affiliated with the Kansas Jayhawk Community College Conference and NJCAA Region 6), Goodland, KS 67735; 800-316-4127; www.nwktc.edu; no football program
- Northwest Mississippi Community College Rangers (Mississippi Association of Community & Junior Colleges and NJCAA Region 23), Senatobia, MS 38668; 662-562-3200; http://northwestms.net; plays football in the MACJC
- Odessa College Wranglers (Western Junior College Athletic Conference and NJCAA Region 5), Odessa, TX 79764; 432-335-6400; www.odessa.edu; no football program
- Olney Central College Blue Knights (Great Rivers Athletic Conference and NJCAA Region 24), Olney, IL 62450; 618-393-2982; www.iecc.edu/occ; no football program
- Otero Junior College Rattlers (NJCAA Region 9), La Junta, CO 81050; 719-384-6831; www.ojc.edu; no football program
- Palm Beach State College (Palm Beach Community College) Panthers (Southern Conference, Suncoast Conference, and NJCAA Region 8), Lake Worth, FL 33461; 561-868-3350; www.palmbeachstate.edu; no football program
- Panola College Ponies (NJCAA Region 14), Carthage, TX 75633; 903-693-2000; www.panola.edu; no football program
- Paris Junior College Dragons (NJCAA Region 14), Paris, TX 75460; 903-785-7661; www.parisjc.edu; no football program
- Pasco-Hernando Community College Conquistadors (Florida Community College Activities Association, Suncoast Conference, and NJCAA Region 8), New Port Richey, FL 34654; 727-847-2727; http://phcc.edu; no football program
- Pearl River Community College Wildcats (Mississippi Association of Community & Junior Colleges and NJCAA Region 23), Poplarville, MS 39470; 601-403-1000; www.prcc.edu; plays football in the MACJC
- Pensacola State College (Pensacola Junior College) Pirates (Panhandle Conference, Florida Community Colleges Activities Association, Suncoast Conference, and NJCAA Region 8), Pensacola, FL 32504; 850-484-1000; www.pensacolastate.edu; no football program
- Pitt Community College Bulldogs (NJCAA Region 10), Winterville, NC 28590; 252-493-7200; www.pittcc.edu; no football program
- Polk State College (Polk Community College) Vikings (Suncoast Conference and NJCAA Region 8), Winter Haven, FL 33881; 863-297-1000; www.polk.edu; no football program
- Potomac State College (West Virginia University) Catamounts (Pennsylvania Collegiate Athletic Association and NJCAA Region 20), Keyser, WV 267261; 304-788-6820; www.potomacstatecollege.edu; no football program
- Pratt Community College Beavers (Kansas Jayhawk Community College Conference and NJCAA Region 6), Pratt, KS 67124; 620-672-9800; http://prattcc.edu; no football program
- Ranger College Rangers (North Texas Junior College Athletic Conference and NJCAA Region 5), Ranger, TX 76470; 254-647-3234; www.rangercollege.edu; no football program
- Redlands Community College Cougars (Oklahoma Collegiate Athletic Conference, Bi-State Conference and NJCAA Region 2), El Reno, OK 73036; 405-262-2552; www.redlandscc.edu; no football program
- Richard J. Daley College (one of the City Colleges of Chicago) Bulldogs (Arrowhead Conference and NJCAA Region 4), Chicago, IL 60652; 773-838-7500; http://daley.ccc.edu; no football program
- Roane State Community College Raiders (Tennessee Junior and Community College Athletic Association and NJCAA Region 7), Harriman, TN 37748; 865-354-3000; www.roanestate.edu; no football program
- Rockingham Community College Eagles (NJCAA Region 10), Wentworth, NC 27375; 336-342-4261; www.rockinghamcc.edu; no football program
- Rose State College Raiders (Bi-State Conference and NJCAA Region 2), Midwest City, OK 73110; 405-733-7673; www.rose.edu; no football program

- St. Charles Community College (Midwest Community College Athletic Conference and NJCAA Region 16), Cottleville, MO 63376; 636-922-8000; www.stchas.edu; no football program
- St. Johns River Community College Vikings (Florida Community College Activities Association, Suncoast Conference, and NJCAA Region 8), Palatka, FL 32177; 386-312-4200; www.sjrcc.edu; no football program
- St. Petersburg College Titans (Florida Community College Activities Association, Suncoast Conference, and NJCAA Region 8), St. Petersburg, FL 33733; 727-341-4772; www.spcollege.edu; no football program
- Salt Lake Community College Bruins (Scenic West Athletic Conference and NJCAA Region 18), Salt Lake City, UT 84123; 801-957-7522; www.slcc.edu; no football program
- San Jacinto College, Central, Ravens (NJCAA Region 14), Pasadena, TX 77505; 281-476-1501; www.sanjac.edu/future-students/about-san-jac/why-san-jac/campuses/central-campus; no football program
- San Jacinto College, North, Gators (NJCAA Region 14), Houston, TX 77049; 281-458-4050; www.sanjac.edu/future-students/about-san-jac/why-san-jac/campuses/north-campus; no football program
- San Jacinto College, South, Coyotes (NJCAA Region 14), Houston, TX 77089; 281-484-1900; www.sanjac.edu/future-students/about-san-jac/why-san-jac/campuses/south-campus; no football program
- Santa Fe College Saints (Florida Community College Activities Association, Suncoast Conference, and NJCAA Region 8), Gainesville, FL 32606; 352-395-5000; www.sfcollege.edu; no football program
- Sauk Valley Community College Skyhawks (Arrowhead Conference and NJCAA Region 4), Dixon, IL 61021; 815-288-5511; www.svcc.edu; no football program
- Seminole State College of Florida Raiders (Florida Community College Activities Association, Mid-Florida Conference and NJCAA Region 8), Sanford, FL 32773; 407-708-4722; www.seminolestate.edu; no football program
- Seminole State College Trojans (Oklahoma Collegiate Athletic Conference, Bi-State Conference, and NJCAA Region 2), Seminole, OK 74868; 405-382-9950; www.sscok.edu; no football program
- Seward County Community College Saints (Kansas Jayhawk Community College Conference and NJCAA Region 6), Liberal, KS 67905; 620-624-1951; www.sccc.edu; no football program
- Shelton State Community College Buccaneers (Alabama Community College Conference and NJCAA Region 22), Tuscaloosa, AL 35405; 205-391-2211; www.sheltonstate.edu; no football program
- Sheridan College Generals (NJCAA Region 9), Gillette, WY 82718; 307-686-0254; www.sheridan.edu; no football program
- Snead State Community College Parsons (Alabama Community College Conference and NJCAA Region 22), Boaz, AL 35957; 256-593-512; www.snead.edu; no football program
- Snow College Badgers (Scenic West Athletic Conference and NJCAA Region 18), Ephraim, UT 84627; 435-283-7000; www.snow.edu; plays football in the Western States Football League
- South Florida Community College Panthers (Southern Conference, Suncoast Conference, and NJCAA Region 8), Avon Park, FL 33825; 863-453-6661; www.southflorida.edu; no football program
- South Georgia College Tigers (Georgia Collegiate Athletic Association and NJCAA Region 17), Douglas, GA 31533; 912-260-4200; www.sgc.edu; no football program
- South Georgia Technical College Jets (Georgia Collegiate Athletic Association and NJCAA Region 17), Americus, GA 31709; 229-931-2394; www.southgatech.edu; no football program
- South Plains College Texans (Western Junior College Athletic Conference and NJCAA Region 5), Levelland, TX; 79336; 806-894-9611; www.southplainscollege.edu; no football program
- Southeastern Community College Blackhawks (Iowa Community College Athletic Conference and NJCAA Region 11), West Burlington, IA 52655; 866-722-4692; www.scciowa.edu; no football program
- Southeastern Illinois College Falcons (Great Rivers Athletic Conference and NJCAA Region 24), Harrisburg, IL 62946; 618-252-5400; www.sic.edu; no football program
- Southern Union State Community College Bisons (Alabama Community College Conference and NJCAA Region 22), Wadley, AL 36276; 256-395-2211; www.suscc.edu; no football program
- Southern University at Shreveport Jaguars (MISS-Lou Junior College Conference and NJCAA Region 23), Shreveport, LA 71107; 318-670-6000; http://web.susla.edu; no football program

- Southwest Mississippi Community College Bears (Mississippi Association of Community & Junior Colleges and NJCAA Region 23), Summit, MS 39666; 601-276-2000; www.smcc.cc.ms.us; plays football in the MACJC
- Southwest Tennessee Community College Saluqis (Tennessee Junior and Community College Athletic Association and NJCAA Region 7), Memphis, TN 38134; 901-333-5000; www.southwest.tn.edu; no football program
- Southwestern Christian College Rams (Texas Junior College Athletic Conference and NJCAA Region 5), Terrell, TX 75160; 972-524-3341; www.swcc.edu; no football program
- Southwestern Illinois College Blue Storm (Great Rivers Athletic Conference and NJCAA Region 24), Belleville, IL 62221; 618-235-2700; www.swic.edu; no football program
- Spartanburg Methodist College Pioneers (NJCAA Region 10), Spartanburg, SC, 29301; 864-587-4000; http://smcsc.edu; no football program
- State College of Florida (Manatee-Sarasota) (Manatee Community College) Manatees (Florida Community College Activities Association, Suncoast Conference, and NJCAA Region 8), Bradenton, FL 34207; 941-752-5000; www.scf.edu; no football program
- State Fair Community College Roadrunners (NJCAA Region 16), Sedalia, MO 65301; 877-311-7322; www.sfccmo.edu; no football program
- Surry Community College Knights (NJCAA Region 10), Dobson, NC 27017; 336-386-8121; www.surry.edu; no football program
- Tallahassee Community College Eagles (Florida Community College Activities Assoc., Suncoast Conference, and NJCAA Region 8), Tallahassee, FL 32304; 850-201-6200; www.tcc.fl.edu; no football program
- Temple College Leopards (North Texas Junior College Athletic Conference and NJCAA Region 5), Temple, TX 76504; 254-298-8282; www.templejc.edu; no football program
- Texarkana College Bulldogs (NJCAA Region 14), Texarkana, TX 75599; 903-832-5565; www.texarkanacollege.edu; no football program
- Three Rivers Community College Raiders (Midwest Community College Athletic Conference and NJCAA Region 16), Poplar Bluff, MO 63901; 877-879-8722; www.trcc.edu; no football program
- Tri-County Technical College Hawks (NJCAA Region 10), Pendleton, SC 29670; 864-646-1500; www.tctc.edu; no football program
- Trinidad State Junior College Trojans (NJCAA Region 9), Trinidad, CO 81082; 800-621-8752; www.trinidadstate.edu; no football program
- Trinity Valley Community College Cardinals (NJCAA Region 14), Athens, TX 75751; 903-677-8822; www2.tvcc.edu; plays football in the Southwest Junior College Football Conference
- Tyler Junior College Apaches (NJCAA Region 14), Tyler, TX 75701; 903-510-2200; www.tjc.edu; plays football in the Southwest Junior College Football Conference
- University of South Carolina, Lancaster, Lancers (NJCAA Region 10), Lancaster SC 29720; 803-313-7000; http://usclancaster.sc.edu; no football program
- University of South Carolina, Salkehatchie, Indians (NJCAA Region 10), Allendale, SC 29810; 803-584-3446; http://uscsalkehatchie.sc.edu; no football program
- University of South Carolina, Sumter, Fire Ants (NJCAA Region 10), Sumter, SC 29150; 803-775-8727; www.uscsumter.edu; no football program
- Utah State University, College of Eastern Utah, Eagles (Scenic West Athletic Conference and NJCAA Region 18), Price, Utah 84501; 435-613-5000; www.ceu.edu; no football program
- Vernon College Chaparrals (North Texas Junior College Athletic Conference and NJCAA Region 5), Vernon, TX 76384; 940-552-6291; www.vernoncollege.edu; no football program
- Vincennes University Trailblazers (NJCAA Region 12), Vincennes, IN 47591; 800-742-9198; www.vinu.edu; no football program
- Volunteer State Community College Pioneers (Tennessee Junior and Community College Athletic Association and NJCAA Region 7), Gallatin, TN 37066; 615-452-8600; www.volstate.edu; no football program
- Wabash Valley College Warriors (Great Rivers Athletic Conference and NJCAA Region 24), Mt. Carmel, IL 62863; 618-262-8641; www.iecc.edu/wvc; no football program
- Wallace Community College, Dothan (George C. Wallace Community College-Dothan) Governors (Southern Conference and NJCAA Region 22), Dothan, AL 36303; 334-983-3521; www.wallace.edu; no football program

- Wallace Community College, Selma, Patriots (NJCAA Region 22), Selma, AL 36703; 334-876-9227; www.wccs.edu; no football program
- Wallace State Community College Lions (Alabama Community College Conference and NJCAA Region 22), Hanceville AL, 35077; 866-350-9722; www.wallacestate.edu; no football program
- Walters State Community College Senators (Tennessee Junior and Community College Athletic Association and NJCAA Region 7), Morristown, TN 37813; 423-585-2600; www.ws.edu; no football program
- Waycross College Swamp Foxes (Georgia Collegiate Athletic Association and NJCAA Region 17), Waycross, GA 31503; 912-449-7600; www.waycross.edu; no football program
- Weatherford College Coyotes (North Texas Junior College Athletic Conference and NJCAA Region 5), Weatherford, TX 76086; 817-594-5471; www.wc.edu; no football program
- Westchester Community College Vikings (Mid Hudson Conference and NJCAA Region 15), Valhalla, NY 10595; 914-606-6600; www.sunywcc.edu; no football program
- Western Nebraska Community College Cougars (NJCAA Region 9), Scottsbluff, NE 69361; 308-635-3606; www.wncc.edu; no football program
- Western Nevada College Wildcats (Scenic West Athletic Conference and NJCAA Region 18), Carson City, NV 89703; 775-445-3000; www.wnc.edu; no football program
- Western Oklahoma State College Pioneers (Oklahoma Collegiate Athletic Conference, Bi-State Conference and NJCAA Region 2), Altus, OK 73521; 580-477-2000; www.wosc.edu; no football program
- Western Texas College Westerners (Western Junior College Athletic Conference and NJCAA Region 5), Snyder, TX 79549; 325-573-8511; www.wtc.edu; no football program
- Western Wyoming Community College Mustangs (NJCAA Region 9), Rock Springs, WY 82901; 307-382-1600; www.wwcc.wy.edu; no football program
- Wharton County Junior College Pioneers (NJCAA Region 14), Wharton, TX 77488, 979-532-4560; www.wcjc.edu; no football program
- Wilkes Community College Cougars (NJCAA Region 10), Wilkesboro, NC 28697; 336-838-6100; www.wilkescc.edu; no football program
- Williston State College Tetons (Mon-Dak Athletic Conference and NJCAA Region 13), Williston, ND 58801; 701-774-4200; www.willistonstate.edu; no football program
- Yavapai College Roughriders (Arizona Community College Athletic Conference and NJCAA Region 1), Prescott, AZ 86301; 928-445-7300; www.yc.edu; no football program

NJCAA Division II Schools

There are 127 Division II teams in the NJCAA that play in 24 different regions.

- Alfred State College (SUNY College of Technology) Pioneers (Western New York Athletic Conference and NJCAA Region 3), Alfred, NY 14802; 607-587-4111; www.alfredstate.edu; plays football in the Northeast Football Conference
- Alpena Community College Lumberjacks (Michigan Community College Athletic Association and NJCAA Region 12), Alpena, MI 49707; 989-356-9021; www.alpenacc.edu; no football program
- Ancilla College Chargers (Michigan Community College Athletic Association and NJCAA Region 12), Donaldson, IN 46543; 574-936-8898; www.ancilla.edu; no football program
- Baltimore City Community College Panthers (Maryland Junior College Athletic Conference and NJCAA Region 20), Baltimore, MD 21202; 410-986-5599; www.bccc.edu; no football program
- Bismarck State College Mystics (Mon-Dak Athletic Conference and NJCAA Region 13), Bismarck, ND 58506; 701-224-5400; www.bsc.nodak.edu; no football program
- Black Hawk College, Moline, Braves (Arrowhead Conference and NJCAA Region 4), Moline, IL 61265; 309-796-5000; www.bhc.edu; no football program
- Brown Mackie College, Salina, Lions (NJCAA Region 6), Salina, KS 67401; 785-825-5422; www.brownmackie.edu; mo football program
- Burlington County College Barons (Garden State Athletic Conference and NJCAA Region 19), Pemberton, NJ 08068; 609-894-9311; www.bcc.edu; no football program
- Carl Sandburg College Chargers (Arrowhead Conference and NJCAA Region 4), Galesburg, IL 61401; 309-344-2518; www.sandburg.edu; no football program

- Cecil College Seahawks (Maryland Junior College Athletic Conference and NJCAA Region 20), North East, MD 21901; 410-287-1000; www.cecil.edu; no football program
- Central Community College Raiders (NJCAA Region 9), Columbus NE 68602; 402-564-7132; www.cccneb.edu; no football program
- Chandler, Gilbert, Community College Coyotes (Arizona Community College Athletic Conference and NJCAA Region 1), Chandler, AZ 85225; 480-732-7000; www.cgc.maricopa.edu; no football program
- Cincinnati State Technical & Community College Surge (Ohio Community College Athletic Conference and NJCAA Region 12), Cincinnati, OH 45223; 513-569-1500; www.cincinnatistate.edu; no football program
- Coastal Bend College, Beeville, Cougars (NJCAA Region 14), Beeville, TX 78102; 361-358-2838; www.coastalbend.edu; no football program
- College of Lake County Lancers (Illinois Skyway Collegiate Conference and NJCAA Region 4), Grayslake, IL 60030; 847-543-2000; www.clcillinois.edu; no football program
- College of Southern Maryland Hawks (Maryland Junior College Athletic Conference and NJCAA Region 20), La Plata, MD 20646; 301-934-2251; www.csmd.edu; no football program
- College of the Albemarle Dolphins (NJCAA Region 10), Elizabeth City, NC 27906; 252-335-0821; www.albemarle.edu; no football program
- Columbus State Community College Cougars (Ohio Community College Athletic Conference and NJCAA Region 12), Columbus, OH 43215; 614-287-5353; www2.cscc.edu; no football program
- Community College of Baltimore County, Catonsville, Cardinals (Maryland Junior College Athletic Conference and NJCAA Region 20), Baltimore, MD 21228; 443-840-2222; www.ccbcmd.edn/directory/cat/catonsville.htm; no football program
- Community College of Baltimore County, Dundalk, Lions (Maryland Junior College Athletic Conference and NJCAA Region 20), Baltimore, MD 21222; 443-840-2222; www.ccbcmd.edu/directory/dundalk/d_maps.html; no football program
- Community College of Baltimore County, Essex, Knights (Maryland Junior College Athletic Conference and NJCAA Region 20), Baltimore, MD 21222; 443-840-2222; www.ccbcmd.edu/directory/essex/index.html; no football program
- Community College of Beaver County Titans (Western Pennsylvania Collegiate Conference, Pennsylvania Collegiate Athletic Association, and NJCAA Region 20), Monaca, PA 15061; 724-480-2222; www.ccbc.edu; no football program
- Community College of Rhode Island Knights (NJCAA Region 21), Warwick, RI 02886; 401-825-1000; www.ccri.edu; no football program
- Cottey College Comets (NJCAA Region 16), Nevada, MO 64772; 417-667-8181; www.cottey.edu; no football program
- County College of Morris Titans (Golden State Athletic Conference and NJCAA Region 19), Randolph, NJ 07869; 973-328-5000; www.ccm.edu; no football program
- Cuyahoga Community College Challangers (Ohio Community College Athletic Conference and NJCAA Region 12), Cleveland, OH 44115; 800-954-8742; www.tri-c.edu; no football program
- Dakota College at Bottineau (Minot State University, Bottineau) Lumberjacks (Mon-Dak Athletic Conference and NJCAA Region 13), Bottineau, ND 58318; 701-228-5488; www.dakotacollege.edu; plays football as an independent team
- Danville Area Community College Jaguars (Mid-West Athletic Conference and NJCAA Region 24), Danville, IL 61832; 217-443-3222; www.dacc.edu; no football program
- Danville Community College Knights (NJCAA Region 10), Danville, VA 24541; 434-797-2222; www.dcc.vccs.edu; no football program
- Dean College Bulldogs (NJCAA Region 21), Franklin, MA 02038; 877-879-3326; www.dean.edu; plays in the Northeast Football Conference
- Delaware Technical and Community College Roadrunners (NJCAA Region 19), Georgetown, DE 19947; 302-856-5400; www.dtcc.edu; no football program
- Delaware Technical & Community College, Stanton/Wilmington Spirit (NJCAA Region 19), Wilmington, DE 19801; 302-571-5300; http://www.dtcc.edu/stanton-wilmington; no football program
- Delta College Pioneers (Michigan Community College Athletic Association and NJCAA Region 12), University Center, MI 48710; 989-686-9000; www.delta.edu; no football program

- Des Moines Area Community College Bears (Iowa Community College Athletic Conference and NJCAA Region 11), Boone, IA 50036; 515-432-7203; http://go.dmacc.edu/boone; no football program
- Edison Community College Chargers (Ohio Community College Athletic Conference and NJCAA Region 12), Piqua, OH 45356; 937-778-8600; www.edisonohio.edu; no football program
- Elgin Community College Spartans (Illinois Skyway Collegiate Conference and NJCAA Region 4), Elgin, IL 60123; 847-697-1000; www.elgin.edu; no football program
- Ellsworth Community College Panthers (Iowa Community Conference Athletic Association and NJCAA Region 11), Iowa Falls, IA 50126; 641-648-4611; www.iavalley.edu/ecc; plays football in the Midwest Football Conference
- Erie Community College Kats (Western New York Athletic Conference and NJCAA Region 3), Buffalo, NY 14203; 716-851-1001; www.ecc.edu; plays football in the Northeast Football Conference
- Essex County College Wolverines (Garden State Athletic Conference and NJCAA Region 19), Newark, NJ 07102; 973-877-3000; www.essex.edu; no football program
- Frederick Community College Cougars (Maryland Junior College Athletic Conference and NJCAA Region 20), Frederick, MD 21702; 301-846-2400; www.frederick.edu; no football program
- Genesee Community College Cougars (Western New York Athletic Conference and NJCAA Region 3), Batavia, NY 14020; 585-343-0055; www.genesee.edu; no football program
- Glen Oaks Community College Vikings (Michigan Community College Athletic Association and NJCAA Region 12), Centreville, MI 49032; 269-467-9945; www.glenoaks.edu; no football program
- Glendale Community College Gauchos (Arizona Community College Athletic Conference and NJCAA Region 1), Glendale, AZ 85302; 623-845-3000; www.gc.maricopa.edu; plays football in the Western States Football League
- Gogebic Community College Samsons (NJCAA Region 13), Ironwood, MI 49938; 906-932-4231; www.gogebic.edu; no football program
- Grand Rapids Community College Raiders (Michigan Community College Athletic Association and NJCAA Region 12), Grand Rapids, MI 49503; 616-234-4000; www.grcc.edu; plays football in the Midwest Football Conference
- Harcum College Bears (NJCAA Region 19), Bryn Mawr, PA 19010; 610-525-4100; www.harcum.edu; no football program
- Heartland Community College Hawks (Mid-West Athletic Conference and NJCAA Region 24), Normal, IL 61761; 309-268-8000; www.heartland.edu; no football program
- Henry Ford Community College Hawks (Michigan Community College Athletic Association and NJCAA Region 12), Dearborn, MI 48128; 800-585-4322; www.hfcc.edu; no football program
- Hesston College Larks (a two-year college of the Mennonite Church USA that is associated with the Kansas Jayhawk Community College Conference and NJCAA Region 6), Hesston, KS 67062; 800-995-2757; www.hesston.edu; no football program
- Highland Community College Scotties (Kansas Jayhawk Community College Conference and NJCAA Region 6), Highland, KS 66035; 785-442-6000; www.highlandcc.edu; plays football in the KJCCC
- Howard Community College Dragons (Maryland Junior College Athletic Conference and NJCAA Region 20), Columbia, MD 21044; 443-518-1200; www.howardcc.edu; no football program
- Illinois Central College Cougars (Mid-West Athletic Conference and NJCAA Region 24), East Peoria, IL 61635; 309-694-5422; www.icc.edu; no football program
- Illinois Valley Community College Eagles (Arrowhead Conference and NJCAA Region 4), Oglesby, IL 61348; 815-224-2720; www.ivcc.edu; no football program
- Iowa Central Community College Tritons (Iowa Community College Athletic Conference and NJCAA Region 11), Fort Dodge, IA 50501; 800-362-2793; www.iccc.cc.ia.us; plays football in the Midwest Football Conference
- Iowa Lakes Community College Lakers (Iowa Community College Athletic Conference and NJCAA Region 11), Estherville, IA 51334; 712-362-2604; www.iowalakes.edu; no football program
- Jackson Community College Jets (Michigan Community College Athletic Association and NJCAA Region 12), Jackson, MI 49201; 517-787-0800; www.jccmi.edu; no football program
- Jamestown Community College (State University of New York) Jayhawks (Western New York Athletic Conference and NJCAA Region 3), Jamestown, NY 14702; 716-338-1000; www.sunyjcc.edu; no football program

- Jamestown Community College, Cattaraugus (State University of New York), Jaguars (Western New York Athletic Conference and NJCAA Region 3), Olean, NY 14760; 716-376-7500; www.sunyjcc.edu/cattaraugus; no football program
- John Wood Community College Trail Blazers (Mid-West Athletic Conference and NJCAA Region 24), Quincy, IL 62305; 217-224-6500; www.jwcc.edu; no football program
- Johnson County Community College Cavaliers (Kansas Jayhawk Community College Conference and NJCAA Region 6), Overland Park, KS 66210; 913-469-8500; www.jccc.edu; no football program
- Johnston Community College Jaguars (NJCAA Region 10), Smithfield, NC 27577; 919-934-3051; www.johnstoncc.edu; no football program
- Kalamazoo Valley Community College Cougars (Michigan Community College Athletic Association and NJCAA Region 12), Kalamazoo, MI 49007; 269-373-7800; www.kvcc.edu; no football program
- Kellogg Community College Bruins (Michigan Community College Athletic Association and NJCAA Region 12), Battle Creek, MI 49017; 269-965-3931; www.kellogg.edu; no football program
- Kirkwood Community College Eagles (Iowa Community College Athletic Conference and NJCAA Region 11), Cedar Rapids, IA 52404; 319-398-5517; www.kirkwood.edu; no football program
- Kirtland Community College Firebirds (Michigan Community College Athletic Association and NJCAA Region 12), Roscommon, MI 48653; 989-275-5000; www.kirtland.edu; no football program
- Kishwaukee College Kougars (Arrowhead Conference and NJCAA Region 4), Malta, IL 60150; 815-825-2086; www.kishwaukeecollege.edu; no football program
- Lackawanna College Falcons (NJCAA Region 19), Scranton, PA 18509; 877-346-3552; www.lackawanna.edu; plays football in the Northeast Football Conference
- Lake Michigan College Indians (Michigan Community College Athletic Association and NJCAA Region 12), Benton Harbor, MI 49022; 269-927-8100; www.lakemichigancollege.edu; no football program
- Lakeland Community College Lakers (Ohio Community College Athletic Conference and NJCAA Region 12), Kirtland, OH 44094; 440-525-7000; http://lakelandcc.edu; no football program
- Lansing Community College Stars (Michigan Community College Athletic Association and NJCAA Region 12), Lansing, MI 48901; 517-483-1957; www.lcc.edu; no football program
- Lewis & Clark Community College Trailblazers (Mid-West Athletic Conference and NJCAA Region 24), Godfrey, IL 62035; 618-468-7000; www.lc.edu; no football program
- Lincoln College Lynx (Mid-West Athletic Conference and NJCAA Region 24), Lincoln, IL 62656; 217-732-3155; www.lincolncollege.edu; no football program
- Lincoln Land Community College Loggers (Mid-West Athletic Conference and NJCAA Region 24), Springfield, IL 62794; 217-786-2200; www.llcc.edu; no football program
- Louisiana State University, Eunice, Bengals (MISS-Lou Junior College Conference and NJCAA Region 23), Eunice, LA 70535; 337-457-7311; www.lsue.edu; no football program
- Luna Community College Roughriders (Western Junior College Athletic Conference and NJCAA Region 5), Las Vegas, NM 87701; 800-588-7232; www.luna.edu; no football program
- Macomb Community College Monarchs (Michigan Community College Athletic Association and NJCAA Region 12), Warren, MI 48088; 586-445-7999; www.macomb.edu; no football program
- Manor College Blue Jays (NJCAA Region 19), Jenkintown, PA 19046; 215-885-2360; www.manor.edu; no football program
- Massasoit Community College Warriors (NJCAA Region 21), Brockton, MA 02302; 508-588-9100; www.massasoit.mass.edu; no football program
- Metropolitan Community College, Penn Valley, Scouts (NJCAA Region 16), Kansas City, MO 64111; 816-604-4000; http://mcckc.edu/explore/campuses/pennvalley; no football program
- McHenry County College Scots (Illinois Skyway Collegiate Conference and NJCAA Region 4), Crystal Lake, IL 60012; 815-455-3700; www.mchenry.edu; no football program
- Mercer County Community College Vikings (Garden State Athletic Conference and NJCAA Region 19), Trenton, NJ 08608; 609-570-3100; www.mccc.edu/welcome_kerney.shtml; no football program
- Monroe Community College (State University of New York) Tribunes (Western New York Athletic Conference and NJCAA Region 3), Rochester, NY 14623; 585-292-2000; www.monroecc.edu; no football program
- Moraine Valley Community College Cyclones (Illinois Skyway Collegiate Conference and NJCAA Region 4), Palos Hills, IL 60465; 708-974-4300; www.morainevalley.edu; no football program

- Morton College Panthers (Illinois Skyway Collegiate Conference and NJCAA Region 4), Cicero, IL 60804; 708-656-8000; www.morton.edu; no football program
- Mott Community College Bears (Michigan Community College Athletic Association and NJCAA Region 12), Flint, MI 48503; 810-762-0200; www.mcc.edu; no football program
- Muskegon Community College Jayhawks (Michigan Community College Athletic Association and NJCAA Region 12), Muskegon, MI 49442; 231-773-9131; www.muskegoncc.edu; no football program
- New River Community College Knights (NJCAA Region 10), Dublin, VA 24084; 540-674-3600; www.nr.edu; no football program
- Niagara County Community College Thunder Wolves (Western New York Athletic Conference and NJCAA Region 3), Sanborn, NY 14132; 716-614-6222; www.niagaracc.suny.edu; no football program
- North Arkansas College Pioneers (Bi-State Conference and NJCAA Region 2), Harrison, AR 72601; 870-391-3000; www.northark.edu; no football program
- North Central Missouri College Pirates (NJCAA Region 16), Trenton, MO 64683; 660-359-3948; www.ncmissouri.edu; no football program
- North Iowa Area Community College Trojans (Iowa Community College Athletic Conference and NJCAA Region 11), Mason City, IA 50401; 641-423-1264; www.niacc.edu; no football program
- Northern Virginia Community College (NJCAA Region 20), Alexandria, VA 22311; 703-257-6600; www.nvcc.edu; no football program
- Oakland Community College Raiders (Michigan Community College Athletic Association and NJCAA Region 12), Bloomfield Hills, MI 48304; 248-341-2000; www.oaklandcc.edu; no football program
- Oakton Community College Raiders (Illinois Skyway Collegiate Conference and NJCAA Region 4), Des Plaines, IL 60016; 847-635-1600; www.oakton.edu; no football program
- Olive-Harvey College (one of the City Colleges of Chicago) Panthers (North Central Community College Conference and NJCAA Region 4), Chicago, IL 60628; 773-291-6100; http://oliveharvey.ccc.edu; no football program
- Orange County Community College (State University of New York, SUNY Orange) Colts (NJCAA Region 15), Middletown, NY 10940; 845-344-6222; www.sunyorange.edu; no football program
- Owens Community College Express (Ohio Community College Athletic Conference and NJCAA Region 12), Toledo, OH 43699; 567-661-7000; www.owens.edu; no football program
- Paradise Valley Community College Pumas (Arizona Community College Athletic Conference and NJCAA Region 1), Phoenix, AZ 85032; 602-787-6500; www.pvc.maricopa.edu; no football program
- Parkland College Cobras (Mid-West Athletic Conference and NJCAA Region 24), Champaign, IL 61821; 217-351-2200; www.parkland.edu; no football program
- Patrick Henry Community College Patriots (NJCAA Region 10), Martinsville, VA 24112; 276-638-8777; www.ph.vccs.edu; no football program
- Phoenix College Bears (Arizona Community College Athletic Conference and NJCAA Region 1), Phoenix, AZ 85013; 602-285-7800; www.pc.maricopa.edu; plays football in the Western States Football League
- Pima Community College Aztecs (Arizona Community College Athletic Conference and NJCAA Region 1), Tucson, AZ 85709; 520-206-4500; www.pima.edu; plays football in the Western States Football League
- Prairie State College Pioneers (Illinois Skyway Collegiate Conference and NJCAA Region 4), Chicago Heights, IL 60411; 708-709-3500; http://prairiestate.edu; no football program
- Prince George's Community College Owls (Maryland Junior College Athletic Conference and NJCAA Region 20), Largo, MD 20774; 301-336-6000; www.pgcc.edu; no football program
- Rappahannock Community College Gulls (NJCAA Region 20), Warsaw, VA 22572; 804-333-6700; www.rappahannock.edu; no football program
- Rend Lake College Warriors (Great Rivers Athletic Conference and NJCAA Region 24), Ina, IL 62846; 618-437-5321; www.rlc.edu; no football program
- St. Clair County Community College Skippers (Michigan Community College Athletic Association and NJCAA Region 12), Port Huron, MI 48061; 810-984-3881; www.sc4.edu; no football program
- St. Louis Community College, Meramec, Archers (Midwest Community College Athletic Conference and NJCAA Region 16), St. Louis, MO 63122; 314-498-7500; www.stlcc.edu/mc; no football program

- Salem Community College Oaks (Garden State Athletic Conference and NJCAA Region 19), Carneys Point, NJ 08069; 856-299-2100; www.salemcc.edu; no football program
- Schoolcraft College Ocelots (Michigan Community College Athletic Association and NJCAA Region 12), Livonia, MI 48152; 734-462-4400; www.schoolcraft.edu; no football program
- Scottsdale Community College Fighting Artichokes (Arizona Community College Athletic Conference and NJCAA Region 1), Scottsdale, AZ 85256; 480-423-6000; www.sc.maricopa.edu; plays football in the Western States Football League
- Shawnee Community College Saints (Mid-West Athletic Conference and NJCAA Region 24), Ullin IL 62992; 618-634-3200; www.shawneecc.edu; no football program
- Sinclair Community College Tartan Pride (Ohio Community College Athletic Conference and NJCAA Region 12), Dayton, OH 45402; 800-315-3000; www.sinclair.edu; no football program
- South Mountain Community College Cougars (Arizona Community College Athletic Conference and NJCAA Region 1), Phoenix, AZ 85042; 602-243-8000; http://southmountaincc.edu; no football program
- South Suburban College Bulldogs (North Central Community College Conference and NJCAA Region 4), South Holland, IL 60473; 708-596-2000; www.ssc.edu; no football program
- Southeast Community College Storm (Nebraska Community College Athletic Conference and NJCAA Region 9), Lincoln, NE 68520; 402-471-3333; www.southeast.edu; no football program
- Southeastern Community College, Whiteville, Rams (NJCAA Region 10), Whiteville, NC 28472; 910-642-7141; www.sccnc.edu; no football program
- Southwestern Community College Spartans (Iowa Community College Athletic Conference and NJCAA Region 11), Creston, IA 50801; 641-782-7081; www.swcciowa.edu; no football program
- Spoon River College Mudcats (Mid-West Athletic Conference and NJCAA Region 24), Canton, IL 61520; 309-647-4645; www.src.edu; no football program
- Stanly Community College (NJCAA Region 10), Albemarle, NC 28001; 704-982-0121; www.stanly.edu; no football program
- Tohono O'odham Community College Jegos (Arizona Community College Athletic Conference and NJCAA Region 1), Sells, AZ 85634; 520-383-8401; www.tocc.cc.az.us; no football program
- Triton College Trojans (North Central Community College Conference and NJCAA Region 4), River Grove, IL 60171; 708-456-0300; www.triton.edu; no football program
- United Tribes Technical College Thunderbirds (Mon-Dak Athletic Conference and NJCAA Region 13), Bismarck, ND 58504; 701-255-3285; www.uttc.edu; no football program
- Vance-Granville Community College Vanguards (NJCAA Region 10), Henderson, NC 27536; 252-492-2061; www.vgcc.edu; no football program
- Wake Technical Community College Eagles (NJCAA Region 10), Raleigh, NC 27603; 919-866-5000; www.waketech.edu; no football program
- Waubonsee Community College Chiefs (Illinois Skyway Collegiate Conference and NJCAA Region 4), Sugar Grove, IL 60554; 630-466-7900; www.waubonsee.edu; no football program
- Wayne County Community College Wildcats (Michigan Community College Athletic Association and NJCAA Region 12), Detroit, MI 48226; 313-496-2600; www.wcccd.edu; no football program
- Wilbur Wright College (one of the City Colleges of Chicago) Rams (North Central Community College Conference and NJCAA Region 4), Chicago, IL 60634; 773-777-7900; http://wright.ccc.edu; no football program

NJCAA Division III Schools

There are 122 Division III teams in the NJCAA that play in 24 different regions.

- Adirondack Community College (State University of New York, SUNY Adirondack) Timberwolves (Mountain Valley Athletic Conference and NJCAA Region 3), Queensbury, NY 12804; 888-786-9235; www.sunyacc.edu; no football program
- Anne Arundel Community College Pioneers (Maryland Junior College Athletic Conference and NJCAA Region 20), Arnold, MD 21012; 410-777-2222; www.aacc.edu; no football program
- Anoka-Ramsey Community College Golden Rams (Minnesota College Athletic Conference and NJCAA Region 13), Coon Rapids, MN 55433; 763-433-1100; www.anokaramsey.edu; no football program

- Atlantic Cape Community College Buccaneers (Garden State Athletic Conference and NJCAA Region 19), Mays Landing, NJ 08330; 609-625-1111; www.atlantic.edu; no football program
- Atlanta Technical College (no mascot) (NJCAA Region 17), Atlanta, GA 30310; 404-225-4400; www.atlantatech.edu; no football program
- Benjamin Franklin Institute of Technology Shockers (NJCAA Region 21), Boston, MA 02116; 617-423-4630; www.bfit.edu; no football program
- Bergen Community College Bulldogs (NJCAA Region 19), Paramus, NJ 07652; 201-447-7100; www.bergen.edu; no football program
- Borough of Manhattan Community College (City University of New York) Panthers (CUNY Athletic Conference), New York, NY, 10007; 212-220-8000; www.bmcc.cuny.edu; no football program
- Bristol Community College Bees (NJCAA Region 21), Fall River, MA 02720; 508-678-2811; www.bristol.mass.edu; no football program
- Bronx Community College (City University of New York) Broncos (CUNY Athletic Conference and NJCAA Region 15), Bronx, NY 10453; 718-289-5100; www.bcc.cuny.edu; no football program
- Brookdale Community College Jersey Blues (Garden State Athletic Conference and NJCAA Region 19), Lincroft, NJ 07738; 732-224-2345; www.brookdalecc.edu; no football program
- Brookhaven College Bears (Metro Athletic Conference and NJCAA Region 5), Farmers Branch, Dallas, TX 75244; 972-860-4700; www.brookhavencollege.edu; no football program
- Broome Community College Hornets (Mid-State Athletic Conference and NJCAA Region 3), Binghamton, NY 13905; 607-778-5000; www.sunybroome.edu; no football program
- Bucks County Community College Centurions (Eastern Pennsylvania Collegiate Conference and NJCAA Region 19), Newtown PA 18940; 215-968-8000; www.bucks.edu; no football program
- Bunker Hill Community College Bulldogs (NJCAA Region 21), Boston, MA 02129; 617-228-2000; www.bhcc.mass.edu; no football program
- Butler County Community College Pioneers (Pennsylvania Collegiate Athletic Association and NJCAA Region 20), Butler, PA 16002; 724-287-8711; www.bc3.edu; no football program
- Caldwell Community College & Technical Institute Cobras (NJCAA Region 10), Hudson, NC 28638; 828-726-2200; www.cccti.edu; no football program
- Camden County College Cougars (NJCAA Region 19), Blackwood, NJ 08012; 856-227-7200; www.camdencc.edu; no football program
- Catawba Valley Community College Buccaneers (NJCAA Region 10), Hickory, NC 28602; 828-327-7000; www.cvcc.edu; no football program
- Cayuga Community College Spartans (State University of New York) (Mid-State Athletic Conference and NJCAA Region 3), Auburn, NY 13021; 315-255-1743; www.cayuga-cc.edu; no football program
- Community College of Allegheny County, Allegheny, Cougars (Pennsylvania Collegiate Athletic Association and NJCAA Region 20), Pittsburgh, PA 15212; 412-237-2525; www.ccac.edu; no football program
- Cedar Valley College Suns (Metro Athletic Conference and NJCAA Region 5), Lancaster, TX 75134; 972-860-8201; www.cedarvalleycollege.edu; no football program
- Central Carolina Community College Cougars (NJCAA Region 10), Pittsboro, NC 27312; 919-545-8044; www.cccc.edu; no football program
- Central Lakes College, Brainerd, Raiders (Minnesota College Athletic Conference and NJCAA Region 13), Brainerd, MN 56401; 218-855-8000; www.clcmn.edu; plays football in the MCAC
- Century College Wood Ducks (NJCAA Region 13), White Bear Lake, MN 55110; 651-779-3300; www.century.edu; no football program
- Clinton Community College (State University of New York) Cougars (Mountain Valley Athletic Conference and NJCAA Region 3), Plattsburgh, NY 12901; 518-562-4200; www.clinton.edu; no football program
- College of DuPage Chaparrals (North Central Community College Conference and NJCAA Region 4), Glen Ellyn, IL 60137; 630-942-2800; http://home.cod.edu; plays football in the Midwest Football Conference
- Columbia-Greene Community College (State University of New York), Twins (Mountain Valley Athletic Conference and NJCAA Region 3), Hudson, NY 12534; 518-828-4181; www.sunycgcc.edu; no football program

- Community College of Allegheny County, Boyce, Saints (Pennsylvania Collegiate Athletic Association and NJCAA Region 20), Monroeville, PA 15146; 724-327-1327; www.ccac.edu; no football program
- Community College of Allegheny County, North (no mascot) (Pennsylvania Collegiate Athletic Association and NJCAA Region 20), Pittsburgh, PA 15237; 412-366-7000; www.ccac.edu; no football program
- Community College of Allegheny County, South, Tigers (Pennsylvania Collegiate Athletic Association and NJCAA Region 20), West Mifflin, PA 15122; 412-469-1100; www.ccac.edu; no football program
- Corning Community College Red Barons (Mid-State Athletic Conference and NJCAA Region 3), Corning, NY 14830; 607-962-9222; www.corning-cc.edu; no football program
- Craven Community College Panthers (NJCAA Region 10), New Bern, NC 28562; 252-638-7200; www.cravencc.edu; no football program
- Cumberland County College Dukes (Garden State Athletic Conference and NJCAA Region 19), Vineland, NJ, 08362; 856-691-8600; www.cccnj.edu; no football program
- Davidson County Community College Storm (NJCAA Region 10), Lexington, NC 27293; 336-249-8186; www.davidsonccc.edu; no football program
- Delaware County Community College Phantoms (Eastern Pennsylvania Collegiate Conference and NJCAA Region 19), Media, PA 19063; 610-359-5000; www.dccc.edu; no football program
- Dutchess Community College (State University of New York) Falcons (Mid-Hudson Conference and NJCAA Region 15), Poughkeepsie, NY 12601; 845-431-8000; www.suny dutchess.edu; no football program
- Eastfield College (Dallas County Community College) Harvesters (Metro Athletic Conference and NJCAA Region 5), Mesquite, TX 75150; 972-860-7100; www.efc.dcccd.edu; no football program
- Fashion Institute of Technology (State University of New York) Tigers (NJCAA Region 15), New York, NY 10001; 212-217-7999; http://fitnyc.edu; no football program
- Finger Lakes Community College Lakers (Mid-State Athletic Conference and NJCAA Region 3), Canandaigua, NY 14424; 585-394-3522; www.flcc.edu; no football program
- Fond du Lac Tribal and Community College Thunder (Minnesota College Athletic Conference and NJCAA Region 13), Cloquet, MN 55720; 218-879-0800; www.fdltcc.edu; plays football in the MCAC
- Fulton-Montgomery Community College Raiders (Mountain Valley Athletic Conference and NJCAA Region 3), Johnstown, NY 12095; 518-736-3622; www.fmcc.edu; no football program
- Gateway Community College Lions (NJCAA Region 21), 88 Bassett Road, North Haven, CT 06473; 203-285-2000; www.gwcc.commnet.edu; no football program
- Georgia Northwestern Technical College Bobcats (Georgia Collegiate Athletic Association and NJCAA Region 17), Rock Spring, GA 30739; 706-764-3510; www.gntc.edu/about/campuses/campus_walker.php; no football program
- Gloucester County College Roadrunners (Garden State Athletic Conference and NJCAA Region 19), Sewell, NJ 08080; 856-468-5000; www.gccnj.edu; no football program
- Harper College Hawks (North Central Community College Conference and NJCAA Region 4), Palatine, IL 60067; 847-925-6707; http://goforward.harpercollege.edu; plays football in the Midwest Football Conference
- Herkimer County Community College Generals (Mountain Valley Athletic Conference and NJCAA Region 3), Herkimer, NY 13350; 315-866-0300; www.herkimer.edu; no football program
- Hibbing Community College Cardinals (Minnesota College Athletic Conference and NJCAA Region 13), Hibbing, MN 55746; 218-262-7200; www.hibbing.edu; no football program
- Holyoke Community College Cougars (NJCAA Region 21), Holyoke, MA 01040; 413-538-7000; www.hcc.edu; no football program
- Hostos Community College (City University of New York) Caimans (CUNY Athletic Conference and NJCAA Region 15), Bronx, NY 10451; 718-518-4444; www.hostos.cuny.edu; no football program
- Hudson Valley Community College Vikings (Mountain Valley Athletic Conference and NJCAA Region 3), Troy, NY 12180; 518-629-4822; www.hvcc.edu; plays football in the Northeast Football Conference
- Itasca Community College Vikings (Minnesota College Athletic Conference and NJCAA Region 13), Grand Rapids, MN 55744; 218-322-2300; www.itasca.edu; plays football in the MCAC
- Jefferson Community College (State University of New York) Cannoneers (Mid-State Athletic Con-

ference and NJCAA Region 3), Watertown, NY 13601; 315-786-2200; www.sunyjefferson.edu; no football program
- Joliet Junior College Wolves (North Central Community College Conference and NJCAA Region 4), Joliet, IL 60431; 815-729-9020; www.jjc.edu; plays football in the Midwest Football Conference
- Kingsborough Community College (City University of New York) Wave (CUNY Athletic Conference and NJCAA Region 15), Brooklyn, NY 11235; 718-265-5343; www.kbcc.cuny.edu; no football program
- Lakes Region Community College Centurians (NJCAA Region 21), Laconia, NH 03246; 603-524-3207; www.lrcc.edu; no football program
- Lamar State College Seahawks (NJCAA Region 14), Port Arthur, TX 77641; 409-983-4921; www.lamarpa.edu; no football program
- Lehigh Carbon Community College Cougars (Eastern Pennsylvania Collegiate Conference and NJCAA Region 19), Schnecksville, PA 18078; 610-799-2121; www.lccc.edu; no football program
- Lincoln College of New England (formerly Briarwood College) Wildcats (NJCAA Region 21), Southington, CT 06489; 800-825-0087; www.lincolncollegene.edu; no football program
- Lorain County Community College Commodores (Ohio Community College Athletic Conference and NJCAA Region 12), Elyria, OH 44035; 800-995-5222; www.loraincc.edu; no football program
- Madison Area Technical College (Madison College) Wolfpack (North Central Community College Conference and NJCAA Region 4), Madison, WI 53704; 608-246-6100; http://matcmadison.edu; no football program
- Manchester Community College Cougars (NJCAA Region 21), Manchester, CT 06045; 860-512-3000; www.mcc.commnet.edu;; no football program
- MassBay (Massachusetts Bay) Community College Buccaneers (NJCAA Region 21), Wellesley Hills, MA 02481; 781-239-3000; www.massbay.edu; no football program
- Mesabi Range Community and Technical College Norse (Minnesota College Athletic Conference and NJCAA Region 13), Virginia, MN 55792; 218-741-3095; www.mr.mnscu.edu; plays football in the MCAC
- Mid-South Community College Greyhounds (Bi-State Conference and NJCAA Region 2), West Memphis, AR 72301; 870-733-6722; www.midsouthcc.edu; no football program
- Middle Georgia Technical College Titans (Georgia Collegiate Athletic Association and NJCAA Region 17), Warner Robins, GA 31088; 478-988-6800; www.middlegatech.edu; no football program
- Middlesex County College Colts (Garden State Athletic Conference and NJCAA Region 19), Edison, NJ 08818; 732-548-6000; www2.middlesexcc.edu; no football program
- Milwaukee Area Technical College Stormers (North Central Community College Conference and NJCAA Region 4), Milwaukee, WI 53233; 414-297-6282; www.matc.edu; no football program
- Minnesota State Community & Technical College Spartans (Minnesota College Athletic Conference and NJCAA Region 13), Fergus Falls, MN 56537; 218-736-1500; www.minnesota.edu/fergusfalls; plays football in the MCAC
- Minnesota West Community & Technical College Bluejays (Minnesota College Athletic Conference and NJCAA Region 13), Pipestone, MN 56164; 800-658-2330; www.mnwest.edu; plays football in the MCAC
- Mohawk Valley Community College (State University of New York) Hawks (Mountain Valley Athletic Conference and NJCAA Region 3), Utica, NY 13501; 315-792-5400; www.mvcc.edu; no football program
- Montgomery College, Germantown, Gryphons (Maryland Junior College Athletic Conference and NJCAA Region 20), Germantown, MD 20876; 240-567-5000; http://cms.montgomerycollege.edu; no football program
- Montgomery College, Rockville, Knights (Maryland Junior College Athletic Conference and NJCAA Region 20), Rockville, MD 20850, 240-567-5000; http://cms.montgomerycollege.edu; no football program
- Montgomery College, Takoma Park–Silver Spring, Falcons (Maryland Junior College Athletic Conference and NJCAA Region 20), Takoma Park, MD 20912; 240-567-5000; http://cms.montgomerycollege.edu; no football program
- Montgomery County Community College Mustangs (NJCAA Region 19), Blue Bell, PA 19422; 215-641-6300; www.mc3.edu; no football program

- Mountain View College (Dallas County Community College District) Lions (Metro Athletic Conference and NJCAA Region 5), Dallas, TX 75211; 214-860-8680; www.mvc.dcccd.edu; no football program
- Nassau Community College Lions (NJCAA Region 15), Garden City, NY 11530; 516-572-7501; www.ncc.edu; plays football in the Northeast Football Conference
- North Country Community College (College of Essex & Franklin, State University of New York) Saints (Mountain Valley Athletic Conference and NJCAA Region 3), Saranac Lake, NY 12983; 518-891-2915; www.nccc.edu; no football program
- North Lake College (Dallas County Community College District) Blazers (Metro Athletic Conference and NJCAA Region 5), Irving, TX 75038; 972-273-3000; http://www.northlakecollege.edu; no football program
- Northampton Community College Spartans (NJCAA Region 19), Bethlehem, PA 18020; 610-861-5300; www.northampton.edu; no football program
- Northern Essex Community College Knights (NJCAA Region 21), Haverhill, MA 01830; 978-556-3000; www.necc.mass.edu; no football program
- Northland Community & Technical College Pioneers (Minnesota College Athletic Conference and NJCAA Region 13), Thief River Falls, MA 56701; 218-683-8800; www.northlandcollege.edu; plays football in the MCAC
- Ocean County College Vikings (Garden State Athletic Conference and NJCAA Region 19), Toms River, NJ 08754; 732-255-0400; www.ocean.edu; no football program
- Onondaga Community College (State University of New York) Lazers (Mid-State Athletic Conference and NJCAA Region 3), Syracuse, NY 13215; 315-498-2622; www.sunyocc.edu; no football program
- Oxford College of Emory University Eagles (Georgia Collegiate Athletic Association and NJCAA Region 17), Oxford, GA 30054; 770-784-8888; http://oxford.emory.edu; no football program
- Passaic County Community College Panthers (Garden State Athletic Conference and NJCAA Region 19), Paterson, NJ, 07505; 973-684-6868; www.pccc.cc.nj.us; no football program
- Pennsylvania Highlands Community College Black Bears (Western Pennsylvania Collegiate Conference and NJCAA Region 20), Johnstown, PA 15904; 814-262-6400; www.pennhighlands.edu/richland; no football program
- Queensborough Community College (City University of New York) Tigers (CUNY Athletic Conference and NJCAA Region 15), Bayside, NY 11364; 718-631-6262; www.qcc.cuny.ed; no football program
- Quinsigamond Community College Wyverns (NJCAA Region 21), Worcester, MA 01606; 508-853-2300; www.qcc.edu; no football program
- Rainy River Community College Voyageurs (Minnesota College Athletic Conference and NJCAA Region 13), International Falls, MN 56649; 218-285-7722; www.rrcc.mnscu.edu; no football program
- Raritan Valley Community College Lions (Garden State Athletic Conference and NJCAA Region 19), Branchburg, NJ 08876; 908-526-1200; www.raritanval.edu; no football program
- Richland College (Dallas County Community College District) Thunderducks (Metro Athletic Conference and NJCAA Region 5), Dallas, TX, 75243; 972-238-6100; www.rlc.dcccd.edu; no football program
- Ridgewater College Warriors (Minnesota College Athletic Conference and NJCAA Region 13), Willmar, MN 56201; 320-222-5200; www.ridgewater.edu; plays football in the MCAC
- Riverland Community College Blue Devils (Minnesota College Athletic Conference and NJCAA Region 13), Austin, MN 55912; 507-433-0600; www.riverland.edu; no football program
- Rochester Community & Technical College Yellowjackets (Minnesota College Athletic Conference and NJCAA Region 13), Rochester, MN 55904; 507-285-7210; www.rctc.edu; plays football in the MCAC
- Rock Valley College Eagles (North Central Community College Conference and NJCAA Region 4), Rockford, IL 61114; 815-921-7821; www.rockvalleycollege.edu; no football program
- Rockland Community College (State University of New York) Hawks (NJCAA Region 15), Suffern, NY 10901; 845-574-4000; www.sunyrockland.edu; no football program
- Roxbury Community College Tigers (NJCAA Region 21), Roxbury Crossing, MA 02120; 617-427-0060; www.rcc.mass.edu; no football program

- St. Cloud Technical & Community College (Minnesota College Athletic Conference and NJCAA Region 13), St. Cloud, MN 56303; 320-308-5000; www.sctcc.edu; no football program
- Sandhills Community College Flyers (NJCAA Region 10), Pinehurst, NC 28374; 910-692-6185; www.sandhills.edu; no football program
- Schenectady County Community College Royals (State University of New York) (Mountain Valley Conference and NJCAA Region 3), Schenectady, NY 12305; 518-381-1200; www.sunysccc.edu; no football program
- Southern Crescent Technical College Tigers (Georgia Collegiate Athletic Association and NJCAA Region 17), Griffin, GA 30223; 770-228-7348; www.sctech.edu; no football program
- Southwest Wisconsin Technical College Chargers (NJCAA Region 13), Fennimore, WI 53809; 608-822-3262; www.swtc.edu; no football program
- Southwestern Oregon Community College Lakers (Northwest Athletic Association of Community Colleges and NJCAA Region 18), Coos Bay, OR 97420; 541-888-2525; www.socc.edu; no football program
- Springfield Technical Community College Rams (Massachusetts Community College Athletic Association and NJCAA Region 21), Springfield, MA 01102; 413-781-7822; www.stcc.edu; no football program
- State University of New York at Delhi Broncos (SUNY Delhi) (Mountain Valley Athletic Conference and NJCAA Region 3), Delhi, NY 13753; 800-963-3544; www.delhi.edu; no football program
- Suffolk County Community College, Selden (State University of New York) Sharks (NJCAA Region 15), Selden, NY 11784; 631-451-4316; www.sunysuffolk.edu; no football program
- Sullivan County Community College (State University of New York) Generals (NJCAA Region 15), Loch Sheldrake, NY 12759; 845-434-5750; www.sullivan.suny.edu; no football program
- Sussex County Community College Skylanders (Garden State Athletic Conference and NJCAA Region 19), Newton, NJ 07860; 973-300-2100; http://sussex.edu; no football program
- Thaddeus Stevens College of Technology (Eastern Pennsylvania Collegiate Conference and NJCAA Region 19), Lancaster, PA 17602; 800-842-3832; www.stevenstech.org; plays football in the Seaboard Conference
- Tompkins Cortland Community College (State University of New York) Panthers (Mid-State Athletic Conference and NJCAA Region 3), Dryden, NY 13053; 607-844-8211; www.tc3.edu; no football program
- Ulster County Community College (State University of New York, SUNY Ulster) Senators (NJCAA Region 15), Stone Ridge, NY 12484; 845-687-5000; www.sunyulster.edu; no football program
- Union County College Owls (Garden State Athletic Conference and NJCAA Region 19), Cranford, NJ 07016; 908-709-7000; www.ucc.edu; no football program
- University of Connecticut at Avery Point Pointers (NJCAA Region 21), Groton, CT 06340; 860-405-9000; www.averypoint.uconn.edu; no football program
- Vermilion Community College Ironmen (Minnesota College Athletic Conference and NJCAA Region 13), Ely, MN 55731; 800-657-3608; www.vcc.edu; plays football in the MCAC
- Wentworth Military Academy & College Red Dragons (Missouri Community College Conference and NJCAA Region 16), Lexington, MO 64067; 800-962-7682; http://wma.edu; no football program
- West Georgia Technical College Golden Knights (Georgia Collegiate Athletic Association and NJCAA Region 17), Waco, GA 30182; 770-537-6000; www.westgatech.edu/locations/murphy.htm; no football program
- Western Technical College Cavaliers (Wisconsin Junior College Athletic Association and NJCAA Region 13), La Crosse, WI 54601; 608-785-9200; www.westerntc.edu; no football program
- Westmoreland County Community College Wolfpack (Pennsylvania Collegiate Athletic Association and NJCAA Region 20), Youngwood PA 15697; 724-925-4000; www.wccc.edu; no football program
- Williamson Free School of Mechanical Trades Mechanics (United States Collegiate Athletic Association and NJCAA Region 19), Media, PA 19063; 610-566-1776; www.williamson.edu; plays football in the Seaboard Conference
- Wytheville Community College Wildcats (NJCAA Region 10), Wytheville, VA 24382; 276-223-4700; www.wc.cc.va.us; no football program
- Yakima Valley Community College Yaks (Northwest Athletic Association of Community Colleges and NJCAA Region 18), Yakima, WA.98902; 509-574-4600; www.yvcc.edu; no football program

NJCAA Region 1

(16 colleges; seven football programs) (Arizona Community College Athletic Conference); Director: Greg Silcox, Paradise Valley Community College, 18401 North 32nd Street, Phoenix, AZ 85032; Telephone: 602-787-6622; Email: greg.silcox@pvmail.maricopa.edu; Web site: http://www.accac.org; National NJCAA Office: 1755 Telstar Drive, Suite 103, Colorado Springs, CO 80920; Telephone: 719-590-9788; Fax: 719-590-7324; Web site: http://www.njcaa.org

- Arizona Western College Matadors (Arizona Community College Athletic Conference), Yuma, AZ 85366; 928-317-6000; www.az western.edu; plays football in the Western States Football League
- Central Arizona College Vaqueros (Arizona Community College Athletic Conference), Coolidge, AZ 85128; 800-237-9814; www.centralaz.edu; no football program
- Chandler-Gilbert Community College Coyotes (Arizona Community College Athletic Conference), Chandler, AZ 85225; 480-732-7000; www.cgc.maricopa.edu; no football program
- Cochise College Apaches (Arizona Community College Athletic Conference), Douglas, AZ 85607; 520-364-7943; www.cochise.edu; no football program
- Eastern Arizona College Gila Monsters (Arizona Community College Athletic Conference), Thatcher, AZ 85552; 800-678-3808; www.eac.edu; plays football in the Western States Football League
- Estrella Mountain Community College Mountain Lions (Arizona Community College Athletic Conference), Avondale, AZ 85392; 623-935-8000; www.estrellamountain.edu; no football program
- GateWay Community College Geckos (Arizona Community College Athletic Conference), Phoenix, AZ 85034; 602-286-8000; www.gatewaycc.edu; no football program
- Glendale Community College Gauchos (Arizona Community College Athletic Conference), Glendale, AZ 85302; 623-845-3000; www.gc.maricopa.edu; plays football in the Western States Football League
- Mesa Community College Thuderbirds (Arizona Community College Athletic Conference), Mesa, AZ 85202; 480-461-7000; www.mesacc.edu; plays football in the Western States Football League
- Paradise Valley Community College Pumas (Arizona Community College Athletic Conference), Phoenix, AZ 85032; 602-787-6500; www.pvc.maricopa.edu; no football program
- Phoenix College Bears (Arizona Community College Athletic Conference), Phoenix, AZ 85013; 602-285-7800; www.pc.maricopa.edu; plays football in the Western States Football League
- Pima Community College Aztecs (Arizona Community College Athletic Conference), Tucson, AZ 85709; 520-206-4500; www.pima.edu; plays football in the Western States Football League
- Scottsdale Community College Fighting Artichokes (Arizona Community College Athletic Conference), Scottsdale, AZ 85256; 480-423-6000; www.sc.maricopa.edu; plays football in the Western States Football League
- South Mountain Community College Cougars (Arizona Community College Athletic Conference), Phoenix, AZ 85042; 602-243-8000; http://southmountaincc.edu; no football program
- Tohono O'odham Community College Jegos (Arizona Community College Athletic Conference), Sells, AZ 85634; 520-383-8401; www.tocc.cc.az.us; no football program
- Yavapai College Roughriders (Arizona Community College Athletic Conference), Prescott, AZ 86301; 928-445-7300; www.yc.edu; no football program

Western States Football League

The Western States Football League is a junior college football league for schools in the states of Arizona, New Mexico and Utah and was formed in 1984 when six Arizona Community College Athletic Conference (ACCAC) schools joined four schools from the Intermountain Collegiate Athletic Conference (ICAC). The original members were Mesa Community College (Mesa, AZ), Phoenix College (Phoenix, AZ), Scottsdale Community College (Scottsdale, AZ), Glendale Community College (Glendale, AZ), Arizona Western (Yuma, AZ), Eastern Arizona (Thatcher, AZ), Dixie College (St. George, UT), Snow College (Ephraim, UT), Eastern Utah (Price, UT), and Ricks College (Rexburg, ID).

Current WSFL schools:

- Arizona Western College Matadors (Yuma, AZ)
- Eastern Arizona College Gila Monsters (Thatcher, AZ)
- Glendale Community College Gauchos (Glendale, AZ)

- Mesa Community College Thunderbirds (Mesa, AZ)
- New Mexico Military Institute Broncos (Roswell, NM)
- Phoenix College Bears (Phoenix, AZ)
- Pima Community College Aztecs (Tucson, AZ)
- Scottsdale Community College Artichokes (Scottsdale, AZ)
- Snow College Badgers (Ephraim, UT)

Western States Football League Champions

Year	School
1985	Snow College (UT)
1986	Ricks College (ID)
1987	Dixie State College of Utah (UT)
1988	Glendale Community College (AZ)
1989	Mesa Community College (AZ)
1990	Dixie State College of Utah (UT)
1990	Glendale Community College (AZ)
1990	Ricks College (ID)
1991	Glendale Community College (AZ)
1992	Ricks College (ID)
1993	Ricks College (ID)
1994	Ricks College (ID)
1995	Dixie State College of Utah (UT)
1996	Dixie State College of Utah (UT)
1996	Snow College (UT)
1997	Ricks College (ID)
1998	Ricks College (ID)
1999	Dixie State College of Utah (UT)
2000	Glendale Community College (AZ)
2001	Dixie State College of Utah (UT)
2002	Dixie State College of Utah (UT)
2003	Dixie State College of Utah (UT)
2004	Scottsdale Community College (AZ)
2005	Glendale Community College (AZ)
2006	Snow College (UT)
2007	Snow College (UT)
2008	Snow College (UT)
2009	Arizona Western College (AZ)
2010	Snow College (UT)

Arizona Community College Athletic Conference / NJCAA Region 1 / Western States Football League Coach of the Year

Year	Coach	School
2003	Greg Croshaw	Dixie State College of Utah (UT)
2003	Joe Kersting	Glendale Community College (AZ)
2004	Ken Giovando	Scottsdale Community College (AZ)
2005	Joe Kersting	Glendale Community College (AZ)
2006	Joe Kersting	Glendale Community College (AZ)
2007	Steve Coburn	Snow College (UT)
2007	Dan Dunn	Mesa Community College (AZ)
2008	Steve Coburn	Snow College (UT)
2009	Tom Minnick	Arizona Western College (AZ)
2010	No Information Available	

Arizona Community College Athletic Conference / NJCAA Region 1 / Western States Football League Offensive Player of the Year

Year	Player	School
2002	J. Copeland	Glendale Community College (AZ)
2003	Brian Hare	Pima Community College (AZ)
2004	Dexter Hill	Scottsdale Community College (AZ)
2005	Tim Brockwell	Glendale Community College (AZ)
2006	Collin Boulay	Glendale Community College (AZ)
2007	Dax Crum	Mesa Community College (AZ)
2007	Pat Riley	Eastern Arizona College (AZ)
2008	Robert Benjamin	Phoenix College (AZ)
2009	Reggie Bullock	Arizona Western College (AZ)
2010	Reggie Bullock	Arizona Western College (AZ)

Arizona Community College Athletic Conference / NJCAA Region 1 / Western States Football League Defensive Player of the Year

Year	*Player*	*School*
2002	C. McKenzie	Glendale Community College (AZ)
2003	Dale Robinson	Glendale Community College (AZ)
2004	Mickey Pimental	Pima Community College (AZ)
2005	Luis Vasquez	Arizona Western College (AZ)
2006	Morris Wooten	Glendale Community College (AZ)
2007	Rico Brooks	Eastern Arizona College (AZ)
2007	Colby Clawson	Snow College (UT)
2007	Tevita Finau	Phoenix College (AZ)
2008	Tevita Finau	Phoenix College (AZ)
2008	Winston Venable	Glendale Community College (AZ)
2009	Prince Ryans	Eastern Arizona College (AZ)
2010	Alonzo Highsmith	Phoenix College (AZ)

NJCAA Region 2

(14 colleges; two football programs) (Bi-State Conference; Little Rock, AR); National NJCAA Office: 1755 Telstar Drive, Suite 103, Colorado Springs, CO 80920; Telephone: 719-590-9788; Fax: 719-590-7324; Web site: http://www.njcaa.org

- Arkansas Baptist College Buffaloes (Bi-State Conference), Little Rock, AR 72202; 501-370-4000; http://arkansasbaptist.edu; plays football as an independent team
- Carl Albert State College Vikings (Oklahoma Collegiate Athletic Conference, Bi-State Conference), Poteau, OK 74953; 918-647-1200; www.carlalbert.edu; no football program
- Connors State College Cowboys (Oklahoma Collegiate Athletic Conference, Bi-State Conference), Warner, OK 74469; 918-463-2931; http://connorsstate.edu; no football program
- Eastern Oklahoma State College Mountaineers (Oklahoma Collegiate Athletic Conference, Bi-State Conference), Wilburton, OK 74578; 918-465-2361; www.eosc.edu; no football program
- Mid-South Community College Greyhounds (Bi-State Conference), West Memphis, AR 72301; 870-733-6722; www.midsouthcc.edu; no football program
- Murray State College Aggies (Oklahoma Collegiate Athletic Conference, Bi-State Conference), Tishomingo, OK 73460; 580-371-2371; www.mscok.edu; no football program
- North Arkansas College Pioneers (Bi-State Conference), Harrison, AR 72601; 870-391-3000; www.northark.edu; no football program
- Northeastern Oklahoma A&M College Golden Norseman (Oklahoma Collegiate Athletic Conference, Bi-State Conference), Miami, OK 74354; 918-542-8441; www.Neo.edu; plays football as an independent team
- Northern Oklahoma College Jets (Oklahoma Collegiate Athletic Conference, Bi-State Conference), Enid, OK 73702; 580-242-6300; www.north-ok.edu; no football program
- Northern Oklahoma College, Tonkawa, Mavericks (Oklahoma Collegiate Athletic Conference, Bi-State Conference), Tonkawa, OK 74653; 580-628-6200; www.north-ok.edu/Tonkawa; no football program
- Redlands Community College Cougars (Oklahoma Collegiate Athletic Conference, Bi-State Conference), El Reno, OK 73036; 405-262-2552; www.redlandscc.edu; no football program
- Rose State College Raiders (Bi-State Conference), Midwest City, OK 73110; 405-733-7673; www.rose.edu; no football program
- Seminole State College Trojans (Oklahoma Collegiate Athletic Conference, Bi-State Conference), Seminole, OK 74868; 405-382-9950; www.sscok.edu; no football program
- Western Oklahoma State College Pioneers (Oklahoma Collegiate Athletic Conference, Bi-State Conference), Altus, OK 73521; 580-477-2000; www.wosc.edu; no football program

NJCAA Region 3

(26 colleges, three football programs) (Mid-State Athletic Conference, Mountain Valley Athletic Conference, Western New York Athletic Conference); Web site: http://www.region3athletics.org/;

National NJCAA Office: 1755 Telstar Drive, Suite 103, Colorado Springs, CO 80920; Telephone: 719-590-9788; Fax: 719-590-7324; Web site: http://www.njcaa.org

- Adirondack Community College (State University of New York, SUNY Adirondack) Timberwolves (Mountain Valley Athletic Conference), Queensbury, NY 12804; 888-786-9235; www.sunyacc.edu; no football program
- Alfred State College (SUNY College of Technology) Pioneers (Western New York Athletic Conference), Alfred, NY 14802; 607-587-4111; www.alfredstate.edu; plays football as an independent team
- Broome Community College Hornets (Mid-State Athletic Conference), Binghamton, NY 13905; 607-778-5000; www.sunybroome.edu; no football program
- Bryant & Stratton College Bobcats (Western New York Athletic Conference), Syracuse, NY 13203; 315-472-6603; www.bryantstratton.edu/Locations/New-York/Syracuse.aspx; no football program
- Cayuga Community College Spartans (State University of New York) (Mid-State Athletic Conference), Auburn, NY 13021; 315-255-1743; www.cayuga-cc.edu; no football program
- Clinton Community College (State University of New York) Cougars (Mountain Valley Athletic Conference), Plattsburgh, NY 12901; 518-562-4200; www.clinton.edu; no football program
- Columbia-Greene Community College (State University of New York), Twins (Mountain Valley Athletic Conference), Hudson, NY 12534; 518-828-4181; www.sunycgcc.edu; no football program
- Corning Community College Red Barons (Mid-State Athletic Conference), Corning, NY 14830; 607-962-9222; www.corning-cc.edu; no football program
- Erie Community College Kats (Western New York Athletic Conference), Buffalo, NY 14203; 716-851-1001; www.ecc.edu; plays football in the Northeast Football Conference
- Finger Lakes Community College Lakers (Mid-State Athletic Conference), Canandaigua, NY 14424; 585-394-3522; www.ucc.edu; no football program
- Fulton-Montgomery Community College Raiders (Mountain Valley Athletic Conference), Johnstown, NY; 12095; 518-736-3622; www.fmcc.edu; no football program
- Genesee Community College Cougars (Western New York Athletic Conference), Batavia, NY 14020; 585-343-0055; www.genesee.edu; no football program
- Herkimer County Community College Generals (Mountain Valley Athletic Conference), Herkimer, NY 13350; 315-866-0300; www.herkimer.edu; no football program
- Hudson Valley Community College Vikings (Mountain Valley Athletic Conference), Troy, NY 12180; 518-629-4822; www.hvcc.edu; plays football in the Northeast Football Conference
- Jamestown Community College (State University of New York) Jayhawks (Western New York Athletic Conference), Jamestown, NY 14702; 716-338-1000; www.sunyjcc.edu; no football program
- Jamestown Community College, Cattaraugus (State University of New York), Jaguars (Western New York Athletic Conference), Olean, NY 14760; 716-376-7500; www.sunyjcc.edu/cattaraugus; no football program
- Jefferson Community College (State University of New York) Cannoneers (Mid-State Athletic Conference), Watertown, NY 13601; 315-786-2200; www.sunyjefferson.edu; no football program
- Mercyhurst North East Saints (Western New York Athletic Conference), North East, PA 16428; 814-725-6100; 866-846-6042; http://northeast.mercyhurst.edu; no football program
- Mohawk Valley Community College (State University of New York) Hawks (Mountain Valley Athletic Conference), Utica, NY 13501; 315-792-5400; www.mvcc.edu; no football program
- Monroe Community College (State University of New York) Tribunes (Western New York Athletic Conference), Rochester, NY 14623; 585-292-2000; www.monroecc.edu; no football program
- Niagara County Community College Thunder Wolves (Western New York Athletic Conference), Sanborn, NY 14132; 716-614-6222; www.niagaracc.suny.edu; no football program
- North Country Community College (College of Essex & Franklin, State University of New York) Saints (Mountain Valley Athletic Conference), Saranac Lake, NY 12983; 518-891-2915; www.nccc.edu; no football program
- Onondaga Community College (State University of New York) Lazers (Mid-State Athletic Conference), Syracuse, NY 13215; 315-498-2622; www.sunyocc.edu; no football program
- Schenectady County Community College Royals (State University of New York) (Mountain Valley Conference), Schenectady, NY 12305; 518-381-1200; www.sunysccc.edu; no football program

- State University of New York at Delhi Broncos (SUNY Delhi) (Mountain Valley Athletic Conference), Delhi, NY 13753; 800-963-3544; www.delhi.edu; no football program
- Tompkins Cortland Community College (State University of New York) Panthers (Mid-State Athletic Conference), Dryden, NY 13053; 607-844-8211; www.tc3.edu; no football program

Northeast Football Conference

As currently configured, the NFC consists of two teams from NJCAA Region 3 (Erie Community College, Hudson Valley Community College), one team from NJCAA Region 10 (Louisburg College), two teams from NJCAA Region 15 (ASA, Nassau Community College), one team from NJCAA Region 19 (Lackawanna College), and one team from NJCAA Region 21 (Dean College).

Northeast Football Conference Champions

Year	*Champion*
1997	Lackawanna College (PA)
1998	Lackawanna College (PA)
1999	Canton (State University of New York) (NY)
1999	Dean College (MA)
1999	Morrisville State College (NY)
2000	Lackawanna College (PA)
2001	Hudson Valley Community College (NY)
2001	Lackawanna College (PA)
2002	Morrisville State College (NY)
2003	Erie Community College (NY)
2003	Hudson Valley Community College (NY)
2003	Morrisville State College (NY)
2004	Hudson Valley Community College (NY)
2005	Nassau Community College (NY)
2006	Lackawanna College (PA)
2007	Dean College (MA)
2008	Dean College (MA)
2009	Dean College (MA)
2010	Nassau Community College (NY)

Northeast Football Conference Coach of the Year

Year	*Coach*	*School*
1997	Tom Namisniak	Cayuga Community College (NY)
1998	Bob Jojo	Hudson Valley Community College (NY)
1998	Tom Namisniak	Cayuga Community College (NY)
1999	Jack Charney	Dean College (MA)
2000	Mark Duda	Lackawanna College (PA)
2001	Tim Mickle	Canton (State University of New York) (NY)
2002	Terry Dow	Morrisville State College (NY)
2003	Bob Jojo	Hudson Valley Community College (NY)
2004	Bob Jojo	Hudson Valley Community College (NY)
2005	Mick Caba	Alfred State College (NY)
2005	Todd Vasey	Dean College (MA)
2006	Mark Duda	Lackawanna College (PA)
2007	Todd Vasey	Dean College (MA)
2008	Todd Vasey	Dean College (MA)
2009	Oji Fagan	Hudson Valley Community College (NY)
2009	Todd Vasey	Dean College (MA)
2010	Jermaine Miles	Nassau Community College (NY)

Northeast Football Conference Offensive Player of the Year

Year	*Player*	*School*
1997	Leroy Collins	Alfred State College (NY)
1997	Sean Higgins	Cayuga Community College (NY)
1998	Marco Burke	Cayuga Community College (NY)
1999	Kwazi Leverette	Morrisville State College (NY)
2000	Alan Jones	Lackawanna College (PA)
2001	Shawn Miller	Hudson Valley Community College (NY)
2002	Jeffery Duggins	Alfred State College (NY)
2003	Emmanuel Marc	Hudson Valley Community College (NY)
2004	Calvin Hall	Hudson Valley Community College (NY)

Year	Player	School
2005	Anthony Rodriguez	Morrisville State College (NY)
2006	Cory Christopher	Nassau Community College (NY)
2007	Aaron Valentin	Erie Community College (NY)
2008	No Information	
2009	Terence Kerns	Lackawanna College (PA)
2010	Steven Miller	Nassau Community College (NY)

Northeast Football Conference Defensive Player of the Year

Year	Player	School
1997	Lamere Corley	Lackawanna College (PA)
1998	Chris Gray	Alfred State College (NY)
1998	Abdul Wilks	Morrisville State College (NY)
1999	Jason Knighton	Lackawanna College (PA)
2000	Derrick Black	Hudson Valley Community College (NY)
2001	Alex Lewis	Morrisville State College (NY)
2002	Chad Rowe	Morrisville State College (NY)
2003	Jamar Atkinson	Morrisville State College (NY)
2004	Jonal St. Dic	Hudson Valley Community College (NY)
2005	Josh Jennings	Dean College (MA)
2006	Antoine Holmes	Lackawanna College (PA)
2007	Mike Balogun	Lackawanna College (PA)
2008	No Information	
2009	Curtis Weatherspoon	Dean College (MA)
2010	Josh Francis	Lackawanna College (PA)
2010	Siriki Diabati	Nassau Community College (NY)

NJCAA Region 4

(30 colleges; three football programs) (Arrowhead Conference, North Central Community College Conference, Illinois Skyway Collegiate Conference—http://www.illinoisskyway.org/); National NJCAA Office: 1755 Telstar Drive, Suite 103, Colorado Springs, CO 80920; Telephone: 719-590-9788; Fax: 719-590-7324; Web site: http://www.njcaa.org

- Black Hawk College, East, Warriors (Arrowhead Conference), Galva, IL 61434; 309-854-1700; Kewanee, IL 61443; 309-854-1875; www.bhc.edu; no football program
- Black Hawk College, Moline, Braves (Arrowhead Conference), Moline, IL 61265; 309-796-5000; www.bhc.edu; no football program
- Carl Sandburg College Chargers (Arrowhead Conference), Galesburg, IL 61401; 309-344-2518; www.sandburg.edu; no football program
- College of DuPage Chaparrals (North Central Community College Conference), Glen Ellyn, IL 60137; 630-942-2800; http://home.cod.edu; plays football in the Midwest Football Conference
- College of Lake County Lancers (Illinois Skyway Collegiate Conference), Grayslake, IL 60030; 847-543-2000; www.clcillinois.edu; no football program
- Elgin Community College Spartans (Illinois Skyway Collegiate Conference), Elgin, IL 60123; 847-697-1000; www.elgin.edu; no football program
- Harper College Hawks (North Central Community College Conference), Palatine, IL 60067; 847-925-6707; http://goforward.harpercollege.edu; plays football in the Midwest Football Conference
- Harry S Truman College (Truman College) (one of the City Colleges of Chicago) Falcons (Arrowhead Conference), Chicago IL 60640; 773-907-4000; www.trumancollege.edu; no football program
- Highland Community College Cougars (Arrowhead Conference), Freeport, IL 61032; 815-235-6121; www.highland.edu; no football program
- Illinois Valley Community College Eagles (Arrowhead Conference), Oglesby, IL 61348; 815-224-2720; www.ivcc.edu; no football program
- Joliet Junior College Wolves (North Central Community College Conference), Joliet, IL 60431; 815-729-9020; www.jjc.edu; plays football in the Midwest Football Conference

- Kankakee Community College Cavaliers (North Central Community College Conference), Kankakee, IL 60901; 815-802-8100; www.kcc.edu; no football program
- Kennedy-King College (one of the City Colleges of Chicago) Statesmen (North Central Community College Conference), Chicago, IL 60621; 773-602-5000; http://kennedyking.ccc.edu; no football program
- Kishwaukee College Kougars (Arrowhead Conference), Malta, IL 60150; 815-825-2086; www.kishwaukeecollege.edu; no football program
- Madison Area Technical College (Madison College) Wolfpack (North Central Community College Conference), Madison, WI 53704; 608-246-6100; http://matcmadison.edu; no football program
- Malcolm X College Hawks (North Central Community College Conference), Chicago, IL 60612; 312-850-7000; http://malcolmx.ccc.edu; no football program
- McHenry County College Scots (Illinois Skyway Collegiate Conference), Crystal Lake, IL 60012; 815-455-3700; www.mchenry.edu; no football program
- Milwaukee Area Technical College Stormers (North Central Community College Conference), Milwaukee, WI 53233; 414-297-6282; www.matc.edu; no football program
- Moraine Valley Community College Cyclones (Illinois Skyway Collegiate Conference), Palos Hills, IL 60465; 708-974-4300; www.morainevalley.edu; no football program
- Morton College Panthers (Illinois Skyway Collegiate Conference), Cicero, IL 60804; 708-656-8000; www.morton.edu; no football program
- Oakton Community College Raiders (Illinois Skyway Collegiate Conference), Des Plaines, IL 60016; 847-635-1600; www.oakton.edu; no football program
- Olive-Harvey College (one of the City Colleges of Chicago) Panthers (North Central Community College Conference), Chicago, IL 60628; 773-291-6100; http://oliveharvey.ccc.edu; no football program
- Prairie State College Pioneers (Illinois Skyway Collegiate Conference), Chicago Heights, IL 60411; 708-709-3500; http://prairiestate.edu; no football program
- Richard J. Daley College (one of the City Colleges of Chicago) Bulldogs (Arrowhead Conference), Chicago, IL 60652; 773-838-7500; http://daley.ccc.edu; no football program
- Rock Valley College Eagles (North Central Community College Conference), Rockford, IL 61114; 815-921-7821; www.rockvalleycollege.edu; no football program
- Sauk Valley Community College Skyhawks (Arrowhead Conference), Dixon, IL 61021; 815-288-5511; www.svcc.edu; no football program
- South Suburban College Bulldogs (North Central Community College Conference), South Holland, IL 60473; 708-596-2000; www.ssc.edu; no football program
- Triton College Trojans (North Central Community College Conference), River Grove, IL 60171; 708-456-0300; www.triton.edu; no football program
- Waubonsee Community College Chiefs (Illinois Skyway Collegiate Conference), Sugar Grove, IL 60554; 630-466-7900; www.waubonsee.edu; no football program
- Wilbur Wright College (one of the City Colleges of Chicago) Rams (North Central Community College Conference), Chicago, IL 60634; 773-777-7900; http://wright.ccc.edu; no football program

Midwest Football Conference

(Commissioner: Thom McDonald; commissioner@iccac.org); http://www.midwestfootballconference.org

The Midwest Football Conference (comprised of NJCAA schools in the midwest United States) was formed when the North Central Community College Conference merged with the Iowa Conference in 2005. As currently configured, the MFC is made up of two divisions, four schools in each division:

East Division: College of DuPage Chapparals (NJCAA Region 4), Grand Rapids Community College Raiders (NJCAA Region 12), Harper College Hawks (NJCAA Region 4), and Joliet Junior College Wolves (NJCAA Region 4); *West Division*: Ellsworth Community College Panthers (NJCAA Region 11), Iowa Central Community College Tritons NJCAA Region 11), Iowa Western Community College Reivers (NJCAA Region 11), and North Dakota State College of Science Wildcats (NJCAA Region 13)

Midwest Football Conference Champions

Year	*Division*	*Team*
2010	MFC-East	Grand Rapids Community College (MI)
2010	MFC-West	Iowa Western Community College (IA)

NJCAA Region 5

(28 colleges; two football programs); Web site: http://www.njcaaregion5.com/; Metro Athletic Conference, North Texas Junior College Athletic Conference, Western Junior College Athletic Conference; National NJCAA Office: 1755 Telstar Drive, Suite 103, Colorado Springs, CO 80920; Telephone: 719-590-9788; Fax: 719-590-7324; Web site: http:www.njcaa.org

- Brookhaven College Bears (Metro Athletic Conference), Farmers Branch, Dallas, TX 75244; 972-860-4700; www.brookhavencollege.edu; no football program
- Cedar Valley College Suns (Metro Athletic Conference), Lancaster, TX 75134; 972-860-8201; www.cedarvalleycollege.edu; no football program
- Cisco College Wranglers (North Texas Junior College Athletic Conference), Cisco, TX 76437; 254-442-5000; www.cisco.edu; plays football in the Southwest Junior College Football Conference
- Clarendon College Bulldogs (Western Junior College Athletic Conference), Clarendon, TX 79226; 806-874-3571; www.clarendoncollege.edu; no football program
- Collin College (formerly known as Collin County Community College) Cougars (North Texas Junior College Athletic Conference), McKinney, TX 75071; 972-548-6790; www.collin.edu; no football program
- Eastfield College (Dallas County Community College) Harvesters (Metro Athletic Conference), Mesquite, TX 75150; 972-860-7100; www.efc.dcccd.edu; no football program
- El Paso Community College Tejanos (Western Junior College Athletic Conference), El Paso, TX 79925; 915-831-3722; www.epcc.edu; no football program
- Frank Phillips College Plainsman (Western Junior College Athletic Conference), Borger, TX 79008; 806-457-4200; www.fpctx.edu; no football program
- Grayson County College Vikings (Western Junior College Athletic Conference), Denison, TX 75020; 903-465-6030; www.grayson.edu; no football program
- Hill College Rebels (North Texas Junior College Athletic Conference), Hillsboro, TX 76645; 254-659-7500; www.hillcollege.edu; no football program
- Howard College Hawks (Western Junior College Athletic Conference), Big Spring, TX 79720; 432-264-5000; www.howardcollege.edu; no football program
- Luna Community College Roughriders (Western Junior College Athletic Conference), Las Vegas, NM 87701; 800-588-7232; www.luna.edu; no football program
- McLennan Community College Highlanders (Western Junior College Athletic Conference), Waco, TX 76708; 254-299-8000; www.mclennan.edu; no football program
- Midland College Chaparrals (Western Junior College Athletic Conference), Midland, TX 79705; 432-685-4500; www.midland.edu; no football program
- Mountain View College (Dallas County Community College District) Lions (Metro Athletic Conference), Dallas, TX 75211; 214-860-8680; www.mvc.dcccd.edu; no football program
- New Mexico Junior College Thunderbirds (Western Junior College Athletic Conference), Hobbs, NM 88240; 575-392-4510; www.nmjc.edu; no football program
- New Mexico Military Institute Broncos (Western Junior College Athletic Conference), Roswell, NM 88201; 800-421-5376; www.nmmi.edu; plays football in the Western States Football League
- North Central Texas College Lions (North Texas Junior College Athletic Conference), Gainesville, TX 76240; 940-668-7731; www.nctc.edu; no football program
- North Lake College (Dallas County Community College District) Blazers (Metro Athletic Conference), Irving, TX 75038; 972-273-3000; http://www.northlakecollege.edu; no football program
- Odessa College Wranglers (Western Junior College Athletic Conference), Odessa, TX 79764; 432-335-6400; www.odessa.edu; no football program
- Ranger College Rangers (North Texas Junior College Athletic Conference), Ranger, TX 76470; 254-647-3234; www.rangercollege.edu; no football program

- Richland College (Dallas County Community College District) Thunderducks (Metro Athletic Conference), Dallas, TX, 75243; 972-238-6100; www.rlc.dcccd.edu; no football program
- South Plains College Texans (Western Junior College Athletic Conference), Levelland, TX; 79336; 806-894-9611; www.southplainscollege.edu; no football program
- Southwestern Christian College Rams (North Texas Junior Athletic Conference), Terrell, TX 75160; 972-524-3341; www.swcc.edu; no football program
- Temple College Leopards (North Texas Junior College Athletic Conference), Temple, TX 76504; 254-298-8282; www.templejc.edu; no football program
- Vernon College Chaparrals (North Texas Junior College Athletic Conference), Vernon, TX 76384; 940-552-6291; www.vernoncollege.edu; no football program
- Weatherford College Coyotes (North Texas Junior College Athletic Conference), Weatherford, TX 76086; 817-594-5471; www.wc.edu; no football program
- Western Texas College Westerners (Western Junior College Athletic Conference), Snyder, TX 79549; 325-573-8511; www.wtc.edu; no football program

NJCAA Region 6

(22 colleges, eight football programs) (all schools play in the Kansas Jayhawk Community College Conference, http://www.kjccc.org); National NJCAA Office: 1755 Telstar Drive, Suite 103, Colorado Springs, CO 80920; Telephone: 719-590-9788; Fax: 719-590-7324; Web site: http:www.njcaa.org

- Allen County Community College Red Devils (Kansas Jayhawk Community College Conference), Iola, KS 66749; 620-365-5116; www.allencc.edu; no football program
- Barton Community College Cougars (Kansas Jayhawk Community College Conference), Great Bend, KS 67530; 620-792-2701; www.bartonccc.edu; no football program
- Brown Mackie College Lions, Salina, KS 67401; 785-825-5422; www.brownmackie.edu; no football program
- Butler Community College Grizzly Bears (Grizzlies) (Kansas Jayhawk Community College Conference), El Dorado, KS 67042; 316-321-2222; www.butlercc.edu; plays football in the KJCCC
- Cloud County Community College Thunderbirds (Kansas Jayhawk Community College Conference), Concordia, KS 66901; 800-729-5101; www.cloud.edu; no football program
- Coffeyville Community College Ravens (Kansas Jayhawk Community College Conference), Coffeyville, KS 67337; 620-251-7700; www.coffeycille.edu; plays football in the KJCCC
- Colby Community College Trojans (Kansas Jayhawk Community College Conference), Colby, KS 67701; 785-462-3984; www.colbycc.edu; no football program
- Cowley County Community College Tigers (Kansas Jayhawk Community College Conference), Arkansas City, KS 67005; 620-442-0430; www.cowley.edu; no football program
- Dodge City Community College Conquistadors (Kansas Jayhawk Community College Conference), Dodge City, KS 67801; 620-227-9310; www.dc3.edu; plays football in the KJCCC
- Fort Scott Community College Greyhounds (Kansas Jayhawk Community College Conference), Fort Scott, KS 66701; 800-874-3722; www.fortscott.edu; plays football in the KJCCC
- Garden City Community College Broncbusters (Kansas Jayhawk Community College Conference), Garden City, KS 67846; 620-276-7611; www.gcccks.edu; plays football in the KJCCC
- Hesston College Larks (a two-year college of the Mennonite Church USA that is associated with the Kansas Jayhawk Community College Conference), Hesston, KS 67062; 800-995-2757; www.hesston.edu; no football program
- Highland Community College Scotties (Kansas Jayhawk Community College Conference), Highland, KS 66035; 785-442-6000; www.highlandcc.edu; plays football in the KJCCC
- Hutchinson Community College Blue Dragons (Kansas Jayhawk Community College Conference), Hutchinson, KS 67501; 620-665-3500; www.hutchcc.edu; plays football in the KJCCC
- Independence Community College Pirates (Kansas Jayhawk Community College Conference), Independence, KS 67301; 620-331-4100; www.indycc.edu; plays football in the KJCCC
- Johnson County Community College Cavaliers (Kansas Jayhawk Community College Conference), Overland Park, KS 66210; 913-469-8500; www.jccc.edu; no football program
- Kansas City Kansas Community College Blue Devils (Kansas Jayhawk Community College Conference), Kansas City, KS 66112; 913-334-1100; www.kckcc.edu; no football program

- Labette Community College Cardinals (Kansas Jayhawk Community College Conference), Parsons, KS 67357; 620-421-6700; www.labette.edu; no football program
- Neosho County Community College Panthers (Kansas Jayhawk Community College Conference), Chanute, KS 66720; 620-431-2820; www.neosho.edu; no football program
- Northwest Kansas Technical College Mavericks (affiliated with the Kansas Jayhawk Community College Conference), Goodland, KS 67735; 800-316-4127; www.nwktc.edu; no football program
- Pratt Community College Beavers (Kansas Jayhawk Community College Conference), Pratt, KS 67124; 620-672-9800; http://prattcc.edu/; no football program
- Seward County Community College Saints (Kansas Jayhawk Community College Conference), Liberal, KS 67905; 620-624-1951; www.sccc.edu; no football program

Kansas Jayhawk Community College Conference Champions

Year	*School*
2001	Butler Community College (KS)
2001	Garden City Community College (KS)
2002	Butler Community College (KS)
2003	Butler Community College (KS)
2004	Butler Community College (KS)
2005	Butler Community College (KS)
2006	Butler Community College (KS)
2006	Coffeyville Community College (KS)
2007	Butler Community College (KS)
2008	Butler Community College (KS)
2009	Fort Scott Community College (KS)
2010	Butler Community College (KS)

Kansas Jayhawk Community College Conference Coach of the Year

Year	*Coach*	*School*
2002	John Rosetti	Dodge City Community College (KS)
2003	Troy Morrell	Butler Community College (KS)
2004	Troy Morrell	Butler Community College (KS)
2005	Troy Morell	Butler Community College (KS)
2006	Rion Rhoades	Fort Scott Community College (KS)
2007	Troy Morrell	Butler Community College (KS)
2008	Troy Morrell	Butler Community College (KS)
2009	Jeff Sims	Fort Scott Community College (KS)
2010	Steve Carson	Independence Community College (KS)

Kansas Jayhawk Community College Conference Offensive Player of the Year

Year	*Player*	*School*
2002	Walter Washington	Dodge City Community College (KS)
2003	Chad Wilmott	Butler Community College (KS)
2004	Zac Taylor	Butler Community College (KS)
2005	No Information	
2006	No Information	
2007	Greg Cross	Fort Scott Community College (KS)
2008	La'Darrian Page	Hutchinson Community College (KS)
2009	Jasmin Hopkins	Fort Scott Community College (KS)
2010	Zach Mettenberger	Butler Community College (KS)

Kansas Jayhawk Community College Conference Defensive Player of the Year

Year	*Player*	*School*
2002	Darrell Shropshire	Coffeyville Community College (KS)
2003	Dashon Goldson	Coffeyville Community College (KS)
2004	David Dixon	Hutchinson Community College (KS)
2005	No Information	
2006	No Information	
2007	Markus White	Butler Community College (KS)

Year	*Player*	*School*
2008	Eugene Kinlaw	Hutchinson Community College (KS)
2009	Scott Smith	Butler Community College (KS)
2010	Cornellius Carradine	Butler Community College (KS)

NJCAA Region 7

(10 colleges; no football schools); Tennessee Junior and Community College Athletic Association; National NJCAA Office: 1755 Telstar Drive, Suite 103, Colorado Springs, CO 80920; Telephone: 719-590-9788; Fax: 719-590-7324; Web site: http:www.njcaa.org

- Chattanooga State Community College Tigers (Tennessee Junior and Community College Athletic Association), Chattanooga, TN 37406; 423-697-4404; www.chattanoogastate.edu; no football program
- Cleveland State Community College Cougars (Tennessee Junior and Community College Athletic Association), Cleveland, TN 37320; 423-472-7141; www.clevelandstatecc.edu; no football program
- Columbia State Community College Chargers (Tennessee Junior and Community College Athletic Association), Columbia, TN 38401; 931-540-2722; www.columbiastate.edu; no football program
- Dyersburg State Community College Eagles (Tennessee Junior and Community College Athletic Association), Dyersburg, TN 38024; 731-286-3200; www.dscc.edu; no football program
- Jackson State Community College Generals (Tennessee Junior and Community College Athletic Association), Jackson, TN 38301; 731-424-3520; www.jscc.edu; no football program
- Motlow State Community College Bucks (Tennessee Junior and Community College Athletic Association), Lynchburg, TN 37352; 931-393-1500; www.mscc.edu; no football program
- Roane State Community College Raiders (Tennessee Junior and Community College Athletic Association), Harriman, TN 37748; 865-354-3000; www.roanestate.edu; no football program
- Southwest Tennessee Community College Saluqis (Tennessee Junior and Community College Athletic Association), Memphis, TN 38134; 901-333-5000; www.southwest.tn.edu; no football program
- Volunteer State Community College Pioneers (Tennessee Junior and Community College Athletic Association), Gallatin, TN 37066; 615-452-8600; www.volstate.edu; no football program
- Walters State Community College Senators (Tennessee Junior and Community College Athletic Association), Morristown, TN 37813; 423-585-2600; www.ws.edu; no football program

NJCAA Region 8

(23 colleges, no football schools) (Suncoast Conference); National NJCAA Office: 1755 Telstar Drive, Suite 103, Colorado Springs, CO 80920; Telephone: 719-590-9788; Fax: 719-590-7324; Web site: http:www.njcaa.org

- Brevard Community College Titans (Florida Community College Activities Association), Cocoa, FL 32922; 321-632-1111; www.brevard.cc.fl.us; no football program
- Broward College (Broward Community College) Seahawks (Florida Community College Activities Association), Fort Lauderdale, FL 33301; 954-201-7350; www.broward.edu; no football program
- Chipola College Indians (Florida Community College Activities Association), Marianna, FL 32446; 850-526-2761; www.chipola.edu; no football program
- College of Central Florida (Central Florida Community College) Patriots (Florida Community College Activities Association), Ocala, FL 34474; 352-873-5800; www.cf.edu; no football program
- Daytona State College (Daytona Beach Community College) Falcons (Mid-Florida Conference, Florida Community College Activities Association), Daytona Beach, FL 32114; 386-506-3000; www.daytonastate.edu; no football program
- Florida State College at Jacksonville Stars (Mid-Florida Conference), Jacksonville, FL 32246; 904-646-2205; www.fscj.edu; no football program
- Gulf Coast State College (Gulf Coast Community College) Commondores (Florida Community College Activities Association), Panama City, FL 32401; 850-769-1551; www.gulfcoast.edu; no football program
- Hillsborough Community College Hawks (Florida Community College Activities Association), Tampa, FL 33614; 813-253-7000; www.hccfl.edu; no football program

- Indian River State College (Indian River Community College) Pioneers (Florida Community Colleges Activities Association), Fort Pierce, FL.34981; 772-462-4772; www.irsc.edu; no football program
- Lake Sumter Community College (Florida Community College Activities Association), Leesburg, FL 34788; 352-787-3747; www.lscc.edu; no football program
- Miami Dade College Sharks (Florida Community College Activities Association), Miami, FL 33132; 305-237-8888; www.mdc.edu; no football program
- Northwest Florida State College Raiders (Florida Community College Activities Association), Niceville, FL 32578; 850-678-5111; www.nwfsc.edu/Niceville; no football program
- Palm Beach State College (Palm Beach Community College) Panthers (Southern Conference), Lake Worth, FL 33461; 561-868-3350; www.palmbeachstate.edu; no football program
- Pasco-Hernando Community College Conquistadors (Florida Community College Activities Association), New Port Richey, FL 34654; 727-847-2727; http://phcc.edu; no football program
- Pensacola State College (Pensacola Junior College) Pirates (Panhandle Conference, Florida Community College Activities Association), Pensacola, FL 32504; 850-484-1000; www.pensacolastate.edu; no football program
- Polk State College (Polk Community College) Vikings (Suncoast Conference), Winter Haven, FL 33881; 863-297-1000; www.polk.edu; no football program
- St. Johns River Community College Vikings (Florida Community College Activities Association), Palatka, FL 32177; 386-312-4200; www.sjrcc.edu; no football program
- St. Petersburg College Titans (Florida Community College Activities Association), St. Petersburg, FL 33733; 727-341-4772; www.spcollege.edu; no football program
- Santa Fe College Saints (Florida Community College Activities Association), Gainesville, FL 32606; 352-395-5000; www.sfcollege.edu; no football program
- Seminole State College of Florida Raiders (Florida Community College Activities Association, Mid-Florida Conference), Sanford, FL 32773; 407-708-4722; www.seminolestate.edu; no football program
- South Florida Community College Panthers (Southern Conference), Avon Park, FL 33825; 863-453-6661; www.southflorida.edu; no football program
- State College of Florida (Manatee-Sarasota) (Manatee Community College) Manatees (Florida Community College Activities Association), Bradenton, FL 34207; 941-752-5000; www.scf.edu; no football program
- Tallahassee Community College Eagles (Florida Community College Activities Association), Tallahassee, FL 32304; 850-201-6200; www.tcc.fl.edu; no football program

NJCAA Region 9

(21 colleges, no football schools) (Mon-Dak Athletic Conference); National NJCAA Office: 1755 Telstar Drive, Suite 103, Colorado Springs, CO 80920; Telephone: 719-590-9788; Fax: 719-590-7324; Web site: http:www.njcaa.org

- Casper College Thunderbirds, Casper, WY 82601; 307-268-2100; www.caspercollege.edu; no football program
- Central Community College Raiders, Columbus NE 68602; 402-564-7132; www.cccneb.edu; no football program
- Central Wyoming College Rustlers, Riverton, WY 82501; 307-855-2000; www.cwc.edu; no football program
- Dawson Community College Buccaneers, Glendive, MT 59330; 406-377-3396; www.dawson.edu; no football program
- Eastern Wyoming College Lancers, Torrington, WY 82240; 866-327-8996; http://ewc.wy.edu; no football program
- Gillette College Pronghorns, Gillette, WY 82718; 307-686-0254; www.sheridan.edu/site/gc; no football program
- Lamar Community College Runnin' Lopes, Lamar, CO 81052; 719-336-2248; www.lamarcc.edu; no football program
- Laramie County Community College Golden Eagles, Cheyenne, WY 82007; 800-522-2993; www.lccc.wy.edu; no football program

- Little Big Horn College Rams, Crow Agency, MT 59022; 406-638-3100; www.lbhc.edu; no football program
- McCook Community College Indians (Nebraska Community College Athletic Conference), McCook, NE 69001; 308-345-8100; www.mpcc.edu/mccook_college.html; no football program
- Miles Community College Pioneers (Mon-Dak Athletic Conference), Miles City, MT 59301; 406-874-6100; www.milescc.edu; no football program
- North Platte Community College Knights, North Platte, NE 69101; 308-535-3600; www.mpcc.edu/North_Platte_Community_College.cfm; no football program
- Northeast Community College Hawks, Norfolk, NE 68701; 402-371-2020; www.northeast.edu; no football program
- Northeastern Junior College Plainsmen, Sterling, CO 80751; 800-626-4637; www.njc.edu; no football program
- Northwest College Trappers (Wyoming Community College Athletic Conference), Powell, WY 82435; 800-560-4692; www.nwc.cc.wy.us; no football program
- Otero Junior College Rattlers, La Junta, CO 81050; 719-384-6831; www.ojc.edu; no football program
- Sheridan College Generals, Gillette, WY 82718; 307-686-0254; www.sheridan.edu; no football program
- Southeast Community College Storm (Nebraska Community College Athletic Conference), Lincoln, NE 68520; 402-471-3333; www.southeast.edu; no football program
- Trinidad State Junior College Trojans, Trinidad, CO 81082; 800-621-8752; www.trinidadstate.edu; no football program
- Western Nebraska Community College Cougars, Scottsbluff, NE 69361; 308-635-3606; www.wncc.edu; no football program
- Western Wyoming Community College Mustangs, Rock Springs, WY 82901; 307-382-1600; www.wwcc.wy.edu; no football program

NJCAA Region 10

(34 colleges, one football program) (Carolinas Junior College Conference); National NJCAA Office: 1755 Telstar Drive, Suite 103, Colorado Springs, CO 80920; Telephone: 719-590-9788; Fax: 719-590-7324; Web site: http:www.njcaa.org

- Aiken Technical College Knights, Graniteville, SC 29829; 803-593-9231; www.atc.edu; no football program
- Brunswick Community College Dolphins, Bolivia, NC 28422; 910-755-7300; www.brunswickcc.edu; no football program
- Caldwell Community College & Technical Institute Cobras, Hudson, NC 28638; 828-726-2200; www.cccti.edu; no football program
- Cape Fear Community College Sea Devils, Wilmington, NC 28401; 910-362-7000; http://cfcc.edu; no football program
- Catawba Valley Community College Buccaneers, Hickory, NC 28602; 828-327-7000; www.cvcc.edu; no football program
- Central Carolina Community College Cougars, Pittsboro, NC 27312; 919-545-8044; www.cccc.edu; no football program
- Clinton Junior College Golden Bears, Rock Hill, SC 29730; 803-327-7402; www.clintonjuniorcollege.edu; no football program
- College of the Albemarle Dolphins, Elizabeth City, NC 27906; 252-335-0821; www.albemarle.edu; no football program
- Craven Community College Panthers, New Bern, NC 28562; 252-638-7200; www.cravencc.edu; no football program
- Danville Community College Knights, Danville, VA 24541; 434-797-2222; www.dcc.vccs.edu; no football program
- Davidson County Community College Storm, Lexington, NC 27293; 336-249-8186; www.davidsoncc.edu; no football program
- Denmark Technical College Panthers, Denmark, SC 29042; 803-793-5176; www.denmarktech.edu; no football program

- Florence-Darlington Technical College Stingers, Florence, SC 29502; 843-661-8324; www.fdtc.edu; no football program
- Guilford Technical Community College Titans, Jamestown, NC 27282; 336-334-4822; www.gtcc.edu; no football program
- Johnston Community College Jaguars, Smithfield, NC 27577; 919-934-3051; www.johnstoncc.edu; no football program
- Lenoir Community College Lancers, Kinston, NC 28502; 252-527-6223; www.lenoircc.edu; no football program
- Louisburg College Hurricanes, Louisburg, NC 27549; 919-496-2521; www.louisburg.edu; plays football in the Northeast Football Conference
- New River Community College Knights, Dublin, VA 24084; 540-674-3600; www.nr.edu; no football program
- Patrick Henry Community College Patriots, Martinsville, VA 24112; 276-638-8777; www.ph.vccs.edu; no football program
- Pitt Community College Bulldogs, Winterville, NC 28590; 252-493-7200; www.pittcc.edu; no football program
- Rockingham Community College Eagles, Wentworth, NC 27375; 336-342-4261; www.rockinghamcc.edu; no football program
- Sandhills Community College Flyers, Pinehurst, NC 28374; 910-692-6185; www.sandhills.edu; no football program
- Southeastern Community College, Whiteville, Rams, Whiteville, NC 28472; 910-642-7141; www.sccnc.edu; no football program
- Spartanburg Methodist College Pioneers, Spartanburg, SC, 29301; 864-587-4000; http://smcsc.edu; no football program
- Stanly Community College, Albemarle, NC 28001; 704-982-0121; www.stanly.edu; no football program
- Surry Community College Knights, Dobson, NC 27017; 336-386-8121; www.surry.edu; no football program
- Tri-County Technical College Hawks, Pendleton, SC 29670; 864-646-1500; www.tctc.edu; no football program
- University of South Carolina, Lancaster, Lancers, Lancaster, SC 29720; 803-313-7000; http://usclancaster.sc.edu; no football program
- University of South Carolina, Salkehatchie, Indians, Allendale, SC 29810; 803-584-3446; http://uscsalkehatchie.sc.edu; no football program
- University of South Carolina, Sumter, Fire Ants, Sumter, SC 29150; 803-775-8727; www.uscsumter.edu; no football program
- Vance-Granville Community College Vanguards, Henderson, NC 27536; 252-492-2061; www.vgcc.edu; no football program
- Wake Technical Community College Eagles, Raleigh, NC 27603; 919-866-5000; www.waketech.edu; no football program
- Wilkes Community College Cougars, Wilkesboro, NC 28697; 336-838-6100; www.wilkescc.edu; no football program
- Wytheville Community College Wildcats, Wytheville, VA 24382; 276-223-4700; www.wc.cc.va.us; no football program

NJCAA Region 11

(13 colleges, three football programs); Iowa Community College Athletic Conference, 414 Northwestern Ave, Suite #1, Ames, IA 50010; Telephone: 515-460-8081; Fax: 866-587-0121; Email: iccac@iccac.org; Web site: http://www.iccac.org; National NJCAA Office: 1755 Telstar Drive, Suite 103, Colorado Springs, CO 80920; Telephone: 719-590-9788; Fax: 719-590-7324; Web site: http://www.njcaa.org

- Des Moines Area Community College Bears (Iowa Community College Athletic Conference), Boone, IA 50036; 515-432-7203; http://go.dmacc.edu/boone; no football program
- Eastern Iowa Community College (Scott Community College) Cougars (Iowa Junior College Athletic

Association), Bettendorf, IA 52722; 563-441-4001; www.eicc.edu/general/scott/index.html; no football program

- Ellsworth Community College Panthers (Iowa Community College Athletic Conference), Iowa Falls, IA 50126; 641-648-4611; www.iavalley.edu/ecc; plays football in the Midwest Football Conference
- Indian Hills Community College, Centerville, Falcons (Iowa Community College Athletic Conference), Centerville, IA 52544; 800-726-2585; www.ihcc.cc.ia.us/about/locations/centerville.html; no football program
- Indian Hills Community College, Ottumwa, Warriors (Iowa Community College Athletic Conference), Ottumwa, IA 52501; 800-726-2585; http://www.ihcc.cc.ia.us/about/locations/ottumwa.html; no football program
- Iowa Central Community College Tritons (Iowa Community College Athletic Conference), Fort Dodge, IA 50501; 800-362-2793; www.iccc.cc.ia.us; plays football in the Midwest Football Conference
- Iowa Lakes Community College Lakers (Iowa Community College Athletic Conference), Estherville, IA 51334; 712-362-2604; www.iowalakes.edu; no football program
- Iowa Western Community College Reivers (Iowa Community College Athletic Conference), Council Bluffs, IA 51503; 712-325-3200; www.iwcc.edu; plays football in the Midwest Football Conference
- Kirkwood Community College Eagles (Iowa Community College Athletic Association), Cedar Rapids, IA 52404; 319-398-5517; www.kirkwood.edu; no football program
- Marshalltown Community College Tigers (Iowa Community College Athletic Conference), Marshalltown, IA 50158; 641-752-7106; www.iavalley.edu/mcc; no football program
- North Iowa Area Community College Trojans (Iowa Community College Athletic Conference), Mason City, IA 50401; 641-423-1264; www.niacc.edu; no football program
- Southeastern Community College Blackhawks (Iowa Community College Athletic Conference), West Burlington, IA 52655; 866-722-4692; www.scciowa.edu; no football program
- Southwestern Community College Spartans (Iowa Community College Athletic Conference), Creston, IA 50801; 641-782-7081; www.swcciowa.edu; no football program

NJCAA Region 12

(28 colleges, one football program) (Michigan Community College Athletic Association, Ohio Community College Athletic Conference); with the exception of Vincennes University; National NJCAA Office: 1755 Telstar Drive, Suite 103, Colorado Springs, CO 80920; Telephone: 719-590-9788; Fax: 719-590-7324; Web site: http://www. njcaa.org

- Alpena Community College Lumberjacks (Michigan Community College Athletic Association), Alpena, MI 49707; 989-356-9021; www.alpenacc.edu; no football program
- Ancilla College Chargers (Michigan Community College Athletic Association), Donaldson, IN 46543; 574-936-8898; www.ancilla.edu; no football program
- Cincinnati State Technical & Community College Surge (Ohio Community College Athletic Conference), Cincinnati, OH 45223; 513-569-1500; www.cincinnatistate.edu; no football program
- Columbus State Community College Cougars (Ohio Community College Athletic Conference), Columbus, OH 43215; 614-287-5353; www2.cscc.edu; no football program
- Cuyahoga Community College Challangers (Ohio Community College Athletic Conference), Cleveland, OH 44115; 800-954-8742; www.tri-c.edu; no football program
- Delta College Pioneers (Michigan Community College Athletic Association), University Center, MI 48710; 989-686-9000; www.delta.edu; no football program
- Edison Community College Chargers (Ohio Community College Athletic Conference), Piqua, OH 45356; 937-778-8600; www.edisonohio.edu; no football program
- Glen Oaks Community College Vikings (Michigan Community College Athletic Association), Centreville, MI 49032; 269-467-9945; www.glenoaks.edu; no football program
- Grand Rapids Community College Raiders (Michigan Community College Athletic Association), Grand Rapids, MI 49503; 616-234-4000; www.grcc.edu; plays football in the Midwest Football Conference
- Henry Ford Community College Hawks (Michigan Community College Athletic Association), Dearborn, MI 48128; 800-585-4322; www.hfcc.edu; no football program

- Jackson Community College Jets (Michigan Community College Athletic Association), Jackson, MI 49201; 517-787-0800; www.jccmi.edu; no football program
- Kalamazoo Valley Community College Cougars (Michigan Community College Athletic Association), Kalamazoo, MI 49007; 269-373-7800; www.kvcc.edu; no football program
- Kellogg Community College Bruins (Michigan Community College Athletic Association), Battle Creek, MI 49017; 269-965-3931; www.kellogg.edu; no football program
- Kirtland Community College Firebirds (Michigan Community College Athletic Association), Roscommon, MI 48653; 989-275-5000; www.kirtland.edu; no football program
- Lake Michigan College Indians (Michigan Community College Athletic Association), Benton Harbor, MI 49022; 269-927-8100; www.lakemichigancollege.edu; no football program
- Lakeland Community College Lakers (Ohio Community College Athletic Conference), Kirtland, OH 44094; 440-525-7000; http://lakelandcc.edu; no football program
- Lansing Community College Stars (Michigan Community College Athletic Association), Lansing, MI 48901; 517-483-1957; www.lcc.edu; no football program
- Lorain County Community College Commodores (Ohio Community College Athletic Conference), Elyria, OH 44035; 800-995-5222; www.loraincc.edu; no football program
- Macomb Community College Monarchs (Michigan Community College Athletic Association), Warren, MI 48088; 586-445-7999; www.macomb.edu; no football program
- Mott Community College Bears (Michigan Community College Athletic Association), Flint, MI 48503; 810-762-0200; www.mcc.edu; no football program
- Muskegon Community College Jayhawks (Michigan Community College Athletic Association), Muskegon, MI 49442; 231-773-9131; www.muskegoncc.edu; no football program
- Oakland Community College Raiders (Michigan Community College Athletic Association), Bloomfield Hills, MI 48304; 248-341-2000; www.oaklandcc.edu; no football program
- Owens Community College Express (Ohio Community College Athletic Conference), Toledo, OH 43699; 567-661-7000; www.owens.edu; no football program
- St. Clair County Community College Skippers (Michigan Community College Athletic Association), Port Huron, MI 48061; 810-984-3881; www.sc4.edu; no football program
- Schoolcraft College Ocelots (Michigan Community College Athletic Association), Livonia, MI 48152; 734-462-4400; www.schoolcraft.edu; no football program
- Sinclair Community College Tartan Pride (Ohio Community College Athletic Conference), Dayton, OH 45402; 800-315-3000; www.sinclair.edu; no football program
- Vincennes University Trailblazers, Vincennes, IN 47591; 800-742-9198; www.vinu.edu; no football program
- Wayne County Community College Wildcats (Michigan Community College Athletic Association), Detroit, MI 48226; 313-496-2600; www.wcccd.edu; no football program

NJCAA Region 13

(26 colleges, 12 football programs) (Minnesota College Athletic Conference, Mon-Dak Athletic Conference); National NJCAA Office: 1755 Telstar Drive, Suite 103, Colorado Springs, CO 80920; Telephone: 719-590-9788; Fax: 719-590-7324; Web site: http://www. njcaa.org

- Anoka-Ramsey Community College Golden Rams (Minnesota College Athletic Conference), Coon Rapids, MN 55433; 763-433-1100; www.anokaramsey.edu; no football program
- Bismarck State College Mystics (Mon-Dak Athletic Conference), Bismarck, ND 58506; 701-224-5400; www.bsc.nodak.edu; no football program
- Central Lakes College, Brainerd, Raiders (Minnesota College Athletic Conference), Brainerd, MN 56401; 218-855-8000; www.clcmn.edu; plays football in the MCAC
- Century College Wood Ducks, White Bear Lake, MN 55110; 651-779-3300; www.century.edu; no football program
- Dakota College at Bottineau (Minot State University, Bottineau) Lumberjacks (Mon-Dak Athletic Conference), Bottineau, ND 58318; 701-228-5488; www.dakotacollege.edu; plays football as an independent team
- Dakota County Technical College Blue Knights (Minnesota College Athletic Conference), Rosemount, MN 55068; 651-423-8301; www..dctc.edu; no football program

- Fond du Lac Tribal and Community College Thunder (Minnesota College Athletic Conference), Cloquet, MN 55720; 218-879-0800; www.fdltcc.edu; plays football in the MCAC
- Gogebic Community College Samsons, Ironwood, MI 49938; 906-932-4231; www.gogebic.edu; no football program
- Hibbing Community College Cardinals (Minnesota College Athletic Conference), Hibbing, MN 55746; 218-262-7200; www.hibbing.edu; no football program
- Itasca Community College Vikings (Minnesota College Athletic Conference), Grand Rapids, MN 55744; 218-322-2300; www.itasca.edu; plays football in the MCAC
- Lake Region State College Royals (Mon-Dak Athletic Conference), Devils Lake, ND 58301; 701-662-1600; www.lrsc.edu; no football program
- Mesabi Range Community and Technical College Norse (Minnesota College Athletic Conference), Virginia, MN 55792; 218-741-3095; www.mr.mnscu.edu; plays football in the MCAC
- Minnesota State Community & Technical College Spartans (Minnesota College Athletic Conference), Fergus Falls, MN 56537; 218-736-1500; www.minnesota.edu/fergusfalls; plays football in the MCAC
- Minnesota West Community & Technical College Bluejays (Minnesota College Athletic Conference), Pipestone, MN 56164; 800-658-2330; www.mnwest.edu; plays football in the MCAC
- North Dakota State College of Science Wildcats, Wahpeton, ND 58076; 701-671-2401; www.ndscs.edu; plays football in the Midwest Football Conference
- Northland Community & Technical College Pioneers (Minnesota College Athletic Conference), Thief River Falls, MA 56701; 218-683-8800; www.northlandcollege.edu; plays football in the MCAC
- Rainy River Community College Voyageurs (Minnesota College Athletic Conference), International Falls, MN 56649; 218-285-7722; www.rrcc.mnscu.edu; no football program
- Ridgewater College Warriors (Minnesota College Athletic Conference), Willmar, MN 56201; 320-222-5200; www.ridgewater.edu; plays football in the MCAC
- Riverland Community College Blue Devils (Minnesota College Athletic Conference), Austin, MN 55912; 507-433-0600; www.riverland.edu; no football program
- Rochester Community & Technical College Yellowjackets (Minnesota College Athletic Conference), Rochester, MN 55904; 507-285-7210; www.rctc.edu; plays football in the MCAC
- St. Cloud Technical & Community College (Minnesota College Athletic Conference), St. Cloud, MN 56303; 320-308-5000; www.sctcc.edu; no football program
- Southwest Wisconsin Technical College Chargers, Fennimore, WI 53809; 608-822-3262; www.swtc.edu; no football program
- United Tribes Technical College Thunderbirds (Mon-Dak Athletic Conference), Bismarck, ND 58504; 701-255-3285; www.uttc.edu; no football program
- Vermilion Community College Ironmen (Minnesota College Athletic Conference), Ely, MN 55731; 800-657-3608; www.vcc.edu; plays football in the MCAC
- Western Technical College Cavaliers (Wisconsin Junior College Athletic Association), La Crosse, WI 54601; 608-785-9200; www.westerntc.edu; no football program
- Williston State College Tetons (Mon-Dak Athletic Conference), Williston, ND 58801; 701-774-4200; www.willistonstate.edu; no football program

Minnesota College Athletic Conference Champions

Year	*School*
1996	Vermilion Community College (MN)
1997	Rochester Community and Technical College (MN)
1998	Rochester Community and Technical College (MN)
1999	Rochester Community and Technical College (MN)
2000	Rochester Community and Technical College (MN)
2001	Minnesota State Community and Technical College, Fergus Falls (MN)
2002	Minnesota State Community and Technical College, Fergus Falls (MN)
2003	Rochester Community and Technical College (MN)
2004	Rochester Community and Technical College (MN)
2005	Rochester Community and Technical College (MN)
2006	Vermilion Community College (MN)
2007	Rochester Community and Technical College (MN)

Year	School
2008	Mesabi Range Community and Technical - College (MN)
2009	Central Lakes College, Brainerd (MN)
2010	Rochester Community and Technical College (MN)

NJCAA Region 14

(23 colleges, five football programs) (Southwest Junior College Football Conference), National NJCAA Office: 1755 Telstar Drive, Suite 103, Colorado Springs, CO 80920; Telephone: 719-590-9788; Fax: 719-590-7324; Web site: http:// www. njcaa.org

- Alvin Community College Dolphins, Alvin, TX 77511; 281-756-3500; www.alvincollege.edu; no football program
- Angelina College Roadrunners, Lufkin, TX 75904; 936-639-1301; www.angelina.edu; no football program
- Blinn College Buccaneers, Brenham, TX 77833; 979-830-4000; www.blinn.edu; plays football in the Southwest Junior College Football Conference
- Bossier Parish Community College Cavaliers, Bossier City, LA 71111; 318-678-6000; www.bpcc.edu; no football program
- Coastal Bend College, Beeville, Cougars, Beeville, TX 78102; 361-358-2838; www.coastalbend.edu; no football program
- Galveston College Whitecaps, Galveston, TX 77550; 409-944-4242; www.gc.edu; no football program
- Jacksonville College Jaguars, Jacksonville, TX 75766; 903-586-2518; www.jacksonville-college.edu; no football program
- Kilgore College Rangers, Kilgore, TX 75662; 903-984-8531; www.kilgore.edu; plays football in the Southwest Junior College Football Conference
- Lamar State College, Port Arthur, Seahawks, Port Arthur, TX 77641; 409-983-4921; www.lamarpa.edu; no football program
- Laredo Community College Palominos, Laredo, TX 78046; 956-794-4000; www.laredo.edu; no football program
- Lee College Runnin' Rebels, Baytown, TX 77522; 281-427-5611; www.lee.edu; no football program
- Lon Morris College Bearcats, Jacksonville, TX 75766; 903-589-4000; www.lonmorris.edu; no football program
- Navarro College Bulldogs, Corsicana, TX 75110; 800-628-2776; www.navarrocollege.edu; plays football in the Southwest Junior College Football Conference
- Northeast Texas Community College Eagles, Mt. Pleasant, TX 75456; 903-434-8100; www.ntcc.edu; no football program
- Panola College Ponies, Carthage, TX 75633; 903-693-2000; www.panola.edu; no football program
- Paris Junior College Dragons, Paris, TX 75460; 903-785-7661; www.parisjc.edu; no football program
- San Jacinto College, Central, Ravens, Pasadena, TX 77505; 281-476-1501; www.sanjac.edu/future-students/about-san-jac/why-san-jac/campuses/central-campus; no football program
- San Jacinto College, North, Gators, Houston, TX 77049; 281-458-4050; www.sanjac.edu/future-students/about-san-jac/why-san-jac/campuses/north-campus; no football program
- San Jacinto College, South, Coyotes, Houston, TX 77089; 281-484-1900; www.sanjac.edu/future-students/about-san-jac/why-san-jac/campuses/south-campus; no football program
- Texarkana College Bulldogs, Texarkana, TX 75599; 903-832-5565; www.texarkanacollege.edu; no football program
- Trinity Valley Community College Cardinals, Athens, TX 75751; 903-677-8822; www2.tvcc.edu; plays football in the Southwest Junior College Football Conference
- Tyler Junior College Apaches, Tyler, TX 75701; 903-510-2200; www.tjc.edu; plays football in the Southwest Junior College Football Conference
- Wharton County Junior College Pioneers, Wharton, TX 77488, 979-532-4560; www.wcjc.edu; no football program

Southwest Junior College Football Conference

The SJCFC is currently made up of seven teams, five from NJCAA Region 14, one from NJCAA Region 2 (Northeastern Oklahoma A&M College) and one from NJCAA Region 5 (Cisco College).

Southwest Junior College Football Conference Champions

Year	*School*
2006	Blinn College (TX)
2007	Navarro College (TX)
2008	Blinn College (TX)
2009	Blinn College (TX)
2010	Navarro College (TX)

Southwest Junior College Football Conference Coach of the Year

Year	*Coach*	*School*
2006	Brad Franchione	Blinn College (TX)
2007	Ray Woodward	Navarro College (TX)
2008	Brad Franchione	Blinn College (TX)
2009	No Information	
2010	Nick Bobeck	Navarro College (TX)

Southwest Junior College Football Conference Player of the Year

Year	*Player*	*Position*	*School*
2006	John David Weed	Quarterback	Tyler Junior College (TX)
2007	Jocques Crawford		Cisco College (TX)
2008	Terrance Cain	Quarterback	Blinn College (TX)
2009	Chase Ford	Tight End	Kilgore College (TX)
2010	Josh Johnson	Running Back	Trinity Valley Community College (TX)

Southwest Junior College Football Conference Offensive Player of the Year

Year	*Player*	*Position*	*School*
2006	John David Weed	Quarterback	Tyler Junior College (TX)
2007	Bo Bowling		Northeastern Oklahoma A&M College (OK)
2008	Anthony Morgan	Guard	Navarro College (TX)
2009	Chad Winbush	Running Back	Trinity Valley Community College (TX)
2010	Jacob Morgan		Cisco College (TX)

Southwest Junior College Football Conference Defensive Player of the Year

Year	*Player*	*Position*	*School*
2006	Terrance Gadson	Outside Linebacker	Northeastern Oklahoma A&M College (OK)
2007	Donald Booker		Navarro College (TX)
2008	Jared Price	Defensive End	Blinn College (TX)
2009	Brad Graham	Linebacker	
2010	Princeton Jackson		Blinn College (TX)

NJCAA Region 15

(17 colleges, four football programs) (Mid-Hudson Conference); National NJCAA Office: 1755 Telstar Drive, Suite 103, Colorado Springs, CO 80920; Telephone: 719-590-9788; Fax: 719-590-7324; Web site: http://www.njcaa.org

- ASA College Avengers, Brooklyn, NY 11201; 718-522-2547; www.asa.edu; plays football in the Northeast Football Conference
- Borough of Manhattan Community College (City University of New York) Panthers (CUNY Athletic Conference), New York, NY, 10007; 212-220-8000; www.bmcc.cuny.edu; no football program
- Bronx Community College (City University of New York) Broncos (CUNY Athletic Conference), Bronx, NY 10453; 718-289-5100; www.bcc.cuny.edu; no football program

- Dutchess Community College (State University of New York) Falcons (Mid-Hudson Athletic Conference), Poughkeepsie, NY 12601; 845-431-8000; www.sunydutchess.edu; no football program
- Fashion Institute of Technology (State University of New York) Tigers, New York, NY 10001; 212-217-7999; http://fitnyc.edu; no football program
- Globe Institute of Technology Knights, New York, NY 10018; 212-349-4330; www.globeinstitute.org; plays football as an independent team
- Hostos Community College (City University of New York) Caimans (CUNY Athletic Conference), Bronx, NY 10451; 718-518-4444; www.hostos.cuny.edu; no football program
- Kingsborough Community College (City University of New York) Wave (CUNY Athletic Conference), Brooklyn, NY 11235; 718-265-5343; www.kbcc.cuny.edu; no football program
- Monroe College Mustangs, Bronx, NY 10468; 718-933-6700; www.monroecollege.edu; no football program
- Nassau Community College Lions, Garden City, NY 11530; 516-572-7501; www.ncc.edu; plays football in the Northeast Football Conference
- Orange County Community College (State University of New York, SUNY Orange) Colts, Middletown, NY 10940; 845-344-6222; www.sunyorange.edu; no football program
- Queensborough Community College (City University of New York) Tigers (CUNY Athletic Conference), Bayside, NY 11364; 718-631-6262; www.qcc.cuny.ed; no football program
- Rockland Community College (State University of New York) Hawks, Suffern, NY 10901; 845-574-4000; www.sunyrockland.edu; no football program
- Suffolk County Community College, Selden (State University of New York) Sharks, Selden, NY 11784; 631-451-4316; www.sunysuffolk.edu; no football program
- Sullivan County Community College (State University of New York) Generals, Loch Sheldrake, NY 12759; 845-434-5750; www.sullivan.suny.edu; no football program
- Ulster County Community College (State University of New York, SUNY Ulster) Senators, Stone Ridge, NY 12484; 845-687-5000; www.sunyulster.edu; no football program
- Westchester Community College Vikings (Mid Hudson Conference), Valhalla, NY 10595; 914-606-6600; www.sunywcc.edu; no football program

NJCAA Region 16

(17 colleges, no football programs) (Missouri [Midwest] Community College Athletic Conference); National NJCAA Office: 1755 Telstar Drive, Suite 103, Colorado Springs, CO 80920; Telephone: 719-590-9788; Fax: 719-590-7324; Web site: http://www. njcaa.org

- Cottey College Comets, Nevada, MO 64772; 417-667-8181; www.cottey.edu; no football program
- Crowder College Roughriders, Neosho MO 64850; 417-451-3223; www.crowder.edu; no football program
- East Central College Falcons (Midwest Community College Athletic Conference), Union, MO 63084; 636-584-6500; www.eastcentral.edu; no football program
- Jefferson College Vikings (Midwest Community College Athletic Conference), Hillsboro, MO 63050; 636-797-3000; www.jeffco.edu; no football program
- Metropolitan Community College, Blue River, Trail Blazers, Independence, MO 64057; 816-604-6500; mcckc.edu/explore/campuses/blueriver/welcome.asp; no football program
- Metropolitan Community College, Longview, Lakers, Lee's Summit, MO 64081; 816-604-2000; mcckc.edu/explore/campuses/longview/welcome.asp; no football program; no football program
- Metropolitan Community College, Maple Woods, Monarchs, Kansas City, MO 64156; 816-604-3000; mcckc.edu/explore/campuses/maplewoods/welcome.asp; no football program
- Metropolitan Community College, Penn Valley, Scouts, Kansas City, MO 64111; 816-604-4000; http://mcckc.edu/explore/campuses/pennvalley; no football program
- Mineral Area College Cardinals (Midwest Community College Athletic Conference), Park Hills, MO 63601; 573-431-4593; www.mineralarea.edu; no football program
- Missouri State University, West Plains, Grizzles, West Plains, MO 65775; 417-255-7255; http://wp.missouristate.edu; no football program
- Moberly Area Community College Greyhounds, Moberly, MO 65270; 660-263-4110; www.macc.edu; no football program

- North Central Missouri College Pirates, Trenton, MO 64683; 660-359-3948; www.ncmissouri.edu; no football program
- St. Charles Community College (Midwest Community College Athletic Conference), Cottleville, MO 63376; 636-922-8000; www.stchas.edu; no football program
- St. Louis Community College, Meramec, Archers (Midwest Community College Athletic Conference), St. Louis, MO 63122; 314-498-7500; www.stlcc.edu/mc; no football program
- State Fair Community College Roadrunners, Sedalia, MO 65301; 877-311-7322; www.sfccmo.edu; no football program
- Three Rivers Community College Raiders (Midwest Community College Athletic Conference), Poplar Bluff, MO 63901; 877-879-8722; www.trcc.edu; no football program
- Wentworth Military Academy & College Red Dragons (Missouri Community College Conference), Lexington, MO 64067; 800-962-7682; http://wma.edu; no football program

NJCAA Region 17

(22 colleges, two football programs) (Georgia Junior College Athletic Association — Demorest, GA); National NJCAA Office: 1755 Telstar Drive, Suite 103, Colorado Springs, CO 80920; Telephone: 719-590-9788; Fax: 719-590-7324; Web site: http://www. njcaa.org

- Abraham Baldwin Agricultural College Golden Stallions (Georgia Collegiate Athletic Association), Tifton, GA 31793; 229-391-5001; www.abac.edu; no football program
- Albany Technical College Titans (Georgia Collegiate Athletic Association), Albany, GA 31701; 229-430-3500; www.albanytech.edu; no football program
- Andrew College Fighting Tigers, Cuthbert, GA 39840; 229-209-5270; www.andrewcollege.edu; no football program
- Atlanta Metropolitan College Red-Eyed Panthers, Atlanta, GA 30310; 404-756-4000; www.atlm.edu; no football program
- Atlanta Technical College (no mascot), Atlanta, GA 30310; 404-225-4400; www.atlantatech.edu; no football program
- Central Georgia Technical College Cougars (Georgia Collegiate Athletic Association), Macon, GA 31206; 478-757-3400; www.centralgatech.edu; no football program
- Chattahoochie Technical College Golden Eagles (Georgia Collegiate Athletic Association), Marietta, GA 30060; 770-528-4545; www.chattahoocheetech.edu; plays Club Football in the National Club Football Association
- Darton College Cavaliers (Georgia Collegiate Athletic Association), Albany, GA 31707; 229-317-6000; www.darton.edu; no football program
- East Georgia College Bobcats (Georgia Collegiate Athletic Association), Swainsboro, GA 30401; 478-289-2017; www.ega.edu; no football program
- Georgia Military College Bulldogs, Milledgeville, GA 31061; 478-387-4900; www.gmc.cc.ga.us; plays football as an independent team
- Georgia Northwestern Technical College Bobcats (Georgia Collegiate Athletic Association), Rock Spring, GA 30739; 706-764-3510; www.gntc.edu/about/campuses/campus_walker.php; no football program
- Georgia Perimeter College Jaguars, Clarkston, GA 30021; 678-891-3200; http://jobs.gpc.edu; no football program
- Gordon College Highlanders, Barnesville, GA 30204; 678-359-5555; www.gdn.edu; no football program
- Middle Georgia College Warriors, Cochran, GA 31014; 478-934-6221; www.mgc.edu; no football program
- Middle Georgia Technical College Titans (Georgia Collegiate Athletic Association), Warner Robins, GA 31088; 478-988-6800; www.middlegatech.edu; no football program
- North Georgia Technical College Eagles, Clarkesville, GA 30523; 706-754-7700; www.northgatech.edu/pages/visitors_alumni/campuses/clarkesville.aspx; no football program
- Oxford College of Emory University Eagles (Georgia Collegiate Athletic Association), Oxford, GA 30054; 770-784-8888; http://oxford.emory.edu; no football program
- South Georgia College Tigers (Georgia Collegiate Athletic Association), Douglas, GA 31533; 912-260-4200; www.sgc.edu; no football program

- South Georgia Technical College Jets (Georgia Collegiate Athletic Association), Americus, GA 31709; 229-931-2394; www.southgatech.edu; no football program
- Southern Crescent Technical College Tigers (Georgia Collegiate Athletic Association), Griffin, GA 30223; 770-228-7348; www.sctech.edu; no football program
- Waycross College Swamp Foxes (Georgia Collegiate Athletic Association), Waycross, GA 31503; 912-449-7600; www.waycross.edu; no football program
- West Georgia Technical College Golden Knights (Georgia Collegiate Athletic Association), Waco, GA 30182; 770-537-6000; www.westgatech.edu/locations/murphy.htm; no football program

NJCAA Region 18

(12 colleges, one football program) (Northwest Athletic Association of Community Colleges, Scenic West Athletic Conference); National NJCAA Office: 1755 Telstar Drive, Suite 103, Colorado Springs, CO 80920; Telephone: 719-590-9788; Fax: 719-590-7324; Web site: http://www. njcaa.org

- Clackamas Community College Cougars (Northwest Athletic Association of Community Colleges), Oregon City, OR 97045; 503-594-6000; www.clackamas.edu; no football program
- College of Southern Idaho Eagles (Scenic West Athletic Conference), Twin Falls, ID 83303; 208-733-9554; www.csi.edu; no football program
- College of Southern Nevada Coyotes (Scenic West Athletic Conference), Henderson, NV 89002; 702-651-3000; www.csn.edu/about/locations/henderson.asp; no football program
- Colorado Northwestern Community College Spartans (Scenic West Athletic Conference), Rangely, CO 81648; 800-562-1105; www.cncc.edu; no football program
- Highline Community College Thunderbirds (Northwest Athletic Association of Community Colleges), Des Moines, WA 98198; 206-878-3710; www.highline.edu; no football program
- North Idaho College Cardinals (Scenic West Athletic Conference), Coeur d'Alene, ID 83814; 208-769-3300; www.nic.edu; no football program
- Salt Lake Community College Bruins (Scenic West Athletic Conference), Salt Lake City, UT 84123; 801-957-7522; www.slcc.edu; no football program
- Snow College Badgers (Scenic West Athletic Conference), Ephraim, UT 84627; 435-283-7000; www.snow.edu; plays football in the Western States Football League
- Southwestern Oregon Community College Lakers (Northwest Athletic Association for Community Colleges), Coos Bay, OR 97420; 541-888-2525; www.socc.edu; no football program
- Utah State University, College of Eastern Utah, Eagles (Scenic West Athletic Conference), Price, UT 84501; 435-613-5000; www.ceu.edu; no football program
- Western Nevada College Wildcats (Scenic West Athletic Conference), Carson City, NV 89703; 775-445-3000; www.wnc.edu; no football program
- Yakima Valley Community College Yaks (Northwest Athletic Association of Community Colleges), Yakima, WA 98902; 509-574-4600; www.yvcc.edu; no football program

NJCAA Region 19

(30 colleges, three football programs) (Garden State Athletic Conference — Dover, DE); National NJCAA Office: 1755 Telstar Drive, Suite 103, Colorado Springs, CO 80920; Telephone: 719-590-9788; Fax: 719-590-7324; Web site: http://www. njcaa.org

- Atlantic Cape Community College Buccaneers (Garden State Athletic Conference), Mays Landing, NJ 08330; 609-625-1111; www.atlantic.edu; no football program
- Bergen Community College Bulldogs, Paramus, NJ 07652; 201-447-7100; www.bergen.edu; no football program
- Brookdale Community College Jersey Blues (Garden State Athletic Conference), Lincroft, NJ 07738; 732-224-2345; www.brookdalecc.edu; no football program
- Bucks County Community College Centurions (Eastern Pennsylvania Collegiate Conference), Newtown PA 18940; 215-968-8000; www.bucks.edu; no football program
- Burlington County College Barons (Garden State Athletic Conference), Pemberton, NJ 08068; 609-894-9311; www.bcc.edu; no football program

- Camden County College Cougars, Blackwood, NJ 08012; 856-227-7200; www.camdencc.edu; no football program
- County College of Morris Titans (Garden State Athletic Conference), Randolph, NJ 07869; 973-328-5000; www.ccm.edu; no football program
- Cumberland County College Dukes (Garden State Athletic Conference), Vineland, NJ, 08362; 856-691-8600; www.cccnj.edu; no football program
- Delaware County Community College Phantoms (Eastern Pennsylvania Collegiate Conference), Media, PA 19063; 610-359-5000; www.dccc.edu; no football program
- Delaware Technical and Community College Roadrunners, Georgetown, DE 19947; 302-856-5400; www.dtcc.edu; no football program
- Delaware Technical & Community College, Stanton/Wilmington Spirit, Wilmington, DE 19801; 302-571-5300; http://www.dtcc.edu/stanton-wilmington; no football program
- Delaware Technical and Community College, Terry, Hawks, Dover, DE 19904; 302-857-1100; ww.dtcc.edu/terry; no football program
- Essex County College Wolverines (Garden State Athletic Conference), Newark, NJ 07102; 973-877-3000; www.essex.edu; no football program
- Gloucester County College Roadrunners (Garden State Athletic Conference), Sewell, NJ 08080; 856-468-5000; www.gccnj.edu; no football program
- Harcum College Bears, Bryn Mawr, PA 19010; 610-525-4100; www.harcum.edu; no football program
- Lackawanna College Falcons, Scranton, PA 18509; 877-346-3552; www.lackawanna.edu; plays football in the Northeast Football Conference
- Lehigh Carbon Community College Cougars (Eastern Pennsylvania Collegiate Conference), Schnecksville, PA 18078; 610-799-2121; www.lccc.edu; no football program
- Manor College Blue Jays, Jenkintown, PA 19046; 215-885-2360; www.manor.edu; no football program
- Mercer County Community College Vikings (Garden State Athletic Conference), Trenton, NJ 08608; 609-570-3100; www.mccc.edu/welcome_kerney.shtml; no football program
- Middlesex County College Colts (Garden State Athletic Conference), Edison, NJ 08818; 732-548-6000; www2.middlesexcc.edu; no football program
- Montgomery County Community College Mustangs, Blue Bell, PA 19422; 215-641-6300; www.mc3.edu; no football program
- Northampton Community College Spartans, Bethlehem, PA 18020; 610-861-5300; www.northampton.edu; no football program
- Ocean County College Vikings (Garden State Athletic Conference), Toms River, NJ 08754; 732-255-0400; www.ocean.edu; no football program
- Passaic County Community College Panthers (Garden State Athletic Conference), Paterson, NJ, 07505; 973-684-6868; www.pccc.cc.nj.us; no football program
- Raritan Valley Community College Lions (Garden State Athletic Conference), Branchburg, NJ 08876; 908-526-1200; www.raritanval.edu; no football program
- Salem Community College Oaks (Garden State Athletic Conference), Carneys Point, NJ 08069; 856-299-2100; www.salemcc.edu; no football program
- Sussex County Community College Skylanders (Garden State Athletic Conference), Newton, NJ 07860; 973-300-2100; http://sussex.edu; no football program
- Thaddeus Stevens College of Technology (Eastern Pennsylvania Collegiate Conference), Lancaster, PA 17602; 800-842-3832; www.stevenstech.org; plays football in the Seaboard Conference
- Union County College Owls (Garden State Athletic Conference), Cranford, NJ 07016; 908-709-7000; www.ucc.edu; no football program
- Williamson Free School of Mechanical Trades Mechanics (United States Collegiate Athletic Association), Media, PA 19063; 610-566-1776; www.williamson.edu; plays football in the Seaboard Conference

NJCAA Region 20

(29 colleges, no football programs) (Pennsylvania Collegiate Athletic Association) (Maryland Junior College Athletic Conference); National NJCAA Office: 1755 Telstar Drive, Suite 103, Colorado Springs, CO 80920; Telephone: 719-590-9788; Fax: 719-590-7324; Web site: http://www. njcaa.org

- Allegany College of Maryland Trojans (Maryland Junior College Athletic Conference), Cumberland, MD 21502; 301-784-5000; www.allegany.edu; no football program
- Anne Arundel Community College Pioneers (Maryland Junior College Athletic Association), Arnold, MD 21012; 410-777-2222; www.aacc.edu; no football program
- Baltimore City Community College Panthers (Maryland Junior College Athletic Conference), Baltimore, MD 21202; 410-986-5599; www.bccc.edu; no football program
- Butler County Community College Pioneers (Pennsylvania Collegiate Athletic Association), Butler, PA 16002; 724-287-8711; www.bc3.edu; no football program
- Community College of Allegheny County, Allegheny, Cougars (Pennsylvania Collegiate Athletic Association), Pittsburgh, PA 15212; 412-237-2525; www.ccac.edu; no football program
- Community College of Allegheny County, Boyce, Saints (Pennsylvania Collegiate Athletic Association), Monroeville, PA 15146; 724-327-1327; www.ccac.edu; no football program
- Community College of Allegheny County, North (no mascot) (Pennsylvania Collegiate Athletic Association), Pittsburgh, PA 15237; 412-366-7000; www.ccac.edu; no football program
- Community College of Allegheny County, South, Tigers (Pennsylvania Collegiate Athletic Association), West Mifflin, PA 15122; 412-469-1100; www.ccac.edu; no football program
- Community College of Baltimore County, Catonsville, Cardinals (Maryland Junior College Athletic Conference), Baltimore, MD 21228; 443-840-2222; www.ccbcmd.edn/directory/cat/catonsville.htm; no football program
- Community College of Baltimore County, Dundalk, Lions (Maryland Junior College Athletic Conference), Baltimore, MD 21222; 443-840-2222; www.ccbcmd.edu/directory/dundalk/d_maps.html; no football program
- Community College of Baltimore County, Essex, Knights (Maryland Junior College Athletic Conference), Baltimore, MD 21222; 443-840-2222; www.ccbcmd.edu/directory/essex/index.html; no football program
- Cecil College Seahawks (Maryland Junior College Athletic Conference), North East, MD 21901; 410-287-1000; www.cecil.edu; no football program
- Chesapeake College Skipjacks (Maryland Junior College Athletic Conference), Wye Mills, MD 21679; 410-822-5400; www.chesapeake.edu; no football program
- College of Southern Maryland Hawks (Maryland Junior College Athletic Conference), La Plata, MD 20646; 301-934-2251; www.csmd.edu; no football program
- Community College of Beaver County Titans (Western Pennsylvania Collegiate Conference, Pennsylvania Collegiate Athletic Association), Monaca, PA 15061; 724-480-2222; www.ccbc.edu; no football program
- Frederick Community College Cougars (Maryland Junior College Athletic Conference), Frederick, MD 21702; 301-846-2400; www.frederick.edu; no football program
- Garrett College Lakers (Maryland Junior College Athletic Conference), McHenry, MD 21541; 301-387-3000; www.garrettcollege.edu; no football program
- Hagerstown Community College Hawks (Maryland Junior College Conference), Hagerstown, MD 21742; 240-500-2000; www.hagerstowncc.edu; no football program
- Harford Community College Fighting Owls (Maryland Junior College Athletic Conference), Bel Air, MD 21015; 443-412-2000; www.harford.edu; no football program
- Howard Community College Dragons (Maryland Junior College Athletic Conference), Columbia, MD 21044; 443-518-1200; www.howardcc.edu; no football program
- Montgomery College, Germantown, Gryphons (Maryland Junior College Athletic Conference), Germantown, MD 20876; 240-567-5000; http://cms.montgomerycollege.edu; no football program
- Montgomery College, Rockville, Knights (Maryland Junior College Athletic Conference), Rockville, MD 20850, 240-567-5000; http://cms.montgomerycollege.edu; no football program
- Montgomery College, Takoma Park–Silver Spring, Falcons (Maryland Junior College Athletic Conference), Takoma Park, MD 20912; 240-567-5000; http://cms.montgomerycollege.edu; no football program
- Northern Virginia Community College, Alexandria, VA 22311; 703-257-6600; www.nvcc.edu; no football program
- Pennsylvania Highlands Community College Black Bears (Western Pennsylvania Collegiate Conference), Johnstown, PA 15904; 814-262-6400; www.pennhighlands.edu/richland; no football program

- Potomac State College (West Virginia University) Catamounts (Pennsylvania Collegiate Athletic Association), Keyser, WV 267261; 304-788-6820; www.potomacstatecollege.edu; no football program
- Prince George's Community College Owls (Maryland Junior College Athletic Conference), Largo, MD 20774; 301-336-6000; www.pgcc.edu; no football program
- Rappahannock Community College Gulls, Warsaw, VA 22572; 804-333-6700; www.rappahannock.edu; no football program
- Westmoreland County Community College Wolfpack (Pennsylvania Collegiate Athletic Association), Youngwood PA 15697; 724-925-4000; www.wccc.edu; no football program

NJCAA Region 21

(17 colleges, one football program) (Massachusetts Community College Athletic Association—Boston, MA); National NJCAA Office: 1755 Telstar Drive, Suite 103, Colorado Springs, CO 80920; Telephone: 719-590-9788; Fax: 719-590-7324; Web site: http://www.njcaa.org

- Benjamin Franklin Institute of Technology Shockers, Boston, MA 02116; 617-423-4630; www.bft.edu; no football program
- Bristol Community College Bees, Fall River, MA 02720; 508-678-2811; www.bristol.mass.edu; no football program
- Bunker Hill Community College Bulldogs, Boston, MA 02129; 617-228-2000; www.bhcc.mass.edu; no football program
- Community College of Rhode Island Knights, Warwick, RI 02886; 401-825-1000; www.ccri.edu; no football program
- Dean College Bulldogs, Franklin, MA 02038; 877-879-3326; www.dean.edu; plays in the Northeast Football Conference
- Gateway Community College Lions, 88 Bassett Road, North Haven, CT 06473; 203-285-2000; www.gwcc.commnet.edu; no football program
- Holyoke Community College Cougars, Holyoke, MA 01040; 413-538-7000; www.hcc.edu; no football program
- Lakes Region Community College Centurians, Laconia, NH 03246; 603-524-3207; www.lrcc.edu; no football program
- Lincoln College of New England (formerly Briarwood College) Wildcats, Southington, CT 06489; 800-825-0087; www.lincolncollegene.edu; no football program
- Manchester Community College Cougars, Manchester, CT 06045; 860-512-3000; www.mcc.comment.edu; no football program
- MassBay (Massachusetts Bay) Community College Buccaneers, Wellesley Hills, MA 02481; 781-239-3000; www.massbay.edu; no football program
- Massasoit Community College Warriors, Brockton, MA 02302; 508-588-9100; www.massasoit.mass.edu; no football program
- Northern Essex Community College Knights, Haverhill, MA 01830; 978-556-3000; www.necc.mass.edu; no football program
- Quinsigamond Community College Wyverns, Worcester, MA 01606; 508-853-2300; www.qcc.edu; no football program
- Roxbury Community College Tigers, Roxbury Crossing, MA 02120; 617-427-0060; www.rcc.mass.edu; no football program
- Springfield Technical Community College Rams (Massachusetts Community College Athletic Association), Springfield, MA 01102; 413-781-7822; www.stcc.edu; no football program
- University of Connecticut at Avery Point Pointers, Groton, CT 06340; 860-405-9000; www.averypoint.uconn.edu; no football program

NJCAA Region 22

(18 colleges, no football programs) (Alabama Community College Conference—400 South Union Street, Suite 425, Montgomery, AL 36104; Telephone: 334-262-4560; Fax: 334-262-4561; Web site: http://www. acccsports.org); National NJCAA Office: 1755 Telstar Drive, Suite 103, Colorado Springs, CO 80920; Telephone: 719-590-9788; Fax: 719-590-7324; Web site: http://www. njcaa.org

- Alabama Southern Community College Eagles, Monroeville, AL 36461; 251-575-3156; www.ascc.edu; no football program
- Bishop State Community College Wildcats, Mobile, AL 36603; 251-405-7000; www.bscc.cc.al.us; no football program
- Calhoun Community College Warhawks (Alabama Community College Conference), Decatur, AL 35609; 256-306-2500; www.calhoun.edu; no football program
- Central Alabama Community College Trojans (Alabama Community College Conference), Alexander City, AL 35010; 256-234-6346; www.cacc.edu; no football program
- Chattahoochee Valley Community College Pirates (Alabama Community College Conference), Phenix City, AL 36869; 334-291-4900; www.cv.edu; no football program
- Enterprise State Community College Boll Weevils (Enterprise-Ozark Community College), Enterprise, AL 36330; 334-347-2623; www.escc.edu; no football program
- Faulkner State Community College Sun Chiefs (Alabama Community College Conference), Bay Minette, AL 36507; 251-580-2100; www.faulknerstate.edu; no football program
- Gadsden State Community College Cardinals (Alabama Community College Conference), Gadsden, AL 35903; 256-549-8200; www.gadsdenstate.edu; no football program
- Jefferson Davis Community College Warhawks, Brewton, AL 36427; 251-867-4832; www.jdcc.edu; no football program
- Lawson State Community College Cougars (Alabama Community College Conference), Birmingham, AL 35221; 205-925-2515; www.ls.cc.al.us; no football program
- Lurleen B. Wallace Community College Saints (Alabama Community College Conference), Andalusia AL 36420; 334-222-6591; www.lbwcc.edu; no football program
- Marion Military Institute Tigers (Alabama Community College Conference), Marion, AL 36756; 800-664-1842; www.marionmilitary.edu; no football program
- Shelton State Community College Buccaneers (Alabama Community College Conference), Tuscaloosa, AL 35405; 205-391-2211; www.sheltonstate.edu; no football program
- Snead State Community College Parsons (Alabama Community College Conference), Boaz, AL 35957; 256-593-512; www.snead.edu; no football program
- Southern Union State Community College Bisons (Alabama Community College Conference), Wadley, AL 36276; 256-395-2211; www.suscc.edu; no football program
- Wallace Community College, Dothan (George C. Wallace Community College, Dothan) Governors (Southern Conference), Dothan, AL 36303; 334-983-3521; www.wallace.edu; no football program
- Wallace Community College, Selma, Patriots, Selma, AL 36703; 334-876-9227; www.wccs.edu; no football program
- Wallace State Community College Lions (Alabama Community College Conference), Hanceville AL, 35077; 866-350-9722; www.wallacestate.edu; no football program

NJCAA Region 23

(19 colleges, 14 football programs) (MISS-Lou Junior College Conference — New Orleans, LA) (Mississippi Association of Community & Junior Colleges); Meridian Community College had been a member of both MLJCC and MACJC but left the conferences in 2002 and 2007, respectively. National NJCAA Office: 1755 Telstar Drive, Suite 103, Colorado Springs, CO 80920; Telephone: 719-590-9788; Fax: 719-590-7324; Web site: http://www. njcaa.org

- Baton Rouge Community College Bears (MISS-Lou Junior College Conference), Baton Rouge, LA 70806; 225-216-8000; www.mybrcc.edu; no football program
- Coahoma Community College Tigers (Mississippi Association of Community & Junior Colleges), Clarksdale, MS 38614; 662-627-2571; www.ccc.cc.ms.us; plays football in the MACJC
- Copiah-Lincoln Community College Wolfpack (Wolves) (Mississippi Association of Community & Junior Colleges), Wesson, MS 39191; 601-643-5101; www.colin.edu; plays football in the MACJC
- Delgado Community College Dolphins (MISS-Lou Junior College Conference), New Orleans, LA 70119; 504-671-5000; www.dcc.edu; no football program
- East Central Community College Warriors (Mississippi Association of Community & Junior Colleges), Decatur, MS 39327; 601-635-2111; www.eccc.edu; plays football in the MACJC

- East Mississippi Community College Lions (Mississippi Association of Community & Junior Colleges), Scooba, MS 39358; 662-476-5000; www.eastms.edu; plays football in the MACJC
- Hinds Community College Eagles (Mississippi Association of Community & Junior Colleges), Raymond, MS 39154; 601-857-5261; www.hindscc.edu; plays football in the MACJC
- Holmes Community College Bulldogs (Mississippi Association of Community & Junior Colleges), Goodman, MS 39079; 662-472-2312; www.holmes.cc.ms.us; plays football in the MACJC
- Itawamba Community College Indians (Mississippi Association of Community & Junior Colleges), Fulton, MS 38843; 662-862-8000; www.iccms.edu; plays football in the MACJC
- Jones County Junior College Bobcats (Mississippi Association of Community & Junior Colleges), Ellisville, MS 39437; 601-477-4000; www.jcjc.edu; plays football in the MACJC
- Louisiana State University, Eunice, Bengals (MISS-Lou Junior College Conference), Eunice, LA 70535; 337-457-7311; www.lsue.edu; no football program
- Meridian Community College Eagles, Meridian, MS 39307; 601-483-8241; www.mcc.cc.ms.us; no football program
- Mississippi Delta Community College Trojans (Mississippi Association of Community & Junior Colleges), Moorhead, MS 38761; 662-246-6322; www.msdelta.edu; plays football in the MACJC
- Mississippi Gulf Coast Community College Bulldogs (Mississippi Association of Community & Junior Colleges), Perkinston, MS 39573; 601-928-5211; www.mgccc.edu; plays football in the MACJC
- Northeast Mississippi Community College Tigers (Mississippi Association of Community & Junior Colleges), Booneville, MS 38829; 800-555-2154; www.nemcc.edu; plays football in the MACJC
- Northwest Mississippi Community College Rangers (Mississippi Association of Community & Junior Colleges), Senatobia, MS 38668; 662-562-3200; http://northwestms.net; plays football in the MACJC
- Pearl River Community College Wildcats (Mississippi Association of Community & Junior Colleges), Poplarville, MS 39470; 601-403-1000; www.prcc.edu; plays football in the MACJC
- Southern University at Shreveport Jaguars (MISS-Lou Junior College Conference), Shreveport, LA 71107; 318-670-6000; http://web.susla.edu; no football program
- Southwest Mississippi Community College Bears (Mississippi Association of Community & Junior Colleges), Summit, MS 39666; 601-276-2000; www.smcc.cc.ms.us; plays football in the MACJC

No information available on MACJC champions or annual awards

NJCAA Region 24

(19 colleges, no football programs) (Great Rivers Athletic Conference) (Mid-West Athletic Conference — Springfield, IL); National NJCAA Office: 1755 Telstar Drive, Suite 103, Colorado Springs, CO 80920; Telephone: 719-590-9788; Fax: 719-590-7324; Web site: http://www. njcaa.org

- Danville Area Community College Jaguars (Mid-West Athletic Conference), Danville, IL 61832; 217-443-3222; www.dacc.edu; no football program
- Heartland Community College Hawks (Mid-West Athletic Conference), Normal, IL 61761; 309-268-8000; www.heartland.edu; no football program
- Illinois Central College Cougars (Mid-West Athletic Conference), East Peoria, IL 61635; 309-694-5422; www.icc.edu; no football program
- John A. Logan College Volunteers (Great Rivers Athletic Conference), Carterville, IL 62918; 618-985-3741; www.jalc.edu; no football program
- John Wood Community College Trail Blazers (Mid-West Athletic Conference), Quincy, IL 62305; 217-224-6500; www.jwcc.edu; no football program
- Kaskaskia College Blue Devils (Great Rivers Athletic Conference), Centralia, IL 62801; 618-545-3000; www.kaskaskia.edu; no football program
- Lake Land College Lakers (Great Rivers Athletic Conference), Mattoon, IL 61938; 217-234-5253; www.lakeland.cc.il.us; no football program
- Lewis & Clark Community College Trailblazers (Mid-West Athletic Conference), Godfrey, IL 62035; 618-468-7000; www.lc.edu; no football program
- Lincoln College Lynx (Mid-West Athletic Conference), Lincoln, IL 62656; 217-732-3155; www.lin colncollege.edu; no football program
- Lincoln Land Community College Loggers (Mid-West Athletic Conference), Springfield, IL 62794; 217-786-2200; www.llcc.edu; no football program

- Lincoln Trail College Statesman, Robinson, IL 62454; 618-544-8657; www.iecc.edu/LTC; no football program
- Olney Central College Blue Knights (Great Rivers Athletic Conference), Olney, IL 62450; 618-393-2982; www.iecc.edu/occ; no football program
- Parkland College Cobras (Mid-West Athletic Conference), Champaign, IL 61821; 217-351-2200; www.parkland.edu; no football program
- Rend Lake College Warriors (Great Rivers Athletic Conference), Ina, IL 62846; 618-437-5321; www.rlc.edu; no football program
- Shawnee Community College Saints (Mid-West Athletic Conference), Ullin IL 62992; 618-634-3200; www.shawneecc.edu; no football program
- Southeastern Illinois College Falcons (Great Rivers Athletic Conference), Harrisburg, IL 62946; 618-252-5400; www.sic.edu; no football program
- Southwestern Illinois College Blue Storm (Great Rivers Athletic Conference), Belleville, IL 62221; 618-235-2700; www.swic.edu; no football program
- Spoon River College Mudcats (Mid-West Athletic Conference), Canton, IL 61520; 309-647-4645; www.src.edu; no football program
- Wabash Valley College Warriors (Great Rivers Athletic Conference), Mt. Carmel, IL 62863; 618-262-8641; www.iecc.edu/wvc; no football program

Northwest Athletic Association of Community Colleges (NWAACC)

Formed in 1946 as the Washington State Junior College Athletic Conference and renamed the Washington Athletic Association of Community Colleges in 1964, today's NWAACC consists of 35 community colleges in the states of Washington and Oregon as well as the Canadian province of British Columbia. While each of its members schools offer a wide variet of sports programs for both men and women, the NWAACC does not support football and none of its members offer football programs.

As currently configured, the NWAACC is divided into four regions: Northern (10 teams), Southern (eight teams), Eastern (eight teams) and Western (nine teams).

- Bellevue College Bulldogs (Northern Region), Bellevue, WA 98007; 425-564-1000; http://bellevuecollege.edu
- Big Bend Community College Vikings (Eastern Region), Moses Lake, WA 98837; 509.793.2222; www.bigbend.edu
- Blue Mountain Community College Timberwolves (Eastern Region), Pendleton, OR 97801; 541-276-1260; www.bluecc.edu
- Centralia College Trailblazers (Western Region), Centralia WA 98531; 360-736-9391; www.centralia.edu
- Chemeketa Community College Storm (Southern Region), Salem, OR 97309; 503-399-5000; www.chemeketa.edu
- Clackamas Community College Cougars (Southern Region), Oregon City, OR 97045; 503-594-6000; www.clackamas.edu
- Clark College Penguins (Western Region), Vancouver, WA 98663; 360-699-6398; www.clark.edu
- Columbia Basin College Hawks (Eastern Region), Pasco, WA 99301; 509-547-0511; www.columbiabasin.edu
- Community Colleges of Spokane Sasquatch (Eastern Region), Spokane, WA 99217; 509-533-7000; www.ccs.spokane.edu
- Douglas College Royals (Northern Region), New Westminster, British Columbia V3M 5Z5, Canada; 604-527-5400; www.douglas.bc.ca
- Edmonds Community College Tritons (Northern Region), Lynwood, WA 98036; 425-640-1459; www.edcc.edu
- Everett Community College Trojans (Northern Region), Everett, WA 98201; 425-388-9100; www.everettcc.edu
- Grays Harbor College Chokers (Western Region), Aberdeen, WA 98520; 360-532-9020; www.ghc.edu

- Green River Community College Gators (Western Region), Auburn, WA 98092; 253-833-9111; www.greenriver.edu
- Highline Community College Thunderbirds (Western Region), Des Moines, WA 98198; 206-878-3710; www.highline.edu
- Lane Community College Titans (Southern Region), Eugene, OR 97405; 541-463-3000; www.lanecc.edu
- Linn-Benton Community College Roadrunners (Southern Region), Albany, OR 97321, 541-917-4811; www.linnbenton.edu
- Lower Columbia College Red Devils (Western Region), Longview, WA 98632; 360-442-2311; www.lowercolumbia.edu
- Mt. Hood Community College Saints (Southern Region), Gresham, OR 97030; 503-491-6422; www.mhcc.edu
- Olympic College Rangers (Northern Region), Bremerton, WA 98337; 360-792-6050; www.olympic.edu
- Peninsula College Pirates (Northern Region), Port Angeles, WA 98362; 360-452-9277; www.pc.ctc.edu
- Pierce College Raiders (Western Region), Lakewood, WA 98498; 253-964-6500; www.pierce.ctc.edu
- Portland Community College Panthers (Southern Region), Portland, OR 97280; 971-722-6111; www.pcc.edu
- Seattle Community College Storm (Northern Region), Seattle, WA 98103; 206-934-3600; www.sccd.ctc.edu
- Shoreline Community College Dolphins (Northern Region), Shoreline, WA 98133; 206-546-4101; www.shoreline.edu
- Skagit Valley College Cardinals (Northern Region), Mount Vernon, WA 98273; 360-416-7600; www.skagit.edu
- South Puget Sound Community College Clippers (Western Region), Olympia, WA 98512; 360-754-7711; www.spscc.ctc.edu
- Southwestern Oregon Community College Lakers (Southern Region), Coos Bay, OR 97420; 541-888.2525; www.socc.edu
- Tacoma Community College Titans (Western Region), Tacoma, WA 98466; 253-566-5000; www.tacomacc.edu
- Treasure Valley Community College Chukars (Eastern Region), Ontario, OR 97914; 541-881-8822; www.tvcc.cc.or.us
- Umpqua Community College Riverhawks (Southern Region), Roseburg, OR 97470; 541-440-4600; www.umpqua.edu
- Walla Walla Community College Warriors (Eastern Region), Walla Walla, WA 99362; 509-522-2500; www.wwcc.edu
- Wenatchee Valley College Knights (Eastern Region), Wenatchee, WA 98801; 509-682-6800; www.wvc.edu
- Whatcom Community College Orcas (Northern Region), Bellingham, WA 98226; 360-383-3000; www.whatcom.ctc.edu
- Yakima Valley Community College Yaks (Eastern Region), Yakima, WA 98902; 509.574.4600; www.yvcc.edu

Index

www.ingramcontent.com/pod-product-compliance
Ingram Content Group UK Ltd.
Pitfield, Milton Keynes, MK11 3LW, UK
UKHW051928100926
8556IPUK00022B/1441

9 780786 44867